..K MARKET TOWN...
..NS IN 1801, INCLUDING THE SIX ASSIZE AND
AND INCLUDING THE FOUR SEAPORT
ALSO 25
CW01305527
CLEY-NEXT-THE-SEA
547
Cley
Weybourne
Cromer
676
Cromer
HOLT
1004
Holt
Southrepps
Bacton
NORTH SEA
Aldborough
North Walsham
Walsham
1959
Briston
Worstead
Aylsham
1667
Aylsham
Foulsham
Scottow
Ingham
Cawston Sheep Show
Cakerow
Coltishall
R. ANT
R. THURNE
WENSUM
[Horsham] St Faith
Horning
R. BURE
Ludham
The Northern Broads
GREAT YARMOUTH
14,845
Dereham
NORWICH
36,832
Tombland [Norwich]
Magdalen [Sprowston]
Acle
R. BURE
Yarmouth
R. YARE
Norwich
Bishop Bridge [Norwich]
R. YARE
Hingham
1203
Wymondham
1563
Wymondham
R. CHET
Loddon
799
Loddon
R. WAVENEY
Hempnall
Forncett
Attleborough
1333
The Southern Broads
New Buckenham
New Buckenham
664
Pulham St Mary Magdalen
Banham
Gissing
Harleston with Redenhall
1459
Kenninghall
Harleston
Diss
Diss
2246
Scole
SUFFOLK
N

front endpaper

Market towns were distributed fairly evenly across the English countryside. In theory in the 18th century, in support of efficient wholesale and retail markets, no one lived further than 12 miles from a market town. Conversely, to protect the markets and provide a profitable sales area, the towns were not too close to one another.

Itinerants relied on these towns to provide support services. Bishops on their visitations; Collectors of Excise and Receivers General of the Land Tax; Wesleyan Methodist itinerant preachers stationed on their circuits: all needed a market town base during their tours.

Although Norfolk had a very long coastline there were only four ports with a customs house. The twin harbours of Blakeney and Cley, near the Hardys' Letheringsett base, were served by the customs house at Cley.

The county assizes were held in Lent at Thetford, and in the summer in Norwich. To spare parish officers and other litigants a long trip to Norwich, the county quarter sessions were also held by adjournment in October and January (Old Michaelmas and Old Christmas) at Holt and King's Lynn, and in April/May and July (Old Lady and Old Midsummer) at Little Walsingham and Swaffham.

Fairs held a very important place in working people's lives as a time of reunion with family and friends.

Attendance at the home fair or at the local fair near the workplace was prized by farm servants and maidservants as a customary right to be granted by employers as annual holiday.

In some years the Hardys' brewery apprentice Henry Raven was allowed time off for both Hempton Green (the fair near his family home at Whissonsett) and Holt (the fair nearest to his brewery workplace).

There was also a strong retail element, the map displaying the Norfolk fairs' distribution in locations not well served by market towns

[*map © Margaret Bird 2013*]

THE EDITOR

Margaret Bird has been an honorary research fellow in the History department of Royal Holloway, University of London since 2006.

Born in central London in 1946, she read Modern History at St Anne's College, Oxford and gained her master's degree in Modern History at Royal Holloway. For both degrees she specialised in aspects of English history in the eighteenth century.

She has lived in Kingston upon Thames in Surrey since 1970 and was a partner with her husband Tony in the economic consultancy they founded and ran for 22 years.

She has a deep love of the landscape and waterways of the Norfolk Broads in eastern England. All her life she has spent as much time as possible on the family boat, at first with her parents and later with her husband and three sons

The Diary of Mary Hardy 1773–1809

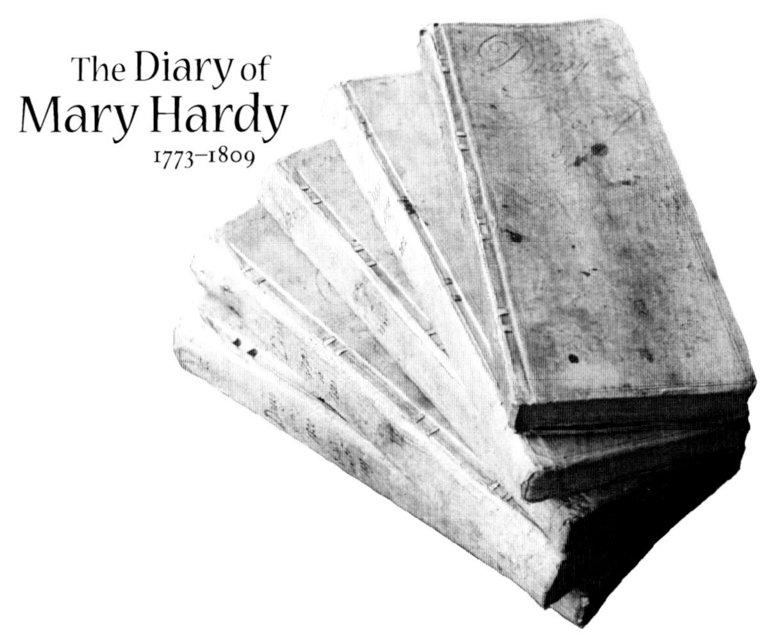

title page Beer barrels occupy a dark corner of Lacock Abbey's brewhouse of *c*.1639. These traditionally coopered and hooped casks were given to the National Trust for its restoration of the brewhouse in 1971 by Wadworths Brewery, of Devizes, Wilts

half-title The five huge ledgers in which Mary Hardy wrote her diary for nearly 36 years are held privately in the Cozens-Hardy Collection
[*photographs Margaret Bird 2001, 1989*]

The Diary of Mary Hardy 1773–1809

Diary 3 *1793–1797*

Farm, maltings and brewery

with the diary of
Henry Raven

edited by
MARGARET BIRD

BURNHAM PRESS
KINGSTON UPON THAMES
2013

BURNHAM PRESS
2013
KINGSTON UPON THAMES

www.burnham-press.co.uk

Published by
Burnham Press, Burnham Lodge,
193 Richmond Road, KINGSTON UPON THAMES,
Surrey, KT2 5DD, United Kingdom

First published 2013

Design and typesetting in Adobe InDesign by Margaret Bird
Main text set in Plantin MT Pro 9½ on 11½
Sidenotes in Plantin Light 8½ on 9
Captions in **Adobe Caslon Pro** semibold 9 on 9¾
Display text Nueva Standard and **Adobe Caslon Pro**
Printers' floral ornaments by the Norwich Press 1796

www.biddles.co.uk

FSC
www.fsc.org

MIX
Paper from responsible sources
FSC® C018575

Printed and bound in the UK by Biddles, part of the MPG Books Group, Bodmin and King's Lynn, 24 Rollesby Road, Hardwick Industrial Estate, KING'S LYNN, Norfolk, PE30 4LS, United Kingdom on 115 gsm Vancouver matt-coated paper woodfree and FSC accredited

ISBN for *Diary 3* as an individual volume:
ISBN 978-0-9573360-2-5

A CIP record for this title is available from the British Library

Diary 3 is one of four individual volumes in the set *The Diary of Mary Hardy 1773–1809*, published 2013

ISBN for the complete set of four Diary volumes:
ISBN 978-0-9573360-4-9

Mary Hardy websites

maryhardysdiary.co.uk

and

maryhardysworld.co.uk

Contents

Diary 3

page

Preliminaries	Editorial introduction	vii
	Contractions, conventions, conversions	xiv
	Digressions from the Letheringsett record	xv
	Figure D3.1 · The Hardys and the Ravens	xvi
DIARY TRANSCRIPTIONS The diary of Mary Hardy 16 August 1793–26 October 1797 *with* The diary of Henry Raven 10 October 1793–25 October 1797 both at Letheringsett, Norfolk	**A family register**	1
	The diary texts	3
	Endnotes and maidservants	403
Appendices	D3.A Figures D3.2–D3.6 Family trees	413
	D3.B A clerical brewer's method	419
	D3.C A chronology of the Hardys' lives 1793–1797	423
Endmatter	Glossary of terms, weights and measures	424
	Bibliography	429
	Index to the diary text of Mary Hardy	433
	Index to the diary text of Henry Raven	474
Companion volumes	The full set of Mary Hardy volumes	550
Forthcoming publication	*Mary Hardy and her World 1773–1809*	551

Figures	FAMILY TREES	
D3.1	The Hardys and the Ravens	xvi
D3.2	Shopkeepers and farmers: the Ravens of Whissonsett, and Foxes of Horningtoft and Brisley	app. D3.A
D3.3	Farmers: the Smiths of Stanfield	app. D3.A
D3.4	Farmers and schoolteachers: the Ravens of Whissonsett Hall	app. D3.A
D3.5	Grocers: the Raven and Hawkins families of Whissonsett and Norwich	app. D3.A
D3.6	Farmers: the Goggs family of Whissonsett and Colkirk	app. D3.A

The Diary of Mary Hardy 1773–1809 Burnham Press, 2013

The four-volume edition of the original manuscripts

***Diary 1* · 28 Nov. 1773–5 Apr. 1781**
Public house and waterway

The Coltishall years (full text)

***Diary 2* · 5 Apr. 1781–16 Aug. 1793**
Beer supply, water power and a death

The early years at Letheringsett (abridged text)

***Diary 3* · 16 Aug. 1793–26 Oct. 1797**
Farm, maltings and brewery

The middle years at Letheringsett (abridged text) with the diary of Henry Raven (full text)

***Diary 4* · 26 Oct. 1797–21 Mar. 1809**
Shipwreck and meeting house

The later years at Letheringsett (abridged text)

The preface and acknowledgments appear at the beginning of *Diary 1* only. Each *Diary* volume has an editorial introduction and list of conventions, a glossary, and its own bibliography and index.

References to entries contained in other *Diary* volumes in the set are cited in the editorial sidenotes as *Diary 1* etc, followed by the date of the diarist's entry: eg 'see *Diary 4*: 8 Oct. 1804'

The Remaining Diary of Mary Hardy 1773–1809 Burnham Press, 2013

The entries 1781–1809 not included in the four-volume edition of the manuscripts

For details of this companion volume see the listing of the full Mary Hardy series on page 550.

In the editorial sidenotes in the four-volume edition these excised entries are cited as Diary MS

Sources: the original manuscripts held privately in the Cozens-Hardy Collection

The diary of Mary Hardy

Ledger 1 · 28 Nov. 1773–6 Jan. 1778

Ledger 2 · 7 Jan. 1778–22 Sept. 1782

Ledger 3 · 23 Sept. 1782–20 July 1790

Ledger 4 · 21 July 1790–7 May 1800

Ledger 5 · 8 May 1800–21 Mar. 1809

The diary of Henry Raven

10 Oct. 1793–25 Oct. 1797

Mary Hardy divided her volumes randomly, leaving off on reaching the end of a ledger and starting a new one immediately. Henry Raven probably took a second ledger with him when his brewing pupillage with the Hardys ended in 1800

Introduction: the brewer's apprentice

by Margaret Bird

IN THE THIRD OF THE DIARY VOLUMES Mary Hardy (1733–1809) steps back a pace, her role being pared down in this editorial abridgment. She yields centre stage to her nephew Henry Raven (1777–?1825), who under his cousin William Hardy junior's supervision embarks on a possibly unique survival: a daily diary by an eighteenth-century brewery apprentice. The diarists lived in the one household, their texts dovetailing through the pages of *Diary 3*.

Henry was born to striving and uncertainty. At the time of his birth in August 1777 his father was mentally ill and undergoing specialist medical care in a Norwich physician's private house, as chronicled in *Diary 1*. Henry's mother Ann valiantly kept the farm going at Whissonsett Hall while looking after her clutch of small children; her eighth was born shortly before her husband's death in 1783 (Figures D3.3 and D3.4 in Appendix D3.A). The opening offered by his aunt's family helped to secure Henry's future from the time he came to live with them in 1792, and he stayed under training at Letheringsett until 1800.

Henry was well placed to record the labours of others, for he experienced them. The working day and the working year were extremely long, as will be demonstrated in the workforce chapter in Volume 2 of the commentary, *Mary Hardy and her World*. Young Henry had little time to himself. He was frequently excluded from the social life of his cousins William and Mary Ann—themselves by no means idle during these years of painstaking consolidation for the Hardys. The careful log of daily tasks constructed by Henry and published here in its 73,000-word entirety is his monument.

Apart from explanatory comments in the *Diary* sidenotes the analysis of the content and significance of the diaries will be reserved for the commentary. As well as fleshing out the terse entries in this set of four *Diary* volumes it will contain large numbers of tables and graphs.

above William Hardy, aged 66. While his brewing pupil Henry Raven was writing his diary and carrying out the strenuous work of floor maltster and apprentice the brewer's son was preparing to take over ownership. William had for years been joint manager with his father, and sole head brewer.

The brewery mortgage was paid off in Sept. 1796. Brewery expansion had been effected in the 1780s; major land acquisition followed in 1800. Much of the Hardys' success rested on the annually hired men and the quality of their work—as logged by Henry in his four-year diary [*portrait by Immanuel 1798, detail: Cozens-Hardy Collection*]

The diarists

Aunt and nephew were born in the village of Whissonsett in central Norfolk. Mary Hardy lived all her life in her home county, but on the ending of his brewing pupillage with the family Henry Raven moved away and worked in London breweries. Nothing is known of their schooling, but in the manner of other members of the family, including Mary Hardy's daughter, they are likely to have been educated partly by their parents and partly in the nearby market town of Fakenham. Their writing style is plain, forthright and unpretentious, introducing us to the world of the small farmer and small manufacturer unadorned.

By keeping the record they illuminate the lives of the unrecorded: the annually hired farm servants who worked on the farm and in the maltings and brewery and journeyed up to 125 miles a week delivering the beer. Mary Hardy tells us of the spread of the Methodists, and of the gradual withering of her adherence to the Established Church. After experimenting with the Anglican Evangelicals she was at her death on 23 March 1809 a Wesleyan.[1]

Editorial method

This work has involved casting into printed form a very large number of entries, at times hastily scrawled, from two diaries. Some abridgment has been necessary. The list on page vi, opposite the start of this introduction, sets out the divisions of the *Diary* volumes and of the original manuscripts. Another list, at the end of *Diary 3* after the indexes, gives the structure of the commentary with its 39 constituent chapters.[2]

The *Diary* divisions and indexes

The periods covered by the four *Diary* volumes do not follow the random dating divisions of the six ledgers. The published work compresses these ledgers into four *Diary* divisions, the breaks reflecting significant events in the diarists' lives:

In 1781 the move to the small village of Letheringsett, in north Norfolk, when William Hardy moved from tenant farmer to freeholder and from manager to owner of a long-established maltings and brewery;

[1] *diarists* The commentary *Mary Hardy and her World 1773–1809* will describe the family background as well as covering these aspects and more. An outline family tree for the diarists, with the occupations of their close relatives, is given on p. xvi (fig. D3.1). Five other family trees, covering the extended Hardy and Raven families, appear in an appendix and are listed on p. vi.

Highlights from Mary Hardy's diary have been published in works by her great-great-grandson Basil Cozens-Hardy: B. Cozens-Hardy, ed., *Mary Hardy's Diary* (Norfolk Record Soc., vol. 37 (1968)), and his earlier work *The History of Letheringsett in the County of Norfolk* (Jarrold & Sons, Norwich, 1957)

[2] *the volumes* For clarity, and to avoid overlap, the following terms are used for the total of nine volumes forming the proposed Burnham Press edition of Mary Hardy's diary:

ledger An individual MS diary volume

Diary An individual volume of the published diary; cited as '*Diary 1*, *Diary 2*' etc

volume An individual volume of the commentary, when published; cited as '*World*, vol. 1' etc

book One of the nine parts into which the commentary *Mary Hardy and her World 1773–1809* will be divided, each containing a number of chapters; each volume has two to three books

In 1793 Mary Hardy's near-fatal illness when she was unable to write her diary for two months, her illness coinciding with the start of her nephew Henry's diary;

In 1797 William Hardy's retirement, when he handed over the business to their son; at the same time Henry Raven's surviving ledger ends.

Both Mary Hardy and Henry Raven inserted endnotes in their ledgers. These notes have been rearranged in the published edition to reflect the new breaks. The register of maidservants, maintained after Mary Hardy's death by other family members, is similarly reordered in the *Diary* volumes to relate to the period of each individual volume.[1]

Each *Diary* has its own editorial index.[2] Each reference in these indexes relates not to a page number but to the date of a diary entry, for two reasons. Firstly a diary entry offers a more precise location, so that the reader does not have to search the whole page. Secondly the index becomes a database in its own right. From the index alone we can observe certain frequencies, calculate seasonal fluctuations, or merely check an individual date.

When abridging (in *Diary 2*, *Diary 3* and *Diary 4*) no excision is made within an individual entry, thus maintaining the rhythm of the diarist's prose. Where entries are omitted the cuts are signalled by '. . .' at the end of the previous day's entry.[3]

1 *maidservants* The register of 90 maidservants is summarised as a table in *World*, vol. 1, app. 1.C

2 *index* In *Diary 3* each of Henry Raven's diary entries is transcribed under the same date as his aunt's so that they can be read together, but their entries are indexed separately

3 *excised extracts* Published separately: M. Bird, ed., *The Remaining Diary of Mary Hardy 1773–1809* (Burnham Press, Kingston upon Thames, 2013)

above The former Pitt Arms at Burnham Market, renamed *c.*1811 the Hoste Arms. Henry Raven and his aunt separately record the accident on 9 Dec. 1796 when the farm servant Thomas Baldwin broke his leg under the wagonwheel on his long journey home from a beer delivery here. His place in the workforce was kept open for him in the three months it took him to recover [*MB* · *2007*]

The technicalities of the transcription

The diaries have been transcribed on the principle that the text should resemble the original manuscript as closely as possible, even though the printed page might become tricky to read at first. The diarists' spelling and grammar yield valuable information, and have as a consequence been retained at the risk of slowing down a reader yet to become familiar with the writers' idiosyncracies. A document of this extraordinary length by a woman with probably only a basic formal education is a rarity, and the manuscripts of Mary Hardy (499,727 words long) and Henry Raven (73,159 words) have been approached with editorial humility. For the sake of clarity a few overrides have had to be applied, and this section goes into the technical details.

Both diarists' spelling is left unchanged. Spelling was not then standardised—although Mary Hardy's did settle into more modern forms over her 36-year span, as will be explained in the analytical study. Both often spell phonetically, their versions offering clues to their speech and distinctive Norfolk vowel sounds, as when Henry Raven writes 'planen dales' for planing deals (planing timber planks).[1] If the meaning is not obvious the modern spelling is inserted in square brackets on its first appearance, as with 'Harron [Herring]', 'savants [servants]'.

Where the word is not spelt in an orthodox manner but the meaning is clear, as in 'A Fast by Procklimation',[2] there is no editorial insertion of '[*sic*]' after the problematic word; otherwise every entry would be spattered with *sic*.

The diarists only rarely use commas, hyphens and full points. Each of their sentences tends to run into the next. In the interests of clarity the minimum of punctuation has been introduced. In such entries as 'Dawson's lad painting H Raven in brewhouse' and 'John Ramm trashing Thomas Boyce in garden', Henry Raven's omission of commas after 'painting' and 'trashing' (the latter meaning threshing as well as thrashing) might give the reader a mistaken impression.[3]

Occasionally Mary Hardy uses apostrophes, but when doing so she may place them where the modern reader would regard them as commas, eg preach,d; bath,d. In the transcription her apostrophes have been placed in the conventional position: preach'd; bath'd. If the diarist has not used an apostrophe none has been introduced into the transcription. If the diarist has left a space to show the possessive this is respected, eg at Mr Ellis s.

The two diarists' abbreviations and contractions are retained, as in 'B H' for brewhouse, 'do' or 'd^{o}' for ditto; both use the ampersand '&' for 'and'. A list of those used most frequently appears at the end of this section. However one of their favourite shorthand forms has been transcribed in full. The 'a' with a flourish at the tail of the letter to signify 'at' is transcribed as 'at'.

The diaries reflect the style of the period in which they were written, and every effort has been made to reproduce that style. Like his aunt, Henry Raven habitually

[1] *planing deals* 'Thomas Youngman's lad planen dales' (26 Jan. 1795)

[2] *proclamation* Mary Hardy's entry for 9 Mar. 1796. Henry writes 'savants' for servants 25 Dec. 1796

[3] *Dawson's lad etc* Henry Raven's entries for 1 Aug. 1797 and 10 Oct. 1794.
His entry for 9 Feb. 1796, 'Bransby dressing John Ramm in malthouse', refers to the thresher Joseph Bransby dressing corn [in the barn]; John Ramm was working as a maltster in the malthouse. An editorial full point is therefore inserted after 'dressing'. When on 25 Sept. 1794 Henry writes 'John Ramm trashing Gunton Thompson's corn', the verb means to thresh, and not to injure or destroy

below **16-year-old Henry Raven's use of superscripts, or superior letters. On 'Saturday 25th' Oct. 1794 he notes that Thomas Baldwin 'Bro^{t} home 1000 tiles'. 'Bro^{t}' is his standard contraction for 'brought'. His aunt, confusingly, employs it for both 'brought' and 'brother'**
[*Cozens-Hardy Collection*]

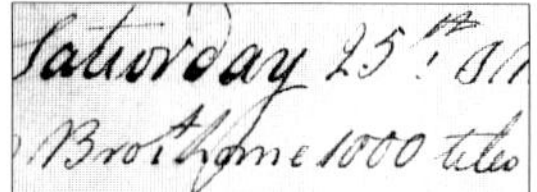

employs superior letters: 'Jno' for John, 'Capt' for Captain, 'for^{n}', 'after^{n}' for forenoon and afternoon, among others. These have been retained. Capital letters were then far more common at the beginning of words, and these too appear in the transcript as the diarists wrote them even though they will seem distracting to the modern reader.

Mary Hardy and Henry Raven favoured the eighteenth-century form known as the 'long s' which resembles a modern 'f' without the full crossbar: 'ſ', as in 'dreſsing graſs seeds' (illustrated for 22 April 1795). This has been modernised to 'dressing grass seeds'. William Hardy—though with rare exceptions not his wife, and never Henry—often uses the Middle English thorn in his entries, as in 'þ^{e}' for 'the'. This has been transcribed as 'y^{e}'.[1]

Mary Hardy occasionally writes the monetary denominations *£ s d* above or below the sums of money to which they refer, as though forming columns. To maintain a disciplined layout they are transcribed in prose style, as in 'bought 30 acres of grass at £95 0*s* 0*d*'.

If she records a sum of money in an abbreviated form it has for clarity been transcribed more fully: '4/' appears as 4/- or 4*s*, using the pre-decimal conventions for writing four shillings. Similarly the sum '7—15—5½' is transcribed £7 15*s* 5½*d*. Where Mary Hardy enters sums of money in the margins of her manuscript these have been placed within the text at the entries to which they refer. A conversion table from pre-decimal to decimal coinage appears at the end of this introduction.

One of her commonest forms of shorthand occurs in references to the time of day. She uses 'M' (morning) to denote the hours from midnight to noon and 'E' (evening) to denote the hours from noon to midnight. She probably adopted her husband's style, these conventions appearing in excise officers' diaries. 'Henry Raven went to Whissonsett M5' means that her nephew set off at 5 am; 'William came home E10' means that her son returned at 10 pm.[2]

The term 'morning' written without a figure can denote the period between the start of the men's working day and breakfast, roughly from 6 am to 9 am. The forenoon ('foornoon') is the period between breakfast and the midday meal (dinner), lasting from 9.30 am to noon or 1 pm.[3]

[1] *the thorn* By the end of the 18th century the thorn was starting to die out, and it does not usually appear in printed books and newspapers. Although written to resemble a 'y', the character was pronounced 'th' as in 'that', not 'y' as in 'yacht'

[2] *excise diaries* Long extracts from these are given in the minutes of the Excise Board held in the National Archives: Public Record Office (TNA: PRO). CUST 47/198–CUST 47/463 cover the years 1752–1809.

The laconic, staccato nature of the diaries of Mary Hardy and Henry Raven echoes the style of the excise diaries, as will be explained in *World*, vol. 1.

Yorkshire-born William Hardy served as an excise officer 1757–69, being in the service at the time of his marriage in 1765. In those 12 years he had six postings round England and twice suffered dismissal before resigning

[3] *forenoon* At first Henry Raven does not adopt the Hardys' usage, and he omits the forenoon. Only during the summer of 1794 does he adjust his log of the day's tasks to resemble William Hardy jnr's division of the first part of the day into morning and forenoon (a usage retained in today's Royal Navy). In the early months Henry's 'morning' extends to the dinner break, as noted against his entry for 24 Apr. 1794; his new style is illustrated under 22 Apr. 1795

Text in bold type in the transcription denotes editorial intrusion. This usually takes the form of a heading to give some structure to the text, as under 24 January 1794, when William Hardy copies out a newspaper report into his wife's diary: '**The anti-war amendment**'.[1]

above Whissonsett Parish Church. Here Mary Hardy was christened and married and Henry christened; here too their parents and others in the family lie buried.

The non-resident rectors left maintenance of the parish registers to a series of conscientious non-resident curates [*MB*·*2000*]

Calendar dates, ages and names

For ease of reference the dating of the diary entries is given in small capitals following a set editorial pattern as 'JANUARY 1, WEDNESDAY', although Mary Hardy and Henry Raven style the date in a more compressed form. Mary Hardy's marginal dating glosses are transcribed in italics after the date in her own spelling, as in '*Whit Sunday*', '*Xmas Day*'.

Following convention all dates before the alteration of the calendar in 1752, with the consequent loss of eleven days, are adjusted to the New Style by altering the year date but not the day. William Hardy was born 26 January 1731 (Old Style). This is given as 26 January 1732; not 26 January 1731/2, nor 6 February 1732.[2]

The religious feasts and legal quarterdays of Michaelmas and Lady Day were kept not on 29 September and 25 March but eleven days later in October and April. Leases expired principally at Old Michaelmas and Old Lady Day, while rents fell due on the four Old Quarterdays. A Christmas service was held in the parish church on 25 December, but Christmas celebrations such as the family's huge workforce dinners in the early nineteenth century could at times merge with Twelfth Night. The New and Old Style quarterdays forming the dominant business backdrop to the diaries are:

Michaelmas 29 September	*Old Michaelmas* 10 October
Christmas 25 December	*Old Christmas* 5 January
Lady Day 25 March	*Old Lady Day* 5 April
Midsummer 24 June	*Old Midsummer* 5 July

Dates of birth, baptism, marriage, death and burial given in the editor's marginal annotations and indexes are often taken from parish registers and the Norwich newspapers. Where those sources conflict with the diary and where the diarist can be trusted to be accurate they are

1 *The anti-war amendment* Entries such as these, interrupting the flow of the narrative, are classed as digressions from the daily record and are listed at the end of this section on p. xv

2 *the calendar* Although born on 12 Nov. 1733 Mary Hardy commemorated her birthday on 23 Nov., this adjustment obviously appealing to her sense of order and method (*Diary 1*: 23 Nov. 1777).

Her husband, father and brother adhered to the New Style dating (26 Jan. 1776, 26 Jan. 1777, 22 Dec. 1775)

overridden, as in the case of the false labour on 24 February 1794 of the day labourer's wife Betty Hall, Mary Hardy going on to record that the child was born and died on 12 March. But Ann Hall's baptism and burial appear in the Letheringsett register under 4 and 7 *January* 1794.[1]

Ages can cause difficulty. In theory if the diarist, the register, the memorial inscription or press report states that a woman died 'in her 60th year' she is likely to have died aged 59. However the practice at times seems to be that the 60th year is taken as meaning 60 years old. Some of the ages quoted in the marginal notes may thus be inaccurate by one year.

We are on shifting ground even with names. Some clergy still favoured Latin transliteration even though Latin had given way to English as the language of public record in 1733, the year of Mary Hardy's birth. In the registers we meet Anna for Ann, Maria for Mary, Susanna for Susan. We see from her small headstone that Mary Hardy's sister, who died young at Whissonsett in 1739, was named Rose Ann. The parish register records a version more suited to an operatic heroine: Rosanna.

In his father's lifetime Mary Hardy's younger son styled himself William Hardy junior, and this is the name adopted throughout. For clarity it is retained in this work even after his father's death, although from the moment that William Hardy died on 18 August 1811 his heir would have dropped the suffix 'junior'.[2]

The hundreds of names in the Acknowledgments in *Diary 1* attest to the size of the debt I owe. Some individuals have been at my side since the beginning in 1988. The project would have proved impossible without the greatly valued access granted by the custodians of the Cozens-Hardy Collection in Norfolk and London. Above all, I have delighted in the unflagging participation of my family.

From this wide circle I give especial thanks to four principal players: Beryl Cozens-Hardy, Jeremy Cozens-Hardy, David Mayes and Michael Sparkes. I am grateful to them for believing in this exciting mission through the years. For exciting it is. Beneath their unprepossessing exterior these documents are humming with life.

[1] *parish records* For the Halls see *Diary 3*, notes for 14 Oct. 1793, 24 Feb. 1794. Mary Hardy was a stickler for the record, and her long text is a gauge of the accuracy of registers in the areas she knew. We can find errors and omissions by the clergy, but on the whole they prove reliable when checked against her dates.

She also shows us that, in her parts of Norfolk, baptism followed very soon after birth, usually within a day or two; and it is this private baptism (not the public ceremony later in church) which is noted in most of the local registers.

Family historians, at least when researching rural Norfolk, can conclude that the lag between birth and christening is likely to be minimal in the period before the Evangelicals, with their severer notions about ceremonies, became dominant. These issues are explored in *World*, vol. 1, in the chapter on children, and in *World*, vol. 3, in the chapters on the parish clergy, preachers and flock

[2] *names* It is impossible to be certain over variant styles and spellings, but on the whole the version preferred by the holder or the family is adopted in this work: Myles, not Miles; Neale, not Neal; Phillis, not Phyllis. In the same spirit I have chosen to call the Hardys' son neither William Hardy the Younger nor, in the style of many modern business histories, William Hardy II

Contractions, conventions, conversions

The diarists' usage

Mary Hardy's family

MA, Miss H	Mary Ann Hardy
M[r] Hardy, M[r] H	William Hardy senior
W[m], WH	William Hardy junior

The Hardys' workforce

GT	William Gunton Thompson
HR	Henry Raven, brewing pupil
JR	John Ramm
JT	John Thompson, labourer, driver
RB	Robert Bye
TB	Thomas Baldwin
WL	William Lamb

The Hardys' family business

B C *or*	B Cart	brew cart [beer cart]
B H	B House	brewhouse
F C		Furze Closes [fields]
L C	L Cart	little cart
M C	M Cart	muck cart
M H	M[t] House	malthouse
M T		mash tun [in brewery]
W H	W[t] Hall	white hall [in brewery]

Brewing notation

X, XX	strong beer, of varying strengths [eg nog, porter, mild, sixpenny]
`/, `//	first parti-gyle, second parti-gyle [in brewing: see the glossary]

Currency symbols and conversion

£ s d = pounds, shillings, pence

pre-decimal		*decimal*	
one pound	= 20*s* =	100p	= £1.00
one shilling	= 12*d* =	5p	= £0.05
2*s* 6*d* =	2/6[d] =	12½p	= £0.125
5*s* 0*d* =	5/- =	25p	= £0.25
£1 1*s* =	one guinea =	105p	= £1.05

Editorial conventions

Parentheses, brackets and headings

(porter)	diarists' text in their own parentheses
[ ]	diarists have left text blank
[.....]	MS illegible
...	editor's excision from MS
[Briningham]	editor's explanation or correction
«cart»	editor's conjecture, where text omitted in the MS
{all}	superfluous words: usually the diarists' repetitions
[[3 Inserted text]]	text entered in the MS by others, an editorial note identifying the hand
Display type **Bold type**	editorial heading, subhead

Biographical abbreviations

b./d.	born / died
bapt.	baptised
bur.	buried
educ.	educated
marr.	married
matric.	matriculated [at university]

Sources and citations

Alum. Cantab.	*Alumni Cantabrigienses*
Alum. Oxon.	*Alumni Oxonienses*
Diary	Another volume in this edition, eg *Diary 4*
Diary MS	*The Remaining Diary of Mary Hardy*
Norw. Merc.	*Norwich Mercury*
NRO	Norfolk Record Office
TNA: PRO	The National Archives: Public Record Office
Univ. Brit. Dir.	*Universal British Directory*
World	*Mary Hardy and her World*

Digressions from the daily record

The middle years at Letheringsett 1793–1797

From the newspaper	The anti-war amendment 1794	41
From the newspaper	Wartime taxation and an accident 1794	44
Mary Hardy's visit to Whissonsett	15–23 February 1795	148
Mary Hardy's visit to Whissonsett	19–21 May 1795	173
Mary Hardy's visit to Whissonsett	17–22 August 1795	199
Mary Hardy's visit to Whissonsett	4–9 January 1796	240
Mary Hardy's visit to Whissonsett	24–28 May 1796	274
Mary Hardy's visit to Whissonsett	2–7 November 1796	313
Mary Hardy's visit to Whissonsett	13–18 March 1797	346
Mary Hardy's visit to Whissonsett	17–22 July 1797, and Norfolk v. All England at cricket	378

left Ledger 4 of Mary Hardy's diary, covering the period 21 July 1790 to 7 May 1800. Her husband has inscribed it on the vellum cover 'Dairy N° 4, 1790': his was the most elegant writing in the family.

As with Henry Raven's diary, Mary Hardy's huge ledgers are strongly bound. This measures 15⅝ inches by 6½ by 1⅝ thick (403 mm x 167 x 48), and weighs 4 lb 5 oz (1·95 kg) [*Cozens-Hardy Collection*]

FIGURE D3.1

The Hardys and the Ravens

The diarists Mary Hardy (writing 1773–1809) and Henry Raven (writing 1793–97) are shown in capitals in italic type. Mary Hardy's husband and three children all made entries in her diary and are also shown in italic

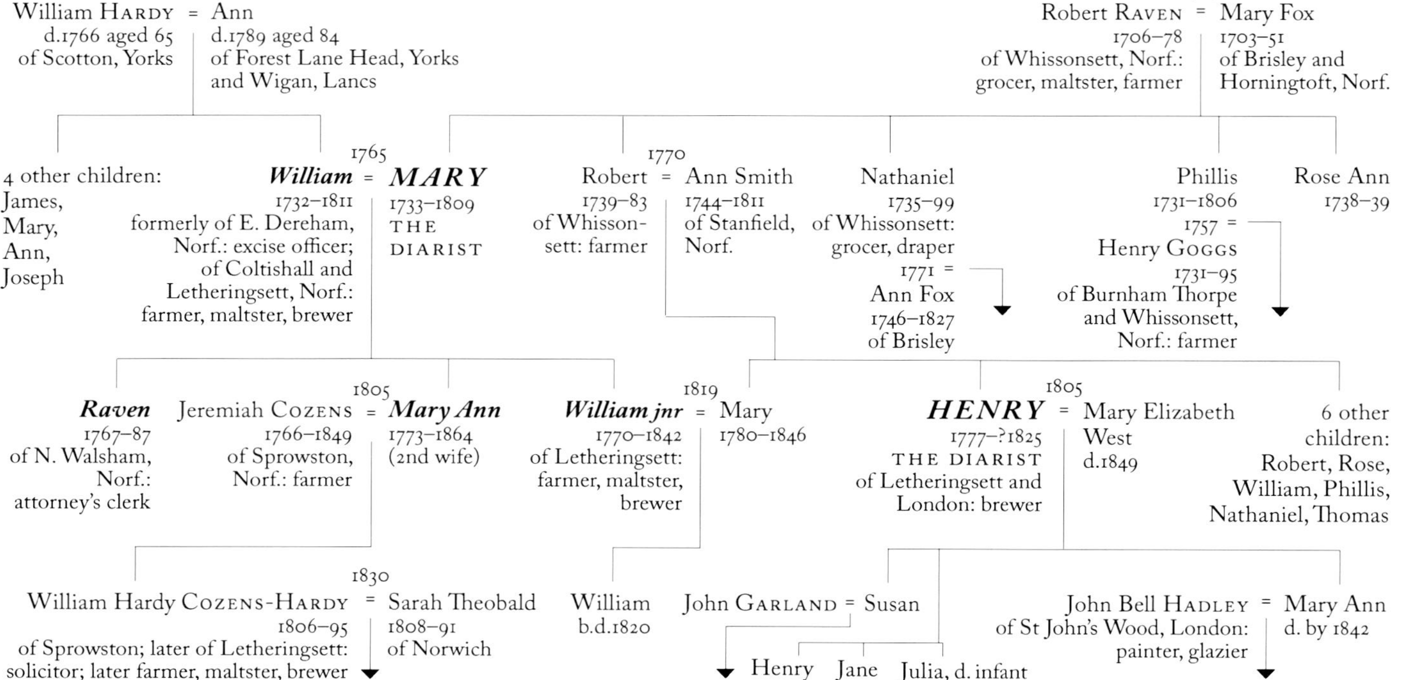

MB13 20
HARDY
RAVEN
William HARDY = Ann
d.1766 aged 65
of Scotton, Yorks
d.1789 aged 84
of Forest Lane Head, Yorks and Wigan, Lancs
1729
Robert RAVEN = Mary Fox
1706–78
of Whissonsett, Norf.: grocer, maltster, farmer
1703–51
of Brisley and Horningtoft, Norf.
4 other children: James, Mary, Ann, Joseph
1765
William = MARY
1732–1811
formerly of E. Dereham, Norf.: excise officer; of Coltishall and Letheringsett, Norf.: farmer, maltster, brewer
1733–1809
THE DIARIST
1770
Robert = Ann Smith
1739–83
of Whissonsett: farmer
1744–1811
of Stanfield, Norf.
Nathaniel
1735–99
of Whissonsett: grocer, draper
1771 =
Ann Fox
1746–1827
of Brisley
Phillis
1731–1806
1757 =
Henry GOGGS
1731–95
of Burnham Thorpe and Whissonsett, Norf.: farmer
Rose Ann
1738–39
Raven
1767–87
of N. Walsham, Norf.: attorney's clerk
1805
Jeremiah COZENS = Mary Ann
1766–1849
of Sprowston, Norf.: farmer
1773–1864
(2nd wife)
1819
William jnr = Mary
1770–1842
of Letheringsett: farmer, maltster, brewer
1780–1846
1805
HENRY = Mary Elizabeth West
1777–?1825
THE DIARIST
of Letheringsett and London: brewer
d.1849
6 other children: Robert, Rose, William, Phillis, Nathaniel, Thomas
1830
William Hardy COZENS-HARDY = Sarah Theobald
1806–95
of Sprowston; later of Letheringsett: solicitor; later farmer, maltster, brewer
1808–91
of Norwich
William
b.d.1820
John GARLAND = Susan
Henry
Jane
Julia, d. infant
John Bell HADLEY = Mary Ann
of St John's Wood, London: painter, glazier
d. by 1842

The Diary of Mary Hardy

Diary 3 · 16 August 1793–26 October 1797
The middle Letheringsett years (abridged text)

with

The Diary of Henry Raven

10 October 1793–25 October 1797 (full text)

Mary Hardy's manuscript ledger 4 (*cont.*)

21 July 1790–7 May 1800

A FAMILY REGISTER [1]

WILLIAM,[2] Son of William Hardy & Ann his Wife, was Born January 26 1732 at Scotton in Yorkshire and Married Mary,[3] youngest daughter of Robt Raven & Mary his Wife of Whissingsett [Whissonsett] in Norfolk, Farmer, December 22 1765, she was Born November 12 1733

RAVEN,[4] Son of the aforesaid William Hardy and Mary his Wife, was Born November 9 1967 at East Dereham in Norfk & Baptised at the same place

WILLIAM,[5] Second Son of the above Willm & Mary Hardy, was Born April 1 1770 at Litcham in Norfolk & Baptised there

MARY ANN,[6] Daughter of the above Willm & Mary Hardy, was Born Novr 3 1773 at Coltishall in Norfolk & Baptised there

---

HENRY RAVEN [*from Mary Hardy's diary, 6 Sept. 1777*]

Recd a Letter from Whissensett, Sister [Sister-in-law] at the Hall brought to Bed with a Boy last Sunday [31 August], Christend on Monday by the name of HENRY

[1] *register* At the end of ledger 1 of Mary Hardy's MS diary, in her hand, following her entry for 6 Jan. 1778; here repeated. See also the family tree on the facing page

[2] *William Hardy* He died at Sprowston, his daughter's home near Norwich, on 18 Aug. 1811 and was buried in his home village at Letheringsett, Norfolk, 22 Aug.

[3] *Mary* The diarist. She died at Letheringsett on 23 Mar. 1809 and was buried there 29 Mar.

[4] *Raven* Articled in 1783 as an attorney's clerk at N. Walsham, Norfolk, he died of tuberculosis at Letheringsett on 12 Feb. 1787 and was buried there 16 Feb.

[5] *William* He followed his father into the family business, greatly expanding it after taking over in 1797. He married his cousin Mary Raven at Letheringsett on 17 Nov. 1819, died there 22 June 1842 and was buried 27 June

[6] *Mary Ann* She married Jeremiah Cozens at Letheringsett 12 Nov. 1805, died in Norwich 28 Oct. 1864 and was buried there 2 Nov.

right A page from Henry Raven's diary for 20–23 June 1796. The two cousins make the entries: Henry for the first day, then William Hardy jnr for the next three while Henry takes a short holiday at his Whissonsett home. William notes 21 June that 'HR rode to Whissonsett Morning.'

In Oct. 1793 William, aged 23, had started off the diary for 16-year-old Henry, who used William's entries as his model. When Henry took breaks at home at Christmas and midsummer William maintained the record for him.

Like the other diarists William uses the 'long s', as in Whiſsonsett, but different contractions are adopted. Here Henry gives 'Cha^{n}' for chaldrons (of coal and cinders); William gives 'Ch'. On 20 June the second parti-gyle of beer (`//) is cleansed (the yeast head being removed and the beer run into casks, ending primary fermentation); the strong beer (X) is cleansed next day in the cool of the morning before breakfast.

The style is largely the same. Both chart the men's movements and tasks, and their own. William calls at the military camp at Weybourne on 21 June, and the next day the beer cart supplies the anti-invasion forces ranged on the coast [*Cozens-Hardy Collection*]

facing page The Letheringsett brewery, and Henry's domain: a detail from an amendment of the late 1930s to a parish plan of 1935. In Apr. 1936 the brewhouse had been destroyed by fire; the hatched malthouse and malt-kilns (to the right) and the tun room and stables (to the left) survived. The shaded area shows a proposed widening of the main road, the Council taking the opportunity of the ruined brewery to improve a dangerous bend.

The waterwheel of 1784, in the underground tunnel built by William Hardy, is labelled 'turbine'. This tunnel carried an offshoot of the River Glaven which he had diverted under the malthouse from a sluice. The gate to Letheringsett Hall, the diarists' old home, is shown opposite [*Cozens-Hardy Collection*]

1793

Our men emptied the cask called Nectar de Vie

MARY HARDY, 15 NOV. 1793

R. Bye, Thomas Baldwin cleaning home cask

HENRY RAVEN, 15 NOV. 1793

[LETHERINGSETT]

AUGUST 16, FRIDAY

Mary Hardy [1] A Showry day. Mr Hardy,[2] Wm,[3] MA,[4] Miss Simonds[5] & P Raven[6] drank tea at Mr Forsters.[7] I poorly, could not go.

⟦ [8] From this time to 17 Oct, a period of Sixty two Days, the Writer of this Book was Afflicted with a Most severe Illness, so Much so that no one had the least Hopes of Her Recovery. ⟧

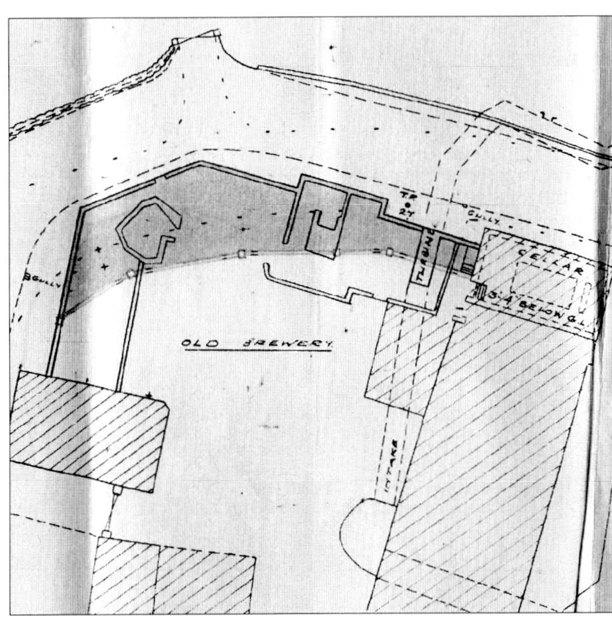
OLD BREWERY
CELLAR

[1] *Mary Hardy* Integrated with this abridgment of the diary of Mary Hardy [*MH*], continued from *Diary 2*, is a full transcription of the diary of her nephew Henry Raven [*HR*]. It was kept at Letheringsett under the initial guidance of her son William Hardy jnr [*WHj*].

Mary Hardy's diary had broken off after her entry for 16 Aug. 1793 when she described herself as poorly, and did not resume until 17 Oct. 1793. A week earlier William had begun Henry's record in a separate ledger

[2] *Mr Hardy* Mary Hardy's husband William, the 'Mr H' of Henry Raven's MS

[3] *William* Mary Hardy's son; 'WH' in Henry's MS

[4] *Mary Ann* Mary Hardy's daughter; 'Miss H' in Henry's MS

[5] *Miss Symonds* Phillis (d.1805 aged 26), only daughter of the Gt Yarmouth grocer and merchant Jonathan Symonds (see note for 18 May 1794). She was staying with the Hardys at the time her hostess was taken ill. She married Gt Yarmouth 28 Nov. 1797 the attorney Edmund Preston

[6] *P. Raven* Henry's sister Phillis (bapt. Whissonsett 12 Jan. 1779, d. 20 May 1844): see notes for 6 June 1794 and 4 Aug. 1797

[7] *Forster* Thomas, a farmer: see note for 6 Oct. 1796

[8] In William Hardy's hand

Henry Raven's manuscript ledger

10 October 1793–25 October 1797

OCTOBER 10, THURSDAY

William Hardy jnr [[[1] Robt Bye at home all day,[2] Luke Bassham mending harness.[3] W Platton went to Runton. Jno Ram [4] & R Barton in Brewhouse,[5] put the Cleanse of Beer into Cask.[6] Mr H at home forenoon, at Clay [Cley] afternoon. T Atwood came afternoon [7] & Order'd 3 Nog & 1 `//.[8]

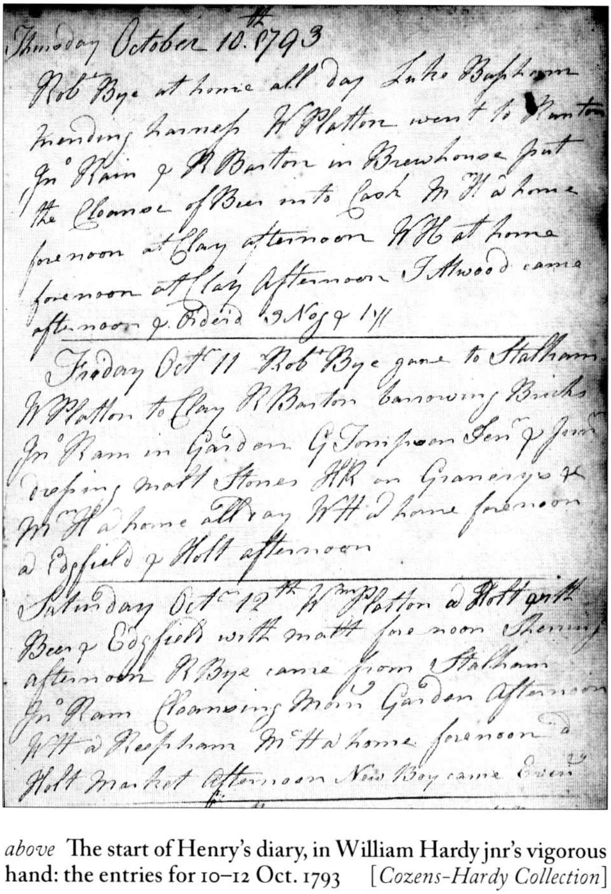

above **The start of Henry's diary, in William Hardy jnr's vigorous hand: the entries for 10–12 Oct. 1793** [*Cozens-Hardy Collection*]

[1] In William Hardy jnr's hand, Henry Raven not taking over until 18 Oct.

[2] *Bye* The Hardys' farm servant, brewer and drayman; his wife Mary had died 11 July 1790 after a year of marriage. He was dismissed 24 Dec. 1795

[3] *Basham* Luke (b. 3 July 1763, bapt. Fakenham 7 July); Holt harnessmaker and collarmaker, and briefly innkeeper of the Black Boys at Holt 1792. He married Holt 13 Sept. 1791 Philippa Spencer and died 10 years later aged 38 (see the illustration overleaf)

[4] *Ramm* John (bur. Letheringsett 20 Dec. 1813 aged 86), head maltster and later thresher; his wife Abigail also worked for the Hardys

[5] *Barton* He was about to be laid off at the end of the hiring year, 10 Oct. being Old Michaelmas Day

[6] *cleanse of beer* Cleansing, now archaic as a term, ended primary fermentation; secondary fermentation continued in the cask

[7] *Atwood* Thomas (bur. Holt 6 May 1805 aged 78), innkeeper from 1784 of the Dolphin on Fish Hill, Holt: see note for 1 Apr. 1794

[8] *nog* Strong beer; Norfolk Nog was a Hardy speciality. The order for four barrels was delivered on 12 Oct. A barrel in London and Norfolk then held 36 gallons (163·7 litres), as it does today nationally. `// was a chalk mark on the vessel for the second, weaker brew

above The grounds of Whissonsett Hall, the home which Henry left at the age of 14 to live with his aunt at Letheringsett. The mediaeval moat, bridged on the approach to the house, the great flint barn built by his grandfather Robert Raven in 1773, and the long drive leading north to the village centre remain features he would recognise; the house was rebuilt in the mid-19th century.

Henry's brother William (b.1776) had left the Hardys in 1791 after only two and a half months as a brewing pupil [*MB · 1998*]

OCTOBER 11, FRIDAY

WHj Rob[t] Bye gone to Stalham,[1] W Platton to Clay.[2] R Barton barrowing Bricks, Jn[o] Ram in Garden. G Tompson Sen[r] & Jun[r] dressing malt Stones,[3] HR on Granerys [granaries] &c.[4] M[r] H at home all day, WH at home forenoon,[5] at Edgfield & Holt afternoon.

[1] *Stalham* Delivering beer to the Maid's Head, run by Robert Staff—a two-day return journey of 50 miles. This was the most distant of the Hardys' tied houses (rear endpaper). William Hardy had taken the house with him from Coltishall

[2] *Cley* The King's Head was the only house supplied by the Hardys at the port and was tied probably continuously from 1792 until 1896

[3] *Thompson* William Gunton (known as Gunton or Gun Thompson), the Hardys' miller 1792–98 for their water-powered corn-mill and water-powered malt-mill in the brewery; also his son Gunton Chapman Thompson. Dressing stones by recutting the grooves was a skilled millwright's job. See notes for 25 July, 28 July 1794, 25 July 1795 and 16 Aug. 1796

[4] *HR* Henry Raven was still on trial before his formal indenture as the brewing pupil, or brewery apprentice, on 19 July 1794.

Henry left 27 Dec. 1800, having lived and worked at Letheringsett since 1792. After William Raven's problems the Hardys took pains to avoid a second failure (*Diary 2*)

[5] *at home* Both William and Henry use the phrase to mean that they or William Hardy snr were across the road from the maltings and brewery, in the area of the house and garden. Mary Hardy's usage includes the working areas as well

above The Fishing Boat, on the Norfolk coast at E. Runton, received the first beer delivery of the new diary on 10 Oct. Unlike most of the Hardys' outlets the Fishing Boat enjoyed some continuity, Robert Hill being innkeeper from before 1789 until after 1800. The Hardys' houses and innkeepers, supplied with and without tie (as charted on the rear endpaper), are listed in the gazetteer in *Mary Hardy and her World*, volume 2 [*MB · 1994*]

OCTOBER 12, SATURDAY

WHj Wm Platton at Holt with Beer & Edgfield with malt forenoon, Sherring^m^ afternoon.[1] R Bye came from Stalham. Jno Ram Cleansing Morng, Garden Afternoon. WH at Reepham. M^r^ H at home forenoon, at Holt Market Afternoon. New Boy came Even^g^.

OCTOBER 13, SUNDAY

WHj G Tompson drew off Beer in Morng,[2] R Bye loaded Cart for Brampton afternoon.[3] Mr Margetson, Holt, came with a friend to ask for Maid's head, [North] Walsham.[4] M^r^ H at home all day. WH & HR at Holt Church afternoon.

OCTOBER 14, MONDAY

WHj R Bye gone to Brampton. W Platton & Boy at harrow, Jno Ram in Brewhouse, G Tompson grinding Malt for brew. T Hall half day after Bricks.[5] M^r^ H at Thursford. WH at home all day, Bot [bought] Barley of [off] Webb & Blomfield at 15/-.[6] Williams of Weybourn came with Rent.[7] Mr Boswell here in forenoon.[8]

[1] *Sheringham* Delivering beer to the Crown, another tied house, with Samuel Sanderson as innkeeper

[2] *drew off beer* This task and loading the carts could be performed fairly discreetly behind the walls of the brewery, Sunday working being an offence

[3] *Brampton* The Queen's Head, a tied house, with Meshack Ives (d. 1 Jan. 1816 aged 64) as innkeeper

[4] *Maid's Head* On 28 June 1793 Nathaniel Berry had absconded owing rent to the Hardys, Thomas Scott later taking over—perhaps the friend referred to here

[5] *Hall* Thomas 'Captain' Hall (bur. Letheringsett 24 June 1808 aged 86), day labourer; he marr. 12 Sept. 1787 Elizabeth (Betty), daughter of the Hardys' former maltster at Coltishall and Letheringsett, William Frary. Hall's first wife, Mary Bircham (marr. Letheringsett 1741), was bur. there 22 May 1785, Mary Hardy noting her death 19 May aged 62 (Diary MS: 19 May 1785). See also note for 24 Feb. 1794

[6] *barley* Priced per coomb (half a quarter); at Norwich prices were 26*s* to 30*s* a quarter (13*s* to 15*s* a coomb) (*Norw. Merc.* 19 Oct. 1793)

[7] *Williams* He may have been paying rent for the Crown at Weybourne, the innkeeper Edward Hall then being in financial trouble: see note for 3 Jan. 1795

[8] *Boswell* Andrew, an Edgefield farmer (bur. there 18 Nov. 1815 aged 80)

OCTOBER 15, TUESDAY

WHj Bye hurt his leg coming home from Brampton & not able to do any thing. W Platton & Jn° Ram carting Quicks of [off] the Hill Close & Boy harrowing all day.[1] G Tompson dressing Wheat Stones. WH went to Brinton & Thornage afternoon.

OCTOBER 16, WEDNESDAY

WHj Jno Ram & Boy in Brewhouse. WH D° [ditto] Brewing, went to Holt in Eveng to Johnsons.[2] HR at Brinton in Morning with Horse. W Platton at the Black boys Holt forenoon,[3] half Ch^{n} lime [half a chaldron of lime from] Mr Forsters & Jobs afternoon.[4] M^{r} H at Clay Morn^{g}, at Holt Afternoon. Robt Bye not able to work.

OCTOBER 17, THURSDAY

WHj Jn° Ram at Cromer with head team.[5] W Platton, Capt Hall, G Tompson Junr carting Muck of the heap at Hill Close. G Tompson Cleansd `//, laid down Wheat Stones. HR at home. M^{r} H at Quarter sessions Holt all day, WH home forenoon. M^{r} & Miss Raven came morng, all went to Holt afternoon. R Bye no work.]]

were discharged.—It appears the dispute arose at the billiard table.

On Monday last as Mr. Basham, a collar-maker, at Holt, was returning home from a neighbouring village, perfectly sober, he fell from his horse, and was found lying in the road on Tuesday morning by some harvest men—he died on Thursday.

above The death on 10 Sept. 1801 of Luke Basham, the Holt harnessmaker used by William (entry for 10 Oct. 1793). The news report states pointedly that the 38-year-old tradesman was 'perfectly sober' at the time of his fall. His daughter Sarah, born six months later, lived two months. The early Norfolk directories show that Luke Basham's widow and children carried on the business for another half century, Philippa Basham dying in 1846 aged 84 and being buried, like her husband, at Holt [*Norwich Mercury, 12 Sept. 1801: Norfolk Heritage Centre, Norwich*]

[1] *quicks* Couch grass (*Agropyron repens*). Hill Close was one of the Furze Closes: land lying in Saxlingham opposite Bayfield Hall and farmed by the Hardys. See note for 12 Aug. 1794

[2] *Johnson* Revd William Tower (d. Holt 18 May 1799 aged 61/62, bur. there 28 May), of Holt, Curate of Twyford 1766, Rector of N. Barningham 1767–99, Rector of Beeston Regis 1772–99, and holder of other curacies

[3] *Black Boys* Adjoining the Shirehouse, it had been bought copyhold by William Hardy for his son Raven 22 Dec. 1783 for 100 guineas (NRO: ACC Cozens-Hardy 20/3/1973, Holt manor court book). The register shows that James Skiffins (son-in-law of the Dolphin's innkeeper Thomas Atwood) had taken over from Luke Basham (NRO: C/Sch 1/16). See also note for 1 Apr. 1794

[4] *lime* The Bayfield limekiln is shown on Faden's map of 1797 on rising ground on the east bank of the Glaven upstream of Bayfield Hall. Thomas Forster supplied lime worth £37 7*s* to John Soane for his building work at Gunthorpe Hall (Sir John Soane's Museum archives: O–XXV, Account book 1789–91, abstract of bills)

[5] *head team* Of horses. John Ramm had taken the wagon (not a one-horse cart) to deliver beer to the Cromer Hotel, the tied house run by Mrs Sanderson and formerly called the King's Arms: see also note for 13 Dec. 1793

[Mary Hardy resumes her entries after her long illness]

Mary Hardy [1] A Close foggy Day.[2] Mr Hardy walkd up to Holt after breakfst to the quarter Sessions, dind at Mr Moores,[3] came home even 9.[4] Brother Raven and Mary came to dinner, we all rid up to Holt afternoon, came home to tea [5] . . .

OCTOBER 18, FRIDAY

[Henry Raven takes over from William Hardy junior]

Henry Raven [6] Jno Ram pumping liquor in Steep Morning,[7] Briston with Beer afternoon.[8] Platton, Capt Hall, G Thompson Junr carting muck in Hill close morning, whent up with one load, braught home turnips Afternoon. HR, G Thompson Gathering appels. Mr H at home all day. WH at home Morning, Whissonsett afternoon. P Williams came to order beer.[9]

CLEY
Wiveton
Bridge
Wiveton Mill
Glanford Mill
Glanford
Summer House
Bayfield Hall
Bayfield
Brick Kiln
Hall
HOLT

[1] *Mary Hardy* After more than two months of silence she resumes the record begun in 1773. She may have been recovering from a stroke or heart attack

[2] *close* Cloudy; overcast

[3] *Moore* James (bur. Letheringsett 5 Aug. 1815 aged 52), Holt attorney. See also note for 3 Jan. 1794

[4] *even 9* 9 pm; 'morn 9' would be 9 am

[5] *Raven* Mary Hardy's brother Nathaniel Raven (b. 22 Dec. 1735, bapt. Whissonsett 1 Jan. 1736, d. Litcham 28 Jan. 1799, bur. Whissonsett 5 Feb.), of the grocer's shop at Whissonsett at what is now Church Farm, east of the church. With him was his daughter Mary (b.1772, bapt. Whissonsett 28 June 1773).

They left with William the following day. See also note for 6 Mar. 1794

[6] The entries for 18 Oct.–21 Nov. are by Henry Raven

[7] *pumping liquor in steep* Pumping water for malting into the 40-coomb cistern at the south end of the malthouse. Here the barley was soaked (steeped) at the start of the manufacturing process, this being the opening day of the 1793–94 malting season. Liquor is the trade term for water used in brewing

[8] *Briston* To the Three Horseshoes, bought by William Hardy in 1792 for £350 and let on a seven-year lease to Francis Longden (*Diary 2*: 6 June 1792)

[9] *Williams* Peter (bur. Thornage 28 Feb. 1801 aged

above The former Black Boys, in the neighbouring village of Thornage. It had been tied to William Hardy's predecessor as Letheringsett brewer, Henry Hagon (d.1780), but the tie was not resumed until William Hardy jnr bought the house copyhold in 1804 for £400 (*Diary 4*). On buying the maltings and brewery in Nov. 1780 William Hardy could not afford to keep all the tied houses built up by Henry Hagon, nor all his extensive farmland other than at Letheringsett and Saxlingham [*MB · 2001*]

facing page Detail from William Faden's map published in 1797 but surveyed 1790–94, showing Letheringsett at the junction of the Holt–Fakenham road with the Blakeney and Cley road. The parsonage (actually the Burrell family's own home) and brewery ('Brew Office') are shown, also what was then Letheringsett Hall (from *c*.1800 Hall Farm) north of the village centre. The Bayfield lime-kiln serving the London architect John Soane's workmen is marked (see 16 Oct. 1793). The hachures to the west identify the possible position of Hill Close in the Hardys' fields called the Furze Closes [*Faden's Map of Norfolk 1797: Larks Press 1989*]

75), innkeeper of the Black Boys at Thornage and the parish clerk. He married Thornage 16 Oct. 1746 Margaret Strutt (bur. Thornage 11 Mar. 1805 aged 76). They had 10 children over 22 years, the eldest, Margaret, being bapt. 26 Dec. 1746 when Mrs Williams was aged 16; the youngest, Joshua, was bapt. 8 Oct. 1768. Six died young

OCTOBER 19, SATURDAY

HR G Thompson Clensed. Jno Ram sowing wheat, Platton ploughing, Capt^t^ Hall spreading muck.[1] R Bye at Thornage with beer afternoon. HR, G Thompson Junr gathering appels. M^r^ H at home morning, Holt mar^t^ [market] afternoon.[2]

OCTOBER 20, SUNDAY

HR G Thompson, Platton car^d^ [carried] three Bar^s^ [barrels] to R^d^ Mays morning.[3] M^r^ H at home all day.

---

1 *muck* Animal manure

2 *market* Holt market was held on Saturdays. As with many other market towns in this arable county it was not only a pitched market for foodstuffs but a sample market, where farmers, maltsters and millers met in the afternoon and evening in public houses to negotiate sales and purchases of barley and wheat (*World*, vol. 3, chap. 7)

3 *Richard Mayes* (Bapt. Letheringsett 28 Mar. 1717, son of Richard and Susan, d. there 30 Jan. 1800); he was buried, according to the register, 4 Mar. 1800. His wife Mary (d. 8 Aug. 1790), née Guttridge, was buried at Fakenham aged 72 (*Diary 2*: 8 Aug., 11 Aug. 1790).

The men worked within sight of the rector and the church while flouting the law, but the beer delivery did not clash with the church service which that day was at 5 pm, as Mary Hardy was careful to note (Diary MS)

right Sheringham Park: the temple designed by Humphry Repton *c.*1811 —but not built until 1975— while he was working on the new house seen in the distance. This was built for Abbot and Charlotte Upcher, Cook Flower's successors at Sheringham. The Old Hall belonging to the Flowers lay on the slope to the right.

William and Mary Ann were on friendly terms with the Flowers (22 Oct.), who had married at Cromer 25 Aug. 1791, the 19-year-old bride Sarah Ditchell Sibbs being the daughter of the vicar. Cook Flower shared William Hardy jnr's passion for tree planting, both establishing shelter belts on hilltops [*MB · 1996*]

OCTOBER 21, MONDAY

HR W Platton, Jn° Ram ploughing, Capt Hall spreading muck half day. R Bye at Gunthorp afternoon,[1] G Thompson Grinding Malt for brew. T Atwood came foornon [forenoon] to order beer. M^{r} H at home all day. WH at home morning, road [rode] out afternoon, Holt Assembly Evining.

MH A Close day. W^{m} went to Clay afternoon to look at some repairs doing there, came home to tea, went to Assembly at Holt eveng 8, came home morn 3. Mr Hardy & I rid out afternoon round by Kelling & Salthouse Heath. Mr Newstead came aftern, paid £30.[2]

OCTOBER 22, TUESDAY

HR Platton at Sheringham morning, black boys Holt afternoon. Jn° Ram ploughing morning, steep [steeping] afternoon. Capt Hall spreading muck half day. M^{r} H {at} Out all day, WH at home all day. R Bye no work.

[1] *Gunthorpe* To the Cross Keys, bought in 1792 by William Hardy for £300 (*Diary 2*: 16 Aug. 1792). Robert Pleasance was the innkeeper

[2] *Newstead* Robert, innkeeper of the Dun Cow at Salthouse, a tied house (*Diary 2*: 20 May 1786, 14 Nov. 1788); he was presumably paying for rent and beer that day. The two entries for 21 Oct. illustrate the complementary nature of the diaries. Henry was not aware of what his uncle was doing that day and often neglects the Hall side; his aunt under-reports the farm and brewery

MH A Close day. W^m^ breakfstd & dind at Mr Burrells.[1] M^r^ & Mrs Flower of Sheringham,[2] M^r^ and Mrs Burrell here all the foornoon. M^r^ & M^rs^, Matt & M Davy,[3] M^r^

below Detail of a less polished 1838 version of Josiah Manning's map of Letheringsett, surveyed in 1834; the display version is the frontispiece to the year 1796 in this volume. The River Glaven flows north-west through the village centre towards Bayfield.

South-east of the cross-hatched church [151] stands the Hardys' house [1], by then in extensive grounds. In Henry's time at Letheringsett the main road had run west–east right past the windows of the south front, the great southern bend being created by William in 1808. The riverside malthouse is the long thin building; the malt-mill and brewhouse against the road form the angle of the brewery yard [75], with a narrow opening to the yard south of the tun room. The King's Head [76], moved here in 1808, lies east of the Brewhouse Pightle [74]. The rector's former house, barn and grounds [98], west of the basin containing the brewing liquor [73], are by the road junction to the west [*James Oxley-Brennan Collection*]

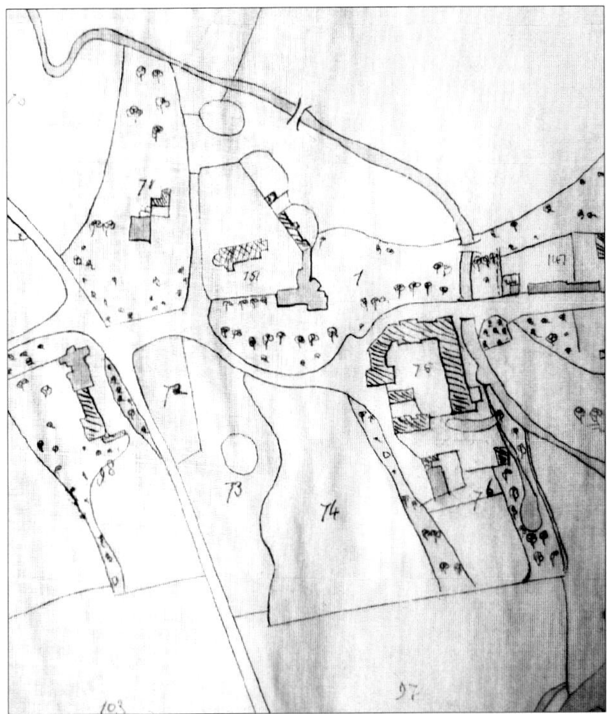
71
151
1
76
72
73
74

[1] *Burrell* Revd John (b. and bapt. Letheringsett 20 Sept. 1761, bur. there 18 Nov. 1825); he had succeeded his father, also John, as rector on the latter's death in 1786.

He lived with his wife Elizabeth Anna Maria (d. 16 Nov. 1795, bur. Letheringsett 21 Nov.), née Garrett, at the house later called The Lodge, this being the rector's own house as the parish's small parsonage had long been demolished. He served also as Curate of Hunworth with Stody and later of Langham and Wiveton

[2] *Flower* Cook (d. W. Beckham, bur. there 29 May 1842 aged 77). His wife Sarah (b. and bapt. Cromer 4 Dec. 1772) died at St Andrew's, Norwich, 7 June 1819 (*Norw. Merc.* 12 June) and was bur. W. Beckham; her father Revd Richard Sibbs held the livings of Cromer and Sheringham.

After selling their Sheringham estate the couple lived for a time at Southrepps. See also notes for 2 Dec. 1795 and 14 Oct. 1796

[3] *Davy* John (d. 2 Dec. 1805 aged 69/70, bur. 6 Dec.), Holt grocer and draper. He marr. Holt 6 Nov. 1774 his second wife Mary (d. 17 Feb. 1820 aged 80, bur. 24 Feb.), sister to the Cawston grocer Matthew Starling. With them on 22 Oct. were two children: Matthew, and Mary (bur. Holt 29 July 1820 aged 43). The widowed Mrs Davy ran the shop, handing over to Matthew Davy in 1808, but he was soon bankrupted (*Norw. Merc.* 8 Nov. 1810)

& M^rs^ & Miss Baker [1] & Mr Wade drank tea here.[2] Mr Hardy went with Mr Moore to Blakeney, dind & drank tea at Mr Chaplins & recond [reckoned],[3] came home even past 10 . . .

OCTOBER 23, WEDNESDAY

HR Jno Ram & Boy in Brewhouse, WH D^o^ Brewing. Platton to Fakenham & Syderstone with beer,[4] Capt Hall ploughing in hill close. M^r^ H at home all day. R Bye no work.

OCTOBER 24, THURSDAY

HR W Platton to Wells.[5] G Thompson Clensed `//. Jno Ram empty«ing» the steep morning, on Grannerys afternoon. M^r^, M^rs^ H at Hildolwestone all day, WH at D^o^ [ditto].[6] R Bye no work.

below The Maid's Head at Hindolveston: part of the valuation plan by Messrs Spelman of Norwich following the death of Mary Hardy's grandson William Hardy Cozens-Hardy in Apr. 1895, his executors immediately putting the maltings, brewery and tied houses up for sale. This house was valued at £550 freehold and was sold with the whole to Morgans Brewery of Norwich in Mar. 1896. The new owners speedily ended beer production at Letheringsett [*Cozens-Hardy Collection*]

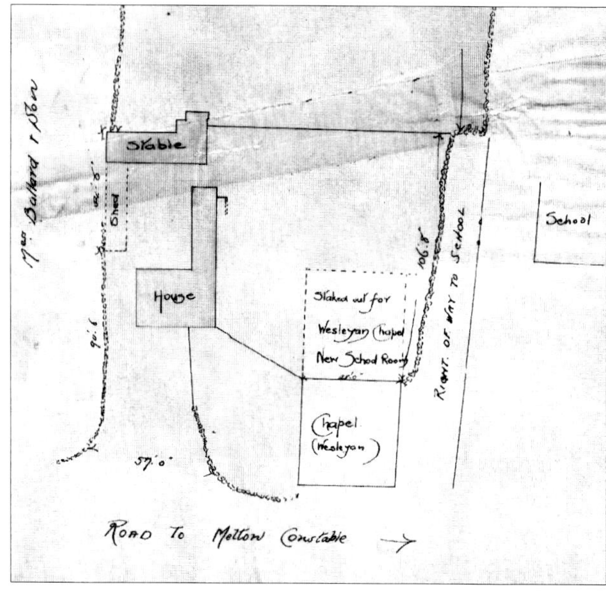
Stable
Shed
House
School
Staked out for
Wesleyan Chapel
New School Room
Chapel
(Wesleyan)
Right of way to School
Road to Melton Constable

[1] *Baker* John (b. 28 Aug. 1727, d. Holt 30 June 1804), ironmonger. Formerly of Gt Yarmouth and Wells, he married (1) 13 Sept. 1757 Ellen Minns (d. 1 Nov. 1759); (2) Holt 28 Sept. 1760 Priscilla Custance (b. 21 Nov. 1734, d. Holt 26 Dec. 1810, bur. 30 Dec.) (NRO: ACC Cozens-Hardy 4/1/80, Baker family tree by M. Brenda Baker, 20 Apr. 1975). For John Baker's only daughter Margaret see note for 18 Jan. 1794

[2] *Wade* John, of Holt Windmill—then newly built but soon to burn down: see notes for 8 May 1794, 11 Sept. 1795 and 7 Mar. 1796

[3] *Chaplin* Henry (d. 18 May 1794), of Cley and Blakeney, merchant, from whom William Hardy had hired the Cromer Hotel/King's Arms since 1781 (*Diary 2*)

[4] *Fakenham and Syderstone* Delivering to the Bell at Fakenham, run until his death in 1802 by John Gathercole, and the Buck at Syderstone, run until 1798 by the widowed Jane Hazel.

William Hardy jnr had bought both houses copyhold from Booty's Binham brewery in 1792 (*Diary 2*)

[5] *Wells* To the Fighting Cocks at the top of Staithe Street, bought in 1789 for £250 (*Diary 2*). John Walden was innkeeper, handing over on 18 Oct. 1796 to William Silence

[6] *Hindolveston* The family may have dined at the tied house, the Maid's Head (illustrated), then kept by the widowed Mrs Prior (NRO: C/Sch 1/16)

above The former Maid's Head at Hindolveston. The diarists could not hit on a spelling of the village which satisfied them and it appears in a variety of guises, as on 24 Oct. On the 1895 plan (illustrated opposite) the Methodist chapel next door, with its proposed schoolroom to the rear, is shown against the main street. The public house is set well back, as seen above, with a large front yard and with the shed and stables behind the house [*MB* · *2002*]

MH A very fine day. Mr Hardy, I & W^m^ rid to Hildonveston Morn 9, they measured the Timber, we dind there & came home even pst 5. Mr Bird of Thornage & Mr Williams drank tea here & confirmd the bargain for Albro [Aldborough] publick House.[1] M^r^ T Temple drank tea & Supt here.[2]

OCTOBER 25, FRIDAY

HR W Platton to Hindonvestone with beer and Foulsham for Barrels. Jno Ram dressing cumbs morning,[3] on Granaries afternoon. Capt Hall half a day. M^r^ H {at} out all day. WH out morning, home afternoon. Bye no work.

MH A Close drisley day. Mr Hardy went to Walsingham to a Sale of A Publick House at Dalling, Mr Bidden of Saxlingham bought them [?], came home eve 11.[4]

[1] *bargain* Deal, or agreement; the attorney and magistrate John Gay, of Aldborough, and Mr Bird and William Williams, of Thornage, appear to have acted as agents. William Hardy paid Mr Bird 300 guineas (£315) for the Black Boys 8 Apr. 1794, although beer deliveries did not begin until 24 Nov. 1795. Thomas Chamberlin served as innkeeper until his goods were seized in lieu of rent by William Hardy jnr and Mr Williams 23 Feb. 1798 (*Diary 4*)

[2] *Temple* Thomas, a Thornage farmer

[3] *culms* Also cumbs/coombs, defined as 'the little sprouts and roots of malted barley, withered, turned dry and separated by the screen' (R. Forby, *The Vocabulary of East Anglia* (London, 1830), vol. 2, p. 206). The shoots, rich in nitrogen, were used in poultry- and cattle-feed as a by-product of malting, and also as fertiliser (*Diary 3*: 10 Jan. 1794, 4 Apr. 1796).

Dressing, as in dressing flour, removed impurities and foreign bodies

[4] *Dalling* Field Dalling. The Heart or Hart, later the Jolly Farmers, was for sale that day at the Black Lion, Lt Walsingham 'with the orchard adjoining, in the occupation of James Reeve, at the rent of £5 15*s* 6*d*' (*Norw. Merc.* 12 Oct. 1793). John Bidden was a Saxlingham farmer. William Coe, a Field Dalling farmer, had bought the house by 1797, and let it to the Hardys: see note for 9 May 1797

right Part of the west wall of Letheringsett's 18th-century malthouse, facing the brewery yard. The two maltsters were at opposite ends of their working lives, Ramm then being 66 and Henry aged 16. Both must have been physically robust to take the strain of the punishing job (29 Oct. 1793).

This fine flint-and-brick building is of six bays, plus the lean-to for the steep; with the kilns it measures in total 148 feet by 36 (45 by 11 metres) [*MB · 2001*]

OCTOBER 26, SATURDAY

HR W Platton to Overstrand.[1] G Thompson Clensed morning, Jn° Ram on granaries. Mr H at home morning, Holt market afternoon. WH «at» N° Walsham.

MH A Cold Windy day. Wm sett of for N Walsham morng past 9 to see after the Maids Head, Berry having shut it up & run away, he came home eveng 8. Mr Hardy went to Markt, came home even 7 . . .

OCTOBER 28, MONDAY [2]

HR W Platton to Kettlestone with beer,[3] R Bye harrowing in hill close. G Thompson Grinding malt for brew, Jn° Ram in malt house. Mr, Mrs H at Whissonsett, WH at home all day.

OCTOBER 29, TUESDAY

HR Thos Balden [Baldwin] to Corpusta.[4] R Bye to Clay, brout home Chald Coles [chaldron of coals]. W Platton, Thos Hall in the yards all day. Mr H {at} not home, WH at home morning, Clay afternoon. Jn° Ram, H Raven in malt house all day.

---

1 *Overstrand* Delivering to the White Horse, kept by Thomas Thirst/Thurst

2 *Monday* Sundays at first went unrecorded by Henry, perhaps because he did not wish to provide evidence of Sunday working. He altered his practice 16 Feb. 1794

3 *Kettlestone* To the Plough, run by Matthew Pearce, which George Chad of Thursford Hall had bought from William Hardy in 1791 for £80 (*Diary 2*: 28 Apr. 1791)

4 *Corpusty* Henry Raven's spelling suggests the way it was pronounced locally. On 16 Jan. 1784 William Hardy had bought the Horsehoes leasehold from William Wiggett Bulwer (1730–93), of Heydon Hall, and had sublet it to the innkeeper Robert Wagstaff (*Diary 2*).

It was one of the four houses transferred from Coltishall (rear endpaper)

OCTOBER 30, WEDNESDAY

HR Platton, Jno Ram, Boy in Brewhouse. T Balden «at» Edgefield morning,[1] Holt afternoon to Bullin with beer, bro^t [brought] home nine coomb barley.[2] R Bye «at» hinderingham,[3] W^m H at Brewing. G Thompson, Platton rung pigs afternoon.[4]

OCTOBER 31, THURSDAY

HR T Balden «at» Walsham, W Platton ploughing in Bells acre.[5] G Thompson Clensed `//, R Bye in brewhouse all day. W Tinker and man at work all day.[6] Jno Ram and HR in malt house, WH at home all day. Capt Hall all day at work.

above The south wall of the 18th-century tun room, as reclad by William Hardy jnr in 1814. The flints, as good insulators, kept the casks at an even temperature. The tun room or vat house led from the brewery's 'white hall' (2 Nov. 1793) [*MB · 2008*]

[1] *Edgefield* Delivering to the Three Pigs, kept by James Dyball until 1804 or later

[2] *Bulling* William (bur. Holt 14 Apr. 1805 aged 51), of the Bull at Holt, bought 1804 by William Hardy for £205 (*Diary 4*). By Sept. 1794 Joseph Baker had taken over from Bulling, to be succeeded *c.*1797 by William Dyball.

The barley may have come from Bulling's farm on the edge of Holt Heath, acquired by William Hardy 15 Nov. 1796 in part payment for Bulling's debts

[3] *Hindringham* The Hardys supplied two of the village's three houses: the Duke's Head, run by John Wisker, and the Falgate, run by William Chapman. See note for 21 Dec. 1793

[4] *rung pigs* Presumably ringed their noses

[5] *Bell's Acre* Many villages had fields with this name. It may have been church land farmed to support the church bell, as at Hunworth for Thornage Church (NRO: DN/VIS 29/6, Holt deanery visitation 1784, Revd John Astley's return for Thornage). Small parcels of land were scattered about the pre-enclosure open fields, Letheringsett having a large open field on the Saxlingham side of the parish

[6] *Tinker* William (d. 5 May 1830 aged 75, bur. Letheringsett 8 May), the village carpenter; he had worked on alterations to the Hardys' house and brewery 1787–90 (*Diary 2*). See also note for 27 Dec. 1793

NOVEMBER 1, FRIDAY

Henry Raven T Balden to Clay [Cley] Chaldron half Coles [for a chaldron and a half of coals] from Mr Elliss.[1] R Bye to Study morning,[2] Dawlin [Field Dalling] afternoon.[3] Platton ploughing all day, Capt Hall in the yards. Wm Tinker and man at work all day. Jno Ram, HR in malthouse. WH home all day.

NOVEMBER 2, SATURDAY

HR T Balden to Clay for Coles from Mr Elliss morning, Cinders afternoon from Mr Manns.[4] R Bye ploughing in wheat stuble Furze close. Platton in brew house all day. G Thompson got clense beer into great cask

below Screened malt (4 Nov. 1793) is seen alongside Norfolk barley still in the ear, before threshing. This malt has been only lightly kilned and is suitable for pale ales. It can be roasted until it is dark chocolate in colour, as is required for porter and stout. Both are shown lifesize [*malt courtesy Woodforde's Norfolk Ales*]

[1] *Ellis's* John Ellis (d. 12 Aug. 1836 aged 67), a Cley merchant, and dealer in coal and cinders (coke)

[2] *Stody* Delivering to the Red Lion; John Carr was innkeeper of the house known by 1806 as the Three Horseshoes. Its 18th- and 19th-century history is well documented in the manor court book and the deeds (NRO: NRS 16609, 32 D5; BR 160/35, 1729–1896).

It continued tied to Letheringsett until 1896, when it was bought by Morgans of Norwich

[3] *Field Dalling* In addition to the Hart, the Crown at Field Dalling was supplied from Letheringsett, with Samuel Coker as innkeeper

[4] *Mann* John (d. Norwich 16 Aug. 1794 aged 44, bur. Cley 19 Aug.), a prominent Cley merchant.

Cinders gave off a gentle, non-sulphurous heat and were used in the malt-kiln furnaces in preference to coal, which would have tainted the malt.

The coal was imported from the North-East and converted to coke in the cinder ovens on the quays of the Norfolk ports and on Broadland staithes. John Mann owned cinder ovens, his Cley property also including 'spacious malt-houses, granaries, coal houses, coalyards, quays . . .' (*Norw. Merc.* 30 Aug. 1794).

See also notes for 17 Aug. and 30 Sept. 1794

above The former Red Lion at Stody, remodelled after its days as a public house owned by William Hardy's brewery.

The copyhold property is described 30 Dec. 1784 in the manor court book as adjoining the churchyard and the main Brinton road on land measuring 90 feet by 36 feet (27·5 by 11 metres). On that day William Hardy's purchase of the house on behalf of his 14-year-old son William was confirmed, and this small outlet was bound for the first time under a brewer's yoke [*MB · 1993*]

in white hall Morning, clensd afternoon.[1] Jno Ram in malthouse. M^r^, M^rs^ H {at} came from Whissonsett morning.[2] WH at [and] HR help^t^ [helped] with the Beer. W Tinker and man all day.

NOVEMBER 4, MONDAY

HR Thos Balden skreining malt morn.[3] R Bye, Bal^d^ [and Baldwin] ploughing afternoon. G Thompson Grinding malt for brew, Jno Ram in malt house. M^r^ H at holt [Holt] morning, home afternoon, WH at home all day.

NOVEMBER 5, TUESDAY

HR T Balden to Briston and Study with beer. R Bye to Clay, tooke up ¼ Chal^d^ Lime from Mr Johnson's [4] for Lines,[5] brot home 2 Chal^d^ Cinders from Mr Manns. M^r^, M^rs^ H at [and] Miss «and» WH at Holt to dine.

Mary Hardy A very Showry day. We all dind at Mr Bartells, Edmd Bartell & his Wife there, they came home with us & drank tea here. [6]

[1] *white hall* The racking room where the beer was drawn into barrels or into one of the great casks, its name presumably deriving from the whitewash on the walls (14 Nov. 1793, 8 June 1795). Double doors led into the tun room to make draying easier. The great casks, for maturing and conditioning the beer, ranged in capacity from 100 barrels to 208 barrels (*Diary 2*)

[2] *from Whissonsett* Mary and William Hardy had spent a busy few days visiting relatives, Mary Hardy noting over the next two days in her diary that she felt very poorly

[3] *screening malt* Sieving it through a hand-operated machine to remove shoots and foreign bodies

[4] *Johnson* Probably John Johnson of Cley, who had called at the Hardys' in 1786 over the lease of the Crown at Weybourne. Like so many industrial sites his lime-kiln is not marked on Faden's map of Norfolk

[5] *Lynes* John (d.1800 aged 63), of the King's Head at Cley. He and his wife Edny/Edna (d.1800 aged 62) were buried in the same grave, the register noting that they died within eight hours of each other. Mary Hardy gives their date of death as 26 Jan. 1800; the register gives their date of burial as 7 Jan. (NRO: PD 270/5).

They had 11 children baptised at Cley 1762–79

[6] *Bartell* The Hardys' medical practitioner Edmund

Bartell (d. 13 July 1816 aged 72), of Holt, and his wife Sarah (d. 19 Nov. 1828 aged 82), née Dacke; their elder son Edmund (d. 27 May 1855 aged 85), and his first wife Margaret (d. 13 Dec. 1836 aged 67), née Wadsworth, whom he had married at Howe 15 July 1793. See also notes for 13 Dec. 1793 and 2 Aug. 1796

above Stained and painted glass at Letheringsett Hall, dating from William Hardy jnr's remodelling of the east front 1832–34.

This is almost certainly the work of his great friend Edmund Bartell jnr (5 Nov. 1793), a surgeon and artist at Brooke and later at Cromer, who took a great interest in mediaeval glass. He and his parents lie buried near the chancel steps at Swannington Church, mural tablets commemorating the family [*MB · 1993*]

NOVEMBER 6, WEDNESDAY

HR Thos Balden and Boy in Brewhouse, WH Do [ditto] Brewing. RB [Robert Bye] to Jordens with beer and Clay for 1½ Chald Coles from Mr Elliss.[1] T Youngman mending flour Mill.[2] Mr H at home all day. Jno Ram in Malt House.

MH A Showry day. Wm Brew'd, Mr Hardy at home all day. Mr Mason of Brinton here foorn, bought some Bark which came from Hildonveston.[3]

---

[1] *Jordan* John (who died on or just before 12 June 1795), of the Blue Bell at Wiveton.

He was bur. Wiveton 15 June aged 52, the curate (and Cley rector) paying tribute to the man who had been 'clerk of the parish of Wiveton above seven years'. Mary Jordan—possibly his daughter (b. 26 Feb. 1767, bapt. Edgefield 1 Mar.)—continued to run the house for a few months until Edward Taylor took over; supplies from Letheringsett then ceased (NRO: C/Sch 1/16). See also note for 12 June 1795

[2] *Thomas Youngman* (Bur. Letheringsett 22 Nov. 1834 aged 76), the Letheringsett millwright. He and his wife Lydia (bur. 6 Jan. 1828 aged 68) lived in one of the houses fronting the main street. He later built for himself the Hill House, on the corner of Workhouse Lane and the main road

[3] *Mason* John, listed in the *Universal British Directory* as a tanner and one of Brinton's two principal traders; bark was used in tanning (*Univ. Brit. Dir.*, vol. 3 (1794), p. 280)

NOVEMBER 7, THURSDAY

HR Thos Balden to Sherrington and Bale,[1] R Bye to Dawling and Bale.[1] G Thompson Clense'd `//. Mr Mason sent a load Barley, tooke home a load Bark. W Tinker and man all day. Capt Hall helpen [helping] men to load Bark, Jno Ram in Malt house. Mr H at home all day, WH at home all day.

NOVEMBER 8, FRIDAY

HR R Bye to Sheringham, Thos Balden to Walsingham.[3] Capt Hall all day. Mr Mason, Brinton, sent for a load of Bark. G Thompson dressing flour for Sea.[4] Mr H at home all day, WH at Edgefield with Mr Moore.

NOVEMBER 9, SATURDAY

HR R Bye to Fakenham. Thos Balden in B«r»ewhouse morning, ploughing wheat stuble Furze close. G Thompson Clensed morning. Mr H at home morning, Holt market af«t»ernoon. WH at home morning, Holt market afternoon. Jno Ram in Malt house.

[1] *Sharrington* To Mrs Hannah Porter, innkeeper of the Swan until after 1803

[2] *Bale* To the Angel, where the recently widowed Ann Howlett was soon to hand over to Thomas Claxton

[3] *Walsingham* Until 1794 the Hardys supplied the Maid's Head, one of Lt Walsingham's seven public houses; it was kept by Clement Jacob. They very briefly supplied another: see note for 11 Nov. 1793

[4] *for sea* For shipping. Letheringsett, west of Holt, lay near the seaport of (Blakeney and) Cley: see the front endpaper map

below The interior of the malthouse: the same length of the west wall as that seen earlier from the yard (page 14). The wide door enabled large loads to be carried through; the position of the old wooden stairway to the upper malting floor can be seen. The holes for the massive floor joists remain above the lower louvred opening [*Christopher Bird 1999*]

FEATHERS HOTEL
COOKE
Residential
Hotel

MH A Showry day. Mr Hardy went to Holt market Morng 11, dind at Mr Moores, drank tea at Mr Bartells & came home eveng past 9. W^{m} rid [rode] up afternoon. Mrs Sheppard of Holt let her House to a Mr Coe from Yarmouth [1] . . .

NOVEMBER 11, MONDAY

HR R Bye to Syderstone, Thos Balden to wells [Wells], Jno Ram in malt House. M^{r} H hom«e» all day, WH home all day.

MH A fine morng, a Stormy windy after«noon». Mr Hardy at home all day. Mr Rust from Walsingham dind here [2] . . .

NOVEMBER 12, TUESDAY

HR Thos Balden to Cromer, Rb^{t} Bye to Holt afternoon. Jno Ram & Bye skren'd [screened] malt, G Thompson Grinding malt for brew. M^{r} H home all day, WH at home morning, Road [rode] out with Miss H at afternoon.

NOVEMBER 13, WEDNESDAY

HR Thos Balden & boy in Brewhouse all day, WH Brewing. R Bye to Waybourn & Runton,[3] G Thompson dressing wheat stones. Jno Ram in malthouse. M^{r} H home all day.

MH A fine day but cold. W^{m} brewd. Mr Hardy at home all day. M^{r} & Mrs Burrell, M^{r} & Mrs Sheldrake drank tea here [4] . . .

[1] *Mrs Sheppard* Elizabeth (bur. Holt 20 Oct. 1816 aged 77), née Main. She had run Holt's premier inn, the Feathers, since the death of her husband John in 1780. She announced in the *Norwich Mercury* 16 Nov. 1793 that she had let the house to William Coe from Christmas, but the letting fell through. She advertised again 4 Jan. 1794 and was then successful: see note for 26 June 1794

[2] *Rust* Charles, innkeeper *c.*1792–94 of the Crown at Lt Walsingham (NRO: C/Sch 1/16). This visit is the only recorded link between the Hardys' brewery and the Crown

[3] *Weybourne* See notes for 14 Oct. 1793, 3 Jan. 1794. The Crown stood on the main street in the village centre, Ordnance Survey grid references being given in the gazetteer of public houses (*World*, vol. 2)

[4] *Sheldrake* John, of Holt, had taken over from

facing page The Feathers was rebuilt in 1709, the year after the great fire at Holt. By 1793 the widowed Elizabeth Sheppard had run it single-handed for 13 years (9 Nov. 1793). Here it is seen in 1922, with spectacular window boxes and signwriting [*Norfolk Heritage Centre, Norwich*]

below Nectar de Vie: Mary Hardy's entry for 15 Nov. 1793. Like ships and swords, great casks bore names. A further snippet which Henry does not give us is the name of a second cask, Bountiful (9 Dec. 1793). More usually, as on 22 Nov., his aunt's laconic entries bear little relation to the hectic schedule over the road at the maltings and brewery [*Cozens-Hardy Collection*]

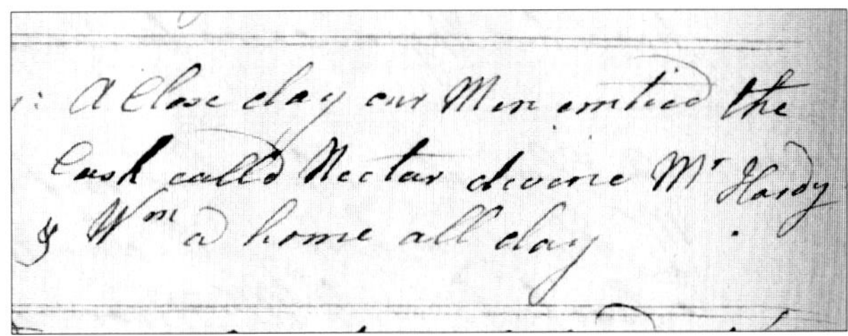
A Close day our Men emtied the Cask calld Nectar deverie Mr Hardy & Wm a home all day.

Edward Cox Tooby as officer of Holt 1st Ride in Lynn Excise Collection. He had survived the massive reorganisation of the Excise in 1789 while he was at Fakenham. From 15 Oct. 1795 he served also as Inspector of Weights and Balances for the hundred of Holt (NRO: C/S 1/15, Holt Quarter Sessions).

He was posted 15 May 1798 to Hitchin, Herts, to succeed Robert Forster as officer of Hitchin 1st Division in Bedford Collection. The Excise Board in London granted his application to leave the service 13 May 1803 (TNA: PRO CUST 47/363, pp. 58–60; CUST 47/406, p. 106; CUST 47/433, p. 64)

NOVEMBER 14, THURSDAY

HR Mr H, WH [Mr Hardy and William Hardy junior] Drawing of [off] Beer. R Bye, T Balden in Tunn Rooom [tun room], ploughing in wheat stuble Furze Close afternoon. G Thompson laid down wheat stones & Clense'd '//, Jno Ram in Malt house.

NOVEMBER 15, FRIDAY

HR R Bye, Thos Balden cleaning home Cask morning, ploughing afternoon in wheat stuble Furze close, Jno Ram in Malt house. Mr H at home all day, WH at home all day.

MH A Close day. Our Men emtied the Cask calld Nectar deverie [de Vie]. Mr Hardy & Wm at home all day . . .

NOVEMBER 16, SATURDAY

HR R Bye at Holt morning to skiffins [Skiffins'] & Bullings.[1] T Balden to P Williams morning, ploughing afternoon in wheat stuble Furze Close {afternoon}. Boy to Dawsins [Dawson's] for 100 tiles afternoon.[2] G Thompson Clense'd morning. Mr H at home morning, holt market afternoon, WH & Miss H home morning, holt market afternoon.

[1] *Skiffins* Of the Black Boys at Holt: see note for 16 Oct. 1793

[2] *Dawson* The Dawsons were builders and cartwrights at Holt. This may have been George (d. 16 May 1809 aged 78), or George jnr (bur. Holt 10 May 1840 aged 80), or John (see 24 Feb. 1794); none is listed under Holt in the *Universal British Directory* 1794. The contract for building Letheringsett's house of industry was awarded to George Dawson snr 15 Jan. 1796.

The phrase '100 tiles' may mean one hundredweight (112 lb/50·8 kg): Mary Hardy's usage at Coltishall, and one used generally at the time

NOVEMBER 18, MONDAY

HR R Bye to Stalham. Thos Balden in Brewhouse morning, ploughing afternoon. G Thompson Grinding malt for brew. Jas Bambry & boy all day.[1] Mr H at home all day. WH at home morning, Holt Asembly Evening. Jno Ram in Malt house.

MH A fine day. J Bolton breakfasted & dind here, he & Wm walkd up to Holt foornoon.[2] Mr Hardy at home all day. Wm went to Holt Assembly even 8, came home Morn 3 [3 am] . . .

NOVEMBER 19, TUESDAY

HR R Bye came home from Stalham, T Baldn [Baldwin] ploughing all day, G Thompson dressing flour for sea. Jas Bambry and boy all day. Mr H at home morning, Holt afternoon. Wm H at home morning, Holt afternoon.

NOVEMBER 20, WEDNESDAY

HR R Bye to Edgefield and Corpusta [Corpusty]. T Balden «in» Brewhouse and to holt with beer to Johnson. Wm H at Brewing, Mr H at Gunthorp. Jno Ram in malt house.

NOVEMBER 21, THURSDAY

HR R Bye to Branton [Brampton] and Walsham. Thos Balden in Brewhouse morning, Gunthorp afternoon and took 6 Bushels malt to Mr Sturleys & 2 Coomb [2 coombs of malt] & 42 lb Hoops [hops] to Gunthorp.[3] G Thompson Clensed `//, Grinding malt for brew. Mr H at home all day. WH at home morning, holt afternoon to Davys.

[[[4] NOVEMBER 22, FRIDAY

William Hardy jnr R Bye came from Walsham. T Baldwin in Brewhouse forenoon, Screening Wheat in afternoon. HR went to Whissonsett M5 [5 am]. Jno Ram in M house [malthouse], GT & Boy in Brewhouse. Jno Lines [Lynes] of Clay here afternoon & order'd 4 [barrels] Nog, 1 [barrel] `//. Mr Carr, a Brewer, calle'd afternoon from Dereham.[5] WH Painted the Cowl forenoon, mended pump afternoon. Mr, Mrs, Miss Baker here evening. T Baldwin lit the fire E7 [7 pm] to Brew.

MH A fine day. Mr Hardy & Wm at home all day. Mr & Mrs & Miss Baker drank tea here.

[1] *Bambry* A Holt bricklayer and roofer, presumably laying the roof tiles

[2] *John Bolton* A former excise officer at Holt, or his son of the same name

[3] *malt* By contrast Mary Hardy's diary rarely refers to retail sales. The farmer John Sturley had taken over *c*.1787 from Thomas Hewitt as occupier of Thornage Hall. Mr Sturley was also a butcher, who took on apprentices (TNA: PRO IR 1/67, 3 Mar. 1791).

The malt and *hops* (barrel *hoops* were sold by the bunch, whereas small amounts of hops were sold by weight, Henry being misled by William Hardy snr's Yorkshire accent) were for Gunthorpe Hall, where Charles Collyer's private brewhouse had recently been designed and built by John Soane (Sir John Soane's Museum archives: 29/4A/2–4). Mr Collyer bought malt retail (eg 5 Mar., 24 Apr. 1794). See also note for 5 Dec. 1793

[4] In Henry's absence the entries for 22–26 Nov. are by William Hardy jnr, giving a wealth of detail

[5] *Carr* The new owner of an E. Dereham brewery, Messrs Rayner & Chastney having recently announced they were declining business. Their large concern had 12 draught horses and mares accustomed to farm work as well as draying (*Norw. Merc.* 21 Sept. 1793).

For the E. Dereham breweries see the directory of breweries in *World*, vol. 2

left **'William Hardy [jnr] painted the cowl forenoon' (22 Nov. 1793). Letheringsett's two revolving malt-kiln cowls, newly restored in June 2001, seen from the north. The diary entry suggests there was only one kiln in 1793** [*MB · 2001*]

NOVEMBER 23, SATURDAY

WHj R Bye went to Whissonsett M3 & from thence with HR to Winch for Colts.[1] T Baldwin in Brewhouse Morn^{g}, to Clay [Cley] after^{n} with Beer & Bro^{t} home 1½ Ch [chaldrons] Cinders from Jno Manns. G Tompson Cleans'd Morning, Brewing & dressing Flour. WH in B House [brewhouse] all day & Boy, Jno Ram in Mt House [malthouse]. M^{r} H at Holt Market Afternoon.

MH A Cold dry day. Wm Brew^{d}. Mr Hardy & MA walkd up to Holt Mark^{t}, MA drank tea at Miss Alps, came home even 9 [2] . . .

NOVEMBER 24, SUNDAY

WHj G Tompson & Baldwin Cleans'd `// Morning. WH went to Thornage afternoon, HR & Robt Bye came home in the Evening with the Colts.

NOVEMBER 25, MONDAY

WHj R Bye to Fakenham with Beer. T Baldwin Ploughing all day, Jno Ram & HR in M^{t} house all day. G Thompson at the Fair afternoon.[3] M^{r} H & WH at the Fair Morning, dined at home, & Holt after. WH Bo^{t} [bought] 1 Last Wheat of Barwick at 21/-.[4] T Thurst orderd the Cart this week, F Longden Orderd the Cart [beer cart] Thursday at longest.

MH A very fine day. Mr Hardy rid up to Holt Horse fair foornoon, walkd up Afternoon, came home even 11. W^{m} walk^{d} up foornoon & afternoon, came home even 8. I & MA rid up foornoon, bought 5 St. 9 lb Beeff at 3^{d} pr lb [5] . . .

---

[1] *colts* Returning from their summer grazing at E. or W. Winch, near King's Lynn

[2] *Miss Alpe* Mary Alpe (d. 20 Nov. 1798 aged 51) had been Mary Ann's schoolmistress at Holt 1781–83: see note for 4 Aug. 1797

[3] *fair* Holt Fair, held twice a year on the fixed dates of 25 Apr. and 25 Nov.; the morning was devoted to a horse and cattle fair. The Overstrand and Briston innkeepers combined attendance with placing urgent beer orders

[4] *Barwick* John, innkeeper 1783–*c.*1790 of the Thatched House Tavern, Brinton (*Diary 2*); he had moved to a farm at Gunthorpe, where he is listed in the 1806 Norfolk pollbook. Wheat at Norwich market was 40*s* to 43*s* a quarter (20*s* to 21*s* 6*d* a coomb); coal was 29*s* 4*d* a chaldron (*Norw. Merc.* 9 Nov. 1793). With a last of corn equalling 20 coombs, William owed the farmer £21

[5] *beef* This figure converts to 3*s* 6*d* a stone, the bulk price of beef remaining fairly constant since the early Coltishall years

NOVEMBER 26, TUESDAY

WHj R Bye to Hildonveston with Beer, T Baldwin to Wells d°.[1] G Tompson, Boy, Mr H & WH put beer into Cask & Cleans'd forenoon. WH at Holt in Evening, supt with Mr Thomas.[2] HR & Jn° Ram in M house [malthouse].]]

NOVEMBER 27, WEDNESDAY

Henry Raven [3] T Baldin to Briston with beer. R Bye skreening Malt for brew, G Thompson Grinding Malt for D°. Mr H at Aldborough with Mr Bird. WH home morning, holt Evening. HR, Jn° R in Malt house.

MH A Wet morng, close day. Mr Hardy & Mr Bird of Thornage went to Albro [Aldborough] Morng 9, came home even past 3. Maids & M Loades Washd 4 weeks linnen.[4] Wm drank tea & Supt at Mr Bartells, came home eveng 12.

NOVEMBER 28, THURSDAY

HR R Bye to Overstrand with beer, T Baldin to Study [Stody] with beer. HR, Jno Ram in Malthouse. Mr H home foornoon, Mr Burrells Evening. WH home morning, Mr Burrells Evening. Cademy bro^t^ a load Timber.[5]

MH A close mild day. Mr Hardy & Wm at Mr Burrells in the eveng to meet Messrs Thomas, Morgan & Moore, came home eve past 10 [6] . . .

NOVEMBER 29, FRIDAY

HR Thos Balden to Cromer with beer. G Thompson, R Bye & Boy in Brewhouse, WH brewing. Mr H at home all day. HR, Jno Ram in Malt house.

NOVEMBER 30, SATURDAY

HR R Bye to Sheringham. Thos Baldin in brewhouse morning, Edgefield afternoon. Boy in brew house morning, ploughing afternoon in five acre's [the Five Acres]. G Thompson Clensed `// & put beer into home Cask. HR, Jno Ram in Malt house. Cademy brott [brought] a load of Timber from Hindolvestone. Mr H home morning, Holt market afternoon with Miss H. WH home morning, Holt market Do.[7]

[1] *ditto* ie to Wells with beer

[2] *Thomas* Revd William, Curate of Holt *c.*1790–96; he married Holt 21 Jan. 1793 Mary Winn of Holt

[3] Henry Raven takes over again until 12 Jan. 1794

[4] *M. Loades* Mary (bapt. Letheringsett 27 Aug. 1758, bur. there 22 Nov. 1824—aged, according to the register, 68), daughter of Michael and Lucy. Mary Loades' illegitimate six-year-old daughter Ann was to die of rabies 2 Sept. 1796

[5] *Cademy* John Cademy and his wife Hannah, née Porter (possibly the daughter of the Sharrington innkeeper of the same name), appear in the Letheringsett registers

[6] *at Mr Burrell's* The clergymen formed a close-knit group. The Rector of Letheringsett conducted William Thomas's marriage earlier that year, and was to conduct the marriage 31 Mar. 1795 of one of the witnesses, Susannah Johnson of Holt, daughter of Revd William Tower Johnson. At her wedding to Revd James Morgan (d.1803), of Shipdham, William Thomas stood witness. Mr Morgan then officiated 2 Aug. 1796 at the widowed John Burrell's own wedding to Mary, another of Revd Mr Johnson's milliner daughters. See note for 31 Mar. 1795

[7] *ditto* ie Holt market afternoon. Henry too delighted in dittos

DECEMBER 2, MONDAY

Henry Raven Thos Baldin to Wiverton with beer, brot home 1½ Chald Cinders from Jno Manns. G Thompson Clense'd & grinding malt fro [for] brew, R Bye & boy in brew house all day. W Tinker & man did a job to the Waggon in morning. Capt Hall Carting muck out «of the» Street. HR, Jno Ram in Malt house. Mr H & WH at home all day.

DECEMBER 3, TUESDAY

HR G Thompson, T Balden & Boy in Brewhouse, WH at Brewing. R Bye ploughing in five Acres. W Tinker «and» man mending the waggon. Capt Hall carting muck in yard morning. HR, Jno Ram in Malt house. Mr H at home all day.

DECEMBER 4, WEDNESDAY

HR R Bye in Brewhouse morning, Holt to Skiffins afternoon. Thos Balden to Walsingham. G Thompson Clens'd '// morning, put Beer in home Cask afternoon. W Tinker & man mending little cart. Mr H at home all day. WH & Miss H at Sheringham to Mr Flowers. HR, Jno Ram in Malt house.

Mary Hardy A rime frost, very fine day. Mr Hardy at home all day. Wm & MA went to Mr Flowers at Sheringham to dinner & to celebrate Mrs Flowers birth day she being now 21 Years of age, they staid all Night.

DECEMBER 5, THURSDAY

HR R Bye to Wells with 15 Sacks flour. T Balden, G Thompson drawing of [off] Sixpeny morning,[1] Balden at holt afternoon. Boy to Gunthorp to Mr Colliers with beer.[2] Mr H at home all day. WH & MH [Miss Hardy] came from Mr Flowers. HR, Jno Ram in Malt House.

MH A fine bright day. Mr Hardy at home all day. Wm & MA came home in Mr Flowers Whisky even 6 having broke down our Cart foornoon going to [West] Beckham [3] . . .

DECEMBER 6, FRIDAY

HR R Bye in Brewhouse all day. Thos Balden ploughing and loaded for Syderstone. G Thompson Clense'd morning, dressing flour afternoon. H Raven to Sheringham afternoon, Jno Ram in Malt House. Mr H, WH at home all day.

[1] *sixpenny* The strongest of the Hardys' brews. Nog, a popular Norfolk beer, and porter were classed as fourpenny, and the weakest of the brews twopenny. These were historic names signifying the retail price per quart.
For brewing methods see *World*, vol. 2, chap. 7

[2] *Collyer* Charles (d.1830 aged 75), of Gunthorpe Hall (see notes for 16 Oct. and 21 Nov. 1793), son of Daniel (d.1773). The father, 'serious, sensible, successful' (St Mary's, Wroxham, mural tablet on north wall of chancel), had been a merchant and vintner in the City of London.
Charles was brother to Revd Daniel Collyer (1752–1819), Vicar of Wroxham 1776–1801, builder of Wroxham Hall 1799. Both brothers were educated at Eton and became barristers before entering the Church.
Charles was ordained deacon Norwich 1796, priest 1796; Rector of Gunthorpe with Bale 1798–1830, Rector of Thornage with Brinton (on John Astley's death) 1803–26; Rector of Cley 1828–30 (*Alum. Cantab.*); he served also as an active JP on the Holt bench.
References to retail sales of beer direct from the brewery are very rare

[3] *whiskey* A light, two-wheeled gig. Henry Raven returned the whiskey to Sheringham the following day and collected the Hardys' cart

right Two Shire horses quietly pull a single-furrow plough through the stubble in the driving rain of 9 Sept. 2001 at the Tunstead Trosh. This traditional farming festival is held close by the Tunstead public house supplied by William Hardy from Coltishall. Samson, a bay aged 22 years, and Lad, a grey aged 16, were raised at nearby Skeyton. In the first winter recorded by Henry Raven ploughing ceased on 28 Dec. 1793 and resumed 14 Feb. 1794. The work usually stopped for between four and eight weeks in the worst of the winter weather [*MB · 2001*]

facing page Revd Charles Collyer's seat of Gunthorpe Hall, set in its own park south-east of the main Holt–Fakenham road. The Hardys sold malt and beer retail to the Hall as well as supplying their tied house the Cross Keys, shown (but not labelled) on the road leading to the south-east gate of the park. This public road was later closed, presumably affecting trade [*Faden's Map of Norfolk 1797: Larks Press 1989*]

DECEMBER 7, SATURDAY

HR Thos Balden to Syderstone with beer. R Bye and Boy ploughing morning, R Bye took out of Barn 17 Coomb Barley & ploughing afternoon. G Thompson Grinding malt for brew. MH [Mr Hardy], WH at home morning, Holt Market afternoon. HR, J Ram in Malt House.

DECEMBER 9, MONDAY

HR G Thompson & Boy in Brewhouse. R Bye, Thos Balden Cleaning small cask in W Hall [white hall]. WH at D^o^ Brewing. HR, Jno Ram in Malt House. Mrs Lines came to order 4 Nog, 1 Six [four barrels of nog, one barrel of sixpenny]. Walden came to Settle with M^r^ H «who was» at home all Day.[1]

MH A Close cold day. Wm Brewd & emtyed the Cask Bountifull. Mr Hardy at home all day, Mr Walden from Wells dind here.

---

[1] *Walden* John: see note for 24 Oct. 1793. The entry shows that there must have been an additional ledger recording payments. Neither Mary Hardy's diary nor Henry's was used at Letheringsett to note the innkeepers' cash payments

DECEMBER 10, TUESDAY

HR Thos Balden in Brewhouse Morning, jobs in yard afternoon. R Bye in Brewhouse morning, Clay afternoon, Brot home 1½ Chald Cinders from Mr Manns. WH, HR got Clense Beer into home cask morning, empted great cask in W Hall afternoon. Jno Ram in Malt house. MH [Mr Hardy] at home all day.

MH A dry day. Mr Hardy & Wm at home all day. Thompson went to Aylsham to receive a Legacy left him by a Relation . . .

DECEMBER 11, WEDNESDAY

HR Thos Balden to Briston. R Bye & boy ploughing in 5 Acres. WH {at} gone to Whissonsett. MH [Mr Hardy] at hom all day. HR, J Ram in Malt house.

DECEMBER 12, THURSDAY

HR G Thompson Clense'd morning, dressing wheat stones afternoon. R Bye ploughing all day in field. Thos Balden to Holt for empty Barrels morning, to Do [Holt] to Crawfers afternoon with beer.[1] Mr H home fornoon, Holt afternoon, WH at Whissonset.

DECEMBER 13, FRIDAY

HR R Bye to Fakenham with beer. T Balden in Brewhouse, G Thompson Grinding Malt for brew. HR & Jno Ram in Malt house. WH & Mr Goggs came from Whissonsett.[2] Miss Wymer [3] & Miss Bartle came to «dinner» & whent to Mr Temples with Mr H & Miss H.[4]

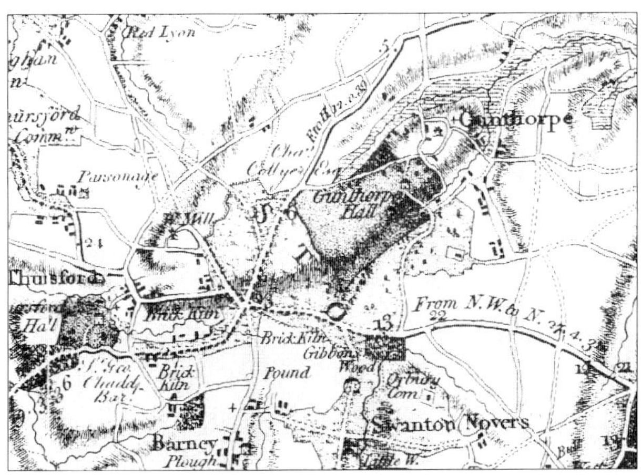
Red Lyon
Gunthorpe
Parsonage
Mill
Gunthorpe Hall
Thursford
Brick Kiln
From N.W. to N.
Pound
Swanton Novers
Barney
Plough

[1] *Crafer* Henry, innkeeper 1791–97 of the King's Head at Holt; he and his wife Elizabeth, née Coe, appear in the Holt registers for the baptism and burial of their children. Crafer failed in business 9–10 Nov. 1796 owing debts to William Hardy and was bankrupted: see note for 4 May 1797

[2] *Goggs* Mary Hardy's entry shows him to be the Whissonsett farmer Henry Goggs jnr (b. Whissonsett 1 Jan. 1767, bapt. 4 Jan., bur. there 27 Mar. 1827), son of her sister Phillis (1731–1806) and Henry Goggs (1731–95), farmer, of Whissonsett and formerly of Burnham Thorpe: see app. D3.A, fig. D3.6.

Henry marr. Whissonsett 5 Dec. 1797 Martha Buscall (d. 1846 aged 74), of London; they had 13 children

[3] *Miss Wymer* Clara, daughter of George Wymer, a Norwich attorney; she marr. St Gregory's, Norwich 28 Sept. 1797 Lieut. Thomas Stirling of the Marines (*Norw. Merc.* 30 Sept. 1797)

[4] *Miss Bartell* Charlotte, only daughter of Edmund and Sarah Bartell (see note for 5 Nov. 1793), Henry Raven recording the name phonetically. Charlotte marr. Holt 19 Aug. 1807 the widowed William Bircham jnr (1769–1853) of Hackford, of the Reepham brewing family. His first wife Charlotte Quarles of Foulsham, whom he had marr. 12 Dec. 1793, had died 9 Nov. 1803 (*Norw. Merc.* 14 Dec. 1793, 12 Nov. 1803)

facing page 'Mr Hardy . . . measured great cask in white hall evening' (17 Dec.).

As a former excise officer William Hardy was able to cope with the task himself. This manual of 1793 by a Collector of Excise, a man at the head of his profession, gives instructions on calculating the capacity of vessels such as malting steeps and brewing squares as both dry measures (eg in bushels) and wet (eg in gallons) [*W. Symons, The Practical Gager or the Young Gager's Assistant (1793): Bodleian Libraries, Oxford*, Vet. A5 e.3751, pp. 56–57]

MH A very wet foornoon, fine Afternoon. Miss Wymer & Miss Bartell dind here. Mr Hardy & MA, Mr Bakers & Mr Bartells family drank tea & Supt at Mr Temple of Thornage, came home even 12. Wm & H Goggs came home to tea. Mrs Sanderson came eveng 10 [1] . . .

DECEMBER 14, SATURDAY

HR T Balden to Sheringham with beer. R Bye to Thornage with beer morning, ploughing afternoon. Mr H at home morning, holt market afternoon. WH at home morning, holt market afternoon with Miss Wymer & Miss Bartle & Miss Hardy. HR, Jno Ram in malt house.

DECEMBER 16, MONDAY

HR R Bye, Thos Balden Cleaning great Cask in W Hall. G Thompson & Boy in Brewhouse, WH Brewing. HR, J Ram in Malt House. Mr H at home all day. W Tinker & Man at work afternoon.

DECEMBER 17, TUESDAY

HR R Bye to Dawling and Kettlestone with beer, Thos Balden to Runton with beer. G Thompson Clens'd `//. WH at home morning, Holt afternoon. Mr H at home all day & measured great Cask in W Hall evening. H Raven, Jno Ram in Malt House. W Tinker & man half a day.

DECEMBER 18, WEDNESDAY

HR Thos Balden to Edgefield & Corpusta, R Bye to Salthouse. G Thompson & WH got Beer in to home Cask. Mr H at home all day. Mr «and» Mrs Flower came morning, whent to Holt Assembly with WH & Miss H.[2] HR, J Ram in M House.

DECEMBER 19, THURSDAY

HR R Bye to Wells with beer. T Balden in Brewhouse morning, Holt afternoon. G Thompson Clense'd morning, Grinding malt for bin afternoon. Mr H, WH at home all day. Mr, Mrs Flower whent home Evening. H Raven, Jno Ram in M House.

DECEMBER 20, FRIDAY

HR T Balden to No [North] Walsham with beer, R Bye to Gunthorp with beer, G Thompson Grinding Malt for brew. H Raven, Jno Ram in M House. Sawers [sawyers] at work afternoon. Mr H home all day. WH at holt morning, home afternoon. Mr Moore came to dine.

---

1 *Mrs Sanderson* Mary: see note for 17 Oct. 1793. She ran the Cromer Hotel following the death of her husband Thomas on 17 May 1793 aged 41, and was the fourth visitor staying at Letheringsett 13–14 Dec. 1793. Her husband's bankruptcy was still being administered. A further meeting of the bankruptcy commissioners was held in Norwich 1 Dec. 1795, and the final dividend was paid to the creditors in Mar. 1798 (*Norw. Merc.* 28 Nov. 1795, 24 Mar. 1798)

2 *Mr Flower* Not Cook: Mary Hardy writes, 'Mrs Flower and Mr S. Flower dined here.' Samuel Flower announced in the *Norwich Mercury* 29 Aug. 1795 that he was leaving his rented house at Upper Sheringham; he appears to have

56 Of finding Factors, &c.

In like manner were the other factors for circles found, which are inserted in the following table.

ART. III.

To find factors for squares.

THIS is done by dividing of unity by the solid capacity of each gallon, bushel, foot, pound, *&c.* See the following examples.

282.	1,000000	,003546	Common factors for squares.	Ale gallons.
231.	1,000000	,004329		Wine gall.
268.8	1,000000	,003720		Malt gall.
2150.42	1,000000	,000465		Malt bush.
227.	1,000000	,004405		Mash tun g.

And in like manner were all the other factors for squares found, which are inserted in the following table.

ART. IV.

To find gage points for squares.

THOSE gage points are no other than the square roots of the solid capacities of each gallon, bushel, *&c.* therefore extract the square root from the number of inches to a gallon or bushel, *&c.* and it is done. As for example:

The square roots of		are	The square gage points for
282.		16.79	Ale gallons.
231.		15.19	Wine gallons.
268.8		16.39	Malt gallons.
2150.42		46.37	Malt bushels.
227.		15.07	Mash tun gallons.

ART.

(57)

ART. V.

A Table of Factors.

Multipliers, Divisors, and Gage points, for Squares and Circles.	Factors for		Divisors for		Gage points for	
	Squares	Circles.	Squares	Circles.	Squares	Circles.
Inches the area of unity	1	,785398	1	1.27324	1	1.128
A superficial foot	,006944	,005454	144.	183.34	12.	13.54
A solid foot	,000578	,000454	1728.	2200.16	41.57	46.91
Ale gallon	,003546	,002785	282.	359.05	16.79	18.95
Wine gallon	,004329	,003399	231.	294.12	15.19	17.15
Malt or corn bushel	,000465	,000365	2150.42	2738.00	46.37	52.32
Malt gallon	,003720	,002922	268.8	342.24	16.39	18.5
Mash tun gallon	,004405	,00346	227.	289.	15.1	17.07
A pound of hard soap cold	,036845	,028939	27.14	34.56	5.21	5.88
A pound of hot soap	,035714	,028050	28.0	35.65	5.29	5.97
A pound of green soap	,038956	,0306	25.67	32.68	5.06	5.72
A pound of white soft soap	,039123	,030731	25.56	32.54	5.05	5.7
A pound of tallow net	,031844	,025101	31.4	39.98	5.6	6.32
A pound of green starch	,028736	,022565	34.8	44.32	5.9	6.66
A pound of dry starch	,024813	,019491	40.3	51.3	6.35	7.16
A pound of flint glass	,094697	,074405	10.56	13.44	3.25	3.69
A pound of white glass	,071123	,05586	14.06	17.9	3.74	4.32
A pound of green glass	,082102	,064516	12.18	15.5	3.48	3.94

Having found proper factors and divisors both for squares and circles, as in the above table, the area of any square or circular figure may be found in any of the

D 5

DECEMBER 21, SATURDAY

HR R Bye to Brampton with beer, T Balden came from Walsham. Boy whent to Furze Closes for Load Turnips and a Load sand morning. G Thompson, WH got 10 Bar^{s} [barrels of] Beer in great Cask W Hall. Sawers at work all day. Mr Chapman came to Order 4 Nog, 18 `//.[1] Jno Ram, HR in M House. M^{r} H home morning, Holt market afternoon. WH at Holt market afternoon.

DECEMBER 22, SUNDAY

MH A Wet day. All went to our Church afternoon. Mr Burrell read a Lecture . . .

DECEMBER 23, MONDAY

HR T Balden to Hinderingham with beer. G Thompson, R Bye, Boy in Brewhouse, WH Brewing. M^{r} H, Jno Ram, R Bye got 22 Bar^{s} Beer in great Cask W [white] Hall moved to Lower Sheringham (see 10 Aug. 1796)

[1] *Chapman* William, innkeeper of the Falgate on the Walsingham road at Hindringham (note for 30 Oct. 1793). This inordinately large order (6336 pints) was for a very small house, but only four of the 22 barrels were of strong nog.

A landowner or cleric giving a frolic may have been determined to keep to a minimum the quantity of strong beer on offer

afternoon.[1] HR, Jn° Ram in M House. Sawers at work. W Tinker came morning to set box fast in brew Cart.[2]

DECEMBER 24, TUESDAY

HR R Bye to Waybourn with beer, Thos Balden to Edgefield with beer and Holt. G Thompson Clense'd `// morning, dressing flour afternoon. Jn° Ram, HR in M House. Mr H, WH home all day. T Youngman mending the Crane, Sawers at work.[3]

DECEMBER 25, WEDNESDAY

HR G Thompson, HR put 18 Bars Beer in great Cask W Hall. Mr H home all day. WH, HR home morning, Holt afternoon. Sarvants & famaly [farm servants and their families] came to get a Xtmas [Christmas] dinner.

MH Chrismas Day A close dry day. We all went to our Church foornoon, A Communion. Our Labourers & Wives dind here. Wm & H Raven walkd up to Holt afternoon, drank tea at Mr Moors, came home eveng 7. Mrs Dunns Mother Died [4] . . .

DECEMBER 26, THURSDAY

HR T Balden to Cromer with beer, R Bye home all day. G Thompson Clense'd morning, dresd folur [dressed flour] afternoon. Mr H at home all day, WH road out morning & afternoon. Miss Custance [5] & Miss A Raven [6] & N Raven came from Whissonsett.[7]

[1] *Mr Hardy* Henry's entries show that Mary Hardy habitually under-records her husband's participation in the work of the brewery. She had noted under 23 Dec. merely that he was 'at home all day'—a phrase which, although accurately reporting that he was not absent, is nevertheless open to misinterpretation

[2] *box* An iron sleeve lining the stock at the centre of the hub; similarly a sleeve for a pump (15 Feb. 1796)

[3] *crane* Its first mention; it was presumably for the logs

[4] *died* The entry has been added later, suggesting that the deceased was from outside the village. There is no corresponding entry in the Letheringsett register

[5] *Miss Custance* Frances (b. 7 May 1771, priv. bapt. Fakenham 9 May, publicly 25 Sept.), daughter of Mary Hardy's first cousin Phillis, wife of William Custance (d. 31 Aug. 1816 aged 77), a Fakenham joiner and cabinetmaker; Frances's aunt was Mrs Priscilla Baker.

She married 30 July 1800 William Bennett, a draper of Twickenham, Middx. See note for 11 July 1794; also app. D3.A, fig. D3.2

[6] *Ann Raven* Anna, known as Ann (bapt. Whissonsett 5 Sept. 1773, bur. there 19 Dec. 1814), younger daughter of Mary Hardy's brother Nathaniel. See note for 17 Feb. 1794; also app. D3.A, figs D3.2, D3.5

[7] *Nathaniel Raven* (b. and bapt. Whissonsett 25 Apr.

facing page A 20th-century one-horse cart in a front garden at Rockland St Mary on the Norfolk Broads. As with most carts the floor is cross-boarded (stretching the width of the cart), for strength; muck carts however were long-boarded, to allow for easier unloading and washing down. The Hardys used carts daily to carry coal, cinders, hay, malt, turnips and muck as well as the beer barrels, yet there are surprisingly few references to repairs to carts and wagons (23 and 27 Dec. 1793).

Here the 'ladders' enable loads to be built higher than the plank sides of the cart [*MB · 1989*]

overleaf 16-year-old Henry Raven's entries for 31 Dec. 1793–3 Jan. 1794. Already his record covers more than the work of the farm, maltings and brewery, and he has taken to noting social events—even though he is rarely included in them. Like his aunt he uses @ to represent 'at': 'Mr H. @ home all day'. His spellings are often phonetic: 'Balden' for Baldwin, one of the farm servants; 'Study' for Stody village. His prime task is to record the everyday tasks, from which we can plot the men's working year. Henry and the miller were tunning beer even on Christmas morning 1793 [*Cozens-Hardy Collection*]

DECEMBER 27, FRIDAY

HR R Bye ploughing all day. T Balden in Brew house, G Thompson grinding malt for brew. M^{r} H, WH at home all day. Sawers at work, Jno R, HR in M House. Ja^{s} Tinker came to mend wggon [wagon] morning.[1]

DECEMBER 28, SATURDAY

HR R Bye, T Balden ploughing all day. WH, G Thompson got Clense beer in W Hall. Jno R, HR in M House. RB, T Balden got D^{o} Beer [cleansed beer] in great Cask. WH, M^{r} H at home morning, holt market with the Ladies afternoon. Sawers at work.

DECEMBER 30, MONDAY

HR R Bye to Sheringham with beer. G Thompson, T Balden & Boy in Brewhouse, WH Brewing. W Tinker & man at work, Sawers at work. M^{r} H at home all day. WH at & Miss H & Miss Custance & Miss Raven at Holt Ball. HR, J Ram in M House.

DECEMBER 31, TUESDAY

HR R Bye to Hindonvestone with beer, T Balden to Briston with beer. G Thompson Clense'd `//. M^{r} H, WH at home all day. Jno Ram, HR in M House. W Tinker & Man, Sawers at work.

1781), the diarist Henry's youngest surviving brother (app. D3.A, fig. D3.4). He and his wife Sarah settled in the isolated hamlet of Sefter Green in the parish of Pagham on the Selsey peninsula in Sussex, where he ran the National School founded in 1825 at Sefter Green. Four children were baptised at Pagham: Edward, 5 Sept. 1829; Elizabeth, 7 Jan. 1832; Robert, 6 Apr. 1834; and William Hardy, 17 Dec. 1837. Nathaniel's cousin William Hardy jnr remembered him in his will

---

[1] *James Tinker* A Letheringsett carpenter, like his brother William; their parents William Tinker of Matlaske and Barbara Money of Briston had marr. Edgefield 27 Oct. 1747. James marr. Letheringsett 12 Nov. 1793 Mary Jeckell, the bride signing her name and the groom making his mark. There is some doubt about the wedding date: see Mary Hardy's marriage register in the endnotes. William Tinker had by contrast signed on his second marriage 12 Oct. 1790. Four children were born at Letheringsett to James and Mary Tinker: Barbara (b. and bapt. 17 Nov. 1794); Thomas (b. and bapt. 7 Nov. 1796); William (b. and bapt. 18 Nov. 1799); and Martha (b. 30 Aug. 1804 and bapt. 4 Sept.). James Tinker was employed in the rebuilding of Letheringsett Hall's east front 1832–34

Tuesday 31st R Bye to Winoonestone with beer I Balden to Brixton with beer G Thompson Clensed ff Mr H W H a home all day Jno Ham H R in M House W Tinker & Man Sawers at work

Wednesday Jany 1st 1794 I Balden to Studey with beer R B ye jobs morning Muck Cart afternoon ~~G Thompson Clensed~~ ff Mr H Wm H a home all day Mr Mrs Miss Temple & Miss Johnson Miss Hannant Miss Bartle Mr R Raven Mr N Raven came to drink tea

Thursday 2nd I Balden to Bale with beer morning much cart afternoon R Bye in brew house morning Do G Thompson Clensed morning dressing wheat stones afternoon W Tinker & man hear in morning shiffins Do Jno R H R in M House sawers at work Mr H a home all day W H a walked to Mr Temples with ladies morning

Friday 3rd I Balden R Bye at much cart & got a load Turnips home & carried 2 Hog to Mr Marp G Thompson laid down wheat Stones & grinding Malt for brew Jno R H R in M House Tinker & man at work at shiffings sawers at work Mr H a home all day Mr Dal gex came to look at Minor W H gone to Foulsham

1794

T. Baldwin to Beckhithe with beer, broke his arm coming home by falling down under the wheel

HENRY RAVEN, 23 DEC. 1794

JANUARY 1, WEDNESDAY

Henry Raven T Balden to Study with beer. R Bye jobs morning, Muck Cart afternoon. M^r H, W^m H at home all day. M^r, M^rs & Miss Temple & Miss Johnson,[1] Miss Hannant,[2] Miss Bartle, M^r R Raven,[3] M^r N Raven came to drink tea.[4]

JANUARY 2, THURSDAY

HR T Balden to Bale with beer morning, muck cart afternoon. R Bye in brew house morning, D^o.[5] G Thompson Clense'd morning, dressing wheat stones afternoon. W Tinker & man hear [here] in morning, Skiffins D^o. Jno R, HR in M House. Sawers at work. M^r H at home all day, WH {at} walked to Mr Temples with Ladies morning.

Here Lyeth the Body of Thoms
Smith Millwright he departed
this life April ye 16 in 1725
Aged 82 Years

left 'G. Thompson ... dressing wheatstones' (2 Jan.). Tools and a newly dressed stone are depicted at nearby Wiveton on this fine headstone to an earlier millwright Thomas Smith, who died in 1725 aged 82 and who lies by the north door [*MB · 2001*]

[1] *Miss Johnson* Mary (b. and bapt. Plumstead-by-Holt 12 Nov. 1767, bur. Letheringsett 11 Oct. 1833), one of the milliner daughters of Revd William Tower Johnson. She married the widowed Revd John Burrell: see note for 2 Aug. 1796

[2] *Miss Hannant* Mary Hardy spells the name as Hanault

[3] *Robert Raven* Henry's eldest brother (bapt. Whissonsett 30 Oct. 1771), who farmed at Whissonsett Hall: see the family tree at app. D3.A, fig. D3.4

[4] *Nathaniel Raven* (b. and bapt. Whissonsett 6 Aug. 1774, bur. there 4 Sept. 1851), only son of Mary Hardy's brother Nathaniel. He took over the running of the grocery and farm on his father's death in 1799, and married 25 Nov. 1802 his cousin Mary Fox (app. D3.A, figs D3.2, D3.5)

[5] *ditto* At muck cart in the afternoon

JANUARY 3, FRIDAY

HR T Balden, R Bye at muck cart & got a load Turnips home & carried 2 [barrels] Nog to Mr Mays. G Thompson laid down wheat Stones & grinding Malt for brew. Jno R [Ramm], HR in M House. Tinker & man at work at Skiffings, Sawers at work. M^r H at home all day. M^r Da^l [Daniel] Jex came to look at Minor.[1] WH gone to Foulsham. R Raven, NR Junr, N Raven gone home.[2]

Mary Hardy A Sharp rime frost. Mr Hardy at home all day. Robt & the 2 Nath^ls [two Nathaniels] went away Morng 11. W^m went to Foulsham at same time to look at a Publick House, came home eveng 5.[3] The 2 Miss Jennes^s drank tea here [4] . . .

JANUARY 4, SATURDAY

HR R Bye to Viverton [Wiveton] with beer & Clay for sinders to Mr Manns, T Balden to Gunthorp. M^r H, WH at home morning, Holt market with the Ladies. HR, Jno Ram in M House. Sawers at work.

JANUARY 6, MONDAY

HR T Balden to Walsingham with beer. R Bye, G Thompson in Brewhouse & Boy & got 10 Bar^s Beer in home Cask, WH at D^o Brewing. Jno Ram, HR in M House. M^r H at home all day. Ladies to Holt «to» Mr Bartles. J Graveland turning over muck.

[1] *Minor* One of the horses. The Jexes were Letheringsett blacksmiths, and probably farriers as well

[2] *NR jnr* Nathaniel, son of Mary Hardy's brother Nathaniel. To distinguish her two nephews named Nathaniel Raven, Mary Hardy would call Nathaniel's son 'NR from the shop' and Robert's son 'NR from the Hall'. The mothers, both Mrs Ann Raven, were 'Sister Raven' and 'Sister Raven from the Hall'

[3] *Foulsham* None of the market town's public houses was advertised in the press at this time. The Ship Inn, with its bowling green, had been tied to the Guist brewer Thomas Brooke (d. July 1790 aged 67), and had been let in 1788 at £30 a year (*Norw. Merc.* 29 Mar. 1788). Two of his others, the Swan Inn at Guist and the Falgate at Stibbard, were to be acquired by John Day's brewery in St Martin-at-Oak, Norwich (*Norw. Merc.* 11 Oct. 1794).

As with John Blanchflower at the Ship, the other innkeepers at Foulsham had stable tenure in the 1790s—Thomas Frost at the Bull, and Christopher Sherringham at the King's Arms (NRO: C/Sch 1/16, Alehouse register 1789–99)

[4] *two Miss Jennises* Mary and Elizabeth. Their sister Ann had married the Holt attorney James Moore at Holt 18 Mar. 1790. She had died 12 Dec. 1792 aged 24 and was bur. Cley 15 Dec., leaving two daughters. Her elder surviving sister, Mary

Pleasance Jennis (bapt. Cley 7 Jan. 1774), married 8 Feb. 1798 Revd John Glover of Wymondham (*Norw. Merc.* 10 Feb. 1798), the witnesses being her sister Elizabeth Jennis (bapt. Cley 17 Sept. 1779) and the Master of Holt's Free Grammar School, Thomas Atkins. (The Holt register gives the marriage date as 1 Feb.)

James Moore married Swaffham 31 Dec. 1799 Mary Marcon. By 1802 he had run heavily into debt (*Diary 4*; see also note for 23 May 1794)

MH A Sharp frost, very little sunshine. Mr Hardy at home all day, was poorly. Wm Brew'd. I went to speak to Mrs Burrell afternoon, she was very poorly. The Girls walkd to Holt afternoon, drank tea at Mr Bartells. Heard Ann Davy was Maried last June in London [1] . . .

JANUARY 7, TUESDAY

HR R Bye to Wells with beer. T Balden & Boy to Holt with beer & to Hempsted for Stones. Sawers at work, J Graveland turning muck. Jno R, HR in M House. Mr H at home all day. WH at home morning, Holt Evening with Ladies. G Thompson Clensed `//.

[1] *Ann Davy* Daughter of the shopkeeper John Davy of Holt by his first wife Elizabeth (bur. Holt 12 Dec. 1773). In 1787 Ann had been apprenticed to a milliner in Woodbridge, Suff. (*Diary 2*).

From Mary Hardy's later entries (eg *Diary 4*: 29 Aug. 1798) it is likely Ann Davy had become Mrs Hooper

facing page and *top* 'Sawyers at work', records Henry Raven through late December and early January.

At Gunton Park Sawmill some volunteers from the Norfolk Industrial Archaeology Society turn to primaeval technology—the Hardys' sawyers at least had a crane—while preparing for one of the mill's regular open days. Oak from Sheringham Park, Cook Flower's former estate, is given to the Society by the National Trust for sawing into planks on open days using the water-powered reciprocating saw in this thatched watermill; the sawn timber is then returned for use in Trust properties. The vertical blade marks are valued in architectural restorations: modern circular saws leave unauthentic marks.

The mill was built *c.*1823 for the Gunton estate by the Saxthorpe ironfounder William Hase [*MB · 1999*]

facing page The Brewhouse Pightle at Letheringsett (15 Jan. 1793): a panoramic view looking north-east. Over the generations this pightle (a small enclosed field or meadow) was indissolubly linked to the maltings and brewery in all sales of the property.

To the left is the south front of Letheringsett Hall as rebuilt by William Hardy jnr; in the centre the massive tun room he had remodelled in 1814; and to the right his malt-kilns, with one of the cowls just visible above the roof line, and the squat brewery stables. The basin supplying the brewing liquor lies behind the trees to the far left.

In 1808 the King's Head, the brewery tap (out of the picture to the right), was moved south of the stables from its position on the main road opposite the Hall. Richard Mayes (13 Jan. 1793) served here as innkeeper from before 1757 until 26 Mar. 1794 [*MB · 2001*]

JANUARY 8, WEDNESDAY

HR R Bye at home all day. T Balden at home morning, Holt afternoon. G Thompson, WH got Clense Beer into home cask. Jn° R, HR in M House. Sawers at work. MH [Mr Hardy] at home all day.

JANUARY 9, THURSDAY

HR R Bye to Fakenham with beer. T Balden in Brewhouse morning, Holt afternoon with beer & fetching gravil to B [Black] Boys. G Thompson Clensed. Jn° R, HR in M House. Mr H, WH at home all day. Mr, Mrs Sheldrake & Mr Josh [Joseph] Davy & Mrs D & Miss Davy came to drink tea.[1] Sawers at work.

JANUARY 10, FRIDAY

HR R Bye to Briston. T Balden in Brewhouse morning, Sowing Cumbs afternoon.[2] G Thompson Grinding Malt for brew. Jn° R, HR in M House. MH [Mr Hardy] at home all day. WH at home morning, Holt afternoon with Ladies. M [Mr] Youngman put up a though [trough] in Tun Roome.

JANUARY 11, SATURDAY

HR T Balden to Cromer with beer. R Bye & Boy sowing Soot morning, got away wheat afternoon.[3] Sawers at work. Jn° R, HR in M House. Mr H & WH at home morning, Holt market afternoon with the Ladies.

[[[4] JANUARY 12, SUNDAY

William Hardy jnr H Raven sett off for Whissonsett on Minor M4. We all went to Church before breakfast. A Raven, Miss Custance & I Walked to Holt afternoon.

---

[1] *Miss Davy* Mary Hardy includes in the party Miss Alpe and both Elizabeth (Bett) Davy and Susan Davy. Elizabeth, Mrs Mary Davy's stepdaughter, marr. Holt 28 Oct. 1794 Edward Robinson, a linen draper from the City of London, and they settled in Hackney (see note for 28 Oct. 1794).

Her brothers John, also a linen draper in the City, and Joseph were living and working in London

[2] *culms* As a fertiliser: see note for 25 Oct. 1793

[3] *soot* Also used as a fertiliser, as noted by 18th-century agriculturalists. Soot and ash had for centuries been prized for their nourishment of the soil

[4] William resumes, writing in the first person, until Henry takes over on 20 Jan. on his return from his short break at Whissonsett. Henry had not lost a minute, setting off at 4 am despite the frost and dark of midwinter

MH A small frost. We all went to our Church qrtr before ten in Morng, Mr Burrell preach'd.[1] W^{m} & the Girls walk'd up to Holt afternoon, came back to tea. Mrs Forster calld aftern.[1] Henry Raven went to Whissonsett . . .

JANUARY 13, MONDAY

WHj T Baldwin, Wm Hardy, G Tompson & Boy Brewing, R Bye to Corpusty with beer. Jno Ram in Mt House, Sawyers at work. Mr Moor dined here. A [Ann] Raven, Miss Custance, Miss Hardy & Mr Moor walke'd to Holt to Tea at Mr Bakers, W Hardy rode up in the Even^{g}. The Purse Club feast at Mr Mayses, a great dispute with them, at last resolved to remove it to Holt.[3] M^{r} H at home all day.

JANUARY 14, TUESDAY

WHj T Baldwin poorly part of the forenoon, at Ja^{s} Reeve's with beer after^{n}.[4] R Bye & G Tompson Cleansd `//, drew beer off in W^{t} Hall & Loaded Waggon for Stalham. J Ram in Mt House, Sawyers here, T Youngman's Boy here afternoon. Pet^{r} Williams came Morn^{g} & order'd 3 [barrels] Nog tomorrow. M^{r} H at home all day, M^{rs} H Washing.

[1] *church* Taken with William's note that the family went to church before breakfast it is evident the Hardys could sometimes have a very late breakfast on Sundays

[2] *Mrs Forster* Wife of Thomas (see note for 16 Aug. 1793). She was the sister of John Buckle (d.1818 aged 70), a Norwich ironmonger and tobacconist, then serving as mayor

[3] *purse club* Also known as a box club, a mutual benefit society for working men. Mary Hardy first recorded a meeting of the Letheringsett purse club at the King's Head 15 Mar. 1790 (*Diary 2*). See also note for 21 Jan. 1794

[4] *Reeve* At the Hart, Field Dalling; his house was soon to be renamed the Jolly Farmers

JANUARY 15, WEDNESDAY

WHj Thos Baldwin & G Tompson got the beer into Wt Hall forenoon & put it into the Cask afternoon. R Bye gone to Stalham. Thos Hall shoveling muck up in Pightle afternoon.[1] Sawyers at work. Jno Ram in Mt House. Mr & Wm H at home all day. A Dobson here in Morn after furnace Bars.[2] T Youngman here eveng after the Rollers.[3]

JANUARY 16, THURSDAY

WHj T Baldwin at Petr Williams in Morng,[4] G Tompson & he Cleans'd afternoon. Sawyers here. Thos Hall spreading muck on Bells Acre, Jno Ram Mt House. T Youngman all day after Rollers. Mr & WH home all day, Jno Wade drank tea here this afternoon. R Bye came from Stalham.

JANUARY 17, FRIDAY

WHj T Baldwin verry Ill. R Bye to Sherringham with beer, Jno Ram in Mt House. Thos Hall spreading muck foren, T Youngman after Rollers. Mr H & Mrs H at Holt forenoon. Miss Raven, Miss Hardy & WH drank tea at Mr Davys. Sawyers finished their work.

MH A small frost, fine day. Mr Hardy & I rid up to Holt foornoon in L [little] Cart, I fitted on a gown at Miss Bacons, came home to dinner. Wm, MA & A Raven rid up to Holt afternoon, drank tea at Mr Davys …

[1] *Pightle* The Brewhouse Pightle, on the western slope above the brewery.
All William Hardy's dispersed arable fields, meadows and pasture lay west of the River Glaven

[2] *Dobson* Abraham (bapt. Letheringsett 8 Apr. 1753, bur. there 6 May 1807), of Holt; son of William (d.1767) and Elizabeth, née Mayes. His repair of the ironwork of the malt-kiln or brewing copper furnaces indicates that he was a blacksmith.
His brother William (privately bapt. Letheringsett 26 Apr. 1741, publicly 10 May, bur. there 12 May 1820 aged, according to the register, 82) was to take over Letheringsett King's Head from Richard Mayes —possibly a relative on his mother's side—on 25 Mar. 1794, Lady Day.
A third brother, Richard (bapt. Letheringsett 30 June 1739), innkeeper of the White Lion at Holt 1781–84, had left Holt 1 Apr. 1784 when bankrupted

[3] *rollers* Metal cylinders for crushing grain in a malt-mill, although the Hardys seem customarily to have used grindstones

[4] *Peter Williams* William's earlier phrasing (14 Jan.) suggested that the order for Thornage was urgent, especially as the innkeeper had called before breakfast. With one drayman 25 miles away at Stalham the order for three barrels of nog was not despatched until two days later, again before breakfast

left A winter dawn in the centre of Holt: the Georgian elegance of the house named High Silver. Holt was largely refaced after the destruction of the 1708 fire and has beautiful buildings. Its shops, services and sample market proved a magnet for the Hardys; its winter subscription assemblies were regularly advertised and were held monthly in the Shirehouse (20 Jan. 1794) [*MB · 1998*]

facing page The site of the Black Boys at Holt, adjoining the Shirehouse. James William Skiffins was innkeeper 1793–95, placing a large order for nog 20 Jan. 1794 which was delivered the next day. In the mid-19th century, when the Black Boys had long ceased trading, Mary Hardy's grandson erected this building in its place as a Methodist manse for the Wesleyan Reformers [*MB · 2003*]

JANUARY 18, SATURDAY

WHj T Baldwin to Edgefield with beer. R Bye to Clay with d° & Bro^t^ home 2 C^h^ [two chaldrons] Cinders from Jn° Manns. G Tompson grinding M^t^ with Rollers, T Youngman «at work» forenoon & finished Rollers. Jn° Ram in Mt House. M^r^ H at hom forenoon, Holt Afternoon. Miss Custance, Miss Baker & Adam [Baker] here Morng,[1] Mrs Forster & W Herring drank tea.[2] WH at home all day.

JANUARY 19, SUNDAY

WHj G Tompson & men drew off Beer & Loaded Cart for Siderstone. All at Church morning. Ann Raven, M [Mary Ann] Hardy & WH walkd to Holt Church afternoon.]]

JANUARY 20, MONDAY

Henry Raven T Balden to Siderstone. G Thompson, R By & Boy in Brewhouse all day, WH Brewing. HR, RR & Miss M Raven came from Whissonsett. Jn° Ram in M House. M^r^ H at home all day. Ja^s^ Skiffins came & Orderd 5 Nog. The Company gone to the Ball.[3]

---

[1] *Miss Baker and Adam* Margaret (1765–1830) and Adam Calthorpe Baker (1773–1810), two of John and Priscilla Baker's three surviving children. Neither was to marry

[2] *Herring* Mary Hardy names him as William Herring. He was possibly the son of James Herring (d.1803 aged 45), of Norwich, linen and woollen draper, hatter and hosier, who was neighbour in the Haymarket to Mrs Forster's mayoral brother John Buckle. Or this may be Mrs Forster's great-nephew: John Buckle's daughter Rebecca (d.1827 aged 81) was the wife of John Herring (d.1810 aged 61), who was to serve as Mayor of Norwich 1799

[3] *ball* Henry was the only one of the young cousins not to go to the assembly

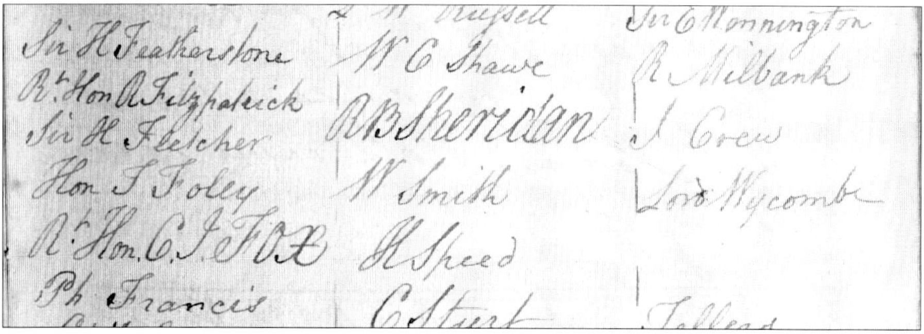

above From William Hardy's entry in his wife's diary, 24 Jan. 1794. A Foxite Whig, his highlighting of R.B. Sheridan and C.J. Fox (both stridently anti-war) shows where his sympathies lay: with the 'virtuous' MPs voting against a conflict so damaging to manufacturing and trade [*Cozens-Hardy Collection*]

MH A very fine day. Wm Brew^d^. Robt & M Raven came to dinner, Henry came home with them. Robt, W^m^, MA & the 2 Miss Ravens went to the Ball at Holt eveng 6.

JANUARY 21, TUESDAY

HR R Bye to Overstrand with beer. T Balden in Brewhouse morning, Holt afternoon with beer. G Thompson, Jno Ram & Boy pumping beer in home cask afternoon. M^r^ H at Holt all Day, WH & Ladies drank tea at Holt. R Staff came morning.

MH A fine day. Robt Raven went away Morng 8. Mr Hardy walkd to Holt foornoon, dind at Mr Moores, met the Purse Club at the Kings Head Afternoon, came home eve 10.[1] Mrs Flower of Sheringham & M Johnson came from Holt foornoon. Robt Staff & Son came foornoon, Slept here. W^m^ & the Girls drank Tea at Miss Johnsons, Holt, came home eveng 9.[2] The Parliament met . . .

JANUARY 22, WEDNESDAY

HR R Bye Drunk all day, T Balden to Salthouse with beer. Jno R & HR in M House. R Raven came Evening. WH & Ladies at holt afternoon, M^r^ H at Holt all day.

JANUARY 23, THURSDAY

HR R Bye & T Balden Drunk all day. GT & Jno R & Boy Clensed morning. HR, Jno R in M House. M^r^ H at Holt all day to Quarter Sessions, WH at home all day. R Raven put his hobby in wiskey & drove it up to Holt & after dinner whent home with Miss MR [Mary Raven] & A Raven.[3] R Staff whent home morning.[4]

[1] *purse club* Mary Hardy makes it clear that this was now meeting at the King's Head, Holt, having moved from the King's Head, Letheringsett. Holt had its own provident society, which met at the Feathers and was described in May 1795 as newly formed: 'It is for creating a fund for the payment of an annuity of £20 per annum to the widow and children of each deceased member,' (*Norw. Merc.* 2 May 1795). That figure, and the fact that its meetings were held at 1 pm, suggests that the Feathers' club was not for the ordinary labouring man

[2] *Misses Johnson* See notes for 28 Nov. 1793, 1 Jan. 1794 and 31 Mar. 1795

[3] *hobby* A small horse. The whiskey had been borrowed from Mr Branford (Diary MS: 22 Jan. 1794), the Branfords being a Horningtoft, Godwick and Oxwick farming family: see note for 17 Feb. 1794

[4] *Staff* It took the Stalham innkeeper and his son three days to call on their brewer, whose draymen gave the visitors an unfortunate impression of working habits at the brewery

JANUARY 24, FRIDAY

HR R Bye in Brewhouse morning, Edgefield afternoon with beer. T Balden to Runton with beer. Jn° R, HR in M House. G Thompson Grinding Malt for Brew. Mr H & WH {at} Out all day.

MH A Cold windy day. Mr Hardy & Wm went to Foulsham Morng 10.

From the newspaper

The anti-war amendment 1794

⟦ *Wm Hardy* [1] On Tuesday ye 21st Instant the Parliament met and the Kings Speech being read a Voat of Thanks was proposed but an Amendment was wished for in order to put an end to the French War. The Following Members being the Minority Voated for ye Amendment [2] . . .

These are the 62 Vertuous Membrs who Voted in this great contest for PEACE, against 277. ⟧

[LETHERINGSETT]

JANUARY 25, SATURDAY

HR R Bye to Wells & cart broke down. T Balden to Gunthorp morning, Briston afternoon with beer. Boy taken ill afternoon. Jn° R & HR in M House. Mr H & WH at home morning, Holt afternoon.

MH Wind high, Stormy day, frose at Night & some snow fell. Mr Hardy & Wm walkd to Holt Markt aftern, came home eveng 10. Robt Buy went to Wells, broke down his Cart at Warham, did not git home till Morng 10 . . .

JANUARY 27, MONDAY

HR R Bye to Wells with Beer & Jn° Jex & A Dobson with him to Bring home Brew Cart.[3] G Thompson & T Balden in brew house, WH at Brewing. HR & Jn° Ram in M House. Mr H at home morning, Holt afternoon. Boy ill.

JANUARY 28, TUESDAY

HR G Thompson Clensed `// morning. R Bye, T Balden drayed away Clense beer in White Hall D° [morning] & turned [?tunned] them up afternoon & HR turnd [?tunned] them into Great Cask. G Thompson, WH draying beer afternoon.

---

1 In William Hardy's hand, as he makes clear. At Coltishall he had championed the insertion in the diary of items of significance from the press, but that tradition had largely died

2 *members* William Hardy then lists the names of the 12 members of the House of Lords and 62 of the House of Commons who voted in favour of the anti-war amendment to the speech from the throne which had been moved in the Lords. The full list of names was not given in the Norwich papers, so was obtained from the London press. Among the anti-war MPs were Thomas William Coke, his brother Edward, and the brewer Samuel Whitbread jnr. Charles James Fox moved the anti-war amendment in the Commons, where William Windham spoke in *support* of the Government (having been fiercely against the American war): see note for 11 July 1794.

War was one of the defining political issues of the day, and is covered in *World*, vol. 4, chaps 6, 7, 8

3 *John Jex* (d. 26 June 1797 aged 52, bur. Letheringsett 29 June), formerly of Stody, Letheringsett blacksmith and grandfather of the village's eminent whitesmith, blacksmith and clockmaker Johnson Jex (1778–1852).

John Jex's widow Sarah was bur. Letheringsett 4 Feb. 1821 aged 74

JANUARY 29, WEDNESDAY

HR R Bye, T Balden at muck Cart morning, getting hay over & carried 1 Bar^{l} `// to T Atwood afternoon. W Tinker mending Carts afternoon, Jno Jex laying iron arm in Brew Cart.[1] Jno R, HR in M House. M^{r} H & WH at home all day. Wm Dobson from Holt came to look at Kings head.[2]

JANUARY 30, THURSDAY

HR R Bye & T Balden at Muck Cart all day, G Thompson Clensed & Grinding Malt for brew. W Tinker all day after Cart. M^{r} H & WH at home all day. Jno Ram & HR in M House.

JANUARY 31, FRIDAY

HR R Bye & T Balden muck Cart all day. Jno Ram in M House. WH & HR drove Molly in Malt Cart to Wells.[3] W Tinker & Man mending Stable doors & Brew Cart. G Thompson grinding Malt for Brew. M^{r} H at home all day, W^{m} H & Miss H at Holt Evening.

MH A dry windy day. W^{m} & HR drove the Mare Molly in Turnip Cart as far as Wells, came home even 4. He [William] & MA drank tea & Supt at Mr Moores at Holt, came home morng 3. Mrs Temple of Thornage brought to Bed with a Girl [4] . . .

FEBRUARY 1, SATURDAY

Henry Raven R Bye to N^{o} Walsham with Beer. T Balden to Viverton with Beer & Clay for Cinders fron [from] Jno Mann's. Jno Ram & HR in M House. M^{r} H & WH at stacking dales.[5] R Raven Came from Whissonsett.

FEBRUARY 2, SUNDAY

Mary Hardy A fine day. All went to our Church foornoon, Mr Burrell preach'd. Robt Raven went away after dinner, Henry rid with him as far as Fakenham. W^{m} went to Holt Church Afternoon, came home to tea . . .

FEBRUARY 3, MONDAY

HR T Balden to Cromer with beer, G Thompson dressing flour. R Bye & Boy in Brewhouse, WH Brewing. Capt Hall spreading Muck in Furze Close. M^{r} H & M^{rs} H rode to Mr Temples & Miss H at Holt at Mr Bakers. HR & Jno Ram in M House.

[1] *arm* The spindle upon which the wheel turns; the earlier broken arm might have been of timber.

Mending the beer cart proved a tricky operation involving specialists who devoted three days to the task

[2] *Dobson* See note for 15 Jan. 1794. Richard Mayes's dispute with the purse club may well have occasioned his departure from the King's Head

[3] *Molly* She had gone missing as a young filly in Apr. 1792. After searching the countryside William had managed to trace her to Raynham, four miles south of Fakenham

[4] *Mrs Temple* The register suggests the little girl was born slightly earlier. Martha, daughter of Thomas Temple and Mary, née Beverley, was bapt. Thornage 24 Jan. 1794.

There had been a double marriage in the Temple–Beverley families. Michael Beverley of Tibenham had married Mary Temple at Thornage in Dec. 1778 [date illegible]; both were single and both signed

[5] *dales* Deals; sawn planks, presumably the fruit of the sawyers' efforts. If so this was unseasoned wood which had to be stacked for years in the open, each plank separated by shallow risers to allow full aeration and prevent rot.

Henry's spelling reflects his Norfolk speech

right The Furze Closes, across the Blakeney road from Bayfield Park, showing the crumbly texture of this light, well-drained arable soil; here the ground has been prepared for potato drilling. Robert Bye borrowed the Bayfield Hall flag harrow as early as 5 Feb. 1794 to prepare the ground.

Barley was sown in the spring, in April and early May; wheat in the autumn. According to Mary Hardy's daily weather entries in her diary the only snow during the mild winter of 1793–94 fell on 25 Jan. [*MB · 2001*]

FEBRUARY 4, TUESDAY

HR R Bye to Fakenham with beer. G Thompson Clens'd `// morning & got Beer in Cask afternoon. T Balden at home all day. Mr H at home with gught [gout], WH & HR to Gunthorp. Jno R in M House.

FEBRUARY 5, WEDNESDAY

HR T Balden to Brampton with beer. R Bye Whent to Mr Forsters for Flag harrow morning, at harrow afternoon in Furze Close.[1] Jno R & HR in M House. Mr H & WH at home all day. Mr Moore & Mr Thomas dine'd hear.

FEBRUARY 6, THURSDAY

HR T Balden in Brewhouse morning, to Blakeny for 1½ Chald Coles from Mr Chaplins afternoon. R Bye at Harrow all day, G Thompson Clense Do [cleansed all day] & Grinding Malt for Brew. Mr H very Bad. WH at home morning, at Holt afternoon. Jno R & HR in M House.

MH A very fine day. Mr Hardy confind with the Gout. Wm at home all day.

FEBRUARY 7, FRIDAY

HR R Bye to Walsingham with beer, T Balden to Briston & Holt with beer. Capt Hall & G Thompson throwing mould out River.[2] Jno R, HR in M House. Mr Hardy very bad. Miss Custance came to dine & whent to Mr Forsters with WH & Miss Hardy.

MH A close Morng, wet afternoon. Mr Hardy worse then yesterda«y». Miss Custance came to dinner. Wm, MA & Miss Custance went to tea to Mr Forsters, came home eveng 10.

[1] *flag* Defined by William Marshall as 'the furrow turned' (W. Marshall, *The Rural Economy of Norfolk*, vol. 2 (London, 1787), p. 379). The fields had be harrowed to break up the clumps of soil; see also note for 10 Mar. 1796

[2] *throwing mould* Mould is a synonym for earth; in this context it is dredged silt. The River Glaven powered three waterwheels within a two-mile stretch: at Letheringsett corn watermill; the Hardys' malt-mill, brewery pumps and cornmill; and at Glandford corn watermill. The river and the brewery waterwheel culvert needed regular clearing and sluicing

From the newspaper

Wartime taxation and an accident 1794

From the News papers,[1] New Taxes to be ras^{d} this year to pay the Interest of Eleven Millions:[2]

	[£]
an aditional Tax on Bricks,[3] Tiles & Pavements [4] [of] 1*s* 6*d* pr 1000	70,000
Ditto on Slate pr ton Coastwise Ditto on Stones pr ton [5]	30,000
Ditto on Crown Glass Ditto on Plate do [glass] [6]	52,000
Brittish Spirits 1^{d} pr Gallon	107,000
Forigm [foreign] Rum pr Gall [gallon] F [French] Brandy pr Gall [gallon] [7]	136,000
Young Attorneys [8]	25,000
Surplus of the Year 1793	428,000
Paper [9]	63,000
making together	911,000
to pay the Interest	11,000,000

A Malencholy Accident happend last Monday eveng at the little Theater in the Hay Market. 14 Persons were troden & Squezd to death & many others much hurt in going down to the Pitt [10] . . .

above **Pamments; terracotta floor tiles known to Mary Hardy as 'pavements' in her Coltishall diary and when recording the rise in duty to help fund the French war (7 Feb. 1794). Made locally in brick-kilns they were particularly useful in areas subject to wet, such as kitchens, laundries and brewhouses** [*MB · 2011*]

1 *newspapers* Mary Hardy gives a very truncated summary of the proposals of the Prime Minister, William Pitt, in the Budget debate in the House of Commons

2 *interest* The figure was interest on £11 million of government borrowing, with a proportional increase in the Sinking Fund of £650,000. The new rates all related to *additional* levels of duty

3 *bricks etc* An additional duty of 1*s* 6*d* per thousand

4 *pavements* Floor tiles

5 *slate* and *stones* An additional 10*s* per ton on slate; 2*s* 6*d* per ton on stones

6 *crown glass* and *plate glass* An additional 8*s* and 10*s* 8*d* per hundredweight respectively

7 *French brandy* An additional 10*d* per gallon

8 *young attorneys* Articled clerks: £100 on every apprenticeship indenture, and £100 on each admission to practise

9 *paper* As a consequence of the new level of duty the two Norwich newspapers had to raise their retail prices as from 28 June 1794 from 3½*d* to 4*d*

10 *theatre* The King and Queen were present at the Haymarket Little Theatre in London, but were not aware of the accident until after the end of the performance

[LETHERINGSETT]

FEBRUARY 8, SATURDAY

HR R Bye to Sherington [Sharrington] & Hinderingham with beer, T Balden to Thornage & Study [Stody] with beer. G Thompson Grinding M [malt] for brew. Jere More throwing mould out River [1] & sinking Cart House with T Hall.[2] Jn° R, HR in M House. Mr H very bad. WH & Miss Custance & Miss Hardy at Holt market.

FEBRUARY 9, SUNDAY

MH A very fine day. Mr Hardy some thing better. We all went to our Church eveng 4 . . .

FEBRUARY 10, MONDAY

HR R Bye to Corpusta with beer. G Thompson, T Balden & Boy in Brewhouse, WH brewing. HR & Jn° R in M House. Mr H at home all day. Mr & Mrs & Miss Bartle came to drink tea. T Atwood came & Orderd 4 Nog.

FEBRUARY 11, TUESDAY

HR R Bye, T Balden got Clense Beer in W Hall morning, afternoon D°, whent to Weybourn with beer. WH, G Thompson, Jn° Cobb, R Bye, HR got Clense Beer in Great Cask.[3] Jn° Ram in Malt House. Mr H at home, WH at Holt Evening.

FEBRUARY 12, WEDNESDAY

HR T Balden to Holt with beer & Brot home 7 Hundred [? hundredweight] Bricks from Dawsons. R Bye very ill. Jere Moore, Capt Hall sinking Cart house, W Tinker & man all day. Jn° R & HR in M House. Mr & WH at home all day.

MH A very fine day. Mr Hardy rather lame in both feet. Wm at home all day . . .

FEBRUARY 13, THURSDAY

HR R Bye to Bale & Kettlestone with beer. T Balden at harrow morning, in brew house aftern, Boy at D° afternoon. Capt Hall in ⟦[4] Brewhouse⟧ all day. G Thompson Clensed morning, Grinding malt for brew Evening. Jn° & HR in M House. WH at Fakenham, Mr H at home all day. Jn° Cobon kild [killed] pig Morning.[5]

FEBRUARY 14, FRIDAY

HR R Bye ploughing all day. T Balden to Clay with beer & Brot home 2 Chald Cinders from Mr Manns. G Thompson grinding malt for brew. Jn° R & HR in M House. Mr [Hardy] at home all day, WH [ ].

[1] *Jeremiah Moore* (Bur. Letheringsett 13 Sept. 1818 aged 68). He specialised in river and marsh management, having dredged the river for the Hardys in 1786 and surveyed the Salthouse marshes with them 1789–90 (*Diary* 2).

He and his wife Ann (bur. Letheringsett 25 Oct. 1806), née Clarke, first appear in the parish register for the baptism of their daughter Ann in 1781. Six other children were bapt. 1784–96: Sarah, Esther, Maria, Jeremiah, David, David. They already had an older son (entry for 20 May 1794).

Moore married Letheringsett 21 Dec. 1807 Hannah Overton (bur. there 16 Mar. 1843 aged 71), whose four illegitimate children had already died: see note for 20 May 1794

[2] *sinking cart house* Laying the foundations for the cart house about to be built beside the river

[3] *John Cobb* Probably John Cobon (13 Feb.)

[4] William has erased 'ditto' in Henry's original entry 'Captain Hall in ditto all day', and substituted 'Brewhouse'. He may at the same time have asked his cousin to cut down on his lavish and confusing use of dittos. Absent for a time, they reappeared in strength two months later

[5] *John Cobon* (Bur. Letheringsett 28 Nov. 1812); described in the register as 'formerly a farmer in this parish'

MH A fine day. Mr Hardy very poorly, lame in both feett.[1] M Ann walk'd up to Holt aftern, drank tea at Mr Johnsons,[2] H Raven went for her eveng 8 in L Cart. A Total Eclipse in the Moon.[3] Wm came home from Whisonsett eveng 8 . . .

FEBRUARY 15, SATURDAY

HR R Bye & T Balden ploughing in Furze close, Jno Ram & HR in M House. Boy whent for load turnips morning. Mr H at home all day. WH at home morning, Holt market afternoon. Mr Moore Dine'd here.

FEBRUARY 16, SUNDAY [4]

HR G Thompson, R Bye, T Balden, Capt Hall & Boy got Clense Beer in home cask morning. Mr H at home all day. WH at home morning, Holt Church afternoon. G Thompson, HR walked out afternoon.[5] Jno R in M House.

FEBRUARY 17, MONDAY

HR R Bye & Boy in Brewhouse all day, T Balden at plow in Furze Close. WH Brewing & whent to the Ball. Jno R, HR in M House. G Thompson Dressing W Stones [wheatstones]. N Raven Junr came afternoon. R Raven, Jno Branford call'd Evening.[6]

MH A wet day. Wm Brewd, Mr Hardy somthing better. Nathl Raven came eveng 3. Wm, MA & Nathl went to the Ball at Holt, came home morng 3, Mrs Flower came home with them & Slept here . . .

FEBRUARY 18, TUESDAY

HR T Balden at plough all day. R Bye in Brewhouse morning, Edgefield with Beer afternoon. G Thompson Clense'd `// morning, layd down W Stones afternoon. Mr H at home all day. WH & N Raven walked to Holt morning, Company at tea afternoon. Jno R, HR in M House. T Youngman & Lad after water Wheel afternoon, T Boyce after ditch in Brewhouse pitol [Pightle].[7]

FEBRUARY 19, WEDNESDAY

HR R Bye, T Balden fetching stones from Lime Kiln morning & Lime afternoon. Mr Custance, Miss Custance calld here afternoon,[8] N Raven whent Home afternoon. Jno R, HR in M House. Mr H at home all day. WH dined at Mr Bakers, Holt. T Boyce after Ditch in pitol.

---

1 *Mr Hardy* By the next day he could not walk at all, and by 18 Feb. the gout had spread to his knee

2 *Johnson* Revd William Tower: see note for 16 Oct. 1793

3 *eclipse* 'Greater than will happen for some years to come,' the *Norwich Mercury* had forecast on 8 Feb. 1794

4 From this date Henry usually records Sundays

5 *walked out* Went for a walk

6 *Branford* John Bell Branford (d. 30 Nov. 1861 aged 98, bur. Horningtoft from Oxwick 7 Dec.); he is listed as a Godwick farmer in the 1806 county pollbook, and later farmed at Oxwick. He was engaged for 10 months 1804–05 to Nathaniel Raven's daughter Ann (*Diary 4*), but the engagement was broken off and each died without marrying

7 *Thomas Boyce* (Bur. Letheringsett 18 Feb. 1855 aged 89), a gardener and jobbing labourer who became the Hardys' farm servant when Thomas Baldwin had an accident during a beer delivery: see 23 and 24 Dec. 1794. Boyce had married the Hardys' former maidservant Sarah Jeckell at Letheringsett 22 Dec. 1791: see notes for 6 Sept. 1794 and 3 Oct. 1796

8 *Mr Custance* Shown by Mary Hardy to be Mr G. [George] Custance (b. 2 Apr. 1767, privately bapt. Fakenham 7 Apr., publicly 10 June), son of William and her cousin Phillis Custance, née Myles

left A drayhorse eases his muscles in front of a brewery dray and driver, his tack on the ground.

This was almost certainly a larger animal than the Hardys would have used. Tall Shires and Percherons needed great quantities of hay, a commodity the Hardys were usually short of in the arable country around Coltishall and Letheringsett.

Henry Raven very rarely calls the beer cart a dray (20 Aug. 1795), although the term was in use in the 18th century. Instead he uses the verb, as when the men are draying the beer around the brewery (eg 22 Apr. 1794, 27 Apr. 1797) [*drawing by Ibbotson; engraving by Tookey 1799*]

FEBRUARY 20, THURSDAY

HR T Balden, G Thompson gitting wheat out barn morning, TB to Briston afternoon with beer. R Bye ploughing in 5 Acres morning, in Brewhouse afternoon. GT Clensed afternoon, Jn° R, HR in M House. T Boyce finnished the ditch. T Bulling kild 52 Rats in barn. Mr H & WH at home all day.

FEBRUARY 21, FRIDAY

HR R Bye at home morning, Gunthorp afternoon with beer & Brot Load oziers to Mr Chamfers.[1] G Thompson Grinding Malt for Brew. T Balden ploughing morning, drawing of [off] Porter afternoon. Jn° R & HR in M House. T Boyce skreening wheat & dressing Cumbs [culms]. Mr H & WH at home all day.

[1] *Chamfer* Probably James Canfor, a Holt basketmaker (*Univ. Brit. Dir.*, vol. 3 (1794), p. 280). Osiers are flexible willow wands and twigs, or the trees themselves, the best being from the species *Salix viminalis.* They were grown commercially in osier carrs beside streams for the basket trade.

The ones carried by the drayman could have come from the headstream of the Glaven by the Cross Keys at Gunthorpe, or from the banks of the Glaven itself. William Hardy jnr planted his own osier bed in the riverside meadow at Letheringsett Hall Farm (*Diary 4*: 14 Mar. 1805)

FEBRUARY 22, SATURDAY

HR R Bye to Sheringham with beer, T Balden to Wells with beer, T Boyce throwing muck up in yards.[1] Jno R, HR in M House, porterd morning. Boy whent for load turnips. M^r^ H at home all day. WH at home morning, Holt market afternoon.

FEBRUARY 24, MONDAY

HR T Balden, G Thompson & Boy in Brew house, WH Brewing. Mr Bunnets men pulling Mr Mays stable down,[2] R Bye fetching Bricks & tiles & pavements from Jno Dawsons.[3] Jno R, HR in M House. T Boyce helping Bricklayers, Capt Hall loading Bricks. M^r^ H at home all day. Mr Bartell slept here.

MH A Close day. Wm Brew'd. Mr Hardy much as yesterday. Mr Bartell came «to» attend Eliz Hall in Labour, supt & Slept here, Mr Burrell drank tea here.[4]

[1] *muck* Piles of manure are liable to overheat and become a fire hazard if not properly managed. Unfortunately for Boyce and the others in the yard it was, according to Mary Hardy, a windy day

[2] *Bunnett* It is not clear if this was the father or son, both Holt builders. The elder John was bur. 29 Jan. 1829 aged 83; the younger 10 Feb. 1855 aged 81.

John Bunnett jnr married Holt 20 Nov. 1798 Mary Browne, signing with an elegant flowing hand. One of the witnesses was the Holt plumber William Haddon, who also worked for the Hardys

[3] *Dawson* See note for 16 Nov. 1793

[4] *Elizabeth Hall* (Bur. 24 June 1818 aged about 56), wife of 'Captain' Thomas Hall (see note for 14 Oct. 1793). The entry for 12 Mar. 1794 would suggest the premature labour of 24 Feb. was a false alarm. It might have injured the baby, Ann Hall living only three hours (although the parish registers recorded Ann's baptism and death 4 Jan. and her burial 7 Jan. 1794 —evidently an error, as

MASTER SAMSON,

THE PROPERTY OF

MESSRS COZENS-HARDY & SON,

Is at the Service of the Public this Season at £1 5s. each Mare, or £4 for 4 Mares. Groom's Fee, 2s. 6d. each Mare.

MASTER SAMSON is a beautiful brown, six years old, stands 16¾ hands high, has short legs, possesses immense power and substance, is perfectly sound, very active, good tempered, an excellent worker, and a sure Stockgetter. He obtained the £5 Prize as a yearling at the Norfolk Agricultural Show held at Fakenham, in June, 1875, and the First Prize at the North Walsham Show, in October, 1878.

His Sire—that noted horse SAMSON—the property of Mr. C. Cozens-Hardy, was a dark brown, standing 17 hands high.

His Grandsire — SAMSON — the property of Mr. R. K. Folley, of Long Sutton, was a beautiful dark brown, standing 17½ hands high, and for symmetry and activity was unrivalled.

His Dam—by Mr. G. Pearson's celebrated brown horse PRINCE — is a splendid brown cart mare, the winner of the £2 Prize as a Brood Mare at the North Walsham Show in October, 1874.

Master Samson will travel in the neighbourhood of Holt, Aylsham, St. Faith's, Coltishall, North Walsham, Bodham, Cley, and Binham.

The money to be paid to the Groom the second week in June.

Letheringsett Brewery,
March, 1880.

E. J. Playford, Printer, Holt.

right The Letheringsett brewery later had a fine heavy horse of 16¾ hands named Master Samson. His sire and grandsire, both also Samson, were even taller at 17 and 17½ hands.

Mary Hardy's grandson William Hardy Cozens-Hardy and his eldest son Clement, his partner in the brewery, offer prize-winning Master Samson's services as a stud horse in Mar. 1880 [*Cozens-Hardy Collection*]

left The Brewhouse Pightle, seen from the 18th-century roadside site of the King's Head. Here Thomas Boyce was working in the ditch probably connecting the brewery with the Hardys' liquor basin up the slope (18–20 Feb.) [*MB · 1993*]

FEBRUARY 25, TUESDAY

HR T Balden to Holt & Waybourn with beer. R Bye fetching sand morning, T Boyce casting sand morning. Jn° R, HR in M House. G Thompson, WH & R Bye & T Balden & Boy got Beer in Cask Evening.

MH A very fine morng, very wet afternoon. Mr Hardy something better, Wm at home all day. Mr Bartell went away after breakfast, came again to Supper & Slept here.

FEBRUARY 26, WEDNESDAY

HR R Bye to Stalham. T Balden to Clay for Cinders morning & Thornage afternoon with beer. T Boyce cleaning Bricks, Boy gitting wood out yard. Jn° R & HR in M House. WH gone to Norwich.

MH A fine day. Wm sett of for Norwich morn 8, Mr Bartell went with him, they Slept at Mr G Wymer.[1] Mr Hardy something better, got up Stairs at Night with his Crutches.

FEBRUARY 27, THURSDAY

HR T Balden to Dawling & Holt with beer & got two lode [loads] of sand home. G Thompson Clensed & Grinding Malt for Brew. Jn° Ram in M House. T Boyce cleaning Bricks, Boy got home lode turnips. R Bye came from Stalham, WH from Norwich. Mr H at home all day.

explained in the editorial introduction). The couple had an unhappy history of child-rearing. Since their marriage in 1787 they had also lost John in 1788 aged four months. Their third and last child John was to die in 1795 aged 10 weeks.

Betty Hall supported herself by spinning; she was convicted in 1803 of reeling false yarn and was fined (*Norw. Merc.* 30 Oct. 1803)

1 *Wymer* George (d. in St Stephen's parish, Norwich, 27 Aug. 1809 aged 72), attorney, of the Stamp Office at 42 St Giles's: see note for 13 Dec. 1793. The elaborate eulogy to his wife (d. 10 May 1795) suggests she was already suffering her fatal malady by 1794: 'An indefatigable attention to every conjugal and maternal duty rendered her inestimable as a parent and wife, whilst a peculiar serenity of disposition and pliability of mind conducted her through a series of complicated suffering . . .'

Less than six months later the sorrowing widower remarried: at Newton Flotman 3 Nov. 1795, to Miss Harrold (*Norw. Merc.* 16 May, 7 Nov. 1795)

MH A very fine day. Mr Hardy just able to git up & down Stairs on his Crutches. W^m^ & Mr Bartell came home from Norwich even 5.

FEBRUARY 28, FRIDAY

MH A Wet foornoon, fine afternoon. Mr Hardy much as yesterday. A Fast Day by Proclamation. Service at our Church Afternoon, MA went to Church, M^r^ & Mrs Forster came to our Church.[1] W^m^ went up to Holt foornoon, dind at Mr Moores, they both came to tea, Moore Supt here, Wm Herring Dind & Supt here . . .

MARCH 1, SATURDAY

Henry Raven R Bye to Overstrand with beer, T Balden fetching lime, sand & marl. Mr Bunnets Men all day. Jno Ram, HR in M house. T Boyce cleaning bricks. M^r^, M^rs^ H rode to Holt morning, WH & Miss «to» Holt market afternoon.

MARCH 3, MONDAY

HR T Balden to Runton with beer. R Bye, G Thompson & Boy in brew house, WH brewing. Jno Ram & HR in M house. W Tinker, J Tinker & man all day. Bricklayers came morning but whent away after breakfast. T Boyce sinking a place for stable.

Mary Hardy A very wet day. Mr Hardy much as yesterday. Wm Brewd. Workmen pulling down & clearing the rubish at Mays^s^ [2] . . .

MARCH 4, TUESDAY

HR T Balden to Syderstone with beer, R Bye to Hindonvestone. G Thompson Clensed `// morning, dressing flower afternoon. Bunnets men morning, one labourer all day. Tinker & men fornoon. Jno R in M house.

MARCH 5, WEDNESDAY

HR R Bye to Holt morning, Edgefield afternoon, bro^t^ home 10 Coomb 1 Bushel Barley from Mr Bozwells. T Balden at home all day, Boy to Gunthorp with Malt. Bunnets men all day, T Boyce all day. Jno Ram, HR in M house.

MH *Ash Wednesd«ay»* A fine day. Mr Hardy something better, W^m^ at home all day. Bricklayers began building a Stable at R Mays's . . .

[1] *fast day* 'A general fast and humiliation before Almighty God . . . for obtaining pardon of our sins, and for averting those heavy judgements which our manifold provocations have most justly deserved; and imploring His blessing and assistance on the arms of His Majesty by sea and land, and for restoring and perpetuating peace, safety and prosperity to himself, and to his kingdoms' (Suffolk Record Office (Ipswich): HA 24/50/19/4.5 (1), Bacon Longe Collection, Printed copy of the form of prayer to be used in all churches and chapels throughout England and Wales, 28 Feb. 1794).

Only Mary Ann attended from the Hardy family.

Henry made no entry in the brewery diary, although this does not necessarily indicate a holiday for the men as he may have been cautious about recording work on a day dedicated by royal proclamation to fasting and humiliation.

On some earlier fast days William Hardy had not honoured the requirement to let his men off work

[2] *workmen* Taken together, the two diaries explain the builders' hours that day. They arrived early, managed to carry out some demolition work at the King's Head, stopped for breakfast and were then prevented by the rain from doing further work

left The burnt-out shell of the Letheringsett brewery (centre), viewed from the west and captured by Basil Cozens-Hardy shortly after the fire of 24 Apr. 1936; the tun room (right) and the malthouse and kilns survived. When Henry Raven recorded building work in 1794 the King's Head stood in the foreground, gable end to the road.

William Hardy jnr moved both road and public house in 1808 [*Cozens-Hardy Collection*]

MARCH 6, THURSDAY

HR T Balden to Fakenham with beer, R Bye ploughing all day. Boyce & Boy «and» G Thompson got Beer in home cask & Clensed. Jno R & HR in M house. Bricklayers all day, two trowel men, one Laboror.[1] WH at home all day. Mr, Mrs Raven from Whissonsett afternoon.[2] W Tinker & two men all day.

MARCH 7, FRIDAY

HR T Balden to Clay for 2 Chaldns Cinders from Mr Manns morning, at home afternoon. R Bye ploughing morning, Briston afternoon. Jno Ram in M house, A Dobson Cutting straw. 2 trowel men & 2 Laborors all day, J Tinker & Man all day. WH & Mrs H & Mr Raven rode to Holt morning, Mr H & Mr Raven rode to Holt afternoon.[3]

MARCH 8, SATURDAY

HR R Bye ploughing all day. T Balden, T Hall, T Bulling & Boy got stack in.[4] 2 trowel men & 2 Labourours. Jno Ram in M House. J Tinker & man all day. WH at home morning, Holt market afternoon. Mr, Mrs Raven gone home morning. T Boyce at work in yard.

MARCH 10, MONDAY

HR R Bye to Wells with beer. T Balden got Load of Stones & to Corpusta with beer. 2 trowel men & two Labourours all day. T Boyce at work in Yard, Jno Ram in M house. WH gone to Norwich.

1 *trowelmen* Skilled bricklayers, as opposed to unskilled labourers. Henry was keeping a detailed record as the men would have been paid by the day

2 *Mrs Raven* Ann (bapt. Brisley 4 Jan. 1746, d. 28 Sept. 1827, bur. Whissonsett), née Fox, wife and first cousin of the diarist's brother Nathaniel (app. D3.A, figs D3.2, D3.5). She was ill during the visit and did not go out. She and the diarist were particularly close, Mrs Raven coming to live at Letheringsett Hall 1806–09 and providing companionship for Mary Hardy after Mary Ann's marriage in Dec. 1805 and Mary Raven's in Apr. 1806

3 *rode* In Nathaniel Raven's chaise

4 *got stack in* Moved the stacked barley into the barn

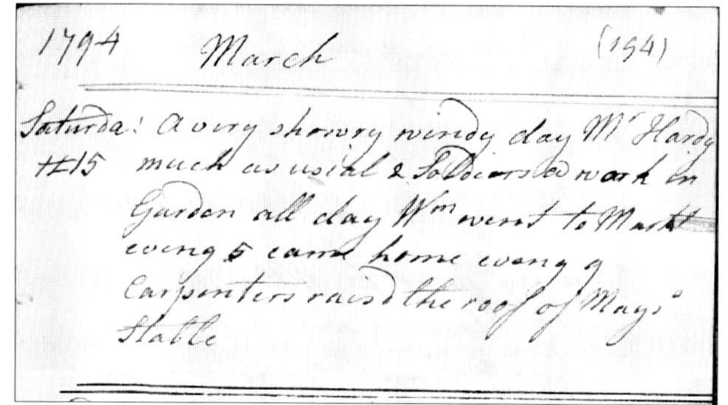
1794 March (154)

Saturday 15 A very showry windy day Mr Hardy much as usual & 2 Soldiers at work in Garden all day Wm went to Markt eveng & came home eveng 9 Carpenters raisd the roof of Mays' Stable

right '2 Soldiers at work in Garden all day': Mary Hardy's entry for 15 Mar. 1794. Henry too was aware of their presence (18 Mar.).

The coastal areas were in a ferment over defence preparations. These would have been Regulars, billeted locally, the men not camping under canvas until early summer. The Army evidently preferred to see their men busy—even if it meant gardening for civilians hostile to the war—rather than drinking in that family's alehouses [*Cozens-Hardy Collection*]

MARCH 11, TUESDAY

HR R Bye ploughing all day. T Balden in Brew house & got 1½ Chal^{n} Lime. G Thompson & Boy in Brewhouse, WH Brewing. Jno Ram in M house. 1 trowel men [man] & 1 Laboror [labourer] all Day. T Boyce sinking Mr Mays yard. W^{m} & Ja^{s} Tinker & man all day.

MARCH 12, WEDNESDAY

HR R Bye ploughing all day. T Balden in brewhouse morning, to Studdy [Stody] afternoon. G Thompson Clense'd `// & got Beer into home cask. Wm Tinker & man all day, Ja^{s} Tinker half a day, 2 trowel men & two laborers all day. Jno R & HR in M house. WH at home all day.

MH A fine Morng, raind afternoon. Mr Hardy continue very lame. We Irond linnen. MA & I went to our Church foornoon.[1] Bricklayers & Carpenters at work at R Mays^{s}. Eliz Hall brought to Bed, the Child died soon after it was born, Mr Bartell breakfasted & Dind here [2] . . .

MARCH 13, THURSDAY

HR T Balden ploughing all day, R Bye at Brampton with beer. Jno Ram in M House. 2 trowel men & 2 Laborours all day. WH at home all day. W Tinker & men all day, T Boyce at work in yards.

MARCH 14, FRIDAY

HR R Bye & T Balden & T Boyce & HR to Mr Forsters for two load of hay.[3] G Thompson grinding Malt for Brew. 2 trowel men & 2 laborers all day. Jno Ram in M House. WH at home all day. Mr Orsborn came and orderd Beer.[4] W Tinker & two men all day.

---

1 *church* Mother and daughter attended some of the Wednesday morning services throughout Lent. Their menfolk did not

2 *Elizabeth Hall* See note for 24 Feb. 1794

3 *two loads* A precise imperial measure, one load equalling 36 trusses. This would have been old hay, at 56 lb (25·4 kg) to the truss; new hay, with a greater moisture content, was 60 lb (27·2 kg) to the truss. The four men thus collected approximately 1829 kg of hay (1·83 metric tonnes) from the Bayfield estate

4 *Mr Osborne* He is not listed as an innkeeper in the county alehouse register under any of the villages receiving deliveries over the next few days (NRO: C/Sch 1/16). He may have been provisioning the military

MARCH 15, SATURDAY

HR T Balden to Overstrand with beer. R Bye to Sherington & Bale morning, Holt afternoon. Jn° Ram in M house, T Boyce at work in yards. 1 trowel man & 1 Laborer all day. Mr H at home all day. WH at home morning, Holt market afternoon. W Tinker & two men all day.

MH A very showry windy day. Mr Hardy much as usial. 2 Soldiers at work in Garden all day.[1] Wm went to Markt eveng 5, came home eveng 9. Carpenters raisd the roof of Mayss Stable . . .

MARCH 16, SUNDAY

HR T Balden Loaded for N° Walsham. WH & Miss Hardy walked to Holt Church afternoon, H Raven rode to Clay Evening. G Thompson Out afternoon. Mr H at home all Day.

MARCH 17, MONDAY

HR T Balden to N° Walsham with beer. R Bye got 3 Chaln Lime from Mr Forsters. T Boyce at work in yard morning, casting sand afternoon. Jn° Ram & H Raven in M house. G Thompson & Boy in Brewhouse all day, WH Brewing. 2 trowelmen & 2 Laborers all day. Mr H at home all Day, Miss Hardy at Holt afternoon.

MARCH 18, TUESDAY

HR T Balden to Sheringham with beer, R Bye Gunthorp with beer & Clay for Cinders from Mr Manns. Jn° Ram & HR in M House. T Boyce stopping gaps all day.[2] 2 trowel men & 2 Laborers all day. G Thompson Clensed `//. 2 Soldiers at work in Garden. WH & Mr H at home all Day. W Tinker all Day & man half a Day.

MARCH 19, WEDNESDAY

HR R Bye to Salthouse with beer & Clay for Cinders from Mr Manns. T Balden ploughing morning & Thornage afternoon, Boy at harrow afternoon. 2 trowelmen & 2 Laborers all day. G Thompson, RB & TB, Boy got Clense beer in H [home] cask. Tinker & 2 men all Day. Jn° Ram in M house. HR rode to Holt & Thornage morning. Company at Tea. T Boyce stopping gaps morning, at work in yard.

MH A very fine day. Mr Hardy finely. 2 Soldiers at work in Garden afternoon. Mrs Raven from Norwich & 3 Children, Miss Wymer, Mr & Mrs Bartell & Miss B

[1] *two soldiers* They had begun gardening the day before, and continued daily until 22 Mar. As reported in the *Norwich Mercury*, John Richard Dashwood, Sheriff of Norwich, called for action 'for the internal defence and security of this kingdom', the call being taken up at huge gatherings around Norfolk.

On 12 Apr. 1794 William Windham gave an impassioned speech at the Shirehall, Norwich, against France and in support of the Volunteers, his words being countered by the anti-war T.W. Coke. Mary Hardy's pro-defence friends and neighbours contributed to the funds, her nephew Robert Goggs of Colkirk giving £2 2*s* (*Norw. Merc.* 19 Apr. 1794).

The Hardys' names do not appear in the published lists of donors. Like very many Norfolk farmers and manufacturers they supported Coke's trenchant views.

Large numbers of Norfolk clergy supported the government's measures and contributed towards local defence funds. The larger landowners gave handsomely, Sir George Chad of Thursford, Sir Berney Brograve of Worstead and Henry Jodrell of Bayfield each giving £100 (*Norw. Merc.* 19 Apr.).

By 26 Apr. 1794 the county had collected £7020 (*Norw. Merc.*)

[2] *stopping gaps* In the hedges

drank tea here.[1] W^m^ went to the Ball at Holt eveng 9, came home M3 . . .

MARCH 20, THURSDAY

HR G Thompson & T Balden Clensed morning, harrow afternoon. R Bye, HR in M house, Jn° Ram very ill & no work. 2 trowelmen & 2 Laborers all Day, W Tinker & men all Day. T Boyce at work in yard. WH at home all Day & Company at tea.

MARCH 21, FRIDAY

HR R Bye to Hinderingham with beer, T Balden at Home all day. Boy for 2½ Hun^d^ [hundredweight] tiles. G Thompson grinding Malt for brew, Jn° Ram in M house. W Tinker & 2 men morning, 2 trowel men & 2 Laborers all Day. M^r^ H at holt all Day. WH & Miss Hardy Out all Day at Sherringham.

MARCH 22, SATURDAY

HR R Bye to Walsingham, T Balden to Cromer with beer. W Tinker & 2 men, 2 trowel men & 2 Laborers all Day. T Boyce at work in yard. M^r^ H & WH at home all Day, at Holt Evening. Jn° R, HR in M house.

[[MARCH 23, SUNDAY

William Hardy jnr HR sett off at 5 in the morn^g^ for Whissonsett & returned in the Even^g^. Jn° Wade called in the forenoon. Mr Burrell preached in afternoon. Ja^s^ Moor came & drank Tea. M^r^, M^rs^, Miss [Hardy] & WH at Church.]]

MARCH 24, MONDAY

Henry Raven R Bye to Holt & Briston with beer. G Thompson, Balden & Boy in brewhouse, WH Brewing. Jn° R, HR in M house. 2 trowelmen & 2 laborers all Day, W Tinker & 1 man all Day. M^r^ H at home all Day. T Boyce at work in yard.

MH A fine day, turnd hasy afternoon. Wm Brew'd. Mr Hardy at home all day. Carpenters & Bricklayers began repairing R Mays^s^ House.

MARCH 25, TUESDAY

HR R Bye at harrow in Furze close all Day. T Balden helping in M house & brewhouse, G Thompson Clensed `//. Boy getting home sand & half Chal^n^ Lime. T Boyce dig«g»ing sand & barrowing bricks, 2 trowel men & 2 Laborers all Day, W Tinker & 2 men. W Dobson began

[1] *Mrs Raven* Wife of Henry Raven (not known to be a relation), innkeeper of the King's Head in Norwich Market Place; his first wife Sarah, née Baldwin, also a friend of the Hardys and Bartells, had died in 1786 aged 25.

The innkeeper Henry Raven features in Parson Woodforde's diary, the Weston rector choosing to stay at the King's Head when in the city

above The King's Head at Letheringsett, as rebuilt on its new site in 1808 when it was set well back from the road (and from the Hardys' south-facing windows). William Dobson replaced Richard Mayes as innkeeper 25–26 Mar. 1794.

It is seen here across the Brewhouse Pightle while it was hosting the large gathering after Beryl Cozens-Hardy's funeral on Friday 14 Oct. 2011 [*MB · 2011*]

above Southrepps: the former Crown, viewed from its back yard, part of which used to be a large bowling green. At £600 this was the most expensive public-house purchase recorded by Mary Hardy, and at £40 Robert Summers' annual rent was the highest of the tied-house rentals in 1797.

To the left, across Crown Loke, can be seen another former Morgans' tied house, the New Inn. When the Norwich brewers bought the Letheringsett tied estate in 1896 they acquired a competitor to their existing house next door. The Crown lost out and was closed by 1904 [*MB · 2001*]

to draw beer on his own account. Mr, Mrs & WH sett out in Mrs Shephards coach at 8 oClock in morning.

MH A very foggy Morng, fine day. Mr Hardy, I & Wm went to Southreps morng 8 in Mrs Sheppards post Chaise, dind there, did not agree for the House, came home eveng past 7, Mr Moore of Holt met us there.[1] Mr Creamer of Beeston was Maried to Miss Buckell of Cringleford.[2]

MARCH 26, WEDNESDAY

HR R Bye & Boy at harrow all Day. R Bye [?], HR in M house. G Thompson dressing W [wheat] Stones. T Balden to Runton with beer & Cromer for winderframes.[3] W Tinker & 2 men, 2 trowelmen & 2 Laborers all Day.

[1] *Southrepps* The Hardys were to buy the Crown at Southrepps 3 Apr. 1794, this freehold being the one quoted by William Hardy jnr as his electoral qualification in 1802 and 1806. Despite her very restricted social life since her illness Mary Hardy made the effort to be present at important negotations over the purchase of the inn; James Moore of Holt acted as the Hardys' attorney

[2] *Cremer* Cremer Cremer (b. 11 June 1768, d. 29 Apr. 1808). Formerly Cremer Woodrow, of Beeston Hall, on the coast at Beeston Regis, he had been adopted by his great-uncle Edmund Cremer and took his surname in 1785. His wife Ann (d. 21 Dec. 1860 aged 88, having been a widow 52 years), was the daughter of Thrower Buckle (d. 5 Feb. 1795 aged 62), of Cringleford, Norwich. Her uncle John Buckle (see note for 12 Jan. 1794), then Mayor of Norwich, was a political supporter of Mr Cremer's neighbour William Windham of Felbrigg; her aunt was Mrs Forster of Bayfield. The Cremers' fortunes are recounted by their descendant R.W. Ketton-Cremer in *Felbrigg: The story of a house* (Futura Publications, London, 1982), pp. 267–86. See also note for 6 Feb. 1795

[3] *window frames* Percy Millican refers to this local pronunciation: 'Horstead House then [1814] passed to . . . Edmund Henry Lyon, who is said to have rejoiced

in the nickname of Dandy Lyon. He later added the name of Winder to his own which necessitated the change of nickname to Beau Winder!' (P. Millican, *A History of Horstead and Stanninghall, Norfolk* (Norwich, 1937), p. 119)

---

[1] *getting malt over* From the storage area in the huge roof space of the malthouse to the malt-mill between the malthouse and brewhouse

[2] *quicks* An unwanted creeping weed: see note for 15 Oct. 1793

[3] *cow* The cows and dairy were the women's responsibility (*World*, vol. 1, chap. 8). The red cow was probably a Norfolk Red, of a deep mahogany colour

[4] *evening* Mary Hardy explains that William could not go to market until the workmen had left off

Southrepps
Parsonage
A
M
Crown
Ale Ho.
Direction
Post

above **The Crown at Southrepps, south of the church, is marked as an alehouse on Faden's map; Mary Hardy calls it an inn (3 Apr. 1794)** [*Faden's Map of Norfolk 1797: Larks Press 1989*]

R Bye at harrow afternoon, Jno Ram came in M house at noon. WH at home all Day, Mr H at home all Day. Mr, Mrs & Miss Baker drank tea here afternoon.

MH A fine day. Mr Hardy & Wm at home all day. Hannah Bone came to dinner. Mr & Mrs & Miss Baker drank tea here. Wm Dobson took R Mays's House . . .

MARCH 27, THURSDAY

HR R Bye, T Boyce at harrow all Day. G Thompson Clense'd morning, began «grinding» Malt for brew. T Balden & Boy got Beer in home Cask & help«ed» to Clense morning & clearing fat [vat] «and» getting M Over afternoon.[1] Jno Ran [Ramm] & HR in M house. W Tinker & 1 man all Day, 2 trowel men & 2 Laborers all Day. Mr H & WH at home all Day.

MARCH 28, FRIDAY

HR T Balden ploughing morning, Clay with beer afternoon, R Bye to Fakenham with beer. G Thompson grinding M [malt] for brew. W Tinker & man all Day, 2 trowel men & 2 Laborers all Day. J Ram, H Raven in M house. Mr H & WH at home all Day, T Boyce at work in yard. Capt Hall, HR & Boy Burning quicks afternoon.[2]

MH A fine day. Wm at home all day. Mr Hardy, I & MA drank tea at Mr Bartells. Mr Atwood at work in Garden Afternoon. Spotted Cow Calf'd, the red Cow Calfd in the Night [3] . . .

MARCH 29, SATURDAY

HR R Bye to Kettlestone with beer, T Balden to Sheringham with beer. W Tinker & man, 2 trowel men & 2 Laborers all Day. T Boyce at work in yards. Jno Ram & HR in M house. Mr H, WH at home all Day, WH at Holt market Evening.[4]

MARCH 31, MONDAY

HR T Balden to Wells with beer. R Bye, G Thompson & Boy in Brewhouse, WH brewing. Jno Ram & H Raven in M house. 2 trowelmen & 2 Laborers all Day, W Tinker & 2 men all Day. Mr H at home all Day, Mr Moore drank tea here. T Boyce at work in yard.

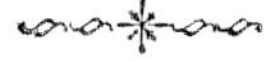

APRIL 1, TUESDAY

Henry Raven T Balden ploughing all Day. R Bye help«ing» to Clense `// & onloded Cinders morning & to Clay with beer, bro[t] home 2 Chal[d] Cinders from M[r] Manns. 2 trowelmen & 2 Laborers all day, W Tinker & 2 men. T Boyce at work in yards. Boy whent for 1 Chal[d] Lime. T Atwood & Skiffins at work in garden.[1] Jn[o] Ram & HR in M house. M[r] H & WH at home all Day.

APRIL 2, WEDNESDAY

HR R Bye ploughing morning, T Balden & Boy at harrow morning. G Thompson, R Bye, T Bal[d] & D[o] [the boy] got Clense Beer in home Cask afternoon. Tinker all day, 2 trowel men & 1 Laborer all Day. M[r] H & WH at home all Day. Jn[o] Ram & H Raven in M house. Boyce at work in yard, T Atwood at work in Garden.

APRIL 3, THURSDAY

HR T Balden to Edgefield with beer & drawing of [off] Porter. G Thompson Clensed morning, begun «grinding» Malt for brew. R Bye & Boy help«ing» to Clense & clearing fat [vat] & drawd of [drew off] Porter. Jn[o] Ram & HR in M house, T Boyce at work in yard. 2 trowelmen & 2 Laborers all Day, W Tinker & 1 man all Day. M[r] H at home morning, Holt afternoon, WH at home all Day. M[r] Moore Dine'd here.

Mary Hardy A fine Morng, Wet afternoon. M[r] Moore dind here, M[r] Hardy & he rid up to Holt afternoon to meet M[r] Grey & Mr Summers of Southreps, bought the Crown Inn of Southreps for £600, to take possession at Micheal-mas next.[2] Mr H supt at M[r] Moores & came home even past 10 . . .

APRIL 4, FRIDAY

HR R Bye to Waybourn morning, W Dobsons afternoon. T Balden fetching 4 Load sand morning & lime afternoon. G Thompson grinding M for Brew. Jn[o] Ram & HR in M house. W Tinker & 1 Man all Day, 2 trowelmen & a Laborer{s} all Day. M[r] H & WH at home all Day. T Boyce at work in yard.

APRIL 5, SATURDAY

HR R Bye to Syderstone with beer, T Balden ploughing morning in Furze Close & to Briston with beer afternoon. T Boyce at work in yard, Boy ploughing after-

[1] *Atwood and Skiffins* See note for 16 Oct. 1793.
James William Skiffins married at Blakeney 1788 Ann, daughter of Thomas Atwood; they were the parents of the Hardys' maidservant 1808–10 Mary Ann (b.*c.*1788) and of their boy 1807–08 James William jnr (b.1791). James snr moved in 1795 from the Black Boys to the White Lion at Holt, the house across the road from his father-in-law at the Dolphin. There he failed in business in 1806, his two principal creditors being William Hardy jnr and Samuel Love, to whom he signed over all his estate and effects (*Norw. Merc.* 22 Mar. 1806). He sold up from the White Lion 3 Oct. 1808 (*Diary 4*).
I am grateful to Elaine Ulph of Old Costessey, Norwich, and Helen Rees of Tasmania for details of the Skiffins family tree

[2] *Crown Inn* Then the only public house in this large village of 571 persons (1801 census), south of Cromer; it lay 13 miles from the brewery (rear endpaper map). John Summers was the inn-keeper (10 Oct. 1794) and perhaps owner (11 Oct.), and was present at the transaction at Holt. The Crown was valued by Messrs Spelman of Norwich in 1895 at £800 freehold (Cozens-Hardy Collection: Valuation of estates 1895).
See also notes for 10 Sept. and 21 Oct. 1794

above Wells, East Quay: the former Jolly Sailor (far left) faces north out to sea. The Everitt family running the house was heavily indebted. John Everitt, shipwright and publican, was released from Norwich Castle in July 1794 under the provisions of the Insolvency Act as his debts did not exceed £1000. William Hardy had Nicholas Everitt, presumably his visitor of 7 Apr. 1794, arrested for debt 21 Sept. 1795 [*MB · 2001*]

noon. Jn° Ram, H Raven in M house. 2 trowel men & 2 Laborers all Day, Tinker & 2 men all Day. M^r H at home all Day. M^rs H & Miss Hardy at Holt afternoon. WH at home all Day, at Holt Evening.

MH A fine day. Mr Hardy at home all day. I & MA walkd up to Holt afternoon, went to Fleggs Sale a little while,[1] drank tea at Mr Davys, bought some Sheets. W^m came for us in L Cart after tea, came home eveng past 9. Jo^s Davy sett of for London yesterday . . .

APRIL 6, SUNDAY

HR G Thompson, R Bye, T Balden & Boy got Beer in home Cask. M^r H & WH at home all Day. Famaly all whent to Church afternoon.

APRIL 7, MONDAY

HR T Balden, G Thompson, Boy in Brewhouse all Day. R Bye to Beckhigh with beer.[2] W Hardy brewing. Jn° Ram, HR in M house. 2 trowelmen & 2 Laborers all Day, W Tinker & 3 Men all Day. M^r H at home all Day, 2 Gentlemen from Wells.

---

[1] *Flegg* John, tailor and shopkeeper, had assigned his estate and effects for the benefit of his creditors, and his stock and household furniture were sold 4–5 Apr. at the King's Head, Holt.

He remained in business, trading as a tailor, habit-maker and staymaker at Holt (*Norw. Merc.* 29 Mar., 17 May 1794)

[2] *Beckhithe* A small fishing station at the foot of the cliff in the parish of Overstrand. It had no public house of its own, and it is likely that Bye was calling at the White Horse at the Beckhithe end of Overstrand. Henry uses the two place names interchangeably (eg 1 Mar. 1794)

MH A Showry day. Wm Brewd, Mr Hardy at home all day. Mr Everett & Mr Horsefall drank tea here.[1]

APRIL 8, TUESDAY

HR T Balden help to Clense `// & to Thornage with beer morning, Holt afternoon, G Thompson clense'd `// morning. Boy got a Load thornes to Meadow, Jno Fox stopping gaps.[2] Ja^{s} Tinker all Day, 1 trowel men [man] & 1 Laborer all Day. Jno Ram, HR in M house. M^{r} H at home fornoon, Holt after. WH at home all Day.

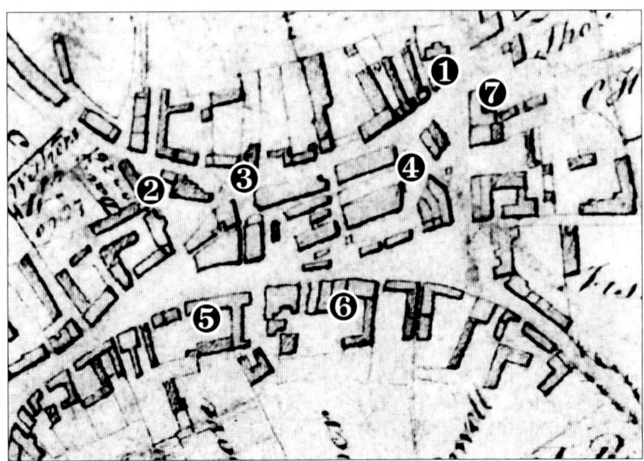
1
2
3
4
5
6
7

above Holt town centre, from the enclosure map of 1810 by Charles Burcham. Seven public houses were supplied from Letheringsett for some or all of the time 1781–1809, and are listed here with the names of their innkeepers in 1793–94. Only the Black Boys and possibly the White Lion were also tied to Letheringsett by 1793. An eighth house in business in 1793–94, the Three Mariners, with Thomas Harvey as innkeeper, had no link to the Hardys. Numbers are here superimposed on the enclosure map for the purposes of the list:

1. *Angel*	Henry Goggle (supply by the Hardys had ceased *c.*1789)
2. *Black Boys*	James William Skiffins
3. *Bull*	William Bulling, followed by Joseph Baker
4. *Dolphin*	Thomas Atwood
5. *King's Head*	Henry Crafer
6. *Three Feathers*	Elizabeth Sheppard
7. *White Lion*	John Howard

[TNA: PRO MR1/257, *Holt enclosure map 1810, detail*]

[1] *Horsfall* Revd Samuel, Curate of Barney 1784 and of Wells, succeeded the Hardys' friend Revd Benjamin Crofts as Rector of Gressenhall 1 July 1797. He was one of the bevy of 'literates' (non-graduate clergy) in the diocese (*World*, vol. 3, chap. 1). His companion was probably Nicholas Everitt of the Jolly Sailor (note for 21 Sept. 1795), who was tied by mortgage to William Hardy; the carpenter John Wordingham paid off the mortgage 3 Jan. 1797.

The *Norwich Mercury* of 12 July 1794 announced John Everitt's release from prison, stating that his debts did not exceed £1000. Insolvency Acts permitted the clearing of selected categories of debtors from gaols if their principal creditors lodged no formal objection. The Curate of Wells may have been standing surety or acting as intermediary in a more general capacity.

The subject of debt and in particular the innkeepers' lack of liquidity is covered in *World*, vol. 2, chap. 11

[2] *John Fox* (Bapt. Aylmerton 7 Apr. 1751, bur. Letheringsett 25 Dec. 1832 'aged 83'), a day labourer formerly of Hempstead-by-Holt; he marr. Letheringsett 7 Nov. 1775 Elizabeth, née Bransby (bur. there 15 Dec. 1824 aged 74), a Quaker. See also *Diary 2*: 17 Dec. 1784. I am grateful to Elaine Ulph of Old Costessey for help with the Fox family tree

facing page Letheringsett Hall, the Hardys' home with its 1809 Greek Doric portico, viewed from the south-west corner of the tun room (right).

The lopsided telegraph pole stands on the site of the old King's Head, where teams of builders spent weeks at work after William Dobson's arrival as innkeeper in 1794. The brewery stands across the road from the church, the tower of which can be seen behind the Hall portico.

The draymen were put to work 20 Apr. 1794—Easter morning, the holiest day in the Christian calendar. The timing of that beer delivery to the King's Head did not clash with the church service, but the following week's may have done [*MB · 2001*]

MH A very fine day. We washd 4 weeks linnen. W^m^ at home all day. Mr Hardy rid to Mr Moores at Holt afternoon, paid Mr Bird of Thornage for Albro [Aldborough] Publick House 300 Guineas, came home eveng 7[1] . . .

APRIL 9, WEDNESDAY

HR T Balden to Wells with beer. R Bye ill morning, ploughing afternoon, Boy ploughing all Day. Jno Ram, HR in M house. W Tinker & 3 Men all Day, 1 trowel men [man] & 2 Laborers all Day. M^r^ H at home all Day. WH at home morning, at Blakeny afternoon. M^r^, M^rs^ & Miss Bartell & Mr Wade drank tea here. Jno Fox stoping gaps.

APRIL 10, THURSDAY

HR R Bye at Thornage & Hindonvestone with beer. G Thompson & Boy to Holt for winder frames & Clense'd morning, begun «grinding» Malt for brew. W Tinker & 3 Men all Day, 2 trowelmen & 2 Labo^s^ [labourers] all Day. Jno R, HR in M house. Jno Fox stoping gaps. M^r^ H & WH at home all Day.

MH A cold Showry day. Mr Hardy & W^m^ at home all Day, Bottled some red Port in eveng, 10 Doz.[2] Raind in Night . . .

APRIL 11, FRIDAY

HR R Bye helping in M house morning & to Sheringham with beer. T Balden ploughing in Furze Close, G Thompson grinding M for Brew. W Tinker & 3 Men all Day, 2 trowel men & 2 Laborers all Day. Jno Ram & HR in M house. M^r^ H & W [William] at home all Day. Jno Fox stoping gaps.

APRIL 12, SATURDAY

HR T Balden to Brampton with beer. R Bye ploughing morning, Edgefield after noon. Jno Ram, HR in M house. HR set of to Whissonsett Evening six. 2 trowel men & 2 Laborers all Day. W Tinker & 3 men morning, 2 men afternoon. Jno Fox stoping «gaps». M^r^ H at home all Day. WH at home morning, Holt Market afternoon.

APRIL 13, SUNDAY

HR R Staff came for Cart.[3] R Bye Loaded for Stalham afternoon & sett of at 10 oClock Evening. HR & R [Robert] Raven came from Whissonsett.

---

[1] *Aldborough* The Black Boys: see note for 24 Oct. 1793

[2] *10 dozen* 120 bottles

[3] *for cart* For a delivery by the beer cart; an urgent order, to judge from the response. By waiting for nightfall the drayman could hope to avoid the attention of the magistrates over Sunday working.

The Stalham innkeeper stayed for dinner and supper at the Hardys', thus presumably being able to guide Robert Bye on the 25-mile journey in the dark to the far-flung outpost (rear endpaper map)

APRIL 14, MONDAY

HR G Thompson, T Balden & Boy in brew house all Day, WH Brewing Porter. Jn° Ram, HR in M house. W Tinker & 3 men all Day, 1 trowel man & 2 Laborors all Day. Mr H & WH at home all Day. Boy whent for 1 Chald Lime.

APRIL 15, TUESDAY

HR T Balden to Corpusta with «beer», R Bye home from Stalham. Jn° Ram, HR in M house. G Thompson Clensed `// morning, striping Male afternoon.[1] W Tinker & 1 man all Day, 2 trowel men & 1 Laborer morning, 2 laborers afternoon. Mr H & WH at home all Day, WH Rode to Brinton Evening. Jn° Fox at work in yard.

MH A fine day. Mr Hardy at home all day. «I» Went to Speak to Mrs Burrell in eveng. Wm went to Fokers of Briston [Brinton] after tea with the Mare Molly to go to Norwich Fair tomorrow to be sold [2] . . .

APRIL 16, WEDNESDAY

HR R Bye to Walsham with beer, T Balden to Fakenham with beer. Jn° Ram, HR in M house. W Tinker & 1 man all Day, 2 trowelmen & 2 Laborers all Day. Jn° Fox at work in yard. Mr H at home all Day. WH at home morning, Bodham afternoon. Recd of W Bulling sow & 7 pigs at £3.

[1] *stripping male* Cleaning or sifting meal, the second of the four grades of flour. Henry's Norfolk vowel sound is reflected in his spelling of meal

[2] *Norwich Fair* Held on the Thursday before Good Friday in Tombland, the broad open space outside the west end of Norwich Cathedral's precincts. Molly did not find a purchaser in Norwich (1 May).

Norfolk's fairs, which played an important social as well as commercial role, are located on the front endpaper map.

The diarists record 25 places where fairs were held, but the actual number of events noted by them was greater, many towns and villages holding two a year, such as Holt, or even three, such as Cawston. See *World*, vol. 3, chap. 10

above **The Hardys' maltings in the spring, with the River Glaven running along the east wall of the malthouse and kilns** [*MB · 1993*]

APRIL 17, THURSDAY

HR T Balden to Runton with beer. R Bye fetching 3 Chal^{d} Lime morning, sand afternoon. Jno Ram, H Raven in M house. W Tinker & 1 man all Day. GT & WH Clensed Porter morning. 2 trowelmen & 2 Laborers all Day. Jno Fox casting gravle [gravel]. M^{r} H at home all day, WH at Clay afternoon.

MH A very fine day. Mr Hardy at home all day. W^{m} went to Cley with Mr Moore to see the New Bath, dind & drank tea at Mr Ellis's, came home eveng 10.[1] Moore supt here, M^{r} & Mrs Bartell supt here . . .

APRIL 18, FRIDAY

HR R Bye to Study & Briston with beer & Mr Forsters for 1 Load of Hay. G Thompson Grinding M for brew. T Balden & Boy at harrow all Day. Jno Fox at work in yard morning, burning quicks afternoon. Jno Ram, H Raven in M house. M^{r} H & WH at home all Day. Capt Hall whent with R Bye for Load of Hay. W Tinker & 1 man, 2 trowelmen & 1 Laborer all Day.

APRIL 19, SATURDAY

HR T Balden to Cromer with beer. R Bye to Bullins [Bulling's] with beer & Skiffins & got 16 Coomb barley out barn. Jno Ram & H Raven in M house, Jno Fox at work in yard. W Tinker & 1 man all Day, 2 trowel men & 2 laborers all Day. M^{r} H at home all Day. WH at home morning, Holt afternoon with Miss Hardy.

APRIL 20, SUNDAY

HR T Balden, R Bye carrd 2 Nog [carried two barrels of nog] to Dobsons morning. Famaly all whent to Church afternoon.

APRIL 21, MONDAY

HR G Thompson, R Bye & Boy in brewhouse. WH Brewing & supt at Dobsons. 2 trowel men & 2 Laborers all Day. T Hall at harrow morning in Furze Close. T Balden at harrow morning, ploughing afternoon. Jno Ram & HR in M house. W Tinker & 2 men all Day. Capt Hall at harrow afternoon in 5 Acres.[2] M^{r} H at home all Day, T Temple drank tea here.

MH A very warm dry day. Mr Hardy at home, W^{m} brewd Porter. A Town meeting at Dobsons, M^{r} H & W^{m} supt there, came home past 11.[3] Atwood at work in Garden . . .

---

[1] *new bath* Robert Anthony had taken over: 'Cley new and elegant saltwater baths' were to open 16 June for public bathing; 'NB hot baths will be provided' (*Norw. Merc.* 7 June 1794). He was a Cley shopkeeper; his wife Ann became Mary Hardy's friend and fellow member of the Methodist congregation at Cley (*Diary 4*)

[2] *'Captain' Hall* He is the same labourer as the Thomas Hall who was harrowing elsewhere that morning

[3] *town meeting* Letheringsett held its parish meeting on Easter Monday, when new officers were elected for the year

APRIL 22, TUESDAY

HR Luke Basham mending harnes«s». WH & R Bye dray'd Clense Beer into W Hall. G Thompson, Jno Fox, M^r^ H & Boy put Clense Beer in Cask W Hall. T Balden at plough all Day, T Hall at harrow all Day. Jno Ram, HR in M house. W Tinker & 3 Men D^o^ [all day], 2 trowel men & 2 Laborers all Day.

APRIL 23, WEDNESDAY

HR T Balden to Thornage with beer morning, Sowing & ploughing afternoon, T Hall ploughing in barley all Day. R Bye to Salthouse & Sheringham with beer. Jno R & HR in M house. Jno Fox at work in yard morning, spreading outholling in B house pitol [Brewhouse Pightle] afternoon.[1] W Tinker & 3 men all day, 2 trowelmen & 2 Laborers all Day. M^r^ H & M^rs^ H & Miss Hardy to Mr Forsters to tea, WH at home all day.

MH A fine warm day. Mr Hill dind here. Mr Hardy, I & MA drank tea at Mr Forsters of Bayfield. W^m^ at home all day.

APRIL 24, THURSDAY

HR R Bye & T Balden ploughing morning, T Balden to Clay with beer afternoon. Boy to Gunthorp with 4 Coomb malt. G Thompson Grinding M for brew. Jno Ram & H Raven in M house. Tinker & 3 men all Day. 2 trowelmen all Day, 2 Laborers till 10 oClock, only 1 till night.[2] M^r^ H at home all Day. WH to Sheringham. Jno Fox at work in yard morning spreading gravil in yard. Ja^s^ Lee came for fat^ng^.[3]

MH A hot dry day. Mr Hardy at home all day. W^m^ rid to Mr Flower at Sheringham foornoon, he was not at home, went from thence to lower Sheringham,[4] came home eveng 6, went to the Assembly at Holt eveng 8, came home M3 . . .

APRIL 25, FRIDAY

HR R Bye to Beckhigh with beer. Balden, T Hall ploughing in Furze Close. Boy burning quicks afternoon & to Holt fair. HR whent to see pig waid [weighed]. Jno R in M house. Tinker & 3 men morning, 2 men afternoon. M^r^ H at home all Day. WH & Miss H at holt afternoon. 1 trowel men [man] & 1 Laborer all Day.

[1] *outholling* Scour; silt. The derivation appears to be from *holl*, the Anglo-Saxon word for a ditch; thus to outholl is to scour or shovel out a ditch. Here John Fox was spreading the outholling—fertile silt from the bed of the ditch—over the meadow. See W. Marshall, *The Rural Economy of Norfolk*, vol. 1, p. 101; vol. 2, pp. 76–7, 385; also R. Forby, *The Vocabulary of East Anglia*, vol. 2, p. 240.

The use of dialect words by Henry and his fellow diarists is listed in *World*, vol. 1, app. 1.A

[2] *till night* For the moment Henry, unlike his aunt and cousin, divides the day into morning (before noon), afternoon and evening, with no forenoon between the first two. 'Night' may mean nightfall or denote the end of a normal working day (about 6–7 pm). His practice soon changes (eg 7, 9, 11, 12 July 1794)

[3] *fattening* The fattening pig, which Henry was to see being weighed the next day. The pigs were kept in the brewery and fed on brewer's grains

[4] *Lower Sheringham* The coastal, fishing part of the village, where the Crown perched precariously on the cliff edge; as with Beckhithe and Overstrand to be distinguished from its hinterland of Upper Sheringham, where Cook Flower's house stood on rising ground exposed to the north and east winds

above St Michael-at-Plea, Norwich. John Wells, the owner of the Coltishall maltings and brewery which William Hardy had managed, his wife Elizabeth and many of their children lie buried beneath the chancel step. On 26 Apr. 1794 Mary Hardy learned that her cousin had married John Wells's daughter. The name of the church derives from its former role as the Court of Common Pleas for the Archdeacons of Norwich [*MB · 2011*]

APRIL 26, SATURDAY

HR T Balden to Edgefield & Bale with beer. R Bye & Cap[t] Hall ploughing, Boy at harrow morning. Jn[o] Ram & HR in M house. Tinker & 1 man all Day, 1 trowel men & 1 Laborer all Day. M[r] H & M[rs] & Miss H at Holt afternoon. WH rode to Holt morning, at home afternoon.

MH A very warm dry day. M[r] Hardy, I & MA rid up to Holt Mark[t], drank tea at M[r] Bakers, home even 8. W[m] rid up after tea, came home eveng 10. Heard Peter Raven was Maried last Thursday to Miss Wells of Norwich.[1]

APRIL 27, SUNDAY

HR R Bye & T Balden Car[d] 4 Bar[s] Beer in[to] Dobsons.[2] Famaly all whent to Church morning, WH at Holt afternoon.

MH A Showry day. All went to our Church foornoon, a Communion, no Sermon.[3] W[m] went to Holt Church Afternoon, drank tea at M[r] Moores & he came home with him & Supt here . . .

[1] *Peter Raven* Son of the diarist's first cousin Peter Raven (1738–1805), of the Horningtoft branch, and Elizabeth (d.1800 aged 59), he was bapt. Litcham 12 May 1765. Father and son were surgeons at Litcham; the family tree is in *Diary 2*: app. D2.A, fig. D2.3.

The bride's father John Wells (1735–1823), merchant and manufacturer, and his wife Elizabeth (d.1834 aged 89), née Money, lived in the parish of St Michael-at-Plea, Norwich, where he was serving as Sheriff of Norwich 1793–94. The marriage was conducted by Revd John Wells, possibly the son of Thomas, great-uncle of the bride's father. The Wells brewing dynasty is charted in *World*, vol. 2, chap. 8, where there is a family tree. Revd Mr Wells is not listed in *Alum. Cantab.* or *Alum. Oxon.*, suggesting he was a non-graduate clergyman.

Peter Raven jnr and Elizabeth Money Wells (b.1767) had one son, Peter Wells Raven (bapt. Litcham 29 June 1796, bur. there 5 Aug. 1796). The young mother was buried at Litcham on 4 July 1797, according to the register. However the *Norwich Mercury* announced 8 July that she had died on 6 July

[2] *car[d]* The sentence reads, 'R. Bye and T. Baldwin carried 4 barrels of beer into Dobson's'

[3] *Communion* This was the 1st Sunday after Easter, there being no Communion on Easter Day itself

APRIL 28, MONDAY

HR T Balden, G Thompson & Boy in Brewhouse all Day, WH Brewing. R Bye, T Hall finnish [finished] sowing Barley. Jn° Ram & HR in M house. Tinker & 3 men all Day, 1 trowel man & 1 Laborer all Day. Mr H at home all Day. Mr Tempel's 2 men turning muck.

MH A cold windy stormy day. Wm brew'd Porter. Mr Hardy at home all day.

APRIL 29, TUESDAY

HR T Balden, G Thompson got Clense Beer in W Hall morning, got it in Cask afternoon. Jn° Ram, HR in M house. WH helping Beer in to cask. Capt Hall, R Bye p«l»oughing all day. W Tinker Junr all Day, W Tinker morning.[1] 2 trowel men & 2 Laborers all Day. Mr H at home all Day.

MH A Cold windy day. Mr Hardy & Wm at home all day. Mr T Temple drank tea here, bought the Muck in our yards for 30 Guineas . . .

APRIL 30, WEDNESDAY

HR T Balden to Fakenham with beer. R Bye sowing seeds morning, in brewhouse afternoon.[2] W Tinker all Day, 2 trowel men & 2 Laborers all day. Jn° Ram & HR in M House. G Thompson Cleanse'd. Mr H & WH at home all day. Mr Youngmans man & Lad here morning.

[1] *William Tinker jnr* Son of the carpenter's first wife Mary (bur. Letheringsett 17 Sept. 1787 aged 31), née Brett. William jnr was learning his father's trade early, having been bapt. 11 Mar. 1783. A carpenter of the same name, presumably this same son, carried out much of the rebuilding of the Hall under William Hardy jnr 1832–34, as recorded in William's diary (held in the Cozens-Hardy Collection)

[2] *seeds* Probably grass seed. The various types were of great interest to farmers and agriculturalists, and to the rector John Burrell who, as 'J.B.' of Letheringsett, had a letter published in the *Norwich Mercury* 21 June 1794. He described the properties of a grass, the heart trefoil or clover, growing on Benjamin Barcham's land (by the sea) at Sheringham, 'the produce of a bag of seed cast upon the sea-beach more than 40 years ago' and far superior to the ordinary variety

left Another dawn view of the maltings, where Henry worked alongside experienced John Ramm. The brewer, miller and millwright William Gunton Thompson lived with his wife Ann in the cottage seen here, built by William Hardy in 1792 against the south-east corner of the malthouse.

A sluice by the north wall of the cottage (glimpsed behind the trunk of the small tree) controls the entry to the culvert which carries river water under the malthouse to the brewery yard and thence to the waterwheel [*MB · 1998*]

right In the waterwheel tunnel running under the main road, looking towards its southern opening in the brewery yard; 11-year-old Christopher Bird has to duck under the low roof. This photograph was taken from close to the site of the wheel, called by the Hardys their 'slave'—as we learn from William Stones's long poem of *c.*1823, *The Garden of Norfolk* [*MB · 1989*]

facing page In the same spirit Henry Raven records in his MS that after working on the wheel the millwright 'set [the] waterwheel at liberty' on 6 May 1794 [*Cozens-Hardy Collection*]

MAY 1, THURSDAY

Henry Raven R Bye to Wells with beer. T Balden to Waybourn & Viverton [Wiveton] with beer & Clay for 1 Chald Cinders from Mr Manns. 2 trowelmen & 2 Laborers all day, W Tinker & 2 men all day. G Thompson grinding M [malt] for brew, Jno Ram & HR in M house. M^r^ H & WH at home all day, whent to Mr Temples to tea, M^rs^ H & Miss at Mr Temples to tea.

Mary Hardy A Cold dry day. A London rider came in Morng [1] to look at the Molly Mare,[2] did not agree for her. We all drank tea at Mr Temples of Thornage, Mr Moore supt here . . .

MAY 2, FRIDAY

HR R Bye to Sheringham & Runton with beer, T Balden to Sherington & Kettlestone with beer. 2 trowel men & 2 Laborers all day, Tinkers 2 men all Day. Jno Ram & HR in M house. Boy Carting gravil to headyard & mucking Out pigs hous. G Thompson grinding M for brew. WH & H Raven painting Dobson's Dining Room, MH [Mr Hardy] at home all day.

MAY 3, SATURDAY

HR R Bye to Hinderingham & Walsingham with beer. G Thompson, T Balden, Jno Ram, HR & Boy put Clense Beer in great Cask in W Hall. M^r^ H & M^rs^ «at» Holt market afternoon. 2 trowelmen & 2 Laborers all Day. Mr Youngman«'s» man & Lad hanging gate. WH at home all day, Miss H at Holt afternoon.

MH A fine day. Mr Hardy, I & MA rid up to Holt afternoon, drank tea at Mr Bartells, a Meeting at the Shirehouse for raising Volenteers by Subscription for the defence of the Country.[3] W^m^ at home all day . . .

---

[1] *rider* A firm's travelling representative. Had he acquired Molly she would have had to complete a punishing daily mileage

[2] *the Molly mare* The mare named Molly

[3] *Volunteers* See note for 15 Mar. 1794. The administrative units, the hundreds, were now forming cavalry as well as infantry units of Volunteers. Regular reports appeared in the press throughout May, many of the Hardys' friends (but not the Hardys themselves) adding to the figure which by 31 May had reached £10,737 for Norfolk. The Holt attorney William Brereton gave £5 5*s*, Revd John Burrell £2 2*s*, Charles Collyer £21, John Ellis £2 2*s*, Mary Hardy's

MAY 4, SUNDAY

HR R Bye & T Balden car[d] [carried] 2 Nog to W Dobsons morning, Famaly whent to Church afternoon. Miss Bartle, Miss Raven & R Bartle walked down here after tea.[1]

MAY 5, MONDAY

HR R Bye, T Balden, G Thompson in brew house. WH Brewing & rode to Holt Evening. Cap[t] Hall & Boy at harrow, 2 trowel men & 2 Laborers all Day. Jn[o] Ram & H Raven in M house. M[r] H at home all day.

MAY 6, TUESDAY

HR R Bye, G Thompson Clense'd `// morning, drawing of Beer afternoon, WH helping to draw of beer. Jn[o] Ram & H Raven in M house. 1 trowel man & 1 Laborer all Day. T Balden ploughing in field [open field], Cap[t] Hall & Boy at Harrow all day. HR whent to Saxlingham with Byes Horse morning.[2] M[r] Youngman & Lad came to set water wheel at Liberty afternoon.

MAY 7, WEDNESDAY

HR R Bye & T Hall «at» stone Cart, T Balden at Syderstone with beer. G Thompson dressing W [wheat] Stones & Clense'd, Jn[o] Ram & HR in M house. 2 trowelmen & 2 Laborers all day. M[r] Youngman at work here afternoon. WH helping to Cleanse, M[r] H at home all day.

brother Nathaniel Raven £3 3*s*, her cousins Ben Raven and Thomas Raven £2 2*s* and £1 1*s*, Zebulon Rouse £1 1*s*, the Holt shopkeeper Charles Sales £1 1*s*, Revd Joshua Smith of Holt £5 5*s*, the Thornage farmer Thomas Temple £2 2*s*. The Norwich units tended to receive the most detailed coverage in the local press (*Norw. Merc.* 19 Apr., 26 Apr., 3 May, 10 May, 31 May 1794)

---

1 *Bartell* Robert (publicly bapt. Holt 3 July 1783, died there 10 Feb. 1801 aged 19 or 21, bur. 15 Feb.), younger son of Edmund Bartell snr

2 *to Saxlingham* Probably to the horse doctor John Hammond (28 Jan. 1795): perhaps the farrier of 1813 who was a Calvinistic Methodist (NRO: DN/VIS 46/7, Holt deanery visitation 1813, Saxlingham return)

MAY 8, THURSDAY

HR R Bye ploughing morning in field. T Balden, Capt Hall at gravil cart morning, TB carting stones out «of» Dobson yard into rode [road]. G Thompson Grinding M for brew. Bricklayers here 2 hours in Morning. WH at Holt all day. Jno Ram in M house, HR at Holt morning. Mr H at home all day. Mr Wade's Mill burnt down in about 4 hours.[1] Bumpsted came for Pig.[2]

MH A Cold showry day, wind high. Mr Wades Mill at Holt Burnt down, took fire by accident Morng 9. Wm went up, dind at Mr Bartells, came home eveng 4, drank tea at Mr Burrells. Mr H at home all day.

MAY 9, FRIDAY

HR R Bye ploughing in Field. T Balden at work in Dobsons yard morning, to Gunthorp afternoon with beer. Jno Ram & HR in M house, Capt Hall at work in yards. G Thompson Laid down W Stones. Mr Youngman after Palisade. T Atwood came & Orderd 4 Nog, Pleasance came & Orderd 7 Nog.[3]

MH A fine Morng but cold, Wet afternoon. Mr Hardy, I & MA rid up to Holt field foornoon to see the ruins of the Mill. Wm at home all day . . .

MAY 10, SATURDAY

HR R Bye to Holt morning with beer & Thornage & Stody afternoon. T Balden, G Thompson & Boy in brew house, WH Brewing & Painting Palisade. T Youngman's Lad at work here all day. Jno Ram & HR in M house. Mr H, Mrs H & Miss H at Holt afternoon, WH drank tea at Mr Burrels.

MAY 11, SUNDAY

HR R Bye & T Balden Loaded waggon & Cart afternoon. Famaly all whent to Church morning, HR to Holt Church afternoon. WH to Holt Church afternoon & Rode out after tea.[4]

MAY 12, MONDAY

HR R Bye to Stalham with beer, T Balden to Syderstone with beer. G Thompson Grinding Malt for brew, Jno Ram & H Raven in Malt house. WH rode out, Mr H at home all Day. T Youngmans Lad Painting ¾ day. Mr Gathercole came morning,[5] Gentleman cald [called] morning 7.

[1] *mill* See note for 22 Oct. 1793; John Wade's mill had been built only in May 1786, according to Mary Hardy (*Diary 2*). It was owned in 1792 by Charles Kendle of Holt, Wade being the tenant miller. 'The accident was caused by the friction giving so much heat to the gudgeons [the sockets into which the pins fit] as to set the woodwork on fire'; the stock of flour was also lost (*Norw. Merc.* 10 May 1794). Letheringsett Watermill, rebuilt 1798, has a bell to warn the miller if the stones are grinding too close. Were they to touch, the resulting sparks would set fire to the timbers.

A new tower mill (illustrated opposite) was built at the start of the Cley road, but John Wade moved to a mill at Gt Ryburgh (entry for 11 Sept. 1795). Although competitors, he and William Hardy jnr appear to have been on friendly terms, going together to Newcastle the previous summer to expand their market for flour

[2] *Bumpstead* John, a pig dealer

[3] *Pleasance* The large order for Robert Pleasance of Gunthorpe was despatched immediately. He and the Holt innkeeper perhaps expected extra business from sightseers on their way to or from the ruins

[4] *rode out* William's mother noted that he went to Mr Bird at Thornage

[5] *Gathercole* Of Fakenham Bell: note for 23 Oct. 1793

left Holt Windmill in 1916, successor to John Wade's mill, which burned down in four hours in a high wind on 8 May 1794. William Hardy jnr and Henry Raven were in Holt as it was destroyed, and William and Mary Hardy and Mary Ann saw the ruins the following day. It was replaced by this five-floor brick mill with its Norfolk boat-shaped cap; its sails were removed 1925 and it was demolished 1974 [NRO: MC 2043/9, 909x6, *Checkley Collection*]

below A cast-iron window of 1846 at the former St Nicholas Ironworks, Dereham: both an ornament and a protection in the event of fire. The rose at each boss (below left) is identical to the bosses at Letheringsett Watermill, which William Hardy jnr bought in 1827 [*MB · 2011*]

MAY 13, TUESDAY

HR R Bye home from Stalham, T Balden to Brampton with beer. G Thompson Clensed morning & grinding M for Brew, Jno Ram & HR in M house. Youngmans Lad Painting & help to Clense morning. M^r^ H at home all day, W & Miss Hardy rode out morning. Mr Wagstaff came morning.[1] Youngman came to git plug out «of» great Cask.

MAY 14, WEDNESDAY

HR R Bye, T Balden Cleaning H [home] Cask & got Beer in to cask. G Thompson & Boy in Brewhouse, WH brewing. Youngmans Lad Painting. Jno Ram, HR in M house. M^r^ H at home all day.

MAY 15, THURSDAY

HR T Balden to Clay with beer & in brewhouse, R Bye to Fakenham with beer. G Thompson Clensed `//, Jno Ram & HR in M House. Mr Raven & Miss R Raven came Evening.[2] M^r^ H & M^rs^ H at home all Day.

[1] *Wagstaff* Of the Horseshoes at Corpusty: see note for 29 Oct. 1793

[2] *Rose Raven* Henry's sister (bapt. Whissonsett 13 Dec. 1773); she married there 23 June 1797 Thomas Skrimshire (note for 18 June 1797; also app. D3.A, fig. D3.4). On 25 Aug. 1829 at Syderstone Parsonage, where her husband ran a school, she died suddenly 'to the irreparable grief of her family and regret of her friends' (*Norw. Merc.* 29 Aug.). Her daughter Ann served as companion 1842–46 to Mary Hardy, Henry and Rose's youngest sister and widow of William Hardy jnr

MH A fine day. Mr Hardy, I & MA rid up to Holt afternoon, drank tea at Mr Davys, Miss Leak show'd her fashions.[1] Brot Raven & Rose Raven came Eveng 8.

MAY 16, FRIDAY

HR G Thompson & R Bye Card [carried] Clense Beer off. R Bye to Corpusta with beer, T Balden to Sheringham & Runton with beer. Jno Ram & HR in M house. Mr Raven & W Hardy gone to Whissonsett. Mr H & Mrs H & Miss Hardy and Miss Raven, WH & Mr Raven rode out morning.

MH A very fine day. We all to [took] a ride to the Seaside at Salthouse foornoon, came home to dinner. Brot Raven & Wm went to Whisonsett after tea . . .

MAY 17, SATURDAY

HR R Bye to Holt & Briston with beer. T Balden in Brewhouse morning & Blackney for Cinders. Jno Ram in M house. G Thompson Clense'd morning & grinding Malt for brew. Mrs H & Miss H & Miss Raven to Holt after tea. G Dawson gone to Whissonsett & from thence tomorrow to Setch.[2]

MAY 18, SUNDAY

HR G Thompson Grinding M for brew, R Bye & T Balden card 2 Nog to Dobsons. Mr & Miss Symonds came from Yarmouth.[3] Famaly all whent to Church afternoon. Geor Dawson came from Setch.

HOLT.

S. and M. JOHNSON return thanks to their Friends for the liberal encouragement they have experienced, and inform them and the Public, that S. JOHNSON will return from London with a fashionable Assortment of MILLINERY, which they beg leave to offer to their attention on Tuesday, May 15. (779

MILLINERY.

A. LEAK returns her sincere thanks for favours already received, and begs leave to inform the Ladies of Holt and its environs, that she will return from London with a fashionable Assortment of MILLINERY, which will be ready for their inspection on Thursday the 17th inst. when all favours will be gratefully acknowledged.

HOLT, May 12, 1792. (776

right Two Holt millineries advertise the latest London fashions in the *Norwich Mercury* of 12 May 1792.

Susan and Mary Johnson, daughters of the Revd William T. Johnson, were to marry clergymen serving Shipdham and Letheringsett. Ann Leak, later in partnership with her sister Bell, would every May tell customers of her return from the capital with the new styles. She 'showed her fashions' to William and Mary Hardy and Mary Ann at Holt on 15 May 1794 [*Norfolk Heritage Centre, Norwich*]

[1] *Miss Leak* Ann (bur. Holt 17 Jan. 1803 aged 61, 'pauper'), a milliner in the town

[2] *Setchey* Pronounced Setch; a small village south of King's Lynn where the River Nar joins the Gt Ouse. George Dawson jnr (see note for 16 Nov. 1793) was probably arranging summer grazing for the Hardys' colts, Setchey also offering lush pasture for the Scottish drovers' cattle before the autumn fairs at Setchey, St Faiths, Harleston and Hempton Green

[3] *Symonds* Jonathan (d. Ormesby St Margaret 9 Aug. 1803 aged 65), grocer, wharfinger and Common Councilman, Gt Yarmouth; see note for 16 Aug. 1793.
The Hardys' Coltishall wherry had berthed at his wharf 1776–81 (*Diary 1*)

left Elegant header-bond brickwork at Ormesby St Margaret Old Hall, rebuilt 1735 for Cotton Symonds, to which the Gt Yarmouth merchant, grocer and the Hardys' old friend Jonathan Symonds was shortly to retire. His daughter Phillis was taken ill with fits while staying at Letheringsett in May 1794 [*MB · 2001*]

MAY 19, MONDAY

HR T Balden to Viverton & Waybourn with beer. R Bye to Thornage morning, Dawling afternoon. G Thompson dressing flower [flour], Jn° Ram in M house. Jeremiah Moore at work in River downstream.[1] M[rs] & two Miss Davys drank tea here.[2] Jn° Fox at work in shrubery.

MAY 20, TUESDAY

HR R Bye to N° Walsham with beer. Balden, G Thompson & Boy in brewhouse. WH Brewing & walk'd to Holt with M[r] Symonds.[3] Jn° Ram & HR in M house, Jere Moore & Son at work in River down Stream.[4] M[r] & Miss H & Miss Symonds, Miss Raven & M[r] Symonds whent to Sheringham afternoon. Jn° Fox diging in shrubery.

MAY 21, WEDNESDAY

HR T Balden to beckhige [Beckhithe] with beer. R Bye at work in brewhouse morning, Kettlestone afternoon D° [with beer]. Jn° Ram & HR in M house. Jere Moore & Son at work in River in Garden. M[r] H at home all day, WH & Miss Raven Rode out Evening.

[1] *downstream* In the area of the Hall shrubbery and cascade

[2] *Miss Davys* Bett and Susan

[3] *William Hardy* [*jnr*] He had returned 19 May from Whissonsett. Jonathan Symonds left on 21 May

[4] *Moore and son* See note for 8 Feb. 1794. There is no record in the Letheringsett registers of Moore's first marriage, nor this son's baptism. Before her 1807 marriage to the widowed Moore, Hannah Overton (of the King's Head at Holt, publicly bapt. Holt 4 Aug. 1771) had had four illegitimate children: Thomas, bur. Holt 1791; Elizabeth and John, born 12 Sept. 1802 and 29 May 1805, bapt. Letheringsett and bur. Holt; and John, bur. Holt 1807. All lived only a few months.

No father was named, but the careful Mr Burrell noted Hannah's parish of settlement as Thursford; she resided at Letheringsett under a certificate. Quarter sessions records show that on 3 Jan. 1795 she had been removed by magistrates'

right A fine monumental mason was working in the Blakeney area at this time. This headstone in the churchyard records the death of 32-year-old Henry Smith, who 'Launched into the Ocean of Eternity' after falling from his horse 'into a Rivulet of Time' at Cley Watering 24–25 May 1794; the merchant was returning very late at night from Holt market.

A poignant piece of evidence emerged from the inquest of 27 May at Blakeney: 'Verdict: accidental death. His dog, which lay by him when found, had torn his hat in pieces in endeavouring to pull him out of the water' (*Norwich Mercury*, 31 May 1794) [*MB* · *2000*]

to the Memory of
SMITH
who fell from his Horse
into a Rivulet of Time
from thence he Launched
into the Ocean of Eternity

order from Holt to Thursford, John Spaul (bur. Letheringsett 18 June 1820 aged 44) being the subject of a bastardy order for Hannah 23 July 1802 (NRO: C/S 1/15, C/S 1/17). On 12 Nov. 1804 Spaul married the Hardys' former maidservant Elizabeth Wortley (*Diary 4*)

MAY 22, THURSDAY

HR T Balden to Wells with beer. R Bye to Edgefield with beer, took 5 Coomb Malt for A Boswell, & to Holt afternoon. G Thompson grinding M for brew. Jere Moore & Son at work in River in garden. Jn° Clark sent for Hoggs [hogs]. Jn° Ram & HR in M house. Mr H & WH at home all Day. Mr & Mrs Sheldrake drank tea here.

MAY 23, FRIDAY

HR R Bye & T Balden at work in brewhouse, G Thompson grinding M for brew & gitting beer in Home cask. Jn° Ram & HR in M house. Mr H & WH at home all day, Ladies walkd to Holt to tea. Skiffins in Garden, Jere Moore at work in River.

MH A cold Showry day. Mr Hardy & Wm at home all day. The Girls walk'd up to Holt afternoon, drank tea at Mrs Jennis's.[1] From the News Papers, The British Troops Defeated with great loss in France.[2] Many people taken up in England for Sedition & Treason, the Heabeas Corpus Act Suspended.[3]

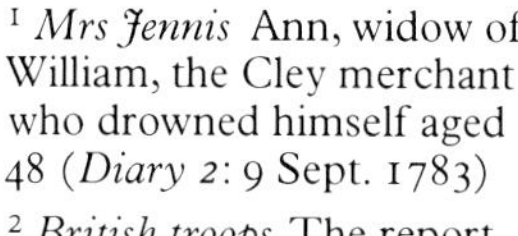

[1] *Mrs Jennis* Ann, widow of William, the Cley merchant who drowned himself aged 48 (*Diary 2*: 9 Sept. 1783)

[2] *British troops* The report is likely to have been from a London paper as the Norwich papers came out on Saturdays. For the defeat, see note for 25 May 1794

[3] *Habeas Corpus* The controversial suspension was to allow political suspects to be held without trial.

This time of ferment, the papers being full of alarms over alleged treason and sedition, naval and military engagements and the Terror, is covered in M. Bird, *Mary Hardy and her World* ('*World*'), vol. 4, chaps 6, 7

MAY 24, SATURDAY

HR T Balden to Runton, Cromer & Beckhigh with beer. R Bye in brew house morning, Salthouse afternoon with beer. G Thompson & Boy in brew house all day, WH brewing. Jere Moore at work all day. Jn° Ram & H Raven in M house. Mr & Mrs H & Ladies at Holt Market afternoon. Jn° Fox at work in Shrubery all Day.

MH A cold day. Mr Hardy rid to Holt afternoon, came home eveng 11. Wm Brew'd. I, MA, Miss Symonds & Rose Raven walkd up to Holt Markt, drank tea at Miss Leakes, walkd home. Mr Smith of Blakney was killd going home from Markt Morn 2, fell from his Horse in a little run of Water in the lane going from Holt to Cley.[1]

MAY 25, SUNDAY

HR R Bye & T Balden card 2 Nog to Dobsens morning, Famaly all whent to Church morning. R [Robert] Raven came from Whissonsett.

MH A cold day. All went to our Church foornoon, Mr Burrell preachd. Robt Raven came to dinner, went home after tea, Mrs Forster came an hour in the eveng. The British Troops & Allies defeated in Flanders yesterday & this day sennet [se'nnight] [2] . . .

above 'John Clark sent for hogs' (22 May 1794), hogs being adult male pigs. The Hardys sold their surplus pigs fattened on the by-products from brewing known as brewer's grains. These four-month-old Large Blacks are seen at Gressenhall Farm and Workhouse, the Museum of Norfolk Rural Life [*MB · 2011*]

[1] *run of water* Known as Cley Watering, just north-west of Holt Hall; the beck runs south-west to join another tributary of the Glaven at Hall Farm, west of Workhouse Lane. Henry Smith's son James was born posthumously, buried with him, and is commemorated on the same headstone

[2] *Flanders* Then still part of the Austrian Netherlands.

A se'nnight (seven nights) was a week, the form being preserved today in the fourteen-night fortnight.

This more detailed item would have been written up from the extensive coverage in the Norwich papers. The Austro–British action at Tourcoing, near Lille, 17–18 May was led by HRH the Duke of York (1763–1827), second son of George III, but the Allies were heavily outnumbered by the victorious French and the Duke had to flee the field.

The Allies lost 4000 men killed or wounded; 1500 were captured. Although the Prussian Field Marshal Mollendorff reported a victory over the French at Kayfers-Lautern on 23 May the First Coalition (Britain, Hanover, Austria and Prussia) then collapsed.

Tourcoing is commmeorated in the nursery rhyme, 'Oh, the grand old Duke of York/He had ten thousand men . . .' The Duke, at first victorious at Beaumont in Apr. 1794, faced numerous logistical difficulties. His striking administrative ability and leadership later came to the fore over home defence

MAY 26, MONDAY

HR R Bye & T Balden at work in brew house morning, D° [R Bye] to Sheringham with beer afternoon, T Balden ploughing in field afternoon. Jere Moore & Son at work in River in yard.[1] Mr H at home all Day. WH at home all day, at Holt in Evening, Ladies at Holt afternoon. Jn° Ram & HR in M house. Boy whent for 1 Chald Lime from Mr Forsters morning & mucking out Hoggs house's afternoon. Youngmans Lad making Center.[2]

MAY 27, TUESDAY

HR R Bye & T Balden ploughing all day. G Thompson Cleansed morning, Jn° Ram & HR in M house. Jere Moore & Son at work in River in yard. Mr H at home all day, Wm H at Mr Forsters to tea with the Ladies. Jn° Fox half a day.

MH A cold showry day. Mr Hardy at home all day. Wm, MA, Miss Symonds went to Mr Forsters of Bayfield to tea. Miss Symonds was taken in fitts & could not git home till past 11, was very bad till morng 2, the 2 Maids set [sat] up with her. Mr Farthings son fell from his Horse last night coming from Briston Fair.[3]

MAY 28, WEDNESDAY

HR R Bye ploughing all day. T Balden at work at home morning, ploughing afternoon. Jere Moore & Sone [son] at work in River in yard, Bunnets 4 Men turning arch over River. Jn° Fox half day, Mr Youngman ¾ day. Jn° Ram in M house. G Thompson set of for N° Walsham at 5 in Morning.[4] Mr H & WH at home all day, Miss Symonds very ill morning. Capt Hall cleaning Bricks afternoon.

MH A cold drisly day. Mr Hardy & Wm at home all day, Miss Symonds very poorly all day with fitts. From the News papers, a Victory gaind over the French near Tournay.

MAY 29, THURSDAY

HR R Bye ploughing morning, at harrow afternoon. T Balden ploughing morning & whent for load Bricks afternoon & got over Malt for Brew. Jn° Ram in M house. Jn° Fox at work morning, Mr Youngman afternoon mending waterwheel, Jere Moore at work in River. Mr

[1] *river in yard* The waterwheel culvert, emerging from under the malthouse, opens into the yard before curving north to pass under the malt-mill house

[2] *centre* A timber frame supporting the arch which the bricklayers were about to alter (29 May), the culvert openings having brick arches set into the flint cobbles. When the lime mortar was set the centre would be struck. It seems a testing job for a millwright's lad, although 'lads' were more experienced assistants than 'boys'

[3] *Briston Fair* Not shown in the printed list in Crouse and Stevenson's memorandum book 1790, nor is it in the Norwich directories of 1783 and 1802. Robert Farthing (d.13 Nov. 1806 aged 65), a coal and cinder merchant at Blakeney, was later bankrupted: see note for 8 June 1797

[4] *North Walsham* Not with a beer delivery, but probably to attend the Ascension Day fair, suggesting the miller had family connections there. The men were sometimes allowed time off to attend their home fairs

above 'Jeremiah Moore and son at work in river in yard' (26 May 1794). The waterwheel culvert emerges briefly into the brewery yard from under the ivy on the west wall of the malthouse (right) before heading north to power the wheel. A much later building (centre) stands above it close to the site of the malt-mill. The huge doorway into the malthouse was made in the mid-20th century to allow farm equipment to be stored [*MB · 2001*]

facing page The culvert from the River Glaven, constructed by William Hardy, enters the brewery yard from under the malthouse; the pipe, restricting the flow, was installed in the 1970s long after the end of the waterwheel's active life. Moore and the builders seem to have been adjusting the flow in 1794 [*MB · 1993*]

Bunnet & 3 men all Day. M^r^ H & WH at home all Day. Ja^s^ Dyball came morning.[1] Townspeople when [went] the bounds of the Parrish afternoon.[2] Capt Hall cleaning Bricks all Day.

MH Assention Day A fine day. Mr Hardy & W^m^ at home all day, we all went to our Church afternoon, Mr Burrell & Church Wardens went the bounds of the Parish. The Bricklayers turning an Arch in the B«rew» House yard. Miss Symonds finely . . .

[1] *James Dyball* From the Three Pigs at Edgefield

[2] *bounds* Beating the bounds at Rogationtide, when the rector, parish officers, villagers and children walked the parish boundary (*World*, vol. 2, chap. 3). 'The parish [in 1784] extends about ten furlongs [1¼ miles] from east to west and about nine furlongs from north to south, the outlines remarkably irregular. It comprehends 28 houses; has no family of note in it . . .' Ten years later that rector's son gave the circumference as about 10 miles, with 40 houses, and still no families of note (NRO: DN/VIS 29/6, DN/VIS 33a/4, Holt deanery visitations 1784, 1794, Letheringsett returns by Revd John Burrell snr and jnr)

above **William Hardy, by Huguier 1785. It had been his bold decision to convert to water power in 1784** [*Cozens-Hardy Collection*]

MAY 30, FRIDAY

HR R Bye at home morning, ploughing afternoon in Field. T Balden at home morning, at Sheringham D^o [afternoon], Jno Ram in M house. 1 trowel man and 1 Laborer all Day, Jno Fox covering the Arch. Boy at harrow afternoon. M^r H & WH at home all Day & Skiffins in Garden. Capt Hall days Work, Jere Moore & Sone at work in River all Day.

MAY 31, SATURDAY

HR T Balden to Stody & Edgefield with beer, R Bye to Branton [Brampton] with beer. G Thompson grinding M [malt] for Brew. Jno Ram & HR in M house. 1 trowelman & 1 Laborer all Day, Capt Hall Days work, Boy at harrow morning. M^r H & WH at Holt market afternoon, Ladies at Holt afternoon. Jere Moore at work in River all Day.

JUNE 1, SUNDAY

Henry Raven R Bye & T Balden Car^d [carried] Cleanse beer off morning. Famaly all whent to Church afternoon. Rob Raven & Miss Raven whent home after tea, HR rode to Fakenham with them.[1]

JUNE 2, MONDAY

HR Rob Bye to Hindonvestone with beer, T Balden to Fakenham with beer, Capt Hall at work in Pitol. Jno Fox in Furze Close diging for clay.[2] M^r H at home all Day, WH to Norwich to buy a Chaise. Jno Ram & HR in M house. M Pleasance came morning.[3] Boy Ploughing in Field all Day, Jere Moore at work in River.

Mary Hardy A very fine day. W^m sett of for Norwich Morng 4 to look at a one Horse Chaise to sell [to be sold] at the Maids Head in St Symonds [St Simon's], he dind & drank tea at M^r G Wymers, bought the Chaise for [ ] & came home eveng 10 . . .

---

[1] *Miss Raven* Robert took Rose home, having brought their sister Phillis to Letheringsett on 31 May: see note for 16 Aug. 1783

[2] *clay* Clay was used to line ('puddle') watercourses such as canals and would have been needed for the basin in the Brewhouse Pightle (21 June 1794).
The waterwheel culvert is brick lined

[2] *M. Pleasance* Either an error for Mr Pleasance, or a relative of his from the Cross Keys at Gunthorpe

---

ONE-HORSE CHAISE.
TO BE SOLD,
A Very Neat London-Built SINGLE-HORSE CHAISE, with Harness, the whole plated, and in good condition, with a driving-box, and trunk, price 20l.
To be seen at Mr. Baldry's, Maid's Head, Norwich.

right **'A one-horse chaise to sell at the Maid's Head . . .' (2 June). The advertisement attracting the Hardys supplies the price—£20** [*Norwich Mercury, 31 May 1794: Norfolk Heritage Centre, Norwich*]

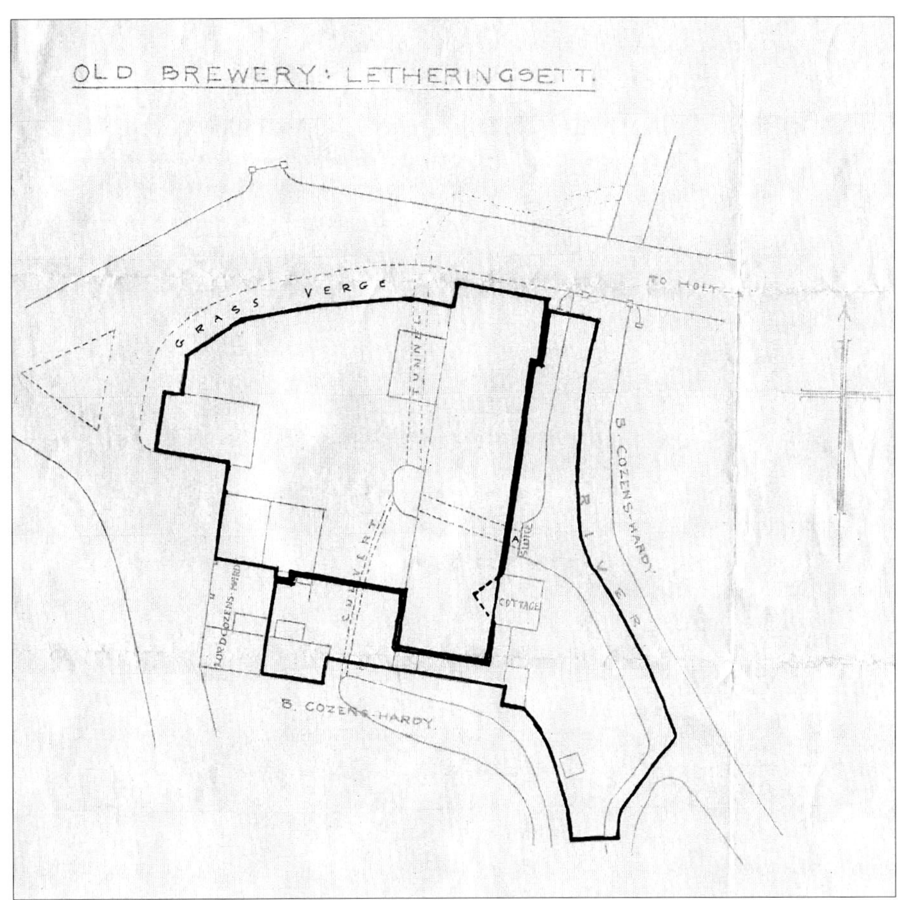
OLD BREWERY: LETHERINGSETT.
GRASS VERGE
TO HOLT
B. COZENS-HARDY
RIVER
COTTAGE
CULVERT
B. COZENS-HARDY

JUNE 3, TUESDAY

HR R Bye & T Hall at Muck cart all Day. T Balden, G Thompson & Boy in brewhouse all Day, WH Brewing. Jere Moore at work in River, Jn° Ram in M house. Mr H at home all Day.

JUNE 4, WEDNESDAY

HR R Bye at muck cart morning & to Clay with beer & Brot home 2 Chal'd [?«cinders»] from Mr Manns. Capt Hall filling muck «cart» morning, weeding «afternoon». G Thompson Cleansed `//. T Balden helping at home morning, at Bale & Sherrington with beer afternoon. Jn° R & HR in M house, Jere Moore at work in River. WH walkd to Holt morning, Mr H at home all Day.

above A plan by Francis Hornor & Son, of Norwich, of the maltings, brewery site and watercourses. It accompanies a conveyance of 14 Apr. 1943 defining the new road boundary: see the earlier plan illustrated under the diary entry for 16 Aug. 1793.

Double dotted lines denote subterranean culverts; the opening into the yard is shown in the centre [*Cozens-Hardy Collection*]

facing page 'Went to church forenoon and took a walk to Brother Raven's' (11 June 1794). The Whissonsett farmhouse, later known as Church Farm, where Nathaniel Raven lived; his grocery shop had stood front left. The property had earlier belonged to his uncle, another Nathaniel Raven (1711–84), and to Mary Hardy's grandparents Henry and Rose Raven. Apart from the excitement of their raffle winnings Mary Hardy and her son spent their visit to her home village 9–14 June on the usual round of calls on the Goggs and Raven families [*MB · 2011*]

JUNE 5, THURSDAY

HR T Balden ploughing. Rob Bye spread{l}ing muck & onloaded Cinders morning, whent to Briston with beer afternoon. Jere Moore at work in River in Pitol.[1] Jn° Ram & HR in M house, Gun Thompson grinding M for brew, Capt Hall Weeding. M^r H & WH at home all Day. Mrs Prier came from Hindonvestone.[2]

JUNE 6, FRIDAY

HR T Balden to Runton with beer. R Bye helping to Cleanse morning, to Clay for Cinders afternoon, G Thompson Cleansed D° [morning]. Jn° Ram & HR in M house, Jere Moore at work in River. WH whent to Sheringham with Ladies afternoon, M^r H at home all Day. Dawsons Carpentar at work.

MH A fine morng, showry afternoon. Mr Hardy at home all «day». Our new Chaise came home in morng. MA & Miss Symond«s» & P Raven rid to Sheringham afternoon in Chaise, W^m on Minor, came home half past 9.[3] M^r & Mrs Bartell drank tea here . . .

JUNE 7, SATURDAY

HR R Bye, G Thompson & Boy in brew house, WH brewing. Jn° Ram & HR in M house. T Balden whent to Holt for new Cart & to Creffer [Crafer] with beer morning, to Hunworth with Cart wheels afternoon. Jere Moore at work in River. Dawsons Carpentar all Day. HR rode to Hunworth morning. M^r H at home all Day.[4] Mr Temples men begun the muck.

JUNE 8, SUNDAY

HR R Bye & T Balden Car^d Cleanse beer off morning. Famaly all went to Church morning. WH & HR whent to Holt afternoon. G Thompson rode to Birmmingham afternoon.[5]

[1] *in river in Pightle* Moore may have been working on the watercourse linking the brewery reservoir (the pond) by gravity to the brewery down the slope.

Brewing liquor was softened, or ameliorated, in the open pond for brews such as porter requiring soft water (*World*, vol. 1, chap. 10; vol. 2, chap. 7)

[2] *Mrs Prior* See note for 24 Oct. 1793; this was not Mary Hardy's trusted friend and servant Molly Prior. Mrs Prior's husband Thomas had died in late 1792 or early 1793, and his widow was about to hand over the Maid's Head at Hindolveston to Philip Thacker

[3] *Phillis Raven* See note for 16 Aug. 1793. At the age of 18 she became assistant mistress at Miss Alpe's school at Holt 1797–98: see note for 4 Aug. 1797.

She married Whissonsett 19 Sept. 1806 Joseph Thompson (1780–1846), of Brandon, Suff., a schoolmaster; he later ran the Guildhall Academy at E. Dereham. Phillis and her sister Rose Skrimshire both had the task of looking after their husbands' boarders in addition to their own children

[4] *at home* His wife noted that Mr Hardy walked to Holt market

[5] *Birmingham* Briningham was pronounced locally Birmingham or Burningham, from its former name; neighbouring Brinton had likewise once been Burnton

JUNE 9, MONDAY

HR R Bye to Syderstone with beer. T Balden to Hunworth for Cart wheels & then to Thornage with beer. Jn° Ram & HR in M house. Carpenter at work in morning. WH & M^rs^ H set out for Whissonsett morning.[1] Temples men «at» muck Cart.

JUNE 10, TUESDAY

HR T Balding [Baldwin] helping to Cleanse, G Thompson Cleanse«d» morning. Jn° Ram in M house. M^r^ H at home all Day. Boy came home at night.

JUNE 11, WEDNESDAY

HR R Bye to Stalham with beer, T Balden ploughing in Field, T Hall spreading muck. G Thompson Dressing flour, Jn° Ram in M house. M^r^ H at home all Day. Tempels me«n» at muck Cart.

MH [at Whissonsett] A hot dry day. Went to Church foornoon & took a walk to Bro^t^ Ravens, dind at Sister Goggs, drank tea at Bro^t^ Ravens. W^m^ raffled & won a piece for a Gown, I won a square of Muslin. Supt & Slept at Mr Goggs . . .

JUNE 12, THURSDAY

HR R Bye home from Stalham, T Balden to Corpusta with beer. Jn° Ram & HR in M house. Tempels Men at muck Cart, Jere Moore at work in River. T Hall ploughing morning, weeding afternoon. M^r^ H at Mr Tempels with the Ladies to tea.

1 *Whissonsett* Mary Hardy and William travelled in the new chaise, which explains why the boy was needed to take the horse back to Letheringsett on 10 June

above **Brinton and Briningham have the same root in Burnton/Brunton and Burningham. An ancient poppyhead bench end in Brinton Church makes a play on the village name in this burning tun** [*MB · 2011*]

above '. . . Dined at William Dobson's at the housewarming, . . . had but little company' (18 June). The King's Head at Letheringsett, rebuilt in 1808 south of its old site, is seen here from the Brewhouse Pightle. Over recent years a popular, award-winning house, its new innkeeper William Dobson had a shaky start in 1794, his housewarming not proving a success. Brewers subsidised such parties for their tied outlets [*MB · 2010*]

JUNE 13, FRIDAY

HR R Bye to Clay for Cinders from Mr Ellis forenoon, at harrow & onloading Coles. G Thompson grinding Malt for brew, Jno Ram & HR in M house. Jere Moore ¾ Day in River, Jno Gidney all Day,[1] W Platten & W Parsons half Day in River.[2] Mr Tempels men at muck Cart. Mr H at home all Day. Mr Wade & Miss Jennis drank tea here. Mr Pleasance came & orderd a load of Beer. T Balden to Walsingham with beer.

JUNE 14, SATURDAY

HR T Balden Carr«y»ing muck into Field, Capt Hall filling muck cart. R Bye to Gunthorp morning, filling muck cart afternoon. G Thompson finnish«ed» grinding Malt, Jno Ram & HR in M house. Jere Moore & W Platten at work in River. Mrs H & WH came from Whissonsett with N Raven, Mr H at home all Day.[3] Mr Tempels men at muck cart.

1 *Gidney* Probably John jnr (bapt. Letheringsett 20 Sept. 1761—the same day as the future rector, bur. there 8 Mar. 1822), son of John (bur. there 13 Mar. 1823 aged 88) and Frances (bapt. there 30 Sept. 1739, buried there 28 Feb. 1831 'aged 94'), née Stangroom; Fanny Gidney used to help Mary Hardy on washing days 1784–92. John jnr married 18 Jan. 1791 Ann Barber (bur. 20 May 1821 aged 49), of Letheringsett, and their children appear in the registers. One of their sons, Robert (bapt. 28 Nov. 1792), was accidentally killed at the age of 24, Revd John Burrell annotating the burial entry 15 Sept. 1817: 'NB This man met Death by falling under the wheels of a waggon' (NRO: PD 547/44)

2 *Parsons* William, husband of Elizabeth (bur. Letheringsett 22 May 1807), formerly Mrs Eldritch, née Bastard; their children are in the registers. William married there 1 Aug. 1815 William Lamb's widow Susan, the Hardys' former maidservant Susan Ward 1788–89 and washerwoman 1799–1802, whose skull was fractured in an attack by the miller Zebulon Rouse 24 Nov. 1804 shortly before his temporary confinement in Bethel (*Diary 4*). William Parsons was brought from Heigham, Norwich, for burial 20 Apr. 1842 aged 75.

See also notes for 4 Feb., 5 June and 7 Sept. 1795

3 *N. Raven* Probably Henry's cousin Nathaniel: he is *Mr* Raven on 16 June

JUNE 15, SUNDAY

HR R Bye & T Balden Car^d Cleanse beer off morning. Famaly all whent to Church afternoon.

JUNE 16, MONDAY

HR Gun Thompson, T Balden & Boy in Brew house. WH brewing & walkd to Holt with Mr Raven. R Bye at muck cart morning, ploughing afternoon. T Hall filling muck cart morning, spreading muck afternoon. Jno Ram & HR in M house, Mr Tempels men at muck Cart. M^r H at home morning, at Holt afternoon, N Raven whent home Evening 7. Thos Atwood & Matt Peirce came and Orderd 4 Nog Each.[1]

MH [at Letheringsett] A fine day, cool. W^m brewd. Mr Hardy walk'd up to Holt afternoon, drank tea at Mr Bartells. W^m & NR walkd up to Holt afternoon, came back to tea, N Raven went away after tea. M^r & Miss Symonds went away after Breakfast [2] . . .

JUNE 17, TUESDAY

HR R Bye ploughing in turnipseed morning, whent to Holt noontime & got to work at 5 oClock afternoon.[3] T Balden helping to Cleanse `// & to Holt & Edgefield with beer, Gunton Thompson Cleans«d» `//. Jno Ram, HR in M house. Jere Moore at work in River, Mr Tempels men at muck Cart. M^r H at home all Day. WH, Miss H & Miss Raven to Guestwick afternoon. Mrs Howlet sent an Order for a load of Beer.[4]

JUNE 18, WEDNESDAY

HR R Bye to Kettelstone & Fakenham with beer, T Balden to Sheringham & Dawling with beer. Jere Moore at work in River. Mr Tempels men finnish'd muck Cart afternoon 3 oClock. Jno Ram & H Raven in Malt house. M^r H & WH rode to Edgefield morning to look at some hay & Dined at W Dobsons with a Party of Gentelmen. Thos Hall brewing meadow.[5]

MH A very fine day. Mr Hardy & W^m rid to Edgefield foornoon to look at some Hay, did not buy, Dind at Wm Dobsons at the Housewarming. W^m came home eveng past 11, M^r H came home morn past 1, had but little company. Mrs Forster came to speak to us in eveng . . .

[1] *Pearce* Of the Plough at Kettlestone: see note for 28 Oct. 1793

[2] *Miss Symonds* She had been ill again with fits on 1 and 5 June, according to her hostess

[3] *Robert Bye* A very rare instance of a long dinner break, evidently frowned upon by Henry. The drayman would have hoped to escape notice as William Hardy jnr was away at Mr Keeler's of Guestwick.

There were problems with workforce morale and discipline. Robert Bye and Thomas Baldwin were drunk all day on 19 June during William's absence at Aldborough

[4] *Mrs Howlett* Ann, widow of Stephen Howlett, of the Angel at Bale: see note for 7 Nov. 1793

[5] *brewing meadow* ? In the Brewhouse Meadow (the Brewhouse Pightle)

right William Hardy jnr (1770–1842), in an unsigned portrait of *c.*1826. With his cousin Henry Raven away in Whissonsett for a midsummer holiday he maintained the diary 21–29 June. Just as his father had written the other family diary for his mother in the early months 1773–74, so William showed Henry the way in Oct. 1793.

This is thought to be the only surviving likeness of the enterprising farmer and brewer. In 1993, contemplating William's clear features, long straight nose and appraising eyes in this large painting then hanging at Letheringsett Hall, Beryl Cozens-Hardy observed that he resembled her father Edward, 3rd Lord Cozens-Hardy, William's great-great-nephew [*Cozens-Hardy Collection*]

below 'National School Erected In 1825': the date stone on the old schoolhouse at Sefter Green in Pagham parish, on the Selsey Peninsula in Sussex, where Henry's brother Nathaniel was to serve as master [*MB · 1998*]

JUNE 19, THURSDAY

HR Rob[t] Bye & T Balden Drunk all Day. G Thompson Cleanse'd morning, grinding Malt for brew afternoon, Jn[o] Ram & HR in Malt house. Jere Moore at work in river. M[r] H at home all Day, WH to Alborough.

JUNE 20, FRIDAY

HR R Bye to Wells with beer, T Balden ploughing all Day. Jere Moore at work in River morning. G Thompson grinding Malt for brew, Jn[o] Ram & H Raven in Malt house. M[r] H at home all Day, WH at home morning, Holt afternoon.

[[JUNE 21, SATURDAY

William Hardy jnr T Baldwin at Siderstone & Fakenham, Rob[t] Bye at Brampton with beer. Cap[t] Hall ploughing, W Dobson sew [sowing] turnips in the Field. J Moore heaving mud out of the Pond.[1] H Raven & Phillis went to Whissonsett afternoon, Nat[l] came in Morn[g] for them.[2]

JUNE 22, SUNDAY

WHj All went to our Church forenoon. M[r], M[rs] & Miss Bartell, M[r] Geo Wymer Sen[r] drank tea & Supt here.

---

[1] *Moore* William helpfully gives more information than his cousin. Jeremiah Moore was dredging and puddling the pond in the Brewhouse Pightle and either making a new watercourse to it or enlarging an existing one

[2] *Nathaniel* Henry and Phillis's youngest brother from Whissonsett Hall, the future Sussex schoolmaster

JUNE 23, MONDAY

WHj R Bye, G Tompson & Boy brewing. T Baldwin at Salthouse with beer & bro^t^ home 1½ Ch Cinders from Jno Manns forenoon, at Briston with Beer in afternoon. T Boyce at work in the Yard, Capt Hall ½ day carting Mud from the Pond, J Moor in the Pond. Mr Keeler, Mr Everett, Mr Jarvis & Mr Nobbs came after dinner & settled, Sup^t^ & went away at 12 oClock.

MH A fine day. Mr Hardy at home all day, Wm Brew'd. Mr Keeler, Mr Everet, Jarvis & Nobs drank tea & Supt here & reck'd for Barley.[1] MA rid up to Holt with Mrs Forster . . .

JUNE 24, TUESDAY

WHj T Baldwin at Beckhigh with beer, R Bye to Wiverton & Weybourn with D^o^ & lost a barrell. G Tompson & WH Cleansd `// in Morning. M^r^, M^rs^, Miss & Wm Hardy at Sherring^m^, dined with Cook Flour [Flower].[2] T Boyce in Yard part of the day, Capt Hall carting Mud part of day, J Moor in the Pond.

JUNE 25, WEDNESDAY

WHj T Baldwin at Cromer. R Bye at Hinderingham forenoon, Stody & Thornage afternoon with beer. G Tompson Cleansd X. WH at home forenoon, at Hempstead afternoon. Capt Hall Carting Mud, T Boyce in the Yard, J Moor in Pond.

JUNE 26, THURSDAY

WHj T Baldwin & R Bye at Plough in furrze Close. J Moor in Pond, T Boyce in Yard, Capt Hall carting mud. J Dawson came in evening to alter Brewcart. Mr Banyard at Dobson's even'g & gave orders for Beer.[3] G Tompson Grinding Malt for Brew.

JUNE 27, FRIDAY

WHj T Baldwin at Gunthorp with Malt & Sherrington [the Swan at Sharrington] with beer forenoon, at Mud cart afternoon. R Bye at Holt with beer forenoon, Mud Cart afternoon, Capt Hall filling mud «cart», T Boyce in Yard. Mr Hardy at Holt Mill forenoon, Mrs Hardy taken very Ill forenoon. G Tompson finished grinding Malt.

MH A very fine day. Mr Hardy rid to Holt foornoon to look at some stuff at Wades Mill, did not buy any, came

[1] *reckoned for barley* The malting season had ended on 20 June, enabling Henry to have a brief holiday at home and the suppliers to calculate their final claims.

The visitors were arable farmers, three of them from Guestwick: Robert Everitt, who sold up from his farm in Sept. 1801, Thomas Keeler and Mr Jarvis.

[2] *Sheringham* William and Mary Hardy travelled in the chaise, their children on horseback. Mary Ann was probably mounted pillion as, like her mother, she was no horsewoman

[3] *Banyard* Charles (d. King's Lynn 4 Nov. 1808 aged 54) had newly come to the Feathers at Holt and was sizing up the competition.

He and William Dobson moved into their public houses at Lady Day, 25 Mar. 1794, Mrs Sheppard having again advertised the Feathers (*Norw. Merc.* 4 Jan. 1794) after the letting to William Coe had fallen through: see note for 9 Nov. 1793. Son of Charles and Elizabeth Banyard of E. Dereham, he came to Holt from the Three Tuns at King's Lynn and was to return to Lynn in 1802 to run the prestigious Duke's Head in the Tuesday Market (*Norw. Merc.* 1 Feb. 1794, 6 Nov. 1802). His wife, formerly Miss Harwin, appears as both Mary and Elizabeth in the Holt register. Charles Banyard's headstone is lined up along the south wall in the south-west corner of St Nicholas' churchyard at Dereham

home to dinner. I taken with dimness in my Eyes, sent for Mr Bartell, he came & din'd here [1] . . .

JUNE 28, SATURDAY

WHj T Baldwin, Bye & Capt Hall at mud cart all day, T Boyce in Yard. Mr Hardy & WH at market afternoon.

JUNE 29, SUNDAY

WHj All at our Church afternoon. G Tompson & Family went to Weybourn.]]

[[[2] JUNE 30, MONDAY

? Nathaniel Raven of Whissonsett Hall T Balden in brewhouse, WH brewing, Gun Thompson & Boy in D^o. R Bye to Corpusta & Clay with beer, Bro^t home 1½ Chal^d Coles. Capt Hall at mud Cart. Jno Ram in Malt house & Mowing borders. H Raven came from Whissensett Evening 8, G Thompson road to Edgefield after noon. M^r H at home all Day, WH & Miss H road to Holt Evening.]]

MH A Hot day. W^m brewd. Maids & Betty Loades washd 4 weeks Linnen.[3] Mr Hardy at home all day. Began cutting Hay in fur Closes.

Monday 30th. T Balden in brewhouse WH brewing
Gun: Thompson & Boy in D^o. R Bye to Corpusta
& Clay with beer Bro^t. home 1½ Chal^d. Coles
Capt Hall at mud Cart Jno Ram in Malt house

& Mowing borders H Raven came from Whissensett
Evening 8 G Thompson road to Edgefield after
noon M^r H at home all Day WH & Miss H road to Holt
Evening

[1] *eyes* She recovered next day from this latest bout of pain and impaired vision

[2] There is no record in either MS of a young relative coming back with Henry from Whissonsett, nor was anybody staying with the Hardys at the time. The childish hand may well be that of Nathaniel Raven, Henry's brother

[3] *Betty Loades* Elizabeth (bapt. Letheringsett 24 Mar. 1770), daughter of Michael and Lucy; she had helped on earlier washing days and continued to do so until 1807. Her illegitimate daughter Ann, sworn to R. Clarke, alias Cunningham, of Cley, was to be born and bapt. Letheringsett 30 Apr.

JULY 1, TUESDAY

Henry Raven T Balden to Runton with beer. R Bye at mud cart, T Hall & Jn° Ram filling mud cart. G Thompson dressing W [wheat] Stones & Cleansed `//, HR tending Kiln.[1] Mr H, WH at home all Day. Jere Moore at work in Pond. Sharpen from Briston came & Bot Molly wisker & Left Black 2 year old filly.[2] T Boyce mowing grass.

JULY 2, WEDNESDAY

HR R Bye & T Balden ploughing all Day, T Hall mud cart, Jere Moore at work in pond. Jn° Ram haymaking. G Thompson, H Raven & Mr H Cleansed. G Thompson Dressing W Stones, T Boyce Mowing grass. WH at home all Day, HR road to Bodham Evening.

JULY 3, THURSDAY

HR T Balden ploughing all Day. R Bye to Edgefield forenoon with beer, got up half load hay & Loaded Cart for Stalham afternoon. G Thompson dressing W Stones. Hall at mud cart forenoon, chopping Sticks afternoon, Jn° Ram Dressing Combs [culms]. Mr H & Mrs H set out for Gressenhall morning, got as far as Swanton [Novers], Horse tumble'd down, Brews [bruised] Mrs H face & Broke one String of Shaise [chaise].[3] WH put little Mare in Malt Cart Evening.[4]

Mary Hardy A wet morng, cleard up morng 8. Mr Hardy & I sett of for Gresenhall in our Chaise morng past 8, got as far as Swanton & the Horse fell down with us, brues'd my head & hurt Mr Hardys side, broke one of the Shafts of the Chaise, had the Chaise mend'd & came back eveng 2.

JULY 4, FRIDAY

HR R Bye to Stalham with beer. T Balden ploughing forenoon, hay making & to Holt with beer, G Thompson grinding Malt for brew. T Hall, T Boyce & Boy

facing page **The entry in Henry's diary for 30 June 1794, spread over two pages, is in a round, childish hand. This is probably 13-year-old Nathaniel Raven, writing at his brother's dictation, with Henry's distinctive spelling of Baldwin, Corpusty and rode.**

Like Henry, the scribe gives the conventional version of the miller's name, Thompson. William Hardy jnr, by contrast, habitually adopted the spelling of the Norwich brewing dynasty, Tompson [*Cozens-Hardy Collection*]

1801 [?actually 1802] and buried there 25 Oct. 1802.

She married the Letheringsett labourer William Overton 21 Feb. 1814 and was buried 29 Mar. 1816

---

[1] *kiln* Further confirmation that there was at this time only one malt-kiln (and thus one cowl: see 22 Nov. 1793). At the end of the malting season the kiln and furnace had to be cleaned thoroughly and the terracotta kiln tiles with their daisy-patterned perforations had to be pricked clean (illustrated overleaf)

[2] *Sharpen* The 1806 Norfolk pollbook shows Thomas Sharpens as a Briston farmer. Wisker and Whisker do not appear in the dialect dictionaries, and may have been a pet name for Molly; or she may have come from the Hardys' long-serving Hindringham innkeeper, John Wisker

[3] *string* Mary Hardy calls it the shaft. Henry uses the word still employed today in architectural and nautical circles, a stringer being a long piece of timber used as a supporting beam in houses or as a brace to strengthen the hull of a ship

[4] *little mare* The new filly (1 July) was being introduced to work as a draught horse as well as a riding horse.

Like colts, fillies were not put to severe work until they were fully developed as adult horses

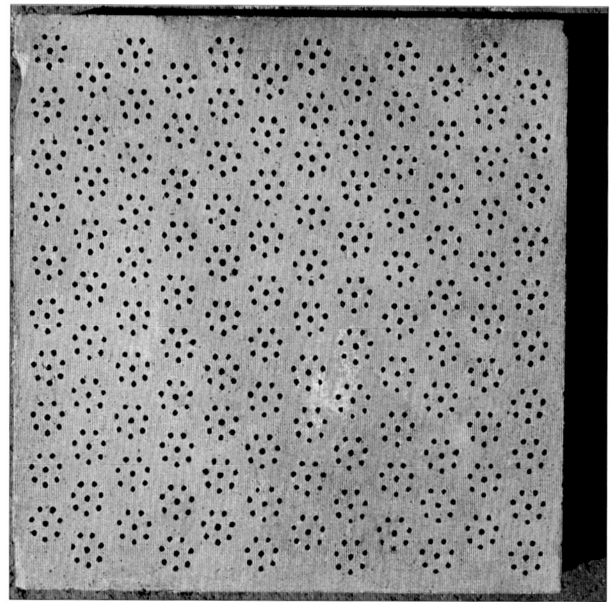

right 'Henry Raven tending kiln' (1 July). This tile, of a standard 18th- to 20th-century type, was salvaged by the Letheringsett estate gardener David Mayes when 19th-century heated greenhouses in the Hall grounds were demolished in 1985. It had been set with others on top of the pipes to diffuse the heat.

It almost certainly came from the Hardy malt-kilns, having been made redundant when later wedge-wire kiln floors were installed [*MB · 2011*]

haymaking. M^rs^ & Miss & HR to Confirmation, Holt. M^r^ H & WH at Holt afternoon. W Bulling came morning & Orderd 5 Nog.[1]

MH A Hot day. I, MA & H Raven went to Holt morng 11 in the Chaise, MA & HR was confirm'd by Bishop Sutton.[2] We dind & drank tea at Mr Bartells, came home even 8.

JULY 5, SATURDAY

HR R Bye home from Stalham. T Balden to Sheringham with beer & Help'd to Carry Cleanse beer of [off] with WH. HR & G Thompson & WH cleaned Hop Cham^r^ [chamber]. T Boyce & Jno Ram haymaking forenoon, at work in yard afternoon, T Hall at work in front yard. M^r^ H at home all Day, WH at Holt afternoon.

MH A hot dry day. W^m^ went to Market eveng 4, came home evng 9. Mr Hardy & I rid up to fir Closes in L [little] Cart foornoon to look at some Hay . . .

JULY 6, SUNDAY

HR R Raven came morning, whent home Evening. Famaly whent to Church morning, a Lecture Evening. Mr Wade drank tea & supt here.

---

1 *nog* The Bull's innkeeper anticipated good business from the confirmation candidates' families, the order being delivered that same day by Thomas Baldwin. Revd Robert Thomlinson, Rector of Cley, noted in his parish register that on 4 July 1794 the Bishop confirmed 50 candidates from Cley, and 11 from Wiveton (where Mr Thomlinson served as curate). 400 in total were confirmed at Holt that day: see *World*, vol. 3, chaps 1, 2

2 *Bishop Sutton* Rt Revd Dr Charles Manners Sutton (1755–1828), Bishop of Norwich and Dean of Windsor. Grandson of the 3rd Duke of Rutland, a descendant of Edward III, and enjoying the favour of George III, he had been appointed to the see of Norwich in 1793 following the death of Rt Revd Dr George Horne (1730–92)

left **The underside of the malt-kiln tile, showing the holes feeding the heat from the furnace to the topside perforations. It measures 12 inches by 12 by 2 (30·5 cm x 30·5 x 5)** [*MB · 2011*]

JULY 7, MONDAY

HR R Bye to Kettlestone with beer. T Balden to Briston with beer forenoon, help«ed» to get up hay afternoon. Jn° Ram howing D° [hoeing forenoon], after hay afternoon. G Thompson, T Boyce getting up hay afternoon. Mr H & WH at home all Day.

MH Excesive hot dry day. Mr Hardy at home all day. Wm went to Holt Bowling Green after tea, came home eveng 10.[1]

JULY 8, TUESDAY

HR T Balden to Fakenham with beer. R Bye, G Thompson & Boy in Brewhouse, WH Brewing. Jn° Ram howing turnips in Field, T Boyce at work in yard. Mr H begun to Paint best Parlor.

MH Excesive Hot day. Mr Hardy at home & poorly with pain in his side from his fall. Wm Brew'd.

JULY 9, WEDNESDAY

HR R Bye, T Balden, T Boyce & Boy got up two Load of hay fornoon. T Balden to Waybourn with beer, R Bye to Bale with beer afternoon. T Boyce at work in yard afternoon, Jn° Ram howing turnips in Field. G Thomp-

after only two years as Bishop of Norwich. As Dean of Windsor he was responsible directly to the monarch as St George's Chapel, Windsor Castle, was a Royal Peculiar, free from episcopal oversight.

The visit to Holt was part of Bishop Sutton's primary visitation. There had been no opportunity for confirmation in the Holt deanery since June 1787 when William Hardy jnr was confirmed at 17; Mary Ann and Henry were now aged 20 and 16 respectively.

As well as granting access to the spiritual solace of Holy Communion, confirmation was for the candidates a necessary preliminary for compliance with the Test Act. Only Anglican communicants could go to university and take up most types of public office

[1] *bowling green* William was starting to attend bowls at the Feathers (see 27 Aug. 1795). This was possibly a new venture by Charles Banyard; Monday-evening bowls had in earlier years been held at the King's Head, Holt

son, H Raven Cleansed `// forenoon, Best afternoon.[1] Mr H whent to Mr Kings [2] & Bot 6 Load of Hay,[3] WH & T Boyce whent to look of it Evening.

MH A cool close day. Mr Hardy & I rid in L Cart into Holt field, lookd at some Hay of Mr Kings, then rid to Coopers at Holt Lawn,[4] his hay was spoke for, call«ed» at Mr Kings coming back & bought 53 Cocks for £21 0*s* 0*d*, came home to tea. Wm rid to look at the Hay after tea . . .

JULY 10, THURSDAY

HR R Bye to Syderstone with beer. T Balden, T Boyce, Jno Ram & Boy getting up hay. G Thompson, H Raven & T Hall onloded hay, E Hall raking after Waggon.[5] Mr H at home all Day, WH & Miss H rode to Holt after tea.

JULY 11, FRIDAY

HR R Bye, T Balden, T Boyce & Boy after Hay forenoon. Jno Ram at work in field, T Do [Boyce] at work in yard afternoon. Capt Hall at mud cart all Day. Mr H & WH at home all day. Mr, Mrs & Miss Bartell drank tea here. Mr Bare came after Hindonvestone house.

below **Holt Lawn lies north of Holt (9 July) beside the rivulet known as Cley Watering, which flows south-west into Letheringsett and in which Henry Smith died (24 May). The Hardys' brewery ('Brewhouse') is shown in the village centre west of the River Glaven; the 'Hall' is Letheringsett Hall Farm**
[*Bryant's Map of Norfolk 1826: Cozens-Hardy Collection*]

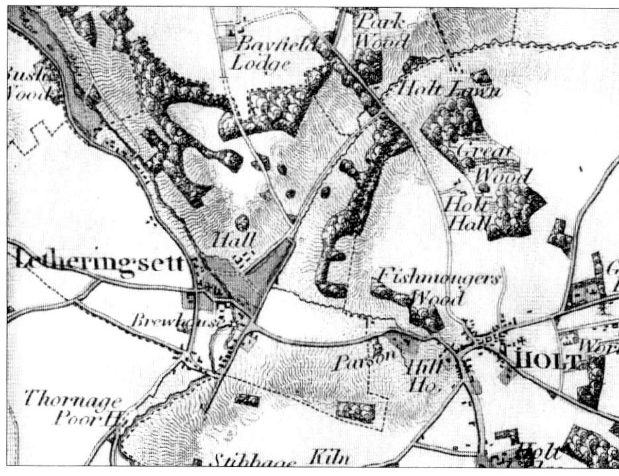
Park Wood
Bayfield Lodge
Holt Lawn
Great Wood
Holt Hall
Hall
Fishmongers Wood
HOLT
Kiln

[1] *best* As in best bitter; best mild

[2] *King* Robert, farmer and tanner. On leaving Sheepwalk Farm at Holt the previous summer he had advertised a sale of his flock of 460 sheep of the Norfolk breed 'equal to any hard-keeping' and reared on Holt Sheepwalk 'which consists of about 1600 acres of hard ling heather' (*Norw. Merc.* 10 Aug. 1793).

'Holt Field' was the pre-enclosure open field, as was the field in Letheringsett to which Henry Raven refers, eg 8 and 9 July 1794

[3] *hay* New hay: see note for 14 Mar. 1794. As at Southrepps on 25 Mar. 1794, Mary Hardy was making an effort to take an active part once more in the family concern. Taking the two diary entries together it can be calculated there were 216 trusses of hay in 53 cocks, there being usually four trusses to the cock or stook (where the bundles of newly-mown grass are propped against one another to form a cone as they dry in the sun). The six loads, already cocked, weighed 5878·6 kg, or 5·88 metric tonnes, costing £21

[4] *Holt Lawn* Marked on Faden's map of 1797 and on Bryant's of 1826, north of Holt and east of Cley Watering

[5] *Elizabeth Hall* Performing a similar task to the one she and her mother had carried out at harvest time for the Hardys at Coltishall 20 years earlier

above Norwich Cathedral, the cloisters. Mary Ann Hardy and Henry Raven were confirmed at Holt on 4 July 1794 by Bishop Manners Sutton, who in 1805 was appointed Archbishop of Canterbury—the only occasion on which the Primate has been appointed direct from Norwich. The 1794 tour of his new diocese was the Bishop's primary visitation, occupying him without a break from 6 June (Newmarket) to 18 July (Norwich) and then long into the autumn. The visitation returns of 1794, filled in by the clergy from every parish in the huge see and now housed in the Norfolk Record Office, yield precise and detailed data on each of the 1296 parishes [*MB · 2011*]

MH A very Hot day. Mr Hardy & W^m^ at home all day. M^r^ & M^rs^ & Miss Bartell drank tea here. Mr Windham vacantd his seat in Parliment by accepting a Place of Secretary of the War department [at War], A oppersition likely to take place for a Member of Parliment for Norwich between Windham & Counsellor Mingay of Thetford, the Ellection to be to Morrow.[1] Mrs Custance & Mrs Robt Raven came to Holt to Mr Bakers.[2]

[1] *an opposition* A contest. William Windham (1750–1810), of Felbrigg Hall, was required to present himself to his constituents for re-election after accepting the government post. Cllr James Mingay was nominated by the opponents of 'Weathercock Windham', but they failed to consult their man in advance and he polled 700 as against Windham's 1236. The surprising strength of the unwitting candidate's vote reflected the electorate's disquiet over their Member's political allegiance since the 1790 general election. The vote was even more surprising as Mingay was a last-minute choice after the Norwich banker Bartlett Gurney's refusal to stand as the peace candidate. On hearing of the election result Mingay declared that he was anyway ineligible to stand (*Norw. Merc.* 19 July 1794).

Many of the MP's manufacturing and trading supporters had been anti-war from principle in 1790, and 'Windham's change of front, from a liberal-minded Whig to a furious anti-Jacobin, had not pleased them at all' (R.W. Ketton-Cremer, *Felbrigg*, p. 226)

[2] *Mrs Custance and Mrs Raven* The sisters Phillis (bapt. Whissonsett 7 Apr. 1737, bur. there 14 Feb. 1812: note for 26 Dec. 1793) and Hannah (bapt. Whissonsett 20 Sept. 1739, bur. there 17 Dec. 1794). They were the daughters of Mary Hardy's aunt Phillis Raven,

who had married Paul Myles in 1732.

Phillis Custance's husband William was in dire straits, his cabinet-making business about to be stopped (26 July 1794) and his bankruptcy declared (9 Aug.). The bankruptcy proceedings lasted until May 1796, when the creditors received their final dividend (*Norw. Merc.* 7 May 1796).

Hannah, widow (and cousin) of Robert Raven of Tunstead, was to die five months after this diary entry. On his father's death in 1792 their son Myles Raven had inherited the Tunstead farm held copyhold from Sir John Berney, Bt. Myles gave up Norfolk farming in Oct. 1797, the sale of the farming stock and household furniture taking four days (*Norw. Merc.* 16 Sept. 1797).

See the family trees in app. D3.A, fig. D3.2, and in *Diary 2*: app. D2.A, fig. D2.3

above 'Walked a-farming after tea' (13 July 1794). Ripening barley sways in the wind at Lamas, near Coltishall. Walking the crops was a tradition introduced to William by his father, who would take his young sons on evening strolls at Horstead [*MB · 2011*]

JULY 12, SATURDAY

HR R Bye to Hindonvestone with beer & help«ed» to Cleanse fat [vat], T Balden to Thornage & Stody with beer, T Boyce at work in yard. T Hall at mud cart forenoon, Jn° Ram at mud cart all Day. Mr H at home all Day. WH, Mrs H & Miss H at Holt after tea. Mr Betts dined here.

MH A very Hot dry day. Mr Hardy at home all day. Wm, I & MA rid up to Holt in L Cart after tea. An Ellection for a Member of Parliment for Norwich at Norwich, Mr Windham was again rechosen after an obstinate oppersition with Mr Mingay . . .

JULY 13, SUNDAY

HR Famaly all whent to church afternoon. WH, HR & G Thompson walked afarming after tea.[1]

[1] *walked a-farming* An engaging phrase for examining the crops' progress; today it is more usually called walking the crops.

Here it conveys a sense of the comfortable relations between the young brewer, the new apprentice and the experienced miller as they strolled round the Hardys' scattered fields in the warm evening sunshine—'an excessive hot day', noted Mary Hardy

JULY 14, MONDAY

HR T Balden ploughing up turnips & sowing. Robt Bye ploughing forenoon, to Dawling [Field Dalling] with beer afternoon, Boy at harow afternoon. G Thompson grinding Malt for Bin & brew. M^r H road to Holt afternoon, WH to Cromer. T Boyce at work in yard. Jno Ram finnish^d getting away mud & cleard the wood from Pond & got stones out brewhouse yard.

MH A close morng, very hot afternoon. W^m went to Cromer & Southreeps Morng 7, came home eveng 9. Mr Hardy, I & MA drank tea at Dobsons at the Kings Head, met Mr Burrells & Mr Bartells Family [1] . . .

JULY 15, TUESDAY

HR T Balden to Corpusta with beer. Robt Bye to Wiverton with beer forenoon, to Holt with waggon to be mended & got up 1 Load of Mirgin from Lime Kiln, Boy fetching mirgin.[2] G Thompson grinding Malt for brew. T Boyce at work in yard, Jno Ram howing turnips in Field. M^r & M^rs & Miss Hardy dined at Mr Bakers. WH to Wells, HR roade to Edgefield.

JULY 16, WEDNESDAY

HR T Balden to Edgefield with beer & at work in yard, R Bye at work in yard. Jno Ram howing turnips in Furze Close, T Boyce at D^o in D^o [at work in yard]. Gun^t Thompson grinding Malt for brew. Boy to Birmingham [Briningham] with good [? goods] morning. M^r & WH road out afternoon.

JULY 17, THURSDAY

HR T Balden, G Thompson, H Raven & Boy in brewhouse, WH brewing. R Bye fetching mirgin & whent to Holt for waggon. T Boyce at work in yard, Jno Ram howing turnips. M^r, M^rs & Miss Baker & M^rs [Hannah] Raven Dined here. M^r, Mrs Burrell & Miss Leake & Miss Flower Drank tea here.[3] M^rs & Miss & N Raven came from Whissonsett afternoon.[4]

JULY 18, FRIDAY

HR R Bye to Wells with beer, T Balden to Walsingham with beer. G Thompson, WH & H Raven Cleans^d `// forenoon, Strong [beer] afternoon. T Boyce at work in yard. Jno Ram howing turnips half day. Mrs Forster & Mrs Harron [Herring] drank tea here. M^r H at home all Day.

1 *King's Head* This is the first time the families have been recorded patronising the brewery tap, suggesting that following the rebuilding and under the new tenant it had gone rather more upmarket. Small country public houses as well as the market town inns could be frequented socially by the clergy and well-to-do

2 *mergin* Also mirgin: cement, Marshall defining it as 'the mortar or cement of old walls' and describing it also as a much coveted manure (W. Marshall, *The Rural Economy of Norfolk*, vol. 2, p. 383; vol. 1, p. 30).

The Hardys may have valued it as a lime-based cement to line or puddle the liquor pond

3 *Miss Flower* See note for 14 Oct. 1796

4 *Miss Raven* Identified by Mary Hardy as Henry's youngest sister Mary (b. Whissonsett Hall 22 Apr. 1780, bapt. Whissonsett 23 Apr., marr. Letheringsett 17 Nov. 1819 her first cousin William Hardy jnr, d. Letheringsett 24 Dec. 1846, bur. 30 Dec. in the Hardy family vault). Their only child William died a few weeks after his birth and was bur. Letheringsett 21 Mar. 1820.

On her husband's death in 1842 she lived at The Lodge, formerly the house of John Burrell snr and jnr.

14-year-old Mary arrived with her mother Ann and brother Nathaniel for the signing of Henry's indentures as brewery apprentice 19 July

above **The diarists record an assortment of gardeners: innkeepers, soldiers, labourers, farm servants (eg 23, 31 July). An itinerant preacher writes of hollyhocks at the Hall *c*.1823** [*MB · 2011*]

JULY 19, SATURDAY

HR R Bye to Sheringham with beer, T Balden & T Boyce at work in yard, Jn° Ram howing turnips in Field. WH laid down gutter Bricks & whent to Market after tea.[1] Mrs Raven whent home after tea, HR roade to Thursford with them. Mr H at home all Day.

MH Very hot day, no rain. Mr Hardy at home all day. Sister Raven & Childrn went away after tea. Wm went to Market eveng 5, came home eveng 9. H Raven bound himself apprentice . . .

JULY 20, SUNDAY

HR Famaly all whent to Church forenoon, WH & HR whent to Holt afternoon. G Thompsons Famaly whent to Walsingham.

JULY 21, MONDAY

HR Robt Bye to Runton with beer, T Balden to Cley with beer & Brot home 1½ Chald Coles from Mr Ellis s. Boy whent to Sherington for 100 & 50 Brace of fish.[2] Jn° Ram howing turnips, T Boyce at work in yard. Mr H at home all Day, WH at Sherington. Robt Pleasance came for 1 Bar Beer.[3] T Youngmans Lad Painting. HR road to Edgefield.

MH A dry day, not so hot as yesterday. Mr Hardy at home all day. Wm & MA rid up to Holt in Chaise after tea. Wm went to Bowling green, came home eveng 9 . . .

JULY 22, TUESDAY

HR Robt Bye to Fakenham with beer, T Balden to Gunthorp & Kettlestone with beer. T Boyce at work in yard, Jn° Ram howing turnips. T Youngmans Lad painting, G Thompson grinding Malt for Bin. Mr H at home all Day, WH road out afternoon.

JULY 23, WEDNESDAY

HR Robt Bye to Salthouse with beer, came home by Cley for 1½ Chald Cinders & To Thornage with beer. T Balden to Holt & Edgefield with beer, G Thompson grinding Malt for brew. T Boyce at work in yard, Jn° Ram howing turnips & work in garden. Mr H at home all Day, Mr J [Joseph] Davy drank tea here. WH at home all Day. T Youngmans Lad Painting.

JULY 24, THURSDAY

HR T Balden at Mirgin & gravil cart. R Bye to Shering-

---

[1] *gutter bricks* Purpose-moulded concave bricks channelling spillages and enabling thorough sluicing

[2] *150 brace of fish* 300 fish, to stock the Brewhouse Pightle pond, which must have been finished by 21 July. A small headstream of the Glaven runs from west to east through Sharrington. In his undated poem Stones refers to the reservoir as 'the larger pond, where sportive fishes play' (W. Stones, *The Garden of Norfolk, or The rural residence* (Norwich, [*c*.1823]) p. 51)

[3] *one barrel of beer* A small order would not have pleased the brewer, the delivery hardly being an economic proposition

ton with beer & «at» gravil cart. G Thompson grinding Malt for brew, T Boyce at work in yard. Jno Ram howing turnips & work in garden. Mr H & WH at home all Day. Mr J Ellis drank tea here.

JULY 25, FRIDAY

HR R Bye to Brampton with beer. T Balden & Boy at gravel forenoon, Hinderingham with beer afternoon. T Boyce at work in yard, J Ram in garden. G Thompson & wife to Clay.[1] Mr H at home all Day, WH roade out afternoon. Chapman Brot 20 geese.[2]

MH A fine day. Mr Hardy at home all day. Wm rid to Hildonveston [Hindolveston] afternoon, came back to tea. Sarah went to Clay fair.[3] Chaplin [Chapman] of Hindrinham brought us 22 Geese.

JULY 26, SATURDAY

HR Robt Bye to Walsham with beer, T Balden to Syderstone with beer. T Boyce at work in yard, Jno Ram in garden. Mr H & WH at Holt morning, at Market afternoon. H Raven whent to Whissensett.

MH A fine foornoon, Showry aftern. Mr Hardy walkd up to Holt foornoon, came home eveng 4. We all walkd up «to Holt» to tea, drank tea at Mr Davys, rid home in L Cart. H Raven rid to Whisonsett in the eveng, hard [heard] Mr Custance of Fakenham was stopt.[4]

Back Common
Common
Whissonset
Dir. Post
Whissonset Hall
Godwick in Ruins
Godwick Hall
Tittleshall cum Godwick
Old Hall Grove
Stanfield

left **Whissonsett lies five miles south of Fakenham, its common by the Wensum headstream still unenclosed in 1794. Whissonsett Hall, Henry's home, is marked. His mother Ann was from neighbouring Stanfield** [*Faden's Map of Norfolk 1797: Larks Press 1989*]

[1] *to Cley* Presumably, like the maid Sarah Turner, to attend the fair held towards the end of July to mark the eve of the festival (Old Style) of St Margaret of Antioch, the church's patron saint. Thompson's wife Ann was buried Letheringsett from Walsingham 2 Mar. 1800—'aged about 50', recorded Mary Hardy in her register (*Diary 4*)

[2] *Chapman* William, of the Falgate at Hindringham

[3] *Sarah* The first time either of the maids has been named since the reopening of Mary Hardy's diary on 17 Oct. 1793. Her register (in the endnotes) shows that Sarah Turner and Hannah Dagliss were hired 11 Oct. 1793: Sarah at £3; Hannah at £2 15*s*. Both stayed the year. Sarah served again 1795–96, at £3 10*s*; Hannah served continuously Feb. 1795–May 1797 at £3 3*s* a year, and after three further periods of service left the Hardys on 10 Oct. 1801.

For the Hardys' maidservants see *World*, vol. 1, chap. 8, and vol. 1, app. 1.C

[4] *Custance* See notes for 26 Dec. 1793 and 11 July 1794

[1] *church* This was the day Thomas Boyce's daughter Maria and Jeremiah Moore's son David were received publicly into the church; they had been privately baptised in January and March just after birth. Maria was buried at Letheringsett on 13 Dec. 1834 at a time of sickness, there being 23 burials between 10 May and 30 Dec. 1834. Although the cause of Maria's death is not stated, 11 infants and young children died of scarlet fever 12 Oct.–21 Dec. 1834 (NRO: PD 547/44)

[2] *Gunton Thompson jnr* The case did not go to quarter sessions. Since neither Henry nor his aunt gives the reason for the young man's arrest it may have been on a delicate matter such as a paternity case. If so, the justices could have found in his favour, for he did not marry for another 19 months; or enough money was found to offer sureties to the parish responsible for the mother and child.

It is unlikely to have been a disputed settlement case, as he must have been in good health to be helping with the maltstones and harvest and was not a burden on the parish. On marrying Ann Starling (the Hardys' maid 1791–93), of Letheringsett, on 5 Nov. 1795 he was declared to be of Edgefield. The groom signed and the bride made her mark; see also note for 5 Nov. 1795. William Hardy jnr was evidently a parish officer: perhaps overseer of the poor, or constable

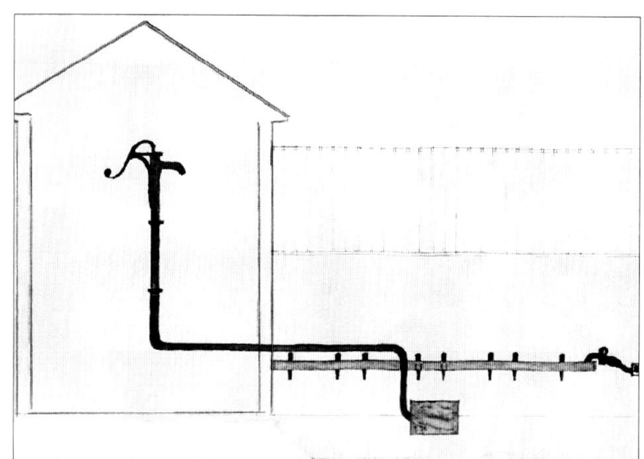

JULY 27, SUNDAY

HR Famaly whent to Church afternoon,[1] H Raven came from Whissensett Evening.

MH A fine day. All went to our Church Afternoon, Mr Burrell read a Lecture on the Sacrament. H Raven came home eveng 9.

JULY 28, MONDAY

HR Robt Bye & Boy in Brewhouse, T Balden to Corpusta with beer. WH Brewing, took [arrested] G Thompson Junr morning, «Gunton Thompson jnr» was took to the Justices forenoon, father whent with him.[2] T Boyce stoping gaps morning, at work in yard, J Ram howing turnips. Mr H out all Day. Mr Youngmans lad painting.

MH A very fine day. Maids & Eliz Loades washd 4 weeks Linn [linen]. Mr Hardy walkd up to Holt foornoon on business, dind at Mr Moores, drank tea at Mr Bakers, went to the purse Club at the Kings Head & came home eveng 11 . . .

JULY 29, TUESDAY

HR Robt Bye at home morning, Sheringham afternoon. T Balden in bed forenoon, to Holt & help«ed» to Cleanse. G Thompson & HR Cleanse'd `// forenoon, strong afternoon, Jno Ram howing turnips. T Boyce finnish«ed» brewhouse yard & work«ing» in garden. Mr H at home all Day, WH at Holt afternoon. Youngmans lad painting.

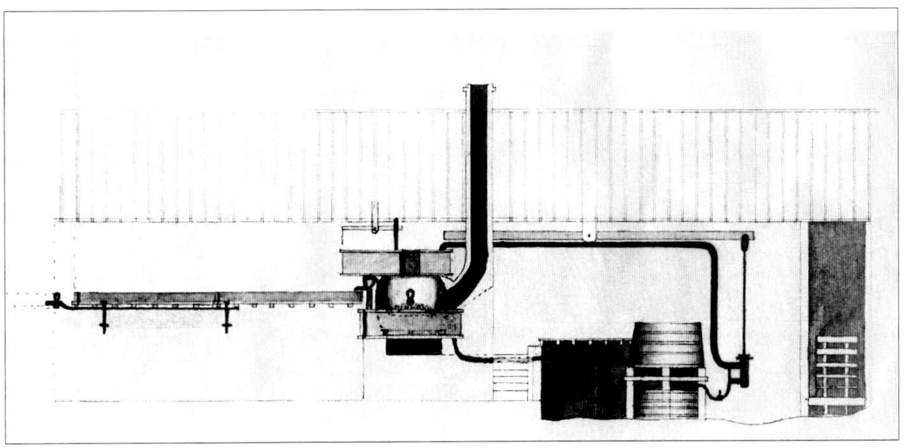

facing page and *above* Henry Raven's mother and his youngest sister and brother were present when his indentures were signed on 19 July 1794. The village malthouse, kilns, brewhouse, white hall, tun room and counting house became his realm until 1800. This depiction of the Letheringsett brewery is almost certainly by William Hardy jnr's architect William Mindham in the period 1808–14; the accompanying plan is overleaf.

The workings, which begin with the waterwheel in its channel (above, far right), and end in the tun room with its huge pump for filling the casks, are explained in more detail in *Diary 2*, under 4 Apr. 1782, and *World*, volume 2, chapter 7. The brewing process is charted from the coopered mash tun and underback across to the copper (with the flue) and thence to the shallow coolers (left) with cocks opening to the fermenting tuns (not depicted). Racking, with cocks for eight barrels, takes place in the 'white hall' next to the tun room. Vertical timber boarding is much in evidence [*Cozens-Hardy Collection*]

JULY 30, WEDNESDAY

HR Robt Bye to Waybourn & Bale with beer. T Balden to Briston with beer & Corpusta & Edgefield with `// & Grains.[1] T Boyce in garden, Jno Ram howing turnips. G Thompson & Son laid down Malt Stones. M^r^ H at Holt Venison feast, WH & Miss Hardy at Holt Evening.[2]

MH A fine day. Finishd ironing Eveng 3. Mr Hardy went to a Veneson feast to dinner at the Kings head at Holt, came home even 10.

JULY 31, THURSDAY

HR R Bye & Boy cleaning barn & Cleard fat [vat]. T Boyce in garden, Jno Ram howing turnips. M^r^ H & WH out all Day. T Balden ill. Mr Youngman mending watergate.[3]

[1] *grains* The only time brewer's grains are mentioned. A cattle-feed, pig-feed and fertiliser, these by-products of brewing are the sediment left behind in the fermenting vessel

[2] *venison feast* The stewards were Thomas Forster and James Moore (*Norw. Merc.* 26 July 1794)

[3] *watergate* The sluice gate by the malthouse to control the flow from the Glaven to the waterwheel culvert

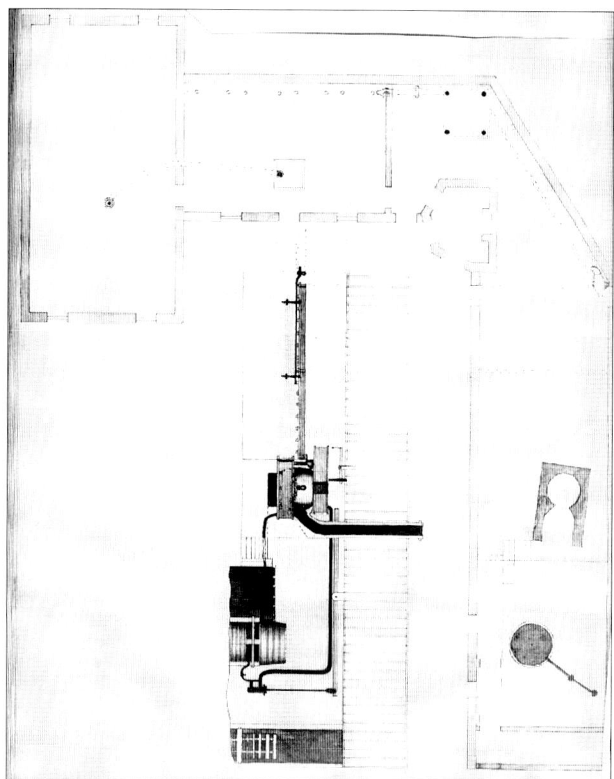

right The plan shows the brewing equipment aligned to the north front facing the main road (far right); the white hall and tun room lie to the west (top). Basil Cozens-Hardy, who cut these drawings into fragments and pasted them into an album, labelled the little room with two windows facing south-east into the yard as the counting house. His father Sydney (b.1850) was given six months' training as brewer at Henry Raven's age until deciding against that career, and it was probably Sydney who guided Basil over the labelling. Henry's farming and brewing diary would have been stored with other ledgers and petty cash in a secure room such as this [*Cozens-Hardy Collection*]

facing page The 17th-century Communion rails at Ranworth Church on the Norfolk Broads are a fairly rare survival, as Victorian restorers took churches in hand to reflect their own views on ritual. These 'Prayer Book Church' features honour post-Reformation injunctions issued 1549–1662.

In 1794 most of the Hardy family worshipped at Letheringsett and were frequently present for Communion on the four occasions it was offered during the year (3 Aug.). Family worship changed in the 1790s as Methodism spread [*MB · 2011*]

MH A Close day. Mr Hardy & W^m^ went to Southreps in our Chaise Morng 9 to meet a Man from Norwich to hire that publick House, did not let it, came home by Cromer eveng 10. M^r^ & Miss Bartell drank tea here. Skivens [Skiffins] at work in Garden . . .

AUGUST 1, FRIDAY

Henry Raven Robt Bye to Wiverton with beer & Clay for Cinders, T Balden to Cromer with beer. G Thompson grinding Malt for brew, T Boyce in garden, Jno Ram howing turnips. M^r^ H & WH at home all Day.

AUGUST 2, SATURDAY

HR Robt Bye to Kettlestone with beer, card of [carried off] Cleanse beer. T Balden & Boy at gravil cart forenoon, onloading coles & card of beer. G Thompson grinding Malt for brew. T Boyce in garden, Jn° Ram howing turnips. Mr H at home all Day. WH, Mrs & Miss H at Holt afternoon.

AUGUST 3, SUNDAY

HR Famaly all whent to Church forenoon, WH & HR whent to Holt afternoon. Mr Burrel preach«ed» a Lecture Evening.

Mary Hardy A fine day. All went to our Church foornoon, A Communion.[1] Wm & HR went to Holt Church afternoon, Mr T Fisher preachd.[2] We had a Lecture at our Church eveng 7.

AUGUST 4, MONDAY

HR T Balden, G Thompson, H Raven & Boy in brewhouse, WH Brewing. R Bye stoping gaps forenoon,[3] to Blakeny for 1½ Chald Coles afternoon. Jn° Ram howing turnips, T Boyce in garden. Mr Dawson came & took boxes out «of the» brew cart.[4] Mr H & WH at Balkny [Blakeney].

MH A Cold stormy day. Mr Hardy & Wm rid to Blakney afternoon to buy some Coales of Mr Chaplins selling at 23/- pr Chaldrn, Wm came home to tea.[5] Mr Hardy rid

[1] *Communion* This may have been the Whitsun Communion running very late, or, unusually, a fifth administration of the Sacrament in the year. In answer to the new Bishop's question, the rector had replied four weeks earlier that he administered the Sacrament four times a year (Easter, Whit, Michaelmas and Christmas) to about 30 communicants (NRO: DN/VIS 33a/4, Holt deanery visitation 1794, Letheringsett return)

[2] *Fisher* Revd Thomas (bapt. Sharrington 1768, d. Holt 10 Nov. 1806); his mother Mary (d. Holt 19 Nov. 1807), née Southgate, was sister to the brewer Henry Hagon's second wife Elizabeth, and his father Thomas had farmed at Sharrington before moving to Holt.

He was admitted Christ's College, Cambridge 1787, ordained deacon Ely 1792, priest 1792; Curate of Linton, Cambs 1792, of Holt 1794, of Chesterford, Essex 1795; Rector of Girton, Cambs 1800–06.

He died at his father's house, his father dying 11 days later (*Alum. Cantab.*; *Diary 4*)

[3] *stopping gaps* In hedges

[4] *boxes* See note for 23 Dec. 1793

[5] *coals* This rate was considerably cheaper than the 29*s* 4*d* a chaldron quoted at Norwich in the winter (note for 25 Nov. 1793). Coal sold more cheaply in the summer months when demand slackened; also

to Langham, drank tea at Mr Frosts, came home eveng 8.[1] I taken poorly with pain in my Stomack . . .

AUGUST 5, TUESDAY

HR Robt Bye & T Baldin Brot 9 Chaldr Coles from Blakeny, T Boyce & Boy onloden Coles. J Ram howing turnips. H Raven, G Thompson, WH Cleansed `// forenoon, Strong afternoon. Mr H at home all Day.

AUGUST 6, WEDNESDAY

HR R Bye & T Balden brot 9 Chald Coles from Blakeny, T Boyce & Boy onloding Coles. J Ram howing turnips in field. WH out all Day, Mr & Mrs & Miss Hardy drank tea at Mr Burrels.

MH A Close Morng, begun to rain eveng 4, continued till eveng 8. A dry night. Wm went with Mr Moore to Sheringham morng 8, dind at Mr Cremers at Beeston, came home eveng 10. Mr Hardy, I & MA drank tea at Mr Burrells, Mr H staid till eveng 12 . . .

AUGUST 7, THURSDAY

HR Bye to Fakenham with beer, T Baldin to Walsingham & Dawling with beer. Jno Ram howing turnips. G Thompson & Boy onloaded two load Coles afternoon. Mr & WH at home all Day.

AUGUST 8, FRIDAY

HR Robt Bye to Wellse with beer. T Baldin to Blakeny for 2 load Coles, one for G Thompson. Jno Ram howing turnips, G Thompson grinding Malt for brew. Nath Raven came with Mr Watson, WH & Mr H whent to Holt with them afternoon.[2] Miss H gone to Norwich with Miss Bartell.[3]

AUGUST 9, SATURDAY

HR T Baldin to Runton with beer. R Bye to Blakeny for 1½ Chald Coles from Mr Braetons [Brereton's] & got up 2 Load gravil.[4] G Thompson grinding Malt for bin, Jno Ram howing turnips. Mr & WH at home morning, Holt Market afternoon. N Raven gone home afternoon 3 oClock.

MH A fine day. N Raven went away after dinner. Mr Hardy walkd to Holt Markt, drank tea at Mr Bartells. Wm rid up to Holt, drank tea at Widw Fishers, both came home eveng 9. Mr Custance of Fakenham made a Bankrupt [5] . . .

extra costs were incurred in river transport to Norwich.

The men spent five days 4–8 Aug. shifting the unusually large purchase from Blakeney, and a further day collecting coal from another merchant. The Hardys then had to consider new security measures (12 Sept. 1794)

---

[1] *Frost* The 1806 Norfolk pollbook lists Stephen Frost as a gentleman of Langham. A farmer, he made diary jottings in printed memorandum books 1768–1816 and was a passionate hare courser (NRO: MC 120/11–120/85, 593X3–594X5)

[2] *Watson* He was unknown to Mary Hardy, who notes him as *a* Mr Watson of Mileham; he had come to Holt 'to be admitted to a small estate in Mileham'

[3] *Miss H* Mary Ann Hardy and Charlotte Bartell seized the opportunity of taking a postchaise returning empty to the city—a 'returned postchaise'

[4] *Brereton* Robert (bapt. Brinton 14 Oct. 1759, d. 11 June 1831, bur. in the family vault at Blakeney), merchant, and until 1789 a Brinton farmer; son of John (1725–85), he came from the Brinton family which had founded the Letheringsett brewery. By Apr. 1795 he was one of William Custance's assignees, the other being Nathaniel Raven (*Norw. Merc.* 4 Apr. 1795)

[5] *bankrupt* The *Norwich Mercury* on 16 Aug. 1794 announced the commission

HOME CIRCUIT.

	From London to			
	Hoddeſdon, p. 187		—	17
c.	Hertford		4	21
	Epping		13	34
	Ongar		7½	41½
c.	Chelmsford		11½	53
	Graveſend, p. 258		22½	75½
a.	Rochester		9	84½
a.	Maidſtone, p. 8		8½	93
	Tunbridge, p. 305		14	107
l.	Grinſtead		15	122
a.	Croydon		19	141
c.	Kingſton		10	151
	London, p. 23		11½	162½

The Summer Aſſizes are holden alternately, at Guildford and Croydon for Surry; and at Lewes and Horſham for Suſſex.

MIDLAND CIRCUIT.

	From London to			
c.	Northampton, p. 140		—	66
	Wellingborough		11	77
	Kettering		7	84
c.	Oakham, p. 153		21	105
	Stamford		11½	116½
	Bourn		11	127½
c.	Lincoln, p. 180.		36	163½
	Newark.	p. 270	17½	181
	Southwell	p. 270	7	188
c.	Nottingham	p. 270	14	202
c.	Derby, p. 269		15½	217½
	Loughbro'	p. 140	17	234½
c.	Leiceſter	p. 140	11	245½
	Hinkley	p. 225	14	259½
c.	Coventry	p. 225	13¼	272¾
c.	Warwick	p. 225	10	282¾

The Aſſizes in the Midland Circuit, ſometimes begin at Oakham, and end at Warwick; at other Times they begin at Warwick, ending ſometimes at Northampton, and ſometimes at Lincoln.

NORFOLK CIRCUIT.

	From London to			
l.	Ayleſbury	p. 103	—	40½
	Winſlow	p. 103	10	50½
s.	Buckingham	p. 103	6¾	57¼
	Newport Pagnel		14	71¼
c.	Bedford		13¼	84½
	Eaton		11½	96
	Bugden		6	102
c.	Huntingdon		4	106
c.	Cambridge	p. 290	15	121
	Newmarket	p. 290	12	133
c.	BurySt.Edm.	p. 290	14½	147½
s.	Thetford	p. 199	12	159½
l.	Norwich	p. 199	29	188½
	London	p. 199	109	297½

OXFORD CIRCUIT.

	From London to			
l.	Reading, p. 60		—	39
c.	Oxford, p. 330.		27½	66½

left 'Henry Raven and Mr Hardy went to Norwich Assizes morning 8' (12 Aug. 1794). Daniel Paterson's 1794 table of the judges' circuits contains errors (*A New and Accurate Description of all the Direct and Principal Cross Roads in England and Wales*). The Thetford Assizes were held not in summer ['*s*'] but in March ['*l*' for Lent], and the Norwich Assizes in August ['*s*', not '*l*']. The Norfolk Circuit wound through several counties for nearly 300 miles.

['*c*'] marks those towns where assizes were held constantly every circuit, ['*a*'] assizes held alternately with another town or city [*Paterson's Roads (10th edn, 1794), cols 377, 378*]

AUGUST 10, SUNDAY

HR Famaly all whent to Church afternoon. R Bye, J Ram & T Baldin dine'd here being the begining of harvest.

AUGUST 11, MONDAY

HR G Thompson, HR, R Bye & Boy in brewhouse, WH Brewing. Jn° Ram, T Baldin reeping wheat in hill close. Mr H at home all Day. Mr, Mrs Bartell drank tea here. ⟦[1] R Bye to Edgfield in Afternoon with beer.

AUGUST 12, TUESDAY

William Hardy jnr Jn° Ram & R Bye reaping in Hill close, T Baldwin at Holt, Thornage & Briston with beer. G Tompson, Boy, WH Cleansd X & \`//. R Bartell spent the afternoon here. HR & Mr H went to Norwich Assises M8.

of bankruptcy issued against William Custance, cabinetmaker, ironmonger, dealer and chapman; his affairs were being handled by the Fakenham solicitor William Stokes

[1] William Hardy jnr takes over during Henry's visit to Norwich 12–13 Aug.

MH A very fine day. Mr Hardy set of for Norwich in the Chaise & H Raven on the little Mare morng 8, W^m^ at home all day. We rid up to fir Closes afternoon, JR & R Bey shear'g wheat there.[1] Robt Bartell here afternoon.

AUGUST 13, WEDNESDAY

WHj Jno Ram & Boy reaping, T Baldwin ill. R Bye at Stalham, G Tompson dressing W [wheat] Stones. WH at home all day, HR came from Norwich.]]

MH A Hot dry day. W^m^ at home all day, we rid up to fir Closes afternoon to the Shearers. H Raven came home from Norwich eveng past 9. Baldin Ill. Robt Buy went to Stalham.

AUGUST 14, THURSDAY

Henry Raven Jno Ram & Boy reaping, R Bye home from Stalham. G Thompson Dressing flour, T Baldin ill. Duke reaping in Bells Acre.[2] WH at home all Day.

MH A hot dry day. J Ram & Boy Shearing Wheat in fir Closes, got one Load home. Balding Ill. Miss Mighles[3] & Bell Leak drank tea here.[4]

AUGUST 15, FRIDAY

HR T Baldwin to Clay with beer & got up three load wheat & one Barley. R Bye to Hindolvestone with beer, & G Thompson, R Bye, WH Car^g^ [carrying] wheat & barley. HR grinding M for brew, Jno Ram & Boy reaping.

MH A hot dry day. JR & Boy shear'g in fir Closes. W^m^ at home all day, Caried some Wheat & 1 Load of Barley from the fir Closes.

AUGUST 16, SATURDAY

HR R Bye to Sheringham with beer, T Balden to Brampton with beer. Jno Ram, Sam Platton, G Thompson & Boy reaping.[5] HR grinding M for Brew. WH at home all Day.

MH A very hot dry day. W^m^ at home all day. JR, S Platton mowing Wheat in fir Closes. Mr Hardy & MA came home from Norwich eveng 11.

AUGUST 17, SUNDAY

HR Famaly whent to Church morning and alecture Evenining [evening].

MH A very hot dry day. All went to our Church foornoon, Mr Burrell preachd & read a Lecture in the eveng. W^m^ went to Holt Church Afternoon, heard Mr Man of

[1] *Furze Closes* The entries of mother and son taken together show this Hill Close to be one of the sloping fields in Saxlingham opposite Bayfield Park (part of William Hardy's original purchase in 1780).
Another Hill Close, bought by William Hardy jnr as part of the Letheringsett Hall Farm estate in 1800, was a 12-acre field north of the farmhouse

[2] *Duke* Thomas 'Duke' Humphrey (bur. Letheringsett 25 Oct. 1795 as 'an aged husbandman'). His nickname Duke derived presumably from a local saying adopted by Parson Woodforde: 'Dined with Duke Humphrey, that is, no dinner at all' (J. Woodforde, *The Diary of a Country Parson*, ed. J. Beresford, vol. 3 (Oxford Univ. Press, 1927), p. 365, 1 Aug. 1792). Duke had worked in the Hardys' garden 1781–92 and had run errands when needed

[3] *Miss Mighells* She had come to board with the Burrells in Sept. 1790. In later years two members of this prominent Lowestoft family lived in the village: Elizabeth (bur. Letheringsett 12 Feb. 1818 aged 68), and Anne (bur. 2 Oct. 1827 also aged 68)

[4] *Bell Leak* See note for 15 May 1794

[5] *Platten* Samuel (bur. Letheringsett 22 Sept. 1817 aged 75), gamekeeper to Mrs Jodrell at Bayfield Hall

above 'R. Bye, J. Ramm & T. Baldwin dined here being the beginning of harvest' (10 Aug. 1794). This harvest panorama on the Holt–Letheringsett border dates from the early years of the 20th century. The photograph, entitled by Basil Cozens-Hardy 'View from Pereers Hills', shows corn stooks left to air before being stacked in the open or stored in the barn, and presents an August scene familiar to Henry Raven. The brewing pupil, who did not usually help with work on the farm, lent a hand with getting up the wheat (18 Aug.) [*Cozens-Hardy Collection*]

Clay died Suddenly at Norwich last Night which provd true.[1]

AUGUST 18, MONDAY

HR Robt Bye to Beckhigh with «beer». G Thomp^n, H Raven, T Balden & Boy in brewhouse & got up four load wheat, WH Brewing. M^r H road to the furze Closes. Jno Ram mowing wheat in Bells Acre & furze Close barley. W Dobson D^o [mowing] in bells acre morning, M Gallant gathering wheat morning.

MH A hot dry day. Men finishd cutting Wheat. Mr Hardy & W^m at home all day, I & MA walkd up to Holt after tea. Brewd . . .

AUGUST 19, TUESDAY

HR G Thompson & T Baldwin got up one load wheat & Cleansed `// morning, mowing afternoon. GT & HR Cleansed X afternoon. Robt Bye, Jno Ram & W Dobson mowing. M^r H & WH at home all Day.

[1] *Mann* Mary Hardy added the last sentence later. See notes for 2 Nov. 1793 and 30 Sept. 1794. John Mann marr. Gt Yarmouth 23 Jan. 1776 Priscilla Carr, who after his death went to live at Holt.

His will is held with the deeds of the Fishmongers' Arms at Cley, which he owned copyhold 1789–94 (NRO: BR 17/7/4), his widow and son Isaac being two of the executors of the complex estate. A voluminous Mann archive 1770–1857 also rests in the county record office (NRO: ACC Cozens-Hardy, 11/2/1976).

Jonathan Hooton devotes a chapter to John Mann in more prosperous times 1771–85 (J. Hooton, *The Glaven Ports: A maritime history of Blakeney, Cley and Wiveton in north Norfolk* (Blakeney History Group, Blakeney, 1996), pp. 194–8), and also gives a study of the merchant Henry Chaplin and his ships (pp. 198–9)

AUGUST 20, WEDNESDAY

HR T Baldwin to Syderstone with beer. Robt Bye mowing, to Corpusta with beer afternoon. Jno Ram mowing, Boy raking bells Acre & Furze Close foorenoon, G Thompson helpt to get them [the rakings] up afternoon. WH road out foorenoon, Mr H at home all Day.

MH A fine day. J Ram Mowing Barley. R Buy & T Baldin out with Brew Cart, brought home all the Wheat. Mr Hardy at home all day. Wm rid to Mr Butters' of Briston foornoon, dind there, came home eve 1 [morning 1] . . .

AUGUST 21, THURSDAY

HR Jno Ram & T Baldwin mowing forenoon, getting up barley afternoon. G Thompson, HR & Boy Do [getting] up four load Barley Do [afternoon]. Mr & WH at home all Day. Robt Bye ill, Jno Thompson riding mare on goft afternoon.[1]

AUGUST 22, FRIDAY

HR T Baldwin to Fakenham & Kettlestone with beer, Jno Ram mowing morning. G Thompson, Boy & Jno Ram got up three load barley, H Raven grinding M for brew. Mr H at home all Day, WH road out all Day.

AUGUST 23, SATURDAY

HR T Baldwin to Sherrington morning, Thornage & Stody afternoon with beer. Jno Ram mowing Do [morning], drag raking afternoon. H Raven grinding Malt for brew & bin. Mr H at home all Day. WH at home morning, Holt Market afternoon. R Bye ill.

MH A Showry Morng, dry afternoon. Mr Hardy at home all day. Wm went to Holt Markt afternoon, heard Mr Mann of Cley died in very bad Circumstances, very much in debt . . .

AUGUST 24, SUNDAY

HR Mr, Mrs Sales came & drank tea & whent to Church with famaly.[2] Mr, Mrs Forster calld in Evening. Mr, Mrs & Miss Bartell & Miss Stannard calld in Do [evening],[3] Robt Bartell & A Gwiyn [? Gwynn] walk'd down Evening.

AUGUST 25, MONDAY

HR Robt Bye, Jno Ram & Boy got up one load barley morning,[4] Do [Robert Bye] to Dawling afternoon. Jno Ram at work in hay howse & putting up wheat. G Thompson, H Raven, T Baldwin in brewhouse, WH

[1] *goft* Also goaf and goaft; a stack of corn, here loaded on the cart or wagon drawn by the Hardys' mare. While Forby describes a goaf (plural goaves) as the stack in the barn, as opposed to one left out in the open, Henry Raven and his aunt regard the stack as a goft if *intended* for the barn, even though it is still in the process of being carried there (R. Forby, *The Vocabulary of East Anglia*, vol. 2, p. 134)

[2] *Sales* Charles (d. 7 Jan. 1821 aged 68, bur. Holt 11 Jan.), a Holt draper and grocer, and his wife Ann (bur. Holt 5 July 1821 aged 65), née Legge; they had married Holt 8 Jan. 1782. Their headstone to the left of the path to the west door is one of the most legible of the stones of this period in Holt churchyard.

Mary Hardy often gives the name as Seales, apparently over-compensating for the Norfolk vowel sound in which 'deals' and 'meal' are pronounced dales and male

[3] *Miss Strannard* Daughter of Joseph Stannard of Norwich

[4] *one load* Mary Hardy reported thundery showers from 8 am onwards

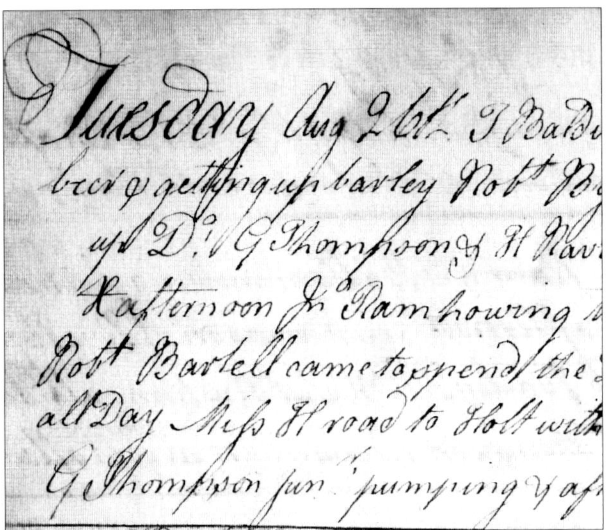
Tuesday Aug 26th T Baldw
beer & getting up barley Robt By
up Do G Thompson & H Rav
X afternoon Jno Ram howing t
Robt Bartell came to spend the
all Day Miss H road to Holt with
G Thompson Jun pumping & af

above Detail of Henry Raven's entry for 26 Aug. 1794 showing, in line 4, his notation for XX (very strong beer). The system at the Letheringsett brewery was to use bars, as on medals, to denote repetition; hence XX was written as X̶. The notation was well suited to making swift chalk marks on barrels and casks [*Cozens-Hardy Collection*]

brewing. Mr H at home all Day. Jane Reeve came for brew cart, Skiffins in garden.[1]

AUGUST 26, TUESDAY

HR T Baldwin to Waybourn with beer & getting up barley. Robt By, Jno Ram & Boy getting up Do [barley]. G Thompson & H Raven Cleansed `// morning, XX afternoon, Jno Ram howing turnips morning. Robt Bartell came to spend the Day. Mr & WH at home all Day. Miss H road to Holt with Mrs Forster Evening. G Thompson Junr pumping & after barley afternoon.

MH A very fine day. Maids & Eliz Woods washd 4 weeks linnen.[2] Men carried Barley out of 6 Acres. Mr Hardy at home all day. Mrs Smith of Cley & a Lady with her drank tea here.[3] MA rid up to Holt with Mrs Forster.

AUGUST 27, WEDNESDAY

HR R Bye to Sheringham with beer, took one [barrel] for Bulling at Holt. T Baldwin clearing fat [vat] & Skreen-

[1] *Jane Reeve* Presumably the wife or daughter of James Reeve of the Hart at Field Dalling. Her request was met immediately

[2] *Elizabeth Woods* Not bapt. Letheringsett, but possibly the daughter of John Woods (bur. there 18 July 1786 aged 60) and Elizabeth (bur. 26 Oct. 1787), dying of a putrid fever (*Diary 2*: 24 Oct. 1787); both were classed in the register as paupers and thus excused payment of duty. Elizabeth had been indicted before the Holt magistrates with four other Letheringsett women 16 Oct. 1788 for 'living out of service', a legal term for prostitution (NRO: C/S 1/14, Quarter sessions order book)

[3] *Mrs Smith* Elizabeth (d. 21 Sept. 1803, bur. Cley 25 Sept.), formerly Mrs Hunt, wife of the Hardys' lawyer John Smith of Cley, whom they had used in legal disputes until turning increasingly to James Moore.

In 1799 Mrs Smith, 'gentlewoman', registered a purpose-built Methodist chapel at Cley. She was active in registering other Cley properties for meetings (NRO: DN/DIS 1/2, ff. 75, 45, 69, 98, 24 Oct. 1799, 7 Jan. 1792, 3 Jan. 1799, 4 Oct. 1802). Her widowed husband married Cley 1 Feb. 1804 Pleasance Harrison, also of the Methodist society at Cley; John Smith did not attend meetings.

For the significance of Elizabeth Smith's promotion of Wesleyanism, see *World*, vol. 3, chaps 2–4

ing Malt. Jno Ram drag raking & Skreening Malt & turning Barley with T Baldwin.[1] M^r H & WH at home all Day.

MH A very Showry day, no Corn carried. Mr Hardy drank tea at Mr Burrells, W^m at home all day.

AUGUST 28, THURSDAY

HR T Baldwin to Hinderingham with beer & getting up barley, H Raven to Guestwick with Malt. Jno Ram, Robt Bye, T Baldwin & G Thompson Junr turning & getting up barley, Boy & T Youngman«'s» Lad & Mr Thompson after D^o [barley] afternoon.[2] Boy Cornwall raking after waggon, Jno Thompson riding mare on goft. M^r H at home all Day, WH driving.

MH A dry day. Finishd Harvest except the rakins . . .

AUGUST 29, FRIDAY

HR R Bye to Briston with beer & drag raking. T Baldwin, Jno Ram drag raking foorenoon, getting up rakin [rakings] afternoon. G Thompson grinding Malt for brew. M^r, M^rs & Miss H at Holt to tea, WH at home all Day.

AUGUST 30, SATURDAY

HR R Bye to Bale with beer, T Baldwin to Salthouse with beer. Jno Ram in garden forenoon, Boy & all of them gathering largis afternoon.[3] G Thompson grinding M for brew morning. M^r & WH at Holt afternoon.

AUGUST 31, SUNDAY

HR Famaly all whent to Church morning & a lecture Evening. WH at Holt afternoon.[4]

MH A Wet day. All went to our Church foornoon, Mr Burrell preach'd. W^m went to Holt Church afternoon, drank tea at Mr Davys, Matt Davy from London there, came home eve 8. Mrs Jodrill of Bayfield died this Morng [5] . . .

SEPTEMBER 1, MONDAY

Henry Raven G Thompson, H Raven, R Bye & Boy in Brewhouse, WH brewing. T Baldwin to Cromer with beer, Jno Ram howing turnips in Field. R Bye to Holt at night with beer.

SEPTEMBER 2, TUESDAY

HR R Bye «to» Wiverton with beer foorenoon, help«ed» to Cleanse & load for Syderstone. G Thompson, WH,

---

[1] *turning barley* It was important to air the barley while it stood in stooks in the open to keep it from rotting when wet. As Henry does not record the weather it is useful to consult Mary Hardy's diary to learn why virtually no work was done in the fields that day

[2] *Mr Thompson* William Gunton, the miller. He may have been granted a polite prefix to distinguish him from his son who was also at work; or he may have been looking through the huge ledger and ragging Henry about showing a little more respect

[3] *largess* End-of-harvest tips from neighbouring, comfortably-off families.

Henry, as an indentured pupil and belonging to his master's family, and 'Mr' Gunton Thompson—skilled miller and millwright foremost and farm labourer second—would not have joined the harvesters

[4] *church and a lecture* This was Henry's 17th birthday. The entry reads somewhat joylessly, but the Hardys' birthdays similarly passed without jollification

[5] *Mrs Jodrell* Elizabeth, who died aged 79, was the owner of Bayfield Hall in her own right by purchase, the daughter of Richard Warner of N. Elmham, and widow of Paul (1713–51), whom she had married in 1744 and who had sat as MP for the notorious rotten borough of Old Sarum in Wiltshire. See notes for 15 Sept. 1794 and 2 Jan. 1795

left Lewknor, in Oxfordshire: the Jodrell chapel in St Margaret's Church. Arrangements for a funeral halfway across the kingdom took time, and Elizabeth Jodrell's hearse and long procession of mourners could not set off from Bayfield Hall until two weeks after her death. This marble monument, by P. Bazzanti of Florence, was erected in the Jodrell chapel in 1833 to her eldest son, the Norfolk landowner, classical scholar, dramatist and MP Richard Paul Jodrell (1745–1831); her own monument is illustrated in *Diary 2* [*Christopher Bird 1996*]

T Baldwin & Boy Cleansed `// forenoon, X afternoon. TB got out one load muck, Jn° Ram howing turnips. Mr H at home all day. Mr, Mrs Burrell drank tea here. HR to Birmingham [Briningham] forenoon, Edgefield afternoon.

SEPTEMBER 3, WEDNESDAY

HR R Bye to Syderstone with beer. T Baldwin at work in yard forenoon, Skreening Malt for brew & Holt with beer, G Thompson keeping tally.[1] Jn° Ram Trashing barley.[2] Famaly at Holt, WH at turtle feast.[3]

SEPTEMBER 4, THURSDAY

HR R Bye at muck Cart forenoon, Edgefield afternoon. T Baldwin D° [at muck] Cart D° [forenoon], Gunthorp D° [afternoon]. G Thompson Grinding M for brew Evening. Jn° Ram Trashing forenoon, howen [hoeing] turnips afternoon. WH & Miss H at Cromer. Jas Dybal, David Pleasance came and Orderd beer.[4]

[1] *tally* For the malt. No new malt was made in the summer, and a careful record had to be kept of stock until the new season began in October

[2] *trashing* Threshing. Henry's grandfather Robert Raven, his aunt Mary Hardy and cousin William used the old Norfolk word 'tasking'; Henry is moving towards the modern term.

While some dictionaries refer to the origin of 'trash' as obscure, Henry's spelling offers a likely derivation of the synonym for rubbish or unwanted matter

[3] *turtle feast* Mary Hardy records that it was held at the Shirehouse at Holt. The previous year it had been held at the Feathers, under the distinguished stewards William Windham and Thomas William Coke (*Norw. Merc.* 21 Sept. 1793)

[4] *James Dyball* [*and*] *David Pleasance* Their beer orders were despatched with impressive speed to Edgefield and Gunthorpe

Mary Hardy A very fine day. W^m^ & MA rid to Cromer foornoon with the Davys & came home eveng past 9. Geo^r^ Wymer from Reepham & his Clarke Slept here.[1] Mr Hardy at home all day. M^r^ & Mrs Todhunter calld here after tea in their way to Wells.[2]

SEPTEMBER 5, FRIDAY

HR R Bye to Fakenham with beer, T Baldwin to Wells with beer, Jno Ram Trashing & howing turnips. M^r^, WH at home all Day. Mr Davys famaly dined & drank tea here.

MH A Wet day. Mr Davy & 2 Sons & Mr Edwd Roberson [Robinson] dind & drank tea here,[3] Mrs Davy, Bett & Miss Riches drank tea here.[4]

SEPTEMBER 6, SATURDAY

HR T Baldwin to Corpusta with beer, R Bye at muck cart. Jno Ram trashing & howing turnips, G Thompson dressing flower. M^r^ H, M^rs^ & Miss H whant [went] to Norwich in Banyards chaise. Harvest supper at W Dobsons. WH at Holt market, sup't at {at} Dobsons, HR sup't at D^o^ [Dobson's]. T Boyces boy getting muck of pitol [muck off the Pightle].[5]

SACRED
To the Memory of
GEORGE WYMER Gent.
Who departed this Life 26th July 1839
In the 75th Year of his Age.
Also of
ELIZABETH his wife
who died Feb. 17th 1847
Aged 81 Years.

[1] *George Wymer* (d. 26 July 1839 aged 74/75), Reepham attorney and son of the Norwich attorney George Wymer. His brother Francis William, a Norwich brandy merchant, announced that day in the *Norwich Mercury* (published 6 Sept.) that he was in financial difficulty and had handed over the management of his affairs to their father

[2] *Todhunter* William, Wells excise supervisor and port surveyor for Wells and Cley; he was succeeded 15 May 1797 by Robert Brunskill (d. at Holt 26 Apr. 1799: see *Diary 4*) (TNA: PRO CUST 47/402, p. 91)

[3] *Robinson* The City of London draper and Bett Davy's betrothed: see notes for 9 Jan. and 28 Oct. 1794

[4] *Miss Riches* Mary, a friend of the Hardys, Davys, Bartells and Burrells, and probably the daughter of Robert Riches, farmer, of the tiny settlement of Alethorpe, near Fakenham

[5] *Boyce's boy* It is unlikely that a day labourer could afford to employ an assistant. This may be his elder stepson, eight-year-old James. His wife Sarah (bapt. Letheringsett 27 Nov. 1766, bur. there 31 May 1857), née Jeckell, had given birth to the first of her three illegitimate children in Mar. 1783. William, son of the Hardys' innkeeper Richard Mayes, lived only a few days (*Diary 2*), but the other sons James (b.1786) and William (b.1789) had survived

left John Opie's portrait *c.*1801 of the former Mayor of Norwich John Herring, shawl manufacturer and Whig. The Hardys made a one-day trip to see Mr Herring 6 Sept. 1794. Shortly afterwards beer deliveries to the city began, lasting to Michaelmas 1796; the Herrings may have taken to Letheringsett brews. The British expeditionary troops seen here are a reminder of the swift, practical aid given them by the mayor in the aftermath of the Helder campaign of 1799 [*Norfolk Museums & Archaeology Service* (*Norwich Castle Museum & Art Gallery*)]

facing page This tablet to the attorney George Wymer jnr (see 4 Sept. 1794) and his wife Elizabeth (d. 17 Feb. 1847 aged 81) is in the north aisle, Reepham St Mary [*MB · 2011*]

MH A very Showry day. Mr Hardy, I & MA sett of for Norwich in Banyard«'s» Post Chaise Morng 6, got to Norwich morn 10, Breakfastd at [and] dind at Mr Geo^r^ Wymers, drank tea at Mr John Herrings & set out from Norwich ½ after 6 o Clock, got home eveng 11.[1] Our Men had their Harvest frollick at Dobsons . . .

SEPTEMBER 7, SUNDAY

HR Famaly all whent to Church afternoon, WH at Holt Evening.

SEPTEMBER 8, MONDAY

HR G Thompson, H Raven, R Bye & Boy in brewhouse all Day, WH brewing. Jno Ram howing turnips. T Baldwin all {all} [?ill all] Day. Mr Skelton came with 14½ Last bran & Pollard.[2] M^r^ H at home all day. T Boyces boy getting muck of Pitol. H Goggs came from Whissonsett.

[1] *John Herring* (d. 22 Sept. 1810 aged 61), Sheriff of Norwich 1786, Mayor 1799; his career is summarised by B. Cozens-Hardy and E.A. Kent, *The Mayors of Norwich 1403 to 1835* (Jarrold & Sons, Norwich, 1938), p. 145; see also note for 18 Jan. 1794. John, William and Robert Herring are listed as merchants in Gildengate Street, Norwich, in the *Universal British Directory*, vol. 4 (1798). All three became mayor

[2] *bran and pollard* The coarsest grades of flour and used largely for livestock feed; the other grades were flour, meal, and supers or middling. This was a very large quantity. With 10 quarters (20 coombs) to the last, it would have totalled approx. 29 metric tonnes

SEPTEMBER 9, TUESDAY

HR Robt Bye helpt to Car^{y} of Cleanse, whent to Walsingham with beer. T Baldwin helpt D^{o} [helped to carry off cleanse beer] & Cleanse«d» `// & to Holt with beer & Cleanse«d» X. G Thompson D$^{o}$ [cleansed] `// forenoon, X afternoon. M^{r} H at home all day. WH walk^{d} to Holt morning, H Goggs whant away Evening. R Hill came & orderd 4 Nog.

SEPTEMBER 10, WEDNESDAY

HR R Bye at muck cart & loaded for Norwich, T Baldwin to Runton with beer, G Thompson dressing Wheat stones. H Raven Botteling of sispenny afternoon.[1] M^{r}, M^{rs} & Miss Hardy drank tea at Thos Tempels. WH road to Holt afternoon, Mr Summers call^{d} afternoon.[2] Raven from Walsingham came after Walsham Maids head.[3]

SEPTEMBER 11, THURSDAY

HR R Bye to Norwich with beer.[4] T Baldwin at home forenoon, Clay with beer & loaded for Southrepps afternoon. G Thompson dressing W stones, H Raven grinding Malt for brew. Boy to Holt with one barrell beer. M^{r} H at home all Day, WH out forenoon, at home afternoon. G Thompson, HR & WH took up bees.

SEPTEMBER 12, FRIDAY

HR T Baldwin to Southrepps with beer, G Thompson grinding M for brew & laid down W Stones, HR & Boy gathering Appels. R Bye not from Norwich. M^{r}, M^{rs}, Miss & WH at Holt afternoon. Mr Youngman put a lock on cole [coal] house door.

SEPTEMBER 13, SATURDAY

HR Robt Bye came home morning two oClock & came to work at noon & car^{d} of Cleanse beer. T Baldwin putting beer in cask forenoon, Car^{d} of D^{o} [cleanse beer] afternoon & riddle«d» a load of gravel.[5] G Thompson, H Raven put beer into great cask. M^{r} H at Holt all Day, M^{rs} H & Miss at Holt afternoon. WH road out morning, Holt afternoon. T Youngman's Lad Painting.

MH A Close day. Mr Hardy dind at the Justice sitting at Holt, came home eveng 8. I & MA walk'd up after«noon», drank tea at Mrs Jinnis's, came home eveng past 7. W^{m} rid up, drank tea with us, came home eveng 10. Raind in eveng . . .

[1] *bottling off sixpenny* The first reference to bottled beer since the early days at Coltishall. Being a strong brew, sixpenny would have good keeping qualities and may have been destined for Norwich (11 Sept. 1794)

[2] *Summers* See note for 3 Apr. 1794. Beer deliveries were about to begin to the Crown at Southrepps, which until then may have done its own brewing, John Summers being a small-scale publican brewer. He advertised all his household furniture for sale from the Crown, including a brewing copper and all the equipment needed for brewing from 10 bushels to 5 coombs (*Norw. Merc.* 4 Oct. 1794)

[3] *Raven* He was unsuccessful in securing the tenancy of the Maid's Head at N. Walsham, held by James Dew in 1795. There is no entry in the register for the Maid's Head at Michaelmas 1794, suggesting that it was then without a tenant (NRO: C/Sch 1/16)

[4] *to Norwich with beer* A great coup for Letheringsett, as the city was awash with powerful brewers. This was the first time the Hardys had delivered to the city, and eight further consignments were to follow over two years. The two-day 44-mile round trip was hardly economic, especially as loading the beer wagon occupied part of a third day

[5] *riddle* A coarse sieve. A load of gravel, as a precise volume, equalled one cubic yard (0·76 cubic metre)

left Riddles, or sieves, were also used in the brewhouse (13 Sept.). This coarse sieve stands inside the cooler in the 18th-century brewhouse at the National Trust's Charlecote Park, Warwickshire. The wort from the copper flows along the wooden channel (foreground) into the large, shallow, unlined cooler. The riddle was used for screening malt to remove the culms (unwanted shoots), Charlecote's being a private operation akin in scale to John Summers' at the Crown, Southrepps (10 Sept.).

The Hardys would have used a commercial appliance to screen their malt [*MB* · *2000*]

SEPTEMBER 14, SUNDAY

HR Famaly to Church afternoon & a lecture Evening. WH at Holt afternoon.

SEPTEMBER 15, MONDAY

HR R Bye to Dawling & Briston with beer. T Baldwin, G Thompson, H Raven & Boy in brewhouse, WH brewing. Jn° Raven, A [Adam] Baker, Miss Wigg & Miss Bartell dined and drank tea here.[1] M^r^ H at home all Day. Jn° Ram trashing.

MH A very fine Morng, A Showr abt Noon, a fine afternoon. Mrs Joddril was carried thro Town in their way to Oxfordshire to be buried. A Hearse & Six, 2 Mourning Coaches with 6 Horses each, 2 other Carriages & all her Tenents on Horseback form'd the Procession.[2] Wm Brew'd, Mr Hardy at home all day. Mr John Raven from Tunstead, Adam Baker, Miss Bartell & Miss Wigg Dind & drank tea here . . .

[1] *John Raven* Son of Mary Hardy's cousins Robert and Hannah Raven of Tunstead: see note for 11 July 1794

[2] *Mrs Jodrell* She was interred in the Jodrell family chapel at Lewknor Church, Oxon. Her eldest son Richard Paul Jodrell owned Salle in Norfolk and lived at the family seat at Lewknor, and inherited many of the Jodrells' Norfolk estates including the manors of Sharrington and Saxlingham. His hand is evident in some of the careful annotations to the Jodrell papers 1290–1948 in the Norfolk Record Office (NRO: WHT).

Her second son Sir Paul was physician to the Nabob of the Carnatic and lived in Madras. Her daughter Elizabeth married Richard Warburton Lytton of Knebworth, Herts. See also note for 2 Jan. 1795 on Mrs Jodrell's son Henry, the Hardys' new neighbour.

The Bayfield estate papers 1461–1897 are also held in the NRO (MC 632)

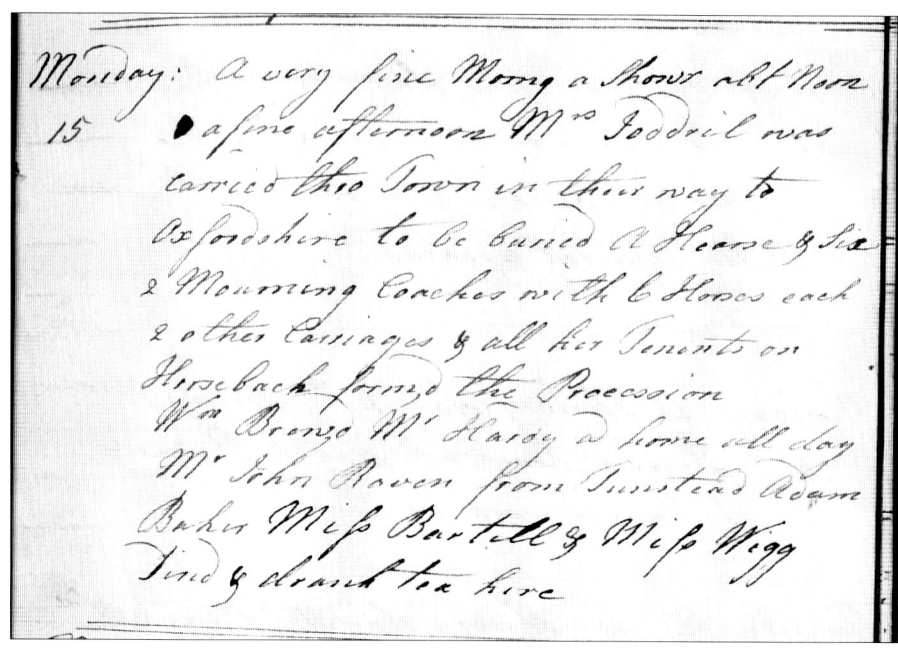
Monday: a very fine Morng a Shower abt Noon
15 a fine afternoon Mrs Joddril was
carried thro Town in their way to
Oxfordshire to be buried A Hearse & Six
2 Mourning Coaches with 6 Horses each
2 other Carriages & all her Tenants on
Horseback formd the Procession
Wm Brewd Mr Hardy at home all day
Mr John Raven from Tunstead Adam
Baker Miss Bartell & Miss Wigg
Dind & drank tea here

above 15 Sept. 1794: Mary Hardy gives what seems to be an eye-witness account of the departure of her eminent neighbour to join Paul Jodrell in his last resting place after 43 years of widowhood; the Hardys' dinner guests had probably come from Holt to watch the procession too. The families were not on visiting terms. Mrs Jodrell had called on Mary Hardy once in 13 years—over hiring a maidservant in 1791 [*Cozens-Hardy Collection*]

facing page The arms of Elizabeth Jodrell, Lewknor Church, Oxon. She left Bayfield to her youngest (and posthumous) son Henry (1752–1814), JP, MP, barrister, Recorder of Gt Yarmouth, who in 1795 erected an elaborate memorial to his mother of which this forms the base [*MB · 1996*]

SEPTEMBER 16, TUESDAY

HR R Bye to Hindolvestone with beer, T Baldwin Kettlestone with beer. G Thompson, WH Cleansed `// forenoon, X beer Evening. Mr Bartell & two Friends call^{d} here morning. M^{r}, WH dined with D^{o} [Mr Bartell]. Jno Ram trashing & dressing Wheat.

SEPTEMBER 17, WEDNESDAY

HR T Baldwin to Thornage & Stody with beer & Swanton [Novers] for tiles.[1] R Bye to Sheringham D^{o} D^{o} [with beer], Boy to Edgefield with beer. M^{r} H & Thos Tempell to Wells, WH at home all Day. D Pleasance came forenoon. Fox from Hindolvestone came with a sample of Barley.[2] Jno Ram Mowing.

[1] *tiles* Probably from John Dew's brickworks at Swanton Novers, used in the past by the Hardys and valued for its white bricks

[2] *Fox* John, listed in the 1806 Norfolk pollbook as a Hindolveston farmer

MH A dry day, wind very high aftern. Mr Hardy & W^m^ at home all day.[1] Skivens in the Garden. Mrs Ives from Branton [Brampton] & her Sister came morng past 9, Breakfstd & dind here, went away eveng 3.[2] Hannah Boone went away after tea [3] . . .

SEPTEMBER 18, THURSDAY

HR R Bye to Wells with beer, took Jack & bro^t^ home a horse from Walden's.[4] T Baldwin to Edgefield & Waybourn with beer. Boy spreading muck forenoon, ploughing afternoone in 5 Acre's, G Thompson & H Raven skreening & grinding Malt for brew. M^r^ & WH at home all Day. Bunnets two men, trowel man & Laborer. Mrs Ives came & orderd a load beer. Buck from Foulsham came with sample of barley. Jno Ram mowing.

SEPTEMBER 19, FRIDAY

HR T Baldwin to Brampton with beer. Boy gathering Apples forenoon, to Bale with beer afternoon, G Thompson & HR skreening & grinding Malt. M^r^ & WH to Cromer. R Bye at Dobsons all Day, Jno Ram Mowing. Skiffins in garden, T Boyce half a day in garden. Bricklayers all Day.

MH A fine day. Mr Hardy & W^m^ went to the Justice sitting at Cromer, dind there, drank tea «at» Mr Flowr of Sheringham, came home eveng 11.[5]

[1] *at home* An example of an inconsistency between the two diaries. Henry's version, that William Hardy went to Wells, is likely to be the more accurate; he may also be right over the date of Mrs Ives's order (18 Sept.)

[2] *Mrs Ives* Of the Queen's Head, Brampton, she was undertaking a 29-mile round trip. The headstone in St Peter's churchyard at Brampton shows that Ann, wife of Meshack Ives, died 1 Aug. 1836 aged 75.

Mrs Ives's reception was by 1794 a rarity. In the days at Coltishall 1773–81 the innkeepers and their families had been handsomely entertained. By the 1790s, and especially after Mary Hardy's illness, they more usually called at the brewery across the road, and Mary Hardy appears not to know they had come

[3] *Hannah Boone* She had arrived the previous evening

[4] *Jack* One of the horses. Unless another was named in his honour, Jack stayed with the Hardys and was valued by William Hardy in Sept. 1797 at £12—the cheapest of the four riding horses named in the accounts. The eight farm and brewery draught horses were valued at £8 each (*World*, vol. 2, chap. 2)

[5] *sitting* The sessions for alehouse licences for N. Erpingham hundred

SEPTEMBER 20, SATURDAY

HR T Baldwin to Cromer & Beckhigh with beer, Boy to Bale & gunthorpe with beer & Malt, G Thompson & HR grinding Malt. 1 trowelman & 1 Laborer all Day. Jno Ram drag raken forenoon, in garden afternoon, T Boyce in garden.[1] WH & Miss H at Holt Market, M^{r} H at home all Day. Thos Atwood came & Orderd beer. R Bye no work.

MH A very showry day. Mr Hardy at home all day. W^{m} & MA rid up to Holt afternoon in the Chaise, drank tea at Widow Fishers, came home eveng 8. W^{m} bought a Mare of Mr Banyard for to run in the Chaise . . .

SEPTEMBER 21, SUNDAY

HR Famaly all whent to Church afternoon. Robt Raven came from Whissonsett.

SEPTEMBER 22, MONDAY

HR T Baldwin to Sheringham & Holt with beer. Robt Bye, G Thompson, H Raven & Boy in brewhouse, WH Brewing. Jno Ram & T Boyce in garden. M^{r} H at home all Day. 1 trowelman & 1 Laborer all Day.

SEPTEMBER 23, TUESDAY

HR Robt Bye to Runton with beer, T Baldwin to Holt & Wiverton with beer. G Thompson, HR Cleansed `// morning, X beer Evening. Jno Ram & T Boyce in garden. 1 trowel man & one Laborer all Day. M^{r} & WH at home morn, to Gunthorp & Holt afternoon. Jno Walden came forenoon.

[1] *drag-raking* The aftermath: the early-autumn crop of hay which John Ramm had started to mow on 17 Sept.

facing page Riverside Farm (as it later became known), Letheringsett, viewed in 1892 from upstream where the lane to Lt Thornage fords the Glaven south of the farmhouse. Owing to modern embanking the ford is now rather narrower at this point, and consequently deeper at times.

The farmhouse owned by Charles Kendle was described as 'new-built' in the *Norwich Mercury* when the 112-acre farm was offered for sale 10 Feb. 1798. William Hardy jnr negotiated unsuccessfully for it, and James Cobon bought the estate two weeks later for £3160 (*Diary 4*) [*photograph Gerald C-H. Willans 1892: Cozens-Hardy Collection*]

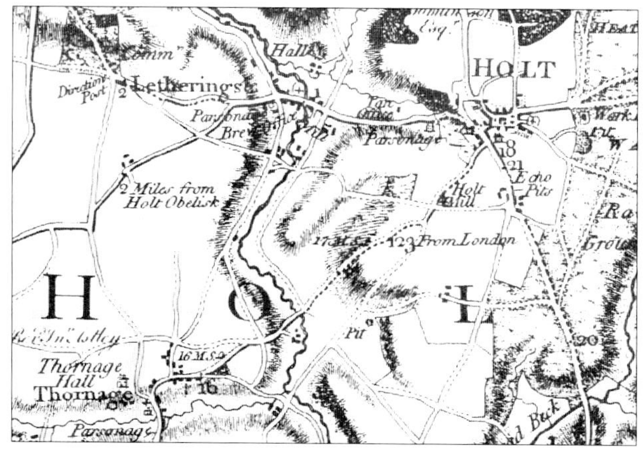
HOLT
Hall
Letherings
Direction Post
Parsonage
Brew
2 Miles from Holt Obelisk
Holt Mill
Echo Pits
123 From London
Thornage Hall
Thornage
Parsonage
Pit
H
O
L

right Faden's map: the Glaven flows north towards Letheringsett Watermill and the Hardys' 'Brew Office'. Charles Kendle's farmhouse and barn are depicted as two buildings immediately south of the watermill. 'Holt Mill', seen on the main road close by the 123-mile milestone from London, is a different mill from Charles Kendle's [*Faden's Map of Norfolk 1797: Larks Press 1989*]

SEPTEMBER 24, WEDNESDAY

HR R Bye to Syderstone with beer, T Baldwin to Sherington [Sharrington] with beer & after jobs. G Thomps^{n} & HR Dressing flower. WH at Holt morning, Mr Wade dined here. Jno Ram & Thos Boyce after hay part of foorenoon, in garden afternoon. 1 trowel man & 1 Laborer all Day. M^{r} H at Reefham with Mr Bartell.[1]

SEPTEMBER 25, THURSDAY

HR R Bye to Corpusta with beer, helpd to ring pigs morning. T Baldwin ringing pigs morning & to Sheringham with beer, took Black filly. T Boyce in garden, Jno Ram trashing [threshing] G Thompsons corn. GT & H Raven begun «grinding» Malt for brew. M^{r} H at home all Day. WH & Miss H at Holt afternoon. 1 trowel man & 1 Laborer all Day.

SEPTEMBER 26, FRIDAY

HR Thos Baldwin to Fakenham with beer. R Bye to Salthouse with beer & got one load clay from Mr Kendals pit.[2] Jno Ram trashing, Thos Boyce in garden. M^{r} H at home all Day, WH & Miss H at Holt afternoon.

[1] *Reepham* Mary Hardy records that her husband accompanied Mr and Mrs Bartell in the White Lion's postchaise at 6.30 am.

The trip was probably in connection with timber (eg 30 Mar., 12 July 1796)

[2] *Kendle* Charles, Holt farmer and later auctioneer, and owner of the ill-fated windmill at Holt. He had bought Riverside Farm at Letheringsett from the estate of his father William (d.1792), of Thornage, who had rebuilt the farmhouse towards the end of his life (B. Cozens-Hardy, *The History of Letheringsett*, p. 160).

Further details of that acquisition are held with Basil Cozens-Hardy's deposits in the NRO, a deed of 14 Dec. 1792 showing that Charles Kendle paid £2500 to his father's executors John Davy of Holt and Thomas Kendle of Sharrington; the miller Richard Rouse was still occupier of the farm in 1792 (NRO: ACC Cozens-Hardy 4/1/1980; see also MS 19830, Z 2D, Thornage with the Members court book 1786–1812, pp. 116–17).

An estate map of 1798 is held in the Cozens-Hardy Collection (illustrated in *Diary 4*: 1 Jan. 1798).

The claypit (26 Sept. 1794) probably lay due east of the nearby ford and west of the Common Hills, as a field there is named Claypit Piece on the rear endpaper map of Basil Cozens-Hardy's *The History of Letheringsett*

SEPTEMBER 27, SATURDAY

HR Rob[t] Bye & Tho[s] Baldwin car[d] of Cleanse beer & draw[d] of [drew off] Sixpenny foorenoon, after other jobs afternoon. Jn[o] Ram trashing, Tho[s] Boyce in garden. Boy to Holt Sessions afternoon,[1] WH & Miss at Holt afternoon.

SEPTEMBER 28, SUNDAY

HR Famaly to Church & alecture afternoon.

SEPTEMBER 29, MONDAY

HR G Thompson, H Raven, T Baldwin & Boy in brewhouse, WH brewing. Jn[o] Ram after hay, T Boyce after hay. R Bye ill foorenoon, to Hindolveston afternoon. M[r] & Miss Fishers here at tea. M[r] & M[rs] H at Cley all Day.[2]

SEPTEMBER 30, TUESDAY

HR Rob[t] Bye ploughing till 2 oClock & then loaded for Stalham, T Baldwin to Holt & Briston with beer. G Thompson & H Raven Cleansed `//. Jn[o] Ram trashing, T Boyce in garden. M[r] & W Hardy at Clay all Day.

MH A Close day, reather raind towards eveng. M[r] Hardy & W[m] rid to the Sale to Cley, bought [ ] Tiles, [ ], came home eveng 8.

OCTOBER 1, WEDNESDAY

Henry Raven Rob[t] Bye to Stalham. T Baldwin help[t] to Cleanse & whant [went] to Cley with beer & bro[t] home load tiles. Jn[o] Ram in Barn, T Boyce in garden, G Thompson & HR Cleansed morning. M[r] & WH at Cley all Day.

Mary Hardy A Close hasy day. M[r] Hardy & W[m] rid to the Sale at Cley foornoon, bought a pair of Pistols at £1 1*s* 0*d*, A Cheese Wagon 7*s*,[3] some tart press s 2*s*,[4] 1 Barrell & 1 half Barrell at [ ].

OCTOBER 2, THURSDAY

HR T Baldwin to Waybou[n] [Weybourne], G Thompson & H Raven grinding Malt for brew. Jn[o] Ram in barn, T Boyce in garden. Rob[t] Bye came from Stalham. M[r], M[rs] & WH at Cley all Day.

MH A very Close foggy day. M[r] Hardy & I rid to the Sale at Cley in Chaise foornoon, W[m] rid on Horseback, we bought 2 Books, Drelingcourt on Death & Sherlock on

---

[1] *Holt sessions* Hiring sessions, held just before the great exodus of maidservants, farm servants and farm boys from their old places at Old Michaelmas. A second sitting was needed, presumably owing to the press of numbers (4 Oct.).

We never learn this boy's name, nor that of his two successors; but we do know their wide range of tasks

[2] *Cley* For the five-day sale of the late John Mann's household furniture, farming stock and merchandise, auctioned by William Custance [jnr] of Walsingham, son of Mary Hardy's cousin Phillis Custance. Mary and William Hardy had attended the first day on 29 Sept. Their former cinder merchant owned a huge stock, this tying up of capital being perhaps partly responsible for the 'bad circumstances' of his business (23 Aug. 1794).

The sale included eight cart horses, various colts and fillies, wagons, '200 chaldrons of excellent coals' and a large quantity of tiles; the Fishmongers' Arms was also for sale (*Norw. Merc.* 27 Sept. 1794).

Cley's Collector of Customs, Peter Coble, had previously owned this public house. It never became a Hardy tied house, instead going to the Wiveton common brewers James and John Ramm (NRO: BR 17/7, which contains a mass of information on John Mann's properties)

[3] *wagon* Serving trolley

[4] *tart presses* Pastry moulds

above Cley: the former Fishmongers' Arms. The alehouse register in the Norfolk Record Office suggests that this house, known in the 20th century as Sunbeams, changed its name from the White Horse in 1789–90. Cley's saltwater baths were situated close by (*Norwich Mercury*, 27 Sept. 1794). This public house formed part of John Mann's extensive estate which had to be disposed of when he died 'very much in debt', as Mary Hardy had reported on 23 Aug. 1794. The Hardys attended all five days of the sale from 29 Sept., but did not buy this outlet [*MB* · *1998*]

Judgment for 3/-,[1] bought the Kitchen Range & Oven for £8 11*s* 0*d*, dind at Mr Smiths & came home before 7 in eveng.

OCTOBER 3, FRIDAY

HR T Baldwin to Cromer with beer, R Bye to Edgefield with beer. G Thompson Grinding Malt, HR & Boy gathering Apples afternoon. Mr H at Cley all Day, WH & Miss H at Holt Evening. Jno Ram in barn, T Boyce in garden.

MH A very fine day. Mr Hardy went to the Sale at Cley foornoon, bought a Celeret for £1 14*s* 6*d*,[2] Dind at Mr Ellis's, came home even past 11 . . .

OCTOBER 4, SATURDAY

HR T Baldwin card of Cleanse beer & to Sheringham with beer. R Bye card of Do [carried off cleanse beer] & to Cley for aload of firnature. Jno Ram in barn, T Boyce in garden. Mr & WH at Cley, Boy at Holt Sessions.

[1] *books* Charles Drélincourt (b. Sedan 1595, d. Paris 1669), French Protestant divine and author of *Consolations against the Fears of Death*. Also either William Sherlock (*c*.1641–1707), Dean of St Paul's, London, author of the famous *Practical Treatise on Death*, first published in London in 1692 and running to many editions; or his son Bishop Thomas Sherlock (1678–1761), of the sees of Bangor, Salisbury and London, whose *Tryal of the Witnesses of the Resurrection of Jesus* (first published 1729) was a popular volume in which argument over the Day of Judgment and the Resurrection was presented in the form of a judicial trial.

Mary Hardy, who almost never mentions books, was now interesting herself in devotional works

[2] *cellaret* A case, cabinet or sideboard for holding wine bottles

above Letheringsett Mill, rebuilt 1798 by Zebulon Rouse, elder brother of Peter and Sally (5 Oct. 1794); the family had lived at the farm just upstream. This mill straddled the Glaven uncomfortably close to the water-powered brewery. Zebulon's father Richard also worked the watermill at Glandford [*MB* · 2000]

OCTOBER 5, SUNDAY

HR Famaly to Church afternoon.[1] Peter & Miss Rouse drank tea here,[2] Mr Bartells famaly drank tea & Supt here.

OCTOBER 6, MONDAY

HR R Bye, G Thompson, HR & Boy in brewhouse all Day, WH Brewing. T Baldwin to Southrepps with beer, T Boyce in garden. Jno Ram on grannerys & dressing wheat. Mr H at home all Day.

MH An exceeding Wet cold day. Mr Hardy at home all day. Mr Custances Sale of New Furniture at Fakenham begin to Day [3] . . .

OCTOBER 7, TUESDAY

HR Robt Bye ploughing, T Baldwin to Thornage after jobs. G Thompson & H Raven Cleansed `// & dressing flower, T Boyce in garden. Mr & Mrs Flower & W & Miss H whent to Holkham, Mr H at home all Day. Jno Ram in barn forenoon.

---

1 *church* According to Mary Hardy, only she herself, Mary Ann and the ladies attended the service

2 *Peter and Miss Rouse* The younger children of the farmer and miller Richard Rouse (d.1816 aged 84) and his wife Mary Ann (d.1826 aged 81), née Fitt. Peter (d. Holt 2 Feb. 1830 aged 58, bur. there 8 Feb.), married Elizabeth Goulty of W. Beckham and became a farmer at Lt Thornage. His sister Sally (Sarah, bapt. Letheringsett 28 May 1777), in 1801 married Thomas Drosier (d.1835 aged 61) of Blakeney (*Diary 4*: 21 Dec. 1801). Trained as a Holt attorney under William Withers, Drosier was bankrupted as a miller at Blakeney Mill (*Norw. Merc.* 24 Feb. 1827).

See also notes for 5 Oct. 1795, 23 June, 25 Oct. 1796

3 *new furniture* From his workshop, and not the far more usual sales of used furniture following moves, bankruptcies and deaths. Like other merchants and manufacturers of the time, William Custance held large stocks: numerous pieces of mahogany furniture including 144 chairs; timber 'comprising upwards of 10,000 feet of fine dry mahogany in boards and planks, 6000 feet of wainscot in boards . . .' and a good timber drug and two carts.

House and land were also for sale: 'A new substantial brick-built modern dwelling house . . . with workrooms . . .', also a barn and pasture (*Norw. Merc.* 20 Sept. 1794)

above Holkham Hall: the garden front of 1734–53, the local pale brick looking from a distance like freestone. The visit of 7 Oct. was 'to see the Hall and Gardens', writes Mary Hardy, Tuesday being open day for tourists [*MB · 2001*]

OCTOBER 8, WEDNESDAY

HR Robt Bye ploughing, «? Thomas Baldwin» at home all Day. T Boyce in garden, G Thompson & H Raven Cleansed X beer. M^r^ & WH at home all Day, M^r^ & Mrs Flower whent home Evening. Jo^s^ Baker came & orders [ordered] aload of beer.[1]

OCTOBER 9, THURSDAY

HR Robt Bye ploughing all Day. T Baldwin it [at] Clay cart forenoon, at Holt with beer & got over brew of M [a quantity of malt for brewing] afternoon. G Thompson dressing Wheat Stones, HR grinding Malt for brew. WH set of to Whissonsett forenoon, M^r^ H at home all Day.

MH A fine day. W^m^ sett of for Whisonset & a round by Burnham Morng 9.[2]

OCTOBER 10, FRIDAY

HR Robt Bye ploughing & whent to Briston with beer, T Baldwin to Holt with beer. Jno Ram trashing [threshing], T Boyce in garden. G Thompson laid down Wheat Stones, H Raven grinding Malt & whent to Edgefield afternoon. Boy whent away after dinner, Maids after tea, New one [new maid] came Evening.[3] M^r^ H very poo{o}rly.

[1] *Joseph Baker* He had newly taken over from William Bulling at the Bull, Holt (NRO: C/Sch 1/16). He may be the builder Joseph Baker who married Holt 1 May 1804 Susanna Dawson, of the building family. George Dawson [? jnr] stood witness; bride, groom and witnesses signed neatly

[2] *a round* A tour of the public houses

[3] *new one* Ann Brown

MH A fine day. Maids & Boy went away Afternoon. Ann Brown from Holt came to live here, Ann Brown came to live here upper Servt.[1]

OCTOBER 11, SATURDAY

HR T Baldwin to Gunthorp with beer & in brewhouse, R Bye to Stody & Kettlestone with D^{o} [beer]. T Boyce in garden, G Thompson & HR dressing flower. M^{r} H at home forenoon, Holt afternoon. Mr Summers dinde [dined] here.

MH A fine day. Mr Hardy rid to Holt afternoon with Mr Summers & paid him for the Publick House at Southreeps, drank tea at Mr Moores & came home eveng 7. W^{m} did not come home from Whisonset . . .

OCTOBER 12, SUNDAY

HR Famaly to Church foorenoon, WH came from Whissonsett Evening.

OCTOBER 13, MONDAY

HR G Thompson, HR, T Baldwin & Boy in brewhouse, WH Brewing. R Bye to Hindolvestone with beer, T Baldwin to Holt afternoon. Jno Ram in barn, T Boyce in garden half day. Jo^{s} Bakers two men half a day. Mr Williams from Thornage Call'd afternoon.

MH A very fine day. Wm Brewd. Mr Hardy at home all day, bought 2 Cows of Wm Bullin of Holt for £10 . . .

OCTOBER 14, TUESDAY

HR R Bye to Fakenham & Syderstone with beer, T Baldwin to Hinderingham & Edgefield with beer. G Thompson, WH & HR Cleanse'd `// forenoon, Grinding Malt for brew. Jno Ram in brewhouse & Sleep't [steeped]. M^{r} H at home all day, HR to Birmingham afternoon. Jere Moore here afternoon.

OCTOBER 15, WEDNESDAY

HR T Baldwin to Cromer with beer. R Bye at home forenoon, to Bale afternoon with beer. G Thomp^{n} Cleanse'd D^{o} [forenoon], Jno Ram in brewhouse all Day. T Boyce in garden, H Raven grinding Malt for brew. 1 trowel man & 1 Laborer.

MH A very fine day. Mr Hardy & W^{m} rid to Gunthorp foornoon, sold a Cottage to Mr Collier [Collyer] for £100 0*s* 0*d*, came home to Dinner.[2] 2 Miss Jenniss drank tea here.

[1] *Ann Brown* She was hired at £2 15*s* a year, with an additional 5*s* for good behaviour. She stayed only a few months, leaving on 31 Jan. 1795. The second maid hired in Oct. 1794, Frances Thompson, was paid £3, with an additional 3*s*. She lasted the full year

[2] *a cottage* This was not the Cross Keys at Gunthorpe, which William Hardy had bought for £300 in 1792 (*Diary 2*: 16 Aug. 1792). It may have been a property adjoining the public house and its grounds

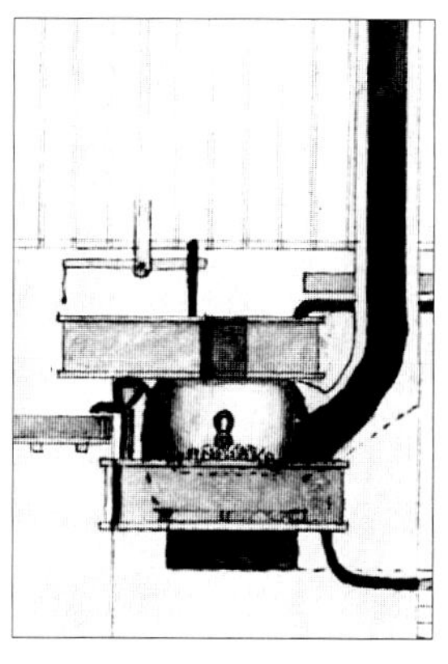

above The brewing copper and its flue: detail from the early-19th-century drawings seen for July 1794. Although the new malting season had begun with the first steep on 14 Oct., Robert Bye was probably lighting the fire for the brewing copper on 17 Oct., and not the malt-kiln furnace [*Cozens-Hardy Collection*]

OCTOBER 16, THURSDAY

HR R Bye got over brew of Malt & whent to Corpusta with beer, T Baldwin ploughing & harrowing. Jn° Ram trashing, T Boyce in garden. Mr & WH road out forenoon. 1 trowl Man & 1 Laborer all Day.

MH A fine day. Mr Hardy at home all day. Wm went up to Holt forenoon, was on the Jury at the Qrtr Sessions,[1] dind at Mr Bartells, came home eveng 4. I & MA walkd up to Holt Afternoon, drank tea at Mr Davys, came home eveng 7. 2 Bricklayers at work altering the Kitchen Chimney.[2]

OCTOBER 17, FRIDAY

HR G Thompson, H Raven & Boy in brewhouse, WH brewing. R Bye kindled the fire & whent to Walsingham with beer, T Baldwin to Sherringham with beer. Jn° Ram in brewhouse, T Boyce in garden. 1 trowelman & 1 Laborer all Day.

MH A fine day. Robt Hill of Runton dind here. 2 Bricklayers at work in Kitchen. Wm Brewd, Mr Hardy at home all day. Rain in Night . . .

OCTOBER 18, SATURDAY

HR R Bye to Runton, T Baldwin to Hindolvestone & Edgefield with beer. Jn° Ram dressing wheat & tending Malthouse, T Boyce in garden. G Thompson & HR Cleansed `//. Mr Hardy at home all Day, W & Miss H at Holt afternoon. 1 trowelman & 1 Laborer all Day.

OCTOBER 19, SUNDAY

HR G Thompson, H Raven, W Hardy, T Balden & R Bye Cleansed foorenoon. Famaly whent to Church afternoon.

OCTOBER 20, MONDAY

HR T Baldwin to Syderstone with beer, R Bye to Fakenham with be«e»r. G Thompson Grinding Malt for brew. Jn° Ram in Malthouse, T Boyce in garden. 1 trowel man & 1 Laborer all Day. WH & Mr H at home all Day.

OCTOBER 21, TUESDAY

HR R Bye ploughing all Day, T Baldwin to Holt with beer. Jn° Ram in Malthouse, T Boyce in garden. G Thompson & HR grinding Malt for brew. Robt Foulger came & orderd aload of beer.[3] Mr H road to Mr Forsters forenoon, WH at home all Day, brick layers all Day.

[1] *jury* If this were the grand jury, which examined whether there were sufficient grounds to bring a case before the magistrates, the diarist would have said so. This was probably the petty jury, the panel of 12 which brought in a verdict; the JPs passed sentence.

While at Whissonsett the previous week William could have been briefed about one of the items of business: James Williamson was found guilty of leaving his wife and child chargeable to Whissonsett parish.

The minutes show there was little business to be transacted at Holt's Michaelmas Quarter Sessions (the county quarter sessions held at Holt by adjournment), although there were a few cases relating to alleged assaults (NRO: C/S 1/15)

[2] *bricklayers* They were probably installing John Mann's kitchen range and oven (2 Oct.), for which they had to alter the flue

[3] *Foulger* Robert, on his first visit to Letheringsett to order beer after taking over the Crown at Southrepps at Old Michaelmas 1794 (see notes for 3 Apr., 10 Sept. 1794). His tenure was an unhappy one, for he died a few months later after a long illness (*Norw. Merc.* 4 Apr. 1795).

By Sept. 1795 the register was showing Esther Foulger, presumably his widow, as innkeeper (NRO: C/Sch 1/16). Robert Summers then took over

Sunday Octr 19. 1794 G Thompson H Raven W Hardy J Baldin & R Bye Cleansed forenoon famaly whent to Church afternoon

Monday 20th J Baldwin to Syderstone with beer R Bye to Fakenham with beer G Thompson grinding malt for brew fr Ram in malthouse J Boyce in garden three men & 1 Laborer all Day W H & Mr H at home all Day

Tuesday 21st R Bye ploughing all Day J Baldwin to Holt with beer fr Ram in malthouse J Boyce in garden G Thompson & H R grinding malt for brew Robt Foulger came & orderd a bar of beer Mr H rode to Mr Forsters forenoon W H at home all Day brick layers all Day

Wednesday 22d R Bye to Southrepps with beer J Baldwin G Thompson H R & Boy in brewhouse W H brewing fr Ram in malthouse J Boyce in garden Mr H at home all Day brick layers all Day

above Henry Raven's diary for 19–22 Oct. 1794, marking the completion of the first year. It now ran to 19,135 words (not counting his aunt's separate diary), of which he had written 17,368 words. The task of training was taken seriously, and Henry was experiencing all the work of the maltings and brewery.

In the early years of his pupillage Henry was excluded from most of the visits, parties and balls enjoyed by his cousins and their friends. Almost his sole recorded leisure activity was to go to Sunday service—and the Sabbath was often a working day, as shown on 19 Oct. His aunt would nonetheless have appreciated his companionship of an evening if others in the family were absent, for she led a quiet social life in the months following her severe illness [*Cozens-Hardy Collection*]

OCTOBER 22, WEDNESDAY

HR R Bye to Southrepps with beer. T Baldwin, G Thompson, HR & Boy in brewhouse, WH brewing. Jn° Ram in Malthouse, T Boyce in garden. Mr H at home all Day, brick layers all Day.

MH A fine Morn, close afternoon, wet Night. Br«i»cklayers at work in Kit«c»hen & finishd. Wm Brewd. Mr Hardy went afternoon to see Mr Forster, found him much better, drank tea there.[1]

OCTOBER 23, THURSDAY

HR R Bye Car'd of Cleanse beer & help to Cleanse `// forenoon, loaded for Stalham & whent to Dawling afternoon. T Baldwin ill. Jn° Ram in Malthouse. T Boyce muckt out pigs house & at work in garden. G Thompson cleansd `// morning. Mr & WH at home all Day.

MH A very wet day. Wm at home all clay. Mr Hardy, I & MA drank tea at Mr Burrells. I was taken with dimness in my Eyes after Supper . . .

OCTOBER 24, FRIDAY

HR R Bye to Stalham with beer, T Boyce to Wells with beer. T Baldwin helping to Cleanse'd [cleanse] & got over brew of Malt. G Thompson & HR Cleansed forenoon, Jn° Ram in Malt house. Mr & WH at home all Day.

OCTOBER 25, SATURDAY

HR T Baldwin to Holt & Cley with beer & Brot home 1000 tiles, R Bye came from Stalham.[2] T Boyce in garden, Jn° Ram in Malthouse. G Thompson began to grind M [malt] for brew. Mr & WH at Holt afternoon, H Raven to Whissonsett.

MH A fine day. Mr Hardy & Wm went to Holt Markt in Chaise. Wm went to T Johnsons Funeral, was Pall bearer, came home eveng 9.[3] Henry Raven went to Whisonsett eveng 4. Dimness in my Eyes.

OCTOBER 26, SUNDAY

HR Famaly to Church forenoon, WH at Holt afternoon. T Baldwin loaded for Brampton. HR came home Evening.

MH A dry day. All went to our Church foornoon, A Communion. Wm went to Holt Church Afternoon, drank tea at Mr Bartells. Henry Raven came home from Whisonsett eveng 8 . . .

[1] *Mr Forster* He had been ill since 19 Oct.

[2] *1000 tiles* From John Mann's sale (30 Sept.)

[3] *funeral* Thomas, son of Revd William Tower Johnson, of Holt, and Mary, née Dack, had died 21 Oct. aged 19 (*Norw. Merc.* 8 Nov. 1794); he had been baptised (publicly) at Holt 8 Sept. 1778. He had attended a large party at the Hardys' on 20 Mar. 1794 (Diary MS)

above The 13th-century font at Holt. Baptisms here need to be interpreted with great care: the rector, Joshua Smith, noted only *public* baptisms. Further, both he and his townsfolk persisted in bringing children very late to public baptism—even aged 10, which was drawing close to confirmation age. Thomas Johnson, a clergyman's son (25 Oct. 1794), had been christened here aged three [*MB · 2011*]

OCTOBER 27, MONDAY

HR T Baldwin to Brampton, R Bye to Cromer with beer. Jn° Ram in M house, T Boyce after jobs. G Thomp. grinding Malt. WH to Sherringham, Mr H road out afternoon.

OCTOBER 28, TUESDAY

HR T Baldwin to Wiverton & Waybourn with beer, Bye to Briston with beer. T Boyce in garden, Jn° Ram in Malthouse. Mr & W Hardy to South Repps. Mr Youngmans Lad mending Warter wheel [waterwheel] part of forenoon.

MH A fine day. Mr Hardy & Wm sett of for Southreps Morng 8, came home by Cromer Eveng 10. Eliz Davy of Holt was Married to Edwd Robinson, Linnen Draper from London. As soon as the Ceremony was over they sett of for London.[1] Maids & Betty Woods washd 4 Weeks Linn . . .

OCTOBER 29, WEDNESDAY

HR G Thompson, R Bye & Boy in brewhouse, Jn° Ram & H Raven in Malthouse, WH brewing. T Baldwin at harrow forenoon, Sowing Vetches & Loaded for Beckhigh. T Boyce in garden. Mr H at home all Day.

OCTOBER 30, THURSDAY

HR T Baldwin to Beckhigh with beer, R Bye Sowing Vetches & loaded for South Repps with beer. Jn° Ram in Malt house, T Boyce in garden. G Thompson & H Raven Cleanse'd `//. Mr & WH at home all day.

OCTOBER 31, FRIDAY

HR Robt Bye to South Repps with beer, T Baldwin to Salthouse with beer & Cley for tiles. T Boyce in garden morning & kild & flea'd [?flayed] the Walden Horse.[2] Jn° Ram in Malt house. G Thompson, H Raven & WH Cleanse'd forenoon. Mr H at home all Day.

NOVEMBER 1, SATURDAY

Henry Raven T Baldwin to Sherringham & Thornage with beer, R Bye Sowing Vetches. T Boyce in garden & help't to Clear fat [vat] morning. Jn° Ram in Malthouse, G Thompson & H Raven Skreening & grinding Malt for brew. W & Miss H at Holt market afternoon, Mr Hardy at home all Day.

[1] *Robinson* See note for 9 Jan. 1794. The service was conducted at Holt by the Letheringsett rector Revd John Burrell, the witnesses being Matthew and Joseph Davy, Mary Riches, and the newly retired innkeeper of the Feathers, Elizabeth Sheppard

[2] *Walden horse* The horse named Walden, possibly acquired from John Walden of the Fighting Cocks at Wells (18 Sept. 1794).

If by 'kild' Henry means 'killed' the animal was evidently slaughtered and his hide stripped (flayed, or 'flea'd'). But this seems a rather too specialised task for the day labourer and jobbing gardener.

The verb 'kild' may derive from the Norfolk noun 'kell', defined by Forby as 'the omentum or cawl of a slaughtered beast', the omentum being a large fold of peritoneum hanging over the intestines; it may also relate to 'kelter', meaning condition (R. Forby, *The Vocabulary of East Anglia*, vol. 2, p. 179).

In other words Boyce may have given the horse some conditioning or worming drench to try to correct an internal disorder, and then have proceeded to bleed or fleam ('flea'd') the unfortunate animal

left 'Elizabeth Davy of Holt was married to Edward Robinson, linen draper, from London' (28 Oct. 1794). The Holt register gives the groom's parish as St Stephen Walbrook, with its Wren City of London church seen here. The central dome south of the tower was a trial run by the architect 1672–87 before he embarked on the more ambitious scheme at St Paul's.

By 1800 the Robinsons and their daughter Betsy were settled in the new suburb of Hackney, with easy access to the City.

Bett Davy came from a family with strong London links. Four or more of the Holt draper and grocer's children went to live there, and in the early 19th century many more of Mary Hardy's acquaintance were drawn to London. Increasingly, visits to and from the capital were undertaken in the Hardys' circle [*drawing by Thomas H. Shepherd 1829*]

NOVEMBER 2, SUNDAY

HR Famaly all whent to Church morning, WH to Thornage afternoon.

Mary Hardy A fine Morng, raind towards eveng. All went to our Church foornoon, no Sermon. W^m^ walkd to Thornage Church Afternoon, drank tea at J Kendles, home eveng past 7 . . .

NOVEMBER 3, MONDAY

HR R Bye to Fakenham with beer, T Baldwin to Hindolvestone with beer. Jn° Ram ill, H Raven in Malthouse. T Boyce in garden. G Thompson grinding D° [malt] for brew. M^r^ & Mrs Raven from Whissonsett came to dine.[1] M^r^ & WH at home all Day.

[1] *Mr and Mrs Raven* Mary Hardy's brother Nathaniel and his wife; for the latter see note for 6 Mar. 1794. This was Mary Ann's 21st birthday, which—unlike William in 1791—she was celebrating very quietly.

Visits possibly planned for her birthday had to be cancelled: see note for 6 Nov.

above A pantiled roof on the 18th-century Coltishall King's Head, such tiles being produced in numerous local brick-kilns; the Hardys' men were busy unloading pantiles 6 Nov. 1794. The play of light and shade on their wavy form creates an interesting texture [*MB·2008*]

NOVEMBER 4, TUESDAY

HR G Thompson, T Baldwin & Boy in brewhouse, WH brewing. R Bye to Edgefield with beer. T Boyce in garden, Jno Ram & H Raven in Malthouse. M^{r} H at home all Day. Meach. Ives came afternoon.[1] Mr Sheldrake Sup^{t} here.

NOVEMBER 5, WEDNESDAY

HR Robt Bye & T Baldwin after jobs all Day, G Thompson & H Raven Cleanse'd `//. Jno Ram in Malthouse, T Boyce cleaning chaise harness afternoon. M^{r} H & WH at home all Day, Revnd Burrell drank tea here.

NOVEMBER 6, THURSDAY

HR T Baldwin to Corpusta with beer & took 300 Pan tile [pantiles]. R Bye to Sherrington & Bale with beer forenoon, unloading tile afternoon. T Boyce helping to Cleanse and D^{o} [unloading] tiles. Jno Ram in Malthouse, G Thompson & HR Cleanse'd. M^{r} & WH at home all Day. Mr Nath Raven road to Fakenham. M^{r}, M^{rs} & Miss Sheldrake drank tea here.

MH A fine Morng, very wet afternoon. Bro^{t} & Sister was going away but the rain prevented, Bro^{t} rid to Fakenham & came back even 6. M^{r} & Mrs Sheldrake drank tea & Supt here, Mrs Sheldrake slept here on acct of the heavy rain [2] . . .

NOVEMBER 7, FRIDAY

HR R Bye to Dawling with beer & to Blakney for two Chal^{d} Cinders from Mr Farthings. T Baldwin to Sheringham with beer. Jno Ram in Malthouse, T Boyce in garden. M^{r} & WH at home all Day. M^{r} & Mrs Raven gone home this morning.

NOVEMBER 8, SATURDAY

HR R Bye to Blakney for 2 Ch. Cinders from Robt Farthings, T Baldwin to Stody & Holt with beer. Jno Ram in Malthouse, T Boyce in garden. G Thompson grinding Malt for brew. M^{r} & M^{rs} & WH at Holt afternoon. Boy got aload of turnips for cows.

NOVEMBER 9, SUNDAY

HR Famaly all whent to Church forenoon, M^{rs} H was taking very poorly at church. Mr Forster drank tea.

MH A very fine day. All went to our Church foornoon, Mr Burrell preach^{d}. I poorly with pain in my head &

---

1 *Meshack Ives* See note for 13 Oct. 1793

2 *heavy rain* The rain had also prevented the Hardys and Ravens from going to Thomas Forster at Bayfield on 3 Nov. and to Cook Flower at Sheringham on 5 Nov.—an 'excessive wet day', noted Henry's aunt. The workforce continued with their duties despite the dreadful weather, although no work was done in the fields during this period

dimness in my eyes. Mr Fisher, hop mercht from London, calld here aftern. Mrs Forster & three Nephews drank tea here.

NOVEMBER 10, MONDAY

HR G Thompson, H Raven, R Bye & Boy in brewhouse, WH Brewing. T Baldwin to Cromer with beer, H Raven whent to Thornag«e» with Malt. WH whent to Holt Asembly & S Sharpe [?Sharpens] came home with him & Slept here. Mr H at home all Day.

MH A fine day. Mr Hardy at home all day. Wm Brewd & went to Holt Assembly in eveng, came home Morng 3. Mr Sharp from Brinton [?Briston] came home with him & Slept here . . .

NOVEMBER 11, TUESDAY

HR R Bye Cleanse'd `// & to Holt with beer, T Baldwin ploughing in Furze Close. G Thompson & HR Cleansed `// & dressing flower [flour]. Jno Ram in Malthouse, T Boyce in garden. Mr, Mrs, Wm & Miss Hardy whent to Mr Forsters to tea. D [David] Pleasance came & Orderd beer.

NOVEMBER 12, WEDNESDAY

HR T Baldwin & R Bye to Gunthorp with beer & Brot home timber. G Thompson, WH & H Raven Cleanse'd X forenoon. Jno Ram in Malt house, T Boyce in garden. Boy ran away.[1] Mr & WH at home all Day. Mr & Miss Bartell & Miss Baker drank tea here. Bricklayers all Day.

NOVEMBER 13, THURSDAY

HR R Bye to Runton with beer, T Baldwin at home all Day. Jno Ram in Malthouse, T Boy«c»e in garden. G Thompson grinding Malt for brew. WH & Miss Hardy gone to Whissonsett, HR whent as far as Snoring. 1 trowelman & 1 Laborer all Day.

NOVEMBER 14, FRIDAY

HR T Baldwin got up aload of Furze and whent to Edgefield with beer & brot home 17 Cs [coombs] barley from Boswell's. R Bye helpt to get up aload of Furze & after other jobs. G Thompson grinding Malt, Jno Ram in Malthouse, T Boyce in garden. Capt Hall trashing. Mr H at home all Day. Mr Wymer [? of Reepham] cald here.

[1] *Boy ran away* He may have had difficulty adjusting to his exacting role in the busy household. Mary Hardy makes no reference to his disappearance, and there is no word that anyone went looking for him.
His replacement arrived on 24 Nov.

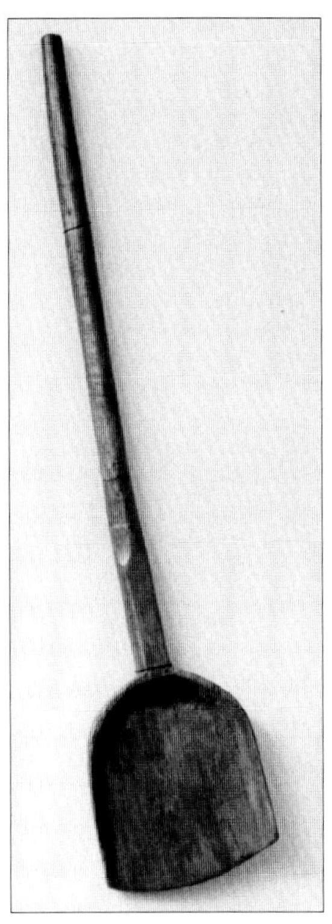

above **A long-handled malting shovel, its surfaces and edges smoothed to prevent damage to the grain** [*Ian P. Peaty Collection*]

NOVEMBER 15, SATURDAY

HR R Bye to Blakeny with beer to put on board aship for London, T Baldwin at home all Day. Jn° Ram in Malthouse, T Boyce in garden. Capt Hall trashing, G Thompson dressing Wheat Stones. WH came home afternoon & Bro^t^ [bought] Mary Raven home with him.[1]

NOVEMBER 16, SUNDAY

HR Famaly all whent to Church afternoon, Mr Burrell preache'd.

NOVEMBER 17, MONDAY

HR G Thompson & Baldwin in brewhouse, WH Brewing. R Bye to wells [Wells] with beer, T Boyce in garden. Capt Hall trashing, H Raven in Malthouse. M^r^ H at home all Day. Thos Press drank tea here.[2]

NOVEMBER 18, TUESDAY

HR T Baldwin to Waybourn with beer, R Bye in Malthouse morning after jobs. G Thompson & WH cleansed `//, H Raven & Jn° Ram in Malthouse. Capt Hall trashing, Thos Boyce in garden. Skiffins came with a mare to sell. Mr Davy drank tea here. Mr Hardy at home all Day. Bunnets too [two] men at Waybourn.

MH A very cold dry day. Mr Hardy & W^m^ home all day. Mr Skivens dind here. Mr Davy drank tea here & recknd. A Sharp wind, frosty night. T Boyce in Garden . . .

NOVEMBER 19, WEDNESDAY

HR R Bye to Holt with beer forenoon & afternoon. T Baldwin at home all Day, help^t^ to Cleanse. Gunton Thompson & H Raven Cleansed XX forenoon. Jn° Ram in Malthouse, Thos Boyce in garden. Capt Hall trashing. Bunnets 2 men gone to wor«k» at public house, Waybourn. WH road out, M^r^ H at home all Day.[3]

NOVEMBER 20, THURSDAY

HR T Baldwin to Kettlestone with beer, R Bye to Hinderingham with beer. HR got over part of abrew of Malt, G Thompson grinding Malt for brew. Jn° Ram in Malthouse, Thos Boyce in garden. M^r^ & WH at home all day.

NOVEMBER 21, FRIDAY

HR Thos Baldwin ploughing and whent to Holt. R Bye got up aload of turnips, setting up furze in yard [4] and whent to Holt with bar. [barrel] Staves [5] & bro^t^ home 10 Coombs Oats & new waggon. Jn° Ram in Malthouse,

---

[1] *Mary Raven* Henry's sister; William's future wife

[2] *Thomas Press* (b.*c*.1762, bur. Weston 1836), farmer (Cozens-Hardy Collection: letter of 22 May 1972 from his descendant Martin Press to Basil Cozens-Hardy). He, his wife Elizabeth, née Carter, and their children occupied the later-named Piggotts Farm (opposite) near the main Holt road. They left 10 Oct. 1801 for Gimingham, the owner James Cobon then moving to Piggotts from Letheringsett Hall Farm and giving vacant possession to William Hardy jnr

[3] *rode out* To view the repairs being carried out at Weybourne, according to Mary Hardy's diary

[4] *setting up furze* Gorse was bound into faggots to form a temporary fence. The expedient intrigued and impressed William Marshall as he watched the process 28 Oct. 1782: 'This morning I observed some workmen fencing a rick-yard with furze-faggots, alone—a species of fence I have not met with before . . . Furze faggots, thus placed, are a fence against every kind of stock; even hogs and hares; and, in a country overstocked with the latter, might frequently be used, as a temporary fence, with great advantage' (W. Marshall, *The Rural Economy of Norfolk*, vol. 2, pp. 362–3)

[5] *staves* Pieces of wood shaped to form a barrel and held in place by the hoops and ends

left **Piggotts Barn, Letheringsett, opposite the turning to the watermill; part of the barn's roadside wall dates from the early 17th century. William Hardy jnr bought the farm from James Cobon in 1839. His nephew demolished the farmhouse next to the barn *c.*1869 to build 'Fear One Cottages' in 1870 [*MB·2001*]**

Thos Boyce in garden. G Thompson grinding Malt for brew & bin. Mr H at home all day, WH road out Evening.

NOVEMBER 22, SATURDAY

HR Thos Baldwin to Sheringham with beer, R Bye at home all day. Jno Ram in Malthouse, Thos Boyce in garden. Mr & Mrs, WH & Mary Raven at Holt afternoon.

NOVEMBER 23, SUNDAY

HR T Baldwin & R Bye card of [carried off] Beer. Famaly all whent to Church forenoon and alecture Evening. Robt Bartell drank tea, Supt & Slept here.[1]

NOVEMBER 24, MONDAY

HR Thos Baldwin to Fakenham with beer, R Bye to Syderstone with beer. Jno Ram in Malthouse, T Boyce in garden. WH at home all day. New boy came home morning.[2]

NOVEMBER 25, TUESDAY

HR T Baldwin to Cromer with beer. R Bye got up aload of turnips & whent to Briston with beer.[3] H Raven whent to Holt with his Sister, WH at Holt. Mr Everitt & Mr Keeler dine'd here. Mr H at Holt.

MH A close foggy day. Mr Hardy & Wm rid up to Holt fair foornoon, came home to Dinner. Mr Everet & Mr Keeler dind here, went away eveng 4. Mr Hardy & Wm, H Raven & M Raven went to the Fair, drank tea & Supt at Mr Bartells, came home eveng 10.

---

1 *Robert Bartell* He stayed overnight on account of the rain, according to his hostess

2 *came home* Although this suggests that the runaway boy had returned (12 Nov.), it is more likely that Henry was using the Norfolk phrase for an arrival. Bags of hops came home, just as new servants came home to their new place (*World*, vol. 1, app. 1.A, Dictionary of Norfolk speech)

3 *Baldwin and Bye* The men were kept well away from the local fair, whereas the lack of an entry for the other members of the workforce suggests they were given the day off—Henry included. Bye's heavy drinking on 1–3 Dec. may have been as a protest against being banned by the Hardys from attending Holt Fair, something he would have regarded as his right. The workforce at Coltishall had similarly reacted when prevented from going to their local Whit Monday fair (*World*, vol. 2, chap. 1)

facing page **Holt Church. Edmund and Sarah Jewell lie buried under the chancel steps, with an altar recently placed above them in this central position liturgically. An active JP, he had as Captain of the local Volunteers been interred with military honours in 1784. His widow was one of only four gentry resident at Holt, as listed in the *Universal British Directory* at this time** [*MB · 2011*]

NOVEMBER 26, WEDNESDAY

HR T Baldwin to Hindolvestone with beer. R Bye, G Thompson, HR & Boy in brew house, WH brewing. T Boyce stopping gaps, Jno Ram in Malthouse. M^r H roade to Briston.

MH A very fine day. Maids & Betty Woods wash'd 4 weeks linnen. Mr Hardy went to Briston to meet J Grooms Executor, came home eveng 6. I taken with dimness in my Eyes eveng past 9 . . .

NOVEMBER 27, THURSDAY

HR R Bye to Cley with beer, T Baldwin ploughing. Jno Ram in Malthouse, T Boyce in garden. G Thompson & H Raven Cleansed `//. M^r H & WH at home all Day. Capt Hall trashing.

NOVEMBER 28, FRIDAY

HR R Bye to South Repps with beer, T Baldwin to Brampton with beer. Jno Ram in Malthouse, Capt Hall trashing. G Thompson & H Raven Cleansed X beer. M^r & WH at home all day. T Baldwin hurt his Leg.

NOVEMBER 29, SATURDAY

HR R Bye to Edgefield & Holt with beer, Jno Ram in Malthouse. Capt Hall trashing, T Boyce at work in furze Close. Thos Baldwin no work. Boy got up aload of turnips.

NOVEMBER 30, SUNDAY

HR Famaly all whent to Church Evening. WH, HR & Mary Raven whent to Holt D^o [Church]. M^r & Mrs Forster drank tea here.

MH A fine day but cold. W^m, HR & MR rid up to Holt Church afternoon in our Chaise with a Horse for trial of Mr Dybals of Edgefield. M^r & M^rs & young Forster came to our Church eveng 4, drank tea here.

DECEMBER 1, MONDAY

Henry Raven G Thompson & H Raven grinding Malt for brew, C [Captain] Hall trashing. Thos Boyce at work in furze Close. M^r & M^rs & Mary Raven at Holt all Day, WH at Holt afternoon. R Bye drunk.

Mary Hardy A Chearly day, Wet eveng. Mr Hardy, I & M Rav^n rid up to Holt to Mrs Jewells Sale foornoon, a stop was put to the Sale [1] on Acct of a Letter from the Ld

---

[1] *Mrs Jewell* Sarah (d. 3 Nov. 1794 aged 70/76, bur. Holt 10 Nov.), née March; her husband Edmund had died 10 Nov. 1784 aged 65. On his death she had assumed his manorial lordships, eg Briston Hall, Meliors and Chosells (NRO: MC 1825/8, Manor court book 1771–94, p. 1, 22 Oct. 1771, sidenote).

The sale proceeded afresh 9–10 Jan. 1795. The Lord Chancellor 1793–1801 was Lord Loughborough. 18 months later the Norwich paper gave the reason for the delay. A Chancery case over Edmund Jewell's estate, defended by William Brereton (Sarah Jewell's executor), had just ended in London: 'To be peremptorily sold, pursuant to a decree of the High Court of Chancery, made in a cause Chicheley against Brereton, in the Public Sale Room, in Southampton Buildings, Chancery Lane, London, on 11th July 1796, all the . . . estates of Edmund Jewell . . .' (*Norw. Merc.* 22 Nov. 1794, 11 June 1796)

EDMUND JEWELL Esq.
one of his Majesty's Justices
of the Peace which he executed
with strict Honour.
tenth of November
1784
Aged 65.

Chancellor, Mr Chrismas' goods were sold.[2] We dind & drank tea at Mr Bartells, home eveng past 8.

DECEMBER 2, TUESDAY

HR G Thompson grinding Malt for brew, H Raven in Malthouse. T Boyce at work in furze Close, Capt Hall trashing. Boy got up aload of turnips, R Bye drunk. M^r & M^rs, WH & Mary Raven at Holt afternoon. M^r & Mrs Flower & Miss Fisher Cald [called] here.

MH A Close drisly day. M^r H, I & MR [Mary Raven] rid up to the Sale after dinner, drank tea at Mr Sheldrakes, came home eveng 9. Bricklayer put up the Water Cistern in Kitchen [2] . . .

DECEMBER 3, WEDNESDAY

HR Jo^s Bakers too men at work & Bunnets too men at work in kitchen. H Raven in Malthouse, Jno Ram ill, R Bye ill. Thos Baldwin whent to Holt & bro^t home 6 Bar^s [barrels] from the Coopers & things from Mrs Juells.[3] G Thompson grinding barley,[4] T Boyce at work in furze Close. Capt Hall trashing. M^r & M^rs & Miss Bartell, M^r & M^rs & Miss Sheldrake & Mr Smith [of Cley] drank tea here.

[1] *Christmas* William, the former attorney at Coltishall and Harleston, who had run into financial difficulties necessitating the sale. He marr. Holt 2 Feb. 1790 Edmund Jewell's niece Dorothy Gallant Chicheley (b.*c.*1774, publicly bapt. Holt 23 July 1784 [!]), daughter of Henry Chicheley, of Gt Yarmouth, and Elizabeth, née Gallant.

Mrs Christmas was due to inherit the large estate under the terms of Mrs Jewell's will, but her relations were trying to wrest her inheritance from her (NRO: ANW (1785) W 76, f. 113, Will of Edmund Jewell of Holt, dated 18 Sept. 1784, proved 10 Nov. 1784; NRO: NCC (1794) 251 Coe, Will of Sarah Jewell of Holt, dated 22 Dec. 1789, with codicil 30 Apr. 1792, proved 8 Dec. 1794). Mr Christmas's goods were not part of the Chancery action

[2] *cistern* The tank feeding running water by gravity to the kitchen, supplied probably from the Brewhouse Pightle pond or a well beside it, as described in *World*, vol. 1, chap. 7, under the section 'Drinking filtered ancestor' (the pipes crossing the churchyard)

[3] *barrels* Confirmation that the brewery did not have its own cooperage at this time. Under William Hardy jnr a cooperage was to be built behind the brewery stables

[4] *grinding barley* Grain failing to make malting grade was ground for animal feed: eg 12 Nov. 1795, 18 Sept. 1797

[1] *carpenter* Mary Hardy notes that he was working in the kitchen

[2] *Mr Hardy cleansed* One of his rare appearances in the brewery

[3] *stage coach* This was a reintroduction of a service instituted by private subscription in 1784 following William Pitt's new duties on riding and carriage horses; the route was Wells–Holt–Aylsham–Norwich. The service had been withdrawn in 1786, and the coach, horses and harness sold at Holt (*Diary 2*)

[4] *Ellis* Mary Hardy records that the Cley merchant and her husband attended a sale at Holt of land belonging to the late John Mann

above Whissonsett Hall, where Henry spent his midwinter holiday, was rebuilt in the mid-19th century. This part of the garden wall survives probably from the Ravens' time there [*MB·1998*]

DECEMBER 4, THURSDAY

HR R Bye to Hindolvestone with beer. G Thom^{n}, T Baldwin & Boy in brewhouse, Jno Ram & HR in Malt house. Capt Hall trashing, T Boyce at work in furze close. Carpenters & bricklayers at work. WH brewing. T Baldwin whent for aload of faggots. M^{r} H at home all day.

DECEMBER 5, FRIDAY

HR R Bye gone to Stalham. T Baldwin helping to Cleanse `// and whent to Cley for too Chal$^{d}$ Cinders from M$^{r}$ Farthings. G Thompson & H Raven cleanse `//, Capt Hall trashing. T Boyce at work in furze close, Jno Ram in Malthouse. WH & Mary Raven whent to Whissonsett, HR road to Snoring with them. Carpenter at work all Day.[1]

DECEMBER 6, SATURDAY

HR T Baldwin to Dawling & Salthouse with beer, R Bye came from Stalham. G Thom^{n} & M^{r} H Cleansed.[2] H Raven Stripping Meal. Jno Ram in Malthouse, Capt Hall trashing, T Boyce at work in furze close. M^{r} H at Holt market afternoon.

DECEMBER 7, SUNDAY

HR Famaly to Church morning. W & Miss Hardy & Robt Raven came from Whissonsett afternoon.

DECEMBER 8, MONDAY

HR R Bye ploughing. T Baldwin to thornage forenoon with beer, at work at home afternoon. Jno Ram in Malthouse, T Boyce at work in furze close. M^{r} & WH at home all Day.

MH A fine day. W^{m} & R Raven walkd up to Holt foornoon, came home to dinner, R Raven went away after dinner. Mr Hardy at home all day. The Stage Coach from Wells to Norwich began to run.[3] W^{m} went to Holt Assembly, came home Morng 3 . . .

DECEMBER 9, TUESDAY

HR R Bye ploughing all Day, T Baldwin to Holt with waggon wheels & after jobs. G Thompson grinding Malt for brew, Jno Ram in Malthouse. T Boyce at work in furze close. M^{r} H at Holt afternoon. Mr Ellis dine'd here.[4]

DECEMBER 10, WEDNESDAY

HR R Bye to Corpusta with beer, T Bald^{n} to Stody with beer forenoon. Jno Ram in Malthouse, Capt Hall trashing. T Boyce in furze close, G Thompson grinding Malt. Mr & WH & H Raven whent to Cley to Bottle of a pipe of wine.[1]

DECEMBER 11, THURSDAY

HR T Baldwin ploughing. R Bye, G Thompson, H Raven & Boy in brewhouse, WH brewing. Jno Ram in Malthouse, Capt Hall trashing. Mr H at home all Day.

DECEMBER 12, FRIDAY

HR R Bye ploughing. T Baldwin to Wiverton with beer & Blakeny for too Chald [two chaldrons] cinders from Mr Farthins. Jno Ram in Malthouse, Capt trashing. WH at Holt afternoon. G Thompson & HR Skreening Malt. Mr H at home all Day.

DECEMBER 13, SATURDAY

HR R Bye ploughing, T Baldwin to Holt with beer & after jobs. Jno Ram in Malt house, T Boyce at work in furze close, Capt Hall trashing. Mr & WH at Holt market afternoon. Mr Woodcock cald here forenoon.[2]

Mary Ann Hardy ⟦ [3] A fine mild day. Mr Hardy and Wm rode to Holt Market after dinner, came home eveng 10.⟧ I taken with dimness in my eyes . . .

DECEMBER 14, SUNDAY

HR Famaly all whent to Church afternoon, Mr Burrell preach«ed».

DECEMBER 15, MONDAY

HR R Bye to Fakenham with beer, Thos Baldwin clearing fat [vat] & whent to Bale with Do [beer]. Jno Ram in Malthouse, Capt Hall trashing. G Thompson & H Raven got over abrew of Malt. Mr & WH at home all Day.

MH A very fine day. Mr Hardy at home all day. Wm rid up to Holt with the Banking Book eveng 4, drank tea at Mr Seales, came home eveng 9.[4]

DECEMBER 16, TUESDAY

HR T Baldwin to Cromer with beer, R Bye to Holt & Edgefield with beer. G Thompson grinding Malt for brew, Jno Ram in Malthouse, Capt Hall trashing. Mr & WH at home all Day. My Brother Nath [Nathaniel Raven] came from Whissonsett. Thos Temple came & Orderd a load of Mild for Ricd Temple of Barmore [Barmer].[5]

[1] *pipe* A wine measure: two hogsheads or 126 gallons (572·8 litres); half a tun.

Mary Hardy states that although they drew off the whole pipe they kept only one eighth for themselves—approx. an anker and a half (15¾ gallons)

[2] *Woodcock* Possibly the Briston grocer (*Univ. Brit. Dir.*, vol. 3 (1794), p. 281), although Mary Hardy does not mention his visit. This may alternatively have been a builder of the same name, who had worked for the Hardys in 1787 (*Diary 2*)

[3] The entries for 11–13 Dec. in Mary Hardy's diary are in Mary Ann's hand, perhaps to relieve her mother of the task while her eyes were troubling her

[4] *banking book* William Hardy snr had been engaged in discussions with Gurneys shortly before the bank's Holt branch was established in 1792 (*Diary 2*). A local branch was an extremely useful facility for a brewer dealing in large volumes of cash

[5] *load of mild* A retail sale, and not to a public house, it is also a rare reference to the variety of beer ordered. The delivery was made 27 Dec. to the farmer, who was to borrow £120 from the Hardys 18 Sept. 1797; Richard Temple sold up at Barmer in Sept. 1801 (*Diary 4*).

Mild could, like bitter, be brewed in varying strengths

MH A fine day. Nath[l] Raven from the Hall came eveng 4. M[r] Hardy went to a Club at Dobsons for the first time, came home Morng 1, W[m] went a little while. M[r] Hardy changd our Chaise Mare for a Horse & the little Mare for a Cart Mare . . .

DECEMBER 17, WEDNESDAY

HR R Bye to Runton with beer. T Baldwin got up aload of turnips, a D[o] [load] of Clay & A D[o] [a load] of gravill. Jn[o] Ram in Malthouse, Cap[t] Hall trashing. M[r] W & Miss H & N Raven to Sherringham.[1] M[r] Woodcocks Apprentice drank tea here.

DECEMBER 18, THURSDAY

HR R Bye to Blakeny for too Chal[d] Cinders from M[r] Farthins. Jn[o] Ram in Malthouse, Cap[t] Hall trashing. M[r] H at home all Day. WH & N Raven rode to Blakeny morning & WH whent to Holt afternoon. M[r] & M[rs] Temple & a Lady drank tea here.

MH A rime frost. M[r] Hardy at home all day. W[m] dind at the Feathers at Holt at the School feast, drank tea at M[r] Bartells, came home eveng 9.[2] M[r] & M[rs] Temple & M[rs] Booth from Norwich drank tea here . . .

DECEMBER 19, FRIDAY

HR R Bye & Baldwin at muck cart all Day. Jn[o] Ram in Malthouse, Cap[t] Hall trashing. T Boyce at work in furze close. M[r] & M[rs], Miss & WH & N Raven to M[r] Temples afternoon.

DECEMBER 20, SATURDAY

HR R Bye to Holt & Sherrington with beer. T Baldwin, G Thompson, Boy & HR in brewhouse. Jn[o] Ram Malthouse, Cap[t] Hall trashing. T Boyce at work in furze close. Henry Goggs & M[r] H whent to Holt market, WH brewing.

DECEMBER 21, SUNDAY

HR H Goggs whent away morning after breakfast. Famaly all when [went] to Church forenoon. G Thompson Cleansed `//.

DECEMBER 22, MONDAY

HR R Bye to Sherringham with beer. T Baldwin to Cromer & cart broke down. Jn[o] Ram in Malthouse, Cap[t] Hall trashing. M[r] & WH at home all day. G Thompson & H Raven «and» WH Cleansed XX.

[1] *Sheringham* William, Mary Ann and Nathaniel went for dinner and tea at Cook and Sarah Flower's

[2] *school feast* An annual event, combined with speech day. William Hardy jnr had attended the Free Grammar School, Holt only very intermittently 1781–83

above Distinctive ventilation holes in the barn belonging in the late 18th century to the Aufreres of Hoveton St Peter and now part of the very popular attraction Wroxham Barns.

The Hardys had only one barn, plus their granaries and store chambers within the maltings and brewery. Their 72-year-old labourer Thomas 'Captain' Hall spent the last months of 1794 threshing in the barn [*MB · 2011*]

above A Norfolk farm wagon with unshod wheels, the wooden rims not being protected by iron tyres. Thomas Baldwin had a bad time on the icy roads on his beer delivery to Cromer on 22 Dec. The following day, on another delivery, one of the huge wagonwheels ran over his arm on his 26-mile round trip. He did not return to work until 14 Feb. 1795, the labourer Thomas Boyce being promoted to his place in the intervening weeks
[*photograph pre-1937 by Miss F. Foster: Norfolk Heritage Centre, Norwich*]

DECEMBER 23, TUESDAY

HR T Baldwin to Beckhigh [Beckhithe] with beer, broke his arme comeing hom by fallen down under the wheel, R Bye to Holt with beer & whent to meet Baldwin. Jn° Ram in Malthouse. Mr & WH at home all day.

MH A Sharp frost. Mr Hardy went to Dobsons Club in eveng, came home eveng 9. Wm rid up to Holt in eveng to hear how Jos Davy did who is very bad. Old Mrs Hipkins died Sudenly last Night. Thos Balden broke his Arm coming from Sheringham.

DECEMBER 24, WEDNESDAY

HR R Bye to Gunthorpe & Clay with beer, T Boyce to Waybourn with beer, C Hall trashing. Mrs Flower came to dine. Mr & WH at home all day, Jn° Ram in Malthouse.

MH A very sharp frost, wind high, began to Snow eveng 4, a very bad Night. Mrs Flower came to Dinner & staid all Night. Mr Hardy & Wm at home all day.

DECEMBER 25, THURSDAY

HR Being Christmas day Sarvants & Laborers & Wives dined here.[1] Famaly to Church afternoon, M[r] Burrell preached.

MH *Chris May* [*Christmas Day*] A-Snowd almost all {all} day, M[rs] Flower could not git home. We all went to our Church Afternoon, M[r] Burrell preach[d]. Our Labourers & their Wifes dind here.

DECEMBER 26, FRIDAY

HR R Bye to upper Sheringham with beer & Loaded for Syderstone & Barmer.[2] T Boyce got up aloade of Turnips, Cap[t] Hall trashing. G Thompson & H Raven got over brew of Malt & began to grind, Jn[o] Ram in Malthouse. M[r] H at home all Day, WH roade to Holt morning.

MH Thawd. M[rs] Flower could not git home . . .

DECEMBER 27, SATURDAY

HR R Bye & T Boyce gone to Syderstone & Barmer with beer. Jn[o] Ram in Malthouse, Cap[t] Hall trashing. M[r] & WH at Holt Market. M[rs] Flower gone home.

[[DECEMBER 28, SUNDAY

William Hardy jnr Family all at Church forenoon.[3] WH at Holt Church afternoon, drank Tea at M[r] Bakers. HR & Nat[l] Raven set off for Whissonsett M7.

DECEMBER 29, MONDAY

WHj R Bye brewing & Holt with beer, T Boyce Jobs in Yard. Cap[t] Hall tasking, Jn[o] Ram in M H [malthouse], GT grinding all night.[4] M[r] H & WH at home.

MH A Close cold day. M[r] Hardy drank tea at M[r] Burrells. W[m] at home all day & Brew'd . . .

DECEMBER 30, TUESDAY

WHj R Bye to Wells with beer, T Boyce help[d] in brewhouse to Cleanse `// & Jobs in the Yard, Jn[o] Ram in MH. M[r] & WH at home all day, loaded Cart for Southreeps [Southrepps].

MH A fine day. We Washd 5 weeks Linn [linen]. M[r] Hardy & W[m] at home all day. I taken poorly with pain in my Side.[5]

DECEMBER 31, WEDNESDAY

WHj R Bye to Southreeps with beer. T Boyce at Thornage with beer forenoon, Carting gravel in afternoon.

[1] *servants and labourers* Unlike his aunt, Henry here uses precise language. He tells us that the annually hired men (the farm servants) were included in the festivities, as also the labourers hired by the day or week such as Captain Hall and, until just recently, Thomas Boyce.

Mary Hardy, by contrast, uses the loose umbrella term 'labourers', although it was strictly inaccurate. She was under great strain with the snow and intense cold; Sarah Flower was imprisoned in her house; and five weeks' laundry loomed—in weather hopeless for drying.

Further, she and her husband were about to suffer flare-ups of old ailments

[2] *Upper Sheringham* Presumably delivering to Cook Flower: another unusual reference to direct sales

[3] *at church* William's mother recorded that there was a Communion, but no sermon

[4] *tasking* Threshing. William, who took over diary-keeping during his cousin's holiday at Whissonsett 28 Dec.–4 Jan., adopted the usage of his mother and grandfather

[5] *in my side* The diarist deleted 'Stomack' and substituted 'Side'

above 'Gunton Thompson grinding all night' (29 Dec. 1794). The gable end of the miller and millwright's cottage is seen jutting forward at the south-east corner of the malthouse at Letheringsett (right). Built 1792 by William Hardy it was intended for his brewery clerk, but the Hardys dispensed with clerks and instead installed Gunton Thompson and his family 1792–98. The cottage was refaced in 1870 by William Hardy Cozens-Hardy.

The malthouse steep stands in the lean-to with the pantiled roof beside the cottage; the sawpit and cooperage built by William Hardy jnr are partially seen just to the left.

The photographer, Sydney Cozens-Hardy or his 15-year-old son Basil, took this view in the spring of 1901 from the front of their new home. Standing across the Glaven from the maltings this was Letheringsett Watermill's Mill House, built a century earlier for the Rouses and newly renamed Glavenside by the Cozens-Hardys. A watering place for stock runs down behind the railings to the left [*Cozens-Hardy Collection*]

GT, WH & boy Cleansed X morning, Capt Hall tasking. WH at a Ball, Holt, in Evening for the benefit of Mrs Overton.[1] Mr H at home all day with Gout in his Hand, Mrs H verry poorly.

MH {A} some Snow in the Morng, very fine day. Mr Hardy got alittle of the Gout in one of his hands, I poorly with pain in my Side.

[1] *Mrs Overton* Mary, née Hayton. She or her husband John (bur. Holt 13 Jan. 1799 aged 77), formerly of the King's Head, may have met some misfortune. They marr. Holt 13 Nov. 1759; he signed the register

below Mary Hardy aged 51: her portrait in 1785 by Huguier, a Frenchman staying at Holt. She is dressed in pale blue and dove grey for a visit to the 'playhouse' at Holt, where a company of travelling players performed in a barn behind the White Lion; her cap might be one of Ann Leak's advertised 'London fashions'.

No reference to a portrait of Henry Raven has been found in the Hardy and Cozens-Hardy archives; he may never have sat for one [*Cozens-Hardy Collection*]

above Mary Hardy aged 64: her portrait in 1798 by Immanuel, the Jewish artist whom she had befriended. She was by then a paid-up member of the Wesleyan Methodist society (congregation) at Cley, as perhaps she wished to proclaim by the sobriety of her dress and tall cap. The lace is delicately depicted, as also the rich sherry-coloured velvet of her gown.

The face remains recognisably the same across the divide of 13 years; it is her air that has changed. The diarist started attending Methodist meetings in 1795: at Briston (Calvinistic at first) from 4 Jan., and at Cley (Wesleyan) from 8 Nov.; Wesleyanism was supplanting Lady Huntingdon's Calvinistic Methodism across the area.

Henry regularly accompanied his aunt as driver of the open cart, and presumably joined her at the meetings. His parents, brothers and sisters were not drawn to Nonconformity, and there is no reason to suppose he was personally so inclined. Indeed his aunt's new-found Methodism seriously cut into his precious free time [*Cozens-Hardy Collection*]

1795

Mr Hardy and William went to Weybourne and Sheringham to get the serving the Camp with beer

MARY HARDY, 1 JUNE 1795

JANUARY 1, THURSDAY

William Hardy jnr R Bye at Edgfield & Stody with beer, T Boyce carrying deals into M [malt] Chamber forenoon & jobs in afternoon, Capt Hall tasking. 2 Carpenters here sawing &c [etc], G Thompson Grinding Malt for the brew. Jno Ram in M H [malthouse].

Mary Hardy A very sharp rime frost. Mr Hardy & W^{m} at home all day. My Side some thing better, we Irond. I taken with dimness in my eyes very bad eveng 8 . . .

JANUARY 2, FRIDAY

WHj R Bye at Hindolveston with beer, T Boyce & boy got home 2 Load of Furrze from Mr Jodrells hill.[1] Capt Hall tasking. A Cow calv'd in Morning. 2 Carpenters at work. G Thompson finish'd grinding Malt, Jno Ram in M H. M^{r} H at home all day, M^{rs} & WH rode out in Morning.[2] M^{r} & Mrs Burrell drank Tea here. R Bye loaded Waggon for Fakenham & Siderstone in Even^{g}.

JANUARY 3, SATURDAY

WHj R Bye to Fakenham & Siderstone with beer, T Boyce at Briston with beer. Jno Ram in M H, 2 Carpenters at

[1] *Jodrell* Henry (b. 1752, marr. 2 Sept. 1802 Johanna Elizabeth, daughter of John Weyland of Woodeaton, Oxon, d. 11 Mar. 1814), JP, the new owner of Bayfield Hall: see note for 15 Sept. 1794. A barrister, he served as Recorder of Gt Yarmouth 1792–1813. A Tory, he was elected Oct. 1796 MP for Gt Yarmouth, defeating Adm. Sir John Jervis and serving with Maj. Gen. William Loftus in the seat previously held by Brig. Gen. Howe (who had died at Port Royal, Jamaica, 20 July 1796). Defeated 1802 at Gt Yarmouth he swiftly secured the nomination for Bramber, Sussex, which seat he held 1802–12. He was appointed Deputy Lieutenant for Norfolk in 1803. For his role as a JP and advocate see *World*, vol. 3, chap. 6

[2] *rode out* 'For an airing', reported Mary Hardy. She had also been visited by the rector's wife in the morning

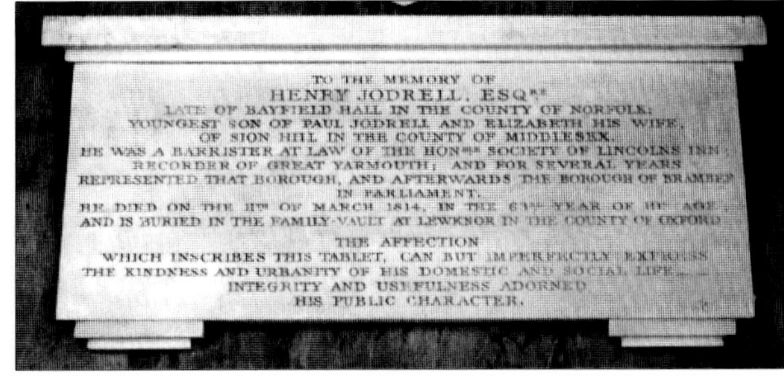
TO THE MEMORY OF
HENRY JODRELL, ESQ.RE
LATE OF BAYFIELD HALL IN THE COUNTY OF NORFOLK;
YOUNGEST SON OF PAUL JODRELL AND ELIZABETH HIS WIFE,
OF SION HILL IN THE COUNTY OF MIDDLESEX.
HE WAS A BARRISTER AT LAW OF THE HON.BLE SOCIETY OF LINCOLNS INN;
RECORDER OF GREAT YARMOUTH; AND FOR SEVERAL YEARS
REPRESENTED THAT BOROUGH, AND AFTERWARDS THE BOROUGH OF BRAMBER
IN PARLIAMENT.
HE DIED ON THE 11TH OF MARCH 1814, IN THE YEAR OF HIS AGE,
AND IS BURIED IN THE FAMILY-VAULT AT LEWKNOR IN THE COUNTY OF OXFORD
THE AFFECTION
WHICH INSCRIBES THIS TABLET, CAN BUT IMPERFECTLY
THE KINDNESS AND URBANITY OF HIS DOMESTIC AND SOCIAL LIFE,
INTEGRITY AND USEFULNESS ADORNED
HIS PUBLIC CHARACTER.

left **The memorial to Henry Jodrell in Letheringsett Church bears near-identical wording to that in Lewknor Church, Oxon, except for the addition of the final personal tribute probably by his widow Johanna. She remained at Bayfield Hall and married George Nathaniel Best** [*MB · 2011*]

above The inn board and spectacular ironwork of the former White Lion at Holt. James William Skiffins moved from the Black Boys at Holt in 1795 to take John Howard's place at the White Lion (4–5 Jan.), Mr Clark and then Francis Wakefield taking over at the Black Boys. The White Lion was one of Holt's leading inns, patronised by the justices, with a playhouse–barn, and having a postchaise for hire. Howard was moving to an even more prominent Hardy establishment elsewhere [*MB · 2011*]

work. Edwd Hall here in forenoon with a Clock.[1] M^r^ & WH at Holt Market afternoon.]]

JANUARY 4, SUNDAY

Henry Raven M^rs^ & WH whent to Briston. H Raven came from Whissonsett Evening.

MH A Sharp frost, fine day. All went to our Church foornoon, Mr Burrell preach'd. Mr Hardy rid up to Holt foornoon to settle some buesiness with Howard at the Lion, came back to dinner.[2] I & W^m^ went to Meeting at Briston afternoon, came home eveng 5. H Raven came home even 8. Dimness in my eyes eveng 7.

JANUARY 5, MONDAY

HR R Bye to Brampton with beer, T Boyce to Wiverton & Salthouse with beer. Jno Ram in Malthouse. Boy got up aloade of turnips & whent to Mr Sturleys with Malt. M^r^ H gone to Burnham [Market] with Howard, WH & Miss H gone to Mr Flowers.

MH A sharp frost, fine day. Mr Hardy set of for Burnham with Mr Moor in Howds Post Chaise Morng 8 to settle Howard in A Publick House there, did not come home that Night. W^m^ & MA went to Mr Flow-

[1] *Edward Hall* (Bur. Weybourne 25 Jan. 1797), innkeeper of the Crown; his first wife Anne, née Cranefield, had been bur. 19 Mar. 1792 aged 37. Five children (Samuel, Edward, Elizabeth, Elizabeth, Samuel) were bapt. Weybourne 1780–89; only Edward and the younger Elizabeth survived infancy. In 1791 Hall had assigned his estate and effects for his creditors (*Norw. Merc.* 9 Apr. 1791).

Hall marr. (2) 1794 Martha Hardy, of Weybourne. The widowed Mrs Hall may have tried to run the Crown (see entry for 9 Oct. 1797), but the register shows that by Old Michaelmas 1797 Stephen Eade had taken over (NRO: C/Sch 1/16). The house then lost its connection with Letheringsett. See also notes for 14 Oct. and 13 Nov. 1793

[2] *Howard* John, innkeeper of the White Lion at Holt from 1786, his children appearing in the Holt registers; he was about to move to the Pitt Arms (later the Hoste Arms) at Burnham Market. His wife Mary, née Cawdwell, was buried Burnham Market 16 Feb. 1806 aged 47. He took over at Burnham from Elizabeth Ballard, widow of William. William (bur. there 3 Mar. 1794 aged 56) is shown in the alehouse register 1792, Elizabeth 1794 (NRO: C/Sch 1/16); she was bur. 28 Dec. 1794 aged 48.

At the end of 1794 Mrs Ballard was winding up her affairs, calling in all the money owed to her; she

ers at Sheringham Morng 11 to a Ball there.[1] Dimness in my eyes in the night. A Sale at the late Mrs Jewells at Holt [2] . . .

JANUARY 6, TUESDAY

HR R Bye to Corpusta with beer, T Boyce unload«ing» furze & chopping sticks. G Thompson dressing Wheat Stones, H Raven grinding Malt for Bin. Mr Kendals [Kendle's] men Carting Muck out of Yard. Jno Ram in Malthouse, Capt Hall trashing. Mr H came home from Burnham, W & Miss H came home from Mr Flowers.

JANUARY 7, WEDNESDAY

HR R Bye, Boy & H Raven in brewhouse, G Thompson dressing Wheat stones, WH brewing. Thos Boyce after jobs, Capt Hall trashing, Jno Ram in Malthouse. Mr & Mrs Sheldrake drank tea here.

JANUARY 8, THURSDAY

HR R Bye to Cromer with beer, Thos Boyce to Blakney for seven bags of Hops.[3] Jno Ram in M H, Capt Hall trashing. H Raven & G Thompson Cleansed `//. Mr H at home all day, WH whent to Holt Evening. Boy verry ill.

died suddenly a few days later (two notices, *Norw. Merc.* 3 Jan. 1795). See also note for 28 Oct. 1796

[1] *ball* This was 21-year-old Mary Ann's last recorded dance; William was still dancing in 1808. Mother and daughter adopted a rather more austere lifestyle

[2] *sale* It resumed over the four days 5–6 and 9–10 Jan., 'the former impediments being now removed' (*Norw. Merc.* 3 Jan. 1795)

[3] *bag of hops* A sack weighing 2½ cwt (127 kg), and measuring 7½ feet high by 8 feet in circumference (2·3 and 2·4 metres). Seven bags would prove a testing errand for one man

left Briston: the successor to the chapel attended by Mary Hardy (4 Jan.). A new Calvinistic Methodist chapel for Briston had been built in 1783 by Thomas Mendham on this site; this Wesleyan successor dates from 1811–12. Mendham died in 1793, and his meeting later adopted the Arminian Methodism of the Wesleyans. Briston's young local preacher Josiah Hill (b.*c.*1773) soon became a full-time itinerant Wesleyan preacher.

The convoluted tale of Briston Methodism is told in volume 3 of *Mary Hardy and her World* [*MB* · *2011*]

JANUARY 9, FRIDAY

HR R Bye to Kettlestone with beer, T Boyce helping to Cleanse & got up aloade of Clay. G Thompson, H Raven & WH Cleansed X. Boy went home verry ill. Jn° Ram in M H, Capt Hall tasking. Mr & Miss & WH at Holt afternoon.

MH A Close drisley day. Mr Hardy, MA & Wm went to A Sale of the late Mrs Jewells at Holt afternoon, drank tea at Mr Sheldrakes, came home past 9. MA bought a sett of China Ornement for a Chimney piece for 4/-.

JANUARY 10, SATURDAY

HR R Bye to Sherringham with beer. T Boyce got up aloade of turnips, a D° [load] of Clay & other jobs. Jn° Ram in Malthouse, Capt Hall dressing barley. Chas Kendals man Carting muck out of Yard. Mr, Mrs & Miss Hardy at Holt to dine, WH at Holt Market afternoon.

MH A very Sharp frost, fine day. Mr Hardy, I & MA walkd to the Sale at Holt foornoon, bought 13 Silver Table Spoons at 5/3d pr ounce, 31 oz 10 «?drams» £7 15*s* 5½*d*, a pair of Salts at 5/2d 3 oz £9 1*s* 10*d*, 4 Salt Spoons at 7/2d pr ounce, Cost 6/9½d [6*s* 9½*d*].[1] We drank tea at Mr Bartells, came home eveng 9, Mr Hardy came home eveng 11 . . .

JANUARY 11, SUNDAY

HR Mrs H & H Raven whent to Briston, Mr & WH to Holt Church, no prayers at our Church.

JANUARY 12, MONDAY

HR R Bye to Holt with beer & jobs. T Boyce here in Morning, whent to his Club.[2] Jn° Ram in M House, G Thompson grinding Malt for brew. Mr H at Mr Burrells Audit.[3] W & Miss H at Holt to tea at Johnson's. Mr Wood, a Rider, Cal'd here forenoon.

JANUARY 13, TUESDAY

HR T Boyce at work in brewhouse, R Bye after jobs & Loaded for Burnham. HR whent to Edgefield with Malt. Jn° Ram in Malthouse, Capt Hall trashing. Mr H at home all Day. WH roade to Gresham & Sheringham.

JANUARY 14, WEDNESDAY

HR R Bye to Burnham with beer. G Thompson, H Raven & T Boyce in brewhouse, WH brewing. Jn° Ram in M House, Capt Hall trashing. Mr H at home all day.

[1] *tablespoons etc* The MS is very difficult to decipher. The diarist has inserted additions to the text above each line without marking where these are to appear; the writing is cramped, and the significance of the figures unclear. As well as itemising the purchases she gives their weight and their cost per ounce, there being 16 drams to the ounce

[2] *club* It is not stated whether this is a new purse or box club, or the old one which had left the King's Head at Letheringsett after the dispute with Richard Mayes (13 Jan. 1794)

[3] *audit* A tithe frolic, held usually at the King's Head at Letheringsett. It lasted over 12 hours, William Hardy setting off in time for dinner and arriving home past 2 am

[4] *rider* Probably the rider *for* Mr Wood, the London chemist (note for 17 June 1795)

MH A Sharp frost. Mr Hardy at home all day, Wm Brewd. Some Snow fell in the Night. Mrs Burrell taken Ill . . .

JANUARY 15, THURSDAY

HR R Bye to Hindolvestone with beer, T Boyce to Cley with beer & Bro^t^ home 3½ Hun^d^ ruff tiles [3½ hundredweight of roof tiles].[1] Jno Ram in Malthouse, G Thompson, HR & WH Cleansed `//. Capt Hall trashing. M^r^ H at home all Day.

JANUARY 16, FRIDAY

HR R Bye to Edgefield with beer, T Boyce at work at home. G Thompson, HR, WH & M^r^ H Cleansed XX. Jno Ram in M House, Capt Hall tasking.

JANUARY 17, SATURDAY

HR R Bye to Runton &. Cromer with beer, T Boyce at work at home. Jno Ram in M H, Capt Hall tasking. M^r^ & WH at Holt Market.

MH A Sharp frost, frequent storms of Snow. Mr Hardy & W^m^ walkd up to Holt Markt afternoon, came home eveng past 9. Snow in the Night. Mrs Burrell very bad, Dr Heath sent for from Fakenham.[2]

JANUARY 18, SUNDAY

HR M^r^ & WH at Holt afternoon, no prayers at our Church.

MH A Sharp frost, snow drifted, no service at our Church. Mr Hardy & W^m^ walkd up to Holt afternoon expecting to go to Church but there was no service, came home to tea.

JANUARY 19, MONDAY

HR R Bye to Stody & loaded for Stalham, T Boyce after jobs. Jno Ram in Malthouse, Capt Hall trashing. M^r^ H at home all Day. W & Miss H to Holt morning, WH roade out afternoon.

MH A sharp frost, close day. Mr Hardy at home all day. W^m^ & MA rid up to Holt foornoon in Chaise, came back to dinner. W^m^ went up afternoon to carry the Banking Book & some other business, drank tea at Mr Bartells, came home eveng 9.

JANUARY 20, TUESDAY

HR R Bye to Stalham with beer, T Boyce to Holt with beer & jobs. Jno Ram in M H, Capt Hall trashing. WH & Miss H at Holt afternoon, M^r^ H at home all Day.

facing page **The magnificent tower of Fakenham Church can be seen for miles around, but in the town itself it is hemmed in by the market place and surrounding houses. Dr John Heath attended both Elizabeth Burrell and Mary Hardy in their last months.**

Unusually for rural areas a physician rather than a surgeon, he was to bury his young wife and stillborn child in the sanctuary of this church [*MB · 1999*]

---

[1] *roof tiles* Possibly 350 tiles but more probably 3½ cwt of tiles, hundred being a synonym for hundredweight

[2] *Dr Heath* John Heath, MD, of Fakenham. His ledger stone in the parish church shows that he 'died at Bath after a lingering illness' on 9 June 1823 in his 60th year and was buried in his brother's church at Inkberge [Inkberrow], Worcs.

He attended Mary Hardy in her final illness a few months before and then after the death of his 33-year-old wife while giving birth to a stillborn daughter 13 July 1808; they had married 4 Sept. 1807.

Mrs Frances Heath, daughter of Charles Money of Raynham, and her child lie under the sanctuary step at St Peter and St Paul, Fakenham (*Norw. Merc.* 16 July 1808; *Diary 4*: 16 July 1808)

MH A very Sharp frost, snowd great part of the Day. W^m^ & MA met some Company at Mrs Jenes's [Jennis's] at Holt, home evg 9. Mr Hardy went to Dobsons Club, home 9 . . .

JANUARY 21, WEDNESDAY

HR R Bye home from Stalham, T Boyce to Waybourn with beer. Jno Ram in M H [malthouse], Capt Hall trashing. WH, G Thompson & HR rightsided the workshop.[1] Ja^s^ Skiffins came & Orderd 4 Nog. M^r^ H at home all Day.

JANUARY 22, THURSDAY

HR R Bye to Holt with beer, T Boyce after Jobs. Mr Youngmans lad planing dales [deals]. Jno Ram in M House, Capt Hall trashing. M^r^ H at Holt all Day, WH at Holt afternoon.

MH Extreme sharp day, snowd almost all day. Mr Hardy walkd up to Holt foornoon to the Quarter Sissions, was on the Grand Jury, dind at the Lion.[2] W^m^ went up after dinner, drank tea at Mr Bartells, both came home eve 9 . . .

JANUARY 23, FRIDAY

HR R Bye very ill, T Boyce after Jobs. G Thompson Grinding Malt for brew, Water Wheel froze.[3] Jno Ram in M House, Capt Hall trashing. M^r^ & WH at home all Day. Mr Youngmans lad planing dales.

[1] *rightsided* Possibly set to rights or put in order, but it is more likely to mean that they balanced the accounts.
Robert Forby writes that 'to right' is to set to rights, whereas 'to rightside' is to state and balance an account, the phrase being 'very familar in the mouths of those who can neither keep nor even read a written account; but by mere exercise of memory can *rightside* it with the utmost precision, though it consist of a multitude of minute particulars' (R. Forby, *The Vocabulary of East Anglia*, vol. 2, pp. 276–7). The fact that William had been busy with the banking book two days earlier may lend weight to Forby's definition

[2] *grand jury* See note for 16 Oct. 1794

[3] *froze* Froze up; froze solid. This would happen to the pumps as well

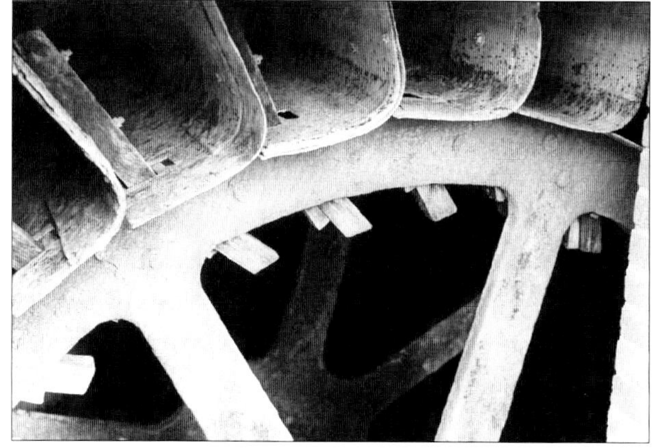

right 'Waterwheel froze', (23 Jan. 1795). The brewery wheel, installed by William Hardy in 1784, was destroyed in the 1936 fire. This wheel powers Letheringsett Watermill, the mill rebuilt by Richard Rouse's son Zebulon in 1798. The wheel appears from its design to have been rebuilt in the 19th century [_MB · 1989_]

above The downstream end of the brewery waterwheel tunnel emerges under the arch to the right and rejoins the Glaven by the 1818 road bridge at Letheringsett, the height of the cascade echoing the drop in the tunnel by the wheel. The arch marks the southeast corner of the Hardys' garden in 1795 [*MB · 1998*]

JANUARY 24, SATURDAY

HR R Bye very ill, T Boyce after jobs, G Thompson at work in Water wheel. Jn° Ram in M H, Capt Hall trashing. T Youngmans lad planing dales. Mr & WH at Holt market afternoon.

MH Extreme sharp frost, bright day, snow very deep. Mr Hardy walkd to Holt Market, Wm rode, came home eveng 9. I walkd to speak to Mrs Burrell . . .

JANUARY 25, SUNDAY

HR Famaly all to Church afternoon. WH & HR whent to Hempsted to Skate & drank tea at Mr Bartells.[1]

JANUARY 26, MONDAY

HR G Thompson, H Raven, T Boyce in brewhouse, WH brewing. R Bye to Briston with beer. Thos Youngmans lad planen dales [planing deals]. Jn° Ram in Malthouse, Capt Hall after jobs.

JANUARY 27, TUESDAY

HR R Bye to Wells with beer, T Boyce to Dawling [Field Dalling] with beer. Jn° Ram in M H, G Thompson, H Raven & WH Cleanse'd `// morning. Capt Hall muck-

[1] *to skate* Probably on the frozen Glaven. Upriver at Hempstead-by-Holt it is a smaller stream, named the Hempstead Beck, which comes down from Baconsthorpe to be augmented later by other headstreams at Hunworth and Thornage

ing out pigs houses, Thos Youngmans lad planen dales. M^{r} H at home all Day. Deb Ram married forenoon.[1]

MH A very fine thaw. Mr Hardy went to Holt afternoon to see to the valuing Howards goods.[2] W^{m} went up after tea, came home Eveng past 9. Deb Ram was Maried . . .

JANUARY 28, WEDNESDAY

HR T Boyce after jobs, R Bye drunk. Jno Ram in MH, Capt Hall trashing. G Thompson, HR & WH Cleanse'd XX. M^{r} H at home all Day. Hammon from Saxlingham cal^{d} morning to bleed a horse.[3] T Youn^{gn} Lad finnish planen Dales [finished planing deals].

JANUARY 29, THURSDAY

HR R Bye & T Boyce at muck cart morning, whent to Holt with beer & Loaded for South Repps. Jno Ram in M H, Capt Hall tasking. M^{r} & M^{rs}, Miss & WH at Holt afternoon. Mr Young^{s} [? Mr Youngman's lad] at work part of Day.

above The mechanism for raising and closing the sluice gate at the entrance to the waterwheel tunnel, an offshoot from the Glaven towards the south end of the malthouse's east wall. From this point the culverted channel flows north-west under the malthouse to the yard, thence to the site of the wheel, and finally under the busy road to the main river again [*MB · 1989*]

1 *Deb Ramm* It was very unusual for Henry to include snippets of village news, but Deborah Ramm was the daughter of the senior maltster, his old boss in the malthouse 1793–94. She was bapt. Letheringsett 16 Feb. 1765 and had two illegitimate sons: Samuel (b. and bapt. 24 Sept. 1784), and William (b. 18 Dec. 1788, bapt. 26 Jan. 1789, bur. 23 Aug. 1789), William's burial entry noting that his mother had sworn William Margetson as father. Her elder son, who called himself Samuel Wright (bur. 15 Nov. 1816), worked as a Letheringsett labourer.

Deb and Rebecca Ramm (bapt. Letheringsett 17 Aug. 1768) were reported in the *Norwich Mercury* of 20 Oct. 1792 to be 'notorious prostitutes' held on remand in Walsingham Bridewell. Rebecca's parents Matthew and Sarah had died in 1773 and 1774. Deb married 27 Jan. 1795 Thomas Balls, single, of St Nicholas, King's Lynn; both made marks and seem then to have left the parish. William Dobson stood witness, and there is no suggestion in the diary that John Ramm had time off to attend the wedding

2 *Howard's goods* Furniture and fittings in a public house belonged usually to the innkeeper. If he did not take them with him they would be offered for sale to the new tenant or to the public following a valuation

3 *Hammond* See note for 6 May 1794

JANUARY 30, FRIDAY

HR R Bye & T Boyce to South Repps with beer, Jno Ram in M House. Ja^s^ Broughton Casting & Skreening of cumbs [culms].[1] Mr Thompson grinding Malt for brew.[2] M^r^ H at home all day.

MH A severe frost, bright day. Mr Hardy & W^m^ at home all day. Our 2 Men went to Southreps with Beer, the roades being almost impassible did not git home till 3 in the morng.

JANUARY 31, SATURDAY

HR R Bye got 3 Bar^s^ [barrels] beer in at Dobson's, T Boyce got up aload of turnips. Ja^s^ Broughton after jobs, Jno Ram in Malthouse. M^r^ & WH at Holt market afternoon, Miss H walked to Holt afternoon.

MH A very sharp frost, close day. Mr Hardy & W^m^ walkd to Holt Mark^t^ Afternoon, came home eveng past 9, MA walkd up & came home to tea. Ann Browne went away . . .

FEBRUARY 1, SUNDAY

Henry Raven R Bye cleaned the Copper, G Thompson got up Liquor for brew. Famaly all to Church forenoon.

FEBRUARY 2, MONDAY

HR R Bye, Ja^s^ Broughton, G Thomp^n^ & H Raven in brewhouse, WH brewing. Jno Ram in Malthouse, Thos Boyce to Fakenham with beer. Capt Hall tasking. M^r^ H at Home all Day.

FEBRUARY 3, TUESDAY

HR R Bye to Cromer with beer, T Boyce to Bale & Thornage with beer. Jno Ram in Malthouse, Ja^s^ Broughton after jobs. G Thompson, HR & WH Cleansed `//. M^r^ H at Holt all Day. Mr Youngman at work half a day.

Mary Hardy Snowd all day. Mr Hardy walkd up to Holt foornoon to meet Howard, came home 10. W^m^ at home all day. Levi the Jew & his Son drank tea here.[3] Maids & Betty Woods washd 5 weeks Linn.

FEBRUARY 4, WEDNESDAY

HR R Bye to upper Sherringham with beer, T Boyce to Wiverton with beer & Blakeny for 1½ Chald. coles from Z Rouse's.[4] Jno Ram in M H, Ja^s^ Broughton after jobs.

[1] *Broughton* James Broughton snr, labourer, was buried Letheringsett 23 June 1813 aged 'between 70 and 80'. He was probably the father of the labourer of the same name, father or son working for the Hardys in the 1790s when they were short-staffed.

James jnr became a weekly labourer for the Hardys 16 Oct. 1797. His wife Mary, née Waterson, was buried Letheringsett 2 Aug. 1805; their children are recorded in the registers. On their marriage at Thornage 8 Nov. 1801 he had signed with a shaky hand

[2] *'Mr' Thompson* Perhaps a continuation of a private joke between pupil and miller, Gunton Thompson calling for a little more respect (see note for 28 Aug. 1794)

[3] *Levi* Jacob Levi, a Wells auctioneer. There was no mention in the press of an auction at the White Lion, and he and his son may have been helping with the valuation

[4] *Rouse* Zebulon (bur. Cley 27 Sept. 1840 aged 75), variously Blakeney coal merchant, Letheringsett miller and Cley land surveyor, elder son of Richard and nephew of the Hardys' trusted farm servant, of the same name, at Coltishall (see note for 5 Oct. 1794). He marr. Cley 8 Mar. 1808 Lydia Starling, spinster, of Cley, described by Mary Hardy as Mr Kalière's daughter (*Diary 4*; she was presumably stepdaughter to the Dutch surgeon and

former bath owner: see note for 10 Oct. 1796).

Children bapt. at Cley were: Mary Ann, 10 June 1808; Sarah Anne, [?31] Oct. 1809 (bur. 31 Dec. 1809); Richard, 8 Aug. 1812; Thomas, 14 Mar. 1814; John, 15 Apr. 1815 (bur. 20 July 1815); John, 19 Nov. 1816 (bur. 5 Dec. 1816); Tabitha, 17 Nov. 1817; Lydia, 21 Sept. 1819 (bur. 6 Dec. 1819); Peter Fitt, 9 Dec. 1820 (bur. 10 Jan. 1821); and Ruth, 11 June 1825.

In 1798 Zeb Rouse, a Methodist, introduced singing into Letheringsett Church, rebuilt Letheringsett Watermill, and registered its granary as a meeting house (*Diary 4*). Bankrupted *c.*1800, he was held in the King's Bench Prison, Southwark. He was confined in the Bethel at Norwich in 1804: see note for 13 June 1794

G Thompson, HR & WH Cleanse'd X. M[r] & WH whent to Sherringham.

MH A very sharp frost, snow very deep. A bright foornoon, snowd all the Afternoon. M[r] Hardy & W[m] went to lower Sheringham in the Chaise, sold M[r] Barcham asmall piece of Land for a Coal Yard,[1] had a cruel Journey home, the snow being very deep & drifted, came home eveng 7.

FEBRUARY 5, THURSDAY

HR R Bye & T Boyce to Hindolvestone with beer, Jn[o] Ram whent home ill afternoon. Ja[s] Broughton at work here forenoon, G Thompson grinding M for brew. M[r] & WH at home all Day.

MH Sharp frost, Chearly day. M[r] Hardy & W[m] at home all day. The Snow the deepest that have been known for many years.[2]

[1] *Barcham* Benjamin, shopkeeper and merchant. In 1802 he declined shopkeeping, selling that part of his business to Charles Woodrow, liquor merchant, from Hindolveston; Barcham still continued with the timber, coal and skin trade at Sheringham (*Norw. Merc.* 16 Oct. 1802). His yard adjoined the Hardys' Crown, being handy for the colliers which would beach on an ebbing tide to be unloaded. See also note for 30 Apr. 1794

[2] *snow* The harsh winter and late spring were to lay the foundations for the

FEBRUARY 6, FRIDAY

HR R Bye to Corpusta & Edgefield with beer, T Boyce to Holt with beer & filld aload of muck. Ja^s^ Broughton at work in garden. Jno Ram gone home ill, HR in M House. G Thompson grinding Malt for brew. M^r^ H at home all Day, WH drank tea at Mr Forsters.

MH A very sharp frost, bright day. Mr Hardy at home all day. W^m^ drank tea at Mr Forsters of Bayfield, came home eveng past 10, heard Mr Buckle of Cringleford, Bro^t^ [brother] to Mrs Forster, was dead [1] . . .

FEBRUARY 7, SATURDAY

HR R Bye at muck cart forenoon, to Gunthorp afternoon. T Boyce D^o^ D^o^ D^o^ [at muck cart] all Day, Ja^s^ Broughton & Boy filling. M^r^ & WH at Holt afternoon. Jno Ram in Malthouse.

FEBRUARY 8, SUNDAY

HR R Bye loaded for Syderstone. Famaly all to Church afternoon. Mr Chrismas & Mr Banyard calld here.

FEBRUARY 9, MONDAY

HR R Bye to Syderstone with beer, G Thomp. kendle'd [kindled] the fire to brew. T Boyce in brewhouse forenoon, to Salthouse afternoon. HR & Boy in brewhouse, WH brewing. Jas Broughton «at» jobs, Jno Ram in M H. M^r^ H at home all Day.

FEBRUARY 10, TUESDAY

HR R Bye & T Boyce car'd of Cleanse of beer & loaded for Burnham. Jno Ram in M H, Capt Hall dressing. Ja^s^ Broughton at work in garden, G Thomp. Cleanse'd `//. M^r^ H at Dobsens [Dobson's] Evening, WH at home all Day. Mr Forster drank tea here.

MH The thaw still continue, Water very high in the River & Meadows. Mr Hardy at home all day.

FEBRUARY 11, WEDNESDAY

HR R Bye and Thos Boyce to Burnham with beer, Ja^s^ Broughton & Boy at work in garden. Jno Ram in M H. G Thompson, M^r^ & WH Cleansed X beer, H Raven Stripping Meal. Capt Hall dressing.

MH A Close dry day. Mr Hardy & W^m^ at home all day. T Boyce, J Broughton & Boy getting Muck into Garden . . .

facing page The iconic Norfolk image: Cley Mill, seen across the reedbeds of the silted Glaven estuary.

The Customs House, coal wharves, cinder ovens, malthouses and granaries of the port used to straggle along the hard beside this mill, which was built soon after Mary Hardy's death.

After a highly colourful early career, the former coal merchant and miller Zeb Rouse settled down in Cley with his wife and growing family to pursue his new profession of land surveyor.

He was from a family of millers. The lasting legacy Zeb gave the Glaven Valley is the towering brick watermill erected by him at Letheringsett in 1798.

From the late 1980s, under Michael Thurlow, it has followed its old calling of producing stoneground flour by water power [*MB · 2011*]

---

failure of the 1795 harvest, and thus for the bread riots of Dec. 1795 and Jan. 1796

---

1 *Mr Buckle* Thrower; he had died the previous day: see note for 25 Mar. 1794.

His widow died 21 Apr. 1806 aged 76 (*Norw. Merc.* 7 Feb. 1795, 26 Apr. 1806)

facing page Letheringsett, 26 Aug. 1912: the maltings in the severe floods. Smoke drifts up from Thompson's old cottage (centre), the fire lit perhaps in an attempt to embark on drying operations; the twin cowls of the malt-kilns are silhouetted against the sky.

The photographer—probably Sydney or Basil Cozens-Hardy, or perhaps a professional from Holt—is standing in the gardens of Glavenside on what was usually the lawn, the ornamental rustic bridge (centre right) clearly marking the River Glaven's accustomed channel. Floods and high water levels are sometimes recorded by Mary Hardy, as on 10 Feb. 1795 [*Cozens-Hardy Collection*]

FEBRUARY 12, THURSDAY

HR R Bye & Thos Boyce got barley out of barn & got over brew of Malt & Loaded for Wells. Jas Broughton spreading Muck, Jno Ram in M H. Capt H dressd & got away his corn, G Thompson grinding Malt for brew. WH whent of for Whissonsett forenoon 10.[1]

FEBRUARY 13, FRIDAY

HR R Bye to Wells with beer. T Boyce to Cley with Do [beer] & brot home 2 Chald Cinders from Mr Elliss [Ellis's]. Jno Ram in M H, Jas Broughton spreading muck. G Thompson finnish'd grinding Malt for brew. H Raven to Holt afternoon, Mr H at home all day.

MH A Close day. Mr Hardy at home all day. Wm came & Robt Raven came home from Whisonsett eveng 9, Mr Goggs of Whisonsett Died this Afternoon abt 4 oClock Aged 63. Froze at Night.

FEBRUARY 14, SATURDAY

HR Bye to Sherringham with beer, Thos Boyce to Hinderingham with beer. Jno Ram in M H, Jas Broughton spreading Muck. T Baldwin to Holt forenoon with beer.[2] WH, Miss H & Robt Raven at Holt morning, Mr H, WH & R Raven at Holt market afternoon.

MH A Sharp frost. MA rid up to Holt foorn, came home to dinner. Mrs Sheldrake came aftern to alter & repair my Gowns, Slept here.[3] Mr Hardy & Wm walkd to Holt Market aftern, came home Even 9.

Mary Hardy's visit to Whissonsett

15–23 February 1795

FEBRUARY 15, SUNDAY

HR [at Letheringsett] Mr & Mrs Hardy & Robt Raven sett of for Whissonsett forenoon 11 oClock. R Bye & T Boyce Card 4 «barrels» of Nog to Dobsons keeping room.[4] Chymnay [chimney] got on fire about Noon. Miss & WH & H Raven whent to Church forenoon.

MH A very Close day. Mr Hardy & I set of for Whisonsett Morng 11, got there evng past 1, Dind, drank tea, Supt & Slept at Sister Goggs.

FEBRUARY 16, MONDAY

HR R Bye, G Thompson, H Raven & boy in brewhouse, WH brewing. T Boyce to Beckhigh with beer, Jno Ram

[1] *Whissonsett* Mary Hardy noted that William was also calling at Gunthorpe and Fakenham (on market day)

[2] *Baldwin* Thomas Baldwin had broken his arm on 23 Dec. 1794. William took care to give him undemanding tasks in the early days back at work, while retaining Baldwin's replacement Thomas Boyce

[3] *gowns* Probably mourning dresses. The diarist had not worn mourning since her severe illness of Aug.–Oct. 1793, and she may have lost weight

[4] *keeping room* Sitting room; the cellar at the King's Head could have flooded

in Malthouse. Capt Hall at work in garden. Mrs Sheldrake drank tea here. Stonemason came & swept the keeping Room Chymney morning. Mr Goggs buried to Day.

MH [at Whissonsett] A very close foggy day. We were at Mrs Goggs all day, Mr Goggs was Buried.

FEBRUARY 17, TUESDAY

HR R Bye to Edgefield with beer. T Boyce ploughing forenoon, to Holt with beer afternoon. G Thomn, HR & T Baldwin Cleanse'd `//. Jno Ram in M H, Capt Hall trashing. WH at Gunthorp.

MH A sharp wind frost. We dind & drank tea at Brother Ravens, supt & slept at Mr Goggs.[1]

FEBRUARY 18, WEDNESDAY

HR R Bye & T Boyce to Briston for two Loade of Hay. G Thompson & HR Cleanse'd X. Jno Ram in M H, Capt Hall trashing. T Baldwin came. WH to Sharringham [Sheringham].

MH A very sharp wind frost. We drank tea at Sister Ravens at the Hall. Heard Mr Bengm Crofts of Gresnal [Gressenhall] was killd by a fall from his Horse [2] . . .

FEBRUARY 19, THURSDAY

HR R Bye & T Boyce to Briston for hay. Jno Ram in M H, Capt Hall tasking. G Thompson grinding M for brew. WH at home all Day.

[1] *Mr Goggs's* The former Henry Goggs jnr (see the family tree at app. D3.A, fig. D3.6). The younger son was quickly granted his father's style, 'Mr', and inherited the Whissonsett farm

[2] *Crofts* Benjamin jnr, the younger son of the Hardys' old friend Revd Benjamin Crofts (Rector of Gressenhall, also Rector of Whissonsett 1789–95), the younger Benjamin serving as Curate of Whissonsett.

Educ. Scarning School, he went to Caius College, Cambridge 1774 aged 19, matric. 1777, BA 1779; ordained deacon 1777, priest 1785. His curacy of Gressenhall 1777 was his first; later curacies included Themelthorpe, Twyford, E. Bradenham (where his brother John was rector: see note for 23 Aug. 1795), also Horningtoft (serving Robert Forby), Brisley, and Billingford. The visitation returns show stipends in the region of £25–30 p.a (eg DN/VIS 33a/1, Brisley deanery visitation 1794, Horningtoft return). In 1791 he married Penelope Cobb of Hoe.

The *Norwich Mercury* reported the accident 28 Feb. 1795 in terms which although strictly correct—the father as the elder Revd Mr Crofts not requiring any initial—could have made it unclear to readers which clergyman had died: 'On Wednesday se'nnight as the Revd Mr B. Crofts was returning from Fakenham to Gressenhall he fell from his horse between Whissonsett and Oxwick, by which he fractured his head and dislocated his neck, and was found dead early on Thursday morning, with his horse standing near him. His cash, some bills, and watch, being all found safe, leaves no reason to suppose that any person had molested him, but that he certainly fell down in a fit.'

For the Crofts family this was the third death in a few months. Revd John's eldest daughter had died at Fakenham in July 1794, and his brother-in-law Peter Elwin jnr of Briston had died aged 43 that same month (*Norw. Merc.* 2 Aug., 19 July 1794). Added to these misfortunes their sister Betsy's husband Revd John Wilson was as usual in straitened circumstances, turning to brother clergy for loans (J. Woodforde, *The Diary of a Country Parson*, ed. J. Beresford (Oxford Univ. Press, 1929), vol. 4, pp. 198, 265, 15 May 1795, 12 Mar. 1796)

FEBRUARY 20, FRIDAY

HR R Bye to Holt with beer forenoon, doing nothing afternoon. T Boyce got up a load of turnips forenoon, nothing afternoon.[1] Jn° Ram M H, Cap[t] Hall tasking, G Thompson grinding M for brew. WH at home all Day.

FEBRUARY 21, SATURDAY

HR R Bye & T Boyce at muck cart & whent to Thornage with beer Evening. Ja[s] Broughton & Boy filling muck «cart». Jn° Ram M H, Cap[t] Hall trashing. WH at Holt afternoon.

FEBRUARY 22, SUNDAY

HR Famaly to Church afternoon. R Bartle drank tea here, H Raven whent to Whisonsett. M[r] Webster from Norwich.

MH A frosty morng, a slow thaw Afternoon. We went to Church foornoon. M[r] Hardy dind & drank tea at Bro[t] Ravens. M[r] Goggs & I rid to Fakenham afternoon, went to the Chappel & went back to Whisonsett to tea.[2]

---

1 *nothing afternoon* The weather may have prevented outdoor work. At Whissonsett Mary Hardy recorded high winds and snowfalls

2 *chapel* On 20 July 1773 'a certain house belonging to Mary Frankling, spinster, commonly called the New Chapel' was registered as a meeting house; her sister Elizabeth Franklin's house at Hunworth was similarly registered 9 June 1774 (NRO: DN/DIS 1/2, p. 23, f. 25). (Elizabeth Franklin, later Mrs Grieves, also founded the Briston chapel of 1775 as part of Lady

FEBRUARY 23, MONDAY

HR R Bye unloading hay & to Holt with beer, T Boyce to Fakenham with beer. Broughton & Boy unloading [?the hay] & after jobs. G Thompson dressing flower & T Baldwin filling hopper. M^{r} & M^{rs} H & H Raven came from Whissonsett. Mr Webster & WH trye'd the horse, Mr Webster gone home.

MH The thaw still continue, Close day. We sett of for home abt Noon, got home eveng past 3. Mr Webster from Norwich came last Night & Slept here.

[LETHERINGSETT]

FEBRUARY 24, TUESDAY

HR R Bye to South Repps with beer. Ja^{s} Broughton spreading Muck, T Boyce ploughing. WH & Miss H roade to Holt afternoon in Chaise. Jno Ram in Malthouse, Capt Hall trashing.

MH A very close day, thaw still continue. Mr Hardy & W^{m} at home all day, changd our Chaise Horse with Mr Webster & gave him 11 Guineas in exchange, he went away foornoon.

Huntingdon's Connexion, with Thomas Mendham as minister, that chapel adopting Independency in 1783).

The Calvinistic Methodists active in the management of the Fakenham chapel, which still stands in the town centre, included Henry Goggs snr and jnr and Charles Case snr (father-in-law of Mary Ann Hardy's future sister-in-law Elizabeth, née Cozens: see note for 20 July 1797).

Henry Goggs snr was admitted as copyhold tenant 10 Nov. 1779, and his son as trustee 20 July 1795 (NRO: MS 15403, 44B, Fakenham Lancaster manor court book, pp. 66–8). For Mary Parker, née Franklin, and Thomas Mendham see *World*, vol. 3, chaps 3 and 4

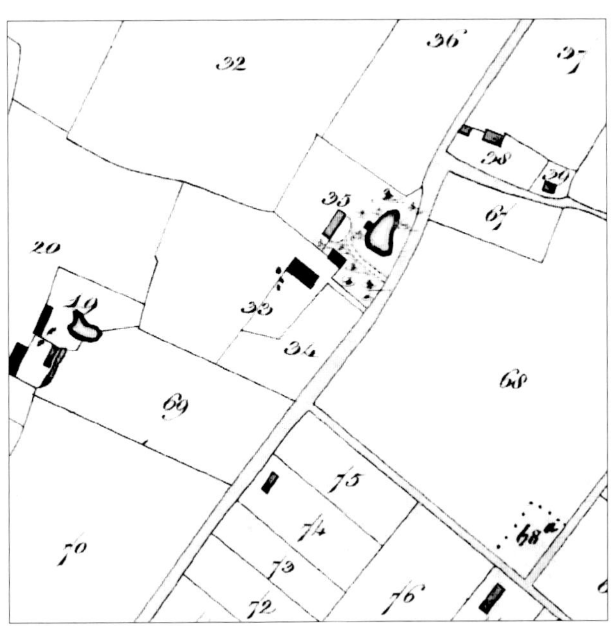
32
36
37
38
39
35
67
20
19
33
34
68
69
75
74
73
72
76
70
68a

facing page **The Goggses' farm at Whissonsett. As was common in Mary Hardy's family, male ultimogeniture was practised, not primogeniture. Henry, the younger son, got the farm outright. His elder brother Robert had years earlier been established as a tenant farmer at nearby Colkirk** [*MB · 2011*]

left **Hamrow, the northern hamlet of Whissonsett where the Goggs family lived, from the tithe map surveyed in 1838. The farmhouse [35] has a large pond at the front, now filled in** [TNA: PRO IR 30/23/629, *tithe map 1843, detail*]

THE NORFOLK PLOUGH AT WORK.

above The Norfolk plough, an illustration in Nathaniel Kent's analysis of Norfolk farming for the Board of Agriculture, published in London in 1796. Ploughing began in the Hardys' Five Acres on 7 Mar. 1795, ready for barley sowing on 30 Apr. [*N. Kent, General View of the Agriculture of the County of Norfolk, facing p. 36*]

facing page Fakenham: the former Calvinistic Methodist chapel of 1773, promoted by the Goggs family of Whissonsett and attended by Mary Hardy 22 Feb. 1795, by which time it was being shared with the Wesleyans [*MB · 2000*]

FEBRUARY 25, WEDNESDAY

HR Being Faste day no work, Miss H & H Raven whent to Church afternoon. Sharpan Came with a Horse, WH bought it. M^{r} & M^{rs} & Mr Thos Forster drank tea here.[1] M^{r} & WH roade to Holt morning.

MH A close mild day. A Publick fast by Authority. M^{r} & Mrs Foster came to our Church Afternoon, drank tea here. MA & H Raven at our Church . . .

FEBRUARY 26, THURSDAY

HR Robt Bye to Cromer with beer. T Boyce in brewhouse morning, at work in garden all Day. G Thompson, H Raven & Boy in brewhouse, WH brewing. M^{r} & Miss H at Mr Forsters, HR whent for them Evening.

FEBRUARY 27, FRIDAY

HR R Bye to Gunthorp with beer & loaded for Burnham. T Boyce to Hindolvestone with beer, T Baldwin after jobs. Gunton, HR & Boy Cleansed `//,[2] Thompson laide down W [wheat] Stones. Thos Youngman triming the Mill geers [trimming the mill gears].

FEBRUARY 28, SATURDAY

HR R Bye & Thos Baldwin to Burnham with beer. Thos Boyce spreading muck «and at» jobs. G Thompson, HR & WH Cleanse'd X. Jno Ram in M H, WH & Miss H at Holt afternoon.

---

1 *Mr Thomas Forster* Thomas Forster jnr

2 *Gunton* Gunton Thompson jnr

MARCH 1, SUNDAY

Henry Raven R Bye Loaded for Brampton, T Baldwin for Norwich. H Raven & M^rs H whent to Briston, WH at Holt afternoon.[1]

MARCH 2, MONDAY

HR R Bye to Brampton, T Baldwin to Norwich with beer. Boy to Blakney for ½ Chal. Cinders from Mr Farthings. Jno Ram in M H, T Boyce turning up muck & tying fagots. M^r H drank tea at Mr Burrels, Mrs Forster drank tea here.

MARCH 3, TUESDAY

HR R Bye loaded for Syderstone, T Baldwin came from Norwich. T Boyce tying faggots. Jno Ram in M H, G Thompson grinding Malt for bin. M^r H & WH at home all Day.

Mary Hardy A close cold day. Mr Hardy rid up to Holt Afternoon to speak to Mr Clark who is going into the black Boys, came home to tea.[2]

MARCH 4, WEDNESDAY

HR R Bye to Syderstone with beer, took 4 Bar^s [barrels] for Mr Temple of Barmer.[3] T Baldwin to Waybourn with beer & got up a Load of turnips. G Thompson grinding Malt for brew, Jno Ram in M H. Boy asleep all Day, Thos Boyce at work in front yard. H Raven to Holt afternoon, M^r & WH at home all Day.

MH A Close cold day. Mr Hardy, I & MA went to our Church foornoon, W^m at home all day . . .

MARCH 5, THURSDAY

HR R Bye after jobs forenoon, to Stody with beer afternoon. T Baldwin to Blakeny for 2 Chal. Cinders from M^r Fa«r»things. Jno Ram in Malthouse, T Boyce at work in garden. Boy very ill. M^r & WH at home all Day.

MARCH 6, FRIDAY

HR R Bye in brewhouse & whent to Bale with beer. T Boyce in brewhouse, WH brewing. T Baldwin to Sherrington & Kettlestone with «beer». H Raven in Malthouse, Jno Ram {in} ill, Boy ill. M^r, M^rs & Miss Bartell drank tea here, M^r & Mrs Sheldrake drank tea here.

MARCH 7, SATURDAY

HR R Bye & Capt Hall ploughing in five Acres. T Boyce in garden, T Baldwin after jobs. G Thompson Cleansed

[1] *Briston* As on 4 Jan. 1795, they were attending the Calvinistic Methodists' meeting in the chapel which Mendham had built for them in 1783. William Hardy jnr was at Holt Church. Only in the years after his mother's death did he fully embrace Wesleyan Methodism

[2] *Black Boys* The alehouse register indicates that James Skiffins was replaced by Francis Wakefield, but Mr Clark[e] could have spent a few months as innkeeper between the two (NRO: C/Sch 1/16)

[3] *4 barrels* This seems a surprisingly large amount for a private individual rather than a licensed outlet. With 36 gallons (163·7 litres) to the barrel the order represented 1152 pints (nearly 655 litres). Yet the tiny settlement of Barmer was ill fitted to supporting a large frolic or audit

'//, Jno Ram in M H. W & Miss H at Holt market afternoon. Mr Smith in garden forenoon.

MARCH 8, SUNDAY

HR H Raven & M^{rs} H whent to Briston, M^{r} & Miss & WH to Church afternoon. G Thompson, HR & WH Cleanse'd X.

MARCH 9, MONDAY

HR R Bye ploughing in Furze Colse [Closes], T Baldwin at Harrow in D^{o}. Jno Ram in Malthouse, Capt H tasking. G Thompson & H Raven Dressing flowr, Boy got up aload of turnips. M^{r} & WH set of for South Repps, Beckhigh & Cromer. Mr Woodcock came afternoon & Settled, Mr Barwick came morning to Settle. T Boyce in garden.

MH A very close Morng, provd a very Wet day. Mr Hardy & W^{m} set of for Southreps Morn 10. Maid & Eliz Woods washd 5 Weeks linnen & baked.

MARCH 10, TUESDAY

HR R Bye to Holt with beer forenoon, ploughing afternoon, T Baldwin to Runton with beer. Capt Hall trashing, Jno Ram in Malthouse, G Thompson dressing flower. HR road to Birninham [Briningham] & Settled with Mr Bissell. T Boyce in garden. M^{r} & WH came home afternoon, Sam. Sanderson [

].

MH A fine day. Mr Hardy & W^{m} came home eveng 4. S Sanderson & a Mr Johnson Came to hire the Crown at lower Sheringham, wet eveng, they Slept at Mr Dobsons [1] . . .

MARCH 11, WEDNESDAY

HR R Bye ploughing all Day, T Bald^{n} to Cromer with beer. T Boyce in garden, Capt Hall trashing, Jno Ram in M H. M^{r} H at home all Day, WH & Miss H at Holt afternoon at Mr Bartells. Bunnets two men here part of forenoon doing something to Dobsons House.

MARCH 12, THURSDAY

HR T Baldwin to Corpusta with beer, R Bye ploughing in lower furze close. T Boyce in garden, Jno Ram in M H. Capt Hall trashing, G Thompson grinding Malt for brew. WH & H Raven planting furze & triming up threes [trees] afternoon. M^{r} H at work in garden. M^{r}

[1] *Crown* Robert Johnson took over from Samuel Sanderson, who moved to run the military canteen at Weybourne Camp (see note for 1 June 1795). Johnson stayed two years before abandoning the public house: see the diary entries 30 Sept.–25 Oct. 1796.

Turnover was extremely high in a trade beset by debt. It was also characterised by mobility, Johnson moving to the north coast of the county from Attleborough, a market town in south central Norfolk (16 Mar.). The public houses and their problems are covered in *World*, vol. 2, chaps 9–11

above **Cabbage after rain. Flowers are not mentioned by Henry, and almost never by his aunt. The kitchen garden, vital to supplying the household's needs, was probably the principal focus of William Hardy and Thomas Boyce's attentions (eg 12 Mar., 16 Mar. 1795)** [*MB · 2011*]

Youngmans man & lad sawying forenoon, Boy got up a loade of turnips.

MARCH 13, FRIDAY

HR R Bye & T Baldwin driving muck upto furze close & Bells acre, T Boyce & Boy filling. Jno Ram in M H, Capt^t^ Hall dressing. M^r^ H at home all Day, WH upt [?upped] to furze close.[1] Mr Youngmans man & lad sawying forenoon. Mr Chas Sales drank tea here.

MARCH 14, SATURDAY

HR R Bye to Fakenham with beer, T Baldwin to Blakeny for 2 Chal^d^ Cinders from Mr Fathings. Jno Ram in M H, Capt^t^ H dressing. M^r^ H at home all Day. Two men from South Repps Dine'd here.[2]

MH A very sharp windy day. Mr Hardy at home all day. W^m^ went to Holt Market afternoon & to the Play in Eveng, came home eveng 11.[3] Began to Snow eveng 4, continued greatest part of the Night . . .

MARCH 15, SUNDAY

HR Famaly all to Church forenoon, WH & H Raven to Holt afternoon.

MARCH 16, MONDAY

HR T Baldwin, G Thompson, H Raven & Boy in brewhouse, WH brewing. R Bye very porley. Jno Ram in Malthouse, Capt^t^ Hall dressing. T Boyce at work in garden & unloaded Cinders. Sam. Sanderson & Mr Johnson Dined here. M^r^ H at Holt afternoon. Geo. Dawson here afternoon mending Coach at Jexes.

MH A Cold Wet day. Wm Brew'd. S Sanderson & Mr Johnson from Atlebourg [Attleborough] dind here & agreed for the Crown at Sheringham. Mr Hardy went up to Holt with them, came home eveng 10 . . .

MARCH 17, TUESDAY

HR R Bye at harrow afternoon & car^d^ of [carried off] Cleanse beer, T Baldwin after jobs. T Boyce in garden, G Thompson Cleanse'd `//. Jno Ram in M H, Capt^t^ Hall trashing. Robt Staff came afternoon. [. . . .] [?Luke] Basham & Lad cleaning coach & mending harness.

MARCH 18, WEDNESDAY

HR R Bye to Edgefield with beer, T Bald^n^ to Salthouse with D^o^. T Boyce spreading muck & at work in garden, Jno Ram in M H. G Thompson & WH Cleanse'd XX.

[1] *upped* Went up, presumably

[2] *two men* They may have brought the news that Robert Foulger at the Crown was dying: see note for 21 Oct. 1794. Henry Raven's record increasingly reveals the omissions in his aunt's

[3] *play* David Fisher and Company had been 'licensed to perform plays within the parish of Holt for 24 days, *vide* petition'. Fisher (1760–1832), actor–manager of the travelling Company of Comedians, appears to have received an extension to his licence as the performances lasted from 14 Mar. or earlier until 25 Apr. or later. His troupe then moved to Lt Walsingham (licensed for 20 days) and Fakenham (24 days) (NRO: C/S 1/15, Holt Quarter Sessions, 22 Jan. 1795; Walsingham Quarter Sessions, 23 Apr. 1795).

On his next tour David Fisher bypassed Holt, and none of the Hardys was recorded as attending plays in 1796. The magistrates Charles Collyer and Henry Lee Warner granted the company a licence 'to perform tragedies etc' at Fakenham for 20 days between 1 July and 31 Oct. 1796, provided the approbation of Revd Dixon Hoste (another JP, of Godwick Hall) and 'the principal inhabitants' of Fakenham were obtained (C/S 1/15, Walsingham Quarter Sessions, 14 Apr. 1796)

Rob[t] Staff & WH roade to Blakney afternoon. Luke Basham & Lad mending harness ¾ day. M[r] H at home all Day.

MH Very sharp, north wind high & Storms of Snow & sleet. M[r] Hardy at home all day. W[m] rid to Blakney with M[r] Staffe Aftern, came home to tea. T Boyce opening drains in Garden.

MARCH 19, THURSDAY

HR R Bye to Dawling with beer & Loaded for Stalham, T Baldwin to Hindolvestone with beer. T Boyce in garden, Jn[o] Ram in M H, Cap[t] Hall trashing. M[r] H & WH at home all Day.

MH A fine chearly day, wind cold. M[r] Hardy & W[m] at home all day. T Boyce cutting a drain across the Garden . . .

MARCH 20, FRIDAY

HR R Bye to Stalham, T Baldwin to Gunthorp. Jn[o] Ram in M H, T Boyce making under drain in garden.[1] WH & HR taking up Chasenut tree & seting it in Phitle [chestnut tree and setting it in Pightle].[2] Cap[t] Hall trashing. M[r] H at h«o»me all Day, G Thompson grinding Malt for brew.

MARCH 21, SATURDAY

HR R Bye came home from Stalham. T Bald[n] at harrow forenoon, to Holt afternoon, Boy at harrow aftern. T Boyce in garden, Jn[o] Ram in M H. Cap[t] Hall set thorns round a tree in Phitle.[3] M[r] H at [ ] afternoon, WH at Holt Market & Play Evening.

MARCH 22, SUNDAY

HR M[rs] H & H Raven at Briston afternoon, M[r] & Miss & WH at own church afternoon.

MARCH 23, MONDAY

HR R Bye & Boy in brew house, G Thompson & H Raven in brewhouse, WH brewing. T Baldwin to lower Sheringham with beer, R Bye to Cley with beer.[4] Jn[o] Ram in M H, Cap[t] Hall trashing. M[r] H at home all Day.

MARCH 24, TUESDAY

HR R Bye to Cromer with beer, T Baldwin to Wells with beer. Jn[o] Ram in M H, Cap[t] Hall trash[g]. M[r] & Miss & Nath Raven came from Whissonsett. Boy gitting stone from M[r] Burrels, G Thompson & H Raven Cleanse'd `//.

[1] *underdrain* William Marshall (1787) was a firm advocate of underdraining, '. . . a practice which is not of long standing in the district' (W. Marshall, *The Rural Economy of Norfolk*, vol. 1, p. 148). He describes the method in detail in his minutes, and notes that the deep trenches, triangular in section, could be filled with wood or stones before the topsoil was replaced (vol. 2, pp. 1–4). See also note for 26 Jan. 1797.

The system evidently held good for horticultural purposes, draining presumably being helped by the slight slope from the Hall to the river

[2] *chestnut tree* The Brewhouse Pightle is full of great shady trees, and it is no longer possible to identify this particular tree—if indeed it has survived. It may have been planted at the bottom of the slope, beside the brewery. Draymen at Elgoods Brewery in Wisbech, Cambs, used to stand the beer barrels under the shade of a chestnut in the brewery yard while the casks were waiting to be loaded (archive photograph exhibited in the brewery's museum, May 2001)

[3] *thorns* To protect the newly planted tree from the predations of the livestock

[4] *Lower Sheringham* To the Crown, perched perilously on the cliff edge. Upper Sheringham, further inland, also had a public house, the Red Lion, but it was not supplied from Letheringsett. The innkeepers (Celia

above No view survives of Letheringsett Hall before William Hardy jnr's remodellings of 1808–09 (see the Chronology). In 1795 the Hardys' garden covered the grounds shown here, running from the east front of the Hall to the River Glaven in the foreground. The church's round tower stands just out of view north-west of the Hall [*MB* · 2002]

MH A close morng, fine day. T Boyce in Garden. Mr Hardy & Wm at home all day. Brother Raven & Ann & Nathl Raven from the Hall came to dinner. Mr Hardy poorly . . .

MARCH 25, WEDNESDAY

HR R Bye ploughing all Day, T Baldwin to Thornage & loaded for South Repps. T Boyce in garden, Jno Ram in M H, Capt Hall trashing, G Thompson & HR Cleanse'd XX. Mr, Mrs, Miss & W Hardy, Mr Raven & Miss R, Nath Raven & Mr Wade roade to Cley. Boy whent to Edgefield with malt. Mr Wade dined here.

MARCH 26, THURSDAY

HR R Bye ploughing forenoon, to Briston aftern, G Thompson grinding Malt for brew. T Baldwin to South Repps with beer, T Boyce in garden, Jno Ram in M H,

Shepherd (1789, 1790) and William Shepherd (1792–99, and probably beyond)) do not feature in the diaries, nor in the Hardys' accounts 1797–1804 (*Diary 4*).

The Upper Sheringham deliveries (eg 4 Feb., 23 July 1795) were almost certainly to the Flowers at the Hall

[1] *Whissonsett* Mary Hardy records that Ann Raven went home with the rest of the party and that William returned to Letheringsett on the evening of 28 Mar.

[2] *7 nog* Seven barrels of nog, the strong brew that was a Norfolk and Norwich speciality

---

below right 'Mr Hardy at Holt forenoon to settle Alsop's business' (31 Mar. 1795). The final dividend in the bankruptcy of Isaac Alsop, William Hardy's former innkeeper at the King's Arms at Cromer, was to be paid by the bankruptcy commissioners at the Feathers, Holt 31 Mar. (*Norw. Merc.* 21 Mar. 1795).

However a second notice appeared a few weeks later, placed by William Hardy 23 Apr. and published 2 May (illustrated here), showing that matters had not been settled on 31 Mar. and inviting Alsop's creditors to call at the brewer's house to receive their payments.

This was a protracted affair. Alsop, who had also run a butcher's shop at Cromer, had been declared a bankrupt in Aug. 1790, William Hardy becoming assignee. Thomas Sanderson took over the King's Arms in 1791 and renamed it the Cromer Hotel, but he too failed in business [*Norwich Mercury, 2 May 1795: Norfolk Heritage Centre, Norwich*]

Capt Hall trashing. Mr Raven, Nath & WH set of for Whissonsett aftern.[1]

MARCH 27, FRIDAY

HR R Bye ploughing in furze close, T Baldwin ploughing in Bellsacre for^{n} [forenoon], to Holt with beer after^{n}. G Thompson grinding Malt for brew, Jno Ram in Malthouse, Capt Hall trashing. M^{r}, M^{rs} & Miss H at Holt aftern^{n}. Clarke came & Orderd 7 Nog.[2]

MARCH 28, SATURDAY

HR R Bye & T Baldwin ploughing, Boy at harrow. T Boyce in garden, Jno Ram in M H, Capt Hall trashing. M^{r} H at Holt after^{n}.

MARCH 29, SUNDAY

HR R Bye & Thos Baldwin car^{d} of Cleanse beer. Famaly to Church afternoon, WH & HR to Holt afternoon.

MARCH 30, MONDAY

HR R Bye ploughing, Boy at harrow after^{n}. T Baldwin, G Thompson & H Raven in brewhouse, WH brewing. M^{r} H at home all Day. Jno Ram in Malthouse, Capt Hall trashing.

MARCH 31, TUESDAY

HR R Bye ploughing forenoon, to Waybourn aft^{r}. T Baldwin ploughing foornoon, to Wiverton with beer & Blakney for 2 Chal^{d} cinders from Mr Fathings. Jno Ram in Malthouse, Capt Hall trashing, G Thompson took up W [wheat] Stones. M^{r} H at Holt all Day. M^{r}, M^{rs} & Miss Bartell drank tea here. T Boyce stopping gaps in furze close, Jno Ram ill.

FINAL DIVIDEND in ALSOP's BANKRUPTCY.

ALL ſuch Creditors as have duly proved their Debts under the Commiſſion of Bankrupt, awarded and iſſued forth againſt ISAAC ALSOP, late of Cromer, in the county of Norfolk, Dealer and Chapman, may receive a Final Dividend on their reſpective Debts, any time after the 4th day of May next, by applying to Mr. Wm. Hardy, the aſſignee under the ſaid Commiſſion, at his dwelling-houſe, in Letheringſett, near Holt.

N. B. Letters addreſſed to Mr. Hardy (poſt paid) will be duly anſwered.——*Letheringſett, April* 23, 1795. (657

AYLSHAM NAVIGATION.

AS 160,000. of the beſt hard burnt Bricks, 72

MH A foggy morng, fine day. Mr Morgan & Susan Johnson were Married at Holt.[1] Mr Hardy at Holt foornoon to settle Alsops buisiness, came home to dinner eveng 5.[2] Mr, Mrs & Miss Bartell drank tea here. A foggy eveng.

APRIL 1, WEDNESDAY

Henry Raven R Bye & T Baldwin ploughing & Loaded for South Repps, T Boyce stopping gaps. Capt Hall trashing, H Raven in M H. Mr & WH at Holt aftern. Miss Mary Raven spent the Day here. G Thompson & WH Cleansed X. Duke tieing faggots.

Mary Hardy A foggy Morn, fine day. M Raven from Whissonsett came & spent the day with us. She was bride Maid yesterd«ay» to Miss Johnson, they set of for Shipden [Shipdham] morng ½ past 6. I, MA & MR went to our Church foornoon . . .

APRIL 2, THURSDAY

HR R Bye to South Repps with beer, T Baldwin ploughing, Boyce stopping gaps. HR in M H, G Thom. grinding Malt for bin. Boy carting thornes in furze Close, Capt Hall dressing for last time.[3] Mr H at home all Day, WH road to furze Close morning.

APRIL 3, FRIDAY

HR R Bye & T Baldwin after jobs & Loded for Syderstone & Barmer. Capt Hall dressing, HR in Malthouse, T Boyce stopping gaps. Mr, Mrs, Miss & W Hardy at Church fornn, WH & Miss H roade to Stody aftern.

APRIL 4, SATURDAY

HR R Bye & T Baldwin to Syderstone & Barmer with beer, T Boyce stopping gaps. Jno Ram in Malthouse. Boy to Holt forn, got up aloade turnips aftern [a load of turnips afternoon]. Mr H at Holt all Day. WH at Hindolvestone forn, at Holt aftr.

MH A Close foggy cold day. Mr Hardy rid up foornoon to the Justice Sitting to fix on a Plan for raising Soldiers for Goverment according to an Act of Parliment lately made «for» that purpose,[4] dind no were [dined nowhere], drank tea at Mr Bartells. Wm went to Market afternoon, both came home eveng past 10.

[1] *Mr Morgan* See note for 28 Nov. 1793. On her marriage Susan Johnson must have sold her share of the partnership in the Holt millinery to her sister Deborah, for Deborah's name was attached to the notice advertising the latest London fashions to be brought back by their sister Mary on 11 May (*Norw. Merc.* 2 May 1795)

[2] *Alsop* Isaac, the former innkeeper and butcher: see caption opposite

[3] *last time* The barley- and wheat-threshing had come to an end, having occupied Thomas Hall during much of the winter

[4] *raising soldiers* The diarist should have written 'sailors'. Two Quota Acts were passed in March (for quotas from the counties and from the seaports) and a third in April (for Scotland), all part of an entirely new scheme to augment naval recruiting. Reliance on volunteers, on the press gang and on convicted felons and vagrants was proving inadequate. For a well-documented study of the operation of the Quota Acts at local level, in N. Yorkshire, see C. Emsley, with A.M. Hill and M.Y. Ashcroft, *North Riding Naval Recruits: The Quota Acts and the Quota men 1795–97* (North Yorkshire County Council, 1978).

Throughout Apr. 1795 the *Norwich Mercury* gave details of the manner of implementing the first Act in Norfolk. The parishes of Holt hundred (including

above Mary Hardy records 4 Apr. 1795 her husband's attendance at a magistrates' sitting to fix on Holt hundred's means of raising its quota of seven landsmen, the Quota men, to serve in the Royal Navy (and not as 'Soldiers') [*Cozens-Hardy Collection*]

APRIL 5, SUNDAY

HR H Raven & Mrs Hardy to Briston, Mr, Miss H at own Church aftr, WH at Holt. T Baldwin & G Thompson loded for Beckhigh.

MH *Easter Sunday* A moist cold morng, dry afternoon. I & H Raven went to Briston meeting, home eveng past 5.[1] Mr Hardy, Wm & MA went to our Church afternoon, Mr Burrell preach'd. Mrs Forster at Church.

APRIL 6, MONDAY

HR R Bye to Beckhigh with beer, T Baldwin helpd to Cary of [carry off] part of Cleanse beer & whent to Thornage & Holt with beer. T Boyce card of [carried off] part of Cleanse beer & at Work behinde Stable. Mr & WH whent to Lower Sherringham.

MH A Wet morng, dry afternoon. Mr Hardy & Wm rid to Sheringham to settle with Mr Saunderson & Mr Johnson who is now taken the House, they drank tea at Mr Flower at upper Sheringham, came home eveng 10.

APRIL 7, TUESDAY

HR R Bye & Thos Baldwin ploughn in furze Close, T Boyce stopping gaps in Do. Jno Ram in M H, Capt Hall at work in garden & stopping gaps in 6 Acres. Jno Ram in M H. Mr H a Holt all Day, WH at Holt aftr.

Letheringsett) had to raise seven men in total; S. Erpingham hundred (including Coltishall) ten; and Launditch (including Whissonsett) nine, the justices' sittings for these hundreds being held at the Feathers at Holt, the Black Boys at Aylsham and the Bull at Litcham. Bounties of 20 or 25 guineas (£21 or £26 5*s*) were promised to landsmen prepared to serve, such recruits being classed as volunteers and not as pressed men. These inducements attracted the requisite numbers, and by 18 Apr. Norwich had nearly reached its quota of 32. Small villages banded together to find volunteers, the parishes of Thornage, Stody, Hunworth, Melton Constable and Swanton Novers having to produce one Quota man between them. Such strategems probably formed part of the 'Plan' which William Hardy was debating at Holt on 4 Apr.

Foxite readers of the *Norwich Mercury* would not have looked favourably on the government scheme. The newspaper had given prominence to the petition from Norwich for peace 27 Jan. 1795. See also *World*, vol. 4, chaps 6 and 7

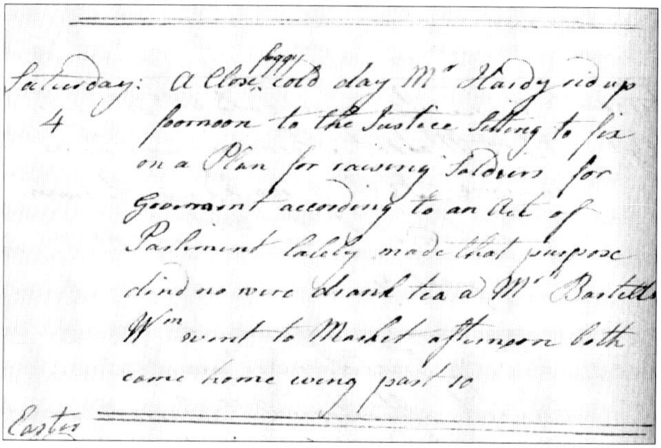

---

[1] *Briston meeting* Mary Hardy, with her family, attended Easter Communion at Letheringsett Church the following Sunday, thus proclaiming herself a practising Anglican still. The Briston meeting house of 1783 was still for sale,

MH A moist morng, close day. Mr Hardy & W^{m} walkd up to Holt afternoon. Mr Hardy came home eveng 8 & went to the town meeting at Dobsons, came home eveng 11.[1] W^{m} went to the Play, supt at Mr Bartells, came home ½ past 11 . . .

APRIL 8, WEDNESDAY

HR R Bye & T Baldwin ploughing, T Boyce stoping gaps. Capt Hall in garden for^{n}, stoping gaps in six Acres. Jno Ram in M H, Boy got up two load of turnips.

APRIL 9, THURSDAY

HR T Baldwin to Fakenham with beer, R Bye ploughing. Capt Hall stoping gaps in six Acres, T Boyce in garden, Jno Ram in M H. M^{r} H at Holt for^{n}.

MH A Close cold day. Mr Hardy at home all day. W^{m} rid up to Holt after tea, came home 9. Mr Robt Garret & Bride came to Mr Burrells [2] . . .

APRIL 10, FRIDAY

HR R Bye & G Thompson in brewhouse. Boy in Brewhouse for^{n}, at harrow aft^{r} in furze Close. WH Brewing & drying of [off] Porter Malt. Jno Ram & H Raven in M H, Capt Hall stoping gaps, T Boyce at work in

with Arminian Methodists being invited to make an offer at the sale on 8 Apr.: 'The above premises . . . are worthy the attention of that respectable society in particular who approve of the doctrines of the late Rev. John Westley [*sic*], MA' (*Norw. Merc.* 28 Mar. 1795).

It was bought after an interval by Joseph Hill, a local farmer, and shortly become Wesleyan. Mary Hardy does not mention the sale

[1] *town meeting* As was usual at Letheringsett, although by no means universally, the annual parish meeting was held at an hour which suited working men

[2] *Robert Garrett* Probably Mrs Burrell's brother

Wood
White
Holland B.
Horse
Shoes
Green
Briston
Common
Union
Mills
Cramers

left The Three Horseshoes at Briston faces the main road running east to Aylsham and Norwich. Renamed *c.*1977 the John H. Stracey, the name was changed in 2008 to the Stracey Inn and reverted in 2012 to the Three Horseshoes. Tied to the Letheringsett brewery for over a century, it was bought copyhold by William Hardy in 1792 for £350 and sold to Morgans in 1896 when valued at £800. The innkeeper Francis Longden was to fall into debt in 1799 and his goods were seized by William Hardy jnr (*Diary 4*).

It was at the Horseshoes that the 1783 Calvinistic Methodist chapel at Briston was offered for sale on 8 Apr. 1795, no purchaser having been found since Mendham's death in Feb. 1793. Nonetheless weekly services were still being held during the interregnum [*Bryant's Map of Norfolk 1826: Cozens-Hardy Collection*]

garden. M^r H at home all Day. M^r & Mrs Sheldrake drank tea here, HR whent to Holt for^n for shrubs to Mr Moors.[1]

APRIL 11, SATURDAY

HR R Bye to Cromer, left two Bar^s [barrels] at Carafors [Crafer's], Holt, T Baldwin to Sharrington & Stody. Jno Ram in M H, Capt Hall stoping gaps in Meadow. Boy got up aload of turnips. G Thompson & H Raven Cleanse'd `//. M^r H at home all Day, WH at Holt aft^n. Mr Burrell & M^r & Mrs Garratt took awhalk in our shruberys & garden.[2] T Boyce stoping gaps.

MH A chearly day. Mr Hardy walkd upto Holt foornoon to the Justice sitting,[3] dind at Mr Moores, went to the Play, came home after midnight. W^m went to Mark^t afternoon, drank tea & Supt at Mr Bartells, went to the Play, came home after mid«night». Mr Burrell & Family here foornoon.

APRIL 12, SUNDAY

HR H Raven & M^rs H when«t» to Briston aft^n, Famaly all at own Church for^n. G Thompson, HR Cleanse'd XX.

MH A Moist morng, close day. All went to our Church foornoon, no Sermon, A Communion. I & HR went to meeting at Briston, came home half past 5 . . .

APRIL 13, MONDAY

HR R Bye & Thos Baldwin ploughing, G Thompson & H Raven strip«p»ing Meal. Jno Ram in Malt House, T Boyce in garden. Capt Hall stoping gaps & scraping muck up in yard.[4] WH at Holt aft^n, M^r H at home all Day. M^r & M^rs & Miss H at Mr Burrells Evening, WH at Holt aft^n.

APRIL 14, TUESDAY

HR T Baldwin to Burnham, R Bye to Blakney for 2 Chas [chaldrons] Cinders from Mr Farthing. Jno Ram in Malthouse, T Boyce in garden. Capt Hall & Boy skreening Malt for^n, diging aplace for atree in shrubberry. G Thompson dresst flower for^n, grinding Malt for bin aftr^n. WH, J Ram & H Raven drying of porter Malt.

APRIL 15, WEDNESDAY

HR R Bye to Bale for^n, plough^g & sowing Barley aft^r in Wheat stubble furze Close. T Baldwin, T Boyce, Capt Hall & Boy carting stones of new lay furze close.[5] G Thomp-

[1] *shrubs* These are likely to have come from the garden of the Gressenhall House of Industry where the attorney James Moore's father, of the same name, had been governor and nurseryman. He had died the previous July, owning 'many volumes of books'. A quantity of fruit trees and shrubs had been for sale at Gressenhall 6 and 8 Apr. (*Norw. Merc.* 12 July 1794, 4 Apr. 1795)

[2] *our shrubberies* After three years at his aunt's Henry had come to identify himself with the Letheringsett family

[3] *sitting* For the Quota men for the Navy. This first convening of the petty sessions had been advertised in the *Norwich Mercury* 4 Apr. 1795. William Hardy was at the justices' sitting at Holt the following Saturday as well, presumably in connection with the naval quota

[4] *Capt. Hall* Thomas and Elizabeth Hall's son John was born and privately bapt. Letheringsett that day, 13 Apr. 1795; he was buried there 23 June 1795

[5] *new lay* Also ley: meadow or pasture newly converted from arable. A field of grass of one year's standing is a one-year ley; of two years' standing a two-year ley.

One- and two-year leys formed part of the crop rotation: see *World*, vol. 2, chap. 4

son dress«ing» flower, Jn° Ram in M H. Jo^{s} Bakers man & Boy at Work here all Day, M^{r} H at home all Day.

APRIL 16, THURSDAY

HR R Bye ploughing & sowing Barley, T Baldwin to Sherringham, came by Waybourn for Drum. T Boyce in garden. Capt Hall skreening Malt «and» unloading Cinders for^{n}, at harrow aft^{n}. M^{r} H at home all Day, HR at Holt Evening. G Thompson grinding Malt for Brew.

MH A very fine day. Mr Hardy & W^{m} at home all day. Mr Benfield the Musition & Mr Sheldrake drank tea here [1] . . .

APRIL 17, FRIDAY

HR R Bye to Edgefield & Corpusta with beer, T Baldwin to Holt, Cley & Briston with D°. T Boyce ploughing in barley for^{n}, in garden aft^{n}. Capt Hall stoping gaps in furze close, G Thompson finnish«ed» grinding Malt, Jn° Ram in M H. WH, HR and Boy sett arange of Hurdels in Phitle [a range of hurdles in Pightle]. Boy at Harrow after^{n}, Jos^{h} Bakers man & Lad all Day.

APRIL 18, SATURDAY

HR R Bye to Runton, T Baldwin to Hindolveston & Holt with beer. Boy got up two loads of turnips, T Boyce in garden. Capt Hall stoping gaps in furze close, Jn° Ram in M H. M^{r} H at Holt all Day, W & Miss H at Holt aftr^{n}.

APRIL 19, SUNDAY

HR R Bye & Thos Baldwin car^{d} of nine Bar^{s} Beer. Famaly all at own Church aftr^{n}. G Thompson set of for N Walsham 5 OClock morning.

MH Some small showers. All went to our Church Afternoon, Mr Burrell preach'd. Thompson went to N Walsham to look at the Publick House, came home eveng 8 [2] . . .

APRIL 20, MONDAY

HR R Bye ploughing & sowing in Wheat stubble furze close, T Boyce ploughing in field. T Baldwin, G Thompson & Boy in brewhouse, WH brewing. T Hall stoping gaps in furze close, Jn° Ram in Malthouse. M^{r} H at home all day, Mr Ralph call^{d} afternoon.

APRIL 21, TUESDAY

HR R Bye & Thos Boyce ploughing & sowing barley in lower close furze [Lower Furze Close]. T Baldwin to

IM 1777

above Gressenhall House of Industry: the incised brick by the main entrance has the intertwined initials and foundation date 'IM 1777' for the Hardys' old friend James Moore, the first governor and nurseryman. The Hardys bought garden plants apparently transported from the house of industry (10 Apr. 1795).

A cottage garden complete with old varieties is open to the public at Gressenhall Farm and Workhouse [*MB · 2011*]

---

[1] *musician* Possibly from David Fisher's company: see note for 14 Mar. 1795. Travelling players boarded and lodged in public houses and with local residents, and Mr Benfield may have been staying with the excise officer while performing at Holt.

The company was not named in the *Norwich Mercury*, nor were its Holt performances advertised, but it received complimentary reviews (eg in the edition of 16 May 1795)

[2] *N. Walsham* To check on the Maid's Head, which was still standing empty: see note for 11 May 1795

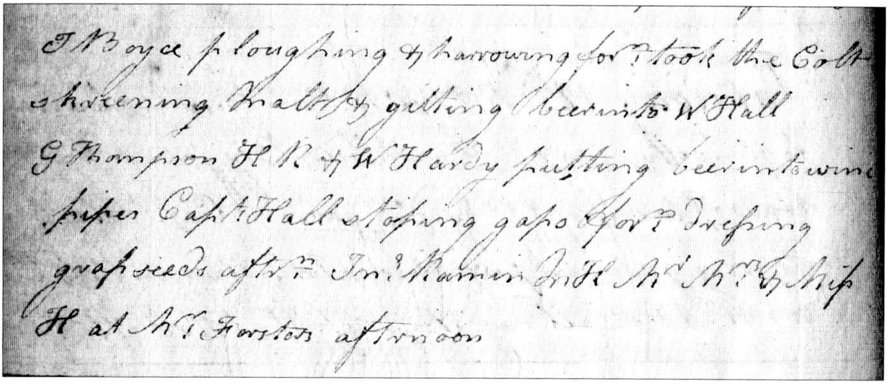

above **Part of 17-year-old Henry's entry for 22 Apr. 1795, referred to in the editorial introduction as exemplifying the writing style of the time: 'for^{n}' for forenoon; the 'long s' in 'drefsing grafs seeds'; 'Jno' for John; 'M H' for malthouse. At first he did not distinguish morning from forenoon, but after a few months he adopted the Hardys' practice** [*Cozens-Hardy Collection*]

Hinderingham, G Thompson Cleansed `//, Jno Ram in M H. Capt Hall stoping gaps in furze close, T Boyce at harrow aftr^{n}. M^{r} H at home all day.

APRIL 22, WEDNESDAY

HR R Bye to Burnham with beer, T Baldwin to Thos Atwoods, Clarkes & Crawfers D^{o} D^{o} [with beer]. T Boyce ploughing & harrowing for^{n}, took the Colt, skreening Malt & getting beer into W Hall [white hall]. G Thompson, HR & W Hardy putting beer into wine pipes.[1] Capt Hall stoping gaps for^{n}, dressing grass seeds aftr^{n}. Jno Ram in M H. M^{r}, M^{rs} & Miss H at Mr Forsters aft«e»rnoon.

MH A very fine day. W^{m} at home all day. Mr Hardy, I & MA walkd to Bayfield afternoon to look at Mr Jodrils [Jodrell's] new Plantations,[2] I drank tea at Mr Forsters, Mrs Herring from Norwich there . . .

APRIL 23, THURSDAY

HR R Bye to Gunthorp with beer for^{n}, ploughing aft^{n}. T Baldwin & Thos Boyce to Mr Temples for one load of hay for^{n}, D^{o} [Thomas Boyce] at mould Cart aftr^{n}, T Baldwin ploughing aft^{n}. Capt Hall & Boy at Mould cart in 5 Acres aftr^{n}.

1 *wine pipes* This expedient indicates a severe shortage of beer barrels; local fairs must have strained coopers' and brewers' stocks. Henry had been recording an upsurge in beer deliveries to Holt in the days preceding Holt Fair, held 27 Apr. 1795 (on the Monday) to avoid clashing with market day

2 *new plantations* These were treated exceedingly unfavourably by Edmund Bartell jnr in his unpublished MS of 1809, 'Notes chiefly descriptive of Picturesque Effects as relating to Scenery and Buildings . . .' (Cozens-Hardy Collection).

They eradicated a landscape which had delighted him as a boy: 'Bayfield . . . has of late years undergone a revolution under the hands of a modern landscape gardener, who appears to have expended a great sum in destroying those natural beauties, [for] the loss of which his art has not been able to compensate . . .' See *World*, vol. 1, chaps 9 and 10, on gardens and grounds

APRIL 24, FRIDAY

HR R Bye G Thompson & Boy in brewhouse, WH brewing. T Baldwin & Thos Boyce ploughing & sowing barley in furze close. Jno Ram in M H, Capt Hall stoping gaps in furze close. Mr, Mrs Forster & Mrs Herring drank tea here.

MH A fine day, some Small showers of rain. Mr Hardy at home all day, Wm Brew'd Porter. Mr & Mrs Forster & Mrs Herring drank tea here.

APRIL 25, SATURDAY

HR R Bye sowing seeds, T Boyce ploughing, Boy harrowing. T Baldwin to Wells with beer, G Thompson Cleanse'd `//. Mr H at Holt aftrn. Capt Hall stoping gaps, Jno Ram in M H. Josh Baker cam«e» & orderd load of Beer.

MH A cold windy day. Mr Hardy walkd to Holt Markt. Wm & MA rid up «in» Chaise, drank tea «at» Mrs Jennes's, they all went to the Play, came home eveng 12. A Wet eveng till 8 oclock then the Wind blew a perfect Hurracane till Morng. I very poorly . . .

below Bayfield Park, by Humphry Repton, Sept. 1779; two men are engaged in a rough shoot at the start of the season. Bayfield Hall lies in the valley near the ruined parish church (right); Glandford Church, on the far hill, was also partially ruinous. After his mother's death in 1794 Henry Jodrell embarked on schemes of improvement. He closed the road through the park in 1797, and, as Mary Hardy noted on 22 Apr. 1795, created new plantations.

Repton was not the expert assigned to the task, but a man named Richard Creed (d.1803 aged 44), brought in from the Jodrell estate at Syon Hill, Isleworth, Middlesex (*Diary 4*) [*Norfolk Museums & Archaeology Service* (*Norwich Castle Museum & Art Gallery*)]

APRIL 26, SUNDAY

HR T Boyce & M^{rs} H whent to Briston aftr^{n}. M^{r}, WH & Miss H at own Church.[1]

APRIL 27, MONDAY

HR R Bye to Cromer with beer, T Boyce at harrow for^{n}. Capt Hall stoping gaps for^{n}, T Baldwin to Blakney for 2 Chal^{d} Cinders from Mr Farthing. HR & Nath Raven came from Whissonsett for^{n}. Mr Flower & Mr Walden dine'd here. All whalk'd to fair aftr^{n}, M^{r} H sold 2 Cows & Bot [bought] one.[2]

above Cattle grazing beside a tributary of the River Wensum at Gressenhall, where they are in the care of the Norfolk Museums Service. The morning of Holt Fair was always devoted to farm livestock and horses, William Hardy selling two heifers and buying a cow on 27 Apr. 1795. Mary Hardy, with a direct housekeeping interest in the family's small dairy herd, is far more specific about these transactions than Henry Raven [*MB · 2011*]

facing page, top The former Half Moon at Bintree. It was for sale in Apr. 1795 from the Norwich brewer John Day's country estate of 31 tied houses and was visited 7 May 1795 by William Hardy snr and jnr, who appear to have been considering buying the Half Moon and also the Falgate at Stibbard and the Swan at Guist. In the end they bought none of them. The Half Moon stood gable end to the old meandering main Norwich–Wells road; the modern road now runs nearby. The old Swan and old Falgate stand full square against the modern road which at these points follows the course of the old highway [*MB · 2001*]

1 *own church* As well as attending Letheringsett in the morning with the rest of his family William went to Holt Church in the afternoon. His cousin, who was at Whissonsett that weekend, never expresses his feelings about attending Methodist meetings. At first Henry probably went out of kindness to his aunt, serving as her driver. Once it became plain that meetings were no longer an experiment but part of a new way of life he handed over the driving to others so that he could attend Anglican services once more.

Like William, he was particularly drawn to Evening Prayer at Holt Church

2 *fair* By his emphasis on 'forenoon', Henry implies that Boyce and Hall were employed 27 Apr. only until dinnertime. Baldwin's task would also have taken only half the day, but Bye would have been away much of the day on his 23-mile trip. John Ramm, Gunton Thompson and the farm boy are not mentioned at all.

The inference is that the last three were granted a full day at the fair and that three others missed only the horse and cattle fair. Henry fails to record any work done by Robert Bye for the following day and a half. Bye was either still recovering from the final hours of the fair or perhaps from subsequent imbibing to neutralise his resentment at missing it

MH A very Windy day. Henry Raven & Nath[l] from the Shop came Morn p [past] 11.[1] M[r] Hardy rid up to Holt fair foornoon, sold 2 Heefers for 10 Guineas, bought a Cow for £5 15*s* 6*d*, came home to dinner. M[r] Flower & M[r] Walden of Wells Dind here. M[r] H, W[m], MA & N Raven went to the Fair Afternoon, drank tea at M[r] Davys, came home eveng past 8 . . .

APRIL 28, TUESDAY

HR T Baldwin to Dawling with beer, T Boyce to harrow all day in field. Cap[t] Hall barrowing muck into garden, onloaded Cinders & stubing Roots, Jn[o] Ram in M H.[2] Nath R, WH & HR whent to the play.

APRIL 29, WEDNESDAY

HR R Bye to Salthouse with beer aftr[n]. T Baldwin, G Thompson, H Raven & Boy in brewhouse & clean'd great Cask.[3] Cap[t] Hall & T Boyce ploughing all day in field. M[r] H at home all «day». M[rs] & Miss H at M[r] Forsters, I whent for them evening. M[r] Nath Raven whent away after tea. WH road to Stody.

APRIL 30, THURSDAY

HR T Baldwin to Kettlestone & putting Porter into home-cask. R Bye & Tho[s] Boyce ploughing & sowing barley in 5 Acres. Capt Hall stubbing Roots & putting beer in home Cask. G Thompson, HR & WH putting porter into H [home] Cask. M[r] H at home all day, Master Herring drank tea here.

1 *Nathaniel* Son of Mary Hardy's shopkeeping brother Nathaniel Raven

2 *stubbing roots* Digging the stumps up: '*stub*, an old root, or stump; also to grub such roots up' (J.O. Halliwell, *Dictionary of Archaic Words* (Bracken Books, London, 1989; 1st pub. 1850)). For the novelist Anthony Trollope it was Herefordshire dialect and required explanation: 'They have already begun to cut down, or what they call stubb up, Barnton Spinnies' (A. Trollope, *The Prime Minister* (1st pub. 1876), chap. 75)

3 *in brewhouse* Mary Hardy notes that William was also brewing that day

below **The 'Furlgate' or Falgate at Stibbard (7 May) is labelled on Faden's map. Standing some way from the village centre it served travellers on the main road** [*Faden's Map of Norfolk 1797: Larks Press 1989*]

SEVERALS
Stibbard Green
Stibbard
Work Ho
Stibbard Furlgate
COMMON
STIBBARD
Guist Common

above A skittish colt enjoying summer grazing on a hot day. Although a brewing pupil, Henry also carefully records work on the farm.

We learn on 22 Apr. 1795 that the colt was put to ploughing and harrowing, and on 20 May to delivering beer, presumably to accustom the young animal to being harnessed and in the shafts. It is unusual to hear of the Hardys employing their colts, who were customarily sent to lush pastures in the summer and were not expected to earn their keep [*MB · 2011*]

MAY 1, FRIDAY

Henry Raven R Bye to Stalham with beer, T Baldwin to Sherringham & Edgefield with D°. Capt Hall tying faggots, T Boyce ploughing & sowing Barley. Jn° Ram in Malthouse. M^{r} H at home all day. Jo^{s} Baker & Mr Banyard cl'd [called] evening.

MAY 2, SATURDAY

HR R Bye came for [from] Stalham, H Raven whent to Walsham. T Baldwin in brewhouse & whent to Holt with beer, Capt Hall after jobs, T Boyce plough & sowing barley. G Thompson in brewhouse, Boy at harrow.

Mary Hardy A fine day. Wm Brewd Porter. Mr Hardy walkd to Holt Mark^{t} aftern, came home eveng 8 . . .

MAY 3, SUNDAY

HR R Bye Loaded for Fakenham & Syderstone, T Baldwin D° for Brampton. Famaly at Church. Miss Jennis & Miss D^{r} [Deborah] Johnson drank tea here.

MAY 4, MONDAY

HR R Bye to Fakenham & Syderstone with beer, T Baldwin to Brampton. Capt Hall jobs, Jn° Ram in M H, G Thompson began grinding Malt for brew. T Boyce ploughing, finnish«ed» 5 Acres. M^{r}, Mrs Flower dine'd & drank tea here.

MAY 5, TUESDAY

HR R Bye & T Boyce ploughing & sowing barley in field, T Baldwin to Thornage & Holt with beer & loaded for Southrepps. Jn° Ram in M H, Capt Hall skreening Wheat. M^{r} & WH to Southrepps. Mrs Goggs & Miss Raven came for^{n}.

MH A very fine warm day. Mr Hardy & W^{m} went to Southreps Morng 6, came home eveng 8. Sister Goggs & M Raven came Morng 11, the Man went home in the eveng with the Horses . . .

MAY 6, WEDNESDAY

HR R Bye, G Thompson, HR & Boy in brewhouse, T Baldwin to Southrepps with beer. T Boyce ploughing for^{n}, harrowing aftr^{n}. Jn° Ram in M H, Capt Hall [ ]. WH Brewing, M^{r} H at home all Day. Mrs Herring, M^{r}, M^{rs} & Miss Bartell drank tea here.

MAY 7, THURSDAY

HR R Bye sowing cloverseed.[1] T Boyce harrowing, made

[1] *clover seed* The diary is rarely specific over the types and varieties of grass sown, although it was a topic hotly debated at the time: see note for 30 Apr. 1794

an end of Barley sowing for^{n}, in garden after^{n}. Jno Ram in M H, T Baldwin helping to put Porter in home cask & whent to Briston aftr^{n}. R Bye to Wayborn with beer aftr^{n}. M^{r} & WH to Guist & Bintree. G Thom^{n}, H Raven put cleanse Porter into cask for^{n}.

MH A fine day, not so hot as yesterday. Mr Hardy & W^{m} rid [rode] to Stibbard & Guist to look at some publick Houses of Mr Days that are to be sold, came home eveng 6.[1]

MAY 8, FRIDAY

HR T Baldwin helping to Cleanse & whent to Blakney for 2 Chas [chaldrons] Cinders from M^{r} fathings, R Bye after jobs. Capt H at work in shrubberry, T Boyce in garden. G Thompson & H Raven cleansd morning. M^{r}, W & Miss H set of for Norwich mor^{g} ten, Miss Raven spent the Day at Holt.

MH A Close cold day, wind high. Mr Hardy & MA sett of for Norwich in our Chaise Morng 10, W^{m} went by Reepham.[2] M Raven spent the day at Miss Johnsons at Holt . . .

MAY 9, SATURDAY

HR R Bye to Cromer with beer. T Baldwin to Wiverton with beer for^{n}, Rolling barley aftr^{n}.[3] Jno Ram in M H, T Boyce in garden. G Thompson grinding Malt for brew, Capt Hall at work in shrubberrys.

MAY 10, SUNDAY

HR M^{rs} H, Mrs Goggs & Miss Raven to own Church for^{n}, D^{o} & D^{o} [Mrs Hardy & Mrs Goggs] to Briston aftr^{n}. M^{r}, W & Miss H came from Norwich Evening 8.

MH A Cold windy chearly day. Sister Goggs, I, M Raven & H Raven went to our Church foornoon, Mr Burrell preach'd. Sister & I & H Raven went to Briston meeting Afternoon, came home even 6. Mr Hardy, W^{m} & MA came home eve 8. Mrs Wymer of Norwich Died this Night[4] . . .

MAY 11, MONDAY

HR G Thompson, T Boyce, Boy & H Raven in brewhouse.[5] T Baldwin to Sherringham with beer, R Bye Drunk at Waybourn. Capt Hall in shrub^{y} [shrubbery]. M^{r} H whent to Walsham with Mr Dew, T Baldwin loaded for Walsham.[6]

[1] *Stibbard and Guist* To see the Falgate and the Swan. With the Half Moon at Bintree (the village named by Henry) they formed part of the brewery estate of the late John Day: see the captions on the previous pages and overleaf

[2] *Reepham* There was no public house belonging to Day's in the town. Mary Hardy may be referring to the Foldgate at neighbouring Whitwell, which was still for sale by Day's executor (*Norw. Merc.* 11 Oct. 1794 (illustrated overleaf), 25 Apr. 1795)

[3] *rolling barley* Marshall was scathing in his criticism of the lightweight, inadequate rollers used before and after sowing (W. Marshall, *The Rural Economy of Norfolk*, vol. 2, pp. 58, 145)

[4] *Mrs Wymer* See note for 26 Feb. 1794

[5] *in brewhouse* Mary Hardy names William as brewer

[6] *Dew* James, arriving in post just in time for the Ascension Day fair, probably the best day of the year for sales. He is shown in the register in 1795 as the new man at the Maid's Head, N. Walsham; by 1798 William Smith had taken over (NRO: C/Sch 1/16). The interregnum had been a long one. The last beer delivery had been on 26 July 1794, and the house is not listed in the register for Sept. 1794. Dew may later have moved to the Bushel, in St Augustine's, Norwich: see Mary Hardy's endnotes

TO BE SOLD,

ST. MARTIN's BREWERY, NORWICH,

(The Property of Mr. JOHN DAY, Beer and Porter Brewer, and Wool and Yarn Factor, deceaſed.)

Lot I. THE Capital DWELLING-HOUSE, Gardens, Orchards, Stables, Coach-Houſe, and Appurtenances, in ST. MARTIN's AT OAK.

The BREWING-OFFICE adjoining, and ſeveral ſpacious and new-erected large and convenient Edifices and Buildings for Tun-Rooms, Store-Rooms, Malt and Hop Lofts, Mill-Houſe, Counting-Houſe, &c. forming a complete premiſſes for conducting an extenſive trade.

The new-erected VAT-HOUSE and STORE-CELLARS adjoining or near the Brewing-Office, which will contain about 5000 barrels.

And Three ſubſtantial MALTING-OFFICES, near the Brew-houſe, that will wet upwards of 130 Cooms of Barley, with the ſpacious WOOL-HALL, lately erected, and large Store-Rooms for Corn, and Stabling for 20 Horſes.

Alſo, the following ESTATES in NORWICH, late of Mr. DAY, connected and intended to be ſold with this Lot:

Celler Houſe - - - - -	St. Martin's at Oak	Black Friars and Dwelling-houſes adjoining - -	St. George Colegate
Buck and Tenements - -	Same	Wherry and Tenements -	St. Peter per Mountergate
Queen Caroline - - - -	Same	Prince Ferdinand & Tenements	St. Julian
Dolphin - - - - - -	St. Mary	Black Swan and Tenements	St. Andrew
Crown and Sceptre - - -	St. Michael Coſlany	Roſe - - - - - - -	St. Peter per Mountergate
Two Brewers - - - -	St. George Colegate	King Alfred - - - - - -	St. John Timberhill
White Lion - - - - -	St. Paul	Half Moon and Tenements	St. Peter Southgate
Fountain - - - - - -	St. Benedict	Tiger and Tenements - -	St. Stephen
Globe - - - - - - -	Heigham	Caſtle and Tenements - -	St. James
Lord Camden - - - -	St. Gregory	King's Head - - - - -	St. Benedict
Roe Buck - - - - -	Same	Shoulder of Mutton & Tenements - - - - - -	St. Stephen
Horns - - - - - - -	St. Julian	Horſe and Groom - - -	Back of Inns
Trumpet and Tenements -	St. Stephen	Chequer - - - - - - -	St. Gregory
Toft's Gardens - - - -	St. Clement	Robin Hood and Tenements	Pockthorpe
Bird Cage - - - - - -	St. Swithin	Eight Ringers and Tenements	St. Michael Coſlany
Black Horſe - - - - -	St. George Tombland	Pheaſant Cock and Tenements	Ber-ſtreet.
St. John's Head - - - -	St. Michael Coſlany		

The above Premiſſes are in excellent repair, of the yearly value of 900l. and upwards, the greater part Freehold, and the remainder Leaſehold for long terms of years.

Alſo the LEASEHOLD INTEREST of the ſaid Mr. DAY, for ſundry ſhort Terms of Years, of and in the undermentioned ESTATES in NORWICH:

Dolphin - - - - - - -	Heigham	Cow and Hare - - - -	Heigham
Two valuable Meadows at the back of Brewing-Office	Same	White Lion - - - - -	St. Mary
Boar's Head - - - - -	On the Quay ſide	George Inn - - - - -	St. Stephen
Red Well - - - - - -	St. Michael at Plea	Two Quarts - - - - - -	Same
City of Norwich - - - -	All Saints	Jack Newberry & Dwelling-Houſe - - - - - -	St. Clement
Golden Ball - - - - -	Caſtle Ditches	Greenland Fiſhery - - -	St. Mary Coſlany
DoveTavern, Dwellinghouſes and Shops - - - -	St. Lawrence	Jolly Farmers - - - - -	St. Martin's Palace
King's Arms - - - - -	St. John's Sepulchre	Dun Cow, & a capital Malthouſe in Fuller's hole, 60 cooms ſteep - - -	St. Martin's Gates
Roe Buck - - - - - -	St. Martin's Palace	Hope and Anchor - - -	St. Lawrence
Elephant and Chambers -	St. Saviour	Turk's Head and Stands -	Weaver's Lane
Bellman - - - - - -	St. Peter Mancroft	Anchor - - - - - - -	St. Martin at Oak
Wheel of Fortune - - -	St. Edmund's	Golden Lion - - - - -	Brazen Doors.
Cock - - - - - - -	Lakenham		

There are Twenty other PUBLIC-HOUSES in NORWICH, connected with the Office hired by Mr. DAY from year to year; and the preſent number of Drawers for the Office in Norwich is Eighty.

Together with this Lot will be ſold EIGHTY-THREE LICENCES, appropriated (with the conſent of the Corporation of Norwich) to St. Martin's Brewing-Office, with the valuable ſtock of Porter and Nog, Beer, Malt, Hops, Coals, Horſes, Carts, Coppers, Maſhtun, Coolers, ſix new Vats, as fixed in Vat-Houſe, for near 3000 barrels, Pumps, Implements, Utenſils, Fixtures, Signs and Settles at Drawing-Houſes in Norwich, and all and every other the Stock in Trade uſed in the Brewery.

The ſituation and extent of theſe Premiſſes being ſo well known render any further deſcription unneceſſary. They certainly offer ſingular advantages to any perſon wiſhing to carry on an extenſive Trade, being capable of brewing and vending FIFTEEN THOUSAND BARRELS yearly.

Alſo, the following FREEHOLD *and* COPYHOLD ESTATES *in* NORFOLK, *late of* Mr. DAY, *in ſeparate Lots:*

Lot 2	White Horſe - - -	Croſtwick	Lot 15	Wodehouſe's Arms -	Wicklewood
3	White Horſe - - -	St. Faith	16	White Horſe - - -	Cawſton
4	Cock - - - - -	Upton	17	King's Head - - -	Hoveton
5	Falcon - - - - -	Limpenhoe	18	White Horſe - - -	Trowſe
6	Recruiting Serjeant -	Dereham	19	Adam and Eve - -	Carlton
7	Swan - - - - -	Coſteſſey	20	Queen's Head - -	Banwell
8	George - - - -	Catton	21	Chequer - - - -	Hoe
9	Foldgate - - - -	Whitwell	22	Ram Inn - - - -	Bawdeſwell
10	Horſe Shoes - - -	Baſſingham	23	White Horſe - - -	Edgefield
11	Swan - - - - -	Guieſt	24	Foldgate - - - -	Stibbard
12	George - - - -	Elmham	25	Horſe Shoes - - -	Worthing
13	Bull - - - - -	Tuddenham	26	Greenland Whale Fiſhery	Yarmouth.
14	Roſe and Crown -	Wyndham			

The ſeveral Parcels of Land belonging to each Country Eſtate will be ſold therewith. Many of theſe Country Houſes have been lately rebuilt, are now all in excellent repair, and together of the yearly value of 330l.

Alſo, the LEASEHOLD INTEREST *of the ſaid* Mr. DAY, *for ſhort Terms of Years, in the following* ESTATES *in* NORFOLK, *in Lots:*

Lot 27	Red Lion - - -	Eaton	Lot 30	Blue Boar - - -	Sprowſton
28	Black Horſe - - -	Swannington	31	White Horſe - -	Aylſham.
29	King's Head - -	Acle			

For Terms, Prices and Particulars enquire of Mr. Ganning, ſole Executor of Mr. Day, or Mr. John Grand, Solicitor, St. Giles's ſtreet, Norwich.

☞ The Premiſſes may be viewed (with Tickets) by applying as above. (1791

facing page and *above* On his death John Day's brewery in St Martin-at-Oak, Norwich, was put up for sale in Oct. 1794. His was a valuable business, the third largest in Norwich in 1794 after Tompson's and Finch's, with steeping capacity in the maltings totalling 130 coombs (when the Hardys had 40 coombs) and brewing *capacity* of 15,000 barrels a year (when the Hardys brewed 2000). He also had impressive 'new-erected' storage for long-maturing brews. 111 innkeepers or 'drawers' were tied to Day's.

His executor Daniel Ganning (d.1810 aged 63) stepped in to run the business and offer it as a going concern, but wished early to shed the country houses. In the event the city maltings, brewery and outlets were not bought by John Morse (1745–1837) until 1797.

The notice in the *Norwich Mercury* 25 Apr. 1795 additionally included as part of Day's country estate the Half Moon at Bintree, nearly 17 miles away from the manufacturing base. The houses at Hoe and Guist lay 18½ miles from Norwich; the Falgate at Stibbard 20 miles; the Greenland Whale Fishery lay an inconvenient 22 miles away at Gt Yarmouth.

Ganning, an alderman of Norwich, may have regarded the country estate as uneconomic. He announced its sale, to be held in separate lots on 9 May 1795 at noon at the Angel Inn, Norwich Market Place. William Hardy snr and jnr were in the city that day. But neither diarist divulges the reason for the 44-mile trip [*Norwich Mercury, 11 Oct. 1794: Norfolk Heritage Centre, Norwich*]

MAY 12, TUESDAY

HR T Baldwin to Walsham with beer. R Bye came about ten OClock & whent to Corpusta D^{o} D^{o} [with beer], T Boyce in garden. Capt Hall at work in shrubberry for^{n}, Jno Ram in Malthouse. W & Miss H & Miss Raven whent to Sherringham to tea, M^{r} H at home all day.

MAY 13, WEDNESDAY

HR G Thompson set of for Walsham morning 5. T Baldwin to T Atwoods & Clarks at Holt, R Bye to Cley & Bale with beer. T Boyce in garden, Jno Ram in M H, H Raven began to grind Malt for brew. M^{r} & M^{rs} H, Mrs Goggs, Miss Raven & Miss H at Mrs Forsters aftr^{n}, WH at home all Day.

MH A Cold windy day, small rain foornoon. We all drank tea at Mr Forsters except W^{m}. MR & W^{m} walkd to Holt foornoon, John Herring from Norwich came here foornoon.[1] G Thompson & Wife had our Cart & old Mare to Walsham Fair . . .

MAY 14, THURSDAY

HR R Bye to Norwich with beer, T Baldwin to Runton with beer. T Boyce in garden, Capt Hall in shrubberys. Jno Ram in M H, H Raven grinding Malt for Brew. M^{r} H at home all day, WH at Holt evening. Miss H & [Miss] Raven drank te«a» at Mr Sheldrakes.

MAY 15, FRIDAY

HR R Bye came from Norwich, Baldwin to Fakenham with beer. T Hall at work in shrubbery, T Boyce in garden, G Thompson came from N Walsham. M^{r} H & W [William] at home all Day. Miss H & Miss Raven at Holt aftr^{n}, WH whent for them Evening.[2]

MAY 16, SATURDAY

HR R Bye, G Thompson, HR & Boy in brewhouse, T Baldwin to J Bakers with beer & at work in brewhouse, WH brewing. M^{r} H at home all Day. Capt H in shrubberrys, T Boyce in garden, Jno Ram in M H. Mrs Goggs & Miss Raven whent away after tea. Mr Huson cal^{d} aftr^{n}.[3]

MH A Chearly day, wind Cold. Mr Hardy at home all day, Wm Brewd. M^{r} [ ] came to take the Southreps House to rebuild. Sister Goggs & M Raven went away eveng 5, heard Robt Raven had left his Mother last Sunday [4] . . .

[1] *John Herring* The absence of the prefix 'Mr' suggests he was not the future mayor (6 Sept. 1794). This was probably 'Master Herring' (30 Apr. 1795), inviting the Hardys to the Forsters at Bayfield or bringing the order for beer: the delivery was made the following day

[2] *Holt* Mary Hardy records that the family and visitors were having tea at the Forsters' (at Bayfield)

[3] *Huson* Possibly Peter Hudson, who was to move in Oct. 1795 from the Three Tuns at Wells to take over from John Metcalf at the Fleece, on Wells quay, with its 'neat postchaises and careful drivers'. William Pearson, the Wells carrier, gave up carrying to take over at the Three Tuns (*Norw. Merc.* 10 Oct. 1795)

[4] *Robert Raven* This would have been a tremendous blow, and must have caused shock waves through the family. Robert, the eldest son, had helped his mother, the copyhold farmer, run Whissonsett Hall Farm since his father's death in 1783 after a long illness; Robert was then only 12. The next son, William, had probably left home soon after his abortive brewing pupillage at Letheringsett in 1791. Henry was indentured to the Hardys; and the youngest surviving son, Nathaniel, was then 13.

Robert returned home on 1 Aug. 1795. His aunt does not record what he had done in the intervening months, and his brother Henry does not make any

above In the heart of the town of Fakenham, away from the traffic and the shops, can be found a series of narrow, winding lanes with glimpses of the soaring church tower and of cascades of pantiled roofs, gabled dormers, and tumbled-in brickwork on gable ends.

It was symptomatic of the family feeling of William and Mary Hardy for the anxious Ravens that they should set off for Whissonsett very shortly to give what support they could during the crisis reported on 16 May. They paused at Fakenham only on their return journey on 21 May, a market day.

Henry makes no mention of the anguish he must have been feeling at his brother's abandonment of the family farm [*MB* · *2001*]

MAY 17, SUNDAY

HR R Bye, T Baldwin, G Thompson & Boy Cleansed `//. M^{rs} H & H Raven whent to Briston aftr^{n}.[1]

MAY 18, MONDAY

HR R Bye to Sharrington with beer & Edgefield aftr^{n}. T Baldwin to Roll [rolling] in morning, to Holt for Wheels to Carry to Clay & Bro^{t} home 1 Chal^{d} Lime from Mr Johnsons. T Boyce in garden, G Thompson Cleanse'd X. Capt Hall at work in meadow, Jno Ram in M H, WH to South Repps.

comment in his professional journal of record.

Whissonsett, her home for nearly half her life, inspired Mary Hardy's deep and lasting love. In the years 1795–1807 she saw some of the Ravens' old links wrenched asunder; they lost the Hall and farm (already much diminished by 1795) in 1805. The story is told in *Diary 4* and in *World*, vol. 1, chaps 2–4

Mary Hardy's visit to Whissonsett

19–21 May 1795

MAY 19, TUESDAY

HR T Baldwin to Beckhigh. R Bye in brewhouse for^{n}, to Holt aft^{r} with beer, G Thompson grinding Malt for brew. T Boyce in garden, Capt Hall in Meadow, J Ram in Malthouse. M^{r} & M^{rs} H & H Raven sett of for Whissonsett morning nine.

1 *Briston* They returned from the meeting in time for afternoon service at Letheringsett Church

[1] *engine* The pumped jet of water was fed through the shrubbery: see *World*, vol. 1, chap. 10 on pleasure grounds

[2] *man from Norwich* Revd Mr Burrell identified him in the burial register 24 May 1795: 'William Telley of the parish of St Gregory, Norwich, killed by a fall from an overthrown cart near my garden wall, by which he dislocated his neck . . .' (NRO: PD 547/2)

above St Gregory, Norwich, the parish church of the Hardys' friend and attorney George Wymer, whose daughter Clara was married here in Sept. 1797.

Its parishioner William Telley was buried not in its tiny churchyard but in the village where he met his fatal accident 21 May 1795. Long-distance carriage of a body could be prohibitively expensive for the poor [*MB · 2001*]

MH A warm dry day. Maids & Betty Woods wash'd 5 Weeks Linnen. I & Mr Hardy & H Raven sett of for Whissonsett, got to Mr Goggs at Noon, drank tea at Bro^t^ Ravens, Slept at Mr Goggs.

MAY 20, WEDNESDAY

HR R Bye to Cromer with beer. T Baldwin to Wells with beer, took the Colt. Capt Hall in Meadow, Jno Ram in M H, G Thompson grinding malt for brew & Bin. H Raven came from Whissonsett fore^n^, WH whalk^d^ to Holt evening.

MH [at Whissonsett] A Hot dry day. Mr Hardy & Bro^t^ lookd over the Hall Farm foornoon, found it in very bad condition. I walkd up to the Hall foornoon, dind & drank tea at Mr Goggs.

MAY 21, THURSDAY

HR [at Letheringsett] T Baldwin, G Thompson, H Raven & Boy in brewhouse. R Bye after his harness for^n^, got up 2 Loads of sand aftr. J Ram in M H part of day, diging in shrubberry & Carting sand, Capt Hall at work in Meadow. Luke Basham & Boy mend^g^ harness. M^r^ & M^rs^ H came home Evening. Play'd the engine in garden Evening.[1]

MH A Hot dry day. We dind at Bro^t^ Ravens & set of for home eveng past 3. Bro^t^ & Sister Raven went with us to Fakenham Market were [where we] drank tea at the Crown & came home even near 9. A Man from Norwich dislocated his Neck with being overturnd in a Cart near Mr Burrells.[2]

[LETHERINGSETT]

MAY 22, FRIDAY

HR R Bye in brewhouse fore^n^, to Blakeny with beer to put on board ship. T Baldwin to Thornage for^n^, Loaded for Barmer & Syderstone aftn. J Ram in M H part of day & part in shrubberry. Capt Hall in Meadow, T Boyce in garden & fore Yard. WH whent to Blakney for^n^, M^r^ H at home all Day. A{m} Stranger got amischief last night comeing from Atwoods sale.

MH A Hot dry day. W^m^ rid to Blakney foornoon, came home to dinner, Mr Hardy at home all day. The Man

left 'Mr Hardy and Brother [Nathaniel] looked over the Hall Farm forenoon, found it in very bad condition' (20 May 1795). Whissonsett Hall was rebuilt in the mid-19th century on the site of the Ravens' ancient moated manor house. This west front, with its sweeping views over the fields towards Godwick, had a formal entrance from the pre-enclosure track leading south to Tittleshall.

The pronouncement on the state of the farm can hardly have cheered the four women and 13-year-old boy left in command when 23-year-old Robert Raven left his family and the farm on 10 May. The Hall was to be occupied by the Ravens for only 10 more years [*MB · 1998*]

Died at Mr Dobsons eveng 10 that got a Mischief last Night . . .

MAY 23, SATURDAY

HR R Bye & T Baldwin to Syderstone & Barmer with beer. T Boyce in garden, Capt Hall in Meadow. Jno Ram in Malthouse & Brewhouse all Day, G Thompson grinding Malt for brew. M^{r} H at Holt aftr^{n}, WH, Miss & M^{rs} H at Holt aftr^{n}.

MAY 24, SUNDAY

HR H Raven & M^{rs} H at Briston aftr^{n}, WH at Holt aftr & famaly at own Church Evening.

MAY 25, MONDAY

HR R Bye to Stalham with beer, T Baldwin to Sherringham with beer. G Thompson, H Raven & Boy in Brewhouse, WH brewing. Capt Hall nowork, T Boyce in garden forn [forenoon]. M^{r} H at home all Day. Miss M & S Davy drank tea here.

below The Whissonsett enclosure map of 1816 shows the Hall partially encircled by its moat, and the great barn of 1773 to the north [NRO: C/Sca 2/325, *detail*]

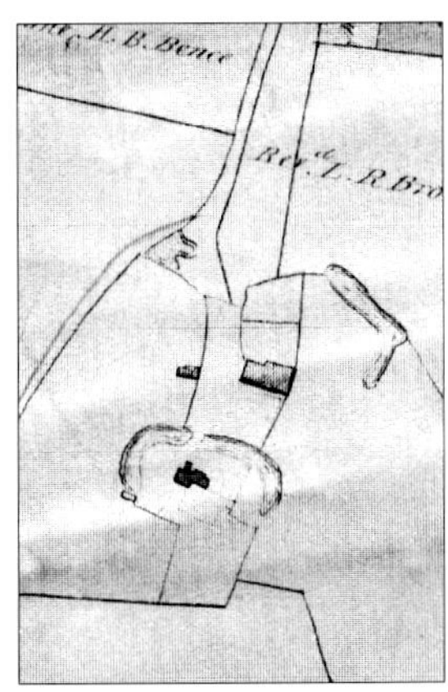
H. B. Bence

MAY 26, TUESDAY

HR T Baldwin to Brampton with beer, R Bye in brewhouse & whent to Holt. G Thompson Cleansed `// & cleard throughs [troughs], T Boyce after jobs forn. M^r^ H at home all day, Miss & WH set of for Whissonsett foren [forenoon].

MAY 27, WEDNESDAY

HR T Baldwin to Corpusta with beer, R Bye to Hindolvestone with beer, G Thomp^n^ grinding Malt for brew. M^r^ H at home all Day, G Thompson & H Raven Cleansd X morning.

MAY 28, THURSDAY

HR R Bye to Fakenham with beer, T Baldwin to Edgefield aftr^n^. Capt Hall in Meadow, Jno Ram after jobs. T Boyce in garden aftr^n^, G Thompson grinding Malt for brew. M^r^ H at home all Day, WH came from Whissonsett.[1]

MAY 29, FRIDAY

HR R Bye in brewhouse forenoon, to Dawling with beer aft^r^, T Baldwin to Briston & Holt with D^o^. T Boyce in garden, Capt Hall no work. Jno Ram trimming Malt & Wheat for^n^,[2] in brewhouse aftr^n^. G Thompson, H Raven & Boy in D^o^ [brewhouse], WH brewing. M^r^ H at home all day.

MAY 30, SATURDAY

HR T Baldwin to South Repps with beer, R Bye helping to Cleanse'd [cleanse] `// & whent to Gunthorp with beer. Jn^o^ Ram cleaning barn, sleept [steeped] & working in shrubberry, T Boyce in garden. G Thompson & HR Cleanse'd `//. M^r^ H & WH at Holt aftr^n^.

MAY 31, SUNDAY

HR G Thompson, H Raven, R Bye, T Baldwin & Boy Cleanse'd X morning. M^rs^ H & HR whent to Briston after^n^, M^r^ H & WH at Holt after^n^.[3]

JUNE 1, MONDAY

Henry Raven R Bye to Sherringham with beer, T Baldwin twice to Blakney for 3 Chalds Coles [3 chaldrons of coals] from Mr Farthings. G Thompson grinding Malt for brew, T Boyce in garden. M^r^ & WH at Waybourn & Sherringham.

[1] *Whissonsett* Mary Ann was staying with Henry Goggs; she came home on 6 June

[2] *trimming* This was near the end of the malting season, and haymaking and harvest were also approaching. John Ramm was probably putting the sacks of malt and wheat in order, to set in order being one of the many definitions of the verb 'to trim' (J.O. Halliwell, *Dictionary of Archaic Words*)

[3] *Briston* The pattern of church and meeting house attendance—one diverging from the rest of the family—which was to characterise the last 14 years of Mary Hardy's life has begun to develop. She notes her husband and son at Letheringsett Church on the afternoon of 31 May (whereas Henry has them at Holt), and the implication is that her Briston meeting clashed with Letheringsett's church service. The previous week (24 May) Mary Hardy and Henry had returned from Briston meeting in time to join all the rest of the family for Evening Prayer at Letheringsett, held that day at 6 pm.

It is not clear at what point she switched from Calvinistic to Wesleyan Methodism at Briston, but Mendham's old meeting seems to have changed in the second half of 1795.

When William Kilburn set up his meeting in 1800 (note for 2 June 1795) she made no mention of it. By May 1797 she was attending the *Wesleyans* at Briston

above and *top* **Mary Hardy (1 June) and Henry Raven (6 June) record the securing of the beer contract for the Army camp on the cliffs at Weybourne—which had for centuries been regarded as an invasion point—followed by the first delivery to the Royal Horse Artillery. An advance party was to stay overnight at E. Dereham on 6 June and march for the camp the next day. The Hardys did not permit their anti-war principles to interfere with a promising business opportunity** [*Cozens-Hardy Collection*]

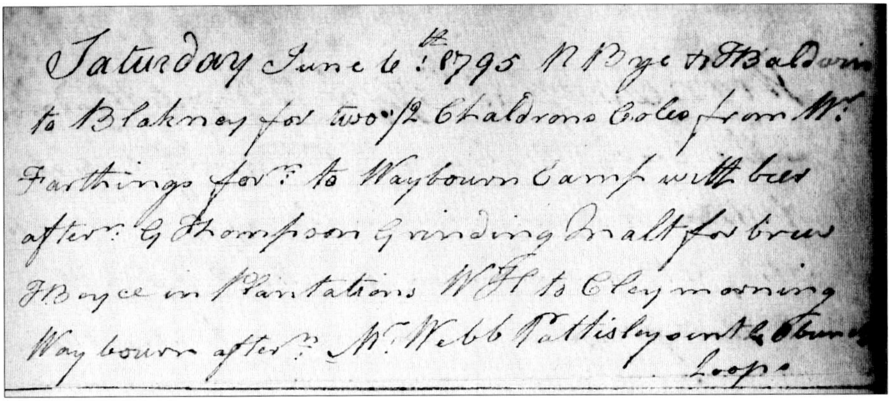

Mary Hardy A dry windy day. Mr Hardy & Wm went to Weyborn & Sheringham to git the serving the Camp with Beer, came home eveng past 11.[1] Mrs Forster drank tea here . . .

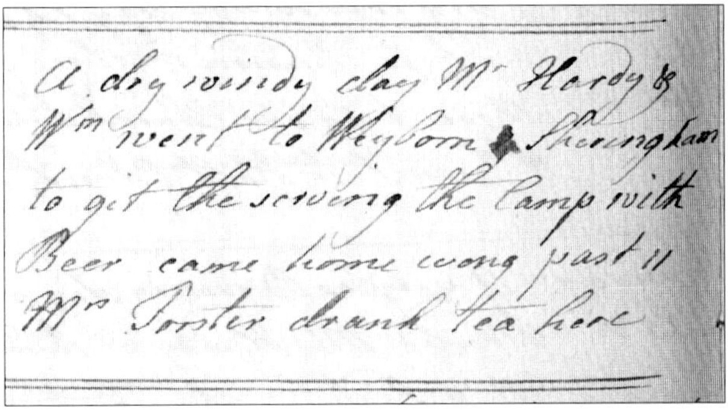

JUNE 2, TUESDAY

HR R Bye to Waybourn with beer, T Baldwin to Southrepps with beer. T Boyce in garden, G Thompson finnish«ed» grinding Malt for bru [brew] morning. Mr H drank tea at Mr Burrells, WH at home all Day. Mrs Mendham & Mrs Killburn drank tea here.[2]

[1] *camp* The Royal Horse Artillery were coming, to be joined for part of that summer by the Queen's Bays and on field days by the Norfolk Rangers, the troop of Volunteers raised by Lord Townshend of Raynham Hall. The beer would not have been for the soldiers alone. Weybourne's resident population of 323 (in 1801) was on field days augmented to thousands (*Norw. Merc.* 13 June, 29 Aug. 1795). See also notes for 26 June, 24 Aug. and 22 Oct. 1795

[2] *Mrs Kilburn* Wife of the Calvinistic Methodist William Kilburn, who had been a hotpresser in St Martin-at-Oak, Norwich, when on 24 Nov. 1775 he registered the new-built meeting house at Loddon belonging to the grocer William Crisp. On 27 May 1800 he similarly registered his own dwelling house at Briston as set apart for the worship of Protestant Dissenters, by which time the Wesleyans were firmly established in Mendham's 1783 chapel (NRO: DN/DIS 1/2, ff. 26, 83). Mrs Mend-

JUNE 3, WEDNESDAY

HR T Baldwin, G Thompson, H Raven & Boy in brewhouse, WH brewing. R Bye at Roll after«noon» & onloaded coles, T Boyce in garden. M^{r} H at home all day.

JUNE 4, THURSDAY

HR R Bye whent for aload of bricks & after jobs, T Baldwin after jobs.[1] G Thompson & H Raven Cleansed X, T Boyce in garden. M^{r} H & WH at home all Day.

JUNE 5, FRIDAY

HR T Baldwin to Cley & Wiverton with beer. R Bye in brewhouse fore^{n}, whent to Holt & got up 2 loade of Stones from Chas Lamb after^{n}.[2] T Boyce in gardens & Plantations, G Thom^{n} grinding M for brew. W Tinker here after^{n}.

MH A Hot dry day. Mr Hardy set of for Gresenhall & Whisonset Morng 9, John Thompson went with him. M^{r} & M^{rs} & M^{r} S Flower drank tea here & M^{r} & Mrs Sheldrake.[3]

ham was probably Elizabeth, widow of Thomas.

Mary Hardy does not mention the visitors

---

[1] *bricks* Probably for use as plinths for the new backs (18 and 24 June) built by William Tinker, John Bunnett and their men in June; the brewery would urgently have needed extra capacity to meet the needs of the camp. Unusually large numbers of men were put to work on the project: as many as ten 23–26 June. The Hardys were in a hurry

[2] *Charles Lamb* (Bapt. Letheringsett 1 Aug. 1766), eldest son of William Lamb (who was bur. there 5 Mar. 1814 aged 73) and his first wife Alice (bur. Letheringsett from Sharrington 20 Jan. 1784 aged 42), née Walker: see note for 13 June 1794. Charles marr. Letheringsett 2 Dec. 1789 Ann (Nanny) Lines or Lynes, who like her stepmother-in-law Susan worked as the Hardys' washerwoman. She was probably daughter to John and Edny Lynes of the King's Head at Cley, across the road from the Customs House (right).

The 1806 Norfolk pollbook shows the Tory-voting Charles Lamb as a Letheringsett cordwainer; he lived in a cottage on the main street near the Glaven. When his wife was buried at Letheringsett 19 Aug. 1824 aged 68 he was a customs officer once more

[3] *S. Flower* Samuel: see note for 18 Dec. 1793

JUNE 6, SATURDAY

HR R Bye & T Baldwin to Blakney for two ½ [two and a half] Chaldrons Coles from Mr Farthings forn, to Waybourn Camp with beer aftern. G Thompson Grinding Malt for brew, T Boyce in Plantations. WH to Cley morning, Waybourn aftern. Mr Webb, Pattisley, sent 40 bunches «of» hoops.[1]

MH A very hot dry morng, A Thunder Storm & raind great part of the afterno«on». Mr Hardy & MA came home from Whisonsett eveng past 9. Wm rid upto Holt Markt after tea . . .

JUNE 7, SUNDAY

HR R Bye & T Baldwin card [carried] off Cleanse beer. H Raven & Mrs H whent to Briston aftern, famaly all to Church forn.

JUNE 8, MONDAY

HR R Bye to Cromer with beer, T Baldwin to Waybourn with beer. H Raven in Malthouse, T Boyce in garden, G Thompson whitening tun room.[2] WH & Miss H whent to Holt forenoon. W Tinker half a day.

MH A Cold drisly day. Mr Hardy at home all day. Wm & MA rid up to Holt foornoon to see a Rejement of Artillary come into town which are to be Encamped at Weyborn near the Sea. They dind at Mr Bartells, came home to tea.

JUNE 9, TUESDAY

HR R Bye to Runton, cart broke down at Holt. T Baldwin to Beckhigh with beer, T Boyce in garden. Mr & Mrs H at Holt, WH & Miss H whent to Birmingham [Briningham] to meet the Atillery. H Raven in M H.

MH A very Close foggy day. Mr Hardy & I walkd up to Holt foornoon to se another Regiment of Artillerry expected at Holt, they did not come. We dind & drank tea at Mr Bartells, Wm drank tea there.

facing page The old Customs House at Cley, seen from the main street. Charles Lamb, son of the Hardys' farm servant, maltster, drayman and coachman William Lamb, served in the customs service at Cley as a tidewaiter (known later as preventive officer, and responsible for boarding and inspecting ships entering port). He seems to have lived beside the sea in 1795, the Hardys' men collecting two loads of stones from him on 5 June [*MB · 1998*]

above The bridge over a Wensum headstream, looking towards Pattesley.

This rivulet runs close to the border of Whissonsett and the long decayed settlement of Pattesley, from where the Hardys obtained barrel hoops on 6 June [*MB · 2011*]

---

1 *Pattesley* Comprising the southern part of Oxwick parish, and little more than one large farm. The hoops, for barrels, could have been of bark, not iron. In William Hardy's inventory of Sept. 1797, compiled when he was handing over to his son, he had in stock 180 iron-bound barrels valued at 9*s* each and 280 bark-bound barrels at 4*s* each (*World*, vol. 2, chap. 11)

2 *whitening* Whitewashing; also called whiting in the diaries

facing page 'Heard Jordan of Wifton was dead' (12 June). The Wiveton Bell stands across the green from the church where the innkeeper John Jordan also served as parish clerk. His daughter Mary took over until she married Edward Taylor at Cley in Oct. 1796, a few days after the last Letheringsett delivery [*MB* · *2002*]

JUNE 10, WEDNESDAY

HR R Bye to Hindolveston with beer. T Baldwin to Salthouse & got up aload of Stones. W Tinker & man all Day. HR whent to Stody, T Boyce in garden. M^r^, M^rs^, W & Miss H whent to Holt forenoon. Clarkson [Claxton] from Bale cald Evening.[1]

MH A Wet cold Morng, foggy afternoon. Mr Hardy, I & MA rid up to Holt in Chaise foornoon to se the Rejiment of Artillary come in, we came home to dinner. NB The Rejiment Lodgd at Holt that Night.

JUNE 11, THURSDAY

HR T Baldwin to Sherringham with beer. R Bye, G Thompson & Boy in brewhouse, HR in M H, WH brewing. W Tinker & man all Day, T Boyce in garden. M^r^ & M^rs^ & Miss H whent to Waybourn morning.

MH A fine pleasant Morng, foggy afterday. Mr Hardy on Horse back, I & MA in Chaise morng 8 followed the Rejiment from Holt to the Camp at Weyborn, came home eveng 2. Wm Brew'd.

JUNE 12, FRIDAY

HR R Bye to Bale & Thornage with beer, T Baldwin after jobs, T Boyce in garden. H Raven in M H. W Tinker & man all day. G Thompson Cleansed `//. M^r^ H at home all Day.

MH A very cold dry day. Heard Jordan of Wifton was dead, W^m^ rid to Wifton afternoon.[2] Mr Hardy at home all day.

JUNE 13, SATURDAY

HR R Bye to Edgefield & Waybourn with beer, T Baldwin helping to Cleanse & whent «to» Waybourn with beer. T Boyce in garden, W Tinker & 3 men all day. G Thompson & H Raven Cleansed X morning. Famaly all to Holt afternoon.

MH A cold dry day. Mr Hardy, I & MA walkd up to Holt Mark^t^, I & MA drank tea at Mr Davy^s^, came home eveng 8. W^m^ rid to Weyborn afternoon to the Camp, came home eve 9.

[1] *Claxton* Thomas Claxton, from the Angel at Bale (also known as the Angel and Oak), north of the church, had taken over from Ann Howlett, widow of Stephen Howlett. He stayed until 1804 or later, paying the modest annual rent in 1797 of £5

[2] *Jordan* See note for 6 Nov. 1793. Martha, née Middleton, wife of John Jordan, had been bur. Wiveton 25 Apr. 1792 aged 59. Four of their children were baptised at Edgefield: Ann (1765, bur. 1767); Mary (1767, the licensee in Sept. 1795); Anne (1769); John (b. 6 Nov. 1771, bapt. 17 Dec. 1771), who as 'Little Jordan' served as the Hardys' boy 1792–93 and married Cley 22 Oct. 1795 Elizabeth Jeckell of Cley, both signing. A third daughter, Martha, was bapt. Wiveton 20 Mar. 1775 and married there 7 Apr. 1795 John Coe of Wiveton, both making marks. By 1797 'Little Jordan' was innkeeper of the Hardys' tied house the Dun Cow at Salthouse: see note for 24 Feb. 1796.

At the time that William Hardy bought the Letheringsett brewery in 1780 the Blue Bell at Wiveton was owned by Henry Hagon, John Jordan paying rent of £6 10*s*. When the house was offered for sale by the brewer's executors William Hardy did not buy it and the tie was broken (*Norw. Merc.* 23 June 1781). It was for years still *supplied* from Letheringsett, the last beer delivery recorded by Henry Raven being on 3 Oct. 1796

WIVETON BELL

JUNE 14, SUNDAY

HR M^rs^ H & T Boyce whent to Briston. M^r^, W & Miss H at own Church aft^r^. H Raven whent to Waybourn.

MH A cold dry day. T Boyce went with me to Briston Meeting after, H Raven went to the Camp afternoon. W^m^ went to Holt Church afternoon, Mr Hardy & MA went to our Church aftern. Heard Mr Temple of Weyborn was Dead [1] . . .

JUNE 15, MONDAY

HR R Bye to Stody & Corpusta with beer, T Baldwin to Kettlestone with D^o^. W Tinker & 2 men fore^n^ & 3 after^n^, T Boyce in garden, G Thompson grinding Malt for brew. Mr Burrell, Mr Todhunter & Mr Sheldrake drank tea here. M^r^ H at home all Day.

JUNE 16, TUESDAY

HR R Bye to Syderstone with beer. Thos Baldwin to Cley for the Wheels & 1 Chal^d^ coles from Mr Ellis s, T Boyce in garden. M^r^ H at home all Day, WH & H Raven whent to Holt evening. W Tinker & 3 men all day.

JUNE 17, WEDNESDAY

HR T Baldwin, G Thompson, HR & Boy in brewhouse, WH Brewing. M^r^ & Miss H whent to the Camp after dinner. R Bye to Cley for 1½ Chaldn Coles from Mr Cooks,[2] H Raven painted the gate, T Boyce only half a day. Mr Woods cal^d^ here for^n^. W Tinker & 3 men all day.

1 *Temple* 'Died, on 13 June, aged 58, Mr Robert Temple, a respectable farmer at Weybourn' (*Norw. Merc.* 20 June 1795). The Weybourne register gives his *burial* date as 13 June

2 *Cooke* Probably the merchant Corbett Cooke: 'This chapel was bought in the year 1808 from Mr Corbett Cooke, merchant, Cley' (William Gilpin, the itinerant preacher on the Walsingham Circuit and also Chairman of the Norwich District, writing 18 Aug. 1809: NRO: FC 18/1, Record of members in the Methodist Connexion in the Walsingham Circuit).

At first a local (part-time) preacher and leader of the Wesleyan Methodist society at Cley, Corbett Cooke became an itinerant (full-time) within the Wesleyan Connexion: see *World*, vol. 3, chaps 3 and 4

facing page, far right All Saints, Bale, where the daughter of the Letheringsett brewer Henry Hagon lies buried by the chancel step. Elizabeth Southgate Hagon (1775–1802) was the last child to be born at Letheringsett Hall until the birth of William Hardy jnr's son William in 1820. She eloped with the 23-year-old Curate of Holt, Revd William Wright Wilcocks, to Gretna Green on the Scottish border where they married on 20 June 1795, following this with an English ceremony at Catton, Norwich, on 10 Aug. 1795. When living at Bale House she died aged 27, 'to the inexpressible grief of her family and the irreparable loss of her infant children, to whom she was a most attentive and affectionate mother' (*Norwich Mercury*, 24 Dec. 1802) [*MB · 2001*]

MH A drisly Morng, cold windy Afternoon. Wm Brewd. A Mr Wood, Chemist from London, calld here foornoon.[1] Mr Hardy & MA rid to the Camp at Weyborn Afternoon to se the Troops exercise, came home Eveng past 6.

JUNE 18, THURSDAY

HR T Baldwin to Stody & Briston, R Bye to Wells with beer, T Boyce no work. W Tinker & 3 men all day, Bunnets men came morning. G Thompson cleansd `//.

MH A very Wet cold day. Mr Hardy & W^m^ at home all day. Carpenters Building a New Back.

JUNE 19, FRIDAY

HR R Bye to Waybourn & Sharringham with beer, T Baldwin to the Camp with D^o^. W Tinker & 4 men all day, Bunnets 2 men all day. M^r^ H & WH at home all day, G Thom^n^ began grinding Malt for brew.

MH A very Cold day like March, wind very high at North, Cut the Vegetables in Garden very much. The Cliff at Sheringham against our Publick House much damag'd by A High Tide.

JUNE 20, SATURDAY

HR R Bye to Holt & Edgefield with beer, T Baldwin to Fakenham with d^o^. W Tinker & 4 men all day, T Boyce in garden, G Thompson grinding Malt for brew & Bin. WH to Sharringham, M^r^ H at home all day.

MH Wind high & as cold as Yesterday. W^m^ set of for Sheringham to see the breach the Sea have made,[2] Din'd at Mr Flowrs of Sherringham then went to the Camp & came home by Holt eveng 8. Mr Hardy at home all day. Heard Mr Wilcocks was gone of to Scotland with Miss Hagon.[3]

[1] *Wood* As a hop-dealer and chemist he sold brewing equipment such as brewer's yeast. The Hardys called on him in May 1800 in London, when either his shop or his house, or both, were in Wilderness Row beyond the Tower. If this was the chemist and brewing supplier Matthew Wood he also sold colourings and adulterants: see P. Mathias, *The Brewing Industry in England 1700–1830* (Cambridge Univ. Press, 1959), pp. 420–23; also *World*, vol. 2, chap. 7

[2] *Sheringham* The Crown had been endangered by storms and high tides 1788–92 and was to fall into the sea 22 Oct. 1800 (*Diary 4*). The unseasonal weather would have affected the quality of the wheat and barley at a time when they were turning from green to burnished gold in the field

[3] *Miss Hagon* Elizabeth Southgate (bapt. Letheringsett 4 Apr. 1775, d. Bale 20 Dec. 1802), only child of Henry Hagon by his second wife Elizabeth (d.1787), formerly Mrs Wilson, née Southgate. The orphaned Elizabeth was in the care of her mother's relatives, the Fishers. The English ceremony at Catton, Norwich, seven weeks after the elopement was apparently with the permission of her uncle 'James' [? Thomas] Fisher of Holt (*Norw. Merc.* 27 June, 15 Aug. 1795).

The groom Revd William Wright Wilcocks was a very colourful character (Mary Hardy's entry for 17 Jan.

below Exquisite mid-15th-century Norwich glass in the south window by Mrs Wilcocks' vault in Bale Church. Her fine ledger stone has a very large blank space for her husband or children; it was never filled [*MB · 2011*]

JUNE 21, SUNDAY

HR Mrs H & H Raven whent to Briston after. Mr, W & Miss H whent to Holt Church aftern. Miss Stannard cald [called] here morning.

MH A fine day. No service at our Church. Mr Hardy, Wm & MA went to Holt Church afternoon, home to tea. I & H Raven went to Briston meeting. Heard John Davy of London was Maried.[1]

JUNE 22, MONDAY

HR R Bye & T Baldwin getting up sand & loaded for Burnham, T Boyce in garden, W Tinker & 4 men all Day. H Raven whent to Gunthorp aftern, Mr & WH at home all Day. Boy getting Building Stones out of Holt lane.

MH A close day, reather cold. Mr Hardy at home all day, Wm went to Holt Bowling Green after tea.

1797). Son of William Wilcocks of Norwich, educ. Bungay, he was admitted 1789 to Caius College, Cambridge; scholar 1789–90, migrated 1790 to Trinity, BA 1794, MA 1820; ordained deacon Norwich 1794, priest 1806; Curate of Field Dalling 1801, of Wiveton 1801–04, of Thornage with Brinton 1806 (living at Thornage Rectory), Vicar of Barney 1806–46, Rector of Pudding Norton (a sinecure) 1807–46 (*Alum. Cantab.*; also the visitation returns). He was heavily in debt (*World*, vol. 2, chap. 11; vol. 3, chap. 1)

[1] *John Davy* [*jnr*] His wife Elizabeth died three years later, leaving him with two children: see note for 4 July 1795

above Dried whole hops (*Humulus lupulus*), seen greatly reduced in size. On securing the Weybourne Camp beer contract William Hardy jnr installed a hop back (24 June 1797), a vessel containing hops and perforated at the bottom to form a coarse sieve through which the wort passes from the copper to the cooler, thus removing the solids.

Ever a moderniser, his enhancement of the brewing process would have made his operation more efficient [*MB · 2011*]

JUNE 23, TUESDAY

HR W Tinker & 5 men all day. R Bye, G Thompson, HR & Boy in brewhouse, WH brewing. T Baldwin to Burnham with beer, Bunnets 4 men all day. M^r^ H at home all day.

MH A fine day, small Showr towards Eveng. Wm Brew'd. Mr Hardy at home all day. Mr Sheldrake & Mr Hill dind here, Mr Gathercole calld Aftern.

JUNE 24, WEDNESDAY

HR R Bye to Runton with beer, T Baldwin after Jobs. W Tinker & 5 men all day, Bunnets 4 men all day. W & M^r^ H at home all day, T Boyce in garden.

MH A fine day. Mr Hardy & W^m^ at home all day. Carpenters finishd the Back & began a Hop Back . . .

JUNE 25, THURSDAY

HR T Baldwin to Holt with beer & got up 1 load of Stones, R Bye to Holt with beer & bro^t^ home lime & loaded for Walsham, W Tinker & 5 men all day. WH to Gunthorp to Mr Clollier [Collyer], M^r^ H at home all day. H Raven whent to Gueastwick [Guestwick] for^n^. Bunnets 4 men all day, T Boyce in G [garden].

right A Second World War pillbox defies the battering of the surf at Weybourne Hope. Over the centuries there have been fears of an invasion force taking advantage of this deep-water anchorage. As a result Weybourne has one of the greatest concentrations of 20th-century fixed defences in the country [*Christopher Bird 2011*]

above The end of the cliffs at Weybourne Hope. A Second World War heavy-machine-gun post is dug into the clifftop commanding the defile, its cavernous loophole visible only from on shore. The diarists do not state where the Artillery camp was pitched, but it may have been on Muckleburgh Hill, west of the village centre, used in the 20th century as a military camp and now housing the Muckleburgh Collection open to the public.

If the mounted troops, resplendent in blue with red facings and formed only in Feb. 1793, had been apprehensive of their reception in a famously Jacobin county they had little to fear. The Foxite William Hardy and his family turned out on 11 June to join the procession to the coast, jostling with six-pounders and howitzers. The military stood outside the brewing regulatory system, and there were no applications to JPs for licences—a welcome change for a busy brewer [*Christopher Bird 1998*]

JUNE 26, FRIDAY

HR R Bye to Walsham with beer, T Baldwin to Holt with D^o^ & after jobs. W Tinker & 5 men only for^n^. HR grinding Malt for brew, G Thompson dressing W Stones. Mr Keeler, Mr Everitt & Miss Billings came & Dined here & whent to Camp with our famaly. Bunnets 4 men only half aday, T Boyce in garden half day.

MH A close day & some small Showers, turnd very cold towards eveng. Mr Everet, Mr Keeler & Miss Billins dind, drank tea & Supt here, they all went to the Camp afternoon with Mr Hardy, W^m^ & MA, being field day the Cannon were fired [1] . . .

[1] *field day* The Hardys delighted in visiting the camp, and were to take parties of friends and relations; even Henry managed to get to it occasionally.

The Lord Lieutenant Marquis Townshend had been pressing the Government for Weybourne to be defended, the background to and organisation of home defence being analysed in *World*, vol. 4, chap. 7. For local detail, see P. Kent, *Fortifications of East Anglia* (Terence Dalton, Lavenham, 1988), pp. 178–9, 185–90; also B. Lavery, *We shall fight on the Beaches: Defying Napoleon and Hitler, 1805 and 1940* (Conway, London, 2009), pp. 128–35, 158–9, 163. Basil Cozens-Hardy further sets the context with a document of 1587 detailing preparations to withstand an earlier attack: 'Norfolk coastal defences in 1588', *Norfolk Archaeology*, vol. 26 (1938), pp. 310–14

JUNE 27, SATURDAY

HR R Bye & T Baldwin to Camp with beer, T Boyce in garden. Bunnets 2 men half Day & 2 all Day. G Thompson laid down W Stones. M^{r} H at Holt after^{n}. Boy getting stones out of Street. WH at Holt after tea.

JUNE 28, SUNDAY

HR R Bye Loaded for Stalham. H Raven & M^{rs} H whent to Briston aft^{r}.[1]

JUNE 29, MONDAY

HR R Bye to Stalham with beer, T Baldwin to Sherringham with beer. T Boyce in garden, J Ram all Day.[2] M^{r} & WH at home all Day.

JUNE 30, TUESDAY

HR T Baldwin to Holt for^{n}, in yards after^{n}, T Boyce in garden. R Bye came from Stalham, J Ram all Day. M^{r} & WH at home all Day.

MH A close dry morng, Wet afternoon. Mr Hardy at home all day. W^{m} rid to Mr Colyers afternoon, bought some small Timber, drank tea there, came home eveng past 9…

JULY 1, WEDNESDAY

Henry Raven T Baldwin, G Thompson & Boy in brewhouse, WH d^{o} [in brewhouse] Brewing. T Boyce in garden, R Bye whent for aload of Wood. M^{r} H at home all Day. Mr Banyard & Mr Moore dine'd here. Jobbers came & Bot [bought] six piggs.[3]

JULY 2, THURSDAY

HR T Baldwin to Thornage with beer & Gunthorp for aload of Wood. R Bye to Hinderingham with beer, T Boyce in garden. G Thompson Cleanse'd `// for^{n}, XX aft^{r}.[4] WH whent to Gunthorp, Mr H at home all Day.[5] J Tinker & Barnes all Day.

JULY 3, FRIDAY

HR R Bye to Sherringham with beer, T Baldwin to Waybourn with beer. T Boyce in garden, W Tinker & 3 men all Day. M^{r} & WH at home all Day.

JULY 4, SATURDAY

HR T Baldwin & R Bye to Cley with beer & Bro^{t} home 3 Chal^{d} Coles from Mr Cookes, T Boyce at work in river. G Thompson grinding Malt for brew, W Tinker & 3 men all Day. M^{r} H at home all Day, WH at Holt aftr^{n}.[6]

---

[1] *Briston* Henry Raven left for Whissonsett after the meeting; William Hardy snr and jnr and Mary Ann attended Letheringsett Church that afternoon

[2] *all day* The diary is useful in showing which workers were paid by the day. John Ramm must have been paid off at the end of the malting season and then have been classed as a day labourer

[3] *jobber* A dealer acting on his own account as a principal; on this occasion as a dealer in livestock

[4] *cleansed* At the height of the summer both brews, the weaker and the stronger, were cleansed the day after brewing. During the colder months September–June cleansing seems to have been spread over two days following brewing day

[5] *Gunthorpe* 'After the timber,' noted Mary Hardy

[6] *Holt* William and Mary Ann went up to the shopkeeper to meet John Davy jnr and his new wife Elizabeth. They were to have two children: John (b. 1 June 1796, bapt. 28 June) and Elizabeth (b. 9 Nov. 1797 and bapt. 6 Dec.). Mrs Davy was buried 24 May 1798 in the north vault at All Hallows', Bread Street, in the City of London, where they lived.

John Davy jnr was to bring his second wife on a bridal visit to his father 12 Mar. 1802 (*Diary 4*)

left Basil Cozens-Hardy (1885–1976), in a studio portrait of *c*.1933. In that year he completed his typescript of brief highlights from his great-great-grandmother's diary which were published by the Norfolk Record Society in 1968 as *Mary Hardy's Diary*.

A Norwich solicitor all his long working life, except for service in the First World War during which he was badly wounded, he sorted and preserved huge numbers of documents now held in the Cozens-Hardy Collection and the Norfolk Record Office. From boyhood he was a keen photographer. Some of his images, with the permission of his family, are seen in these volumes.

Possessing a strong topographical sense, he is best known for his articles and books on Norfolk history which, like those by his friends Robert Wyndham Ketton-Cremer and Percy Millican, combine scholarship with lively readability.

A powerful illustration of Basil Cozens-Hardy's forethought in preserving family correspondence appears overleaf [*Cozens-Hardy Collection*]

JULY 5, SUNDAY

HR Famaly all to Church for^{n}, M^{rs} H at Briston aft^{n}. H Raven came from Whissonsett.[1]

Mary Hardy A Chearly day till towards eveng then turnd hasy, Wind cold. All went to our Church foornoon, Mr Burrell preach'd. T Boyce went with me to Briston meeting, a Mr Hill from Snoring preach'd there.[2]

JULY 6, MONDAY

HR T Baldwin to Cromer with beer. T Boyce in garden for^{n}, haymaking aft^{rn}. M^{r} & WH at home all Day. J Ram cutting grass, R Bye no work.

MH A dry close cold day. Mr Hardy & W^{m} at home all day. M^{r} & M^{rs} & Jo^{s} & Mary & M^{r} & Mrs John Davy [jnr] drank tea here . . .

JULY 7, TUESDAY

HR T Baldwin to Edgefield & Holt with beer, R Bye to the Camp. T Boyce in garden for^{n}, haymaking aftr^{n}, Boy haymaking after^{n}. M^{r} & WH at home all Day, Jno Ram cutting grass. Mr Jarves [Jarvis] came & Settled.

[1] *Henry Raven* He had set off on 28 June for Whissonsett, where he would have been needed for haymaking in his brother Robert's absence. He still maintained the brewery diary, presumably using notes made by William and writing them up on his return

[2] *Hill* The Hills were prominent in Methodist circles, Joseph Hill buying the 1783 Briston chapel (note for 5 Apr. 1795); a mural tablet to his wife Ann (d. 12 Nov. 1812 aged 42) is in its successor of 1812. *Josiah* Hill, farmer, and Ann, housewife, are listed in 1798 as paid-up members of the Lt Snoring Wesleyan society, this being the first year for which the lists have

above and *right* This unusual archival scrap of paper sheds light on Mary Hardy, as in it we learn how she was regarded by an acquaintance. The letter, on one sheet of paper, was written at Milford in S. Wales on 20 July 1842. It is a former Wesleyan Methodist itinerant preacher's letter of condolence to Mary Ann's son William Hardy Cozens on the death of his uncle, William, the previous month.

Josiah Hill had recently retired: 'I sensibly feel the advantage of freedom from the labours and anxieties of itinerancy . . .' He was then aged 68, and had begun preaching when aged about 21 as a Wesleyan Methodist, although he had been baptised into Calvinism in 1773 at Guestwick Independent Church. He had evidently known Thomas Mendham, who had been forced out of the Calvinistic Methodist Chapel of 1775 at Briston with which Guestwick became closely linked in 1783. He asks William Hardy Cozens to return one or two letters of 'poor Mendham' which he had lent him; and he ends, 'My best love to my relatives in Briston'.

He remembers Mary Hardy and Mary Ann as being 'at the commencement of my ministry amongst my most constant and attentive hearers'. He is the first Methodist preacher, apart from Mendham, to be named by Mary Hardy (5 July 1795); she goes on to record more than 40 other Nonconformist preachers over the next 14 years. Josiah Hill died in 1844.

The letter is transcribed in full in *Mary Hardy and her World*, volume 3, chapter 3 [*Cozens-Hardy Collection*]

JULY 8, WEDNESDAY

HR T Baldwin, G Thompson, H Raven & Boy in brewhouse, WH A-brewing. T Boyce cutting grass, Jn° Ram cutting grass. Mr & Mrs Hardy, Mr Goggs & Steward all whent to the Camp aftern.[1] Jn° Rolfe [ ].[2]

below **From Mostyn John Armstrong's history of Norfolk (1781). The Hardys kept a copy in their counting house, as we know from the 1797 inventory. He calls in an earlier war for a military camp of Regulars or Militia to be established at Weybourne. If, as the diaries suggest, the arrival of the troops in 1795 was a novelty, it could explain the way the soldiers were feted. Mary Hardy and Henry Raven record 14 visits to the camp that summer by their family and friends—quite apart from the beer deliveries** [*M.J. Armstrong, The History and Antiquities of the County of Norfolk (Norwich, 1781), Holt hundred, p. 117, detail*]

H O L T. 117

At a place here called Waborne Hope, was a fortification; the ſhore is ſtony, and the ſea ſo deep that ſhips may ride here, and lie againſt it: the Danes are ſaid to have landed here on their invaſions.

This Waborne Hope, or Waborne Hoop, as it is now corruptly called, is the moſt dangerous place, and moſt open to an enemy, of any on the Norfolk coaſt: the ſhore is the boldeſt of any, and tranſport-ſhips may approach it ſo very near as almoſt to land an army without the aſſiſtance of flat-bottomed boats. It is an object worthy of conſideration, eſpecially at the preſent time, when an invaſion from France is ſo much threatened, whether it would not be proper to renew the fortification, and to erect a fort of modern conſtruction, with batteries of heavy cannon to defend it. When ſo many camps were formed in the year 1778, of regulars and militia, in different parts of the kingdom, it muſt be preſumed that government apprehended an invaſion ſomewhere, and therefore the moſt acceſſible places on the Britiſh coaſt, and this is one of the moſt acceſſible, ought to have been particularly guarded. It ſtill remains unnoticed, and in its defenceleſs ſituation ſeems to invite an enemy, and to court the attack.

survived in the (Wesleyan) Walsingham Circuit. In 1799 James Hill, shopkeeper, and Harrison Hill were in the Fakenham society; also a single woman, Ann Hill, housekeeper. In 1801 Harrison Hill, then of Hempton, was a local preacher (NRO: FC 18/1); Mary Hardy was to hear him at Briston in 1804 (*Diary 4*).

Josiah and Harrison, the sons of Joseph Hill, of Salle, farmer, and his wife Mary, were born 13 Nov. 1773 and 17 Apr. 1775 and bapt. 30 Nov. 1773 and 26 Apr. 1775 by Revd James Kirkpatrick of the Guestwick Independents (NRO: FC 11/1, Guestwick Independent Church book 1694–1854, p. 149). The preacher at Briston on 5 July 1795 is almost certainly this Josiah Hill, admitted that month on trial as a Wesleyan itinerant preacher (*Minutes of the Methodist Conferences*, vol. 1 (London, 1812), p. 302).

Mary Hardy heard Josiah at Briston, Cley and Fakenham 1798–1803 (*Diary 4*)

---

[1] *Steward* Farm steward to Henry Goggs; they had arrived the previous day

[2] *John Rolfe* A Coltishall builder whom the Hardys had first used 20 years earlier. He had also worked on their Cley malthouse in 1781 and installed the new brewing copper at Letheringsett in 1790. As Mary Hardy does not mention his visit it is likely that he stayed in the village at the King's Head

MH A close cold day. Wm Brew'd. Mr Hardy, I, Mr Goggs & Servt went to the Camp afternoon, it was field day, we came home to tea, Mr Goggs went home after tea. Mr Tooby drank tea here [1] . . .

JULY 9, THURSDAY

HR R Bye to Runton with beer, T Baldwin to Wiverton with D^o^ & helping to Cleanse. G Thompson & H Raven Cleansed `// & XX. W Tinkers two men all day, Bunnets two men all day, T Boyce cutting grass. M^r^ H at home all Day, WH at Holt to dine at Mr Bartells. W Tinker began to take down the backs.

JULY 10, FRIDAY

HR R Bye to Corpusta with beer, T Baldwin to the Camp & Loaded for Syderstone & Barmer. T Boyce cutting grass, Jno Ram, Boy & H Raven haymaking. W Tinker & two men all Day, Bunnets two men all Day. M^r^ & WH at home all Day.

MH A cold close day, wind high. Mr Hardy & W^m^ at home all day gitting up the new Backs . . .

JULY 11, SATURDAY

HR R Bye & Thos Baldwin to Barmer & Syderstone with beer, T Boyce cutting grass. W Tinker & two men all Day, Bunnets two men all Day. Jno Rolfe putting in furnes [furnace] bars. M^r^ & WH at home all Day. H Raven whent to Gu«e»stwick, Boy to Dawling & Holt with beer. Miss H Dine'd & drank tea at Holt.

JULY 12, SUNDAY

HR M^rs^ H & H Raven whent to Briston afternoon. M^r^, W [William] & Miss H at own Church afternoon.[2]

JULY 13, MONDAY

HR R Bye to Brampton with beer, T Baldwin to South Repps with D^o^. W Tinker & two men all Day, Bunnets two men all Day. T Boyce, Jno Ram, Boy & H Raven haymaking. M^r^ & WH at home all Day, G Thompson grinding Malt for brew.

MH A very Cold windy day. Mr Hardy & W^m^ at home all day. I very Ill with A Cold.

JULY 14, TUESDAY

HR R Bye to Waybourn with beer,[3] T Baldwin to Briston with D^o^. Jno Ram in shrubbery for^n^, haymaking after^n^. T Boyce in garden for^n^, haymaking after^n^. W Tinker &

[1] *Tooby* Edward Cox Tooby had taken over from John Bolton as excise officer in Holt District in the massive excise reorganisation of 1789 (*Diary 2*); his place was later taken by John Sheldrake. He was in 1795 officer of Fakenham Ride, Lynn Excise Collection, and was posted 10 Aug. 1798 to become officer of Northampton 1st Division, Northampton Collection, only to return to Norfolk six months later as officer of Norwich 8th Division at his own request (TNA: PRO CUST 47/408, p. 38; CUST 47/410, p. 95). He died 5 June 1834 aged 74, his headstone at Dereham recording he was 'many years Supervisor of Excise'

[2] *own church* Mary Hardy recorded William at Holt Church that afternoon. The family was regularly divided between three places of worship

[3] *to Weybourne* To the Crown; Henry is careful

Exciſe. (*Ale, &c.*) 41

of exciſe, or two juſtices, on proof thereof, ſhall diſcharge the duties thereon impoſed by this act. ſ. 16.

And every dealer in and retailer of *cyder* and *perry*, and other perſon receiving into his cuſtody either of them for ſale, and every perſon who ſhall buy any fruit to make into cyder or perry for ſale, ſhall make entry of his ſtorehouſes, cellars, and other places, at the exciſe office within the diſtrict; on pain of 50 l. 1 G. 3. c. 3. ſ. 21.

Places to be entred.

By the 15 G. 2 c. 11. No common brewer, innkeeper, victualler, or other retailer of beer or ale, ſhall without firſt giving notice at the next office of exciſe, or to the commiſſioners or ſubcommiſſioners, or one of them, erect, alter, or enlarge, any tun, fat, back, cooler, or copper, and make uſe thereof for brewing or making any beer, ale, or worts; on pain of 50 l. And every other perſon, in whoſe occupation any houſe, out-houſe, or other place ſhall be, where any ſuch private tun, fat, back, cooler, or copper ſhall be found, ſhall alſo forfeit 50 *l.* And the ſame together with all beer, ale, or worts therein, ſhall be taken up, ſeized, and forfeited. ſ. 1.

Notice and entry of places for brewing beer or ale.

And by the 5 G. 3 c. 43. If any common brewer ſhall *alter* the poſition of any tun, batch, float, cooler, or copper, after the ſame hath been ſet up and fixed, without firſt giving notice thereof in writing to the officer; or ſhall place any boards, ſtone, wood, or any other materials at the dipping place; or ſhall by any other means prevent or hinder the gager from taking true dips and gages of beer, ale, or worts; he ſhall forfeit 20 l. ſ. 25.

And the officer of exciſe in the day-time, and in the preſence of a conſtable, where he ſhall have juſt ſuſpicion, that any private back, tun, or other concealed veſſel or receptacle are uſed by any brewer, maker, or retailer of exciſeable liquors, on requeſt firſt made, and cauſe declared, may break open the door, or any part of his brewhouſe, warehouſe, or other room in his poſſeſſion, and enter, and break up the ground in ſuch houſe or room, or ground near adjoining in his poſſeſſion, to ſearch for ſuch back, tun, or other veſſel, or any pipe or conveyance leading thereto; and if he finds any private pipe or other conveyance, he may ſearch and follow the ſame, and if it ſhall lead into any ground, houſe, or place in the poſſeſſion of any other perſon, on like requeſt, and with a conſtable, he may enter the ſame, and break open the ground, or any part of the houſe if occaſion ſhall be, to follow ſuch private pipe, in order to find out ſuch concealed back, tun, or veſſel, making good the ground or houſe ſo broken up, or giving reaſonable ſatisfaction to the

facing page The tower of Coltishall Church, from the north-west; Mary Hardy had recorded the local builder John Rolfe 'mending the steeple' at Coltishall in July 1774. The Hardys must have thought highly of Rolfe's expertise, for they called him over to Letheringsett for major work on the brewing backs and furnaces in July 1795. He seems to have specialised in the installation of kilns, furnaces and ovens [*MB · 2001*]

left From Burn's *Justice of the Peace*, a work owned by the Hardys and listed in the inventory of Sept. 1797 (*Diary 2*, app. D2.C). Burn devotes 239 pages to the Excise. Here he sets out the statutory obligations of a common brewer making alterations to his equipment.

When he called on 8 July 1795 Edward Cox Tooby—probably deputed as he was *not* the excise officer on the spot—would have been checking the recent work and looking for concealed pipework designed to defraud the Revenue [*J. Burn, The Justice of the Peace and Parish Officer, 16th edn (1788), vol. 2, p. 41*]

two men all Day, Bunnets two men all Day. G Thompson finnish«ed» grinding Malt for brew. Mr & Mrs Raven came from Whissonsett morning, whent to the Camp with Mr & Miss H & H Raven afternoon. Mrs H very Porly.

to differentiate between deliveries to the public house and to the camp

MH A tolerable day, wind cold. Mr Hardy & Wm at home all day. Brot & Sister Raven came morn 11, they & Mr Hardy & H Raven rid to the Camp afternoon, came home to tea. I very poorly with a Cold . . .

JULY 15, WEDNESDAY

HR R Bye to Cromer, Baldwin to Wells with beer. W Tinker all day, Matt Booth & man all Day.[1] T Boyce in garden, Jno Ram in Shrubberry. Mr & WH at home all Day.

JULY 16, THURSDAY

HR R Bye, T Baldn, Boy, G Thompson & HR in brewhouse, WH brewing. W Tinker all Day, T Boyce & Jno Ram haymaking. Mr H at home all day. Baldwin whent to Holt with beer afternoon.

MH A fine day. Wm Brewd. Mr Hardy & MA, Brot & Sister Raven rid to Lower Sheringham by the Camp Afternoon, drank tea there & came home eveng past 9. I poorly with a Cold . . .

JULY 17, FRIDAY

HR R Bye to Hildolvestone with beer, T Baldwin to Sheringham with beer. G Thompson & H Raven Cleansed `// & X. WH & Mr H at home all Day, Mr Raven whent home last night.[2]

JULY 18, SATURDAY

HR R Bye to Holt & Dawling, T Baldwin to Fakenham. Jno Ram cutting Vetches, T Boyce in garden. Mr & WH at Holt market afternoon, G Thompson Dressing flower.

JULY 19, SUNDAY

HR Mrs H & H Raven whent to Briston aftern, famaly all at own Church morning.

JULY 20, MONDAY

HR R Bye to Kettlestone with beer, T Baldwin very ill. T Boyce at work in River & in garden, G Thompson & H Raven grinding Malt for brew. WH to South Repps. Mr Mann, Miss Baker & Miss Man drank tea here, Mrs Smith drank tea here.[3]

JULY 21, TUESDAY

HR R Bye, Jno Ram & Boy after Hay. H Raven dressing Malt Stones, G Thompson [ ]. Mr H at home all Day, WH whent out aftn to buy some hay. Jno Ram in Shruy [shrubbery].

[1] *Matthew Booth* A Holt plumber and glazier, these being allied trades: see note for 25 Oct. 1796. Joseph Booth is also given as a Holt plumber and glazier at this time (*Univ. Brit. Dir.*, vol. 3, p. 279)

[2] *Mr Raven* The MSS are at times at variance over dates and movements. Mary Hardy records that her brother and sister-in-law left after tea on 17 July (Diary MS)

[3] *Mann* John and Priscilla Mann's son Isaac (bapt. Cley 4 Sept. 1777), who in 1795 was living at Holt at his mother's and who later had a long career in the W. Indies. Having attended the grammar schools at King's Lynn (under Mr Lloyd) and Holt (Mr Atkins) he was preparing to go up to Cambridge, being admitted to Caius College in 1796; BA 1800; ordained deacon 1800, priest Norwich 1801.

He married 6 Jan. 1801 Miss Leaky/Lecky of Gt Russell Street, London, and served the curacies of Holt, Aylmerton (where his young son was scalded to death in 1803: see *Diary 4*, note for 27 Sept. 1801), and Hemsby 1805–06. In Jamaica he served as Rector of Vere 1807, St Catherine's 1808, and Kingston 1813–28. He died 31 Oct. 1828 aged 51.

With him on 20 July was Miss Mann, probably his sister Sarah Anne (bapt. Cley 5 Jan. 1782), the Manns' only daughter; she did not marry. Another son, John, had died aged about nine months in Dec. 1779

MH A very fine day. Maids & Betty Woods wash'd 5 Weeks linnen. Mr Hardy & W^m^ at home all day. Wheat Meal 3/- pr Stone [1] . . .

JULY 22, WEDNESDAY

HR R Bye, G Thompson & Boy in brewhouse, H Raven dressing Malt Stones.[2] WH D^o^ brewing, M^r^ H at home all Day. Jno Ram in Shrubberry all Day.

JULY 23, THURSDAY

HR R Bye helping to Cleanse `// & whent to Holt & upper Sherringham with beer. Jn^o^ Ram in Shrubberry all Day, G Thomp^n^ & H Raven Cleansed `// & XX. W Tinker & two men all Day. WH & M^r^ H at home all Day. D Pleasence came & Orderd aload of beer.

JULY 24, FRIDAY

HR R Bye to Salthouse & Waybourn with beer. Jno Ram, G Thompson & Boy got up two load of hay. W Tinker & two men all Day. M^r^ & WH at home all Day.

MH A Showry day. Mr Hardy & W^m^ walkd to Thornage to look at some Hay, got very Wet.

JULY 25, SATURDAY

HR R Bye to Gunthorp fornoon, getting up hay after^n^. G Thomp^n^, Jno Ram & Boy got up 5 load of hay. Mrs Thomp^n^, E Hall & H Thompson haymaking.[3] W Tinker & two men all Day. Mr & WH at home all Day, H Raven finnis [finished] Malt Stones.

MH A very fine day. Our people got up all our Hay. Mr Hardy & W^m^ at home all day . . .

JULY 26, SUNDAY

HR Famaly all to Church aftern, H Raven whent to Waybourn aftern.

JULY 27, MONDAY

HR T Baldwin to Bale with beer forenoon, ploughing afternoon. R Bye to gitting up Vetches forn [forenoon], to the Camp afternoon. Jno Ram whent to plough & after Vetches for^n^, W Tinker & two men all Day. W Hardy & Miss H whent to Sherringham afternoon. G Thompson grind«ing» Malt for brew.

MH A fine day till towards eveng then raind great part of the Night. M^r^ & Mrs Baker drank tea here. W^m^ & MA rid to the Camp & Sheringham, drank tea at Mr Flowers, came home Eveng past 9.

[1] *wheat meal* The diarist gives the first hint of the wheat famine which was to strike nationally (see entries for 17–21 Dec. 1795).

On the orders of the Privy Council the Norwich magistrates introduced a series of emergency measures, including a ban on producing flour (as opposed to lower-grade meal) until 1 Oct. (NRO: C/S 1/15, Norwich Quarter Sessions, 15 July 1795).

The unfolding story of high wheat prices and bread riots is told in *World*, vol. 3, chap. 6

[2] *maltstones* From 21 July 1795 Henry Raven was to share with Gunton Thompson the task of dressing the Hardys' maltstones, but not the wheatstones

[3] *Mrs Thompson etc* Probably Ann, wife of the miller (see note for 25 July 1794), with their daughter Harriet Gunton Thompson and with Elizabeth Hall.

Harriet married Letheringsett 20 Feb. 1797 James Riches Moy of Ingworth. Their first child Harriet Gunton Moy was born 23 May 1797 and bapt. Letheringsett 24 May; they then moved to Ingworth

facing page The Swan at Whissonsett stood at the crossroads opposite Mary Hardy's old home on the corner and at the start of the long drive south to the Hall. It closed in 2006 [*MB · 2000*]

above 'Robert Raven returned home to his mother' (1 Aug. 1795). Although William and Mary Hardy stayed at Nathaniel Raven's 17–22 Aug. they very unusually did not call at Whissonsett Hall or see any of that side of the family. Relations may have been strained following William Hardy's unfavourable verdict on the farm (20 May). This panorama on the approach to the farm from the north-west is of wheatfields heavy with grain. In the summer of 1795 the precious wheat was wiped out, leading to the food riots recorded by the two diarists that winter [*MB · 2011*]

JULY 28, TUESDAY

HR T Baldwin to Sherringham with beer,[1] R Bye ploughing in 5 Acres all Day. Jn° Ram in Shrubberry, W Tinker all Day. Mr & WH at home all Day.

MH A fine day. I poorly, dimness in my Eyes. Mr Hardy at home all day. Wm poorly with a Cold & tooth ake, walkd up to Holt afternoon, got his tooth drawn, drank tea at Mr Bartells. A Shower in the eveng.

JULY 29, WEDNESDAY

HR R Bye to Holt & Cley with beer. T Baldwin, G Thompson, H Raven & Boy in brewhouse, WH Brewing. Jas Tinker half a day, Jn° Ram in Shrubberry. Mr Askew dined here. Mr H at home all day.

MH A Showry day. Mr Hardy at home all day, Wm Brewd. Mr Askew, one of the Artillerry Men from the Camp, dind & drank tea here, Mrs Flower came after tea.

1 *Sheringham* The presence of the Artillery seems to have quadrupled Edward Hall's trade at the Crown, one of Weybourne's two public houses at the time, where deliveries shot up from roughly one a month to one a week.

Nearby Sheringham also profited from the new arrivals, and from all those flocking to the field days and other excitements. Deliveries tripled to Robert Johnson at the Crown at Lower Sheringham, rising from three-weekly intervals to weekly

JULY 30, THURSDAY

HR T Baldwin & R Bye at home for^{n}, to Gunthorp after^{n} for a «load of» timber. G Thompson & H Raven Cleansed `// & X beer. M^{r} & WH at home all day.

MH A fine day. Mr Hardy & I rid to Wells foornoon in the Chaise to speak to Mr Everett about some Money he ows Mr Hardy.[1] We dind at Waldens at the Fighting Cocks, came home eveng past 7. W^{m} & MA walkd up to Holt afternoon, drank «tea» at Mr Bartells.

JULY 31, FRIDAY

HR R Bye to Overstrand with beer, T Baldwin after Jobs. Jno Ram in garden, G Thompson to Cley fair after^{n}. M^{r} & WH whent to Edgefield & bot [bought] some hay.

MH A very Showry day. Mr Hardy & W^{m} rid to Edgefield afternoon to look at some Hay of Mr Derbys,[2] bought ab^{t} 5 Loades for Eighteen Guineas,[3] drank tea at Mr Mins's,[4] came home eveng past 8.

[1] *Everitt* See note for 7 Apr. 1794. It is not clear if this is John Everitt, earlier imprisoned for debt, or Nicholas, who was about to be arrested (21 Sept. 1795)

[2] *Darby* John, an Edgefield farmer, had married in 1780 into the Coltishall brewing family whom William Hardy had served as brewery manager. His wife Ann (bapt. Coltishall 21 Sept. 1744, bur. Edgefield 14 Dec. 1800) was co-heiress to her father William Wells (bur. Coltishall 31 May 1751) and owner 1744–97 of two of the tied houses. During her minority and after her father's death her uncle, the former Edgefield farmer Zephaniah Oakes (bur. Coltishall 22 Dec. 1770) acted for her; her mother Sarah, née Oakes, was bur. Coltishall 18 May 1757.

Ann Darby's great-uncle John Wells (d.1736) had probably founded the brewery in the first quarter of the 18th century. See also note for 26 Apr. 1794

[3] *18 guineas* Per load, approx. £3 15*s* 7¼*d*; £18 18*s* is indivisible by five in pre-decimal money. The wet, cold summer would have produced a poor hay harvest. Not self-sufficient in hay at the best of times the Hardys were careful to buy in from outside very early.

The long spell of hot weather in the September enabled them to mow a second small crop of grass

[4] *Minns* John (d. Jan. 1819 aged 85), an Edgefield farmer

right Jamaica *c.*1906; a small settlement outside Port Royal, near Kingston.

The demands of empire took some of Mary Hardy's circle across the world. The young Isaac Mann, son of the Cley merchant (20 July, 4 Aug.), whom she knew as a schoolboy and then as a Norfolk curate, served in Jamaica for most of his adult life. He ended his career as chaplain to the Bishop of Jamaica and as Rector of Kingston 1813–28 [*Editor's collection*]

AUGUST 1, SATURDAY

Henry Raven R Bye to Hindolvestone & Sherrington with beer, T Baldwin to Holt & Runton with D^o^, Jno Ram in garden. M^r^ H at home all Day, WH at Holt market afternoon.

Mary Hardy Very showry day. Mr Hardy at home all day. W^m^ went to Holt Market afternoon, drank tea at Mr Sealess [Sales's], home eveng 9. Robt Raven returnd home to his Mother.[1]

AUGUST 2, SUNDAY

HR Famaly all to own Church forenoon. H Raven whent to Sherrington with J Kendle.[2]

MH Fine Morng, showry afternoon. All went to our Church foornoon, a Communion. I went to Briston Meeting, took the Boy with me. W^m^ went to Holt Church afternoon, drank tea at Mr Sealess.

AUGUST 3, MONDAY

HR R Bye to Waybourn & Thornage with beer, T Baldwin to Sherringham with d^o^. WH to South Repps. Jno Ram in garden, G Thompson grinding Malt for brew. T Baldwin unloaded a load of hay Evening.

[1] *Robert Raven* None of his sisters nor his brother from the Hall came to stay with the Letheringsett relations that summer. Henry, with divided loyalties, would have been placed in a difficult position. However when Robert dined with the Hardys on Holt Fair day 25 Apr. 1796 Mary Hardy was to give no hint of a breach

[2] *J. Kendle* This may be the Thornage farmer John Kendle; but he is more probably James (bapt. 1776) or possibly John (bapt. 1788), sons of Thomas Kendle of Sharrington Hall: see note for 8 Nov. 1795

MH A Showry foornoon, dry afternoon. W^{m} went to Southreps & cromer Morng 9, came home eveng 9. Mr Hardy at home all day. A Ball at Holt for the Camp Officers &c . . .

AUGUST 4, TUESDAY

HR R Bye and T Baldwin at work in yards & unloaded aload of hay, Jno Ram in Garden. M^{r} H whent to Salthouse with Mr Cappa [? Capps] after^{n}, WH out before dinner. I Mann, Miss Mann & Miss Baker drank tea here.

AUGUST 5, WEDNESDAY

HR G Thompson, Jno Ram at Edgefield loading hay, R Bye & Thos Baldwin driving it home. WH whent to Edgefield Morn & afternoon, C Lamb half day.

AUGUST 6, THURSDAY

HR Bye, G Thompson, H Raven & Boy in brewhouse, WH brewing. T Baldwin to Cromer with beer. M^{r} H to Cley afternoon. M^{r}, Mrs Sheldrake drank tea here, Mr Smith of Cley drank tea here.

AUGUST 7, FRIDAY

HR R Bye to Fakenham with beer, T Baldwin to Stody & Briston with d^{o}. Jno Ram in Garden, G Thompson & H Raven Cleansed `// & X beer. M^{r} & WH at home all day.

AUGUST 8, SATURDAY

HR Bye to the Camp and Wiverton with beer, T Baldwin to Sherringham with d^{o}. Jno Ram in garden, Boy to Salthouse for^{n} for two piggs. WH & M^{r} H whent to Holt after^{n}.

AUGUST 9, SUNDAY

HR Famaly all to Church for^{n}, M^{rs} H whent to Briston after^{n}. T Baldwin loaded for Stalham, H Raven whent to Whissonsett morning 6 OClock.

AUGUST 10, MONDAY

HR T Baldwin to Stalham, R Bye to Corpusta & Holt with beer. Jno Ram in Garden. H Raven, NR Junr & Miss Raven came from Whiss. Morning & whent to camp with our famaly.

MH A fine Morng, Showry afternoon. H Raven came home Morng 9, Mary & Nathl Raven came with him, they & W^{m} & MA went to the Camp foornoon being field day & came back Eveng 4. Mr Hardy at home all day . . .

below '. . . Agreed to build a house of industry for the poor' (12 Aug.). A detail from William Hardy jnr's map of Letheringsett Hall Farm as it was in 1800–01, showing (centre right) the new workhouse in the road renamed Workhouse Lane; it was formerly Townhouse Lane.

The Glaven crosses the main road bottom left. A small springwater stream from Holt, named the Frambeck, runs west just south of the workhouse.

This house of industry was built on the site of the parish townhouses on a small patch of common land, enabling it to have a good-sized vegetable garden. As the complete map shows, it stood on its own away from the village centre [*Cozens-Hardy Collection*]

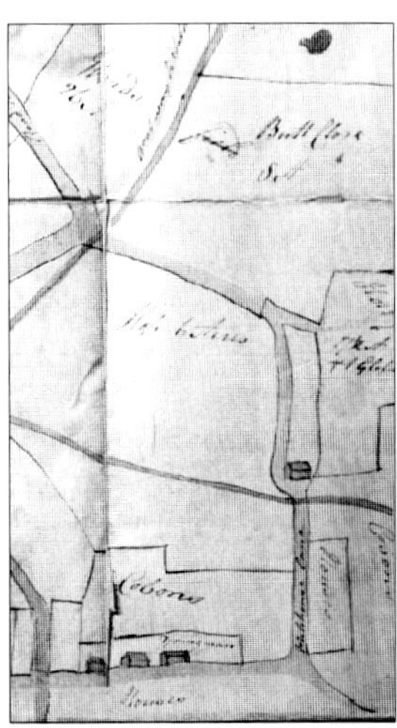

above The former Gressenhall House of Industry. This east wing gives an idea of the imposing scale of these incorporated houses, caring for the poor of a large number of parishes. Letheringsett's was designed just for the poor of the village and housed only a few souls too aged or ill to support themselves [*MB · 2011*]

AUGUST 11, TUESDAY

HR R Bye to Wells with beer, T Baldwin came from Stalham. Jn° Ram in garden, Boy whent to Stody evening. Mr, WH, Miss H & Miss & Mr Raven whent to Holt evening. R Bye loaded for Syderstone.

AUGUST 12, WEDNESDAY

HR R Bye to Syderstone with beer, T Baldwin to Dawling & Holt with beer. Jn° Ram in Garden, Boy to Stody morning. G Thomp. Grinding Malt for brew. Mr H at home all day. W & Miss H, Mr & Miss Raven whent to Camp forn. Tinkers two men part of Day.

MH A Hot dry day. Wm & MA, Nathl & M Raven went to the Camp foornoon, a great number of Strangers went expecting it was a field day but it was not. Ann Johnson dind & drank tea here.[1] Nathl & M Raven went away Eveng past 6. Mr Hardy at A Vestry meeting in the Eveng, agreed to Build a House of Industry for the Poor [2] . . .

AUGUST 13, THURSDAY

HR T Baldwin, H Raven & Boy in brewhouse all Day, G Thompson dressing Wheat Stones, WH brewing. R Bye in brewhouse forn, to Blackney for 1½ Chaldron Coles

1 *Ann Johnson* 'Died on Monday last [24 Aug.], at Holt, suddenly, of apoplexy, much respected, in the 60th year of her age, Anna, third daughter of the Rev. William Tower Johnson, late rector of Beeston Regis and N. Barningham . . .' (*Norw. Merc.* 29 Aug. 1829). She was born 28 Jan. 1769 and bapt. 29 Jan. at Plumstead-by-Holt, and like her sisters became a milliner at Holt.

She suffered the indignity in the pages of the *Norwich Mercury* 3 Feb. 1798 of a hoax announcement of her marriage at Fakenham 2 Feb. to Thomas Lamb; the report was rescinded the following week. She never married, and was buried at Holt 28 Aug. 1829

2 *house of industry* The small house, essentially a pair of semi-detached cottages, was sold by the parish officers in 1837 after the Union took responsibility for Letheringsett's poor under the Poor Law Amendment Act of 1834. Mary

from Mr Farthings. M^r^ H at home all day. W Tinker & two men all day.

AUGUST 14, FRIDAY

HR R Bye helping to Cleanse `// and drove of one load of muck & whent to Waybourn Camp with beer. T Baldwin helping to Cleanse and drove out three load of muck, Jn^o^ Ram filling muck Cart. Tinkers two men part of day. G Thompson and H Raven Cleansed `// & X beer. M^r^ & WH at home all day.

MH A Tempest with abundance of Rain began this Morng between 2 & 3 o Clock, went of [off] in ab^t^ an hour, came on again ab^t^ 6, continued ab^t^ an hour, came on Morng 10, continued till after 1, a great deal of rain. The rain continued all the aftern & Night [1] . . .

AUGUST 15, SATURDAY

HR R Bye to Waybourn with beer, T Baldwin to Edgefield with d^o^. Jno Ram at work in brewhouse half a-day, Tinkers two men part of day. Boy to Guestwick with Malt. WH & Miss H at Holt market afternoon, Mrs Forster & Mrs Herring drank tea here.

AUGUST 16, SUNDAY

HR Famaly all at own Church for^n^. M^rs^ H and H Raven whent to Briston after^n^, WH at Holt afternoon.

Mary Hardy's visit to Whissonsett

17–22 August 1795

AUGUST 17, MONDAY

HR [at Letheringsett] Jno Ram & T [R] Bye ploughing in Hill close, T Baldwin to Brampton with beer. M^r^ & M^rs^ H whent to Whissonsett after tea, WH whent to South Repps. Miss H drank tea at Mr Forsters.

AUGUST 18, TUESDAY

HR R Bye to Southreeps with beer. T Baldwin to Holt for^n^, ploughing afternoon. Jno Ram Ploughing all Day in hill Close, G Thompson grinding Malt for brew. WH at home all Day. Mr Matt Davy, Mr Robbinson, M^r^, Mrs Hooper, Miss Cross & Miss Davys drank tea here. W Tinker & two men all day.

MH [at Whissonsett] A fine day. Mr Hardy & Brother rid to Gresenhall foornoon.[2] I went «to» Sister Goggs, we dind, drank tea & Supt at Bro^t^ Ravens . . .

Ann's husband Jeremiah Cozens bought the house at auction 14 Sept. 1837 for £270 (NRO: ACC Cozens-Hardy 11/2/1976, Draft indenture), and it was rebuilt by their son. For the history of this and the earlier townhouses, see *World*, vol. 3, chap. 6; also B. Cozens-Hardy, *The History of Letheringsett*, pp. 128–30

---

[1] *tempest* Apart from its effect on the men carting beer and manure, this must have damaged the wheat and barley ripening at Letheringsett. The harvest there did not begin until the second latest date recorded in the 36 years of the diary, 31 Aug.; only the 1799 harvest began later, on 2 Sept. Both were famine years. The marked variations in the Hardys' farming year are charted in *World*, vol. 2, chap. 4

[2] *to Gressenhall* Perhaps to gain some advice and ideas from the house of industry built in 1777, although this was a far greater institution than the one proposed for Letheringsett. Gressenhall served the hundreds of Launditch and Mitford and thus took the poor of 51 parishes including those of the market town of E. Dereham. In 1801, a year of particular hardship, it housed 670 inmates, the largest figure in its history (S. Pope, *Gressenhall Farm and Workhouse* (Poppyland Publishing, Cromer, 2006), pp. 9–13, 15, 20)

right The massive tower of St Bartholomew, Brisley, in midwinter sunshine. The Brisley shopkeeper Thomas Fox lies buried alongside his cousins, the Ravens, at Whissonsett. Until he failed in business in 1796 he had owned his parents' grocery and warehouses as well as the Brisley house. He left the shop for a day trip to the camp to join the thousands at the military review on 24 Aug. 1795 [*MB* · *2000*]

AUGUST 19, WEDNESDAY

HR R Bye, G Thompson, H Raven & Boy in brewhouse, WH brewing. Jno Ram finnished ploughing hill close. Mr Herring & Mr Buckle cal'd here for^{n}.[1] Mrs Robinson, Mrs Hooper & the Miss Davys cal'd here afternoon, H Raven drove them up to Holt.

AUGUST 20, THURSDAY

HR R Bye after Jobs for^{n}, to Camp with beer afternoon. T Baldwin after D^{o} [jobs] forenoon, to Gunthorp & Thornage with beer afternoon. G Thom^{n} & H Raven Cleanse'd `// & X beer, WH at home all day. W Tinker & two men all day. Bunnets three men all day sinking the well.[2] Geo. Dawson after Brew dray afternoon.[3]

MH A fine day. Mr Hardy & I, Bro^{t} & Sister Raven rid «to» Horningtoft & Brisley foornoon, dind, drank tea & Supt at Mr Goggs. Mr Hardy & Bro^{t} Raven went to Fakenham Market afternoon.

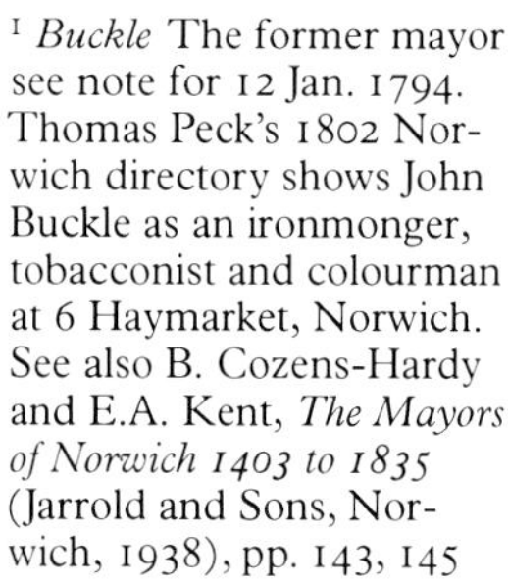

[1] *Buckle* The former mayor: see note for 12 Jan. 1794. Thomas Peck's 1802 Norwich directory shows John Buckle as an ironmonger, tobacconist and colourman at 6 Haymarket, Norwich. See also B. Cozens-Hardy and E.A. Kent, *The Mayors of Norwich 1403 to 1835* (Jarrold and Sons, Norwich, 1938), pp. 143, 145

[2] *well* In the brewery itself as Messrs Hase and Devereux were installing the new pump in the brewhouse (8 Sept. 1795); no visible trace remains.

A well remains beside the basin at the top of the slope in the Brewhouse Pightle. It was used to pump drinking water to the Hall pantry until mains water was installed in the village in 1955: see note for 2 Dec. 1794

[3] *after brew dray* Either repairing the beer cart or collecting it for repair. The Hardys very rarely used the term dray; 'brew cart' was their customary name for the two-wheeled delivery vehicle

AUGUST 21, FRIDAY

HR R Bye & T Baldwin at muck cart all day, Jno Ram & Boy filling D^o. W Tinker & two men all day, Bunnets three men all day. WH at home all day. G Thompson grinding malt for bin, H Raven whent to Saxthorpe.[1]

MH A fine morng, a Thunderstorm eveng 5, a heavy Show^r of rain. Mr Hardy & Bro^t Raven rid to the Greasing grounds at Horningtoft foornoon, dind at Bro^t Ravens.[2] We all rid to Brisley afternoon, drank tea at Mr Foxs [3] . . .

AUGUST 22, SATURDAY

HR R Bye to Cromer with beer. T Baldwin got his horres shoo'd [horses shod] & whent to Hinderingham with beer. Jno Ram in garden & howing [hoeing] turnips. M^r & M^rs H came from Whissonsett, WH at Holt Market afternoon. Mr Huson call'd after^n.

below Silhouetted against the dim interior of the Letheringsett tun room and observed by David Durst, Mary Manning of the Norfolk Industrial Archaeology Society uses a re-fashioned wire coathanger to chart the watercourses under the brewery yard by divining. The small party of industrial archaeologists had some success in tracing the underground drains using the makeshift rods which were leaping and spinning into life, but they did not find the well sunk on 20 Aug. 1795 [*MB · 1993*]

[1] *Saxthorpe* Presumably to tell William Hase, the iron-founder, engineer and clockmaker, that the well had been sunk and the pump could be installed: see entry for 29 Aug. 1795

[2] *greasing grounds* Pasture or grazing grounds for fattening livestock

[3] *Fox* The Brisley grocer and draper Thomas Fox (bapt. Brisley 7 Aug. 1740, d. 23 Aug. 1826 aged 86, bur. Whissonsett 29 Aug.).

The son of Barnaby and Margery Fox of Brisley, he was Mary Hardy's cousin and Nathaniel's Raven's cousin and brother-in-law. He lies with the Ravens, and not at Horningtoft with his parents: see the family tree at app. D3.A, fig. D3.2.

When his business failed in 1796 his shop was put up for sale. He resigned his estate and effects to 'Nathaniel Raven of Whissonsett, grocer and draper' for the benefit of his creditors; 'And the creditors of the said Thomas Fox are to take notice, that unless they forthwith sign the deed, which is left in the hands of the said Nathaniel Raven, they will be excluded from any share of the money arising from the sale of his effects.' The Foxes' 'old-accustomed' shop, with its house, warehouses, chandlery, gardens and orchard, were for sale freehold (*Norw. Merc.* 16 July, 6 Aug. 1796).

The bankrupt Henry Crafer at the King's Head at Holt had a similar deed of trust to that of Thomas Fox (see 10 Nov. 1796)

[LETHERINGSETT]

AUGUST 23, SUNDAY

HR M^rs^ H & H Raven whent to Briston after^n^. M^r^, Miss & WH at own Church after^n^.

MH A very fine day. I & H Raven went to Briston meeting afternoon. Mr Hardy, W^m^ & MA went to Church afternoon. M^r^ & Mrs Crofts from Fakenham came Even 8, Slept here.[1] Mr Faucit [Fawcitt] from Scotten in Yorkshire came [2] . . .

AUGUST 24, MONDAY

HR R Bye to Holt & Salthouse with beer, T Baldwin to Wells with beer. Jno Ram howing turnips, G Thompson & H Raven dressing flowr. M^r^ & WH, Miss Hardy, Mr Raven, Mr Fox & M^r^ & Mrs Crofts whent to Camp.[3]

AUGUST 25, TUESDAY

HR R Bye to Runton with beer, T Baldwin to Holt & Waybourn with beer. Jno Ram howing turnips, G Thompson & H Raven grinding Malt for brew. M^r^ & Mrs Crofts whent to Faken^m^ after tea, Mr Raven & Mr Fox set of for Whiss. after tea. Graveland turning over muck half day.

[1] *Crofts* Revd John (d. 11 Sept. 1828 aged 80, buried under the chancel, Whissonsett Church, 17 Sept.), elder son of Revd Benjamin Crofts: see note for 18 Feb. 1795. Educ. Scarning School and Caius College, Cambridge, and Fellow of Caius 1774–77; ordained deacon 1771, priest 1772; after brief curacies he served as Curate of Fakenham (living at the rectory) 1777–1810, Vicar of E. Bradenham 1782–97, Rector of Stratton Strawless 1784, and Rector of Whissonsett 1797–1828, where he succeeded his father.

He married (1) Elizabeth Elwin (d. Fakenham 23 Feb. 1787), of Booton; (2) Susanna Oxenborow (bapt. Wells 17 Oct. 1765, d. Wells 18 Nov. 1845 aged 80, bur. Whissonsett 22 Nov.), daughter of the Wells merchant Edward Oxenborow. The children of both marriages are recorded in the Fakenham and Whissonsett registers

[2] *Scotton* William Hardy's childhood home: a township in the parish of Farnham, near Knaresborough, N. Yorks; the name Fawcett or Fawcitt appears in the Knaresborough registers. This may be Simon Fawcitt, husband of Sarah. Their daughter Jane was bapt. Knaresborough 1 Mar. 1778 while the family was living in Farnham parish

[3] *camp* For the field day and review by Marquis Townshend, who 'expressed the greatest satisfaction to the Commanding Officer,

AUGUST 26, WEDNESDAY

HR R Bye to Briston with beer. T Baldwin, G Thompson, H Raven & Boy in brewhouse, WH D° Brewing. Jn° Ram howing turnips. Mr H at home all day. T Baldwin road to Longdens evening conserning a dispute in the reckening.[1] Graveland turning over muck.

[1] *Longden* At the Horseshoes at Briston; he had received a beer delivery from Robert Bye earlier in the day. The Hardys had confidence in Baldwin to resolve the problem

facing page Knaresborough Castle, N. Yorkshire (23 Aug.). During part of her long widowhood Mary Hardy's mother-in-law Ann lived on the far bank from the Castle at Forest Lane Head. Although William Hardy left his home county for the Excise in 1757 he kept in touch with many in the area, and his Knaresborough nephew came to stay for three months in 1796 [*MB · 2008*]

below Lord Townshend (sixth from the left) at a Militia review in Norfolk in the Seven Years War. With a long, distinguished war record (he had assumed command on Wolfe's death at Quebec in 1759) he actively promoted home defence as Lord Lieutenant of Norfolk. His review of the Artillery at Weybourne on the field day of 24 Aug. 1795 attracted more than 3000 spectators [*'Review of the Western Norfolk Battalion of Militia', commissioned in 1760 and ascribed to 'The Circle of David Morier', detail; reproduced courtesy the 8th Marquess Townshend*]

Major Judson'; Lord Walpole was also present (*Norw. Merc.* 29 Aug. 1795).

Mary Hardy was as noncommittal as her nephew, but neither diarist was present. We do at least learn from her that it was a hot day (Diary MS).

(Lord Townshend, the first holder of the peerage, styled himself Marquis and not, in the manner of his successors, Marquess Townshend)

AUGUST 27, THURSDAY

HR R Bye in brewhouse for^{n}, to Kettlestone with beer afternoon. T Baldwin in brewhouse for^{n}, to Cley with beer & Brot [brought] home 1½ Chald. co«a»ls from Mr Cooks. Jno Ram finnished howing turnips, G Thompson & H Raven Cleansed `// & X beer. WH at Holt after tea, M^{r} H at home all Day. Graveland turning over muck.

MH A very fine day. Mr Hardy at home all day. W^{m} went to Banyards Bowling green after tea. Mr Fauset dind here . . .

AUGUST 28, FRIDAY

HR Bye to Camp with beer, T Baldwin to Fakenham with D^{o}, Jno Ram in garden. Boy whent to Dawling with beer, Graveland turning over muck. H Raven painting G Thompson's house, G Thompson grinding Malt for Bin. M^{r} & WH at home all day.

AUGUST 29, SATURDAY

HR R Bye to Blakeny for 1½ Chald. coles from Thos Bonds, T Baldwin to Blakeny for 3 Chalds coal^{s} from M^{r} D^{o} [Bond]. Jno Ram in garden. M^{r} H whent to Holt to dine. W, M^{rs} & Miss H at Holt after^{n}. Mr Hase calle'd here morning.[1]

MH A very fine day. Mr Hardy went up to Holt foornoon with Mr Burrell to Justice sitting concerning the House of Industry to be Built, dind & drank tea at Mr Moores. I & W^{m} & MA rid up afternoon, drank tea at Mr Bartells, came home eveng 8 . . .

AUGUST 30, SUNDAY

HR Famaly all at own Church forenoon. M^{rs} H & H Raven whent to Briston afternoon, WH at Holt afternoon. R Bye loaded for Barmer & T Baldwin for Burnham. Mr Sheldrake had the old mare to go to Byburch.[2]

AUGUST 31, MONDAY

HR R Bye to Barmer, T Baldwin to Burnham with beer. Jno Ram & Capt Hall mowing barley in furze close,[3] G Thompson & H Raven grinding Malt for brew. M^{r} & M^{rs}, Miss & WH at Cook Flower Esqr to spend the day. H Raven to Holt forenoon, Graveland turning over muck.

[1] *Hase* William (1767–1841), third of that name at the Saxthorpe smithy of his father and grandfather; they both died in 1787. His brother Thomas (1783–1860) appears to have specialised as an iron-founder 1800–60, whereas William had a variety of skills of which engineering was one. For a detailed study of William and Thomas Hase and their work, see D. Durst, 'Hase: ironfounder of Saxthorpe', *Journal of the Norfolk Industrial Archaeology Society*, vol. 6, no. 1 (1996), pp. 69–87.

In the same issue David Durst identifies, for the first time, William Hase as the designer of the water-powered sawmill at Gunton Park built in 1823–24 for Lord Suffield and restored to working order in 1988 (D. Durst, 'Craftsmen at Gunton Sawmill', vol. 6, no. 1 (1996), pp. 88–95). It is illustrated here under the entries for 3–7 Jan. 1794

[2] *Byburch* Probably Ryburgh rather than Bylaugh, as Henry Raven later writes Ryburgh as Ryburch (11 Sept. 1795)

[3] *mowing barley* This was the first day of harvest (see note for 14 Aug. 1795), and also Henry's 18th birthday.

Neither diarist mentions wheat during the 1795 harvest: the crop had failed.

The Hardys employed almost no additional labourers as harvestmen, indicating there was so little to get home that the regular

SEPTEMBER 1, TUESDAY

Henry Raven R Bye to Corpusta with beer, T Baldwin to Sherringham with beer. Capt Hall mowing Barley, Jno Ram ill from breakfast time till night.[1] WH to South Repps, Mr H at home all day.

SEPTEMBER 2, WEDNESDAY

HR R Bye, G Thompson, H Raven & Boy in brewhouse, WH brewing. T Baldwin to Holt with beer foren, mowing Barley. Jno Ram & Capt Hall mowing Barley.

Mary Hardy A very hot bright day. Wm Brew'd. Mr Hardy & I went to Fakenham Morng past 8, dind & drank tea at Mr Crofts, met Brot & Sister Raven there, went home with them to Whisonset.

SEPTEMBER 3, THURSDAY

HR R Bye to Camp with beer & loaded for Syderstone & Barmer, T Baldwin to Thornage & Stody with beer & loaded for South Repps. Jno Ram & Capt Hall mowing Barley, G Thompson & H Raven Cleansed `// & X beer. W Hardy drank tea at Holt, Mr & Mrs H came from Whissonsett. Mr Baker«'s» two Sons (all day).[2]

MH [at Whissonsett] A very hot bright day. Went to Sister Goggs after breakfast, dind & drank tea at Brot Ravens, set of for home Eveng 5, got home eveng 8.

SEPTEMBER 4, FRIDAY

HR R Bye to Syderstone & Barmer with beer, T Baldwin to South Repps with Do. Jno Ram & Capt Hall mowing Barley. Bunnets two men all day, Joh Baker['s] Son all Day. G Thompn Dressing flower. Mr & WH at home all day, Boy to Cley for [ ].

MH Hot morng, close windy day. We all drank tea at Mr Dobsons, met Mr & Mrs Forster, Mr & Mrs Seales, Mr & Mrs Banyard, Mrs Fisher, Mr N Burrell,[3] Miss M Johnson, Miss Mighles, Miss B Leake.

SEPTEMBER 5, SATURDAY

HR R Bye to Waybourn foren with beer, Carrying barley afternoon. T Baldwin to Holt with beer foren, Carrying Barley afternoon. Jno Ram & Capt Hall mowing Barley morning & then whent to gather Barley ready to Carry. Mr Baker at work all Day, Bunnets two men all day. Mr H at Holt Market aftern, WH at home all day. G Thompson after Barley.

workforce of farm servants and trusted labourers could cope with the task. Casual labourers relied on harvest work for a boost to their income. Its loss was to add to their distress as wheat prices shot up that autumn and winter

---

[1] *from breakfast time* John Ramm had thus been able to do a morning's work, from daybreak until about 8 or 9 am

[2] (*all day*) These are Henry's parentheses; he and his aunt used them very sparingly. The entry for 4 Sept. shows these were the sons of the Holt builder Joseph Baker

[3] *N. Burrell* Revd John Burrell's younger brother Nathaniel (bapt. Letheringsett 3 Dec. 1762, bur. there 15 May 1818), a Holt surgeon. The presence of many connected with the rector, among them his future wife Mary Johnson, suggests that the meeting at the King's Head had been called by him. It may have been concerned with the establishment of the house of industry in the village.

If so, it is noticeable that eight women (three single, four married and a widow) were actively involved in its financing or administration. Also it was socially wholly acceptable for unaccompanied women to join mixed company in a small, unpretentious public house

MH A very fine day. Mr Hardy went to Holt Mark^t^ afternoon, came home eving 9. Our Men fetching Barly from fur Closes.

SEPTEMBER 6, SUNDAY

HR Famaly all at own Church after^n^, M^rs^ H & H Raven to Briston. R Bye & T Baldwin carried of Beer morning.[1]

MH A very Hot day. I & H Raven went to Briston afternoon. We all went to our Church after Six o Clock, Mr Burrell preach'd.

SEPTEMBER 7, MONDAY

HR R Bye, T Baldwin, G Thompson, T Hall & W Dobson after Barley in furze close. Jno Ram, Boy & F Jeckell in barn,[2] Su^n^ Lamb gathering Barley.[3] M^r^ & WH at home all day, Mr Baker at work all day.

MH A very hot dry day. Men fetching Barly from the fur Closes. Mr Hardy & W^m^ at home all day.

SEPTEMBER 8, TUESDAY

HR Jno Ram & Capt Hall drag raking. R Bye to Bale with beer & after Barley, T Baldwin & Boy after barley. G Thompson whiting brewhouse, Mr Hase at work after the engine all Day. M^r^ & WH at home all day, Mr Baker all day.

[1] *Robert Bye and Thomas Baldwin* William Hardy would have been sorely tempted to gather in the harvest while the hot dry weather lasted. It is perhaps a measure of his respect for the law regarding Sunday observance that the men were instead put to discreet tasks hidden behind the brewery walls

[2] *F. Jeckell* Probably Francis (bapt. Letheringsett 11 Mar. 1772), son of the blacksmith of the same name (bur. 22 Oct. 1786) and his wife Mary. Francis jnr marr. 8 June 1803 Mary Joyce of Letheringsett, the groom signing. Their children were baptised elsewhere, suggesting that the Jeckells had left the village, but three infant sons all named William were buried at Letheringsett 26 Aug. 1809, 1 Apr. 1810 and 17 Nov. 1811

[3] *Susan Lamb* William Lamb's second wife: see note for 13 June 1794. As Susan Ward she served as the Hardys' maidservant 1788–89 at a time when the widowed William Lamb was live-in coachman (*Diary 2*). She marr. Lamb 4 June 1790 at Letheringsett, and their daughter Elizabeth was born at Weybourne 14 Aug. 1790 and publicly bapt. Letheringsett 24 Apr. 1791

MH A fine Hot day. Mr Hardy & W^m at home all day. Mr Hase from Saxthorp came to put up a New Pump in B House [brewhouse].

SEPTEMBER 9, WEDNESDAY

HR R Bye, T Baldwin, Jno Ram, Capt^t Hall & Boy gitting up barley, G Thompson & H Raven grinding Malt for brew. Mr Deverrech from Norwich & Matt Booth & Mr Hase after engine,[1] J Baker & E Baker all day. M^r H at home all day, WH roade out with Mr Henderson.[2]

top 'We all went to our church after six o'clock' (6 Sept. 1795). The interior of Letheringsett Church *c.*1901, viewed from the south door towards the chancel (right), pulpit (centre) and the north aisle (left). This photograph from Basil Cozens-Hardy's albums shows the low-hanging candelabra which had recently been given by Sir Alfred Jodrell of Bayfield Hall. Lighting afternoon services proved a problem, and Mary Hardy records the fluctuating times of Evening Prayer in winter and summer, the start of the service varying bewilderingly from 1.45 pm to 7 pm [*Cozens-Hardy Collection*]

facing page Letheringsett Church was restored by William Butterfield in the 1870s and much has been altered since Mary Hardy's time, but these corbel grotesques have looked worshippers in the eye—and winked at them—since the 14th century [*MB · 2011*]

[1] *Devereux* Edmund, shown 1798 as a plumber, painter and glazier in Gildengate Street, Norwich (*Univ. Brit. Dir.*, vol. 4), and in the 1802 Norwich directory at 73 and 4 Gildengate Street.

He died 4 Dec. 1814 aged 63/64, a ledger stone commemorating him and his wife Sarah (d.1827 aged 80) by the sanctuary steps, St George Colegate, Norwich. Henry's spellings suggest that the plumber adopted an anglicised pronunciation of his name.

Neither Henry nor his aunt identifies the work carried out in the brewery, but the pump was probably for the new well (20 Aug.)

[2] *Henderson* Shown 1798, with no forename, as a baker and flour merchant in Newcastle upon Tyne (*Univ. Brit. Dir.*, vol. 4). He

called upon three millers: William Hardy, William Cook of Thornage Watermill, and John Wade, of Gt Ryburgh, formerly of Holt Windmill. He also visited the local ports though which the flour could be shipped. Such movements out of the area in which the flour was produced caused widespread resentment and was perceived locally as aggravating shortages and pushing up prices. Millers who shipped coastwise and by inland waterway were to prove the target of attack

MH A Hot dry «day». Mr Hardy at home all day. 5 Men at Work in B House. Mr Henderson from N«ew» Castle came to Dinner. W^m went to Thornage with Mr Henderson to speak to Mr Cook.[1] M^r & Mrs Bartell, M^r & Mrs Barnham from London drank tea here.

SEPTEMBER 10, THURSDAY

HR T Baldwin to Holt & Edgefield with beer. R Bye, Jno Ram & C [Captain] Hall howing turnips, Boy got up some rakings. Mr Hase & Mr Deverich after new engine. WH roade out with Mr Henderson, M^r H at home all day. J Baker at work all day.

MH A fine day. W^m & Mr Henderson rid to Cley & Blakeney foornoon, came home to dinner.

SEPTEMBER 11, FRIDAY

HR R Bye to Bick high [Beckhithe] with beer. T Baldwin, Jno Ram & Capt Hall mowing Barley in 5 Acres. Mr Hase & Mr Deverichs got new engine to work, J Baker & E Baker at work all day. M^r H whent to Whiss^t with Mr Henderson by Ryburch [Ryburgh], WH at home all day.

MH A fine day. Mr Hardy went with Mr Henderson in a Post Chaise to Ribourg [Ryburgh] to speak to Mr Wade, he was not at home & they went to Whisonsett, dind & drank tea at Bro^t Ravens, brought Sister Goggs home with them Eveng 7. The Men finishd the Pump.

SEPTEMBER 12, SATURDAY

HR T Baldwin, G Thompson & Boy in brewhouse, H Raven whent to Aylsham with Mr Devericks, WH brewing. M^r H to wells [Wells], Mr Henderson with him. R Bye to Runton with beer, T Baldwin to Holt with beer after^n. Jno Ram & C Hall mowing Barley.

MH A Close dry day. Mr Hardy & Mr Henderson set of for Wells in our Chaise morng 9, expected M^r H [Hardy] home in eveng, did not come. Wm Brewd. MA walkd up to Holt afternoon . . .

SEPTEMBER 13, SUNDAY

HR Famaly all to Church fore^n. H Raven drove M^rs H & Mrs Goggs to Briston, WH at Holt after^n. G Thompson Cleansed `//.

SEPTEMBER 14, MONDAY

HR T Baldwin to Camp & Sherringham with beer, R Bye to Cromer with d^o. G Thompson & H Raven Cleansed

---

[1] *Cook/Cooke* William (d.1826), of Thornage Watermill. He was admitted 29 Apr. 1784 into Briston Independent Meeting by Revd John Sykes. He marr. Thornage 7 Oct. 1789 Mary Sturley (d.1848), both signing; some of their children were baptised by Mr Sykes. William Cook jnr is shown by the Independents in 1825 at Glandford (perhaps at the watermill); his wife died in 1835 (NRO: FC 11/1).

The Cooks were alluded to by Revd John Astley of Thornage in 1784: 'There is one family who dissent from the Established Church—millers by occupation—and they attend at a meeting in Hunworth . . . The name of their teacher is [ ] Sykes. They are very sober in life and industrious' (NRO: DN/VIS 29/6, Holt deanery visitation 1784, Thornage return). See also notes for 15 Nov. 1795 and 13 Apr. 1796

XX beer. Jn° Ram mowing grass, Capt Hall tasking. Mr H at home all day, WH to Sherringham afternoon.

SEPTEMBER 15, TUESDAY

HR R Bye & T Baldwin to Cley with beer & brot home 3 Chald Coals from Mr Jacksons,[1] G Thompson & H Raven grinding Malt for brew. Jn° Ram mowing grass, Capt Hall tasking. Mr & WH at home all day. Mr Ellis from Cley drank tea here, Josh Baker Called here afternoon.

SEPTEMBER 16, WEDNESDAY

HR R Bye to Sherrington [Sharrington] & the Camp with beer, T Baldwin to Wells with D°. G Thompson, H Raven & Boy in brewhouse, WH Brewing. Capt Hall tasking part of Day & laying bottom for Stack. Mr H at home all day. Mr, Mrs Sheldrake drank tea here.

SEPTEMBER 17, THURSDAY

HR R Bye, T Baldwin, G Thompson, Capt Hall after Barly. C Lamb, James the Miller [?], D Mays & T Jickell [Jeckell] got to help to git up barly,[2] finnished all the dwarth Corn 14 Load.[3] Mr, Mrs and Miss H & Mrs Goggs to Mr Forster to tea.

SEPTEMBER 18, FRIDAY

HR R Bye to Holt with beer forenoon & Waybourn & Sheringham afternoon, T Baldwin to Stalham. G Thompson & H Raven Cleansed X beer, Capt Hall tasking. Mr H & Mrs Goggs to Camp aftern, WH at home all day.

SEPTEMBER 19, SATURDAY

HR R Bye to Fakenham with beer, T Baldwin returned from Stalham. Capt Hall & Boy gathering Barley rakings forenoon, got them up & one load of Hay from Furze close. G Thompson & H Raven grinding Malt for brew. Mr H at Holt all «day», WH & Sister at Holt afternoon.

MH A very Hot dry day. Mr Hardy walkd to Holt foornoon to the Justice sitting for Licences, dind with them, came home Eveng 11 [4] . . .

SEPTEMBER 20, SUNDAY

HR Mrs H & Mrs Goggs & H Raven whent to Briston afternoon. WH at Holt, I Mann came home with him and drank tea. R Bye loaded for Syderstone. WH parted from Boy.[5]

[1] *Jackson* In her endnotes (*Diary 4*) Mary Hardy notes the death of Mr Jackson snr of Cley 28 Oct. 1802 aged 67. Thomas Jackson (d. 8 Oct. 1833 aged 73) is listed as a merchant at Cley in the 1806 county pollbook; he married Martha Ellis at Cley 23 Jan. 1783

[2] *Mayes* David (bapt. Letheringsett 22 Feb. 1735), cordwainer, son of William and Amy, née Coe. His wife Mary Ann, née Whitaker, was born 1734 and bur. 14 Dec. 1798; their children are recorded in the Letheringsett registers. He and his brother William (bapt. 29 June 1728) were Nonconformists, David attending Wesleyan Methodist meetings at Briston and Cley with Mary Hardy in 1804 (*Diary 4*). William was to belong to the Briston Independents, into whose church he was received 1 July 1796 at a time when others were being excluded for supporting Arminians (the Wesleyans). He married Susanna Westby, and their children were baptised into Independency (NRO: FC 11/1). William Mayes's house at Letheringsett was registered as a meeting house 16 Dec. 1795 (NRO: DN/DIS 1/2, f. 54). Mary Hardy did not attend that meeting, and it was probably Independent

[3] *dwarth corn* Possibly dwarf corn: stunted barley

[4] *licences* Innkeepers', issued at petty sessions

[5] *parted from* Gave notice to. William is unlikely to

SEPTEMBER 21, MONDAY

HR R Bye to Syderstone, T Baldwin to Waybourn & Holt with beer. Jno Ram mowing grass. M^{r} H to Walsingham & Wells, WH at home all day. Mrs Davy & M^{r} & Mrs Davy drank tea here. G Thompson & H Raven got brewing things ready.

MH A fine day. Mr Hardy went to Wells in the Chaise, took John Thompson with him, came home eveng past 10, had Nicholas Everet of Wells Arested.[1] W^{m} at home all day. Mr John Davy & Wife, M^{rs} & M Davy drank tea here . . .

SEPTEMBER 22, TUESDAY

HR R Bye to Holt & Briston with beer. T Baldwin, G Thompson, Jno Ram & H Raven in brewhouse, WH brewing. HR, TB [Thomas Boyce] & Jno Ram got up 5 Acres of Rakeing. M^{r}, M^{rs} & Miss Hardy & Mrs Goggs to Holt to tea. Mr Wilkin called here afternoon. J Graveland turning over muck.

SEPTEMBER 23, WEDNESDAY

HR R Bye in brewhouse forenoon, to Thornage after^{n} with beer. T Baldwin to Cromer with D^{o}. G Thompson & H Raven Cleanse'd `// foren^{n}. Mr Jno Davy Senr & M^{r} J Davy Junr whent shootting foren^{n} & came & dine'd here. Jno Ram Mowing Grass. J Graveland turning over muck morning, tasking the rem^{r} [remainder or remaining] part of day. M^{r}, M^{rs} & Miss Hardy & Mrs Goggs to Southrepps in Banyards Chaise.

MH A fine morng, a little lowering before noon, a fine afternoon. Mr Davy & Son John came here foornoon shooting Partriges, dind & drank tea here. Mr Hardy, I, Sister Goggs & MA set of in Banyards Post Chaise for Southreps, Breakfstd there, went to Cromer, Dind & drank tea there, came home Eveng 9 [2] . . .

SEPTEMBER 24, THURSDAY

HR R Bye harrowing furze close, T Baldwin helping to Cleanse & set of for Burnham with beer. Jno Ram at Work in brewhouse all Day, J Graveland tasking till 5 OClock then got to turning over Muck. G Thompson & H Raven Cleansed XX beer & got over ten coomb of Malt for brew. M^{r} H at home all day, W & Miss H to Sherringham with aparty.

have dismissed the boy on the spot only three weeks before the date for moving on; indeed the two diarists noted that the boy actually went away 10 Oct. 1795

---

[1] *Everitt* See note for 7 Apr. 1794. John Everitt is shown in the alehouse register for 1789 and 1790, Elizabeth Everitt for 1792 and 1794, and Nicholas Everitt was newly registered as innkeeper in Sept. 1795 (NRO: C/Sch 1/16). Nicholas was also a shipbuilder, his yard soon being for sale (*Norfolk Chronicle*, 2 Jan. 1796; see also M. Stammers, *Shipbuilding at Wells in the 18th and 19th Centuries* (Wells Local History Group, 2011), pp. 3, 18)

[2] *Sister Goggs* Phillis Goggs left Letheringsett the next afternoon

SEPTEMBER 25, FRIDAY

HR R Bye to Cromer & Wiverton with beer, T Baldwin Ret[d] [returned] from Burnham & Loaded for Corpusta & Hindolvestone. Jn[o] Ram tasking, J Graveland turning over Muck part of day. M[r] H to Guestwick, WH at home all day.

SEPTEMBER 26, SATURDAY

HR R Bye to Sherringham with beer, T Baldwin to Edgefield, Corpusta & Hindolvestone with D[o]. G Thompson & H Raven grinding Malt for brew. M[r] & WH at Holt Market after[n]. Jn[o] Ram at Work in brewhouse forenoon, gathering Largess after[n]. Harvast supper at Dobsons Evening.

SEPTEMBER 27, SUNDAY

HR Famaly all at own Church fore[n], M[rs] H & H Raven to Briston aftern.

SEPTEMBER 28, MONDAY

HR R Bye to Brampton with beer, T Baldwin to Camp & Waybourn with D[o]. G Thompson, H Raven & Boy in brewhouse, WH Brewing, Jn[o] Ram in brewhouse.

SEPTEMBER 29, TUESDAY

HR R Bye to Edgefield with beer, T Baldwin to Runton with D[o]. Jn[o] Ram tasking forenoon, got up one load of hay. G Thompson & H Raven Cleansed `//. M[r] & W[m] H at home all day. T Baldwin Loaded for Barmer, Boyce in Garden.

MH A very fine day. Maids & Betty Woods washd 5 weeks linnen. M[r] Branford from Godwick Dind here.[1] M[r] Hardy & W[m] at home all day . . .

SEPTEMBER 30, WEDNESDAY

HR T Baldwin to Barmer, R Bye to Bale and Kettlestone with beer. G Thompson & H Raven Cleansed X beer. Jn[o] Ram tasking, Boy to Salthouse with A Barrell of Beer. M[r] H at home all day, WH at home for[n], Out afternoon. T Boyce in Garden all Day.

OCTOBER 1, THURSDAY

Henry Raven R Bye to Hindolveston with beer, T Baldwin to Holt with beer. J Ram tasking, T Boyce in garden, G Thompson & H Raven grinding Malt for brew. M[r] & WH at home all day.

above The old Round Hill plantation behind Letheringsett Hall Farm, viewed from the end of the Hardys' garden. There was little cover for game (23 Sept. 1795) on the Hardys' land until William Hardy jnr embarked on his planting schemes in the early 19th century [*MB · 2002*]

facing page The side entrance to the former Jolly Sailor at Wells, its memory preserved in the name of this lane. William Hardy had its innkeeper, the shipbuilder Nicholas Everitt, arrested for debt 21 Sept. 1795 [*MB · 2001*]

[1] *Branford* John Bell: see note for 17 Feb. 1794.

William Hardy had also dined with Mr Keeler of Guestwick 25 Sept. 1795, perhaps to arrange purchases of barley ready for the new malting season

OCTOBER 2, FRIDAY

HR T Baldwin to Runton with beer. R Bye, G Thompson, H Raven & Boy in brew house, WH brewing. J Ram tasking, T Boyce in Garden. M^r^ H at home all day. Mrs Forster, Miss Jenniss [? Miss Jennises] drank tea here.

OCTOBER 3, SATURDAY

HR R Bye to Beckhigh with beer, T Baldwin to Holt & Thornage with D^o^. G Thompson & H Raven Cleansed `// & X beer. M^r^, M^rs^, Miss & W Hardy to Holt afternoon, H Raven to Holt ball.

Mary Hardy A very close warm day, began to rain Eveng 6, a very Wet Night. Mr Hardy, W^m^ & MA walk'd up to Holt afternoon, drank tea at Mr Sheldrakes.[1] M^r^ H came home eveng 8, W^m^ & MA came home past 9. H Raven went to Mr Browns Ball in Eveng [2] . . .

OCTOBER 4, SUNDAY

HR Famaly to own Church afternoon. T Baldwin loaded for Burnham.

OCTOBER 5, MONDAY

HR T Baldwin to Burnham with beer, R Bye to Wakefields & Thos Atwoods with beer, T Boyce in Garden.[3] Jno Ram dressing Barley, got it on Granary & Steep^t^ [steeped] afternoon. WH to Whiss., M^r^ H to Cley afternoon.

[1] *Mr Sheldrake* The excise officer was appointed Inspector of Weights and Balances for Holt hundred 15 Oct. 1795, the appointment being regularly renewed (NRO: C/S 1/15, Holt Quarter Sessions)

[2] *Mr Browne's ball* The annual ball given at Holt by John Browne (d. Thorpe St Andrew Aug. 1799: *Norw. Merc.* 10 Aug. 1799), the visiting dancing master from Norwich who had taught William and Mary Ann. This event, known as the Children's Ball, was his opportunity to show off to his pupils' families and friends the skills acquired by the children, although there is no evidence to suggest that Henry had been his pupil unless perhaps at school in Fakenham

[3] *Wakefield* Francis, at the Black Boys at Holt

OCTOBER 6, TUESDAY

HR R Bye to Cromer. T Baldwin after Malt for^{n}, to Salthouse after^{n}, G Thompson & H Raven Grinding Malt for brew & bin. WH came from Whissonsett, M^{r} H to Cley after^{n}. T Boyce in Garden, Jno Ram ill all day.

MH A fine day. Mr Hardy rid up to Holt afternoon to hire a Horse to go to Norwich, could not git one, drank tea at Mr Bartells, home eve 7. W^{m} came home from Whisonsett Eveng 8.

OCTOBER 7, WEDNESDAY

HR R Bye to Sheringham with beer, T Baldwin brewing & whent to Stody. Boy, G Thompson & H Raven in brew house, WH brewing. T Boyce in garden. M^{r} & Miss H to Norwich.[1]

MH A fine day. Mr Hardy & MA set of for Norwich in our own Chaise morng 8, W^{m} at home all day . . .

above The Letheringsett steep 29 Dec. 2001, taken from the west end, with (left) one of the two arched openings shown in the photograph opposite. This view shows the steep as a lean-to built against the south end of the malthouse. It was enlarged in 1814, as signalled by a roughly incised date stone on the far side of the steep's east wall. Over time this huge brick cistern became a convenient rubbish receptacle, Basil Cozens-Hardy referring 2 Sept. 1950 in a letter to the farmer who was his tenant at the brewery site to 'the strange collection of inflammable junk in the old steep'. He wanted it cleared away for roof repairs [*MB · 2001*]

[1] *Norwich* The churchwardens and overseers of Letheringsett were appealing against those of Edgefield over an order by the JPs Henry Jodrell and Charles Collyer for Mary, wife of Abraham Ford, and their three children to be removed to Letheringsett. The Letheringsett parishioners won, the order being quashed by the four Norwich justices 7 Oct. 1795.

The Norwich JPs continued to be anxious about 'the present high price of corn'. They appointed a committee to enquire into the causes, and instructed the chairman to report directly to the Privy Council in London (NRO: C/S 1/15, 7 Oct. 1795)

facing page 'John Ramm dressing barley, got it on granary and steeped afternoon' (5 Oct. 1795). The Letheringsett malthouse, looking south towards the access points to the single-storey steep (beyond the far wall), from the top of the staircase by the kilns. Light would not have flooded in from the steep when this was a working malthouse; this photograph was taken 29 Dec. 2001 when the roof and wall were falling in. Until then the steeping area had been extremely dark, being visible only with torches. The granary was in the roof of the malthouse, away from the rats [*Christopher Bird 2001*]

OCTOBER 8, THURSDAY

HR R Bye to Southrepps with beer, T Baldwin to Cley & the Camp with beer. T Boyce in Garden forenoon, helping Boy to clear fat [vat] &c. G Thompson & H Raven Cleansed `// & skreening Malt for brew, WH whiting the brewhouse. Mrs Harison from Cley dined here, Pleasance came & Orderd a load of beer.

OCTOBER 9, FRIDAY

HR T Baldwin to Stalham. R Bye to Gunthorpe with beer & Bro^t home nine Coomb of Barley. Jno Ram Steep^t, G Thomp^n & H Raven began to Grind Malt for brew. W Tinkers two men half a day. M^r & Miss H came from Norwich afternoon.

OCTOBER 10, SATURDAY

HR R Bye to Holt forenoon, to Dawling & Morston with beer after^n.[1] T Baldwin return'd from Stalham, Jno Ram after Jobs, T Boyce in Garden. Boy whent away after Dinner. H Raven Grinding Malt for brew, W Tinker & two men all day. M^r H to Holt afternoon. Mr Sharpe from Brinton call'd. WH at Holt after tea.

[1] *Morston* There was then only one public house in this tiny coastal village (population 99 in 1801): the Chequers, kept by Edmund Balls. William Hardy and Raven had called there 18 Apr. 1781 on first coming to Letheringsett, suggesting that it had been supplied by Henry Hagon. William Hardy hired the house 30 Mar. 1782, but deliveries had since ceased (*Diary 2*). The Chequers was supplied once more from 10 Oct. 1795 and Balls must have re-hired it about then, for the Hardys' accounts show his *rental* payments from 1797 or earlier to 1804 or later (*World*, vol. 2, chap. 11; *Diary 4*, app. D4.B)

facing page **The malthouse east wall, of brick and flint, May 2001. 54-year-old William Lamb was hired as maltster for the 1795–96 season (12 Oct.); he had in earlier years served as farm servant. On Bye's dismissal at Christmas 1795 Lamb took his place on 27 Dec. and John Ramm, at 68, again took up his malt shovel** [*MB · 2001*]

MH A Close hasy day. Mr Hardy walk'd to Holt Markt afternoon, came home Eveng past 12. Wm rid up, came home eveng 10. Frances Thompson & the Boy went away [1] . . .

OCTOBER 11, SUNDAY

HR Famaly all to own Church forenoon, WH & HR at Holt afternoon.

OCTOBER 12, MONDAY

HR R Bye to Syderstone with beer, T Baldwin to Hinderingham with do. T Boyce in Garden, J Ram tasking. W Lamb in Malthouse, G Thompson dressing flower.[2] Mr & WH at home all day.

OCTOBER 13, TUESDAY

HR R Bye in brewhouse forn, to Briston with beer aftern. G Thompson, HR & Boy in brew house, T Boyce after Jobs and in brew house, WH brewing. Mr H at home all day. An examineer Call'd with Mr Sheldrake, Mr & Mrs Sheldrake drank tea here.[3]

OCTOBER 14, WEDNESDAY

HR R Bye to Fakenham with beer, T Baldwin «to» North Walsham with Do.[4] T Boyce ploughing in Hill Close, J Ram tasking. W Lamb in Malthouse, G Thomn & H Raven Cleansed `//. WH whent of to Southrepps 6 OClock morning, Mr H at home all day.

OCTOBER 15, THURSDAY

HR R Bye to Waybourn with beer, T Baldwin helping to Cleanse & whent to Thornage with beer. T Boyce ploughing in furze Close, J Ram tasking. W Lamb in Malthouse, G Thompson & H Raven Cleanse'd X beer. H Goggs Came morning & whent to Holt Quarter sessions. WH at home all day, Mr H at Holt all day.

MH A Showry day. Mr Goggs came to breakfast, went to the qrtr Sessions at Holt, came back Eveng 4 & went home. Mr Hardy walk'd up to Holt foornoon, dind with the Justices, came home eveng 8 . . .

[1] *went away* Hannah Dagliss stayed, at £3 3*s* p.a., and was joined by Sarah Turner, at £3 10*s* (Mary Hardy's register, endnotes)

[2] *William Lamb* See notes for 13 June 1794, 5 June and 7 Sept. 1795. At 54 he was 14 years younger than Ramm, who would have found malting ever more testing as he grew older

[3] *examiner* A senior excise officer, at the same level as supervisor, posted to a District for specific tasks. On this occasion he would have been inspecting recent alterations to the brewery

[4] *N. Walsham* See the note for 11 May 1795. After the flurry of activity in May and the last delivery of Letheringsett beer on 26 June 1795 the Maid's Head may have closed again until hired by James Dew at Old Michaelmas

above **Letheringsett's malt-kiln furnace bars, complete with dead rat at the back** [*MB · 2001*]

above Morston Creek. The Chequers, on the coast road at Morston, began again to be supplied with Letheringsett beer on 10 Oct., but evidently did not have many drinkers. Henry Raven recorded only 17 deliveries in two years [*MB · 1995*]

OCTOBER 16, FRIDAY

HR R Bye to Holt & Edgefield with beer, T Baldwin to Holt with beer & Blakeny for 2 Chaldron Cinders from Mr Farthings. T Boyce ploughing in furze Close, Jno Ram tasking. W Lamb in Malthouse, G Thompson & H Raven dressing flour. M^r^ H at home all day, WH at Holt afternoon. Mr Jarvis from Guestwick came after his Barley & found it different half apeck in a Coomb.[1] A Rider from London call'd forenoon.

OCTOBER 17, SATURDAY

HR R Bye to Hindolvestone with beer, T Baldwin [ ], T Boyce ploughing. J Ram tasking, W Lamb in Malthouse, G Thomp^n^ & H Raven gathering apples. WH at Holt aftern, H Raven whent to Whiss [Whissonsett].

OCTOBER 18, SUNDAY

HR Famaly all to Church aftern. H Raven came from Whiss^t^.

OCTOBER 19, MONDAY

HR R Bye to Well^s^ with beer, T Baldwin to Cley for three Chaldron Coals from Mr Cooks. T Boyce ploughing, Jno Ram tasking. W Lamb in Malthouse, G Thompson grinding Malt for brew. WH road to Cley for^n^.

OCTOBER 20, TUESDAY

HR R Bye to Cley for 2 Chal^d^ Cinders from Mr Elliss [Ellis's]. T Baldwin, G Thompson, HR & Boy in brewhouse, WH Brewing. W Lamb in Malthouse, Jno Ram part of day, T Boyce harrowing. M^r^ H at home all day.

MH A fine day. Wm Brew'd, Mr Hardy at home all day. M^r^ & Mrs Baker & Mrs Custance of Fakenham drank tea here . . .

OCTOBER 21, WEDNESDAY

HR R Bye to Waybourn & Camp with beer, T Baldwin after Jobs. G Thompson & H Raven Cleanse'd `//. W Lamb in Malthouse, T Boyce harrowing, Jno Ram part of day. WH road to Bale for^n^, M^r^ H at home all day.

OCTOBER 22, THURSDAY

HR R Bye to Sherringham with beer, T Baldwin to Norwich, T Boyce ploughing. W Lamb in Malthouse, G Thompson & H Raven Cleanse'd X beer. WH to Waybourn afternoon, M^r^ H at home all day.

---

[1] *Jarvis* All grain was measured by volume and not by weight.

With four pecks to the bushel, and four bushels to the coomb, the difference would have been just noticeable—the grain was out by one thirty-second, roughly 3%. If Mr Jarvis had sent £20 worth of barley, the difference would have totalled 12*s* 6*d*. The barley could have dried out and shrunk between harvesting at Guestwick and its arrival at Letheringsett.

The glossary at the end of this volume explains weights and measures

MH A Wet morng, fine afternoon. Mr Hardy at home all day. W^m rid to the Camp & from thence to Mr Flowers at Sheringham, drank tea there, came home eveng past 9 [1] . . .

OCTOBER 23, FRIDAY

HR R Bye to Fakenham with beer, T Baldwin came from Norwich Evening. W Lamb in Malthouse, T Boyce ploughing in furze close, G Thompson & H Raven skreening Malt for brew. WH at home all day, M^r H at home all day.

OCTOBER 24, SATURDAY

HR T Baldwin to Holt to Crafers & Banyards & to Stody with beer. R Bye to Salthouse with beer & Cley for two Chal^d Lime from Mr Johnsons. W Lamb in Malthouse, G Thompson & H Raven Grinding Malt for brew. M^r H at Holt markett, WH to Salthouse, Cley & Holt Market. T Boyce ploughing.

OCTOBER 25, SUNDAY

HR Famaly all to Church forenoon, M^rs H & H Raven to Briston after^n.[2] The men Carried of [off] Cleanse Beer morning.

OCTOBER 26, MONDAY

HR R Bye, G Thompson, HR & Boy in Brewhouse, WH brewing. T Baldwin to Waybourn & Holt with beer, T Boyce ploughing. W Lamb in Malthouse, Jno Ram tasking. Mr Youngmans Man after Cleansing pump forenoon.[3]

OCTOBER 27, TUESDAY

HR R Bye to Dawling & Thornage with beer, T Baldwin to Cromer with D^o. G Thompson & H Raven Cleansed `//, W Lamb in Malthouse. T Boyce harrowing forenoon & rakeing quicks of [off] the Land afternoon. J Ram tasking, Boy raking quicks of Land. M^r & WH at home all day.

OCTOBER 28, WEDNESDAY

HR R Bye to Runton with beer, T Baldwin to Holt & the Camp with d^o. J Ram tasking, W Lamb in Malthouse, T Boyce rakeing of quicks of Land. G Thompson & H Raven Cleansed X beer. M^r & WH at home all day.

MH A fine day. Mr Hardy & W^m at home all day. Mr Burrell here in Eveng.

[1] *camp* In a week's time the regiment was to move to winter quarters and the beer contract be ended: see note for 1 June 1795. The camp was struck on 31 Oct., and the following day a crowd of 2000 people could be seen ranged on the Castle Ditches watching the Artillery pass through Norwich on their way from Weybourne to Woolwich (*Norw. Merc.* 7 Nov. 1795).

The diarists and the press are rather vague about the military. We know from the careful Rector of Cley that (as well as the Artillery) the Royal Horse Artillery were stationed on the coast that summer. Mr Thomlinson noted two members of that regiment marrying Cley women by licence 17 Oct. and 20 Oct. 1795, just before their departure. He entered the grooms' camp, Weybourne, as their home parish (NRO: PD 270/9, Cley marriages 1754–1812)

[2] *Briston* Mary Hardy did not go to a Briston meeting again until 7 May 1797. By then Thomas Mendham's 1783 chapel had changed from the Calvinistic Methodists to the Wesleyans, under whose ministry it is recorded from 1798 in the Wesleyan lists for Walsingham Circuit (NRO: FC 18/1). Meanwhile Mary Hardy had begun to attend the Wesleyan Methodists at Cley (8 Nov. 1795)

[3] *after cleansing pump* In pursuit of; ie repairing the pump from the fermenting tun. It needed attention again on 15 Feb. 1796

facing page 'William dined at the Feathers at Holt at the bowling green frolic' (29 Oct. 1795).

The elegant first-floor windows of the Feathers: their thin glazing bars may date from the early 18th century, when the Feathers was rebuilt after the 1708 Holt fire.

Following Thomas Baldwin's delivery of 24 Oct. William's brew would have been served at the bowls frolic [*MB · 1999*]

below right Letheringsett, the south churchyard: the grave of Elizabeth Bullock (left), formerly Mrs Milligen, who served for some time as Mary Hardy's washerwoman; the headstone is deeply incised.

It may have been Mrs Milligen who introduced her employer to Cley meeting (8 Nov. 1795). She was an active Wesleyan by 1808, when she hosted the cottage meeting established by Mary Hardy (*Diary 4*). She was to serve as Mary Hardy's cook and dairymaid 1803–04.

In 1799 she signed the register on her second marriage, to the labourer John Bullock, whose wife had died in 1797 and whose 18-year-old son had drowned in 1785 while bathing at Glandford (*Diary 2*).

Mrs Bullock died in 1832 aged 76 [*MB · 2011*]

OCTOBER 29, THURSDAY

HR R Bye to upper Sherringham & the Camp with beer. T Baldwin Carting of quicks for^{n}, to Holt with beer afternoon. W Lamb in Malthouse, Jno Ram tasking. G Thomp^{s} & «? H Raven» Skreen'd the brew of Malt. M^{r} H at home all day, WH at Holt Bowling green feast afternoon.

MH A Windy Stormy day. Mr Hardy at home all day. W^{m} dind at the Feathers at Holt at the Bowling Green Frollick, came home Even 10 . . .

OCTOBER 30, FRIDAY

HR R Bye & T Baldwin carting muck, T Boyce & Boy filling Muck cart. G Thompson & H Raven grinding Malt for Brew, W Lamb in Malthouse, J Ram tasking. M^{r} H at home all day. WH home for^{n}, road [rode] out afternoon.

OCTOBER 31, SATURDAY

HR R Bye to Burnham with beer. T Baldwin got Barley out of Barn, got up a load of sand & whent to Wiverton with beer & Cley for 1½ Chal^{d} Coals for Mr Thompson [William Gunton Thompson]. W Lamb in Malthouse, J Ram tasking. T Boyce after Job«s» for^{n}, raking of quicks of Land in furze close.

MH A Windy day, some Storms of rain. W^{m} went to L [Lower] Sheringham foorn, dind at Mr Flowers & came to Holt Mark^{t} afternoon, came home Eveng 9. Mr Hardy rid up to Mark^{t} aftern, drank tea at Mr Moores, came home Eveng 10 . . .

RAC

NOVEMBER 1, SUNDAY

Henry Raven Famaly all at own Church afternoon. Robt Bartell spent the day here.

NOVEMBER 2, MONDAY

HR T Baldwin, G Thompson, H Raven & Boy in brewhouse, WH brewing. Boyce cleaning yard, J Ram tasking, W Lamb in Malt house. M^{r} H at home all day. R Bye to Corpusta with beer. WH whalk'd to Holt morning, J Mason drank tea here.

NOVEMBER 3, TUESDAY

HR R Bye to Cley with beer & Bro^{t} home 2 Chal^{d} Cinders from Mr Ellis's, Baldwin to Beckhigh with beer. W Lamb in Malthouse, J Ram tasking, T Boyce after Jobs for^{n}. WH whent of to Brook morning,[1] M^{r} H at home all day. G Thompson & H Raven Cleansed `//.

Mary Hardy A Windy dry day till Eveng 4 then Stormy. W^{m} set off Morng 8 for Norwich & Brooke, Mr Hardy at home all day. Maids & Eliz Milegan Washd 5 Weeks Linnen [2] . . .

NOVEMBER 4, WEDNESDAY

HR R Bye to Cromer with beer, T Baldwin to Holt & Waybourn with beer. Lamb in Malthouse, J Ram tasking, T Boyce spreading Muck. G Thompson & H Raven Cleanse'd X beer. M^{r} H at home all day.

[1] *Brooke* A large village six miles south-east of Norwich, where William's friend Edmund Bartell jnr practised as a surgeon

[2] *Elizabeth Milligen* (d. 21 Dec. 1832 aged 76, bur. Letheringsett 22 Dec.). Her first husband Thomas had been the subject of a case occupying William Hardy during Apr. to July 1783. Brought from London to Letheringsett under a vagrancy order, Milligen was sentenced to a term in Walsingham Bridewell. The Letheringsett parish officers had to attend quarter sessions across the county at King's Lynn and Swaffham in connection with the case (*Diary 2*).

Thomas Milligen and Elizabeth Jeckell, both single and of Letheringsett, had married at Letheringsett 18 Sept. 1774. Their son Miles was bur. 15 Dec. 1775 aged a few weeks; their daughter Maria (bapt. there 7 July 1777) served as the Hardys' maidservant 1797–98. Milligen's widow married Letheringsett 12 Nov. 1799 the widowed labourer John Bullock (bur. 24 Dec. 1803); at his death he was described in the register as a 'labouring pauper'.

In 1808 Elizabeth Bullock was living in a rented cottage on the north side of the main street through the village; this dwelling house hosted the Wesleyans (NRO: DN/DIS 1/2, f. 127, 18 Nov. 1808)

NOVEMBER 5, THURSDAY

HR R Bye to Sherrington & Holt with beer. T Baldwin setting about muck in furze close, T Boyce & Jn° Ram filling.[1] Lamb in Malthouse, G Thompson took up wheatstones. G Thompson Junr was married in the morning before Breakfast.[2]

NOVEMBER 6, FRIDAY

HR R Bye to Syderstone with beer, T Baldwin to Southrepps with D°. J Ram tasking, W Lamb in Malthouse, T Boyce after Jobs. G Thompson & H Raven skreening Malt for Brew. WH came from Brook, M^r H at home all Day.

MH A Wet Morng, fine day. Water in River very high. Sister Raven from Whisonsett came to dinner, went away Eveng past 3. W^m came home Eveng 6, heard Geo^r Wymer was Married last Tuesday [3] . . .

NOVEMBER 7, SATURDAY

HR R Bye & T Baldwin carrd of [carried off] Cleanse beer for^n. R Bye to Muck cart afternoon, T Boyce filling Muck cart. J Ram tasking, W Lamb in Malthouse, G Thomp. Grinding Malt for brew. WH at Holt market afternoon, M^r H at home all day. T Baldwin very ill afternoon.

NOVEMBER 8, SUNDAY

HR Famaly all at own Church forenoon, M^rs H to Cley afternoon. H Raven to Sherrington after^n.

MH A fine day. All went to our Church foornoon, Mr Burrell preach'd. I rid to Cley Afternoon to the Meeting, took the Boy with me, came home before 5.[4] H Raven went to Mr Kend«l»es of Sherington to tea.[5] W^m went «to» Holt Church afternoon, came home to tea . . .

NOVEMBER 9, MONDAY

HR R Bye and T Baldwin driving out muck [cart], J Ram filling, T Boyce ploughing in Wheat. M^r H at home all Day, WH at Sherringham all day. Boy filling muck Cart.

NOVEMBER 10, TUESDAY

HR R Bye & T Baldwin ploughing in Wheat, T Boyce & Boy spreading muck. J Ram dressing for^n, W Lamb in Malthouse. M^r H poorly with Gout, WH at home all day. Mr Woods rider Call'd forenoon. G Thompson whiting the small beerhouse [?small-beer house].

---

1 *filling* The muck cart

2 *G. Thompson jnr* See note for 28 July 1794. Henry's note of the early hour is interesting as marriage registers do not give times. The ceremony must have been performed at about 8 am, the earliest permitted canonical hour, given that a weekday breakfast would be no later than 9. There is no further mention of Gunton Chapman Thompson and his wife in the Letheringsett registers, suggesting that they moved elsewhere

3 *George Wymer* See note for 26 Feb. 1794

4 *Cley* Mary Hardy's first attendance at Cley meeting, held at Mrs Elizabeth Smith's home and licensed 7 Jan. 1792 (see note for 26 Aug. 1794). Mary Hardy, housewife, is listed in July 1798 in the earliest surviving Wesleyan Methodist congregation register at Cley, part of the newly formed Walsingham Circuit (NRO: FC/1). Wesleyanism is covered in *World*, vol. 3, chaps 2–4

5 *Kendle* Thomas, of Sharrington Hall, farmer. He married Sharrington 1775 Maria Chambers, and 13 children were baptised there 1776–94: James, Thomas, Maria, Martha, William Chambers, John, Sarah, John, Robert, Mary Ann, Elizabeth, Mary Ann and Susanna (see note for 2 Aug. 1795).

Thomas Kendle had taken out a 14-year lease on Sharrington Hall and farm from Mrs Elizabeth Jodrell

SHARRINGTON
ANTIQUES

above Sharrington Hall, where there were boys of Henry Raven's age and where he was starting to have a social life of his own (8 Nov.). The lease from Mrs Jodrell, who owned the Hall and farm in her own right, shows that it had a malthouse attached; her tenants, the Kendles, could have sought advice from Henry [*MB · 2001*]

NOVEMBER 11, WEDNESDAY

HR R Bye & Thos Baldwin plowing in Wheat, T Boyce spread«ing» Muck. W Lamb in Malthouse, J Ram tasking. WH at Holt afternoon. Nath. Raven came from Whissonsett, whent to Holt afternoon. Mr H very poorly with Gout.

MH A fine day. M & Nathl Raven from Whisonsett came to dinner, they went to Holt afternoon, Wm went with them, drank tea at Miss Johnsons. Wm & Nathl came home Eveng 9. Mr Hardy quite confind with the Gout . . .

NOVEMBER 12, THURSDAY

HR T Baldwin & Thos Boyce finnis [finished] Sowing Wheat forn, began to plough Barley Stubble. R Bye to Sherringham with beer, G Thompson Grinding Barley for Horses. WH & N Raven whalk«ed» out forenoon, road out afternoon.

NOVEMBER 13, FRIDAY

HR R Bye, G Thompson, H Raven & Boy in brewhouse, WH brewing. T Baldwin & T Boyce ploughing in barley stubble. Miss Riches Dine'd here,[1] Mr, Mrs Sheldrake & Mr Forster drank tea here. Miss Raven & Miss Jenniss [the Misses Jennis] whalk'd to Letht [Letheringsett] forenoon. Mr N Raven whent away after dinner.

---

20 Oct. 1785 at £300 p.a. (NRO: WHT 3/2/6, Jodrell estate papers)

---

[1] *Miss Riches* Mary Hardy gives her name as Richards (as does Henry 5 Sept. 1797), noting that she was staying with the Forsters. This was therefore not Mary Riches of Alethorpe

NOVEMBER 14, SATURDAY

HR R Bye helping to Cleanse `// & whent to Bale & Holt with beer, T Baldwin to Fakenham with beer. T Boyce tying faggots, G Thompson & HR Cleansed `//. WH & Miss H at Holt after^{n}, M^{r} H very poorly with Gout.

NOVEMBER 15, SUNDAY

HR M^{rs} H to Hunworth Morning, no prayers at own Church aft^{n}. WH at Holt after^{n}.

MH A shower in morng, fine afternoon. I went to Hunworth Meeting foornoon,[1] no service at our Church on acct of Mrs Burrell being a Dying. Mr Hardy better. M Raven & Deb Johnson calld here afternoon.

NOVEMBER 16, MONDAY

HR R Bye to Wells with beer, T Baldwin to Kettlestone with D^{o}. T Boyce cleaning the yard, J Ram tasking, W Lamb in Malthouse. H Raven drove Miss Hardy to Holt, WH at Sherringham & spent the Evening at Holt. M^{r} H poorly with Gout.

MH A Close day. Mr Hardy much as yesterday. W^{m} went to Sheringham foornoon, came home eveng 4. Mr Smith of Cley here afternoon. MA went up to Holt foornoon, Dind & drank tea at Miss Johnsons. Mrs Burrell Died ab^{t} 10 this Eveng [2] . . .

NOVEMBER 17, TUESDAY

HR R Bye to Salthouse with beer, T Baldwin to Holt & Briston with D^{o}. T Boyce paving the piggs' yard forenoon, Cleaning great yard afternoon. W Lamb in Malthouse, J Ram tasking. G Thomp^{n} & H Raven skreening Malt & began to grind for brew. A Boswell came & Orderd Malt, WH at home all day.

NOVEMBER 18, WEDNESDAY

HR R Bye & T Baldwin to Gunthorp with beer & brought home two loads of Timber, T Boyce to Gunthorp after timber. W Lamb in Malthouse, J Ram tasking. WH at Gunthorp, G Thompson & H Raven grinding Malt for brew.

MH A very Stormy day, Wind very high. Mr Hardy finely. W^{m} went to Gunthorp foornoon to Load some Timber he bought of Mr Colyer, both the Wagons went, came home eveng 4. A small Shock of an Earthquake was felt at Holt, Fakenham & many other places in the Kingdom between 11 & 12 oClock at Night . . .

[1] *Hunworth meeting* Thomas Mendham had registered Elizabeth Franklin's house at Hunworth 9 June 1774 (presumably as a Calvinistic Methodist meeting). However Mary Hardy was probably attending Charles Swallow's; he had registered his house 19 July 1792 (NRO: DN/DIS 1/2, ff. 25, 47). By 1798 the Hunworth meeting may have ceased to exist, for Charles Swallow, gamekeeper, led the Briston (Wesleyan Methodist) congregation that year (NRO: FC 18/1). He is listed as a Hunworth gunsmith in the 1806 county pollbook

[2] *Mrs Burrell* A brief death announcement appeared in the *Norwich Mercury* 21 Nov.

Her burial date was not given in the parish register, but Mary Hardy notes it as 21 Nov. The bereaved husband entered the date of death only: 'Elizabeth Anna Maria Burrell, wife of John Burrell, Rector, (late E.A.M. Garrett, spinster, daughter of John Garrett of Brinton, formerly of Briston), died

NOVEMBER 19, THURSDAY

HR T Baldwin, G Thompson, H Raven & Boy in brewhouse, WH d° brewing. R Bye ploughing & loaded for Stalham, J Ram tasking. T Boyce stopping Gaps in furze Close, W Tinker & two men all day. Miss H spent the day at Bayfield.

NOVEMBER 20, FRIDAY

HR R Bye to Stalham with beer, T Baldwin to Holt & Edgefield with beer & Malt & Brought back 13 Coomb barley. J Ram tasking, W Lamb in Malthouse, T Boyce in Garden. WH at Sherringham forenoon, G Thompson & HR cleansed `//. Miss Raven & Miss Bartell dine'd, drank tea & Sup[t] here.

NOVEMBER 21, SATURDAY

HR T Balden to Holt with beer. J Ram tasking forenoon, in Malthouse after[n]. R Bye came from Stalham. W Lamb in Malthouse for[n], T Boyce in Garden. G Thompson & H Raven Cleansed XX, M[r] H whalk'd into brewhouse fore[n].[1] M[rs] Flower dine'd here, WH at Holt Market.

MH A sharp rime frost. M[rs] Flowr dind & drank tea here, MA rid up to Holt with her in Eveng. M[r] Hardy at home all day. W[m] walkd to Holt Market aftern, came home eveng 9. M[rs] Burrell was buried . . .

NOVEMBER 22, SUNDAY

HR M[rs] H & H Raven to Cley after[n], no service at Own Church. WH at Holt afternoon.

NOVEMBER 23, MONDAY

HR R Bye to Wells with beer & Brought home ten Bags of hops, T Baldwin to Burnham with beer. G Thomp[n] & H Raven skreening Malt & grinding for brew. W Lamb in Malthouse, J Ram tasking. WH at home all day, T Boyce in garden. Miss Johnson & Miss Raven whalk'd down here forenoon.

NOVEMBER 24, TUESDAY

HR R Bye to Aldborough with beer, T Baldwin came from Burnham & to S Sandersons.[2] T Boyce in Garden, J Ram in Barn, W Lamb in Malthouse. G Thompson & H Raven in brewhouse, WH brewing. M[r] H at home all day. M[r] & M[rs] Raven came Evening, Miss H at Holt afternoon.[3]

facing page 'No service at our church on account of Mrs Burrell being a-dying' (15 Nov.). Basil Cozens-Hardy's undated photograph shows the Burrells' family home at Letheringsett; there was no parsonage. The rector's wife died here on 17 Nov., and would have been buried in the Burrell vault in the church.

John Burrell married the Holt milliner Mary Johnson the following August [*Cozens-Hardy Collection*]

Nov[r] 17, 1795' (NRO: PD 547/2)

---

[1] *Mr Hardy* Possibly an ironic remark by Henry, his master's appearances in the brewery being so rare as to merit special mention. However William Hardy had been confined to the house, his gout permitting not even minor sorties

[2] *Sanderson* This entry relates probably to 25 Nov., not 24 Nov. Henry made a few crossings-out at this point and evidently forgot to erase the beer delivery which he later entered for the following day. Samuel Sanderson had been running the canteen at Weybourne Camp; this was the last beer delivery of the year to him

[3] *Mr and Mrs Raven* Mary Hardy's brother Nathaniel and his wife Ann

BLACK

[1] *mill* The squat, stumpy brick windmill stands between the coast road and the sea at Blakeney. It was built before 1769 and was later raised or 'hained' to four storeys.

In 1786 it was occupied by Samuel Fromow, and in 1806 by William Marsh. A full account of its history is given by Harry Apling: *Norfolk Corn Windmills* (Norfolk Windmills Trust, Norwich, 1984), pp. 189–92.

Zebulon Rouse's brother-in-law Thomas Drosier, husband of Sally, was bankrupted 17 Jan. 1827 while running the mill: see note for 5 Oct. 1794

NOVEMBER 25, WEDNESDAY

HR R Bye after Jobs forenoon, T Baldwin to Waybourn with beer & to S Sandersons. W Lamb in Malthouse, J Ram tasking. T Boyce in Garden, G Thompson & H Raven Cleansed '//. Mr Raven & WH whent to Holt fair forenoon, Mrs Flower dine'd here. HR whent to Holt afternoon.

NOVEMBER 26, THURSDAY

HR R Bye to Hindolvestone with beer, T Baldwin to Sherringham with beer. G Thompson & H Raven Cleanse'd X beer. W Lamb in Malthouse, J Ram helping to Cleanse & clear fatt [vat]. T Boyce in garden. Mr H at home all day, WH & Mr Raven rode to Blackeny to the sale.

MH A Sharp rime frost. Brot Raven & Wm went to Blakney foornoon to a Sale at the Mill, came home eveng 5.[1] Sister Ravn & MR & MA walk'd up to Holt foornoon, came back to dinner. Miss M Johnson drank tea here . . .

NOVEMBER 27, FRIDAY

HR R Bye to Southrepps with beer, W Lamb in Malt house, J Ram tasking. T Boyce [?T. Baldwin] in Brewhouse, G Thompson & H Raven grinding Malt for Brew. T Boyce to Blakeney afternoon, WH to Sherringham after^{n}. M^{r} & Mrs Raven whent of for Whiss^{t} after dinner. Mr Willm Carting away muck.[1]

NOVEMBER 28, SATURDAY

HR R Bye to Cley for 2 Chaldron Cinders from Mr Ellis's. G Thompson, H Raven & Boyce & Wodehouse in brewhouse,[2] WH brewing & Whent to Holt Markett. W Lamb in Malthouse, J Ram tasking. M^{r} H at home all Day. Mr Williams carting away muck.

NOVEMBER 29, SUNDAY

HR Mrs Hardy & Mrs Youngman Whalk'd to Cley afternoon,[3] WH & Miss H at Holt Church after^{n}, M^{r} H at home all day. No prayers.

MH A Sharp rime frost. No service at our Church, I & Mrs Youngman walk'd to Cley meeting afternoon. W^{m} & MA walkd to Holt Church afternoon, Mr Burrell preachd there. Mr Hardy at home all day. Thawd in the Night . . .

[1] *Mr William* Presumably the lawyer William Williams of Thornage (28 Nov.)

[2] *Woodhouse* Nicholas (4 Dec. 1795), the Hardys' 'great boy': ie a little older, given more responsibility—and a name; he left 10 Oct. 1796. He may be the son of Christopher Woodhouse of Lt Thornage and Susanna, née Bulwer or Buller; their son Thomas was buried Letheringsett 5 Apr. 1797, shortly followed by Mrs Woodhouse herself 12 Apr. 1797. See also notes for 4 Dec. 1795, 11 Apr. 1797

[3] *Mrs Youngman* Lydia (bur. Letheringsett 6 Jan. 1828 aged 68), wife of Thomas; the two women had a return walk of 7½–8 miles. She had at times helped the Hardys with sewing, and occasionally attended Cley and Briston Methodist meetings with Mary Hardy until 1806. Like Elizabeth Bullock she is not listed as a member of either society: we cannot judge the number of worshippers by paid-up membership alone

facing page Aldborough, the Black Boys. Although William Hardy had bought this public house for the large sum of 300 guineas on 8 Apr. 1794 the first record of the monthly beer deliveries from Letheringsett came on 24 Nov. 1795. It is possible the house had until then had a publican brewer whose craft was to be made obsolete by the thrusting common brewer armed with the tie [*MB · 1992*]

left Blakeney Mill (26 Nov.), also known as Friary Mill, is 'one of only a few Norfolk brick tower mills that can be given an 18th-century date' (H. Apling, 1984) [*MB · 2011*]

NOVEMBER 30, MONDAY

HR R Bye to Brampton with beer, T Baldwin to Stody with D^o^ & Loaded for Barmer. T Boyce after jobs. W Lamb in M House, Jno Ram tasking. G Thompson & H Raven Cleansin«g» & Got Cleanse of beer into great cask in White Hall, T Baldwin, W Lamb & Wodehouse help'd to get Beer into Cask. WH rode to Cley forenoon, M^r^ H at home all Day.

DECEMBER 1, TUESDAY

Henry Raven T Baldwin to Barmer, R Bye to Holt with beer. W Lamb in Malthouse, Jno Ram tasking, G Thompson & H Raven dressing flower. WH to Sherringham, M^r^ H at home all Day. Mr Burrell drank tea here.

DECEMBER 2, WEDNESDAY

HR T Baldwin came from Barmer & whent to Thornage with beer, R Bye to Runton with D^o^. G Thompson & H Raven grinding Malt for brew, W Lamb in M house. J Ram tasking, T Boyce in Garden. Mr Flower sent for some furze threes [? fir trees].[1]

[1] *fir trees/furze trees* Since Cook Flower's successor Abbot Upcher (1784–1819) quickly set about planting both fir trees and furze (gorse) in the light soil, it is difficult to interpret the meaning here (S. Yaxley, ed., *Sherringhamia: The journal of Abbot Upcher 1813–16* (Larks Press, Guist Bottom, 1986), pp. 5, 12–13, entries for 12 Jan. 1813 and for Mar.–May 1814). William Hardy jnr's spelling 29 Dec. 1795, when Cook Flower ordered 150 *fir* trees, might suggest the order of 2 Dec. was also for conifers.

At the time of the sale on 10 July 1811 to Upcher for £52,500 the Sheringham (Old) Hall estate had 150 acres of arable and meadow, 127 acres of woods and plantations, 45 of furze and underwood (for protecting newly planted saplings), and 102 acres of other land (NRO: UPC 13/6, 639X4, Sale agreement, Cook Flower to Abbot Upcher). The lawyer was William Repton. His father Humphry was to transform the estate at the end of his career

below 'R. Bye drunking': Henry Raven's note, squeezed in at the end of the entry for 3 Dec. 1795, gives a hint of trouble to come.

Robert Bye was dismissed on Christmas Eve 1795, just before the festive dinner laid on for the workforce. Bye had worked long hours for the Hardys over many years, Sundays included, but loyal service did not save him. It was the serious accident suffered by his old team-mate Thomas Baldwin a year later which brought Bye back into the regular team on 15 Dec. 1796 [*Cozens-Hardy Collection*]

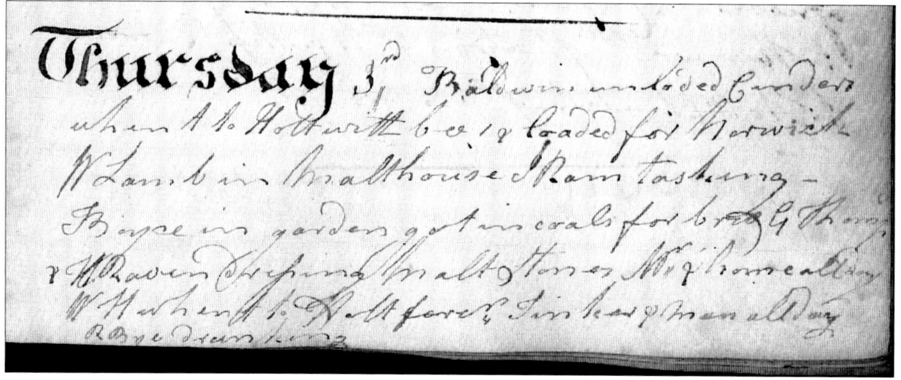
Thursday 3rd [illegible] Baldwin unloded Cinders [illegible] to Holt with beer & loaded for Norwich
W Lamb in Malthouse J Ram tasking –
T Boyce in garden got in coals for brew G Thomp[son]
& H Raven [illegible] Malt [illegible] [illegible]
W H went to Holt forenoon [illegible] at home all Day
R Bye drunking

above The view from Sheringham Heath, looking towards Beeston and a sea busy with shipping, by a youthful Humphry Repton *c.*1779; he has only slightly exaggerated the sloping terrain of the Cromer ridge. The foreground shows the scrub and gorse which flourishes on thin heathland soil. The wooded estate of Sheringham (Old) Hall, seat of William's friend Cook Flower and earlier his father, lies out of sight to the left (2 Dec. 1795) [*Norfolk Museums & Archaeology Service* (*Norwich Castle Museum & Art Gallery*)]

DECEMBER 3, THURSDAY

HR T Baldwin unloded Cinders, whent to Holt with beer & loaded for Norwich. W Lamb in Malthouse, J Ram tasking. T Boyce in garden, got in coals for brew. G Thomp^{n} & H Raven dressing Malt Stones. M^{r} & [Mr Hardy at] home all day, WH whent to Holt fore^{n}. Tinker & man all day. R Bye drunking.

Mary Hardy A fine day. W^{m} walkd up to Holt foornoon with John Davy, came home to dinner. M Raven came from Holt to Stay . . .

DECEMBER 4, FRIDAY

HR T Boyce, HR & G Thompson in brewhouse, WH D^{o} brewing. T Baldwin to Norwich with beer, R Bye to Wiverton & Cley for 2 Chald. Cinders from Mr Ellis's. J Ram tasking, W Lamb in Malthouse. Mich^{s} Woodhouse whent away with swell^{d} leg's.[1] W Tinker & 2 Men all Day.

DECEMBER 5, SATURDAY

HR R Bye to Holt & Hindolvestone with beer, T Baldwin came from Norwich. W Lamb in Malthouse, G Thompson & H Raven Cleanse'd `// & dressing Malt

[1] *Mich^{s}* Usually Michaelmas; here probably an error for Nicholas, the 'great boy' (note for 28 Nov. 1795).

He may be the Nicholas Woodhouse who, with his wife Mary, was the subject of a removal order from Weybourne to Bayfield in Jan. 1798, an order which was quashed 18 Apr. 1798 when Bayfield appealed (NRO: C/S 1/15, Quarter sessions held at Holt and Norwich).

Such an order could be applied for if the subject had a disability causing him/her to become chargeable to the parish of residence. Nicholas's swollen legs may have developed into a disabling condition

Stones. Mr H at Holt, W & Miss Hardy & Miss Raven to Holt afternoon. J Ram tasking, T Boyce in Garden. Tinkers two men all Day.

DECEMBER 6, SUNDAY

HR G Thompson, H Raven Cleanse'd morning, R Bye, T Baldwin & T Boyce assisted in Cleansing. Mrs H & H Raven whent to Hunworth afternoon, WH & Miss Raven to Holt Church afternoon.

MH A Close day, drisly Morng. I & H Raven went to Hunworth Meeting. All went to our Church eveng 7, Mr Burrell preachd.[1] Wm & MR walk'd to Holt Church aftern.

DECEMBER 7, MONDAY

HR R Bye to Cromer with beer, T Baldwin to Holt with Do to Atwoods & Wakefields. T Boyce in Garden, W Lamb in Malthouse. J Ram at work half a day, W Tinker & two Men all day. G Thompson laid Down Malt Stones, Mr Williams carting muck.

MH A Close foggy day. Mr Hardy & Wm at home all day. Mr Burrell & Miss Leake drank tea here.

DECEMBER 8, TUESDAY

HR T Baldwin to Edgefield with beer & clean'd the Copper, R Bye ploughing in furze close. W Lamb in Malthouse, Jno Ram tasking. T Boyce in Garden, G Thompson & H Raven Grinding Malt for brew. W Tinker & two Men all Day. Mr H at home all Day, Mr Williams carting away muck.

MH A Close foggy day. Mr Hardy went to Mr Burrells after tea, Wm at home all day. Maids & Eliz Milegan washd 5 Weeks linnen.

DECEMBER 9, WEDNESDAY

HR T Baldwin, G Thompson & H Raven in brewhouse, WH Do brewing. R Bye ploughing. T Boyce in brewhouse morning, in Garden all Day. J Ram tasking part of Day, W Lamb in Malthouse. Mr Williams Carting away muck, Mr H at home all Day.

MH Frosty morng, close afternoon. Wm Brew'd. Mr Hardy & M Raven went to Mr Burrells after tea . . .

DECEMBER 10, THURSDAY

HR R Bye & T Baldwin to Cley for six Chaldron Coals from Mr Cook's. W Lamb in Malthouse, J Ram tasking.

1 *Mr Burrell* In the weeks following his wife's death the pattern of the rector's services changed. Instead of taking a single weekly alternating morning and afternoon service he started to take two services on Sundays (eg 13 Dec.), and at varying times (6 Dec., 13 Dec.)

above 'H. Raven painted the gate in Pightle' (14 Dec.). The Brewhouse Pightle field gate, near the tun room and beside the King's Head until William moved his tied house in 1808. Apart from work in the fields at harvest, Henry Raven's duties in the maltings and brewery generally insulated him from events outside. As he painted the gate beside the main road he would have been aware of the rumblings of disquiet over the price of wheat which on 14 Dec. were to break out into open revolt [*MB* · *2002*]

G Thompson & HR Cleanse'd `//, Mr Williams Carting away muck. M^r & Mrs Sheldrake drank tea here. M^r & WH at home all day. T Boyce unloaded a load of Cinders in Morning & then whent into Garden. H Raven & WH trimm'd the Chaise horse afternoon.

DECEMBER 11, FRIDAY

HR R Bye to Bale with beer, T Baldwin unloading coals & whent to Holt with beer. W Lamb in Malthouse, J Ram in brewhouse, G Thompson & H Raven Cleansed X beer. Mr Williams carting away muck. W & Miss Hardy & Miss Raven whent to Sherringham.

DECEMBER 12, SATURDAY

HR T Baldwin to Salthouse with beer & Cley for 2 Chald. Cinders from Mr Ellis's, R Bye to Morston & Cley with beer. W Lamb in Malthouse, T Boyce in garden, J Ram after Jobs. M^r H at Holt afternoon. W & Miss & Miss Raven came from Sherringham evening.

DECEMBER 13, SUNDAY

HR M^rs H & H Raven whent to Hunworth Morning, famaly to Church afternoon & Evening.

MH A fine morng, showry afternoon. I & H Raven went to Hanworth [Hunworth] foornoon. All went to our Church afternoon, Mr Burrell preachd & preachd again Even 6, we all went . . .

DECEMBER 14, MONDAY

HR R Bye to Sherringham with beer, T Baldwin to Briston and Corpusta with D^o. W Lamb in Malthouse, T Boyce in garden. J Ram in Brewhouse, G Thompson & H Raven grinding Malt for brew & Bin. M^r, M^rs & Miss Hardy & Miss Raven drank tea at Mr Burrells. WH rode to Holt after tea then whent to Mr Burrell evening. H Raven painted the gate in Phitle [the Brewhouse Pightle].

DECEMBER 15, TUESDAY

HR R Bye to Holt with beer Morning, to Cley after^n with D^o & Bro^t home 2 Chal^d Cinders from Mr Ellis's, T Baldwin to Fakenham with D^o [beer]. W Lamb in Malthouse, J Ram tasking, T Boyce in Garden. M^r H rode to Bayfield morning.[1] Miss Hardy & Miss Raven at Holt afternoon, WH at Holt Evening. S Sanderson Call^d here after^n.

[1] *Bayfield* Like most of his neighbouring north Norfolk JPs (eg Sir Edward Astley, Bt, Charles Collyer, Revd Dixon Hoste and Lord Townshend) Henry Jodrell was at home; T.W. Coke soon came to Norfolk. The justices led attempts to suppress the protests without further inflaming the situation, while yet protecting the property of the farmers and millers. As the great majority of the JPs based themselves in their local community and did not move to London or Bath for the season they understood local grievances and laboured to defuse the crisis; even so, they were to need the support of the military (15 Dec.).

In the aftermath the judicial penalties directed at the rioters were largely lenient (note for 20 Dec. 1795). At Norwich 17 grand jurors and many of the justices issued statements in sympathy with the plight of the people and resolved to reduce wheat consumption in their own families (*Norw. Merc.* 16 Jan. 1796)—a somewhat lacklustre response to severe shortages. There were no hearings relating to the north Norfolk riots at Holt Quarter Sessions on 21 Jan. 1796 (NRO: C/S 1/15), those cases being heard in the city where sentences could be made consistent countywide.

Magisterial leadership is examined in *World*, vol. 3, chap. 6, as also the course of the riots and the nature of the response

[1] *riot* The first of the area's bread riots which became widespread as wheat prices rose following the failure of the harvest. Since 28 Nov. 1795 the *Norwich Mercury* had been giving detailed bulletins on the scarcity of wheat and flour. At Norwich and Gt Yarmouth on 28 Nov. wheat was 68*s* to 74*s* a quarter; by 5 Dec. it had risen to 78*s* to 80*s*. For comparison, prices at Norwich and Gt Yarmouth 10 Jan. 1795 were 48*s* to 55*s*.

London prices were far higher. Wheat at Mark Lane Corn Exchange 3 Dec. 1795 was 84*s* to 93*s*. For the moment the price of barley remained more stable.

The soldiers seen by Mary Hardy as they passed her house were a company of the Pembroke Militia, quartered at Holt. They were ordered to Warham, beyond Wells, to be held in reserve until needed.

The object of the rioters was to prevent the shipping of flour out of the local area, and the women on the quayside at Wells had to be dispersed at bayonet point.

At Mildenhall Bridge, Suff., one man let the water out of the lock, stranding the barges carrying wheat bound for Cambridge. At night 150 people took the wheat, leaving untouched the barley on board. Three men and two women were arrested out of the 150: one of the features of the disturbances was the high number of women trying to draw attention to the plight of their starving children (*Norw. Merc.* 19 Dec. 1795)

above **Letheringsett Hall: part of the south front, viewed from the Brewhouse Pightle. Until William Hardy jnr's 1808 road diversion, creating the great loop for the south lawn, the main road led in a nearly direct line right against the south-facing windows. The Hardys, who were farmers and millers as well as maltsters and brewers, were extremely vulnerable to rioters** [*photograph A.E. Coe, of Norwich, 1880: Cozens-Hardy Collection*]

MH A fine day. Mr Hardy at home all day. MA & M Raven walkd to Holt afternoon, drank tea at Miss Johnsons, W^m^ went for them with the Chaise in Eveng. The Soldiers from Holt sent for to Wells to Quell a Riot went past Morng 7.[1]

DECEMBER 16, WEDNESDAY

HR R Bye, G Thompson, J Ram & H Raven in Brewhouse, WH D^o^ brewing. W Lamb in Malthouse, T Baldwin ploughing. M^r^ H at home all day, Miss H & Miss Raven drank tea at Holt. Mr Nath Raven Junr came Evening. H Raven whent to Holt evening for the Ladys. Robt Staff came from Stalham. T Boyce in Garden & whent to Bayfield evening with Malt.

MH A very fine day till Eveng past 4 then raind. Mr Hardy at home all day, Wm Brew'd. MA & MR walkd up to Holt afternoon, drank tea at Mr Davys, H Raven

Riots. Rivers Navigable.

RIOTS.

It seems clear, that every sheriff, under sheriff, and also every other peace officer, as constables and like officers, may, and ought to do all that in their power lies towards the suppressing of a riot, and may command all persons whatsoever to assist them therein. 1 *Hawk.* c. 65. s. 11.

If twelve* or more persons unlawfully and riotously assemble, a justice, sheriff, mayor, or other head officer of any town corporate, on notice of such assembly, shall come as near them as he can with safety, and make the following proclamation:—

Our Sovereign Lord the King charges and commands all persons assembled, immediately to disperse themselves, and peaceably depart to their habitations, or lawful business, on pain of imprisonment, or the penalties inflicted by the Act made in the first year of the reign of King George I. for preventing tumults and riotous assemblies.
God save the King.

If within an hour after this proclamation is made, the rioters do not disperse, or if they hinder the proclamation or him who makes it, it is felony without benefit of clergy; and the constables, with proper assistance, may seize and carry them before a justice.

left Reading the Riot Act did not always suffice, as reported in the *Norwich Mercury* 19 Dec. 1795: 'The proclamation was read, which was attended by nothing but menaces and uproar; and it being read a second time in vain, the Pembroke Militia marched into the town [Wells], and was ordered to protect the flour and [its] embarkation. Every resistance was made; when the men with equal spirit and caution advanced with their bayonets to protect both the flour and the ship . . .' A large number of women had assembled over some days at Wells to stop the flour being shipped.

Once reading the Riot Act failed, the justices had to rely on fixed bayonets [*The Whole Duty of Constables, by an acting magistrate* (*2nd edn Norwich, 1815*), *p. 57*]

went for them in the Chaise Eveng 8. Nath[l] Raven came to tea. The Soldiers returnd from Wells to Holt.

DECEMBER 17, THURSDAY

HR T Baldwin helping to Cleanse `// & whent to Sharrington with beer. W Lamb in Malthouse half Aday, J Ram a days work. G Thompson & H Raven Cleansed `//. R Bye drunk all day. M[r] & Miss Raven & W & Miss Hardy whalkd to Holt morning, Company at tea afternoon. H Raven to Sherringtons [Sharrington] in Evening on Account of Mob.

MH A fine day. M[r] Hardy at home all day. The young people walkd up to Holt foornoon, came back to dinner. 2 Miss Jenness [Jennises], Miss M & S Davy & Miss D Johnson drank tea here. Some poor people stopt 5 Loades of Flower [flour] at Sherington [Sharrington] belonging to Z Rouse of Glanford going to Lynn.[1]

[1] *Lynn* Zebulon Rouse would have been trying to bypass the Wells riots by shipping through the port of King's Lynn, although he would have done well selling his flour there. Wheat prices at Lynn were even higher than in Norwich—78*s* 8*d* on 28 Nov., as against 48*s* 4*d* on 10 Jan. 1795 (*Norw. Merc.* 28 Nov., 5 Dec. 1795). It is hard to imagine what Henry could have done when faced by a starving mob. He may have gone to Sharrington as a witness in the future court

DECEMBER 18, FRIDAY

HR T Baldwin ploughing in five Acres, R Bye ploughin«g» in field & loaded for Syderstone. W Lamb in Malthouse, J Ram a days work after Jobs. G Thompson & H Raven Cleanse'd X beer. WH set of for Fakenham morng 6 OClock, M^{r} H at Sherrington. M^{r} & Miss Raven set of for Whissonsett forenoon.

MH A very fine day. W^{m} set of for Siderston Morng 7. M & N Raven went away Morng 11, Mr Hardy went with them as far as Sherington. A great many people gather'd together there unloaded the flower & sett it in a House, The Justices could not perswade them to give it up.[1]

DECEMBER 19, SATURDAY

HR R Bye to Syderstone with beer, T Baldwin to Sherrington with D^{o} & unloaded Cinders & whent to Holt with D^{o} [beer].[2] W Lamb in Malthouse, J Ram a days work after Jobs, G Thompson dressing Wheatstones. M^{r} H at Holt. WH came from Whiss^{t} [Whissonsett], whent to Holt Evening.

part of. The Justices sat great part of the day to settle the Mob but nothing was done & no other business was transacted. They sent for a Troop of Horse from Norwich & a party of Foot Soldiers from Aylsham they arived at Holt about 8 oclock on Sunday Morng

Sunday: 20 A very fine day. The Soldiers march through our Town about 10 Clock went to Sherington & set a guard over the Flower that was seizd took up a Man namd Bone suposd to be one of the ringleaders of the Mob returnd to Holt about 3 oClock

right Extracts from Mary Hardy's entries for 19 and 20 Dec. 1795. The infantry must have marched the 12 miles from Aylsham through the cold December night. Her diary and Henry's are two of very few records of these riots, the Norwich Quarter Sessions minutes merely listing the charges against the ringleaders, the verdicts, and, for those convicted, the sentences [_Cozens-Hardy Collection_]

proceedings or to give his support to the Kendles, whose fine farmhouse lay not far from the road: the rioters were venting their wrath and despair on farmers and millers

[1] *flour* The house in which it was stored was the Swan, on the main Lynn road at Sharrington (and supplied by the Hardys), as we learn from Henry Jodrell's official reports to Lord Townshend, the Lord Lieutenant, and to the Government (TNA: PRO HO 42/37, ff. 306, 308, 311–14, dated 16 Dec., 22 Dec., 23 Dec. 1795). These are quoted at length in *World*, vol. 3, chap. 6

[2] *Sharrington* There had been a beer delivery to the village only two days previously. The deliveries of 19 and 21 Dec. could have been to supply the troops posted to guard the flour. Both war and civil unrest were good for business

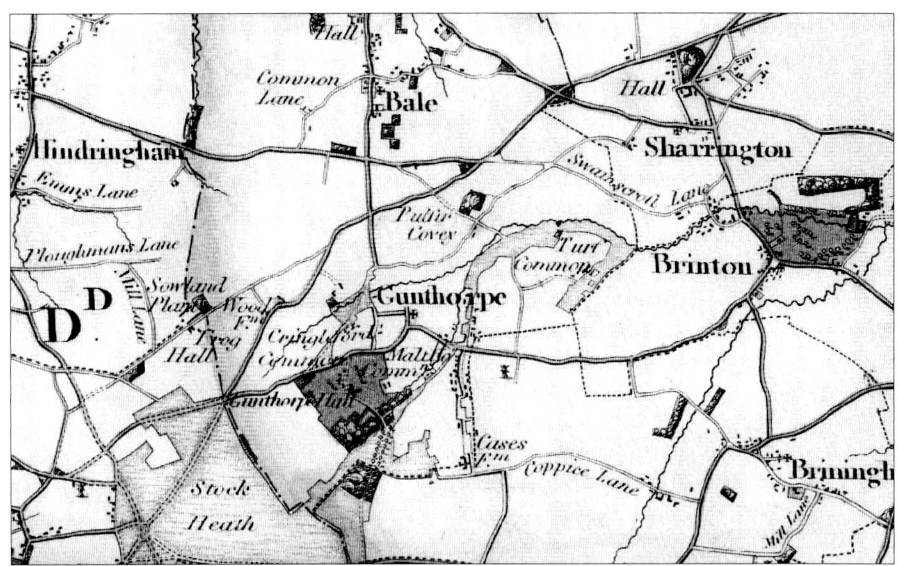
Hall
Common
Lane
Bale
Hall
Sharrington
Brinton
Gunthorpe
Turf
Common
Mill Lane
D
D
Frog
Hall
Cases
Fm
Coppice Lane
Stock
Heath
Mill Lane

above The main road from Cromer and Holt to Fakenham and King's Lynn runs south-west through Sharrington. The Swan, which became the focus of the unrest as the flour was put under armed guard there, stands north of the main road just north-west of Sharrington Hall. The flour was on the move again on 21 Dec. 1795. By this time the ringleaders, all local, had been arrested and the farmers and other members of the Loyal Holt Association could escort it from Sharrington to Stock Heath, south of Gunthorpe. William Hardy rode with them [*Bryant's Map of Norfolk 1826: Cozens-Hardy Collection*]

MH A Stormy day, wind high. Mr Hardy rid up to Holt foorn, dind at Mr Vickerys,[1] drank tea at Mr Bartells, came home Eveng past 9. Wm came home from Whisonset to tea, rid up to Holt Markt, home eveng past 9. The Justices sat grat [great] part of the day to settle the Mob but nothing was done & no other buisiness was transacted. They sent for a Troop of Horse from Norwich & a party of Foot Soldiers from Ay«l»sham, they arivd at Holt about 8 oclock on Sunday Morng.[2]

DECEMBER 20, SUNDAY

HR Famaly to Church forenoon. Soldiers pass'd through here about 1 OClock on their way to Sherrington. Mrs H at Cley afternoon, WH rode to Sherrington afternoon.

[1] *Vickery* Caryar Vickery, a Holt surgeon. His wife Catherine, née Munnings, died at Holt 22 May 1793 (Diary MS: 22 May) and was bur. there 27 May aged 32; their nine-month-old daughter Mary Ann had been bur. Holt 6 Mar. 1793. He ran off in 1798 with the wife of the Curate of Holt: see note for 4 Dec. 1796; also *World*, vol. 1, chap. 4, on marriage and separation

[2] *troop of horse* Dragoons from the Inniskilling Regiment were quartered in Norwich (*Norw. Merc.* 5 Dec. 1795). Neither the Regulars from Ireland nor the Militia from S. Wales recruited from anywhere near E. Anglia. It was deliberate policy not to deploy against the local citizenry any serving troops raised in the area, for fear of a clash of loyalties

right The *Norwich Mercury* of 26 Dec. 1795 reports the events of 21 Dec. near Holt [*Norfolk Heritage Centre, Norwich*]

We are happy to hear that a tumult which arofe in the neighbourhood of Holt, in this county, by a mob feizing fome flour that was going to Lynn, has, by the vigilance and activity of the Magiftrates, fubfided.

On Monday morning Mr. Jodrell of Bayfield, and Mr. Collyer, by notices fent out to the different towns in the hundred, affembled with the High Conftables and nearly 100 of the Gentlemen and Yeomanry in the neighbourhood, met on horfeback, in the Market-place of Holt, and conducted the flour fafely through the hundred. Too much praife cannot be given to the activity of the Magiftrates and the exertions of the Gentlemen and Yeomanry on this occafion. On Tuefday an affociation was entered into at Holt called the Loyal Holt Affociation, the terms of which as propofed to the meeting by Mr. Jodrell and Mr. Collyer were as follows: "We the Loyal Holt Affociation, whofe names are underwritten, do hereby pledge ourfelves that in cafe of any tumult or difturbance to the public peace, we will inftantly come forward in our perfons to affift the Civil Power in the due execution of the laws, each man mounted on horfeback with his ftaff." More than 150 of the Gentlemen and Yeomanry who affembled on this occafion, figned their names to this affociation.—This plan, which feems well calculated to fupprefs civil commotion and preferve the public peace, is adopting the conftitutional authory of the Poffe Comitatus, and reflects the higheft credit on the worthy Magiftrates who propofed it; each affociator is to receive a ftaff from the High Conftable, with a device emblematical of the affociation. We are happy to find that feveral refpectable Clergymen have joined the above affociation with a fpirit that becomes them.

MH A very fine day. The Soldiers marchd through our Town about 1 oClock, went to Sherington & set a guard over the Flower that was seizd, took up a Man namd Bone suposd to be one of the ringleaders of the Mob, returnd to Holt about 3 o Clock.[1] We all went to our Church foornoon, Mr Burrell preachd. I went to Cley meeting afternoon, T Boyce went with me, home eveng 5. W^m went to Sherington afternoon, back to tea. All went to our Church even 6, prayers & Sermon.

[1] *ringleaders* The minutes of the quarter sessions at Norwich 13 Jan. 1796 record the fate of the rioters. The JPs sitting that day were Henry Jodrell, Hon. Henry Hobart, Sir Edmund Bacon, Bt, Sir John Wodehouse, Bt, and Sir John Lombe, Bt. The case of the rioters at Diss and Blo Norton, in south Norfolk, was heard first.

For the Sharrington riots the appellants were Zebulon Rouse and Richard Rouse [millers], and the defendants Thomas Bunn [the 'Bone' referred to by Mary Hardy 20 Dec.], of 'Gunton' [Gunthorpe], Thomas Harris or Harry of Field Dalling, Thomas Fuller, Robert Park or Parke of Saxlingham [-by-Holt], and Martha, wife of David Pleasance, 'for a riot' [Mrs Pleasance being the daughter-in-law of the Hardys' innkeeper at the Cross Keys, Gunthorpe]. The jury found them guilty, but they received light sentences. Bunn and Parke were committed to Aylsham Bridewell for six months and were to find sureties; Harry and Fuller were committed to Wymondham Bridewell for six months and were to find sureties; Martha Pleasance was fined 20*s* and had to find sureties.

Importantly, the five

DECEMBER 21, MONDAY

HR T Baldwin to Sherrington & Holt with beer, R Bye Clearing Mash fat [vat]. W Lamb in Malthouse, J Ram tasking. WH at home all Day. A Large company of Farmers came through Letherst on their way to Sherrington, M^{r} H whent with them.[1]

MH A very Wet day. The Soldiers & Justices & alarge party of Farmers went through the town Morng 11 to Sherington & guarded the Flower which was seizd as far as Stock Heath.[2] Mr Hardy went with them part of the way, came back to dinner.

DECEMBER 22, TUESDAY

HR R Bye ploughing forenoon, to Holt with beer afternoon, T Baldwin to Fakenham with D^{o}. W Lamb in Malthouse, J Ram taking up Patatoes.[3] WH dine'd at Holt, M^{r} H at home all day. G Thompson & H Raven grinding Malt for Brew & an«d» Bin.

above Letheringsett Hall, its south front long buffered by lawn and hedge from the main road. The building's foundation lines and L-shape remain largely the same as in 1795; the Greek Doric portico by the dining room dates from 1809. Mary Hardy had a ringside seat when watching processions of rioters, Regulars, Militia and the local 'loyal' farmers [*MB · 1990*]

were not sent before the assizes, which had greater sentencing powers. However two other defendants, far from the north Norfolk riots, were committed to appear at Thetford's Lent Assizes (NRO: C/S 1/15).

The *Norwich Mercury* of 16 Jan. 1796 reported the Sharrington case and added, 'Ann Horne, Mary Horne, Peter Sutton and others were acquitted': leniency was to the fore

---

[1] *farmers* From the newly formed Loyal Holt Association (as illustrated facing page)—an example of the swift way new institutions could be formed to respond to emergencies. Structures were dynamic in nature, and by no means fossilised

[2] *flour* Prices continued to rise. At Norwich and Gt Yarmouth wheat stood at 110*s* to 114*s* a quarter and barley at 35*s* to 37*s*; Mark Lane wheat prices were lower at 96*s* to 108*s*, and more volatile for barley at 34*s* to 39*s* (*Norw. Merc.* 9 Jan. 1796). These prices show that the rioters' fears proved justified: by exporting wheat to London the capital's crisis was eased at the expense of the grain-producing counties

[3] *potatoes* The first time these have been mentioned since the Hardys' move to Letheringsett in 1781. The poor wheat harvest could have encouraged growers to turn to this other staple carbohydrate crop

MH A fine day. W^m walkd up to Holt, dind with the Justices & Farmers at the Shire House,[1] met to examine Witneses concerning the Riot, came home eveng past 9. Mr Hardy at home all day.

DECEMBER 23, WEDNESDAY

HR R Bye to Cromer with beer, T Baldwin to Runton with D^o. G Thompson & H Raven grinding Malt for brew, J Ram tasking, W Lamb in Malthouse. M^r H at home all Day. Mr Williams Carting away Muck. [[[2] Robt Bye Left the Team.]]

MH A fine day. W^m rid to Sheringham Afternoon, calld us at Mr Seales s [Sales's] at Holt eveng 8, we walkd up & the Chaise came for us.

DECEMBER 24, THURSDAY

HR T Boyce to South Repps with beer, G Thompson & H Raven in Brewhouse. T Baldwin to Beckhigh with d^o. Lamb in Malthouse, J Ram tasking. WH brewing, M^r H at home all day. Mr Williams Carting away muck.

MH A Wet day. Wm Brewd, Mr Hardy at home all day. Robt Buy turnd away.[3]

DECEMBER 25, FRIDAY

HR G Thompson & H Raven Cleansed `//. This being Christmas Day the Laborers all dine'd here. M^rs H & H Raven whent to Cley after^n.

MH *Xmas Day* A very fine day. Mr Hardy, I & MA went to our Church foorn, only prayers. Our Labourers & Wifes dind here. I & H Raven went to Cley Afternoon, home to tea. We went to Church in eveng. W^m & HR drank tea at Mr Bartells, Holt . . .

[[DECEMBER 26, SATURDAY

William Hardy jnr T Boyce to Hinderingham with beer, T Baldwin to Holt foren^n, to Thornage after^n. G Tompson Cleansd X, W Lamb in M^t H [malthouse], Jno Ram in Brewhouse & Jobs. Mr Hardy at Market afternoon, WH to Aldborough & Southreeps. H Raven went to Whissonsett in Even^g, M^rs & Miss Hardy Holt Morn^g.

DECEMBER 27, SUNDAY

WHj WH at Holt Church afternoon & Family at our Church in Eveng. M^rs H rode to Clay with T Boyce. W Lamb left M^t H & took the Team & Jno Ram the M^t H, new Boy W^m came home.

[1] *justices* The JPs at the first quarter sessions held at Holt after the riots were Henry Jodrell, Charles Collyer, John Gay and Zurishaddai Girdlestone (NRO: C/S 1/15, 21 Jan. 1796).

This day, 22 Dec., was William and Mary Hardy's 30th wedding anniversary

[2] Written in William's hand; he was perhaps mistaking the day. As Henry did not return from Whissonsett until 3 Jan. he must have used William's notes to compile the diary for 30 Dec.–3 Jan.

[3] *turned away* Dismissed; like her son, Mary Hardy gives no reason for it. Bye's place in the team was taken for a few days by Thomas Boyce, to whom the Hardys had turned when Baldwin broke his arm, but on 27 Dec. 1795 William Hardy jnr reintroduced Lamb to the team and Boyce reverted to his more humble role as a day or weekly labourer.

By 15 Oct. 1796 Bye had been taken on again as a casual. He was reinstated in the team 15 Dec. 1796 when Baldwin broke his leg, indicating that Bye had not found a settled place elsewhere. He stayed with the team, even when Baldwin returned to work three months later, until June 1797; he appears then to have been demoted to day labourer and to have moved to a new post at Old Michaelmas 1797. Bye is not mentioned thereafter, and he was not buried at Letheringsett

DECEMBER 28, MONDAY

WHj WL & TB to Sherringham's with beer & Carting Rocks to the Jetty work.[1] Jno Ram in M^{t} H, boy clearing M T [mash tun]. WH rode to Sherringham afternoon, M^{r} H & Mr Burrell at Clay all day. E^{d} Hall here forenoon. W Tinker & Ben at Work after M T Bottom.

MH A Showry morng, fine day. Mr Hardy & Mr Burrell rid to Cley in his Wisky [whiskey] morng 10, bought some timber for fencing the Industry House Garden,[2] dind & drank tea at Mr Ellis's, came home eveng past 9 & went to the Town meeting at Dobsons about an hour. W^{m} rid to Sheringham afternoon, drank tea at Mr Barchams, came home Eveng past 9. Our 2 Men & teams at Sheringham laying large Stones against the bank to prevent the Sea from taking it away . . .

DECEMBER 29, TUESDAY

WHj T Baldwin Jobs & to Burnham in Afternoon with beer, W Lamb to Holt twice with beer. Jno Ram in M^{t} H, boy cleaning the Yard & Jobs. W Tinker & Ben all day. Mr Flower sent for 150 Fir tress [trees]. M^{r} & WH at home all day.]]

DECEMBER 30, WEDNESDAY

Henry Raven W Lamb to Aldborough with beer, T Baldwin came from Burnham. G Thompson grinding Malt for brew. W Tinker & Ben finnis [finished] the M Tun [mash tun] foren^{n}, Jobs after^{n}, J Ram in Malthouse. M^{r} & WH at home all Day. Love came to See the filly on account of her being ill.[3]

DECEMBER 31, THURSDAY

HR T Baldwin, G Thompson & Boy in Brewhouse, WH brewing. W Lamb to Holt forenoon, after Jobs afternoon. J Ram in M H, M^{r} H at home all Day.

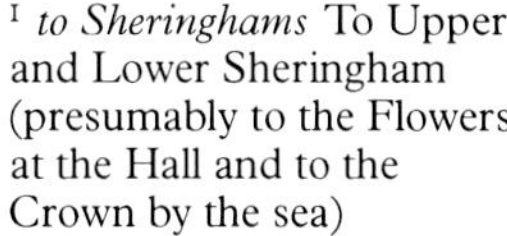

[1] *to Sheringhams* To Upper and Lower Sheringham (presumably to the Flowers at the Hall and to the Crown by the sea)

[2] *garden* The long frontage of the house of industry's garden against the lane would give passers-by the opportunity to talk over the fence to those working in the garden, somewhat reducing the isolation of the inmates in this remote north-eastern corner of the village.

As the house was not built until the summer of 1796 the entry suggests that the garden was enclosed early, enabling spring sowing to be undertaken for the occupants who were to move in later.

More than 200 years later the enclosure is cared for in private hands as a fruit and vegetable garden

[3] *Love* A horse doctor from Holt. This was probably Samuel Love (bur. Holt 26 Sept. 1822 aged 59), who ran the King's Head at Holt 1797–1804, and the Feathers from 1804 until 1808 or later. See also note for 18 Apr. 1797

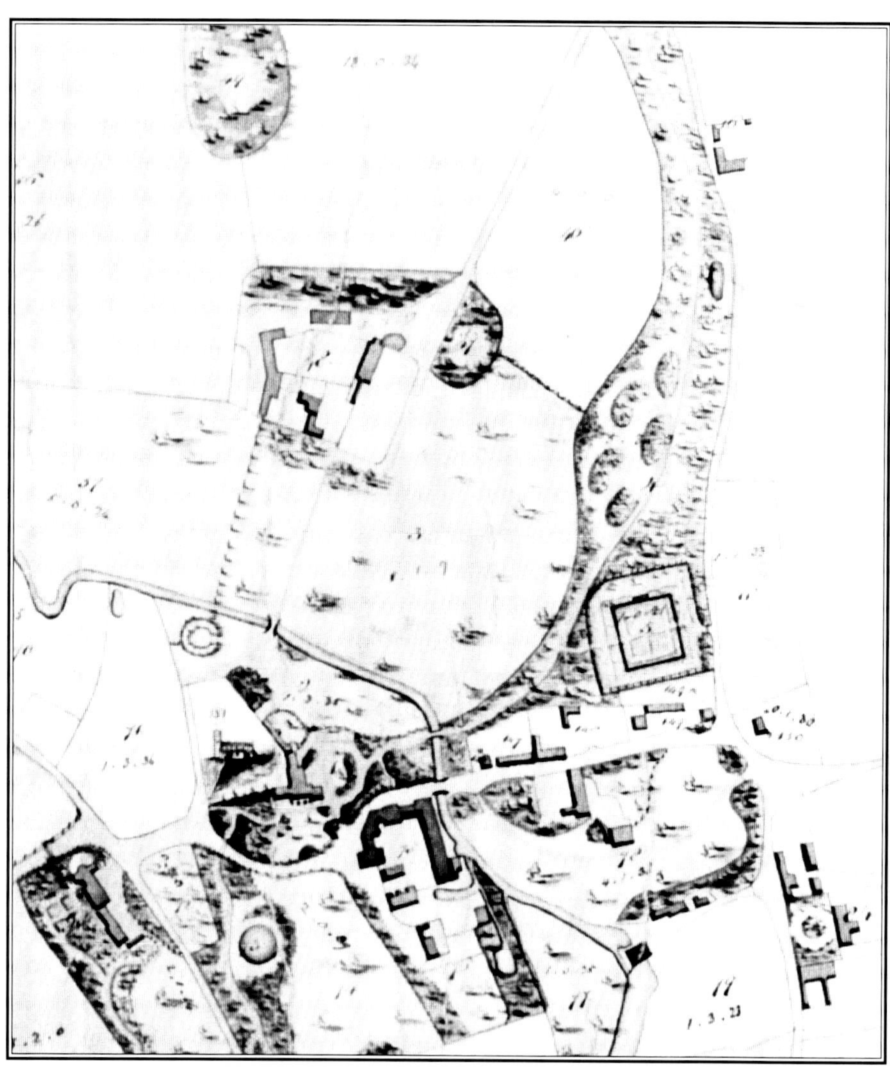

above A detail from Josiah Manning's display map of Letheringsett 1834. (The village centre is seen in his 1838 version under the entry for 22 Oct. 1793.) This shows at top right [16] the parish's little house of industry of 1796 with its enclosure to the north—the fenced garden referred to by Mary Hardy 28 Dec. 1795. Just south of the property is what appears to be a pond fed by the Frambeck, a stream of spring-water running from the Spout Hills at Holt. In the 20th century, and probably earlier, there was also a well for the residents.

William Hardy jnr's carriage drive [4] sweeps along the west side of Workhouse Lane through his new plantations. He also built the great walled kitchen garden [5].

To the west [48] are the farmhouse and farm buildings of Letheringsett Hall Farm, the manorial seat which William was to buy in 1800 [*Cozens-Hardy Collection*]

1796

Mr Hardy and William met at Mr Howard's at Rudham, paid off the mortgage on the brewing office £1000 MARY HARDY, 13 SEPT. 1796

JANUARY 1, FRIDAY

Henry Raven T Baldwin helping to Cleanse `// & whent to Waybourn with beer, W Lamb ploughing in six Acars [Acres]. G Thompson Cleansed `//, J Ram in Malthouse. M^r H at Cley all Day, WH at home all Day.

JANUARY 2, SATURDAY

HR W Lamb to Wells with beer & bro^t home 7 Baggs of hops, T Baldwin to Edgefield with beer for^n, to Dawling after^n with D^o. G Thompson Cleansed X beer, J Ram in M H. M^r & WH at home forenoon, at Market after^n.

Mary Hardy A very fine day. I & Mrs Youngman walkd to a meeting at Sherington, came home to tea.[1] Mr Hardy & W^m walkd to Holt Mark^t, came home eveng 10.

JANUARY 3, SUNDAY

HR Carried 1 Bar^l Six [one barrel of sixpenny] to W Dobsons. Famaly at Church forenoon. M^rs H whent Cley after^n, WH at Holt afternoon. H Raven came from Whissonsett.

MH A very fine day. We all went to our Church foornoon, a Communion.[2] I & Mrs Youngman & John Thompson went to Cley in the Chaise aftern. We all went to our Church in the Eveng . . .

JANUARY 4, MONDAY

HR W Lamb & T Baldwin Carting out Muck all day, Joseph Bransby & Boy filling Muck cart.[3] Jno Ram in malthouse. M^r & W Hardy at home all Day.

[1] *Sharrington* The dwelling house of William Bangay, cordwainer, was registered for Nonconformist meetings 18 May 1793 (NRO: DN/DIS 1/2, f. 48). It is not clear if this is William Bangay [jnr], who kept the Chequers from before 1789 until after 1799 (NRO: C/Sch 1/16), or William Bangay snr, who by 1792, and aged 71, had farmed his own estate at Sharrington for 40 years, as he deposed in a contested tithe case (TNA: PRO E 134/32 Geo. 3 HIL 2, f. 122, 23–25 Jan. 1792).

Bangay's meeting is not listed among the Wesleyan societies in the Walsingham Circuit in 1798 and beyond (NRO: FC 18/1); it may by then have been subsumed into the active meeting at neighbouring Brinton. It was however Wesleyan Methodist. William Denton, Gent., of Gt Walsingham, registered Bangay's dwelling in 1793. He was one of the two itinerant preachers stationed on the Walsingham Circuit 1792 and 1793 (*Minutes of the Methodist Conferences*, vol. 1, pp. 250, 266)

[2] *Communion* Christmas Communion; the Sacrament could be offered days or even weeks after the actual feast day

[3] *Joseph Bransby* He marr. Letheringsett 17 July 1792 Elizabeth Lighten (d. Dec.

1793). Both were widowed and from the parish; the groom signed while Mrs Lighten made her mark.

His first wife, also Elizabeth, was buried Letheringsett 18 June 1791. His second wife, when married to James Lighten, had given birth to twin daughters Elizabeth and Sarah, bapt. Letheringsett 21 Apr. 1765.

See also the note in Mary Hardy's endnotes register

---

[1] *dressing wheatstones* From July 1795 the brewing pupil had shared with the miller Gunton Thompson the task of dressing the maltstones, but this responsibility never extended to the wheatstones

[2] *Sister Raven's* At the Hall: the Hardys' first recorded contact with Henry Raven's side of the family, apart from Henry himself, since William Hardy's indictment of the farm 20 May 1795

Mary Hardy's visit to Whissonsett
4–9 January 1796

JANUARY 5, TUESDAY

HR [at Letheringsett] T Baldwin & W Lamb Carting out Muck, Bransby & Boy filling. M^r^ & Mrs Hardy set of for Whiss^t^ forenoon, HR whent with them. J Ram in Malthouse, WH at home all day.

MH A fine day. Mr Hardy & I set of for Whisonset morng 11, got to Whisonset eveng 2, dind at Bro^t^ Ravens, drank tea, Supt & Slept at Mr Goggs . . .

JANUARY 6, WEDNESDAY

HR T Baldwin helping to empty Mash tun & waighing [weighing] hops & whent to Briston with beer, W Lamb helping to clear M T [mash tun] & whent to plough & to Holt with beer. G Thomp^n^ dressing Wt [wheat] stones & Grinding Malt for brew.[1] J Bransby tasking, J Ram in Malthouse, T Boyce half a days work. H Raven came from Whiss^t^, WH at home all Day. M^rs^ & Mr Sheldrake drank tea here.

JANUARY 7, THURSDAY

HR W Lamb to Sherringham with beer, T Baldwin to Corpusta with D^o^. Bransby heaping up muck forenoon & spreading D^o^ after^n^. J Ram in M H, T Boyce after Jobs all day. WH planting in Phitle [Pightle], Tinkers two men all day. G Thompson laid down W [wheat] Stones, H Raven grinding Malt for Brew.

JANUARY 8, FRIDAY

HR W Lamb, G Thompson, H Raven & Boy in Brewhouse, WH D^o^ brewing. T Baldwin to Cromer with beer, Tinkers too men all day, T Boyce after Jobs. H Raven whent to Whiss^t^ Evening. Mr Bartell & Miss Wymer drank tea here. J Ram in Malthouse.

MH [at Whissonsett] A fine day. Breakfst«ed», dind & Supt at Bro^t^ Ravens, drank tea at Sister Ravens, Mrs Goggs there.[2] Henry Raven came to Whisonset for us.

JANUARY 9, SATURDAY

HR W Lamb to Stody with beer forenoon, ploughing afternoon. T Baldwin after Jobs forenoon & whent to Holt with beer. J Ram in Malthouse, G Thomp. Cleansed `//. Bransby half a day spreading muck. M^r^ & Mrs Hardy & H Raven came from Whiss^t^, WH at Holt market after^n^.

above **Whissonsett: the magnificent barn beside the farmhouse and grocer's shop which belonged to Mary Hardy's uncle and later her brother, both named Nathaniel Raven. As usual, the Hardys spent a good deal of time 'at Brother Raven's'** [*MB · 1995*]

MH A fine day. We set of from Whisonset morng 11, calld at Mr Custances at Fakenham & got home Eveng past 2. W^m^ went to Holt Mark^t^, came home eveng 9.

[LETHERINGSETT]

JANUARY 10, SUNDAY

HR Famaly at Church evening, WH at Holt church after^n^. W Lamb Loaded for Brampton.

MH A very fine day. I & J Thompson & Lydia Youngman went to Cley Meeting afternoon, home even pst 5. W^m^ at Holt Church afternoon, drank tea at Mr Bartells. All went to our Church Eveg 6, Mr Burrell preach'd . . .

JANUARY 11, MONDAY

HR W Lamb to Brampton with beer,[1] after Jobs fore^n^ & whent to Sherrington with beer after^n^.[2] H Raven in M H, T Boyce planting fir trees part of forenoon & whent to his Club. G Thompson grinding Malt for brew, Bransby tasking. M^r^ H at Clay forenoon, WH at home all day. Miss Wymer & Miss Dowson dine'd & drank tea here.[3]

[1] *Lamb* As Brampton lay 14½ miles away, requiring a round trip of nearly 30 miles, it would have been impossible for Lamb to carry out all these tasks in the one day. Henry probably omitted to note that it was Thomas Baldwin who was doing the jobs and delivering to Sharrington

[2] *Sharrington* Once the excitement of the dragoons, the loyal farmers and the escort of the flour through the rioters had died down, beer deliveries to Mrs Porter at the Swan settled back again to their pattern of roughly nine a year.

However in the three months mid-Apr. to mid-July 1797 she took nine deliveries, perhaps to serve those working on the enclosure. The Bill had been before Parliament in the summer of 1796 for the enclosure of the 'very extensive and rich common of Sharrington' (*Norw. Merc.* 7 May 1796; see also *Norw. Merc.* 24 Sept. 1796).

Anger and anxiety over the proposed enclosure may have further inflamed the rioters and made this small village a flashpoint

[3] *Miss Dowson* Henry usually spells her name Dowson; Mary Hardy gives it as Dewson (eg Diary MS: 11 Jan. 1796)

JANUARY 12, TUESDAY

HR T Baldwin, G Thompson, H Raven & Boy in brewhouse, WH D° Brewing. W Lamb after Jobs, J Ram in Malthouse, Bransby tasking. M^r^ H at home all Day. A hop rider calld evening.

JANUARY 13, WEDNESDAY

HR T Baldwin to Fakenham with beer & brought hom«e» a Hop presser which came from Brisley.[1] W Lamb drayin beer into Whitehall forenoon & put it in to Cask after^n^. G Thompson & H Raven cleansed `// & put beer into Cask, WH & Boy helping to put beer in to D°. Jn° Ram in Malthouse, Bransby tasking.

JANUARY 14, THURSDAY

HR T Baldwin to Holt with beer & Loaded for Barmer, W Lamb to Thornage & Loded for Syderstone. Jn° Ram in Malthouse, Bransby tasking. G Thompson & H Raven Cleansed X beer. M^r^ H at home all day, WH out all day. A Rat man came & laid some poison for Rats. [[[2] WH at Thurga«r»ton & Cromer.]]

JANUARY 15, FRIDAY

HR W Lamb to Syderstone with beer, T Baldwin to Barmer with D°. Bransby tasking, J Ram in Malthouse, G Thompson grinding Malt for brew. M^r^ & WH at home all day. Mr Bartell, Miss Wymer & Miss Dowson drank tea here. H Raven clean'd the Lumber Chamber.[3]

[[[4] The Workhouse put out to build to Dawson of Holt.]]

JANUARY 16, SATURDAY

HR T Baldwin to Salthouse, W Lamb to Hindolvestone with beer. Jn° Ram in Malthouse, Bransby tasking. M^r^, M^rs^, Miss & W Hardy at Holt Market afternoon.

MH A very fine day. We all walk'd up to Holt Mark^t^, all drank tea at Mr Bartells excep«t» Mr Hardy, came home eveng past 8.

JANUARY 17, SUNDAY

HR Famaly to Church forenoon, WH & H Raven at Holt after^n^, M^rs^ H at Cley after^n^. T Baldwin Loaded for Southrepps.

MH A beautiful day. All went to our Church foornoon, Mr Burrell preachd. I went to Cley afternoon with J Thompson, home eveng 5 . . .

---

[1] *hop-presser* Not a person, but a device for tightly packing the dried hops into their bags or sacks. Without such a press the hops would have to be stamped and trodden down by the men into the sacks, as much air as possible needing to be removed to prevent deterioration. As the hop-weighing of 6 Jan. suggests, the Hardys may have needed the equipment to bag the hops for onward sale in small quantities.

The hop-presser could have come from Thomas Fox's shop at Brisley, at a time when he was running further into debt (note for 21 Aug. 1795)

[2] In William Hardy jnr's hand

[3] *lumber chamber* Although this could be a store room in the brewery there was a box room in the house, called by William Hardy in his 1797 inventory the 'dark chamber' (*Diary 2*, app. D2.C). It contained assorted bed hangings, sheets, boxes, bird cages and half-barrels.

An earlier dark chamber had by 1797 become Mary Ann's dressing room: see note for 22 Mar. 1796

[4] In William Hardy jnr's hand

JANUARY 18, MONDAY

HR W Lamb, H Raven, Gunto«n» Thompson & Boy in brewhouse, T Baldwin to Southrepps with beer. J Ram in Malthouse, Bransby tasking. M^{r} H at home all day, WH brewing.

JANUARY 19, TUESDAY

HR W Lamb to Sherringham with beer, T Baldwin to Holt with beer & Loaded Lambs Waggon for Stalham. J Ram in Malthouse, Bransby tasking, G Thompson & H Raven Cleansed `//. M^{r} & M^{rs} & Miss Hardy & WH at Mr Forsters to tea.

MH A very fine day. Mrs Smith of Cley dind here, she brought Mrs Thaqur to Mr Dobsons.[1] We walkd to Mr Forsters of Bayfield to tea, the Chaise came for us in the eveng, W^{m} came after tea . . .

JANUARY 20, WEDNESDAY

HR W Lamb to Stalham with beer, J Ram in Malthouse, Bransby tasking. G Thompson & H Raven Cleansed X beer, Baldwin drunk all day. M^{r} & M^{rs}, Miss & W Hardy drank tea & Sup^{t} at Mr Bartells, Holt. Miss Riches dined here.

JANUARY 21, THURSDAY

HR T Baldwin to Runton with beer, W Lamb came from Stalham. J Ram in Malthouse, Bransby tasking. W Hardy on the grand Jury Quarter Sessions, M^{r} H at Holt.[2] H Raven whent to Fakenham with Miss H.[3]

JANUARY 22, FRIDAY

HR W Lamb & Baldwin to Gunthorpe with beer & Bro^{t} home too Lodes [two loads] of timber. J Ram in Malthouse, Bransby tasking. WH to Walsham, M^{r} H to Gunthorpe. H Raven out all night at Althorpe [Alethorpe], G Thompson grinding Malt for Brew.

JANUARY 23, SATURDAY

HR T Baldwin to Hindolvestone with beer, W Lamb to Waybourn with D^{o} & Cley for 2 Chald^{n} cinders from Mr Ellis's. J Ram in Malthouse, Bransby tasking. M^{r} & M^{rs} & WH at Holt Market afternoon.

MH A dry windy day. Mr Wade of Rybro [Ryburgh] dind here. We all walkd to Holt afternoon, drank tea at Mr Sheldrakes. Chaise came for us Eveng 8, W^{m} came home eve 9.

[1] *Mrs Thaqur* Presumably the wife of Peter Thurgar, a local preacher within the Walsingham Circuit. He was based at Holt in 1801; by 1809 he was based at Wells, his name being given as Thurgar, and in 1811 he was still at Wells. In the register of chapels at the end of the register Peter Thurgur of Wells, pattenmaker, is noted as one of the trustees of the Wells Wesleyan chapel built in 1808 (NRO: FC 18/1).

His wife Ann, née Dobson, was probably related to William Dobson, the innkeeper of Letheringsett King's Head, whom she was visiting. The Thurgars' daughter Ann, aged seven years, and son James, four months, were buried at Holt on 15 and 17 Feb. 1801

[2] *quarter sessions* As the tumults of the previous five weeks had been dealt with at Norwich (note for 20 Dec. 1795) the sessions at Holt had to consider only the usual routine matters: bastardy and vagrancy cases, appeals over removal orders and against poor rates, and desertion of his family by the breadwinner; there was also a case of fraud (NRO: C/S 1/15)

[3] *Miss Hardy* Mary Ann was visiting William Custance at Fakenham in the chaise. Thursday being market day, Henry would have had the opportunity of meeting many of his family and old friends

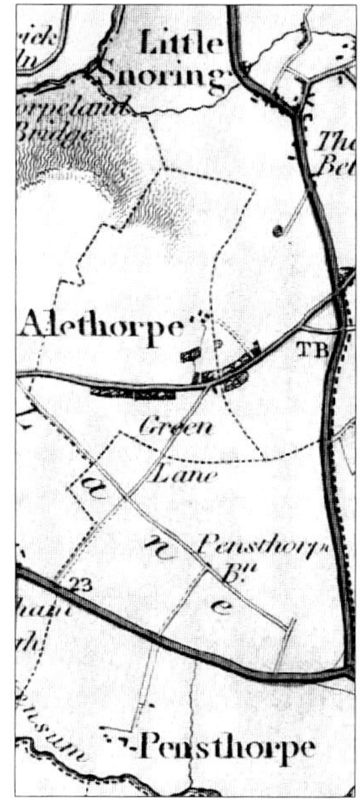
Little
Snoring
Alethorpe
TB
Green
Lane
23
Pensthorpe

above 'H. Raven out all night at Alethorpe' (22 Jan. 1796). This tiny settlement two miles north-east of Fakenham was too small to appear on Faden's map of 1797. The sole voter in 1806 was the farmer Robert Riches, who held land in Field Dalling. Henry was probably staying overnight at the Riches' farmhouse, a further instance of his creation of an independent social life of his own [*Bryant's Map of Norfolk 1826: Cozens-Hardy Collection*]

JANUARY 24, SUNDAY

HR M^{rs} H at Cley afternoon. Famaly to Church evening, WH at Holt after^{n}.

MH A dry windy day. I with John Thompson went to Cley meeting Afternoon, came home to tea. All went to our Church even 6 . . .

JANUARY 25, MONDAY

HR W Lamb to Briston & Morston with beer. T Baldwin, G Thompson, Boy & H Raven in Brewhouse, WH D^{o} Brewing. J Ram in Malthouse, Bransby tasking. M^{r} H at home all day.

JANUARY 26, TUESDAY

HR T Baldwin to Cromer with beer, W Lamb helping to cleanse `// & whent to Edgefield with beer. G Thompson & H Raven Cleansed `//. H Raven in Malthouse, J Ram very ill. Bransby tasking. WH to Fakenham, M^{r} H at home all day.

MH A fine Morng, Stormy afternoon, Wind high. W^{m} set of for Fakenham Assembly morng 11, Mr Hardy at home all day.

JANUARY 27, WEDNESDAY

HR W Lamb to Holt twice with beer forenoon & drove out five Lodes of Muck afternoon, Boy filling Muck cart. T Baldwin helping to Cleanse X beer foren^{n} & filling Muck cart after^{n} & Loded for Burnham. H Raven in Malthouse, J Ram ill. Bransby tasking. Mr Hardy Poorly with gout. W Tinker & Ben all day sawing.

MH A fine day. Mr Hardy poorly with a cold, at home all day.

JANUARY 28, THURSDAY

HR T Baldwin to Burnham with beer, W Lamb to Sheringham with D^{o}. J Ram in Malthouse, Bransby tasking. W Tinker & too men all day. M^{rs} H & H Raven drank tea and sup^{t} at Mr Temples, WH came from Fakenham to Mr Temples. M^{r} H very Poorly with Gout.

MH A very Showry day. Mr Hardy poorly with the Gout. I & H Raven went to Mr Temples at Thornage to tea & Supper, Miss Wymer & Miss Dewson went with me in the Chaise. W^{m} came to us from Whisonset Eveng 7, came home eve 12. A Woman brought to Bed at Mr Dobsons, she is Married [1] . . .

---

[1] *she is married* And thus less likely to be a charge on the parish, especially as the baby was not baptised at Letheringsett

JANUARY 29, FRIDAY

HR W Lamb driving out Muck, T Baldwin & Boy filling. J Ram in Malthouse, Bransby tasking. W Tinker & Man all day, T Boyce at Work in Garden. G Thompson & H Raven grinding Malt for Brew. Mr H Poorly with Gout. WH at home all day & whent to Holt with Miss Wymer & Miss Dewson evening.

JANUARY 30, SATURDAY

HR W Lamb & T Baldwin got too lodes of Clay for garden & then whent one to Cley with beer & Brot home 2 Chald cinders from Mr Ellis's & the other to Wiverton with beer & Blakeny for empty Barrels. J Ram in M H, Bransby tasking. W Tinker & man all day. WH at Holt Market aftern, G Thompson & H Raven cleaning Wheat Chamber. Mr H Poorly with gout.

JANUARY 31, SUNDAY

HR Famaly all at own Church forenoon, Mrs H to Clay aftern. H Raven whent to Waybourn afternoon for the Boy.[1]

MH A Close day. All went to our Church foornoon except Mr Hardy who was very poorly with the Gout. I went to Cley meeting afternoon, home even 5.[2] Wm went to our Church in eveng.

FEBRUARY 1, MONDAY

Henry Raven T Baldwin to Wells with beer. W Lamb, G Thompson & H Raven & Boy in brewhouse, WH Do Brewing. Nicks [Nicholas] Woodehouse came morning & whent to Harrow, W Tinker & too men all day. J Ram in M H, Bransby tasking. Mr H Poorly with Gout. Boy Wm whent away after dinner.

Mary Hardy A very fine day. Mr Hardy better. Wm Brew'd. Mr Burrells Audit.

FEBRUARY 2, TUESDAY

HR W Lamb to Corpusta with beer, T Baldwin helping to Cleanse `// and whent to Stody with beer. T Boyce in garden, H Raven in Malthouse, Bransby tasking. G Thompson Cleansed `//, W Tinker & two men all day. WH at Holt drawing of [off] wine, Mr H poorly with Gout. Thos Atwood came & Orderd A Lode of Beer.

[1] *boy* The new boy replaced 'Boy William', who had lasted just over a month (27 Dec. 1795, 1 Feb. 1796)

[2] *All went . . . I went . . .* Mary Hardy's attendance at meetings independently of her family may have given back her old confidence and vigour after the long period of convalescence since 1793. She had become noticeably more active, both physically in her walks and socially in the round of calls she had started to make (eg 16 Jan., 19 Jan., 7 Feb. 1796)

above Lt Walsingham Methodist Church, built in 1793–94, became the mother chapel of the Wesleyan circuit formed that year.

Most of the full-time Wesleyan itinerant preachers heard by Mary Hardy in north Norfolk from 1795 were based here [*MB · 2000*]

above Letheringsett Parish Church: the lectern and Bible.

The beginning of 1796 marked Henry's severance from Methodist meetings. He had last attended meetings at Briston, Cley and Hunworth all towards the end of 1795. From January 1796 he attended only Church of England services at Letheringsett and Holt, and presumably at Whissonsett when at home.

Without Henry to drive her, Mary Hardy relied on John Thompson and Thomas Boyce and, when necessary, on walking [*MB · 2011*]

MH A very fine day. Mr Hardy finely in the day but bad in eveng with pain in his knee. Wm went to Holt foornoon to draw of 1 eaith [one eighth] of a Pipe of Wine, dind at Banyards at the Feathers, came home eveng 9.

FEBRUARY 3, WEDNESDAY

HR T Baldwin to Holt twice with beer, W Lamb to Edgefield with Do & got up a lode of gravil. G Thompson & HR Cleansed X beer, J Ram in Malthouse. Bransby tasking, T Boyce in garden. WH & H Raven spent the evening at Mr Bartells, Mr H Poorly with Gout. H Craffer sent for small beer.

MH A fine day. Mr Hardy very poorly with the gout in his Knee. Wm & HR went to Mr Bartells in the eveng to meet some young people, supt there & came home past Midnight . . .

FEBRUARY 4, THURSDAY

HR W Lamb & T Baldwin ploughing in furze close, J Ram in Malt house, Bransby tasking. T Boyce mending the rode [road] comeing in to yarde, G Thompson dressing Wheatstones. WH at home all day, Mr [Mr Hardy] Poorly with Gout. Mr & Mrs Sheldrake drank tea here.

FEBRUARY 5, FRIDAY

HR W Lamb & T Baldwin skreening Malt forenoon & ploughing afternoon. J Ram in Malthouse, Bransby tasking. G Thompson dressing Wheatstones, H Raven grinding Malt for Brew. WH at home all day, Mr H Poorly. Boyce in garden.

FEBRUARY 6, SATURDAY

HR W Lamb to Aldborough with beer, T Baldwin ploughing. J Ram in Malthouse, Bransby tasking, T Boyce in garden. WH at Holt afternoon, Mr H poorly.

FEBRUARY 7, SUNDAY

HR Famaly at own Church evening. H Raven to Sherrington. Matt Peirce [of Kettlestone] came & Orderd a lode of Beer.

MH A Close dry day. Mr Hardy poorly. I & J Thompson went to Cley meeting afternoon, home eveng 5. Wm went to Holt Church afternoon. Wm & I went to our Church eveng 6, Mr Burrell preach'd. H Raven went to Mr Kendles of Sherington to dinner. M [Mr] Hardy had a very bad night . . .

FEBRUARY 8, MONDAY

HR W Lamb to Kettlestone with beer. T Baldwin, G Thompson, H Raven & Boy in Brewhouse, WH brewing & drying Porter Malt. J Ram in Malthouse, Bransby tasking, T Boyce helping to dry porter Malt. M^{rs} & Miss Bartell, Miss Wymer & Miss Dowson drank tea here. M^{r} H Poorly.

FEBRUARY 9, TUESDAY

HR W Lamb to Salthouse with beer, took half a loade of straw, and to Cley for 2 Chaldron Cinders from Mr Ellis's. T Baldwin after Jobs all day, Bransby dressing. J Ram in Malthouse, G Thompson & H Raven Cleansed `//. WH at home all day, Mr Hardy finely.

FEBRUARY 10, WEDNESDAY

HR W Lamb to Waybourn with beer, T Baldwin to Bale with D^{o} & got up a loade of Clay. J Ram in Malthouse, WH drying of Porter malt, Bransby tasking. M^{r} H finely.

FEBRUARY 11, THURSDAY

HR W Lamb, T Baldwin, G Thompson, H Raven & Boy gitting in the Stack into Barn, WH at home all day. J Ram in Malthouse. M^{r} H finely. Bransby in barn. W Lamb to Holt after^{n} with beer, T Baldwin Loded for Southrepps. G Thompson & H Raven Skreene'd some Malt.

MH A very fine morng, close aftern. W^{m} at home all day. Mr Hardy finely. W^{m} got the Stack of Barly into Barn.

FEBRUARY 12, FRIDAY

HR W Lamb to Sherringham with beer, T Baldwin to Southrepps with D^{o}. J Ram in Malthouse, Bransby tasking. T Boyce in Garden, G Thompson grinding Malt for brew. WH at home all day, M^{r} H got better with gout.

MH A Cold stormy day. Mr Hardy finely, got into garden. W^{m} at home all day. Miss Wymer, Miss Bartell & Miss Dewson dind & drank tea here.

FEBRUARY 13, SATURDAY

HR T Baldwin to Thornage with beer & ploughing. W Lamb, T Boyce, G Thompson, H Raven & Boy in Brewhouse, WH brewing & whent to Holt afternoon. J Ram in malthouse, Bransby tasking. M^{r} H finely. H [home] Cask was Cleaned.

below The blade of a long-handled mashing oar, from the National Trust property of Charlecote Park, Warwickshire. In small brewhouses this was used to stir the hot mash of grist malt and liquor at the start of brewing, but the Hardys probably used mechanised paddles. William Tinker had been working on the mash tun bottom in late December 1795 [*MB · 2000*]

HOLT, NORFOLK.

WM. PAGE,

Stationer, Perfumer, Glaſs and Hardwareman,

HAVING declined buſineſs in favor of Mr. JOSEPH ERRATT, takes this method of returning his moſt grateful thanks to his Friends and the Public in general, for the liberal ſupport and patronage he experienced for near 20 years, and of which he begs a continuance to his ſucceſſor, whom he flatters himſelf will merit their approbation.

J. ERRATT,

Printer, Bookſeller, Stationer and Bookbinder,

RESPECTFULLY begs leave to inform the Ladies and Gentlemen of HOLT and its vicinity, that he has entered upon the premiſſes of Mr. Wm. Page, and humbly ſolicits a continuance of thoſe favours his predeceſſor was honoured with, to merit which it will ever be his greateſt ambition.

To the variety which ſo juſtly diſtinguiſhed Mr. Page's ſhop, J. E. has added a freſh aſſortment of every article in the Perfumery, Hardware and Cutlery branches, alſo an elegant collection of Satin-wood and Ivory Tea Caddies, Mahogany and Japan Tea Boards, Waiters, &c. likewiſe a choice ſelection of Tea and Coffee Urns, of the moſt modern taſte, with a variety of goods too numerous to be here inſerted, which, from his connection with the firſt houſes in the above branches, he is enabled to offer to the Public at the London prices.

PRINTING

Executed with neatneſs, accuracy and diſpatch, on the moſt reaſonable terms.

BOOKBINDING,

In all its various branches, done in a plain or elegant manner; merchants' accompt books made and ruled to any pattern; Libraries regulated and repaired.

J. E. propoſes eſtabliſhing a CIRCULATING LIBRARY, for which purpoſe he has procured a collection of the moſt approved Novels, Romances, Plays, &c. a Catalogue of which will be publiſhed in a ſhort time.

Magazines, Reviews, and all Periodical Publications regularly ſerved, and every order in the Bookſelling and Stationary line punctually attended to.——☞ Muſic and Muſical Inſtruments, with every reputable Patent Medicine.

WINTER EVENINGS RATIONAL AMUSEMENT.

MH A fine day. Mr Hardy at home all day. Wm went to Markt afternoon, came home eveng 9, Wheat 50*s* Comb [a coomb], Barly 15*s* pr Comb.[1]

[1] *wheat etc* Expressed in quarters, these Holt prices are 100*s* and 30*s* respectively (see notes for 15, 17 and 21 Dec. 1795). By 20 Feb. 1796 wheat was 106*s* to 110*s* at Norwich, while barley, which had been harvested before the late summer storms, remained stable; on 5 Mar. wheat was 116*s* to 120*s* and barley still low at 32*s* to 35*s*, the Mark Lane prices being in line with these figures (*Norw. Merc.*).

At Westminster the House of Commons committee enquiring into the high price of corn was hearing evidence. Charles Dundas, MP, of Newbury, Berks, called for a single national unit of measurement—not the Winchester bushel, as volume, but a new unit of *weight*—to prevent fraud. Other MPs wanted to regulate agriculture and bemoaned the consolidation of small farms into large ones, which enabled 'the large farmers . . . to withhold their grain from the market, and keep up the price'.

By Apr. 1796 these shortages had eased. Prices at Norwich and Gt Yarmouth were quoted as wheat 72*s* to 76*s*; barley 28*s* to 29*s*. At Mark Lane wheat was 68*s* to 76*s* and barley 29*s* to 32*s* (*Norw. Merc.* 30 Jan., 20 Feb., 5 Mar., 9 Apr. 1796)

FEBRUARY 14, SUNDAY

HR Famaly all to Church forenoon. M^rs H at Cley afternoon, WH at Holt Church afternoon. W Lamb loaded for Burnham, G Thompson Cleansed `//.

MH A very fine morng, reather stormy afternoon & night. All went to our Church foornoon, Mr Burrell preachd. I & J Thompson went to Cley meeting. W^m & I went to our Church in eveng, heard a Lecture.

FEBRUARY 15, MONDAY

HR W Lamb to Burnham with beer, J Ram in Malthouse, Bransby tasking. G Thompson & H Raven Cleanse'd XX beer. Mr Youngman came & drew the boxe out of Cleansing Pump.[1] WH to Whiss^tt, M^r H finely.

MH A Stormy morng. Mr Hardy at home all day. W^m set of for Fakenham to a Sale at Mr Greens at the Mill[2] . . .

FEBRUARY 16, TUESDAY

HR T Baldwin to Sherrington with beer foren^n & Ploughing after^n. W Lamb Harrowing forenoon & Ploughing D^o [in the afternoon]. J Ram in Malthouse, Bransby tasking. M^r & WH at home all Day. Boy whent to Mr Forsters for 4 C^o [coombs] Wheat. G Thompson grinding Malt for brew.

FEBRUARY 17, WEDNESDAY

HR T Baldwin, G Thompson, H Raven & Boy in brewhouse, WH D^o brewing. J Ram in Malthouse, Bransby tasking, W Lamb ploughing. M^r H at home all day. Baldwin to Holt afternoon with beer. Miss Wymer, Miss Bartell & Miss Dowson whalk'd down here after^n.

FEBRUARY 18, THURSDAY

HR W Lamb & T Baldwin driving Out Muck, T Boyce filling. J Ram in Malt House, Bransby tasking forenoon. G Thompson, H Raven Cleansed `// & got 13 Bar^ls X beer into Home cask & clear'd the througfs [troughs]. M^r & WH at home all Day.

MH A very fine day. Mr Hardy & W^m both at home all day. Miss Wymer went away from Mr Bartell to Reepham[3] . . .

FEBRUARY 19, FRIDAY

HR W Lamb to Wells with beer, T Baldwin to Fakenham with D^o. J Ram in Malthouse, Bransby tasking. G Thompson & H Raven Cleansed X beer. WH whent to Cromer, M^r H at home all Day. T Boyce in garden.

facing page The *Norwich Mercury* of 28 Nov. 1795: William Page hands over to Joseph Erratt (entry for 24 Feb. 1796). The new man wished to establish a circulating library at Holt but failed to prosper, coming to stay overnight with the Hardys when his business collapsed (30 Sept. 1797). His stock in trade was for sale 14–16 Feb. 1798, by which time he had diversified into small items of furniture such as portable writing desks
[*Norfolk Heritage Centre, Norwich*]

---

1 *box* See note for 23 Dec. 1793

2 *mill* All the live and dead stock of William Green of Fakenham Watermill (distinct from Hempton Watermill, just upstream on the Wensum) was for sale by auction 15 and 16 Feb., '. . . consisting of five capital cart horses, a riding mare, two mares aged, a hobby, a colt, two cows, five pigs, two wagons, a breast cart, two flour carts, two one-horse carts, five tumbrils, harness, saddles, bridles etc, two stacks of exceeding good hay, about 50 sacks of flour and a quantity of fine pollard etc . . .' (*Norw. Merc.* 6 Feb. 1796). There is no suggestion by either diarist that William bought any of these items

3 *to Reepham* Presumably to stay with her brother, the attorney George Wymer jnr

FEBRUARY 20, SATURDAY

HR W Lamb to Holt with beer forenoon, Ploughing afternoon, T Baldwin Ploughing all Day. G Thompson grinding Malt for brew. M^r^ & M^rs^ H at Holt afternoon. T Boyce in Garden. WH at Holt after^n^.

MH A close day. Mr Hardy & I rid to Holt Mark^t^ afternoon, I drank tea at Mr Sheldrakes, Mr Hardy drank tea at Mr Bakers. W^m^ went to Mark^t^ after tea, Wheat 56*s*, Barly 17.

FEBRUARY 21, SUNDAY

HR M^rs^ H at Cley afternoon. Famaly to Church evening, WH at Holt afternoon.

MH A close dry day. I & J Thompson went to Cley meeting afternoon, home eveng 5. All went to our Church in eveng, Mr Burrell read a Lecture.

FEBRUARY 22, MONDAY

HR W Lamb to Syderstone with beer, T Baldwin to Holt & after Jobs. G Thompson & H Raven & Boy got the Beer into H cask, J Ram in Malthouse, Bransby tasking. WH, Miss H & Miss Custance Whalk'd to Holt forenoon, Mr Hardy at home all Day.

MH A close dry day. Mr Hardy at home all day, Wm Brew'd. H Raven went to Fakenham with the Chaise for MA & Miss Custance, they came home eveng past 4 [1] . . .

FEBRUARY 23, TUESDAY

HR W Lamb to Syderstone with beer, T Baldwin to Holt twice with beer. G Thompson, H Raven & Baldwin got beer into Home cask & Cleansed `//. J Ram in Malthouse, Bransby tasking. M^r^ H at home all Day. WH, Miss Hardy & Miss Custance whalk'd to Holt morning.

FEBRUARY 24, WEDNESDAY

HR W Lamb Ploughing in five Acres. T Baldwin driving out Muck, T Boyce filling Muck cart, J Ram in Malthouse. G Thompson & H Raven Cleansed XX beer morning. [[[2] M^r^ & M^rs^, Miss & W Hardy & Miss Custance drank tea at Holt.]] Mr Erratt came down in evening & Orderd half a Barrell beer.[3] Mr Roberts from Salthouse & Jas Skiffins from Holt came & Order«ed» beer.[4]

[1] *Mary Ann and Miss Custance* A moderately rare instance of the two diarists' records failing to tally. It looks as though Henry Raven duplicated his entries for 22 and 23 Feb., precipitating the omission of the brewing day on 22 Feb. The duplication suggests that, like his aunt, he compiled his diary from rough notes

[2] This sentence is in a smaller and slightly more ornate hand than Henry's. It may be Frances Custance's, noting the entry in which she appeared that day. It is more probably that of Henry's young brother Nathaniel Raven, making his second entry in the diary. Both Henry and his aunt note Nathaniel's departure 25 Feb.; neither had noted his arrival

[3] *Erratt* Joseph Erratt had taken over William Page's shop at Holt in Nov. 1795, introducing into its wide-ranging retail business of stationery, perfumery, glass and hardware the trade of the more specialist printer, bookseller and bookbinder; he also supplied music, musical instruments and patent medicines and wished to establish a circulating library—probably Holt's first

[4] *Roberts* He appears to have taken over from John Clarke at the Dun Cow. By Sept. 1797 John Jordan was in charge (note for 12 June 1795). In the space of eight years 1789–97 the Dun Cow had six innkeepers

FEBRUARY 25, THURSDAY

HR W Lamb to Salthouse with straw & some spars & by Cley for 2 Chal[d] Cinders from M[r] Elliss. T Baldwin driving out Muck, T Boyce filling Muck D[o] [muck cart] & turning muck up in yard. J Ram in Malthouse. Bransby spreading muck forenoon, tasking afternoon. M[r] H at home all day. WH rode to Salthouse afternoon, Nath Raven whent away afternoon.

FEBRUARY 26, FRIDAY

HR W Lamb to South repps with beer, T Baldwin to Runton with D[o]. J Ram in Malthouse, Bransby tasking, T Boyce turning muck up in yard. G Thompson, H Raven & Boy got the Cleanse beer into Cask. M[r] & M[rs] Flower spent the day here, Miss Bartell & Miss Baker dined & drank tea.

MH A Cold Windy day. M[r] Hardy & W[m] at home all day. M[r] & M[rs] Flower dind & drank tea here, M[rs] Flower staid all Night . . .

FEBRUARY 27, SATURDAY

HR T Baldwin to cromer & Beckhigh with beer, W Lamb to Hinderingham & Holt with d[o] [beer]. T Boyce, G Thompson, H Raven & Boy in brewhouse, WH d[o] [in brewhouse] brewing. M[r] & Miss Hardy & Miss Custance at Holt after, WH at Holt Evening.[1]

John Ives
1729

[1] *at Holt* Mary Hardy notes that her husband, daughter and Miss Custance were at Holt market. This was the day that the (first) bankruptcy of the Coltishall brewer Chapman Ives (1758–1804) was announced in the press: see *Diary 1*, *Diary 2*.

The news would have been the talk of every market town in the county and beyond; yet the diarist does not mention it. Ives's maltings, porter brewery and tied outlets represented a very considerable concern for a rural business, his grandfather Clement Ives having acquired 13 tied houses by 1722. For an analysis of Ives's, see *World*, vol. 2, chap. 8; the tied houses are tabulated in vol. 2, chap. 9

left **This solid silver tobacco tin, inscribed 1729, belonged to Chapman Ives's father, the Coltishall brewer John Ives (d.1766). It measures 4 inches by 2½ by 1¼ inches deep (10·5 x 6·5 x 3 cm).**

The tin came to the late Audrey Wilson, née Church, through the Ives family, her grandmother Charlotte Fuller (*c.*1848–1931) being a granddaughter of George Ives.

Mrs Wilson was brought up at Coltishall at Hazelwood House, formerly Ives's brewery; her mother was born at the King's Head across the road

[*photograph MB · 1992; courtesy Audrey Wilson*]

above The bridge over the Wensum linking Gt and Lt Ryburgh. John Wade's watermill, shown on Faden's county map of 1797, stood a short way downstream. William called at the mill 7 Mar. 1796 to ask Wade to act as a witness at the Lent Assizes opening at Thetford on 11 Mar.; those court records have not survived.

The mill was rebuilt in 1890 and demolished in 1925. A second mill, built by the maltster Frederick E. Smith in 1860, stood nearby [*drawing by F. Stone; lithograph by D. Hodgson 1831*]

FEBRUARY 28, SUNDAY

HR Mrs Hardy & Miss Custance to Cley afternoon, WH & H Raven at Holt afternoon.

FEBRUARY 29, MONDAY

HR W Lamb to Burnham with beer. T Baldwin after Jobs forenoon, ploughing after^n^. G Thompson & H Raven cleansd X beer. M^r^ & WH at home all day. J Ram in Malthouse, Bransby tasking.

MARCH 1, TUESDAY

Henry Raven Thos Baldwin to Corpusta with beer. W Lamb after jobs foreno^n^, to Cley with beer & 2 Chal^d^ cinders from Mr Elliss. Baldwin loaded for Norwich, J Ram in Malthouse, B[ ].[1] M^r^ & WH at home all day. G Thompson & H Raven grinding Malt for brew.

MARCH 2, WEDNESDAY

HR T Baldwin to Norwich with beer. G Thompson, H Raven & Boy in brewhouse, WH D^o^ brewing. Jno Ram in M H, Bransby tasking, W Tinkers too men all day. W Lamb whent to Holt with beer & loded for Stalham. M^r^ H at home all day.

1 *B* Joseph Bransby's tasks go unrecorded by Henry

MARCH 3, THURSDAY

HR W Lamb to Stalham with beer, G Thompson & H Raven Cleanse'd `//. Jn° Ram in Malthouse, Bransby tasking. Mr & Mrs Bartell & Mr & Mrs Templl [Temple] drank tea and supt here. Mr H rode to Cley, WH rode to Gunthorpe. T Baldwin came from Norwich.

Mary Hardy A Cold dry day. Wm rid foornoon to Mr Colyers at Gunthorp, came home eve 3. Mr Hardy rid to Cley afternoon to speak to Mr Smith, came home eveng 5. Mr & Mrs Bartell, Mr, Mrs & Miss Temple drank tea & Supt here . . .

MARCH 4, FRIDAY

HR T Baldwin helping to Cleanse & whent to Edgefield with beer, W Lamb came from Stalham. G Thompson & HR cleanse'd XX. Jn° Ram in Malthouse, Bransby tasking, T Boyce in garden. Mr & WH at home all day.

MARCH 5, SATURDAY

HR Thos Baldwin to Brampton with beer, W Lamb to Morston, Thornage & Stody with D°. Jn° Ram in M H, Bransby after Jobs. G Thompson & H Raven grinding Malt for Brew. Mr, WH, Miss H & Miss Custance at Holt afternoon.

MH A frosty, very cold day. Mr Hardy rid up to Holt Markt afternoon. Miss Custance, MA & Wm walkd up to Holt, drank tea at Mr Davys, came home eveng past 9. Wheat 58/-, Barly 17*s*.

MARCH 6, SUNDAY

HR Mrs H & Miss Custance at cley afternoon, WH at cley aftern. Mr H at home all day.

MH Snowd a good deal foornoon, dry aftern. Miss Custance & I went to Cley meeting afternoon. Wm went with us to speak to Mr Smith, came home half past 5.[1]

MARCH 7, MONDAY

HR T Baldwin & Thos Boyce ploughing in six Acres, W Lamb to Holt twice with beer, J Ram in Malthouse. Mr H at home all day, WH to Ryburch [Ryburgh]. W Tinkers too men all day, himself half a day.[2] Miss Hardy spent the day at Holt.

MH A sharp frost, close cold day. Miss Custance went away to Holt to Mr Bakers, MA dind & drank tea there. Wm went to Ribro [Ryburgh] to speak to Mr Wade to go to Thetford as an evidence, came home even 9.[3]

[1] *to speak to Mr Smith* Thus William was not attending the meeting at Cley

[2] *himself* An engaging term for the governor or boss, as in 'Is himself at home?'

[3] *Thetford* To appear as a witness at the Lent Assizes. Presumably the visit to the local JP Charles Collyer on 3 Mar. and the flurry of activity with the Cley attorney John Smith was also in connection with the riots. Six of the 43 prisoners held for trial were accused of rioting and related misdemeanors (*Norw. Merc.* 27 Feb., 19 Mar. 1796); none came from north Norfolk.

The only mill in Gt and Lt Ryburgh at this time, and thus presumably the former Holt miller John Wade's, was the watermill on the Gt Ryburgh bank downstream of the bridge. It stood beside a later mill with *eight* pairs of stones, built in 1860 and owned by Frederick Edgar Smith (b.1827), who by 1861 was living at the Mill House; he was the founder of the firm of F. & G. Smith, the Gt Ryburgh, Wells and E. Dereham maltsters (later Crisp Malting Ltd).

I am grateful to Barré Funnell of Poringland for his detailed account of the two watermills (his letter to me of 25 Sept. 2002). The story of Ryburgh Mill under the Smiths is given in Betty Wharton's *The Smiths of Ryburgh: 100 years of milling and malting* (Crisp Malting Ltd, Gt Ryburgh, 1990), pp. 5–28

MARCH 8, TUESDAY

HR Thos Baldwin, G Thompson, H Raven & Boy in brewhouse, WH d^{o} Brewing. W Lamb & Thos Boyce ploughing, J Ram in Malthouse. M^{r} H out after^{n}, WH at Holt afternoon. W Tinker & too men all day. M^{r} & Mrs Sheldrake drank tea here.

MH A Sharp frost. Maids & Eliz Milegan washd 4 Weeks Linnen. Wm Brew'd. Mr Hardy went to Cley afternoon to speak to Mr Smith, came home by Holt eveng 8. M^{r} & M^{rs} & M Sheldrake drank tea here.

MARCH 9, WEDNESDAY

HR G Thompson, H Raven, Thos Baldwin, W Lamb, Thos Boyce & Boy got the beer into great cask forenoon, being fast day no work done the afternoon.[1] M^{rs} & Miss Hardy whent to Cley aftern.[2] WH rode to Sherringham afternoon, M^{r} H at home all day.

MH A very cold hasy day. A Fast by Procklimation, service at our Church afternoon. I & MA went to Cley meeting afternoon, came home eveng 5. W^{m} rid to Sheringham, dind & drank tea there, came home eveng 8.

MARCH 10, THURSDAY

HR W Lamb & Thos Baldwin laying the flags forenoon & ploughing afternoon,[3] Thos Boyce laying the flag in

B——m *dibbled** ſeven pecks of white peas an acre, on ***olland,*** once-plowed, in flags, "as wide as he could whelm them." Two rows of holes on each flag; the holes about three inches apart in the rows; namely, "four holes in the length of the foot," one pea in each hole. Gave 4s. 6d. an acre for "dabbing;" and hired "droppers" by the day (children belonging to the pariſh); which coſt him about 4s. an acre more. The men offered to dibble and drop for 9s.—The ſoil free from ſtones. Finiſhed 27 Feb.

above Marshall's observations of 1782 on dibbling peas during spring sowing. The Hardys' men were 'to dibble and drop' [*W. Marshall, The Rural Economy of Norfolk (1787), vol. 1, p. 249*]

[1] *fast day* The Hardys' men were unobtrusively busy in the morning and thus in breach of what the authorities expected on this solemn day; they were however let off in time for the afternoon service at Letheringsett, a service ignored by all the Hardy family. The Rector of Weston, feeling ill in the bitter cold, likewise failed to attend prayers, his curate deputising for him (J. Woodforde, *The Diary of a Country Parson*, ed. J. Beresford, vol. 4 (Oxford Univ. Press, 1929), pp. 264–5, 9 Mar. 1796)

[2] *Miss Hardy* A major event: Mary Ann's first attendance at Cley meeting

[3] *laying the flags* Turning over the furrows in the ploughed fields: see note for 5 Feb. 1794. The men were preparing the ground for sowing peas, a process described in great detail by William Marshall in *The Rural Economy of Norfolk*, vol. 1, pp. 248–251: 'Lays are seldom plowed more than once for peas; and the seed is, in general, dibbled in, upon the flag of this one plowing' (p. 251). He mentions many ways of sowing peas, but does not refer to the Hardys' method of brushing or 'bushing' the seed in (11–12, 14 Mar. 1796). In the illustrated extract (right) he records that children of the parish were sometimes entrusted with dibbling. However, apart from their farm boy, the Hardys rarely relied on child labour, in this or in other farming operations

6 Acres. J Ram in M H, G Thompson took up Wheat Stones. M^r H & WH at home all day, Wm Tinker & too men all day. Mr Ellis came & slept here.

MH A frost, shearly [chearly] day. Mr Hardy at home all day. W^m went up to Holt after tea. Mr Ellis Supt & Slept here in order to sett of for Thetford in the Morng. Mrs Prior came.[1]

MARCH 11, FRIDAY

HR W Lamb laying the flag, rolling and brush^d in the peas. Thos Baldwin to Aldborough with beer, J Ram in Malthouse. Gunton Thompson laid down wheat Stones, H Raven grinding Malt for brew and bin. Ed^m Balls & man dibbling peas, Thos Boyce at work in six Acres. Wm Tinker & too men all day. WH & Mr Ellis set of for Thetford morning 7 OClock, M^r H at home all day.

MH A very fine day. W^m & Mr Ellis set of for Thetford Assises Morng past 6. Mr Hardy at home all day . . .

MARCH 12, SATURDAY

HR W Lamb to Salthouse with beer & Cley for too Chaldrons of Cinders from Mr Ellis's, Thos Baldwin rolling and Bushing in the Peas. Thos Boyce at work in six Acres, Balls & Mann [man] dibbling Peas. J Ram in Malthouse, Bransby tasking. Wm Tinker & too men all day. M^r H at home all day, Miss H at Holt.

MARCH 13, SUNDAY

HR Famaly all at own Church forenoon, M^rs H whent to Hunworth afternoon. WH came home evening. W Lamb loaded for Burnham.

MH A beautiful day. We all went to our Church foornoon, Mr Burrell preachd. I & J Thompson went to Hunworth meeting afternoon. W^m came home from Thetford assises Eveng past 8 . . .

MARCH 14, MONDAY

HR W Lamb to Burnham, Thos Baldwin to Runton with beer, Thos Boyce at work in six Acres. J Ram very ill, H Raven in Malthouse. Boy laying the flag & Bushing in Peas, Ball{d}s & his man dibbling. WH to Gunthorpe, M^r H at home all day.[2] Miss Custance and Miss Baker drank tea here. Wm Tinkers too men half a day.

above **St Peter, Belaugh, its tower stairway leading to commanding views over the Bure valley. 'Goody Moll' Prior, who came to stay on 10 Mar. 1796, used at times to take the Hardy children across the fields to services here** [*MB · 2001*]

[1] *Mrs Prior* Mrs Mary (Molly) Prior, of Belaugh and later of Hoveton or Wroxham, who had loyally supported Mary Hardy during the Coltishall years when she helped with the three young Hardy children and stood in for absent maidservants; the children had also stayed with her occasionally in the 1770s.

This visit was her last recorded contact with the Hardys

[2] *Gunthorpe* William was dining at Charles Collyer's (Diary MS). He was pre-

sumably briefing the JP on the outcome of the assize hearing—intelligence denied to us as Mary Hardy remains silent and as the Norfolk assize series in the National Archives does not cover these years

MARCH 15, TUESDAY

HR W Lamb, G Thompson & Boy in Brew house, Thos Baldwin ploughing, Thos Boyce ploughing all day, WH brewing. Jno Ram in Malthouse, Bransby tasking. H Raven whent to Gunthorpe & Brunton [Brinton], Mr H at home all day. Mrs Bartell came here Evening.

MARCH 16, WEDNESDAY

HR Thos Baldwin Ploughing forenoon & whent to Waybourn with beer afternoon, W Lamb to Gunthorpe with beer. Jno Ram in Malthouse, Bransby tasking. W Tinker & Man all day, Bunnets too trowelmen & too Laborers all day taking down the counting Room in yard. G Thompson & H Raven Cleansed `// and dressing flower.

MH A very fine day. Mr Hardy & Wm at home all day, took down the Counting House in the fore yard.[1] I poorly with dimness in my Eyes . . .

MARCH 17, THURSDAY

HR Thos Baldwin to Wells with beer, W Lamb bushing in Peas forenoon, to Holt with beer afternoon. J Ram in Malthouse, Bransby tasking. G Thompson & H Raven Cleansed X beer, G Do [Thompson] whent to Thornage aftern. WH to North Walsham, Mr Hardy at home all day. Bunnets too trowelmen & too Laborers all day. Mr & Miss Raven came from Whissonsett.[2]

MARCH 18, FRIDAY

HR W Lamb & Thos Baldwin at muck cart, Wm Tinker all day. Thos Boyce painting in Garden, Bunnets 4 men all day. Jno Ram in Malthouse, Bransby tasking.

MARCH 19, SATURDAY

HR W Lamb to Edgefield & Stody with beer. Thos Baldwin, G Thompson, H Raven & Boy in Brewhouse, WH do brewing. Jno Ram in M H, Bransby tasking. Bunnets 4 men all day, Tinker & one man all day.

MARCH 20, SUNDAY

HR G Thompson & men Cleansed `// & clard throughfs [cleared troughs]. Famaly at own church Evening, Mrs H at Cley afternoon.

MH A Cold close day. I & J Thompson went to Cley meeting Afternoon, home even 5. All went to our Church eveng past 6, Mr Burrell read a Lecture.

---

[1] *counting house* Neither diarist makes it clear which of the two counting houses this was: in the family home, or across the road at the brewery.

This is likely to have been the counting house at the Hall, the one at the brewery being rebuilt in Sept. 1797. Just as the Hardys' men did not rely on the *skipper* to load and unload their wherry at Coltishall but did the tasks themselves (*Diary 1*), so the *clients'* workforce collected building materials from far afield for John Bunnett and his team.

The demolition was part of a further reconstruction of the house, in addition to those of 1781 and 1787–88, as a result of which Mary Ann was to gain a suite of rooms: her bedroom above the kitchen, and a dressing room (entry for 22 Mar. 1796). The full inventory is transcribed in *Diary 2*, app. D2.C

[2] *Mr and Miss Raven* Identified by Mary Hardy as her brother and his daughter Mary; they left on 19 Mar.

Kitchen Chamber & Dressing Room

	£	s	d
Carv'd Mahog^y Bedstead Crimson Silk damask Hangings Feath^r Bed 3 Blankets Bolster Pillows and bedding compleat	42	-	-
an Old Feather bed	2	10	-
Festoon Window Curtains	5	5	-
4 Chairs	-	12	-
Dressing Table & Cover	-	10	-
Large Glass	2	10	-
Washing Stand Bottle &c	-	10	6
pair Bed side Carpets	-	10	-
Swing Glass	-	15	-
Stove Bright & Fire Irons	1	11	6
Chimney Jars	-	10	-

left Part of William Hardy's domestic inventory and valuation made 12 and 13 Sept. 1797, as recorded by his wife in her diary. In Mar. 1796 their daughter was aged 22, and Mary Ann would have been helping her mother as housekeeper of a busy household.

During the alterations of 1796 she was given the best bedroom—and perhaps the warmest, being above the kitchen; alone of the family she had a dressing room. She could offer tea and coffee and have overnight guests in her well-equipped private suite [*Cozens-Hardy Collection*]

MARCH 21, MONDAY

HR Thos Baldwin to Sherringham with beer & Brot home alode of paving stones, W Lamb to Holt twice with beer & got a lode of sand. G Thompson & H Raven Cleanse'd X beer. J Ram in Malthouse, Bransby stopping gaps part of day & tasking. Bunnets 4 men all day, Tinkers man half a day. WH at home all day, Mr H at Holt afternoon.

MH A Cold dull day. Mr Hardy rid to Holt afternoon to speak to Mr Atthow about the Bull Publick House,[1] drank tea at Mr Bartells, came home eveng 9.

MARCH 22, TUESDAY

HR W Lamb to Hindolvestone with beer & loaded for Barmer, Thos Baldwin got three loads of Mirgin & one loade of sand & loaded for Syderstone. Jno Ram in M H, Bunnets 4 men all day. W Tinker & Ben all day, Jas Tinker half a day. Mr & WH at home all day. G Thompson & H Raven grinding Malt for brew. Dawsons lad Painting.

MH A fine day. Mr Hardy & Wm at home all day, opend the dark Chamber to make a dresing room for MA.[2]

[1] *Athow* Thomas (d. 3 Oct. 1812 aged 89), Holt cooper and timber merchant; he served as Holt churchwarden 1786–1812. He sold the Bull at Holt to William Hardy jnr in 1804 for £205 (*Diary 4*: 9 Oct. 1804).

He served in 1795 as treasurer of Holt Friendly Society, incorporated 10 Jan. 1757. Many of the Hardy's circle from Holt and the surrounding villages were members, including craftsmen and innkeepers (NRO: ACC Cozens-Hardy 11/2/1976, *Articles . . . of the Friendly Society meeting at . . . the Mariners in Holt* (E. Dereham, 1795) [printed, unpag.]); see also *World*, vol. 2, chap. 11

[2] *dressing room* See note for 15 Jan. 1796

facing page **'Carpenters at work in garden putting up rails to tie the fruit trees to' (23 Mar. 1796). These pears near Thornage churchyard are carefully trained to absorb the sun's light and warmth. 'Nailing' fruit trees is urged in the gardening book written by William Hardy for Mary Ann and still held in the family's collection** [*MB · 2011*]

MARCH 23, WEDNESDAY

HR W Lamb to Barmer with beer, Thos Baldwin to Syderstone with Do, J Ram in Malthouse. Bunnets 2 men all day, W Tinker & 2 men all day. Mr & WH at home all day. Gunton Thompson & H Raven draying of [off] beer, Dawsons lad Painting.

MH A fine day. Bricklayers at work in dark Chamber. Carpenters at work in Garden putting up rails to tye the Fruit Trees to{o}.[1] Mr Hardy at home all day . . .

MARCH 24, THURSDAY

HR Thos Boyce, G Thompson, H Raven & Boy in Brewhouse, WH brewing & whent to Holt to tea. WL to Cley for 3 Chaldron lime from Mr Johnsons, Thos Baldwin harrowing & whent to Holt with beer. Bunnets 4 men all day, Tinker & 2 men all day. Mr & Miss H at Holt to tea.[2] Boyce at work in yard, Dawsons lad painting.

MARCH 25, FRIDAY

HR W Lamb to harrow forenoon, to Thornage & Stody with beer afternoon. Thos Baldwin helping to Cleanse `//, J Ram in Malthouse, Bransby tasking. Bunnets 4 men all day, W Tinker & 2 men all day. Mr & WH at home all day. G Thompson Cleansed `//, T Boyce at work in yard.

MH A Cold dry day. Bricklayers & Carpenters at work in Chamber. Mr Hardy went to Mr Bartells eveng 8, Slept there in order to go to Norwich with them.

MARCH 26, SATURDAY

HR Thos Baldwin to Cromer with beer, W Lamb at sand cart. G Thompson & H Raven Cleansed X beer, T Boyce at work in yard. Bunnets 4 Men at work all day, Tinker & too men all day. WH at home all day & at Holt Evening, Mrs & Miss Hardy at Cley afternoon. J Ram in Malthouse, Bransby dressing. Boy carting Bricks out of yard.

MH A Cold close foornoon, a small rain aftern. I & MA went to Cley in Chaise aftern, drank tea at Mr Smiths, Mr Easto preach'd there.[3] Came home eveng 7, Mr Hardy came home Morn past 1.

MARCH 27, SUNDAY

HR Famaly at own Church forenoon. Mrs Hardy to Cley afternoon, WH at Holt Church afternoon.

---

[1] *fruit trees* William Hardy jnr's dining chairs *c.*1823 were made from cherry trees on the estate, and his walled garden had apple, pear and cherry trees (W. Stones, *The Garden of Norfolk*, pp. 84, 92)

[2] *at Holt* With William to supper with the Bartells

[3] *Easto* Samuel Eastaugh or Easthaugh of Hempton had an interesting career as a Methodist local preacher. At first he adhered to Calvinistic Methodism and officiated at Fakenham's 1773 chapel; its founder Mary Parker, née Franklin, gave him a legacy in 1788 on condition that he keep preaching (NRO: ANF (1789) W9, f. 302, Archdeaconry of Norfolk, will of Mary Parker, dated 20 Nov. 1788, proved 22 Jan. 1789). By 1795 he was a Wesleyan. In 1809 he was still at Fakenham, as one of the Wesleyan circuit's seven local preachers; in 1811 he was one of ten (NRO: FC/1). He married Catherine Child at Fakenham 7 Nov. 1799

MH A very cold day, frequent Storms of Snow. All went to our Church foornoon, a Communion.[1] I went to Cley meeting afternoon with JT . . .

MARCH 28, MONDAY

HR Thos Baldwin to Waybourn with beer & helping to Clear the throughfs, W Lamb to Edgefield with D^{o} & help^{d} to carry of Cleanse of beer. G Thompson & H Raven grinding Malt for brew, J Ram in Malthouse. W Tinker & too men all day, Bunnets too men all day. M^{r} & WH at home all day.

MARCH 29, TUESDAY

HR W Lamb to Burnham with beer. Thos Baldwin, G Thompson, H Raven & Boy in brewhouse, WH D^{o} brewing. J Ram in malthouse, Thos Boyce in garden. W Tinker & too men all day, Bunnets 4 men all day. M^{r} H at home all day, Mr Bartell call^{d} here afternoon.

MH A Cold close day. Mr Hardy at home all day, went to Town meeting to Dobsons, Supt there, came home eveng 11. Carpenters & Bricklayers at work in Chamber. Wm Brew'd.

MARCH 30, WEDNESDAY

HR W Lamb carting gravil into yard from Mr Williams Pit, Thos Boyce, Charles Moore & Boy filling.[2] Thos Baldwin to South Repps with beer, J Ram in Malthouse. Bunnets 4 men all day, W Tinker & too men all day. WH at home all day, M^{r} H whent out early in morning.

MH A Close drisly day. Mr Hardy went to Reepham with M^{r} & Mrs Bartell to sett out some Timber to fell, Slept at Mr Wymers.[3] W^{m} at home all day. Bricklayers & Carpenters at work . . .

MARCH 31, THURSDAY

HR Thos Baldwin Carting gravil, Chas Moore & Boy filling gravil cart, Thos Boyce at work in yard. Bunnets 4 men all day, W Tinker & too men all day. J Ram in Malt H, G Thompson & H Raven grinding Malt for brew. WH at home all day. W Lamb to Corpusta with beer forenoon & Holt with D^{o} afternoon.

APRIL 1, FRIDAY

Henry Raven Thos Baldwin to Fakenham with beer. W Lamb, G Thompson, H Raven & Boy in brewhouse,

[1] *Communion* This was Easter Day. Mary Hardy and Mary Ann had not attended their customary Wednesday services at Letheringsett Church during Lent, nor a Good Friday service; it is unlikely that Mr Burrell did not offer them that year. The entry demonstrates Mary Hardy's 'doublemindedness'. An Anglican communicant on Easter morning, she attended a Nonconformist meeting only a few hours later. As a result both rector and Methodist preacher could count her as one of their flock

[2] *Charles Moore* William, son of Charles Moore and Elizabeth, née Waller, was bur. Letheringsett 21 June 1804

[3] *Reepham* William Hardy's accounts of 25 Sept. 1797 (*World*, vol. 2, chap. 11)

WH D^o^ Brewing. W Tinker & two men all day, Bunnets 4 men all day, J Ram in Malthouse. M^r^ H at home all day, T Boyce at work in yard.

APRIL 2, SATURDAY

HR Thos Baldwin helping to put beer into Cask forenoon, at harrow after^n^. W Lamb after beer & carting gravil. Thos Boyce carting gravil forenoon, at work in yard after^n^, Char^s^ Moore Carting and filling gravil. Bunnets 2 men all day, W Tinkers too men all day, himself half a day. G Thompson, HR & Boy got the Cleanse beer int«o» Cask in W H [white hall].

Mary Hardy A fine mild day. Ann & Rose & Nathl Raven dind here in their way to Holt. We all went to Holt afternoon. Mr Hardy, I & MA drank tea at Mr Bartells. I & MA came home eveng 7, M^r^ H, W^m^ & Nathl came home eveng 9.

APRIL 3, SUNDAY

HR Gunton Thompson, H Raven Cleansed X beer. Famaly at own Church after^n^, M^rs^ H at Cley after^n^.

MH A fine warm day. I & J Thompson went to Cley meeting afternoon. Mr Hardy, W^m^ & MA went to our Church afternoon, Mr Burrell preach'd. W^m^, N Raven & H [Henry] drank tea at Mr Burrells, Miss Johnsons & Miss Ravens there [1] . . .

APRIL 4, MONDAY

HR Thos Baldwin sowing kiln Cumbs [culms] & whent to Cley for 2 Chal^d^ cinders from Mr Ellis's, Thos Boyce sowing Cumbs & at work in yard.[2] W Lamb ploughing forenoon, to Holt with beer Afternoon. J Ram in Malthouse, G Thompson & H Raven grinding Malt for brew. M^r^ & WH at home all day, Wm Tinker at work all day.

APRIL 5, TUESDAY

HR W Lamb to Wiverton with beer & Cley for 2 Chal^d^ cinders from Mr Elliss. Thos Baldwin, G Thompson, H Raven & Boy in brewhouse, WH D^o^ Brewing. J Ram in Malthouse, Bransby tasking, Thos Boyce in garden.

APRIL 6, WEDNESDAY

HR Thos Baldwin & W Lamb ploughing in furze close, G Thompson & H Raven Cleansed `//. Thos Boyce at work in yard, J Ram in Malthouse, Bransby tasking. M^r^

show that the timber was at Kerdiston, the parish adjoining Reepham. He valued it, together with timber at Blakeney, at £40

---

[1] *Miss Johnsons* The Misses Johnson were shortly to announce that they were 'leaving off millinery at Holt'; the milliners S. and M. Ditchell at the same time applied to the public for their patronage. Ann Leak's millinery was still in business, with the latest London fashions being brought to Holt (*Norw. Merc.* 30 Apr., 7 May 1796)

[2] *sowing kiln culms* See notes for 25 Oct. 1793 and 10 Jan. 1794.

Henry's diary yields a large amount of industrial archaeological data. Both his diary and his aunt's have been used as sources in detailed, well-illustrated surveys by David W. Durst, entitled 'Letheringsett: Industrial archaeology in a rural setting' and published in six parts in the *Journal of the Norfolk Industrial Archaeology Society*:
1: 'The introduction', vol. 5, no. 3 (1993); revised and updated in vol. 8, no. 2 (2007);
2: 'The watermill', vol. 5, no. 4 (1994);
3: 'Hall Farm sawmill', vol. 5, no. 5 (1995);
4: 'The brewery', vol. 7, no. 4 (2004) [this also covers the maltings];
5: 'Water systems', vol. 8, no. 1 (2006);
6: 'Notes on Johnson Jex', vol. 8, no. 2 (2007)

& M^rs^ H at home all Day, WH & Mr Moore to Gressinghall [Gressenhall]. M^r^ & Mrs Sheldrake drank tea & Sup^t^.

MH A fine day but cold. W^m^ rid to Gresenhall with Mr Moore to get some Shrubs & plants out of the Workhouse Garden, came home eveng 9. M^r^ & Mrs Sheldrake drank tea & supt here. Mr Hardy at home all day. I, MA & M^rs^ S went to meeting in eveng [1] . . .

APRIL 7, THURSDAY

HR Thos Baldwin ploughing forenoon, filling Muck cart after^n^. W Lamb at harrow forenoon, driving out Muck. Thos Boyce at work in yard, J Ram in Malthouse, Bransby tasking. G Thompson & H Raven began to grind Malt for brew. M^r^ H at home all day, Bunnets two men all day.

APRIL 8, FRIDAY

HR Thos Baldwin to Wells with beer. W Lamb sowing Vetches & spreading Muck forenoon, to Holt twice with beer after^n^. J Ram in Malthouse, Bunnets two men all day. Bransby tasking, G Thompson Grinding Malt for brew. Boy spreading Muck morning. M^r^ & WH at home all day.

APRIL 9, SATURDAY

HR Thos Baldwin to Sherringham with beer & Bro^t^ home a lode of paving Stones. W Lamb in brewhouse & whent to Bale with beer. G Thompson, H Raven & Boy in Brewhouse, WH D^o^ Brewing. Bunnets 4 men all day. W Tinkers two men all day, himself half a day. Mr Sanderson dine'd here. M^r^ & WH at Holt Market after^n^, J Ram in Malthouse.

MH A Cold reather stormy day. Wm Brew'd & drank tea at Miss Leakes at Mr Burrells,[2] walkd up to Holt Mark^t^ eveng 6, home pst 10. Mr Hardy walkd up afternoon, drank tea at Mr Bartells.

APRIL 10, SUNDAY

HR Famaly at Church forenoon, Mrs Hardy at Cley afternoon. H Raven whent to Sherringham with a Party.

MH A Cold dry day. All went to our Church foornoon, Mr Burrell preachd & read a Lecture in the eveng. I went to Cley meeting afternoon, Mr Bartell drank tea here afternoon. H Raven went to Sheringham after-

[1] *meeting* Further evidence that women rather than men were drawn to Methodism in the 1790s, as discussed in *World*, vol. 3, chap. 4. The register of meeting houses shows that Mrs Susanna Winn's home had been registered at Letheringsett 28 Mar. 1796; William Mayes's certificate (almost certainly for the Independents) was dated 16 Dec. 1795 (NRO: DN/DIS 1/2, f. 54—for both). Mrs Winn, formerly Mrs Dix, née May [?Mayes], was bur. Letheringsett 16 Oct. 1798. On the day she died, 13 Oct., Zebulon Rouse registered his granary at Letheringsett Watermill as the village (Wesleyan Methodist) meeting house (DN/DIS 1/2, f. 66).

The rector may have felt particularly aggrieved with Mrs Winn as she was the widow of his parish clerk, James Winn (d. 12 Jan. 1793 aged 59, bur. 15 Jan.), who with Mary Hardy had been active in helping to run the village's Church of England Sunday school from 1786. It was a cause dear to the rector's heart (*Diary 2*)

[2] *at Mr Burrell's* The entry for 10 May 1796 confirms that both the Misses Leak had taken rooms at the rector's house. They could also have helped to keep house for Mr Burrell following his wife's death. It was very difficult for a man with a demanding career to run a household—but Ann and Bell Leak themselves had a Holt business of their own to run

noon with his Sister & Cousin & Miss Johnsons & others, came home eveng 10.[1] Mr Burrell kick'^{d} up a dust with the Methodist in the Eveng.

APRIL 11, MONDAY

HR W Lamb to Beckhigh with beer, Thos Baldwin to Holt twice with D^{o}, J Ram in M H. Bunnets 4 men all day, W Tinker & two men all day. G Thompson & H Raven grinding Porter malt. M^{r} H to Norwich with Mr Bartell. Miss Hardy spent the day at Holt, WH to Holt Evening.

MH A very cold windy day.[2] Bricklayers & Carpenters at work ab^{t} the store room.[3] Mr Hardy sett of for Norwich in Banyards Post Chaise with M^{r} & Mrs Bartell morn 6, did not return this Night. MA walkd up to Holt foornoon, dind & drank tea at Miss Johnsons, W^{m} went up for her after tea in the Chaise . . .

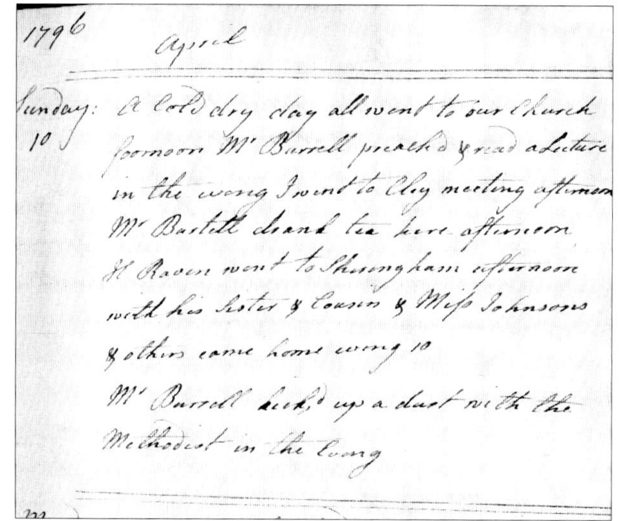
1796 April

Sunday 10 A cold dry day all went to our Church foornoon Mr Burrell preach'd & read a Lecture in the eveng I went to Cley meeting afternoon Mr Bartell drank tea here afternoon H Raven went to Sheringham afternoon with his Sister & Cousin & Miss Johnsons & others came home eveng 10 Mr Burrell kick'd up a dust with the Methodist in the Eveng

above 'Mr Burrell kicked up a dust with the Methodist in the evening' (10 Apr. 1796). Mary Hardy's entry reveals the undercurrent of tension running in the village four days after she and Mary Ann attended their first Nonconformist meeting on John Burrell's turf. Susanna Winn, widow of the rector's former parish clerk, had just registered her dwelling house 'for the worship of Protestant Dissenters' [*Cozens-Hardy Collection*]

1 *sister and cousin* Rose and Ann Raven

2 *cold windy day* Confirmed by Parson Woodforde, who pithily described the day as 'Very cold, barren, growless'. Mary Hardy refers in some of her entries to the cold, very dry April, this occasioning some anxiety for farmers after the recent bad harvests caused in part by cold, late springs. At last the rain came at the end of the month. Mary Hardy wrote 30 Apr., 'A fine rain in the night'. James Woodforde recorded one of his gentle, spontaneous thanksgivings on 1 May: 'A most gracious rain almost the whole night. Lord make us grateful for the same. All vegetation seems at the height of growing' (J. Woodforde, *The Diary of a Country Parson*, ed. J. Beresford, vol. 4, pp. 270, 275)

3 *store room* According to the 1797 valuation (*Diary 2*, app. D2.C) this was on the ground floor near the kitchen and was used for storing china and earthenware, basins, pots and pans; it also housed a large mahogany dining table.

Following William Hardy jnr's remodelling of the Hall from 1809 the store room was on the south side between the dining room and the kitchen (W. Stones, *The Garden of Norfolk*, p. 88). Beryl Cozens-Hardy told me in Jan. 1989 that the five ledgers of Mary Hardy's MS diary had been stored there in very large drawers until the 1970s

above Sykes's meeting: Briston's former Calvinistic Methodist meeting house of 1775, which in 1783 had adopted Independency; the manse (right) had been Mendham's. Three days after Mr Burrell's confrontation with the unnamed Methodist preacher at Letheringsett on 10 Apr. 1796 the Revd John Sykes, the Independent minister from this chapel, came to preach at a Letheringsett meeting. This may have been the newly registered Wesleyan Methodist meeting, for Mary Hardy and Mary Ann were there to hear him. The diarist records other instances of interdenominational Nonconformist worship [*MB · 2011*]

APRIL 12, TUESDAY

HR Tho[s] Baldwin, G Thompson, H Raven & Boy in brew-house, WH D[o] Brewing Porter. W Lamb to Briston with beer & loaded for Stalham. J Ram in malthouse, Bunnets 4 men all day, W Tinker and two men all day. M[r] H came from Norwich.

APRIL 13, WEDNESDAY

HR W Lamb to Stalham with beer. G Thomp[n], Tho[s] Baldwin, H Raven & Boy Cleansed `//, got the Cleanse Beer into great cask. J Ram ill, Bransby tasking. Bunnets 4 men all day, W Tinker & two men all day. M[r] & WH at home all day.

MH A very fine day. M[r] Hardy & W[m] at home all day. We Irond. M[rs] Forster drank tea here. I & MA went to the meeting, M[r] Sikes preachd there.[1]

[1] *Sykes* Revd John, of the Guestwick, Briston and Hunworth Independent meetings: see note for 9 Sept. 1795. He served as minister of Guestwick Independent Church 1776–1824 and of Briston Chapel 1783–1824; the church book holds a great deal of material about him (NRO: FC 11/1). Guestwick Church had only 10 pastors 1652–1872, of whom he was the ninth. He was trained by 'Mr Scott' in Yorkshire (NRO: FC 58/8/3, Deeds of Guestwick Chapel and manse), and when he arrived on trial on the resignation of Revd James Kirkpatrick in Apr. 1776 the Guestwick Independent Church had 20 members. They took five months to decide they wished him to stay, and he was confirmed in office 29 Oct. 1776 (FC 11/1, p. 149).

Mr Sykes, a careful recordkeeper, minuted the transfer of the Briston Chapel (illustrated above) from Lady Huntingdon's Connexion in 1783. After a pastorate of 48 years he died 27 Mar. 1824. He was interred 2 Apr. in the burial ground of his Guestwick chapel, now in private hands; his widow Frances (d.1841) and six of their children lie with him. His ministry is described in *World*, vol. 3, chap. 3.

Interestingly Joseph Hill, who later owned the 1783 Briston chapel, was one of the signatories inviting John Sykes to Norfolk in 1776 (NRO: FC 58/8/3)

[1] *hay* It was unusual for the Hardys to sell hay to others, especially as they were not fully stocked themselves despite their purchases the previous summer: they had to buy in more hay 23 Apr.

[2] *Thomas Boyce* The labourer took over in the malthouse when John Ramm fell ill. Malting, a continuous process, cannot be left unattended other than overnight, but Henry Raven might have been the more likely deputy for his old comrade

[3] *Thomas Baldwin* On this day, 18 Apr., Elizabeth, the daughter of Thomas Baldwin and Elizabeth, née Bell, his wife, was buried at Holt aged 24. She could be the farm servant's sister or daughter, but neither diarist mentions a bereavement and on the funeral day the Hardys' man was far away on a 35-mile round trip

above **Burnham Market's Hoste Arms, then known as the Pitt Arms, to which Baldwin was delivering on 18 Apr.** [*MB · 1999*]

APRIL 14, THURSDAY

HR Thos Baldwin to Holt with beer & whent with the mare to Loves. G Thompson, H Raven grinding malt for Brew. Bunnets 4 men all day, W Tinker & two men all day. Thos Boyce at work in garden, Mr & WH at home all day. W Lamb came from Stalham.

MH A fine day. Mr Hardy & Wm at home all day. Qrtr [Quarter] Sessions at Walsingham. Carpenters & Bricklayers at work in Store room.

APRIL 15, FRIDAY

HR W Lamb, G Thompson & Boy in brewhouse. H Raven in Malthouse, J Ram ill. Thos Boyce in grarden [garden] & helping in M H, Thos Baldwin to Bale & Gunthorpe with beer. Bunnets 4 men all day, W Tinker & two men all day. WH brewing Porter, Mr H at home all day. Ann & R Raven whalkd from Holt Morning.

MH A fine day. Bricklayers & Carpenters at work. Wm Brewd Porter, Mr Hardy at home all day . . .

APRIL 16, SATURDAY

HR W Lamb to Thornage with beer & card [carried] a lode of hay to Holt for Thos Atwood.[1] G Thompson, H Raven & Boy got the Cleanse beer into W H [white hall] foren & into Cask afternoon & Cleansed Porter. Mr H at Holt afternoon. Bunnets 4 men all day. J Ram ill, Thos Boyce in Malthouse, Bransby tasking.[2] Ann & Rose Raven dined here & whalkd to Holt with Miss Hardy, WH at Holt after tea. Thos Baldwin to Runton with beer.

APRIL 17, SUNDAY

HR Famaly at Church afternoon, Mrs H at Cley Afternoon, WH at home all day. Thos Baldwin loaded for Burnham.

MH A very fine day. I & JT went to Cley meeting afternoon. Mr Hardy, Wm & MA at our Church afternoon, Mr Burrell preach'd. A & R Raven & the Johnsons'S dind & drank tea at Mr Burrells . . .

APRIL 18, MONDAY

HR Thos Baldwin to Burnham with beer,[3] W Lamb to Cromer with Do. J Ram in Malt H, Bransby tasking. G Thompson, H Raven grinding man [malt] for brew, Bunnets 4 men all day. Mr H at home all day, Mr Bartell calld here Evening. WH at home all day.

APRIL 19, TUESDAY

HR Thos Baldwin, G Thompson, HR & Boy in brew-house, WH brewing Porter. W Lamb to Holt twice fore-noon & Rolling aftern. J Ram in Malthouse, Bransby tasking, Thos Boyce at work in grarden [garden]. W Tinker all day.

MH A very fine dry day. Wm Brewd Porter, Mr Hardy at home all day. Bricklayers at work & finish'd.

APRIL 20, WEDNESDAY

HR Thos Baldwin to Cley with beer & Brot home 1½ Chald Coles from Mr Jacksons forenoon, to plough aftern. W Lamb ploughing all Day & sowing Barley. G Thompson, H Raven & Boy got Cleanse beer into great Cask, Thos Boyce in garden. Mr & WH at home all day. J Ram in Malthouse, Bransby tasking. H Raven whent to Holt Ball.[1]

MH A fine day. Mr Hardy dind with the Collector, came home even 8.[2] Mrs Sheldrake here . . .

APRIL 21, THURSDAY

HR W Lamb & Baldwin ploughing & sowing Barly. J Ram in Malthouse, Bransby tasking, Thos Boyce in garden. Mr & WH at home all day. G Thompson Drawing of X beer. Miss Ravens came here Evening.[3]

APRIL 22, FRIDAY

HR W Lamb to Holt, Stody & Salthouse with beer, Thos Baldwin to Alborough with Do. Boy ploughing in field forenoon, J Ram in Malt house. Bransby tasking, Thos Boyce in garden. Mr H at home all day. Mrs, Miss & W Hardy & Miss Ravens to Mr Forsters to tea. Mr Sales calld here Afternoon.

APRIL 23, SATURDAY

HR Thos Baldwin to Corpusta with beer & Brot a lode of Hay from Jas Dyballs. W Lamb to Sherington with beer morning & Sherringham with Do. J Ram in Malt-house, Bransby tasking. G Thompson & Boy got part of Cleanse beer into W Hall. Thos Boyce in garden, H Raven to Edgefield. Mr, WH & Miss Hardy at Holt afternoon, Miss R & Ann Raven at Holt.

APRIL 24, SUNDAY

HR H Raven, G Thompn, W Lamb, Boyce, Baldwin & Boy got Cleanse Porter into cask. Famaly at Church

[1] *Holt ball* This was advertised as being held on *21* Apr. (*Norw. Merc.* 16 Apr. 1796); it was not the annual Children's Ball given by the dancing master in the autumn. Henry's social life was now noticeably less limited than in his early years with the Hardys

[2] *Collector* The Collector of Excise, the most senior official at local level in the excise service. Norfolk, with north Suffolk, was divided into two excise collections: Norwich to the east, and Lynn to the west; Holt, on the border, was moved from one to the other as required by the pressure of business.

Under the major excise reorganisation of 13 Jan. 1789 Holt District, with four rides, had stayed within Norwich Collection (TNA: PRO CUST 47/363, pp. 69–71). But three months later there was a change of heart, and Holt, now with merely two rides (malt and hides), was transferred to Wells District within Lynn Collection (CUST 47/365, p. 95, 3 Apr. 1789). Cooke Watson was confirmed in his existing post as the Collector of Lynn and is the Collector referred to by Mary Hardy on 20 Apr. 1796; he was still in post in 1799 (CUST 47/411, p. 63, 16 May 1799)

[3] *Miss Ravens* The cousins Rose and Ann, who had come that day from Holt to stay with their Letheringsett relations

aftr^{n}, M^{rs} H to Cley. M^{r}, WH & Miss H at Holt, Ann & R Raven at Holt aftrn. H Goggs came aftr.

MH A drisly Morng, fine afternoon. All went to our Church foornoon, Mr Burrell preach'd. I & JT went to Cley meeting afternoon, came home to tea. Mr Hardy & W^{m} & the Girls went to Holt Church afternoon. H Goggs came eveng 5.

APRIL 25, MONDAY

HR Thos Baldwin to Wells with beer. W Lamb at harrow forenoon, to Holt fair after^{n}. J Ram in Malthouse, Bransby tasking, Thos Boyce in garden forenoon. M^{r} & W Hardy and Mr Goggs to Holt forenoon. M^{r} & Mrs Todhunter & Mr Sheldrake dined here, Robt Raven came foren^{n}. Famaly whalk^{d} to Holt after tea.

MH A dry Cold Windy day. Holt Fair. M^{r} H, Mr Goggs went up to the fair foornoon, came home to dinner. M^{r} & Mrs Todhunter, Mr Sheldrake & Robt Raven dind here. H Goggs went away Eve 4, W^{m} & the Girls went to Holt after tea. R [Robert] Raven went away Eve 9.

APRIL 26, TUESDAY

HR W Lamb, G Thompson, H Raven & Boy in brewhouse, WH D^{o} Brewing. Thos Boyce in garden, J Ram in Malthouse, Bransby tasking. M^{r} & M^{rs} & Miss Hardy & the Miss Ravens drank tea at Holt. Thos Kendle drank tea with WH, H Raven whalk^{d} to Holt Evening.[1]

MH A Cold close day. Wm Brew'd. Mr Hardy, I & the Girls walkd up to Holt afternoon, drank tea at Mr Sheldrakes. Mr Hardy went to the Feathers ab^{t} Skivens business in the Eveng, came home eveng past 10 . . .

APRIL 27, WEDNESDAY

HR W Lamb to Waybourn with beer forenoon & sowing seeds & harrowing afternoon. Thos Baldwin to Edgefield with D^{o} & got up a lode of turnips. G Thompson & H Raven Cleansed `//. J Ram in M H, Bransby tasking, Thos Boyce in garden. WH, Miss Hardy & the Miss Ravens spent the day at Mr Flowers. H Raven at Holt Evening.

APRIL 28, THURSDAY

HR W Lamb & Baldwin to Holt with beer morning & the Camp with D^{o} afternoon.[2] Boyce in garden, Bransby tasking, J Ram very ill. G Thompson & H Raven Cleansed

[1] *Thomas Kendle* The absence of a prefix suggests this was not Mr Kendle of Sharrington Hall but his son Thomas jnr (b.1777), who was exactly Henry Raven's age: see note for 8 Nov. 1795

[2] *camp* An advance party must have arrived for the summer. The main body of the Artillery did not pitch camp until June, with the next beer delivery being made on 13 June.

William would have had the opportunity of renewing the beer contract for Weybourne Camp during his visit to Sheringham the previous day

X beer. Famaly whalk[d] to Bayfield morning. H Raven in Malthouse. M[r] & M[rs] Bartell drank tea here, WH at home all Day.

APRIL 29, FRIDAY

HR W Lamb to Sherringham with beer & Loaded for Barmer. Tho[s] Baldwin to Holt with D[o], got the Barley out of Barn & loded for Syderstone. Jn[o] Ram in Malthouse, Bransby finnis [finished] tasking. M[r] & WH at home all day, Miss Ravens & HR whalk[d] to Holt morning. M[rs] & Miss Davy, Miss Jennis & Miss Baker drank tea here, M[r] Roxby & M[r] Harriss drank tea here.[1] Tho[s] Boyce in garden.

APRIL 30, SATURDAY

HR W Lamb & Baldwin to Barmer & Syderstone with beer, Tho[s] Boyce in garden. J Ram in Malthouse, G Thompson & H Raven grinding Malt for brew. Boy got the Barrel Stuff out of Rices.[2] M[r] & WH at Holt after[n]. Nath[l] & the Miss Ravens whent of for Whissonsett.

MAY 1, SUNDAY

Henry Raven M[rs] Hardy to Cley after[n]. M[r], WH & Miss Hardy at Holt Church afternoon. W Lamb loaded for Southrepps.

MAY 2, MONDAY

HR W Lamb to Southrepps with beer, took two Bar[ls] [barrels] for Thaxter of Walsham.[3] T Baldwin, G Thomp., H Raven & Boy in brewhouse, WH D[o] Brewing. Jn[o] Ram in Malthouse, T Boyce in garden. M[r] & M[rs] Forster & M[r] John & M[rs] Herring drank tea here. T Baldwin whent to Kettlestone with beer. M[r] Hard{a}y at home all day.

MAY 3, TUESDAY

HR W Lamb to Cley for two Chaldrons of Cinders from M[r] [ ], to Holt with beer & Loaded for Burnham afternoon. T Baldwin to Hindolvestone with beer. G Thompson, H Raven & Boy Cleansed `//. Jn[o] Ram in Malthouse, Boyce in garden. M[r] H at home all day, W & Miss H rode out afternoon.

MAY 4, WEDNESDAY

HR W Lamb to Burnham with beer, T Baldwin to Briston & Thornage with D[o]. T Boyce at work in shrubbery,

facing page **Sunrise, from the top of Muckleburgh Hill between Weybourne and Kelling. As Repton's *View from Sheringham Heath* shows (illustrated for 2 Dec. 1795) this is hilly country, and the many visitors to the camp would have enjoyed raked viewing on these wide heaths as they watched the military exercises by the sea to the north.**

Viewers on the summit of the hills today look down on gorse bushes and tree tops below [*MB · 2011*]

---

[1] *Roxby* A London hop-factor with whom the Hardys had regularly dealt in the past (*Diary 2*). Mr Harris was presumably his assistant, Mary Hardy referring to her visitors as 'Mr Roxby and a young gentleman with him' (Diary MS)

[2] *Rice's* The MS is unclear: Henry may have written 'Rixes' (Rix's)

[3] *Thaxter* A puzzling entry. The alehouse register for Michaelmas 1795 and 1796 shows no innkeeper of that name at any of N. Walsham's 15 public houses (NRO: C/Sch 1/16). He may have opened up the Maid's Head briefly for the fair, assuming that James Dew had by then left and that William Smith (first listed in 1798) had not yet taken over; the alehouse records for 1797 have not survived

facing page N. Walsham: the market cross, with the parish church behind the row of shops and inns to the left.

Mary Hardy's cousin Neale Raven was a draper, tailor and grocer in the market place until his death in 1789 (*Diary 1*).

Part of the church tower collapsed in May 1724 following prolonged bell-ringing to accompany the town's Ascension Day fair; until then the tower and spire had been the tallest edifice in the county after Norwich Cathedral steeple.

The Hardys granted their miller William Gunton Thompson a good deal of time off for fairs. In 1796 he attended not only his local fair (at Holt on 25 Apr.) and his home fair (N. Walsham on 5 May), but also the fairs at Weybourne on 17 May and Cley on 29 July [*drawing by J.B. Ladbrooke c.1824*]

Boy turning up mush [muck] in yard. J Ram in Malthouse, H Raven Cleansed X beer. G Thompson whent off to Walsham morning 4 oC[. . .] [o'clock].[1] M^r^ & WH at home all day. Dawsons lad painting.

MAY 5, THURSDAY

HR W Lamb & Baldwin ploughing turnep ground & Bells Acre, Thos Boyce at work in garden. Boy turning up muck forenoon, Carting gravill afternoon. J Ram ill, H Raven look'd after the Malthouse. M^r^ «Hardy» at home all day. Dawsons lad painting. WH at home all Day.

MAY 6, FRIDAY

HR W Lamb ploughing forenoon, at harrow afternoon, T Baldwin ploughing all day. T Boyce at work in garden, Boy Carting gravil & got one lode of Mirgin. H Raven in brewhouse & tended the Malthouse. M^r^ H at home all day. Dawsons Lad Painting. WH at home all day.

MAY 7, SATURDAY

HR T Baldwin to Brampton with beer, W Lamb to Runton with D^o^. T Boyce helping in Malthouse & in garden, Matt Booth mending the Pipes.[2] H Raven in Malthouse. M^r^ & WH at Holt Market afternoon, M^rs^ & Miss H at Holt after^n^.

MAY 8, SUNDAY

HR Famaly at own Church forenoon. H Raven to Sherington [Sharrington] to Dine, Mr Wade dined here. W Lamb & T Baldwin Carried of Part of Cleanse of beer.

Mary Hardy A Wet morng, fine afternoon. All went to our Church foornoon, Mr Burrell preachd & read a Lecture in the Eveng. I & J Thompson went to Cley meeting afternoon, came home to tea. Mr Wade here all the Afternoon.

MAY 9, MONDAY

HR T Baldwin to Wiverton with beer & Cley for 1½ Chal^d^ Coles from Mr Jacksons. W Lamb in brewhouse part of Day & whent to Holt & Waybourn with beer. G Thomp. & Boy in Brewhouse, H Raven whent to Guestw«ic»k with Malt. M^r^ H at home all day, WH brewing & whent to Holt. Thos Boyce in garden.

MH A very Showry day. Wm Brew'd, Mr Hardy at home all day. A Town meeting in the Eveng [3] . . .

---

[1] *Walsham* The Ascension Day fair fell that year on 5 May, a popular month for fairs. These are charted on the front endpaper

[2] *Booth* The Holt plumber and glazier: see notes for 15 July 1795 and 25 Oct. 1796

[3] *town meeting* Probably in connection with the parish house of industry. There was normally only one meeting a year, on Easter Monday, to set the rates

MAY 10, TUESDAY

HR W Lamb to Fakenham with beer, T Baldwin to Beckhigh with D°. G Thompson & H Raven Cleansed `// & dressing Maltstones, Thos Boyce in garden. Mr H at home all day, WH at home all day.

MAY 11, WEDNESDAY

HR T Baldwin to Sherringham with beer, W Lamb to Bale & Hinderingham with D°. T Boyce in garden, G Thompson & H Raven dressing Maltstones. Mr & WH at home all day. G Thompson Cleansed X beer.

MAY 12, THURSDAY

HR T Baldwin to Hindolveston with beer. W Lamb & Boy got up two loades of Firs & got some lifts into furze Close.[1] G Thompson & H Raven dressing Maltstones, T Boyce at work in garden. Mrs [?Mr] H at home all Day, WH at holt aftern, HR at Holt Evening.

MAY 13, FRIDAY

HR W Lamb to Alborough with beer, T Baldwin Sitting [setting] lifts in furze Close & ploughing. T Boyce in

[1] *lifts* '*lift*: a sort of coarse rough gate of sawn wood, not hung, but driven into the ground by pointed stakes, like a hurdle, used for the same purposes of sub-dividing lands, stopping gaps in fences &c, and deriving its name from the necessity of *lifting* it up for the purpose of passing through . . .' (R. Forby, *The Vocabulary of East Anglia*, vol. 2, pp. 194–5)

THE
BLACK
LION
HOTEL

right The Black Lion, in the Friday Market at Lt Walsingham, stands aside from the bustle of the town.

One of the town's leading inns, the Black Lion served additionally as the excise office. Here on 13 May 1796 William Paul held the auction attended by William Hardy for the second Sharrington public house. Later known as the Chequers, Mary Hardy calls it the Chequer, under which name it was advertised in the *Norwich Mercury* of 7 May 1796. Her husband did not acquire it, and William Bangay [jnr] remained as occupier on a lease renewable annually [*MB · 2002*]

garden, Boy sitting lifts & ploughing. WH to Cromer, Mr Hardy to Walsingham afternoon. G Thompson laid Down Malt Stones.

MH A Cold windy Stormy day. W^m^ went to Cromer morng 8 with Mr Moore, came home eveng 11.[1] Mr Hardy rid to Walsingham afternoon to a Sale of the Checkquer Publick House at Sherington, came home eveng 11.

MAY 14, SATURDAY

HR Thos Baldwin to Southrepps with beer, W Lamb to Morston with D^o^ & ploughing in five Acres. Thos Boyce in garden, G Thompson & H Raven grinding Malt for brew. Mr Ellis Dine'd here & supt. M^r^ & M^rs^, W & Miss Hardy to Holt after tea. Boy ploughing after^n^. W Tinker & Ben all day.

MH A Showry day. Mr Ellis of Cley dind, drank tea & Supt here. We all walkd up to Holt after tea. I & MA came home eveng 8, J Thompson met us with the Chaise. Mr Hardy & W^m^ came home Even 10 . . .

MAY 15, SUNDAY

HR Famaly at own Church afternoon, H Raven at Holt. W Lamb & T Baldwin carried of the Cleanse of Beer morning. Mrs Hardy at Cley afternoon.

MAY 16, MONDAY

HR T Baldwin, G Thompson, H Raven & Boy in brewhouse, WH D^o^ brewing. W Lamb carting Murgen [mir-

[1] *Cromer* The presence of William's attorney suggests they may have been looking over the New Inn, which was to be advertised for sale in the *Norwich Mercury* on 14 and 28 May (notice illustrated opposite).

William did not attend the auction at Aylsham on 31 May: he was busy at Holt during the general election campaign

gin]. M^r H at home all day. T Boyce in garden half a day. Lamb, Baldwin & G Thompson Dined here being Whitsom [Whitsun] Monday.[1]

MAY 17, TUESDAY

HR W Lamb, Baldwin & G Thompson Cleansed `// & X beer & then whent to Waybourn fair,[2] H Raven whent to Hempton fair aftern.[3] M^r & WH at home all day. GT dressing Wheat Stones.

MH A very fine day. Mr Hardy & W^m at home all day. Ann Ives aged 18 having been poorly was walking up «to» Holt to the Doctor, was taken very bad on the road & Died in about 3 hours [4] . . .

MAY 18, WEDNESDAY

HR G Thompson dressing Wheat Stones, T Boyce in garden. Lamb and Baldwin no work. W & Miss H set of for Whissonsett forenoon, M^r H at home all day.

CROMER.

To be SOLD by AUCTION,

By Mr. BACON,

At the Black Boys, at Aylſham, on Tueſday the 31ſt day of May, 1796, at Three o'clock in the afternoon,

THE LEASE (of which 27 years are unexpired) of a large and commodious HOUSE, with coach-houſes, ſtables, &c. known by the name of the NEW INN or HOTEL, at Cromer, the moſt delightful and romantic part of the Norfolk coaſt, and at preſent one of the beſt frequented and faſhionable Bathing Places in England.

The ſituation is extremely well adapted to the reception of families who may ſeek temporary retirement from the purſuits of pleaſure or the fatigues of buſineſs.

The houſe commands a proſpect of the German Ocean, and directly under the cliff on which it is ſituated the bathing machines are every morning drawn out upon the ſands. (822

For further particulars apply to Foſter, Son and Unthank, attornies, in Norwich.

above This notice in the *Norwich Mercury* 28 May 1796 describes Cromer's tourist credentials in glowing terms (13 May). William Hardy was to hire the New Inn at Cromer from Mrs Chaplin of Blakeney in May 1798; it is not clear if she had bought the lease in 1796 at this auction. The notice fails to mention that John Wilson was innkeeper. He moved to the Cromer Hotel (the old King's Arms) in 1802, and the New Inn became Tucker's Hotel under George Cooke Tucker [*Norfolk Heritage Centre, Norwich*]

1 *Whit Monday* The first record of a special dinner offered to the workforce at Whitsuntide. Mary Hardy does not mention it, which may suggest either that Mary Ann and the maids were primarily responsible for the preparations or that the burden of feeding only three additional mouths was negligible. At Coltishall the men had usually been let off work for the Whit Monday fair, but had not been given dinner first. The yearly farm servants were given Whit Monday dinners in 1797 and 1798, Christmas dinners resuming in Dec. 1798

2 *Weybourne Fair* This does not appear in the printed lists of county fairs, eg in the Norwich directories of 1783 and 1802 and in N. Kent, *General View of the Agriculture of the County of Norfolk* (1796), pp. 166–7.

The fair must have been a good one, Lamb and Baldwin being in no state to work the next day

3 *Hempton Green Fair* One of the biggest stock fairs in the county, and Henry's home fair, held twice a year on Whit Tuesday and on the fixed date 22 Nov.

4 *Ann Ives* Daughter of Clement Ives and Anne, née Lighten or Lighton, who had married at Letheringsett 14 Dec. 1775; the burial register gives her age as 17. She was not baptised at Letheringsett, unlike her brothers Robert and Francis (bapt. 12 May 1777 and 18 Sept. 1778) and her sister Jane (bapt. 2 Aug. 1785)

right Part of the very long notice which is likely to have been the reason for the day trip to Norwich by the Hardys and their lawyer on 21 May. Chapman Ives of Coltishall had been bankrupted earlier in the year; the conversion of an early-18th-century brewery to steam power might have led to his downfall.

He, his mother Rose in his minority, his father and grandfather had built up the tied estate which here forms 27 of the 28 lots. The Ship at Tuttington (lot 4) had been tied to Wells's during William Hardy's time as manager at Coltishall, and was later to become part of the Letheringsett tied estate [*Norwich Mercury, 14 May 1796, detail: Norfolk Heritage Centre, Norwich*]

To be SOLD by AUCTION,
By WM. BURT,
On Saturday the 21ſt day of May inſt. at Three o'clock in the afternoon preciſely, at the Maid's Head, in St. Simon's, Norwich—IN TWENTY-EIGHT LOTS,

Lot 1. ALL that valuable & new-erected BREW-HOUSE, ſituate at Coltiſhall, in Norfolk; containing three coppers, two maſh-tuns, under-back, four working tuns, ſtillions, which will work off about 150 barrels, with 14 ſtore vats, and other convenient utenſils, together with a ſteam engine, and forcing and lifting pumps, on the moſt improved principles;—there are alſo two Malt-houſes adjoining the ſaid Brew-houſe, one of which wets 30 quarters at a time, and has a plate kiln; and the other wets 15 quarters, and has a tile kiln, with ſuitable working floors and lofts, and very capacious granaries. The plant likewiſe comprizes a cooperage, with two large ſtore rooms, vat rooms, and working ſtore houſe, with a large yard, three ſtables, cart lodge, and piggery, capable of feeding and lodging 200 ſwine, with a meadow of about four acres adjacent thereto. There is likewiſe a Dwelling-houſe, with a garden thereto, and another malt houſe, with a 15-quarter ciſtern, and very extenſive granaries belonging thereto, all adjoining the water, and cottages for the maltſters, with a piece of garden ground to the ſame.—All freehold.

But there is a free rent of 5s. 7d. per annum, payable to the manor of Coltiſhall.

N. B. The purchaſer of this lot will be required to take the utenſils employed in the ſaid brewery, together with the ſtock in trade, at a valuation to be fixed by two indifferent perſons, one to be choſen by the vendors, and the other by the purchaſer; and in caſe ſuch two perſons ſhall not agree, then by a third perſon, to be named by ſuch two perſons.

Lot 2. The King's Head, at Coltiſhall, and a ſmall Cottage adjoining.

Lot 3. The White Horſe, at Great Hautbois.

Lot 4. The Ship, at Tuttington, with an acre of Land, and double Cottage near thereto, &c.

Lot 5. The Vats, in St. Peter's Southgate, Norwich, with Granaries, Coal Binns, Cellars, Stables, &c.

Lot 6. A Dwelling-houſe, with four acres of Land and two Marſhes, at Smallburgh.

below Coltishall King's Head (lot 2), acquired by Chapman Ives after taking over John Browne's Coltishall maltings, brewery and outlets *c.*1787 [*MB · 2010*]

MAY 19, THURSDAY

HR W Lamb to Stalham with beer, T Baldwin to Holt & Briston with D°. T Boyce in garden, Boy clearing fat [vat] & turning up muck in yard, G Thompson dressing Wheat Stones. Mr H at home all day, W & Miss H came from Whissonsett in Evening.

MH A very fine day but windy. Mr Hardy at home all day. M Ives of Branton [Brampton] dind here, & Mr Wade in his way home from London. Wm & MA came home from Whisonsett Eveng 9.

MAY 20, FRIDAY

HR W Lamb came from Stalham, Thos Baldwin to Wells with beer, T Boyce at work in River making a dam across River. W Tinker all day. WH drew the Water out of River & Pond & took out the fish. G Thompson laid down Wheat Stones. M^r^ H at home all day.

MH A very fine day. Mr Hardy {Hardy} at home all day. Miss Leake & Mrs Sheldrake drank tea here. Mr Smith of Cley came in the Eveng to go to Norwich with Mr Hardy to Morrow, Slept here. Ann Ives was Buried.

MAY 21, SATURDAY

HR Thos Baldwin to Cromer with beer, W Lamb to Corpusta, Holt & Edgefield with D^o^. Thos Boyce at work in river, W Tinker & Mr Youngman Mending Water gate & Wheel.[1] G Thompson grinding Malt for Brew. M^r^, Miss & W Hardy & Mr Smith set out for Norwich morning eight OClock, home at 12 OClock.[2]

MH A very Showry day. Mr Hardy, Mr Smith & MA sett of for Norwich in Crafers Post chaise Morng 7, W^m^ on Horse Back, they came home a little before 12 a Night. Mr Smith Slept here.

MAY 22, SUNDAY

HR Famaly all at own Church forenoon, M^rs^ H to Cley afternoon. M^r^ & WH at holt Church afternoon.

MH A fine day. Mr Smith went away after Breakfast. We all went to our Church foornoon, Mr Burrell preach'd. I & J Thompson went to Cley meeting afternoon & all except W^m^ went to Church in Eveng to hear a funerall Sermon.[3]

MAY 23, MONDAY

HR W Lamb, G Thompson, HR & Boy in Brewhouse, WH D^o^ brewing. Thos Baldwin to Sherringham with beer, Thos Boyce in garden. M^r^ H at home all day. W Tinker & two men all day, Dawsons lad Painting.

MH A Close drisly day. Mr Hardy at home all day, Wm Brew'd. I & MA began hanging her new dressing Room & Bed Chamber.[4]

[1] *watergate and wheel* The work evidently involved the culvert powering the waterwheel; also, fish may have got into the pipes from the basin in the Brewhouse Pightle (7 and 20 May 1796). The watergate was the sluice from the Glaven by the malthouse east wall

[2] *Norwich* Chapman Ives's brewery and 23 remaining tied houses were to be sold by auction at the Maid's Head (opposite); the public houses are listed in full in *World*, vol. 2, chap. 8. As though trying to shield the ambitious young manufacturer from public exposure before the gaze of putative future readers of her diary Mary Hardy never mentions any of the financial disasters which were to beset the Coltishall attorney, farmer, maltster and brewer, then aged 38 and with a young family.

The Hardys would have grieved for their old friend and competitor whom they had known from his youth

[3] *funeral sermon* This could have been for a well-known figure, and not necessarily for someone local. The five persons buried at Letheringsett during the previous 12 months had been the Norwich carter William Telley; the Halls' 10-week-old son John; the Hardys' former gardener 'Duke' Humphrey; the rector's wife Elizabeth Burrell; and Ann Ives

[4] *hanging* With wallpaper. The Hardys often undertook domestic redecoration themselves

above Horningtoft Church, the west front. The nave arch was filled in after the tower's collapse in 1796; the bell-cote dates from 1871. John Moy served for 30 years as churchwarden [*MB · 1999*]

Mary Hardy's visit to Whissonsett
24–28 May 1796

MAY 24, TUESDAY

HR [at Letheringsett] W Lamb to Gunthorpe with beer & helping to Cleanse, Thos Baldwin helping to Cleanse `// & whent to Holt with beer. G Thompson & H Raven Cleansed `// & XX beer. Thos Boyce in garden & Malt-house, Boy turning Over Muckheap in five Acres. M^r^ & M^rs^ H set of for Whiss^t^ forenoon. HR to Cley Evening, WH at home all day. W Tinker & man all day.

MH A fine day. Mr Hardy & I sett of for Whissonsett Morng 10, got there Eveng 1, Dind, drank tea, Supt & Slept at Mr Goggs . . .

MAY 25, WEDNESDAY

HR W Lamb to Salthouse with beer & home by Cley for 1½ Chaldron coles from Mr Jacksons forenoon, to Stody with beer afternoon. Thos Boyce in garden & Malthouse, Nicholass turning over the muck heap in 5 Acres.[1] Thos Baldwin very ill. WH at home all day. W Tinker all day.

MAY 26, THURSDAY

HR W Lamb ploughing forenoon, at Muck cart afternoon. Baldwin at harrow all Day. Nich^s^ turning over muck foren^n^, fillin Muck cart afternoon. Thos Boyce half a day. WH at home, H Raven helping Miss Hardy to hang the room. WH & Miss H drank tea at Mr Burrells. W Tinker & man all day, Dawsons Lad Painting.

MAY 27, FRIDAY

HR W Lamb to Waybourn & Edgefield with beer, Baldwin to Runton with D^o^. G Thom^n^ grinding Malt for brew, Thos Boyce in garden part of Day. Dawson Lad Painting. W Tinker & man all day. H Raven helping to hang the room. M^r^ & M^rs^, Miss & Edm Bartell & Mr Dowson drank tea here.

MH [at Whissonsett] A fine day. Sister Raven & I walkd to Horning«toft» to speak to Mrs Moy.[2] Mr Hardy & Bro^t^ Raven rid to Brisly and Worden [Worthing], came back to Dinner. We drank tea at Mrs Ravens at the Hall.

MAY 28, SATURDAY

HR W Lamb carting muck forenoon, spreading D^o^ afternoon. Baldwin filling Muck cart forenoon, ploughing

---

[1] *Nicholas* Like his aunt Henry usually refers to labourers by their surname or by initial and surname, and to boys either by their forename or, more usually, to the 'boy'. Henry seems to have been in some doubt how to refer to a 'great boy' like Nicholas Woodhouse

[2] *Mrs Moy* Judith, née Fox (bapt. Brisley 2 Aug. 1738, d. Whissonsett 3 Sept. 1814, bur. Horningtoft 8 Sept.), Mary Hardy's first cousin (app. D3.A, fig. D3.2). She marr. Brisley 11 Aug. 1761 John Moy (d. 24 Dec. 1806 aged 75), a farmer and maltster at Horningtoft until retiring to Litcham

afternoon in Bells Acre. Nich[s] spreading Muck after[n]. Tho[s] Boyce in Malthouse, G Thompson grinding Malt for brew. M[r] & M[rs] Hardy came from Whissonsett, M[r] & WH at Holt afternoon.

MH A fine day. Sett of from Whisonsett Morng 10, got home Eveng 1. M[r] Hardy & W[m] went to Holt Mark[t], came home Eveng past 9. M[r] Heath preach'd in Town.[1]

[LETHERINGSETT]

MAY 29, SUNDAY

HR Famaly at own Church afternoon, M[rs] Hardy to Cley afternoon. M[r] H at home all day. M[r] Kendle call[d] evening.

MH A Showry day, Wind high. M[r] Hardy & MA did not go to Church service aftern. W[m] went to Holt Church, came home to tea. I & J Thompson went to Cley meeting.

MAY 30, MONDAY

HR T Baldwin, G Thompson, H Raven & Boy in brewhouse, WH Do brewing. W Lamb to Cley {for} with beer & Bro[t] home [ ] Chaldrons of Cinders from M[r] Ellis's, Tho[s] Boyce in Malthouse. M[r] H at Holt Evening.

MH A very boistrus stormy day. Another Candidate put up for the County Ellection, A M[r] Hare. M[r] Burrell gave a Supper at Dobsons on behalf of him & Woodhouse [Wodehouse].[2] W[m] Brew'd. M[r] Hardy rid up to Holt after tea, home even 10.

MAY 31, TUESDAY

HR W Lamb to Syderstone with beer, Tho[s] Baldwin to Norwich with D[o]. Tho[s] Boyce in Malthouse, G Thompson & H Raven Cleansed `//. M[r] H at home forenoon, to Holt afternoon. Nich[s] trimming of Malt afternoon. WH at Holt afternoon.

MH A fine day. M[r] Hardy walkd up to Holt afternoon, drank tea at M[r] Bartells. The Feathers & Kings Head [at Holt] opend for M[r] Cokes friends. MH [Mr Hardy] came home eveng 9, heard the contest was given up by M[r] Hare.

JUNE 1, WEDNESDAY

Henry Raven W Lamb helping to Cleanse morning then whent to rowl [roll] forenoon, helped to unlode cinders

[1] *Heath* He was attending the Letheringsett meeting, 'town' denoting Letheringsett parish. William Heath was one of the two Wesleyan Methodist itinerant preachers stationed on the Walsingham Circuit in the connexional years 1794–95 and 1795–96 (*Minutes of the Methodist Conferences*, vol. 1, pp. 285, 304). The minutes enable us to follow the preachers' stations.

Heath had come from Colchester, Essex, and in 1796 was posted to Pontefract, Yorks (pp. 266, 333)

[2] *county election* The Tory candidates were Thomas Hare, JP, of Stow Bardolph, and Sir John Wodehouse (1741–1834), Bt, of Kimberley Hall, MP for Norfolk 1784–97 until he was raised to the peerage as 1st Baron Wodehouse of Kimberley. Thomas William Coke of Holkham (the Foxite Whig) and Sir John had announced their candidacy 21 May, Coke pledging to continue with his long-held policies: he had been against the American war and was against the present war with France. But Mr Hare withdrew early from the contest, and the sitting members were returned unopposed on 3 June; the possibility of two Tory members and no Whig representing the county was thus removed. The two weekly Norwich papers, the *Norfolk Chronicle* and the *Norwich Mercury*, followed every turn of event with their usual close attention

& whent to rowl afternoon. Thos Baldwin came from Norwich, Thos Boyce in Malthouse. G Thompson & H Raven Cleanse'd X beer & Dressing flower. WH to Sherringham, Mr H at home all day. Mr Huson calld in morning. Mr & WH supt at the Kings head with a party of Cookes friends.[1]

Mary Hardy A Showry day. Mr Hardy rid up to Holt to tea. [[[2] Mr H & Wm spent the evng at dobsons, met Mr Cookes Friends.]]

JUNE 2, THURSDAY

HR W Lamb to Briston with beer forenoon & Sherrington with Do afternoon. T Baldwin to Cley for 1½ Chaldrons coles from Mr Jacksons afternoon, Thos Boyce in Malthouse. Mr Hardy at home all day, WH to Norwich with Mr Kendle. Boy tremming [trimming] Malt forenoon.

MH A fine foornoon, Showry afternoon. Mr Burrell & Chas Lamb went to Norwich in his Whiskey to the Ellection, came home eveng 11. Wm went to Norwich with Chas Kendle Morng past 6, Thos Youngman & J [John] Jex went.[3] A Wet Night.

[1] *King's Head* At Letheringsett, as Mary Ann's entry shows. The licensee had the freedom—despite the firm Whig principles of the owner William Hardy—to host election meetings in both the Tory and Whig interests (30 May, 1 June). Business was business

[2] In Mary Ann's hand, repairing her mother's omission

[3] *to the election* The groupings are interesting, revealing party loyalties. No poll was taken as the election was uncontested (showing the value of Mary Hardy's record in naming six of the village's potential electorate).

The county pollbook 10 years later shows John Burrell and Charles Lamb plumping for the Tory candidate while William Hardy jnr and Thomas Youngman voted for the Whigs. Supporters of opposing candidates in 1796 did not co-operate over transport. Charles Lamb's Tory allegiance proved no bar to his working for the Hardys (5 June), indicating acceptance of political independence. Mr Burrell's hosting of a Tory supper at the King's Head may have exacerbated the existing tensions between rector and brewer.

Norwich had held its customary disorderly election on 25 May, when the Hon. Henry Hobart (1622 votes) and Rt Hon. William Windham (1159) were victorious over the Quaker banker Bartlett Gurney (1076 votes)

facing page The Glaven cascade at the bridge where a serious accident befell a rival brewer's drayman in the swollen ford on 4 June 1796. In Sept. 2011 the river was not in spate, yet the force seen here, reflecting the parallel fall under the maltings, was considerable [*MB · 2011*]

above The floods, 26 Aug. 1912: Letheringsett's Glaven Farm lies to the right, Lt Thornage to the left. The footbridge over the ford in Riverside Road resembles a footbridge downstream under which Mrs Booty's drayhorse was drowned in 1796 [*Cozens-Hardy Collection*]

JUNE 3, FRIDAY

HR WH came from Norwich evening. W Lamb & Baldwin carried of Cleanse beer. G Thompson grinding Malt for brew, Thos Boyce in Malthouse. Mr H at home all Day. A very wet Day.[1]

MH Raind insesently all day. Mr Hardy at home all day. Wm came home Eve 10 very Wet indeed. Mr Coke & Woodhouse brought in without oppersition. Raind all Night.

JUNE 4, SATURDAY

HR A very wet Day. No work done except helping to get Mrs Bootys horses out of the River which were taken under the Bridge with the stream, one mare was lost.[2] Thos Boyce in Malthouse forenoon, J Ram afternoon. WH whent to Holt, Mr H at home all day.

MH A Wet Morng, the Water higher in the River then ever was remembered. Mrs Bootys Brew Cart attempting to pass through was drawn under the Bridge & one of the Horses drowned. A Man who was riding on the Cart was thrown into the River (for the Cart Overturnd) «and» was providentily sav'd. Mr Hardy at home all day, Wm went to Market Eveng 4.

[1] *very wet* The first time in two and a half years that Henry has recorded the weather, and a masterpiece of understatement. The floods in Norwich were the worst since 1767 (*Norw. Merc.* 11 June 1796)

[2] *Mrs Booty* The Hardys' competitor at the brewery at Binham and widow of John Booty who had died in 1794 (*Norw. Merc.* 27 Sept. 1794). Until 1792, when William Hardy jnr bought them copyhold, the Bell at Fakenham and the Buck at Syderstone had been owned by the Bootys (*Diary 2*).

By 1805 the brewery had closed, William Booty's sale particulars showing it was a relatively small concern (*Norw. Merc.* 3 Aug. 1805)

JUNE 5, SUNDAY

HR Famaly all at own Church forenoon. Mrs Hardy to Cley Afternoon, WH at Holt afternoon. W Lamb loded for Southrepps, Abraham Dobson & Chas Lamb in Malthouse Afternoon.

MH A fine day. We all went to our Church foornoon, Mr Burrell preachd. I & J Thompson went to Cley afternoon, home to tea. Mr Hardy & W^m^ walkd to Holt Church afternoon, came home to tea. Mr Burrell read a Lecture in the eveng.

JUNE 6, MONDAY

HR W Lamb to Southrepps with beer, Thos Baldwin to Corpusta with D^o^. Thos Boyce & H Raven in Malthouse, Nick^s^ at work in River forenoon. Mr Gathercole came & Orderd a lode of beer.[1] M^r^ H at home all day, WH at Holt after tea.

MH A very fine day. I very poorly with dimness in my Eyes & pain in my head. Mr Hardy at home all day. W^m^ went to Holt Bowling green after tea, came home Eveng 9.

JUNE 7, TUESDAY

HR W Lamb in brewhouse morning, to Sherringham with beer. G Thompson, H Raven & Boy in Brewhouse, WH D^o^ brewing. Thos Baldwin to Fakenham with beer & Bro^t^ home 18 bunches of hoops. Thos Boyce in Malthouse. Mr Hardy at home all day.

MH A fine day. Mr Hardy & W^m^ at home all day. I but poorly, Mr Bartell bled me. Took a walk in the Eveng to look at the New Work House . . .

JUNE 8, WEDNESDAY

HR W Lamb to Holt twice with beer & got up a lode of Stones out of rode [road]. Thos Boyce in Malthouse, Thos Baldwin to Burnham with beer, G Thompson & H Raven Cleansed `//. WH & Miss Hardy to Holt after tea, Mr Hardy at home all day.

JUNE 9, THURSDAY

HR W Lamb to Wells with beer. Thos Baldwin carting iron Cinders into river forenoon,[2] to Cley for 1½ Chaldrons coles from Mr Jacksons. Thos Boyce in Malthouse. Nick^s^ helping Baldwin forenoon, at work in garden afternoon. G Thompson & H Raven Cleanse'd X

[1] *Gathercole* See note for 23 Oct. 1793. The Fakenham innkeeper called only four times at Letheringsett in the four years 1793–97. His visit on this occasion may have been no coincidence. He probably wanted to hear all about the accident to the Binham dray which until 1792 had supplied his public house

[2] *iron cinders* Glistening clinker bricks, to provide a hard and lasting lining for the bed of the ford. The calcined surface would offer some grip and thus prevent the type of mishap which befell Mrs Booty's dray; see also note for 11 Sept. 1797. The footbridge had been rebuilt 1790 in a dangerous position *down*-stream of the ford. As a result people and horses could be swept under.

William Hardy jnr's garden bridge of *c.*1801 downstream of the footbridge had flints and clinkers built into the parapet as an ornament as well as for a weatherproof coping (W. Stones, *The Garden of Norfolk*, pp. 55–6, 67). The poet explains that at the estate brickyard 'by accident / Were made the shining cinders on the bridge; / Large, finely figured, and of colours gay.'

As the technicalities of the process presumably did not lend themselves to verse, he added a footnote: 'These cinders . . . were made by a kiln of bricks being accidentally heated so hot as to melt the bricks into one common mass' (p. 67)

beer. Mr & WH at home all Day. Mr Joddrels gardener call«ed» to look at frewtt [fruit] trees.

JUNE 10, FRIDAY

HR W Lamb filling muck cart forenoon, driving out Do aftern. Thos Baldwin carting out muck forenoon, whent to Thornage with beer & filling muck Do [cart] afternoon, Nicks filling muck cart all Day. Thos Boyce in Malthouse, G Thompson grinding Malt for brew. Mr & WH at home all Day. Mr Rouse's men began [ ].[1]

JUNE 11, SATURDAY

HR W Lamb to Aldborough with beer. Thos Baldwin to Holt morning & spreading muck forenoon, ploughing afternoon. Thos Boyce in M H, W Tinker all Day mending brew cart. G Thompson grinding Malt, Jere Moore & son half a day in River. Nicks spreading muck half a day. Mr H at home all day, WH at Holt afternoon.

MH A very fine day. Wm walkd to Holt Markt afternoon, came home eveng past 8. Mr Hardy at home all day. I & MA went to meeting, Mr Witham preach'd.[2]

JUNE 12, SUNDAY

HR WH & H Raven at Holt Church afternoon, Mr & Mrs H to Cley afternoon. Service at six in Evening.

MH A very fine day. I somthing better. Mr Hardy & I went to Cley meeting afternoon,[3] drank tea at Mr Smiths, came home eveng 6. Service at our Church Even 6, Mr Hardy went. Wm went to Holt Church afternoon.

JUNE 13, MONDAY

HR W Lamb to Waybourn & S Sandersons with beer & loded for Overstrand.[4] Thos Baldwin in brewhouse forenoon, to Kettlestone with beer aftern. G Thompson, HR & Boy in brewhouse, WH Do brewing. W Tinker half a day. Thos Boyce in Malthouse, J Ram in garden half a day. Mr H at home all day.

MH A fine day. Mr Hardy at home all day. Wm Brew'd & went up to Holt after tea to the Bowling Green. Mr & Mrs Baker drank tea here . . .

JUNE 14, TUESDAY

HR W Lamb to Overstrand with beer, Thos Baldwin to Runton with Do. Thos Boyce in Malthouse, Gunton Thompson & H Raven Cleanse'd `//. J Ram at work in

[1] *Mr Rouse* Either Zebulon or his father Richard: see note for 5 Oct. 1794

[2] *Witham* 'John Wittam' is listed with William Heath as one of the two itinerant preachers stationed on the Walsingham Circuit by the Wesleyan Methodist Conference held at Manchester from 27 July 1795; the connexional years lasted from one conference to the next, the conferences being held in different cities in England every July/August (*Minutes of the Methodist Conferences*, vol. 1, p. 304). In 1794 Wittam was serving on the Northampton Circuit; at the 1796 conference he was posted to the St Ives Circuit, Hunts (*Minutes*, vol. 1, pp. 285, 331).

Mary Hardy understood the hardships of itinerancy, with the strains imposed on family ties, on children, and on the support mechanisms of loving relatives and close friends: in 1765 she had married into itinerancy in the form of the excise service. In future years she was to offer meals and overnight accommodation to the Methodist preachers

[3] *Cley meeting* The first time William Hardy had attended a Nonconformist meeting since hearing Thomas Mendham's funeral sermon at Briston for Selina, Countess of Huntingdon (*Diary 2*: 31 July 1791)

[4] *S. Sanderson's* The canteen at Weybourne Camp, where the Artillery were to arrive on 17 June

garden, Jere Moore & Son in River in garden. M^{r} & WH at home all Day. W Lamb loaded for Aldborough, Baldwin for Southrepps.

JUNE 15, WEDNESDAY

HR W Lamb to Aldborough with beer, Thos Baldwin to Southrepps with D^{o}. Thos Boyce in Malthouse, Jere Moore & Son at work in River. Nick^{s} carting gravel out of garden, G Thompson & H Raven Cleanse'd XX beer. W Tinker all Day. M^{r} & W Hardy at Holt afternoon, the Artillery came to Holt.

JUNE 16, THURSDAY

HR W Lamb ploughing forenoon, Carting muck afternoon of [off] muck heap in 6 Acres. Baldwin ploughing forenoon, whent to Edgefield with beer afternoon. Nick^{s} spreading muck fore^{n}, filling D^{o} after^{n}. Boyce in Malthouse. M^{r} & WH at home all Day. Jere Moore & Son at work in River.

JUNE 17, FRIDAY

HR W Lamb & Baldwin at muck cart all Day & got up one lode of Mirgin, Nick^{s} filling Muck cart. Thos Boyce in Malthouse, Jere Moore & Son in river, G Thompson grinding Malt for brew. M^{r} H at home all Day, WH whent to Waybourn with the Artillery.

MH A fine Morng, raind alittle afternoon. Mr Hardy at home all day. W^{m} walkd up to Holt foornoon to see the Artillerary March out of Town, walkd to Weybon to the Camp, Dind at Mr Erritts at Holt, came home even 4. Plattons Wife taken in a fitt & speechless this Eveng [1] . . .

JUNE 18, SATURDAY

HR W Lamb to Brampton with beer, Baldwin ploughing in five Acres, Nick^{s} spreading muck. Thos Boyce in Malthouse, G Thompson grinding Malt for brew. Jere Moore & Son at work in River. M^{r} & WH at Holt afternoon. Mr Richard Temple dined here. Jere Moore & Son all Day.

JUNE 19, SUNDAY

HR Famaly all at Own Church forenoon. M^{r} & WH at Holt Afternoon, M^{rs} H to Cley aftern. H Raven at Holt.

JUNE 20, MONDAY

HR Thos Baldwin to Sherringham with beer. W Lamb in brewhouse forenoon, to Salthouse with beer & Cley for

[1] *Platten's wife* Mary Hardy notes that the Bayfield Hall gamekeeper's wife died at about 5 o'clock the following afternoon and was buried 21 June. The Letheringsett register, apparently in error, records the burial of Mary, wife of Samuel Platten, as taking place on 6 June 1796. In her endnotes register Mary Hardy records that Mrs Platten died suddenly 'aged about 50'. Her husband married the widowed Mary Stimson at Saxlingham on 13 Oct. 1801, both making marks

below **After the floods the river specialist Jere Moore and his son worked for the Hardys 11–20 June, presumably repairing the banks.**

This early-20th-century postcard shows the Glaven with boarded banks just downstream of the cornmill [*Preston Bros, Holt, detail: Cozens-Hardy Collection*]

2 Cha^{n} [chaldrons] Cinders from Mr Ellis's Afternoon. G Thompson & H Raven & Nich^{s} in Brew house, WH D^{o} brewing. Boyce in Malthouse, Jere Moore & Son all Day in River. M^{r}, M^{rs} & Miss Hardy drank tea at Mr Forsters.

[[JUNE 21, TUESDAY

William Hardy jnr Thos Baldwin to upper Sherringham forenoon & Holt afternoon, WL to Bale & Whiverton with beer & bro^{t} home 1½ Ch Coles from Mr Cooks. T Boyce in M H, GT Cleansd `//, Nic^{s} after gravel in garden. WH rode to Camp after Tea, HR rode to Whissonsett Morning.

MH A Close Morng, fine afternoon. Mr Wood, Drugist from London, dind here. Mr Hardy at home all day. W^{m} rid to the Camp after tea, came home pst 9. S Plattons Wife Buried . . .

JUNE 22, WEDNESDAY

WHj Thos Baldwin to Morston with beer forenoon & jobs in garden afternoon. W Lamb to Weybourn forenoon with beer & garden afternoon, Cleansd X Morning. Nic^{s} in garden, T Boyce in M H. M^{r} H at home all day. WH at Brampton & Edgefield, bo^{t} 9 Acres of Grass of Danby [Darby] for £19.

above The drawings of the county bridges (those maintained out of the county rate) by the county surveyor Francis Stone depict closely observed scenes of life on the waterside 1830–31.

Here, at Setchey on the River Nar, four men are staithing the banks. The one on the left appears to be standing in a lighter; two are hammering home the planks; and a fourth fetches more timber from across the bridge.

The results of their efforts, on the right-hand bank, look remarkably similar to the boarding at the Rouses' former Mill House at Letheringsett nearly a century later (illustrated opposite) [*drawing by F. Stone; lithograph by D. Hodgson 1831*]

JUNE 23, THURSDAY

WHj T Baldwin at Corpusty foren^{n}, Sowing Bell's Acre afternoon. W Lamb Ploughing & harrowing all day, Nic^{s} Jobs in Yard, T Boyce in Malthouse. M^{r} & Mrs Flower dined & «drank» Tea here with Miss Goulty.[1] M^{r} & Mrs Coke, Holkham, call^{d} in Evening.[2]

JUNE 24, FRIDAY

WHj T Baldwin & Lamb at Plough all day & Nic^{s} Spreading Muck in 5 Acres forenoon, to Edgfield for Barley after^{n}. GT began grinding malt for Brew afternoon. Mr Wade dined here. WH rode to Barningham [Briningham] afternoon & Hunworth. M^{r} H home all day.

MH A fine day. Mr Hardy at home all day. W^{m} rid to Briningham after dinner, came home to tea.

JUNE 25, SATURDAY

WHj T Baldwin to Siderstone & Lamb to Barmer with beer. T Boyce «in» M H, N^{s} [Nicholas Woodhouse] Jobs at home. G To Grin'g Malt [Gunton Thompson to grinding malt] & «to» Mr Cooks for pollard. M^{r} H, WH & Miss H at market after^{n}.]]

[1] *Miss Goulty* Possibly Elizabeth Page Goulty, of W. Beckham (bur. Holt 14 Nov. 1862 aged 85), future wife of Peter Rouse: see note for 5 Oct. 1794. Their daughter Elizabeth Goulty was born 11 Aug. 1810, privately bapt. the next day at Letheringsett, publicly 21 Aug. 1810. Elizabeth Goulty, presumably Peter Rouse's mother-in-law, was bur. Holt from Beckham 26 Aug. 1826 aged 74; his presumed father-in-law Robert was bur. Holt from Beckham 29 Sept. 1828 aged 78.

The Flowers had W. Beckham connections and were later to move there: see note for 22 Oct. 1793

[2] *Mrs Coke* Jane (b. Sherborne, Gloucs, 29 Nov. 1753, marr. Sherborne 25 Oct. 1775 Thomas William Coke, d. Bath 2 June 1800, bur. Tittleshall 16 June), daughter of James Lennox Dutton of Sherborne and sister to James, 1st Lord Sherborne, who had married Coke's sister Elizabeth. The timing of the visit suggests this was a post-election call to thank their supporters (*World*, vol. 4, chap. 6). Mary Hardy gives the visit even less attention than her son, and notes that only Mr Coke called (Diary MS).

Jane Coke died leaving three daughters, the youngest aged five; she had had a stillborn son in 1776. Coke married Lady Anne Keppel in 1822, with whom he had five sons and a daughter

MH A very hot day. Mr Hardy & MA walkd up to Holt Mark^t^, MA drank tea at Mr Bakers, Mr Hardy at Mr Bartells. M^r^ & Mrs Smith of Cley drank tea here. M^r^ S & W^m^ walkd to Holt after tea, M^rs^ S, I & MA went to meeting in the Eveng.[1] M^r^ & M^rs^ S went away eveng past 9 . . .

JUNE 26, SUNDAY

Henry Raven Mrs Hardy to Cley afternoon, WH at Holt afternoon. M^r^ & Miss H to own Church afternoon.

JUNE 27, MONDAY

HR Thos Baldwin to Norwich with beer, W Lamb to the camp with beer & Holt with D^o^, Thos Boyce in Malthouse. M^r^ & WH at home all Day. Mr Keeller & Mr Everett came afternoon to Settle for years Barley.

MH A fine day but not hot. Mr Hardy & W^m^ walkd to Mr Forsters to buy some hay, did not agree for it, came home to tea. Mr Keeler, Mr Everitt & Mr Ladle came to recon, drank tea & Supt here, Mr Forster Supt here, all went away before 12.

[1] *meeting* Neither William nor Henry troubled to report Mary Hardy's attendance at meetings other than on Sundays. Preoccupied with work, they may at times have been unaware of her activities during the week. Were it not for her diary her early experiments with weekday Methodism would have gone unrecorded

facing page Jane Coke (23 June) was buried at Tittleshall, close to Godwick, by Whissonsett, where the Cokes had settled in the 16th century. Opposite this marble monument to her on the south wall of the chancel at Tittleshall is a huge memorial to James I's Lord Chief Justice Sir Edward Coke [*MB* · 2011]

below '. . . Calm and unassuming in the ordinary offices of social life. But inflexible and unwearied in the discharge of all its nobler and more arduous duties . . .': the epitaph to Jane Coke was composed by her husband for her 1805 monument by Nollekens. She would actively champion her husband's cause at election time [*MB* · 2011]

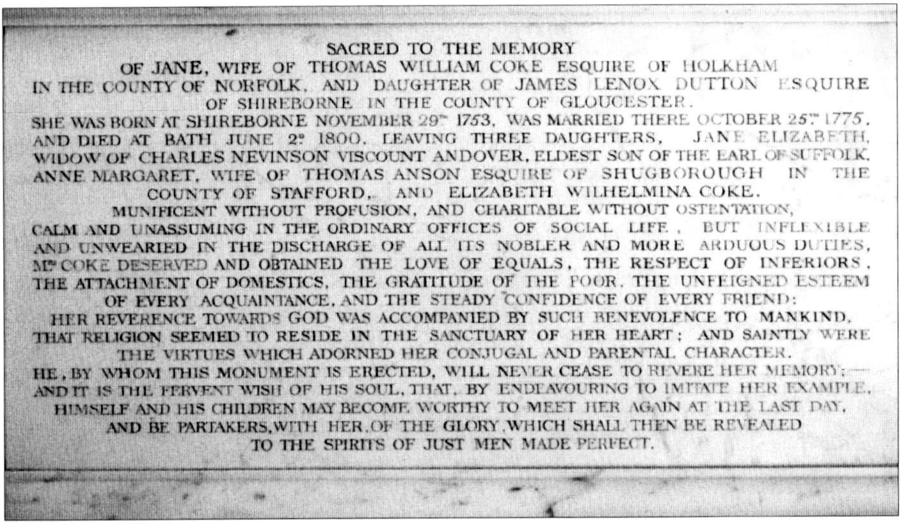

SACRED TO THE MEMORY
OF JANE, WIFE OF THOMAS WILLIAM COKE ESQUIRE OF HOLKHAM
IN THE COUNTY OF NORFOLK, AND DAUGHTER OF JAMES LENOX DUTTON ESQUIRE
OF SHIREBORNE IN THE COUNTY OF GLOUCESTER.
SHE WAS BORN AT SHIREBORNE NOVEMBER 29TH 1753, WAS MARRIED THERE OCTOBER 25TH 1775,
AND DIED AT BATH JUNE 2^D^ 1800, LEAVING THREE DAUGHTERS, JANE ELIZABETH,
WIDOW OF CHARLES NEVINSON VISCOUNT ANDOVER, ELDEST SON OF THE EARL OF SUFFOLK,
ANNE MARGARET, WIFE OF THOMAS ANSON ESQUIRE OF SHUGBOROUGH IN THE
COUNTY OF STAFFORD, AND ELIZABETH WILHELMINA COKE.
MUNIFICENT WITHOUT PROFUSION, AND CHARITABLE WITHOUT OSTENTATION,
CALM AND UNASSUMING IN THE ORDINARY OFFICES OF SOCIAL LIFE, BUT INFLEXIBLE
AND UNWEARIED IN THE DISCHARGE OF ALL ITS NOBLER AND MORE ARDUOUS DUTIES,
M^RS^ COKE DESERVED AND OBTAINED THE LOVE OF EQUALS, THE RESPECT OF INFERIORS,
THE ATTACHMENT OF DOMESTICS, THE GRATITUDE OF THE POOR, THE UNFEIGNED ESTEEM
OF EVERY ACQUAINTANCE, AND THE STEADY CONFIDENCE OF EVERY FRIEND:
HER REVERENCE TOWARDS GOD WAS ACCOMPANIED BY SUCH BENEVOLENCE TO MANKIND,
THAT RELIGION SEEMED TO RESIDE IN THE SANCTUARY OF HER HEART; AND SAINTLY WERE
THE VIRTUES WHICH ADORNED HER CONJUGAL AND PARENTAL CHARACTER.
HE, BY WHOM THIS MONUMENT IS ERECTED, WILL NEVER CEASE TO REVERE HER MEMORY;—
AND IT IS THE FERVENT WISH OF HIS SOUL, THAT, BY ENDEAVOURING TO IMITATE HER EXAMPLE,
HIMSELF AND HIS CHILDREN MAY BECOME WORTHY TO MEET HER AGAIN AT THE LAST DAY,
AND BE PARTAKERS, WITH HER, OF THE GLORY, WHICH SHALL THEN BE REVEALED
TO THE SPIRITS OF JUST MEN MADE PERFECT.

JUNE 28, TUESDAY

HR W Lamb, G Thompson & Nick^s^ in brew house, WH D^o^ Brewing. Thos Baldwin came from Norwich, bro^t^ home 10 Qr^s^ Wheat.[1] Boyce in M H, J Ram in garden. M^r^ H at home all Day, H Raven came from Whiss^t^.

MH A fine day. H Raven came home Morng 11. Mr Hardy & W^m^ at home all day, Wm Brew'd. Mr Hardy walkd to Mr Forsters after tea, bought 30 Acr^s^ of Grass at £95 0*s* 0*d*, came home eve 10 [2] . . .

JUNE 29, WEDNESDAY

HR W Lamb to Fakenham with beer. Thos Baldwin ploughing & harrowing forenoon, sowing turnips afternoon. Thos Boyce in garden, H Raven in M H, Nich^s^ Skreening a last «of» wheat. G Thompson & H Raven Cleanse'd `// morning & X beer evening. M^r^, Miss Raven [3] & Mrs Cozens came forenoon,[4] dined & whent to Camp & Lower Sherringham. M^r^, M^rs^, Miss & W Hardy whent to Sherringham to tea.

JUNE 30, THURSDAY

HR W Lamb to Stalham with beer, Thos Baldwin to Sherringham with D^o^, Thos Boyce in M H. M^r^, Miss Raven & Mrs Cozens whent away after tea. Nick^s^ clearing fat. M^r^ & WH at home all day.

[1] *10 quarters of wheat* The weekly returns in the *Norwich Mercury* show that wheat was then selling at 70*s* to 82*s* a quarter, a marked reduction from the Norwich peak of 116*s* to 120*s* of 5 Mar. 1796. The Hardys' purchase thus cost in the region of £35 to £41

[2] *grass* At £3 3*s* 4*d* an acre this was considerably more expensive than the deal of £2 2*s* 2½*d* an acre negotiated by William at Edgefield on 22 June; hence presumably William Hardy's initial reluctance to 'agree' on 27 June

[3] *Miss Raven* Identified by Mary Hardy as Mary, daughter of her brother Nathaniel

[4] *Mrs Cozens* Described by Mary Hardy as 'of Norwich'. She may have been Sarah (d.1825), née Brown, wife of James Cozens (1770–1864), a Norwich maltster.

She is more likely to have been Mary (d. 9 July 1842 aged 75), wife of John Cozens (b. 14 Jan. 1769, bapt. Westwick 16 Feb., d. 10 July 1841). They married 1 Oct. 1793 shortly after the dissolution of his partnership with Jonathan Davey and before he had entered into partnership

right The 'Mrs Cozens' who features prominently in the diary in Mary Hardy's last years: her daughter Mary Ann, from 1805 the wife of Jeremiah Cozens, mother of William Hardy Cozens (b.1806), and stepmother to her husband's two children by his first, shortlived marriage. The artist and portrait date are unknown [*Cozens-Hardy Collection*]

left The Old Meeting, off Colegate, Norwich, a strongly Nonconformist part of the city; it was built 1693 for the Independents. John Cozens, the Norwich wholesale and retail grocer with property in Sprowston, was known as 'the Sprowston Fox' for his radicalism, which matched that of Charles James Fox.

He and his wife Mary, née Hawkins, whom we first meet on 29 June 1796, lie buried here. They are also commemorated by a very simple mural tablet on the south wall of the ground floor [*MB · 2001*]

---

with John Copeman. She was the daughter of another radical Norwich grocer Thomas Hawkins, whose shop stood at the corner of Tombland and Queen Street and who was an elder of St Mary's Baptist meeting under Joseph Kinghorn.

Mary Cozens' brother, the London sugar-factor Thomas Druery Hawkins (1774–1861), supplied John Cozens' shop in Norwich Market Place (NRO: BR 28/6, 28/7, Cozens & Copeman, bought books 1790–1811).

Mary Cozens was not only Mary Raven's future sister-in-law. James and John Cozens were the brothers of Mary Ann Hardy's future husband Jeremiah (1766–1849). See the family trees in *Diary 4*, app. D4.A, figs D4.3, D4.5

MH A very fine day. Brother & Daughtr & Mrs Cozens went away eveng 6. Mr Hardy went to look at the Hay he bought of Mr Forster foornoon, went to a [manor] Court at Saxlingham in the eveng, came home eveng past 9. W^m^ up to Holt foornoon, home aftern.

JULY 1, FRIDAY

Henry Raven W Lamb came from Stalham. Thos Baldwin to Briston with beer forenoon, ploughing and sowing turnips afternoon. Nich^s^ ploughing aftern, John Thompson harrowing & rolling in five Acres. Boyce in M H, G Thompson began to grind malt for brew. M^r^ & WH roade out forenoon, WH rode to Edgefield afternoon.

right The Old Brewery House, formerly Dial House, dating from 1700. This and the King's Arms across the market place are in the parish of Hackford, but the adjoining parishes of Reepham, Kerdiston, Whitwell and Hackford are often thought of as the one town called Reepham. This usage is sometimes adopted by Mary Hardy, but at other times she is more precise.

Bircham's brewery was a large concern in the late 18th century, with a tied estate which, like Booty's of Binham, stretched into the area covered by the Hardys.

Charlotte, daughter of the Holt surgeon Edmund Bartell, was to marry the widowed William Bircham jnr in 1807 and settled at The Ollands, also in Hackford. Like William Bircham snr's first wife Frances, Charlotte Bartell's mother was a Dacke [*MB · 2006*]

Mary Hardy A fine day. Mr Hardy & W^m^ rid to look at the Hay foornoon, came home to dinner. W^m^ rid to Edgefield aftern to look at some Hay he bought of Mr Derby, came home to tea. M^r^ & Mrs Forster & 2 young Herrings drank tea here.[1]

JULY 2, SATURDAY

HR W Lamb to Camp with beer & Stody with D^o^, Thos Baldwin to Waybourn with D^o^ & sowing turnips, Nich^s^ ploughing all day. Boyce in Malthouse & put a snit onto cherry tree,[2] G Thompson grinding Malt for brew. M^r^ & WH at Holt Afternoon, Miss H very poorly.

MH A fine day. MA very poorly with a bilious complaint. Mr Hardy & W^m^ went to Holt Mark^t^, came home Eveng 10.

JULY 3, SUNDAY

HR Famaly all at own Church forenoon, WH & H Raven at Holt afternoon. Mr Sheldrake supt here.

MH A fine day. MA very poorly. All went to our Church excep«t» MA foornoon, Mr Burrell preachd. W^m^ went to Holt Church afternoon, came home to tea. Mr Hardy went to our Church in the Eveng, I went to meeting. Mrs Smith came after tea . . .

---

[1] *two young Herrings* Presumably John Herring jnr and William Herring jnr: see entry for 15 Aug. 1796

[2] *snit* The MS is unclear. It might read 'net' (to protect the fruit from the birds). If Henry did intend 'snit' this is presumably a variant of sneck or snick, defined as an iron fastening, as on a door latch (R. Forby, *The Vocabulary of East Anglia*, vol. 2, pp. 310–11). In the Hardys' case it could be an iron staple or truss to support the cherry tree

JULY 4, MONDAY

HR Thos Baldwin, G Thompson, H Raven & Boy in brewhouse, whent haymaking aftern, Wm H Do [in brewhouse] brewing. W Lamb to Holt forenoon, haymaking Aftern. Thos Boyce in M H, Mrs Thompson & Daughter haymaking Afternon. Mr H at home all Day.[1]

JULY 5, TUESDAY

HR Thos Baldwin making hay «and» sowing turnips, W Lamb to Southrepps with beer. G Thompson & H Raven Cleanse'd `// morning, whent a hay making & Cleanse'd X beer evening. Mrs Thompson & Harriot, two Maids & Nich hay making. Mr & WH at home all Day.

MH A Showry day. Mr Hardy & Wm after the Hay but little good was done. Mr J Davy of Holt drank tea here & recon'd . . .

JULY 6, WEDNESDAY

HR Thos Baldwin to Burnham with beer, W Lamb at Holt morning, whent after hay but the weather prevented their doing any thing,[2] came home & whent to Holt with beer. Thos Boyce in garden. Mr H at home all Day, WH rode to Edgefield.

JULY 7, THURSDAY

HR Baldwin to Edgefield with beer, W Lamb to Runton with Do, Thos Boyce in garden. Mrs Thompson, Harriot, Nick & John Ram hay making afternoon, H Raven in Malthouse. Robt, Rose, Phillis, Mary Raven & Miss Rowden came from Whissonsett forenoon & Whalk'd to Holt evening.[3]

JULY 8, FRIDAY

HR Baldwin to Cromer with beer, W Lamb to Sherringham with Do, Thos Boyce in garden. Mr T, Nick, John Ram & Mrs Thompson & Harriot haymaking part of day.[4] Mr H at home all day. WH, H Raven & His Brothers & Sisters all rode to the camp & Sherringham, Mr Robt Raven & his party whent away after tea. Mrs Sheldrake, Miss Baker & Miss Mack drank tea here.

JULY 9, SATURDAY

HR W Lamb to the Camp with beer, Baldwin to Waybourn with Do & got up a lode of Vetches. Thos Boyce in garden, H Raven in Malt H [malthouse]. Mr & WH at Holt Market afternoon, Nick after jobs.

1 *Mr Hardy* His wife says he was 'after the hay' all day

2 *weather* Mary Hardy noted showery conditions every day, the worrying weather at haymaking being crowned by a thunderstorm on the night of 15–16 July when the mown grass was cocked in the fields to dry

3 *from Whissonsett* With the exception of Miss Rowden (presumably Julia Rowden, a witness at Rose Raven's wedding less than a year later) these were Henry's brothers and sisters. His brother Nathaniel was also in the party, according to Mary Hardy. The absence of Henry's remaining sibling William suggests that he had already left home.

Henry was being allowed more time off than in his early years as brewing pupil

4 *Mr T* The miller William Gunton Thompson

above **Mary Ann Hardy ('MA'), aged 11, by Huguier** [*Cozens-Hardy Collection*]

facing page Mary Proudfoot is the only recorded example in Mary Hardy's diary of a woman preacher (17 July 1796). As well as preaching at Cley on 17 July Mary Proudfoot, wife of a Wells limeburner, appears also to have led the meeting at Letheringsett the following day. It was extremely unusual for William Hardy to attend a meeting; he may have been intrigued by the prospect of a woman preacher.

Mary Proudfoot is listed in 1798 as a member of the Wells Wesleyan Methodist congregation; Hannah Proudfoot, single, mantuamaker, was also of the Wells meeting. Of the 23 Methodists at Wells that year, 13 were women; by 1799 the numbers had risen to 16 women out of 22.

'Sister Proudfoot', as John Wesley called her in 1781, had begun her mission under Mary Franklin as a Calvinistic Methodist in the 1770s. She was probably the 'young woman' of Wells whom Wesley met and much admired 30 Oct. 1781, as he recorded in his journal; she is also mentioned in his letter of 3 Apr. 1782 to Thomas Carlill as Sister Proudfoot [*Cozens-Hardy Collection*]

JULY 10, SUNDAY

HR Mrs Hardy to Cley afternoon. M^r^, Miss, WH & H Raven at own Church afternoon.

JULY 11, MONDAY

HR W Lamb to Corpusta with beer. T Baldwin, G Thompson, H Raven & Nick in brewhouse. WH D^o^ brewing, whalk'd to Holt evening. Boyce in garden. M^r^ & Mrs Bartell drank tea here, M^r^ H at Mr Forsters afternoon.

JULY 12, TUESDAY

HR G Thompson & H Raven cleanse'd `//, W Lamb to Aldborough with beer, Thos Baldwin to Hindolvestone with D^o^. G Thompson, Nick, Thos Boyce haymaking half a day, M^rs^ D^o^ [Thompson] & Harriot all Day. M^r^ H out, WH rode to Edgefield.

MH A very fine day. Mr Hardy sett of Morng 8 to Reepham to Measure Timber for Mr Bartell, slept there. Maids & Betty Milegan washd 4 Weeks Linnen. Our people after Hay . . .

JULY 13, WEDNESDAY

HR Thos Baldwin to Wells with beer. W Lamb cleaning out hay house forenoon, whent to Cley with beer & bro^t^ home 1½ Chal^d^ coles from Mr Cooks. G Thompson, wife & Daughter, Nick & Thos Boyce haymaking half a day. WH to Reepham, Mr Hardy came home Evening.

JULY 14, THURSDAY [1]

MH A drisly morning, fine day till even 7 then raind. W^m^ went to Reepham with Mr Bartell, came home even 10, Mr Hardy came home with him.

JULY 15, FRIDAY

HR W Lamb & Baldwin cleaning out hay house & laying the bottom of the Stack, Boyce in garden. G Thompson & Nick after hay afternoon, J Ram drag raking all Day. M^r^ & WH at home all day. A very havy [heavy] tempest in the night.

MH A very hot day. Mr Hardy busy after the Hay, W^m^ rid to Edgefield to look at the Hay there after tea. A terible Night of Lightning & some thunder . . .

JULY 16, SATURDAY

HR W Lamb to Sherringham with beer, Thos Baldwin after jobs forenoon. Mr Thompson, Nick & Baldwin

---

[1] This day was omitted by Henry, who seems to have muddled some of the Reepham dates

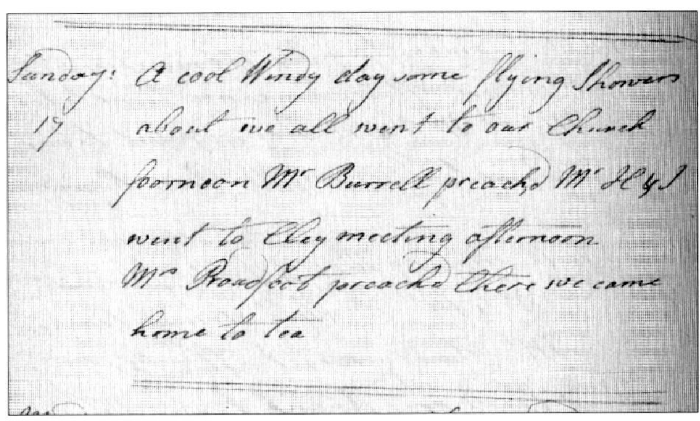
Sunday: A cool Windy day some flying Showers
17 about we all went to our Church
foornoon Mr Burrell preachd Mr H & I
went to Cley meeting afternoon.
Mrs Proudfoot preachd there we came
home to tea

got up two lodes of hay from furze close afternoon. Boyce in garden, HR grinding Malt for brew. Mr & WH at Holt aftern.

JULY 17, SUNDAY

HR Famaly all at own Church morning, Mr & Mrs H at Cley afternoon. WH at Holt afternoon, Robt Bartell drank tea here.

MH A cool Windy day, some flying Showers about. We all went to our Church foornoon, Mr Burrell preach'd. Mr H & I went to Cley meeting afternoon, Mrs Proudfoot preachd there, we came home to tea.[1]

JULY 18, MONDAY

HR W Lamb, Nick in brewhouse forenoon, G Thompson, C Lamb, Nick in field. Baldwin driving & unpitching, W Lamb helping After hay, got up eight Lode. Thos Boyce stacking, W Dobson on stack. WH brewing, H Raven in brewhouse all day. Mr H at home all Day.

MH A fine cool day. Wm Brewd. Mr Hardy busy after the Hay, got some home. Mrs Smith & Mrs Proudfoot drank tea here & held a meeting in the eveng at the Widow Winns. A Town meeting in the eveng. Norwich Assises began . . .

JULY 19, TUESDAY

HR Thos Baldwin to Morston & Holt with beer. W Lamb to Stody & Holt with Do, got up a lode of Vetches & helpt to Cleanse. G Thompson & H Raven Cleanse'd `// morning, X beer evening. Thos Boyce in garden. Mr & WH at home all day. Mrs & Mr H Goggs came afternoon, Mr G whent away Evening.

[1] *Mrs Proudfoot* Mary (d. 5 Feb. 1833 aged 90), wife of Isaac Proudfoot (d. 22 July 1809 aged 58); their headstone was by 2001 propped against the east wall of the old churchyard of the parish church of St Nicholas, Wells-next-the-Sea. Both practising Methodists, their epitaph obliquely describes them as saints:
Blessed are the dead that die in the Lord; Precious in the sight of the Lord is the death of his saints.

Isaac Proudfoot, labourer, had married Mary Vaux at Wells 2 Mar. 1778; both were single and both signed. Their daughter Elizabeth was bapt. Wells 1 Dec. 1778 and buried there 17 July 1780. Isaac is entered as a limeburner and member of the Wells meeting in 1799 (NRO: FC 18/1); in the 1806 Norfolk pollbook he is listed as a Wells labourer.

Women do not seem to have taken the oaths and declarations required of male preachers, and thus Mrs Proudfoot was not registered as a preacher; but most of the preachers recorded by Mary Hardy do not appear to have taken the oaths (NRO: C/Sch 1/1/30–32, Oaths and declarations of Dissenting preachers 1796–1822).

Wesley's view of Mary Proudfoot is quoted fully in *World*, vol. 3, chap. 3, and is summarised in N. Virgoe, *The Heavenly Road: John Wesley's journeys in Norfolk and Suffolk* (Larks Press, Guist Bottom, 2011), pp. 99–101

JULY 20, WEDNESDAY

HR Tho[s] Baldwin to Kettlestone with beer. W Lamb, G Thompson, J Ram & Nick got 4 loads of hay from furze close & after whent to Edgefield for 2 D[o] [loads]. M[r] Forster«'s» three teams bro[t] eleven lode. M[r] Forster sent two men unto stack, Boyce stacking, C Lamb all day after hay. M[r] & WH at home all Day, M[r] Elliss drank tea.

JULY 21, THURSDAY

HR W Lamb, Baldwin, G Thompson & C Lamb to Edgefield twice, bro[t] home four Lodes, M[rs] T raking after waggon. M[r] Forsters three teams Bro[t] home 18 lodes from lime kiln field,[1] M[r] F sent three men unto Stack. Boyce stacking, Joseph Bransby on stack. M[r] & M[rs] & Miss H & M[rs] Goggs drank tea at M[r] Forsters, WH at home all day. We were Obliged to prop the Stack up evening.[2]

JULY 22, FRIDAY

HR W Lamb to Salthouse & Waybourn with beer, Baldwin to the Camp with D[o]. M[r] Forster finnis [finished] bringing hay, Boyce Stacking. M[r] D[o] [Forster] sent two men unto Stack, N Woodehouse after hay. M[r] & WH at home all day.

MH A fine day excep«t» a Shower afternoon. M[r] Hardy & W[m] at home all day, finishd Stacking of Hay. A Mad Dog of M[r] Kings of Holt woried 2 of our Cats, bit Dobsons Dog, bit M Loades Child yesterday & was killd in Town.[3] We all walkd up to see the House of Industry afternoon . . .

JULY 23, SATURDAY

HR Baldwin to Overstrand with beer, W Lamb to Hinderingham & Briston with D[o]. Tho[s] Boyce trimming up Stack, G Thompson grinding Malt for brew, H Raven to Guestwick with Malt. M[r] & WH at Holt Markett Afternoon. N[s] [Nicholas] & M[r] T got the loose hay from Stack unto hay chamber.

JULY 24, SUNDAY

HR M[rs] H & M[rs] Goggs to Cley aftern. M[r] & Miss H & H Raven at own Church afternoon, WH at Holt. W Lamb loaded for Syderstone.

[1] *Lime Kiln Field* In Bayfield: see note for 16 Oct. 1793

[2] *to prop the stack up* A quick, simple way was to wedge wooden poles against the side that was listing

[3] *mad dog* As Mary Hardy was soon to record, six-year-old Ann Loades (born and privately bapt. Letheringsett 4 June 1790, publicly 20 June), the illegitimate daughter of her former washerwoman Mary Loades, died 2 Sept. 1796 after falling very ill with what was presumed to be rabies.

The diarist made a careful record of the progress of the illness in her endnotes register, and Mr Burrell made these observations under the entry for Ann's burial 4 Sept.: 'Died of hydrophobia, having been bitten six weeks before and taken 16 doses of Cutting's antidote'. See also note for 31 Aug. 1796.

Parson Woodforde had heard there were many mad dogs running about about that summer (J. Woodforde, *The Diary of a Country Parson*, ed. J. Beresford, vol. 4, p. 289, 18 June 1796). The press also occasionally reported incidents, as when an ostler at the Bear Inn at Gt Yarmouth was bitten by a mad dog and died 'raving mad' at Acle six weeks later (*Norw. Merc.* 4 June 1796)

JULY 25, MONDAY

HR W Lamb to Syderstone with beer. Thos Baldwin, G Thompson, H Raven & N^s in brewhouse, WH d^o brewing. Boyce dressing grass seeds, J Ram «and» Boy spreading dung in Phitle.[1] M^r H Goggs & Mr Cook came from Whiss^t morning, M^r & M^rs H & Mrs Goggs rode with them to Salthouse before dinner. M^r G & M^r C whent away after tea.[2]

JULY 26, TUESDAY

HR W Lamb setting lifts in furze close forenoon,[3] whent to Waybourn with beer afternoon. Thos Baldwin setting lifts forenoon, whent to Edgefield with beer & Malt Afternoon and loded for Fakenham & Syderstone, Boyce howing turnips. M^r & WH at home all Day. G Thompson & HR cleanse'd `// morning, X beer evening.

JULY 27, WEDNESDAY

HR Thos Baldwin to Fakenham & Syderstone with beer, W Lamb to Holt & Hildolvestone with d^o. Boyce howing turnips, Nich^s at work in river & whent to Bayfield with Malt, G Thompson grinding Malt for bin. M^r H at home all day. Mrs Forster drank tea here. Mr Jacobs & a stranger call'd here afternoon.[4]

JULY 28, THURSDAY

HR W Lamb to S«h»arrington with beer forenoon, to Cley for 1½ Chal^n coals from Mr Cooks. Baldwin to Holt with beer foren^n, to Cley for 1½ Chal^n Coles from Mr Cooks Afternoon. Boyce howing turnips, G Thompson grinding Malt for brew. M^r & WH at home forenoon, rode to Kelling after tea. Mr Cubitt dined here.

JULY 29, FRIDAY

HR W Lamb and Nick got up two loads of Sand forenoon. WL whent with M^r H to look at Mr Forster«'s» whole crop & loded for Southrepps Afternoon. Baldwin to Thornage with beer forenoon, after Jobs after^n. Nick whent to Hunworth with half of Milde & then whent to Cley fair, Boyce howing turnips. G Thompson to D^o [Cley] fair Afternoon.[5] WH rode to camp, after came home put the pipe up belonging to the engine.

MH A very fine day. W^m at home all day. Mr Hardy rid [rode] to Cley Fair afternoon, came home Eveng past 11 . . .

[1] *seeds* A portion would be retained after haymaking for next season's sowing on other than meadow land. Some arable was to be ploughed for grass, thus becoming 'new lay'

[2] *Mr Cook* From London, according to Mary Hardy. They went off to the seaside at Salthouse despite the rain. He and his family often visited the Hardys 1798–1808 (*Diary 4*).

William and Mary Hardy and Mary Ann were to board and lodge at the Cooks' at Shoreditch, outside the City of London, for five weeks in 1800, when it was evident that Mr Cook regularly attended meetings and did not go to Church of England services.

Like Henry Goggs he was probably a Calvinistic Methodist, Mary Hardy referring to his Holywell Mount meeting in Shoreditch (which adhered to Lady Huntingdon) (*Diary 4*: 16 May, 13 June 1800)

[3] *setting lifts* See note for 12 May 1796

[4] *Jacobs* Possibly Clement Jacob, innkeeper of the Maid's Head, Lt Walsingham since 1785, although the last delivery to the former tied house had been on 17 Oct. 1794

[5] *Cley Fair* Neither Thompson the miller nor Woodhouse the boy/labourer seems to have been fit for work the following day

JULY 30, SATURDAY

HR W Lamb to Southrepps with beer. Thos Baldwin to Cley for 1½ Chaldrons coals from Mr Cooks forenoon, after Jobs afternoon. Boyce howing turnips. Mr H at Holt Markett afternoon. Mr & Mrs Cory, Mr Erratt, Miss Gooderson & Mr C Cory came here forenoon.[1] WH whent to Holt Afternoon.

JULY 31, SUNDAY

HR Famaly at Church forenoon, Mr H poorly. WH at Holt afternoon.

MH A fine day but many shews for rain. I & MA went to our Church foornoon, Mr Burrell preachd. Wm went to Holt Church afternoon, drank tea at Mr Bartells, came home Eveng 9. I & Sister & MA went to our Church in the eveng, Mr Burrell preach'd. Mr H poorly . . .

AUGUST 1, MONDAY

Henry Raven W Lamb, G Thompson, HR & Nicks in brewhouse, WH Do brewing. Thos Baldwin to Morston with beer & got up a lode of Vetches, Boyce thaching hay stack. Mr H at home all day. Mrs H, Miss H & Mrs Goggs drank tea at Holt, WH whent to Holt Evening.

AUGUST 2, TUESDAY

HR W Lamb & Baldwin to Cley for 6 Chald coals from Mr Cooks, Boyce thaching. G Thompson & H Raven Cleansnd `// & ground Malt for bin. WH to Cromer with Mr Bartell, Mrs Bartells famaly drank tea here. Mr H at home all day. Mr Burrell was «married» this morning at Holt, pass'd through here to Fakenham.[2]

Mary Hardy A very Showry day. Mr Burrell was Married to Miss Mary Johnson of Holt, sett of for Fakenham as soon as Maried. Wm went to Cromer Morn 6, took Mrs Bartell with him in the Chaise, they went to see for a place for Edmd Bartell, they all drank tea here [3] . . .

AUGUST 3, WEDNESDAY

HR W Lamb to Stalham with beer, Thos Baldwin to Cromer with Do. Thos Boyce half a day howing turnips. G Thompson & H Raven Cleanse'd X beer morning, were obligd to take up the Cleansing pump. Mr & WH at home all Day, Miss Leakes drank tea here.

[1] *Mr Cory* Possibly Revd James (d.1864 aged 93), of Kettlestone, Rector of Shereford 1796–1864, Rector of Kettlestone 1796–1864, Curate of Lt Snoring; Revd John Crofts was his curate at Shereford 1784 (NRO: DN/VIS 31/2, Repertory of curates 1784)

[2] *Mr Burrell* See notes for 28 Nov. 1793 and 1 Jan. 1794. The witnesses were the bride's sister Deborah Judith Johnson and J. Moy, presumably Judith or John Moy of Horningtoft; no announcement appeared in the *Norwich Mercury.*

Henry's phrase 'passed through here' suggests that the villagers turned out to line the road. Mr Burrell was back in Letheringsett by 7 Aug., when Mary Hardy records him preaching in church.

The Burrells' eight children were baptised at Letheringsett, the date of the public ceremony in church being omitted here for the first four: Shambrook (b. 9 July 1797, bapt. 11 July); John William (b. and bapt. 9 Dec. 1798); Jane (b. and bapt. 28 Sept. 1800); Mary Amelia (b. and bapt. 28 Feb. 1802); Elizabeth Anna Maria (b. 1 Apr. 1804, publicly bapt. 6 May); Emma Moy (b. 27 Apr. 1806, publicly bapt. 31 Aug.); Deborah Judith (b. 28 Dec. 1808, publicly bapt. 22 Jan. 1809); and Susanna (b. 27 July 1810, publicly bapt. 26 Aug.). All eight grew to adulthood

[3] *Edmund Bartell* See note for 5 Nov. 1793. By the

AUGUST 4, THURSDAY

HR Thos Baldwin unloded a lode of coals then whent to Cley for 1½ Chald coals from Mr [ ] & then whent to Holt with beer. W Lamb came from Stalham, Boyce thaching. Nicks mern'd [?mended, ?mergined] the river bank & unloding coals &c. Mr H at home all day, WH at Holt evening. H Raven painting Afternoon.

AUGUST 5, FRIDAY

HR W Lamb to Waybourn with beer, Thos Baldwin to Sheringham with do, Boyce thaching. G Thompson grinding Malt, Nicks after Jobs. WH & H Raven painted the flappers, Mr H at home all day.[1] Miss H whalk'd to Holt evening. Mr Sales call'd here Afternoon.

MH A fine day. Sister Goggs went away Even 3. Mr Hardy, I & W & MA took a walk to the Workhouse afternoon, MA walk'd up to Holt after tea . . .

AUGUST 6, SATURDAY

HR Thos Baldwin got up 4 lode of Vetches & whent to Camp with beer.[2] W Lamb got up a lode of clay & Bricks from Holt forenoon, after jobs aftern. Boyce finnis thaching forenoon, turnip howin aftn. G Thompson grinding Malt for brew.

AUGUST 7, SUNDAY

HR Mrs H to Cley afternoon, WH at home all Day. H Raven whent to Sharrington aftern.

AUGUST 8, MONDAY

HR W Lamb to Cley for 3 Chald coals from Mr Jacksons. Thos Baldwin, G Thompson, H Raven & Boy in brewhouse, WH Do brewing. W Tinker & two men all day, Boyce part of day. Mr H at home all day.

AUGUST 9, TUESDAY

HR Thos Baldwin after Jobs all day, W Lamb after Jobs. G Thompson & H Raven Cleansed `// morning, X beer evening. Nicks harrowing turnips forenoon & after Jobs. Bunnets two trowel men & two Laborers building walls for bridge, W Tinker & two men all day after bridge in garden.[3] Mr & WH at home all day. Mr Burrells famaly & ours drank tea at work house.

MH A fine day. Mr Hardy, I, Wm & MA & Mr Burrells Family drank tea at the New Workhouse, the Workmen Supt at Mr Dobsons.

time his household furniture at Brooke was advertised (*Norw. Merc.* 6 Aug. 1796) he had already moved to Cromer.

As was William's practice when calling at towns and villages with his outlets he must have checked supplies at the Cromer Hotel: there was a beer delivery the following day

---

[1] *flappers* The timber louvres which when opened gave light and ventilation to malthouses and brewhouses. Many, such as Elgoods of Wisbech, still have them

[2] *camp* It is noticeable that the presence of the military at Weybourne was no longer the great draw it had been in 1795, the diarists recording far fewer visits to watch the field days and exercises in the summer of 1796

[3] *bridge in garden* Mr Bunnett was starting to build the brickwork for the public footbridge on its upstream frontage alongside the main Fakenham–Holt road and the ford; William Tinker was busy that day with the carpentry on the downstream, north-facing front.

Henry's record of days worked suggests either that the Hardys were paying or that a careful note had to be kept for the ratepayers. William Hardy snr or jnr may that year have held the parish office of surveyor of the highways

AUGUST 10, WEDNESDAY

HR Thos Baldwin to Corpusta with beer. W Lamb to Holt for brew cart, took it to Hunworth forenoo«n», to Holt with beer afternoon. G Thompson Stripping Meal. W Tinker & Ben all day, Jas Tinker half a day. Famaly to Sherringham to dine. Bunnets Man and Laborer all day.

MH A Showr in the Morng, very fine day. Mr Hardy, I, Wm & MA dind & drank tea at Mr Flowers of L [Lower] Sheringham.[1]

AUGUST 11, THURSDAY

HR Thos Baldwin to Salthouse with beer & Cley for 1½ Chald coals from Mr Jacksons, W Lamb to Runton with Do, G Thompson dressing flour. W Tinker & one man all day, Jas Tinker ¼ of day. Boyce howing turnips, Bunnets man & lad all day.[2] Mr & WH at home all Day, H Raven to Bodham evening on the Colt.

[1] *Flower* Samuel: see note for 18 Dec. 1793. By 1804 he was living at Sustead, where he was granted a game duty certificate (*Norw. Merc.* 29 Sept. 1804)

[2] *Bunnett's man* Henry has erased 'Bunnets two men' and amended the entry to 'Bunnet's man & lad', demonstrating that his entries had to be specific as they were used for calculating the rates of pay due; hence also the 'quarter of a day' noted. The house of industry would have been funded out of the parish poor rate, probably augmented by charitable donations by those in the diarists' circle: see note for 4 Sept. 1795

All that Brick and tiled Workhouse with a small yard attached together with a dilapidated Cottage adjoining or near And also two small pieces of land belonging thereto, and containing together, by estimation half an acre. The premises are built on waste land without the consent in writing of the Lord of the Manor under Gilberts Act. There are no Trusts affecting the same.
The Workhouse is in good repair, and in the occupation of the Matron only, the last surviving pauper died a few days ago.
The Cottage is dilapidated

right 'Mr Burrell's family and ours drank tea at workhouse' (9 Aug. 1796). The Burrells and Hardys had a celebration tea on the day the building work was finished, the Holt contractors being given supper at the King's Head, Letheringsett. By 1 May 1837, the date of the description of the premises here, the house of industry of 1796 was still 'in good repair'.

It had known only 40 years of active service as the parish workhouse, being supplanted by the Poor Law Amendment Act of 1834, implemented 1836, under which the poor of Letheringsett were sent to the workhouse at W. Beckham serving the Erpingham Union. James Hewitt of Holt is the Lord of the Manor of Letheringsett Laviles referred to here.

This MS statement was entered on the standard printed request form to the Poor Law Commissioners for consent to the sale of the redundant premises. Apart from the matron the workhouse was empty: 'the last surviving pauper died a few days ago' [*Cozens-Hardy Collection*]

left The house of industry was bought by Jeremiah Cozens, Mary Ann's husband, when it was put on the market in 1837. Their son William Hardy Cozens-Hardy (as he became in 1842) remodelled the property in the mid-century as four cottages; this view is of the south front from Workhouse Lane (later Garden Lane).

In 1943, when the future Letheringsett Hall gardener David Mayes moved here as a small child, it was still divided into four cottages. The gardens on the north side, totalling half an acre, were partly carved out of a small common named Townhouse Common: the workhouse's predecessor, the parish townhouses for the poor, had stood here.

The Hardys' maltster John Ramm spent his last years in this house of industry until his death in 1813 aged 86. Also resident in 1808 were Mary Hardy's washerwomen Elizabeth and Mary Loades—the same Mary Loades whose daughter Ann had died of rabies in 1796 (*Holt and Letheringsett Inclosure: A state of the claims* (1808)). They died in 1816 and 1824 [*MB · 2006*]

MH A very fine day. Mr Hardy at home all day. W^{m} went to Holt bowling Green after tea, I & MA walk'd to Bayfield after tea . . .

AUGUST 12, FRIDAY

HR W Lamb to Holt for waggon, after jobs forenoon, to Holt with beer Afternoon & loded for Barmer & whent of [off] evening. Baldwin very ill. Bunnets man & laborer all day, Tinker & man half a day. Boyce howing turnips. M^{r} & WH at home all day, Miss Davys drank tea here.[1]

AUGUST 13, SATURDAY

HR Baldwin to Gunthorpe with beer forenoon, after Jobs after^{n}, W Lamb came from Barmer. Bunnets man & Laborer all day, W Tinker & one man half a day. Nick after Jobs, G Thompson grinding Malt for brew. WH & H Raven to Kelling morning, famaly at Holt market after^{n}. Mr Minn dined here.

---

[1] *Miss Davys* Mary, Sarah and Susan Davy, according to Mary Hardy

[1] *Knaresborough* The market town near Scotton township, where William Hardy grew up: see note for 23 Aug. 1795. His sister Mary, wife of William Thackwray, lived at Forest Lane Head across the River Nidd from Knaresborough.
The Thackwrays' son William was shortly to arrive for a long visit (note for 26 Sept. 1796), and the unknown Mr Green may have been finalising some of the arrangements

[2] *drank tea* As Henry's reference to *Mrs* Burrell shows, this was the bridal visit, one of a series of formal calls on the new bride by her neighbours and friends

above The precious wheat (20 Aug.). The 1796 harvest was a good one, and the poor were spared the shortages of the previous winter [*MB · 2010*]

AUGUST 14, SUNDAY

HR Famaly at own church forenoon. M^rs^ H to Cley afternoon, WH & H Raven at Holt Afternoon.

MH A fine day. All went to our Church foornoon, A Communion. I & JT went to Cley meeting afternoon. A Mr Green from Knasbro [Knaresborough] in Yorkshire here a little while afternoon.[1] We all went to our Church even 6, Mr Burrell preach'd.

AUGUST 15, MONDAY

HR Thos Baldwin to Brampton with beer. W Lamb, G Thompson, H Raven in brewhouse. Nick^s^ in brewhouse forenoon, to Guestwick after^n^ with Malt, Boyce turnip howing. W Tinkers man all day, himself half a day. M^r^ H at home all day, WH brewing & at Holt Evening. Mary Loads in garden Afternoon.

MH A fine day. Mr Hardy at home all day. W^m^ went to Holt Bowling green after tea, came home eve 9. John & Wm Herring calld in the eveng.

AUGUST 16, TUESDAY

HR W Lamb to Bale & Edgefield with Malt, Thos Baldwin to Aldborough with D^o^. Gunton Thompson & H Raven cleansed `// morning, X evening. W Tinker & man all day, Boyce howing turnips. M^r^ & M^rs^ & Miss Hardy drank tea at Mrs Burrells.[2] Nick^s^ after Jobs.

MH A fine day. Maids & Eliz Milegan Wash'd 5 Weeks Linnen. We all except W^m^ drank tea at Mr Burrells, M^r^ & Mrs Sheldrake & Miss Thompson went with us . . .

AUGUST 17, WEDNESDAY

HR W Lamb to Wells with beer, Thos Baldwin to Sheringham with D^o^. W Tinker & Ben all day. G Thompson grinding Malt for brew, Thos Boyce howing turnips. M^r^ & WH at home all Day. G Thomp. took up wheat Stones.

AUGUST 18, THURSDAY

HR Thos Baldwin to Kettlestone with beer, W Lamb to Stody & Briston with d^o^. G Thompson dressing Wheat stone, H Raven grinding Malt for brew and bin. Boyce howing turnips, Nick^s^ at work in river afternoon. M^r^ & WH at home all day.

MH A fine day. Mr Hardy at home all day. W^m^ went to Holt Bowling Green after tea, came home even 9.

AUGUST 19, FRIDAY

HR W Lamb to Syderstone with beer. Baldwin to Blakeny [Blakeney] for oake for Barrels forenoon, to Cley for 1½ Chal^{d} coals from Mr Jacksons after^{n}. G Thompson & H Raven dressing Malt stones, Boyce in garden, Nick^{s} after Jobs. M^{r}, M^{rs}, Miss & W Hardy drank tea at Dobsons.

MH A fine day. Mr Hardy & W^{m} at home. We all drank tea at Wm Dobsons, expected to meet aparty there, nobody there but Mrs Forster, she Supt here . . .

AUGUST 20, SATURDAY

HR W Lamb & Nick^{s} reaping all day.[1] Thos Baldwin reaping forenoon, to Camp with beer after^{n}. Boyce in garden, W Dobson cutting Peas. G Thompson & HR dressing Malt stones. M^{r} & WH at Holt markett, Miss H at Holt after tea. W Tinker & man ¼ days work.

AUGUST 21, SUNDAY

HR M^{rs} H to Cley afternoon. M^{r}, Miss & WH at own Church, HR to Holt.

MH A Hot day. I & J Thompson went to Cley meeting afternoon, Mr Hill began preaching there. Mr Hardy, MA & W^{m} went to our Church afternoon, Mr Burrell preachd . . .

AUGUST 22, MONDAY

HR Thos Baldwin, G Thompson, H Raven & Nick^{s} in brewhouse. W Lamb to Thursford & Holt twice with beer.[2] Boyce & J Ram reaping all day. M^{r} & H [Mr Hardy] home all day, Mr Balls spent the day.[3] WH brewing.

AUGUST 23, TUESDAY

HR Thos Baldwin to Cromer with beer, W Lamb to Fakenham with D^{o}. Thos Boyce & J Ram reaping, G Thompson & H Raven cleanse«d» `// & XX beer. Nick^{s} cutting Peas half a day. M^{r} & WH at home all day.

AUGUST 24, WEDNESDAY

HR Thos Baldwin to Overstrand with beer, W Lamb to Wiverton with D^{o} & Cley for 1½ Cha. coals from Mr Jacksons & pea cutting afternoon. Boyce & J Ram reaping, Nick^{s} cutting Peas. Mr Hardy dined at Holt. M^{rs}, Miss & WH drank tea «at Mr» Bartells. G Thompson laid down Malt stones.

[1] *reaping* Cutting wheat with a sickle; barley was mown with a scythe. The balance of the Hardys' harvest crops was different that year, much more emphasis being placed on wheat—presumably owing to the famine of 1795—and on peas. Harvesting the barley did not begin until 7 Sept.

A bumper harvest for Norfolk had been forecast in midsummer: 'There never was a year in which Plenty reared her fair front . . . than the present', with the promise of an abundance of grass, grains and potatoes, all of which were by early July 'in great forwardness'. Unlike many of the *Mercury*'s harvest prognostications of earlier years this optimism proved justified, prices dropping markedly. By 15 Oct. 1796 wheat stood at 50*s* to 54*s* a quarter at Norwich and Gt Yarmouth, barley 20*s* to 28*s*, and oats 14*s* to 22*s*; malt was 24*s* per coomb (*Norw. Merc.* 2 July, 15 Oct. 1796)

[2] *Thursford* The first time the Hardys had delivered to the Crawfish/Lion. William Girling had been innkeeper since the early 1790s, his predecessor John Griggs last being listed in the alehouse register for 1790 (NRO: C/Sch 1/16). Girling is shown at the Crawfish in 1792 and 1794, and at the Lion 1795–99

[3] *Balls* Mary Hardy notes him as 'young Mr Balls'. This was Thomas Balls jnr, son of the Saxlingham

farmer of the same name. His father had rented their farm 24 Oct. 1791 from Mrs Elizabeth Jodrell on a 10-year lease beginning at Old Michaelmas 1791. The annual rent was £174 for the first year and £182 for the remaining years; also included in the lease was some land at Foulsham—probably a grazing ground (NRO: WHT 3/2/3/1).

Mr Balls snr died suddenly on the night of 21–22 July 1802 (*Diary 4*: 22 July). His son Thomas married at Wells 10 May 1798 Margaret Woodrow of Wells (*Norw. Merc.* 12 May 1798) and continued farming at Saxlingham. The daughter of Henry and Susanna Woodrow, she was bapt. Wells 23 Aug. 1766 and bur. Holt 20 Mar. 1827

AUGUST 25, THURSDAY

HR W Lamb & Thos Baldwin & Nicks cutting peas all day, Boyce & J Ram reaping. Mr & Mrs Wymer, Mr, Mrs & Miss Bartell dined & drank tea here.[1] Mr & WH at home all day.

AUGUST 26, FRIDAY

HR W Lamb, Thos Baldwin, G Thompson & Nick cutting peas, Boyce & J Ram reaping all day. Mr & WH at home all day. H Raven grinding Malt for brew.

AUGUST 27, SATURDAY

HR Thos Baldwin, G Thompson cutting peas, Boyce cutting hase & at work in garden.[2] Nick cutting peas forenoon, in garden afternoon. H Raven grinding Malt for brew, W Lamb to Burnham with beer. WH at Holt after tea, Mr H at home all day.

Sept 2 : Ann Loades between 6 & 7 Years of Age
was bitten by a Mad Dog in the forehead
on the 23 of July she had Antidotes given
her by a person near South Walsham the
Child continued well till Monday the 29 of Augt
near Six Weeks when she was taken with
Sickness in her Stomach & pain in her head
on the Tuesday the 30 she grew worse a
fever with pain in her head & Stomach with
a total loss of Appetite & Sleep on the Wednesday
31 she was in a high Fever & had a violent
Fitt on Thursday Sept 1 she seemed to be better
not so much Fever as yesterday but no
appetite nor any moore Sleep then yesterday
but on the Morng of Friday 2 Septr she
was taken with a Violent Fitt which lasted
near 2 hours the fever ran very high her
Eyes were fixt & seemingly without Sight
another Fitt came on abt 1 oClock but
not so violent as before & a short time
after she died seemingly easy & without
much pain

[1] *Mr and Mrs Wymer* From Norwich; they had been at the Bartells' the previous day. See also note for 10 May 1795

[2] *hase* Both William Marshall and Robert Forby define a *hay* as a clipped hedge. Forby adds it was 'more particularly a clipped quickset [hawthorn] hedge' and explains that it was commonly pronounced as though it were the plural noun *haze*. *To haze* was to expose to dry, such as by hanging linen on a hedge (W. Marshall, *The Rural Economy of Norfolk*, vol. 2, p. 381; R. Forby, *The Vocabulary of East Anglia*, vol. 2, pp. 153, 154)

AUGUST 28, SUNDAY

HR Famaly at own church forenoon, M^rs^ H to Cley afternoon. H Raven whent to Whiss^t^ morning, return'd evening.

AUGUST 29, MONDAY

HR Thos Baldwin to Sharringham [Sheringham] with beer, W Lamb to Hinderingham with d^o^ & got up a loade of Clay. G Thompson setting of shieves after^n^, Nick^s^ after Jobs.[1] M^r^ H out with Mr Smith. HR carried the pipe to Holt twice.[2] M^rs^ & Miss H drank tea at Holt.

MH A Showry foornoon, fine afternoon. Mr Smith from Cley Breakfastd here, he & Mr Hardy went to Thursford in our Chaise Morng, came home even 6.[3]

AUGUST 30, TUESDAY

HR Thos Baldwin to Waybourn with beer & at work in barn. W Lam«b», G Thompson, H Raven & Nick^s^ in brewhouse, WH D^o^ brewing. Mr Hardy at home all day. Jno Rams boy came to work here.[4]

MH A Wet day. Mr Hardy at home all day, Wm Brew'd. Ann Loades taken Ill, suppos'd to be the effects of a bite of a Mad Dog.[5]

AUGUST 31, WEDNESDAY

HR W Lamb to Corpusta with beer, Thos Baldwin at work in barn & turning Peas, Nick after jobs. G Thompson & H Raven cleansed `// morning, X beer evening. M^r^ & WH at home all day. Mr Love came with a mare to sell.

facing page Mary Hardy's eyewitness account of Ann Loades' death aged six from hydrophobia, in the register at the end of her MS diary ledger. A press report on the case implied that the owner of the rabid dog had sought a treatment which, it was hoped, would save the little girl: 'Died, on Friday se'ennight, at Letheringsett, of canine madness, Ann Loads, a child of six years old. The hydrophobia attacked her on the Wednesday preceding, in consequence of a wound she received from a dog about six weeks before in the forehead, although she had taken 16 doses of an antidote prepared by Mr Cutting, of Ranworth, near South Walsham, and every other endeavour that humanity could dictate had been exerted by Mr King, the owner of the dog, to preserve the child from this most dreadful malady' (*Norwich Mercury*, 10 Sept. 1796) [*Cozens-Hardy Collection*]

[1] *setting of sheaves* To dry: it had rained that morning and the previous day, and corn could not be stacked or stored while damp

[2] *carried the pipe* Either carried a wine cask or, more probably, carried a piece of plumbing for one of the pumps

[3] *Thursford* William Hardy may have taken his attorney to arrange the repayments for the £60 bond of the innkeeper William Girling. The brewer's tie took the form of this bond, Girling repaying the Hardys at £3 a year (see the accounts 1798–1804 in *Diary 4*, app. D4.B). The house, named the Crawfish but sometimes the Lion (note for 22 Aug. 1796), stood further south-west along the main Fakenham road from the location of the later Crawfish

[4] *John Ramm's boy* His youngest child, according to the Letheringsett register, was his daughter Blythe, bapt. 13 Sept. 1776. A later son may have been missed out in the register, or this may have been a grandson whom he and his wife Abigail were rearing

[5] *Ann Loades* See note for 22 July 1796. The diarist took a great interest in the course of the illness; once the symptoms had developed it carried off Ann Loades in three and a half days. The text of Mary Hardy's account of the illness, entered in her register, is transcribed in the endnotes

MH A Wet day. Mr Hardy & Wm at home all day. I & MA & Wm went to see the Child Loades, found her very bad.

SEPTEMBER 1, THURSDAY

Henry Raven W Lamb to Runton with beer, Nicks to Thursford for a sow and pigs, G Thompson dressing flour. Mr Love came morning to dock the colt & exchange'd a mare with Mr H for Lamb«'s» old Horse.[1] Baldwin ill with tooth ache. WH at Holt after tea.

Mary Hardy A Showry Morng, fine afternoon. Mr Hardy, I & MA went to see the Child Loades foornoon, found her better.

SEPTEMBER 2, FRIDAY

HR W Lamb, Thos Baldwin & W Dobson turning peas «and» setting of the Wheat forenoon, got up two loads of wheat & whent a reaping afternoon. G Thompson & Nick after peas & Reaping. Mr & WH at home all day. Mr & Mrs Forster & Mrs Herring & Mrs Sales drank tea here.

MH A fine day. Heard in the Morng the Child Loades was very bad. I & MA went to se the Child Loades abt Noon, found her very bad, she died soon after 1 oClock. Mr Hardy & Wm at home all day. Mrs Leales [Sales] & Miss Wall,[2] Mr & Mrs Forster, Mrs Herring & Mrs John Herring from Norwich drank tea here [3] . . .

SEPTEMBER 3, SATURDAY

HR W Lamb & G Thompson reaping all day, Thos Baldwin to the Camp with beer & got up two loads of Wheat, Nick helping Baldwin with wheat.[4] Mr H at home all day, WH at Holt afternoon. H Raven grinding Malt for brew.

SEPTEMBER 4, SUNDAY

HR Mrs H to Cley Afternoon. Mr, Miss & WH at own church aftern, HR at Holt.

MH A fine day. I & JT went to Cley meeting afternoon. Mr Hardy, Wm & MA went to our Church afternoon, Mr Burrell preachd. The Child Loades was Burried . . .

SEPTEMBER 5, MONDAY

HR W Lamb to Briston with beer & whent after peas, Thos Baldwin to Salthouse with beer & after Do [peas].

---

1 *dock* A surgical operation to remove the tail, an insensitive procedure banned in the UK by Act of Parliament in 1949 as it was painful for the animals and meant they could no longer swish flies away

2 *Miss Wall* Possibly the sister of John Claxton Savory's brother-in-law; the Savorys were about to take over the tenancy of Bayfield Hall from the Forsters (see notes for 6 Oct. and 13 Nov. 1796)

3 *Mrs Herring* Possibly the mother of John Herring, Mayor of Norwich 1799; she died 19 Feb. 1803 aged 78 (*Norw. Merc.* 26 Feb. 1803). If so, the 'Mrs John Herring' with her was presumably her daughter-in-law Rebecca (d.1827).

The visitors could alternatively have been the former Mayor's wife with *her* daughter-in-law, the wife of John Herring jnr

4 *helping with wheat* As in 1794 and 1795 the Hardys did not hire outside labourers, 'the harvestmen' of the summers of the 1770s and 1780s, to get in the harvest.

Instead they turned to one or two outsiders to help, such as the innkeeper of the King's Head, William Dobson (2 Sept.)

G Thompson pitching peas, Nick^s & Eli^t Chastney in the Barn, Boy riding horse.[1] HR in brewhouse, M^r & WH at home all day.

SEPTEMBER 6, TUESDAY

HR W Lamb, G Thompson & Thos Baldwin finnis reaping wheat & got up two loads of peas. Nick^s reaping forenoon, H Raven in brewhouse. M^r & WH at home all day. Boy keeping piggs.

SEPTEMBER 7, WEDNESDAY

HR W Lamb to Stody with beer foren^n, mowing after^n. Thos Baldwin, G Thompson, H Raven & Nick^s in brewhouse, WH d^o Brewing. M^r H at home all day.

SEPTEMBER 8, THURSDAY

HR W Lamb, Thos Baldwin & Nich^s got up the remainder of peas & wheat forenoon, whent amowing after^n. G Thompson & H Raven cleansed `// & X beer. M^r H at home all day, WH out all day. HR rode to Dawling with Hammonds bill.

MH A Very fine day. Mr Hardy at home all day. W^m went to Hildonveston, Briston, Corpusty & Saxthorp gathering of Money, came home eveng past 8.[2]

SEPTEMBER 9, FRIDAY

HR W Lamb & Thos Baldwin mowing all day, Nich^s after Jobs & turning up muck. M^r H at home all day, WH out all day. G Thompson in brewhouse.

MH A very fine Harvest day. Mr Hardy at home all day, W^m went Morng 10 to the Camp. The Camp broke up this Morn, they were order'd to Woodbridge in Suffolk. W^m dind at Mr Flowers at Sheringham, went to Lower Sheringham afternoon, came home eveng 9.

SEPTEMBER 10, SATURDAY

HR W Lamb mowing morning, in morning [? afternoon] to Holt & Cley with beer, Baldwin D^o [mowing] & whent to Morston with d^o [beer]. Nick^s after Jobs & turning up muck. M^r & M^rs & Miss Hardy whent out in Crafers chaise, WH out on horse back. Ed^m Balls call^d morning, Mr Walden & Mr Silance call'd morning.[3] Mr Howards Son came and orderd the cart, bro^t £30.[4] H Raven at home all day.

MH A very fine day. Mr Hardy, I & MA sett of Morn 7 for Albro [Aldborough] in Crafers Post Chaise {Morng

[1] *Elizabeth Chasteney* There are numerous Chasteneys in the Letheringsett registers. The Hardys' harvest labourer could have been Elizabeth, second wife of William Chasteney, whose daughter Ann was bapt. 9 Dec. 1781; or Elizabeth, née Sexton, who married Hammond Chasteney 6 Nov. 1794.

She may have been the Elizabeth Chasteney, presumably unmarried, who was hired as the Hardys' cook 11 May 1797 after the sudden dismissal of Hannah Dagliss. She stayed until 10 Oct. 1797

[2] *gathering of money* Hindolveston, Briston and Corpusty had Hardy public houses, but William did not supply beer to the Castle, the only public house at Saxthorpe in 1796. It is likely that he was calling at Hase's Saxthorpe foundry to settle his account for plumbing work at the brewery

[3] *Mr Walden and Mr Silence* John Walden was about to hand over the Fighting Cocks at Wells to William Silence, who was to stay as innkeeper until at least Michaelmas 1804, paying rent to the Hardys of £13 a year (*Diary 4*, app. D4.B)

[4] *ordered the cart* John Howard's son requested a beer delivery to Burnham Market. The request was not met until 15 Sept.

7}, got to Albro Morn half past 8, staid there till near 10, got to Southreps ab^t 10, staid there till half past 1 then went to Cromer to Dinner, met M^r & Mrs Smith, M^r & Mrs Jaxson [Jackson] & Miss Jarvis from Cley. W^m went by Runton & Beckhithe & met us at Cromer, we got home alittle after 8.

SEPTEMBER 11, SUNDAY

HR Famaly all at own Church forenoon, H Raven rode to Thursford forenoon. WH at Holt afternoon.

MH A Wet Morng, fine afternoon. I was taken very poorly with dimness in my Eyes forenoon, was very Ill all day, could not go out all day. Mr Hardy & W^m went to our Church foornoon, M^r H went to our Church in the eveng. M^r H let the Fighting Cocks at Wells to a Mr Silence.

SEPTEMBER 12, MONDAY

HR W Lamb to Bale & Thursford with beer & loded for Syderstone, Thos Baldwin to Edgefield with D^o & got up a lode [load] of Barley. G Thompson, Nich^s got up the barley out of field & a lode out of furze close. M^r H out, WH to Whissonsett. H Raven to Edgefield morning.

MH A very fine day. Mr Hardy & J Thompson sett of in the Chaise for Wells & Siderstone & Slept at Mr Temples at Barmer. W^m sett of for Gunthorp «and» Fakenham Mor«ning» 9 & Slept at Whisonsett. I better than Yesterday.

SEPTEMBER 13, TUESDAY

HR W Lamb to Syderstone with beer, Thos Baldwin to Aldborough with D^o. Nick & G Thomp. got up a lode of barley, HR grinding Malt for brew. M^r & WH came from Rudham.

MH A fine day. I was very poorly. The 2 Miss Leakes drank tea here. Mr Hardy & W^m met at Mr Howards at Rudham, paid of [off] the Mortgage on the Brewing Office £1000, dind [dined] there & came home Eveng past 6 [1] . . .

SEPTEMBER 14, WEDNESDAY

HR W Lamb, Thos Baldwin, Nick in brewhouse morning, the«n» whent after barly. G Thompson, HR in brewhouse, WH d^o brewing. M^r H at home all day.

[1] *mortgage* Both William Hardy 5 Apr. 1781 and his brewing predecessor Henry Hagon in 1779 had mortgaged their house named Rawlings, the maltings and brewery to John Davy, Esq., of Mileham, William Hardy transferring the mortgage on 24 Feb. 1783 to the farmer Thomas Howard, Gent., of W. Rudham; Hagon had had an earlier mortgage from 1758 with the Senkler family of Barwick. Hagon's first mortgage was paid off in 1774; his second, of 1779, was discharged when his executors paid off his debts in 1781 (Cozens-Hardy Collection: Letheringsett Laviles manor court book, pp. 88, 93, 99, 108, 110, 113–14, 122–3).

Thomas Howard [snr] died in 1787 aged 73. The £1000 loan arranged with William Hardy was taken on by Thomas Howard jnr in 1787. The Letheringsett Laviles court book does not record the out-of-court transfers, nor the final paying off of the mortgage; no manor court sat between 6 Nov. 1795 and 8 Dec. 1806. A cursory note in the margin of the court record of 6 Apr. 1781 (p. 114, illustrated) refers merely to the discharge of the debt to John Davy, as noted at the next court held on 16 Jan. 1787.

The manor court book of Thornage with the Members is more helpful, recording the out-of-court agreement of 13 Sept 1796 in which William Hardy snr is shown as a beer and porter brewer: 'Thomas Howard [the son]

SEPTEMBER 15, THURSDAY

HR W Lamb to Wells with beer, Thos Baldwin to Burnham with Do. G Thompson & HR Cleansed `//, Nick & Wm Dobson cleaning out the Bath.[1] Mr & WH at home all day.

MH I [A] very fine day. Mr Hardy & Nick & Wm Dobson cleard the Bath. Wm went to Holt afternoon, drank tea at Mr Bakers, came home even 8.

SEPTEMBER 16, FRIDAY

HR W Lamb to Holt twice forenoon, whent drag raking & got the rakings up. Baldwin to Thornage with beer & after rakings, finnis harvest. Mr & Mrs, Miss & WH to Cromer. G Thompson & H Raven Cleansed X beer.

by a writing under his hand dated the 13th September 1796' submitted at a court held 25 Oct. 1798 that the £1000-mortgage was discharged (NRO: MS 19829, Z 2D, Thornage with the Members 1763–86, p. 169).

William Hardy jnr took over an unencumbered property from his father in 1797

[1] *bath* Mary Hardy had last bathed in 1788 in the open-air brick-lined bath dug in the garden in 1785. She may have considered that her recent ill-heath could be cured by taking up outdoor bathing once more

below From the Letheringsett Laviles manor court book (p. 114): part of the record of the court of 6 Apr. 1781 minuting William Hardy's £1000-mortgage taken out with John Davy of Mileham. It was finally paid off in 1796 [*Cozens-Hardy Collection*]

by the rod, All and every the Messuages Lands Tenements
and Hereditaments whatsoever of him the said William Hardy
holden of the said Manor by Copy of Court Roll with the appurtenances, And the reversion and reversions remainder and
remainders thereof And all the Estate and Interest of him the
said William Hardy of in or to the same premises To the
Use and Behoof of John Davy of Mileham in the County
of Norfolk Esquire his Heirs and Assigns for ever Upon
Condition that if he the said William Hardy his Heirs
Executors Administrators or Assigns do and shall well and tr-
truly pay or cause to be paid unto the said John Davy his
Executors Administrators or Assigns the Sum of One thousand
pounds with lawful Interest for the same of lawful money of
Great Britain upon the fifth Day of June now next ensuing
without any fraud deduction or abatement whatsoever according
to and in full discharge of the proviso or Condition contained
in a certain Indenture of Mortgage by Demise and in or
Appointment bearing Date on the fifth Day of this present
Month of April and made between the said William Hardy
of the one part and the said John Davy of the other part

Discharged 16: Jan: 1787

above **On their visit to Edmund Bartell jnr in his new home at Cromer on 16 Sept. the Hardys walked to the lighthouse. This was the town's first, built on the East Cliffs in 1719 and lit by 15 oil lamps. The Hardys' host depicted the scene in the frontispiece to his book [*Cromer considered as a Watering Place* (*enlarged 2nd edn 1806*), *detail*]**

MH A very fine hot day. I began to Bathe. Mr Hardy & I, W^m^ & MA went to Cromer foornoon, dind & drank tea at Mr Edmd Bartells. I, W^m^ & MA walkd to the Light House afternoon. Came home eveng 9. Finishd Harvest.

SEPTEMBER 17, SATURDAY

HR W Lamb & Thos Baldwin cleard the fat [vat] then whent after larges«s» & had frolic in evening. Nich^s^ after Jobs forenoon. M^r^ H at Holt all day, WH at Holt afternoon. G Thompson in brewhouse.

MH A very hot day. Mr Hardy went to Holt foornoon to Justice Sitting for Licences, dind with the Justices, drank tea at Mr Bartells, came home Eveng 8. Our Men had their Harvest frollick at Dobsons.

SEPTEMBER 18, SUNDAY

HR M^rs^ H to Cley forenoon. M^r^ & M^rs^ & Miss H at own church afternoon, WH & HR to Holt afternoon.

MH A very hot day. I & J Thompson went to Cley meeting Morng 8, Mr Hill preach^d^ there. We all except W^m^ went to our Church Afternoon, Mr Burrell preachd. W^m^ went to Holt Church afternoon & came home to tea. A Wet Night.

SEPTEMBER 19, MONDAY

HR W Lamb to Syderstone & Barmer with beer. Thos Baldwin to Briston forenoon, stopping gaps afternoon. Nich^s^ after jobs foren^n^, turning up muck D^o^ [afternoon]. M^r^ H at home all day, WH & H Raven drove the Colt in cart. G Thompson in brewhouse.

MH A Wet Morng, close dry afternoon. Maids began to Wash 5 Weeks Linnen.[1] Mr Hardy «and» W^m^ try'd the Leader, the Colt, in the little Cart [2] . . .

SEPTEMBER 20, TUESDAY

HR W Lamb & Thos Baldwin car^d^ of [carried off] the beer morning & then whent a harrowing forenoon, after Jobs afternoon. Nich^s^ turning up muck forenoon, at work in Bath aftern. Thos Boyce at work in bath afternoon, Gunton Thompson & H Raven grinding malt for brew. M^r^ & WH at home all day.

SEPTEMBER 21, WEDNESDAY

HR W Lamb to Runton with beer, Thos Baldwin to Kettlestone with do. Nich^s^ after Jobs, G Thompson & H Raven

---

[1] *began to wash* Laundering was spread over two days. Elizabeth Milligen arrived the following day to help the maids with the main bulk of the heavy washing

[2] *the Leader* The colt's name. The accounts show that a year later William Hardy valued Leader at £25, the most expensive of his four riding horses.

Minor was worth £20, a mare lent to Mrs Ann Raven at Whissonsett Hall £15, and Jack £12. On his retirement William Hardy

in brewhouse. Mr H at home all day, W Hardy to Sheringham.

MH A Wet Morng, fine afternoon. Mr Hardy at home all day. Wm went to Bodham foornoon & from thence to Sheringham, dind at Mr Flowers, bought 6 little Piggs at 25*s* each, came home eveng 9 [1] . . .

SEPTEMBER 22, THURSDAY

HR W Lamb to Southrepps with beer, Thos Baldwin in brewhouse morning then whent with Wm Dobson to Mr Flowers, Sherringham, for six piggs. G Thompn, H Raven & Nichs in brewhouse, WH Do brewing. Mr H at home all day. HR put the Leader colt into Chaise.

SEPTEMBER 23, FRIDAY

HR W Lamb to Hindolvestone with beer, Thos Baldwin to Sherringham with Do. G Thompson & H Raven cleansed `//, Nichs after Jobs. Mr H at home all day. WH to Mr Balls, Saxlingham, to tea.

SEPTEMBER 24, SATURDAY

HR W Lamb to Sharrington & Corpusta with beer, Thos Baldwin to Fakenham with Do. Mr & WH at Holt afternoon. G Thompson & HR cleansed X beer.

SEPTEMBER 25, SUNDAY

HR Thos Baldwin loded for Brampton. Mr & Mrs & Miss Hardy at own Church afternoon, WH & HR at Holt.

MH A Very windy dry day. No service at our Church, Mr Burrell being at Norwich, no Meeting at Cley. Wm & H Raven went to Holt Church afternoon, came home to tea. A Wet Night.

SEPTEMBER 26, MONDAY

HR Thos Baldwin to Brampton with beer, W Lamb to Edgefield & Holt with Do. Nichs in brewhouse, Boyce in garden, G Thompson dressing flour. Mr & WH at home all day. Mr Wm T [ ] came evening.[2]

MH A very Wet day. Mr Hardy & Wm at home all day. Wm Thackery from Forrest Lane Head came eveng 6. I Bathd.[3]

SEPTEMBER 27, TUESDAY

HR W Lamb to Overstrand with beer, Thos Baldwin after Jobs & loded for Norwich. G Thompson & HR grinding Malt for brew, Boyce in garden. Wm Holman howing turnips, Nichs after Jobs. Mr, WH & Mr Thack—

retained Leader and Jack as his personal property (tabulated in *World*, vol. 2, chap. 2)

---

1 *six little pigs* Inflation was marked. In Jan. 1775 the Hardys had sold a sow and six piglets for £1 11*s* 6*d*. 21 years later the piglets alone, without their mother, cost £7 10*s* 0*d*. Fetching them took two men most of the working day

2 *William T.* Not William Hardy's brother-in-law William Thackwray, but his young nephew of the same name; Mary Hardy and sometimes Henry Raven do not accord their guest the prefix 'Mr'. He stayed until 1 Jan. 1797, when he set off on his return voyage to Hull.

William Hardy's sister Mary (bapt. Farnham, W. Riding, 27 Jan. 1738 and bur. there 20 May 1799) married William Thackwray at Knaresborough 17 Oct. 1775. Land tax assessments for Bilton with High Harrogate show that the couple settled in a very modest rented property just across the River Nidd at Forest Lane Head in Bilton, outside Harrogate (W. Yorks Archive Service, QE 13/5/6).

Their son William, apparently their only child, was baptised at Knaresborough on 21 July 1779, his parents' place of residence being given as Bilton with Harrogate

3 *I bathed* The diarist also bathed on 22, 23 and 28 Sept.

above Moonlight, a 12-year-old grey mare, one of the Shire horses ploughing at the Tunstead Trosh of 2001.

In the 1797 accounts the Hardys' eight cart horses were valued, with harness, at £8 each. They delivered the beer and toiled in the fields [*MB · 2001*]

whent to Sherringham afternoon & spent the evening at Bayfield, M^rs^ & Miss H drank tea at Bayfield.

MH A fine day. Mr Hardy & W^m^ & Wm Thackery rid to Sheringham afternoon to speak to Johnson, he got out of the way.[1] I & MA walkd to Mr Forsters, Bayfield, they came to us, we drank tea & Supt there, came home eveng 11 . . .

SEPTEMBER 28, WEDNESDAY

HR W Lamb, G Thompson, H Raven & Nich^s^ in brewhouse, WH D^o^ [in brewhouse] Brewing. Thos Baldwin to Norwich with beer, W Holman howing turnips, Boyce in garden. M^r^ H at home all day. M^r^ & Mrs Baker drank tea here, M^r^ & Mrs Forster & the Miss Richards drank tea here.[2]

SEPTEMBER 29, THURSDAY

HR W Lamb to Gunthorpe with beer, Thos Baldwin came from Norwich. G Thompson & H Raven Cleansed `// & X beer, Nich^s^ after Jobs. M^r^ & M^rs^ H at home all day, Miss Leaks drank tea here. WH & HR whent to Holt ball.

MH A dry day. Mr Hardy at home all day. W^m^ & H Raven went to the Childrens Ball, came home Morng 2. A [Ann] Leake Supt here.

SEPTEMBER 30, FRIDAY

HR W Lamb to Cromer with beer. Thos Baldwin ploughing & whent to Holt with beer, Nich^s^ ploughing all day. M^r^ H at home all day. Wm Holman mowing grass, Boyce in garden.

MH A fine day. W^m^ went to L [Lower] Sherringham Morng 7 with Mr Moore, heard Johnson had left the Premises & had given a Judgment to Mr Cubit which was put in Execution, came home Eveng 6. Mr Hardy at home all day. M^r^ & M^rs^ & M Sheldrake & Mr Davy drank tea here. I Bathd.

OCTOBER 1, SATURDAY

Henry Raven W Lamb & Thos Baldwin ploughing in 6 Acres, Boyce in garden. Nich^s^ after Jobs, G Thompson in brewhouse. WH to Sheringham, W Holman mowing grass. M^r^ H & W Thack[ ] to Sheringham, M^rs^ & Miss H at Holt afternoon.

[1] *got out of the way* Evaded them. Robert Johnson had borrowed money from Mr Cubitt on the security of the Crown (30 Sept. 1796); William Hardy had leased the premises to Johnson (16 Mar. 1795)

[2] *Miss Richards* Strictly the Misses Richards: Mary Hardy notes that Mrs Richards and her two daughters came

Mary Hardy A fine day. Mr Hardy & W^m^ went to Sheringham foornoon to speak to Johnson, he was not to be found, they dind at Mr Flowers at upper Sheringham then came to Holt Mark^t^, came home eveng 9. I & MA walkd up to Holt Sessions afternoon, drank tea at Mr Davys, came home eveng 7.[1]

OCTOBER 2, SUNDAY

HR M^rs^ H to Cley forenoon. Famaly at own church afternoon, HR at Holt.

MH A very fine day. I & J Thompson went to Cley foornoon. I, MA & W^m^ & Wm Thackray went to our Church afternoon, Mr Burrell preachd. Mr Hardy rid to Cley expecting to meet Johnson of Sheringham but did not, came home past 6 . . .

OCTOBER 3, MONDAY

HR Thos Baldwin ploughing forenoon, to Holt & loaded for Stalham afternoon. W Lamb Harrowing D^o^ [forenoon], to Wiverton with beer & Blakney for 1½ Chal^n^ coles for G Thompson. W Holman mowing grass, Boyce in garden. Nich^s^ haymaking afternoon with M^rs^ D^o^ [Mrs Boyce].[2] M^r^ H at home all day.

OCTOBER 4, TUESDAY

HR W Lamb to Aldborough with beer, Thos Baldwin to Sherringham & Waybourn with D^o^. Boyce & Holman mowing grass. Nich^s^ after Jobs forenoon, haymaking after^n^. G Thompson & HR grinding Malt for brew. M^r^ H at home all day, WH & W Thackwray at Holt afternoon.

OCTOBER 5, WEDNESDAY

HR W Lamb in brewhouse forenoon, to Stody afternoon with beer. Nich^s^ in D^o^ [brewhouse] forenoon, got up a load of Hay after^n^. G Thompson & H Raven in brewhouse, WH D^o^ brewing. Baldwin to Stalham, W Holman tasking, Boyce in garden. Bunnets man & Laborer, W Tinker & man all day. M^r^ H at home all day, M^r^ & Miss Bartell & Miss Dowson drank tea here.

OCTOBER 6, THURSDAY

HR W Lamb to Brampton with beer, Thos Baldwin ploughing. Boyce in garden, Holman tasking. Wm Tinker at work all day, Bunnets man & Laborer all day. G Thompson & HR cleansed `//. M^r^ H at Bayfield sale, WH rode to Cley.

[1] *Holt Sessions* The Michaelmas petty sessions for hiring servants

[2] *Mrs Boyce* See notes for 18 Feb. and 6 Sept. 1794. Sarah Boyce, daughter of Hammond and Ann Jeckell, had given birth to her fifth child, John, on 26 May 1796; her next, Thomas, was born 23 Oct. 1798.

Mrs Boyce's hours in the field on 3 and 7 Oct. 1796 would have been approx. 1–7 pm, when she was still feeding John herself. As both were fine days the four-month-old could well have accompanied her into the hayfield, unless she left him with a friend who then brought him over for a feed during the afternoon.

Except for Eliza, for whom the rector noted only the public baptism in the register, all seven children born to the Boyces following their marriage were privately and publicly baptised. The parents elected for a public ceremony *en masse* on 6 Feb. 1803 for four of them.

The dates of birth and private baptism are given here: Maria, b. 27 Jan. 1794, bapt. 28 Jan. 1794 (and buried 13 Dec. 1834); John and Thomas (above), bapt. 26 May 1796 and 25 Oct. 1798; Mary Anne, b. and bapt. 27 Dec. 1800; George, b. and bapt. 24 Dec. 1802; Robert, b. 25 Dec. 1805, bapt. 27 Dec. 1805; and Eliza, b. 25 Sept. 1808, publicly bapt. 16 Oct. 1808. All survived infancy

Norwich.—The Sale to begin at Ten o'clock preciſely.

To be SOLD by AUCTION,
On Thurſday the 6th of October, and two following days,
at Bayfield-Hall, near Holt, Norfolk,

ALL the FARMING STOCK, Implements of Huſbandry, Dairy and Brewing Utenſils, ſome feather beds and furniture, of Mr. Thomas Forſter; conſiſting of twenty horſes, eight colts, thirty cows, (about half of the polled breed) two cows, with calves, five ſcore of lambs, ſixty fat crones, and ſome two-ſhear wethers, fifty hogs and pigs, ſeven waggons, two carts, five tumbrels, five ploughs, four pair of harrows, flag ditto, two drill and three other rollers, ſixteen pair of harneſs, &c. thirty dozen hurdles, four dozen lifts, one copper and four ſervants beds. (1599

above The sale 6–8 Oct. 1796 of Thomas Forster's stock was attended by the Hardys over all three days. They bought a cow, a tumbril (a cart which tips backwards to deposit its load) and a roller, but did not take this opportunity of acquiring the flag harrow they had borrowed in Feb. 1794
[*Norwich Mercury, 24 Sept. 1796: Norfolk Heritage Centre, Norwich*]

MH A very fine day. Mr Hardy went to a Sale at Mr Forsters foornoon & rid to Mr Smiths at Cley afternoon, came home eveng 6.[1] Wm went to the Sale foornoon & to Cley, came home to Dinner, went again afternoon, came home even 5. Mr & Mrs Burrell, Mr & Mrs Sheldrake drank tea here. I Bathd.[2]

OCTOBER 7, FRIDAY

HR W Lamb to Thornage & Edgefield with beer, Thos Baldwin to Salthouse & haymaking. Nichs after Jobs, W Holman tasking. Boyce in Garden, G Thompson & Sarah Boyce haymaking Aftern. Mr H at Bayfield all day. Mrs, Miss & WH at Bayfield afternoon.

MH A fine day but cold. Mr Hardy went to Forsters Sale foornoon, bought a Cow for £4 12*s*, A Tumbril & Role [roller] [ ]. I, Wm & MA went afternoon, drank tea at Mr Forsters, came home eveng 7. I Bathd . . .

OCTOBER 8, SATURDAY

HR W Lamb dragraking forenoon, to Thursford with beer aftern. Thos Baldwin ploughing forenoon, to the sale for tumbril & got up lode of hay. Wm Holman tasking, Boyce in garden, Nichs after Jobs. Mr H at the sale, WH & Mr Thackwry at Holt afternoon.

[1] *sale* Thomas Forster was moving from Bayfield Hall to Holt House, a farm on the outskirts of Leziate east of King's Lynn (10 Oct.); the 1845 county directory describes Leziate as a 'small decayed parish' (W. White, *History, Gazetteer, and Directory of Norfolk* (Sheffield, 1845), p. 598). The Forsters seem to have retained some property near their old home, for in the 1806 Norfolk pollbook Thomas Forster—the only voter in the village, and a Whig—is shown living at Leziate but quoting Letheringsett as his qualification.

John Claxton Savory took over the tenancy at Bayfield Hall until moving to Bayfield Lodge (the house later called Bayfield Brecks), which stands alone on the Letheringsett–Cley road. He and his bride started to build their new home 23 Feb. 1797.

John Claxton Savory of Bayfield Hall married E. Rudham 31 Oct. 1796 Mary, eldest daughter of Thomas Howard (the farmer to whom, until the previous month, William Hardy had been mortgaged) (*Norw. Merc.* 5 Nov. 1796). See also note for 13 Nov. 1796

[2] *bathed* Mary Hardy bathed almost every day 3–26 Oct., but not on Sundays

OCTOBER 9, SUNDAY

HR Famaly at own Church forenoon, M^rs^ H to Cley afternoon.

OCTOBER 10, MONDAY

HR Thos Baldwin to Holt & Sherringham with beer, W Lamb to Holt with Do & got up 2 lode of hay & loded for Syderstone. G Thompson & H Raven grinding Malt for brew. Thos Boyce took the garden for £10 per Annum,[1] Nichs Woodehouse & Sarah Turner whent away.[2] Mr & WH at home all day.

MH A dry windy day. Mr Hardy & Wm at home all day. Our great Boy Nichl [Nicholas] & Sarah Turner went away. Mr Forster remov'd from Bayfield to Holt House near Lynn Regus [Regis]. I Bathd . . .

OCTOBER 11, TUESDAY

HR W Lamb to Syderstone with beer, Thos Baldwin to Corpusta with Do. G Thompson, H Raven & W Holman in brewhouse, WH Do brewing. Mr H rode out,[3] W Thackwray shooting with C Kendle. Miss H drank tea at Holt.[4]

OCTOBER 12, WEDNESDAY

HR W Lamb to Runton with beer, Thos Baldwin ploughing. G Thompson & HR cleansed `//, W Holman after Jobs. Mr H at home all day, WH to Salthouse Afternoon.

OCTOBER 13, THURSDAY

HR W Lamb harrowing forenoon, after Jobs afternoon. Boyce gathering apples aftern, Baldwin to Burnham with beer. G Thompson & H Raven Cleansed X beer morning, W Holman After Jobs. Mr H at Holt quarter Sessions, WH & Miss H at Holt Afternoon. Wm Thackwray shooting.

MH A very fine day. Mr Hardy walkd up to Holt foornoon to the qr Sessions, dind at the Kings Head, came home eveng past 5. Wm & MA drank tea at Mr Bartells, came home even 9. I Bathd.

OCTOBER 14, FRIDAY

HR W Lamb to Fakenham with beer, Thos Baldwin ploughing all day, Wm Holman after Jobs. Mr H at Holt, WH & Mr Thackwray to Wells. G Thompson & HR in brewhouse, fat died.[5]

[1] *Boyce* He was thus promoted from the insecurity of life as a day labourer (see note for 24 Dec. 1795), and at a higher (part-time) wage than his predecessor. When 'Duke' Humphrey had taken the garden in Oct. 1787 it was at an annual salary of £7 (*Diary 2*), the difference presumably reflecting Boyce's vigour and willingness to work more hours than 'Old Duke'. Like all those who served the Hardys he had to help out when required, and he continued to work as a labourer, especially after Baldwin's injury on 9 Dec. 1796

[2] *went away* Hannah Dagliss (note for 2 May 1797) stayed on as maidservant, Sarah Turner being replaced by Sarah Starling at £3 a year (Mary Hardy's endnotes). However Sarah stayed only until 18 Apr. 1797 and Hannah was dismissed soon afterwards.

It is possible that Sarah Starling was the mother of Zeb Rouse's future wife Lydia Starling. Lydia, the illegitimate daughter of Sarah Starling, and bapt. Cley 15 Nov. 1784, married Zebulon Rouse at Cley 8 Mar. 1808: see note for 4 Feb. 1795

[3] *rode out* To Lower Sheringham to meet his attorney John Smith, according to Mary Hardy

[4] *Miss Hardy* She and her mother had tea with the Burrells at Mr Sheldrake's

[5] *vat died* ? Cleaned as thoroughly as possible

left Knaresborough Parish Church, in what was then the West Riding of Yorkshire. William Thackwray's parents married here in 1775, and here he was christened in 1779; the family lived over the River Nidd at Forest Lane Head.

As a first-time visitor to Letheringsett the 17-year-old appears somewhat dislocated. He was adopted at first by his uncle and cousin and was taken on their business trips. Coping with indebted innkeepers however seems not to have been to his taste; nor did he take to his aunt's Methodist meetings.

Instead he chose to go shooting—not one of his hosts' pastimes—with Charles Kendle, who otherwise hardly features in the diaries [*Christopher Bird 2007*]

MH A fine day. W^m^ & Wm Thackwray went to Wells in the Chaise morng 9, came home eveng past 5. Mr Hardy went to Holt to meet Mr Bignal & Mr Smith of Cley on Johnsons Acct [1] . . .

OCTOBER 15, SATURDAY

HR Thos Baldwin to Bale & Salthouse with beer, W Lamb ploughing all day. W Holman after Jobs, G Thompson & H Raven in brewhouse. M^r^ H at Holt afternoon, WH at Holt.

OCTOBER 16, SUNDAY

HR Famaly at Own Church afternoon, H Raven to Sharrington afternoon.

MH A very fine day. I went to Cley Meeting foornoon, Mr Hill Preach'd. All went to our Church afternoon, Mr Burrell preach'd . . .

OCTOBER 17, MONDAY

HR W Lamb, Thos Baldwin ploughing all day. W Holman after Jobs, G Thompson began to grind Malt for brew. WH to Blackney & Wells, M^r^ H at home all day. Mr Ellis dined here.

OCTOBER 18, TUESDAY

HR W Lamb to Wells with beer, Thos Baldwin twice to Cley for 2 Last of Malt from Mr Elliss [Ellis's], W Holman after Jobs. M^r^ H at home all day, Mr Walden & Mr Silense came afternoon. G Thompson grinding malt for brew, Boyce in garden. WH at home all day.

MH A Wet Morng, fine after^n^. Mr Hardy & W^m^ at home all day. Mr Walden & Mr Silence came even 4, Walden resig'n'd the Fighting Cocks at Wells to Silence, went away even 7. I Bathd . . .

[1] *Bignal* Probably John Bignold of Norwich, who married Sheringham 1 Nov. 1798 Mary, sister of Cook Flower of Sheringham.

They settled at Cromer, where he held the parish office of surveyor of the highways (A. Campbell Erroll, *A History of the Parishes of Sheringham and Beeston Regis* (Sheringham, 1970), p. 101).

Their headstone in Cromer churchyard shows that he died 4 Nov. 1837 aged 64, and his wife Mary 9 Feb. 1835 aged 64; their son Henry Flower Bignold died 11 June 1820 aged 20 (W. Rye, *Cromer, Past and Present: or, An attempt to describe the parishes of Shipden and Cromer, and to narrate their history* (Norwich, 1889), pp. xvi, xv)

OCTOBER 19, WEDNESDAY

HR W Lamb to Morston forenoon & Holt afternoon. Thos Baldwin, G Thompson & Wm Holman in brewhouse, WH Do brewing. Boyce in garden. Mr H at home all day, Mr Thackwray shooting with C Kendle.

OCTOBER 20, THURSDAY

HR W Lamb to Edgefield forenoon, to Holt Afternoon. Thos Baldwin to Briston forenoon, to Do [Holt] aftern. W Holman after Jobs, Thos Boyce in garden. Mr H at home all day. G Thompson & H Raven Cleanse'd `//. WH, Mr Thackwray & Miss H to Whissonsett. C Kendle bought two piggs at 3½ guineas each.[1]

OCTOBER 21, FRIDAY

HR W Lamb & T Baldwin ploughing all day, G Thompson & H Raven Cleansed X beer. W Holman after Jobs, J Ram & Lad tasking, Boyce in garden. Mr H poorly with gout.[2]

OCTOBER 22, SATURDAY

HR W Lamb to Syderstone with beer, Thos Baldwin to Waybourn & Sherringham with Do, W Holman after Jobs. J Thompson to Cley aftern with 1 Barl [barrel] beer, J Ram tasking, G Thompson in brewhouse. Wm, Miss Hardy & Mr Thackwray came from Whissonsett, Mr H at Holt afternoon.

OCTOBER 23, SUNDAY

HR Mr & Mrs & Miss H to own church forenoon. Mrs H to Cley afternoon, WH at Holt.

MH A Close dry day. Mr Bignold calld here foornoon abt Johnsons affairs. Mr Hardy, I & MA went to our Church foornoon, Mr Burrell preach'd. I & JT went to Cley meeting afternoon, Wm went to Holt Church afternoon . . .

OCTOBER 24, MONDAY

HR W Lamb to Holt with beer & Edgefield for barley, Thos Baldwin to Fakenham with beer. W Holman after Jobs, H Raven in Malthouse, G Thompson in brew Do [brewhouse]. Mr H at home all day, WH to Hindolvestone.[3] HR to Holt forenoon for greens «from» Mr Moors.[4] W Lamb to Cley for 2 Chal cinders from Mr Elliss.

[1] *3½ guineas* £3 13*s* 6*d*

[2] *gout* William Hardy was able to receive Henry Crafer of the King's Head at Holt that day, presumably to discuss the innkeeper's imminent bankruptcy: see note for 9 Nov. 1796.

The King's Head and the White Lion were the two most prestigious inns at Holt after the Feathers. All had chaises or whiskeys for hire, and while the White Lion hosted the travelling players the Feathers and King's Head had bowling greens. Henry Crafer was forced to sell early in 1797, when the King's Head had new stabling for nearly 100 horses (*Norw. Merc.* 7 Jan. 1797). Perhaps that large extension to the stables had strained his finances

[3] *William* Mary Hardy records that he also called on the Misses Leak 'at Crowson' (Croxton, forming a united parish with Fulmodeston), and dined at 'Mr Sanderford's'.

This was Revd Dr Peter Sandiford (d. Fulmodeston 13 Sept. 1835 aged 85), Rector of Fulmodeston and of Thurning, Gresham Professor of Astronomy at Cambridge 1785, Domestic Chaplain to the Archbishop of Canterbury 1799–1805.

The Misses Leak had evidently moved out of Mr Burrell's house before his marriage to Mary Johnson. However Croxton lay inconveniently far from Holt for the milliners

[4] *greens* Evergreens; shrubs

OCTOBER 25, TUESDAY

HR T Baldwin to Southrepps with beer, W Lamb to Overstrand with D^o^, G Thompson grinding Malt for brew. W Holman after Jobs, J Ram tasking. M^r^ H at home all day, WH rode out morning. Mr Smith spent the day here, Mr Bignold dine'd & drank tea here.

MH A very Stormy Morn, fine afternoon. Maids & Eliz Milegan Wash'd 5 Weeks Linn [linen]. Mr Hardy & W^m^ at home all day. Mr Smith came morn 9 to settle Johnsons Buisiness with Mr Begnal, Breakfstd & Dind here.[1] Mr Bignold & a Mr Edwards Dind here, settled the business, B & Mr Edwards hired the Sheringham House [2] . . .

OCTOBER 26, WEDNESDAY

HR T Baldwin to Kettlestone with beer. W Lamb, G Thompson, H Raven & W Holman in brewhouse, WH d^o^ brewing. J Ram in Malthouse. M^r^ H at home all day, Mr Moore supt here.

OCTOBER 27, THURSDAY

HR W Lamb to Hildolvestone with beer, Baldwin to Thornage & Stody with d^o^. W Holman unloded cinders and whent to harrow, G Thompson & H Raven Cleanse'd `//. HR & W Thackwray & Mr Hardy gathering apples afternoon, WH at Holt forenoon. Mr Balls drank tea & supt here.[3]

OCTOBER 28, FRIDAY

HR W Lamb to Sharrington with beer forenoon, setting about muck after^n^. T Baldwin to Holt D^o^, filling muck cart after^n^. W Holman after Jobs fore^n^, filling muck d^o^ [cart] afternoon in six acres. G Thompson & H Raven cleanse'd X beer, J Ram in Malthouse. M^r^ & WH out all day.

MH A very fine day. Mr Hardy & Mr Moore went to Burnham in Crafers post Chaise Morng 8, W^m^ went on Horseback, they went to git some security of Howard at the [ ] for their Debts, came home even 7.[4] W^m^ went «to» Rich'd Temples at Barmer & Slept there . . .

OCTOBER 29, SATURDAY

HR W Lamb to Sherringham with beer, T Baldwin driving out muck, W Holman filling muck cart. J Ram in Malthouse, G Thompson & H Raven in brewhouse.

[1] *Smith* Mary Hardy tends to omit gossip and tittle-tattle from her record; Henry omits it almost entirely. At Norwich Quarter Sessions on 24 Sept. 1796 John Smith had alleged an assault by Thomas Drosier of Holt (presumably Sarah Rouse's future husband: see note for 5 Oct. 1794) and Matthew Booth, the Holt plumber employed by the Hardys 1795–96. Each pleaded guilty at the county quarter sessions in the city 7 Jan. 1797 and each was fined sixpence and discharged.

The level of the fine suggests that the justices considered the affair trivial, but found that a technical assault had indeed taken place (NRO: C/S 1/15)

[2] *Edwards* John; he hired the Crown from the Hardys Oct. 1796–Aug. 1799 and needed to take out a mortgage from them. The innkeeping accounts for Sept. 1797 are in *World*, vol. 2, chap. 11; for Sept. 1798–Sept. 1804 (under William Hardy jnr) in *Diary 4*, app. D4.B.

Often, as here, a new innkeeper is accompanied by another person, about whom we learn very little. This was probably an individual of reputable standing offering sureties

[3] *Balls* Noted by Mary Hardy as Mr T. Balls, and thus likely to be Thomas Balls jnr of Saxlingham

[4] *Howard* See note for 5 Jan. 1795. John Howard had

WH came after^{n}, whent to Holt evening. M^{r} H at Markett, M^{rs}, Miss H & W Thackwray at Holt.

OCTOBER 30, SUNDAY

HR M^{rs} H to Cley forenoon, WH & HR at Holt After^{n}. M^{r} H at home all day.

MH A Close foggy day. I & JT went to Cley foornoon, came home to dinner. Mr Smith of Cley went to Sheringham to speak to Johnson, calld here Even 2, dind here. W^{m} went to Holt Church afternoon & drank tea at Mr Bartells, came home even 7. I, MA & Wm Thack. went to our Church afternoon, Mr Burrell preachd.

OCTOBER 31, MONDAY

HR W Lamb harrowing forenoon, carting out muck afternoon. T Baldwin carting out d^{o} forenoon & harrowing & Loaded for Stalham. W Holman & Boyce filling Muck cart. J Ram in M H [malthouse], G Thompson in brewhouse. Miss Ann & Rose Raven came from Whissonsett. M^{r} & WH to Sharringham.

MH A fine day. Mr Hardy & W^{m} went to Sheringham Morn 9, got a new Tenant into the House, his name is Edwards, & came home even past 6. Ann & Rose & Nathl Raven the younger came even 5.[1] Heard Sister Goggs is very Ill [2] . . .

NOVEMBER 1, TUESDAY

Henry Raven T Baldwin to Stalham with beer. W Lamb driving out muck forenoon, to Holt with beer after^{n}. Boyce filling muck cart forenoon, W Holman filling muck d^{o} [cart] & spreading muck. J Ram in Malthouse, G Thompson dressing Wheatstones. M^{r} H at home all day. WH & Nath Raven rode to Glamford [Glandford]. W Tinker & man all day.

Mary Hardy's visit to Whissonsett

2–7 November 1796

NOVEMBER 2, WEDNESDAY

HR [at Letheringsett] W Lamb to Wells with beer, Baldwin came from Stalham. W Holman after Jobs, J Ram in Malthouse, G Thompson & HR in brewhouse. M^{r} H at home all day, WH to Cley afternoon. W Tinker & man all day.

already run into financial difficulty at the White Lion at Holt in 1792 (*Diary 2*), and matters became worse at the Pitt Arms, Burnham Market. On 27 Jan. 1800 he was taken as a debtor to Norwich Castle (*Diary 4*), and a commission of bankruptcy was issued in May (*Norw. Merc.* 17 May 1800)

[1] *the Younger* The son of Mary Hardy's brother Nathaniel Raven

[2] *Sister Goggs* She recovered her vigour after what may have been a stroke or heart attack, and lived until 1806

above **Whissonsett: a Saxon cross, discovered *c.*1900 during the digging of a grave in the north churchyard where members of the Goggs family lie buried. It now stands inside the church** [*MB · 2011*]

facing page Light pours through clear glass into the nave of Whissonsett Church. The airy, spacious part of the church reserved for the congregation has none of the jewel-dark stained glass which often accompanied Victorian restorations [*MB · 2011*]

below right The worn iron-work and open-grained timbers of the south door date from the 14th century.

Whissonsett had no resident rector during Mary Hardy's lifetime, being served from nearby parishes by curates such as the Revd George Norris (6 Nov.). Mr Norris lived in the cramped rectory at Stanfield, as his incumbent William Davy told the Bishop in 1801: 'I reside at Ingoldsthorpe, and serve my own church at Anmer. The reason of my absence is that the [Stanfield] parsonage is extremely small, and incapable of accommodating a large family, and the value of the living such as not to enable me to build . . . The Revd George Norris resides in the parsonage. I allow him £25 a year, and a small portion of glebe.'

The parsonage of which Mr Davy complained had however for years been the home of his predecessor, the Revd Rash Bird—and both Mr Bird and Mr Norris were family men [*MB · 2011*]

Mary Hardy I [A] wet morng, dry close day. I & Nathl Raven sett of for Whisonsett Morng past 10, got there alittle after 1, found Mrs Goggs very poorly, I dind, drank tea, Supt & Slept there. Sister N [Nathaniel] Raven drank tea there.

NOVEMBER 3, THURSDAY

HR W Lamb & T Baldwin ploughing & sowing Vetches & wheat. Boyce spreading Muck, W Holman after Jobs. J Ram in Malthouse, G Thompson grinding Malt for brew. M^{r} H at home all day, Miss H & Miss Ravens & WH to Holt afternoon.

MH [at Whissonsett] A fine day. Sister Goggs very bad. I took a walk to Bro^{t} Ravens after dinner, came back to tea . . .

NOVEMBER 4, FRIDAY

HR W Lamb ploughing forenoon, to Hinderingham after^{n} with beer. T Baldwin ploughing & sowing wheat. Boyce spreading Muck foren^{n}, in garden after^{n}. W Holman after Jobs, G Thompson grinding Malt for brew, J Ram in M H, W Tinker at work all day. M^{r} & WH at home, Miss Jennis's drank tea here.

NOVEMBER 5, SATURDAY

HR W Lamb ploughing morning & whent to Salthouse with beer & Cley for door &C [etc],[1] Baldwin & W Holman in brewhouse & Malthouse. G Thompson & H Raven in brewhouse, WH D^{o} brewing & whent to Holt after^{n}. M^{r} & Miss H & Miss Ravens to Holt after^{n}, W Thackwray to Holt Evening.

NOVEMBER 6, SUNDAY

HR Famaly all at own church forenoon, H Raven at Holt aftern. Mr Moore & Mr Forster supt here.

MH A Sharp rime frost. Sister Goggs much as yesterday.[2] I went to Church foornoon, Mr Norris Preach'd [3] . . .

NOVEMBER 7, MONDAY

HR W Lamb & Baldwin ploughing all day, T Boyce spreading muck. W Holman after Jobs, J Ram in Malthouse. G Thompson & H Raven cleansed X beer. M^{r} H at home all day, WH at Holt evening. Mr Nath Raven & M^{rs} H came from Whissonsett. Miss Leaks drank tea here.[4]

[1] *door* See the entry for 10 Nov. 1796

[2] *Sister Goggs* Phillis Goggs's condition had improved on 4 Nov., continuing the same on the following day

[3] *Mr Norris* Not Charles (1744–1833), for 44 years Rector of Fakenham. This was George, Curate of Stanfield, who also served as Curate of Whissonsett.

Revd George Norris (b. Wood Norton 6 Oct. 1765, d. Norwich 6 Oct. 1832) lived at Stanfield, his rector there being based near Castle Rising at Ingoldisthorpe (NRO: DN/VIS 36/10, Brisley deanery visitation 1801, Stanfield return). Son of Revd William Norris, Rector of Kilverstone, he was educ. Bury St Edmunds and Norwich; admitted pensioner Caius College, Cambridge 1785, BA 1789, MA 1792; ordained deacon, and priest, Norwich 1789. He marr. Sarah Seaman 22 Mar. 1790 and lived from 1818 at Wood Norton Hall. The Norrises are commemorated on ledger stones in the chancel at Stanfield: George, 'late of Wood Norton, Rector of Bagthorpe, Vicar of Geist', who was bur. 13 Oct. 1832; his wife Sarah (d. 2 May 1803 aged 40); two sons William and Robert; and their eldest son Lieut. George Norris, who was killed 1813 in the siege of San Sebastian aged 22

[4] *Misses Leak* They appear to have returned from Fulmodeston-with-Croxton (24 Oct. 1796). Probably to their relief they settled once more at Holt. Ann Leak still

ran the millinery and continued her visits to London in May to secure the latest fashions for her clients (eg *Norw. Merc.* 6 May 1797)

---

[1] *Crafer* The King's Head innkeeper was bankrupt, John Burcham and John Davy of Holt being appointed his assignees (*Norw. Merc.* 3 Dec. 1796, 7 Jan. 1797). The public house was to be sold on 16 Jan., with its two parlours, small parlour, bar, tea room, dining room, three principal bedrooms, four other bedchambers, four attic rooms, and new stabling for nearly 100 horses. James Moore, acting for the innkeeper, handled Crafer's debts and bankruptcy 1793–96, eg: '1795. Aug. 5. Attending you on the subject of your arrest by Mr Ganning . . .' (NRO: ACC Cozens-Hardy 23/8/76, Attorney's ledger)

[2] *bathed* The diarist bathed almost every day to 2 Dec., the exceptions being Sundays and (sometimes) days of frost, snow or storms

[3] *door into the King's Head* Henry's phrasing suggests this could have been a communicating door

[4] *Mary Ann* Henry left her at Whissonsett, fetching her on 13 Dec. Mary Ann was probably Phillis Goggs's goddaughter. Mrs Goggs, her father Robert Raven and her son Robert had specially journeyed to Coltishall for the church christening (*Diary 1*: 29 Nov., 1 Dec. 1773)

[LETHERINGSETT]

NOVEMBER 8, TUESDAY

HR T Baldwin to Aldborough with beer, W Lamb ploughing & sowing wheat. T Boyce spreading muck part of day & ploughing the rema«i»nder, J Ram in Malthouse. G Thompson in brewhouse, W Holman after Jobs. M^{r} & WH at home all day.

NOVEMBER 9, WEDNESDAY

HR W Lamb to Brampton with beer, T Baldwin to Corpusta with D^{o}. J Ram in Malthouse, G Thompson grinding Malt for brew, W Holman in brewhouse. M^{r} & Miss Ravens, W & Miss Hardy rod«e» to sea side forenoon, M^{r} H at Holt forenoon.

MH A Showry Morng, fine day. Mr Hardy walkd up to Holt before breakfast to speak to Mr Moore about Crafers buisiness, he being oblidgd to stop payment, came home Morng 11.[1] Mr Roxby came with him, he [? William Hardy] bought [ ] Pockets of Hops. Bro^{t} Raven, W^{m} & the Girls rid to Keeling [Kelling] foornoon. I Bathd.[2]

NOVEMBER 10, THURSDAY

HR W Lamb G Thompson & W Holman in brewhouse, WH D^{o} brewing. T Baldwin to Edgefield & Holt with beer. Dawson«'s» man all day, Bunnets man all day putting door into Kings head.[3] M^{r} & Miss Raven & HR whent of to Whisonsett.

MH A Showry morng. Bro^{t} Raven, Daugh^{tr} Rose [Ann], Rose Raven, MA & H Raven sett of for Whisonsett about 12 oClock.[4] Mr Hardy walkd up to Holt afternoon to settle a deed of trust for the benefit of Crafers Creditors but he was not to be found, came home to tea. Wm Brewd. I Bathd . . .

NOVEMBER 11, FRIDAY

HR T Baldwin to Holt morning, at harrow remainder of day. W Lamb, G Thompson & W Holman cleanse'd `//, put beer into home cask & cleanse'd X beer. WL rolling after^{n}, J Ram in M H. M^{r} & WH at home all day, H Raven came from Whissonsett. Dawsons man all day.

NOVEMBER 12, SATURDAY

HR W Lamb rolling & got up two lode of stubble from furze close. Baldwin harrowing wheat stubble forenoon,

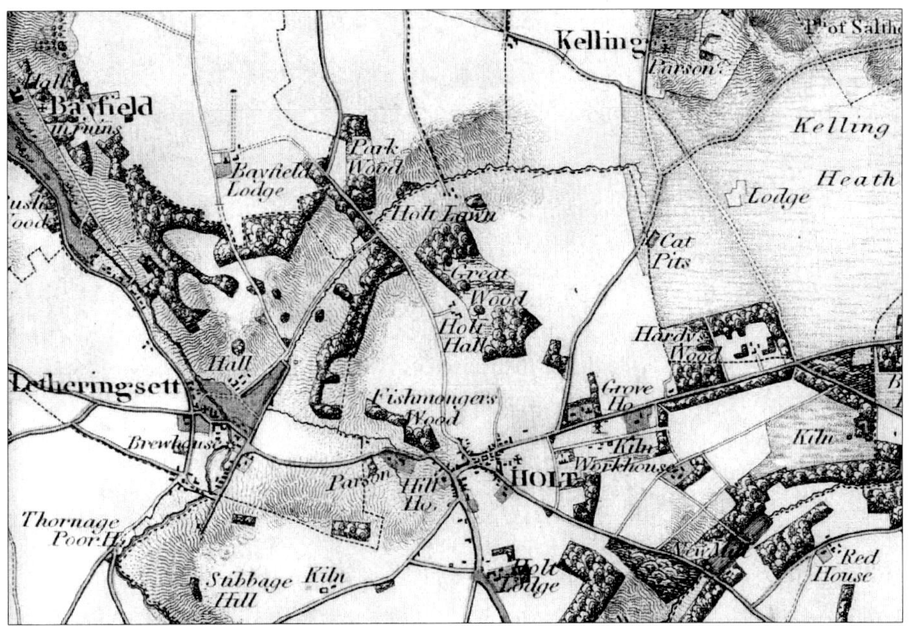
Kelling
Parson
Kelling
Heath
Lodge
Bayfield
Bayfield
Lodge
Park
Wood
Holt Lawn
Cat
Pits
Great
Wood
Holt
Hall
Hardy's
Wood
Hall
Letheringsett
Fishmongers
Wood
Grove
Ho
Brewhouse
Kiln
Workhouse
Kiln
HOLT
Parson
Hill
Ho.
Thornage
Poor H
Stibbage
Hill
Kiln
Holt
Lodge
Red
House

above As part repayment of a debt by an innkeeper, William Hardy acquired a small farm on undernourished light land at Holt on 15 Nov. 1796; this was the 'affair with William Bulling' of the previous day. The purchase marked the prelude to the expansion under William Hardy jnr which was to transform the Hardys' 50-acre holdings of 1781 into the 2930-acre total of 100 years later. Here Hardy's Wood marks the site of the farm, on the Cromer road north-east of the town centre.

Bayfield Lodge, built by the Savorys in 1797, stands in an isolated spot north of William Hardy jnr's plantations [*Bryant's Map of Norfolk 1826: Cozens-Hardy Collection*]

ploughing d^{o} after^{n}, W Holman after D^{o}. Dawsons man all day, J Ram in M H, W Pinchin cleaning harness. M^{r} & M^{rs} & WH at Holt afternoon. G Thompson in brewhouse.

NOVEMBER 13, SUNDAY

HR M^{rs} H to Cley forenoon. M^{r} & M^{rs}, WH & W Thackwray at own Church afternoon. W Lamb Loded for Sherringham, & Baldwin for Barmer.

MH A fine day. I & JT went to Cley meeting in the morning. We all went to our Church afternoon, Mr Burrell preachd. M^{r} & Mrs Savory a [at] Church for the first time.[1]

[1] *Savory* See note for 6 Oct. 1796. Four children were born to the Savorys at Bayfield and baptised privately at Letheringsett: Mary Ann, b. 26 Sept. 1797, bapt. 28 Sept.; Eliza, b. 22 July 1799, bapt. 23 July; Thomas Howard, b. 8 Nov. 1800, bapt. 15 Nov.; and John, b. 10 Nov. 1801, bapt. 16 Nov. Mr Burrell noted that Mary Ann was publicly baptised at Rudham; the other three children had their public ceremony at Letheringsett 26 Sept. 1803.

Mrs Savory died 23 Feb. 1805 aged 32 (*Norw. Merc.* 2 Mar.), Mary Hardy giving the cause as dropsy (*Diary 4*). Her husband moved 11 Oct. 1805 to Syderstone, his brother-in-law Mr Wall taking over Bayfield Lodge. There are ledger stones to the Savory

NOVEMBER 14, MONDAY

HR W Lamb to Sharringham with beer, T Baldwin to Barmer with d°. J Ram in Malthouse, Boyce in garden. W Holman after Jobs, G Thompson & HR in brewhouse. Mr H at Holt & WH at Sherringham.

MH A Close dry day. Wm rid to Sheringham foornoon to look at some Workmen employ«ed» in repairing the Publick House, came home eveng 7. Mr Hardy rid up Holt foornoon to settle an affair with Wm Bullen [Bulling], din'd at Mr Moores, came home eveng 5. I Bath'd.

NOVEMBER 15, TUESDAY

HR W Lamb to Holt forenoon, ploughing afternoon. T Baldwin ploughing all day & loaded for Fakenham, W Holman after Jobs. J Ram in Malthouse, Boyce in garden. Mr H at Holt afternoon. WH to Sherringham forn, came to Holt to dine, H Raven to Holt evening. W Lamb Loded for Burnham.

MH A fine day. Wm rid to Sheringham foornoon & came back to dinner at the Book Club at Holt, came home Even past 8.[1] Mr Hardy rid up to Holt afternoon, settled with Wm Bullen for a debt, he agreed to have apiece of Land upon Holt Heath & took a Bond for £3 pr year for 10 Years,[2] drank tea at Mr Bakers, came home Eveng past 8. I Bathd. I sent Mr Burrell a Letter in contradiction to A Sermon preachd last Sunday . . .

NOVEMBER 16, WEDNESDAY

HR W Lamb to Burnham with beer, T Baldwin to Fakenham with d°. J Ram in Malt H, Boyce in garden. W Holman after Jobs, G Thompson & H Raven grinding Malt for brew. Mr & WH at home all day. HR whent to Holt with the brew horse to Loves.

NOVEMBER 17, THURSDAY

HR T Baldwin in brewhouse forenoon, to Waybourn for beer from Sandersons.[3] W Lamb ploughing forenoon, to Waybourn with beer & brot some home from Sandn. W Holman, G Thompson & HR in brewhouse, WH D° brewing. J Herring tasking, J Ram in Malthouse, Boyce in garden. Mr H at home all day.

NOVEMBER 18, FRIDAY

HR W Lamb & Baldwin came from Waybourn forenoon. Baldwin whent to plough aftern & Lamb to Black-

family in the chancel of Syderstone Church; the family vault is in the churchyard near the south-west corner of the building. Two stones, now almost totally indecipherable, appear to commemorate John and Mary Savory and their sons Thomas and John

---

[1] *book club* At the Feathers; the club may have been formed on the back of Joseph Erratt's circulating library proposed in 1795

[2] *piece of land upon Holt Heath* The heath stretched north-east from Holt. Lying more than two miles east of the brewery and three miles from the Furze Closes at Saxlingham the new farm was inconveniently situated.

William Hardy's accounts for Sept. 1797 show that he held 12 acres at Holt valued at £120; he also had 46 acres at Letheringsett and Saxlingham valued at £1800 (tabulated and analysed in *World*, vol. 2, chap. 2). At £10 an acre for Holt Heath and £39 an acre for the rest the new farm was a poor proposition. It is called by Henry 'Bulling Farm', by his aunt 'Holt Heath Farm', and by William 'Holt Farm'

[3] *beer from Sanderson's* Samuel Sanderson was winding down the camp canteen, selling it 12–13 Jan. 1797. The Hardys' contract was ended with Weybourne Camp

ney for 2 Chal^{d} cinders from Mr Fathings. J Ram in M H, J Herring tasking. Bumpsted came for fat pigg. G Thompson Cleans'd `// & X beer, W Holman after Jobs. H Raven to Waybourn forenoon. M^{r} H at home all day. WH to Wells.

MH A Wet day. W^{m} went to Wells «to» settle with Walden morng 9, came home even 8. Mr Hardy at home all day . . .

NOVEMBER 19, SATURDAY

HR W Lamb & T Baldwin ploughing all day, J Ram in Malthouse. Boyce in garden, W Holman after Jobs. M^{r} & WH at home forenoon, WH at Holt after^{n}. G Thompson in brewhouse, W Pinchin after Jobs.

NOVEMBER 20, SUNDAY

HR Famaly at own church forenoon. M^{rs} H & Mr Thackwray at Cley after^{n}, WH at Holt after^{n}.

NOVEMBER 21, MONDAY

HR W Lamb to Sherringham with beer, T Baldwin to Thursford with d^{o}. J Ram half a day in M H, W Holman after Jobs, W Pinchin after Jobs. M^{r} & WH rod«e» to new farm forenoon.[1] G Thompson in brewhouse. HR in Malthouse afternoon. W Tinker & man all day.

MH A Close foggy day. Mr Hardy & W^{m} went to look at the Land on Holt Heath purchased of Bullin, came home to dinner.

NOVEMBER 22, TUESDAY

HR T Baldwin to Runton & Cromer with beer, W Lamb to Sharringham with D^{o} & ploughing in barley stubble. Jno Ram in Malthouse, W Holman after Jobs. G Thompson & H Raven grinding Malt for Brew. M^{r} H at home all day, WH out all day. Mr Smith dined here, Miss Leaks drank tea here. Ja^{s} Tinker half a day.

MH A fine Morng, close afternoon. W^{m} rid to Sheringham to look at the work Men, came home even 7. Mr Hardy at home all day. I Bath^{d} . . .

NOVEMBER 23, WEDNESDAY

HR T Baldwin to Briston with beer. W Holman, G Thompson & H Raven in brewhouse, WH d^{o} brewing. J Ram in Malthouse, Boyce in garden, J Herring tasking. M^{r} H at home all day. Bumpsted drew a pigg.[2] Ja^{s} Tinker all day.

[1] *new farm* The thin soil was poor and neglected. Over the coming months, from 29 Nov., the Hardys lavished wagonloads of muck on it, also marl and mould (soil). Taking up large quantities of time and labour, the farm diverted them from their other tasks.

The purchase, with further small acquisitions, enabled William Hardy to make a claim when enclosure came: *he* still held the land and had not passed it to his son with the rest of the business in 1797. In *Holt and Letheringsett Inclosure: A state of the claims* (Holt, 1808) he states that he had purchased freehold 'several pieces of land, lying in Holt, containing by estimation 30 acres, more or less,—part whereof, viz. about 13 acres, is inclosed arable land, and the remainder thereof is unenclosed'. He claimed rights of pasture on Holt's warrens, commons and wastes (p. 25, claim 34).

Another item in William Hardy's accounts states that he paid £55 for land at Holt between Sept. 1796 and Sept. 1797. The Bull innkeeper's £30 bond (diary entry for 15 Nov. 1796), which also appears in the accounts, was only in part payment; William Hardy had additionally to make this capital outlay to secure the land. His son was to show little interest in farming it

[2] *drew* Removed the entrails, as in hanged, drawn and quartered

NOVEMBER 24, THURSDAY

HR W Lamb to Holt morning & helping to Cleanse forenoon & ploughing after^{n}, T Baldwin ploughing all day. Boyce in garden, J Ram in M H, W Holman after Jobs. M^{r} H at home all day, WH to Saxlingham after^{n}. G Thompson & H Raven cleansed `// & XX.

NOVEMBER 25, FRIDAY

HR W Lamb to Wells with beer, T Baldwin ploughing all day. W Holman after Jobs, Boyce in garden, J Ram in Malthouse. G Thompson at Holt after^{n}. M^{r} & WH at Holt forenoon, Miss Leakes & Mr Balls dined here.[1]

NOVEMBER 26, SATURDAY

HR T Baldwin to Salthouse with beer & Cley for 1½ Chald cinders from Mr Ellis s, W Lamb ploughing & whent to Thornage with beer. J Ram in M H, W Holman after Jobs. M^{r} H at Holt afternoon, WH to Saxlingham to dine, back to Holt Market.[2] Ed^{m} Hall came & Orderd a lode of beer.[3]

NOVEMBER 27, SUNDAY

HR Mrs Hardy & Mr Thackwray to Cley forenoon, WH & HR to Holt after^{n}, no service at own Church.

NOVEMBER 28, MONDAY

HR T Baldwin ploughing forenoon, loded the waggon with muck after^{n}. W Lamb to Waybourn forenoon, helping TB [Thomas Baldwin] after^{n}. W Holman after Jobs, J Ram in Malthouse. M^{r} H at home all day, WH to Sherringham. G Thompson in brewhouse.

MH A fine day but cold. Mr Hardy went to look at our new purchas'd Land upon Holt Heath, came back to dinner. W^{m} went to Sherringham with T Balls to look at some repairs doing there morng 9, drank tea at Mr Flowers at up«p»er Sheringham & came home eveng past 8. I Bathd . . .

NOVEMBER 29, TUESDAY

HR W Lamb & T Baldwin took two Waggon lode of muck & ploughs to Bulling farm & whent to ploughing, came home when finnish'd piece & Loded the waggons with Muck. W Holman to Bulling farm [the Holt Heath farm] forenoon, after Jobs after^{n}. J Ram in barn, Thos Rayner took the M H.[4] G Thompson grinding Malt for brew.

[1] *Balls* Thomas Balls [jnr] of Saxlingham; William had had tea and supper at the Saxlingham farm the previous day. Mary Hardy noted that Thomas Balls accompanied William to Holt Fair on the afternoon of 25 Nov.

Ann and Bell Leak appear to have shut up shop on fair day, spending the whole time from before dinner until after supper with Mary Hardy

[2] *Saxlingham* Mary Hardy records her son as dining with Mr Savory at Bayfield

[3] *Edmund Hall* Presumably *Edward* Hall, of the Crown at Weybourne

[4] *took the malthouse* Was hired as maltster for the rest of the season

above **A Norfolk plough (29 Nov. 1796), seen here at rest by Salle Church** [*H. Repton 1779, detail: Norfolk Museums & Archaeology Service* (*Norwich Castle Museum & Art Gallery*)]

NOVEMBER 30, WEDNESDAY

HR W Lamb & «Baldwin» carting muck to Bulling farm, W Holman after Jobs. J Ram in barn tasking, Jno [?Thomas] Rayner in Malthouse, G Thompson & HR in brewhouse. M^r^ & WH at home all day.

DECEMBER 1, THURSDAY

Henry Raven W Lamb & Baldwin got six lodes of muck to Bulling farm, W Holman filling muck cart. J Ram in barn tasking, Thos Raynor in M^t^ H [malthouse], G Thompson & H Raven grinding Malt for brew. M^r^ & WH at home all Day. Boyce in garden.

DECEMBER 2, FRIDAY

HR W Lamb to Sherringham with beer. Baldwin, W Holman, G Thompson & H Raven in Brewhouse, WH D^o^ brewing. Thos Raynor in M^t^ H, J Ram in barn, Boyce taking up pittatoes. Mr Hardy at home all day.

Mary Hardy A Sharp frost, chearly day, a deal of snow on the ground, the roades very slippery & dangerous. Wm Brewd, Mr Hardy at home all day. I Bathd . . .

DECEMBER 3, SATURDAY

HR Thos Baldwin to Holt with beer fore^n^ & Cley after^n^ with D^o^ & Bro^t^ home 2 Chaldrons cinders from Mr Ellis s. W Lamb after Jobs forenoon, at muck cart after^n^. W Holman D^o^ forenoon, filling muck cart after^n^. J Ram in Barn ta«s»king, Thos Raynor in M^t^ H, G Thompson & HR Cleansed `// & X beer. M^r^ & WH at Holt afternoon.

DECEMBER 4, SUNDAY

HR Famaly at own church foren^n^ & Holt afternoon. W Lamb Loded for Fakenham.

MH A very sharp frost, roades very slippery. We all went to our Church foornoon, Mr Burrell preachd from John 7 Chap^t^ 24 Verse, a poor composition indeed & pointed.[1] Mr Hardy, I & W^m^ walkd to Holt Church afternoon, Mr Francis preachd, we came home to tea.[2]

DECEMBER 5, MONDAY

HR W Lamb to Fakenham with beer, Thos Baldwin got two waggon lode of muck to Bulling farm. W Holman after Jobs, J Ram tasking. Thos Raynor in Malthouse, Boyce in garden. Mr Hardy at home all day, WH & Mr Thackwray to Holt forenoon scating [skating].

[1] *John 7, v. 24 Judge not according to the appearance, but judge righteous judgment.* In the early years at Coltishall Mary Hardy used to record the text on which the Sunday sermon was based, but she had discontinued the practice in 1776.

Mr Burrell's words must have caused deep offence. Since verse 23 indirectly relates to keeping the Sabbath, it is tempting to speculate whether he had made a less-than-veiled reference to Sunday working at the brewery on a day when Lamb was loading the wagon with beer barrels. Although this activity could not be seen from the road the noise would have been heard

[2] *Francis* Revd Robert Bransby Francis, the son of Revd Bransby Francis and Anne, née Gittins (d.1800, herself a classical scholar and poet); he served as Curate of Holt *c.*1796–98. Brought up at Edgefield Rectory, he was admitted to Corpus Christi College, Cambridge 1785, BA 1790, MA 1794; ordained deacon Norwich 1790, priest 1792; Curate of Edgefield 1790, serving his father; Vicar of Roughton 1814. He held many other curacies, including in 1813 those of Briston and Melton.

His wife Letitia Ann, née Cracroft, left him in 1798 for the Holt surgeon Caryar Vickery (see note for 19 Dec. 1795). Mr Vickery's goods were put up for sale at Holt the following month and Mr Francis jnr's a few weeks later. The surgeon's creditors were invited to send in their demands to Charles Sales of Holt (*Norw. Merc.* 5 Jan., 23 Feb., 7 Sept. 1799).

The Francises were in time reconciled, as described in *World*, vol. 1, chap. 4. Robert Francis was living at E. Carleton when he was buried there 5 May 1850 aged 82; Letitia Ann, also of E. Carleton, was buried there 23 Mar. 1866 aged 88 (NRO: PD 207/6)

MH A Sharp frost, storms of Snow & Hail afternoon, froze again at Night. Mr Hardy & W^m^ at home all day. Mrs Pleasance & a Mrs England came & recond & dind here [1] . . .

DECEMBER 6, TUESDAY

HR W Lamb to Hindolvestone with beer & loded for Syderstone. Baldwin got up a load of muck to Bulling farm & whent to Gunthorpe with beer, W Holman after Jobs. J Ram tasking, Thos Raynor in Malthouse, Boyce in garden. WH at Holt forenoon & evening, M^r^ & M^rs^ H to Holt Afternoon. Mr Thack^y^ shootting with Mr Kendle. Ja^s^ Dyball came & Orderd a lode of beer.

DECEMBER 7, WEDNESDAY

HR W Lamb to Syderstone with beer. Baldwin to Holt with D^o^ forenoon & Edgefield after^n^, Bro^t^ home 5 C^o^ 2 Bu^s^ Barley [5 coombs 2 bushels of barley]. J Ram dressing peas, W Holman after Jobs. Raynor in M^t^ H, G Thompson & HR grinding Malt for brew. M^r^ H at Holt, WH at home all day. Boyce in garden.

below **Part of the plan of the Cross Keys, Gunthorpe for Messrs Spelman's valuation of the Letheringsett brewery in 1895; the house was sold freehold to Morgans for £750. In 1797 Robert Pleasance paid annual rent of £8** [*Cozens-Hardy Collection*]

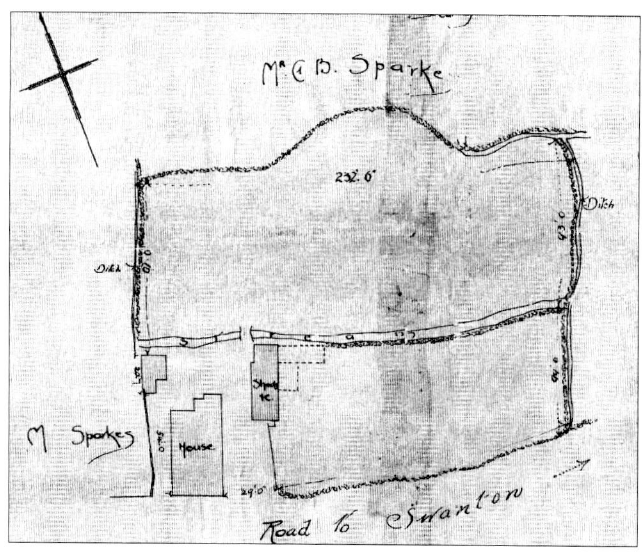
Mr C B. Sparke
Ditch
House
M Sparkes
Road to Swanton

[1] *Mrs Pleasance* As the wife of the innkeeper of the Cross Keys at Gunthorpe she also brought an order for beer, the cart being despatched the next day. Her companion was perhaps the wife of Thomas Waller England, listed in the 1806 Norfolk pollbook under Gunthorpe

left **Gunthorpe: the empty bracket for the inn board at the former Cross Keys** [*MB* · *2002*]

MH A Sharp frost. Mr Hardy walkd up to Holt foornoon, A meeting of the deputy Lievetenents for the augmentation of the Militia according to anew act of Parliment made for that purpose, he drank tea at Mr Bartells & came home eveng 7.[1] It began to thaw ab^t^ 3 in the afternoon & continued part of the night then froze sharp again . . .

DECEMBER 8, THURSDAY

HR W Lamb got two waggon lode of muck to Bulling farm. T Baldwin to Stody with beer & got one lode of muck to Bu^g^ [Bulling] farm & loded for Burnham. J Ram tasking, Raynor in M^t^ house. W Holman after Jobs, Boyce in garden. M^r^ & WH at home all day.

DECEMBER 9, FRIDAY

HR W Lamb, W Holman, G Thompson & H Raven in brewhouse, WH d^o^ brewing. T Baldwin to Burnham, waggon wheel whent over his Leg & broke it coming home.[2] Boyce in garden, J Ram tasking, Raynor in Mt House. M^r^ H at home all day.

MH A sharp frost, bright day. W^m^ at home all day. Mr Hardy dind & drank tea at Mr Burrell being his {his} tithe Audit, came home eveng past 10. Thos Baldin broke his Leg coming from Burnham . . .

[1] *Militia* The year 1797 was to be Britain's Year of Peril.

To defend the country against the feared invasion by France 60,000 men aged 18 to 45 were to be raised to be ready 'on the shortest notice, properly armed and clothed, and in readiness to join the Militia of their counties'; the local press was full of the news for weeks (eg *Norw. Merc.* 29 Oct., 12 Nov., 19 Nov, 3 Dec. 1796; also details of the cavalry 4 Feb. 1797).

Under the Augmentation to the Militia Act passed 11 Nov. 1796 (37 Geo. III, cap. 3), Norfolk with Norwich had to provide 1992 men for the Supplementary Militia; Suffolk had to find 1470, Essex 1756, and Cambridgeshire 646. At the moment of invasion or its immediate expectation they were then to be embodied and serve full-time.

Each parish provided its quota by ballot, but paid substitutes could be accepted and volunteers enrolled. Section 13 of the Act empowered overseers to give a bounty to persons volunteering; if sufficient numbers of volunteers came forward the ballot could be suspended. The overall arrangements were in the hands of the Deputy Lieutenants. See *World*, vol. 4, chap. 7 for details

[2] *Baldwin* Mary Hardy notes that it had snowed

most of the day on 8 Dec. 1796 (Diary MS). Thomas Baldwin set out the next day in these treacherous conditions on his 35-mile return trip delivering beer to Burnham Market. As happened when Baldwin broke his arm on a delivery in Dec. 1794 Thomas Boyce took his place in the team for a while. Robert Bye was then recalled (15 Dec.), his ready availability suggesting either that he had been unemployed after losing his job a year earlier or that he had managed to find only casual work.

Baldwin appears to have made a full recovery. He was up and walking 17 Feb. 1797, took his dinner with the men on 27 Feb. and 4 Mar., and returned to full-time work on 13 Mar.

On his return Baldwin was not at first put to the draying which had cost him a broken arm and a broken leg, but was given steady farm work such as ploughing. Bye stayed on, perhaps as Holt Heath Farm was occupying a great deal of manpower and the Hardys needed an extra man in the team.

After the sea (William's Hardy jnr's sloop *Nelly* being lost with all hands in 1804) the drayhorse posed the greatest danger to the Hardys' men and caused the most injuries.

The industrial accidents suffered by the men are analysed in *World*, vol. 2, chap. 1, which also contains more general labour tables and graphs

DECEMBER 10, SATURDAY

HR W Lamb & T Boyce after Jobs forenoon, got up two lode of clay after^{n}. W Holman after Jobs, J Ram tasking. Thos Raynor in Malthouse, G Thompson & H Raven Cleansed `// & X beer. M^{r} & WH at Holt after^{n}.

DECEMBER 11, SUNDAY

HR M^{rs} H to Cley forenoon. M^{r} H at own Church after^{n}, WH at Holt. Mr Balls [jnr] drank tea here.

DECEMBER 12, MONDAY

HR W Lamb whent to furze close for Lifts forenoon, got up a lode of turnips & carried some beer of [off] throughs [troughs] after^{n}. Boyce in garden & Jobs foren^{n}, helping Lamb afternoon. W Holman after Jobs, J Ram tasking. T Raynor in M^{t} H, G Thompson took up Wheatstones. M^{r} & WH at home all day, Mr Baker drank tea here.

MH A fine thaw. Mr Hardy & W^{m} at home all day, Mr Baker drank tea here. A Meeting of the people liable to be drawn for the Militia to raise a Subscr«i»ption in favour of those that may be drawn at Dobsons, Mr Hardy & «? William» there alittle while in the eveng. Wm Thackwray went to Mr Balls, Saxlingham, foornoon, staid all Night.

DECEMBER 13, TUESDAY

HR W Lamb & Boyce at Mould cart at Bulling farm, W Holman filling D^{o}. J Ram taking [tasking], T Raynor in M^{t} H, G Thompson dressing stones. HR whent to Whissonsett, Mr Thackwray to Saxlingham. M^{r} & WH at home all day.

MH The thaw still continue, a close reather drisly day. Henry Raven set of for Whisonset Morng 11 in the Chaise for MA. Mr Hardy & W^{m} rid to look at the Land on Holt Heath foornoon, M^{r} H got wet in his feet.

DECEMBER 14, WEDNESDAY

HR Boyce driving mould «cart» at Bulling farm, W Lamb & Holman filling mould cart. J Ram tasking, Raynor in Malthouse, G Thompson dressing Wheatstones. M^{r} H at home all day, WH to Cley after^{n}. H Raven & Miss H came from Whissonsett.

MH A very fine morng, close drisly day. Mr Hardy at home all day, MA & H Rav^{n} came home eveng 5. W^{m}

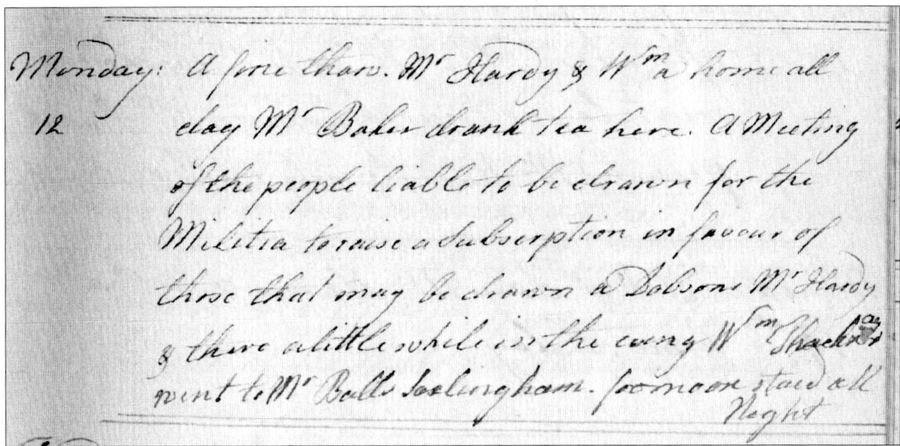

Monday: A fine thaw. Mr Hardy & Wm at home all
12 day Mr Baker drank tea here. A Meeting
of the people liable to be drawn for the
Militia to raise a subscription in favour of
those that may be drawn at Dobsons Mr Hardy
& there a little while in the evening Wm Thackwray
went to Mr Balls Saxlingham. forenoon staid all
Night

above Mary Hardy records 12 Dec. 1796 the meeting at the King's Head, Letheringsett to set up a fund for the payment of substitutes. Holt was to hold a similar meeting at the Feathers on 17 Dec., as announced in the *Norwich Mercury* of 3 Dec. 1796.

The hundred of Holt had to find nine men for the Supplementary Militia. This was to be effected, so the press declared, 'with little inconvenience to individuals', Militiamen being called out to exercise within their own counties for 20 days a year at 1*s* a day, and with their families being maintained during their absence. The support of the families of Militiamen and substitutes fell to the parish, under the supervision of parish officers and JPs. The ballot proved hugely unpopular, provoking riots [*Cozens-Hardy Collection*]

rid to Cley aftern to speak to Mr Jackson to git a friend of his at New Castle to pay Bells groats to keep him in Prison, came home even 8 [1] . . .

DECEMBER 15, THURSDAY

HR W Lamb got three waggon lode of muck to Bulling farm. R Bye at Clay cart, Boyce spreading muck and casting clay with J Herring & Duffield.[2] W Holman filling waggon with muck & after Jobs. Mr & WH at home all day. J Ram tasking, Thos Raynor in Malthouse.

DECEMBER 16, FRIDAY

HR W Lamb got one waggon lode of muck to Bulling farm & whent to Edgefield with beer, R Bye to Wells with beer. Boyce spreading muck at Bulling farm, W Holman spreading Muck in field and after Jobs. J Ram tasking, Raynor in Mt House. Mr H at home all day, WH to Walsingham with Mr Ellis & Mr Balls, J Herring & W Duffield carting clay.

[1] *Bell* Possibly George Bell, of Newcastle upon Tyne, flour-dealer (*Univ. Brit. Dir.*, vol. 4 (1798)). William Hardy jnr and others along the north Norfolk coast had exported flour to Newcastle, where the merchant seems to have been imprisoned for debt

[2] *casting clay* Presumably spreading marl over the starved fields, rather than throwing jambs of marl down to the bottom of a marlpit. The land now forms part of the grounds of Gresham's School

MH A Close dry day. Mr Hardy at home all day. Mr Ellis of Cley & Mr T Balls Junr of Saxlingham Breakfstd here & went with Wm to Walsingham to see Mr Minns new Mill, came home eveng past 9.[1] Mr Ellis Supt here . . .

DECEMBER 17, SATURDAY

HR W Lamb got three waggon lode of muck to Bulling farm, R Bye carting clay at farm. W Holman filling muck waggon & after Jobs, J Herring & Boyce filling clay cart. W Tinker half a day. Mr & WH at Holt Market aftern.

DECEMBER 18, SUNDAY

HR Famaly at own Church forenoon, HR to Sharrington afternoon.

DECEMBER 19, MONDAY

HR R Bye at Clay cart at Bulling farm, Boyce & Herring filling Do. W Lamb to Sherringham with beer, W Holman spreading muck at B [Bulling] farm & after Jobs. J Ram tasking, T Raynor in Mt H. Mr & WH at home all day, W Tinker half a day mending tumbrill.

DECEMBER 20, TUESDAY

HR R Bye, W Holman, G Thompson & HR in brewhouse, W Lamb to Bale with beer & oiling his harness. Boyce in garden, J Ram tasking, T Raynor in Mt H. Mr Scott & man mending Harness.[2] Mr & WH at home all day.

MH A fine day. Mr Hardy rid up to the Holt Heath Farm afternoon. Wm at home all day & poorly with the rumatism.

right 'William Lamb . . . oiling his harness . . . Mr Scott and man mending harness' (20 Dec.).

Mary Hardy generally does not cover these mundane yet essential tasks; it is her nephew who illuminates the men's daily round. This harness is used by the heavy horses at Union Farm, part of the Norfolk Museums Service's land at Gressenhall [*MB · 2011*]

[1] *Minns* Lewis, miller and leading Wesleyan Methodist at Lt Walsingham, where he was one of the trustees of the chapel built 1793–94; he subscribed 10 guineas to the building fund (NRO: FC 18/1), and laid one of the foundation stones. He voted Whig in the 1768 and 1806 county elections, both pollbooks listing him as a Lt Walsingham miller.

Windmills are shown at Walsingham on Faden's county map of 1797. Minns may alternatively have occupied the ancient watermill on the River Stiffkey at Lt Walsingham Priory.

William Gunton Thompson left the Hardys' employment 10 Oct. 1798 to work as a miller at Walsingham, his departure signalling what seems to have been almost the end of cornmilling within the Letheringsett brewery and coinciding with Zebulon Rouse's expansion of the watermill at Letheringsett. Thompson was replaced only briefly by William Hardy jnr (*Diary 4*: 30 Oct. 1798)

[2] *Scott* The Holt saddler Gatzon Scott (*Univ. Brit. Dir.*, vol. 3, p. 280). He is given as a collarmaker in the apprenticeship books, as when he took on Henry

CATHARINA DE II.
ALLEEN HEERSCHERESSE ALLER RUSSEN

left Catherine the Great, whose death Mary Hardy records 22 Dec., five weeks after the event. The diarist mentions only two other foreign monarchs: Queen Caroline Mathilda of Denmark (1775), a British princess who was sister to George III; and Louis XVI, 'beheaded by his own subjects' (1793). She never names Napoleon Bonaparte, instead referring to the threat from 'the French'.

Reiner Winkeles' sumptuous engraving captures the splendour of the ruler of Russia, who had a particular link with Mary Hardy's part of the world through her acquisition in 1779 of the treasures of Houghton Hall amassed by Sir Robert Walpole [*engraving by R. Winkeles 1787*]

DECEMBER 21, WEDNESDAY

HR W Lamb & R Bye after Jobs forenoon, whent to Blakeny for 4 Chal^d^ cinders from Mr Tempes [Temple's].[1] G Thompson & HR cleansed `// & X beer. J Ram tasking, T Raynor in M^t^ H, Boyce in garden. WH at home all day, M^r^ H to Holt after^n^. Miss Leaks drank tea here.

MH A sharp frost. Wm Brewd. Mr Hardy at home all day, the Miss Leakes from Holt drank tea & Supt here. Killd a Pigg, weighd 15&½ Stone.

DECEMBER 22, THURSDAY

HR W Lamb to Brampton with beer. R Bye unlode«d» 2 lode of Cinders & whent for 5 hundred bricks to Holt, loded for Stalham & got some top wood from meadow. W Holman after Jobs, Boyce topping trees in D^o^ [the meadow]. J Ram tasking, T Raynor in Malthouse. M^r^ & M^rs^, Miss & WH drank tea at Mr Savorys, Bayfield. G Thompson dressing flour.

MH A sharp rime frost. Mr Hardy, I, W^m^ & MA drank tea at Mr Savorys of Bayfield. A very sharp Night. From the News paper: the Empress of Rusia died at Petersburg Novr 15.[2]

Woodrow (TNA: PRO IR 1/67, no. 170, 31 May 1794)

---

[1] *Temple* Thomas William Temple (d. 17 Feb. 1816 aged 48), of Blakeney, merchant; his ledger stone lies at St Nicholas' Church, Blakeney at the east end of the south aisle

[2] *Empress of Russia* Catherine II (Catherine the Great); born in 1729 a princess of Anhalt-Zerbst, she had married Tsar Peter III of Russia in 1745 and had ruled alone following the Tsar's death in 1762

facing page The Hardys' malthouse in the grip of winter: the east front, viewed from across the Glaven. Only three of the six bays are visible. It has the traditional louvred openings, the control of light and air to the vast interior being the only means of controlling the temperature for the grain as it germinated. Like most traditional floor maltings it is aligned north–south.

The malt-kilns (right) and the lean-to for the barley steep (out of sight to the left) add to the length of this massive industrial building [*MB* · *2000*]

DECEMBER 23, FRIDAY

HR R Bye to Stalham with beer, Boyce topping trees in Meadow, W Holman after Jobs. J Ram tasking, T Raynor in Malthouse, W Lamb no work. Mr H at home all day, WH at Holt forenoon. Mr Price call'd here.

MH A very sharp frost. Mr Hardy at home all day. Wm attemptd to go to Cromer & Southreps but was not able to he had the rumatism so bad.

DECEMBER 24, SATURDAY

HR T Boyce to Aldborough with beer, R Bye came from Stalham, W Holman after Jobs. J Ram tasking, T Raynor in Mt House, W Lamb no work. Mr & WH to Holt afternoon. J Tinker all day at work. G Thompson in brewhouse.

MH A sharp frost. Mr Hardy & Wm walkd to Holt markt afternoon, drank tea at Mr Davys, came home even 9. Heard young Mr Howard of Burnham, Brot to Mrs Savory of Bayfield, was Dead & young Billins of Rudham died Sudenly.[1]

DECEMBER 25, SUNDAY

HR Being Christmas day savants all dined here.[2] Mrs H whent to Cley forenoon, famaly at own church Afternoon.

MH *Xmas Day* A very sharp rime frost. I & Wm Thackwry went to Cley Meeting foornoon. Our Labourers & their Wifes dind here. Mr Hardy & Wm & MA went to our Church afternoon, Mr Burrell preach'd . . .

DECEMBER 26, MONDAY

HR R Bye to Runton with beer, T Boyce to Holt & Sharrington with Do. J Ram tasking, T Raynor in Mt House. G Thompson in Brewhouse, W Holman after Jobs. Mr & WH at Wells.[3]

DECEMBER 27, TUESDAY

HR R Bye to Fakenham with beer, W Lamb to Briston & Thornage with Do. J Ram tasking, T Raynor in Mt House. G Thompson & HR grinding malt for brew, W Holman after Jobs. Mr & WH at home all day.

DECEMBER 28, WEDNESDAY

HR W Lamb to Overstrand with beer. R Bye, G Thompson, H Raven & W Holman in brewhouse, WH do Brewing. J Ram tasking, T Raynor in Malt house. Mr H at home all day.

---

1 *Howard* Nicholas, aged 27, of Burnham Thorpe, second son of Thomas Howard of Rudham (*Norw. Merc.* 14 Jan. 1797)

2 *savants* Servants; ie the farm servants. The spelling reveals the vowel sound, as in today's 'clark' for clerk, 'Darby' for Derby

3 *Wells* They probably took William Thackwray's trunk to the port, for when he left for Yorkshire on 1 Jan. 1797 he was on horseback, riding pillion

DECEMBER 29, THURSDAY

HR W Lamb & R Bye in Brewhouse fore^{n}, to Blakeny for 4 Chal. cinders from Mr Temples, W Holm. after Jobs. G Thompson & H Raven cleansed `// & X beer, J Ram tasking, T Raynor in Mt H. M^{r} & WH at home.

MH The thaw still continued, much milder then yesterday. I rid as far as Mr Temples of Thornage aftern to look at a very large Hogg they had killd, Weighd 30 St. 12 lb, came home to tea. Mr Thos Balls Junr drank tea & Supt here . . .

DECEMBER 30, FRIDAY

HR W Lamb & R Bye unloding cinders forenoon, got two lode of muck to Bulling farm. W Holman after Jobs, J Ram tasking. T Raynor in Malthouse, G Thompson in brewhouse. M^{r}, M^{rs}, Miss & WH spent the evening at Dr Bartells.[1]

DECEMBER 31, SATURDAY

HR W Lamb to Morston with beer & whent to furze close for a peice of timber, R Bye got three waggon lode of muck to Bulling farm, W Holman after Jobs. J Ram tasking, T Raynor in Malthouse, G Thompson dressing Flour. M^{r} & WH at Holt, Mr Thackwray whalk'd to Stody.[2]

MH A Mild Close day. Mr Hardy walkd up to Holt foornoon to Justice sitting, dind at the Feathers, came home eve 6. W^{m} rid to Holt foornoon, came home to dinner, walkd to Mark^{t} afternoon, came home eveng 9. I & MA rid up to Holt afternoon, came home to tea.

[1] *Dr Bartell* A respectful prefix. He was a surgeon, not a physician, but nevertheless practised medicine in the manner of most country surgeon–apothecaries

[2] *Mr Thackwray* This was his last full day in Norfolk; he did not visit his relatives at Letheringsett again in his aunt's lifetime.

He is mentioned only once more in his aunt's diary, when he was living or staying in London after the death of his mother in 1799. William Hardy had kept in touch with his nephew, for he spent the day with the Hardys at their lodgings in Shoreditch on 16 June 1800 (*Diary 4*)

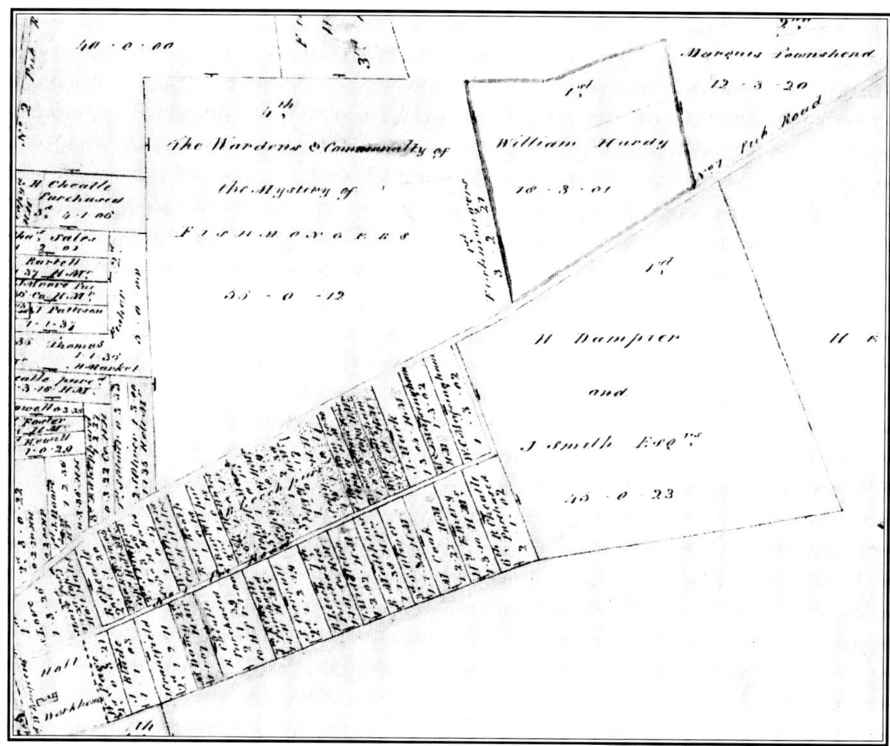
40 · 0 · 00
4th
The Wardens & Communalty of
the Mystery of
Fishmongers
35 - 0 - 12
1st
William Hardy
18 · 3 · 01
Marquis Townshend
12 · 3 · 20
1st
H Dampier
and
J Smith Esq.rs
45 · 0 · 23

above Part of the Holt enclosure map of 1810, by Charles Burcham, showing the area to the north-east of the town centre bisected by the Cromer road ['N° 1 Public Road']. The E-shaped Elizabethan workhouse (to the south-west) stands east of the parish church in present-day Pearsons Road near Grove Lane, but was in 1797 on the edge of Holt Heath.

By 1810 the Hardys had extended their original 12-acre purchase of Holt Heath Farm. William Hardy is marked as the owner of the 18¾-acre parcel of land north of the main road and bordering land held by the trustees of the Free Grammar School ['The Wardens and Communalty of the Mystery of Fishmongers'].

Early in 1797 the Hardys began to plant fir trees suited to the poor soil at what Henry Raven calls 'Bulling farm'; by 1826 the plantation could be labelled 'Hardy's Wood' on Bryant's map (illustrated under mid-November 1796).

Very soon after William Hardy's purchase of this small farm from William Bulling, the indebted former innkeeper of the Bull at Holt, there was talk of a proposed Holt enclosure. After hours of listening to two of its promoters on 30 March 1797 Mary Hardy developed a headache. Enclosure was to prove a long-drawn-out process, requiring two Acts in quick succession in 1807 and 1809 [TNA: PRO MR1/257, *Holt enclosure map 1810, detail*]

1797

Mr Burcham of Holt and young King came . . . to show Mr Hardy the form of an Act of Parliament for enclosing the heath and commons at Holt MARY HARDY, 30 MAR. 1797

[[[1] *J*ANUARY 1, SUNDAY

William Hardy jnr Mr Thackwray set off for Wells behind Jno Tompson Morng 4, H Raven sett off for Whissonsett Morng 5. Mrs, Miss & WH at Church forenoon, WH Holt Church afternoon.

Mary Hardy A Mild foggy day. Wm Thackwry set of for Wells to go to Hull in Blooms Vessel Morng 4, expected the Ship wod [would] sail at 7 but it did not, J Thompson returnd abt Noon.[2] H Raven went to Whisonsett for a Week. I, Wm & MA went to our Church foornoon, a Communion, no Sermon. Wm went to Holt Church afternoon, home to tea . . .

JANUARY 2, MONDAY

WHj W Lamb to Blakney for 10 Bags Hops & to Holt with Waggon, R Bye to Corpusty with beer. T Raynor in M H, Jno Ram in Barn. W Holman in B H [brewhouse] forenoon, Jobs afternoon. WH walkd to Holt Farm Morng, rode with Mr Savory to Edgfield Afternoon. Mr H at home all day.

JANUARY 3, TUESDAY

WHj W Lamb to Wells with beer, R Bye muck Cart to the Furrze Close. T Raynor in M H, Jno Ram in Barn. Mr H at home all day. Mr Wordingham Dined here.[3] Miss H drank tea at Mr Savory, WH went in the Even for her. W Hollman filling Muck «cart».

MH A Mild close day. Mr Wordingham came Morn 10 to pay of Everetts Mortgage, dind here. MA walkd to Bayfield, drank tea at Mr Savorys, Wm went for her in the Chaise in Eveng . . .

[1] The entries for 1–7 Jan. are by William Hardy jnr, during Henry's holiday at home. Henry resumed 8 Jan. and continued without a break until the end of the MS volume on 25 Oct. 1797

[2] *Bloom* It is not clear if this is John Bloom or, possibly, his son James Gardner Bloom (bapt. Wells 19 Dec. 1774), Wells merchants, shipbuilders and Hull traders. John's wife Mary was the daughter of James Gardner, for whom their son was named. Her father had been master of the brigantine *Catherine and Mary*, of Wells, the ship being lost off the harbour 15 Nov. 1773. Capt. Gardner died aged 60; also his 20-year-old son James, and five other members of the crew (NRO: PD 679/6, Note by the rector in the burial register).

James Gardner Bloom was to be both a naval and a military captain as he was later to command the 1st Wells Company of Voluntary Infantry (NRO: MS 66, Lt Col. Metzner's inspection, 8 Nov. 1803, p. 25)

[3] *Wordingham* Identified in William Hardy jnr's accounts as John Wordingham (*Diary 4*, app. D4.B). On his marriage to Mary Ransome at Wells 20 Oct. 1768 he was given as a Wells carpenter. Both signed, and John Bloom stood witness

above A fine yeast head builds on a brew of Butser Bitter at George Gale & Co.'s Brewery, Horndean, Hampshire. 70 barrels of Butser Bitter were brewed 20 Feb. 2002, this photograph being taken on the Brewery History Society's visit of 23 Feb. Like all real-ale breweries Gale's carefully conserved its yeast, this strain dating at least from 1957 and probably much earlier. The fermenting tun was not lined, but painted with brewer's paste.

In early 1797 William Hardy jnr was handing over to Henry Raven as brewer [*MB · 2002*]

JANUARY 4, WEDNESDAY

WHj W Lamb went with a Load muck to Holt farm & bro^t^ home empty Cart, R Bye & he the rest of day Cart^g^ Muck to Furrze Close, W Hollman filling. T Raynor in M H, G Tompson grinding Malt for the Brew. M^r^, M^rs^ H rode in after^n^ to Holt Farm, WH rode to Mr Balls's & Supt there.

JANUARY 5, THURSDAY

WHj W Lamb all day & R Bye part of day Muck Cart^g^ to Furrze Close & Holt in Morn^g^ with beer, W Hollman filling. T Raynor in M H, J Ram in Barn. M^r^ H at home all day, WH at home.

JANUARY 6, FRIDAY

WHj W Lamb & R Bye at muck Cart all day, T Boyce & W Hollman filling. T Raynor in M H, J Ram in Barn. M^rs^ & Miss Davy, Miss Howard & Miss Savory & Mr Bartell drank tea here, M^r^ H at home all day.

JANUARY 7, SATURDAY

WHj R Bye to Burnham with beer, W Lamb to Thursford & Holt with Beer. W Hollman scraping road & Jobs, T Raynor in M H, Jno Ram in barn. W Tinker & Ben sawing. M^r^ & WH to Holt Market in afternoon.]]

JANUARY 8, SUNDAY

Henry Raven Mrs Hardy to Cley forenoon, famaly at own Church after^n^. H Raven came from Whissonsett Evening.

JANUARY 9, MONDAY

HR W Lamb, W Holman, G Thompson & H Raven in brewhouse,[1] R Bye to Salthouse & Cley with beer & Bro^t^ home [ ] Chal^d^ cinders from Mr Ellis's. T Raynor in Mt House, J Ram in barn. M^r^ & W Hardy at home all day. M^rs^ & Miss Sheldrake drank tea here, M^r^ S came evening.

JANUARY 10, TUESDAY

HR W Lamb & R Bye to Gunthorpe for timber to Mr Collyers, W Holman in brewhouse & Jobs. J Ram tasking, T Raynor in Malthouse, G Thompson & H Raven cleansed `//. M^r^ H at home all day, WH dined at Holt book club.

MH A drisly Morng, dry afternoon. Mr Hardy at home all day. W^m^ dind at the Book Club at Banyards at Holt, Mr Ellis of Cley came home with him & Supt here . . .

---

[1] *brewhouse* Although neither Henry nor his aunt says so, this must have been a brewing day. Cleansing the weaker brew (removing the yeast head) was performed the following day, and the strong beer would have been cleansed 11 Jan.

JANUARY 11, WEDNESDAY

HR W Lamb to Holt with beer forenoon, at cravil [gravel] cart afternoon. R Bye in brewhouse D° [forenoon], at gravil D° afternoon. W Holman after Jobs, Raynor in M H, J Ram tasking. M^r H at home all day.

JANUARY 12, THURSDAY

HR W Lamb to Saxlingham with the waggon & after Jobs. R Bye whent to Holt with Dauson gil & whent to Bulling farm with a waggon lode of muck & bro^t home furze.[1] T Raynor in Malthouse, J Ram tasking. M^r H at home all day, WH rode to Waybourn.

MH A sharp frosty morng, thawd in the day & snowd alittle. Mr Hardy at home all day. W^m went to S Sandersons Sale at Weybon foornoon,[2] bought a Bath Stove 5/6^d,[3] 6 Mahogany Chairs 37*s* & some earthen ware, came home eveng 5. M^r T Balls of Saxlingham, M^r & Miss Bartell drank tea & Supt here, settled the Timber Book.

JANUARY 13, FRIDAY

HR W Lamb to Syderstone with beer, R Bye unloded a lode of furze & whent to Bale with beer. T Raynor in Malthouse, J Ram in Barn. M^r, M^rs H & Miss & WH spent the evening at Mr Temples. HR & G Thompson in brewhouse. WH to Waybourn after^n, {WH to Waybourn afternoon}.

MH A sharp frost, began to thaw eveng 4 & was a very Wet Night. W^m went to the Sale of the Canteen at Weybon foornoon, came home eveng 5. We all drank tea & Supt at Mr Temples of Thornage, home eve 12.

JANUARY 14, SATURDAY

HR R Bye to Holt & Waybourn with beer & bro^t home Chairs &c [etc] bought at Sale. W Lamb to Kettlestone with beer & carried 200 fir trees,[4] W Holman to Waybourn for sashes [sash windows]. T Raynor in Malthouse, J Ram tasking, H Raven to Waybourn. M^r H at Holt all day, M^rs & Miss H to Holt to tea, WH whent after tea.

MH A close dry day. Mr Hardy walkd up to Holt, the Militia was drawn, he dind at Mr Thomas, came home eveng 9.[5] I & MA rid up to Holt aftern, drank tea at the Miss Lekes, W^m came for us eveng 8 . . .

[1] *Dauson gil* Dawson's gill or the Dawson gill; Henry implies the possessive similarly in 'Bulling farm'. In his list of provincialisms Marshall defines *gill* as a pair of timber wheels. Bye would have been taking them to the cartwrights at Holt (W. Marshall, *The Rural Economy of Norfolk*, vol. 2, p. 380)

[2] *sale* See note for 17 Nov. 1796. Samuel Sanderson was dismantling the canteen building, even to the point of selling off the sash windows which the Hardys then installed in their house (14 Jan., 23 Mar. 1797).

The Artillery must have decided they were not returning in the foreseeable future and thus had no further use for the camp

[3] *bath stove* A stove grate with two hobs, designed to be set into the fireplace and not to be freestanding. The advantage of such models was that a light meal could be prepared or a kettle boiled on the hobs, putting the coals to dual use.

William Hardy's inventory later that year (*Diary 2*, app. D2.C) shows that the Hardys placed the grate in the counting house; their more expensive model was in the keeping room

[4] *fir trees* These were planted at Holt Heath Farm 25 Feb. 1797

[5] *drawn* The Militia ballot was held for Holt hundred, evidently peaceably. Norwich, like some other parts of the country, had riots (*World*, vol. 4, chap. 6)

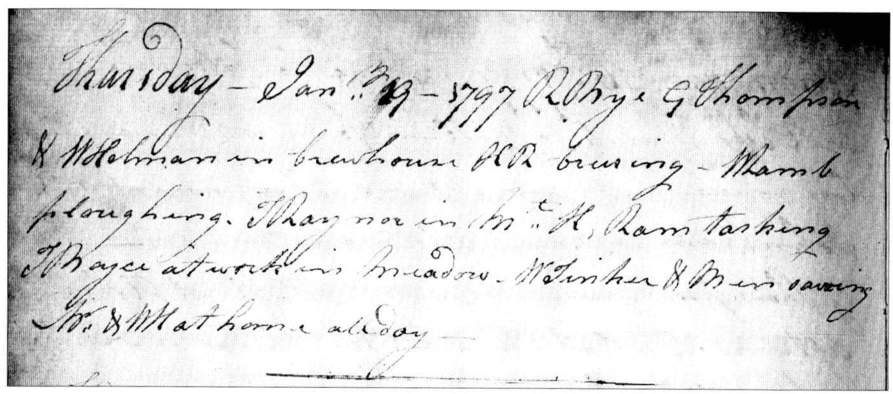

above 'H[enry] R[aven] brewing' (19 Jan.). Exactly two and a half years to the day since the signing of his indentures the brewing pupil records his new status in the brewery
[*Cozens-Hardy Collection*]

JANUARY 15, SUNDAY

HR Famaly at own Church forenoon, WH & H Raven at Holt afternoon. M^r & Mrs Savory calld here morning & whent to Church.

JANUARY 16, MONDAY

HR R Bye to Fakenham with beer, W Lamb to Bulling farm with a waggon lode of muck & bro^t home furze. T Raynor in M^t H, John Ram tasking. W Holman after Jobs, G Thompson grinding barley. M^r H at Holt afternoon, WH at home all day. H Raven weigh'd 10 bags Hops, T Boyce in garden.

MH A very fine day. Mr Hardy walkd to Holt to a Sale of the King Head, it was not sold, came home eveng 6.[1] W^m at home all day.

JANUARY 17, TUESDAY

HR W Lamb to Stody & Edgefield with beer, R Bye & W Holman whent to Bulling farm with a waggon lode muck & bro^t home furze and unloded them. T Raynor in M^t H, John Ram tasking. Gunton Thompson dressing Wheat Stones, H Raven began to grinde Malt for brew evening. Mr Youngman trimming gears &c.[2] M^r & WH at home all day. Thos Boyce at work in Meadow ¾ of day. Mr Wilcocks turn^d his cart over & hurt his leg, stop^t here.[3]

MH A Close day. Mr Hardy & W^m at home all day. Eveng past 10 Mr Wilcocks overturnd his Cart in the field being very much in Liquor & bruisd his Leg & broke both the shafts of his Cart & came here, had our L Cart to go home in . . .

[1] *King's Head* See note for 9 Nov. 1796. Joseph Thompson had bought it by 1798, appearing as the owner–occupier in the land tax assessment (TNA: PRO IR 23/61, p. 38). Samuel Love served as innkeeper from 1798 (NRO: C/Sch 1/16; also *Diary 4*). By the Holt enclosure Love had become owner, with Thomas Waterson as innkeeper in 1808 (*Holt and Letheringsett Inclosure: A state of the claims*, p. 30, claim 47)

[2] *trimming gears* Presumably the cornmill's, temporarily out of action while the stones were dressed

[3] *Mr Wilcocks* Elizabeth Hagon's husband: see note for 20 June 1795

JANUARY 18, WEDNESDAY

HR W Lamb stacking furze forenoon, at harrow after^{n}. R Bye pitching D^{o} [furze] forenoon, got up two lode Clay after^{n} from C Kendles pit.[1] T Raynor in M^{t} H, Jno Ram tasking, W Tinker & man sawing. G Thompson laid down wheatstones, H Raven whent to Holt forenoon. M^{r} & WH at home all day. M^{r} & M^{rs} & Miss Bartell spent the evening hear with Mrs Temple, Mr Wilcocks sarvant came home with cart.

JANUARY 19, THURSDAY

HR R Bye, G Thompson & W Holman in brewhouse, HR brewing.[2] W Lamb ploughing, T Raynor in M^{t} H, Ram tasking. T Boyce at work in Meadow. W Tinker & Ben sawing. M^{r} & WH at home all day.

MH A close day. Mr Hardy went to the Quarter Sessions at Holt, dind at the Feathers, came home eveng 8. Wm Brewd & at home all day. Mr Smith of Cley dind here . . .

JANUARY 20, FRIDAY

HR W Lamb helping to git peas out «of the» Barn & ploughing. R Bye ploughing, whent to Briston with beer after^{n}. G Thompson & H Raven Cleanse'd `//. W Holman in brewhouse forenoon, whent to Holt for barl^{s} [barrels] & Thornage with Malt. M^{r} H at home all day. M^{r} & Mrs Savory, Miss S & Miss Howard drank tea here.

JANUARY 21, SATURDAY

HR W Lamb to Burnham with beer, R Bye to Brampton with D^{o}. T Raynor in M^{t} H, J Ram tasking. W Holman after Jobs, G Thompson & H Raven cleansed X beer. M^{r} & WH at Holt afternoon, W Tinker & Ben sawing.

JANUARY 22, SUNDAY

HR Famaly at Church afternoon, M^{rs} H to Cley forenoon. Miss Leaks drank tea & sup^{t} here.

MH A Close dry day. I & JT went to Cley meeting foornoon. We all went to our Church afternoon, Mr Burrell preachd, a poor Comp«o»sition. The 2 Miss Leekes drank tea & Supt here . . .

JANUARY 23, MONDAY

HR W Lamb to Wells with beer, R Bye to Hildolvestone with d^{o}. T Raynor in M^{t} H, W Holman at work at furze

[1] *Charles Kendle's pit* He owned a lime-kiln (*Holt and Letheringsett Inclosure: A state of the claims*, p. 25, claim 35)

[2] *Henry Raven brewing* Mary Hardy's entries for 19 and 27 Jan. and 2 Feb. 1797 suggest however that William was present with his pupil: 'William brewed'. But Henry does not report his presence. On 16 and 22 Feb. Henry definitely brewed without William's supervision, although his cousin probably retained his status as head brewer. His aunt does not record Henry's promotion to full brewer until 24 Apr. 1797

taurant

above Holt King's Head was not sold following Crafer's bankruptcy (16 Jan.), William Hardy failing to buy it for his brewery.

The house continued to elude him, his brewer's tie being secured more loosely by innkeeper indebtedness [*MB · 1993*]

close. T Boyce in garden, G Thompson dressing flour. M^r H at home all day, WH set of for Sherringham, Cromer &C.[1]

JANUARY 24, TUESDAY

HR W Lamb ploughing all day, R Bye to Thornage with beer & ploughing. T Raynor in M^t H, J Ram tasking, W Holman «at» turnip cart & after Jobs. Boyce in garden, G Thompson & HR in brewhouse. M^r H at home all day, Miss H drank tea at Holt.

JANUARY 25, WEDNESDAY

HR W Lamb to Sharringham with beer, R Bye to Holt twice & carried of [off] some beer, W Holman after Jobs. T Raynor in Malthouse, J Ram tasking, G Thompson grinding Malt for brew. M^r H at home all day, T Boyce half a day.[2]

JANUARY 26, THURSDAY

HR W Lamb to Bulling farm with a waggon lode muck, bro^t back a lode furze. R Bye to Bulling farm with cart D^o [load] muck, bro^t home ling for under drain & got wood out of meadow.[3] T Raynor in M^t H, Ram tasking. T Boyce & W Holman at work in Meadow, G Thomp. dressing flour. M^r H at home,[4] WH came home to tea.

JANUARY 27, FRIDAY

HR W Lamb, W Holman & G Thom. in brewhouse. R Bye & T Boyce whent to bulling farm with a waggon loade muck & bro^t home furze. H Raven brewing, T Raynor in M^t H, J Ram tasking. M^r & WH at home all day, WH whent to Bayfield evening.

MH A frosty morng, Close day. Mr Hardy at home all day. W^m rid to Mr Savorys after tea, came home eveng 10. Wm Brew'd . . .

JANUARY 28, SATURDAY

HR R Bye helping to Cleanse `// & whent to Hinderingham with beer, W Lamb & Holman whent to Bulling farm with a lode Muck & bro^t home furze than [then] whent to meadow for wood. T Raynor in M^t H, J Ram tasking, T Boyce in Meadow. M^r H at Holt all day, WH at Holt afternoon. G Thompson & H Raven Cleansed `// &C.

JANUARY 29, SUNDAY

HR Famaly at own church forenoon, WH & H Raven at Holt afternoon. Robt Bartell drank tea here.

---

[1] *Cromer etc* William also called at Runton and spent the night at Cromer. He went on to Coltishall, his mother noting that he returned from there 26 Jan.

He could have called at Chapman Ives's brewery to see what was still for sale following the auctions of the autumn; the brewery had not found a buyer. Mr Ives's brother-in-law Anthony Ransome was continuing to manage the maltings and brewery for the moment, before moving to Norwich to take over William Latten's failing brewery in St Clement's (*Norw. Merc.* 6 Jan. 1798; also *World*, vol. 2, chap. 8)

[2] *half a day* Henry notes Thomas Boyce's hours 17 and 25 Jan. as though he were on day-labour rates

[3] *ling for underdrain* Heather for top-lining deep-cut drains (see note for 20 Mar. 1795). William Marshall observes that where stones were unavailable wood was generally used for lining the bottom of the drains, with smaller boughs and 'heath' laid on top (W. Marshall, *The Rural Economy of Norfolk*, vol. 2, pp. 2–3).

The heather and furze would have come from the area of open heathland which formed part of Holt Heath Farm, the smaller boughs coming from the meadow where Boyce had been pruning trees

[4] *Mr Hardy* This was his 65th birthday, but neither diarist records any special commemoration

JANUARY 30, MONDAY

HR W Lamb to Corpusta with beer, R Bye to Aldborough with D^{o}. T Raynor in M^{t} H, J Ram finnis'd tasking, T Boyce at work in Meadow. W Holman «at» turnip cart forenoon, getting wood out of meadow afternoon. M^{r} H at home all day, WH to Bulling farm. Mr Temple, Blakeny, drank tea here.

JANUARY 31, TUESDAY

HR R Bye to Sharrington & Edgefield with beer, W Lamb to Southrepps with d^{o}. T Raynor in Mt House, J Ram dressing peas, W Holman after Jobs. Boyce at work in Meadow, G Thompson & HR in brewhouse, W Tinker & man all day. M^{r} & WH at home all day.

FEBRUARY 1, WEDNESDAY

Henry Raven W Lamb & R Bye stacking furze, got peas out of barn & got two lode gravel into Meadow. T Raynor in M^{t} H, Boyce at work in Meadow, G Thompson grinding malt for brew. M^{r} H at home all day, WH whent to Saxlingham to tea & sup«p»er. W Holman after Jobs.

FEBRUARY 2, THURSDAY

HR R Bye, W Holman & G Thompson in brewhouse, H Raven brewing. W Lamb no work, T Raynor in M^{t} house. M^{r} H at home all day. M^{r}, Miss Balls & Miss Mills & Miss Mundha«m» came morning, Miss Howard & Miss Savory call'd afternoon.[1] WH at home all day.

FEBRUARY 3, FRIDAY

HR W Lamb carting gravill into meadow, W Holman & R Bye filling, T Boyce part of day in Meadow. G Thompson & H Raven cleansed `//. M^{r} H at home all day, WH at Mr Savorys.

Mary Hardy A Close dry day. Mr Hardy at home all day. W^{m} drank tea & Supt at Mr Davys at Holt, J Davy from London being there, came home eveng 11 . . .

FEBRUARY 4, SATURDAY

HR R Bye helping to Cleanse morning than whent to Sharringham with beer. W Lamb carting gravel into meadow, T Boyce & W Holman filling D^{o} [gravel cart]. T Raynor in M^{t} H, G Thompson & H Raven cleansed XX. M^{r} & W Hardy at Holt market, HR rode to Thursford forenoon. M^{rs} & Miss H at Holt afternoon.

above Furze: bright yellow gorse (*Ulex europeaus*).

As well as nourishing the hungry land at the new farm with manure, marl ('clay') and topsoil ('mould'), the Hardys' men seem to have been clearing it of the gorse which flourishes on the open heathlands of north Norfolk.

The spiky, prickly spines which pass for leaves would have been awkward to handle, but proved their worth in field drains by denying vermin a rat run and by catching loose debris in the spikes [*MB · 2011*]

[1] *Miss Mundham* Probably Mindham. Ann Mindham signed as one of the witnesses at the Wells wedding of Thomas Balls jnr and Margaret Woodrow on 10 May 1798

FEBRUARY 5, SUNDAY

HR M^rs^ H to Clay forenoon, famaly at own church afternoon. WH drank tea at Bayfield.

FEBRUARY 6, MONDAY

HR W Lamb ploughing at bulling farm, R Bye whent to Saxlingham for Waggon & got two waggon lodes of muck to Bulling farm. T Raynor in M^t^ H, W Holman at work in Meadow, G Thompson in brewhouse. M^r^ & WH at home all day, Mr Balls spent the day here.

FEBRUARY 7, TUESDAY

HR W Lamb to Holt with beer forenoon, to Salthouse with D^o^ & Cley for 1½ Chaldron cinders from Mr Ellis's. T Raynor in Mt House, W Holman after Jobs & spreading gravel in Meadow. WH at home all day. R Bye ill. M^r^ H at Clay. Mrs Custance Senr & Junr drank tea here.[1]

MH A Close foggy day. Mr Hardy & W^m^ at home all day. Mrs Custance from Fakenham, Mrs Wm Custance & Miss Baker drank tea here.

FEBRUARY 8, WEDNESDAY

HR W Lamb carting gravil into Meadow, T Boyce & W Holman filling gravil cart. T Raynor in Malthouse, G Thompson in Brew house. R Bye very ill. M^r^ & WH at home all day, Miss Hardy drank tea at Mr Davys.

MH A Close foggy day. Mr Hardy at home all day, Mr Temple of Blakeny dind & drank tea here. W^m^ & MA drank tea at Mr Davys of Holt, met M^r^ & Mrs Savory there. Mr Hardy very poorly . . .

FEBRUARY 9, THURSDAY

HR W Lamb carting gravil into Meadow forenoon & filling D^o^ cart afternoon. R Bye ill fore^n^, carting gravil afternoon, W Holman & T Boyce filling gravil cart. G Thompson grinding Malt, T Raynor in Malthouse. M^r^ & WH at home all day. Miss Davys & Miss Howard & Miss Savory drank tea here.

FEBRUARY 10, FRIDAY

HR W Lamb to Burnham, R Bye to Wells with beer, T Boyce at work in Meadow. W Hol^n^ after Jobs, T Raynor in Malthouse, G Thompson grinding malt for brew. M^r^ H very poorly, WH at home all day. M^rs^ & Miss Hardy drank tea at Holt.

[1] *Mrs Custance etc* Phillis, wife of William Custance snr of Fakenham: see note for 11 July 1794. Their daughter-in-law Martha (d. 6 May 1857 aged 88) was daughter of Downham Market attorney Thomas Holman; she had married William Custance jnr 14 Jan. 1788 while he was a cabinetmaker and upholsterer at King's Lynn (*Norw. Merc.* 19 Jan. 1788). They later moved to Cambridge, where he practised as a surveyor; he had started his working life as an auctioneer. The Custances were staying with the Bakers at Holt

above The cock from the copper in the National Trust's 18th-century estate brewhouse at Charlecote, Warwickshire.

The wooden chute is loosely strapped to the cock so that the flow can be directed either to the mash tun as hot liquor or to the cooler as hot wort (unfermented beer) [*MB · 2000*]

above The National Trust's Lacock Abbey, Wiltshire. The brewing copper (the boiler) stands at the top of a flight of six steps, the copper's height providing the necessary gravitational flow to other vessels. The open-topped tank, made of copper, hangs inside the rendered outer shell which supports the structure.

The heavy-duty cock controls the flow to the timber channel leading to the wooden, lead-lined cooler (right). As seen also in the Letheringsett drawings (depicted under July 1794) the Lacock cooler has a tension mechanism, the wooden pegs around the edge permitting adjustments to this large, shallow, open tray subject to extremes of temperature [*MB · 2001*]

FEBRUARY 11, SATURDAY

HR W Lamb, G Thompson & W Holman in brewhouse, H Raven Brewing. R Bye got up two lode muck up to Bulling farm, T Boyce in Meadow, T Raynor in M^t^ house. M^r^ H at home all day, WH to Holt.

MH A close foggy day. W^m^ went to Holt foornoon, enterd into sosiety releating to the Cavelry to be raisd, came home to dinner, went to Mark^t^ afternoon, came home eveng 9.[1] Mr Hardy poorly.

[1] *cavalry* As well as the Act for the Supplementary Militia, it was decreed in a second Act of 1796 that home-defence cavalry were to be raised. This Act was 'for enabling His Majesty to raise a provisional force of cavalry to be embodied in case of necessity for the defence of these kingdoms'. As usual, the details were posted in the local press, the county's noticeboard (*Norw. Merc.* 19 Nov. 1796, 4 Feb. 1797).

Once more the civilian population was at the mercy of the ballot and, if well off, at the expense of finding a substitute. Now both horse and horseman were in the ballot.

One horseman, clothed, furnished and mounted, was to be enrolled for service for every 10 horses kept for riding or carriage work (as opposed to the working draught animals). The Act envisaged that those owning fewer than 10 such horses (like William Hardy jnr) would band into groups or 'societies': 'The Act, after providing for the case of persons keeping ten or more such horses, directs that all other persons charged for any number less than ten shall be classed together in such manner as that one horse and horseman shall be provided for, and in respect of every class consisting of ten horses, that the person who is to provide the horse and horseman for every such class shall be chosen by ballot, and afterwards be

FEBRUARY 12, SUNDAY

HR G Thompson Cleansed `//. M^{rs} H to Clay afternoon & WH to Holt afternoon.

MH A fine day. Mr Hardy something better. I & MA went to our Church foornoon, Mr Burrell preachd. I went to Cley meeting afternoon. The 2 Miss Leekes here in the eveng. I taken with dimness in my Eyes [1] . . .

FEBRUARY 13, MONDAY

HR W Lamb to Cromer with beer, R Bye to Overstrand with D^{o}, G Thompson & H Raven Cleansed X beer. W Holman after Jobs, T Raynor in Malthouse, T Boyce in garden. M^{r} H at home all day. WH to Clay afternoon & drank tea at Mr Temples, Thornage.

FEBRUARY 14, TUESDAY

HR R Bye harrowing all day in furze close, W Lamb whent to Holt morning & Clay for 2 last Oats [and Cley for 2 last of oats] from Mr Rouse's. T Raynor in Malthouse, G Thompson in Brewhouse, H Raven whent to Clay. M^{r} & WH at home all day, Mr Balls drank tea here.

FEBRUARY 15, WEDNESDAY

HR R Bye at harrow in furze close, W Lamb at work in Meadow, T Boyce in D^{o}.[2] W Holman in brewhouse, G Thompson grinding Malt for brew, T Raynor in Malthouse. M^{r} & WH at home all day.

MH A Sharp windy day. Mr Hardy & W^{m} at home all day. Mrs Custance of Fakenham, Mrs Wm Custance & Miss Baker dind & drank tea here, Mrs Sturly drank tea here.[3] Red Cow Calvd in the night [4] . . .

FEBRUARY 16, THURSDAY

HR R Bye, W Holman in brewhouse, cleaned great cask in W Hall [white hall]. W Lamb harrowing all day, T Boyce in Meadow. H Raven brewing, G Thompson in brewhouse. M^{r} & W Hardy at home all day, M^{r} & Mrs Bartell drank tea here.

MH A rime frost, fine day. Mr Hardy at home all day. W^{m} walkd up to Holt afternoon, drank tea at Mr Davys, came home eveng. Mr Hardy, I & MA walkd up to Mr Cobens hills.[5] M^{r} & Mrs Bartell drank tea here . . .

FEBRUARY 17, FRIDAY

HR R Bye at work in Meadow fore^{n}, to Briston with beer afternoon, W Lamb & W Holman in Meadow all day.

enrolled for the service by himself or substitute' (*Norw. Merc.* 4 Feb. 1797).

William was again lucky in the ballot, held at Holt 25 Feb. 1797

---

[1] *my eyes* This was an isolated attack; the diarist had not suffered for some months from eye trouble. It is possible that the strain of the day contributed to her illness, for this was the 10th anniversary of her son Raven's death. Her husband, too, was ill in the approach to the anniversary. Mr and Mrs Bartell, who had both supported the Hardys devotedly during Raven's lingering death, came to tea on the anniversary of the funeral on 16 Feb.

[2] *in ditto* Henry sometimes uses 'ditto' as shorthand to signify a repetition of the last-mentioned item rather than as a substitution for the word on the line above. Here he probably intends it to refer to 'Meadow'

[3] *Mrs Sturley* Of Thornage Hall: see note for 21 Nov. 1793

[4] *red cow* She was probably of the local mahogany-red beef cattle breed, the Norfolk Red: ancestor, with the dairy breed the Suffolk Dun, of today's Red Polls

[5] *Mr Cobon's hills* To the north of Letheringsett Hall Farm's farmstead. James Cobon was buried Letheringsett 31 Aug. 1840 aged 84; see also note for 3 Apr. 1797

T Raynor in Malthouse, G Thompson got some beer into W Hall, T Boyce in Meadow. M^{r} H at home all day. T Baldwin came walking to Letheringsett.[1] Mr Temple drank tea here.

FEBRUARY 18, SATURDAY

HR W Lamb to Fakenham with beer. R Bye helping to put beer into Cask, cleansing & whent to Holt with beer, bro^{t} home a lode furze, W Holman D^{o}. T Raynor in Malthouse, G Thompson & H Raven put beer into great cask & Cleansed X. M^{r} H at home all day, WH to Holt market.

FEBRUARY 19, SUNDAY

HR Mrs Hardy to Clay forenoon, Miss & M^{r}, WH & H Raven at own Church afternoon, M^{r} H poorly with gout in his hand.

FEBRUARY 20, MONDAY

HR R Bye unloded furze & whent to Thursford with beer, W Lamb whent to plough on heath but broke his tack. T Raynor in M^{t} H, W Holman after Jobs, G Thompson grinding Malt for brew. M^{r} H to Reefham with Mr Bartell, WH rode to Bale. M^{r} & Mrs Raven came afternoon.

MH A rime frost, very fine day. Mr Hardy sett of for Reepham morng 9 with Mr Bartell in Banyards Post Chaise to measure up some Ash Timber, staid all Night. W^{m} at home all day. Bro^{t} & Sister Raven came eveng past 4. Mrs Seales [Sales] of Holt brought to Bed of a Girl . . .

FEBRUARY 21, TUESDAY

HR W Lamb at harrow & carting of quicks forenoon, to Clay with beer afternoon, bro^{t} home 2 Cha^{l} Cinders from Mr Ellis's, T Raynor in M H, W Holman at work in meadow. H Raven in brewhouse, G Thompson & R Bye no work. M^{r} H came home evening, WH at home all day. M^{r} & Mrs Sheldrake drank tea here.

FEBRUARY 22, WEDNESDAY

HR W Lamb, G Thompson & W Holman in brewhouse, H Raven brewing. R Bye ploughing at Holt forenoon, in furze Close afternoon, T Raynor in Mt H. M^{r} & M^{rs} H & M^{r} & Mrs Raven & Miss H drank tea at Mr Sheldrakes, WH at home all day.

above 'Mr Hardy, I and Mary Ann walked up to Mr Cobon's hills' (16 Feb. 1797).

The Hardys believed in taking the air to restore health and nerves. On the 10th anniversary of Raven's funeral his parents and sister, unusually, rambled on the Bayfield/Letheringsett border. Here the Round Hill plantation is seen from the lane running past the village house of industry and the Savorys' new house at Bayfield [*MB · 2001*]

[1] *Thomas Baldwin* One of the very rare human touches in Henry Raven's diary, reminiscent of the pleasure Mary Hardy took in recording her young children's milestones (*Diary 1*).

The entry suggests that the drayman did not live in the village, unless he had moved away temporarily to be nursed back to health

[1] *new house* The Savorys and their new baby moved into the house 11 Jan. 1798, showing a taste for a traditional vernacular style. The two-storey red-brick house with its central pediment and shaped gables is something of a throwback to the type of house popular in brick regions from the late 17th century until about 1740.
Its name was later changed from Bayfield Lodge to Bayfield Brecks

---

facing page The Bank of England, City of London: 'The Bank of England and all the banks in city and country stopped payment today' (28 Feb.). Fuelling all the other uncertainties of the time, William Pitt's administration took the nation by surprise by ordering the stopping of all cash payments by banks. The Bank of England's Governor and Directors found themselves constrained by a Privy Council order of the night of 26 Feb. 1797.

The period known as the Restriction, then unprecedented, whereby banknotes could not freely be converted into cash, lasted until 1821.

Debtors had long been required by law to repay creditors in cash; hence the large number of bankruptcies and business failures [*drawing by T. H. Shepherd; engraving by W. Tombleson 1827, detail*]

FEBRUARY 23, THURSDAY

HR W Lamb ploughing at Bulling farm, R Bye ploughing in furze close. T Raynor in Malt H, T Boyce in meadow. W Holman after Jobs, G Thompson & H Raven Cleansed `// & dressing flour. M^{r} & Mrs Hardy rode to Bulling farm. M^{r} & Mrs Raven, WH & Miss H drank tea at Mr Johnsons, Holt.

MH A rime frost, very fine day. Bro^{t} & Sister Rav^{n}, Mr Hardy, I, MA & W^{m} took a ride in foornoon up Mr Savorys Closes were his new Farm House is to be Built,[1] call«ed» at Mr Savory at Bayfield, came home to dinner. Mr Hardy & I rid onto Holt Heath afternoon to see the Man at Plow there, came home to tea. Bro^{t} & Sister, W^{m} & MA drank to [tea] at Mr Johnsons at Holt . . .

FEBRUARY 24, FRIDAY

HR R Bye to Syderstone & barmer for empty Barrells, W Lamb to Holt & Hindolvestone with beer. T Boyce in Meadow forenoon, taking up fir threes [trees] afternoon. W Holman after Jobs, G Thompson & H Raven cleansed XX, T Raynor in Mt H. M^{r} & WH at home all day, M^{r} & Mrs Raven whent to Whissonsett.

FEBRUARY 25, SATURDAY

HR W Lamb to Holt, Edgefield & Thornage with beer, R Bye ploughing. T Boyce, J Herring planting fir threes at Bulling farm, W Holman after Jobs. T Raynor in M^{t} H, G Thomp. grinding Malt for brew. M^{r} H at Holt all day. WH at Holt farm forenoon, to market afternoon.

MH A frosty morng, fine day till eveng 4 then turnd very hasy. Mr Hardy & W^{m} went up after breakfast to Holt Heath Farm to plant some fur Trees, Mr Hardy stopt at Holt «to» see the Cavelry drawn & dind there. W^{m} came home to dinner & went to Mark^{t} afternoon, both came home even 9. MA walkd to Bayfield afternoon, drank tea at Mr Savorys . . .

FEBRUARY 26, SUNDAY

HR Famaly at own Church forenoon, WH & HR at Holt afternoon. Mrs Hardy to Clay afternoon.

FEBRUARY 27, MONDAY

HR W Lamb, G Thompson & W Holman in brewhouse, H Raven brewing. R Bye to Waybourn & Gunthorpe, W Lamb whent to Sharrington after^{n}. T Raynor in M^{t} H,

T Boyce in garden. T Baldwin came & got his dinner. Mr H at home all day, Mr & Miss Bartell drank tea here. WH at home all day, Miss Davy & Miss Savory drank tea here.

FEBRUARY 28, TUESDAY

HR W Lamb ploughing in furze close ¾ of day, in Bells Acre remainder of day, R Bye ploughing in bulling farm. T Raynor in Mt H, G Thompson & H Raven Cleansed `//, T Boyce in garden. Mr & WH at home all day, W Holman after Jobs.

MH A rime frost, very fine day. Mr Hardy at home all day. T Balls Junr drank tea & Supt here. NB The Bank of England & all the Banks in City & Country stopt payment to Day.[1]

[1] *Bank of England* The stoppage was triggered principally by fears of invasion. This threat at the end of 1796 had precipitated withdrawals and the hoarding of gold, and in Feb. 1797 'the report of a landing of French troops in Wales caused enough alarm to spur Pitt into protecting the Bank's reserves against panic withdrawals.' As the supply of Bank of England reserves was dangerously low Pitt acted swiftly to protect the stocks from further depletion. On 26 Feb. 'Pitt called a meeting of the Privy Council, and the Directors [of the Bank] were ordered not to pay cash for notes until Parliament had considered the matter' (V.H. Hewitt and J.M. Keyworth, *As Good as Gold: 300 years of British bank note design* (British Museum Publications, London, 1987), pp. 41–42).

On 1 Mar. the Norwich banking firms agreed to issue only notes: R., B. & J. Gurney; Roger Kerrison & Son; Harvey & Hudson; Kett, Hatfeild & Back; and Day, Dalton & Day. Their compliance caused instant problems of cash liquidity.

The Chancellor of the Exchequer swiftly moved in the House of Commons that 'No person shall be arrested, on first process, who tenders banknotes to the amount of his debt' (*Norw. Merc.*, 4 Mar., 1 Apr. 1797). But his injunction was ignored. Bankruptcies remained high, as described in *World*, vol. 2, chap. 11

[1] *church* This was Ash Wednesday, Mr Burrell holding a prayer service

[2] *town* Letheringsett. The itinerant preacher John Saunderson was stationed with Josiah Hill on the Walsingham Circuit; in August he was moved to the Lynn Circuit (*Minutes of the Methodist Conferences*, vol. 1, pp. 331, 365)

above A maltster's hand shovel and fork, at Elgoods Brewery Museum, Wisbech, Cambridgeshire. Wooden shovels were used to turn or 'plough' the barley on the malthouse floor; forks broke up the grain to stop it matting. Powered tools were not introduced until the mid-20th century in many Norfolk maltings.

Thomas Raynor should have hung up his tools on 8 Mar. Instead he and the others were at work [*MB · 2001*]

MARCH 1, WEDNESDAY

Henry Raven W Lamb helping to get beer into cask & whent to Corpusta with beer. R Bye & W Holman, G Thompson & H Raven put beer into cask & cleansed X beer, RB went to plough afternoon. T Raynor in M^{t} H, T Boyce in garden. M^{r} H to Holt after^{n}, WH at Holt afternoon.

Mary Hardy A Close cold day. I & MA went to our Church foornoon,[1] Mr Hardy & W^{m} went to the Holt Heath Farm afternoon, they burnt the Ling. Mr Hardy came home to tea, W^{m} came home eveng 10.

MARCH 2, THURSDAY

HR W Lamb to Southrepps with beer, R Bye to Aldborough with D^{o}, W Holman after Jobs. T Boyce in garden, T Raynor in M^{t} H, G Thompson & H Raven grinding Malt for brew. M^{r} & WH at home all day.

MH A sharp rime frost, fine day. Mr Hardy & W^{m} at home all day. Robt Staff came eveng 3, Slept here . . .

MARCH 3, FRIDAY

HR W Lamb to Wells with beer, R Bye to Runton with D^{o}. T Raynor in Mt House, T Boyce in Meadow. W Holman, G Thompson in brewhouse, H Raven brewing. M^{r} & WH at home all day, M^{rs} & Miss H drank tea at Holt.

MARCH 4, SATURDAY

HR W Lamb to Stody & Sharringham with beer, R Bye to Burnham with D^{o}. T Boyce in Meadow, W Holman at turnip cart & cleard fat [cleared vat]. G Thompson & H Raven cleansed `// & grinding Malt for brew, T Raynor in M H, T Baldwin came & dined here. M^{r} & WH at Market afternoon.

MH A Cold day. Mr Hardy & W^{m} went to Holt Mark^{t} afternoon, came home eve 9. Mr Sanderson preachd in Town.[2]

MARCH 5, SUNDAY

HR G Thompson, H Raven, W Lamb, R Bye & W Holman cleard throughs [troughs] & cleansed XX beer, D^{o} & D^{o} [Lamb and Bye] greaze'd the Beer carts. Famaly at Church afternoon.

MH A Windy cold day. Mr Hardy, W^{m} & MA went to our Church afternoon, Mr Burrell preach'd. W^{m} poorly with the Rumatism . . .

MARCH 6, MONDAY

HR W Lamb to Stalham with beer. R Bye, W Holman & G Thompson in brewhouse, H Raven brewing. T Raynor in Malthouse, T Boyce at work in Meadow. M^r & WH at home all day.

MARCH 7, TUESDAY

HR W Lamb came from Stalham. R Bye, W Holman & G Thompson at work in brewhouse. T Raynor in M^t H, T Boyce at «work» in Meadow. H Raven whent to Walsham morning, Ret^d [returned] evening. M^r & W Hardy at home all day, Mr Bignold & Mr Edwards dined here.

MARCH 8, WEDNESDAY

HR W Lamb, R Bye, W Holman, G Thompson & H Raven got the Cleanse of beer into cask & cl«e»ansed XX the forenoon. W Lamb & RB turning barley afternoon, T Raynor in Malthouse. M^r H at home all day, WH whalk'd to Holt afternoon. GT grinding Malt for brew. This being a general fast Mr Burrell preach'd a Sarmon forenoon.

MH A Close day. Mr Hardy at home all Day. A Fast by Proclamation, M^r H went to Church foornoon.[1] W^m went up to Holt afternoon, drank tea at Mr Moores . . .

MARCH 9, THURSDAY

HR R Bye to Morston & Edgefield with beer. W Lamb, W Holman & G Thompson in Brewhouse, H Raven brewing. T Raynor in M^t H, T Boyce in garden. M^r & W Hardy at home all day, Nath Raven Junr came from Whissonsett.

MARCH 10, FRIDAY

HR W Lamb ploughing at Bulling farm, R Bye harrowing forenoon & ploughing Afternoon. G Thompson Cleansed `//, W Holman at work in brewhouse, T Raynor in Mt H. H Raven & Mr Raven Junr rode to Edgefield & Briston forenoon. Miss Davy & Miss Gay drank tea here.

MH A very cold windy day. Mr Hardy & W^m at home all day. Miss Mary & Susan Davy & Miss Gay of Edgefield drank tea here.[2]

MARCH 11, SATURDAY

HR R Bye to Fakenham with beer. W Lamb helping in brewhouse forenoon, at harrow afternoon. G Thomp-

[1] *fast* As usual, by requiring their men to work on the fast day during the national emergency William Hardy and his son were openly defying the authorities.

William Hardy snr may have sought to deflect attention from what was going on in the barn or granary and in the maltings and brewery by turning up for the church service—the only member of his family to do so. As though in another act of defiance, father and son had put more men than usual to Sunday working on 5 Mar. They were perhaps joining in the undercurrent of protest against the Tory government, this seething discontent spilling into the naval mutinies later in the year.

Instead of engendering cohesion at a time of crisis, recent legislation had caused opinions to become polarised. The explosion of what were regarded as unconstitutional moves, culminating in the Supplementary Militia, Provisional Cavalry, and stopping of cash payments, provoked stormy protests in Norwich by its Whiggish leading citizens and councillors and, county-wide, by JPs, MPs (including Coke) and the county gentry (*Norw. Merc.*, reports Apr.–May 1797)

[2] *Miss Gay* Probably the daughter of Benning Gay, listed in the 1806 county pollbook as an Edgefield farmer with property at Guestwick

son & H Raven Cleansed X beer & grinding Malt for brew, T Raynor in Malthouse. M^{r} H at Holt all day, WH & Mr Nath Raven Junr at Holt Market afternoon. H Raven set of for Whiss^{t} evening 6 OClock.

MH A very cold dry day, wind very high. Mr Hardy walk'd up to Holt foorno^{n} on acct of the Cavelry, W^{m} walkd to Mark^{t} afternoon, they came home eveng 9. H Raven set of for Whissonset Eveng 7 . . .

MARCH 12, SUNDAY

HR Famaly at Own Church forenoon, WH & Mr Raven Junr at Holt afternoon. H Raven came from Whissonsett evening Nine o Clock.

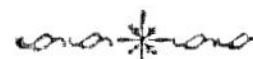

Mary Hardy's visit to Whissonsett
13–18 March 1797

MARCH 13, MONDAY

HR [at Letheringsett] R Bye, W Holman in brewhouse, H Raven brewing. G Thompson dressing wheat Stones, T Raynor in M^{t} H, T Boyce in garden. T Baldwin whent to plough about 2 hours than whent to Holt with brewcart to Dawsons.[1] WH at Holt Afternoon, M^{r} & M^{rs} H & M^{r} R [Raven] Junr set of for Whiss^{t} forenoon.

MH A Cold windy day. Mr Hardy & I set of for Whisonsett morng 10, N Raven went with us, we got there Even 1, Dind & took a walk to Mr Goggs & went back to Bro^{t} to tea . . .

MARCH 14, TUESDAY

HR W Lamb to Briston with «beer» forenoon, helping to clear fat & at work in Meadow, W Holman at work in Meadow. T Baldwin after Jobs, G Thompson laid down wheat Stones. R Bye to Northwalsham with beer.[2] WH at home all day. Dawson came home with new cart.[3]

MARCH 15, WEDNESDAY

HR W Lamb helping to get beer into great cask morning & whent to plough at Bulling farm. R Bye in brewhouse forenoon, got up two lode of thornes afternoon, T Baldwin in brewhouse all day. G Thompson & H Raven got beer into Cask & Cleansed X beer, T Raynor in M^{t} H, Boyce at work in 5 Acres. WH at home all day.

[1] *Dawson* There was no innkeeper of that name at Holt. The dray cart could have needed repairs at the cartwright's, or it may have been replaced (14, 22 Mar.)

[2] *N. Walsham* See note for 11 May 1795. The Maid's Head was back in business, but Henry records only very occasional deliveries: 14 Mar., 29 May, 3 Oct. 1797

[3] *came home with* Delivered

Grove

above William Hardy and his brother-in-law called 17 Mar. on John Shearing of Paxfield, Helhoughton (here given as Packfield Farm). It lay near heaths and commons midway between Lt Rudham and W. Raynham.

They called in connection with Holt Heath. William Hardy may have been seeking advice over farming thin heathland soil
[*Faden's Map of Norfolk 1797: Larks Press 1989*]

MARCH 16, THURSDAY

HR R Bye ploughing at Bulling farm. W Lamb in brewhouse & whent to Holt afternoon with beer. G Thompson & T Baldwin in brewhouse, H Raven Brewing. W Holman & T Boyce at work in Meadow, T Raynor in M^t^ house. W Hardy at home all day. Miss Bartell spent the day here, Mr Balls drank tea & sup^t^.

MH [at Whissonsett] A dry chearly day. Mr Hardy & Bro^t^ Raven went to Gresenhall, dind & drank tea there, came home even 8. I & Sister Raven walkd to Horningtoft foornoon to speak to Mrs Moy, drank tea at Sister Goggs.

MARCH 17, FRIDAY

HR W Lamb to Southrepps with beer, R Bye ploughing at Bulling farm & got up a lode of thornes. W Holman & Baldwin after Jobs forenoon, at harrow a heaping quicks afternoon, T Raynor in Malthouse. T Boyce at work in Meadow, G Thompson & H Raven Cleansed `//. W Hardy at home all day.

MH A dry chearly day. Mr Hardy & Bro^t^ Raven rid to Paxfield to speak to Mr Shearing about some Land on Holt Heath.[1] We all dind & drank tea at Sister Ravens at the Hall . . .

MARCH 18, SATURDAY

HR R Bye to Brampton with beer. W Lamb after Jobs forenoon, ploughing at Bulling farm, Boyce at work in yard. W Holman & T Baldwin after Jobs, T Raynor in M^t^ H, G Thompson & H Raven Cleansed XX. WH at Holt evening, M^rs^ & M^r^ H & Nath Raven came from Whissonsett afternoon.

[LETHERINGSETT]

MARCH 19, SUNDAY

HR Mrs Hardy to Clay forenoon. Famaly at own Church afternoon, H Raven at Holt.

MH A dry chearly day. I & J Thompson went to Cley Meeting foornoon. All except H Raven went to our Church Afternoon, Mr Burrell preachd a Political Sermon, Prov^b^ 24.[2] The Miss Leekes call'd in the Eveng.

[1] *Paxfield* By coincidence the occupier of the farm, John Shearing, was at the same time looking for a tenant at the Red Lion, Fakenham's premier inn (*Norw. Merc.* 18 Mar. 1797). See also Henry Raven's entry for 1 June 1797

[2] *Prov. 24* The diarist has not quoted the verse. This chapter is devoted mostly to the righteousness of the struggle against evil men, and could be interpreted as a justification for taking up arms in time of war. Verse 10 berates the hearer: *If thou faint in the day of adversity, thy strength is small.*

The rector, a confirmed Tory, could have drawn on many other passages to make his point, thereby angering the anti-war Hardys.

He might also have dwelt on the parliamentary majority in support of the Government, verse 6 being capable of an interpretation favouring the ministerial policy of the day: *For by thy wise counsel thou shalt make thy war: and in multitude of counsellors there is safety.*

A few days later Revd Mr Burrell may have appreciated the irony of his neighbours' actions. His recalcitrant anti-war flock were installing in their home some sash windows salvaged from the dismantled military camp canteen (23 Mar. 1797)

MARCH 20, MONDAY

HR W Lamb & Thomas Baldwin ploughing at Bulling farm, R Bye draying away beer & whent to Corpusta with beer. T Raynor in M^{t} H, W Holman in brewhouse forenoon, sowing seeds after^{n} in Meadow. T Boyce in garden, G Thompson grinding Malt for brew. Nath Raven left us the afternoon 3 oClock.

MH A dry chearly day. Mr Hardy at home all day. W^{m} rid to Saxlingham afternoon, drank tea & Supt at Mr Balls, came home after ten. Lame Cow Calv'd. Mr Burrell quareled with Mrs Dobson . . .

MARCH 21, TUESDAY

HR R Bye, W Holman & G Thomp^{n} in brewhouse, H Raven brewing. W Lamb & T Baldwin ploughing at Bulling farm, T Raynor in Malthouse, T Boyce in garden forenoon. Mr Nash from Horsted dined here.[1] Mr Hardy rode to Holt afternoon, WH at home all day.

MARCH 22, WEDNESDAY

HR W Lamb & T Baldwin ploughing at Bulling farm. R Bye to Thursford forenoon, to Sharrington afternoon. T Raynor in Malthouse, W Holman after Jobs, G Thompson Cleansed `//, ground malt for bin & whent to Saxlingham for Mr Hammond. H Raven whent to Guestwick afternoon. M^{r} H at home all day, WH whent to Sharringham.

MH A dry chearly day. Mr Hardy up to Holt Farm foornoon, came home to dinn«er». W^{m} rid to Sheringham in his new Cart, Din'd there, drank tea at Mr Flowers at upper Sheringham, came home even 7.

MARCH 23, THURSDAY

HR W Lamb to Morston & Thornage with beer & helping to Cleanse, R Bye helping to git beer into cask morning & whent to plough at Bulling farm. T Baldwin at harrow at Bulling farm, J Herring sowing Oats forenoon, T Raynor in Mt House. G Thompson & H Raven got the Cleanse beer into cask & Cleansed XX beer, W Holman at work in brewhouse all day. Mr Bunnett & Lad all day putting in sashes in headhom«e»,[2] Dawsons Man all day. W Hardy at home all day, M^{r} H at Bulling farm afternoon. M^{r} & Mrs Sheldrake drank tea here.

[1] *Nash* The Hardys had known many members of the Nash family while at Coltishall (*Diary 1*).

This was probably the prominent Horstead farmer and churchwarden Spooner Nash (bur. Horstead 21 Nov. 1810 aged 72), of Largate Farm; his widow Mary died at Coltishall 11 June 1814 aged 82 and was buried at Horstead 15 June.

His first wife Ann, née Grimes, whose death Mary Hardy recorded in 1779, had been the widow of the miller of Horstead Watermill, William Royall.

The visitor may alternatively have been another Horstead farmer known to the Hardys, Samuel Nash

[2] *headhome* The entries of Henry Raven and Mary Hardy taken together indicate it was a synonym for frontage.

The Hardys were replacing some of their east-facing windows against the front yard, and not the south windows facing the main road; the camp canteen seems to have been quite a substantial structure.

David Yaxley's glossary lists a term closely related to Henry's, *head house*: 'The main part of a dwelling house, particularly the front range as opposed to the backhouse or leanto part' (D. Yaxley, *A Researcher's Glossary of words found in historical documents in East Anglia* (Larks Press, Guist Bottom, 2003), p. 101)

left A Norfolk farm wagon on display at Wroxham Barns. These are heavy vehicles; mercifully when Baldwin was run over by the beer wagon on 9 Dec. 1796 he was returning with empty barrels. He was lucky not to have been killed, the press often reporting fatal cart and wagon accidents.

He was back at work on 13 Mar., but walked behind the plough for only two hours that day. He then took an empty cart to Holt [*MB · 1992*]

MH A dry chearly day. Mr Hardy rid to Holt Farm afternoon, came home to tea. Mr & Mrs & M Sheldrake drank tea here. A small Shower in the eveng. Wm at home. Bricklayers & Carpenter at work putting Sashes into the Yard front. Mrs Mason Died at Godwick.

MARCH 24, FRIDAY

HR R Bye to Wells with beer & loded for Burnham, W Lamb to Waybourn with beer & Clay for [ ] Cinders from Mr Ellis's. T Raynor in Mt H, W Holman in brewhouse. Mr Bunnett«'s» Man & two lads all day, Dawson«'s» Man all day. T Baldwin & J Herring at work at Bulling farm. WH at home all day, Mr H at Holt afternoon.

MH A dry chearly day. Mr Hardy rid to Holt Farm Afternoon, came home to tea. Wm at home all day & poorly . . .

MARCH 25, SATURDAY

HR R Bye to Burnham with beer. W Lamb in brewhouse, whent to Mr Temples for a lode of Straw. W Holman sowing grass seeds in Meadow forenoon, in brewhouse afternoon, T Baldwin ploughing at Bulling farm. G Thompson in brewhouse, HR Brewing, T Raynor in Mt H. Bunnett«'s» Man & two Laborers all day & Dawsons Man all day. Mr & WH at home all day.

below Sash windows in the *headhome*, Henry's dialect word for the main frontage (23 Mar.). The two on the ground floor of the east front, to the right of the entrance porch, are William Hardy jnr's study, the room in which he died on 22 June 1842 [*MB · 1998*]

Beeston
East Runton
Watch Tower

MARCH 26, SUNDAY

HR Mrs Hardy to Clay afternoon, W Hardy at Holt Church afternoon. M^{r} H at home all day.

MH A Windy day & showers afternoon. No service at our Church, I & JT went to Cley meeting Afternoon. W^{m} went to Holt Church afternoon, drank tea at Mr Bartells.

MARCH 27, MONDAY

HR W Lamb ploughing & [at] Bulling farm, R Bye ploughing in barley, T Baldwin sowing & brushing oats at B [Bulling's] farm. W Holman in brewhouse forenoon, at Bulling farm afternoon getting off Stones.[1] Mr Hardy at home all day. WH & Mr Balls whent to Reefham. G Thompson Cleansed XX beer,[2] H Raven rode to Saxlingham morning.

MH A close day, some small showers of Rain. W^{m} & T Balls of Saxlingham went to Reepham in the Chaise Morng 8. W^{m} bought some Timber of Mr Sewill,[3] came home eveng 8, T Balls Slept here. Mr Hardy at home all day . . .

MARCH 28, TUESDAY

HR W Lamb to Sharringham with beer, bro^{t} home 800 Bricks from Mr Creamers Kiln.[4] R Bye ploughing at Bulling farm on old ground,[5] T Baldwin ploughing & sowing Barley at D^{o}. W Holman after Jobs, G Thompson in brewhouse. Mr Hardy at Holt afternoon,[6] H Raven whent to Brinton for Cloverseed. WH & Miss H set of for Whissonsett forenoon 10 OClock.

[1] *getting off stones* The indebted innkeeper would appear to have devoted his time to running the Bull rather than maintaining his small farm. Not only did the soil need bulking up and nourishing with loads of muck and marl, but it had to be cleared of heather, gorse and stones. Such management as Bulling's made expert agriculturalists shake their heads over what they saw as 'moors' instead of productive ground at a time of national shortages; hence the push for efficiency and enclosure

[2] *cleansed XX* Henry now often does not record the cleansing of the weaker brew (`//). Henry's brewing pattern differs from William's. He uses fewer men, and brews more often

[3] *Sewell* Samuel Sewell is listed in the 1806 Norfolk pollbook as a carpenter of Hackford, the parish adjoining Reepham; the two form the town centre

[4] *Mr Cremer's kiln* Marked on Faden's county map of 1797 (illustrated) on the northern edge of Beeston Heath, to the south of Cremer Cremer's Beeston Hall, Beeston Regis

[5] *old ground* Also known as olland and lay-ground: a year of grass as part of the cereal rotation. Bye was ploughing up the grass

[6] *Mr Hardy* According to his wife he spent all the afternoon at Holt Heath Farm

MARCH 29, WEDNESDAY

HR R Bye & Tho[s] Baldwin ploughing in lower furze close. W Lamb & W Holman harrowing & Rolling at Bulling farm forenoon, unloded a lode of Straw & got up a lode of wood afternoon. T Raynor in M[t] H, Dawsons man all day, Bunnett & Lad all day. Gunton Thompson in brewhouse. M[r] Hardy at Thursford with M[r] Smith, M[rs] Dobson drank tea here.

MH A drisly day. I very poorly with dimness in my Eyes & Head Ake all day. M[r] Hardy went with M[r] Smith of Cley to M[r] Girlings at Thursford to settle an affair of Scandal propagated against him, came home eve 8.[1] M[rs] Dobson drank tea here.

MARCH 30, THURSDAY

HR Tho[s] Baldwin & W Lamb ploughing for peas, R Bye sowing peas, W Holman at harrow. Gunton [Thompson] grinding Malt for brew, T Raynor in M[t] H, Dawsons Man all day. M[r] Hardy at M[r] Temples afternoon.

MH A fine day. M[r] Hardy at home all day. M[r] Burcham of Holt & Young King came Eveng past 5 to show M[r] Hardy the form of an Acct of Parliment for inclosing the Heath & Commons at Holt,[2] they drank tea here & staid till eveng 8. I very poorly with pain in my Head . . .

MARCH 31, FRIDAY

HR Tho[s] Baldwin & W Lamb ploughing, R Bye sowing peas. W Holman at harrow ¾ of day then in brewhouse, T Raynor in M[t] H, T Boyce at work in furze close. M[r] H at home all day. G Thompson in brewhouse. M[r] W Hardy & Miss H came from Whissonsett.

APRIL 1, SATURDAY

Henry Raven W Lamb Bushing [brushing in] & rolling the peas, T Baldwin ploughing in furze close. R Bye in brewhouse forenoon, ploughing after[n]. W Holman & G Thompson in brewhouse, H Raven brewing. T Raynor in M[t] H, T Boyce at work in furze close. M[r] & WH at Holt afternoon.

APRIL 2, SUNDAY

HR W Lamb, R Bye, T Baldwin, W Holman & H Raven got the beer into great Cask. M[rs] H at Clay forenoon, M[r] & WH at home all day.

facing page **Cremer Cremer's brick-kiln by the heath at Beeston Regis (28 Mar.)** [*Faden's Map of Norfolk 1797: Larks Press 1989*]

---

[1] *an affair of scandal* The nature of the allegation is not stated, nor is it clear if it was directed at William Hardy or his innkeeper; drinkers—and the Excise—were ever watchful over adulterated beer. In his accounts for the year ending 25 Sept. 1797 William Hardy entered an item, 'Paid for Girling £40 0*s* 0*d*', which may relate to this 'scandal' (*World*, vol. 2, chap. 11).

[2] *Act of Parliament* This was not passed until 1807 (*World*, vol. 2, chap. 3). A meeting had been held at the Feathers, Holt on 31 Aug. 1796 to 'consider the propriety of an application to Parliament for enclosing the heaths, commons, wastes etc of Holt' (*Norw. Merc.* 27 Aug. 1796). By the time of the second meeting at the Feathers, on 14 Mar. 1797, to agree the wording and to nominate commissioners, Letheringsett was included in the draft Bill, creating further scope for claims (*Norw. Merc.* 25 Feb. 1797). Neither meeting was attended by the Hardys.

The visitors of 30 Mar. were the surveyor and valuer John Burcham and the farmer John King (bur. Holt 6 Apr. 1835 aged 69), son of Robert: see note for 9 July 1794

Mary Hardy A Showry day. I & J Thompson went to Cley meeting foornoon. I poorly with dimness in my Eyes afternoon. Mr Hardy & W^m^ at our Church afternoon, M^r^ & Mrs Savory came to our Church Afternoon.

APRIL 3, MONDAY

HR W Lamb to Syderstone with beer, R Bye to Edgefield with beer & ploughing half a day, T Baldwin ploughing in furze close. W Holman helping to Cleanse & after Jobs, T Boyce at work in yard, G Thompson Cleansed X beer. M^r^ H & H Raven sett of for Coltishall Morning, WH at home all day.

MH A Rainy day. Mr Hardy sett of for Horstd & Coltishall with H Raven in the Chaise, dind at Branton,[1] drank tea at M^r^ S Nash^s^ at Horstd, heard Mr Press s Farm was promisd to Mr Coben of this Town,[2] Supt at Mr Hawses at Coltishall & Slept at the W^t^ Horse at Hobbis [White Horse at Great Hautbois].[3] W^m^ at home all day & very poorly.

CAR SALES

[1] *Brampton* William Hardy bought the Cross Keys at Brampton in the year to Sept. 1797, his accounts giving the purchase price as £92; the innkeeper William Doughty paid £5 rent (*Diary 4*, app. D4.B). The public house had been for sale following Chapman Ives's bankruptcy (*Norw. Merc.* 14 May 1796), the purpose of William Hardy's Coltishall visit being presumably to secure what he could from the piecemeal break-up of Ives's concern

[2] *Mr Press's farm* The Letheringsett farm later known as Piggotts, and owned by Mrs Margaret Tryon. The Press family left 10 Oct. 1801. James Cobon, his wife Mary (bur. Letheringsett 1 Feb. 1844 aged 82), née Overton, whom he had married 8 Aug. 1787, and their growing family moved into this farm from Letheringsett Hall Farm (see notes for 17 Nov. 1794 and 16 Feb. 1797).

Spooner Nash's news held great significance for the Hardys, James Cobon's removal giving William jnr vacant possession a year after his purchase of the manor and Hall Farm in Oct. 1800 (*Diary 4*)

[3] *Hawes* Siday (b. Bury St Edmunds, Suff. 8 Oct. 1748, marr. Coltishall 27 Nov. 1786 Elizabeth Porson of E. Ruston, d. Coltishall 6 Oct. 1827, bur. there 12 Oct.), farmer, maltster and brewer; his name rhymes with tidy. He had come to Coltishall in summer 1782 from King's Lynn (*Diary 2*).

facing page Coltishall: the Old House, refronted 1727 by John Wells (d.1736), stands shyly behind high walls and trees on the main road opposite Upper Common. This was from *c*.1801 the home of the farmer, maltster and brewer Siday Hawes. He had taken over from William Hardy in 1782 as manager of the maltings and brewery, beside the river, of the Norwich merchant John Wells (d.1823).

By 1805 Hawes owned the three village breweries William Hardy had known: Wells's, Ives's and Browne's, this last having been bought *c*.1787 by Chapman Ives. Hawes concentrated brewing at this house, where Wells's had been founded nearly a century earlier [*MB · 2001*]

above left '. . . Supped at Mr Hawes's at Coltishall and slept at the White Horse at Hautbois' (3 Apr.).

Ornamental ironwork for the inn board at the old White Horse, Gt Hautbois, where William Hardy and Henry Raven stayed overnight. It faces the main Norwich–N. Walsham road turnpiked in 1797, on the eastern approach to Coltishall Bridge over the Aylsham navigation [*MB · 2002*]

APRIL 4, TUESDAY

HR W Lamb whent to Coltishall early morning, R Bye to Overstrand with beer. T Baldwin ploughing, W Holman stoping gaps. T Boyce at work at furze close, T Raynor in M^{t} H, WH at home all day. M^{r} H & H Raven came from Coltishall by Aldborough.

MH A fine day till eveng 4 then raind. W^{m} sent Wm Lamb to Coltishall to Mr Hardy, he came home eveng 3. W^{m} finely. Maids & Eliz Loades washd 4 Weeks Linnen. Mr Hardy came home Eveng 8 . . .

APRIL 5, WEDNESDAY

HR W Lamb to Thursford & Clay with beer, R Bye After Jobs morning & whent to Hildolvestone with beer. W Holman in brewhouse, G Thompson grinding Malt for brew, T Boyce at work at furze close. T Raynor in M^{t} H, M^{r} & WH at home all day.

APRIL 6, THURSDAY

HR R Bye to Briston forenoon, to Salthouse with beer & Clay for 2 Chaldron Cinders from Mr Ellis's after^{n}. W Lamb, W Holman & G Thompson in brewhouse, HR brewing. T Raynor in M^{t} H, T Boyce at work at furze close. M^{r} & WH at home all day.

MH Dry morng, raind again afternoon. Mr Hardy at home all day, W^{m} very bad with the Rumatism . . .

At the time of his son Robert's death in 1841 the brewery had 53 tied houses (NRO: MS 7351, 7 D4); most of these were the tied estate of the three breweries from which Hawes's was formed. Mrs Hawes (d.1842 aged 86), was sister to Richard Porson (1759–1808), from 1791 Regius Professor of Greek at Cambridge.

The history of Coltishall brewing is charted in *World*, vol. 2, chap. 8

above Coltishall Hall, Chapman Ives's home. The White Horse, where the Letheringsett party stayed, was for sale from his bankruptcy of 1796. It was the only one of the four local public houses with an innkeeper known to William Hardy from his Coltishall years.

This was the first of Henry Raven's two recorded visits to the village where his cousins had spent their early years; the second was in Aug. 1803 [*MB · 2011*]

APRIL 7, FRIDAY

HR W Lamb to Fakenham with beer, R Bye to Cromer with D^{o}. T Baldwin ploughing in five Acres, W Holman after Jobs & harrowing a little time afternoon. G Thompson & H Raven Cleansed `// & X beer, T Raynor in Malthouse, T Boyce at work in furze close. M^{r} H at home all day, WH at Holt Afternoon.

MH A Cold windy day. Mr Hardy at home all day. W^{m} very poorly, rid up to Holt Farm afternoon & drank tea at the Miss Leakes . . .

APRIL 8, SATURDAY

HR W Lamb to Wells with beer, R Bye to Holt & Stody with beer & unloded Cinders. T Baldwin ploughing, W Holman after Jobs forenoon, at harrow afternoon. T Raynor in M^{t} H, G Thompson in brewhouse. M^{r}, M^{rs}, Miss & W Hardy at Holt Afternoon.

APRIL 9, SUNDAY

HR Famaly at Church forenoon. M^{r} & M^{rs} & Miss Forster spent the day here, H Raven at Holt afternoon.

APRIL 10, MONDAY

HR W Lamb & T Baldwin ploughing in 5 Acres, R Bye at harrow at Bells acre, furze close & 5 acres. T Raynor in Malthouse, T Boyce at work at furze close. W Holman after Jobs, G Thompson dressing flour. M^{r} & M^{rs} & Miss Forster whent a way 12 OClock. M^{r} H at home all day, WH at Holt afternoon.

APRIL 11, TUESDAY

HR W Lamb to Aldborough with beer, R Bye & T Baldwin ploughing & sowing barley. W Holman cleaning yard forenoon, at work in furze close afternoon. T Raynor in Mt House, T Boyce at work at furze close, G Thompson in brewhouse. M^{r} & WH at home all day.

MH A Close cold day. Mr Hardy & W^{m} at home all day. Mrs Woodhouse from L [Little] Thornage was Buried, her Son was Burried last Wednesday.[1]

APRIL 12, WEDNESDAY

HR W Lamb & R Bye ploughing & sowing barley in furze Close & Bells acre, Baldwin to Hindringham & Holt with beer, T Boyce at work in furze close. T Raynor in M^{t} H, W Holman in brewhouse, G Thompson grinding Malt for brew. M^{r} H at home all day, W Hardy rode out afternoon.

---

[1] *Mrs Woodhouse* See note for 28 Nov. 1795. Mary Hardy recorded in her endnotes register that Mrs Woodhouse was aged 57 and her son [Thomas] aged 24. Susanna, Christopher Woodhouse's daughter by 'his first wife', was buried Letheringsett 7 Apr. 1804 aged 24. The widowed husband married Thornage 14 Oct. 1800 Catherine Middleton, both making marks

MH A very fine Mild day. Mr Hardy up to Fur Closes foornoon & afternoon. Wm rid up to Holt afternoon, drank tea at Mr Bartells, Edmd Bartell there. Mr & Mrs Bartell went to Norwich Yesterday.

APRIL 13, THURSDAY

HR W Lamb to Southrepps with beer, T Baldwin to Sharrington with beer & ploughing afternoon. R Bye in brewhouse forenoon, ploughing aftern, W Holman & GT in Do [brewhouse], HR brewing. T Raynor in Mt H, T Boyce at work at furze close. W Hardy & Mr Balls to Southrepps, Mr H at home all day.

MH A Very foggy day. Wm & T Balls went to Southreps to pack up a Piano Forteo, did not bring it home on acct of some dispute about it by Mr Baker,[1] they drank tea at Mr Bartells at Cromer & came home eveng 9, Mr Balls supt here.

APRIL 14, FRIDAY

HR W Lamb & T Baldwin ploughing forenoon. W Lamb to Sharringham afternoon, T Baldwin dressing grass seeds & loded for Burnham afternoon. R Bye at harrow & sowing barley forenoon, dressing grass Seeds afternoon. W Holman in brewhouse, T Boyce at work in furze close. T Raynor in Mt H, G Thompson & H Raven [ ].

MH *Good Friday* A Close drisley day. Mr Hardy & Wm at home all day. I went to Cley meeting Afternoon . . .

APRIL 15, SATURDAY

HR W Lamb & R Bye ploughing & sowing Barley in five acres, T Baldwin to Burnham with beer, W Holman at harrow part of day & after Jobs. T Raynor in Mt H, T Boyce in garden. Mr & WH at Holt Afternoon.

APRIL 16, SUNDAY

HR H Raven set of for Whissonsett morning 5 oClock, Mr H at home all day. Mr Burrell very poorly, no prayers. Mrs H to Clay.

MH *Easter Sunday* A very fine day. No service at our Church, I & J Thompson went to Cley Meeting. Mr Hardy, Wm & MA went to Holt Church afternoon, Old Mr Francis preachd there [2] . . .

APRIL 17, MONDAY

HR T Baldwin to Runton & Holt with beer, W Lamb & R Bye ploughing & sowing barley in five acres. W Hol-

[1] *Mr Baker* John, a Southrepps farmer. The incident may be the one leading eventually to a charge of assault brought by John Baker against the innkeeper of the Crown, Robert Summers. The case was heard at the county quarter sessions at Norwich 24 July 1799 and respited 9 Oct. 1799, Summers evidently being let off (NRO: C/S 1/15)

[2] *Old Mr Francis* Revd Bransby Francis (bur. Edgefield 26 July 1829 aged 89), whose son served as Curate of Holt (see note for 4 Dec. 1796). He was born in Norwich, probably the son of Revd John, minister of St Peter Mancroft; admitted 1758 to St Catharine's College, Cambridge; BA 1762, MA 1765; ordained deacon Norwich 1763, priest 1764; Curate of Lakenham 1763; Rector of Edgefield 1764–1829, where he served 65 years as resident priest; Rector of Long Melford, Suff. 1819–29 (*Alum. Cantab.*)

The activities of his Sunday school at Edgefield were recorded in the *Norwich Mercury* long after reports of almost all the other Sunday schools in the county had ceased to receive publicity. The edition of 7 Jan. 1797 contained an account of the Christmas dinner he had provided as usual for the children.

The term 'old' means 'senior'. Mr Francis was then aged 56 or 57, and the diarist 63

man ditching in furze close,[1] T Boyce at furze close. T Raynor in M^{t} H, M^{r} & WH at home all day.

APRIL 18, TUESDAY

HR T Baldwin finnish«ed» ploughing & sowing barley. W Lamb to Holt & Edgefield with beer, Bro^{t} home 6 Coomb barley from Boswells. R Bye at harrow in furze close, T Boyce & W Holman at work at furze close. T Raynor in M^{t} H, G Thompson & H Raven in brewhouse. M^{r} & WH at home all day. M^{r} T Balls Junr & Sisters drank tea here, Mr Love drank tea here & Miss Bartell.[2] Town Meeting at Dobsons.

MH A very fine day. Mr Hardy & W^{m} at home all day. Mr Balls & his 2 Sisters & a Mr Love drank tea here. Mr Hardy Supt at the Town meeting at Dobsons. Sarah Starling went away, Eliz Janry came in her place [3] . . .

APRIL 19, WEDNESDAY

HR W Lamb sowing seeds & harrowing in 5 Acres, T Baldwin at harrow in d^{o} & rolling in furze Close, W Holman at work in furze close. T Boyce in garden, R Bye in brewhouse. G Thompson grinding Malt for brew, T Raynor in Mt House. M^{r} & WH at home all day.

APRIL 20, THURSDAY

HR W Lamb, R Bye & Gunton Thompson in brewhouse, H Raven brewing. W Holman at work in furze close, T Baldwin rolling the newlay &C [etc]. T Boyce in garden, T Raynor in Mt House. M^{r} H at home all day. M^{rs} & WH whent to Fakenham morning, returned Evening.

MH A very fine day. I & W^{m} sett of for Fakenham morng 9, dind & drank tea at Mr Custances, came home Even past 8, W^{m} spoke to Doctr Heath about the Rumatism. Mr Hardy at home all day . . .

APRIL 21, FRIDAY

HR W Lamb to Southrepps with beer, T Baldwin to Corpust«y» & Holt with D^{o}. R Bye in brewhouse, T Raynor in Malthouse. G Thompson & H Raven Cleansed `// & X beer & dressing Maltstones, W Holman at furze close. M^{r} H at home all day, Miss & WH at Saxlingham to tea.

APRIL 22, SATURDAY

HR T Baldwin to Thornage with beer & whent to Holt farm with a lode of muck. W Lamb got 3 lode muck to D^{o}, R Bye filling & after Jobs.[4] T Raynor in M^{t} H,

[1] *ditching* Hedging; Marshall defines it as 'a general term for fencing with hedge and ditch' (W. Marshall, *The Rural Economy of Norfolk*, vol. 2, p. 378). The skilled ditcher usually liked to work with thorn bushes (hawthorn or blackthorn) to produce a dense barrier for livestock

[2] *Love* See notes for 30 Dec. 1795 and 16 Jan. 1797. Samuel Love was about to become the new innkeeper of the King's Head at Holt following Henry Crafer's bankruptcy.

Love moved to the Feathers at Holt in 1804 while retaining ownership of the King's Head, the Feathers then being newly purchased by Mr Taylor of Gt Yarmouth. Mary Hardy records that her husband and Samuel Love signed the lease in Norwich for the Feathers (*Diary 4*: 8 Oct. 1804), suggesting that Love was tied to Letheringsett in some way, such as by bond.

The history of each of the Hardys' 101 public house outlets is summarised in the gazetteer (*World*, vol. 2)

[3] *Elizabeth Jennerys* She stayed until 10 Oct. 1797 and was paid £1 10*s*: see note for 10 Oct. 1796 and Mary Hardy's register of maidservants in the endnotes

[4] *filling* The muck cart

G Thompson & H Raven dressing Malt Stones. M^{r} & WH at Holt Market, Miss H at Holt After^{n}. W Holman at work at furze close,[1] T Boyce in garden.

APRIL 23, SUNDAY

HR Famaly at own Church forenoon. M^{rs} H to Clay afternoon, WH & H Raven at Holt after^{n}. T Baldwin loded for Stalham.

MH A very fine day. All went to our Church foornoon, a Communion, no Sermon. I & JT went to Cley meeting afternoon. W^{m} went to Holt Church afternoon & drank tea at Mr Seales, came home even past 8.

APRIL 24, MONDAY

HR W Lamb got two lode muck to Holt farm forenoon, whent to Briston with beer afternoon. R Bye filling muck cart forenoon, cutting the wood in yard afternoon. T Boyce in garden, T Baldwin to Stalham with beer. Gun^{t} Thompson & H Raven laid down malt stones, M^{r} H at home all day. The Miss Leaks drank tea here, AL [Ann Leak] rode out with WH afternoon.

MH A fine day, a small Showr eveng 6. Mr Hardy & W^{m} at home all day. H Ravn Brewd.[2] The Miss Lekes from Holt drank tea here, we sent them home in the Cart . . .

APRIL 25, TUESDAY

HR W Lamb & R Bye carting thornes into Field forenoon, whent to Holt fair afternoon, T Baldwin came from Stalham. T Boyce in garden, T Raynor in M^{t} H, G Thompson in brewhouse. M^{r} & WH at Holt fair. Mr Temple, Blakeny, dined here. M^{rs}, Miss H and H Raven whent to Holt after tea.

[1] *William Holman* This appears to have been his last day working for the Hardys. Mary Hardy had not mentioned him, showing the value of Henry's record. His labour had been needed since Sept. 1796 in the hard-pressed months when the new farm took up extra time and effort, and after Nicholas Woodhouse's departure in Oct. 1796 there was no farm boy

[2] *Henry Raven* Strangely, the day Mary Hardy first acknowledges her nephew as brewer is not recorded by Henry as a brewing day. He notes 20 and 28 Apr. as brewing days

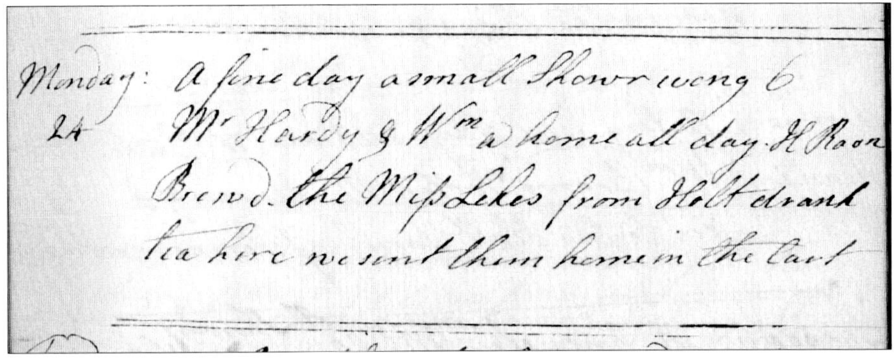
Monday: A fine day a small Showr eveng 6
24 Mr Hardy & W^{m} a home all day. H Ravn
Brewd. the Miss Lekes from Holt drank
tea here we sent them home in the Cart

below **'H. Raven brewed.' Mary Hardy's entry for 24 Apr. raises questions over her accuracy. This is her first reference to Henry's new status. But he had been brewing without supervision for three months—and 24 Apr. seems not to have been a brewing day** [*Cozens-Hardy Collection*]

APRIL 26, WEDNESDAY

HR W Lamb to Edgefield with beer forenoon, whent to Holt farm with a lode muck afternoon. T Baldwin ill, no work.[1] R Bye in brewhouse, T Raynor in Mt H, T Boyce in garden part of day. Mr H at home all day, WH at Holt afternoon. G Thompson & H Raven in brewhouse.

APRIL 27, THURSDAY

HR W Lamb to Holt morning with beer & draying beer from white hall the remainder of day, R By«e» Do from Do.[2] WH drawing of [off] porter in W Hall, H Raven grinding Malt for brew and Bin. T Raynor in Mt H, T Boyce in garden, T Baldwin putting beer into Cask afternoon. G Thompson ill, not able to work.

MH A very Wet morng, close drisly day. Mr T Forster dind here & took MA home with him Eveng past 2 to Holt House near Lynn . . .

APRIL 28, FRIDAY

HR W Lamb to Fakenham & Sharrington with beer. T Baldwin, R Bye & G Thompson in brewhouse, H Raven brewing. T Raynor in Mt H, T Boyce in garden. Mr H at Holt Afternoon, WH at Mr Savorys to tea.

APRIL 29, SATURDAY

HR R Bye in brewhouse all day, W Lamb to Holt morning, in brewhouse remainder of day. T Baldwin to Brampton with beer, G Thompson & H Raven Cleansed `// & XX beer. T Raynor in Malthouse, T Boyce in Garden part of day. Mr & WH at Holt afternoon.

APRIL 30, SUNDAY

HR Men at work in brewhouse morning. Mrs H to Clay morning, famaly at own church Afternoon.

MH A very fine day. I & JT went to Cley meeting foornoon, all went to our Church afternoon. Mr Burrell preachd from Matthew 5 Chaptr 16 Verse, made a very poor hand of it.[3] Mr T Balls Junr came here in the Eveng & Supt here.

MAY 1, MONDAY

Henry Raven W Lamb in brewhouse morning, whent to Holt & ploughing Afternoon. R Bye & G Thompson in Brewhouse, H Raven brewing (Porter).[4] T Raynor in M H, T Boyce in garden, T Baldwin to Sharringham with beer. Mr & WH at home all day.

[1] *ill* This may be Henry's diplomatic way of saying that Baldwin had a hangover after the fair. During the Coltishall years his aunt would note her husband as 'ill' following a long stint at the public house

[2] *ditto from ditto* Bye was draying beer out of the white hall. William seems no longer to be reining in his cousin over his predilection for dittos

[3] *Matt. 5, v. 16 Let your light so shine before men, that they may see your good works, and glorify your Father which is in heaven.*

This could have been a controversial text for Mary Hardy. At the heart of the Calvinist tradition, and thus of Lady Huntingdon and her chaplain George Whitefield, was the belief in salvation not by works but by faith alone.

The Wesleyans however, as Arminians, embraced good works as well as faith, as did the Established Church in the 39 Articles

[4] *brewing (porter)* These are Henry's parentheses, as also on 3 May. He was busy brewing porter in early May 1797, and must have satisfied his cousin.

William was away 10–13 May, and 19-year-old Henry was entrusted not only with brewing, cleansing and casking unsupervised but also with seeing to the plumbers' repairs to the pipework

above The brewhouse site where William and Henry brewed: a photograph by Basil Cozens-Hardy after the fire of 24 Apr. 1936, taken looking north-west across the yard. The horizontal timber louvres ventilating the two floors of the brewhouse were destroyed in the flames, leaving the gap in the flint wall seen here between the malt-mill house to the far right and the racking room ('white hall') to the far left [*Cozens-Hardy Collection*]

Mary Hardy A Very fine day. I Began to Bathe. Wm Brew'd Porter, Mr Hardy & I rid to the Holt Farm afternoon.

MAY 2, TUESDAY

HR R Bye & W Lamb at work in brewhouse, G Thompson & H Raven Cleansed XX & grinding Malt for Brew. T Baldwin ploughing in furze close, T Raynor in M^t H, T Boyce at work in field. M^r & WH at home all day.

MH A fine day, some small Showers. Mr Hardy & W^m at home all day. Doctr Heath & Dr Bartell calld to speak to W^m.[1] Hannah Dagliss went away for leaving the dore open for the Chimney Sweep.[2]

MAY 3, WEDNESDAY

HR W Lamb to Southrepps with beer, Bro^t home the Piano Forte. R Bye, T Baldwin in Brewhouse, Cleaned the great cask. G Thompson in brewhouse, H Raven brewing (Porter). T Raynor in Malthouse, T Boyce at work in field. M^r & WH at home all day.

MH A fine day. I Bathd. Mr Hardy & W^m at home all day, Wm Brewd Porter.

[1] *Dr Heath and Dr Bartell* In view of William's sudden determination to bathe in the sea that summer it is likely the doctors recommended a course of sea-bathing to relieve his rheumatism. As a small boy at Coltishall he had bathed with his mother in the malthouse cistern, but had not shown any desire to bathe in her garden bath at Letheringsett. Mr Bartell's son Edmund enthused over Cromer's provision: 'The bathing machines are very commodious, and the bather [attendant] a careful attentive man. The shore also, which is a firm sand, not only renders the bathing agreeable, but when the tide retires, presents such a surface for many miles as cannot be exceeded' (E. Bartell jnr, *Cromer considered as a Watering Place* (1806), p. 23)

[2] *Hannah Dagliss* Mary Hardy's endnotes register of maidservants gives additional detail. Hannah was dismissed 'for leaving the backhouse door unbarred for the chimney-sweeper and then was saucy'. She was paid £1 16*s* 4*d* for her service so far that year. When the Hardys found themselves suddenly without a maid in 1799 the same saucy Hannah was taken on again (*Diary 4*: 9 Jan. 1799).

She may be the Hannah Dagless born at Edgefield in 1770 and orphaned very young: see the note in the maidservants' register. The disruption caused by the departure of two maidservants within two weeks affected the washing routine. When Elizabeth Milligen came to help on 16 May 1797 a backlog of six weeks' laundry had formed

MAY 4, THURSDAY

HR W Lamb, T Baldwin & R Bye at work in brewhouse & getting beer into great Cask &C [etc]. T Raynor in M^{t} H, G Thompson grinding Malt for brew. H Raven & W Hardy put the Cleanse porter in Cask & Cleansed XX. M^{r} H at Holt to dinner, T Boyce at work in field.

MH A very Wet windy day. Mr Hardy walkd up to Holt foornoon to meet Crafords [Crafer's] Creditors to prevent their segning [signing] his Certificate, dind at the Feathers & came home even 7.[1] W^{m} at home all day . . .

MAY 5, FRIDAY

HR R Bye & G Thompson in brewhouse, W Lamb in brewhouse forenoon, after Jobs in yard after^{n}, H Raven brewing porter. T Baldwin ploughing, T Boyce at work in field, T Raynor in Mt H. M^{r} & WH at home all day. M^{r} & Mrs Savory, Miss Howard & M^{r} & Mrs Hawkins drank tea here.[2]

MAY 6, SATURDAY

HR T Baldwin to Holt with beer & helping to git beer in to greate Cask & whent to plough afternoon. W Lamb & R Bye, G Thompson & H Raven got the Cleanse porter into great cask, WL whent to harrow after^{n}. GT, RB & HR Cleansed X beer after^{n}. T Raynor in M^{t} H, T Boyce at work in field. M^{r} & WH at Holt afternoon.

MAY 7, SUNDAY

HR Famaly at own Church fornoon. M^{rs} H to Clay [Briston] afternoon, WH to Holt afternoon.

MH A Cold chearly day. We all went to our Church foornoon. Mr Burrell preach'd Mathew 5, 8, & made a poor hand of it.[3] I & J Thompson went to Briston Meeting afternoon.[4] W^{m} went to Holt Church afternoon, came home to tea.

MAY 8, MONDAY

HR T Baldwin helping to git the porter into Cask & whent to Hindolvistone with beer, W Lamb to Cromer & Runton with beer. R Bye at work at home forenoon, stoping gaps after^{n}, G Thompson & HR & WH got the Cleanse beer into great Cask. T Raynor in M^{t} H, T Boyce at work in field.

MH A very chearly day, wind cold. Mr Hardy at home all day. W^{m} & I rid to lower Sheringham afternoon to look

---

[1] *certificate* Issued if the third meeting of the bankrupt's commissioners proved satisfactory. This was soon to be debated over another bankrupt, the Blakeney merchant Robert Farthing, who supplied the Hardys with coal and cinders (note for 8 June 1797). A certificate would not be issued at the third meeting of an individual's commissioners if the creditors managed to dissuade them from signing it.

William Hardy was acting decisively on 4 May 1797 to prevent the former King's Head innkeeper Henry Crafer, who must still have owed him money, from being discharged. This bankruptcy was not wound up until 1801, the only dividend from the sale of Crafer's estate and effects being issued at King's Lynn 26 Oct. 1801 (*Norw. Merc.* 26 Sept. 1801)

[2] *Mr and Mrs Hawkins* From Lynn, noted Mary Hardy

[3] *Matt. 5, v. 8 Blessed are the pure in heart: for they shall see God*

[4] *to Briston meeting* A return after the long absence since 25 Oct. 1795

above The former Jolly Farmers at Field Dalling, facing the church: 'Mr Hardy and William went to Mr Coe's of Dalling afternoon, hired a public house in that town known by the name of the Jolly Farmers . . .' (9 May 1797). It had high innkeeper turnover, and was also traded between brewers. Birchams of Reepham numbered this among their tied houses when their brewery with its tied estate was sold to the Norwich brewers, Bullards, in 1878 [*MB · 2001*]

at some Pigs of Mr Pages, Wm bought 5. We drank tea there, came home even 8.

MAY 9, TUESDAY

HR T Baldwin to Sharrington & Bale with beer & at work in brewhouse, W Lamb to Corpusta with Do. R Bye very ill forenoon, not able to work, but whent to Dawling afternoon with Mr Hardys horse.[1] G Thompson grinding Malt for brew, T Raynor in Mt H, T Boyce at work in field. WH set of for Whissonsett after dinner, Mr H whent to Dawling with him.

MH A Close high windy cold day. Mr Hardy & Wm went to Mr Coes of Dalling afternoon,[2] hired a bublick [public] House in that Town known by the Name of the Jolly Farmers, they drank tea there.[3] Wm went from thence to Whisonsett in his way to Mr Forsters at Holt House near Lynn were he intend to go to Morrow for his Sister, Mr Hardy came home eveng past 8. Began to rain Eveng 9, continued all Night. I Bathd . . .

1 *Dalling* William must have taken his father with him in the chaise or cart, Robert Bye then delivering William Hardy's horse for the return journey that evening

2 *Coe* William Coe (d.1804 aged 78), a Field Dalling farmer; his grave is by the south porch. He was a formidable negotiator. He and four other parishioners had appealed at Walsingham 14 Apr. 1796 against the Dalling churchwardens and overseers over the poor rate set on 30 Mar. 1796. The appeal was successful, the rate being quashed 28 July 1796 (NRO: C/S 1/15)

3 *Jolly Farmers* It had not been known by that name for long: see note for 25 Oct. 1793. The Hart, under James Reeves, was not listed in the alehouse register from 1795 onwards, the Jolly Farmers making its first appearance in the official record in 1798 with John Rush as innkeeper; the records for 1797 have not survived. By 1799 Thomas Gravelin/Graveland had taken over (NRO: C/Sch 1/16).

The lease from Mr Coe began at Old Michaelmas 1797, the Jolly Farmers not featuring in William Hardy's accounts of Sept. 1797. For some unexplained reason John Rush paid rent of £8 to the Hardys, while Thomas Gravelin paid £6.

James Moore handled the draft lease for William Hardy (NRO: ACC Cozens-Hardy 23/8/1976, Attorney's ledger 1793–99, p. 23)

MAY 10, WEDNESDAY

HR W Lamb to Clay, bro^{t} home 2 Chal^{d} Cinders from Mr Ellis's & Loded for Syderstone. T Baldwin, R Bye & G Thompson in brewhouse, H Raven Brewing. T Raynor in M^{t} H, T Boyce at work in field. Mr Haddens two men came & Mended the pipe belonging to the backs.[1] M^{r} H at home all day.

MAY 11, THURSDAY

HR W Lamb to Syderstone with beer, T B^{d} [Baldwin] to Aldborough with D^{o}, R Bye in brewhouse. T Raynor in M^{t} H, T Boyce at work in field, G Thompson & H Raven Cleansed `// & XX beer. Mr Balls drank tea here, M^{r} H at home all day. HR whent to Mr Temples after straw.

MH A Wet morng, close hasy day. Mr Hardy at home all day. T Balls drank tea here. Eiz [Eliz] Chastney came as Cook.[2] I Bathd . . .

MAY 12, FRIDAY

HR T Baldwin to Clay for 1½ Chal^{d} coals from Mr Jacksons, unloded them & whent to Holt with beer. W Lamb after Jobs forenoon, whent to Gunthorpe with D^{o} [beer], came home by Sharrington & bro^{t} some straw from Mr Lee's. T Raynor in M^{t} H, T Boyce at work in field. G Thompson dressing flour, H Raven clean'd White hall. Mr Temple, Blackney, drank tea here.

MAY 13, SATURDAY

HR W Lamb to Burnham with beer, T Baldwin to Brampton with D^{o}. T Raynor in Mt House, T Boyce at work in yard. R By ¾ of day in brewhouse, G Thompson grinding Malt for brew. M^{r} H at Holt Markett. WH & Miss Hardy came home from Mr Forsters about 5 oClock, WH whent to Holt evening.

MAY 14, SUNDAY

HR Mrs Hardy to Clay afternoon. M^{r}, Miss Hardy & H Raven at own Church afternoon, WH at Holt. The Master Forsters came morning for parcel which WH bro^{t} from Ash Wicking.[3]

MH A very fine day. I & J Thompson went «to» Cley meeting afternoon, Mr Hardy & MA went to our Church afternoon, Mr Burrell preachd from Mathew 5 Chaptr 3 Verse, made a poor hand of it.[4] W^{m} went to Holt Church afternoon, came home to tea.

[1] *Haddon* William (? d. 1 Mar. 1809 aged 61), a Holt plumber and glazier (NRO: PD 2/4; *Univ. Brit. Dir.*, vol. 3, p. 280). He acted as witness at John Bunnett's marriage (see note for 24 Feb. 1794); as a plumber he would have worked closely with the Holt builder.

On 23 Oct. 1770 Haddon had married Jane Howard at Holt. She may have been related to John Howard, innkeeper of the White Lion and in 1797 of the Pitt Arms, Burnham Market

[2] *Elizabeth Chasteney* See note for 5 Sept. 1796

[3] *Ashwicken* A tiny parish next to the Forsters' hamlet of Leziate. Thomas Forster's younger sons appear to have stayed in the Letheringsett area after their parents' removal in Oct. 1796, perhaps as boarders at the Free Grammar School, Holt

[4] *Matt. 5, v. 3 Blessed are the poor in spirit: for theirs is the kingdom of heaven.*

The sharp reproof is interesting in that it must have come not from the diarist, who was at Cley Methodist meeting that afternoon, but from her husband and daughter—and William Hardy had loyally remained a practising Anglican.

It is hard to imagine how the rector managed to displease his listeners when his preaching centred on Christ's Sermon on the Mount, not perhaps the most hotly disputed area of New Testament theology

MAY 15, MONDAY

HR R Bye & G Thompson in brewhouse all day, W Lamb part of day & whent to Thornage with beer, H Raven brewing. T Baldwin to Overstrand with D^{o}, T Boyce in garden, T Raynor in Malthouse. M^{r} & WH at Holt afternoon.

MH A fine day. Mr Hardy rid up to Holt Farm afternoon, came home even 7. W^{m} went to Bowling green afternoon, came home Eve 9. I Bathd . . .

MAY 16, TUESDAY

HR T Baldwin to Wells with beer, W Lamb to Thursford & Kettlestone with D^{o}, R Bye after Jobs. T Raynor in M^{t} H, T Boyce in garden, G Thompson in brewhouse. M^{r} & WH at home all day.

MAY 17, WEDNESDAY

HR W Lamb to Sharrington & Stody with beer & whent to Kelling with WH morning, T Baldwin to Clay for 2 Chaldron Cinders from Mr Ellis's & after Jobs, R Bye at work in brewhouse. T Raynor in M^{t} H, G Thompson grinding Malt for brew, T Boyce in garden. M^{r} & WH at home all day.

MH A Close showry day. I Bathd. Mr Hardy at home all day. W^{m} went to Mr Balls, Saxlingham, drank tea & Supt there. I Bathd, W^{m} rid to the Seaside to Bathe [1] . . .

MAY 18, THURSDAY

HR W Lamb whent to Blakeny with a last of peas forenoon & bro^{t} home 1½ Chaldrons coals from Mr Temple the same afternoon. R Bye & T Baldwin in brewhouse, HR brewing. G Thompson skreening & putting up peas,[2] T Raynor in M^{t} H, T Boyce in garden. M^{r} H at home all day. M^{r} & Mrs Sheldrake drank tea here, WH at home all day.

MAY 19, FRIDAY

HR W Lamb to Sharringham with beer, T Baldwin to Holt twice & to Briston with D^{o}. T Raynor in Malthouse, R Bye after Jobs in brewhous«e». G Thompson & H Raven Cleansed '// & X beer, HR whent to Brinton afternoon, T Boyce howing [hoeing] furrows. M^{r} & WH at home all day.

MH A very hot day. Mr Hardy, I & MA rid to the Holt Farm afternoon. W^{m} went to the Sea Side to Bathe, I Bath'd . . .

above Kelling sunrise.

On 17 May 1797 William apparently persuaded his drayman William Lamb to join him in an early-morning bathe; they went together again to the sea here on 23 May.

This was William's remedy for a rheumatic complaint which he suffered for a few months in 1796–97 [*Christopher Bird 2009*]

[1] *I bathed* Mary Hardy was using her garden bath; as far as we know she never took to sea-bathing. At Coltishall she and young William had bathed early in the morning in the barley steep—out of the malting season

[2] *putting up* Preserving, ready in this case for shipment from Blakeney

MAY 20, SATURDAY

HR W Lamb to Waybourn with beer forenoon, after Jobs Afternoon. T Baldwin [

]. R Bye at work in brewhouse, T Raynor in Malthouse. T Boyce howing furrows in 6 Acres, G Thompson in brewhouse. M^r^ H at home all day, WH at Holt afternoon.

MAY 21, SUNDAY

HR M^rs^ & Miss H at own Church forenoon, WH at Holt Afternoon. H Raven at Saxlingham Afternoon.

MH A fine Morn, Showry afternoon. I & MA went to our Church foornoon. Mr Burrell preachd from Ecle^s^ 7 Chaptr 4 Verse, mad«e» poorly out.[1] I & JT went to Cley meeting afternoon. W^m^ went to Holt Church afternoon, drank tea at Mr Davys. W^m^ went to the Sea & Bath'd . . .

MAY 22, MONDAY

HR W Lamb & T Baldwin got up 4 lode of Sand & 1 D^o^ [load] of Lime forenoon, at work at Bulling farm afternoon. R Bye in brewhouse, G Thompson grinding Malt for brew. T Raynor in M^t^ H, T Boyce howing furrows. M^r^ H at Holt Afternoon, WH at home all day. Mr Balls drank tea here, H Raven walk'd to furze closes afternoon.

MAY 23, TUESDAY

HR W Lamb whent to Kelling with WH morning & in brewhouse remainder of day. R Bye & G Thompson in brewhouse, H Raven brewing. T Baldwin at work at Holt farm, T Raynor in M^t^ H, T Boyce in garden. M^r^ & M^rs^ H drank tea at Mr Burrells, WH at home all day. Master Collier & the Master Forsters drank tea here.

MH A fine day. W^m^ went to Seaside to Bathe. Mr Hardy, I & MA went to Mr Burrells to tea to meet M^r^ & Mrs Moy of Horningtoft . . .

MAY 24, WEDNESDAY

HR T Baldwin & W Lamb at work at Holt farm, R Bye at work in brewhouse. T Raynor in M^t^ H, T Boyce in garden, H Raven Cleansed `// & XX. M^r^ & WH at home all day. G Thompson set of for North walsham morning 6 oClock.[2] M^r^ & Mrs Moy, M^r^, Mrs Burrell, Mr Sheldrake & M^r^ N Burrell drank tea here.[3]

[1] *Eccles. 7, v. 4 The heart of the wise is in the house of mourning; but the heart of fools is in the house of mirth*

[2] *Thompson* The miller was granted three days' leave for N. Walsham Fair

[3] *Mr and Mrs Moy etc* Also included in the tea party, according to Mary Hardy, were Mrs Johnson and Miss Sheldrake

above 'Mr Burrell preached, ... made poorly out' (21 May). Mary Hardy's most cutting language by far in the pages of her diary is reserved for jibes against the rector.

The preacher needs to be slim to fit comfortably into this diminutive early-17th-century pulpit at Barney, near Fakenham. It is the twin of the one known to Mary Hardy at Horningtoft, where her parents had married in 1729 [*MB · 2011*]

above 'W. Lamb ... got up 2½ chaldrons of lime to the public house' (27 May). Here the barrow ramp for a lime-kiln beside the River Waveney near Beccles has a perilous slope to the staithe. For this vignette Robberds provides a commentary on the geology of Broadland, the substratum of chalk (marl) in some of the river valleys, and the employment given 'to numerous lime-burners' at the kilns (J. Stark and J. W. Robberds jnr, *Scenery of the Rivers of Norfolk*, pt 4 (1834), unpag.).

Letheringsett had marl, and the Hardys also had easy access to lime for their own building operations and for those at their public houses

[*drawing by J. Stark; engraving by R. Wallis 1834*]

MAY 25, THURSDAY

HR W Lamb to Sharrington with beer forenoon, at work at Holt farm afternoon. T Baldwin to Fakenham with beer, R Bye at work in brewhouse. T Boyce [ ], T Raynor in Malthouse, HR in brewhouse. Famaly at Mr Savorys to tea.

MH A very fine day. Mr Hardy, I & MA rid to Savorys new Building & from thence to his House, drank tea there, W^m^ came to us. W^m^ went to Seaside to Bathe . . .

MAY 26, FRIDAY

HR T Baldwin at work at Holt farm all day. W Lamb at D^o^ forenoon, to Corpust«y» with beer afternoon. T Raynor in M^t^ H, R Bye after Jobs, T Boyce no work. M^r^ & WH at home all day. G Thompson came from N^o^ Walsham Evening.

MAY 27, SATURDAY

HR T Baldwin to Holt and Edgefield with beer. W Lamb to Sharringham with D^o^, got up 2½ Chal^d^ Lime to the public house. T Raynor in Malthouse, R Bye after Jobs, G Thompson in brewhouse. M^r^ H at home all day, WH at Holt Afternoon.

MH A fine day. Mr Hardy at home all day. W^m^ went to Seaside to Bathe, {M^r^ Hardy at home all day}. I Bathd . . .

MAY 28, SUNDAY

HR M^rs^ H to Clay forenoon. M^r^ & M^rs^ & Miss H at own Church afternoon, WH at Holt. H Raven drank tea at Mr Temples, T Baldwin loaded for N^o^ Walsham.

MAY 29, MONDAY

HR T Baldwin to Northwalsham with beer, W Lamb to Morston & Holt with D^o^ & loaded for Burnham. T Raynor in M^t^ H, R Bye at work in Meadow. T Boyce in Shrubbery, G Thompson grinding Malt for brew & bin. Mr Hardy at home all day, WH at Sharringham. Dawsons man all day.

MH A fine Morng, small rain afternoon. Mr Hardy at home all day. W^m^ went to Sheringham foorn & Bathd, came back to Mr Bartells, dind & drank tea there. I Bathd.

MAY 30, TUESDAY

HR W Lamb to Burnham with beer, T Baldwin to Runton with D^o^. T Raynor in M^t^ H, R Bye in Meadow & after Jobs. M^r^ H at home all day, T Boyce in garden. WH & Miss H set of for Whissonsett forenoon. G Thompson & HR in brewhouse, Dawsons man all day.

MH A moist morng, cold close day. W^m^ & MA sett of for Whisonsett ½ past 10, MA going to stay with Sister Goggs while Henry [Goggs] is in London.[1] Mr Hardy at home all day . . .

[1] *Mary Ann* This was the supportive extended family in action, and a holiday for Mary Ann. She would have been able to share in the excitement of her cousin Rose's preparations for the first wedding in the younger generation since Robert Goggs's marriage in 1779. Henry Raven was granted leave to attend his sister's wedding, held at Whissonsett on 23 June, 'a showery day'.

Henry Goggs's future wife, Martha Buscall, whom he married at Whissonsett on 5 Dec. 1797, was living in London at the time, the marriage register giving her parish as St George-in-the-East, Middx. This is the massive Hawksmoor church of 1714–26 in what is now Cannon Street Road, London E1

MAY 31, WEDNESDAY

HR W Lamb to Aldborough with beer. T Baldwin, R Bye & G Thompson in brewhouse, H Raven brewing. T Raynor in Malthouse, T Boyce in garden. M[r] H at home all day, WH came from Whissonsett.

JUNE 1, THURSDAY

Henry Raven T Baldwin to Holt and Hinderingham with beer, W Lam«b» at work at Holt farm. R Bye after Jobs & at work in river, G Thompson & H Raven Cleansed `//. T Raynor in M[t] H, T Boyce in garden. WH at home all day, Mas[tr] Collier & Herring drank tea here. M[r] H at home all day, the mares fole died.

Mary Hardy A fine day, some small showers. M[r] Hardy & W[m] at home all day. Mastr Colyer & Master Sherring from the School at Holt drank tea here.[1]

JUNE 2, FRIDAY

HR W Lamb and Baldwin at work at Holt farm, R Bye help'd to Cleanse Morning and at work in meadow. T Raynor in M[t] H, T Boyce at work in river, G Thompson & H Raven Cleansed X beer morning. M[r] H at Holt forenoon, WH at Kelling morning, back by breakfast. The Miss Leekes drank tea here.

MH A very fine day. I Bathd, W[m] went to the Seaside to Bathe. M[r] Hardy rid to Holt farm foornoon, W[m] at home all day. The Miss Leakes drank tea here. Wet Night . . .

JUNE 3, SATURDAY

HR W Lamb to Sharringham with beer, T Baldwin to Brampton with D[o], R Bye whent to Sharrington with 1 Bar[l] `// & after Jobs. T Raynor in M[t] H, T Boyce at work in river, G Thompson in brewhouse. WH at Holt Afternoon, M[r] H at home all day.

JUNE 4, SUNDAY

HR Famaly at own Church forenoon. M[rs] H to Cley afternoon, WH & H Raven at Holt afternoon.

MH *Whit Sunday* A very fine day. All went to our Church foornoon, M[r] Burrell preachd. I & J Thompson went to Cley meeting afternoon. W[m] went to Holt Church afternoon, came home to tea. W[m] went to Seaside to Bathe, I Bathd.

facing page 'The mare's foal died' (1 June). Henry records this loss; his aunt does not. We do not learn which breeds of horse the Hardys kept for work on the farm and for delivering beer, but some agriculturalists refer to the small horses of 18th-century Norfolk.

Ruby, the five-year-old mare seen here, is a Suffolk Punch; the breed may well resemble the Hardys' animals, being smaller than some of the mighty heavy horses. Her sleepy nine-week-old foal Trojan suns himself on their summer grazing as guests at Gressenhall's Union Farm, near William Hardy jnr's birthplace of Litcham.

The Hardys suffered losses of calves and foals, and sometimes the mothers. They relied only on their own rudimentary treatments or, on occasion, those of the local animal doctor. Veterinary medicine would not become a certified profession, with a long training and examinations, until the 20th century [*MB · 2011*]

---

1 *Master Collyer etc* Presumably the son of the future Rector of Gunthorpe with Bale, with the son of John Shearing of Paxfield Farm (notes for 5 Dec. 1793, 17 Mar. 1797)

JUNE 5, MONDAY

HR W Lamb & Baldwin at work at Holt farm forenoon, no work after^{n}. R Bye after Jobs part of forenoon, D^{o} [no work] afternoon. G Thompson grinding Malt for brew, T Raynor in M House, T Boyce in garden half a day. W Lamb, T Baldwin, T Raynor & T Boyce dined here being Whitsun Monday. M^{r} H at home all day, WH at Holt after^{n}. Mrs Smith, M^{r} & Mrs Proudfoot drank tea here.

MH A very fine day. Mr Hardy at home all day. W^{m} went to Bowling Green afternoon to Holt, came home even 8. Mrs Smith of Cley & M^{r} & Mrs Proudfoot from Wells drank tea here.

JUNE 6, TUESDAY

HR W Lamb to Cromer with beer, came home by Runton & Sharringham for money.[1] T Baldwin to Clay for 2 Chal^{d} cinders from Mr Ellis's & to Thornage with beer, T Raynor in Mt House, G Thompson grinding Malt for brew. H Raven whent to Fakenham afternoon, M^{r} & WH at home all day. R Bye no work.[2]

MH A very fine day. Mr Hardy & W^{m} at home all day. H Raven went to Hempton Green Fair afternoon, came home even past 10. W^{m} went to Seaside to Bathe, I Bathd . . .

JUNE 7, WEDNESDAY

HR W Lamb to Thursford & Briston with beer, T Baldwin half a day in brewhouse. T Raynor in M^{t} H, G Thompson in brewhouse. M^{r} & WH dined at Mr Bartells, Holt, came home to tea with M^{r}, M^{rs} & Miss Bartell & M^{r} & Mrs Wood.[3] R Bye no work. Mr Smith drank tea here.

JUNE 8, THURSDAY

HR W Lamb in brewhouse forenoon, to Edgefield with beer & Malt afternoon. R Bye & G Thom^{n} in brewhouse, H Raven brewing. T Baldwin to Syderstone with beer, T Raynor in M^{t} H, T Boyce in garden. M^{r} & WH at home all day. M^{r} & Mrs Wood call'd here morning.

MH A fine morng, very showry afternoon. Mr Hardy at home all day. W^{m} went to Seaside in Morng to Bathe, I Bathd. M^{r} T Temple of Thornage drank tea & Supt here. Heard Mr Farthing of Blakney was broke.[4]

[1] *Lamb* Confirmation that, as at Coltishall, the beer money could be collected by the draymen

[2] *Bye* Henry would presumably have noted if Robert Bye was ill; his wording suggests an unauthorised absence. Bye may have chosen to absent himself for two and a half days as he had not been invited to the farm servants' Whitsun dinner on the Monday—a risky course of action by the brewer and drayman, given the strained relations of the past

[3] *Wood* From London, noted Mary Hardy: see note for 17 June 1795

[4] *Farthing* See note for 27 May 1794. The Blakeney merchant's bankruptcy was notified to creditors in the *Norwich Mercury* on 15 July 1797; the three meetings of the commissioners were to be held at the King's Head, Norwich, where Henry Raven was still innkeeper. After Mr Farthing's debtors had sent in their monies and his creditors had proved their debts, at the third meeting 'the said bankrupt is required to finish his examination and the creditors are to assent to, or dissent from, the allowance of his certificate.'

Such settlements took a long time. It was not until 27 Aug. 1803 that the *Norwich Mercury* carried the notice of a dividend payment to the creditors of 5*s* in the pound (25%) by Messrs Gurney & Peckover, the Fakenham bankers

JUNE 9, FRIDAY

HR W Lamb to Stalham with beer, T Baldwin to Sharrington & Holt with beer. R Bye after Jobs forenoon, whent to the furze close for grass afternoon. G Thompson & H Raven cleansed `//. M^r^ H at home all day, WH to Sharringham.

MH A fine day. Mr Hardy at home all day. W^m^ rid to L [Lower] Sheringham foornoon to look after some alterations doing there, came home eveng past 8.

JUNE 10, SATURDAY

HR W Lamb came from Stalham, T Baldwin to Wells with beer. R Bye after Jobs forenoon & turning up muck in yard afternoon, T Boyce in garden. T Raynor in M^t^ H, G Thompson & H Raven Cleansed XX. M^r^ H at home all day. WH to Sharringham, came home by Markett.

MH A Wet morng, fine afternoon. Mr Hardy at home all day. W^m^ went to L Sheringham foornoon, came home by Holt Market, came home eveng 9. Mr Binfield tuned the Piano Forte, he & Mr Sheldrake supt here.[1] I Bathd.

JUNE 11, SUNDAY

HR M^r^ [Mrs] H to Chapple afternoon,[2] M^r^ H at own Church afternoon & WH & H Raven at Holt. Mr Benfield call'd evening.

MH A very fine day. I & JT went to Briston Meeting afternoon. Mr Hardy went to our Church afternoon, Mr Burrell preachd on the Trinity, not much to the purpose. W^m^ went to Holt Church afternoon, came home to tea. W^m^ went to the Seaside to Bathe [3] . . .

JUNE 12, MONDAY

HR W Lamb to Fakenham with beer, T Baldwin to Southrepps with D^o^. R Bye at work in brewhouse, T Boyce in yard and garden. T Raynor in M^t^ H, G Thompson in brewhouse. M^r^ H at home all day, WH set of for Whissonsett afternoon.

JUNE 13, TUESDAY

HR W Lamb to Hindolvestone with beer and after Jobs, T Baldwin to Corpusta with beer. R Bye turning up muck in yard & after Jobs in house, T Raynor in Malthouse. T Boyce cleaning the plantation and the rode. M^r^ H at home all day. G Thompson grinding Malt

[1] *pianoforte* In the keeping parlour, and valued by William Hardy in Sept. 1797 at £13 (*Diary 2*, app. D2.C). The organ, in the parlour, was valued at £20

[2] *chapel* The only time Henry Raven uses the term 'chapel' for a meeting. The Briston Wesleyans did indeed use a purpose-built chapel, built by Mendham in 1783.

The criticism of Mr Burrell's preaching on 11 June must have come from William Hardy and not from his wife, who was not present at the church service

[3] *seaside* William did not share his mother's scruples about bathing on a Sunday and seems to have converted her to his way of thinking, for on 18 June 1797 Mary Hardy bathed on a Sunday for the first time at Letheringsett

for brew. W & Miss H came from Whiss[t] evening. M[rs] Lynes came & Orderd a lode of beer.

JUNE 14, WEDNESDAY

HR T Baldwin & R Bye in brewhouse. W Lamb to Cley with beer, bro[t] home 2 Chal[d] Cinders from M[r] Ellis's, unloded them & got up a lode of Vetches. H Raven brewing, G Thompson in brewhouse. Boyce at work in road & the River afternoon, T Raynor in Malthouse. M[r] H at home all day, WH to Sharringham.

MH A Showry day. W[m] went to Sheringham foornoon to look at some repairs & bathd, came home even past 8. M[r] Hardy at home all day. I Bathd . . .

JUNE 15, THURSDAY

HR W Lamb to Sharringham with beer. T Baldwin ploughing forenoon, to Edgefield afternoon. R Bye in brewhouse forenoon, ploughing D[o]. G Thompson & H Raven Cleansed `//, T Raynor in M[t] H, T Boyce in garden. M[r] H at home all day, WH at Sharrington Afternoon.[1]

JUNE 16, FRIDAY

HR W Lamb ploughing all day, T Baldwin to Runton with beer. R Bye at work in brewhouse & muck'd out the pigg yards, G Thompson & H Raven Cleansed XX. T Raynor in M[t] H, T Boyce in garden. M[r] & WH to Sharringham afternoon.

JUNE 17, SATURDAY

HR W Lamb to Stody & Salthouse with beer & «to» Clay for 1½ chal[d] coals from M[r] Jacksons, T Baldwin ploughing. T Raynor in M[t] H, T Boyce in garden. G Thompson grinding Malt for brew, R Bye in brewhouse. M[r] H at home all day.

JUNE 18, SUNDAY

HR Famaly at own Church forenoon, WH at Holt Afternoon. M[r] W[m], Tho[s] & G Skrimshire, Rose & P Raven came here Evening, HR walk'd to Sharrington to meet them.[2]

MH A fine morng, very showry afternoon. We all went to our Church foornoon, M[r] Burrell preachd. I went to Cley Meeting afternoon, W[m] went to Holt Church afternoon, came home to tea. 3 M[r] Skrimshires, Rose & Phillis Raven came here eveng ½ past 8, slept here. W[m] went to the Seaside to Bathe, I Bathd.

[1] *at Sharrington* To see Mr Kendle, noted Mary Hardy

[2] *William, Thomas and George Skrimshire* Thomas Skrimshire (d. 24 Mar. 1836 aged 61, bur. Whissonsett 29 Mar. in a coffin tomb by the priest's door) was about to become Henry Raven's brother-in-law: see note for 15 May 1794. He made his first visit to the Hardys with either his father William, a Wisbech surgeon, or more probably a brother of the same name, and with his brother George. On his marriage on 23 June he was given as resident in Wisbech St Peter [and St Paul].

Thomas Skrimshire, LLB, was born at Wisbech and admitted to Clare College, Cambridge 22 Dec. 1791; he migrated to Magdalene, the notices of his ordination as deacon and priest giving Magdalene (*Norw. Merc.* 20 Oct. 1798, 28 Dec. 1799). At the time of his marriage to Rose Raven he was or was soon to become master of the Fakenham Academy, a boys' day and boarding school where Latin and Greek were optional (*Norw. Merc.* 28 Dec. 1799); it had been opened by Mrs Hawes's brother Thomas Porson in 1792 (*World*, vol. 1, chap. 6).

The day after his ordination as deacon at Norwich 14 Oct. 1798 he was licensed as Curate of Whissonsett on the nomination of the rector, John Crofts, with a stipend of £30. He was ordained priest 22 Dec. 1799 and moved swiftly to acquire two livings as

JUNE 19, MONDAY

HR W Lamb to Bale & Holt with beer & carried off Cleanse of Beer, T Baldwin to Aldborough with D^o^. R Bye after Jobs, T Raynor in M^t^ H, T Boyce in yard. Wm Tinker & Lad all day. M^r^ H at home all day. W & Miss H whent to Sharringham with the Mr Skrimshires, Miss Ravens, Robt & H Raven to tea, Robt R & Miss Rowden came forenoon.

MH A fine day. W^m^ & MA, H Raven, Robt, Rose, Phillis & Mary Raven, Miss Rowdon & the 3 Mr Skrimshires went to Sheringham afternoon . . .

JUNE 20, TUESDAY

HR W Lamb, R Bye & G Thompson in brewhouse, H Raven brewing. T Baldwin to Overstrand with beer, T Raynor in M^t^ H, Wm Tinkers two men & lad at work all day. M^r^ & WH at home all day, Mr Skrimshires, Miss Ravens & R Raven & Miss Rowden whent of for Whissonsett after tea.

JUNE 21, WEDNESDAY

HR W Lamb to Gunthorpe with beer, T Baldwin (ill). W Tinkers man & Lad. R Bye in brewhouse, G Thompson Cleansed `// & XX beer, W Lamb to Stody & Thornage with beer afternoon. M^r^ & WH at home all day, T Raynor in M^t^ H.

MH A moist morng, dry, close afternoon. W^m^ went to Seaside to Bathe, I Bathd. Miss Bartell & Miss Jones of Cley drank tea here [1] . . .

JUNE 22, THURSDAY

HR W Lamb to Holt & Waybourn with beer, T Raynor in M^t^ H, T Baldwin (Ill). R Bye after Jobs, G Thompson in brewhouse. M^r^ H at home all day, WH to Holt afternoon. W Tinkers «?man» at work.

JUNE 23, FRIDAY

HR W Lamb to Briston with beer forenoon, at muck cart, T Boyce & J Ram filling Muck cart. T Baldwin at harrow forenoon & filling muck cart after^n^, R Bye after Jobs. M^r^ & WH at home all day, G Thompson dressing flour.

MH A Showry day. Mr Hardy at home all day. W^m^ drank tea at Mr Saverys. Rose Raven of Whisonsett was Maried to a Mr Thos Skrimshire of Wisbeach, they immediately set of for that place [2] . . .

Rector of Testerton and Vicar of Gt and Lt Hockham 1800–36; he was also Vicar of Houghton juxta Harpley 1817–22 on the presentation of Lord Cholmondeley (whom he was to serve as private chaplain, also serving as curate at Houghton 1814–17 and again from 1822); lastly he was Vicar of S. Creake 1817–24.

On leaving Fakenham he became master of Syderstone School at his parsonage house there.

His brother George settled nearby. By 1807 he was a shopkeeper living at Hempton and appeared to help with the administrative side of his brother's schoolmastering. He married 9 Jan. 1809 Elizabeth Hannant, a Fakenham milliner, and entered 16 Jan. upon the stock and trade of Mr Peckover of Fakenham as linen and woollen draper while continuing as liquor merchant; he also supplied malt and hops and undertook funeral arrangements (*Norw. Merc.* 27 June 1807, 14 Jan., 21 Jan. 1809)

[1] *Miss Jones* Probably the daughter of Thomas Jones, Collector of Customs, Cley. On 24 July 1801 Sarah Ann Jones married the Curate of Cley, Revd John Raven of Litcham, son of Nicholas, and a distant relation of the Whissonsett Ravens

[2] *married* The ceremony was conducted by the Curate of Whissonsett, Revd George Norris (see

ERECTED
DIRECTION
W.H.

above '1818. Erected by subscription under the plan and direction of W.H.'. The cast-iron inscription on the road bridge at Letheringsett acknowledges William Hardy jnr's role. Its omits to say that it was designed by William Mindham, whose signature is on the architect's drawing (opposite). He was a man of many talents: paperhanger, organist, organ-builder, architect and builder. Sprowston Villa (1806) and the first Foundry Bridge in Norwich (1810) were among his commissions.

His trademark style of blind arcading, brick pilasters, panels of flint infill, and heavy eaves can be seen at Letheringsett Hall (1809, 1832–34) the malt-kilns, and in two of Holt's Methodist chapels (1813, 1838) [*MB · 2002*]

JUNE 24, SATURDAY

HR W Lamb to Sharringham with beer, T Baldwin carting muck at furze close. R Bye, T Boyce & Jn° Ram filling Muck cart, T Raynor in M^t H, G Thompson in brewhouse. M^r H at home all day, WH at Holt afternoon.

JUNE 25, SUNDAY

HR Famaly at own Church Afternoon, M^r [Mrs] H to Cley. H Raven came from Whissonsett.

JUNE 26, MONDAY

HR W Lamb to Brampton with beer, T Baldwin to Kettlestone & Holt with D°. R Bye in brewhouse, T Raynor in M^t H, J Ram after Jobs. T Boyce [ ], G Thompson & H Raven in brewhouse. M^r H at home all day, WH to Sharringham.

MH Very heavy showers of Rain with Thunder. W^m at home all day. Mr Hardy, I & MA set of for Mr Woodcocks of Briston Morng 11,[1] bought some goods there & went from thence to Guestick [Guestwick], dind & drank tea at Mr Keelers, got home even 9. I Bathd. John Jex Died.

note for 6 Nov. 1796), whom the bridegroom was shortly to supplant as curate. The couple were married by licence, seven members of the Raven and Goggs families, including Henry Raven the diarist, and Julia Rowden acting as witnesses. Henry could have set off for Whissonsett after brewing on 20 June, leaving Gunton Thompson to cleanse the following day. Henry returned on 25 June.

Thomas Skrimshire conducted the marriage of Henry's sister Mary to William Hardy jnr in 1819

[1] *Woodcock* See note for 13 Dec. 1794

JUNE 27, TUESDAY

HR T Baldwin to Fakenham with beer, W Lamb to Southrepps with D^{o}. R Bye in brewhouse, G Thompson grinding Malt for brew. T Raynor in Malthouse, J Ram after Jobs. M^{r} & WH at home all day, Miss A & D Johnson & Miss Davy drank tea here.

MH A fine day. Mr Hardy at home all day. W^{m} rid to Sheringham foornoon to look at some repairs doing at the Publick House, came home to dinner Eveng 2. Miss Ann & Miss Deb Johnson & Miss Davy drank tea here. W^{m} bath^{d} . . .

JUNE 28, WEDNESDAY

HR W Lamb at muck cart. T Boyce filling half the day, began to mow the grass after^{n}. J Ram filling muck cart half the day & spreading half the day, W Tinker & man all day. T Baldwin in brewhouse forenoon, ploughing Afternoon. R Bye & G Thompson in brewhouse, H Raven brewing. T Raynor in M^{t} H, Mr H at home all day & WH D^{o}.

JUNE 29, THURSDAY

HR W Lamb to Thursford & Edgefield with beer, T Baldwin ploughing & sowing turnips. J Ram spreading muck part of day, T Boyce mowing grass, R Bye in brewhouse. G Thompson & H Raven Cleansed `// & X beer, T Raynor in Mt H. M^{r} & WH at home all day. M^{r} T & E Balls & Mr Mendham drank tea here.

MH A fine day. I & W^{m} rid to L Sheringham foornoon, came home to dinner. Wm Bath^{d}. 2 Mr Balls s & a Mr Mendham drank tea here.[1] Mr Hardy at home all day. John Jex Buried. I Bathd . . .

JUNE 30, FRIDAY

HR W Lamb ploughing forenoon, to Clay for 2 Chaldrons cinders from Mr Ellis's After^{n}. T Baldwin to Wells with beer. R Bye spreading Muck forenoon, ploughing afternoon. T Raynor in M^{t} H, J Ram spreading muck. T Boyce mowing grass, G Thompson dressing Maltstones. M^{r} H at home all day, WH at home all day.

JULY 1, SATURDAY

Henry Raven W Lamb & T Baldwin at harrow at Holt farm, R Bye ploughing & sowing turnips at furze close. J Ram

[1] *Mendham* This was Mary Hardy's first meeting with William Mindham of Wells, who was to have an extraordinarily varied career at Wells, Holt and Letheringsett. His patrons in his architectural career were to include William Hardy jnr, William's brother-in-law Jeremiah Cozens of Sprowston, and Jeremiah's brother-in-law Jonathan Davey of Norwich, showing the value of personal connections. He also built organs for the churches at Holt and [*continued overleaf*]

W Mindham

above **A detail from the architect's drawing of the 1818 bridge, showing the unobtrusive signature 'W Mindham' beneath one of the piers. The bridge now bears the heavy traffic of the main route from King's Lynn to Cromer, the A148** [*Cozens-Hardy Collection*]

Edgefield, his career being described in *World*, vol. 1, chap. 7.

The Hardys' visitor may have brought a beer order from the Fighting Cocks, for the beer cart was despatched to Wells the following day. Mindham was Wells born, the son of Robert, a Wells joiner, and Mary Mindham; he was bapt. Wells 21 Sept. 1771 and buried Holt from Swanton Novers 8 Sept. 1843.

He married Wells 21 Dec. 1797 Mary, daughter of the Wells shipbuilder Henry Woodrow and Susanna, née Rice; she was bapt. Wells 2 June 1774 and was sister to Margaret, wife of Thomas Balls jnr of Saxlingham (note for 2 Feb. 1797). Mary Mindham was buried Holt 28 Aug. 1828 aged 54, a year after Margaret Balls

spreading muck foren^{n}, mowing weeds in meadow afternoon. T Boyce mowing grass, T Raynor in M^{t} H, G Thompson laid down Malt Stones. Famaly at Holt afternoon.

Mary Hardy A fine day. W^{m} went to the Seaside to Bathe. M^{r} H, I & MA rid up to Holt after«noon», W^{m} walkd. I & W^{m} drank tea at Miss Leakes, MA drank tea at Mr Johnsons, M H [Mr Hardy] rid up to his Farm.[1] I Bathd . . .

JULY 2, SUNDAY

HR M^{rs} & Miss H at Church forenoon. M^{rs} H to Cley afternoon, WH at Holt afternoon. Wm Raven call^{d} morning, dined here, whent to Holt & came to Supper & stayd all night.[2] M^{r} H at home all day.

JULY 3, MONDAY

HR W Lamb after Jobs all day, T Baldwin & Bye after Jobs. T Raynor in M^{t} H, Thompson & H Raven in brewhouse. M^{r} & WH at home all day, Wm Raven set of for Whissonsett after tea.

---

[1] *his farm* The revealing 'his' (the diarists were not given to using possessive determiners) could indicate that the decision to expand the agricultural side of the business by buying the neglected Holt Heath Farm had been William Hardy snr's alone

[2] *William Raven* Henry's elder brother (b. Whissonsett 2 July 1776, bapt. 3 July); his visit coincided with his 21st birthday. He may have been at Whissonsett for his sister's wedding, although he was not one of the witnesses.

William had begun a brewing pupillage with the Hardys 31 Mar. 1791 and

facing page **Letheringsett: the east front of one of the twin malt-kilns built by William Hardy jnr. No architect's drawing survives, but the building is in William Mindham's characteristic style. In 1797 there was almost certainly only one kiln** [*MB* · *2002*]

MH A very wet day. Mr Hardy & Wm at home all day. Wm Raven went away after tea. H Raven supt & spent the eveng at Mr Errets at Holt. I Bathd.

JULY 4, TUESDAY

HR W Lamb & T Baldwin at work at Holt farm, R Bye ploughing & sowing turnips in furze close. J Ram spreading muck forenoon, mowing weeds afternoon, T Boyce mowing grass. G Thompson grinding Mt for brew, T Raynor in Mt H. Mr H at home all day, WH rode to Holt afternoon.

MH A Showry day. Mr Hardy & Wm after Hay at home all day.[1] Wm rid to Seaside to bathe . . .

JULY 5, WEDNESDAY

HR W Lamb to Aldborough with beer. T Baldwin to Holt with Do forenoon & at Holt aftern getting Lime, sand & Bricks to Black boys. R Bye after Jobs, G Thompson dressing Wheat stones, T Raynor in Mt H. Mr H at home all day, WH at Holt afternoon. J Ram mowing weeds in meadow part of day.

JULY 6, THURSDAY

HR W Lamb in brewhouse & whent to Holt with beer, T Baldwin to Runton with Do. R Bye in brewhouse, HR brewing, G Thompson dressing Wheat Stones. T Raynor in Mt H, T Boyce mowing grass. Mr & WH at home all day. W Tinker & man Sawing.

MH A Showry day. Mr Hardy & Wm at home all day. 2 Miss Leakes drank tea & Supt here, 2 Miss Jeniss [two Miss Jennises] drank tea here, Mr Sheldrake Supt here. Wm rid to Seaside to Bathe . . .

JULY 7, FRIDAY

HR W Lamb & T Baldwin at work at Holt farm, R Bye after Jobs. T Boyce mowing grass, Sarah Boyce haymaking Aftern. G Thompson & HR Cleansed `// & XX beer, T Raynor in Mt H. Mr & WH at home all day. Mr & Mrs Bartell Junr & Senr dined here, Mr Moore & Miss Bartell dined & drank tea here.[3]

had lived with them until 11 June that year, when he left suddenly, breaking the apprenticeship agreement (*Diary 2*). His aunt had not mentioned him since, but the visit suggests that any rift had been healed. He may have joined the Merchant Navy, returning from the W. Indies in 1804 (*Diary 4*: 24 Sept. 1804); his name does not appear in the Royal Navy and Army lists

---

[1] *hay* Despite the showery weather at haymaking William Hardy was able to enter in his accounts 25 Sept. 1797, 'Hay crop exceed last year by £8 0s 0d' (*World*, vol. 2, chap. 11)

[2] *lime, sand and bricks* A further illustration of the the way the Hardys' men were taken off their normal tasks to work alongside the teams of builders

[3] *Moore* Mary Hardy notes the attorney's two children among the party. As he had married in Mar. 1790 the children would have been young, perhaps five and six years old, showing that small children were present at formal meals. Their mother Ann, née Jennis, had died young: see note for 3 Jan. 1794

above Shambrook Burrell's initials on the west gable end of his farmhouse beside the Glaven at Lt Thornage. The rector's first child, he was born Sunday 9 July 1797: 'No service at our church, Mrs Burrell brought to bed of a boy afternoon'. There had been no children by the rector's first marriage. Shambrook was to be the eldest of eight to arrive in brisk succession, the two sons taking up farming in a modest way at Letheringsett [*MB · 2001*]

JULY 8, SATURDAY

HR W Lamb to Burnham with beer, T Baldwin to Sheringham with D°. R Bye after Jobs forenoon, haymaking Afternoon. T Boyce mowing grass, Sarah Boyce haymaking. T Raynor in M^t^ H, G Thompson dressing flour. M^r^, WH & Miss H at Holt afternoon.

MH Showry morng, fine afternoon. Mr Hardy rid to Mr Savorys sheep shearers & to look at the Hay afternoon. W^m^ & MA walkd up to Holt afternoon, drank tea at Mr Bartells. Wm Bathd.

JULY 9, SUNDAY

HR M^rs^ & Miss Hardy to Cley [Briston] afternoon, M^r^ & WH at home all day.

MH A very fine day. No Service at our Church, Mrs Burrell brought to Bed of a Boy afternoon.[1] Mr Hardy at home all day. I & MA went to Briston Meeting after^n^, W^m^ went to Holt Church afternoon. I Bathd.

[1] *Mrs Burrell* The unusually fulsome record spaciously laid out in the parish register testifies to the father's joy at his son's birth. Shambrook was the name of a benefactor of Revd John Burrell who was to leave the rector £1300 (*Diary 4*: 5 Dec. 1799). Despite this legacy neither of the two Burrell sons received the Cambridge education of their father and grandfathers.

Shambrook Burrell was privately bapt. 11 July and publicly 6 Aug. 1797; he was buried at Holt from Fish Hill Lane, Holt, 3 Nov. 1850. He married Letheringsett 13 July 1818 Mary Hastings of Letheringsett, the bride making her mark; their daughter Jemima was born and bapt. 19 Nov. 1818. Their second child, Shambrook, was born 5 June 1821 and bapt. Letheringsett 6 June.

Mary, the daughter of Theophilus Pye Hastings and Jemima, née Barker, was born and privately bapt. Letheringsett 1 Dec. 1796, publicly 28 Oct. 1798. Before her marriage she had two illegitimate daughters, both named Mary. The elder was born 15 Mar. 1815, privately bapt. Letheringsett 16 Mar., and died 17 Apr. 1815; the second Mary was born 8 Apr. 1816, privately bapt. Letheringsett 29 Apr., and died 9 May 1817.

The Burrell family historian made this note on Shambrook Burrell snr 20 Dec. 1942: 'Shambrook turned out badly. Married

JULY 10, MONDAY

HR W Lamb to Thornage with beer forenoon, to Salthouse with D° & Clay for 2 Chal^{d} cinders from Mr Ellis's afternoon, T Baldwin to Corpusta with beer. R Bye after Jobs part of forenoon, haymaking Afternoon. G Thompson, J Ram & Sarah Boyce haymaking D° [afternoon], T Raynor in Mt H. M^{r} H at home all day, W & M^{rs} H to Clay Afternoon. H Raven in brewhouse.

MH A fine morng, a Showr afternoon. Mr Hardy after the Hay till the rain came. W^{m} & I rid to Clay afternoon, drank tea at Mr Smiths, the Bath House Sold for 40 Guineas, bought a small Looking Glass for 2/8^{d}, came home even 9 [1] . . .

JULY 11, TUESDAY

HR T Baldwin got up a Lode of Vetches morning then whent to Briston with beer, W Lamb to Edgefield with D° [beer] and after Jobs after^{n}. R Bye in brewhouse, G Thompson grinding Malt for brew. T Raynor in M^{t} H, T Boyce Mowing grass at Holt farm, J Ram drag raking forenoon. M^{r} H at home all day.

JULY 12, WEDNESDAY

HR W Lamb to Holt morning, haymaking remainder part of day, T Baldwin in brewhouse. G Thompson, R Bye & Sarah Boyce haymaking afternoon, T Boyce mowing grass at Holt farm. H Raven brewing, T Raynor in Malthouse & brewhouse. M^{r} & WH at home all day. Mr Sheldrake dined & Supt here, Miss Howard Supt here.

JULY 13, THURSDAY

HR W Lamb to Brampton with beer, T Baldwin to Holt with D° & haymaking, R Bye haymaking. G Thompson & H Raven Cleansed `// & X beer, T Raynor in M^{t} H & after Jobs, T Boyce mowing grass at Holt farm. M^{r} & WH at home all day.

MH A Hot day, our people making Hay. Mr Hardy at home all day, W^{m} went to Seaside to Bathe. I & MA walkd to Holt afternoon, drank tea at Mr Davys . . .

JULY 14, FRIDAY

HR Thos Baldwin to Sharrington with beer & haymaking, W Lamb haymaking. R Bye, G Thompson, Sarah Boyce & Boy haymaking at Holt farm,[2] T Boyce Mow-

Mary Hastings of Letheringsett, a servant; built a small farmhouse at Little Thornage. He afterwards left his wife and went with a woman from Holt named Edmunds.

His son Shambrook also turned out badly. Enlisted as a common soldier, deserted, escaped to America and died there in great poverty' (NRO: ACC Cozens-Hardy 11/2/1976, Letter to Basil Cozens-Hardy by W. H. Burrell, written from Horsforth, Leeds).

A Peckham carpenter named Shambrook Burrell was a witness 3 Apr. 1848 in a housebreaking case at the Central Criminal Court in London (*Old Bailey Proceedings Online* (www.oldbaileyonline.org, version 6.0, 18 November 2011), April 1848 (t18480403), accessed 18 Nov. 2011). The carpenter could be the father or son

[1] *bath house* The auction was held at the King's Head, Cley. John Smith had the particulars of 'all that handsome and new-erected bath house, with the waterworks and reservoir belonging . . .' (*Norw. Merc.* 24 June 1797)

[2] *boy* The Hardys had taken on a boy again, after nine months of doing without; he left 5 Oct. 1797 and was replaced 12 Oct. by 'William'. There was also a second farm boy during the 1797 harvest (eg 8 Sept.)

ing grass. Mr & WH at home all day. H Raven in brewhouse, T Raynor in Mt H & after Jobs. Mr Ellis drank tea & supt here.

JULY 15, SATURDAY

HR W Lamb to Gresham with beer & haymaking.[1] T Baldwin to Cley with beer, brot home 1½ Chald coles from Mr Jacksons & then whent after hay, R Bye after Jobs. T Raynor finnis'd Malting,[2] G Thompson & H Raven in brewhouse. Mr & WH at Holt afternoon.

MH A very hot day. Wm went to Sea Side to bathe. Mr H & he rid to Holt Markt by Kellen [Kelling] to look at some Hay, did not buy it. I & MA walkd up to Holt, drank tea at Mr Bakers, came home even past 8. I Bathd . . .

JULY 16, SUNDAY

HR Famaly at own Church forenoon, WH at Holt afternoon, Mrs H to Cley afternoon. W Lamb loded for Syderstone, T Baldwin loded for Stalham.

Mary Hardy's visit to Whissonsett

17–22 July 1797, and an early Norfolk County Cricket match: Norfolk v. All England

JULY 17, MONDAY

HR [at Letheringsett] W Lamb to Syderstone, T Baldwin to Stalham. R Bye after Jobs forenoon, haymaking with J Ram aftern. G Thompson grinding Malt for brew & bin. T Boyce mowing grass Morning, in garden remainder of day. Mr, Mrs Hardy set of for Whissonsett Evening after tea.

MH Excesive Hot dry day. Wm at home all day. Mr Hardy & I sett of for Whisonsett Even 6, got there Even 9. Wm went to Seaside to bathe.

JULY 18, TUESDAY

HR W Lamb to Cromer, T Baldwin came from Stalham. R Bye in brewhouse & whent to Edgefield with Malt. T Boyce in garden, G Thompson grinding Malt for brew. Mr Wm H at home all day. Mr Haddon & man painting the keeping Room.

MH [at Whissonsett] A fine day, not so hot as yesterday. Mr Hardy, Brot Raven & Son & Mr Fox went to Swafham M8 to se the Cricket match, came home eveng 12.[3]

---

[1] *Gresham* There was only one public house in this village: the Chequers, run by Thomas Hewitt, who had taken over from Thomas Hirst in 1795 or 1796. He continued to be supplied by the Hardys until 1803 or later, but did not pay rent

[2] *Raynor* Even though the Hardys were soon to be without Thomas Boyce's services (see note for 28 Aug.) the maltster was paid off at the end of the malting season and was not kept on through haymaking, hoeing and harvest. He may have returned to his home village to help on a farm.

He returned to his old Letheringsett job at the start of the next season on 5 Oct. 1797

[3] *cricket match* Thousands came to watch, and the Swaffham inns were overflowing. The selection for the county team had taken place at Hempton 20 June.

Two players named Raven were on the scorecard in the newspaper. One, 'Mr M. Raven', at no. 29, may have been Myles Raven of Tunstead, nephew of Ben Raven of Horningtoft and first cousin once removed of the diarist (*Norw. Merc.* 24 June, and 8, 22, 29 July 1797). Later, one of the county's most famous cricketers, Fuller Pilch (1804–70), who played for Holt in the 1820s and for Norfolk 1820–36, came from Horningtoft.

The other Raven in the 1797 team had the initial R and may be Robert, of

above The cricket match on Swaffham Racecourse attended by William Hardy and some of his in-laws 18 July 1797, from a contemporary engraving. One of the first county cricket matches in Norfolk, it was billed as 'Norfolk against All England', the England XI being ranged against 33 players from Norfolk. The match lasted three days, for a stake of 500 guineas.

The batting was slow. The Norfolk team lost by an innings and 13 runs, the score being Norfolk 1st innings 50, All England 144; Norfolk 2nd innings 81. Two members of the Raven family played in the county team [*The Roger Mann Collection*]

Whissonsett, Henry's elder brother.

See D. Armstrong, *A Short History of Norfolk County Cricket* (Larks Press, Guist Bottom, 1990), p. 5; and P. Yaxley, *Looking back at Norfolk Cricket* (Nostalgia Publications, Toftwood, 1997), pp. 6–8, where the scorecard is illustrated

I, Sister Ravn, Mrs Cozens & M Raven drank tea at Mr Goggs . . .

JULY 19, WEDNESDAY

HR W Lamb in brewhouse & got up a Load of hay, T Baldwin to Kettlestone with beer & got up a Load of hay. R Bye in brewhouse, G Thompson in brewhouse & after hay, H Raven brewing. T Boyce in garden. M^r^ WH at home all day, Miss Leeks drank tea here.

JULY 20, THURSDAY

HR W Lamb, T Baldwin, R Bye & T Boyce getting up hay, G Thompson on haystack. H Raven Cleansed XX beer. WH at home all day & gave the men a gallon of beer after they left work.[1]

1 *a gallon of beer* The only time, apart from references to national celebrations, William Hardy jnr's 21st birthday (1791) and Mary Ann's marriage (1805), that either diarist records such a gift. It is not clear if Henry means a gallon of beer *each*, in which case it is unsurprising that William distributed the bounty at the end of the working day, or a gallon shared *between* the

workforce of six or seven including Henry, which was hardly remarkable, allowing just over a pint each

MH Small showr in morng, A fine «day». M^r & Mrs Cozens went to Toffts to dinner.[1] We all dind & drank tea at Mr Goggs. Little Nathl Raven & his Sister Mary sett of for Wisbeach Morn 4 . . .

JULY 21, FRIDAY

HR W Lamb & T Baldwin carting hay & unpitching it, J Ram Loading D^o. R Bye, G Thompson & T Boyce on Stack. W^m H at home all day, H Raven in brewhouse.

JULY 22, SATURDAY

HR W Lamb to Hindolvestone & Holt with beer, T Baldwin to Wells with D^o. R Bye & G Thompson got up three Load of hay, T Boyce trimming up Stack, J Ram part of forenoon after hay. M^r & M^rs H came from Whissonsett afternoon. H Raven in brewhouse, WH at Holt Evening.

[LETHERINGSETT]

JULY 23, SUNDAY

HR Mrs Hardy to Cley forenoon. M^r, Miss & WH at own Church afternoon. WH & H Raven to Kelling morning.[2]

right 'William Lamb to . . . Bale with beer' (25 July). The former Angel and Oak yard, with its stables, skittle alley and (to the rear) the smokehouse.

Deliveries had restarted that summer after an unexplained four-month break, although demand had slackened generally when Thomas Claxton replaced the widowed Ann Howlett as innkeeper in 1795.

In 1794 there had been 13 deliveries; in 1796 there were eight [*MB · 2001*]

---

1 *Tofts* Toftrees, a tiny parish north-east of Raynham Park. John Cozens' sister Elizabeth (1780–1826) married 22 Oct. 1799 the farmer Charles Case [jnr] of Toftrees Hall (*Norw. Merc.* 26 Oct.). The Cases were active in Calvinistic Methodist circles at Fakenham and in hosting Thomas Mendham's meeting at their house (see note for 22 Feb. 1795; also NRO: DN/VIS 29/7, Toftrees deanery visitation 1784, Toftrees return)

2 *Kelling* Since Mary Hardy recorded William bathing that day it seems the cousins went together to Kelling before breakfast to bathe

left The old Angel and Oak, near Bale Church; the inn board bracket points to its past life. It had been tied to Henry Hagon at Letheringsett before 1781, and the tie was probably unbroken until the house was sold in 1896 to Morgans for £780. Thomas Claxton paid £5 annual rent to William Hardy in 1797 [*MB · 1993*]

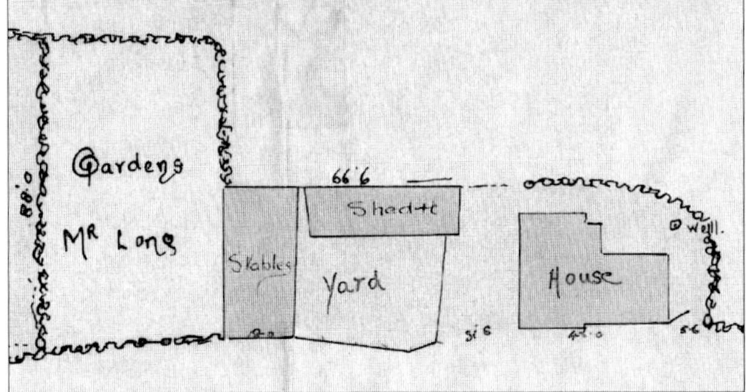
Gardens
Mr Long
66.6
Shed
Stables
Yard
House
well

below left This plan of 1895 shows the well, near the back gate, and the yard edged on two sides by the stables and a shed. The shed was used in the 19th and 20th centuries as a skittle alley (as discovered in 2001 from the owner, Mrs Bettina Carter) [*plan by Messrs Spelman of Norwich: Cozens-Hardy Collection*]

JULY 24, MONDAY

HR W Lamb to Runton with beer, T Baldwin to Thursford & Hinderingham with D°. R Bye & G Thompson carted the Stones from Mr Rouse's Mill forenoon,[1] in brewhouse afternoon. Mr H at home all day, WH to Holt afternoon.

JULY 25, TUESDAY

HR W Lamb to Thornage, Stody, Sharrington & Bale with beer, T Baldwin to Sharringham with D°. R Bye in brewhouse, G Thompson grinding Mt for brew. Mr & WH at home all day, H Raven whent to Sharrington to dine.

MH A fine day. Maids & Eliz Milegan washd 6 Weeks linnen. I poorly with dimness in my Eyes. Mr Hardy & Wm at home all day, Wm went to Sea Side to bathe . . .

[1] *stones* Letheringsett Watermill was being demolished.

The new mill, owned by Zebulon Rouse, then of London, was completed in the autumn of 1798 (*Norw. Merc.* 1 Dec. 1798). As the old mill (rebuilt following the fire of 1744, which had reduced the mill to ruins) was likely to have been built of timber or timber and brick, Henry must mean that the Hardys bought the millstones. They also bought some windows, William Hardy entering in his accounts for the year ending 25 Sept. 1797: 'Z. Rouse sashes etc, stones, £14 0s 0d' (*World*, vol. 2, chap. 11)

above Blakeney: the large brick-vaulted mediaeval undercroft known as the Guildhall was later used by merchants as a coal store. The other warehouses and the granaries were mostly purpose-built and set gable end to the quay [*MB* · *2002*]

JULY 26, WEDNESDAY

HR T Baldwin & R Bye in brewhouse, W Lamb to Corpusta & got up a lode of Vetches. G Thompson dressing flour & at work in brewhouse, H Raven brewing. Mr & WH at home all day. T Boyce howing turnips.

JULY 27, THURSDAY

HR W Lamb ploughing at Holt farm, T Baldwin to Holt morning with beer then whent to work at Holt farm, R Bye after Jobs. G Thompson & H Raven Cleansed `// & X beer, T Boyce howing turnips. Mr Hardy at Holt afternoon, WH at home all day.

MH A fine day, very hot. I Bathd, Wm went to Sea side to Bathe, Mr Hardy & Wm at home all day. The Miss Leakes Supt here . . .

JULY 28, FRIDAY

HR W Lamb to Fakenham, T Baldwin & Robt Bye and Boy at work at Holt farm, G Thompson to Cley afternoon.[1] Mr & WH at Holt afternoon. T Boyce howing turnips, H Raven in brewhouse.

JULY 29, SATURDAY

HR W Lamb ploughing at Holt farm forenoon, to Edgefield with beer afternoon. T Baldwin to Burnham, R Bye & Boy at harrow at Holt farm, G Thompson in brewhouse. Mr & WH at Market afternoon, Mrs & Miss Hardy at Holt afternoon.

JULY 30, SUNDAY

HR Famaly at own Church forenoon. Mrs H to Cley afternoon,[2] H Raven at Holt. Mr & WH at home all day.

JULY 31, MONDAY

HR W Lamb ploughing at Holt farm, T Baldwin mowing & getting up Vetches. R Bye in brewhouse, G Thompson grinding Malt for brew, T Boyce howing turnips. Mr Hardy at home all day, WH whent to Blackney [Blakeney] afternoon. Mrs & Miss H at Holt evening.

MH A few flying Showers. Wm went to sea side to Bathe, I Bathd. Mr Hardy at home all day. I & MA walkd up to Holt after tea, hired an upper Servt Eliz Williams.[3] Wm went to Blakney afternoon to look at some Coales at Mr Farthings, came home even 8 [4] . . .

[1] *to Cley* Presumably for the fair

[2] *to Cley* As on 9 July, Mary Hardy records that she went to *Briston* meeting; John Thompson drove her on 30 July

[3] *Elizabeth Williams* Her name was given as Williamson when she started work for the Hardys on 12 Oct. 1797. She stayed the full year and was paid £3, with 3*s* extra for good behaviour (Mary Hardy's endnotes)

[4] *Farthing* The main sale of the bankrupt's goods was not until 15 Aug. onwards: see note for 16 Aug. 1797

AUGUST 1, TUESDAY

Henry Raven W Lamb & T Baldwin to Blackney 3 times each for 9 Chaldron of Coles from Mr Farthings,[1] R Bye unloded them except two Lode. T Boyce in garden. Mr & WH at home all day. G Thompson grinding Malt for brew, Dawsons Lad painting, H Raven in brewhouse.

AUGUST 2, WEDNESDAY

HR W Lamb in brewhouse forenoon, to Briston afternoon. R Bye & Gunton Thompson in brewhouse, HR brewing. T Baldwin to Aldborough, T Boyce in garden. Mr H at home all day, W Hardy at Holt evening. Mr Balls drank tea here.

Mary Hardy A Showry day but not so bad as yesterday. Mr Hardy at home all day. Mr T Balls drank tea here. Wm rid up to Holt after tea to meet Mr Coe about Dawling publick House, Wm went to Sea side to bathe . . .

AUGUST 3, THURSDAY

HR T Baldwin unloding coals & whent to Holt forenoon, at work at Holt farm afternoon, W Lamb ploughing at Holt farm. R Bye in brewhouse, G Thompson & H Raven Cleansed `// & X beer. Mr & WH at home all day. T Boyce in garden.

[1] *coals* Confirmation that 1½ chaldrons was the maximum preferred load for the carts. Cinders (coke), less dense and thus lighter than coal by volume, could be carried in loads of two chaldrons, a chaldron being a unit of volume, not weight.

The north Norfolk ports therefore used the London measure (26½ cwt), and not the Newcastle measure (the 53-cwt chaldron): there is no way a two-wheeler could bear 79½ cwt (4039 kg). It is estimated that a cart could carry 18–22 cwt (J. Vince, *Discovering Carts and Wagons* (Shire Publications, Princes Risborough, 1987), p. 8), so the Hardys' vehicles, and their horses, were being worked extremely hard with loads of 39¾ cwt.

The contentious subject of coal measure is explored in *World*, vol. 4, chap. 5

left A Newcastle chaldron. The term for a unit of coal measure is derived from the word for a truck: chaldron. Here a replica chaldron rests by the Causey Arch, near Tanfield, Tyne and Wear.

Supplying rural industry with fuel required immense effort in mining the coal, transporting it on a wooden railed wagonway (as here) from pit to staithe, conveying it by collier, unloading it at the port, and carting it inland. Henry's terse entries on coal and cinders record this struggle's final stage [*Christopher Bird 2011*]

right '. . . to Miss Alpe, she hired Phillis for teacher till Christmas next for 4 guineas' (4 Aug. 1797). Mary Hardy's 18-year-old niece Phillis Raven, Henry's sister, took a teaching appointment at Mary Alpe's day and boarding school at Holt. She had left by Jan. 1799, and went for an interview at Burgh Parva with the wife of Jacob Henry Astley.

In answer to this notice the widowed Frances Chase, from King's Lynn, took over the school in Oct. 1800 from Miss Alpe, Mary Alpe's sister (*Diary 4*) [*Norwich Mercury, 2 Aug. 1800: Norfolk Heritage Centre, Norwich*]

TO BE LET,

And Entered upon at Old Michaelmas next,

A Good Spacious MESSUAGE or DWELLNG-HOUSE, fronting the Market-place of the healthy and pleasant town of Holt, with large yard and good garden.—The Dwelling House consists of a good kitchen, a parlour, large school room, hall, four bed-chambers, and four attics, with larder, pantry, wash-house, scullery, and sunk cellar.

The above premises have been many years used as a Boarding School for Young Ladies by the late Mrs. Alpe, and was in very high repute, and will be an excellent situation for a School, (Miss Alpe, the present occupier, intending to decline that line at Michaelmas next,) there being no other Boarding School for Ladies in Holt, nor within ten miles round the same.

For rent and further particulars apply personally or by letters (post paid) to Mr. Withers, attorney, Holt. (1034

AUGUST 4, FRIDAY

HR W Lamb to Syderstone with beer, T Baldwin ploughing at Holt farm, R Bye after Jobs. G Thompson in brewhouse, T Boyce in garden. Mr [Hardy] at home all day. Mr R Raven & Sister came from Whissonsett, whent to Holt aftr tea with Miss & W Hardy.

MH A Showry day. Robt & Phillis Raven came to dinner. We rid up to Holt after tea to speak to Miss Alpe, she hired Phillis for Teacher till Chrismas next for 4 Guineas.[1] I Bathd.

AUGUST 5, SATURDAY

HR W Lamb & T Baldwin at work at Holt farm, R Bye after Jobs. G Thompson in brewhouse, T Boyce in garden. Mr & WH at Holt afternoon.

MH A Showry Morng, fine afternoon. Mr Hardy, Wm & MA rid up to Holt Markt afternoon, Wm & MA drank tea at Miss Leakes. Mrs Smith of Cley drank tea here. Wm went to Seaside to Bathe, I Bathd.

AUGUST 6, SUNDAY

HR Mrs H to Cley afternoon, Miss & W Hardy & H Raven at own Church afternoon. Mr Hardy set of for Norwich afternoon with Mr Moore.

---

[1] *Miss Alpe* Mary: see note for 23 Nov. 1793. With her sister Priscilla and, later, on her own she had run a school for young ladies at Holt for 19 years; it had previously been at Hindolveston (*Norw. Merc.* 28 Mar. 1778). Priscilla Alpe had left the partnership in 1783 on her marriage to the twice-widowed William Bircham (snr) of Reepham.

Phillis appears from the diary to have lived in the schoolhouse, her board and lodging being found by Miss Alpe. As usual the vacancy was not advertised in the press, indicating that Miss Alpe relied on personal enquiry and recommendation when seeking staff

MH A very fine day except a small showr ab^t 1 oClock. Mr Moore here foornoon, Mr Hardy oblidgd to go to Norwich with him in the afternoon to the Assises.[1] I & J Thompson went to Cley meeting.

AUGUST 7, MONDAY

HR T Baldwin to Southrepps with beer, W Lamb ploughing at Holt farm, R Bye after Jobs. G Thompson grinding Malt for brew, T Boyce howing turnips half a day. WH rode out after tea.

MH A fine day. I taken very bad with dimness in my Eyes, sent for Mr Bartell. W^m at home all day. I Bathd.

AUGUST 8, TUESDAY

HR W Lamb to Sharringham & got up Vetches, T Baldwin & Boy at work at Holt farm, R Bye after Jobs. G Thompson grinding Malt & dressing flour, T Boyce howing turnips. M^r W^m H drove Miss H & Miss P Raven to Holt afternoon. Phillis Raven came from Whissonsett to Dinner, whent to Miss Alpes before tea.

MH A very fine day. W^m rid to Holt Farm afternoon. Phillis Raven dind here, she & MA rid up to Holt afternoon, they drank tea there, Phillis took possession of her place as Teacher. Mr Hardy came home from Norwich even 11 . . .

AUGUST 9, WEDNESDAY

HR T Baldwin, R Bye & W Lamb in brewhouse forenoon, getting up brakes afternoon.[2] G Thompson dressing flour, H Raven brewing, T Boyce howing turnips. M^r & WH at home all day. Mr Birde, Mr Nath Raven Junr & Miss Raven came from Whissonsett afternoon.[3]

AUGUST 10, THURSDAY

HR T Baldwin to Holt with beer forenoon, after brakes afternoon. W Lamb cutting Vetches forenoon, after D^o D^o [brakes afternoon]. R Bye after Jobs, G Thompson Cleansed `// & X beer. M^r H at home all day. WH, Miss Hardy, Mr Birde, Nath Raven, Miss Raven & H Raven whent to Sharringham to tea.

AUGUST 11, FRIDAY

HR W Lamb to Gunthorpe & at work at Holt farm, T Baldwin at work at Holt farm, R Bye after Jobs. G Thompson dressed the wheat Stones, T Boyce reaping wheat. Mr Barde [Bird], Nath Raven & Miss R set of

[1] *assizes* The official assize minutes have not survived. Although James Moore's ledger contains notes of his work for William Hardy in 1797 he does not refer specifically to attending the assizes on his behalf. It is possible the case involved Henry Crafer's bankruptcy, which took up a great of deal of time.

It may alternatively have related to the cryptic entry, '[To] Mr William Hardy: 1797 April. Attending you on the subject of Mr Minns' demand on you and advising thereon' (NRO: ACC Cozens-Hardy 23/8/1976, Attorney's ledger 1793–99, p. 23). The compiler of this ledger does not give his name, but by the work and the client list we can identify him as James Moore of Holt

[2] *brakes* Hedging plants such as thorns

[3] *Bird* Of Rudham, noted Mary Hardy; the Miss Raven with him was Nathaniel Raven jnr's sister Mary (from the shop).

During her recent visit to Whissonsett Mary Hardy had recorded that on 19 July 1797 Mrs Cozens and Mary Raven had dined at the house of John Rash Bird, the Rudham surgeon who was possibly the son of Revd Rash Bird (d.1793), the former Curate of Whissonsett.

The house which the surgeon occupied at Rudham was for sale freehold and was described as new built (*Norw. Merc.* 29 July 1797)

for Whissonsett after tea, H Raven rode to Gunthorpe with them.

AUGUST 12, SATURDAY

HR W Lamb & Baldwin at work at Holt farm. R Bye after Jobs forenoon, cutting Vetches afternoon. T Boyce reaping wheat, G Thompson & H Raven in brewhouse. M^r^ H at home all day, WH at Holt after^n^.

MH A fine day. W^m^ went to Mark^t^, went to seaside to Bathe in the Morng. I Taken with dimness in my Eyes. Miss Richards came eve 8.

AUGUST 13, SUNDAY

HR Famaly at own Church forenoon. Miss, W Hardy, Miss Riches & H Raven at Holt Church afternoon. R Bye, W Lamb & T Baldwin dined here being the commencement of harvast.

MH Showers of rain afternoon. All went to our Church foornoon, a Communion. W^m^ & MA & Miss Richard went to Holt Church afternoon. Mr Forster came to Supper & Slept here. I Bathd.

AUGUST 14, MONDAY

HR W Lamb at work at Holt farm, T Baldwin to Gresham & Holt with beer, R Bye after Jobs. T Boyce reaping Wheat, W Dobson cutting peas, G Thompson grinding Malt. H Raven rode to Edgefield forenoon. Mr Forster & Miss Riches whent from here after dinner. Mr Goggs & Mr Cook came from Whissonsett to dinner, they rode to the sea after tea with W & Miss Hardy. WH's gid [? gig] broke down.[1]

MH A fine day. Mr Goggs & Mr Cook from London came to dinner. Mr Forster & Miss Richard dind here & went away Eveng 3. Our young people rid to the Seaside after tea, W^m^ rid to seaside to bathe in the Morng. I Bath'd. Mr Bartell bled me, I laid a blister onto my arm.[2] We began Harvest . . .

AUGUST 15, TUESDAY

HR W Lamb to Beckhigh. T Baldwin to Thornage & Stody forenoon, mowing afternoon. R Bye after Jobs forenoon, mowing after^n^, G Thompson grinding Malt. M^r^ & WH at home all day, Mr Goggs & Mr Cook whent away after dinner.

---

[1] *? gig* This sentence is almost illegible, Henry squeezing it in at the foot of the MS page

[2] *blister* A plaster, to act as a drain where the skin is deliberately punctured.

Parson Woodforde had a blister applied, seemingly successfully, at the start of his severe illness that summer: 'In the night had a blister put between my shoulders which discharged very much indeed in the night and which made me soon better. But before that was put on was all but dead, quite senseless' (J. Woodforde, *The Diary of a Country Parson*, ed. J. Beresford, vol. 5 (Oxford Univ. Press, 1931), p. 37, 13 May 1797).

It was an unpleasant treatment. Parson Forby illustrates the verb *to terrify*: 'To teize [tease]; irritate; annoy. A blister or a caustic is said to *terrify* a patient' (R. Forby, *The Vocabulary of East Anglia*, vol. 2, p. 345)

AUGUST 16, WEDNESDAY

HR W Lamb to Waybourn forenoon, Cley after, bro^t^ home 1½ Chal^d^ coals from Mr Jacksons afternoon. T Baldwin to Kettlestone & got up Vetches & card [carried] beer to Dobson's. G Thompson whent to Waybourn with Lamb. R Bye whent to Kelling forenoon, to Guestwick after^n^.[1] M^r^ & WH whent to Blakney, Mr Farthings Sale.

MH A very showry day. Mr Hardy & W^m^ went to Mr Farthings Sale at Blakney foornoon, bought some Timber & 30 bunches of Lath,[2] came home eve 7. Mrs Sheldrake dind here . . .

AUGUST 17, THURSDAY

HR T Baldwin to Hindolvestone &C [etc]. W Lamb & R Bye & G Thompson in brewhouse, H Raven brewing. M^r^ & W^m^ H at home all day. M^r^ & Mrs Flower dined & drank tea here, M^r^ & Mrs Davy drank tea here.

AUGUST 18, FRIDAY

HR T Baldwin to Morston & helped to Cleanse, W Lamb & R Bye mowing barley. G Thompson & H Raven Cleansed `// & X beer. M^r^ & WH at home all day, drank tea at Dobson's with a party of Ladies & Gentlemen.

MH A Wet Morng, fine day. I Bathd. We all drank tea at Mr Dobsons, met M^r^ & Mrs Seales, M^r^ & Mrs Temple,[3] Mrs Fisher & Mrs Withers of Holt [4] . . .

AUGUST 19, SATURDAY

HR T Baldwin to Runton, W Lamb to Southrepps, R Bye mowing barley. G Thompson & H Raven dressing Maltstones, Boy after Jobs. Mr Hardy at Holt to dinner, WH at Holt afternoon.

AUGUST 20, SUNDAY

HR Mrs Hardy to Clay forenoon. W Lamb & Baldwin Loaded their carts. WH at Holt Church afternoon. H Raven whent to Cromer.

MH Fine day, asmall showr or 2 afternoon exceptd. I & JT went to Cley meeting foornoon, no Preacher there. Mr Hardy & MA at our Church afternoon, W^m^ went to Holt Church. Phillis Raven drank tea here, H Raven went to Cromer afternoon with Mr Banyard & others . . .

AUGUST 21, MONDAY

HR W Lamb to Edgefield & Corpusta with beer, T Baldwin to Hinderingham & Thursford with D^o^. R Bye

facing page **The lofty tower of St Peter and St Paul, Cromer. Henry Raven joined a Sunday outing to Cromer on 20 Aug. organised by the innkeeper of the Feathers.**

During 1797 the brewing pupil had a far more active social life than in the early part of his diary [*MB · 2000*]

---

1 *Kelling* There was no public house in this small village (NRO: C/Sch 1/16), with a population of 132 in 1801. It is likely that Robert Bye was delivering malt to Kelling and Guestwick—perhaps the malt freshly ground the day before

2 *lath* A thin strip of wood used a supporting material, such as a barrel hoop. The sale was held at the merchant's premises at Blakeney. As well as Robert Farthing's house, there were for sale two malthouses, granaries and a coal house: 'The above premises have been erected within a few years' [ie within the last few years]; also a great deal of timber on 15 Aug. and the following few days, and '2000 bunches of laths and a quantity of coals' (*Norw. Merc.* 12 Aug. 1797)

3 *Temple* Thomas Temple's mother was to die the following month aged 93 (*Norw. Merc.* 23 Sept. 1797)

4 *Mrs Withers* Ann (d. 24 Jan. 1835 aged 84), née Trotter. She had married at Holt 13

mowing Barley, G Thompson dressing Wheat Stones. T Youngman at work in Mill part of day, H Raven grinding Malt for binn. Mr & WH at home all day.

AUGUST 22, TUESDAY

HR W Lamb to Fakenham & Salthouse with beer, T Baldwin to Wells with Do. R Bye in brewhouse forenoon, after the wheat afternoon. G Thompson in brewhouse forenoon, after the wheat afternoon. H Raven grinding Malt for brew. Mr & WH at home all day. Mr Gathercole came morning.[1]

AUGUST 23, WEDNESDAY

HR T Baldwin & Bye in brewhouse forenoon, after the wheat afternoon. G Thompson in brewhouse, H Raven brewing. J Ram reaping wheat. Bunnets two men all day. Mr & WH at home all day.

AUGUST 24, THURSDAY

HR W Lamb & R Bye mowing barley in furze close. T Baldwin to Briston forenoon, Do Do [mowing barley] afternoon. G Thompson & H Raven Cleansed `// & XX, Boy after Jobs. Bunnets two men all day. Mr & WH at home all day. Mrs Bartell & Miss Alpe drank tea here.

MH A very showry day. Wm went to Seaside to bathe,[2] Mr Hardy at home all day. [[[3] Miss Alpe and Mrs Bartell drank tea here.]]

AUGUST 25, FRIDAY

HR W Lamb, R Bye & Baldwin mowing barley in five acres, Boy after Jobs. Bunnets two men all day. Mr Hardy at home all day. G Thompson dressing flour. WH at home all day. Mr & Mrs Sheldrake drank tea here.

June 1791 the attorney William Withers (d. Holt 24 Apr. 1827 aged 72/74, bur. there 29 Apr.), who had taken over William Brereton's practice. The inscription on their altar tomb was transcribed by Dew (W.N. Dew, *The Monumental Inscriptions in the Hundred of Holt* (Norwich, 1885), p. 79)

[1] *Gathercole* John Gathercole's beer order for the Bell must have been urgent. He arrived before breakfast, and William Lamb set off immediately for Fakenham

[2] *William* He had also gone sea-bathing on 19, 21 and 23 Aug.

[3] In Mary Ann's shaky hand. She erased her mother's record of the Sheldrakes' visit on 24 Aug., transferred it in her own hand to the next day, and inserted the entry relating to Miss Alpe and Mrs Bartell. Mary Alpe had been her schoolmistress at Holt from May 1781 to Dec. 1783, Mary Ann attending as a day pupil

Thursday: A very showry day Wm went to Seaside
24 to bathe Mr Hardy a home all day
~~Mr & Mrs & M Sheldrake drank tea &~~
~~supt here~~ Miss Alpe and Mrs Bartell drank
tea here

MH A drisly day. W^m went to Seaside to bathe. Mr Hardy at home all day. [[[1] M^r & M^rs & M Sheldrake drank tea & sup^t here]] . . .

AUGUST 26, SATURDAY

HR W Lamb to Sherringham & Edgefield, T Baldwin to Thornage & Cromer. R Bye mowing barley, J Ram reaping Wheat. Bunnets two men all day, G Thompson in brewhouse. M^r H at home all day, WH & Miss Hardy at Holt afternoon. Boy after Jobs.

AUGUST 27, SUNDAY

HR Famaly at own Church forenoon, M^rs H to Briston afternoon, WH at Holt afternoon. Miss Howard call'd evening.

MH A moist Morng, fine day & hot. We all went to our Church foornoon, Mr Burrell preach'd. I, MA & J Thompson went to Briston Meeting afternoon. W^m went to Holt Church afternoon, home to tea . . .

AUGUST 28, MONDAY

HR W Lamb, T Baldwin mowing barley at Holt farm forenoon,[2] when [went] to Kelling afternoon for two lode of Straw. G Thompson & T Boyce mowing barley forenoon at Holt, at work in brewhouse afternoon. Boy after Jobs, R Bye at Mr Cobons instead of T Boyce.[3] M^r & WH at home all day.

AUGUST 29, TUESDAY

HR W Lamb unloded a lode of Straw & whent to Kelling for one lode forenoon, getting up peas afternoon. R Bye & W Dobson in barn, G Thompson pitching peas.

MH A fine Morng, some small Showers afternoon. Our Men caring [carrying] pease till even 5 & then the rain prevented them. Mr Hardy & W^m at home all day, expected Sister Goggs but she did not come. 2 Miss Davy [Two Miss Davys] drank tea here.

AUGUST 30, WEDNESDAY

HR W Lamb to Holt with beer & ploughing & [in] field, got up two lode Barley towards night. R Bye ploughing in D^o [field], helped after the barley. Baldwin to Aldborough. G Thompson turning peas & barley afternoon, Boy after Jobs, Mrs Thompson gathered Bells acre of Barley. M^r & WH at home all day, Miss Howard drank tea here. H Raven in brewhouse.

[1] In Mary Ann's hand

[2] *barley* After the references in the spring to ploughing at Holt Heath Farm this is confirmation that the Hardys had planted arable crops there. They must have been confident that the huge effort put into manuring the soil would make the venture worthwhile. The 1797 harvest brought in more cash than the previous year's, William Hardy noting in his accounts to 25 Sept. 1797: 'Corn crop exceed last year by £60 0s 0d' (*World*, vol. 2, chap. 11). It is unlikely this calculation allowed for the extra labour involved at the Holt farm

[3] *at Mr Cobon's* This explains Thomas Boyce's absence from Henry's diary since 14 Aug. and for much of the rest of the harvest: he had been borrowed by James Cobon for the neighbouring farm's harvest.

Boyce did not return to work at the Hardys' until 25 Sept.—an illustration of the fluidity of the labour market, for he had been hired for an annual (part-time) wage 10 Oct. 1796 as the Hardys' gardener

---

facing page **Mary Ann Hardy corrects the record for 24 Aug.; her mother had mistaken the day on which the excise officer and his family came round. Mary Ann's handwriting never matched the standard of the rest of her family** [*Cozens-Hardy Collection*]

[1] *turning barley* To air it, and prevent it rotting in the fields in the wet weather

[2] *bricks* The brewery counting house was about to be demolished (18 Sept.) and a new one built (20 Oct. 1797). The existing counting house had been completed only recently, on 19 Dec. 1788 (*Diary 2*)

[3] *Mr Sheldrake* Until 1838 excise officers were permitted, within certain carefully defined bounds, to charge for additional tasks such as preparing affidavits; harvesting however was well outside their normal line of duty. Accepting part-time employment from a family whose manufactures it was John Sheldrake's duty to inspect could have compromised the independence and impartiality on which his masters in London insisted.

Offering inducements was prosecuted, with crippling penalties, under statute law: 'And by the 11 G. c.30: If any person liable to the duties of excise [eg William Hardy] . . . shall give or offer to any officer of the said duties [eg John Sheldrake] any bribe, gratuity, or reward, in order to induce him to omit his duty, or to do contrary to it; he shall forfeit £500' (J. Burn, *The Justice of the Peace and Parish Officer* (16th edn, 1788), vol. 2, p. 35)

MH A very fine day. Mr Hardy & W^m^ at home all day. Recd a Letter from Mr Goggs informing me that my Sister is poorly & cant come. Miss Howard drank tea here. I Bathd.

AUGUST 31, THURSDAY

HR W Lamb & Baldwin driving the barley home from furze close, G Thompson pitching D^o^. W Dobson & R Bye in barn, Boy riding the horse in barn, Mary Parr raking after the waggon. H Raven in brewhouse, M^r^ & WH at home all day.

MH A Wet day. Mr Hardy & W^m^ at home all day, no Harvest work done. I Bathd.

SEPTEMBER 1, FRIDAY

Henry Raven W Lamb & Baldwin in brewhouse forenoon, ploughing afternoon. R Bye & G Thompson in Brewhouse forenoon, turning barley afternoon.[1] H Raven brewing, Boy after Jobs. M^r^ & WH at home all day, Mr Sheldrake Supped here.

Mary Hardy A very showry day. Men Brewd. Mr Hardy & W^m^ at home all day . . .

SEPTEMBER 2, SATURDAY

HR W Lamb to Brampton. T Baldwin drag raking forenoon, whent to Holt for 1000 bricks & with beer afternoon.[2] R Bye setting up the wheat, helped to Cleanse & turning barley. G Thompson & H Raven Cleansed '// & XX, Boy after Jobs. M^r^ H at home all day, WH at Holt afternoon.

SEPTEMBER 3, SUNDAY

HR M^rs^ H to Clay afternoon, M^r^ & Miss H at own Church after^n^. WH, H Raven & Nath Raven to Holt Church, Miss Massingham & Miss P Raven came home with us to tea.

MH A fine day. W^m^ went to Seaside to bathe. I & J Thompson went to Briston meeting afternoon, M^r^ H & MA went to our Church afternoon. W^m^ went to Holt Church aftern. Nathl Raven Junr came to dinner, Phillis R & Miss Massingham drank tea here . . .

SEPTEMBER 4, MONDAY

HR G Thompson loading wheat, T Youngman pitching D^o^, Mr Sheldrake helping after wheat half a day.[3] R Bye stacking, T Baldwin & Lamb on Stack, finnish'd the wheat about three OClock than [then] got up two loade of peas. Mr & WH at home all day, H Raven in brewhouse. The Miss Leekes drank tea here.

SEPTEMBER 5, TUESDAY

HR W Lamb, T Baldwin, G Thompson & R Bye got up the remainder of peas & six lode of barley, H Raven in brewhouse. Mr H at home all day, Wm & Miss Hardy whent to Cromer to spend the day. Mr Mendham [Mindham] came afternoon to repair the organ.

MH A very fine day. Wm & MA went to Cromer M10, dind & drank tea at Mr Bartells, came home even 9. A Wet Night. Men Caring [carrying] Barly. Mendham began repairing the Organ . . .

SEPTEMBER 6, WEDNESDAY

HR G Thompson, W Lamb, R Bye & T Baldwin getting up Barley, Mrs Thompson gathering Do. Boy riding horse on goft, T Hall thaching the Wheat Stack. H Raven in brewhouse, Mr Mindham repairing the Organ. Mr & WH at home all day.

SEPTEMBER 7, THURSDAY

HR W Lamb, T Baldwin, R Bye & G Thompson getting up barley out of five acres, H Raven in brewhouse. Boy helping after barley, Mrs Thompson gathering Do. Mr & WH at home all day, Mr Mendham repairing Organ.

SEPTEMBER 8, FRIDAY

HR G Thompson, T Baldwin & R Bye getting the barley from Holt farm, Boy raking after waggon, the other boy keeping piggs.[1] H Raven grinding Malt for brew. Mr & WH at home all day, Mr Mindham after the organ. W Lamb whent to Stalham.

MH A fine day. Men got home the Barly from Holt Farm. I Bathd. Mr Hardy & Wm at home all day.

SEPTEMBER 9, SATURDAY

HR W Lamb came from Stalham. R Bye & G Thompson drag raking forenoon, gathering Larges [largess] aftern. T Baldwin to Syderstone with beer, H Raven grinding Malt for brew, Boy in brewhouse. Mr H at home all day, WH at Holt to dinner.

MH Wind high, raind afternoon. Mr Hardy at home all day. Wm went to Justices sitting at Holt, dind at the Feathers, drank tea at Miss Leekes, came home even 8.

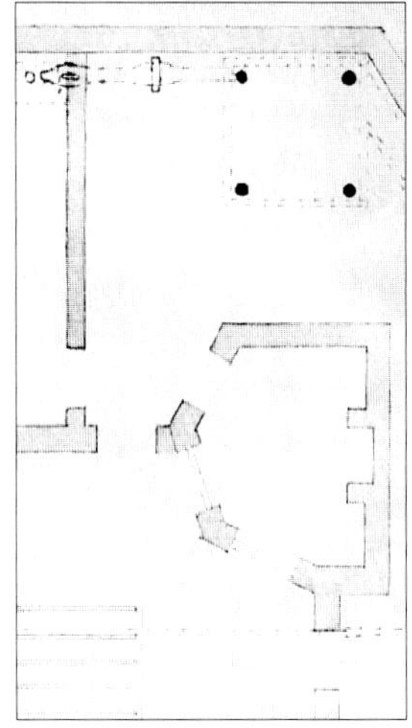

above A small, irregularly shaped (and unheated) room, with two windows onto the yard, is shown in the early-19th-century plan probably by Mindham (reproduced against Mary Hardy's entry for 31 July 1794 and here enlarged) and in the 1935 brewery plan (shown under the entry for 16 Aug. 1793). Basil Cozens-Hardy identified it as the counting house.

Henry's years on the malting floor being over, he was to make the counting house his base (20 Oct. 1797). The rebuilding of this room was the first act by William on taking sole charge of an enterprise which he was to transform between 1797 and 1842 [*Cozens-Hardy Collection*]

[1] *keeping* Tending

SEPTEMBER 10, SUNDAY

HR Famaly at own Church forenoon, M^{rs} H to Clay afternoon. WH to Holt Church afternoon, H Raven at home all day. T Raynor came in the afternoon to speak to M^{r} H (respecting the Malthouse).

MH A very fine day. All went to our Church foornoon, Mr Burrell preachd. I & JT went to Cley meeting afternoon. W^{m} went to seaside, could not Bathe the «sea» being very rough. W^{m} at Holt Church afternoon. I Bathd . . .

SEPTEMBER 11, MONDAY

HR T Baldwin, R Bye & G Thompson in brewhouse all day, H Raven brewing. W Lamb to Gresham with beer. M^{r} H at home all day, WH to Holt evening. Boy barrowing Clinkers to the Cistern.[1]

SEPTEMBER 12, TUESDAY

HR T Baldwin to Holt & Sharringham with beer, W Lamb to Brampton. R Bye in brewhouse & whent to Thornage with Malt, G Thompson & H Raven cleansed `// & XX beer, Boy after Jobs. M^{r} H at home all day, WH at Walsingham.

MH A Windy day, Showry afternoon. Mr Hardy at home all day taking a Valuation «of» our Furniture.[2] W^{m} rid to the Justice Setting at Walsingham, drank tea at Mr Balls, Saxlingham, came home even 8. I bathd.

SEPTEMBER 13, WEDNESDAY

HR W Lamb & R Bye got up 6 acres of rakings forenoon. WL to Hindolvestone afternoon with beer, T Baldwin to Syderstone. R Bye in brewhouse & fenced in the Stack after, Boy after Jobs, G Thompson in brewhouse. H Raven whent to Bale afternoon, WH to Sharringham After^{n}. M^{r} H at home all Day.

MH A Windy day, raind afternoon. Mr Hardy taken [taking] a Valuation of the Furniture. W^{m} rid to Sheringham afternoon to git his Horse shod, drank tea at Mr Flowers, came home even 8 . . .

SEPTEMBER 14, THURSDAY

HR W Lamb to Fakenham with beer. T Baldwin ploughing forenoon, to Edgefield after^{n}. R Bye after Jobs, G Thompson & H Raven in brewhouse. M^{r} & WH at home all day.

[1] *clinkers* Used in various dialects to denote small, well-fired bricks; known also as iron cinders (see note for 9 June 1796). In Shropshire, cradle at Coalbrookdale of new industrial processes including smelting, the word denoted 'a bad sort of coal; a cinder from an iron furnace' (J.O. Halliwell, *Dictionary of Archaic Words*).

Forby describes *clinkers* as 'bricks of a smaller size than usual, burned very hard, and set up on edge to pave stables . . . When thrown togther they do not rattle like common bricks, but make a *clinking*, like the collision of metallic substances; whence their name' (R. Forby, *The Vocabulary of East Anglia*, vol. 1, p. 68).

The Hardys may have used them to form a watertight floor around the large brick cistern in the maltings

[2] *valuation* Preserved in William Hardy's hand and occupying 14 MS pages in Raven Hardy's precedent book; the domestic inventory and valuation are reproduced in full as an appendix to *Diary 2*. He valued the dwelling house, stables, coach house and garden at £600, and the furniture and goods in the three reception rooms (four, if Mary Ann's dressing room is included), the kitchen, back offices, cellars and nine bedrooms and box rooms (two of which were in the attic) at £526 8*s* 6*d*.

The task was for the handover of the business, which he also valued, to

above The Letheringsett brewery after the 1936 fire, looking west. The louvred windows of the brewhouse are seen on the far left; only the foundations remain by the counting house corner. The grounds of Letheringsett Hall are to the right [*Cozens-Hardy Collection*]

SEPTEMBER 15, FRIDAY

HR W Lamb & T Baldwin at work at Holt farm, R Bye in brewhouse & after Jobs afternoon. G Thompson grinding Malt for brew, H Raven in brewhouse. Mr H at Holt farm afternoon, WH at home all day. Boy at Holt farm.

SEPTEMBER 16, SATURDAY

HR W Lamb, T Baldwin, R Bye & Boy at work at Holt farm. G Thompson grinding Malt for brew & grinding sharps.[1] Mr, WH & Miss Hardy at Holt market afternoon, H Raven at home all day.

MH A dry day. Wm went to Seaside to Bathe, I Bath'd. Mr Hardy rid to Holt Farm afternoon. Wm & MA walkd to Holt afternoon, drank tea at Mr Bakers . . .

SEPTEMBER 17, SUNDAY

HR Mrs Hardy to Clay forenoon. Mr, Wm & Miss Hardy at own Church afternoon,[2] Miss Howard drank tea here.

SEPTEMBER 18, MONDAY

HR T Baldwin took 3 barls of Beer to Holt in morning, whent from thence to Holt farm to plough, R Bye & Boy at work at Holt farm. W Lamb to Briston, Thornage & Bale with beer, G Thompson grinding barley for fat Piggs [fattening pigs]. H Raven taking the inside of Countinghouse Down. Mr H at home all day, Mr Moore & Jarvis dine'd here. WH whalked with Mr Moore a shooting. Richd Temple drank tea here.

his son in Oct. 1797. The business accounts of Sept. 1797 are reproduced as tables in *World*, vols 1 and 2

[1] *sharps* Third-grade flour. The best and finest grade was flour, for wheaten bread; the second grade wholemeal; the third, coarse ground for coarse bread and animal feed, was variously called sharps, shorts, supers, middling and stuffins; the fourth grade was bran or pollard. Even within the four divisions there were gradations. Shorts (also known as coarse stuffins) were lower on the scale than sharps (fine stuffins) (J.O. Halliwell, *Dictionary of Archaic Words*)

[2] *our church* As on 1 Oct. 1797, Mary Hardy did not attend an Anglican service even on a day when it did not clash with her meeting

MH A fine day till eveng 6 then a heavy Showr. Mr Hardy & Wm at home all day. Mr Moore of Holt dind & drank tea here, Mr Temple of Barmer drank tea here & borrowed £120.[1] I Bathd.

SEPTEMBER 19, TUESDAY

HR W Lamb, R Bye & Gunton Thompson in brewhouse, H Raven {in} brewing. T Baldwin to Overstrand with beer. Bunnet & three men all day. Mr H at home all day, Wm H to Aylsham & Corpusta.

MH A fine morng, very wet afternoon. Wm rid to Aylsham Justice sitting foornoon, could not git home till even 10 on acct of the rain. Mr Hardy at home all day. Wm began to build a new Counting House [2] . . .

SEPTEMBER 20, WEDNESDAY

HR W Lamb to Thursford with beer & brot home a lode of bricks from Dawsons & whent to Holt with beer, T Baldwin at work at Holt farm, R Bye in brewhouse. Mr Bunnet & Laborer ¾ of day, 2 men all day. Mr & W Hardy at home all day. G Thompson dressing wheat Stones, H Raven Cleansed `// & X beer. Boy after Jobs.

SEPTEMBER 21, THURSDAY

HR W Lamb ploughing at Holt farm, T Baldwin to Salthouse with beer & Clay for 2 Chaldron Cinders from Mr Ellis's & got up a lode of Lime from Holt. R Bye at Holt farm half the day. W Tinker all day, Dawsons man all day, Bunnets two trowel men & two Laborers all day. G Thompson laid down Wheat Stones, H Raven in brewhouse. Mr & W Hardy at home all day. Boy harrow'd the yard aftern,[3] Sam Starling tasking.

MH A fine day. Mr Hardy & Wm at home all day. Bricklayers & Carpenter at work in Counting House . . .

SEPTEMBER 22, FRIDAY

HR W Lamb to Aldborough with beer, T Baldwin & R Bye at work at Holt farm. Bunnets two trowelmen & two Laborers all day, W Tinker all day, Dawson man half the day. Mr H at Holt farm aftern, WH at home all day. G Thompson after Jobs, H Raven painting &C, Starling tasking, the Sawyers at work. The Miss Leekes drank tea here.

SEPTEMBER 23, SATURDAY

HR W Lamb, R Bye & Boy at work at Holt farm. T Baldwin at Holt farm forenoon, then whent to Thornage,

[1] *Temple* £120 was a very large sum to borrow: four years' salary for a cleric with only one or two curacies. The only record of the repaying of the loan came on 4 Apr. 1799, when Mary Hardy recorded that Mr Temple of Barmer paid £20. The last beer delivery to Barmer had been on 14 Nov. 1796, and the empty barrels had been collected 24 Feb. 1797, marking the end of the arrangement.

Mary Hardy was unfamiliar with writing a large sum. She originally wrote it as '£100:20', the way the figure is spoken, before erasing it and substituting the correct version.

Richard Temple may have travelled from Barmer for the burial at Thornage 17 Sept. 1797 of Mary, aged 93, widow of John Temple: see note for 18 Aug. 1797

[2] *new counting house* At the brewery. Mary Hardy entered this sentence as an afterthought

[3] *harrowed* Presumably as a means of sweeping up the rubbish, especially with three building firms simultaneously at work on the new counting house.

The harrow's teeth (the spikes) could afterwards be removed and the main frame dragged along to smooth the surface of the yard

Stody & Sharrington with beer. Bunnets 2 trowelme«n» & two Labourress [labourers] all day, W Tinker all day. G Thompson & H Raven in brewhouse. M^r^, M^rs^ & Miss Hardy at Holt afternoon, WH & Mr Balls whent to Market after tea.

SEPTEMBER 24, SUNDAY

HR Famaly at own Church forenoon. Mrs Hardy to Briston afternoon, WH to Holt church afternoon. M^r^ H at home all day.

MH A foggy morn, turnd to asmall rain, fine towards even. All went to our Church foornoon, Mr Burrell preach'd. I & J Thompson went «to» Briston Meeting afternoon. W^m^ went to Holt Church aftern, came home to tea. I Bathd, W^m^ went to Seaside to Bathe.[1]

SEPTEMBER 25, MONDAY

HR W Lamb, T Baldwin & Boy at work at Holt farm, R Bye in brewhouse. G Thompson began «grinding» the malt for brew, Boyce in garden. W Tinker Making the roof for counting house. Ja^s^ Bambry all day, Bunnetts other man only half the day.[2] M^r^ & WH at home all day. Mr Forster call'd here after dinner & Left Miss Richards.

MH A very Wet Morng, foggy day. Mr Hardy & W^m^ at home all day. Mr Forster brought Miss Richards to dinner, left her here all Night, he went to the Turtle Feast at Holt.[3] I Bathd . . .

SEPTEMBER 26, TUESDAY

HR W Lamb to Burnham with beer. T Baldwin to Morston with D^o^, bro^t^ 1½ Chal^d^ Coals from Mr Temples, Blakeney, forenoon, after Jobs afternoon. R Bye after Jobs, G Thompson grinding Malt for brew & bin. Ja^s^ Bambry cutting bricks.[4] M^r^ & WH at home all day.

SEPTEMBER 27, WEDNESDAY

HR W Lamb to Edgefield forenoon, unloding coals & cinders afternoon. T Baldwin to Clay forenoon, bro^t^ home 1½ Chal^n^ coals from Mr Jacksons & ploughing afternoon. R Bye harrowing the pea stubble forenoon, carting of the stuff afternoon.[5] Boy after Jobs, G Thompson dressing flour. Bunnets two trowelmen & two Laborrers all day. M^r^ & WH whent to Holt afternoon to see the horse rase, Mr Bartell call'd afternoon.

[1] *seaside* The last time William bathed that year; his mother continued to bathe in the garden throughout the winter, Christmas Day included.
She bathed regularly in 1798, the last recorded outdoor bath of her life being on 5 Nov. 1798 (*Diary 4*), when she was nearly 65. William bathed in the sea once in the summer of 1798, and then occasionally in July 1799; he also bathed once at Salthouse in July 1803

[2] *Bambry* A skilled bricklayer: see note for 18 Nov. 1793

[3] *turtle feast* This annual celebration at the Feathers was an expensive affair. The tickets cost 10*s* 6*d* each (*Norw. Merc.* 16 Sept. 1797)—a week and a half's wages for a day labourer

[4] *cutting bricks* Ornamental brickwork was evidently to grace the new counting house. For a study of gauged and cut brick and its use in flutings, pilasters, corbelling etc, see Nathaniel Lloyd's absorbing work *A History of English Brickwork* (Antique Collectors' Club reprint, 1983; 1st pub. London, 1925), pp. 70–82.
East Barsham Manor House, near Walsingham, has a wealth of cut brickwork

[5] *stuff* Builders' materials. Mary Hardy uses the term frequently during the rebuilding of Mary Ann and Jeremiah Cozens' house at Sprowston in 1806 (*Diary 4*)

above The architect's drawing for the cupola and clock at the brewery (opposite) is presumably by Mindham. Cupola and clock crashed down in the 1936 fire [*Cozens-Hardy Collection*]

SEPTEMBER 28, THURSDAY

HR T Baldwin in brewhouse forenoon, to Kettlestone afternoon. W Lamb to Corpusta & got up the second crop grass. R Bye & G Thompson in brewhouse, H Raven brewing. Bunnets two trowel men & two Laborrers all day, W Tinker at work all day. M^r & WH at home all day, Mr Nath Raven came evening.

SEPTEMBER 29, FRIDAY

HR T Baldwin to Sharringham, W Lamb to Runcton [Runton], R Bye after Jobs. G Thompson & H Raven Cleansed `// & XX. Bunnets two trowel men & two Laborrers all day, Boy after Jobs. M^r & WH at home all day, HR whent to the Ball at Holt.

MH A fine day. Mr Hardy & Bro^t took a walk to Mr Savorys Farm House, came home to dinner, went to speak to Mr Burrell aftern, came back to tea. H Raven went to Mr Browns Ball in the eveng. I Bathd.

SEPTEMBER 30, SATURDAY

HR T Baldwin to Southrepps with beer, W Lamb to Wells with D^o. R Bye after Jobs, G Thompson dressing Malt stones. Bunnets two trowel men & two Laborrers all day. M^r H at home all day, WH at Holt after tea. Boy after Jobs. Mr Erratt was here all night, HR whent with him to Holt the next morning.

MH A fine day. Mr Hardy & Bro^t walkd up to Holt foornoon, Bro^t went away Even 3. W^m went to Holt Mark^t after tea, came home even 8. Mr Erret forc'd to give up businiss, Slept here.[1] I Bathd.

OCTOBER 1, SUNDAY

Henry Raven Mrs Hardy to Clay forenoon. Famaly at own Church afternoon, HR at Holt afternoon.

Mary Hardy A very fine day. I & J Thompson went to Cley meeting foornoon, Mr Leggat preachd.[2] Mr Hardy, W^m & MA went to our Church afternoon, Mr Burrell preach'd.

OCTOBER 2, MONDAY

HR W Lamb to Fakenham, T Baldwin to Gressham & Holt. R Bye ploughing forenoon, in brewhouse afternoon. G Thompson laid down Maltstones & began to grind Malt for brew. Boy getting up Lime & Sand,

---

[1] *Erratt* See note for 24 Feb. 1796

[2] *Leggatt* Benjamin (b. near Epworth, Lincs 1 Feb. 1761, d. Deal, Kent 4 Oct. 1822), a local preacher *c.*1782–87, then a full-time Wesleyan Methodist itinerant. He was posted to the Walsingham Circuit from Lynn in Aug. 1797 and was kept there for the ensuing year; he was stationed at Norwich from Gt Yarmouth in 1795. His obituary was minuted in 1823 (*Minutes of the Methodist Conferences*, vol. 1, pp. 365, 331, 400, 304, 285; vol. 5 (London, 1825), pp. 378–9)

above A photograph of perhaps 1895–1910 looking east towards the brewery shows the Hall railings and the corner within which the counting house was set.

The brewhouse chimney and louvred roof opening are beyond, with the malt-kiln cowls just visible on the roof line in the distance. The cupola sits above the white hall; the tun room looms on the right.

The architectural style is all Mindham

[*Cozens-Hardy Collection*]

Bunnets two trowel man & 2 Laborers all day. M^{r} & WH at home. Mr Bartell & Mr Stannard call'd here afternoon, the Miss Leekes drank tea here.

MH A fine day. Mr Hardy & W^{m} at home all day. An Auction of Abr^{m} Dobsons Furniture.[1] The Miss Leakes drank tea & Supt here. I Bath'd . . .

OCTOBER 3, TUESDAY

HR W Lamb to Thornage & twice to Holt with beer, T Baldwin to Walsham with D^{o}. R Bye in brewhouse, Boy after Jobs, G Thompson grinding M^{t} for brew. Bunnets two trowelmen & 2 Laborers all day. M^{r}, M^{rs} & Miss Hardy spent the afternoon at Mr Sales's, Holt, WH whent after tea. Mr Silence call'd forenoon.

OCTOBER 4, WEDNESDAY

HR W Lamb, R Bye & G Thompson in brewhouse, H Raven brewing. T Baldwin ploughing, Boy after Jobs. Bunnets two trowelmen & 2 Laborers all day, W Tinker all day. M^{r} & WH at home all day, T Raynor came morning.

OCTOBER 5, THURSDAY

HR W Lamb to Holt farm for the plough then whent to harrow & ploughing afternoon. R Bye in brew house,

[1] *Abraham Dobson* See note for 15 Jan. 1794. The auction suggests that, like his brother Richard, he had run into financial difficulty at Holt

G Thompson & H Raven Cleansed `// & X beer. Bunnets two trowel men & 2 Laborers all day. Mr Youngman after the Malthouse pump forenoon, Boyce in garden. T Raynor in Malthouse, began to Steep. Mr & W Hardy at home all day. Boy whent away at noon. W Tinker all day, Sawyers at work.

MH A very fine Morng, a foggy aftern & asmall Showr abt eveng 4. Mr Hardy & I rid to Keelling to Mr Ditchells Sale afternoon, came home to tea.[1] I Bathd . . .

OCTOBER 6, FRIDAY

HR W Lamb got up 2 lode of sand & whent to Holt with beer forenoon & ploughing afternoon, T Baldwin ploughing all day. R Bye & Mrs Thompson at Holt farm making hay. Bunnets two trowelmen & 2 Laborers all day, W Tinker at work all day. G Thompson in brewhouse. Mr H & H Raven set of for Southrepps & Cromer morning 8 OClock, W Hardy at home all day.

OCTOBER 7, SATURDAY

HR Bunnets two trowel me«n» & 2 Laborers all day, W Tinker half the day, W Lamb to Alborough with beer. T Baldwin to Dawling with beer, but Coker would not suffer him to leave it so brought it back again & whent to Briston afternoon.[2] R Bye ploughing, G Thompson in brewhouse. WH whent to Holt after tea. Mr H & HR came from Cromer afternoon, Mr H stopped at Holt Market.

OCTOBER 8, SUNDAY

HR Famaly at own Church forenoon. Mrs & Miss Hardy to Briston afternoon, WH & H Raven at Holt afternoon. W Lamb loded for Syderstone.

OCTOBER 9, MONDAY

HR W Lamb to Syderstone with beer, T Baldwin to Cromer with Do, came home by Waybourn & Brot home some beer from Mrs Halls.[3] R Bye after Jobs, G Thompson dressing flour & grinding Barley. T Raynor in Mt house, Bunnets 2 trowelmen & 2 Laborers all day. Mr & WH at home all day, W Tinker all day.

OCTOBER 10, TUESDAY

HR T Baldwin to Hinderham [Hindringham] & Morston with beer, W Lamb to Corpusta & Holt with Do. R Bye after Jobs, whent away at Night.[4] G Thompson grind-

[1] *Ditchell* Anthony, of Kelling. He had successfully appealed to the justices at Holt Quarter Sessions 19 Jan. 1797 against the poor rate set 21 Nov. 1796, alleging that his local JP, Zurishaddai Girdlestone of Kelling Hall, had been underrated by the parish officers (NRO: C/S 1/15)

[2] *Coker* Neither diarist reveals why Samuel Coker rejected the beer. He may have been angered that the Hardys were acquiring the other, rival, public house at Field Dalling, the Jolly Farmers (see note for 9 May 1797). When William Hardy snr and jnr called at Dalling early in the morning of 13 Oct. it was not stated whether they were sorting out matters with Mr Coker at the Crown or taking possession of the Jolly Farmers, or both.

Despite the upset, Samuel Coker continued to be supplied from Letheringsett until he left in 1799. His successor, Samuel May, then broke the link with the Hardys, while the Jolly Farmers continued both tie and supply

[3] *Mrs Hall* Edward Hall of the Crown had died, and the new innkeeper was not supplied from Letheringsett: see notes for 13 Nov. 1793 and 3 Jan. 1795

[4] *R. Bye . . . went away at night* He is not mentioned again by the diarists, and does not appear in future years in the Letheringsett registers

ing Malt, T Raynor in Malthouse. Bunnets trowelman & 1 Laborer all day. Mr Hardy at home all day, WH whent to Aldborough. HR whent to Holt evening.

MH A Close day. Mr Hardy at home all day. Wm went to Albro [Aldborough] foornoon, came home even 5. I Bath'd. Eliz Jennerys & Eliz Chastney went away . . .

OCTOBER 11, WEDNESDAY

HR W Lamb to Thursford & twice to Holt. T Baldwin & G Thompson in brewhouse, H Raven brewing, T Raynor in Malthouse. Bunnets 2 trowelmen & 2 Laborers all day, W Tinker half the day. Mr & WH at home all day.

OCTOBER 12, THURSDAY

HR W Lamb to Sharringham with beer, brot a small bargin of hay from Holt farm.[1] T Baldwin & T Raynor after Jobs & whent to Holt farm for the second crop hay. G Thompson & H Raven Cleansed `// & XX beer. Bunnets 3 trowel men & 2 Laborers all day, Dawson man & W Tinker all day. Mr & WH at home all day, TB loded for Stalham. Boy & Maid sarvant came evening.

MH A very fine day. Eliz Williamson came as upper Servt,[2] Wm [ ] a Lad.[3] Mr Hardy & Wm at home all day. I Bathd.

OCTOBER 13, FRIDAY

HR T Baldwin to Stalham, W Lamb to Stody & Dawling with beer. T Raynor in Mt H, G Thompson dressing Wheat Stones. Bunnets 3 trowel men & 2 laborers all day, W Tinker & Dawsons Man all day. Mr Hardy at home all day, WH whent to Dawling morning. Mr Ellis & Friend calld afternoon.

MH A fine day till Even 6 then raind all Night. Mr Hardy «and» Wm rid to Dawling in the Morng after the Publick House there, came home Morng 10. I Bathd . . .

OCTOBER 14, SATURDAY

HR W Lamb tended the Stock,[4] whent to Salthouse & unloded the hay. T Baldwin came from Stalham, T Raynor in Mt H, G Thompson dressing Wt [wheat] Stones. Youngmans two men mending the water wheel & making a door for counting roan [room] Chamber.[5] Bunnets two trowel men & 2 Laborers all day, W Tinker all day. WH at Holt afternoon, Mr H at home all day. Boy whent to Holt afternoon for Nails.

[1] *bargin* Bargain; an undefined amount. Forby's illustrations accompanying his definition are best quoted in full: '*bargain, s.* an indefinite number or quantity of any thing; not necessarily conveying the idea of purchase and sale. Ex[amples]: "Two good tidy *bargains* of hay from an acre", meaning something less than waggon loads; "A poor *bargain* of wool from three score hoggets"; "A sad *bargain* of lazy chaps"' (R. Forby, *The Vocabulary of East Anglia*, vol. 1, p. 15)

[2] *Elizabeth Williamson* See note for 31 July 1797

[3] *William* His surname is never stated. On his first Sunday he took Mary Hardy to Cley meeting. Like the two maidservants he stayed the full year, leaving 10 Oct. 1798

[4] *tended the stock* Not a task specifically recorded until now; perhaps encompassed by 'after jobs' or 'at jobs' in earlier entries. If Henry is referring to the small dairy herd this was normally a task undertaken by the cook–dairymaid, so William Lamb may have been filling in during the interregnum before Maria Milligen's arrival; looking after the cows was not part of the upper servant's job.

Thomas and Elizabeth Milligen's daughter Maria (bapt. Letheringsett 7 July 1777) was the new cook, at £3 10*s* a year

[5] *counting room chamber* The Hall also had a

counting room chamber, on the first floor, each bedroom being named for the room below.

This entry may suggest that a bedchamber was attached to the brewery counting house—useful perhaps as brewing began in the small hours of the morning with the lighting of the copper for the first mash at 3 or 4 am.

However it is more likely that chamber here means a storage area, as in hop chamber (5 July 1794), and wheat chamber (30 Jan. 1796)

---

[1] *James Broughton jnr* See note for 30 Jan. 1795

[2] *new house* The new counting house. Retail sales were recorded in a separate ledger from the brewery diary. The list of customers can be reconstructed from the Ledger A accounts; the list of innkeepers from Ledger B (*Diary 4*, app. D4.B)

---

facing page **The entrance to Letheringsett Church, viewed from the south door.**

Mothers would kneel inside the church entrance at the start of the service of churching (22 Oct. 1797) [*MB · 2000*]

OCTOBER 15, SUNDAY

HR Mrs Hardy to Clay forenoon. Mr, Miss Hardy & H Raven at own Church afternoon, Wm H at Holt aftern. W Lamb Loded for Brampton.

OCTOBER 16, MONDAY

HR W Lamb to Brampton with beer. T Baldwin to Edgefield forenoon, ploughing afternoon. Bunnets 3 trowel men & 2 laborers all day, W Tinker & Dawsons man all day. Jas Broughton Junr came to work at 7/6d pr wheek.[1] T Raynor in Malthouse, G Thompson & H Raven in brewhouse. Mr & WH at home all day, Mr J Ellis drank tea here. HR whent to Holt evening.

OCTOBER 17, TUESDAY

HR T Baldwin to Fakenham with beer. W Lamb got up one lode of Lime & one lode of sand in forenoon, whent to plough afternoon. Jas Broughton ploughing forenoon, at harrow afternoon. G Thompson grinding Malt for brew, J Ram tasking. Bunnets two trowelmen & two laborers all day, Wm Tinker & Dawsons Man all day. Mr & Wm Hardy at home all day. The Sawyers finnished the timber. Hop Marchant call'd afternoon.

OCTOBER 18, WEDNESDAY

HR W Lamb, Jas Broughton & G Thompson in brewhouse, H Raven brewing. T Baldwin ill, not able to work. Bunnets 2 trowelmen & 2 Laborers all day, W Tinker & Dawsons man all day. T Raynor in Malthouse, J Herring cutting Hay. Mr & Wm Hardy at home all day.

OCTOBER 19, THURSDAY

HR W Lamb & J Broughton ploughing, G Thompson & H Raven Cleansed '// & X beer. Bunnets 2 trowelmen & 2 Laborers all day, W Tinker & Dawsons man all day. T Baldwin ill. Mr H at home all day, T Raynor in Malthouse. WH at Holt afternoon. Mr & Mrs Bartell drank tea here.

OCTOBER 20, FRIDAY

HR W Lamb to Southrepps with beer. T Baldwin ploughing forenoon, after Jobs afternoon in brewhouse. Bunnets 2 trowel man [men] & Labourrer all day, Tinker & Dawson«s» man all day. T Raynor in Malt house, G Thompson in brewhouse. H Raven began to sell goods in {in} new house.[2] Mr H at home all day. WH whent to Holt forenoon, to Bayfield after tea.

MH A very Wet day. Mr Hardy at home all day. W^m atempted to go around [a round] to gather up Mony [money] but the weather prevent'd him from going any further then Holt, he returnd to dinner. I Bathd . . .

OCTOBER 21, SATURDAY

HR W Lamb to Holt twice, Baldwin to Overstrand. J Broughton ploughing all day. Bunnets 2 trowelmen & 2 Laborers all day, W Tinker all day. T Raynor in M^t house, G Thompson in brew house. M^r H at home all day, WH whent to Sherringham.

OCTOBER 22, SUNDAY

HR Famaly at own Church forenoon. M^rs & Miss Hardy to Clay afternoon, WH at Holt afternoon.

MH A very fine day. All went to our Church foornoon, Mr Burrell preach'd. Mrs Savory was Church'd as it is call'd.[1] I, MA & the Lad went to Briston meeting afternoon . . .

OCTOBER 23, MONDAY

HR W Lamb ploughing forenoon, to Edgefield afternoon & Loded for Burnham. T Baldwin to Runton, J Broughton ploughing all day, G Thompson dressing flour. W Tinker & Bunnets 2 men all day. M^r H at home all day, W Hardy to Corpusta &c.[2] M^r & Mrs Sheldrake & Miss P Raven drank tea here.

OCTOBER 24, TUESDAY

HR W Lamb to Burnham, T Baldwin to Holt & Briston, G Thompson grinding Malt for brew and bin. Bunnets 1 trowel man & 1 Laborer all day, T Raynor in Malt house. M^r & W Hardy at home all day. Miss Baker, Miss Bartell & Mr Custance from Portsmouth drank tea here.[3]

OCTOBER 25, WEDNESDAY

HR T Baldwin, G Thompson & J Broughton in brewhouse, T Raynor in Malthouse. W Lamb at harrow in furze close, H Raven brewing. Bunnets 2 men all day. M^r H at home all day, WH whent to Whissonsett. Mr Sheldrake drank tea here. Miss Hardy whent to Holt.

MH A Showry day. Mr Hardy at home all day. W^m sett of for Siderston [Syderstone] & Whisonsett morng 10, slept at Whissonsett. I Bathd. MA drank tea at Mr Bakers at Holt, came home even 8.

[1] *churched* The service of thanksgiving after childbirth derived from the pre-Reformation rite of purification. 'Churched' was a term the diarist had used rather more unselfconsciously during the Coltishall years, suggesting that such services were infrequent at Letheringsett.

Mary Ann Savory had been born 26 Sept. 1797 (see note for 6 Oct. 1796); Mary Hardy and Mary Ann Hardy had called on Mrs Savory on 6 Oct. 1797

[2] *Corpusty etc* Mary Hardy notes that William's tour included Briston

[3] *Mr Custance* Identified by Mary Hardy as Myles Custance (b. 28 Jan. 1769, privately bapt. Fakenham 29 Jan., publicly 19 Sept. 1769), son of William and Phillis Custance of Fakenham

above As we say farewell to Henry as a diarist, and prepare to meet him again in his aunt's diary (*Diary 4*), one tiny image, a mid-20th-century gift to the archive, bids us a more final adieu.

Here all the employees of the Letheringsett maltings and brewery line up in the yard in 1896, some bearing the tools of their trade: the drayman's apron, the malt shovel, the carpenter's tool, the paint tin. Their names are listed in *Mary Hardy and her World*, volume 4.

Adding to the poignancy it was not taken by grateful brewers, the Cozens-Hardys. It looks from its grainy, fuzzy appearance to be a photograph organised by the men to mark the end [*gift of Walter High 1953: Cozens-Hardy Collection*]

OCTOBER 26, THURSDAY

MH A foggy Morng, fine day. Mr Hardy at home all day, W^m^ came home even 9.

[Henry Raven's manuscript ends following his entry for 25 Oct. 1797. Then follow his ENDNOTES, transcribed here after Mary Hardy's]

End of the middle Letheringsett years

Ledger 4 of Mary Hardy's manuscript continues in *Diary 4*

Endnotes, register and maidservants

Mary Hardy's endnotes

Ledger 4: 1793–1797

[These notes and lists were entered at the back of Mary Hardy's manuscript diary ledger 4 and are all in her hand apart from her daughter Mary Ann's insertions and additions, as shown. Where a precise date is given, eg over a death, a related editorial note often appears under that date in the diary transcription]

[no date given]

Jas Dew at the Sign of the Bushell, near the Rose in St Austins [1]

Memorandoms Stocks The 4 pr Cents shut March 8
Dividend to be paid April 5

Books

The Nature, Design & General rules of the United Societies in London, Bristol, Kingswood, Newcastle upon Tine &c [2] abt 6d

A Plain Account of the People call'd Methodists in A Letter to the Revd Mr Perronet, Vicar of Shoreham in Kent [3] abt 1/-

Directions for Renewing our Covenant with God [4] abt 6d

An Extract from the Christian Pattern or A Treatice on the imitation of Christ by Thos A Kempis is published by John Wesley MA abt 2/-

An Appeal or matter of fact & Comon Sense or A Rational Demonstration of Mans Corrupt & lost Estate [5] Abt 3/-

An Earnest Appeal to Men of Reason & Region [*Religion*] By John Wesley MA late fellow of Lincoln Colledge Oxford [6] price abt 3*s*

An Extract from Dr Youngs Night Thoughts on Life, Death & Immortality [7]

The Complaint, or Night Thoughts on Life, death & Immortality [8]

Scripture Prayers for Morng & Eveng for the use of Familys price 1*s* bound

The Parlour preacher, A pack of Cards for those who are determined to win Christ, Phil. III. 8 [9]

[1] *Rose* Peck's 1802 Norwich directory lists John Keymer at the Rose Inn, 2 St Augustine's; at the 1806 general election it was a Whig supporters' house (*Norw. Merc.* 8 Nov. 1806). James Dew may have gone to the Bushel from the Maid's Head, N. Walsham. Not being one of the city's principal inns, the Bushel is not listed in the directory, but it was also in St Augustine's Street, as shown on the Norfolk pubs website <http://www.norfolkpubs.co.uk/norwich/bnorwich/ncbus.htm>, accessed 25 Nov. 2011

[2] *The Nature* By John Wesley (1703–91); it ran to many editions. The only time the diarist refers to Wesley is in this catalogue of tracts which she may have wished to buy

[3] *A Plain Account* By John Wesley (8th edn London 1786)

[4] *Directions* By John Wesley (4th edn 1787; 5th edn 1794)

[5] *An Appeal* By John Fletcher (1729–85), Vicar of Madeley, Salop (4th edn London, 1785); 'sold at the New Chapel [City Road], and at the Revd Mr Wesley's preaching houses in town and country'

[6] *An Earnest Appeal* (1st pub. 1743; 6th edn 1771)

[7] *An Extract* By Edward Young (1683–1765), 1794

[8] *The Complaint* By Edward Young, 1770

[9] *Phil. 3, v. 8 Yea doubtless, and I count all things but loss for the excellency of the knowledge of Christ Jesus my Lord:*

for whom I have suffered the loss of all things, and do count them but dung, that I may win Christ. This text was used by Isaac Watts for his hymn *When I survey the wondrous cross.*

The cards were devised as devotional exercises by W. Mason, a pack being held in the Opie Collection in the Bodleian Libraries, University of Oxford (Opie L 213)

Mary Hardy's register of marriages, deaths and burials at Letheringsett

Ledger 4: 1793–1797

[Caution should be exercised when using Mary Hardy's register. The ages at death tend to be approximate and were arrived at presumably by guesswork and appearance as much as by enquiry. The rector, on the infrequent occasions when he noted it, would have heard the age (or approximate age) from the next of kin.

This selective compilation by the diarist is nevertheless an extremely useful adjunct to the parish registers, at times offering more information than that provided by the rector]

Marriages

1793

Oct. 15 Mr Burrells Man & Maid was Maried [1]
Oct. 22 Ja^s^ Tinker & M Jekell was Married [2]

1794

Oct. 14 John White & Bly [Blythe] Ram was Married [3]

Saturday Jany 19 1833. Bach landing & Laundry floor finished. Jas Tinker putting up Archtrives to doors on the gallery. The Hall windows put in. Garrett doors finished last night. Jno Cookes Stacks burnt Jas Tinker attended with the Engine

above An extract from William Hardy jnr's diary for the week ending 19 Jan. 1833 during the rebuilding of Letheringsett Hall 1832–34. The shadowing on the writing is caused by William's making the entries in pencil and then overwriting them in ink—a feature found in this diary, but not in his entries in Henry Raven's diary 40 years earlier.

Although apparently illiterate at the time of his marriage in 1793 the carpenter James Tinker was responsible for much of the skilled work at the Hall. In Jan. 1833 he was recorded putting up the architraves around the gallery doors. That same week he also took round William's fire engine to a farmer's burning stack: this was a time of rick-burning [*Cozens-Hardy Collection*]

1 *Mr Burrell's man* The groom, William Sandling, and bride, Hannah Chenery, were both single, of Letheringsett, and made marks. Their occupations go unrecorded in the parish register, so the diarist's gloss is interesting

2 *Tinker* Bride and groom were single and of Letheringsett: see note for 27 Dec. 1793. The parish register gives the date as 12 Nov., not 22 Oct.

3 *White* Bride and groom were single, of Letheringsett, and made marks. Blyth or Blythe (bapt. 13 Sept. 1776) was the daughter of John Ramm, the maltster and thresher. The Whites' children are recorded in the Letheringsett registers.

John White's initials are incised very neatly on the tun room west wall, together with those of other members of William Hardy jnr's workforce of 1814. When his son Robert was bapt. 2 Aug. 1818 White's occupation was given as maltster; he thus followed his father-in-law's trade and served the same master. He died aged 79 and was buried on 24 May 1839, the same day as his wife Blythe

1795

Jan. 27 Tho[s] Balls was Maried to Deborah Ram [1]

1797

June 23 M[r] Tho[s] Skrimpshaw of Wisbeach Maried to Rose Raven of Whisonsett, [at Whissonsett], «she» was brought to Bed June 10, 1798 [2]

Register [of deaths or burials]

1793

Oct. 10 W[m] Rowland [aged] ab[t] 70
Dec. 15 M[rs] Bransby near 70 [3]
Dec. 28 M[rs] Dunns Mother 80 [4]

1795

[[[5] *Jan. 19* Mary Woodcock [6]]]
May 24 A Man from Norwich killd with overturning a Cart near M[r] Burrells [7]

1796

May 17 Ann Ives Died Sudenly agd 19
June 18 Plattons Wife Sudenly agd ab[t] 50

Sept. 2 Ann Loades between 6 & 7 Years of Age was bitten by a Mad Dog in the forehead on the 23 of July,[8] she had Antidoates given her by a person near South Walsham, the Child continued well till Monday the 29 of Aug[s] near Six Weeks when she was taken with Sickness in her Stomack & pain in her head, on the Tuesday the 30 she grew worse, a fever with pain in her head & Stomack with a total loss of Appetite & Sleep, on the Wednesday 31 she was in a high fever & had a violent Fitt, on Thursday Sept 1 she seemed to be better, not so much Fever as yesterday, but no appetite nor any moore Sleep then Yesterda«y», but on the Morng of friday 2 Sept[r] she was taken with a Violent Fitt which lasted near 2 hours, the fever ran very high, her Eyes were fixt & seemingly without sight, another Fitt came on abt 1 oClock but not so violent as before & a short time after she died seemingly easy & without much pain

Dec. 26 Mrs Coben from Burnham Aged abt 70 [9]

[1797]

Apr. 5 Young Woodhouse from Thornage aged 24 [10]
Apr. 11 M[rs] Woodhouse from Thornage aged 57
May 19 Christiana Smith Aged [ ] [11]
June 26 John Jex was buried aged [ ] [12]
Oct. [ ] Mary Bullock was Buried Aged [ ] [13]
Susan Ram was Buried aged abt 30 [14]

[1] *Balls* See note for 27 Jan. 1795

[2] *brought to bed* Elizabeth, daughter of Thomas and Rose Shrimshire, was bapt. Fakenham 10 June 1798, the first of a large family

[3] *Mrs Bransby* Elizabeth, late Mrs Lighten, second wife of Joseph, was buried on 7 Dec., so the records do not tally: see note for 4 Jan. 1796

[4] *Mrs Dunn's mother* See note for 25 Dec. 1793

[5] In Mary Ann's hand

[6] *Mary Woodcock* A widow, she was bur. 25 Jan.

[7] *man from Norwich* See note for 22 May 1795

[8] *Ann Loades* See notes for 22 July and 30 Aug. 1796. The diarist had first-hand knowledge, having called on the dying girl

[9] *Mrs Cobon* The parish register confirms that Alice, relict of John Cobon, farmer, was bur. 26 Dec., but does not give her age nor that she had been living at Burnham

[10] *Young Woodhouse* See notes for 28 Nov. 1795, 11 Apr. 1797

[11] *Christiana Smith* Relict of Samuel Smith and aged 86, she was buried 22 May

[12] *Jex* Mary Hardy noted in her diary that the blacksmith had *died* 26 June 1797 and been buried 29 June

[13] *Mary Bullock* The parish register records that *Sarah*, née Dennis, wife of John Bullock, labourer, was bur. 27 Oct.; she is also given as Sarah at the baptism of her children. John Bullock took as his second wife Elizabeth Milligen: see note for 3 Nov. 1795

[14] *Susan Ramm* (Bapt. 9 Jan. 1768, bur. 28 Oct. 1797),

daughter of John and Abigail Ramm. On 16 Oct. 1790 she had married a soldier, George Deighton, who immediately left her. This may explain the use here of her maiden name

Mary Hardy's register of maidservants

Ledger 4: 1793–1797

Servants Wages &c [1]

		£	s	d
	Sarah Turner			
1793				
⟦ *Oct. 10*	Hired Sarah Turner for a Year [at]	**3**	**0**	**0** ⟧
1794				
May 19	Cash	1	6	0
⟦ *Oct. 10*	Cash	1	14	0
	Setled	3	0	0
1795				
Oct. 10	Hired Sarah Turner for a Year [2]	**3**	**10**	**0** ⟧
1796				
Jan. 20	Cash	0	10	6
Feb. 20	Cash	1	1	0
⟦ *Oct. 10*	Cash	1	18	6
	[settled]	3	10	6
	Hannah Dagliss			
1793				
⟦ *Oct. 10*	Hired Hannah Daglass for a Year	**2**	**15**	**0**
1794				
Feb. 8	Cash	0	12	0
Oct. 10	Cash	2	3	0
	[settled]	2	15	0 ⟧

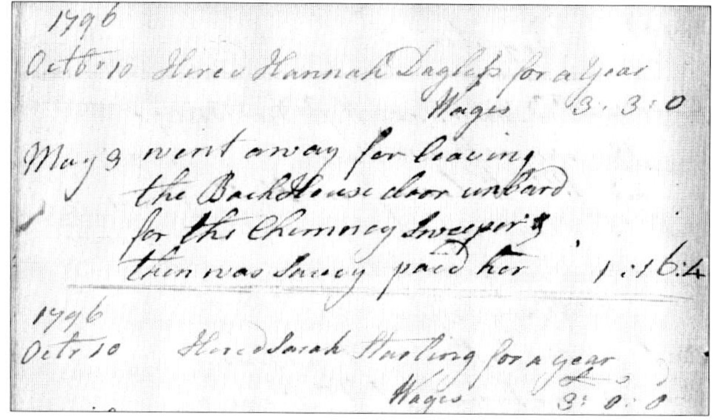

1796
Octr 10 Hired Hannah Daglefs for a Year
Wages 3 . 3 : 0
May 9 went away for leaving
the BackHouse door unbard
for the Chimney Sweeper's
then was Saucy paid her 1 : 16 . 4
1796
Octr 10 Hired Sarah [illegible] for a year
£
Wages 3 : 0 : 0

above Hannah Dagliss, who in 1797 was dismissed for leaving the backhouse door unbarred for the chimney sweep 'and then was Saucy'. Despite the sauce she worked longer for Mary Hardy than any other maidservant [*Cozens-Hardy Collection*]

[1] *servants* From the end of ledger 4 of Mary Hardy's MS diary and, like the register of marriages, deaths and burials, continued from *Diary 2*. The maidservant register began in 1780 and continued without a break until 1821. The 90 maidservants and their wages over this period are tabulated in *World*, vol. 1, app. 1.C.

The accounts for many of the maids reveal how the diarist gave cash advances which she then stopped from the annual total, paying only the balance due at Old Michaelmas (10 Oct.), the end of the hiring year. Wages were paid in arrears apart from interim payments as required. Board and lodging were at the mistress's expense. The entries are by both Mary Hardy and Mary Ann Hardy, indicating that by this time they shared the overall running of the household; the notes in the double square brackets ⟦ ⟧ are by Mary Ann.

The scribbled jottings of the MS have been rearranged in a clearer fashion for this transcription. They are here listed not in date order of each individual payment, but collectively under the name of each maidservant

[2] *Sarah Turner* She worked briefly once more for the Hardys from Dec. 1798 to Jan. 1799 in an interval between maidservants

		£	s	d
	Hannah Dagliss (*cont.*)			
[**1795**]				
[*Feb.*] [1]	Hired Hannah Dagliss at the rate of	**3**	**0**	**0**
⟦*May 2*	Cash	0	8	0
Oct. 10	Setled			
Oct. 10	Hired Hannah Daglass for a Year	**3**	**3**	**0**
Dec. 23	Cash 12 yds & half Muslin 1/6[d] [12½ yards muslin at 1*s* 6*d* a yard]	0	13	6 [2]
1796				
Oct. 10	Setled this Acct ⟧			
Oct. 10	Hired Hannah Daglass for a Year Wages	**3**	**3**	**0**
[**1797**]				
May 3	Went away for leaving the Back House door unbard [unbarred] for the Chimney Sweeper & then was Saucy, paid her [3]	1	16	4
	Frances Thompson			
1794				
⟦*Oct. 10*	Hired Frances Tompson for a year Conditional for good behaviour 3/- ⟧	**3**	**0**	**0**
1795				
Mar. [ ]	Cash	1	1	0
⟦*Oct. 10*	Cash	2	2	0 ⟧
	Ann Brown			
1794				
⟦*Oct. 10*	Hired Ann Brown for a Year Conditional for good behaviour 5*s*; went away a month after Old Christmas [Jan. 1795] ⟧	**2**	**15**	**0**
	Sarah Starling			
1796				
Oct. 10	Hired Sarah Starling for a Year Wages	**3**	**3**	**0**
[**1797**]				
Apr. 11	A Note	1	0	0
Apr. 18	Sarah Starling went away, paid her	0	12	4

[1] *Hannah Dagliss* This entry follows Ann Brown's departure, and thus relates to Feb. 1795

[2] *muslin* If the muslin cost 1*s* 6*d* a yard Mary Ann has miscalculated heavily in the maid's favour: Hannah should have owed 18*s* 9*d*, not 13*s* 9*d*. Mary Ann occasionally makes other slips in the totals, as in the final sum relating to Sarah Turner.

Mary Ann was aged 19 when Mary Hardy was struck down with her prolonged and near-fatal illness in Aug. 1793. She stepped in to assume her mother's housekeeping duties, and continued to do so intermittently either to help her convalescing mother or as Mary Hardy was training her daughter in this exacting role

[3] *Hannah Dagliss* See note for 2 May 1797. She was rehired 9 Jan. 1799, finally leaving the Hardys 10 Oct. 1801. Mary Hardy may have taken pity on her and have treated her more tolerantly than her other maidservants, for Hannah may have been orphaned early. She could be the daughter of Robert and Blyth Dagless of Edgefield, born 3 Mar. 1770, bapt. there on 4 Mar. Her mother was buried there 5 Nov. 1775, leaving a large family; her father was buried 7 Sept. 1777. There were other branches of the Daglass/Dagless/Dagliss family at Edgefield who could have helped to look after the children.

The maidservant may be the Hannah Dagless who married Holt 14 Dec. 1809 John Atwell, both single and of Holt; the groom signed

[1] *if she pleases* If Elizabeth Williamson pleases the Hardys. Elizabeth appears not to have pleased, as the three shillings were not paid

[2] *Maria Milligen* Mrs Elizabeth Milligen's 20-year-old daughter: see note for 3 Nov. 1795

below right Beer production by the Norwich common brewers, as reported in the *Norwich Mercury* for the excise year July 1796–July 1797. Such tables would appear occasionally in a city which prized its manufactures; production figures for country brewers were very rarely reported.

For comparison, Chapman Ives's riverside steam brewery in rural Coltishall was capable of brewing 20,000 barrels a year (*Norwich Mercury*, 9 Oct. 1802).

The *Mercury*, the paper serving the mercantile and manufacturing class, prided itself on its statistical accuracy, pointing out on 3 Aug. 1793 that the table which had been published the previous week in the rival paper was inaccurate; (the *Norfolk Chronicle* was more of a gentry paper).

Henry Raven in his table for beer production 1794–95 (opposite) omitted the columns for table beer and small beer

[*Norwich Mercury, 15 July 1797: Norfolk Heritage Centre, Norwich*]

		£	s	d
	Elizabeth Jennerys			
[1797]				
Apr. 21	Hired Eliz Janry for the remaining part of the Year	**1**	**10**	**0**
[[*Oct. 10*	Cash	1	10	0]]
	Elizabeth Chasteney			
[1797]				
May 11	Hired Eliz Chaseney for the remaining part of the Year at	**1**	**5**	**0**
[[*Oct. 10*	Cash	1	5	0]]
	Elizabeth Williamson			
1797				
[[*Oct. 10*	Hired Eliz Williamson 3/- more if she please's [1]	**3**	**0**	**0**
[1798]				
Apr. 14	Cash	1	1	0]]
Oct. 10	Paid	1	19	0
	[settled]	3	0	0
	Maria Milligen			
1797				
[[*Oct. 10*	Hired Maria Milligan [2]	**3**	**10**	**0**
[1798]				
Apr. 5	Cash	1	11	6]]
Oct. 10	Paid	1	18	6
	[settled]	3	10	0

An account of the number of Barrels of Beer, brewed by the Common Brewers in Norwich, in one year, viz. from the 5th of July, 1796, to July 5, 1797.

	Strong.	Table.	Small.
John Patteson	16139¼	4698¾	852¼
S. and T. Tomson	12176½	——	1882
Peter Finch	8856¾	——	——
Daniel Ganning	8011¼	——	2764
Charles Weston	7696½	——	1773¾
William Latten	230	224½	134¼

Price and new Assize of Bread.—Some of the principal parts of this Bill respect the meal-fac-

Henry Raven's endnotes

Ledger: 1793–1797

[These notes and brewing tables were entered at the front and back of Henry Raven's manuscript diary and are all in his hand [1]]

[no date given]
A receipt [recipe] for destroying Rats
1 lb best wheat Flour
¼ D° [lb] best Lump Sugar
As much sweet wort as will make the above into a past«e» [2]
1½ Ounce of Mercury Subliments Sublimate [3]
21 Drops of Oil of Rodum [4]
Note: the Oil of Rodum is of no use in Sharpe Frost
3 D° [drops] Oil of Cloves
5 D° [drops] Oil of Swallows [5]
2 pennyworth of French figgs cut in to pieces

Boyl them [the figs] in ½ pint of wheat till the wheat breaks with a little coarse Sugar. The Above to be boild in a pint of water or sweet wort. Drain the water or wort from the wheat and also the Figgs—which bury in the Ground

[A recipe for destroying moles]
Take a piece of Oake or Birch bark when dry'd and Curnd [?curled] up 5 Inches long. Lay it over the Moles run. Take a parsnip Scraped like horse Reddish [horseradish], mix it with white arsnick [arsenic] coverd with the Above bark, upon eash [each] of these Biots or [?bights of] Bark.

5 Drops of Oil of Sasafax,[6] Winted [winter] Feed; Spring Feed with the same Bark
5 dew worms tyed together with worsted and staked down in the Runs,[7] sprinkle white arsnack [arsenic] over them with 5 Drops of the oil of Sarsafax—Take a peice of Holley Bark and prick in the Runs

The number of Barrels of Strong beer brewed by the Common Brewers of the City of Norwich betwe«e»n July 5th 1794 and July 5th 1795 *viz.* [8]

		Barrels
Messrs	S & T Thompson [Tompson]	12 851
	Pr [Peter] Finch	8 353
	Dan: Ganning [John Day's executor]	7 341
	J Patterson [John Patteson]	7 277
	C [Charles] Weston	7 188
	Wm Latten	206

[1] *Henry Raven's diary* Henry had reached the end of his ledger; he broke off without explanation. As the spine of his diary is labelled '1793 to 1797 Diary No. 1' a second ledger is likely to have been opened, and may have been taken by Henry to his new employer when his pupillage ended in 1800. It is not in the Cozens-Hardy Collection

[2] *wort* Brewing liquor after mashing and before fermentation. At this stage the beer-to-be is very sweet

[3] *mercury* Obtainable in various forms from the apothecary. The corrosive sublimate mercuric chloride is a crystalline, soluble pesticide and preservative and was used to treat a wide number of human ailments from ulcerated throats to syphilis

[4] *oil of rhodium* Made from rhodium wood, heavily scented, and used in the care of horses

[5] *oil of swallows* An ancient medicinal remedy: a paste made from herbs, cloves, wax, butter and an ox's foot all pounded together with swallows (the birds)

[6] *sassafras* Again part of the apothcary's armoury. The oil, extracted from the dried root of the N. American sassafras tree *Sassafras officinale*, contains camphor, pinene and safrole and was used to treat ailments ranging from rheumatism to syphilis

[7] *dew-worm* A large earthworm visible at night

[8] *common brewers* Stackhouse and Timothy Tompson's brewery lay in King Street; Peter Finch's in Coslany Street; John Patteson's at Pockthorpe in the parish of

St James, on the site of one of the breweries he had acquired; Charles Weston's by St George's Bridge; and William Latten's in St Clement's.

Similar tables appearing in the *Norwich Mercury* on 3 Aug. 1793, 21 July 1798 and 19 July 1800 showed that annual production varied markedly over the decade. By 1800 Patteson had jumped to 20,000 barrels; the Tompsons had fallen to 8800 barrels.

In 1793 John Day's brewery at St Martin-at-Oak had been in third place, producing 10,319 barrels—a little under that of Tompson and Finch. Patteson was about to enter the trade, three concerns he was soon to buy being listed: James Beevor (2636 barrels), Greaves & Co. (1388), and Jehosophat Postle (3512). The partnership between William Latten and Benjamin Suffield was dissolved in June 1797, Latten being declared a bankrupt in Dec. 1797 (*Norw. Merc.* 17 June, 16 Dec. 1797, 6 Jan. 1798). See also the figures on beer production in *World*, vol. 2, chaps 7 and 8

Table by Henry Raven [untitled] [1]

N° 1 – 50	4					
2 – 32	4					
3 – 15	5	R				
4 – 20	5	T				
5 – 40	5	R				
6 – 40	4½					
7 – 35	5½					
8 – 29	5½					
9 – 21	5½					
10 – 40	4					
11 – 35	4					
12 – 38	4½					
13 – 25	4½					
14 – 40	5					
15 – 35	5					
16 – 35	6					
17 – 40	5½	R				
18 – 32	6					
19 – 35	5	R				
20 – 26	6					
21 – 33	5	R				
22 – 39	5½	T				
23 – 28	6½	R		8½		
24 – 25	6	T		8¼		
25 – 30	5½	T		8		
26 – 39	5	T		6		
27 – 25	6½	T		6½		
28 – 40	5			5½		
29 – 24	6			8		
30 – 40	5½			8		
31 – 35	5½			6¼		
32 – 25	6½			6¼		
33 – 30	6			8		
34 – 30	5½			7¼		
35 – 30	6½			6¾		
36 – 20	7			6		
37 – 36	7		A s[t]	8		
38 – 10	15			7¼		
24	12			7¼		
A ran				7½		
				6¼		
				8¾		
				6¾	69½	
				12¼	3½	
				15½	73	
				22	203¼	
				2¾	276¼	10
						3 16
						£13 16

---

[1] *table* These figures, illustrated on the page opposite, are in Henry Raven's hand. They evidently relate to individual brews or gyles (col. 1), followed by the parti-gyles, and may denote the number of barrels drawn off into the large casks (50, 32 etc in col. 2). The totals in a far column possibly show 73 barrels in one cask and 203¼ in the other.

R and T probably denote Running and Tunning: beer for early despatch, such as a light ale; and long-maturing beer, such as porter and nog

The number of Barrels of Strong beer brewed by the Common Brewers of the City of Norwich between July 5th 1794 and July 5th 1795

		Barrels
Messrs. J & T Thompson	12	851
P. Finch	8	353
Dan. Gamming	7	341
J. Patterson	7	277
C. Weston	7	188
W. Latten	7	206

No 1	50	4	23	28	6½	8½
2	32	4	24	25	6	8¼
3	15	5½	25	30	5½	8
4	20	5	26	39	5½	6
5	40	5	27	25	6½	6½
6	20	4½	28	40	5	5½
7	35	5½	29	24	6	8
8	29	5½	30	40	5½	8
9	21	5½	31	35	5½	6½
10	40	4	32	25	6½	6¼
11	35	4	33	30	6	8
12	38	4½	34	30	5½	7¼
13	25	4½	35	30	6½	6¾
14	20	5	36	20	7	6½
15	35	5	37	Ab 26	7	8
16	35	6	38	10	15	7¼
17	40	5½ 69½		22	12	7½
18	32	6 3½		Aver		6¼
19	35	5½ 73				8¾
20	26	6 203¼				6¾
21	33	5½ 276¼				12¼
22	39	5½				15½
						22
						20½

10
3.16
£13.16

previous page Henry's table below that of the principal Norwich brewers is undated.

In his profitability analysis of Sept. 1797 William Hardy assumed a typical brew of 40 barrels and stated that he had brewed 2100 barrels in the year Sept. 1796–Sept. 1797; the previous year the figure was 2000 barrels (tabulated in *Mary Hardy and her World*, volume 2, chapter 11).

Henry's endnotes bring the total length of his diary ledger to 73,159 words, of which he had written 70,215 words and William Hardy jnr 2864 over the four years. Henry's brother Nathaniel Raven wrote 80 words: see the appendix in *Diary 4* tabulating the authorship statistics in Henry's diary and Mary Hardy's [*Cozens-Hardy Collection*]

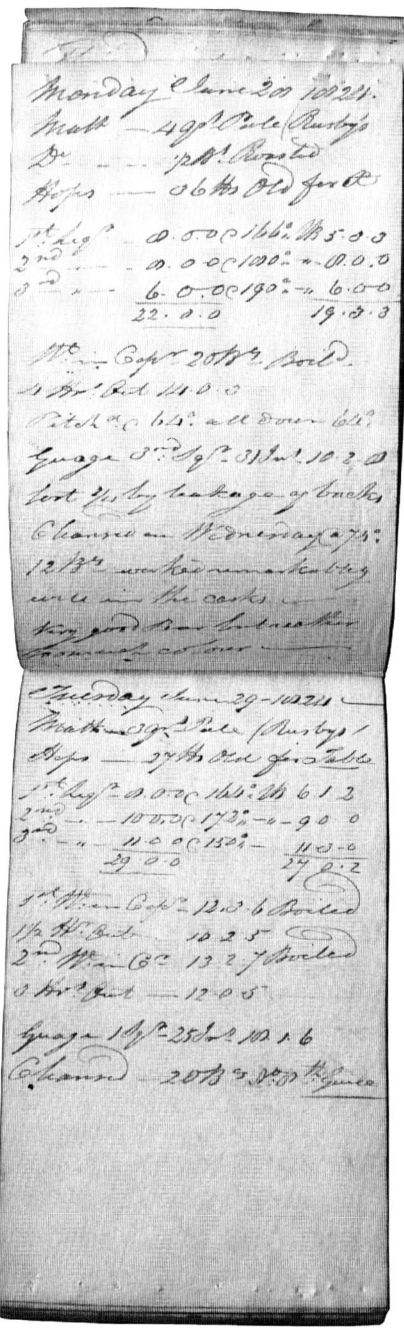

right Two pages, for 28–29 June 1824, from a small brewing book entitled on the cover, 'Hy Raven, Pelican Brewery, Wapping Wall' (beside the Thames, downstream of the City of London). It opens on 11 Feb. 1824. This is Henry Raven himself, head brewer in London first at Smith's, the Plough Brewery, Lambeth 1822–23, and then at Wapping.

He was ill. From Mar. 1824 he worked for 12 weeks as collector and clerk and not at his craft. By 22 Dec. 1824 his writing was very shaky, and he may well have died soon after that last entry.

The book probably came to Letheringsett after Henry's death, Mary Hardy's grandson then using it for his own notes. It was deposited in the Norfolk Record Office in 1976 by Basil Cozens-Hardy's executors [NRO: ACC Cozens-Hardy 11/2/1976]

Appendix D3.A · Figures D3.2–D3.6

Family trees of the diarists' extended family

note A family tree for the immediate family of the diarist Mary Hardy and her diarist nephew Henry Raven appears as fig. D3.1, opposite the register at the opening of this volume. The family trees in this appendix range more widely, but are not exhaustive

figure D3.2 Shopkeepers and farmers: the **Ravens** of Whissonsett, and **Foxes** of Horningtoft and Brisley

D3.3 Farmers: the **Smiths** of Stanfield

D3.4 Farmers and schoolteachers: the **Ravens** of Whissonsett Hall

D3.5 Grocers: the **Raven** and **Hawkins** families of Whissonsett and Norwich

D3.6 Farmers: the **Goggs** family of Whissonsett and Colkirk

above Whissonsett Church, the parish church of Mary Hardy until she was aged 32, and of Henry Raven in his childhood. This forms one of the colourful tapestry and cross-stitch hassocks designed and worked for the church by Margaret Rainbow and a small team of volunteers. The kneeler, which Mrs Rainbow completed in 2000, shows the churchyard yews near the Raven graves; the flag of St George flies on festival days [*MB · 2000*]

FIGURE D3.2

Shopkeepers and farmers: the Ravens of Whissonsett, and Foxes of Horningtoft and Brisley

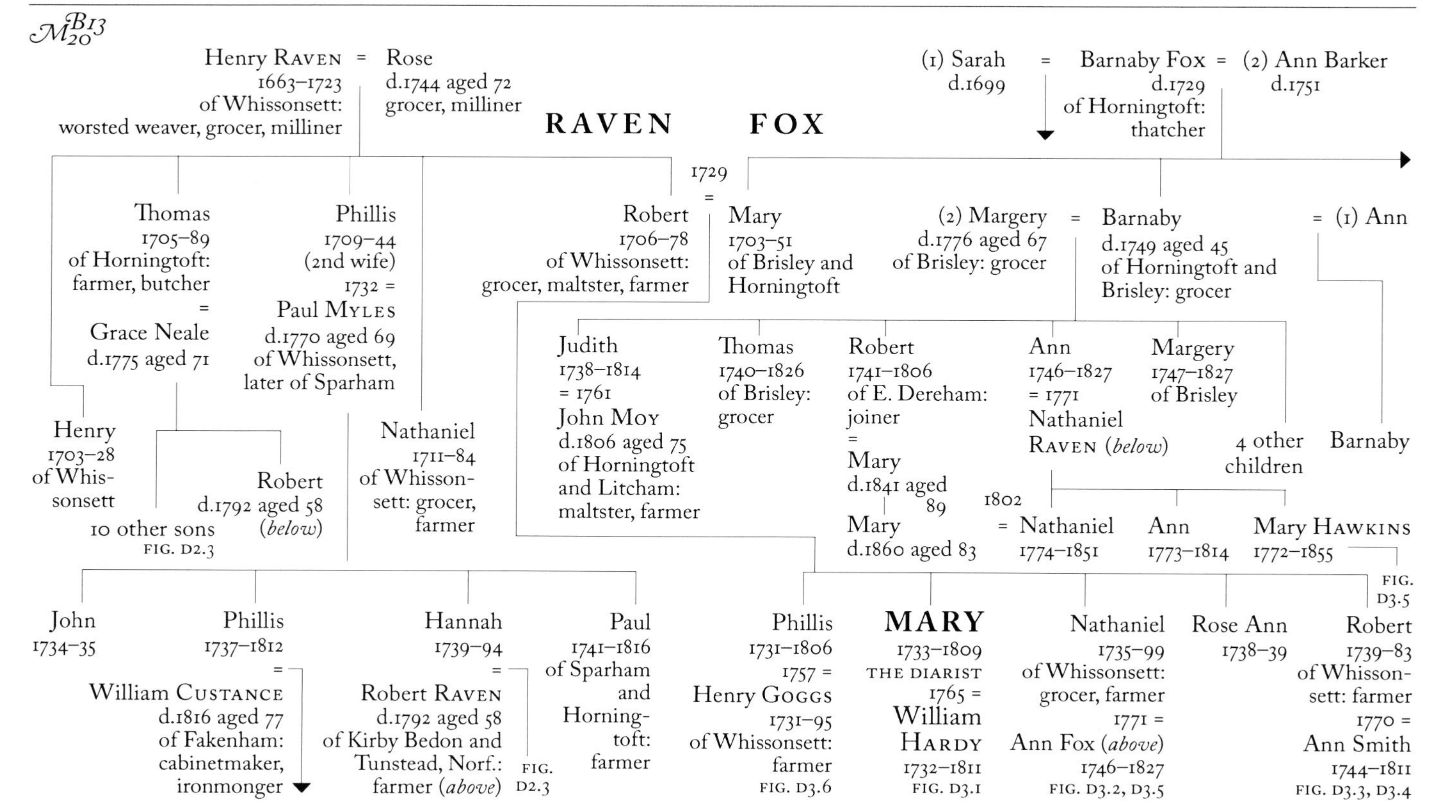

$\mathcal{M}^{B13}_{20}$
Henry Raven = Rose
1663–1723
of Whissonsett:
worsted weaver, grocer, milliner
d.1744 aged 72
grocer, milliner
RAVEN
FOX
(1) Sarah = Barnaby Fox = (2) Ann Barker
d.1699
d.1729
of Horningtoft:
thatcher
d.1751
Thomas
1705–89
of Horningtoft:
farmer, butcher
=
Grace Neale
d.1775 aged 71
Phillis
1709–44
(2nd wife)
1732 =
Paul Myles
d.1770 aged 69
of Whissonsett,
later of Sparham
Robert
1706–78
of Whissonsett:
grocer, maltster, farmer
1729
=
Mary
1703–51
of Brisley and
Horningtoft
(2) Margery = Barnaby
d.1776 aged 67
of Brisley: grocer
d.1749 aged 45
of Horningtoft and
Brisley: grocer
= (1) Ann
Henry
1703–28
of Whis-
sonsett
Robert
d.1792 aged 58
(below)
10 other sons
FIG. D2.3
Nathaniel
1711–84
of Whisson-
sett: grocer,
farmer
Judith
1738–1814
= 1761
John Moy
d.1806 aged 75
of Horningtoft
and Litcham:
maltster, farmer
Thomas
1740–1826
of Brisley:
grocer
Robert
1741–1806
of E. Dereham:
joiner
=
Mary
d.1841 aged
89
Mary
d.1860 aged 83
Ann
1746–1827
= 1771
Nathaniel
Raven (below)
Margery
1747–1827
of Brisley
4 other
children
Barnaby
1802
= Nathaniel
1774–1851
Ann
1773–1814
Mary Hawkins
1772–1855
FIG.
D3.5
John
1734–35
Phillis
1737–1812
=
William Custance
d.1816 aged 77
of Fakenham:
cabinetmaker,
ironmonger
Hannah
1739–94
=
Robert Raven
d.1792 aged 58
of Kirby Bedon and
Tunstead, Norf.:
farmer (above)
FIG.
D2.3
Paul
1741–1816
of Sparham
and
Horning-
toft:
farmer
Phillis
1731–1806
1757 =
Henry Goggs
1731–95
of Whissonsett:
farmer
FIG. D3.6
MARY
1733–1809
THE DIARIST
1765 =
William
Hardy
1732–1811
FIG. D3.1
Nathaniel
1735–99
of Whissonsett:
grocer, farmer
1771 =
Ann Fox (above)
1746–1827
FIG. D3.2, D3.5
Rose Ann
1738–39
Robert
1739–83
of Whisson-
sett: farmer
1770 =
Ann Smith
1744–1811
FIG. D3.3, D3.4

FIGURE D3.3

Farmers: the Smiths of Stanfield

The Smiths showed a deep attachment to Stanfield even when they had moved elsewhere. Baptisms, marriages and burials at Stanfield, and ages shown on Stanfield headstones, are shown in bold type

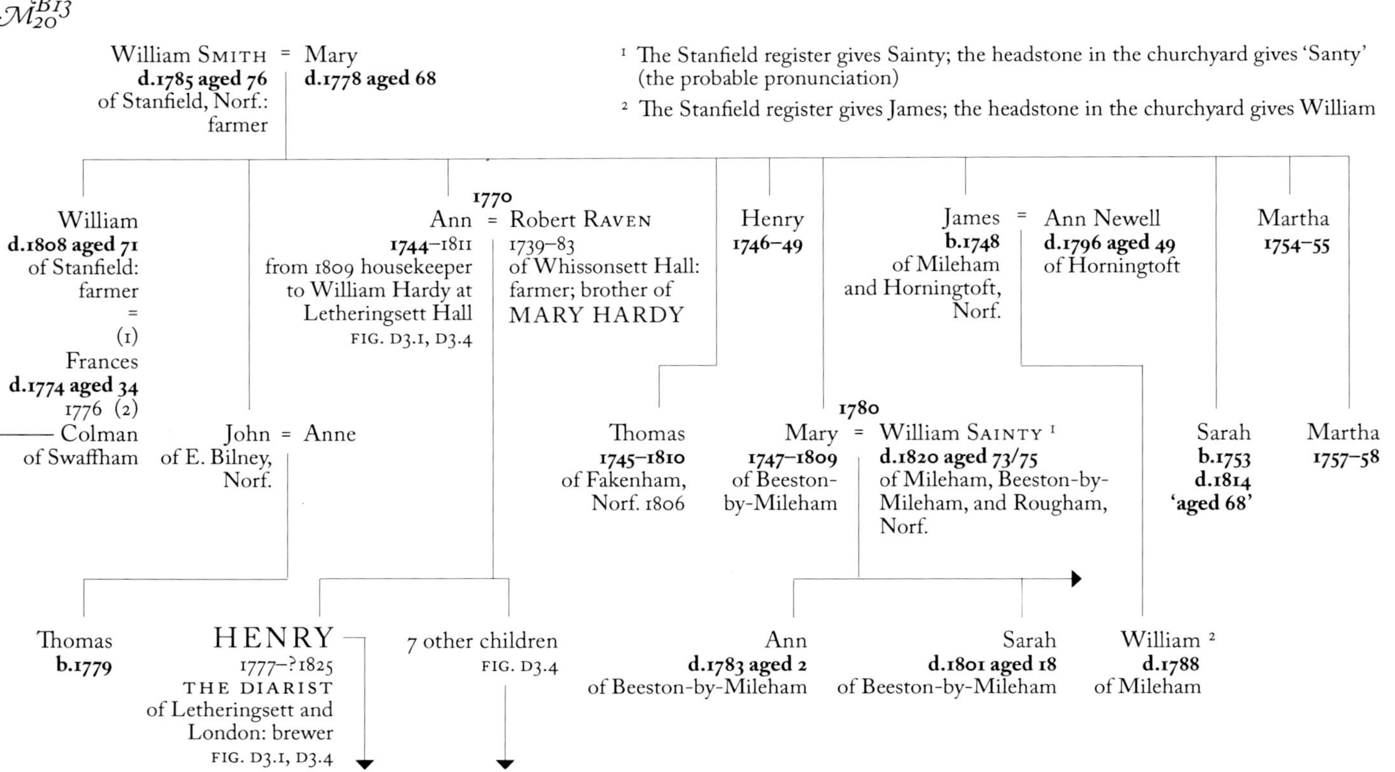

MB13 20
William SMITH = Mary
d.1785 aged 76
of Stanfield, Norf.: farmer
d.1778 aged 68
William
d.1808 aged 71
of Stanfield: farmer
= (1) Frances
d.1774 aged 34
1776 (2) Colman of Swaffham
John = Anne
of E. Bilney, Norf.
1770
Ann = Robert RAVEN
1744–1811
from 1809 housekeeper to William Hardy at Letheringsett Hall
FIG. D3.1, D3.4
1739–83
of Whissonsett Hall: farmer; brother of MARY HARDY
Henry
1746–49
James = Ann Newell
b.1748
of Mileham and Horningtoft, Norf.
d.1796 aged 49
of Horningtoft
Martha
1754–55
Thomas
1745–1810
of Fakenham, Norf. 1806
1780
Mary = William SAINTY 1
1747–1809
of Beeston-by-Mileham
d.1820 aged 73/75
of Mileham, Beeston-by-Mileham, and Rougham, Norf.
Sarah
b.1753
d.1814
'aged 68'
Martha
1757–58
Thomas
b.1779
HENRY
1777–?1825
THE DIARIST
of Letheringsett and London: brewer
FIG. D3.1, D3.4
7 other children
FIG. D3.4
Ann
d.1783 aged 2
of Beeston-by-Mileham
Sarah
d.1801 aged 18
of Beeston-by-Mileham
William 2
d.1788
of Mileham
1 The Stanfield register gives Sainty; the headstone in the churchyard gives 'Santy' (the probable pronunciation)
2 The Stanfield register gives James; the headstone in the churchyard gives William

FIGURE D3.4

Farmers and schoolteachers: the Ravens of Whissonsett Hall

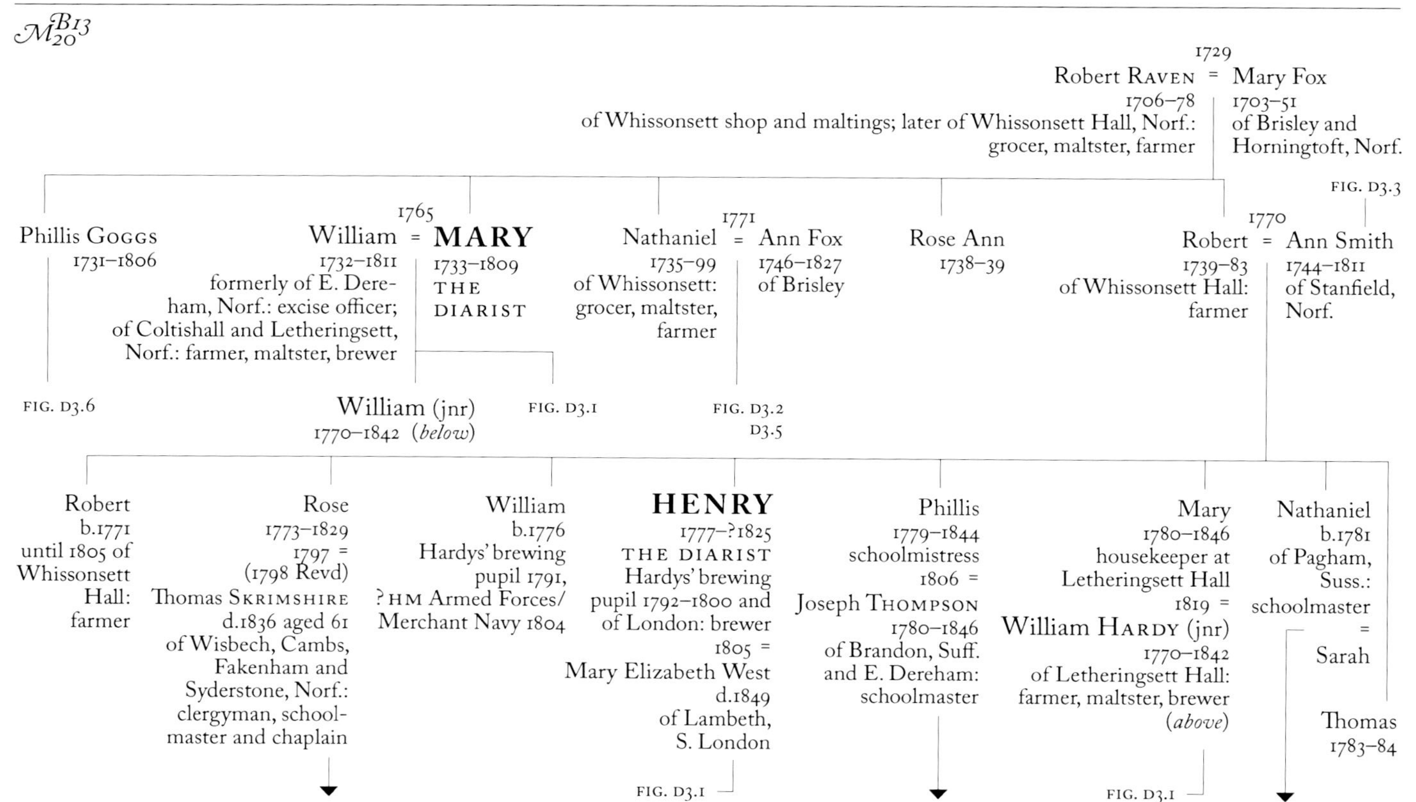

M B13 20
1729
Robert RAVEN = Mary Fox
1706–78
of Whissonsett shop and maltings; later of Whissonsett Hall, Norf.:
grocer, maltster, farmer
1703–51
of Brisley and
Horningtoft, Norf.
FIG. D3.3
Phillis GOGGS
1731–1806
FIG. D3.6
1765
William = MARY
1732–1811
formerly of E. Dereham, Norf.: excise officer;
of Coltishall and Letheringsett,
Norf.: farmer, maltster, brewer
1733–1809
THE DIARIST
FIG. D3.1
William (jnr)
1770–1842 (below)
1771
Nathaniel = Ann Fox
1735–99
of Whissonsett:
grocer, maltster,
farmer
1746–1827
of Brisley
FIG. D3.2
D3.5
Rose Ann
1738–39
1770
Robert = Ann Smith
1739–83
of Whissonsett Hall:
farmer
1744–1811
of Stanfield,
Norf.
Robert
b.1771
until 1805 of
Whissonsett
Hall:
farmer
Rose
1773–1829
1797 =
(1798 Revd)
Thomas SKRIMSHIRE
d.1836 aged 61
of Wisbech, Cambs,
Fakenham and
Syderstone, Norf.:
clergyman, schoolmaster and chaplain
William
b.1776
Hardys' brewing
pupil 1791,
?HM Armed Forces/
Merchant Navy 1804
HENRY
1777–?1825
THE DIARIST
Hardys' brewing
pupil 1792–1800 and
of London: brewer
1805 =
Mary Elizabeth West
d.1849
of Lambeth,
S. London
FIG. D3.1
Phillis
1779–1844
schoolmistress
1806 =
Joseph THOMPSON
1780–1846
of Brandon, Suff.
and E. Dereham:
schoolmaster
Mary
1780–1846
housekeeper at
Letheringsett Hall
1819 =
William HARDY (jnr)
1770–1842
of Letheringsett Hall:
farmer, maltster, brewer
(above)
FIG. D3.1
Nathaniel
b.1781
of Pagham,
Suss.:
schoolmaster
=
Sarah
Thomas
1783–84

FIGURE D3.5

Grocers: the Raven and Hawkins families of Whissonsett and Norwich

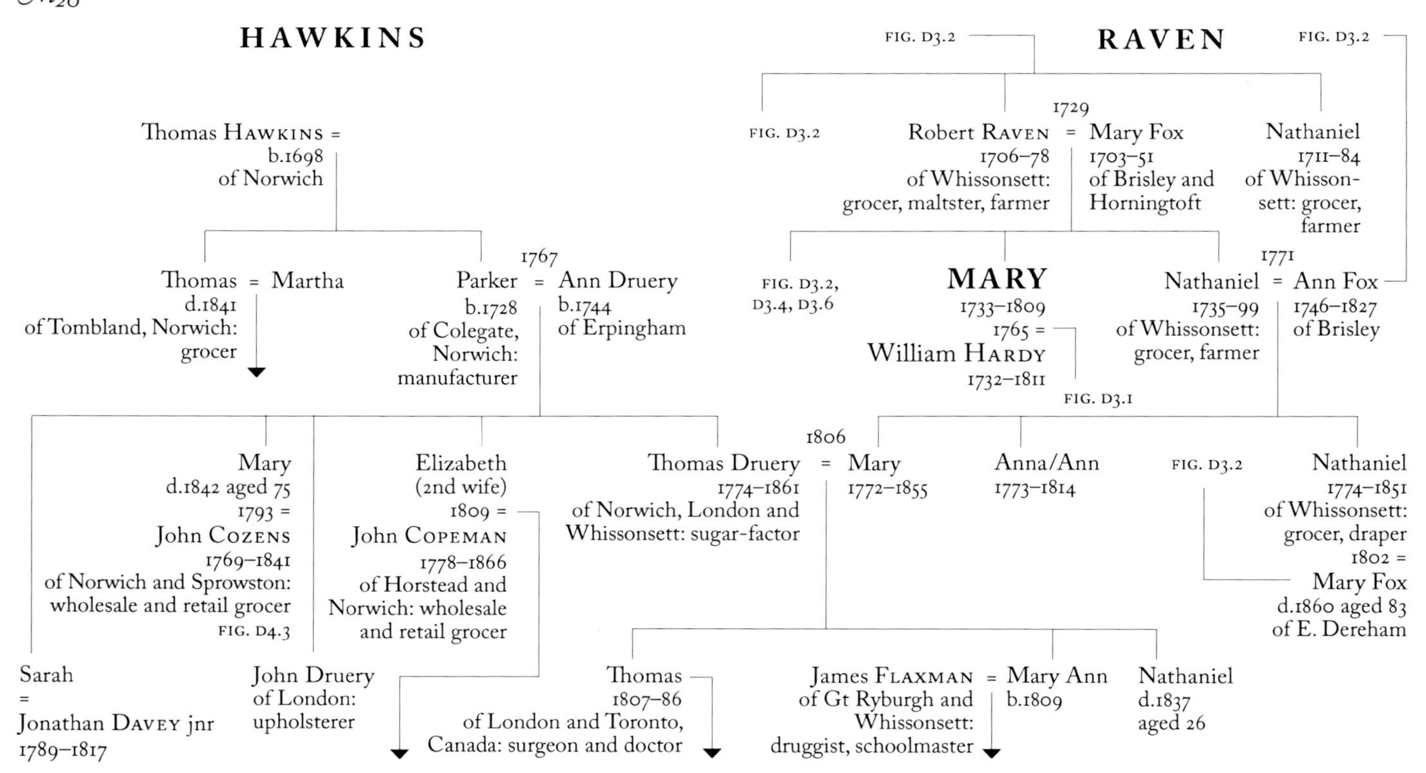

$\mathcal{M}^{B13}_{20}$
HAWKINS
RAVEN
FIG. D3.2
FIG. D3.2
Thomas HAWKINS = b.1698 of Norwich
FIG. D3.2
1729
Robert RAVEN 1706–78 of Whissonsett: grocer, maltster, farmer = Mary Fox 1703–51 of Brisley and Horningtoft
Nathaniel 1711–84 of Whissonsett: grocer, farmer
1767
Thomas d.1841 of Tombland, Norwich: grocer = Martha
Parker b.1728 of Colegate, Norwich: manufacturer = Ann Druery b.1744 of Erpingham
FIG. D3.2, D3.4, D3.6
MARY 1733–1809 1765 = William HARDY 1732–1811
FIG. D3.1
1771
Nathaniel 1735–99 of Whissonsett: grocer, farmer = Ann Fox 1746–1827 of Brisley
Mary d.1842 aged 75 1793 = John COZENS 1769–1841 of Norwich and Sprowston: wholesale and retail grocer
FIG. D4.3
Elizabeth (2nd wife) 1809 = John COPEMAN 1778–1866 of Horstead and Norwich: wholesale and retail grocer
1806
Thomas Druery 1774–1861 of Norwich, London and Whissonsett: sugar-factor = Mary 1772–1855
Anna/Ann 1773–1814
FIG. D3.2
Nathaniel 1774–1851 of Whissonsett: grocer, draper 1802 = Mary Fox d.1860 aged 83 of E. Dereham
Sarah = Jonathan DAVEY jnr 1789–1817
John Druery of London: upholsterer
Thomas 1807–86 of London and Toronto, Canada: surgeon and doctor
James FLAXMAN of Gt Ryburgh and Whissonsett: druggist, schoolmaster = Mary Ann b.1809
Nathaniel d.1837 aged 26

FIGURE D3.6

Farmers: the Goggs family of Whissonsett and Colkirk

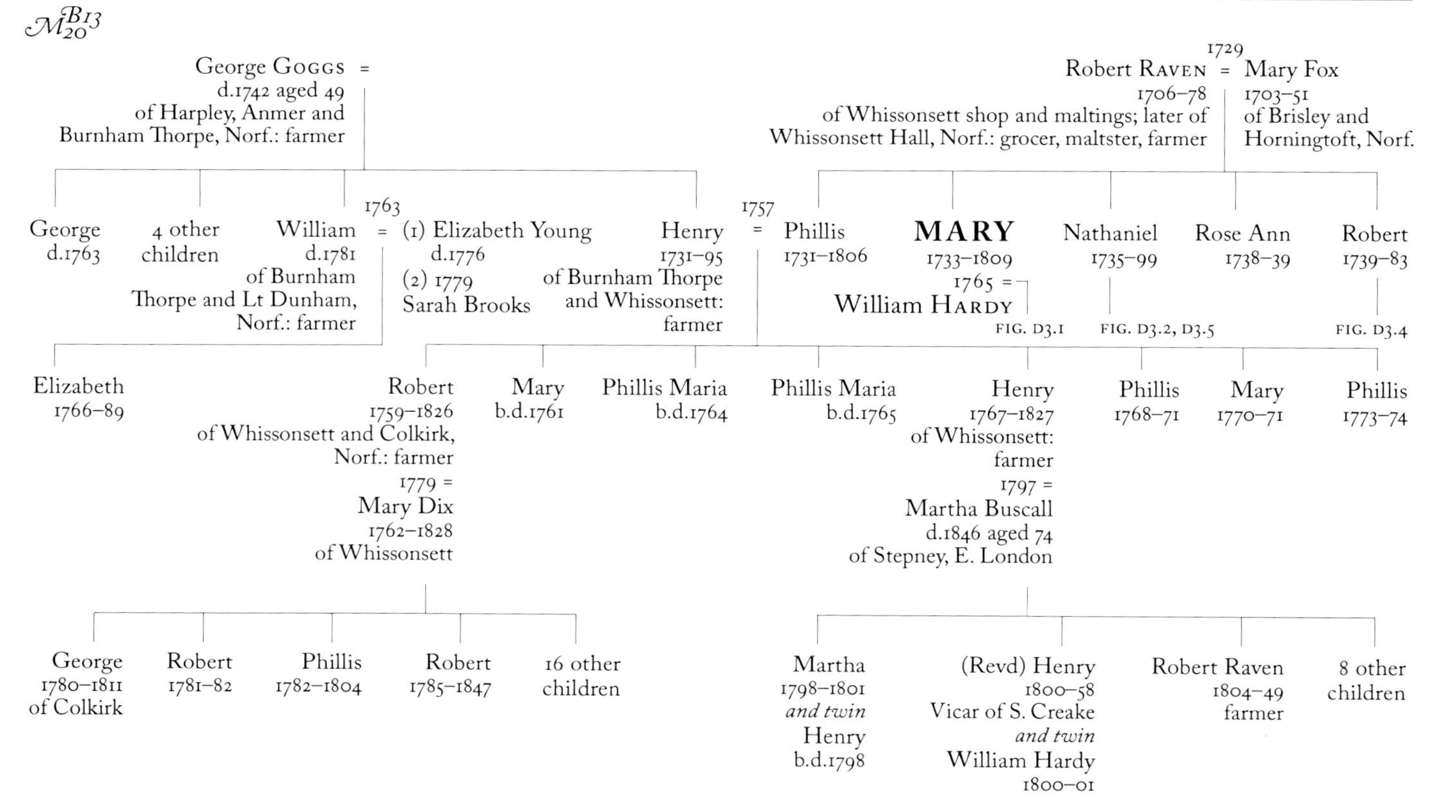

M B13 20
George GOGGS =
d.1742 aged 49
of Harpley, Anmer and
Burnham Thorpe, Norf.: farmer
1729
Robert RAVEN = Mary Fox
1706–78
of Whissonsett shop and maltings; later of
Whissonsett Hall, Norf.: grocer, maltster, farmer
1703–51
of Brisley and
Horningtoft, Norf.
George
d.1763
4 other
children
William
d.1781
of Burnham
Thorpe and Lt Dunham,
Norf.: farmer
1763
= (1) Elizabeth Young
d.1776
(2) 1779
Sarah Brooks
Henry
1731–95
of Burnham Thorpe
and Whissonsett:
farmer
1757
= Phillis
1731–1806
MARY
1733–1809
1765 =
William HARDY
FIG. D3.1
Nathaniel
1735–99
FIG. D3.2, D3.5
Rose Ann
1738–39
Robert
1739–83
FIG. D3.4
Elizabeth
1766–89
Robert
1759–1826
of Whissonsett and Colkirk,
Norf.: farmer
1779 =
Mary Dix
1762–1828
of Whissonsett
Mary
b.d.1761
Phillis Maria
b.d.1764
Phillis Maria
b.d.1765
Henry
1767–1827
of Whissonsett:
farmer
1797 =
Martha Buscall
d.1846 aged 74
of Stepney, E. London
Phillis
1768–71
Mary
1770–71
Phillis
1773–74
George
1780–1811
of Colkirk
Robert
1781–82
Phillis
1782–1804
Robert
1785–1847
16 other
children
Martha
1798–1801
and twin
Henry
b.d.1798
(Revd) Henry
1800–58
Vicar of S. Creake
and twin
William Hardy
1800–01
Robert Raven
1804–49
farmer
8 other
children

Appendix D3.B

A clerical brewer's method 1796

notes These instructions illustrate the craft of brewing practised by a careful and methodical private brewer who lived close to the Hardys' home at Coltishall. They are in the hand of the Revd John Longe jnr, Curate of Henley, near Ipswich, Suffolk,[1] taking dictation from his father the Revd John Longe, resident Rector of Spixworth, near Norwich.[2]

The manuscript is held in the Bacon Longe Collection at the Suffolk Record Office, Ipswich. It is dated 9 July 1796, when the younger man was shortly to leave his curacy to take the living of Coddenham, Suffolk.[3]

John Longe snr appears briefly in the pages of Mary Hardy's diary as the employer of the Hardys' former farm boy William Girling in October 1803 (*Diary 4*). In those few days the clergyman could have drawn on Girling's expertise, gained at the commercial Letheringsett brewery, to guide him through his own brewing processes. The scale and sophistication of a common brewery make a striking contrast with parsonage brewing. A thermometer was in use at Letheringsett, and Henry Raven and his fellow brewers were spared the rector's exertions with his hand-pumping and pails and the re-use of the mash tun as a fermenting vessel.

The spelling and punctuation have been modernised

above Spixworth Rectory, of _c._1780. Here the Revd John Longe instructed his clerical son in the art of brewing. Here too the Hardys' boy William Girling was hired in 1803, only to be called up for the Militia. He hastened back to William Hardy jnr and served as his brewery clerk until dying in 1824 [*MB · 2000*]

[1] *Longe* Revd John (b. 15 Apr. 1765, d. 3 Mar. 1834), elder son of Revd John Longe; educ. Norwich School, admitted Corpus Christi College, Cambridge 1782, migrated to Trinity 1784, scholar 1786, BA 1787, MA 1790, ordained deacon 1787, priest 1789; Curate of Spixworth 1787, later Curate of Henley, Suff., Vicar of Coddenham, Suff. 1797–1834; marr. (1) Charlotte (d.1812), daughter of John Browne of Ipswich, (2) Frances, daughter of Colonel Ward, of Salhouse, Norf. (*Alum. Cantab.*)

[2] *Longe* Revd John (b. Spixworth 1731, d. there 18 Sept. 1806), son of Francis; educ. Eton, admitted Magdalene College, Cambridge 1748, BA 1752, MA 1756, ordained deacon 1754; Rector of Hackford 1755, Rector of Reymerstone 1761, Rector of Spixworth 1756–1806; marr. Dorothy (d.1819 aged 81), daughter of Peter Elwin of Booton and Thurning (*Alum. Cantab.*; mural tablet, south wall of chancel, Spixworth Church)

[3] *source* Suffolk Record Office (Ipswich): Bacon Longe Collection, HA 24/50/19/4.7 (13). In his diary 1796–98, also preserved (HA 24/50/19/4.3 (1), (2)), Revd John Longe jnr notes the dates of the various brews at Coddenham Vicarage.

I am grateful to Derek Manning of Catton and to Joseph Mason of Taverham in his history of Spixworth for drawing my attention to the Coddenham archive (J. Mason, *Spixworth: History and landscape in a Norfolk village* (Norwich, 1998), pp. 17–21)

REVD JOHN LONGE JUNIOR, CURATE OF HENLEY, SUFFOLK: MY FATHER'S DIRECTIONS FOR BREWING

Quantity

5 bushels of malt and 3 lb of hops; fill the copper quite full. When the copper boils take out the fire.

Wet the malt with 8 pailfuls of water—three and a half hot from the copper, and four and a half cold from the gyle tub which stands filled with water ready to supply the copper when emptied.

Add the whole of the hot water from the copper. So set the mash, stirring it well and covering the tub with sacks. Mark the time when the mash is set, and let it stand four hours.

Fill the copper again quite full as before; and when the water is hot steep the hops in the underdeck with a sufficiency of hot water to wet them thoroughly.[1] So leave them till you draw off the first wort.

When the second copper boils cover the fire so as to keep the water hot but not boiling, at least not boiling over.[2] NB Whilst the copper is boiling for the second mash add one pailful of cold water to make amends for what was taken out to steep the hops.

When the first mash has stood four hours begin to draw off, returning the wort gently on the top of the mash till the liquor runs pretty clear; then throw it upon the hops in the gyle tub. Go on drawing off till the wort begins to run slow, but do not drain the mash too close.

Then take the fire quite down and throw the whole copper full of hot water upon the mash tub as before, stirring it well and covering it again.

Then put the first wort with the hops into the copper and make up the fire; watch its beginning to boil, and let it boil briskly for half an hour. Then take down the fire. Run the first wort from the copper through the sieve into the cooler.[3]

Then put the hops into the copper again and draw off the second wort, putting it into the copper to the hops. Raise the fire, watch when it begins to boil, and let it boil half an hour as before. Then take down the fire entirely.

Then carry out the drains, clean the mash tub, and put the second wort from the copper into it, running it through the sieve.

As soon as you have opportunity, set out two or three pailfuls of the first wort abroad in the keelers to cool faster, in order to begin the working with.[4] By this means secure a beginning fermentation, and let the liquor in the cooler be near cold before you add it to the working wort.

When you have taken the first wort from the cooler draw out the second wort from the mash tub and when cool enough return it to the mash tub and set it to work.

NB For the sake of coolness in the summer and warmth in the winter my gyle tub is removed down into the beer cellar and the first wort worked there. The second wort remains all night in the

[1] *underdeck* Underback: the vessel under the mash tun. The brewing process is explained in *World*, vol. 2, chap. 7

[2] *boiling over* This was an open-topped copper

[3] *sieve* To extract the remains of the hops. A commercial brewery like Letheringsett's would have a separate vessel, the hop back; private brewers used simpler equipment

[4] *keelers* Coolers: wide, shallow vessels in which the wort cools after passing from the copper. They were also used in the dairy for cooling milk, the Hardys having six keelers in their dairy and another milk keeler in their bakehouse (*Diary 2*, app. D2.C).

At Spixworth the keelers acted as temporary fermenting tuns, some of the wort being put in them early to 'work'.

Mr Longe does not state that he recycled his yeast, as was customary. He seems to imply here that he allowed wild yeast to begin the fermentation—a far more risky procedure. Almost certainly he would have pitched his own yeast into the vessels and have thus controlled the process

mash tub, and the next day is carried down by pails and mixed with the first wort. Sometimes I fill a 12-gallon cask from the first wort, before mixing, for ale;[1] and then mix for table beer. The effect is scarcely perceptible in the goodness of the main quantity.

With the whole quantity I usually fill one half-barrel, two 12-gallon casks, and five 9-gallon casks—in all 87 gallons.[2]

Memorandum Take off all the froth and yeast before you tun. Fill up that evening, again the next, and once more the third day, when we commonly set the casks right up, as they are to remain. When the head ceases to rise paper the bung holes; and as soon as the paper is no longer forced up by the fermentation bung the casks and stop the vent holes very carefully. The beer will commonly be quite fine in a fortnight.[3]

J.L., SPIXWORTH, JULY 9TH 1796

above **A coopered pail on a stone-flagged floor. This is the private brewhouse at the National Trust's Charlecote Park, Warwickshire. The containers shown here have iron hoops for strength. The Hardys relied on thin lath as well as on iron to hoop their barrels, as revealed by the diaries and inventories** [*MB* · *2000*]

[1] *ale* The rector's term for his lightly-hopped strong beer

[2] *barrel* Very useful evidence that the Norfolk barrel in 1796 contained 36 gallons, not 32 or 34. The rector's 87-gallon calculation is reached by adding *18*, 24 and 45 gallons

[3] *a fortnight* The home brewer drank his beer young; it was not left, like nog and porter, to mature in great casks. Like James Woodforde, Mr Longe used far fewer hops than did the commercial brewers for their ale, thus saving on cost but losing on keeping quality. We know the quantities used in some of William Hardy jnr's recipes of *c.*1830 for his nephew William Hardy Cozens (transcribed in *World*, vol. 2, chap. 7). The comparisons, expressed in bushels and pounds, also show the difference in the size of the copper used in clerical and commercial brewing:

Woodforde's brew (*17 Dec. 1776*)
4 bushels malt, 1½ lb hops

Longe's brew (*1796*)
5 bushels malt, 3 lb hops

Hardy's ale (*c.1830*)
20 bushels malt, 40 lb hops

Hardy's mild beer (*c.1830*)
64 bushels malt, 60 lb hops

Although John Longe jnr as a private brewer was not answerable to the Excise, he did not believe in adulterating his brews with spicy, fruity or metallic additives. He was vituperative about Samuel Child's guide to private brewing which advocated adulteration in 'vile recipes' using 'noxious ingredients' (Suffolk Record Office (Ipswich): Bacon Longe Collection, HA 24/50/19/4.6 (4))

above Letheringsett Hall in William Hardy jnr's time. The earliest surviving image of any of Mary Hardy's homes, it shows the south front and Greek Doric portico viewed from the Brewhouse Pightle.

The dining room is to the left, behind the columns shielding some of the large family portraits from the sun. The parlour or drawing room is to the right, on the site of the keeping parlour or sitting room of Mary Hardy's time.

This undated sketch, signed S.A. Goggs, is by Sarah Ann Goggs (1812–81). She was the daughter of Mary Hardy's nephew, the Whissonsett farmer Henry Goggs (1767–1827). Sarah Ann married in 1839, so the use of her maiden name suggests that it dates from the period *c.*1828–39.

It shows how the road diversion of 1808 enabled William to soften his property with foliage, while not putting a barrier between the Hall and his view of the brewery across the road (out of sight to the right). The open-work fencing, here resembling a timber trellis, is William Hase's iron palisado of 1808. The trees planted by William Hardy jnr on the hills above the Glaven valley are clearly visible from the Pightle slope.

Remodelled on its south side in 1809, this is not the more modest house Henry Raven had known in his years at Letheringsett 1792–1800. In his day the busy Cromer to King's Lynn road passed right by the windows of the south front—so close that passing carters and coachmen could tap on the glass with their whips.

During visits following his marriage and his move to London as a brewer Henry would have seen the changes his cousin was making. This was the home of Henry's sister Mary after her marriage to William in 1819, and before then from 1811 when she was acting as housekeeper at the Hall
[*Cozens-Hardy Collection*]

Appendix D3.C

A chronology of the Hardys' lives 1793–1797

The diarist's family	*The family business*	*Background events*
BREWING AT LETHERINGSETT 1781–1797		
1793 Mary Hardy's life-threatening illness lasts two months from 16 Aug.; she resumes diary 17 Oct.	**1793** With William's help HENRY RAVEN BEGINS FARM AND BREWERY DIARY on 10 Oct.	**1793** Execution of Louis XVI; war with France begins; Jacobins seize power in France
1794 Both diarists lead quiet lives socially at Letheringsett Hall, then called Rawlings; William Hardy supports peers and MPS pressing for peace with France	**1794** Henry Raven with his mother Ann signs articles as William Hardy's brewery apprentice 19 July; he will live with his aunt's family another six years	**1794** Increased taxes and duties to fund war; suspension of Habeas Corpus; treason trials
1795 Mary Hardy starts regular attendance at Methodist meetings; Mary Ann gives up dancing; farm in poor state at Whissonsett Hall, Henry Raven's childhood home	**1795** Hardys secure Weybourne Camp beer contract with Regular Army; new pump and hop back installed in brewery; wheat harvest fails	**1795** Ordnance Survey begin map-making; Seditious Meetings Act; bread riots
1796 Domestic counting house rebuilt; Mary Ann has suite of rooms converted for her use; she starts to join her mother at Methodist meetings; Letheringsett House of Industry opens after parish townhouses rebuilt	**1796** Chapman Ives's steam brewery at Coltishall with maltings and tied houses for sale; William Hardy pays off £1000-mortgage on his own brewery; he buys 12-acre farm at Holt Heath when enclosure first proposed	**1796** General election; Jenner develops smallpox vaccine; Supplementary Militia and Provisional Cavalry established to engage more civilians in anti-invasion measures; Catherine the Great of Russia dies
1797 Piano installed in the Hardys' keeping parlour; William Hardy's itemised inventory values house and garden at £600 and furniture at £526	**1797** Henry Raven brews unsupervised 19 Jan.; William Hardy semi-retires in Sept.; he values total property at £16,274 including outlets; he hands control and ownership to William with annual strong-beer production at 2100 barrels for 42 public houses including 25 tied outlets; HENRY RAVEN'S DIARY ENDS on 25 Oct.	**1797** Year of Peril; banks stop conversion of banknotes into cash; naval mutinies; naval battles of Cape St Vincent and Camperdown; first large-scale county map of Norfolk published by William Faden of London

Glossary

Technical terms, area, weights and measures

This glossary is common to all the four Diary volumes. It relies in part on the published works cited below, and in part on inferences drawn from the diarists' texts as to the Hardys' practice.

Terms and measures varied according to region and even within a county, the imperial standard not being made compulsory until 1826. In some parts of England the statute acre was used; in others the customary acre. Beer barrelage varied, also coal measure. Most produce was measured by volume and not by weight. There were thus wide variations according to the crop and its moisture content. A bushel of barley might weigh from 49 lb to 56 lb; a bushel of wheat from 56 lb to 62 lb.

These terms may have other definitions not given here, the glossary being tailored to the diarists' usage. United States measures, while bearing the same names, often differ markedly from the British, and conversion tables need to be used.

The apprentice or brewing pupil Henry Raven, as a practitioner, uses the farming and manufacturing terms more frequently than his aunt.

Words in italics have their own listed entry.

sources *These sometimes conflict, but guidance has been sought from* C. McCoy, *McCoy's Dictionary of Customs & Excise* (H.H. Greaves, London, 1938); P. Mathias, *The Brewing Industry in England 1700–1830* (Cambridge Univ. Press, 1959); G.E. Mingay, ed., *The Agrarian History of England and Wales: Volume VI 1750–1850* (Cambridge Univ. Press, 1989), pp. 1117–55 (the statistical appendix); and public notices in the *Norwich Mercury*

acre 4840 square *yards* (0·405 hectares): 6 acres = 2·43 hectares, 640 acres = one square mile. Norfolk used the statute acre (4 *roods* to the acre), not the customary acre (3 roods). There were 40 *perches* to the rood, land measure being quoted as '*a r p*'

ale Technically, *unhopped* malted liquor; however by the Hardys' time it was used indiscriminately to mean also hopped liquor (ie *beer*), as a strong brew, made with pale or amber *malt*

alehouse Another name for a public house: on-licensed premises for the sale of *beer* and often for wine and spirits as well, for which additional licences were required. Technically only a tavern had these additional licences, but this distinction had largely faded

assignee A person to whom property is legally transferred so that it can be used for the benefit of the creditors. It differs from a receiver, where the management, but not the ownership, of the debtor's property is vested in a person appointed by a court

back Any coopered vessel used in brewing

bag A sack of *hops*: 2½ *cwt* (127 kg), measuring 7½ *feet* long and 8 feet in circumference (2·3 and 2·4 metres), the canvas weighing 4 *lb*; together with the *pocket* the standard size for selling hops

baiting, bating Pausing (as in bated breath), eg when breaking a journey for refreshment; also (as baiting) setting dogs against other animals for sport, usually in a confined space such as an inn yard

barrel A coopered vessel in which beer is transported. Also a liquid measure:

ale: in theory, from 1531 to 1803, 34 *gallons* in country districts (154·6 litres), 32 gallons in London (145·5 litres); after 1803, 36 gallons nationally (163·7 litres), the figure it remains today;

beer: in theory, from 1531 to 1803, 34 gallons in country districts (154·6 litres), 36 gallons in London (163·7 litres); after 1803, 36 gallons nationally, the figure it remains today.

However many sources show that in 18th-century Norfolk, and earlier, both ale and beer barrels contained 36 gallons (eg *Norw. Merc.* 2 Apr. 1785, 24 Mar. 1787; see also *Diary 3*, app. D3.B, note; *World*, vol. 2, chap. 7)

basin An open reservoir, set high, in which brewing *liquor* can soften (ameliorate) for brews such as *porter* requiring soft water

beer A generic term for such brews as bitter, *fourpenny*, *mild*, *nog*, *porter*, *sixpenny* and *small beer*, all of which were produced commercially using only *liquor*, *malt*, *hops*, yeast and finings. Sugar was not permitted in brewing until 1847

bottle Wine: 5 bottles = one *gallon* after 1803

bran The fourth grade of flour; coarse flour

British spirits Distilled in the British Isles, eg whisky, and not imported, eg brandy; thus subject to excise and not customs duty

bundle See *load*

bushel Until the imperial bushel became the standard in 1824 the Winchester bushel of 1695 was widely used in England and Wales, the measure (the shovel) being round, with an even bottom, 18½ inches wide throughout and 8 inches deep (47 cm and 20·3 cm)
apples: 4 heaped *pecks* or 33 dry quarts
barley: cubic capacity, one bushel = 1¼ cubic *feet* (0·042 cubic metres), with a weight variation range of 49 to 56 *lb* (22·2–25·4 kg)
malt: approx. 42 lb (19·1 kg), malt weighing less than the same volume of barley as its moisture is lost in processing
oats: approx. 38 lb (17·2 kg)
wheat and *meal*: variation range 56 lb to 62 lb (25·4–28·1 kg)

cask A very large closed vessel for storing *beer* undergoing secondary fermentation while it matures. William Hardy's largest cask in 1788 could hold 208 *barrels* (7488 *gallons*, or 59,904 *pints*), but city brewers such as those in Norwich could have much larger casks

chaldron The usual measure for coal; also for the tonnage ('burthen') of 18th-century vessels including those on inland waterways:
nationally: one chaldron = 36 heaped bushels or 12 sacks
north Norfolk: the port of Blakeney and Cley in the Hardys' time used the London measure of 26½ *cwt* (1346·2 kg, or 1·35 metric tonnes) to the chaldron (*Diary 3*: 1 Aug. 1777), not the Newcastle measure of 53 cwt (2692·4 kg, or 2·69 metric tonnes)
Yarmouth, mid-18th century: one chaldron = 20 sacks, each *sack* weighing 137 *lb*; a Broadland chaldron was thus 24½ *cwt* (1242·8 kg). As the Hardys' *wherry William and Mary* was of 12 chaldrons' burthen the vessel can be estimated at either 16 *tons* or 14½ tons, depending on the method of calculating tonnage (R. Clark, *Black-Sailed Traders* (David & Charles, Newton Abbot, 1961), p. 100)

chamber A bedroom, or storage room

cinders Coke; pit coal specially fired in cinder ovens to render it smokeless for roasting barley by slow, even heat and without tainting; (charcoal, with similar properties, is made from wood). Culm, or anthracite, can also be used in *malt*-kilns. Coal can be used for heating the brewing copper, but not in malting as it gives a sulphurous taste to the malt

cistern A very large open-topped tank within the malthouse in which barley is soaked (steeped) at the start of malting: see *steep*

cleansing Removing the yeast head and running the *beer* from the fermentation vessel into *casks*, thus ending primary fermentation

coal meter Coal measurer: a person appointed to measure and weigh coal, *culm* and *cinders* and certify them. If for purposes of levying customs duty the appointment (established 1695) was made by the Commissioners of Customs; it was also a post in an incorporated borough such as Gt Yarmouth. See also *chaldron* and *sack*

colt A young male horse not put to full work

comb, coomb 4 *bushels* or half a *quarter*, and the customary grain measure used by the Hardys: one coomb of barley = approx. 2 *cwt* or 16 *stone* (101·6 kg); one coomb of wheat = approx. 18 stone (114·3 kg)

combs, culms Unwanted shoots from *malted* barley, removed by *screening*; estimated to represent 4% of the weight of the barley on which malt duty had been paid; for culm, see *cinders*

common brewer A licensed wholesale commercial brewer supplying retail outlets (public houses) and who could, with the appropriate licence, also sell retail direct; the later term 'brewer for sale' included the functions of the common brewer

cooler A wide, shallow vessel into which the *wort* passes after boiling in the *copper* and before being run into the fermenting tun; see also *hop back*

copper A closed vessel for boiling the *liquor*, the *grist malt* after *mashing*, and the *hops*, these forming the brew to which yeast is added; in private brewhouses the copper was often an open vessel. When installing the copper the bricklayer had to take care to 'hang' or offset it correctly

couch A separate area within a wooden frame on the malthouse floor near the *steep* where the wetted barley was spread after steeping and was allowed to germinate; here the excise officer gauged the piece of *malt*

counting house Literally accompting house, the room where the books, ledgers and petty cash were stored and business with clients transacted. Both the dwelling house and the brewery complex had counting houses
crone An old ewe
culm, culms See *cinders*; *combs*
cwt See *hundredweight*

drawer A publican (innkeeper or alehouse-keeper), a term particularly applied to those supplied by or tied to a *common brewer*. *Beer* was not pumped up to the parlour but 'drawn' out of the *barrel*
drawing house A public house supplied by a *common brewer* (not therefore one where the innkeeper did his own brewing as a publican brewer), where the house was tied in some way to the brewery: either by direct ownership freehold, copyhold or leasehold and then being let or sublet to the *drawer* by the brewer, or by the drawer being tied to the brewer by a mortgage or bond
dressing Cleaning and removing impurities in grain and *malt*; also recutting grooves in millstones by a trained millwright

engine A pump

faggot Strictly, a piece of wood 3 *feet* long by 24 *inches* in circumference (0·91 by 0·61 metres); loosely, a small length of hewn timber
firkin A butter measure: 56 *lb* (25·4 kg)
foot 12 *inches* or one-third of a *yard* (30·48 cm)
fourpenny (4d) Strong *beer* stronger than *twopenny* but weaker than *sixpenny* and probably classed as *X* by the Hardys; so called from its retail price per quart: see also *nog*; *porter*

gallon Liquid measure: 8 *pints* (4·55 litres)
geneva Gin, a spirit flavoured with juniper
gig A light, two-wheeled vehicle drawn usually by one horse; similar to a *whiskey*
goaf, goaft, goft A rick of corn, usually one being transported by cart or wagon
grist *Malt* crushed in a malt-mill either by metal rollers or by millstones
gyle, gile, guile A brew. It was broken down into two or three parti-gyles. The strongest *beer* came from the first *mash* creating the first parti-gyle (`/), the next strongest from the second (`//), and the weakest from the third (`///). See also *gyle vat*; *mash tun*
gyle vat Another name for a fermenting tun

hop back A vessel containing *hops* and perforated at the bottom to form a coarse sieve through which the *wort* passes from the *copper* to the *cooler*, thus removing the solids
hops *Humulus lupulus*, a native wild hardy perennial climbing plant cultivated for its fruits and first licensed for brewing in England and Wales by Edward VI; when dried and added in brewing the cones give *beer* its distinctive bitter aroma. See *bag* and *pocket*
hundredweight (cwt) 112 *lb* (8 *stone*, or 50·8 kg); 20 cwt = one ton. The rough measure was half a hundredweight = one *bushel* (56 pounds, or 25·4 kg). It was often called 'hundred' at the time, this being the Hardys' usage

inch One-twelfth of a *foot* (2·54 cm)

keel An open commercial Broadland sailing vessel, then often larger than the *wherry*, developed from mediaeval times with a single square sail, centrally positioned mast, winch at the stern, and skipper's cabin at the bow; later ones, from the late 18th century onwards, were sometimes hatched
keeping room The family sitting room, less formal than the parlour

lading Cargo, the bill of lading being the customs certificate of cargo carried whether coastwise (around Britain) or abroad
last 10 *quarters* or 20 *coombs* (approx. 2032 kg or 2 metric tonnes): the largest unit of grain measure
lb See *pound*
liquor Water used in brewing, usually from a spring or well and sometimes left to soften in a *basin* set high at the start of the gravity feed
load A dry measure:
gravel: one cubic *yard* (0·76 cu. metre);
hewn timber: one *ton*
new hay: 19¼ *cwt* (36 trusses of 60 lb each: 977·9 kg);
old hay: 18 *cwt* (36 trusses of 56 lb each: 914·4 kg), new hay weighing more owing to its greater moisture content
rushes: 63 bundles

malt Barley roasted to create fermentable maltose, and crushed or milled for brewing. Different types of malt produce individual *beers*; see also *bushel*; *grist*; *porter malt*
marl A chalky-clay mixture occurring naturally in layers in chalky areas and lying beneath the top layer of clay; quarried in deep

open-cast pits and spread as fertiliser for crops

mash tun A vessel in which the *grist malt* is mixed with hot *liquor*. The strongest brew comes from the first mash; weaker brews from the second, or occasionally third, mashes, the same malt being used for the mashes but with additional hot liquor. See also *gyle*

meal The second grade of flour, less fine than the top grade

meeting A religious service conducted by Methodists and other Protestant Nonconformists on dedicated premises (the meeting house); these might be officially licensed or unlicensed. The premises could range from a purpose-built chapel to a labourer's kitchen or smallholder's outhouse

mild A more lightly hopped *beer* than bitter, allowing a sweeter flavour

mile 1760 *yards* (1·61 km)

muck Farm manure; animal dung

nog A strong, long-maturing *beer* particularly associated with Norfolk and one of the Hardys' staple brews; also called by them *fourpenny* and *X*

ounce (oz) One-sixteenth of a *pound* (weight)

peck One-quarter of a bushel, or 2 *gallons* dry measure

perch A small area of land: 40 perches = one *rood*; 4 roods = 1 *acre*

pint Half a *quart* (0·57 litres), or one-eighth of a *gallon*

pipe A wine cask; also a liquid measure:
port: 138 gallons (627·4 litres)
sherry: 130 gallons (591 litres)
wine: 126 gallons (572·8 litres)

pocket A sack of *hops*: 1¼ cwt (63·5 kg), measuring 7½ feet long by 5¾ feet in circumference (2·3 and 1·75 metres), the canvas weighing 4 *lb*; together with the *bag* the standard size for selling hops

pollard Very coarse, fourth-grade flour suited only to animal feed

porter Strong, long-maturing *beer* of varying strengths (*XX* or, for the Hardys, more usually *X*) with good lasting properties, made from special dark *porter malt*. It first became popular in London in the early 18th century. Owing to the capital costs associated with its large *casks* and slow maturity most village *common brewers* did not attempt to brew it

porter malt Barley further roasted after the process of *malting* has been completed, to darken the colour of the *beer* and enhance its bitter flavour; the chocolate-coloured grain becomes shrunken and very hard

pound (lb: weight) 16 ounces (0·45 kg)

puncheon Liquid measure: *beer*: 72 *gallons* (327·3 litres); wine: 84 gallons (381·9 litres)

quart 2 *pints* (1·14 litres), or one-quarter of a *gallon*

quarter 8 *bushels*, or 2 *coombs*, or one-tenth of a *last*

quicking The process of weeding and destroying, usually by burning, field couch grass or 'quicks' (*Triticum repens*)

quire A paper measure: 24 sheets; 20 quires = one ream (480 sheets)

rider A travelling salesman; the sales representative of a merchant or manufacturer

rood One-quarter of a statute *acre*: 40 *perches* = one rood; 4 roods = 1 *acre*

sack Coal: usually 3 bushels, each sack measuring 50 *inches* by 26 inches (127 by 66 cm); Gt Yarmouth measure 137 lb (62·1 kg); flour or *meal*: 5 *bushels* or 280 *lb* (127 kg)

screening Removing shoots and foreign bodies from grain and *malt*, usually by sieving; all commercially produced malt had to be screened

se'nnight A week (literally seven nights); the parallel contraction, a fortnight, has survived

shearling A young sheep which has had one shearing. A two-year shearling has been shorn twice

sixpenny (6^{d}), the strongest of the Hardys' brews, apparently classed by them XX and comparatively rarely brewed; so called from its high retail price per quart. The Treasury in 1779 regarded it as the product only of 'brewers of fine and particular strong beers and ales' (TNA: PRO CUST 48/20, p. 27)

small beer The weakest *beer*: more commonly brewed by private brewers and brewing victuallers (publican brewers) in country houses, parsonages and public houses, whereas *common brewers* concentrated on varieties of strong beer. See also *gyle*

society The local congregation of paid-up members of a Methodist *meeting house*

staithe A quay or landing place often to be found up cuts ('dykes') and purpose-built canals linking the hinterland to rivers and navigations; sometimes just a grassy bank on the riverside, usually with access to roads, where boats can be loaded and unloaded

steep A *cistern* for soaking barley at the start of *malting*, the process being called steeping. The majority of rural maltings in Norfolk in the 1770s had steeps for 25 or 30 *coombs* of barley (50 or 60 *cwt*/2½ or 3 tons/2·54 or 3·05 metric tonnes), although Letheringsett's in 1780 was 40 coombs. In Norwich at this time brewers often had one or more 50- to 60-coomb steeps (5·08 to 6·1 metric tonnes)
stone (**st.**) 14 *pounds* avoirdupois (6·35 kg). Butcher's meat was often regarded as dead weight and measured at 8 lb to the stone, but Mary Hardy used the avoirdupois reckoning, calculating meat as live weight; otherwise she could not have referred, eg, to '2 St. 12 lb' of beef (*Diary 1*: 19 Aug. 1774)
strong beer *Beer* such as *sixpenny*, best, *nog* and *porter* made from the first *mash* and subject to the highest levels of excise duty, its strength determining the level of duty according to a scale

tandem The harnessing of horses one behind the other and not abreast
tasking Threshing; the tasker is the thresher
tea Black: defined 1767 as Bohea, Congou, Souchong and Pekoe; green: all other varieties
tent Sweet red Spanish wine, technically from the Alicante region
tied house See *drawing house*. A secondary meaning applies to a tenant or subtenant, such as a farm servant, occupying the property only while employed by its owner or tenant, thus guaranteeing him local accommodation. Both parsonages and farm cottages can be tied houses
ton 2240 *lb* or 20 *hundredweight* (1016 kg, 1·016 metric tonnes); in a ship's measure 40 cubic feet or 2000 lb = one ton
trashing Threshing
truss See *load*
tun room A large, lofty store room, also called a *vat* house, where *beer* is left in *casks* to condition or mature; see also '*white hall*'
twopenny (2^{d}), a weak brew, so called from its retail price per quart; the Hardys do not use the term

underback The vessel under the *mash tun* to receive the *wort* before it runs into the *copper*

vat Usually a synonym for a *cask*: a very large closed vessel for storing beer; however see also *gyle vat*

waterman The skipper or mate of a *keel* or *wherry*
wether A castrated male sheep
wharfinger The occupier of a wharf, usually in a sea port or large inland port, such as Norwich, rather than at a village *staithe*
wherry A commercial single-sailed Broadland vessel developed in the 18th century, and then often smaller than the *keel*, with a winch at the bow and skipper's cabin in the stern; by 1800 it was usually hatched to protect the cargo. By the mid-19th century it had superseded the keel owing to its superior design, its mast, placed for'ard, allowing a unique, simple fore-and-aft rig and an uncluttered hold
whiskey A light, two-wheeled vehicle usually pulled by one horse; see *gig*. (Whisky the drink was often called *usquebaugh* or *aqua vitae* at this time: Gaelic and Latin for water of life)
'white hall' A term specific to the Letheringsett brewery: the Hardys' name for the part of the brewery between the fermenting room and *tun room* where the fermented *beer* was run off into *barrels*, for delivery as a young beer, or into a subterranean tank from where it was pumped into the casks if a long-maturing beer
wort Liquid run off from the *mash tun*, *copper* and *cooler*; fermentation has to take place before it can be called *beer* or *ale*

X, XX Strong *beer*—the greater the number of Xs, the stronger the beer. The notation was derived from the chalk marks scribbled on the vessels, *barrels* and *casks*. Brewers would draw a horizontal bar through the letter X to denote XX, and two bars for XXX (X̶, X̶̶)

yard 3 *feet* (0·914 metres)
'I, *'II*, *'III* Parti-gyles: up to three brewings from the one batch of malt. See *gyle*

Bibliography

Manuscript sources

The National Archives of the UK (TNA): **Public Record Office** (PRO)

CUST 47/198–463, Excise Board and Secretariat: Minute books 1751–1809

E 134/32 Geo. 3 hil 2, Exchequer: King's Remembrancer: Depositions taken by Commission 1792

HO 42/37, Home Office: Domestic correspondence, George III, letters and papers 1795

IR 23/61, Land tax assessments 1798: Norfolk

IR 30/23/629, Tithe Commission: Whissonsett tithe map 1843 [surveyed 1838]

IR 1/63, Board of Stamps: Country registers, apprenticeship books 1783–86

IR 1/67, Board of Stamps: Country registers, apprenticeship books 1790–96

MR 1/257, Holt and Letheringsett enclosure: Map by Charles Burcham 1810

Norfolk Record Office (NRO)

ACC Cozens-Hardy 20/3/1973, Holt manor court book, 3 vols, 1774–1850

ACC Cozens-Hardy 11/2/1976: Mann archive 1770–1857

Articles . . . of the Friendly Society meeting at . . . the Mariners in Holt (E. Dereham, 1795)

Henry Raven's brewing book, Pelican Brewery, Wapping Wall, London 1824

Draft indenture for purchase of Letheringsett House of Industry, 14 Sept. 1837

Letter from W.H. Burrell to Basil Cozens-Hardy on Shambrook Burrell, 20 Dec. 1942

ACC Cozens-Hardy 23/8/1976, Attorney's ledger [by James Moore] 1793–99

ACC Cozens-Hardy 4/1/1780, Baker family tree by M. Brenda Baker 1975

ANF (1789) W9, f. 302, Archdeaconry of Norfolk, will of Mary Parker, of Fakenham, proved 22 Jan. 1789

ANW (1785) W76, f. 113, Archdeaconry of Norwich, will of Edmund Jewell, of Holt, proved 10 Nov. 1784

BR 17/7, Copyhold records for the Fishmongers' Arms, Cley-next-the-Sea 1802–72

BR 28/6, 28/7, Cozens & Copeman, bought books 1790–1811

BR 160/35, Copyhold records for the Three Horseshoes, Stody 1772–1896

C/S 1/15, Norfolk Quarter Sessions, minute book 1791–1800

C/S 1/17, Norfolk Quarter Sessions minute book 1805–11

C/Sca 2/325, Enclosure map of Whissonsett, Horningtoft and Stanfield 1816

C/Sch 1/1/30–32, Oaths and declarations of Dissenting preachers 1796–1822

C/Sch 1/16, Register of Norfolk public houses 1789–99

DN/DIS 1/2, Register of meeting houses in the diocese of Norwich 1751–1810

DN/VIS 29/6, Holt deanery visitation 1784

DN/VIS 29/7, Toftrees deanery visitation 1784

DN/VIS 31/2, Repertory of officiating curates in the diocese of Norwich 1784

DN/VIS 33a/1, Brisley deanery visitation 1794

DN/VIS 33a/4, Holt deanery visitation 1794

DN/VIS 36/10, Brisley deanery visitation 1801

FC 11/1, Guestwick Independent Church Book 1694–1854 (incl. Briston Chapel 1783–1854)

FC 18/1, Record of members in the Methodist Connexion in the Walsingham Circuit 1798–1813

FC 58/8, Deeds of Guestwick Chapel and manse 1694–1799

MC 120/11–120/85, 593X3–594X5, Farming diaries and accounts of Stephen Frost of Langham 1768–1816 (44 vols)

MC 632, Bayfield estate papers 1461–1897

MC 1825/8, Briston Hall, Meliors and Chosells manor court book 1771–94

MC 2043/9, 909X6, Checkley Collection: Holt Windmill 1916

MS 66, Lt Col. Metzner's inspection of Norfolk Volunteer companies, vol. 1, 18 Oct.–19 Nov. 1803

MS 15403, 44B, Fakenham Lancaster manor court book 1791–1806

MS 16609, 32 D5, Stody manor court book 1763–1903
MS 19829, Z 2D, Thornage with the Members manor court book 1763–86
MS 19830, Z 2D, Thornage with the Members manor court book 1786–1812
MS 7351, 7 D4, Sale particulars of the Coltishall Brewery, 14 Sept. 1841
NCC (1794) 251 Coe, Norwich Consistory Court, will of Sarah Jewell, of Holt, proved 8 Dec. 1794

PD 2/4, Holt parish register of baptisms and burials 1738–1812, marriages 1738–82
PD 207/6, E. Carleton parish register of burials 1813–1998
PD 270/5, /9 Cley parish registers of baptisms and burials 1779–1814, marriages 1754–1812
PD 547/1–5, /44, Letheringsett parish registers of baptisms, marriages and burials 1653–1996
PD 679/6, Wells-next-the-Sea parish register of baptisms and burials 1754–1801

UPC 13/6, 639x4, Sale agreement for Sheringham (Old) Hall: Cook Flower to Abbot Upcher, 10 July 1811
WHT Jodrell family papers and estates 1290–1948
WHT 3/2/6, Jodrell estate: Lease of Sharrington Hall and farm by Mrs Elizabeth Jodrell to Thomas Kendle, 20 Oct. 1785

Suffolk Record Office (Ipswich)

Bacon Longe Collection:
HA 24/50/19/4.3 (1), (2), Diary of Revd John Longe jnr, Henley and Coddenham, Suff., 1796–99
HA 24/50/19/4.5 (1), Printed copy of the form of prayer for the public fast, 28 Feb. 1794
HA 24/50/19/4.6 (4), Letters of Revd John Longe jnr
HA 24/50/19/4.7 (13), Revd John Longe jnr, My father's directions for brewing, 9 July 1796

West Yorkshire Archive Service (Wakefield)

QE 13/5/6, Land tax assessments 1781–84, Knaresborough and Bilton with High Harrogate

Sir John Soane's Museum

29/4a/2–4, Gunthorpe Hall, Designs for a new house for Charles Collyer 1789–90

Websites

Norfolk Public Houses <www.norfolkpubs.co.uk/norwich/bnorwich/ncbus.htm>, accessed 25 Nov. 2011
Old Bailey Proceedings Online <www.oldbaileyonline.org, version 6.0, 18 November 2011>, April 1848 (t18480403), accessed 18 Nov. 2011

Printed works

Pre-1900 works

Armstrong, M.J., *The History and Antiquities of the County of Norfolk* (Norwich, 1781), Holt hundred
Bartell, E. jnr, *Cromer considered as a Watering Place* (enlarged 2nd edn London, 1806)
Bryant, A., *Map of the County of Norfolk* (London, 1826)
Burn, J., *The Justice of the Peace, and Parish Officer*, 4 vols (16th edn London, 1788)
Chase, W., *The Norwich Directory* (Norwich, 1783)
Crouse, J. and Stevenson, W., *Crouse and Stevenson's Norwich and Norfolk Complete Memorandum Book 1790* (Norwich, 1790)
Dew, W.N., *Monumental Inscriptions in the Hundred of Holt* (Norwich, 1885)
Forby, R., *The Vocabulary of East Anglia*, 2 vols (London, 1830)
Foster, J., *Alumni Oxonienses 1715–1886*, 4 vols (Parker & Co., Oxford, 1888–92)
Holt and Letheringsett Inclosure: A state of the claims (Holt, 1808)
Kent, N., *General View of the Agriculture of the County of Norfolk* (London, 1796)
Marshall, W., *The Rural Economy of Norfolk*, 2 vols (London, 1787)
Minutes of the Methodist Conferences, vol. 1 (London, 1812); vol. 5 (London, 1825)
The Norwich Mercury 1770–1829
Paterson, D., *A New and Accurate Description of all the Direct and Principal Cross Roads in England and Wales* (10th edn London, 1794)
Peck, T., *The Norwich Directory* (Norwich, 1802)
Pigot and Co.'s National Commercial Directory: Norfolk and Suffolk (London, 1830)
The Poll for the Knights of the Shire for the County of Norfolk (Norwich, 1802)
The Poll for the Knights of the Shire for the County of Norfolk (Norwich, 1806)
Rye, W., *Cromer, Past and Present: or, An attempt to describe the parishes of Shipden and Cromer, and to narrate their history* (Norwich, 1889)
Stones, W., *The Garden of Norfolk, or The rural residence* (Norwich, [*c*.1823])

Symons, W., *The Practical Gager or the Young Gager's Assistant* (London, 1793)
The Universal British Directory, 5 vols (London, 1793–98)
White, W., *History, Gazetteer, and Directory of Norfolk* (Sheffield, 1845)
The Whole Duty of Constables, by an acting magistrate (2nd edn Norwich, 1815)

Post-1900 works

Apling, H., *Norfolk Corn Windmills* (Norfolk Windmills Trust, Norwich, 1984)
Armstrong, D., *A Short History of Norfolk County Cricket* (Larks Press, Guist Bottom, 1990)
Bird, M., ed., *The Remaining Diary of Mary Hardy 1773–1809* (Burnham Press, Kingston upon Thames, 2013)
Bird, M., *Mary Hardy and her World 1773–1809*, 4 vols (Burnham Press, Kingston upon Thames [to be published])
Cozens-Hardy, B.,'Norfolk coastal defences in 1588', *Norfolk Archaeology*, vol. 26 (1938)
Cozens-Hardy, B., *The History of Letheringsett in the County of Norfolk with extracts from the diary of Mary Hardy (1773 to 1809)* (Jarrold & Sons, Norwich, 1957)
Cozens-Hardy, B., 'Some Norfolk halls', *Norfolk Archaeology*, vol. 32, pt 3 (1960)
Cozens-Hardy, B., 'Norfolk lawyers', *Norfolk Archaeology*, vol. 33 (1965)
Cozens-Hardy, B., ed., *Mary Hardy's Diary* (Norfolk Record Soc., vol. 37 (1968))
Cozens-Hardy, B. and Kent, E.A., *The Mayors of Norwich 1403 to 1835* (Jarrold & Sons, Norwich, 1938)
Durst, D., 'Craftsmen at Gunton Sawmill', *Journal of the Norfolk Industrial Archaeology Society*, vol. 6, no. 1 (1996)
Durst, D., 'Hase: ironfounder of Saxthorpe', *Journal of the Norfolk Industrial Archaeology Society*, vol. 6, no. 1 (1996)
Durst, D.W., 'Letheringsett: Industrial archaeology in a rural setting', *Journal of the Norfolk Industrial Archaeology Society* (6 pts):
1: 'The introduction', vol. 5, no. 3 (1993); revised and updated in vol. 8, no. 2 (2007)
2: 'The watermill', vol. 5, no. 4 (1994)
3: 'Hall Farm sawmill', vol. 5, no. 5 (1995)
4: 'The brewery', vol. 7, no. 4 (2004)
5: 'Water systems', vol. 8, no. 1 (2006)
6: 'Notes on Johnson Jex', vol. 8, no. 2 (2007)
Emsley, C., with Hill, A.M. and Ashcroft, M.Y., *North Riding Naval Recruits: The Quota Acts and the Quota men 1795–97* (North Yorkshire County Council, 1978)
Erroll, A. C., *A History of the Parishes of Sheringham and Beeston Regis* (Sheringham, 1970)
Faden, W., *Faden's Map of Norfolk* (Larks Press, Dereham, 1989; 1st pub. 1797)
Halliwell, J.O., *Dictionary of Archaic Words* (Bracken Books, London, 1989; 1st pub. 1850)
Hewitt, V.H. and Keyworth, J.M., *As Good as Gold: 300 years of British bank note design* (British Museum Publications, London, 1987)
Hooton, J., *The Glaven Ports: A maritime history of Blakeney, Cley and Wiveton in north Norfolk* (Blakeney History Group, Blakeney, 1996)
Kent, P., *Fortifications of East Anglia* (Terence Dalton Ltd, Lavenham, 1988)
Ketton-Cremer, R.W., *Felbrigg: The story of a house* (Futura Publications, London, 1982)
Lavery, B., *We shall fight on the Beaches: Defying Napoleon and Hitler, 1805 and 1940* (Conway, London, 2009)
Lloyd, N., *A History of English Brickwork* (Antique Collectors' Club reprint, 1983; 1st pub. 1925)
Mason, J., *Spixworth: History and landscape in a Norfolk village* (Norwich, 1998)
Mathias, P., *The Brewing Industry in England 1700–1830* (Cambridge Univ. Press, 1959)
Millican, P., *A History of Horstead and Stanninghall, Norfolk* (Norwich, 1937)
Pope, S., *Gressenhall Farm and Workhouse* (Poppyland Publishing, Cromer, 2006
Stammers, M., *Shipbuilding at Wells in the 18th and 19th Centuries* (Wells Local History Group, 2011)
Venn, J.A., *Alumni Cantabrigienses 1752–1900*, 6 vols (Cambridge Univ. Press, 1940–54)
Vince, J., *Discovering Carts and Wagons* (Shire Publications, Princes Risborough, 1987)
Virgoe, N., *The Heavenly Road: John Wesley's journeys in Norfolk and Suffolk* (Larks Press, Guist Bottom, 2011)
Wharton, B., *The Smiths of Ryburgh: 100 years of milling and malting* (Crisp Malting Ltd, Gt Ryburgh, 1990)
Woodforde, J., *The Diary of a Country Parson*, ed. J. Beresford, 5 vols (Oxford Univ. Press, 1924–31)
Yaxley, D., *A Researcher's Glossary of words found in historical documents in East Anglia* (Larks Press, Guist Bottom, 2003)
Yaxley, P., *Looking back at Norfolk Cricket* (Nostalgia Publications, Toftwood, 1997)
Yaxley, S., ed., *Sherringhamia: The journal of Abbot Upcher 1813–16* (Larks Press, Guist Bottom, 1986)

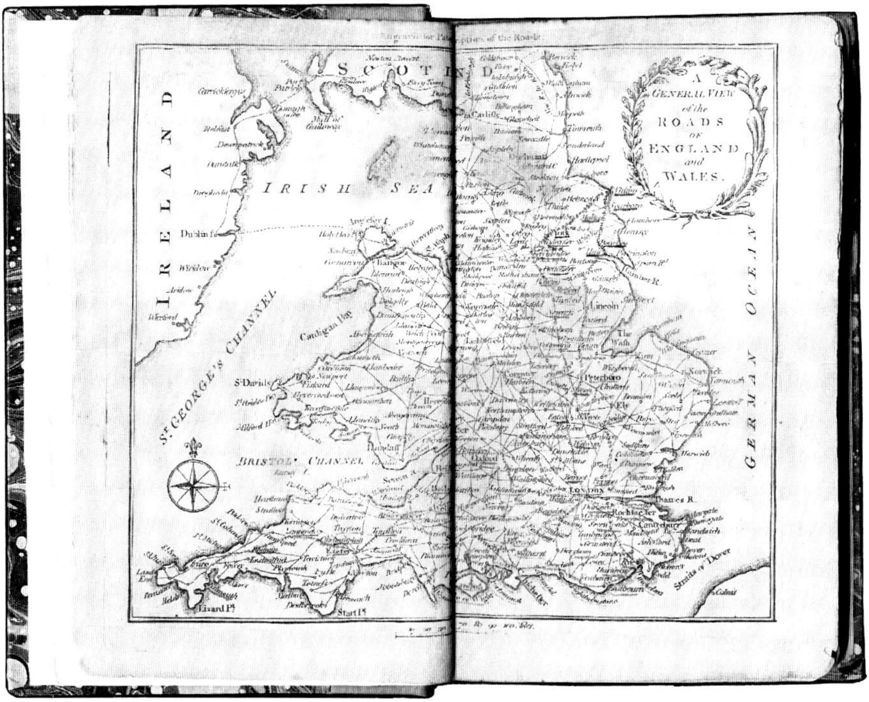

above Daniel Paterson, *A New and Accurate Description of all the Direct and Principal Cross Roads in England and Wales* (10th edn London, 1794). The frontispiece map in this small, well-thumbed road atlas shows the country criss-crossed by fast roads in an age of mail coaches, postchaises and posting inns.

Known for short as Paterson's *Roads*, the work is noted by Mary Hardy at the end of her diary ledger 3, covering the years 1782–1790

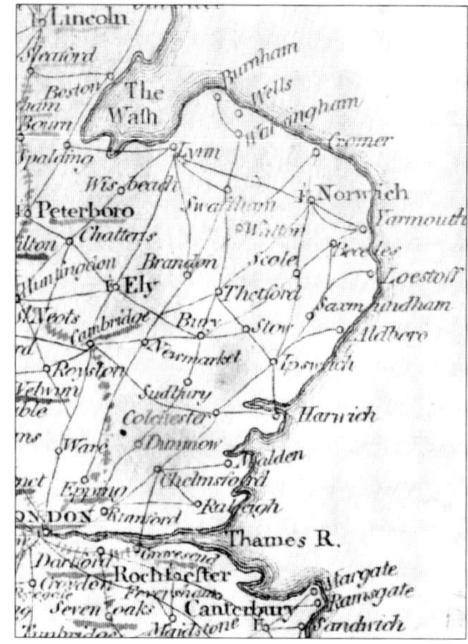
Lincoln
Boston
The
Wafh
Wells
Lynn
Norwich
Peterboro
Yarmouth
Ely
Brandon
Thetford
Cambridge
Newmarket
Sudbury
Colchester
Harwich
Chelmsford
Thames R.
Rochester
Canterbury
Margate
Ramsgate
Sandwich

right This enlargement from the edition of 1794 shows that the Hardys lived in an area not served by any principal road. Almost without exception the main routes to and through Norfolk extended radially from London; those running to the north of the county bypassed Holt, Blakeney and Cley.

The two principal lateral ('cross') roads ran from King's Lynn to Gt Yarmouth via Norwich, and from King's Lynn to Swaffham [*Editor's collection*]

Index to the diary text of Mary Hardy

Diary 3 · 16 August 1793–26 October 1797

The middle Letheringsett years

Editor's index to the abridged diary text of Mary Hardy

Text references are identified not by page number but by date of entry in the diary, eg 24.1.94 *for* 24 January 1794; 1.6.95 *for* 1 June 1795: *ie day, month, year.*

Illustrations, by contrast, are indexed by the page number on which they appear, the page numbers being displayed in bold type, eg **horses**: accidents, **7**, **72**, **276**, **277**; **Skiffins** (Skivens), James William, **39**, **59**, **138**.

Reported events are dated in the index according to their date of entry in the diary and not necessarily according to the date on which they occurred, often reflecting the passage of time between the event itself and the diarist's receipt of the news, eg **Russia**, death at St Petersburg of Empress, 22.12.96 (*the date in December 1796 when Mary Hardy heard the news*), *not* 15.11.96 (*the date of Catherine the Great's death quoted, erroneously, in the press report*).

Index entries in parentheses after the main entry denote the diarist's spelling—and probably her pronunciation—of the word in the manuscript, eg **Baldwin** (Balden, Baldin); **Gressenhall** (Gresenhall, Gresnal); **Guestwick** (Guestick), *although she is not always consistent in the use of such variations. Cross-references are provided where the main entry cannot readily be found, eg* **Dawling**, *see* Field Dalling; **Woodhouse**, Sir John, *see* Wodehouse.

Parentheses after the index entry can also denote the diarist's usage, distinguishing it from the modern term, eg **heather** (ling); **roller** (role).

The diarist's daily entries, endnotes and maidservants' register are indexed; editorial captions, sidenotes and the appendices are not included.

The index to the diary of HENRY RAVEN is compiled separately and follows this index.

These contractions are used in the index:

Hs	*for*	the Hardys
HR		Henry Raven [nephew and brewing pupil]
MA		Mary Ann Hardy [daughter]
MH		Mary Hardy
WH		William Hardy [husband]
WHj		William Hardy jnr [son]

A

accidents, 14 trampled to death at Haymarket theatre, London, 7.2.94
  industrial, **69**: John Wade's windmill at Holt burns down, 8.5.94
  road, **72**, **133**, **174**, **276**, **277**, **349**: cart breaks down with WHj and MA on way to Beckham, 5.12.93; beer cart breaks down with Robert Bye at Warham, 25.1.94; Henry Smith of Blakeney killed in fall from horse near Holt, 24.5.94; Robert Farthing's son falls from horse on way from Briston Fair, 27.5.94; WH and MH injured and chaise damaged when horse falls at Swanton Novers, 3.7.94; Thomas Baldwin breaks arm on way from Sheringham, 23.12.94; Revd Benjamin

accidents, road (*cont.*)
  Crofts jnr killed in fall from horse, 18.2.95; Norwich driver dies from injuries after cart overturns at Letheringsett, 21–22.5.95 and MH's register, endnotes; Mrs Booty's beer cart swept under Glaven bridge in floods, 4.6.96; Thomas Baldwin breaks leg on way from Burnham Market, 9.12.96; Revd Mr Wilcocks injured after cart overturns in Hs' field, 17.1.97

Acres, *see* Six Acres

Acts, *see* Parliament

Aldborough (Albro), Norf., **224**, Messrs Bird and Williams confirm sale of public house, 24.10.93; WH and Mr Bird to, 27.11.93; WH

Aldborough (*cont.*)
pays Mr Bird 300 guineas for public house, 8.4.94; WH, MH and MA to, 10.9.96; WHj to, 10.10.97

Alpe (Alp), Mary (d.1798 aged 51), **384**, Holt schoolmistress; MA to tea, 23.11.93; hires Phillis Raven as teacher, 4.8.97; with Mrs Bartell to tea at Hs', 24.8.97

Alsop, Isaac, **158**, former innkeeper of King's Arms, Cromer; WH at Holt to settle business affairs, 31.3.95

apprenticeship, **120**, **334**, HR bound to Hs, 19.7.94

Army, **52**, **189**, **232**, **266**, two soldiers at work in Hs' garden, 15.3.94, 19.3.94; British troops defeated in France and Flanders, 23.5.94, 25.5.94; WH meets Holt justices over raising soldiers [sailors], 4.4.95; WHj and MA watch regiment of Artillery pass through Holt, 8.6.95; Artillery fails to arrive at Holt, 9.6.95; Hs watch arrival, Artillery stays overnight at Holt, 10.6.95; Hs follow regiment from Holt to Weybourne Camp, 11.6.95; WHj and MA watch troops exercise at Weybourne Camp, 17.6.95; soldiers from Holt sent to Wells to quell riot, 15–16.12.95; Holt justices summon troop of horse from Norwich and foot soldiers from Aylsham to quell riot at Sharrington, 19.12.95; soldiers march through Letheringsett to guard flour at Sharrington, 20.12.95; soldiers escort flour to Stock Heath, 21.12.95; WHj watches Artillery march out of Holt, 17.6.96: *see also* Militia; Volunteers; Weybourne Camp

articles, tax on attorneys' clerks, 7.2.94: *see also* apprenticeship

Artillery, *see* Army; Weybourne Camp

Askew, Mr, of regiment of Artillery at Weybourne Camp; dines with Hs, 29.7.95

assemblies, WHj to:
Fakenham: 26.1.96
Holt: 21.10.93, 18.11.93, 24.4.94, 8.12.94; with Mr Sharp, 10.11.94:
see also balls

assignees, *see* bankruptcy; debt

assizes (assises), **99**:
Norwich: WH and HR to, 12.8.94; opening day, 18.7.96; WH and James Moore to, 6.8.97
Thetford: WHj speaks to John Wade over giving evidence as witness, 7.3.96; WHj from, 13.3.96

Athow (Atthow), Thomas (d.1812 aged 89), Holt cooper and timber merchant; meets WH concerning Bull at Holt, 21.3.96

Attleborough (Atlebourg), Norf., Crown at Sheringham hired from Hs by Robert Johnson of, 16.3.95

attorneys, tax on articled clerks, 7.2.94: *see also individual entries* Christmas, William; Moore, James; Smith, John; Williams, William; Wymer, George; Wymer, George jnr

Atwood, Thomas (d.1805 aged 78), **59**, innkeeper of Dolphin, Holt; at work in Hs' garden, 28.3.94, 21.4.94

auction, Abraham Dobson's furniture, 2.10.97: *see also* sales; valuations

audits, Mr Burrell's, 1.2.96; WH dines at Mr Burrell's tithe, 9.12.96: *see also* frolics

Aylsham, Norf., Gunton Thompson receives legacy at, 10.12.93; Holt justices summon soldiers from to quell riot, 19.12.95; WHj to justices' sitting, 19.9.97

B

backhouse, *see* house, Hs'

backs, *see* brewing equipment

Bacon, Miss, Holt dressmaker; MH to fitting, 17.1.94

Baker, Adam Calthorpe (1773–1810), son of John of Holt; dines with Hs, 15.9.94

Baker, John (1727–1804), Holt ironmonger; with family to tea at Hs', 22.10.93, 23.11.93, 26.3.94, 27.7.95, 20.10.95, 13.6.96, 28.9.96; with family to supper party at Thomas Temple's, 13.12.93; Hs to tea, 26.4.94, 28.7.94, 20.2.96, 25.6.96, 15.9.96, 15.11.96, 15.7.97, 16.9.97, 25.10.97; Mrs Phillis Custance and Mrs Hannah Raven to stay, 11.7.94; Miss Custance to stay, 7.3.96; to tea at Hs', 12.12.96

Baker, John, Southrepps farmer; in dispute with WHj and Thomas Balls jnr over piano at Southrepps, 13.4.97

Baker, Margaret (1765–1830), of Holt, daughter of John of Holt; with family to tea at Hs', 22.10.93, 22.11.93, 26.3.94; with Custances to tea, 7.2.97; with Custances to dinner, 15.2.97

Baker, Mrs Priscilla (1734–1801), née Custance, 2nd wife of John of Holt; with family to tea at Hs', 22.10.93, 22.11.93, 26.3.94, 27.7.95, 20.10.95, 13.6.96, 28.9.96

baking, by Hs' maids and Betty Woods, 9.3.95

Baldwin (Balden, Baldin), Thomas, **133**, **264**, **349**, Hs' farm servant, brewer and drayman; ill, 13–14.8.94; delivering beer, 20.8.94; harvesting wheat, 20.8.94; breaks arm on beer delivery, 23.12.94; breaks leg on beer delivery, 9.12.96

ballots:
Provisional Cavalry: WH at Holt for, 25.2.97
Supplementary Militia, **325**: 12.12.96; WH at Holt for, 14.1.97

Balls, Edmund, ? of Saxlingham; with Thomas Balls jnr and Mr Mindham to tea at Hs', 29.6.97

Balls, Thomas (d.1802), Saxlingham farmer; William Thackwray spends day and night at, 12.12.96; WHj to supper, 20.3.97, 17.5.97; WHj to tea, 12.9.97
Balls, Thomas jnr, Saxlingham farmer; with WHj to Sheringham to inspect workmen's repairs, 28.11.96; with John Ellis to breakfast at Hs', with WHj and John Ellis views Mr Minns' new mill at Walsingham, 16.12.96; to supper, 29.12.96, 28.2.97, 30.4.97; with Bartells to supper at Hs', settles timber book, 12.1.97; with WHj to Reepham, stays overnight at Hs', 27.3.97; with WHj unable to pack up piano at Southrepps as in dispute with Mr Baker, 13.4.97; with WHj to tea at Edmund Bartell jnr's at Cromer, to supper at Hs', 13.4.97; to tea, 11.5.97, 2.8.97, 29.6.97
Balls, Thomas, of King's Lynn; marriage in 1795 to Deborah Ramm noted in MH's register, endnotes
balls:
Holt: WHj, MA and Nathaniel Raven jnr to, 17.2.94; WHj to, 19.3.94; for officers from Weybourne Camp, 3.8.95
John Browne's children's, for pupils: HR to, 3.10.95, 29.9.97; WHj and HR to, 29.9.96
Sheringham: WHj and MA to Cook Flower's, 5.1.95:
see also assemblies
banking, **343**, WHj to Holt with banking book, 15.12.94, 19.1.95; Bank of England and city and country banks stop payment, 28.2.97
bankruptcy, **158**, **335**, **343**, **354**, William Custance, 26.7.94, 9.8.94; Robert Farthing, 8.6.97: *see also* bond; debt
Banyard, Charles (d.1808 aged 54), innkeeper of Feathers, Holt, formerly and later of King's Lynn; postchaise hired by Hs, 6.9.94, 23.9.95, 11.4.96, 20.2.97; WHj buys mare, 20.9.94; WHj to bowling green, 27.8.95; with wife to tea party at King's Head, Letheringsett, 4.9.95; WHj to dinner, 2.2.96; WHj dines at Holt book club, 10.1.97; with HR and party to Cromer, 20.8.97: *see also* Holt, public houses, Feathers
Banyard, Mrs ? Elizabeth, ? Mary, née Harwin, wife of Charles; with husband to tea party at King's Head, Letheringsett, 4.9.95
Barcham, Benjamin, Sheringham shopkeeper and timber, coal and skin merchant; buys land for coal yard from Hs, 4.2.95; WHj to tea, 28.12.95
bark, *see* wood
barley (barly), **16**, **90**:
harvesting: WHj in Furze Closes, 15.8.94; Hs' men, 20.8.94, 5.9.95; Hs' men in Six Acres, 26.8.94; Hs' men in Furze Closes, 5.9.95, 7.9.95; Hs' men at Holt Heath Farm, 8.9.97
barley (*cont.*)
price: per coomb at Holt market, 13.2.96, 20.2.96, 5.3.96
purchase: from Messrs Keeler, Everitt, Jarvis and Nobbs, 23.6.94
storing: stack removed to barn, 11.2.96:
see also corn; harvests
Barmer, Norf., WH and John Thompson stay overnight at Richard Temple's, 12.9.96; WHj stays overnight at Richard Temple's, 28.10.96; Richard Temple borrows £120 from Hs, 18.9.97
barn, Hs', **132**; WHj removes barley stack to, 11.2.96
Barnham, Mr, of London; with wife to tea at Hs', 9.9.95
Barnham, Mrs, with husband to tea at Hs', 9.9.95
barrels, bought by WH and WHj at Cley, 1.10.94: *see also* casks; wood, laths
barrister, *see* Jodrell, Henry
Bartell, Charlotte, daughter of Edmund; dines at Hs', 13.12.93, 15.9.94; with family to supper party at Thomas Temple's, 13.12.93; with family to tea at Hs', 19.3.94, 11.7.94, 31.7.94, 31.3.95; with Clara Wymer and Miss Dewson to dinner, 12.1.96; with father and Thomas Balls jnr to supper at Hs', settles timber book, 12.1.97; with Miss Jones to tea, 21.6.97
Bartell, Edmund (d.1816 aged 72), surgeon-apothecary at Holt; with family to supper party at Thomas Temple's, 13.12.93; stays overnight at Hs', 24–26.2.94; with WHj stays at George Wymer's in Norwich, 26–27.2.94; with family to tea party at King's Head, Letheringsett, 14.7.94; Clara Wymer departs from, 18.2.96; with wife and WH to Norwich, 11.4.96; with WHj to Reepham, 14.7.96; with wife to Norwich, 12.4.97
at Hs': 5.11.93, 12.3.94, 19.3.94, 17.4.94, 6.6.94, 27.6.94, 11.7.94, 31.7.94, 31.3.95, 9.9.95, 3.3.96, 10.4.96, 12.1.97, 16.2.97
Hs at:
1793: 5.11.93, 9.11.93, 27.11.93
1794: 6.1.94, 28.3.94, 3.5.94, 8.5.94, 16.6.94, 9.8.94, 16.10.94, 26.10.94, 1.12.94, 18.12.94
1795: 10.1.95, 19.1.95, 22.1.95, 4.4.95, 7.4.95, 11.4.95, 8.6.95, 9.6.95, 28.7.95, 30.7.95, 29.8.95, 6.10.95, 19.12.95, 25.12.95
1796: 10.1.96, 16.1.96, 21.3.96, 2.4.96, 9.4.96, 31.5.96, 25.6.96, 31.7.96, 17.9.96, 13.10.96, 30.10.96, 7.12.96
1797: 26.3.97, 29.5.97, 8.7.97
hospitality: MH, MA and HR to dinner on confirmation day, 4.7.94; Hs, HR and Mary

Bartell, Edmund, hospitality (*cont.*)
Raven to supper, 25.11.94; WHj and HR to supper party, 3.2.96; WH stays overnight, 25.3.96
medical practice: attends Mrs Hall in labour, 24.2.94, 12.3.94; treats MH for dimness in eyes, 27.6.94; bleeds MH, 7.6.96, 14.8.97; with Dr Heath calls to advise WHj, 2.5.97; treats MH's eyes, 7.8.97; plaster applied to MH's arm, 14.8.97
timber dealings with Hs: with wife and WH to Reepham to decide on timber-felling, 30.3.96; WH measures timber at Reepham, 12.7.96; with daughter and Thomas Balls jnr settles timber book at Hs', 12.1.97; with WH measures ash timber at Reepham, 20.2.97

Bartell, Edmund jnr (d.1855 aged 85), **18**, **304**, of Brooke and Cromer, surgeon; with wife to tea, 5.11.93; WHj with Bartells to Cromer house-hunting for, all to tea at Hs', 2.8.96; Hs to dinner at Cromer, 16.9.96; at parents' house, 12.4.97; WHj and Thomas Balls jnr to tea at Cromer, 13.4.97; WHj and MA to tea, 5.9.97

Bartell, Mrs Margaret (d.1836 aged 67), née Wadsworth, 1st wife of Edmund jnr; with husband to tea at Hs', 5.11.93

Bartell, Robert (d.1801 aged 19/21), son of Edmund; at Hs', 12.8.94

Bartell, Mrs Sarah (d.1828 aged 82), née Dacke, wife of Edmund; with family at Hs', 19.3.94, 17.4.94, 6.6.94, 11.7.94, 31.3.95, 9.9.95, 3.3.96, 2.8.96; with husband and WH to Reepham to decide on timber-felling, 30.3.96; with husband to Norwich, 11.4.96, 12.4.97; with WHj to Cromer house-hunting for Edmund, 2.8.96; with Miss Alpe to tea at Hs', 24.8.97

bathing, **271**, by:
MH in garden bath:
1796: 16.9.96, 26.9.96, 30.9.96, 7.10.96, 6.10.96, 10.10.96, 13.10.96, 18.10.96, 9–10.11.96, 14–15.11.96, 22.11.96, 28.11.96, 2.12.96
1797: 1.5.97, 3.5.97, 9.7.97, 11.5.97, 15.5.97, 17.5.97, 19.5.97, 27.5.97, 29.5.97, 2.6.97, 4.6.97, 6.6.97, 8.6.97, 10.6.97, 14.6.97, 18.6.97, 21.6.97, 29.6.97, 1.7.97, 3.7.97, 9.7.97, 15.7.97, 31.7.97, 4–5.8.97, 7.8.97, 13–14.8.97, 18.8.97, 30–31.8.97, 8.9.97, 10.9.97, 12.9.97, 16.9.97, 18.9.97, 24–25.9.97, 29–30.9.97, 2.10.97, 5.10.97, 10.10.97, 12–13.10.97, 20.10.97, 25.10.97: *see also* baths
WHj at seaside, **363**: 17.5.97, 19.5.97, 21.5.97, 23.5.97, 25.5.97, 27.5.97, 2.6.97, 6.6.97, 8.6.97, 11.6.97, 18.6.97, 21.6.97, 27.6.97, 29.6.97, 1.7.97, 4.7.97, 6.7.97, 8.7.97, 13.7.97, 15.7.97, 17.7.97, 25.7.97, 27.7.97, 31.7.97,

bathing, WHj at seaside (*cont.*)
2.8.97, 5.8.97, 12.8.97, 14.8.97, 24–25.8.97, 16.9.97, 24.9.97; bathes at Sheringham, 29.5.97, 14.6.97; prevented by rough seas from bathing, 10.9.97

baths, **115**, new bath at Cley visited by WHj and James Moore, 17.4.94; MH's garden bath cleaned by WH, Nicholas Woodhouse and William Dobson, 15.9.96; bath house at Cley sold for 40 guineas, 10.7.97

bath stove, *see* fireplaces

Bayfield, Norf., **8**, **110**, **137**, **165**, **207**, **308**, **317**, Hs to tea at Thomas Forster's, 23.4.94, 27.5.94, 22.4.95, 19.1.96, 11.8.96; death of Mrs Elizabeth Jodrell, 31.8.94; Hs view Henry Jodrell's new plantations, 22.4.95; Hs and William Thackwray to supper at Thomas Forster's, 27.9.96; Thomas Forster and family move to King's Lynn area, 10.10.96; Hs to tea at John Claxton Savory's, 22.12.96, 3.1.97, 25.2.97; death of brother of Mrs Savory, 24.12.96; Hs with Mr and Mrs Nathaniel Raven to Mr Savory, 23.2.97: *see also* Forster, Thomas; Jodrell, Mrs Elizabeth; Platten, Samuel; Savory, John Claxton

Beckham, Norf., WHj and MA's cart breaks down on way to, 5.12.93

Beckhithe, Norf., WHj to, 10.9.96

bedding, *see* linen

beef, bought by MH and MA at Holt Fair, 25.11.93

beer, **103**, **177**, **332**, **408**:
porter: brewed by WHj, 21.4.94, 28.4.94, 24.4.95, 2.5.95, 15.4.96, 19.4.96, 1.5.97, 3.5.97
sales: WH and WHj win contract to supply Weybourne Camp, 1.6.95:
see also barrels; brewing; casks

Beeston Regis, Norf., **227**, **350**, marriage of Cremer Cremer, 25.3.94; WHj and James Moore dine with Mr Cremer, 6.8.94

Begnal, *see* Bignold, John

Bell's groats, WHj tries to have Mr Jackson's Newcastle friend to pay, 14.12.96

Benfield (Binfield), Mr, musician; to tea, 15.4.95; tunes Hs' piano, with Mr Sheldrake to supper, 10.6.97

Berry, Nathaniel, innkeeper of Maid's Head, N. Walsham, tied house; abandons Maid's Head, 26.10.93

Bible, *see* sermons

Bidden, John, Saxlingham farmer; buys public house at Field Dalling, 25.10.93

Bignold (Begnal, Bignal), John (d.1837 aged 64), of Cromer; meets WH and John Smith over Robert Johnson's business affairs, 14.10.96; at Hs' over Robert Johnson, 23.10.96;

Bignold, John (*cont.*)
with Messrs Smith and Edwards dines at Hs' and settles Robert Johnson's affairs, with John Edwards hires Crown at Sheringham, 25.10.96
bilious complaint, *see* illness
Bill, *see* Parliament
Billing (Billins), Miss, Guestwick farmer; with Messrs Everitt and Keeler to dinner and supper at Hs' and to Weybourne Camp, 26.6.95
Billing/Billings (Billins), Mr jnr, of Rudham; sudden death, 24.12.96
Binfield, *see* Benfield, Mr
Bird, Mr, of Thornage; with Mr Williams confirms sale of public house at Aldborough to Hs, 24.10.93; with WH to Aldborough, 27.11.93; is paid 300 guineas for Black Boys at Aldborough by WH, 8.4.94
birds, *see* game; geese; shooting
birthday, WHj and MA to Mrs Flower's 21st at Sheringham, 4.12.93
Bishop of Norwich, *see* Manners Sutton, Dr
Black Boys, *see* Aldborough; Holt, public houses
Blakeney (Blakeny, Blakney), Norf., **8**, **72**, **225**, **382**, WH and James Moore dine at Henry Chaplin's, 22.10.93; death of Henry Smith, 24.5.94; WH and WHj buy coal at sale, 4.8.94; WHj and Robert Staff to, 18.3.95; WHj to, 22.5.95; WHj and Mr Henderson to, 10.9.95; WHj and Nathaniel Raven to sale at mill, 26.11.95; Mr Temple at Hs', 8.2.97; bankruptcy of Robert Farthing, 8.6.97; WHj views Mr Farthing's coal, 31.7.97; WH and WHj buy timber and laths at Mr Farthing's sale, 16.8.97
bleeding, as medical treatment; MH by Mr Bartell, 7.6.96, 14.8.97; plaster applied to MH's arm, 14.8.97
Bloom, Capt. [? John, ? James Gardner (b.1774), Wells merchants, shipbuilders and Hull traders]; postpones sailing when William Thackwray booked to sail from Wells to Hull, 1.1.97
Bodham, Norf., WHj to, 21.9.96
Bolton, John ? snr, ? jnr, to breakfast and dinner with Hs, with WHj to Holt, 18.11.93
bond, of £3 a year for 10 years to be paid by William Bulling to WH in part settlement of debt, 15.11.96
Bone/Boone, Hannah, dines with Hs, 26.3.94; departs, 17.9.94
books, by Drélincourt and Sherlock bought by Hs at Cley, 2.10.94; list of religious tracts, MH's endnotes
Holt book club at Feathers, **248**: WHj dines at, 15.11.96, 10.1.97; John Ellis with WHj from, 10.1.97
books (*cont.*)
Hs' ledgers:
banking book: taken by WHj to Holt, 15.12.94, 19.1.95
timber book: settled with Thomas Balls jnr and Bartells, 12.1.97:
see also diary
Boon (Bone), Thomas, ? of Gunthorpe; ringleader of Sharrington mob, arrested by soldiers on suspicion of seizing flour, 20.12.95
Booth, Mrs, of Norwich; with Temples to tea, 18.12.94
Booty, Mrs, **276**, **277**, Binham brewer; beer cart swept under Glaven bridge in floods, horse drowned, 4.6.96
'**Bountiful**' (Bountifull), *see* casks
bowling green, at Feathers, Holt, **219**; WHj to, 7.7.94, 21.7.94, 22.6.95, 27.8.95, 6.6.96, 13.6.96, 11.8.96, 15.8.96, 18.8.96, 15.5.97, 5.6.97; WHj to frolic, 29.10.95
Boyce, Thomas (d.1855 aged 89), Letheringsett labourer employed by Hs; at work in garden, 18.11.94, 24.3.95; shifts muck into garden, 11.2.95; opens drains in garden, 18–19.3.95; with MH to Briston meeting, 14.6.95, 5.7.95; with MH to Cley meeting, 20.12.95
boys (lads), employed by Hs:
boy 17, [unnamed], 1793–94: shearing wheat in Furze Closes, 14–15.8.94; departs, 10.10.94
boy 19, [unnamed], 1794–95: shifts muck into garden, 11.2.95; with MH to Briston meeting, 2.8.95; departs, 10.10.95
boy 20, [unnamed], 1795: with MH to Cley meeting, 8.11.95
boy 22, 'great boy' Nicholas Woodhouse, 1795–96: cleans out MH's bath, 15.9.96; departs, 10.10.96
boy 26, William [no surname], 1797–98: starts work, 12.10.97; with MH and MA to Briston meeting, 22.10.97
Brampton (Branton), Norf., Mrs Ives with sister to breakfast and dinner at Hs', 17.9.94; Meshack Ives to dinner with Hs, 19.5.96; WH and HR dine at, 3.4.97
brandy, *see* spirits
Branford, John Bell (d.1861 aged 98), Godwick farmer, later of Oxwick; dines with Hs, 29.9.95
Bransby, Mrs Elizabeth (d.1793 aged 70), of Letheringsett, formerly Mrs Lighten, burial noted in MH's register, endnotes
brewers, **408**, **411**, *see* Booty, Mrs; Day, John; Hawes, Siday; *for Letheringsett, see* brewing
brewery (brewing office), Hs', at Letheringsett, **116**, **303**, **393**, **397**, **402**; WH and WHj pay off mortgage of £1000 to Thomas Howard, 13.9.96: *see also* brewhouse; brewing

brewhouse, Hs', **3**, **11**, **37**, **49**, **77**, **88**, **94**, **95**, **96**, **201**, **359**, **393**, **397**, **402**, bricklayers turn arch in yard, 29.5.94; William Hase installs new pump, 8.9.95; five men at work, 9.9.95
new counting house, **3**, **391**: building work begins, 19.9.97; bricklayers and carpenter at work, 21.9.97
brewing, at Letheringsett, **332**:
WHj as brewer:
1793: 6.11.93, 13.11.93, 23.11.93, 9.12.93
1794: 6.1.94, 20.1.94, 17.2.94, 3.3.94, 24.3.94, 7.4.94, 24.5.94, 16.6.94, 23.6.94, 30.6.94, 8.7.94, 18.8.94, 15.9.94, 13.10.94, 17.10.94, 22.10.94, 10.11.94, 29.12.94
1795: 14.1.95, 16.3.95, 16.5.95, 11.6.95, 17.6.95, 23.6.95, 8.7.95, 16.7.95, 29.7.95, 2.9.95, 12.9.95, 9.12.95, 16.12.95, 24.12.95
1796: 1.2.96, 22.2.96, 8.3.96, 29.3.96, 9.4.96, 26.4.96, 9.5.96, 23.5.96, 30.5.96, 13.6.96, 28.6.96, 18.7.96, 30.8.96, 10.11.96, 2.12.96, 21.12.96
1797: 19.1.97, 27.1.97
porter: 21.4.94, 28.4.94, 24.4.95, 2.5.95, 15.4.96, 19.4.96, 1.5.97, 3.5.97
HR as brewer, **334**, **357**, **411**: 24.4.97
Hs' men: 1.9.97:
see also beer
brewing equipment, **93**, **94**, **95**, **109**, **118**, **184**, **191**, **247**, **272**, **338**, **339**, backs built by carpenters, 18.6.95, 24.6.95; carpenters build hop back, 24.6.95; backs installed by WH and WHj, 10.7.95: *see also* pump
bricklayers (workmen) [builders], working for Hs:
brewery: turning arch in yard, 29.5.94; in new counting house, 21.9.97
house: altering kitchen chimney, 16–17.10.94; in kitchen, 22.10.94; installing water cistern in kitchen, 2.12.94; in dark chamber, 23.3.96, 25.3.96, 29–30.3.96; in store room, 11.4.96, 14.4.96; at work, 15.4.96, 19.4.96; installing sash windows in yard front, 23.3.97
King's Head, Letheringsett: at demolition work and clearing rubbish, 3.3.94; building new stable, 5.3.94; at work, 12.3.94, 24.3.94
bricks, **163**, additional tax, 7.2.94
Briningham, Norf., **233**, WHj to, 24.6.96
Brinton, Norf., **79**, **233**, Mr Mason at Hs' to buy bark, 6.11.93; Mr Sharp to assembly at Holt and to Hs, 10.11.94
Brisley (Brisly), Norf., **200**, WH, MH and Mr and Mrs Nathaniel Raven to, 20.8.95; Hs and Ravens to tea at Thomas Fox's, 21.8.95; WH and Nathaniel Raven to, 27.5.96
Briston, Norf., WHj to Mr Foker over sale of mare at Norwich, 15.4.94; Mr Farthing's son falls from horse after fair, 27.5.94; WHj dines with Mr Butter, 20.8.94; WH meets John Groom's executor, 26.11.94; WHj collects money, 8.9.96; WH, MH and MA buy goods from Mr Woodcock, 26.6.97
Methodist meeting [? Calvinistic Methodist until mid-1795, then Wesleyan Methodist], **139**, **161**, **188**, **263**: Mr Hill preaches, 5.7.95
attended by MH with: WHj, 4.1.95; HR, 5.4.95, 12.4.95, 21.6.95, 23.8.95, 6.9.95; HR and Mrs Phillis Goggs, 10.5.95; Thomas Boyce, 14.6.95, 5.7.95; boy, 2.8.95, 22.10.97; John Thompson, 7.5.97, 11.6.97, 27.8.97, 24.9.97; MA, 9.7.97, 27.8.97, 22.10.97
Brooke, Norf., WHj to, 3.11.95
Broughton, James (d.1813), Letheringsett labourer; shifts muck into Hs' garden, 11.2.95
Brown/Browne, Ann, of Holt; starts work as Hs' upper servant, 10.10.94; departs, 31.1.95; hire and wages, maidservants' register, MH's endnotes
Browne (Brown), John (d.1799), Norwich dancing master; HR to children's balls for pupils at Holt, 3.10.95, 29.9.97
Buckle (Buckell), Ann (d.1860 aged 88), daughter of Thrower; marriage to Cremer Cremer, 25.3.94
Buckle, Thrower (d.1795 aged 62), of Cringleford; death, 6.2.95
builders, *see* bricklayers
Bull, *see* Holt, public houses
Bulling (Bullen, Bullin), William (d.1805 aged 51), **59**, **317**, **330**, farmer and former innkeeper of Bull, Holt; sells cows to WH, 13.10.94; WH settles business affair with, 14.11.96; WH arranges debt repayment, WH to have land on Holt Heath and 10-year bond, 15.11.96; WH and WHj inspect land bought from, 21.11.96: *see also* Holt Heath Farm
Bullock, Mrs Sarah (Mary) (d.1797), **218**, burial noted in MH's register, endnotes 26.10.97
Burcham, John, Holt auctioneer and surveyor; with Mr King jnr shows WH draft of Holt Enclosure Bill, 30.3.97
burial register, compiled by MH for Letheringsett 1793–97, endnotes
Burnham, Norf., Mrs Cobon brought from in 1796 for burial at Letheringsett, MH's register, endnotes
Burnham Market, Norf., **ix**, **264**, WHj to on tour of public houses, 9.10.94; WH and James Moore establish John Howard in public house, 5.1.95; WH and WHj to with James Moore to get security from John Howard for debts, 28.10.96; Thomas Baldwin breaks leg on return from, 9.12.96

Burnham Thorpe, Norf., death of Nicholas Howard, 24.12.96

Burrell, Mrs Elizabeth Anna Maria (d.1795), **222**, née Garrett, 1st wife of Revd John; with husband at Hs', 13.11.93, 22.10.93; visited by MH when ill, 6.1.94, 15.4.94, 24.1.95; ill, 14.1.95, 17.1.95; Dr Heath summoned, 17.1.95; no service at Letheringsett Church while lies dying, 15.11.95; death, 16.11.95; burial, 21.11.95

Burrell, Revd John (1761–1825), **11**, **222**, **262**, Rector of Letheringsett 1786–1825, Curate of Hunworth with Stody 1786– , Curate of Wiveton 1808–23, Curate of Langham; with Hs and Bartells to tea at King's Head, 14.7.94; Robert Garrett and bride to, 9.4.95; Norwich carter injured outside house, 21.5.95 and MH's register, endnotes; with WH to dinner at John Ellis's, 28.12.95; WHj and cousins at large tea party, 3.4.96; WHj to tea at Misses Leak's at, 9.4.96; has argument with Methodist, 10.4.96; Ann and Rose Raven and Johnsons to dinner, 17.4.96; gives supper party at King's Head in favour of Thomas Hare and Sir John Wodehouse in county election, 30.5.96; takes Charles Lamb in his whiskey to Norwich for election, 2.6.96; marriage to Mary Johnson, they depart for Fakenham, 2.8.96; quarrels with Mrs Dobson, 20.3.97; marriage in 1793 of his manservant and maidservant, MH's register, endnotes

at Hs': 13.11.93, 22.10.93, 24.2.94, 11.4.95, 28.10.95, 7.12.95, 6.10.96

Hs at: 22.10.93, 28.11.93, 8.5.94, 6.8.94, 27.8.94, 23.10.94, 29.12.94, 8.12.95, 9.12.95, 16.8.96, 23.5.97, 29.9.97

parish duties: beats bounds, 29.5.94; unable to take service as absent in Norwich, 25.9.96

house of industry, **294**, **295**: with WH to justices' sitting at Holt over building of, 29.8.95; with WH to Cley to buy fencing for garden, 28.12.95; with family and Hs to tea in, 9.8.96

preaches at Holt: 29.11.95

preaches at Letheringsett:

1794: 12.1.94, 2.2.94, 25.5.94, 17.8.94, 31.8.94, 9.11.94, 25.12.94

1795: 4.1.95, 19.4.95, 10.5.95, 5.7.95, 6.9.95, 8.11.95, 6.12.95, 13.12.95, 20.12.95

1796: 10.1.96, 17.1.96, 7.2.96, 14.2.96, 13.3.96, 3.4.96, 10.4.96, 17.4.96, 24.4.96, 8.5.96, 22.5.96, 5.6.96, 3.7.96, 17.7.96, 31.7.96, 31.7.96, 14.8.96, 21.8.96, 4.9.96, 18.9.96, 2.10.96, 16.10.96, 23.10.96, 30.10.96, 13.11.96, 4.12.96, 25.12.96

1797: 22.1.97, 12.2.97, 5.3.97, 19.3.97, 30.4.97, 7.5.97, 14.5.97, 21.5.97, 4.6.97,

Burrell, Revd John, preaches at Letheringsett, 1797 (*cont.*)

11.6.97, 18.6.97, 27.8.97, 10.9.97, 24.9.97, 1.10.97, 22.10.97

reads evening lectures in church: 22.12.93, 27.7.94, 17.8.94, 21.2.96, 20.3.96, 10.4.96, 8.5.96, 5.6.96

sermons, MH's criticisms, **364**: her letter, 15.11.96; pointed, 4.12.96; poor, 4.12.96, 22.1.97, 30.4.97, 7.5.97, 14.5.97, 21.5.97, 11.6.97; political, 19.3.97

tithe audits: 1.2.96; WH to dinner, 9.12.96

Burrell, Mrs Mary (d.1833 aged 66), **70**, **222**, **376**, Holt milliner, 2nd wife of Revd John, daughter of Revd William Tower Johnson; with Mrs Flower at Hs', 21.1.94; WHj and cousins to at Holt, 21.1.94, 11.11.95; Mary Raven to, 8.5.95; at large tea party at King's Head, Letheringsett, 4.9.95; MA to dinner, 16.11.95, 11.4.96; to tea at Hs', 26.11.95; MA and Mary Raven to tea, 15.12.95; with WHj and Ravens to tea at Mr Burrell's, 3.4.96; with Ravens to Sheringham, 10.4.96; with Ravens to dinner at Mr Burrell's, 17.4.96; marriage to Mr Burrell, they depart for Fakenham, 2.8.96; with husband and Sheldrakes to tea at Hs', 6.10.96; son born, 9.7.97

Burrell, Nathaniel (1762–1818), Holt surgeon; at tea party at King's Head, Letheringsett, 4.9.95

Butter, Mr, of Briston; WHj to dinner, 20.8.94

Bye (Bey, Buy), Robert, **226**, Hs' farm servant, brewer and drayman; beer cart breaks down at Warham, 25.1.94; harvesting wheat, 12.8.94, 20.8.94; delivering beer, 13.8.94, 20.8.94; dismissed, 24.12.95

C

camp, *see* Weybourne Camp

carpenters (workmen), working for Hs:

brewery: building new back, 18.6.95, 24.6.95; building hop back, 24.6.95; in counting house, 21.9.97

garden: putting up rails for fruit trees, 23.3.96

house: in chamber, 25.3.96, 29–30.3.96; in store room, 11.4.96, 14.4.96; at work, 15.4.96; installing sash windows in yard front, 23.3.97

King's Head, Letheringsett: 12.3.94, 24.3.94; raising stable roof, 15.3.94

carriages, *see* chaises; coaches

carts, **30**, WHj and MA break down on way to Beckham, 5.12.93; WH changes little mare for cart mare, 16.12.94; Mr and Mrs Gunton Thompson borrow Hs' and old mare, 13.5.95; Norwich driver injured by overturning cart,

carts (*cont.*)
21.5.95 and MH's register, endnotes; Revd Mr Wilcocks injured and cart damaged overturning in Hs' field, 17.1.97; WHj to Sheringham in new cart, 22.3.97; Misses Leak go home in Hs', 24.4.97
beer cart (brew cart) [dray cart], **47**: Robert Bye's breaks down at Warham, 25.1.94; Robert Bye and Thomas Baldwin carry wheat home in, 20.8.94; Mrs Booty's swept under Glaven bridge in floods, 4.6.96
little cart: Hs to Holt, 17.1.94, 9.7.94, 12.7.94; Hs from Holt in, 14.2.94, 5.4.94, 26.7.94; WH and WHj try colt in, 19.9.96; borrowed by Mr Wilcocks after accident, 17.1.97
tumbril, **308**: bought by WH at Thomas Forster's sale, 7.10.96
turnip cart: WHj and HR to Wells in, 31.1.94: *see also* wagons
casks, **21**, **29**, Hs' men empty great cask called 'Nectar de vie', 15.11.93; WHj empties small cask called 'Bountiful', 9.12.93: *see also* barrels
Catherine II (Empress of Russia) (1729–96), **327**, death reported, 22.12.96
cats, Hs', two attacked by Robert King's mad dog, 22.7.96
cattle, *see* cows
cavalry, *see* Army; Militia
cellaret (celeret), *see* furniture
chairs, *see* furniture
chaises:
Hs', **76**: WHj buys one-horse chaise in Norwich, 2.6.94, 6.6.94; WH and MH injured in accident at Swanton Novers when horse falls and shaft broken, 3.7.94
Hs' journeys: to Sheringham, 6.6.94; MH, MA and HR to Holt for confirmation, 4.7.94; WHj and MA to Holt, 21.7.94, 20.9.94, 19.1.95; WH and WHj to Southrepps, 31.7.94; Hs to Norwich, 12.8.94, 8.5.95, 7.10.95; Hs to Holt market, 25.10.94, 25.4.95; WH and MH to Cley, 2.10.94; WH and WHj to Sheringham, 4.2.95; WH, MH and MA to Holt to watch soldiers, 10.6.95; MH and MA follow regiment to Weybourne Camp, 11.6.95; Hs to Wells, 30.7.95, 12.9.95, 21.9.95; WHj collects family from Holt, 15.12.95, 23.12.95, 11.4.96; HR collects MA and Mary Raven from Holt, 16.12.95; MH, Mrs Youngman and John Thompson to Cley, 3.1.96; Hs collected from Bayfield, 19.1.96, 3.1.97; Hs collected from Holt, 23.1.96; HR drives MH, Clara Wymer and Miss Dewson to Thornage, 28.1.96; HR collects MA and Miss Custance from Fakenham, 22.2.96; MH and MA to Cley,

chaises, Hs', Hs' journeys (*cont.*)
26.3.96; John Thompson collects MH and MA from Holt, 14.5.96; WHj takes Mrs Bartell to Cromer, 2.8.96; WH and John Smith to Thursford, 29.8.96; WH and John Thompson to Wells, Syderstone and Barmer, 12.9.96; WHj and William Thackwray to Wells, 14.10.96; HR to Whissonsett to collect MA, 13.12.96; WHj and Thomas Balls jnr to Reepham, 27.3.97; WH and HR to Horstead and Coltishall, 3.4.97
horses: WHj buys mare from Charles Banyard, 20.9.94; borrowed by Hs from James Dyball on trial, 30.11.94; WH changes chaise mare for horse, 16.12.94; exchanged between Hs and Mr Webster, 24.2.95
postchaises: WH and Mr Henderson to Ryburgh and Whissonsett, 11.9.95
Feathers', Holt (Mrs Sheppard's; Banyard's): Hs to Southrepps, 25.3.94; Hs to Norwich, 6.9.94; Hs and Mrs Phillis Goggs to Southrepps and Cromer, 23.9.95; WH and Bartells to Norwich, 11.4.96; WH and Mr Bartell to Reepham, 20.1.97
King's Head's, Holt (Crafer's): Hs and John Smith to Norwich, 21.5.96; Hs to Aldborough, Southrepps and Cromer, 10.9.96; WH and James Moore to Burnham Market, 28.10.96
White Lion's, Holt (Howard's): WH and James Moore to Burnham Market, 5.1.95
whiskeys:
Mr Burrell's: WH and Mr Burrell to Cley, 28.12.95; Mr Burrell and Charles Lamb to Norwich, 2.6.96
Cook Flower's: WHj and MA from Sheringham, 5.12.93:
see also coaches
chambers, *see* house
chapel services, *see* meetings
Chaplin, Henry (d.1794), Blakeney and Cley merchant; WH and James Moore to dinner and reckon, 22.10.93; WH and WHj buy coal at Blakeney sale, 4.8.94
Chapman (Chaplin), William, innkeeper of Falgate, Hindringham, tied house; brings geese to Hs, 25.7.94
Chasteney (Chastney), Elizabeth, Hs' cook; starts work, 11.5.97; departs, 10.10.97; hire and wages, MH's maidservants' register, endnotes
cheese trolley (cheese wagon), bought by WH and WHj at Cley, 1.10.94
chemist, Mr [? Matthew] Wood of London at Hs', 17.6.95
Chequers (Checkquer), *see* Sharrington

childbirth, individual confinements; daughter born to Mrs Temple, 31.1.94; Mr Bartell attends Mrs Hall in labour, 24.2.94; Mrs Hall's child dies soon after birth, 12.3.94; woman gives birth at King's Head, Letheringsett, 28.1.96; daughter born to Mrs Sales, 20.2.97; son born to Mrs Mary Burrell, 9.7.97: *see also* churching

chimneys, *see* house

china, glass, additional duties on crown and plate glass, 7.2.94; MA buys mantelpiece ornaments at Holt sale, 9.4.94; WHj buys earthenware at sale of Weybourne Camp canteen, 12.1.97; MA and WHj buy small looking-glass at Cley sale, 10.7.97

Christmas (Chrismas), William, former Coltishall and Harleston attorney; goods sold at Holt, 1.12.94

churches, *see* Holt; Letheringsett; Whissonsett

churching, **400**, Mrs Savory at Letheringsett, 22.10.97

cistern, domestic, *see* house, kitchen

Clark, Mr, innkeeper of Black Boys, Holt, tied house; hires Black Boys from WH, 3.3.95

Clay, *see* Cley-next-the-Sea

clergy, *see individual Anglican clergy* Burrell, John; Collyer, Charles; Francis, Bransby; Francis, Robert Bransby; Crofts, Benjamin jnr; Crofts, John; Fisher, Thomas jnr; Horsfall, Samuel; Johnson, William Tower; Manners Sutton, Charles; Morgan, James; Norris, George; Thomas, William; Wesley, John; Wilcocks, William Wright; *for Nonconformists see* preachers; sermons

clerks:
- attorneys': George Wymer's from Reepham stays overnight at Hs', 4.9.94
- brewers' (and Hs' pupil): *see* Raven, Henry

Cley-next-the-Sea (Clay), Norf., **8**, **72**, **115**, **146**, **178**, Henry Smith of Blakeney killed in fall from horse on road to, 24.5.94; sudden death of John Mann, 17.8.94; John Mann heavily in debt, 23.8.94; Mrs Elizabeth Smith to tea at Hs', 26.8.94, 5.6.97, 5.8.97; WHj to with Mr Henderson, 10.9.95; WH and John Burrell buy timber for fencing, 28.12.95; Mrs E. Smith dines with Hs, 19.1.96; WH fails to meet Robert Johnson, 2.10.96; WHj to, 6.10.96; WHj meets Mr Jackson, 14.12.96; Miss Jones at Hs', 21.6.97
- bath house, **115**: WHj and James Moore visit new bath, 17.4.94; sold for 40 guineas, MH and WHj buy mirror at sale, 10.7.97
- fair: Hs' maidservant Sarah Turner to, 25.7.94; WH to, 29.7.96
- John Ellis: WHj and James Moore to dinner, 17.4.94; WH to dinner, 3.10.94; WH and Mr

Cley-next-the-Sea, John Ellis (*cont.*)
Burrell to dinner, 28.12.95; to dinner and supper at Hs', 14.5.96; at Hs' and to Walsingham, 16.12.96; to book club at Holt and supper at Hs', 10.1.97
- John Smith: Hs to dinner, 2.10.94; at Hs', 16.11.95; WH to, 3.3.96, 8.3.96, 6.10.96; WHj to, 6.3.96; MH and MA to tea, 26.3.96; stays overnight with Hs, 20.5.96; WH and MH to tea, 12.6.96; with wife to tea at Hs', 25.6.96; with WH to Thursford, 29.8.96, 29.3.97; with wife, Jacksons and Miss Jarvis dines with Hs at Cromer, 10.9.96; meets WH over Robert Johnson's affairs, 14.10.96; to Sheringham over Robert Johnson, 30.10.96; dines with Hs, 19.1.97; MH and WHj to tea, 10.7.97
- King's Head: WHj supervises repairs, 21.10.93
- Methodist meeting [Wesleyan], **136**, **218**, **289**: none held, 25.9.96
  - attended by MH with: boy, 8.11.95; Mrs Youngman, 29.11.95, 3.1.96, 10.1.96; Thomas Boyce, 20.12.95; HR, 25.12.95; John Thompson, 3.1.96, 10.1.96, 17.1.96, 24.1.96, 7.2.96, 14.2.96, 21.2.96, 20,3.96, 27.3.96. 3.4.96, 17.4.96, 24.4.96, 8.5.96, 22.5.96, 29.5.96, 5.6.96, 14.8.96, 21.8.96, 4.9.96, 18.9.96, 2.10.96, 16.10.96, 23.10.96, 30.10.96, 13.11.96, 22.1.97, 19.3.97, 26.3.97, 2.4.97, 16.4.97, 23.4.97, 30.4.97, 14.5.97, 21.5.97, 4.6.97, 6.8.97, 20.8.97, 10.9.97, 1.10.97; alone, 31.1.96, 10.4.96, 16.10.96, 12.2.97, 14.4.97, 18.6.97; Miss Custance, 6.3.96; MA, 9.3.96, 26.3.96; WH, 12.6.96, 17.7.96; William Thackwray, 25.12.96
  - preachers: Mr Eastaugh, 26.3.96; Mrs Proudfoot, 17.7.96; Mr Hill, 21.8.96, 18.9.96, 16.10.96; preacher fails to come, 20.8.97; Mr Leggatt, 1.10.97
- sales: WH and WHj buy tiles, 30.9.94; WH and WHj buy pistols, cheese trolley, tart presses and barrels, 1.10.94; WH, MH and WHj buy books, kitchen range and oven, 2.10.94; WH buys cellaret, 3.10.94: *see also* Cley, bath house

closes, *see* Furze Closes

cloth, in Whissonsett raffle MH wins muslin and WHj wins dress fabric, 11.6.94; muslin bought for Hannah Dagliss, maidservants' register, MH's endnotes

clothes, fitting for MH's gown at Miss Bacon's, 17.1.94; Mrs Sheldrake stays at Hs' to alter and repair MH's gowns, 14.2.95: *see also* cloth; ironing; washing

clubs:
- Holt:

clubs, Holt (*cont.*)
book club, Feathers, **248**: WHj to dinner, 15.11.96; WHj and John Ellis to dinner, 10.1.97
purse club, King's Head: WH to, 28.7.94
Letheringsett, King's Head: WH to for first time, 16.12.94; WHj to, 16.12.94; WH to, 23.12.94, 20.1.95
purse club: met by WH at King's Head, Holt, 21.1.94:
see also bowling green
coaches, **110**, hearse and mourning coaches in Mrs Jodrell's funeral procession, 15.9.94; Wells–Norwich stage-coach service begins, 8.12.94: *see also* chaises
coal, **382**, **383**, bought by WH and WHj at Henry Chaplin's sale at Blakeney, 4.8.94; land at Lower Sheringham for coal yard sold to Benjamin Barcham by WH and WHj, 4.2.95; WHj views Robert Farthing's coal at Blakeney, 31.7.97
Cobon (Coben), Mrs Alice (d.1796), of Burnham; brought for burial at Letheringsett, MH's register, endnotes
Cobon (Coben), James (d.1840 aged 84), **113**, **127**, **197**, **211**, **238**, **341**, of Letheringsett Hall Farm [then known as Letheringsett Hall], from 1801 of Letheringsett farm later known as Piggotts; WH, MH and MA walk in his hills, 16.2.97; is promised Thomas Press's farm at Letheringsett, 3.4.97
Coe, William (d.1804 aged 78), **361**, Field Dalling farmer; lets Jolly Farmers to WH and WHj, 9.5.97; meets WHj at Holt about public house, 2.8.97
Coe, William, of Gt Yarmouth; hires Feathers, Holt, from Mrs Sheppard, 9.11.93
Coke, Thomas William (1754–1842), **283**, JP, MP, 1st Earl of Leicester of the 2nd creation 1837, of Holkham Hall; Feathers and King's Head at Holt open for his supporters in county election, 31.5.96; WH and WHj to supporters' supper at King's Head, Letheringsett, 1.6.96; returned to Parliament unopposed, 3.6.96
colds, *see* illness
Collector of Excise, *see* excise
Collyer (Collier, Colyer), Charles (d.1830 aged 75), **234**, JP, [Revd Charles 1796], of Gunthorpe Hall, Rector of Gunthorpe with Bale 1798–1830, Rector of Thornage with Brinton 1803–26, Rector of Cley 1828–30; buys cottage from WH and WHj for £100, 15.10.94; WHj loads timber sold by, 18.11.95; WHj to, 3.3.96
Collyer (Colyer), Master, Holt schoolboy, [?son of Revd Charles]; with Master Shearing to tea at Hs', 1.6.97
Coltishall, Norf., **124**, **190**, **251**, **272**, **352**, **354**, WH and HR to supper with Siday Hawes, 3.4.97; William Lamb to, 4.4.97
colts, *see* horses
commons, *see* enclosure
Communion, *see* Letheringsett Church, Sacraments
confirmation, MA and HR at Holt by Bishop of Norwich, 4.7.94
Cook, Mr, of London; with Henry Goggs to dinner with Hs and to seaside, 14.8.97
Cook/Cooke, William (d.1826), Thornage miller; WHj with Mr Henderson to, 9.9.95
cooks, *see* baking; Chasteney, Elizabeth
Cooper, Mr, **88**, of The Lawn, Holt, farmer; WH and MH fail to buy hay from, 9.7.94
copyhold, *see* manor court
corn, none carried in rain, 27.8.94: *see also* barley; mills; wheat
cottage, at Gunthorpe, sold by WH and WHj to Mr Collyer, 15.10.94
counting houses, Hs', *see* brewhouse; house
courts, *see* assizes; justices; manor court; sessions
cows, **166**:
calving: spotted cow and red cow, 28.3.94; red cow, 15.2.97; lame cow, 20.3.97
purchase and sale: WH buys two from William Bulling, 13.10.94; WH sells two heifers and buys cow at Holt Fair, 27.4.95; WH buys cow at Thomas Forster's sale, 7.10.96
Cozens, John (1769–1841), **285**, of Norwich and Sprowston, grocer; with wife dines at Toftrees, 20.7.97
Cozens, Mrs Mary (d.1842 aged 75), **285**, née Hawkins, wife of John; with Nathaniel Raven and Mary Raven departs from Hs, 30.6.96; with MH, Mrs Nathaniel Raven and Mary Raven to tea at Henry Goggs's, 18.7.97; with husband dines at Toftrees, 20.7.97
Crafer (Craford), Henry, **59**, **335**, innkeeper of King's Head, Holt; business stopped, WH consults James Moore over, 9.11.96; absent for signing of deed of trust for creditors, 10.11.96; WH to stop creditors signing discharge certificate, 4.5.97
postchaise hired by Hs, *see* chaises, postchaises: *see also* Holt, public houses, King's Head
Cremer (Creamer), Cremer (1768–1808), **350**, of Beeston Hall, Beeston Regis; marriage to Ann Buckle, 25.3.94; WHj and James Moore to dinner, 6.8.94
cricket, **379**, WH with Nathaniel Raven snr and jnr and Thomas Fox to county match at Swaffham, 18.7.97
Cringleford, Norf., marriage of Ann Buckle to Cremer Cremer, 25.3.94

Crofts, Revd Benjamin jnr (*c.*1755–95), Curate of Gressenhall 1777–95, Curate of E. Bradenham 1784, Curate of Themelthorpe 1784, Curate of Twyford 1784, Curate of Whissonsett 1792–95, Curate of Horningtoft 1793–95, Curate of Billingford 1794, Curate of Brisley 1794; killed by fall from horse, 18.2.95

Crofts, Revd John (d.1828 aged 80), of Fakenham, Curate of Hitcham, Suff. 1771, Curate of Mileham 1772, Curate of Brisley 1777, Curate of Fakenham 1777–1810, Vicar of E. Bradenham 1782–97, Curate of Shereford 1784, Rector of Stratton Strawless 1784–1828, Rector of Whissonsett 1797–1828; with wife stays overnight at Hs', 23.8.95; WH, MH and Mr and Mrs Nathaniel Raven to dinner, 2.9.95

Crofts, Mrs Susanna (1765–1845), née Oxenborow, 2nd wife of Revd John; with husband stays overnight at Hs', 23.8.95

Cromer, Norf., **158**, **271**, **386**, WHj to, 14.7.94, 31.7.94, 28.10.94, 3.8.95; WH to, 31.7.94, 28.10.94; WHj and MA with Davys to, 4.9.94; WH and WHj to justices' sitting and dinner, 19.9.94; Hs and Mrs Phillis Goggs to dinner, 23.9.95; WHj and James Moore to, 13.5.96; Hs to dinner with Smiths, Jacksons and Miss Jarvis, 10.9.96; WHj prevented by rheumatism from going to, 23.12.96; HR, Charles Banyard and party to, 20.8.97

Edmund Bartell jnr, **304**: WHj and Mrs Bartell snr house-hunting for, 2.8.96; Hs to dinner and walk to lighthouse, 16.9.96; WHj with Thomas Balls jnr to tea, 13.4.97; WHj and MA to dinner, 5.9.97

Crown, *see* Fakenham, public houses; Sheringham; Southrepps

Cubitt (Cubit), Mr, in presence of WHj and James Moore takes possession of Sheringham Crown after Robert Johnson's flight, 30.9.96

Custance, Frances (b.1771), of Fakenham, daughter of William; dines with Hs, with WHj and MA to Thomas Forster's, 7.2.94; collected with MA from Fakenham by HR, 22.2.96; with WHj and MA to tea at Mr Davy's, 5.3.96; with MH to Cley meeting, 6.3.96; departs from Hs to stay at Mr Baker's, 7.3.96

Custance, Mrs Martha (d.1857 aged 88), née Holman, wife of William jnr; with mother-in-law and Miss Baker to tea, 7.2.97; with mother-in-law and Miss Baker to dinner, 15.2.97

Custance, Mrs Phillis (1737–1812), née Myles, wife of William, MH's cousin; with sister Mrs Hannah Raven to Mr Baker, 11.7.94; with Bakers to tea, 20.10.95; with daughter-in-law and Miss Baker to tea, 7.2.97; with daughter-in-law and Miss Baker to dinner, 15.2.97

Custance, William (d.1816 aged 77), Fakenham joiner and cabinetmaker; bankrupt, 26.7.94, 9.8.94; stock sale of new furniture at Fakenham, 6.10.94; WH, MH and HR to, 9.1.96; MH and WHj to dinner, 20.4.97

cutlery, Hs buy silver tablespoons, saltspoons and cellars at Holt, 10.1.95

D

Dagliss (Daglass), Hannah (?b.1770), **406**, Hs' maidservant 1793–94, 1795–97, 1799–1801, dismissed for leaving back door open for chimney sweep, 2.5.97; hire and wages, maidservants' register, MH's endnotes

Dalling, *see* Field Dalling

dancing, *see* assemblies; balls

Darby (Derby), John, Edgefield farmer; sells hay to WH and WHj, 31.7.95, 1.7.96

Davy, Ann, daughter of John, marriage in London, 6.1.94

Davy, Elizabeth, *see* Robinson, Mrs

Davy, Mrs Elizabeth (d.1798), 1st wife of John jnr; with family to tea, 6.7.95, 21.9.95

Davy, John (d.1805 aged 69/70), Holt draper and grocer; WHj and MA to Cromer with family, 4.9.94; reckons with Hs, 18.11.94, 5.7.96; with son John dines at Hs' while out shooting, 23.9.95

at Hs': 22.10.93, 5.9.94, 18.11.94, 6.7.95, 5.7.96, 30.9.96

Hs at: 17.1.94, 5.4.94, 15.5.94, 26.7.94, 31.8.94, 16.10.94, 27.4.95, 13.6.95, 16.12.95, 5.3.96, 1.10.96, 24.12.96, 3.2.97, 8.2.97, 16.2.97, 21.5.97, 13.7.97

Davy, John jnr, London linen draper; marriage, 21.6.95; with family to tea, 6.7.95, 21.9.95; with father dines at Hs' while out shooting, 23.9.95; stays at father's, 3.2.97

Davy, Joseph, son of John; departs for London, 5.4.94; very ill, 23.12.94; with family to tea, 6.7.95

Davy, Mary (d.1820 aged 43), of Holt, daughter of John; with family to tea, 22.10.93, 6.7.95, 21.9.95, 17.12.95, 10.3.97: *see also* Davy, Misses

Davy, Mrs Mary (d.1820 aged 80), née Starling, 2nd wife of John; with family to tea, 22.10.93, 5.9.94, 6.7.95, 21.9.95

Davy, Matthew (Matt), of London, son of John; with family to tea, 22.10.93; visits father, 31.8.94

Davy, Misses, of Holt, unnamed daughters of John; to tea, 27.6.97, 29.8.97: *see also* Davy, Mary; Davy, Susanna

Davy, Susanna (Susan) (d.1859 aged 81), of Holt, daughter of John; with sister to tea, 17.12.95, 10.3.97: *see also* Davy, Misses

Dawling, *see* Field Dalling
Day, John (d.1794), **167**, **170**, **171**, owner of St Martin-at-Oak Brewery, Norwich; public houses for sale at Stibbard and Guist visited by WH and WHj, 7.5.95
deals, *see* wood
death register, compiled by MH for Letheringsett 1793–97, endnotes
debt, **58**, **158**, **317**, **335**, **343**, John Mann dies heavily indebted, 23.8.94; WH and MH meet Mr Everitt at Wells over money owed to WH, 30.7.95; Mr Cubitt takes possession of Crown, Sheringham after Robert Johnson's flight, 30.9.96; WH, WHj and James Moore to Burnham Market to get security from John Howard, 28.10.96; WH consults James Moore over stopping of Henry Crafer's business, 9.11.96; Mr Crafer absent for signing of deed of trust for creditors, 10.11.96; William Bulling agrees repayment of debt to WH in form of land at Holt and 10-year bond, 15.11.96; WH to stop Henry Crafer's creditors signing discharge certificate, 4.5.97; Richard Temple borrows £120 from Hs, 18.9.97; Joseph Erratt forced to stop business, 30.9.97: *see also* bankruptcy; mortgages; sales; valuations
Deighton (Ramm), Mrs Susannah (1768–97), of Letheringsett, daughter of John; burial noted in MH's register, endnotes
Derby, John, *see* Darby
Dew, James, of the Bushel, Norwich; noted by MH, endnotes
Dewson, Miss, with MH, Mr and Clara Wymer to supper at Thomas Temple's, 28.1.96; with Charlotte Bartell and Clara Wymer dines at Hs', 12.2.96
diary, MH's, **21**, **52**, **110**, **160**, **177**, **232**, **262**, **289**, **298**, **357**, **388**, **406**, entries by others:
MA, **388**: 11–13.12.94, 1.6.96, 24–25.8.97
WH: 16.8.93, 24.1.94
Dissent/Nonconformity, *see* meetings *under* Briston; Cley-next-the-Sea; Fakenham; Hunworth; Letheringsett; Sharrington; *also* preachers; sermons
Ditchell, Anthony, of Kelling; WH and MH to his sale, 5.10.97
doctors, surgeons, Ann Ives dies on way to calling on, 17.5.96: *see also* Bartell, Edmund; Bartell, Edmund jnr; Heath, John
Dobson, Abraham (1753–1807), Holt blacksmith; auction of furniture, 2.10.97
Dobson, Mrs, wife of William; Mr Burrell quarrels with, 20.3.97; to tea at Hs', 29.3.97
Dobson, William (1741–1820), **54**, **61**, **80**, innkeeper of King's Head, Letheringsett, tied house; takes over from Richard Mayes, 26.3.94; WH and WHj dine at his housewarming, 18.6.94; WH, MH and MA meet Burrells and Bartells over tea, 14.7.94; Samuel Sanderson and Robert Johnson stay overnight, 10.3.95; driver dies from injuries after cart accident, 22.5.95; Hs to tea party, 4.9.95, 18.8.97; Mrs Smith brings Mrs Thurgar to, 19.1.96; woman gives birth at, 28.1.96; his dog bitten by Robert King's mad dog, 22.7.96; workmen finishing Letheringsett workhouse given supper at, 9.8.96; Hs expect large tea party but meet only Mrs Forster, 19.8.96; cleans MH's bath, 15.9.96; meeting over paying substitutes for Supplementary Militia, 12.12.96
club: WH to, 16.12.94, 23.12.94, 20.1.95; WHj to, 16.12.94
election suppers: given by Mr Burrell for supporters of Thomas Hare and Sir John Wodehouse in county election, 30.5.96; given for supporters of T.W. Coke, 1.6.96
Hs' harvest suppers: 6.9.94, 17.9.96
town meetings: WH and WHj to supper, 21.4.94; WH to, 7.4.95, 28.12.95; WH to supper, 29.3.96, 18.4.97:
see also Letheringsett, King's Head
dogs, Robert King's mad dog bites Ann Loades, bites William Dobson's dog and worries cats, is killed in Letheringsett, 22.7.96; Ann Loades taken ill after bite, 30.8.96
Donne, Mrs, *see* Dunn
drains, in Hs' garden, **337**; opened by Thomas Boyce, 18.3.95; underdrain dug by Thomas Boyce, 20.3.95
drapers, marriage of Edward Robinson, London linen draper, to Elizabeth Davy, 28.10.94: *see also* Davy, John; Davy, John jnr; Fox, Thomas; Raven, Nathaniel; Sales, Charles
drays, *see* carts, beer cart
Drélincourt (Drelingcourt), Charles (1595–1669), French Protestant divine; book on death bought by Hs at Cley sale, 2.10.94
dressmakers, *see* clothes
drugs, *see* Bartell, Edmund, medical practice
drunkenness, Revd Mr Wilcocks injured in overturning cart, 17.1.97
Dunn [? Donne], Mrs, death of mother, 25.12.93 and noted in MH's register, endnotes
duties, *see* taxes
Dyball (Dybal), James, innkeeper of Three Pigs, Edgefield; lends horse on trial to Hs, 30.11.94

earthenware, *see* china
earthquake, small shocks felt at Holt and Fakenham, 18.11.95

Eastaugh (Easto), Samuel, **153**, of Hempton, former preacher at Fakenham [Calvinistic] Methodist Chapel; Wesleyan Methodist local preacher by 1795; preaches at Cley meeting, 26.3.96

East Runton, Norf., **6**, **350**, Robert Hill to dinner, 17.10.94; WHj to, 10.9.96

eclipse, total lunar, 14.2.94

Edgefield, Norf., WH and WHj inspect hay, 18.6.94, 15.7.96; Hs accept chaise horse on trial from James Dyball, 30.11.94; WH and WHj buy hay from Mr Darby and to tea with Mr Minns, 31.7.95; Miss Gay to tea with Hs, 10.3.97

Edwards, John, innkeeper of Crown, Sheringham, tied house; with Messrs Smith and Bignold to dinner, settles Robert Johnson's affairs and hires Crown, 25.10.96; installed by WH and WHj, 31.10.96: *see also* Sheringham, Crown

elections, parliamentary:
- 1794 city by-election: precipitated by William Windham's appointment as Secretary for [Secretary at] War, 11.7.94; Windham defeats James Mingay, 12.7.94
- 1796 general election: Thomas Hare put up as candidate for county, Mr Burrell gives supper at King's Head, Letheringsett, for supporters of Hare and Sir John Wodehouse, 30.5.96; Feathers and King's Head at Holt open for T.W. Coke's supporters, Mr Hare withdraws from contest, 31.5.96; Mr Burrell with Charles Lamb to Norwich, WHj with Charles Kendle, Thomas Youngman and John Jex to Norwich, 2.6.96

Ellis, John (d.1836 aged 67), Cley merchant; WHj and James Moore to dinner, 17.4.94; WH to dinner, 3.10.94; WH and Mr Burrell to dinner, 28.12.95; to supper with Hs, 10.3.96, 16.12.96, 10.1.97; stays overnight with Hs, 10.3.96; with WHj to Thetford Assizes, 11.3.96; to dinner and supper, 14.5.96; to Holt Book Club, 10.1.97

elopement, *see* marriages

Empress of Russia, death at St Petersburg reported, 22.12.96

enclosure, **59**, **175**, **295**, **330**, John Burcham and Mr King jnr of Holt show WH draft of parliamentary Bill for enclosing Holt's heaths and commons, 30.3.97

England, Mrs, of Gunthorpe; with Mrs Pleasance to dinner, 5.12.96

entertainments, *see* assemblies; balls; bowling green; clubs; cricket; feasts; frolics; house-warming; music; plays; raffle; shooting

Erratt (Erret, Erritt), Joseph, **248**, Holt printer, bookseller, stationer, bookbinder, perfumer and ironmonger; WHj to dinner, 17.6.96; HR to supper, 3.7.97; forced to stop business, stays overnight with Hs, 30.9.97: *see also* clubs, Holt, book club

Everitt (Everett), Nicholas, **58**, **210**, innkeeper of Jolly Sailor, Wells, tied house; with Mr Horsfall to tea, 7.4.94; visited by WH and MH over money owed to WH, 30.7.95; WH orders arrest, 21.9.95; his mortgage paid off by Mr Wordingham, 3.1.97

Everitt (Everett), Robert, Guestwick farmer; with Messrs Keeler, Jarvis and Nobbs reckons for barley and to supper, 23.6.94; with Mr Keeler to dinner, 25.11.94; with Mr Keeler and Miss Billing to dinner and supper and to Weybourne Camp, 26.6.95; with Messrs Keeler and Ladle to supper and reckons with Hs, 27.6.96

excise, **29**, **191**, **270**, list of new levels of duty taken from newspaper, 7.2.94; WH dines with Collector, 20.4.96: *see also* Sheldrake, John; Todhunter, William; Tooby, Edward Cox

executor, WH meets John Groom's at Briston, 26.11.94

eyes, *see* illness

fairs:
- Briston: Robert Farthing's son falls from horse returning from, 27.5.94
- Cley: Hs' maidservant Sarah Turner to, 25.7.94; WH to, 29.7.96
- Hempton Green: HR to, 6.6.97
- Holt: WH, WHj, HR and Mary Raven to, 25.11.94; Hs and Nathaniel Raven jnr to, 27.4.95; WH, WHj, MA, Henry Goggs, Rose and Ann Raven to, 25.4.96
  - beef fair: MH and MA buy beef, 25.11.93
  - cattle fair: WH sells two heifers and buys cow, 27.4.94
  - horse fair: WH and WHj to, 25.11.93, 25.11.94
- North Walsham, **269**: Mr and Mrs Gunton Thompson to, 13.5.95
- Norwich [Tombland]: Mr Foker to, hoping to sell WHj's mare, 15.4.94

Fakenham, Norf., **140**, **173**, Robert Raven and HR to, 2.2.94; Nathaniel Raven to Hs from, 6.11.94; Dr Heath summoned to Mrs Burrell, 17.1.95; Revd John and Mrs Crofts at Hs', 23.8.95; WH, MH and Mr and Mrs Nathaniel Raven dine at Mr Crofts', 2.9.95; Mrs Phillis Custance at Hs', 20.10.95, 7.2.97, 15.2.97; WH, MH and HR to William Custance, 9.1.96; WHj to assembly, 26.1.96; WHj to sale of Mr

Fakenham (*cont.*)
Green's mill, 15.2.96; HR collects MA and Miss Custance, 22.2.96; Mr Burrell and Mary Johnson to after marriage, 2.8.96; WHj to, 12.9.96; MH and WHj dine at William Custance's, WHj consults Dr Heath, 20.4.97
William Custance's cabinetmaking business: stopped, 26.7.94; bankrupted, 9.8.94; stock sale of new furniture, 6.10.94: *see also* Custance, William
market: WH, MH and Mr and Mrs Nathaniel Raven to, 21.5.95; WH and Nathaniel Raven to, 20.8.95
Methodist meeting, **153**: MH and Henry Goggs to chapel, 22.2.95: *see also* Eastaugh, Samuel
public houses: Hs and Ravens to tea at Crown, 21.5.95: *see also* Gathercole, John
farms, **231**, **232**, **233**, **234**, **238**, WH and Nathaniel Raven find Whissonsett Hall farm in poor condition, 20.5.95; farmers with soldiers and justices escort flour, 21.12.95; WHj dines with farmers and justices at Holt when witnesses give evidence on riot, 22.12.95; Hs and Mr and Mrs Nathaniel Raven view site of John Claxton Savory's new farmhouse, 23.2.97; Thomas Press's farm at Letheringsett to be sold to James Cobon, 3.4.97; WH and Nathaniel Raven to Mr Savory's farmhouse, 29.9.97: *see also* barley; barns; Cobon, James; corn; cows; fields; harvests; hay; Forster, Thomas; Holt Heath Farm; meadows; Packsfield Farm; wheat; workforce
farm servants, *see* workforce
Farthing, Robert (d.1806 aged 65), Blakeney coal and cinder merchant; son falls from horse, 27.5.94; bankrupt, 8.6.97; coal viewed by WHj, 31.7.97; WH and WHj buy timber and laths at sale, 16.8.97
fasts, public, by royal proclamation in support of British troops in wartime; services at Letheringsett, 28.2.94, 25.2.95, 9.3.96, 8.3.97; MH and MA to Cley meeting, 9.3.96
Fawcett (Faucit, Fauset), Mr [? Simon], of Scotton, Yorks; at Hs', 23.8.95; to dinner, 27.8.95
feasts, at Holt; WH to venison feast at King's Head, 30.7.94; WHj to Free Grammar School feast at Feathers, 18.12.94; Thomas Forster to turtle feast, 25.9.97: *see also* audits; frolics
Feathers, *see* Holt, public houses
fences, WH and Mr Burrell buy timber at Cley for fencing house of industry garden, 28.12.95
Field Dalling (Dalling, Dawling), Norf., **361**, public house bought by Mr Bidden, 25.10.93; WH and WHj hire Jolly Farmers from Mr Coe, 9.5.97; WHj and Mr Coe meet at Holt over public house, 2.8.97; WH and WHj to over public house, 13.10.97
field days, *see* Weybourne Camp
fields, Hs', **101**, *see* Furze Closes; meadows; Six Acres; *also* Holt Heath Farm
Fighting Cocks, *see* Wells-next-the-Sea
Fir Closes, *see* Furze Closes
fire, John Wade's windmill at Holt burns down, 8.5.94
fireplaces, WHj buys bath stove grate at sale of Weybourne Camp canteen, 12.1.97
Fisher, Mr, London hop-factor; at Hs', 9.11.94
Fisher, Mrs (Widow), of Holt; WHj to tea, 9.8.94, 20.9.94; MA to tea, 20.9.94; at tea party at King's Head, Letheringsett, 4.9.95, 18.8.97
Fisher, Revd Thomas jnr (1768–1806), of Holt, Curate of Linton, Cambs 1792, Officiating Minister at Holt 1794, Curate of Chesterford, Essex 1795, Rector of Girton, Cambs 1800–06; preaches at Holt, 3.8.94
fits, *see* illness
Flanders, *see* Netherlands
Flegg, John, Holt tailor and shopkeeper; MH and MA buy sheets at sale, 5.4.94
floods, *see* Glaven, River
flour (flower), **231**, **232**, **233**, **234**, five loads intercepted by poor at Sharrington, 17.12.95; stored by rioters to withhold it from justices, 18.12.95; guarded by soldiers against mob, 20.12.95; escorted beyond Sharrington by soldiers, justices and farmers, 21.12.95
meal [second-grade flour]: price 3*s* per stone, 21.7.95:
see also mills; wheat
Flower (Flowr), Cook (d.1842 aged 77), **10**, **227**, of Sheringham [Old] Hall; with wife at Hs', 22.10.93, 5.6.95; WHj and MA to wife's party, 4.12.93; lends WHj and MA his whiskey, 5.12.93; WHj to, 24.4.94, 22.10.95, 28.11.96, 22.3.97, 13.9.97; WH and WHj to, 19.9.94, 6.4.95; WHj and MA to ball, 5.1.95; WHj to dinner, 20.6.95, 31.10.95, 9.9.96, 21.9.96; with WHj to Weybourne Camp, 20.6.95; WHj and MA to tea, 27.7.95; with wife to dinner, 26.2.96; sells WHj six piglets, 21.9.96; WH and WHj to dinner, 1.10.96
Flower, Mrs Sarah Ditchell (1772–1819), **10**, née Sibbs, wife of Cook; with husband at Hs', 22.10.93, 5.6.95; WHj and MA to 21st-birthday party, 4.12.93; with Mary Johnson at Hs', 21.1.94; stays overnight with Hs after ball at Holt, 17.2.94; dines with Hs, prevented by snow from leaving, stays overnight, 24–26.12.94; at Hs', 29.7.95; to dinner, with MA to Holt, 21.11.95; with husband to dinner, stays overnight, 26.2.96

Flower, Samuel, of Sheringham; with Mr and Mrs Cook Flower to tea, 5.6.95; Hs to dinner, 10.8.96

fog, 17.10.93, 25.3.94, 25.11.94, 2.10.94, 16.2.95, 31.3.95, 1.4.95, 4.4.95, 9–11.6.95, 7–8.12.95, 30.10.96, 21.11.96, 1.1.97, 7–8.2.97, 11.2.97, 13.4.97, 25.9.97, 5.10.97

Foker, Mr, Brinton or Briston horse doctor; WHj takes mare Molly to for sale at Norwich Fair, 15.4.94

Forest Lane Head, Knaresborough, Yorks, William Thackwray to Hs, 26.9.96

Forster, Master, son of Thomas; with parents to Letheringsett Church and tea at Hs', 30.11.94

Forster, Mrs, née Buckle, wife of Thomas; at Hs', 12.1.94, 25.5.94, 18.6.94, 1.6.95; with family to Letheringsett Church, 28.2.94, 30.11.94, 25.2.95, 5.4.95; with Hs to Holt, 23.6.94, 26.8.94; to tea, 9.11.94, 30.11.94, 25.2.95, 24.4.95, 13.4.97, 1.7.96, 2.9.96, 28.9.96; death of brother Thrower Buckle, 6.2.95; with husband at tea party at King's Head, Letheringsett, 4.9.95; with Hs to tea at King's Head, to supper with Hs, 19.8.96

Forster, Thomas, **308**, of Bayfield Hall and Holt House, Leziate, near King's Lynn, farmer; Hs, Miss Symonds and Phillis Raven to tea, 16.8.93; WHj, MA and Miss Custance to tea, 7.2.94; with family to Letheringsett Church, 28.2.94, 30.11.94; Hs to tea, 23.4.94, 22.10.94, 13.5.95, 19.1.96, 7.10.96; WHj, MA and Miss Symonds to tea, Miss Symonds taken ill, 27.5.94; recovers from illness, 22.10.94; with family to tea, 24.4.95, 1.7.96, 2.9.96, 28.9.96; with wife at tea party at King's Head, Letheringsett, 4.9.95; WH and WHj fail to buy hay from, 27.6.96; to supper, 27.6.96; sells WH 30 acres of grass, 28.6.96; WH inspects hay bought from, 30.6.96; Hs and William Thackwray to supper, 27.9.96; WH and WHj to sale, 6.10.96; Hs to sale, WH buys cow, tumbril and roller, 7.10.96; moves from Bayfield to Holt House, 10.10.96; dines with Hs and takes MA to Holt House, 27.4.97; WHj collects MA, 9.5.97; to supper and stays overnight, 13.8.97; dines with Hs and takes Miss Richards to Holt House, 14.8.97; takes Miss Richards to Hs, to turtle feast at Holt, 25.9.97

Foulsham, Norf., WHj views public house, 3.1.94; WH and WHj to, 24.1.94

fowls, *see* geese

Fox, Thomas (1740–1826), **200**, Brisley grocer and draper; WH, MH and Mr and Mrs Nathaniel Raven to tea, 21.8.95; with WH and Nathaniel Raven snr and jnr to county cricket match at Swaffham, 18.7.97

France, **40**, **327**, vote on parliamentary amendment to end war with, 24.1.94; defeat of British troops with great losses in, 23.5.94; British victory at Tournai, 28.5.94

Francis, Revd Bransby (d.1829 aged 89), Curate of Lakenham 1763, Rector of Edgefield 1764–1829, Rector of Long Melford, Suff. 1819–29; preaches at Holt, 16.4.97

Francis, Revd Robert Bransby (d.1850 aged 82), son of Revd Bransby, Curate of Edgefield 1790, Curate of Holt *c.*1796–98, Curate of Briston 1813, Curate of Melton 1813, Vicar of Roughton 1814; preaches at Holt, 4.12.96

frolics:
bowling green: WHj to at Feathers, Holt, 29.10.95
harvest: Hs' men's at King's Head, Letheringsett, 6.9.94, 17.9.96:
see also audits; feasts

Frost, Mr [?Stephen], of Langham; WH to tea, 4.8.94

fruit, **259**, carpenters put up rails in garden for tying trees, 23.3.96

funerals, **105**, **110**, Mrs Elizabeth Jodrell's procession through Letheringsett, 15.9.94; WHj pallbearer at Thomas Johnson's at Holt, 25.10.94; WH and MH to Henry Goggs snr's at Whissonsett, 16.2.95; Hs hear funeral sermon at Letheringsett, 22.5.96; MH's Letheringsett burial register 1793–97, endnotes

Fur Closes, *see* Furze Closes

furniture, **248**, **257**, cellaret bought by WH at Cley sale, 3.10.94; William Custance's sale of new stock opens at Fakenham, 6.10.94; WHj buys mahogany chairs at sale of Weybourne Camp canteen, 12.1.97; Hs' valued by WH, 12–13.9.97; auction of Abraham Dobson's, 2.10.97

Furze Closes (Fir, Fur Closes), **43**, Saxlingham fields farmed by Hs; WH to, 12.4.97
harvesting: MH and WHj to shearers, 12–13.8.94; men shearing wheat, 12–15.8.94; WHj carries wheat and barley, 15.8.94; men mowing wheat, 16.8.94; men carrying barley, 5.9.95, 7.9.95
haymaking: 30.6.94; WH and MH inspect hay, 5.7.94:
see also Six Acres

game, *see* shooting; venison

games, *see* bowling green; cricket; entertainments

gardeners, *see* gardens, Hs', men at work

gardens:
Hs', **86**, **87**, **143**, **154**, **157**, **163**, **211**, **230**, **235**, **238**: vegetables cut by north wind, 19.6.95; WH well enough to walk in, 12.2.96
men at work, **52**, **92**: two soldiers, 15.3.94, 19.3.94; Thomas Atwood, 28.3.94, 21.4.94; James Skiffins, 31.7.94, 17.9.94; Thomas Boyce, 18.11.94, 24.3.95; Thomas Boyce, James Broughton and boy shift muck into, 11.2.95; Thomas Boyce working on drains, 18–19.3.95; carpenters put up rails to tie fruit trees, 23.3.96:
see also baths
houses of industry: WH and Mr Burrell buy timber for fencing Letheringsett's, 28.12.95; WHj and James Moore collect shrubs and plants from Gressenhall's, 6.4.96
Garrett (Garret), Robert, with bride to Mr Burrell, 9.4.95
Gathercole, John (d.1802), innkeeper of Bell, Fakenham, tied house; at Hs', 23.6.95
Gay, Miss, of Edgefield; with Misses Davy to tea, 10.3.97
geese, 22 brought by William Chapman to Hs, 25.7.94
George III, King (1738–1820), **327**, amendment to vote of thanks on speech to Parliament, 24.1.94: *see also* fasts
Girling, William, innkeeper of Crawfish/Lion, Thursford, tied house; WH and John Smith at to refute allegations made against WH, 29.3.97
Glandford (Glanford), Norf., **8**, **116**, Zebulon Rouse's flour intercepted by poor at Sharrington on way to Lynn from, 17.12.95
glass, *see* china
Glaven, River (the river), **8**, **11**, **62**, **65**, **66**, **74**, **77**, **112**, **113**, **116**, **143**, **144**, **146**, **149**, **157**, **197**, **238**, **276**, **277**, **280**, **329**, **372**, **373**; water high, 10.2.94, 6.11.95; Mrs Booty's beer cart swept under bridge in floods at Letheringsett, 4.6.96
Godwick, Norf., Mr Branford to dinner, 29.9.95; Mrs Mason dies, 23.3.97
Goggs, Henry (1731–95), Whissonsett farmer, MH's brother-in-law; MH and WHj stay overnight, 11.6.94; death, 13.2.95; burial, 16.2.95
Goggs, Henry jnr (1767–1827), **150**, **151**, **153**, Whissonsett farmer, MH's nephew; to Letheringsett, 13.12.93, 24.4.96; WH and MH to supper and stay overnight, 17.2.95, 19.5.95, 5.1.96, 24.5.96; with MH to Fakenham Chapel, 22.2.95; MH to dinner, 20.5.95; with servant and Hs to Weybourne Camp for field day, departs from Hs, 8.7.95; WH, MH and Mr and Mrs Nathaniel Raven to dinner and supper, 20.8.95; breakfasts with Hs and to Holt Quarter Sessions, 15.10.95; with WH to Holt Fair, departs, 25.4.96; WH and MH to, 13.3.97; MA looks after his mother during his absence in London, 30.5.97; MH, Mrs Nathaniel Raven, Mrs Cozens and Mary Raven to tea, 18.7.97; Hs and family to dinner, 20.7.97; with Mr Cook dines at Hs', with Hs to seaside, 14.8.97; tells MH by letter of his mother's illness, 30.8.97
Goggs, Mrs Phillis (1731–1806), née Raven, wife of Henry, MH's sister; MH and WHj to dinner, 11.6.94; WH and MH to dinner and supper and stay overnight, 15.2.95; WH and MH to husband's funeral, 16.2.95; with niece Mary to Hs, 5.5.95; with MH, Mary Raven and HR to Letheringsett Church and Briston meeting, 10.5.95; departs with Mary, 16.5.95; MH at, 18.8.95; WH and MH at, 3.9.95; taken by WH and Mr Henderson to Letheringsett, 11.9.95; with Hs to breakfast at Southrepps and dinner at Cromer, 23.9.95; with WH and MH to tea at Mrs Robert Raven's, 8.1.96; with Hs to Letheringsett Church, 31.7.96; departs, 5.8.96; very ill, 31.10.96, 2–3.11.96; visited by MH when ill, MH to dinner and supper and stays overnight, Mrs Nathaniel Raven to tea, 2.11.96; recovers, 6.11.96; MH and Mrs Nathaniel Raven to tea, 16.3.97; looked after by MA during son's absence, 30.5.97; too ill to visit Hs, 29–30.8.97
gout, *see* illness
gowns, *see* clothes
grass, WH buys 30 acres from Thomas Forster for £95, 28.6.96: *see also* hay; meadows
greasing grounds, at Horningtoft; WH and Nathaniel Raven to, 21.8.95
Great Hautbois (Hobbis), Norf., **353**, WH and HR stay overnight at White Horse, 3.4.97
Great Ryburgh, *see* Ryburgh
Great Snoring, *see* Snoring
Great Walsingham, *see* Walsingham
Great Yarmouth, Norf., **170**, **171**, Mrs Sheppard lets Feathers, Holt to William Coe of, 9.11.93
Green, Mr, of Knaresborough, Yorks; at Hs', 14.8.96
Green, William, Fakenham miller; WHj to sale at watermill, 15.2.96
Gressenhall (Gresenhall, Gresnal), Norf., **73**, **163**, **166**, **198**, **326**, **366**, WH and MH injured in chaise accident on way to, 3.7.94; death of Revd Benjamin Crofts jnr in fall from horse, 18.2.95; WH and John Thompson to, 5.6.95; WH and Nathaniel Raven to, 18.8.95, 16.3.97; WHj and James Moore collect shrubs and plants from house of industry garden, 6.4.96
Grey, Mr, of Southrepps; sells Crown Inn to WH for £600, 13.4.94

Groom, John (d.1794), of Horseshoes, Briston, tied house; WH meets his executor, 26.11.94
Guestwick (Guestick), Norf., WH, MH and MA dine at Mr Keeler's, 26.6.97
Guist, Norf., **167**, **170**, **171**, WH and WHj view John Day's public house for sale, 7.5.95
guns:
field, **184**, **185**: cannon fired at Weybourne Camp on field day, 26.6.95: *see also* Weybourne Camp
hand: pair of pistols bought by WH and WHj at Cley sale, 1.10.94:
see also shooting
Gunthorpe (Gunthorp), Norf., **27**, **233**, **322**, **323**, WH and WHj at to sell cottage to Mr Collyer, 15.10.94; WHj loads timber bought from Mr Collyer, 18.11.95; WHj to Mr Collyer, 3.3.96; WHj to, 12.9.96

H

Habeas Corpus, *see* Parliament
Hagon, Elizabeth Southgate (1775–1802), **183**, née Hagon, elopes to Scotland with Revd Mr Wilcocks, 20.6.95
hail, storms, 5.12.96
Hall, Mrs Elizabeth (Betty) (d.1818 aged 56), née Frary, wife of Thomas; attended in labour by Mr Bartell, 25.2.94; birth and death of child, 12.3.94
hall, *see* Cobon, James [Letheringsett Hall Farm/ Old Hall]; house [Rawlings/Letheringsett Hall]; Whissonsett, Hall
Hardy, Mary Ann (MA) (1773–1864), **257**, **284**, **287**, MH's daughter; cart breaks down on way to Beckham, 5.12.93; WH and WHj convert dark chamber into dressing room, 22.3.96; wallpapers her dressing room and bedroom, 23.5.96, 26–27.5.96; ill with bilious complaint, 2–3.7.96 walks with parents in James Cobon's hills, 16.2.97; with family tours fields at Bayfield, 23.2.97; goes shopping with parents at Briston, 26.6.97
church and meeting attendance:
Briston meeting, **188**: 9.7.97, 27.8.97, 22.10.97
Cley meeting: 9.3.96, 26.3.96
Holt Church: 21.6.95, 24.4.96, 16.4.97, 13.8.97; confirmed by Bishop of Norwich, 4.7.94
Letheringsett Church: on fast day, 28.2.94, 25.2.95; with family, 25.12.95, 3.4.96, 17.4.96, 2.10.96, 1.10.97; does not attend, 29.5.96
Letheringsett meeting: 6.4.96, 13.4.96, 11.6.96, 25.6.96
diary entries: *see* diary, MH's

Hardy, Mary Ann (*cont.*)
to Holt: 23.6.94, 21.7.94, 18.8.94, 26.8.94, 19.1.95, 14.2.95, 12.9.95, 21.11.95, 26.11.95, 14.5.96, 8.6.96, 31.12.96; Miss Alpe's, 23.11.93, 8.8.97; Mr Bartell's, 28.3.94, 4.7.94, 10.1.95, 8.6.95, 29.8.95, 2.4.96, 13.10.96, 8.7.97; with MH to John Flegg's sale, 5.4.94; Mr Davy's, 5.4.94, 15.5.94, 16.10.94, 27.4.95, 13.6.95, 16.12.95, 5.3.96, 8.2.97, 13.7.97; Mr Baker's, 26.4.94, 7.3.96, 25.6.96, 15.7.97, 16.9.97, 25.10.97; views ruins of John Wade's mill, 9.5.94; views Miss Leak's fashions, 15.5.94; Misses Leak's, 24.5.94, 14.1.97, 5.8.97; Mrs Fisher's, 20.9.94; buys china ornaments and silver at Mrs Jewell's sale, 9–10.1.95; party at Mrs Jennis's, 20.1.95; watches Artillery pass through, 8.6.95, 10.6.95; follows regiment to Weybourne Camp, 11.6.95; Mr Sheldrake's, 3.10.95, 26.4.96; Misses Johnson's, 16.11.95, 15.12.95, 11.4.96; views workhouse, 5.8.96; Revd Mr Johnson's, 23.2.97, 1.7.97; Holt Heath Farm, 19.5.97
balls and dances: with WHj and cousins, 20.1.94, 17.2.94
fair: 25.11.93, 27.4.95, 25.4.96
market: 23.11.93, 26.4.94, 24.5.94, 13.6.95, 25.6.96, 5.8.97
social activities: to Thomas Forster, 16.8.93, 7.2.94, 23.4.94, 27.5.94, 27.9.96, 7.10.96; to supper party at Thomas Temple's, 13.12.93; with WHj and party to Sheringham, 6.6.94; with large party at King's Head, Letheringsett, 14.7.94; to Mr Burrell, 6.8.94, 23.10.94, 23.5.97; with WHj and Davys to Cromer, 4.9.94; to ball at Cook Flower's, 5.1.95; watches troops at Weybourne Camp, 17.6.95, 26.6.95, 16.7.95, 27.7.95, 10.8.95, 12.8.95; to tea at Sheringham, 16.7.95, 19.6.97; to Cook Flower, 27.7.95, 10.8.96; to breakfast at Southrepps and dinner at Cromer, 23.9.95; to John Smith, 26.3.96; with family and John Smith to Norwich for day, 21.5.96; to tea in new Letheringsett house of industry, 9.8.96; to Bayfield, 11.8.96; visits Ann Loades in last illness, 31.8.96, 1–2.9.96; with large party to Aldborough and Southrepps and dinner at Cromer, 10.9.96; to Thomas Forster's sale, 7.10.96; to Mr Savory, 22.12.96, 3.1.97, 23.2.97, 25.2.97, 25.5.97; to dinner with Mr Keeler at Guestwick, 26.6.97; dines with Edmund Bartell jnr at Cromer, 5.9.97
visits: returns with WH from Norwich, 16.8.94; with parents to Norwich, breakfasts and dines at George Wymer's, to tea at Mr Herring's, 6.9.94; with WH to Norwich, 8–10.5.95, 7.10.95; returns with WH from

Hardy, Mary Ann, visits *(cont.)*
Whissonsett, 6.6.95; with Miss Custance collected from Fakenham by HR, 22.2.96; returns with WHj from Whissonsett, 19.5.96; with uncle Nathaniel and cousins to Whissonsett, 10.11.96; collected by HR from Whissonsett, 13–14.12.96; with Thomas Forster to Leziate, 27.4.97; collected by WHj from Leziate, 9.5.97; with WHj to Whissonsett to look after aunt Phillis, 30.5.97

Hardy, Mrs Mary (1733–1809), **136**, **195**, née Raven, the diarist, wife of William, 16.8.93 *and throughout*; *see also* diary, MH's

Hardy, William (Mr Hardy) (1732–1811), **vii**, **40**, **76**, **158**, **257**, **303**, Letheringsett farmer, maltster and brewer, MH's husband, 16.8.93 *and throughout*

Hardy, William jnr (William) (1770–1842), **82**, **113**, **188**, **197**, **332**, **363**, **372**, **374**, **391**, **404**, Letheringsett farmer, maltster and brewer, MH's son, 16.8.93 *and throughout*

Hare, Thomas, JP, of Stow Bardolph; stands as candidate in county election, supporters given supper by Mr Burrell at King's Head, Letheringsett, 30.5.96; withdraws, 31.5.96

harvests, **101**:
1794: MH and WHj to shearers in Furze Closes, 12–13.8.94; men shearing and mowing wheat in Furze Closes, 14–16.8.94; wheat and barley carried from Furze Closes, 14–15.8.94; men finish cutting wheat, 18.8.94; men mowing barley and carrying wheat, 20.8.94; rain prevents work, 27.8.94; all finished except for rakings, 28.8.94; Hs' harvest supper at King's Head, Letheringsett, 6.9.94
1795: men finish carrying barley from Furze Closes, 5.9.95
1796, **296**: fine weather, 9.9.96; ends, 16.9.96
1797: begins, 14.8.97; men carrying peas, 29.8.97; rain prevents work, 29.8.97, 31.8.97; men carrying barley, 5.9.95; men finish carrying barley from Holt Heath Farm, 8.9.97

Hase, William (1767–1841), Saxthorpe blacksmith, ironfounder, clockmaker and water pump engineer; installs new pump in brewhouse, 8.9.95

Hautbois, *see* Great Hautbois

Hawes, Siday (1748–1827), **352**, Coltishall farmer, maltster and brewer; WH and HR to supper, 3.4.97

hay:
making:
1794: cutting begins in Furze Closes, 30.6.94; viewed by MH and WHj in Furze Closes, 5.7.94

hay, making *(cont.)*
1795: ends, 25.7.95
1796: by WH and WHj, weather poor, 5.7.96; by Hs' men, 12.7.96; by WH, 15.7.96, 18.7.96; viewed by WHj at Edgefield, 15.7.96; stacking ends, 22.7.96
1797: by WH and WHj, 4.7.97; viewed by WH, 8.7.97; by WH, rain prevents work, 10.7.97; by Hs' men, 13.7.97
purchase: WH and WHj fail to buy after viewing hay at Edgefield, 18.6.94; Mr King's and Mr Cooper's at Holt viewed by WH and MH, they buy 53 cocks from Mr King for £21, WHj inspects hay, 9.7.94; viewed by WH and WHj at Thornage, 24.7.95; WH and WHj buy five loads for 18 guineas from Mr Darby at Edgefield, 31.7.95; WH and WHj fail to buy from Thomas Forster, 27.6.96; WH views hay bought from Mr Forster, 30.6.96; viewed by WH and WHj, WHj to Edgefield to see hay bought from Mr Darby, 1.7.96; WH and WHj fail to buy after viewing at Kelling, 15.7.97:
see also grass

headache, *see* illness

Heath, Dr John (d.1823 aged 59), **140**, of Fakenham; summoned to treat Mrs Burrell, 17.1.95; consulted over WHj's rheumatism, 20.4.97; with Mr Bartell calls on WHj, 2.5.97

Heath, William, Wesleyan Methodist itinerant preacher; preaches at Letheringsett meeting, 28.5.96

heather (ling), burning by WH and WHj at Holt Heath Farm, 1.3.97

heaths, *see* enclosure; Holt Heath; Holt Heath Farm; Salthouse; Stock Heath

Hempton Green Fair, *see* fairs

Henderson, Mr, Newcastle upon Tyne flour merchant; to dinner, 9–10.9.95; with WHj to William Cook at Thornage, 9.9.95; with WHj to Cley and Blakeney, 10.9.95; with WH to Ryburgh to John Wade, dines at Nathaniel Raven's, with WH and Mrs Goggs to Letheringsett, 11.9.95; with WH to Wells, 12.9.95

Herring, John (d.1810 aged 61), **107**, Norwich merchant and shawl manufacturer, Sheriff of Norwich 1786, Mayor of Norwich 1799; WH, MH and MA to tea, 6.9.94

Herring, John jnr, of Norwich; at Hs', 13.5.95, 15.8.96; with Forsters and William Herring jnr to tea at Hs', 1.7.96

Herring, Mrs [? d.1803 aged 78, mother of John], of Norwich; at tea party at Hs', 2.9.96

Herring, Mrs [? Rebecca (d.1827 aged 81), née Buckle, wife of John]; at Mr Forster's, 22.4.95; with Forsters to tea at Hs', 24.4.95; at tea party at Hs', 2.9.96

Herring, William (?d.1853), to dinner and supper with Hs, 28.2.94; with Forsters and John Herring jnr to tea at Hs', 1.7.96; at Hs', 15.8.96

Hill, Josiah (1773–1844), **139**, **188**, of Snoring, ? former Calvinistic Methodist preacher, from 1795 Wesleyan Methodist itinerant preacher; preaches at Briston meeting, 5.7.95; preaches at Cley meeting, 21.8.96, 18.9.96, 16.10.96

Hill, Robert, **6**, innkeeper of Fishing Boat, E. Runton; to dinner, 23.4.94, 17.10.94, 23.6.95

Hindolveston (Hildonveston), Norf., **12**, **13**, WH, MH and WHj measure timber and dine at, 24.10.93; bark bought by Mr Mason, 6.11.93; WHj to, 25.7.94; WHj collects money, 8.9.96

Hipkins, Mrs, sudden death, 23.12.94

Hobbis, *see* Great Hautbois

hogs, *see* pigs

Holt, Norf., **7**, **8**, **39**, **88**, **112**, **160**, WH dines with James Moore, 17.10.93; Mrs Flower and Mary Johnson to Hs from, 21.1.94; WHj and cousins to tea at Misses Johnson's, 21.1.94; James Moore meets Hs at Southrepps, 25.3.94; MA, Rose Raven and Miss Symonds to tea with Mrs Jennis, 23.5.94; Henry Smith killed by fall from horse on Cley road from, 24.5.94; Mrs Phillis Custance and Mrs Hannah Raven at Mr Baker's, 11.7.94; Hs to tea with Mrs Jennis, 13.9.94; WHj and Mary Ann to tea with Mrs Fisher, 20.9.94; Ann Brown starts work as Hs' upper servant, 10.10.94; WHj enquires after Joseph Davy, 23.12.94; WHj and MA to party at Mrs Jennis's, 20.1.95; WH to tea with Mr Bartell, 4.4.94, 19.12.95, 31.5.96; MA and Mary Raven visit Misses Johnson, 8.5.95; WHj's tooth extracted, 28.7.95; Mary Raven to stay with Hs from, 3.12.95; MA and Mary Raven to Mr Davy, 16.12.95; WH to dinner with Mr Vickery, 19.12.95; WHj and HR to Mr Bartell, 25.12.95; Hs to tea with Mr Sheldrake, 23.1.96; WHj draws off wine, 2.2.96; Miss Custance to stay with Mr Baker, 7.3.96; Ann Ives dies on road to, 17.5.96; WHj dines with Joseph Erratt, 17.6.96; Ann Loades bitten by Mr King's mad dog, 22.7.96; marriage of Mr Burrell and Mary Johnson, 2.8.96; WH dines with Mr Thomas, 14.1.97; Hs to tea with Misses Leak, 14.1.97, 1.7.97; WHj to Mr Davy, 3.2.97; daughter born to Mrs Sales, 20.2.97; Hs and Ravens to Revd Mr Johnson, 23.2.97, 1.7.97; WHj to James Moore, 8.3.97; WHj to Mr Bartell, 12.4.97; HR to supper with Joseph Erratt, 3.7.97; MA and Phillis Raven to, 8.8.97; Mrs Withers at tea party at Letheringsett, 18.8.97; WHj and MA to Mr Baker, 16.9.97, 25.10.97

Holt (*cont.*)

assemblies: *see* Holt, balls *below*

balls and dances: WHj to assembly, 21.10.93, 18.11.93, 24.4.94, 10.11.94, 8.12.94; WHj, MA, Robert, Ann and Mary Raven to, 20.1.94; WHj, MA and Nathaniel Raven jnr to, 17.2.94, 19.3.94; Mr Sharp to assembly, 10.11.94; ball given for officers from Weybourne Camp, 3.8.95; HR to John Browne's children's ball for pupils, 3.10.95, 29.9.96, 29.9.97; WHj to children's ball, 29.9.96

bowling green: *see* Holt, public houses, Feathers

business transacted by Hs: WH buys Crown Inn, Southrepps, 3.4.94; WH pays Mr Bird for Aldborough public house at James Moore's, 8.4.94; WH and MH view Mr King's and Mr Cooper's hay and buy from Mr King, 9.7.94; WHj buys mare from Charles Banyard, 20.9.94; WH pays John Summers for Southrepps public house, 11.10.94; WH buys two cows from William Bulling, 13.10.94; WHj with banking book to, 19.1.95; WH supervises valuation of John Howard's goods, 27.1.95; WH meets John Howard, 3.2.95; WH with Samuel Sanderson and Robert Johnson to, 16.3.95; WH settles Isaac Alsop's business affairs, 31.3.95; WH fails to hire horse, 6.10.95; WH consults James Moore over Henry Crafer's debts, 9.11.96; WH settles deed of trust for Henry Crafer's creditors, 10.11.96; WH settles business affairs with William Bulling, 14.11.96; WH arranges debt repayment and purchase of Holt Heath Farm from William Bulling, 15.11.96; Messrs Burcham and King show WH draft of parliamentary enclosure Bill, 30.3.97; MH and MA hire upper servant Elizabeth Williamson, 31.7.97; WHj meets Mr Coe over Field Dalling public house, 2.8.97; WHj collects money, 20.10.97

clubs: WH meets purse club at King's Head, 21.1.94; WHj dines at book club, 15.11.96

coaches and postchaises: *see* chaises; coaches

fair: *see* fairs

farms: *see* Holt Heath Farm

feasts: *see* Holt, public houses, *below*

Hs to:

1793: 17.10.93, 25.12.93

1794: 6.1.94, 12.1.94, 17.1.94, 17.1.94, 31.1.94, 28.2.94, 3.5.94, 24.5.94, 16.6.94, 23.6.94, 12.7.94, 21.7.94, 26.7.94, 28.7.94, 9.8.94, 18.8.94, 26.8.94, 25.10.94, 8.12.94

1795: 19.1.95, 27.1.95, 14.2.95, 7.4.95, 9.4.95, 9.6.95, 30.7.95, 12.9.95, 3.10.95, 11.11.95, 21.11.95, 26.11.95, 3.12.95, 25.12.95

Holt, Hs to (*cont.*)
1796: 5.3.96, 8.3.96, 10.3.96, 2.4.96, 11.4.96, 26.4.96, 14.5.96, 1.6.96, 30.6.96, 31.12.96
1797: 8.7.97, 13.7.97, 15.7.97, 30.9.97
heath: *see* Holt Heath
market: *see* markets; *also* Holt, Hs to *above*
military activity, **231**, **232**, **233**, **234**, **325**: WHj and MA watch Artillery pass through, 8.6.95; regiment fails to arrive, 9.6.95; Hs watch arrival of regiment, soldiers billeted overnight, 10.6.95; Hs follow regiment to Weybourne Camp, 11.6.95; soldiers sent to quell riot at Wells, 15–16.12.95; justices summon troop of horse from Norwich and foot soldiers from Aylsham to quell riot, 19.12.95; soldiers return after guarding flour and arresting ringleader, 20.12.95; WHj watches Artillery march to Weybourne, 17.6.96; WH to ballot for Supplementary Militia, 14.1.97; WHj joins association for raising Provisional Cavalry, 11.2.97; WH to ballot for cavalry, 25.2.97; WH to over raising cavalry, 11.3.97
playhouse: *see* plays
postchaises: *see* chaises, postchaises
public houses, **59**: Thomas Forster to turtle feast, 25.9.97
Black Boys, **38**: WH meets new innkeeper Mr Clark, 3.3.95: *see also* Skiffins, James William
Bull: WH meets Mr Athow over, 21.3.96: *see also* Bulling, William
Dolphin: *see* Atwood, Thomas
Feathers, **20**, **219**: let by Mrs Sheppard to William Coe, 9.11.93; WHj to bowling green, 7.7.94, 21.7.94, 22.6.95, 6.6.96, 11.8.96, 15.8.96, 18.8.96, 5.6.97; WHj dines at Free Grammar School feast, 18.12.94; WHj to bowling green frolic, 29.10.95; WHj to dinner, 2.2.96; WH to over James Skiffins, 26.4.96; Feathers opens for T.W. Coke's supporters in county election, 31.5.96; WH to dinner on sessions day, 31.12.96, 19.1.97; WHj to dinner on sessions day, 9.9.97: *see also* Banyard, Charles; Sheppard, Mrs Elizabeth
Kings' Head, **335**: WH meets Letheringsett Purse Club, 21.1.94; WH to purse club, 28.7.94; WH to venison feast, 30.7.94; opens for T.W. Coke's supporters in county election, 31.5.96; WH to dinner on sessions day, 13.10.96; not sold at auction, 16.1.97: *see also* Crafer, Henry
White Lion, **138**: WH settles John Howard's affairs, 4.1.95; WH to dinner on sessions day, 22.1.95: *see also* Howard, John

Holt (*cont.*)
riots: *see* Holt, military activity *above*
sales: MH and MA to John Flegg's, 5.4.94; WH, MH and Mary Raven to Mrs Jewell's, 1.12.94; Mrs Jewell's re-opens, 5.1.95; Hs to Mrs Jewell's, 9–10.1.95; WH to King's Head, 16.1.97
schools: *see* schools
sessions: *see* justices; licences; sessions
shirehouse, **39**: meeting to raise Local Defence Volunteers, 3.5.94; WHj dines with justices and farmers, 22.12.95
shopping by Hs, **70**, **248**: MH to fitting for gown at Miss Bacon's, 17.1.94; Hs view Miss Leak's new fashions, 15.5.94
theatre: *see* plays
Volunteers: *see* Holt, military activity, *above*
windmill: John Wade's burns down, 8.5.94; Hs view ruins in Holt Field, 9.5.94; WH fails to buy any goods at sale, 27.6.94

Holt Church, St Andrew, **121**, **129**; Mary Raven to, 30.11.94, 6.12.95; no service held, 18.1.95; MA and HR confirmed by Bishop of Norwich, 4.7.94; WHj acts as pallbearer at Thomas Johnson's funeral, 25.10.94; marriage of Elizabeth Davy and Edward Robinson, 28.10.94; marriage of Susan Johnson and Revd Mr Morgan, 31.3.95; Rose and Ann Raven to, 24.4.96; Miss Richards to, 13.8.97
HR to: 3.8.94, 30.11.94, 25.9.96
MA to: 21.6.95, 29.11.95, 24.4.96, 16.4.97, 13.8.97
MH to: 4.12.96
WH to: 18.1.95, 24.4.96, 5.6.96, 4.12.96, 16.4.97
WHj to:
1794: 2.2.94, 27.4.94, 3.8.94, 17.8.94, 31.8.94, 26.10.94, 30.11.94
1795: 18.1.95, 14.6.95, 21.6.95, 2.8.95, 8.11.95, 29.11.95, 6.12.95
1796: 10.1.96, 7.2.96, 24.4.96, 29.5.96, 5.6.96, 12.6.96, 3.7.96, 18.9.96, 25.9.96, 23.10.96, 30.10.96, 4.12.96
1797: 1.1.97, 26.3.97, 16.4.97, 23.4.97, 7.5.97, 14.5.97, 21.5.97, 4.7.96, 11.6.97, 18.6.97, 9.7.97, 13.8.97, 20.8.97, 27.8.97, 10.9.97, 24.9.97
preachers: Thomas Fisher jnr, 3.8.94; Mr Burrell, 29.11.95; Robert Bransby Francis, 4.12.96; Bransby Francis, 16.4.97

Holt Heath, **330**, WH and Nathaniel Raven meet Mr Shearing over land on, 17.3.97; Messrs Burcham and King show WH draft of parliamentary Bill for enclosing, 30.3.97: *see also* Holt Heath Farm

Holt Heath Farm, **317**, **330**, settled on WH by William Bulling in part payment of debt,

Holt Heath Farm (*cont.*)
15.11.96; inspected by WH and WHj, 21.11.96, 28.11.96, 13.12.96; WH to, 20.12.96, 22.3.97, 24.3.97, 1.5.97, 15.5.97, 19.5.97, 1.7.97, 16.9.97; WH and MH watch ploughing, 23.2.97; WH and WHj plant fir trees, 25.2.97; WH and WHj burn heather, 1.3.97; WHj to, 7.4.97; MH to, 1.5.97, 19.5.97, 8.8.97; MA to, 19.5.97

Holt House, Leziate, Norf., Thomas Forster moves from Bayfield to, 10.10.96; MA with Mr Forster to, 27.4.97; WHj collects MA, 9.3.97

hop back, *see* brewing equipment

hops, **184**, Mr Fisher, hop factor from London, at Hs', 9.11.94

Horningtoft, Norf., **93**, **274**, WH, MH and Mr and Mrs Nathaniel Raven to, 20.8.95; WH and Nathaniel Raven to greasing grounds, 21.8.95; MH and Mrs Nathaniel Raven to Mrs Moy, 27.5.96, 16.3.97

horses:
- accidents, **7**, **72**, **276**, **277**: Henry Smith killed in fall near Holt, 24.5.94; Robert Farthing's son falls after Briston Fair, 27.5.94; WH and MH injured in chaise when horse falls, 3.7.94; Revd Benjamin Crofts jnr killed in fall, 18.2.95; one of Mrs Booty's drayhorses drowned in flooded Glaven when swept under bridge, 4.6.96
- borrowing: WHj, Mary Raven and HR to Holt with chaise horse on trial from James Dyball, 30.11.94; Hs' old mare by Mr and Mrs Gunton Thompson, 13.5.95
- cavalry: *see* Militia
- care, **366**: WHj's shod at Sheringham, 13.9.97
- hire: WH fails to hire horse at Holt for journey to Norwich, 6.10.95
- purchase: WH and WHj to Holt horse fair, 25.11.93; WHj buys chaise mare from Charles Banyard, 20.9.94; WH changes chaise mare for horse and little mare for cart mare, 16.12.94; Hs exchange chaise horses with Mr Webster, 24.2.95
- riding horses: WHj on Minor to Sheringham, 6.6.94; HR to Norwich on little mare, 12.8.94; all Mrs Jodrell's tenants on horseback in funeral procession, 15.9.94; WHj on horseback to Cley, 2.10.94; WH follows regiment to Weybourne Camp on horseback, 11.6.95; WHj on horseback to Norwich, 21.5.96; WHj on horseback to Burnham Market and Barmer, 28.10.96; WHj's shod at Sheringham, 13.9.97
- sale: WHj takes mare Molly to Mr Foker to be sold at Norwich Fair, 15.4.94; London rider fails to buy Molly, 1.5.94

horses (*cont.*)
- working horses, **26**, **47**, **48**, **76**, **152**, **168**, **306**, **326**: WHj and HR drive mare Molly in turnip cart to Wells, 31.1.94; WHj buys one-horse chaise in Norwich, 2.6.94, 6.6.94; six horses to Mrs Jodrell's hearse and each of her mourning coaches, 15.9.94; man taking Mrs Goggs and Mary Raven to Hs returns to Whissonsett with horses, 5.5.95; Hs' two teams reinforce sea wall at Sheringham, 28.12.95; drowning of one of Mrs Booty's drayhorses, 4.6.96; WH and WHj try colt Leader in little cart, 19.9.96:
- *see also* stables

Horsfall (Horsefall), Revd Samuel, of Wells, Curate of Barney 1784, Curate of Wells, Rector of Gressenhall 1797–1805; with Mr Everitt to tea, 7.4.94

Horstead (Horstd), Norf., WH and HR to tea with Spooner Nash, 3.4.97

house, Hs' [Rawlings, later Letheringsett Hall from *c.*1800], **11**, **18**, **37**, **61**, **157**, **230**, **235**, **349**, **393**, **404**, **406**:
- backhouse: Hannah Dagliss dismissed on leaving door unbolted for sweep, 2.5.97 and maidservants' register, MH's endnotes
- chamber: MA's wallpapered by MH and MA, 23.5.96
- chimney: altered by bricklayers in kitchen, 16–17.10.94, 22.10.94
- counting house, in front yard: demolished, 16.3.96
- dressing room, MA's, **257**: created by WH and WHj by opening dark chamber, 22.3.96; bricklayers at work in dark chamber, 23.3.96, 25.3.96, 29–30.3.96; carpenters at work, 25.3.96, 29–30.3.96; wallpapered by MH and MA, 23.5.96, 26–27.5.96
- kitchen: Hs buy range and oven at Cley sale, 2.10.94; bricklayers alter chimney, 16–17.10.94, 22.10.94; bricklayers install cistern, 2.12.94
- store room: bricklayers and carpenters at work, 11.4.96, 14.4.96
- yard: bricklayers and carpenter install sash windows in yard front, 23.3.97:
- *see also* furniture; gardens, Hs'; yards

houses of industry (workhouses), *see* Gressenhall; Letheringsett

housewarming, at public house, **80**; WH and WHj to William Dobson's at King's Head, Letheringsett, few attend, 18.6.94

Howard, John, **ix**, **59**, **138**, innkeeper of White Lion, Holt, and Pitt Arms, Burnham Market; his affairs settled by WH at White Lion, 4.1.95; WH and James Moore in his postchaise to Burnham Market to install him in public

Howard, John (*cont.*)
house, 5.1.95; WH supervises valuation of goods at Holt, 27.1.95; meets WH at Holt, 3.2.95; WH, WHj and James Moore to at Burnham Market to get security from for their debts, 28.10.96
Howard, Miss, daughter of Thomas; to tea, 30.8.97
Howard, Nicholas (d.1796 aged 27), of Burnham Thorpe, son of Thomas; death, 24.12.96
Howard, Thomas, W. Rudham farmer; WH and WHj to dinner and pay off remainder of brewery mortgage of £1000, 13.9.96
HR, *see* Raven, Henry
Hull, Yorks, William Thackwray to Wells to sail for in Capt. Bloom's ship, 1.1.97
Hunworth, Norf., MH to meeting: alone, 15.11.95; with HR, 6.12.95, 13.12.95; with John Thompson, 13.3.96
hydrophobia, *see* illness

I

illness:
bilious complaint: MA, 2–3.7.96
colds: MH, 13–14.7.95, 16.7.95; WHj, 28.7.95; WH, 27.1.96
? epilepsy: *see* fits *below*
eyes: dimness in MH's, 27.6.94, 23.10.94, 25.10.94, 9.11.94, 26.11.94, 13.12.94, 1.1.95, 4–5.1.95, 28.7.95, 16.3.96, 6.6.96, 11–13.9.96, 12.2.97, 29.3.97, 2.4.97, 25.7.97, 7.8.97, 12.8.97; Mr Bartell summoned to treat MH, 27.6.94, 7.8.97
fits: Miss Symonds seized with at Thomas Forster's, is cared for by maids, 27–28.5.94; Mrs Mary Platten seized with and speechless, 17.6.96
gout: WH, 6–7.2.94, 9.2.94, 12.2.94, 14.2.94, 25–27.2.94, 12.3.94, 11.11.95, 15.11.95, 18.11.95, 28.1.96, 31.1.96, 1.2.96; in WH's hand, 31.12.94; in WH's knee, 2–3.2.96, 7.2.96, 12.2.96
headache: MH, 9.11.94, 6.6.96, 29–30.3.97
hydrophobia, **298**: Ann Loades bitten by mad dog, 22.7.96; Ann Loades falls ill, 30–31.8.96, 1.2.96; death of Ann Loades, 2.9.96; account of final stages, MH's register, endnotes
injuries: *see* accidents
rheumatism, **363**: WHj, 20.12.96, 23.12.96, 5.3.97, 6–7.4.97; WHj consults Dr Heath, 20.4.97
side pain: WH, 8.7.94; MH, 30–31.12.94, 1.1.95
stomach pain: MH, 4.8.94
? stroke: *see* fits *above*

illness (*cont.*)
toothache: WHj ill, tooth extracted at Holt, 28.7.95
unspecified:
MH: 25.4.95; ill for 62 days, life despaired of, 16.8.93
WH: 6.1.94, 24.3.95, 31.7.96, 9.2.97, 11.2.97
WHj: 24.3.97, 3–4.4.97
others: Mrs Elizabeth Burrell, 6.1.94, 14.1.95, 1.7.1.95; Thomas Forster, 22.10.94; Joseph Davy, 23.12.94; Dr Heath summoned to treat Mrs Burrell, 17.1.95; Ann Ives, 17.5.96; Mrs Phillis Goggs, 31.10.96, 2–3.11.96, 6.11.96, 30.8.97
workforce: Thomas Baldwin, 13–14.8.94:
see also bathing; bleeding
Independents, *see* Sykes, Revd John
industrial accidents, *see* accidents
industry, houses of, *see* Gressenhall; Letheringsett
injuries, *see* accidents
inns, *see* Holt, public houses; public houses
insolvency, *see* bankruptcy; debt
inventories, *see* valuations
ironing, by Hs, 12.3.94, 30.7.94, 1.1.95, 13.4.96
Ives, Ann (d.1796 aged 17/18), of Letheringsett; dies on Holt road on way to doctor, 17.5.96; burial, 20.5.96 and noted in MH's register, endnotes
Ives, Mrs Ann (d.1836 aged 75), wife of Meshack; with sister to breakfast and dinner at Hs', 17.9.94
Ives, Meshack (d.1816 aged 64), innkeeper of Queen's Head, Brampton, tied house; to dinner, 19.5.96

J

Jackson (Jaxson), Mrs, wife of Thomas; with husband, Hs and party to dinner at Cromer, 10.9.96
Jackson (Jaxson), Thomas, Cley coal merchant; with wife, Hs and party to dinner at Cromer, 10.9.96; consulted by WHj over holding Newcastle upon Tyne contact in prison, 14.12.96
Janry, Elizabeth, *see* Jennerys
Jarvis, Miss, of Cley; with Hs and party to dinner at Cromer, 10.9.96
Jarvis, Mr, Guestwick farmer; with Messrs Everitt, Keeler and Nobbs reckons for barley and to supper with Hs, 23.6.94
Jeckell (Jekell), Mary, of Letheringsett; marriage in 1793 to James Tinker noted in MH's register, endnotes
Jennerys (Janry), Elizabeth, Hs' maidservant; replaces Sarah Starling, 18.4.97; departs,

Jennerys, Elizabeth (*cont.*)
10.10.97; hire and wages, maidservants' register, MH's endnotes

Jennis (Jenes, Jinnis), Mrs Anne, of Holt; MA, Rose Raven and Miss Symonds to tea, 23.5.94; Hs to tea, 13.9.94, 25.4.95; WHj and MA to party, 20.1.95

Jennis (Jennes), Elizabeth (b.1779), of Holt, daughter of Mrs Anne; to tea, 3.1.94, 15.10.94, 17.12.95, 6.7.97

Jennis (Jennes), Mary Pleasance (b.*c*.1774), of Holt, daughter of Mrs Anne; to tea, 3.1.94, 15.10.94, 17.12.95, 6.7.97

Jew, *see* Levi, Jacob

Jewell, Mrs Sarah (d.1794 aged 70/76), **129**, née March, of Holt; Hs to sale of her goods, sale stopped by Lord Chancellor, 1.12.94; sale re-opens, 5.1.95; Hs to sale, MA buys china ornaments, Hs buy silver, 9–10.1.95

Jex, John (d.1797 aged 52), Letheringsett blacksmith; to Norwich for county election, 2.6.96; death, 26.6.97; burial, 29.6.97 and noted in MH's register, endnotes

Jodrell (Joddril, Jodril), Mrs Elizabeth (d.1794 aged 79), **105**, **110**, **111**, **221**, née Warner, of Bayfield Hall; death, 31.8.94; funeral procession through Letheringsett on way to Oxfordshire for burial, 15.9.94

Jodrell (Jodril), Henry (1752–1814), JP, **111**, **137**, **165**, **234**, of Bayfield Hall, barrister, Recorder of Gt Yarmouth 1792–1813, MP for Gt Yarmouth 1796–1802, MP for Bramber. Suss. 1802–12, Deputy Lieutenant of Norfolk 1803, son of Mrs Elizabeth; Hs view his new plantations at Bayfield, 22.4.95

Johnson, Anna (Ann) (1769–1829), Holt milliner, daughter of Revd William Tower; to dinner, 12.8.95; to tea, 27.6.97: *see also* Johnson, Misses

Johnson, Deborah (Deb) Judith (b.1772), Holt milliner, daughter of Revd William Tower; with Mary Raven at Hs', 15.11.95; to tea, 17.12.95, 27.6.97

Johnson, Mary, *see* Burrell, Mrs

Johnson, Misses, Holt milliners, unnamed daughters of Revd William Tower; WHj and cousins to tea, 21.1.94, 11.11.95; visited by Mary Raven, 8.5.95; MA to dinner, 16.11.95, 11.4.96; MA and Mary Raven to tea, 15.12.95; with WHj and Ravens to tea at Mr Burrell's, 3.4.96; with Ravens to Sheringham, 10.4.96; with Ravens to dinner at Mr Burrell's, 17.4.96: *see also* Burrell, Mrs Mary; Johnson, Anna; Johnson, Deborah; Morgan, Mrs Susannah

Johnson, Robert, innkeeper of Crown, Sheringham, tied house, formerly of Attleborough; at Hs' to hire Crown from Hs, stays at King's Head, Letheringsett, 10.3.95; dines with Hs, hires Crown, with WH to Holt, 16.3.95; WH and WHj settle matters with Samuel Sanderson at Sheringham after Crown hired by, 6.4.95; evades WH and WHj at Sheringham, 27.9.96, 1.10.96; abandons Crown, leaving Mr Cubitt in possession, 30.9.96; fails to meet WH at Cley, 2.10.96; WH meets Messrs Bignold and Smith at Holt over affairs of, 23.10.96; Messrs Smith, Bignold and Edwards settle affairs of at Hs', Messrs Bignold and Edwards hire Crown, 25.10.96; meets John Smith at Sheringham, 30.10.96

Johnson, Susannah, *see* Morgan, Mrs

Johnson, Thomas (d.1794 aged 19/21), **121**, son of Revd William Tower; WHj acts as pallbearer at funeral at Holt, 25.10.94

Johnson, Revd William Tower (d.1799 aged 61/62), LLB, of Holt, formerly of Plumstead-by-Holt, Curate of Twyford 1766, Vicar of N. Barningham 1769–99, Rector of Beeston Regis 1772–99, Curate of Bessingham 1784, Curate of Runton 1784; MA to tea, 14.2.94, 1.7.97; WHj, MA, Mr and Mrs Nathaniel Raven to tea, 23.2.97

Jolly Farmers, *see* Field Dalling

Jones, Miss, of Cley; with Miss Bartell to tea, 21.6.97

Jordan, John (d.1795 aged 52), **181**, innkeeper of Blue Bell, Wiveton, formerly of Edgefield; death, 12.6.95

juries, at Holt; WH serves on jury at quarter sessions, 16.10.94; WH serves on grand jury at quarter sessions, 22.1.95

justices, sittings, **191**:
- Aylsham: WHj to, 19.9.97
- Cromer: WH and WHj to and dine, 19.9.94
- Holt, **160**, **325**: WH dines with justices, 13.9.94, 19.9.95, 15.10.95, 17.9.96; WH to over raising soldiers, 4.4.95; WH to, 11.4.95, 31.12.96; WH and Mr Burrell to over building house of industry at Letheringsett, 29.8.95; WH to for licences, 19.9.95, 17.9.96; WHj to, 9.9.97
  - handling of bread riot, **231**, **232**, **234**: poor at Sharrington withhold flour from justices, 18.12.95; all-day sitting to quell riot but nothing done, troop of horse and foot soldiers summoned, 19.12.95; flour escorted past Sharrington, 21.12.95; WHj dines with justices, witnesses examined, 22.12.95
- Walsingham: WHj to, 12.9.97:

see also sessions; *also individual justices* Collyer, Charles; Coke, Thomas William; Hare, Thomas; Jodrell, Henry

K

Keeler, Thomas, Guestwick farmer; to dinner, Hs', 25.11.94; with Mr Everitt and Miss Billing to dinner and supper at Hs' and to Weybourne Camp, 26.6.95; with Messrs Everitt and Ladle to dinner and supper, 27.6.96; Hs to dinner, 26.6.97
Kelling (Keeling, Keelling, Kellen), Norf., **316**, **363**, WH and MH to, 21.10.93; WHj, MA and Ravens to, 9.11.96; WH and WHj fail to buy hay, 15.7.97; WH and MH to Mr Ditchell's sale, 5.10.97
Kendle, John, Thornage farmer; WHj to tea, 2.11.94
Kendle, Thomas, **221**, of Sharrington Hall, farmer; HR to tea, 8.11.95; HR to dinner, 7.2.96
Kerdiston, *see* Reepham
King, *see* George III
King, John (d.1835 aged 69), of Holt, son of Robert; with John Burcham shows WH draft of Holt Enclosure Bill, 30.3.97
King, Robert, **298**, Holt farmer; sells WH and MH 53 cocks of hay for £21, 9.7.94; his mad dog bites Ann Loades and worries animals, 22.7.96
King's Head, *see* Holt, public houses; Letheringsett
King's Lynn (Lynn Regus), Norf., poor at Sharrington intercept flour bound for, 17.12.95; Thomas Forster moves from Bayfield to Holt House near, 10.10.96: *see also* Holt House
kitchen, *see* house
Knaresborough (Knasbro), Yorks, **202**, **310**, Mr Green of at Hs', 14.8.96: *see also* Yorkshire

labourers, employed by Hs, *see* harvests; haymaking; workforce
Ladle, Mr, farmer; with Messrs Keeler and Everitt reckons with Hs, to supper, 27.6.96
lads, *see* boys
Lamb, Charles (b.1766), **178**, Cley tidewaiter and Letheringsett cordwainer, son of William; with Mr Burrell to Norwich for county election, 2.6.96
Lamb, William (d.1814 aged 73), **214**, **326**, **363**, Hs' farm servant, maltster, brewer and drayman; meets WH at Coltishall, 4.4.97
Langham, Norf., WH to tea with Mr Frost, 4.8.94
laundry, *see* ironing; washing
lawyers, *see* articles; attorneys; barrister
L C, *see* carts, little cart
Leader, see horses
Leak (Leake), Ann (d.1803 aged 61), **70**, Holt milliner in partnership with sister Bell; Hs view new fashions, 15.5.94; Hs, Rose Raven and Miss Symonds to tea, 24.5.94; with Mr Burrell to tea, 7.12.95; with Mrs Sheldrake to tea, 20.5.96; to supper, 29.9.96: *see also* Leak, Misses
Leak (Leake), Arabella (Bell), Holt milliner in partnership with sister Ann; with Miss Mighells to tea, 14.8.94; at large tea party at King's Head, Letheringsett, 4.9.95: *see also* Leak, Misses
Leak (Leake, Leeke, Leek), Misses Ann and Arabella (Bell), Holt milliners; boarding at Mr Burrell's, WHj to tea, 9.4.96, 7.4.97, 9.9.97; at Hs', 13.9.96, 12.2.97, 19.3.97, 24.4.97, 2.6.97; to supper, 21.12.96, 22.1.97, 6.7.97, 27.7.97, 2.10.97; back at Holt, MH and MA to tea, 14.1.97; go home in Hs' cart, 24.4.97; MH and WHj to tea, 1.7.97; WHj and MA to tea, 5.8.97: *see also* Leak, Ann; Leak, Arabella
lectures, in evening at Letheringsett Church by Revd John Burrell, 22.12.93, 27.7.94, 3.8.94, 14.2.96, 21.2.96, 20.3.96, 10.4.96, 8.5.96, 5.6.96
ledgers, *see* books
legacy, received by Gunton Thompson at Aylsham, 10.12.93
Leggatt (Leggat), Benjamin, Wesleyan Methodist itinerant preacher; preaches at Cley, 1.10.97
Letheringsett (town), Norf., **8**, **11**, **88**, **101**, **110**, **127**, **238**, **303**, **317**, Mrs Jodrell's funeral procession, 15.9.94; soldiers march through on way to Sharrington, 20.12.95; soldiers, justices and farmers pass through to escort flour past Sharrington, 21.12.95; Mr King's mad dog killed, 22.7.96; Hs walk up to James Cobon's hills, 16.2.97; Thomas Press's farm to be sold to James Cobon, 3.4.97
 house of industry, **197**, **294**, **295**: WH at vestry meeting, decision made to build house of industry for poor, 12.8.95; WH to Holt with Mr Burrell for justices' sitting over building, 29.8.95; WH and Mr Burrell buy timber at Cley for fencing garden, 28.12.95; visited by Hs, 7.6.96, 22.7.96, 5.8.96; Hs and Mr Burrell's family to for tea, workmen to supper at King's Head, 9.8.96
 King's Head, **37**, **49**, **51**, **54**, **61**, **80**, **325**: Hs, Bartells and Burrells to tea, 14.7.94: *see also* Dobson, William; Mayes, Richard
 Methodist meeting [Wesleyan], **218**, **262**, **263**: Mrs Sheldrake to, 6.4.96; Mrs Smith to, 25.6.96; held by Mrs Smith and Mrs Proudfoot at Mrs Winn's, 18.7.96
  attended by MH: with MA, 6.4.96, 13.4.96, 11.6.96, 25.6.96; alone, 3.7.96

Letheringsett, Methodist meeting (*cont.*)
preachers: Mr Sykes, 13.4.96; Mr Heath, 28.5.96; Mr Witham, 11.6.96; Mr Sanderson, 4.3.97
parish (town) government: Mr Burrell and churchwardens beat bounds, 29.5.94
town meetings over supper at King's Head: 9.5.96, 18.7.96; WH to, 21.4.94, 7.4.95, 28.12.95, 29.3.96, 18.4.97; WHj to, 21.4.94
purse club: met by WH at King's Head, Holt, 21.1.94:
see also brewery; brewhouse; Cobon, James [Letheringsett Hall Farm]; fields; Glaven, River; house; Letheringsett Church; meadows; register, MH's, endnotes

Letheringsett Church (our church), St Andrew, **11**, **61**, **137**, **206**, **207**, **218**, **246**, **400**, services regularly attended by Hs and HR: registers of marriages, deaths and burials: *see* MH's register, endnotes
Sacraments attended by Hs, **97**: Easter, 27.4.94, 12.4.95, 27.3.96, 23.4.97; Trinity, 3.8.94, 2.8.95, 14.8.96, 13.8.97; Michaelmas, 26.10.94; Christmas, 25.12.93, 3.1.96, 1.1.97; Mr Burrell reads lecture on, 27.7.94
sermons: Hs hear funeral sermon, 22.5.96: *see also* Burrell, Revd John; lectures
services: none held, 18.1.95, 21.6.95, 15.11.95, 29.11.95, 25.9.96, 26.3.97, 16.4.97, 9.7.97; prayers only, 25.12.95; WH and MA fail to attend, 29.5.96; Mr and Mrs Savory at, 2.4.97
vestry meeting: WH to, agreement reached to build house of industry for poor, 12.8.95: *see also* Burrell, Revd John; lectures; Letheringsett, parish government

Letheringsett Hall [Rawlings], *see* house

Letheringsett Hall Farm [Old Hall], *see* Cobon, James

letters, **158**, sent by MH to Mr Burrell arguing against sermon, 15.11.96; received by MH from Henry Goggs with news of sister's illness, 30.8.97

Levi ('Levi the Jew'), Jacob, Wells auctioneer; with son to tea, 3.2.95

licences, for public houses; WH to Holt for justices' sitting, 19.9.95, 17.9.96

lighthouse, Cromer, **304**, Hs walk to from Edmund Bartell jnr's, 16.9.96

linen, sheets bought by MH and MA at Holt sale, 5.4.94: *see also* cloth; drapers; ironing; washing

ling, *see* heather

Lion, *see* Holt, public houses, White Lion

little cart (L C), *see* carts, little cart

'**Little Nathaniel**', *see* Raven, Nathaniel (b.1781)

Little Ryburgh, *see* Ryburgh

Little Snoring, *see* Snoring

Little Thornage, *see* Thornage

Little Walsingham, *see* Walsingham

livestock, *see* cows; horses; pigs; sheep; *also* geese

Loades, Ann (1790–96), **298**, daughter of Mary; falls ill after bite from mad dog, 30.8.96; visited by Hs while ill, 31.8.96, 1–2.9.96 and MH's register, endnotes; death, 2.9.96; burial, 4.9.96

Loades, Elizabeth (Betty) (1770–1816), **295**, helps Hs with washing, 30.6.94, 28.7.94, 4.4.97

Loades, Mary (d.1824 aged 68), **295**, helps Hs with washing, 27.11.93; daughter bitten by Mr King's mad dog, 22.7.96

London, **70**, **123**, **412**, marriage of Ann Davy, 6.1.94; Joseph Davy to, 5.4.94; Matthew Davy at father's from, 31.8.94; marriage of Edward Robinson, linen draper of, to Elizabeth Davy, they depart for, 28.10.94; marriage of John Davy jnr of, 21.6.95; Mr and Mrs Barnham to tea at Hs', 9.9.95; John Wade returns from, 19.5.96; John Davy jnr at father's at Holt, 3.2.97; Henry Goggs to, 30.5.97; Mr Cook dines with Hs, 14.8.97
merchants and factors: rider looks over WHj's mare Molly, does not buy her, 1.5.94; Mr Fisher, hop-factor, at Hs', 9.11.94; Mr Wood, chemist, at Hs', 17.6.95, 21.6.96

Lord Chancellor [1st Baron Loughborough], stops Mrs Jewell's sale at Holt, 1.12.94

Lord Lieutenant, of Norfolk [1st Marquis Townshend]; WH to meeting at Holt held by Deputy Lieutenants over augmentation of Militia, 7.12.96

Lower Sheringham, *see* Sheringham

Lynn, *see* King's Lynn

M

MA, *see* Hardy, Mary Ann

magistrates, *see* justices

maidservants, Hs', **218**, **406**; maids nurse Miss Symonds through night, 27.5.94; Sarah Turner to Cley Fair, 25.7.94; maids depart, Ann Brown arrives as upper servant, 10.10.94; Ann Brown departs, 31.1.95; Frances Thompson and boy depart, 10.10.95; Hs' great boy and Sarah Turner depart, 10.10.96; Sarah Starling replaced by Elizabeth Jennerys, 18.4.97; Hannah Dagliss dismissed for leaving back door open for chimney sweep, 2.5.97; Elizabeth Chasteney arrives as cook, 11.5.97; MH and MA hire Elizabeth Williamson at Holt as upper servant, 31.7.97; Elizabeth Jennerys and Elizabeth Chasteney depart, 10.10.97; Elizabeth Williamson starts as upper

maidservants (*cont.*)
servant, William as lad, 12.10.97; hire and wages, maidservants' register, MH's endnotes: *see also* Milligen, Maria; Thompson, Frances; *also* menservants; sessions, Holt, hiring; washing
Maid's Head, *see* North Walsham; Norwich
Mann (Man), John (d.1794 aged 44), **115**, Cley merchant; sudden death in Norwich, 17.8.94; died heavily indebted, 23.8.94
Manners Sutton, Right Revd Dr Charles (1755–1828), **89**, Bishop of Norwich 1792–1805, Dean of Windsor 1793–1805, Archbishop of Canterbury 1805–28; confirms MA and HR at Holt, 4.7.94
manor court, WH to at Saxlingham, 30.6.96
manure, *see* muck
mares, *see* horses
markets:
Fakenham: WH, MH and Mrs and Mrs Nathaniel Raven to, 21.5.95; WH and Nathaniel Raven to, 20.8.95
Holt: Rose Raven and Miss Symonds to, 24.5.94; Henry Smith killed returning from, 24.5.94; Hs to, 16.1.96; wheat and barley prices, 13.2.96, 20.2.96, 5.3.96
MA to: 23.11.93, 26.4.94, 24.5.94, 31.1.95, 25.4.95, 13.6.95, 25.6.96, 5.8.97
MH to: 26.4.94, 24.5.94, 13.6.95, 20.2.96
WH to:
1793: 26.10.93, 9.11.93, 23.11.93
1794: 25.1.94, 26.4.94, 9.8.94, 25.10.94, 13.12.94
1795: 24.1.95, 31.1.95, 14.2.95, 25.4.95, 2.5.95, 13.6.95, 5.9.95, 10.10.95, 31.10.95
1796: 2.1.96, 20.2.96, 5.3.96, 9.4.96, 28.5.96, 25.6.96, 2.7.96, 1.10.96, 24.12.96
1797: 4.3.97, 15.7.97, 5.8.97
WHj to:
1793: 9.11.93
1794: 25.1.94, 15.3.94, 26.4.94, 5.7.94, 19.7.94, 23.8.94, 25.10.94, 13.12.94
1795: 24.1.95, 31.1.95, 14.2.95, 14.3.95, 21.3.95, 4.4.95, 11.4.95, 25.4.95, 6.6.95, 1.8.95, 10.10.95, 31.10.95, 21.11.95, 19.12.95
1796: 2.1.96, 9.1.96, 13.2.96, 20.2.96, 9.4.96, 28.5.96, 4.6.96, 11.6.96, 2.7.96, 1.10.96, 24.12.96, 31.12.96
1797: 11.2.97, 25.2.97, 4.3.97, 11.3.97, 15.7.97, 5.8.97, 12.8.97, 30.9.97: *see also* Holt, Hs to
marriages, **123**, **183**, Ann Davy in London, 6.1.94; Edward Robinson to Elizabeth Davy at Holt, 28.10.94; Deborah Ramm at Letheringsett, 27.1.95; Cremer Cremer to Ann Buckle, 25.3.94; Revd Mr Morgan to Susan Johnson at Holt, 31.3.95, 1.4.95; Peter Raven to Miss Wells, 26.4.94; Robert Garrett brings bride to Mr Burrell's, 9.4.95; Revd Mr Wilcocks and Elizabeth Hagon elope to Scotland, 20.6.95; John Davy jnr, 21.6.95; George Wymer of Norwich, 6.11.95; Mr Burrell to Mary Johnson at Holt, 2.8.96; Thomas Skrimshire to Rose Raven at Whissonsett, 23.6.97; register compiled by MH for Letheringsett 1793–97, endnotes
Mary Ann (MA), *see* Hardy, Mary Ann
Mason, John, Brinton tanner; at Hs' to buy bark from Hindolveston, 6.11.93
Mason, Mrs, death at Godwick, 23.3.97
Mayes (Mays), Richard (1717–1800), **37**, **54**, innkeeper of King's Head, Letheringsett, tied house and village lock-up; builders demolishing house and clearing rubbish, 3.3.94; bricklayers build stable, 5.3.94; bricklayers and carpenters at work, 12.3.94; carpenters raise roof of stable, 15.3.94; carpenters and bricklayers repair house, 24.3.94; William Dobson takes over, 26.3.94
meadows, water very high in Glaven, 10.2.94: *see also* fields; greasing grounds; hay
meal, *see* flour
measuring, timber at Hindolveston by WH, MH and WHj, 24.10.93; ash timber at Reepham by WH and Mr Bartell, 20.2.97
medicinal remedies/medicines, *see* Bartell, Edmund, medical practice
meetings [Nonconformist services], *see under individual towns and villages* Briston; Cley-next-the-Sea; Fakenham; Hunworth; Letheringsett; Sharrington: *see also* Methodist
Mendham, Mr, *see* Mindham, William
mending, *see* clothes
menservants, Henry Goggs's accompanies him to Weybourne Camp, 8.7.95; marriage in 1793 of Mr Burrell's manservant and maidservant noted in MH's register, endnotes
Methodism, **136**, **139**, **153**, **245**, **289**, *see* meetings *under* Briston; Cley-next-the-Sea; Fakenham; Hunworth; Letheringsett; Sharrington; *also* preachers; sermons; Wesley, Revd John
Methodist, **262**, **263**, Mr Burrell has argument with, 10.4.96
Mighells (Mighles), Miss, with Bell Leak to tea, 14.8.94; at large tea party at King's Head, Letheringsett, 4.9.95
Militia:
Provisional Cavalry: WHj joins association at Holt for raising, 11.2.97; WH to ballot at Holt, 25.2.97; WH to Holt over, 11.3.97

Militia (*cont.*)
Supplementary Militia, **189**, **203**, **231**, **325**: WH to Holt meeting for augmentation of Militia, 7.12.96; meeting at King's Head, Letheringsett for those liable to be drawn in ballot, 12.12.96; WH to ballot at Holt, 14.1.97
see also Army; Volunteers; Weybourne Camp
millers, *see individual millers and millwrights* Cook, William; Thompson, William Gunton; Youngman, Thomas: *see also* mills
Milligen (Milegan), Mrs Elizabeth (d.1832 aged 76), **218**; helps Hs with washing, 3.11.95, 8.12.95, 8.3.96, 12.7.96, 16.8.96, 25.10.96, 25.7.97
Milligen, Maria (b.1777), Hs' maidservant 1797–98, daughter of Mrs Elizabeth; hire and wages, maidservants' register, MH's endnotes
mills, **33**, **34**, **35**:
Blakeney Windmill, **225**: WHj and Nathaniel Raven to sale, 26.11.95
Fakenham Watermill: Mr Green's, WHj to sale, 15.2.96
Holt Windmill, **69**: John Wade's, burns down, 8.5.94; Hs view ruins in Holt Field, 9.5.94; WH fails to buy any goods, 27.6.94
Walsingham Windmill: WHj, Thomas Balls jnr and John Ellis view Mr Minns' new mill, 16.12.96:
see also millers
Mindham (Mendham), William (1771–1843), **94**, **95**, **96**, **372**, **373**, **374**, **391**, **396**, of Wells, paperhanger, later Holt organ-builder, architect and builder; with Messrs Balls to tea at Hs', 29.6.97; repairs Hs' organ, 5.9.97, 7.9.97
Mingay, James, of Thetford; defeated by William Windham in Norwich by-election, 11–12.7.94
Minns (Mins), John (d.1819 aged 85), Edgefield farmer; WH and WHj to tea, 31.7.95
Minns, Lewis, Lt Walsingham miller; his new mill viewed by WHj, Thomas Balls jnr and John Ellis, 16.12.96
mob, *see* riots
Molly, *see* horses
money, *see* banking; debt; mortgages
moon, total eclipse, 14.2.94
Moore (Moor), James (d.1815 aged 52), **163**, Holt attorney; with Hs and Messrs Thomas and Morgan at Mr Burrell's, 28.11.93; with WHj visits new bath at Cley and to dinner at John Ellis's, 17.4.94; with WHj to Sheringham and to dinner at Cremer Cremer's at Beeston Regis, 6.8.94; with WHj collects shrubs and plants from workhouse garden at Gressenhall, 6.4.96; with WHj to Cromer, 13.5.96
at Hs': to tea, 28.2.94; to supper, 28.2.94, 17.4.94, 27.4.94, 1.5.94; to dinner, 3.4.95
Moore, James (*cont.*)
Hs at: WH to dinner, 17.10.93, 9.11.93, 21.1.94, 28.7.94, 11.4.95, 29.8.95, 14.11.96; WHj and HR to tea, 25.12.93; WHj and MA to tea and supper, 31.1.94; WHj to dinner, 28.2.94; WH to supper, 3.4.94; WHj to tea, 27.4.94, 8.3.97; WH to tea, 29.8.95, 31.10.95
legal practice: with WH to dinner at Henry Chaplin's and reckons, 22.10.93; meets Hs at Southrepps over purchase of Crown, 25.3.94; with WH meets Messrs Grey and Summers to arrange purchase of Crown, Southrepps, 3.4.94; WH pays Mr Bird for Aldborough Black Boys at, 8.4.94; WH to tea at after paying for Crown, Southrepps, 11.10.94; with WH to Burnham Market to establish John Howard in public house, 5.1.95; with WHj to Sheringham after Robert Johnson's surrender of Crown, 30.9.96; with WH and WHj to Burnham Market to get security from John Howard for debts, 28.10.96; consulted by WH over Henry Crafer's debts, 9.11.96; with WH to Norwich Assizes, 6.8.97
Morgan, Revd James (d.1803), of Shipdham; with WH, WHj and Messrs Thomas and Moore at Mr Burrell's, 28.11.93; marriage to Susan Johnson at Holt, 31.3.95
Morgan, Mrs Susannah (Susan) (b.1764), **70**, Holt milliner, daughter of Revd William Tower Johnson; marriage to Revd Mr Morgan at Holt, Mary Raven bridesmaid to, 31.3.95, 1.4.95; departs with husband for Shipdham, 1.4.95: *see also* Johnson, Misses
mortgages, **303**, on Hs' brewery, paid off by WH and WHj to Thomas Howard, 13.9.96; Nicholas Everitt's on Jolly Sailor, Wells paid off by Mr Wordingham, 3.1.97
mourning, hearse and two coaches with six horses each in Mrs Jodrell's procession, 15.9.94
mowing, *see* harvests; hay
Moy, John (d.1806 aged 75), **274**, Horningtoft farmer and maltster; with wife met by Hs at Mr Burrell's, 23.5.97
Moy, Mrs Judith (1738–1814), née Fox, wife of John, MH's cousin; MH and Mrs Nathaniel Raven to, 27.5.96, 16.3.97; with husband met by Hs at Mr Burrell's, 23.5.97
MR, *see* Raven, Mary
muck, in Hs' yard bought by Thomas Temple for 30 guineas, 29.4.94; shifted into Hs' garden by men, 11.2.95
music, WHj and Thomas Balls jnr fail to bring home piano from Southrepps owing to dispute with Mr Baker, 13.4.97; piano tuned by Mr Benfield, 10.6.97; organ repaired by Mr Mindham, 5.9.97, 7.9.97

musician (musition), Mr Benfield at Hs', 16.4.95
muslin, *see* cloth

N

Nash, Spooner (d.1810 aged 72), Horstead farmer; tells WH and HR of forthcoming sale of Thomas Press's farm, 3.4.97
Navy, **160**, WH meets Holt justices over raising 'soldiers' [sailors], 4.4.95
'**Nectar de vie**' (Nectar deverie), *see* casks
Netherlands, defeats of British troops and allies in Flanders, 25.5.94
Newcastle upon Tyne, Northumb., **383**, Mr Henderson at Hs', 9.9.95; WHj speaks to Mr Jackson over contact in prison, 14.12.96
newspapers, extracts from reports, **7**, **40**, **70**, **76**, **158**, **170**, **171**, **234**, **248**, **271**, **272**, **308**, **384**, **408**; new and additional duties and taxes, 7.2.94; defeat of British troops in France, arrests for sedition and treason, suspension of Habeas Corpus, 23.5.94; victory over French at Tournai, 28.5.94; death of Empress of Russia, 22.12.96
Newstead, Robert, innkeeper of Dun Cow, Salthouse, tied house; pays £30 to Hs, 21.10.93
Nobbs (Nobs), Mr, farmer or merchant; with Messrs Everitt, Jarvis and Keeler reckons for barley and to supper, 23.6.94
Nonconformity/Dissent, *see* meetings *under* Briston; Cley-next-the-Sea; Fakenham; Hunworth; Letheringsett; Sharrington; *also* preachers; sermons
Norris, Revd George (d. 1832 aged 67), **314**, **315**, of Stanfield, Curate of Stanfield, Curate of Whissonsett, Rector of Bagthorpe, Vicar of Guist; preaches at Whissonsett, 6.11.96
North Walsham (Walsham), Norf., **269**, WHj checks Maid's Head after Nathaniel Berry absconds, 26.10.93; Gunton Thompson checks public house, 19.4.95; Mr and Mrs Gunton Thompson to fair, 13.5.95
Norwich, Norf., **64**, **89**, **174**, **285**, **408**, **411**, Mrs Raven to tea from, 19.3.94; Mr Foker to sell WHj's mare at fair, 15.4.94; man from fails to hire Crown, Southrepps from Hs, 31.7.94; sudden death of John Mann, 17.8.94; stage-coach service from Wells opens, 8.12.94; Mrs Booth with Temples at Hs', 18.12.94; Mrs Herring at Mr Forster's, 22.4.95; death of Mrs Wymer, 10.5.95; driver from dies of injuries by overturning cart at Letheringsett, 21–22.5.95 and MH's register, endnotes; Holt justices summon troop of horse from, 19.12.95; Mrs Herring to tea, 2.9.96; Mr Burrell at, 25.9.96; Mr and Mrs Bartell to, 12.4.97
Norwich (*cont.*)
  assizes, **99**: open, 18.7.96; WH and James Moore to, 6.8.97
  Hs to, **107**: WHj and Mr Bartell stay overnight at George Wymer's, 26–27.2.94; WHj to dinner with George Wymer, 2.6.94; WH and HR to, 12.8.94; WH and MA from, 16.8.94; WH, MH and MA to for day, to breakfast and dinner at George Wymer's and tea at Mr Herring's, 6.9.94; WH and MA to, 8.5.95, 7.10.95; WH fails to hire horse to go to, 6.10.95; WHj to, 3.11.95; WH with Bartells to, 25.3.96, 11.4.96; WH, WHj, MA and John Smith to for day, 20–21.5.96; Mr Burrell, Charles Lamb, WHj, Charles Kendle, Thomas Youngman and John Jex to election, 2.6.96; WH from, 8.8.97
  newspapers: *see* newspapers
  public houses, **76**, **170**, **171**: WHj buys one-horse chaise at Maid's Head in St Simon's, 2.6.94; James Dew noted at the Bushel, near the Rose in St Augustine's, MH's endnotes: *see also* elections

O

officers, *see* excise
organ, *see* music
oven, kitchen range and oven bought by Hs at Cley sale, 2.10.94
Overstrand, *see* Beckhithe
Oxfordshire, **105**, **110**, **111**, **137**, Mrs Jodrell of Bayfield's funeral procession starts for, 15.9.94

P

Page, Mr, of Lower Sheringham; his pigs viewed by MH and WHj, five bought by WHj, MH and WHj to tea, 8.5.97
pallbearer, *see* funerals
paper, duty levied, 7.2.94: *see also* wallpaper
Parliament, report on opening, 21.1.94; report of vote on amendment to end war, 24.1.94
  Acts, **160**, **330**: justices to organise raising of 'soldiers' [sailors], 4.4.95; suspension of Habeas Corpus, 2.7.94; augmentation of Militia, 7.12.96; Messrs Burcham and King jnr show WH draft of Holt Enclosure Bill, 30.3.97:
  see also elections
partridge, *see* shooting
Paxfield Farm, Helhoughton, Norf., **346**, WH and Nathaniel Raven meet Mr Shearing of over land on Holt Heath, 17.3.97
peace, *see* war
peas (pease), Hs' farm crop, **254**; carried by Hs' men until prevented by rain, 29.8.97

pets, *see* cats; dogs
petty sessions, *see* sessions
piano, *see* music
pigs (piggs), **73**, six piglets bought by WHj from Cook Flower, 21.9.96; killed by Hs, 21.12.96; carcase of 31-stone hog seen by MH at Thomas Temple's, Thornage, 29.12.96; five bought by WHj from Mr Page at Sheringham, 8.5.97
pipes [barrels], *see* wine
pistols, *see* guns
plantations, *see* trees
Platten (Platton), Samuel (d.1817 aged 75), Bayfield Hall gamekeeper; mowing wheat for Hs in Furze Closes, 16.8.94; his wife speechless after fit, 17.6.96; burial of wife, 21.6.96 and MH's register, endnotes
plays, at Holt; WHj to, 14.3.95, 7.4.95; WH and WHj to, 11.4.95; WH, WHj and MA to, 25.4.95
Pleasance, Mrs, of Cross Keys, Gunthorpe, **322**, **323**; with Mrs England dines and reckons with Hs, 5.12.96
ploughing, **26**, **152**, **320**, WH and MH watch ploughman at Holt Heath Farm, 23.2.97
poor, *see* Gressenhall, house of industry; Letheringsett, house of industry; riots
port, *see* wine
porter, *see* beer
postchaises, *see* chaises
preachers, Nonconformist, itinerant and local, **136**, **139**, **153**, **245**, **262**, **263**, **289**: *see individual preachers* Eastaugh, Samuel; Heath, William; Hill, Josiah; Leggatt, Benjamin; Proudfoot, Mary; Saunderson, John; Sykes, John; Witham, John; *see also* sermons
Press, Thomas (*c.*1762–1836), Letheringsett farmer; his farm to be sold to James Cobon, 3.4.97
press, *see* newspapers
Prior, Mrs Mary (Molly), **255**, of Belaugh and Hoveton/Wroxham; stays with Hs, 10.3.96
prison, WHj asks Mr Jackson to get friend at Newcastle upon Tyne to pay Bell's groats to keep him in, 14.12.96
proclamations, *see* fasts
Proudfoot, Isaac (d.1809 aged 58), Wells limeburner; with wife and Mrs Smith to tea, 5.6.97
Proudfoot, Mrs Mary (d.1833 aged 90), **289**, née Vaux, Wesleyan Methodist local preacher, wife of Isaac; preaches at Cley, 17.7.96; with Mrs Smith to tea at Hs' and holds meeting at Mrs Winn's house, Letheringsett, 18.7.96; with husband and Mrs Smith to tea, 5.6.97
Provisional Cavalry, *see* Militia
public houses, hire and purchase, **170**, **171**, **271**, **272**, **335**; Messrs Bird and Williams confirm

public houses, hire and purchase (*cont.*)
sale of house at Aldborough to Hs, 24.10.93; WH fails at Walsingham to buy house at Field Dalling, bought by Mr Bidden, 25.10.93; WHj checks Maid's Head, N. Walsham, after Nathaniel Berry absconds, 26.10.93; Mrs Sheppard lets Feathers, Holt, to William Coe of Gt Yarmouth, 9.11.93; WHj views house at Foulsham, 3.1.94; WH, MH and WHj fail to buy Crown, Southrepps, 25.3.94; William Dobson takes over from Richard Mayes at King's Head, Letheringsett, 26.3.94; WH at Holt buys Crown Inn, Southrepps, for £600, 3.4.94, 11.10.94; WH at Holt pays Mr Bird 300 guineas for Black Boys, Aldborough, 8.4.94; man from Norwich fails to hire Crown, Southrepps from Hs, 31.7.94; WH and James Moore establish John Howard in Pitt Arms, Burnham Market, 5.1.95; Mr Clark hires Black Boys, Holt from Hs, 3.3.95; Hs, Samuel Sanderson and Robert Johnson reach agreement over Johnson's hire of Crown, Sheringham, 16.3.95; Johnson takes over Crown, 6.4.95; WH and WHj view John Day's houses for sale at Stibbard and Guist, 7.5.95; man at Hs' to discuss rebuilding of Crown, Southrepps, 16.5.95; WH meets Mr Athow over Bull, Holt, 21.3.96; WH to Walsingham for sale of Chequers, Sharrington, 13.5.96; WHj collects money from Hindolveston, Briston, Corpusty and Saxthorpe, 8.9.96; WH lets Fighting Cocks, Wells to William Silence, 11.9.96, 18.10.96; Robert Johnson surrenders Crown, Sheringham to Mr Cubitt, 30.9.96; Messrs Bignold and Edwards settle Robert Johnson's affairs and hire Crown, Sheringham, 25.10.96, 31.10.96; King's Head, Holt not sold, 16.1.97; WH and WHj hire Jolly Farmers, Field Dalling from Mr Coe, 9.5.97, 2.8.97; WH and WHj settle matters over Field Dalling house, 13.10.97: *see also* licences; *also under individual towns and villages* Aldborough; Beckhithe; Brampton; Briston; Burnham Market; Cley-next-the-Sea; Cromer; East Runton; Edgefield; Fakenham; Field Dalling; Hindolveston; Holt; Letheringsett; North Walsham; Salthouse; Sharrington; Sheringham; Southrepps; Stalham; Syderstone; Thursford; Wells-next-the-Sea; Wiveton
pump, **94**, **96**, new one installed by William Hase in brewhouse, 8.9.95, 11.9.95
pupillage, *see* apprenticeship; Raven, Henry
purse club, *see* clubs

quarter sessions, *see* sessions

R

rabies, *see* illness, hydrophobia
raffle, at Whissonsett, MH wins muslin and WHj wins dress fabric, 11.6.94
rakings, Hs' harvest finished except for, 28.8.94
Ramm (Ram), Blythe (Bly) (1766–1839), daughter of John; marriage in 1794 to John White, MH's register, endnotes
Ramm (Ram), Deborah (Deb) (b.1765), of Letheringsett, daughter of John; marriage to Thomas Balls, 27.1.95 and MH's register, endnotes
Ramm (Ram), John (d.1813 aged 86), **214**, **295**, of Letheringsett, Hs' farm servant, maltster, brewer and thresher; shearing wheat in Furze Closes, 12.8.94, 14–15.8.94; mowing barley, 20.8.94
Ramm (Ram), Susan, *see* Deighton, Mrs
Raven, Mrs Ann (1744–1811), **93**, née Smith, of Whissonsett Hall, farmer, widow of Robert, MH's sister-in-law, HR's mother; departs with children from Hs, 19.7.94; WH and MH to tea, 18.2.95, 8.1.96, 27.5.96; eldest son Robert leaves home and farm, 16.5.95; Robert returns, 1.8.95; Hs and Ravens to dinner, 17.3.97
Raven, Mrs Ann (1746–1827), née Fox, wife of Nathaniel, MH's sister-in-law; prevented by rain from leaving Hs, 6.11.94; with husband and Hs to Fakenham market, 21.5.95; with husband to Hs, with WH and HR to Weybourne Camp and tea at Sheringham, 16.7.95; with husband and Hs to Horningtoft and Brisley, to dinner and supper at Henry Goggs's, 20.8.95; with husband and Hs to dinner with Revd John Crofts, with Hs to Whissonsett, 2.9.95; dines at Hs', 6.11.95; with MH to Mrs Moy at Horningtoft, 27.5.96, 16.3.97; with MH to tea with Mrs Phillis Goggs, 2.11.96, 16.3.97; with husband to Hs, 20.2.97; with husband and Hs tours Bayfield and to Mr Savory, with husband and Hs to tea with Revd Mr Johnson, 23.2.97; with daughter, MH and Mrs Cozens to tea with Henry Goggs, 18.7.97
Raven, Anna (Ann) (1773–1814), daughter of Nathaniel, MH's niece; with sister Mary and cousins to ball at Holt, 20.1.94; with father and cousin Nathaniel to Hs, 24.3.95; with cousins to dinner, 2.4.96; with Hs to Holt, 2.4.96, 25.4.96; with cousins to tea at Mr Burrell's, 3.4.96; with cousins and Misses Johnson to Sheringham, 10.4.96; with cousin and Johnsons to dinner at Mr Burrell's, 17.4.96; with Hs to Holt Church, 24.4.96; with Hs to tea at Mr Sheldrake's, 26.4.96; with brother and cousin to Hs, 31.10.96; with family to Whissonsett, 10.11.96
Raven, Mrs Hannah (1739–94), née Myles, of Tunstead and Norwich, MH's cousin; with sister Mrs Phillis Custance at Mr Baker's, 11.7.94
Raven, Henry (HR) (1777–?1825), **2**, **32**, **67**, **103**, **120**, **130**, **164**, **221**, **226**, **228**, **244**, **386**, of Whissonsett Hall, Hs' brewery apprentice 1794–1800, son of Mrs Ann Raven, née Smith, nephew of MH; with brother Robert to Fakenham, 2.2.94; to Norwich, 12–13.8.94; to Letheringsett Church on fast day, 25.2.95; to Weybourne Camp, 14.6.95, 14.7.95, 10.8.95; to Mr Kendle of Sharrington, 8.11.95, 7.2.96; with MH to supper at Thomas Temple's, 28.1.96; collects MA and Miss Custance from Fakenham, 22.2.96; with family to Mr Burrell, 3.4.96; with family party to Sheringham, 10.4.96, 19.6.97; not at Letheringsett Church, 19.3.97; to Hempton Green Fair, 6.6.97; with Charles Banyard and party to Cromer, 20.8.97
  farm and brewery work, **332**, **334**, **353**, **354**, **357**, **391**, **411**, **412**: with WHj in turnip cart to Wells, 31.1.94; bound apprentice to Hs, 19.7.94; with WH to Brampton, Horstead and Coltishall, stays overnight at White Horse, Gt Hautbois, 3.4.97; brews as head brewer, 24.4.97
  to Holt: with WHj to tea at James Moore's, 25.12.93; collects MA, 14.2.94, 16.12.95; with MA confirmed by Bishop of Norwich, dines with Mr Bartell, 4.7.94; with WHj to church, 3.8.94, 30.11.94, 25.9.96; with Hs and sister Mary to fair and supper at Mr Bartell's, 25.11.94; to John Browne's children's ball for pupils, 3.10.95, 29.9.96; with WHj to Mr Bartell, 25.12.95, 3.2.96; to supper at Joseph Erratt's, 3.7.97
  Methodist meetings attended with MH, **246**: Briston, 5.4.95, 12.4.95, 10.5.95, 21.6.95, 23.8.95, 6.9.95; Hunworth, 6.12.95, 13.12.95; Cley, 25.12.95
  to and from Whissonsett: 12.1.94, 26–27.7.94, 25–26.10.94, 4.1.95, 27.4.95, 10.8.95, 8.1.96, 28.6.96, 10.11.96, 13–14.12.96, 1.1.97, 11.3.97
Raven, John, son of Mrs Hannah Raven; with Adam Baker and Misses Wigg and Bartell to dinner, 15.9.94
Raven, Mary (MR) (1772–1855), daughter of Nathaniel, MH's niece; with father to Hs, with Hs to Holt, 17.10.93; with cousins to Hs, with sister Ann and cousins to ball at Holt, 20.1.94; at Hs' after acting as bridesmaid to Susan Johnson, 1.4.95; with aunt Phillis to Hs, 5.5.95; to Misses Johnson at Holt, 8.5.95, 15.12.95; with aunts to Letheringsett Church, 10.5.95; with WHj to Holt, 13.5.95; with aunt departs,

Raven, Mary (b.1772) (*cont.*) 16.5.95; with brother and HR to Hs, 10.8.95; with Hs to Weybourne Camp, 10.8.95, 12.8.95; with brother departs, 12.8.95, 18.12.95; with brother dines with Hs and to Holt, 11.11.95; with Deb Johnson at Hs', 15.11.95; with mother and MH to Holt, 26.11.95; from Holt to stay with Hs, 3.12.95; with WHj to Holt Church, 6.12.95; with WH to Mr Burrell, 9.12.95; with MA to Mr Davy, 16.12.95; with father and Mrs Cozens departs from Hs, 30.6.96; with mother and MH to tea with Henry Goggs, 18.7.97

Raven, Mary (1780–1846), of Whissonsett Hall, daughter of Mrs Ann Raven, née Smith, future wife of WHj, MH's niece, HR's sister; with HR and Hs to Holt Fair and supper at Mr Bartell's, 25.11.94; with WHj and HR to Holt Church, 30.11.94; with Hs to Mrs Jodrell's sale at Holt, 1–2.12.94; with Hs to tea at Mr Bartell's, 1.12.94; with family party to Sheringham, 19.6.97; with brother Nathaniel to Wisbech, 20.7.97

Raven, Mrs, of King's Head, Norwich; with children, Clara Wymer and Bartells to tea at Hs', 19.3.94

Raven, Nathaniel (1735–99), **79**, **241**, Whissonsett grocer, draper, farmer and maltster, MH's brother; with WH surveys Whissonsett Hall farm, finds it in poor condition, 20.5.95; with wife to Fakenham market, 21.5.95; with WH to Gressenhall, 18.8.95, 16.3.97; with wife and Hs to Horningtoft and Brisley, to dinner at Henry Goggs's, 20.8.95; with WH to Fakenham market, 20.8.95; with wife and Hs dines with Revd John Crofts, 2.9.95; with WH to Brisley and Worthing, 27.5.96; with WH meets Mr Shearing over Holt Heath land, 17.3.97; with family to Swaffham cricket match, 18.7.97

at Hs': with daughter Mary arrives and to Holt, 17.10.93; with niece Rose arrives, 15.5.94; with Hs to sea at Salthouse, with WHj to Whissonsett, 16.5.94; prevented by rain from leaving, to Fakenham for day, 6.11.94; with daughter Ann and nephew Nathaniel arrives, 24.3.95; with family and Hs to Cley, 25.3.95; departs, 26.3.95, 17.7.95; with wife to Hs, 14.7.95, 20.2.97; with Hs to Weybourne Camp, 14.7.95, 16.7.95; to tea at Sheringham, 16.7.95; with Hs to Letheringsett, 2.9.95; with daughter Mary and Mrs Cozens departs, 30.6.96; with family to Kelling, 9.11.96; with wife and Hs tours Bayfield and to Mr Savory, with wife and Hs to tea with Revd Mr Johnson, 23.2.97; with WH to Mr Savory's farm, dines at Hs', to Mr Bartell, 29.9.97; with WH to Holt, departs, 30.9.97

Raven, Nathaniel (*cont.*)

Hs at: MH and WHj to tea and raffle, 11.6.94; Hs to dinner, 17.2.95, 22.2.95, 21.5.95, 18.8.95, 3.9.95, 5.1.96; Hs to tea, 19.5.95, 3.9.95, 13.3.97; WH and Mr Henderson to dinner, 11.9.95; WH and MH to breakfast, dinner and supper, 8.1.96; MH to, 3.11.96

Raven, Nathaniel jnr (1774–1851), Whissonsett grocer and draper, MH's nephew; with cousins departs from Hs, 3.1.94; to Hs, with cousins to ball at Holt, 17.2.94; departs, 9.8.94; with HR to Hs, with Hs to Holt Fair, 27.4.95; with sister Mary and HR to Hs, 10.8.95; with Hs to Weybourne Camp, 10.8.95, 12.8.95; with sister Mary departs, 12.8.95, 18.12.95; with sister Mary dines with Hs and to Holt, 11.11.95; to tea, 16.12.95; takes sister Ann and cousin to Hs, 31.10.96; with Hs to Whissonsett, 2.11.96, 13.3.97; with family to county cricket match at Swaffham, 18.7.97

Raven, Nathaniel ('Little Nathaniel') (b.1781), **82**, **84**, of Whissonsett Hall, son of Mrs Ann Raven, née Smith, MH's nephew, HR's brother; with brother Robert and cousin departs from Hs, 3.1.94; with WHj to Holt and departs, 16.6.94; to Hs, 16.12.94; with uncle Nathaniel and cousin to Hs, 24.3.95; with sister Rose and cousin dines at Hs', with Hs to Holt, 2.4.96; with WHj, Rose and cousin to tea at Mr Burrell's, 3.4.96; with sister Mary to Wisbech, 20.7.97

Raven, Peter jnr (b.1765), **64**, Litcham surgeon; marriage to Elizabeth Wells, 26.4.94

Raven, Phillis (PR) (1779–1844), **384**, of Whissonsett Hall, Holt schoolteacher, daughter of Mrs Ann Raven, née Smith, MH's niece, HR's sister; with Hs to tea at Thomas Forster's, 16.8.93; with Hs to Sheringham, 6.6.94; with sister Rose and Messrs Skrimshire stays at Hs', 18.6.97; with family party to Sheringham, 19.6.97; with brother Robert to dinner, with Hs meets Miss Alpe at Holt, is hired as schoolteacher until Christmas for four guineas, 4.8.97; dines with Hs, with MA to tea at Holt, takes up post as teacher, 8.8.97; to tea with Hs, 20.8.97

Raven, Robert (b.1771), **175**, **194**, of Whissonsett Hall, farmer, son of Mrs Ann Raven, née Smith, MH's nephew, HR's brother; with brother Nathaniel and cousin Nathaniel departs from Hs, 3.1.94; with HR and cousin Mary to Hs, with cousins at ball at Holt, 20.1.94; departs, 21.1.94; with HR to Fakenham, 2.2.94; dines with Hs, 25.5.95; with WHj to Holt, departs, 8.12.94; with WHj to Hs, 13.2.95; leaves home, 16.5.95; returns to mother, 1.8.95; dines with Hs and departs,

Raven, Robert (*cont.*) 25.4.96; with family party to Sheringham, 19.6.97; with sister Phillis to dinner, with Hs to Holt to meet Miss Alpe, 4.8.97

Raven, Rose, *see* Skrimshire, Mrs

Raven, William (b.1776), formerly of Whissonsett Hall, Hs' former brewery apprentice, son of Mrs Ann Raven, née Smith, MH's nephew, HR's brother; departs from Hs, 3.7.97

Reepham, Norf., **106**, **286**, George Wymer jnr and clerk stay overnight at Hs', 4.9.94; WHj to, 8.5.95; Clara Wymer departs from Mr Bartell's for, 18.2.96; WH with Bartells to over felling timber [?at Kerdiston], WH stays overnight with George Wymer jnr, 30.3.96; WH measures timber for Mr Bartell, stays overnight, 12.7.96; WHj to with Mr Bartell, WH and WHj return from, 14.7.96; WH and Mr Bartell to over measuring ash timber, 20.2.97; WHj and Thomas Balls jnr to, WHj buys timber from Mr Sewell, 27.3.97

registers, **298**, of Letheringsett marriages, deaths and burials 1793–97 and Hs' maidservants 1793–97 compiled by MH, endnotes

rheumatism, *see* illness

Richards, Miss, with Bakers and Forsters to tea, 28.9.96; at Hs', 12.8.97; with Hs to Holt Church, 13.8.97; dines with Hs and departs with Mr Forster, 14.8.97; taken by Mr Forster to stay at Hs', 25.9.97

Riches, Mary, with Davys to tea, 5.9.94

rider, merchant's travelling representative from London, WHj fails to sell mare to, 1.5.94

riots, in bread famine, **228**, **231**, **232**, **233**, **234**, **235**, **325**; soldiers from Holt sent to Wells to quell riot, 15–16.12.95; Zeb Rouse's flour bound for King's Lynn stopped by poor at Sharrington, 17.12.95; mob at Sharrington withhold flour from justices, 18.12.95; all-day sitting at Holt to settle mob but justices do nothing, troop of horse and party of foot soldiers summoned, 19.12.95; soldiers march to Sharrington to guard flour and arrest ringleader, 20.12.95; justices and farmers examine witnesses to riot, 22.12.95

river [Cley Watering], Henry Smith dies in stream on Holt–Cley road after fall from horse, 24.5.94: *see also* Glaven, River

roads, poor conditions, **99**, **165**, **230**, **233**, **353**, **372**, **373**, **393**, **397**; almost impassable, Hs send two men to deliver beer to Southrepps, they return at 3 am, 30.1.95; very difficult in deep snow for WH and WHj returning from Sheringham, 4.2.95; slippery and dangerous in snow, 2.12.96; slippery in frost, 4.12.96: *see also* accidents, road; carts; chaises; coaches; wagons

Robinson, Edward, **123**, London linen draper; with Davys to dinner at Hs', 5.9.94; marriage at Holt to Elizabeth Davy, they depart for London, 28.10.94

Robinson, Mrs Elizabeth (Bett), **123**, née Davy, wife of Edward, daughter of John Davy; with family and future husband to tea at Hs', 5.9.94; marriage at Holt, with husband departs for London, 28.10.94

roller (role), bought by WH at Thomas Forster's sale, 7.10.96

rooms, Hs', *see* house

round, of public houses; by WHj at Burnham Market, 9.10.94

Rouse, Zebulon (Zeb) (d.1840 aged 75), **116**, **135**, **142**, **146**, of Glandford Watermill, Letheringsett Watermill and Cley; his flour intercepted by poor at Sharrington, 17.12.95

Rowden (Rowdon) Miss [?Julia], with Hs, Ravens and Skrimshires to Sheringham, 19.6.97

Rowland, William (d.1793 aged 70), of Letheringsett; burial noted in MH's register, endnotes

Roxby, Mr, London hop-factor; sells hops to WH at Holt, 9.11.96

Royal Family, *see* George III

Royal Navy, *see* Navy

Rudham, Norf., sudden death of Mr Billings jnr, 24.12.96: *see also* West Rudham

rum, *see* spirits

Runton, *see* East Runton

Russia (Rusia), **327**, death at St Petersburg of Empress, 22.12.96

Rust, Charles, innkeeper of Crown, Lt Walsingham; dines with Hs, 11.11.93

Ryburgh (Ribourg, Rybro), Norf., **252**, WH and Mr Henderson meet John Wade at, 11.9.95; John Wade dines with Hs, 23.1.96; WHj to John Wade, 7.3.96: *see also* Wade, John

S

Sacraments, *see* Letheringsett Church

St Petersburg, *see* Russia

St Simon's (St Symond's), *see* Norwich, public houses

Sales (Seales), Mrs Ann (d.1821 aged 65), née Legge, wife of Charles; with husband at tea party at King's Head, Letheringsett, 4.9.95, 18.8.97; to tea party at Hs', 2.9.96; daughter born, 20.2.97

Sales (Seales), Charles (d.1821 aged 68), Holt draper and grocer; WHj to tea, 15.12.94, 1–2.8.95, 23.4.97; with wife at tea party at King's Head, Letheringsett, 4.9.95, 18.8.97; WHj collects Hs from, 23.12.95

sales, Hs to; Mrs Jewell's at Holt stopped by Lord Chancellor, 1.12.94; Mrs Jewell's resumes, 5.1.95; WHj and Nathaniel Raven at Blakeney Mill, 26.11.95; WHj at Fakenham Mill, 15.2.96; Cley bath house sold for 40 guineas, 10.7.97; WH and MH to Mr Ditchell's at Kelling, 5.10.97
agricultural, **308**: WH and WHj buy cow, tumbril and roller at Thomas Forster's at Bayfield, 6–7.10.96
brewery equipment: Hs buy barrels at Cley, 1.10.94; WH and WHj buy bunches of lath at Robert Farthing's at Blakeney, 16.8.97
building materials: WH and WHj buy tiles at Cley, 30.9.94; WH and WHj buy timber at Robert Farthing's at Blakeney, 16.8.97
household goods, **115**: MH and MA buy sheets at John Flegg's at Holt, 5.4.94; William Custance's sale of new furniture begins at Fakenham, 6.10.94; Hs and Mary Raven to William Christmas's at Holt, 1–2.12.94; Hs buy pistols, cheese trolley, tart presses, books, kitchen range, oven and cellaret at Cley, 1–3.10.94; MA buys china ornaments at Mrs Jewell's at Holt, 9.1.95; Hs buy silver spoons and salt cellars at Holt, 10.1.95; WHj buys stove, chairs and earthenware at Mr Sanderson's at Weybourne Camp canteen, 12–13.1.97; MH and WHj buy mirror at Cley bath house, 10.7.97:
see also auction; public houses
Salthouse, Norf., WH and MH to Salthouse Heath, 21.10.93; Hs, Nathaniel Raven and Rose Raven to seaside, 16.5.94: *see also* Newstead, Robert
Sanderson, Mrs Mary (d.1802), innkeeper of King's Arms/Cromer Hotel, Cromer, tied house; at Hs', 13.12.93
Sanderson, Mr, preacher, *see* Saunderson, John
Sanderson (Saunderson), Samuel, innkeeper of Crown, Sheringham, tied house, and keeper of Weybourne Camp canteen; at Hs' to transfer tenancy to Robert Johnson, stays overnight at King's Head, Letheringsett, 10.3.95; dines with Hs, settles transfer, with WH to Holt, 16.3.95; makes final agreement with WH and WHj over transfer, 6.4.95; WHj to sale of Weybourne Camp canteen, 12–13.1.97: *see also* Weybourne Camp
Sarah, Hs' maidservant, *see* Turner, Sarah
sashes, *see* house, yard
Saunderson (Sanderson), John, Wesleyan Methodist itinerant preacher; preaches at Letheringsett meeting, 4.3.97
Savory (Savery), John Claxton (d.1819), **317**, of Bayfield Hall and Bayfield Lodge [later Bayfield Brecks], farmer; with wife to Letheringsett Church, 13.11.96, 2.4.97; Hs to tea, 22.12.96; WHj to, 27.1.97, 23.6.97; with wife to tea at Mr Davy's, 8.2.97; Hs and Mr and Mrs Nathaniel Raven tour site of new farmhouse at Bayfield, 23.2.97; MA to tea, 25.2.97; WH, MH and MA to new farmhouse and to tea at Hall, 25.5.97; his sheepshearers watched by WH, 8.7.97; WH and Nathaniel Raven to farmhouse, 29.9.97
Savory, Mrs Mary (d.1805 aged 32), **400**, née Howard, wife of John Claxton, daughter of Thomas Howard; with husband at Letheringsett Church, 13.11.96, 2.4.97; death of brother Nicholas at Burnham Thorpe, 24.12.96; with husband to tea at Mr Davy's, 8.2.97; churched at Letheringsett, 22.10.97
Saxlingham [Saxlingham-by-Holt], Norf., Mr Bidden buys Field Dalling public house, 25.10.93; WH to manor court, 30.6.96; William Thackwray to Thomas Balls, 12.12.96; Thomas Balls jnr at Hs', 12.1.97; WHj to Thomas Balls, 20.3.97, 17.5.97, 12.9.97; Thomas Balls jnr with WHj to Reepham, 27.3.97: *see also* Furze Closes
Saxthorpe (Saxthorp), Norf., Mr Hase installs new pump for Hs, 8.9.95; WHj collects money, 8.9.96
schools, at Holt:
Miss Alpe's boarding and day school for young ladies, **384**: Phillis Raven hired as teacher, 4.8.97, 8.8.97
Free Grammar School, **330**: WHj to feast at Feathers, 18.12.94; Master Collyer and Master Shearing to tea at Hs', 1.6.97
Scotland, Revd Mr Wilcocks and Miss Hagon elope to, 20.6.95
Scotton (Scotten), Yorks, Mr Fawcett at Hs', 23.8.95
sea, **184**, **185**, **189**, **227**, **271**, **363**, Hs, Nathaniel Raven and Rose Raven to Salthouse, 16.5.94; high tide damages Sheringham cliffs, 19.6.95; WHj inspects breach made at Sheringham, 20.6.95; Hs' men and teams lay large stones against sea bank at Sheringham to prevent undermining, 28.12.95; Hs, Henry Goggs and Mr Cook to, 14.8.97: *see also* bathing, by WHj; ship
sedition, reports of arrests made for treason and, Habeas Corpus suspended, 23.5.94
sermons:
Anglican, **364**: none at Letheringsett, 27.4.94, 2.11.94, 12.4.95, 1.1.97, 23.4.97; funeral sermon at Letheringsett, 22.5.96; MH's criticisms of Mr Burrell's, 15.11.96, 4.12.96, 22.1.97, 19.3.97, 30.4.97, 7.5.97, 14.5.97, 21.5.97, 11.6.97; Revd Robert Bransby

sermons, Anglican (*cont.*)
Francis at Holt, 4.12.96; Revd Bransby Francis at Holt, 16.4.97: *see also* Burrell, Revd John
Independent, **263**: Mr Sykes of Briston and Guestwick at Letheringsett [? at Wesleyan meeting], 13.4.96
Wesleyan Methodist, **188, 289**:
itinerant preachers: Mr Hill of Snoring at Briston, 5.7.95; Mr Heath at Letheringsett, 28.5.96; Mr Witham at Letheringsett, 11.6.96; Mr Hill at Cley, 21.8.96, 18.9.96, 16.10.96; Mr Saunderson at Letheringsett, 4.3.97; no preacher at Cley, 20.8.97; Mr Leggatt at Cley, 1.10.97
local preachers: Mr Eastaugh of Hempton at Cley, 26.3.96; Mrs Proudfoot of Wells at Cley, 17.7.96

servants, *see* maidservants; menservants; *see also farm servants under* boys; workforce

servants in husbandry, Hs', *see* workforce

sessions:
Holt: WH dines with justices, 13.9.94, 19.9.95, 15.10.95, 17.9.96; sitting to organise raising of soldiers [sailors], 4.4.95; WH and Mr Burrell to, 29.8.95; sitting for justices to quell mob, justices send for soldiers, 19.12.95; WH to, 31.12.96; WHj to, 9.9.97
hiring: MH and MA to, 1.10.96
licensing: WH to, 19.9.95, 17.9.96
quarter: WH to, 17.10.93, 13.10.96, 19.1.97; WHj serves on jury, 16.10.94; WH serves on grand jury, 22.1.95; Henry Goggs to, 15.10.95
Walsingham: quarter, 14.4.96:
see also assizes; justices

Sewell (Sewill), Mr [? Samuel], Reepham timber merchant; WHj buys timber, 27.3.97

Sharp, Mr S., of Brinton; with WHj from Holt assembly, stays overnight, 10.11.94

Sharrington (Sherington), Norf., **221, 232, 233, 234, 235, 270**, HR to tea at Mr Kendle's, 8.11.95; poor intercept flour at, 17.12.95; WH, Nathaniel Raven jnr and Mary Raven to, mob unload flour and withhold it from justices, 18.12.95; WHj to, soldiers guard flour seized from mob and arrest ringleader named Bone, 20.12.95; soldiers, justices and farmers escort flour to Stock Heath from, 21.12.95; MH and Mrs Youngman to meeting, 2.1.96; HR dines with Mr Kendle, 7.2.96; WH to Walsingham for sale of Chequers, 13.5.96

Shearing, John, **346**, of Paxfield Farm, Helhoughton; WH and Nathaniel Raven to over land on Holt Heath, 17.3.97

Shearing, Master, Holt schoolboy, [? son of John]; with Master Collyer to tea at Hs', 1.6.97

shearing, *see* harvests; sheep

sheep, WH watches Mr Savory's shearers, 8.7.97

sheets, *see* linen

Sheldrake, John, Holt excise officer and Inspector of Weights and Balances, Holt hundred; with wife and Burrells at Hs', 13.11.93; with wife to supper, 6.11.94, 6.4.96; Hs and Mary Raven to tea, 2.12.94; Hs to tea, 9.1.95, 3.10.95, 23.1.96, 20.2.96; with Mr Benfield at Hs', 15.4.95, 10.6.97; with wife to tea, 5.6.95, 10.12.95, 8.3.96, 6.10.96, 25.8.97; to dinner, 23.6.95, 25.4.96; Hs and Misses Raven to tea at, 26.4.96; with wife, Hs and Miss Thompson to tea at Mr Burrell's, 16.8.96; with wife, daughter and John Davy to tea, 30.9.96; to supper, 6.7.97

Sheldrake, Miss M., daughter of John; with parents to tea, 8.3.96, 30.9.96, 23.3.97; with parents to supper, 25.8.97

Sheldrake, Mrs, Holt dressmaker, wife of John; with husband and Burrells at Hs', 13.11.93; with husband to supper, 6.11.94, 6.4.96, 25.8.97; prevented by rain from leaving, 6.11.94; alters and repairs MH's gown, stays overnight, 14.2.95; with husband to tea, 5.6.95, 10.12.95, 8.3.96, 6.10.96; with MH and MA to Letheringsett meeting, 6.4.96; at Hs', 20.4.96; with Miss Leake to tea, 20.5.96; with husband, Hs and Miss Thompson to tea at Mr Burrell's, 16.8.96; with husband, daughter and John Davy to tea, 30.9.96; to dinner, 16.8.97

Sheppard, Mrs Elizabeth (d.1816 aged 77), **20, 59**, née Main, innkeeper of Feathers, Holt, and excise officekeeper; lets Feathers to Mr Coe, 9.11.93; Hs in her postchaise to Southrepps, 25.3.94: *see also* chaises, postchaises, Feathers'; Holt, public houses, Feathers

Sheringham (Sherringham), Norf., **227**, WHj to, 24.4.94, 31.10.95, 16.11.95, 23.12.95, 9.9.96, 15.11.96; WHj, MA, Phillis Raven and Miss Symonds to, 6.6.94; WHj and James Moore to, 6.8.94; WH and WHj sell land at to Mr Barcham for coal yard, 4.2.95; WH and WHj at to secure beer contract for Weybourne Camp, 1.6.95; WH, MA and Mr and Mrs Nathaniel Raven to tea, 16.7.95; WHj to tea with Mr Barcham, 28.12.95; WHj dines at, 9.3.96; HR to with Rose and Ann Raven, Misses Johnson and others, 10.4.96; Hs dine with Mr Flower of Lower Sheringham, 10.8.96; WHj in new cart to dinner, 22.3.97; MH and WHj buy pigs from Mr Page and to tea, 8.5.97; WHj bathes, 29.5.97, 14.6.97; WHj, MA, HR, Robert, Rose, Phillis and Mary Raven, Miss Rowden and three Mr Skrimshires to tea, 19.6.97; MH and WHj to, 29.6.97; WHj's horse shod, 13.9.97

Sheringham (*cont.*)
Crown: Thomas Baldwin breaks arm returning from beer delivery, 23.12.94; hired by Robert Johnson, 16.3.95; WH and WHj transfer tenancy from Samuel Sanderson to Johnson, 6.4.95; Johnson evades WH, WHj and William Thackwray, 27.9.96, 1.10.96; WHj to with James Moore after Johnson's flight, 30.9.96; WH to Cley hoping to meet Johnson, 2.10.96; Messrs Bignold and Edwards hire Crown, 25.10.96; John Smith meets Johnson, 30.10.96; WH and WHj install John Edwards as new tenant, 31.10.96; WHj checks workmen's repairs and alterations, 14.11.96, 22.11.96, 28.11.96, 9.6.97, 14.6.97, 27.6.97: *see also* Johnson, Robert
Mr and Mrs Cook Flower of [Old] Hall, **10**: at Hs', 22.10.93, 21.1.94; WHj to, 24.4.94, 22.10.95, 28.11.96, 22.3.97, 13.9.97; WH and WHj to tea, 19.9.94, 6.4.95; WHj and MA to ball, 5.1.95; WHj to dinner, 20.6.95, 9.9.96, 21.9.96; WHj and MA to tea, 27.7.95; WHj buys piglets, 21.9.96; WH and WHj to dinner, 1.10.96: *see also* Flower, Cook; Flower, Mrs Sarah
storm damage to cliffs: 19–20.6.95; Hs' men and teams lay stones against sea bank to prevent undermining, 28.12.95

Sherington, *see* Sharrington

Sherlock, Dr [? William (*c.*1641–1707); ? Thomas (1678–1761)], theologian; his book on Judgment bought by Hs at Cley sale, 2.10.94

ship, **227**, William Thackwray to Wells to sail to Hull on board Capt. Bloom's, ship does not sail, 1.1.97

Shipdham (Shipden), Norf., Revd James Morgan and Susan Johnson to after marriage, 1.4.95

shirehouse, *see* Holt

shooting, **165**, partridge by John Davy snr and jnr, 23.9.95

shops, **248**, WH, MH and MA buy goods at Mr Woodcock's at Briston, 26.6.97: *see also* sales; *also individual shopkeepers* Baker, John; Davy, John; Davy, John jnr; Erratt, Joseph; Fox, Thomas; Johnson, Misses; Leak, Misses; Raven, Nathaniel; Raven, Nathaniel jnr; Sales, Charles; Skrimshire, George

side pain, *see* illness

Siderston, *see* Syderstone

Sikes, *see* Sykes, Revd John

Silence, William, innkeeper of Fighting Cocks, Wells, tied house; hires house from WH, 11.9.96; takes over from John Walden, 18.10.96

silver, Hs buy spoons and salt cellars at Holt, 10.1.95

Six Acres, Letheringsett field farmed by Hs; men carrying barley, 26.8.94

Skiffins (Skivens), James William, **39**, **59**, **138**, innkeeper of Black Boys, Holt, tied house, and White Lion, Holt; at work in Hs' garden, 31.7.94, 17.9.94; to dinner, 18.11.94; WH to Feathers over business affairs, 26.4.96

Skrimshire, George, later Fakenham shopkeeper and undertaker, son of William snr; with family party to Hs, stays overnight, 18.6.97; with family party to Sheringham, 19.6.97

Skrimshire, Mrs Rose (1773–1829), wife of Thomas, daughter of Mrs Ann Raven, née Smith, MH's niece, HR's sister; to Hs with uncle Nathaniel, 15.5.94; with Hs to seaside at Salthouse, 16.5.94; with MA and Miss Symonds to tea at Mrs Jennis's, 23.5.94; with Hs to Holt market and tea at Misses Leak's, 24.5.94; with brother Nathaniel and cousin Ann dines at Hs', 2.4.96; with Hs to Holt, 2.4.96, 25.4.96; with family to tea at Mr Burrell's, 3.4.96; with family party to Sheringham, 10.4.96; with cousin Ann and Johnsons to dinner at Mr Burrell's, 17.4.96; with Hs to Holt Church, 24.4.96; with Hs to tea at Mr Sheldrake's, 26.4.96; with cousins to Hs, 31.10.96; with family to Whissonsett, 10.11.96; with sister Phillis and three Mr Skrimshires to Hs, stays overnight, 18.6.97; with family party to Sheringham, 19.6.97; marriage to Thomas Skrimshire, they depart for Wisbech, 23.6.97; her marriage 1797 and birth of child in 1798 noted in MH's register, endnotes

Skrimshire (Skrimpshaw), Thomas (d.1836 aged 61), LLB [Revd Thomas 1798], of Wisbech, Master of Fakenham Academy, Curate of Whissonsett 1798, Curate of Houghton juxta Harpley 1814–17, 1822– ?, Rector of Testerton and Vicar of Gt and Lt Hockham 1800–36, Vicar of Houghton juxta Harpley and Vicar of S. Creake 1817–24, Chaplain to Marquess of Cholmondeley, Master of Syderstone School, son of William snr; with family party to Hs, stays overnight, 18.6.97; with family party to Sheringham, 19.6.97; marriage to Rose Raven at Whissonsett, they depart for Wisbech, 23.6.97 and noted in MH's register, endnotes 26.10.97

Skrimshire, William [? snr, Wisbech surgeon, ? jnr]; with family party to Hs, stays overnight, 18.6.97; with family party to Sheringham, 19.6.97

slate, additional duty on, 7.2.94

Smith, Mrs Christiana (d.1797), burial noted in MH's register, endnotes

Smith, Mrs Elizabeth (d.1803 aged 63), formerly Mrs Hunt, 1st wife of John; to tea, 26.8.94, 5.8.97; dines at Hs', brings Mrs Thurgar to King's Head, Letheringsett, 19.1.96; with husband to tea at Hs', with MH and MA to meeting at Letheringsett, 25.6.96; at Hs', 3.7.96; with Mrs Proudfoot holds Letheringsett meeting at Mrs Winn's, 18.7.96; with husband, Hs and party dines at Cromer, 10.9.96; with Proudfoots to tea, 5.6.97

Smith, Henry (d.1794 aged 32), **72**, **88**, Blakeney merchant; killed in fall from horse returning from Holt market, 24.5.94

Smith, John, Cley attorney; Hs to dinner, 2.10.94; at Hs', 16.11.95; WH to, 3.3.96, 8.3.96, 6.10.96; WHj to, 6.3.96; MH and MA to tea and meeting at, 26.3.96; stays overnight with Hs, 20–22.5.96; WH and MH to tea, 12.6.96; with wife to tea at Hs', 25.6.96; with WHj to Holt, 25.6.96; with wife, Hs and party dines at Cromer, 10.9.96; dines with Hs, 30.10.96, 19.1.97; MH and WHj to tea at on day of bath-house sale, 10.7.97

legal practice: with WH to Norwich, 21.5.96; breakfasts with Hs, with WH to Thursford, 29.8.96; meets WH and Mr Bignold over Robert Johnson's affairs, 14.10.96; breakfasts and dines with Hs, settles Johnson's affairs with Messrs Bignold and Edwards, 25.10.96; meets Johnson at Sheringham, 30.10.96; with WH to Thursford to refute allegations made against WH, 29.3.97

Snoring, Norf., **244**, Mr Hill preaches at Briston meeting, 5.7.95

snow, 25.1.94, 24–25.12.94, 31.12.94, 14.1.95, 17–18.1.95, 20.1.95, 22.1.95, 24.1.95, 3–4.2.95, 14.3.95, 18.3.95, 6.3.96, 27.3.96, 2.12.96; Mrs Flower unable to leave in, 24-25.12.94; two men needed for beer delivery to Southrepps, 30.1.95; deepest known for years, 5.2.95; roads dangerous, 2.12.96

soldiers, *see* Army; Militia; Volunteers; Weybourne Camp

Southrepps (Southreeps, Southreps), Norf., Hs and James Moore to, 25.3.94; WHj to, 14.7.94, 3.8.95; WH and WHj to, 28.10.94, 9.3.95, 5.5.95; WH, MH and MA to, 10.9.96; WHj prevented by rheumatism from going to, 23.12.96

Crown, **55**, **56**, **109**: WH, MH and WHj to dinner, fail to secure purchase, 25.3.94; bought by WH at Holt from Messrs Grey and Summers for £600, 3.4.94; WH and WHj fail to let Crown to Norwich man, 31.7.94; WH pays John Summers for, 11.10.94; two men needed for delivery in snow, 30.1.95; unnamed man at Hs' to hire

Southrepps, Crown (*cont.*)

Crown and rebuild it, 16.5.95; Hs and Mrs Phillis Goggs to breakfast, 23.9.95; WHj and Thomas Balls jnr prevented from collecting piano owing to dispute with Mr Baker, 13.4.97

spirits, additional levels of duty on British spirits, rum and brandy, 7.2.94

sports, *see* bowling green; cricket; shooting: *see also* entertainments

stables, at King's Head, Letheringsett; building begun by bricklayers, 5.3.94; carpenters raise roof, 15.3.94

stacks, **133**, WHj moves barley stack into barn, 11.2.96; Hs Wnish stacking hay, 22.7.96

Staff (Staffe), Robert, innkeeper of Maid's Head, Stalham, tied house; with son stays overnight at Hs', 21.1 94; with WHj to Blakeney, 18.3.95; stays overnight, 2.3.97: *see also* Stalham

Stalham, Norf., Robert Bye delivers beer, 13.8.94: *see also* Staff, Robert

Starling, Sarah, Hs' maidservant 1796–97; replaced by Elizabeth Jennerys, 18.4.97; hire and wages, maidservants' register, MH's endnotes

Stibbard, Norf., **167**, **170**, **171**, WH and WHj view John Day's public house for sale, 7.5.95

stock, *see* cows; horses; pigs; sheep

Stock Heath, Norf., **233**, soldiers, justices and farmers escort flour from Sharrington to, 21.12.95

stocks, financial, noted by MH, endnotes

stomach pain, *see* illness

stones, additional tax on, 7.2.94; laid by Hs' men and teams against sea bank at Sheringham to prevent undermining, 28.12.95

storms, 25.1.94, 28.4.94, 4.8.94, 17.1.95, 18.3.95, 25.4.95, 6.6.95, 14.8.95, 21.8.95, 29.10.95, 31.10.95, 3.11.95, 18.11.95, 19.12.95, 26.1.96, 12.2.96, 14–15.2.96, 27.3.96, 9.4.96, 13.5.96, 30.5.96, 15.7.96, 25.10.96, 5.12.96, 26.6.97

Sturley (Sturly), Mrs, of Thornage Hall; to tea, 15.2.97

Suffolk, soldiers at Weybourne Camp ordered to Woodbridge, 9.9.96

Summers, John, **55**, **109**, innkeeper of Crown, Southrepps, tied house; with Mr Grey at Holt sells Crown to WH for £600, 3.4.94; paid by WH, 11.10.94

Supplementary Militia, *see* Militia

surgeons, doctors, Ann Ives dies on way to calling on, 17.5.96: *see also individual practitioners* Bartell, Edmund; Bartell, Edmund jnr; Heath, John

Sutton, *see* Manners Sutton, Right Revd Dr Charles

Swaffham, Norf., **379**, WH, Nathaniel Raven snr and jnr and Thomas Fox to county cricket match, 18.7.97

Swanton Novers, Norf., **27**, WH and MH injured in chaise accident, 3.7.94

Syderstone (Siderston), Norf., WHj to, 18.12.95, 25.10.97; WH and John Thompson to, 12.9.96

Sykes (Sikes), Revd John (d.1824), **263**, of Guestwick, minister of Guestwick Independent Church 1776–1824, minister of Briston Independent Chapel 1783–1824; preaches at Letheringsett meeting, 13.4.96

Symonds, Jonathan (d.1803 aged 65), **71**, of Gt Yarmouth and Ormesby St Margaret, grocer and merchant; with daughter departs from Hs, 16.6.94

Symonds (Simonds), Phillis (d.1805 aged 26), **71**, daughter of Jonathan; with Hs to tea at Thomas Forster's, 16.8.93; with MA and Rose Raven to tea at Mrs Jennis's, 23.5.94; with Hs to Holt market and tea at Misses Leaks', 24.5.94; seized with fits while at tea at Thomas Forster's with WHj and MA, is nursed by maids, 27.5.94; ill all day with fits, 28.5.94; recovers, 29.5.94; with WHj, MA and Phillis Raven to Sheringham, 6.6.94; with father departs, 16.6.94

T

tart presses, bought by WH and WHj at Cley sale, 1.10.94

taxes, list of new levels of duty taken from newspaper, 7.2.94

teacher, *see* schools

teams, *see* horses, working horses

Temple, Mrs Mary, née Beverley, wife of Thomas; daughter born, 31.1.94; with husband to tea, 18.12.94; with family and Bartells to supper, 3.3.96; with husband at tea party at King's Head, Letheringsett, 18.8.97

Temple, Miss, daughter of Thomas; with parents and Bartells to supper at Hs', 3.3.96

Temple, Richard, Barmer farmer; WH and John Thompson stay overnight, 12.9.96; WHj stays overnight, 28.10.96; to tea at Hs' and borrows £120, 18.9.97

Temple, Robert (d.1795 aged 58), Weybourne farmer; death, 14.6.95

Temple, Thomas, Thornage farmer; to supper at Hs', 24.10.93, 8.6.97; WH, MA, Bakers, Bartells and Clara Wymer to supper, 13.12.93; to tea, buys muck in Hs' yards for 30 guineas, 29.4.94; Hs to tea, 1.5.94; with wife to tea, 18.12.94; MH, HR, Clara Wymer and Miss Dewson to supper, WHj to, 28.1.96; with family and Bartells to supper at Hs', 3.3.96;

Temple, Thomas (*cont.*)
MH views carcase of 31-stone hog, 29.12.96; Hs to supper, 13.1.97; with wife at tea party at King's Head, Letheringsett, 18.8.97

Temple, Thomas William (d.1816 aged 48), Blakeney coal and cinder merchant; to dinner, 8.2.97

Thackwray (Thackery, Thackwry), William (b.*c.*1779), **310**, of Forest Lane Head, Knaresborough, Yorks, WH's nephew; arrives at Hs', 26.9.96; with WH and WHj to Sheringham over Robert Johnson, with Hs to supper at Bayfield, 27.9.96; with Hs to Letheringsett Church, 2.10.96, 30.10.96; with WHj to Wells, 14.10.96; spends day and night at Thomas Balls', 12.12.96; with MH to Cley meeting, 25.12.96; with John Thompson to Wells to set sail aboard Capt. Bloom's ship for Hull, ship does not sail, 1.1.97

theatres:
Holt: *see* plays
London: 14 trampled to death in Haymarket, 7.2.94

Thetford, Norf., James Mingay opposes William Windham in Norwich by-election, 11.7.94
assizes: WHj asks John Wade to appear as witness in trial, 7.3.96; WHj and John Ellis to, 10–11.3.96; WHj from, 13.3.96

Thomas, Revd William, Curate of Holt *c.*1790–96; with WH, WHj and Messrs Morgan and Moore at Mr Burrell's, 28.11.93; WH to dinner, 14.1.97

Thompson, Mrs Ann (d.1800 aged 50), **65**, wife of William Gunton; with husband to N. Walsham Fair in Hs' cart, 13.5.95

Thompson, Frances, Hs' maidservant 1794–95; departs, 10.10.95; hire and wages, maidservants' register, MH's endnotes

Thompson, Miss [? Harriet Gunton, daughter of William Gunton]; with Hs and Sheldrakes to tea at Mr Burrell's, 16.8.96

Thompson, John, with WH to Gressenhall and Whissonsett, 5.6.95; with WH to Wells to arrest Nicholas Everitt, 21.9.95; collects MH and MA in chaise from Holt, 14.5.96; with WH to Wells and Syderstone and stays overnight at Barmer, 12.9.96; takes William Thackwray to Wells, 1.1.97
with MH and others to Wesleyan Methodist meetings:
Briston: 7.5.97, 11.6.97, 27.8.97, 24.9.97
Cley: 3.1.96, 10.1.96, 17.1.96, 24.1.96, 7.2.96, 14.2.96, 21.2.96, 20.3.96, 27.3.96, 3.4.96, 17.4.96, 24.4.96, 8.5.96, 22.5.96, 29.5.96, 5.6.96, 14.8.96, 21.8.96, 4.9.96, 18.9.96, 2.10.96, 23.10.96, 30.10.96, 13.11.96, 22.1.97, 19.3.97, 26.3.97, 2.4.97,

Thompson, John, to Cley meeting (*cont.*) 16.4.97, 23.4.97, 30.4.97, 14.5.97, 21.5.97, 4.6.97, 6.8.97, 20.8.97, 10.9.97, 1.10.97
Hunworth: 13.3.96

Thompson, William Gunton, **33**, **65**, **135**, **149**, **269**, Hs' brewer, miller and millwright 1792–98; to Aylsham to receive legacy, 10.12.93; checks N. Walsham public house, 19.4.95; with wife to N. Walsham Fair in Hs' cart, 13.5.95

Thornage, Norf., **9**, **112**, **259**, **277**, **376**, Mr Bird at Hs' to confirm sale of public house at Aldborough, 24.10.93; Mr Bird with WH to Aldborough, 27.11.93; Hs at large party at Thomas Temple's, 13.12.93; WH pays Mr Bird for Aldborough house, 8.4.94; Hs to Thomas Temple, 1.5.94, 13.1.97; WHj to church and to tea at John Kendle's, 2.11.94; WH and WHj inspect hay, 24.7.95; WHj and Mr Henderson to William Cook, 9.9.95; MH, HR, Clara Wymer and Miss Dewson to supper at Thomas Temple's, WHj to, 28.1.96; MH views carcase of 31-stone hog, 29.12.96; burial of Mrs Woodhouse of Lt Thornage, 11.4.97; Thomas Temple at Hs', 8.6.97: *see also* Temple, Thomas

Thurgar (Thaqur), Mrs Ann, née Dobson, of Wells; brought by Mrs Smith to King's Head, Letheringsett, 19.1.96

Thursford, Norf., **27**, WH and John Smith to, 29.8.96; WH and John Smith at to refute allegations made against WH, 29.3.97

tides, *see* sea

tiles, **44**, **86**, **87**, **124**, bought by WH and WHj at Cley sale, 30.9.94

timber, *see* wood

Tinker, James, **404**, Letheringstt carpenter; marriage in 1793 to Mary Jeckell noted in MH's register, endnotes: *see also* carpenters

tithes, WH dines at Mr Burrell's audit, 9.12.96

Todhunter, Mrs, wife of William; with husband at Hs' on way to Wells, 4.9.94; with husband to dinner, 25.4.96

Todhunter, William, excise supervisor and port surveyor; with wife at Hs' on way to Wells, 4.9.94; with wife to dinner, 25.4.96

Toftrees (Toffts), Norf., Mr and Mrs Cozens dine at, 20.7.97

Tooby, Edward Cox (d.1834 aged 74), **191**, Holt excise officer; to tea at Hs', 8.7.95

toothache, *see* illness

Tournai (Tournay), *see* France

treason, reports of arrests for sedition and, Habeas Corpus suspended, 23.5.94

trees, **317**, **330**, WH, MH and MA visit Henry Jodrell's new plantations at Bayfield, 22.4.95; carpenters put up rails in Hs' garden to tie fruit trees, 23.3.96; WH and WHj plant firs at Holt Heath Farm, 25.2.97: *see also* wood

trial, WHj asks John Wade to give evidence as witness at Thetford Assizes, 7.3.96

tumbril, *see* carts

Tunstead, Norf., **26**, **306**, John Raven dines with Hs, 15.9.94

Turner, Sarah, Hs' maidservant 1793–94, 1795–96; to Cley Fair, 25.7.94; departs, 10.10.96; hire and wages, maidservants' register, MH's endnotes

turnips, WHj and HR in turnip cart to Wells, 31.1.94

turtles, Thomas Forster to turtle feast at Holt, 25.9.97

U

Upper Sheringham, *see* Sheringham

V

valuations, arranged by WH for John Howard's goods, 27.1.95; Hs' furniture by WH, 12–13.9.97

vegetables, **154**, Hs' damaged by north wind, 19.6.95

venison (veneson), WH to feast at King's Head, Holt, 30.7.94

vestry, *see* Letheringsett Church

Vickery, Caryar, Holt surgeon; WH to dinner, 19.12.95

Volunteers, **129**, meeting at Holt Shirehouse for raising by subscription for national defence, 3.5.94

W

Wade, John, **69**, **252**, Holt and Gt Ryburgh miller; with Davys and Bakers to tea, 22.10.93; his windmill at Holt burns down, 8.5.94; WH fails to buy goods at mill, 27.6.94; WH and Mr Henderson to at Ryburgh, 11.9.95; to dinner, 23.1.96; asked by WHj to appear as witness at Thetford Assizes, 7.3.96; at Hs', 8.5.96; dines with Hs on return from London, 19.5.96

wages, maidservants', *see* endnotes

wagons, **133**, **349**, Hs' two wagons collect timber from Gunthorpe, 18.11.95: *see also* carts; cheese trolley

Walden, John, innkeeper of Fighting Cocks, Wells, tied house; to dinner, 9.12.93; WH and MH to dinner, 30.7.95; hands over to William Silence, 18.10.96; WHj settles affairs at Wells, 18.11.96

Wall, Miss [? of Gt Yarmouth], at tea party at Hs', 2.9.96

wallpaper, MH and MA start hanging MA's new dressing room and bedroom, 23.5.96

Walsingham, Norf., **245**, **270**, WH to for sale of Field Dalling public house, 25.10.93; Charles Rust dines with Hs, 11.11.93; quarter sessions, 14.4.96; WH to for sale of Chequers, Sharrington, 13.5.96; WHj to justices' sitting, 12.9.97

war, **40**, **177**, **184**, **185**, **189**, amendment and vote in Parliament to end war with France, 24.1.94; William Windham appointed Secretary for War [Secretary at War], 11.7.94: *see also* Army; fasts; France; Militia; Navy; Netherlands; Volunteers; Weybourne Camp

Warham, Norf., Hs' beer cart breaks down, 25.1.94

washing:
- by Hs' maidservants: 27.11.93, 8.4.94, 30.6.94, 28.7.94, 26.8.94, 28.10.94, 26.11.94, 30.12.94, 3.2.95, 9.3.95, 19.5.95, 21.7.95, 29.9.95, 3.11.95, 8.12.95, 8.3.96, 12.7.96, 16.8.96, 19.9.96, 25.10.96, 4.4.97, 25.7.97
- by others helping maids:
  - Elizabeth Loades: 30.6.94, 28.7.94, 4.4.97
  - Mary Loades: 27.11.93
  - Mrs Elizabeth Millegen: 3.11.95, 8.12.95, 8.3.96, 12.7.96, 16.8.96, 25.10.96, 25.7.97
  - Elizabeth Woods: 26.8.94, 28.10.94, 26.11.94, 3.2.95, 9.3.95, 19.5.95, 21.7.95, 29.9.95:
- *see also* ironing

water, cistern installed in Hs' kitchen, 2.12.94: *see also* pump

watermills, *see* mills

weather, rain interrupts harvest, 27.8.94, 29.8.97, 31.8.97; heavy rain prevents Hs' visitors from departing, 6.11.94; north wind cuts vegetables, high tide damages cliff at Sheringham, 19.6.95; rain interrupts haymaking, 5.7.96, 10.7.97: *see also* earthquake; fog; hail; moon; snow; storms

Webster, Mr, of Norwich; stays overnight, 23.2.95; exchanges chaise horses with Hs, 24.2.95

Wells, Elizabeth Money (1767–97), **64**, of Norwich; marriage to Peter Raven, 26.4.94

Wells-next-the-Sea, Norf., **231**, **289**, WHj and HR to, 31.1.94; Mr and Mrs Todhunter at Hs' on way to, 4.9.94; opening of Norwich stage-coach service from, 8.12.94; WH and Mr Henderson to, 12.9.95; soldiers from Holt sent to quell riot, 15–16.12.95; WH and John Thompson to, 12.9.96; WHj and William Thackwray to, 14.10.96; William Thackwray to with John Thompson to set sail aboard Capt. Bloom's ship for Hull, ship does not sail, 1.1.97; Mr and Mrs Proudfoot to tea with Hs, 5.6.97
- Fighting Cocks: John Walden dines with Hs, 9.12.93; beer cart breaks down during Robert Bye's delivery, 25.1.94; WH and MH dine at, 30.7.95; let by WH to William Silence, 11.9.96; John Walden hands over to William Silence, 18.10.96; WHj settles affairs with Walden, 18.11.96

Wells-next-the-Sea, Fighting Cocks (*cont.*)
- Jolly Sailor, **58**, **210**: WH and MH visit Nicholas Everitt over money owed to WH, 30.7.95; WH and John Thompson to for arrest of Everitt, 21.9.95: *see also* Everitt, Nicholas

Wesley, Revd John (1703–91), **139**, **153**, **245**, **262**, **263**, **289**, founder of Arminian Methodists; MH's list of his tracts, endnotes

West Beckham, *see* Beckham

West Rudham, Norf., WH and WHj pay off brewery mortgage to Thomas Howard, 13.9.96

Weybourne (Weyborn), Norf., death of Robert Temple, 14.6.95: *see also* Weybourne Camp

Weybourne Camp, Norf., **177**, **184**, **185**, **189**, **203**, **266**, WH and WHj to Weybourne and Sheringham to secure beer contract, 1.6.95; WHj and MA watch regiment of Artillery pass through Holt to, 8.6.95; WH, MH and MA follow regiment from Holt to, 11.6.95; WHj to, 13.6.95, 22.10.95, 21.6.96; HR to, 14.6.95; WH and MA watch troops exercise, 17.6.95; WHj to with Cook Flower, 20.6.95; Hs to for field day with Messrs Everitt and Keeler and Miss Billing, cannon fired, 26.6.95; WH, MH, Henry Goggs and servant to for field day, 8.7.95; WH, HR and Mr and Mrs Nathaniel Raven to, 14.7.95; WH, MA and Mr and Mrs Nathaniel Raven to, 16.7.95; WHj and MA to, 27.7.95; Mr Askew, one of artillerymen from, to dinner at Hs', 29.7.95; ball at Holt for officers, 3.8.95; WHj, MA, HR, Nathaniel Raven jnr and Mary Raven to for field day, 10.8.95, 12.8.95; WHj follows Artillery from Holt to, 17.6.96; WHj to as camp breaks up for move to Woodbridge, 9.9.96; WHj to Samuel Sanderson's sale of canteen, buys stove, chairs and earthenware, 12–13.1.97

wheat, **194**, **296**, shearing by Hs' men in Furze Closes, 12.8.94, 14.8.94; carried by WHj from Furze Closes, 15.8.94; mown by men in Furze Closes, 16.8.94; harvesting ends, 18.8.94, 20.8.94; wheat meal 3*s* per stone, 21.7.95
- price per coomb at Holt market: 50*s*, 13.2.96; 56*s*, 20.2.96; 58*s*, 5.3.96:
- *see also* corn; flour; riots

whiskeys, *see* chaises, whiskeys

Whissonsett (Whisonset, Whisonsett), Norf., birthplace of MH and HR, **150**, **151**, **179**, **195**; HR to, 12.1.94, 25.10.94, 1.1.97, 11.3.97; WHj from, 14.2.94, 6.10.95, 19.12.95, 28.1.96; Nathaniel Raven and WHj to, 16.5.94; MH and WHj at, dine at Mrs Phillis Goggs's, to tea at Nathaniel Raven's and win raffle, to supper

Whissonsett (*cont.*)
and stay overnight at Mr Goggs's, 11.6.94; WHj to, 9.10.94, 12.9.96, 9.5.97; WHj fails to return from, 11.10.94; HR from, 26.10.94; WHj and Robert Raven to Hs from, death of Mr Goggs, 13.2.95; WH and MH stay with Mrs Phillis Goggs, 15.2.95; WH to tea at Nathaniel Raven's, 22.2.95; WH, MH and HR to, Hs to tea at Nathaniel Raven's and stay overnight with Henry Goggs, 19.5.95; WH and John Thompson to, 5.6.95; WH and MA from, 6.6.95; WH and MH to with Mr and Mrs Nathaniel Raven, 2.9.95; WH and Mr Henderson dine at Nathaniel Raven's and collect Mrs Phillis Goggs, 11.9.95; Mrs Nathaniel Raven dines with Hs, 6.11.95; Mary and Nathaniel Raven jnr to Hs from, 11.11.95; WH and MH to, dine at Nathaniel Raven's, to supper and stay overnight with Henry Goggs, 5.1.96; HR collects WH and MH, 8.1.96; WHj and MA from, 19.5.96; WH and MH to, to dinner and supper and stay overnight with Henry Goggs, 24.5.96; WH and MH from, 28.5.96; MH and Nathaniel Raven jnr to, Mrs Phillis Goggs very ill, MH stays with Mrs Goggs, 2.11.96; Nathaniel Raven and daughter, Rose Raven, MA and HR to, 10.11.96; HR collects MA, 13.12.96; WH, MH and Nathaniel Raven jnr to, 13.3.97; WH and MH to Henry Goggs and Nathaniel Raven at, 13.3.97; WHj and MA to, MA to look after Mrs Phillis Goggs, 30.5.97; marriage of Rose Raven to Thomas Skrimshire, 23.6.97; WH and MH to, 17.7.97

Church, St Mary the Virgin, **xii**, **313**, **314**, **315**, **413**: MH and WHj to, 11.6.94; WH and MH to, 22.2.95; MH to, Mr Norris preaches, 6.11.96

Hall, **5**, **93**, **130**, **175**, **194**: Nathaniel Raven to Hs, 16.12.94, 24.3.95; WH and MH to tea, 18.2.95, 27.5.96; Mary Raven at Hs', 1.4.95; WH and Nathaniel Raven survey farm, find it in poor condition, 20.5.95; MH to, 20.5.95; Hs and Ravens dine at, 17.3.97; Nathaniel and Mary Raven to Wisbech, 20.7.97: *see also* Raven, Mrs Ann (d.1811); Raven, Robert

Raven's shop, **79**, **241**: Nathaniel Raven jnr at Hs', 27.4.95: *see also* Raven, Nathaniel; Raven, Nathaniel jnr

see also Goggs, Henry jnr

White, John (d.1839 aged 79), Letheringsett maltster; marriage in 1794 to Blythe Ramm noted in MH's register, endnotes

White Horse, *see* Great Hautbois

White Lion, *see* Holt, public houses

Wifton, *see* Wiveton

Wigg, Miss, with Charlotte Bartell, Adam Baker and John Raven to dinner, 15.9.94

Wilcocks, Revd William Wright (d.1846), **183**, of Holt, Bale and Thornage, Curate of Field Dalling 1801, Curate of Wiveton 1801–04, Curate of Thornage with Brinton 1806, Vicar of Barney 1806–46, Rector of Pudding Norton 1807–46; elopes to Scotland with Elizabeth Hagon, 20.6.95; injured in overturning cart while drunk, borrows Hs' cart, 17.1.97

William, MH's son and HR's cousin, *see* Hardy, William jnr

William, [no surname], *see* boys, boy 26

Williams, William, Thornage attorney; with Mr Bird and Thomas Temple to tea, confirms sale of public house at Aldborough, 24.10.93

Williamson (Williams), Elizabeth, Hs' maidservant 1797–98; hired as upper servant by MH and MA at Holt, 31.7.97; starts work, 12.10.97; hire and wages, maidservants' register, MH's endnotes

wills, *see* executor; legacy

Windham, William (1750–1810), MP, of Felbrigg Hall; precipitates Norwich by-election after accepting post of Secretary for War [Secretary at War], 11.7.94; defeats James Mingay in by-election, 12.7.94

windmills, *see* mills

windows, *see* house, yard

wine, WH and WHj bottle 120 bottles of red port, 10.4.94; part of pipe of wine drawn off by WHj at Holt, 2.2.96

Winn, Mrs Susanna (d.1798), **262**, **263**, of Letheringsett, formerly Mrs Dix, née May; Mrs Smith and Mrs Proudfoot hold meeting at her house, 18.7.96

Wisbech (Wisbeach), Cambs, Rose Raven marries Thomas Skrimshire of, they depart for after wedding, 23.6.97 and MH's register, endnotes; Nathaniel and Mary Raven of Whissonsett Hall to, 20.7.97

Witham, John, Wesleyan Methodist itinerant preacher; preaches at Letheringsett meeting, 11.6.96

Withers, Mrs Ann (d.1835 aged 84), née Trotter, of Holt; with Hs at tea party at King's Head, Letheringsett, 18.8.97

Wiveton (Wifton), Norf., **8**, **33**, **181**, death of John Jordan, 12.6.95; WHj to, 12.6.95

Wodehouse (Woodhouse), Sir John (1741–1834), Bt, MP, of Kimberley Hall, 1st Baron Wodehouse 1797; his supporters in county election given supper by Mr Burrell at King's Head, Letheringsett, 30.5.96; returned unopposed as MP for Norfolk, 3.6.96

Wood, Mr [?Matthew], London chemist; at Hs', 17.6.95; to dinner, 21.6.96

wood:
bark: bought by Mr Mason from Hs' Hindolveston plantation, 6.11.93
timber, **34**, **35**: Hs' timber book settled with Thomas Balls jnr and Bartells, 12.1.97
Blakeney sale: WH and WHj buy timber and laths at Mr Farthing's, 16.8.97
Cley sale: bought by WH and Mr Burrell to fence Letheringsett House of Industry garden, 28.12.95
Gunthorpe: bought by WHj from Mr Collyer, collected by Hs' wagons, 18.11.95
Hindolveston: measured by WH, MH and WHj, 24.10.93
Reepham [? Kerdiston]: WH and Bartells decide on trees to be felled, 30.3.96; measured by WH for Mr Bartell, 12.7.96; WH and Mr Bartell measure ash timber, 20.2.97; bought by WHj from Mr Sewell, 27.3.97:
see also trees

Woodbridge, Suff., soldiers at Weybourne Camp ordered to, 9.9.96

Woodcock, Mrs Mary (d.1795), death noted in MH's register, endnotes

Woodcock, Mr, Briston draper and grocer; WH, MH and MA buy goods at, 26.6.97

Woodhouse, Sir John, *see* Wodehouse

Woodhouse, Nicholas, *see* boys, boy 22

Woodhouse, Mrs Susanna (d.1797 aged 57), née Buller, of Lt Thornage; burial after earlier burial of son, 11.4.97 and noted in MH's register, endnotes

Woodhouse, Thomas (d.1797 aged 24); burial, 11.4.97 and noted in MH's register, endnotes

Woods, Elizabeth (Betty), helps Hs' maids with washing, 26.8.94, 28.10.94, 26.11.94, 3.2.95, 9.3.95, 19.5.95, 21.7.95, 29.9.95; helps Hs' maids with baking, 9.3.95

Worden, *see* Worthing

Wordingham, John, Wells carpenter; dines with Hs and pays off Nicholas Everitt's mortgage, 3.1.97

workforce (labourers), Hs', **402**, with wives to dinner, 25.12.93, 25.12.94, 25.12.95, 25.12.96; with teams sent to repair sea bank at Sheringham, 28.12.95
casual: *see* harvests; haymaking
regular, hired by year as farm servants and maltsters: *see* Baldwin, Thomas; Boyce, Thomas; Bye, Robert; Lamb, William; Ramm, John; Thompson, William Gunton; *also hired by year* boys; maidservants; menservants

workhouses (houses of industry), *see* Gressenhall; Letheringsett

Worthing (Worden), Norf., WH and Nathaniel Raven to, 27.5.96

Wymer, Clara, **174**, of Norwich, daughter of George; with Charlotte Bartell to dinner, with Hs, Bakers and Bartells to supper at Thomas Temple's, 13.12.93; with Mrs Raven and Bartells to tea, 19.3.94; with MH, HR and Miss Dewson to supper at Thomas Temple's, 28.1.96; with Charlotte Bartell and Miss Dewson to dinner, 12.2.96; departs for Reepham from Mr Bartell's, 18.2.96

Wymer, George (d.1809 aged 72), **174**, Norwich attorney; WHj and Mr Bartell stay overnight, 26.2.94; WHj to dinner, 2.6.94; Hs to breakfast and dinner, 6.9.94; marriage, 6.11.95

Wymer, George jnr (d.1839 aged 74), **106**, Reepham attorney; with clerk stays overnight, 4.9.94; WH stays overnight, 30.3.96

Wymer, Mrs, of Norwich, 1st wife of George; death, 10.5.95

Y

yards, Hs':
brewhouse, **3**, **66**, **74**, **75**, **77**, **96**, **359**: Thomas Temple buys muck, 29.4.94; bricklayers turn arch, 29.5.94
domestic, **349**: counting house demolished, 16.3.96; bricklayers and carpenter install sash windows in yard front, 23.3.97

Yarmouth, *see* Great Yarmouth

Yorkshire, **202**, **310**, Mr Fawcett of Scotton at Hs', 23.8.95; Mr Green of Knaresborough at Hs', 14.8.96: *see also* Hull; Thackwray, William

Young, Dr Edward (1683–1765), his *Night Thoughts* listed by MH, endnotes

Youngman, Mrs Lydia (d.1828 aged 68), wife of Thomas; with MH to Cley meeting, 29.11.95, 3.1.96, 10.1.96; with MH to Sharrington meeting, 2.1.96

Youngman, Thomas (d.1834 aged 76), **67**, Letheringsett millwright; to Norwich for county election, 2.6.96

Index to the diary text of Henry Raven

Diary 3 · 10 October 1793–25 October 1797

The middle Letheringsett years

Editor's index to the full diary text of Henry Raven

Text references are identified not by page number but by date of entry in the diary, eg 8.5.94 *for* 8 May 1794; 9.1.97 *for* 9 January 1797: *ie day, month, year.*

Illustrations, by contrast, are indexed by the page number on which they appear, the page numbers being displayed in bold type, eg **Fakenham**, **140**, **153**, **173**; **Mindham** (Mendham), William, **94**, **95**, **96**, **372**, **373**, **374**, **391**, **396**.

Index entries in parentheses after the main entry denote the diarist's spelling—and probably his pronunciation—of the word in the manuscript, eg **Beckhithe** (Bickhigh); **Briningham** (Barningham, Birmingham, Birninham); **meal** (male); **windows** (winders), *although he is not always consistent in the use of such variations. Cross-references are provided where the main entry cannot readily be found, eg* **engines**, *see* pumps; **lifts**, *see* gates; **trowelmen**, *see* bricklayers.

Parentheses after the index entry can also denote the diarist's usage, distinguishing it from the modern term, eg **cement** (mergin, mirgin, murgen); **sluice** (watergate); **threshing** (tasking, trashing).

The diarist's daily entries and his endnotes are indexed; editorial captions, sidenotes and the appendices are not included.

The index to the diary of MARY HARDY is compiled separately and precedes this index.

These contractions are used in the index:

Hs	*for*	the Hardys
HR		Henry Raven [brewing pupil]
MA		Mary Ann Hardy [cousin]
MH		Mary Hardy [aunt]
WH		William Hardy [uncle; 'Mr H' in HR's diary]
WHj		William Hardy jnr [cousin; 'WH' in HR's diary]

A

accidents:
domestic: Hs' chimney catches fire, 15.2.95
industrial, **69**: John Wade's windmill at Holt burns down, 8.5.94
road, **133**, **174**, **276**, **277**, **349**: Robert Bye laid off work after hurting leg on beer delivery to Brampton, 15–17.10.93; beer cart breaks down on Robert Bye's delivery to Wells, 25.1.94; MH injured and chaise damaged when horse falls at Swanton Novers, 3.7.94; Thomas Baldwin hurts leg on beer delivery to Brampton, 28.11.94; beer cart breaks down on Thomas Baldwin's delivery to Cromer, 22.12.94; Thomas Baldwin breaks arm under wheel of beer cart on delivery to Beckhithe, 23.12.94; man hurt on way from Holt, 22.5.95; beer cart breaks down on Robert Bye's delivery to Holt, 9.6.95; Mrs Booty's beer cart swept under Glaven

accidents, road (*cont.*)
bridge in floods, horse drowns, 4.6.96; Thomas Baldwin breaks leg under wheel of beer wagon on delivery to Burnham Market, 9.12.96; Revd Mr Wilcocks injured after cart overturns, 17.1.97; WHj's gig breaks down on journey to seaside, 14.8.97

Acres, *see* Bell's Acre; Five Acres; Six Acres

Aldborough (Alborough), Norf., **224**, WH to with Mr Bird, 27.11.93; WHj to, 19.6.94, 26.12.95, 10.10.97; Thomas Baldwin delivers malt, 16.8.96; WH and HR to, 4.4.97
beer deliveries: 24.11.95, 30.12.95, 6.2.96, 11.3.96, 22.4.96, 13.5.96, 15.6.96, 12.7.96, 13.9.96, 4.10.96, 8.11.96, 24.12.96, 30.1.97, 2.3.97, 11.4.97, 11.5.97, 31.5.97, 19.6.97, 5.7.97, 2.8.97, 30.8.97, 22.9.97, 7.10.97
loading: 14.6.96

ale, *see* beer

Alethorpe (Althorpe), Norf., **244**, HR stays overnight, 22.1.96
Alpe, Mary (d.1798 aged 51), **384**, Holt schoolmistress; Phillis Raven to, 8.8.97; with Mrs Bartell to tea at Hs', 24.8.97
apples, *see* fruit
apprentice, Mr Woodcock's to tea at Hs', 17.12.94: *see also* Raven, Henry
arches, Mr Bunnett's four men turning arch over river, 28.5.95; covered by John Fox, 30.5.94: *see also* bricks
Army, **52**, **189**, **232**, **266**, two soldiers at work in Hs' garden, 18.3.94; WHj and MA meet regiment of Artillery at Briningham, 9.6.95; soldiers pass through Letheringsett on way to Sharrington, 20.12.95; Artillery arrives at Holt, 15.6.96; WHj to Weybourne with Artillery, 17.6.96: *see also* Weybourne Camp
arsenic (arsnack, arsnick), used in recipe for destroying moles, HR's endnotes
Artillery, *see* Army; Weybourne Camp
Ashwicken (Ash Wicking), Norf., Master Forsters collect parcel brought by WHj from, 14.5.97
Askew, Mr, of regiment of Artillery at Weybourne Camp; dines with Hs, 29.7.95
assemblies, at Holt; WHj to, 21.10.93, 18.11.93, 10.11.94; Mrs Elizabeth Flower and Samuel Flower, WHj and MA to, 18.12.93; Mr S. Sharpe to, 10.11.94: *see also* balls
assizes, **99**, WH and HR to at Norwich, 12.8.94
attorneys, *see individual entries* Christmas, William; Moore, James; Smith, John; Williams, William; Wymer, George; Wymer, George jnr
Atwood, Thomas (d.1805 aged 78), **59**, innkeeper of Dolphin, Holt; orders beer, 10.10.93, 21.10.93, 10.2.94, 9.5.94, 16.6.94, 20.9.94, 2.2.96; beer deliveries, 29.1.94, 22.4.95, 13.5.95, 5.10.95, 7.12.95; at work in Hs' garden, 1–2.4.94; man hurt returning from sale at, 22.5.95: *see also* Holt, public houses, beer deliveries
audit, WH to Mr Burrell's, 12.1.95
Aylsham, Norf., HR and Edmund Devereux to, 12.9.95; WHj to, 19.9.97

B

backs, *see* brewing equipment
Baker, Adam Calthorpe (1773–1810), son of John; with sister and Miss Custance at Hs', 18.1.94; with John Raven, Miss Wigg & Charlotte Bartell to tea at Hs', 15.9.94
Baker, E., [? son of Joseph]; at work at Hs', 9.9.95, 11.9.95
Baker, John (1727–1804), Holt ironmonger; with family at Hs', 22.11.93, 26.3.94; MA, Ann Raven, Miss Custance and James Moore to tea, 13.1.94; MA at, 3.2.94; WHj to dinner, 19.2.94; Hs to dinner, 15.7.94; with family to dinner at Hs', 17.7.94; WHj to tea, 28.12.94; to tea at Hs', 12.12.96
Baker, Joseph (Joshua), **59**, innkeeper of Bull, Holt, [? also Joseph Baker *below*, builder]; orders beer, 8.10.94, 25.4.95; beer delivery, 16.5.95
Baker, Joseph, Holt builder [? also Joseph Baker *above*, innkeeper]; his two men at work at Hs', 13.10.94, 3.12.94; at Hs', 1.5.95, 15.9.95; his man and boy at work, 15.4.95, 17.4.95; his two sons at work at Hs', 3.9.95; his son at work, 4.9.95; at work, 5.9.95, 7–8,9.95, 10.9.95; with son at work, 9.9.95, 11.9.95
Baker, Margaret (1765–1830), of Holt, daughter of John; with family at Hs', 22.11.93, 18.1.94, 26.3.94, 17.7.94; at Hs', 12.11.94, 20.7.95, 4.8.95, 14.3.96, 29.4.96, 8.7.96, 24.10.97; with Flowers and Charlotte Bartell to dinner at Hs', 26.2.96
Baker, Mrs Priscilla (1734–1801), née Custance, 2nd wife of John; with family at Hs', 22.11.93, 26.3.94, 17.7.94
Baldwin (Balden, Baldin), Thomas, Hs' farm servant, brewer and drayman; to Whit Monday dinner at Hs', 16.5.96, 5.6.97; to Weybourne Fair, 17.5.96; not at work, 18.5.96
brewing:
1793: 6.11.93, 9.11.93, 13–14.11.93, 18.11.93, 20–23.11.93, 30.11.93, 3.12.93, 10.12.93, 13.12.93, 19.12.93, 27.12.93, 30.12.93
1794: 9.1.94, 13.1.94, 21.1.94, 27.1.94, 6.2.94, 10.2.94, 13.2.94, 24.2.94, 11–12.3.94, 24–25.3.94, 7.4.94, 14.4.94, 28.4.94, 5.5.94, 10.5.94, 15.5.94, 17.5.94, 20.5.94, 23.5.94, 26.5.94, 3.6.94, 7.6.94, 16.6.94, 30.6.94, 25.8.94, 15.9.94, 29.9.94, 11.10.94, 13.10.94, 22.10.94, 4.11.94, 17.11.94, 4.12.94, 20.12.94
1795: 16.3.95, 30.3.95, 1.4.95, 20.4.95, 29.4.95, 2.5.95, 16.5.95, 21.5.95, 3.6.95, 17.6.95, 1.7.95, 8.7.95, 16.7.95, 29.7.95, 13.8.95, 26–27.8.95, 12.9.95, 22.9.95, 7.10.95, 20.10.95, 2.11.95, 19.11.95, 9.12.95, 31.12.95
1796: 12.1.96, 25.1.96, 8.2.96, 17.2.96, 8.3.96, 19.3.96, 5.4.96, 12.4.96, 19.4.96, 2.5.96, 16.5.96, 30.5.96, 13.6.96, 4.7.96, 11.7.96, 25.7.96, 8.8.96, 22.8.96, 7.9.96, 14.9.96, 22.9.96, 19.10.96, 5.11.96, 17.11.96, 2.12.96
1797: 16.3.97, 28.4.97, 3.5.97, 10.5.97, 18.5.97, 31.5.97, 14.6.97, 28.6.97, 12.7.97, 26.7.97, 9.8.97, 23.8.97, 1.9.97, 11.9.97, 28.9.97, 11.10.97, 25.10.97

Baldwin, Thomas, brewing (*cont.*)
cleaning vessels: 15.11.93, 9.12.93, 16.12.93, 27.3.94, 14.5.94, 27.8.94, 15.12.94, 29.4.95, 8.12.95, 28.3.96, 17.9.96, 3.5.97
working in brewery: 15.3.97, 4.5.97, 9.5.97, 7.6.97, 20.10.97; in tun room, 14.11.93; lighting fire, 22.11.93; fetching malt, 27.3.94, 9.10.94, 24.10.94, 6.10.95; empties mash tun, 6.1.96; weighing hops, 6.11.96
cleansing beer:
1793: 24.11.93
1794: 16.1.94, 20.3.94, 27.3.94, 8.4.94, 10.6.94, 17.6.94, 29.7.94, 19.8.94, 2.9.94, 9.9.94, 1.10.94, 19.10.94, 24.10.94, 19.11.94, 5.12.94
1795: 17.2.95, 8.5.95, 17.5.95, 13.6.95, 9.7.95, 14.8.95, 24.9.95, 15.10.95, 6.12.95, 17.12.95
1796: 1.1.96, 27.1.96, 2.2.96, 23.2.96, 4.3.96, 25.3.96, 13.4.96, 17.5.96, 24.5.96
1797: 18.8.97
collecting coal and cinders from ports:
1793: 1–2.11.93, 23.11.93, 2.12.93
1794: 1.2.94, 6.2.94, 14.2.94, 26.2.94, 7.3.94, 1.5.94, 17.5.94, 23.6.94, 21.7.94, 5–6.8.94, 5.12.94, 12.12.94
1795: 5.3.95, 31.3.95, 27.4.95, 8.5.95, 1.6.95, 6.6.95, 16.6.95, 4.7.95, 27.8.95, 15.9.95, 16.10.95, 19.10.95, 31.10.95, 10.12.95, 12.12.95
1796: 4.4.96, 20.4.96, 9.5.96, 2.6.96, 9.6.96, 28.7.96, 30.7.96, 4.8.96, 11.8.96, 19.8.96, 26.11.96, 3.12.96
1797: 12.5.97, 17.5.97, 6.6.97, 15.7.97, 1.8.97, 21.9.97, 26–27.9.97
loading and unloading coal and cinders: 2.8.94, 16.3.95, 3.12.95, 11.12.95, 19.12.95, 4.8.96, 12.5.97, 3.8.97
collecting other goods:
barley: 30.10.93, 14.11.94, 31.10.95, 20.11.95, 29.4.96, 7.12.96
barrels, empty: 12.12.93, 3.12.94, 30.1.96; barrel hoops, 7.6.96; barrel oak, 19.8.96
beer: 17.11.96, 9.10.97
bricks: 12.2.94, 2.9.97
cement: 22.3.96, 17.6.96
clay: 17.12.94, 30.1.96, 10.2.96
hay: 29.1.94, 14.3.94, 23.4.95, 3–5.8.95, 23.4.96, 21.7.96, 12.10.97
lime: 19.2.94, 1.3.94, 11.3.94, 4.4.94, 18.5.95, 22.5.97, 21.9.97
sale goods: 3.12.94, 8.10.96
sand: 27.2.94, 1.3.94, 4.4.94, 22.6.95, 31.10.95, 22.3.96, 22.5.97
stones: 7.1.94, 19.2.94, 10.3.94, 17.12.94, 10.6.95, 25.6.95, 21.3.96, 9.4.96
tiles: 17.9.94, 1.10.94, 25.10.94, 31.10.94

Baldwin, Thomas, collecting other goods (*cont.*)
turnips: 3.1.94, 17.12.94, 4.3.95, 27.4.96
vetches: 9.7.96, 1.8.96, 6.8.96, 11.7.97, 31.7.97, 16.8.97
wheat: 20.2.94, 28.6.96
wheels: 9.6.94, 16.6.95
wood: 12.11.94, 4.12.94, 2.7.95, 30.7.95, 18.11.95, 22.1.96
delivering beer, **264**:
1793: 29–31.10.93, 5.11.93, 7–8.11.93, 11–12.11.93, 16.11.93, 20–21.11.93, 23.11.93, 26–30.11.93, 2.12.93, 4–5.12.93, 7.12.93, 11–12.12.93, 14.12.93, 17–21.12.93, 23–24.12.93, 26.12.93, 31.12.93
1794: 1–4.1.94, 6–9.1.94, 11.1.94, 14.1.94, 16.1.94, 18.1.94, 20–22.1.94, 24–25.1.94, 29.1.94, 1.2.94, 3.2.94, 5.2.94, 8.2.94, 11–12.2.94, 14.2.94, 20.2.94, 22.2.94, 25–27.2.94, 3–4.3.94, 6.3.94, 10.3.94, 12.3.94, 15.3.94, 17–19.3.94, 22.3.94, 28–29.3.94, 31.3.94, 3.4.94, 5.4.94, 8–9.4.94, 12.4.94, 15–17.4. 4, 19–20.4.94, 23–24.4.94, 26–27.4.94, 30.4.94, 1–2.5.94, 4.5.94, 7.5.94, 9.5.94, 12–13.5.94, 15–16.5.94, 18–19.5.94, 21–22.5.94, 24–25.5.94, 30–31.5.94, 2.6.94, 4.6.94, 6.6.94, 7.6.94, 9.6.94, 12–13.6.94, 17–18.6.94, 21.6.94, 23–25.6.94, 27.6.94, 1.7.94, 4–5.7.94, 7–9.7.94, 12.7.94, 15–16.7.94, 18.7.94, 21–23.7.94, 25–26.7.94, 28–30.7.94, 1.8.94, 7.8.94, 9.8.94, 12.8.94, 15–16.8.94, 20.8.94, 22–23.8.94, 26.8.94, 28.8.94, 30.8.94, 1.9.94, 3–6.9.94, 9–12.9.94, 16–20.9.94, 22–26.9.94, 30.9.94, 1–4.10.94, 6.10.94, 9–11.10.94, 13–15.10.94, 17–18.10.94, 20–21.10.94, 25.10.94, 27–28.10.94, 30–31.10.94, 1.11.94, 3.11.94, 6–8.11.94, 10.11.94, 12.11.94, 14.11.94, 18.11.94, 20–22.11.94, 24–26.11.94, 28.11.94, 6.12.94, 8.12.94, 10.12.94, 12–13.12.94, 15–16.12.94
1795: 14.2.95, 28.2.95, 2–4.3.95, 6.3.95, 10–12.3.95, 18–21.3.95, 23–27.3.95, 31.3.95, 4.4.95, 6.4.95, 9.4.95, 11.4.95, 14.4.95, 16–18.4.95, 21–22.4.95, 25.4.95, 28.4.95, 30.4.95, 1–2.5.95, 4–7.5.95, 9.5.95, 11–16.5.95, 19–20.5.95, 22–23.5.95, 25–30.5.95, 2.6.95, 5–6.6.95, 8–11.6.95, 13.6.95, 15.6.95, 18–20.6.95, 23.6.95, 25–27.6 95, 29–30.6.95, 2–4.7.95, 6–7.7.95, 9–11.7.95, 13–18.7.95, 27–28.7.95, 1.8.95, 3.8.95, 6–8.8.95, 10–12.8.95, 15.8.95, 17.8.95, 20.8.95, 22.8.95, 24–25.8.95, 27–28.8.95, 31.8.95, 1–5.9.95, 10.9.95, 12.9.95, 14–16.9.95, 18–19.9.95, 21.9.95, 23–26.9.95, 28–30.9.95, 1–3.10.95, 5–10.10.95, 12.10.95, 14–16.10.95, 22–24.10.95, 26–29.10.95, 31.10.95, 3–4.11.95, 6.11.95,

Baldwin, Thomas, delivering beer, 1795 (*cont.*) 14.11.95, 16–18.11.95, 20–21.11.95, 23–26.11.95, 30.11.95, 1–5.12.95, 7–8.12.95, 11–12.12.95, 14–15.12.95, 17.12.95, 19.12.95, 21.12.95, 22–24.12.95, 26.12.95, 28–30.12.95
1796: 1–2.1.96, 6–9.1.96, 11.1.96, 13–16.1.96, 18–19.1.96, 21–23.1.96, 26.1.96, 28.1.96, 30.1.96, 1–3.2.96, 10.2.96, 12–13.2.96, 16–17.2.96, 19.2.96, 22–23.2.96, 26–27.2.96, 1–5.3.96, 11.3.96, 14.3.96, 16–17.3.96, 21.3.96, 23.3.96, 24.3.96, 26.3.96, 28.3.96, 30.3.96, 1.4.96, 8–9.4.96, 11.4.96, 14–16.4.96, 18.4.96, 20.4.96, 22–23.4.96, 25.4.96, 27-30.4.96, 2–4.5.96, 7.5.96, 9–12.5.96, 14.5.96, 19–21.5.96, 23–24.5.96, 27.5.96, 31.5.96, 1.6.96, 6–8.6.96, 10–11.6.96, 13–16.6.96, 20–23.6.96, 25.6.96, 27–28.6.96, 30.6.96, 1–2.7.96, 6–9.7.96, 12–13.7.96, 19–20.7.96, 22–23.7.96, 26–29.7.96, 1.8.96, 3.8.96, 4–6.8.96, 10–11.8.96, 13.8.96, 15.8.96, 17–18.8.96, 20.8.96, 23–24.8.96, 29–30.8.96, 3.9.96, 5.9.96, 10.9.96, 12–13.9.96, 15–16.9.96, 19.9.96, 21.9.96, 23–24.9.96, 26.9.96, 28–30.9.96, 3–5.10.96, 7.10.96, 10.10.96, 13.10.96, 15.10.96, 20.10.96, 22.10.96, 24–28.10.96, 1–2.11.96, 8–11.11.96, 14.11.96, 16.11.96, 21-23.11.96, 26.11.96, 3.12.96, 6–9.12.96
1797: 12–13.4.97, 15.4.97, 17.4.97, 21–22.4.97, 24–25.4.97, 29.4.97, 1.5.97, 6.5.97, 8–9.5.97, 11–13.5.97, 15–16.5.97, 19.5.97, 25.5.97, 27.5.97, 29–30.5.97, 1.6.97, 3.6.97, 6.6.97, 8–10.6.97, 12–13.6.97, 15–16.6.97, 19–20.6.97, 26–27.6.97, 30.6.97, 5–6.7.97, 8.7.97, 10–11.7.97, 13–15.7.97, 17–19.7.97, 22.7.97, 24–25.7.97, 27.7.97, 29.7.97, 2–3.8.97, 7.8.97, 10.8.97, 14–19.8.97, 21–22.8.97, 24.8.97, 26.8.97, 30.8.97, 9.9.97, 12–14.9.97, 18–19.9.97, 21.9.97, 23.9.97, 26–30.9.97, 2–3.10.97, 7.10.97, 9–10.10.97, 13–14.10.97, 16–17.10.97, 21.10.97, 23–24.10.97; not permitted to leave beer at Field Dalling, 7.10.97
delivering other goods: brewer's grains, 30.7.94; bricks, 5.7.97; gravel, 9.1.94; hops, 21.11.93; lime, 5.7.97; malt, 21.11.93, 27.6.94, 20.11.95, 26.7.96, 16.8.96; sand, 5.7.97; tiles, 6.11.94; wheels, 7.6.94, 9.12.94, 18.5.95
drawing off beer:
1793: 5.12.93, 28.12.93
1794: 15.1.94, 28.1.94, 11.2.94, 16.2.94, 21.2.94, 25.2.94, 19.3.94, 27.3.94, 2–3.4.94, 6.4.94, 29.4.94, 3.5.94, 14.5.94, 1.6.94, 8.6.94, 15.6.94, 5.7.94, 2.8.94, 9.9.94, 27.9.94, 4.10.94, 23.11.94

Baldwin, Thomas, drawing off beer (*cont.*)
1795: 29.3.95, 6.4.95, 19.4.95, 30.4.95, 7.5.95, 7.6.95, 6.9.95, 7.11.95, 30.11.95
1796: 23.2.96, 9.3.96, 2.4.96, 13.4.96, 24.4.96, 8.5.96, 15.5.96, 3.6.96, 20.9.96
1797: 2.4.97, 27.4.97, 4.5.97, 6.5.97, 8.5.97
drunkenness: 23.1.94, 19.6.94, 20.1.96
harrowing: 13.2.94, 20.3.94, 2.4.94, 18.4.94, 21.4.94, 16.10.94, 29.10.94, 9.3.95, 21.3.95, 24.3.96, 2.4.96, 26.5.96, 29.6.96, 20.9.96, 31.10.96, 12.11.96, 17.3.97, 23.3.97, 19.4.97, 23.6.97, 1.7.97
harvesting: dines with Hs on first day, 10.8.94, 13.8.97; gathers largess, 30.8.94, 17.9.96; to harvest frolic, 17.9.96
1794: 11.8.94, 15.8.94, 18–19.8.94, 21.8.94, 26–29.8.94
1795: 2.9.95, 5.9.95, 7–9.9 95, 11.9.95, 17.9.95, 22.9.95
1796: 20.8.96, 25–27.8.96, 31.8.96, 2–3.9.96, 5–6.9.96, 8–10.9.96, 12.9.96, 14.9.96, 16.9.96
1797: 15.8.97, 23–25.8.97, 28.8.97, 31.8.97, 2.9.97, 4–8.9.97
haymaking: 4.7.94, 7.7.94, 9–11.7.94, 4–5.7.96, 16.7.96, 18.7.96, 7–8.10.96, 13–15.7.97, 19–21.7.97, 31.7.97
illness: 14.1.94, 17.1.94, 29.7.94, 31.7.94, 13–14.8.94, 23.10.94, 20.7.95, 7.11.95, 25.5.96, 12.8.96, 26.4.97, 21–22.6.97, 18–19.10.97; toothache, 1.9.96
injuries, **133**, **349**: hurts leg, 28.11.94; unable to work, 29.11.94; arm broken under cart-wheel on beer delivery, 22–23.12.94; returns to work, 18.2.95; leg broken under wagon-wheel on beer delivery, 9.12.96; able to walk to Letheringsett, 17.2.97; able to have dinner with men, 27.2.97, 4.3.97; returns to work, 13.3.97
jobs:
1794: 24.9.94, 27.9.94, 7.10.94, 5.11.94, 9.12.94, 13.12.94
1795: 27.2.95, 7.3.95, 17.3.95, 4.6.95, 13.6.95, 24.6.95, 26.6.95, 31.7.95, 20.8.95, 21.10.95, 29.12.95
1796: 9.1.96, 11.1.96, 9.2.96, 22.2.96, 29.2.96, 16.7.96, 29.7.96, 9.8.96, 13.8.96, 20.9.96, 27.9.96
1797: 14.3.97, 17–18.3.97, 17.5.97, 3.7.97, 26.9.97, 12.10.97
working in Hs' yards, 10.12.93, 16.7.94, 19.7.94, 3.9.94, 30.6.95, 4.8.95; at home, 4.2.94, 5.3.94, 21.3.94, 13.11.94, 15.11.94; collects marl, 1.3.94; moves stack into barn, 8.3.94, 1.2.96; malting, 25.3.94, 5.11.96; carting stones and gravel, 8–9.5.94, 24–25.7.94, 2.8.94, 15.4.95, 31.3.96; working in

Baldwin, Thomas, jobs (*cont.*)
King's Head yard, Letheringsett, 9.5.94; collects new cart, 7.6.94; at mud cart, 27–28.6.94; carting cement, 24.7.94; ringing pigs, 25.9.94, 3.4.95; at clay cart, 9.10.94; collects furze, 14.11.94; filling flour hopper, 23.21.95; working in Hs' garden, 16.3.95, 22.6.96; collects drum, 16.4.95; horses shod, 22.8.95; resolves problem with bill at Briston, 26.8.95; carting couch grass, 29.10.95; carting rocks to repair Sheringham jetty, 28.12.95; collects hop press from Brisley, 13.1.96; takes mare to Mr Love, 14.4.96; sets field gates in place, 13.5.96, 26.7.96; carts cinders into river, 9.6.96; cleans hay-house, 15.7.96; lays bottom of haystack, 15.7.96; working in barn, 30–31.8.96; hedging, 19.9.96; collects piglets, 22.9.96; collects malt, 18.10.96; takes ploughs to Holt Heath Farm, 29.11.96; takes beer cart to Mr Dawson, 13.3.97; heaping couch grass, 1.3.97; dressing grass seed, 14.4.97; collects hedging plants, 9–10.8.97; collects straw, 28.8.97
loading beer carts and wagons:
1793: 6.12.93
1794: 16.3.94, 11.5.94, 11.9.94, 26.10.94, 29.10.94
1795: 1.3.95, 25.3.95, 3.4.95, 5.4.95, 3.5.95, 5.5.95, 11.5.95, 22.5.95, 22.6.95, 10.7.95, 9.8.95, 30.8.95, 3.9.95, 25.9.95, 29.9.95, 4.10.95, 30.11.95, 3.12.95
1796: 14.1.96, 17.1.96, 19.1.96, 27.1.96, 11.2.96, 1.3.96, 22.3.96, 17.4.96, 29.4.96, 14.6.96, 26.7.96, 25.9.96, 27.9.96, 3.10.96, 31.10.96, 13.11.96, 15.11.96, 8.12.96
1797: 14.4.97, 23.4.97, 8.5.97, 16.7.97, 20.8.97, 12.10.97
muck carting/spreading:
1794: 2–3.1.94, 29–31.1.94, 14.6.94, 2.9.94, 4.9.94, 19.12.94
1795: 13.3.95, 14.8.95, 21.8.95, 30.10.95, 5.11.95, 9.11.95
1796: 4–5.1.96, 27.1.96, 29.1.96, 18.2.96, 24–25.2.96, 18.3.96, 7.4.96, 28.5.96, 10–11.6.96, 17.6.96, 28–29.10.96, 31.10.96, 28–30.11.96, 1.12.96, 5–6.12.96, 8.12.96
1797: 22.4.97, 23–24.6.97
ploughing:
1793–94: 4.11.93, 9.11.93, 14–16.11.93, 18–19.11.93, 25.11.93, 6.12.93, 28.12.93, 15.2.94, 17–18.2.94, 21.2.94, 13.3.94, 19.3.94, 28.3.94, 1.4.94, 5.4.94, 11.4.94, 21–25.4.94, 6.5.94, 26–28.5.94, 5.6.94, 11.6.94, 26.6.94, 2–4.7.94, 14.7.94
1794–95: 16.10.94, 11.11.94, 21.11.94, 27.11.94, 11.12.94, 27–28.3.95, 31.3.95,

Baldwin, Thomas, ploughing, 1794–95 (*cont.*)
1–2.4.95, 7–8.4.95, 13.4.95, 23–24.4.95, 27.7.95
1795–96: 10–13.11.95, 16.12.95, 18.12.95, 4–6.2.96, 13.2.96, 16.2.96, 20.2.96, 29.2.96, 7.3.96, 10.3.96, 15–16.3.96, 6–7.4.96, 20–21.4.96, 5–6.5.96, 13.5.96, 28.5.96, 11.6.96, 16.6.96, 24.6.96, 29.6.96, 1.7.96
1796–97: 30.9.96, 1.10.96, 3.10.96, 6.10.96, 8.10.96, 12.10.96, 14.10.96, 17.10.96, 21.10.96, 3–4.11.96, 7.11.96, 12.11.96, 18–19.11.96, 24–25.11.96, 28.11.96, 13.3.97, 20–22.3.97, 25.3.97, 28–31.3.97, 1.4.97, 3–4.4.97, 7–8.4.97, 10–11.4.97, 13–14.4.97, 18.4.97, 2.5.97, 5–6.5.97, 15.6.97, 28–29.6.97, 4.8.97
1797–98: 1.9.97, 14.9.97, 18.9.97, 27.9.97, 4.10.97, 6.10.97, 16.10.97, 20.10.97
rolling: 9.5.95, 18.5.95, 12.3.96, 19–20.4.97
screening: malt, 4.11.93, 27.8.94, 3.9.94, 5.2.96; wheat, 22.11.93
sowing: 10.1.94, 23.4.94, 14.7.94, 29.10.94, 24.4.95, 12.11.95, 12.3.96, 4.4.96, 21.4.96, 23.6.96, 29.6.96, 1–2.7.96, 5.7.96, 3–4.11.96, 27–28.3.97, 11.4.97, 18.4.97, 29.6.97
working at Holt Heath Farm: 24.3.97, 22–24.5.97, 26.5.97, 2.6.97, 5.6.97, 4.7.97, 7.7.97, 27–28.7.97, 3.8.97, 5.8.97, 8.8.97, 11–12.8.97, 15–16.9.97, 20.9.97, 22–23.9.97, 25.9.97

Bale, Norf., **183**, **233**, malt deliveries, 20.9.94, 16.8.96; WHj to, 21.10.95, 20.2.97; HR to, 13.9.97
beer deliveries, **380**, **381**:
1793: 7.11.93
1794: 2.1.94, 13.2.94, 15.3.94, 26.4.94, 4.6.94, 9.7.94, 30.7.94, 30.8.94, 19–20.9.94, 15.10.94, 6.11.94, 15.12.94
1795: 3.2.95, 6.3.95, 15.4.95, 13.5.95, 12.6.95, 27.7.95, 8.9.95, 30.9.95, 14.11.95, 11.12.95
1796: 10.2.96, 9.4.96, 15.4.96, 11.5.96, 21.6.96, 12.9.96, 15.10.96, 20.12.96
1797: 13.1.97, 9.5.97, 19.6.97, 25.7.97, 18.9.97:
see also Claxton, Thomas; Howlett, Mrs Ann

Balls, Edmund, ? of Saxlingham; with his man dibbling peas for Hs, 11–12.3.96, 14.3.96; at Hs', 10.9.96; with Thomas Balls jnr and Mr Mindham to tea at Hs', 29.6.97

Balls, Misses, of Saxlingham, daughters of Thomas; at Hs', 2.2.97; to tea at Hs', 18.4.97

Balls, Thomas (d.1802), Saxlingham farmer; WHj to tea, 23.9.96; WHj to supper, 4.1.97

Balls, Thomas jnr, Saxlingham farmer; at Hs', 22.8.96; to supper at Hs', 27.10.96, 16.3.97; dines at Hs', 25.11.96; to tea at Hs', 11.12.96,

Balls, Thomas jnr (*cont.*)
14.2.97, 11.5.97, 22.5.97, 2.8.97; with WHj and John Ellis to Walsingham, 16.12.96; with sister, Miss Mills and Miss Mindham at Hs', 2.2.97; at Hs', 6.2.97; with WHj to Reepham, 27.3.97; with WHj to Southrepps, 18.4.97; with sisters, Mr Love and Charlotte Bartell to tea at Hs', 18.4.97; with Edmund Balls and Mr Mindham to tea at Hs', 29.6.97; with WHj to Holt market, 23.9.97

balls, at Holt; WHj, MA, Miss Custance and Ann Raven to, 30.12.93; party of young people to, 20.1.94; WHj to, 17.2.94; WHj to for Mrs Overton's benefit, 31.12.94; HR to, 3.10.95, 20.4.96, 29.9.97: *see also* assemblies

Bambry, James, Holt bricklayer; with boy at work at Hs', 18–19.11.93; working as Mr Bunnett's bricklayer at Hs', 25–26.9.97

Banyard, Charles (d.1808 aged 54), innkeeper of Feathers, Holt, formerly and later of King's Lynn; at King's Head, Letheringsett, and orders beer from Hs, 26.6.94; Hs hire his postchaise, 6.9.94, 23.9.95; with William Christmas at Hs', 8.2.95; at Hs', 1.5.95; with James Moore to dinner at Hs', 1.7.95; beer delivery, 24.10.95

Barde, Mr, *see* Bird

Bare, Mr, at Hs' in connection with Hindolveston public house, 11.7.94

bark, *see* wood

barley, **16**, **90**:
- carrying: 15.8.94, 28.8.94, 5.9.95, 7–9.9.95, 12.9.96, 14.9.96, 30–31.8.97
- dressing: 10.1.95, 5.10.95
- grinding for livestock, by Gunton Thompson: 3.12.94, 12.11.95, 16.1.97, 18.9.97, 9.10.97
- harvesting: 15.8.94, 21–22.8.94, 25–26.8.94, 1–5.9.95, 7.9.95, 12.9.95, 17.9.95, 19.9.95, 18–19.8.97, 21.8.97, 26.8.97, 5–6.9.97; in Furze Closes, 18.8.94, 31.8.95, 12.9.96, 24–25.8.97, 31.8.97; in Five Acres, 11.9.95, 7.9.97; at Holt Heath Farm, 28.8.97, 8.9.97; in Bell's Acre, 30.8.97
- lifting and turning: 27–28.8.94, 8.3.97, 30.8.97, 1–2.9.97
- ploughing: stubble, 12–13.11.95, 22.11.96; at Holt Heath Farm, 27–28.3.97; in Five Acres, 15.4.97, 17.4.97
- price: 14.10.93
- purchase by Hs: collected from Holt, 30.10.93; wagonload sent by Mr Mason, 7.11.93; from Messrs Webb and Blomfield, 14.10.93; from Mr Boswell, 5.3.94, 14.11.94, 18.4.97; collected from Gunthorpe, 9.10.95; argument with Mr Jarvis over consignment, 16.10.95; collected from Edgefield, 20.11.95, 24.6.96, 24.10.96, 7.12.96; Hs pay Messrs Keeler and Everitt for year's supply, 27.6.96

barley (*cont.*)
- rolling: 9.5.95
- samples: brought by Mr Fox of Hindolveston, 17.9.94; brought by Mr Buck of Foulsham, 18.9.94
- sowing: by Hs' men, 23.4.94, 28.4.94, 15–17.4.95, 1–2.5.95, 5.5.95, 7.5.95, 20–21.4.96, 11.4.97, 14.4.97, 18.4.97; in Furze Closes, 21.4.95, 24.4.95, 12.4.97; in Five Acres, 30.4.95, 15.4.97, 17.4.97; at Holt Heath Farm, 28.3.97; in Bell's Acre, 12.4.97
- stacking: *see* goaft; stacks
- steeping: 5.10.95:
- storing in and fetching from barn: 7.10.93, 19.4.94, 12.2.95, 5.10.95, 31.10.95, 29.4.96: *see also* barn; corn; harvests; malting; straw; threshing

Barmer (Barmore), Norf., Thomas Temple orders load of mild for Richard Temple of, 16.12.94; Robert Bye collects empty barrels, 24.2.97
- beer deliveries: 27.12.94, 4.3.95, 4.4.95, 23.5.95, 11.7.95, 31.8.95, 4.9.95, 30.9.95, 1–2.12.95, 15.1.96, 23.3.96, 30.4.96, 25.6.96, 12–13.8.96, 19.9.96, 14.11.96
  - loading: 26.12.94, 3.4.95, 22.5.95, 10.7.95, 30.8.95, 3.9.95, 29.9.95, 30.11.95, 14.1.96, 22.3.96, 29.4.96, 12.8.96, 13.11.96

barn, Hs', **132**; barley removed, 7.12.93, 19.4.94, 12.2.95, 31.10.95, 29.4.96; wheat removed, 20.2.94; T. Bulling kills 52 rats, 20.2.94; cleaned, 31.7.94, 30.5.95; Hs' men working in, 1–4.10.94, 7.10.94, 13.10.94, 7.9.95, 24.11.95, 11.2.96, 30–31.8.96, 5.9.96, 29.11.96, 2.12.96, 2–3.1.97, 5–7.1.97, 9.1.97, 13.1.97, 29.8.97, 31.8.97; stack taken into, 11.2.96; John Ramm threshing in, 30.11.96, 1.12.96, 3.12.96; peas removed, 20.1.97, 1.2.97; boy riding horse with harvest wagon, 31.8.97: *see also* granaries; threshing

Barnes, Mr, with James Tinker at work at Hs', 2.7.95

barrels, collected from Foulsham, 25.10.93; collected empty from Holt, 12.12.93, 20.1.97; one lost by Robert Bye on beer delivery, 24.6.94; barrel staves delivered to Holt, 21.11.94; six collected from coopers at Holt, 3.12.94; beer stored in wine pipes, 22.4.95; collected empty from Blakeney, 30.1.96; barrel materials collected from Mr Rice, 30.4.96; barrel oak collected from Blakeney, 19.8.96; collected empty from Syderstone and Barmer, 24.2.97; figures for strong-beer barrelage produced by Norwich's common brewers, HR's endnotes: *see also* beer; casks; hoops

Bartell (Bartle), Charlotte, **286**, daughter of Edmund; with Clara Wymer at Hs', with Hs to Thomas Temple, 13.12.93; with Hs to Holt

Bartell, Charlotte (*cont.*)
market, 14.12.93; part of large party at Hs', 1.1.94; with family to tea, 10.2.94, 9.4.94, 11.7.94, 12.11.94, 3.12.94, 6.3.95, 31.3.95, 6.5.95, 8.2.96, 27.5.96, 5.10.96, 27.2.97; at Hs', 4.5.94, 24.8.94, 16.3.97, 7.6.97; with parents to supper, 22.6.94; with MA to Norwich, 8.8.94; with Miss Wigg, John Raven and Adam Baker to dinner at Hs', 15.9.94; with Mary Raven to dinner and supper at Hs', 20.11.95; with Clara Wymer and Miss Dowson at Hs', 17.2.96; with Flowers and Miss Baker to dinner, 26.2.96; with family to dinner, 25.8.96, 7. 7.97; with family and Mrs Temple at Hs', 18.1.97; with Balls family and Mr Love to tea, 18.4.97; with Miss Baker and Myles Custance to tea, 24.10.97

Bartell (Bartle), Edmund (d.1816 aged 72), surgeon-apothecary at Holt; MA and party to, 6.1.94; stays overnight at Hs', 24.2.94; with WH to Reepham, 24.9.94, 20.2.97; with WH to Norwich, 11.4.96; with WHj to Cromer, 2.8.96
at Hs': 10.2.94, 9.4.94, 22.6.94, 11.7.94, 11.8.94, 24.8.94, 16.9.94, 5.10.94, 12.11.94, 3.12.94, 6.3.95, 31.3.95, 6.5.95, 8.1.96, 15.1.96, 3.3.96, 29.3.96, 18.4.96, 28.4.96, 27.5.96, 11.7.96, 25.8.96, 5.10.96, 6.1.97, 18.1.97, 16.2.97, 27.2.97, 7.6.97, 7.7.97, 27.9.97, 2.10.97, 19.10.97
Hs at: 16.9.94, 11.3.95, 9.7.95, 20.1.96, 24.8.96, 30.12.96, 7.6.97; with HR, 25.1.95, 3.2.96

Bartell, Edmund jnr (d.1855 aged 85), **18**, **304**, of Brooke and Cromer, surgeon; with family to tea at Hs', 27.5.96; with family to dinner, 7.7.97

Bartell, Mrs Margaret (d.1836 aged 67), née Wadsworth, 1st wife of Edmund jnr; with husband and his family to dinner at Hs', 7.7.97

Bartell (Bartle), Robert (d.1801 aged 19/21), son of Edmund; at Hs', 4.5.94, 12.8.94, 24.8.94, 26.8.94, 22.5.95, 1.11.95, 17.7.96, 29.1.97; to supper and stays overnight at Hs', 23.11.94

Bartell (Bartle), Mrs Sarah (d.1828 aged 82), née Dacke, wife of Edmund; with family to tea at Hs', 10.2.94, 9.4.94, 22.6.94, 11.7.94, 11.8.94, 24.8.94, 3.12.94, 6.3.95, 31.3.95, 6.5.95, 8.2.96, 28.4.96, 27.5.96, 11.7.96, 2.8.96, 18.1.97, 16.2.97, 7.6.97, 19.10.97; with family to supper at Hs', 22.6.94, 3.3.96; at Hs', 15.3.96; with family to dinner, 25.8.96, 7.7.97; with Miss Alpe to tea, 24.8.97

Barton, R., drawing off beer, 10.10.93; barrowing bricks, 11.10.93

Barwick, John, Gunthorpe farmer; sells wheat to WHj at Holt Fair, 25.11.93; reckons with Hs, 9.3.95

Basham (Bassham), Luke (1763–1801), **7**, Holt harnessmaker and collarmaker; repairs Hs' harness, 10.10.93, 22.4.94; with boy repairs harness, 17–18.3.95, 21.5.95; with boy cleans Hs' chaise, 17.3.95

bath, MH's in garden; cleaned by Nicholas Woodhouse and William Dobson, 15.9.96; Nicholas Woodhouse and Thomas Boyce working in, 20.9.96

battens, *see* wood

Bayfield, Norf., **8**, **110**, **111**, **137**, **165**, **207**, **308**, **317**, MA to, 19.11.95; Hs' men deliver malt, 16.12.95, 27.7.96; WH to, 15.12.95; Hs to, 28.4.96; Hs and William Thackwray to tea, 27.9.96; Hs to sale, 6–7.10.96; Hs to tea at Mr Savory's, 22.12.96; WHj to, 27.1.97, 5.2.97, 20.10.97: *see also* Forster, Thomas; Savory, John Claxton

Beckhithe (Beckhigh, Bickhigh), Norf., Thomas Baldwin breaks arm falling under wheel of beer cart returning from, 23.12.94; WH and WHj to, 9.3.95
beer deliveries: 7.4.94, 25.4.94, 21.5.94, 24.5.94, 24.6.94, 18.8.94, 20.9.94, 30.10.94, 16.2.95, 6.4.95, 19.5.95, 9.6.95, 11.9.95, 3.10.95, 3.11.95, 24.12.95, 27.2.96, 11.4.96, 10.5.96, 15.8.97
loading: 29.10.94, 5.4.95:
see also Overstrand; Thirst, Thomas

beer, **103**, **177**, **332**, **408**, **411**:
collection: from Mr Sanderson at Weybourne, 17.11.96; from Samuel Coker at Field Dalling, 7.10.97; from Mrs Hall at Weybourne, 9.10.97
deliveries: three barrels to Richard Mayes at Letheringsett, 20.10.93; by boy to Charles Collyer at Gunthorpe, 5.12.93; two barrels to Richard Mayes, 3.1.94; one barrel to Thomas Atwood at Holt, 29.1.94; two barrels to William Dobson at Letheringsett, 20.4.94, 4.5.94, 18.5.94, 25.5.94; four barrels to William Dobson, Letheringsett, 27.4.94; Robert Bye loses one barrel on delivery to Wiveton and Weybourne, 24.6.94: *see also* beer, types *below*; *also under individual villages and innkeepers* beer deliveries
gift: one barrel given by WHj to men after work, 20.7.97
orders by innkeepers: Thomas Atwood of Holt, 10.10.93, 21.10.93, 10.2.94, 16.6.94; Peter Williams of Thornage, 18.10.93; John Lynes of Cley, 22.11.93; Mrs Lynes of Cley, 9.12.93; William Chapman of Hindringham, 21.12.93; Peter Williams of Thornage, for delivery next day, 14.1.94; James Skiffins of Holt, 20.1.94, 21.1.95; Robert Pleasance of Gunthorpe, 9.5.94; Matthew Pearce of

beer, orders by innkeepers (*cont.*)
Kettlestone, 16.6.94, 7.2.96; William Bulling of Holt, 4.7.94; Robert Hill of E. Runton, 9.9.94; Mr Clarke of Holt, 27.3.95; Edward Hall of Weybourne, 26.11.96; James Dyball of Edgefield, 6.12.96
shipping: delivered to Blakeney for London, 15.11.94, 22.5.95
storage: *see* bottling; casks; drawing off
types:
best: cleansed, 9.7.94
mild: ordered by Thomas Temple for Richard Temple of Barmer, 16.12.94; half-barrel delivered to Hunworth, 29.7.96
nog:
orders for two barrels: Richard Mayes, 3.1.94; William Dobson, 20.4.94, 4.5.94, 18.5.94, 25.5.94
orders for three barrels: Thomas Atwood, 10.10.93; Peter Williams, 14.1.94
orders for four barrels: John Lynes, 22.11.93; Mrs Lynes, 9.12.93; William Chapman, 21.12.93; Thomas Atwood, 10.2.94, 9.5.94, 16.6.94; Matthew Pearce, 16.6.94; Robert Hill, 9.9.94; James Skiffins, 21.1.95; William Dobson, 15.2.95
orders for five barrels: James Skiffins, 20.1.94; William Bulling, 4.7.94
orders for seven barrels: Robert Pleasance, 9.5.94; Mr Clarke, 27.3.95:
see also beer, types, strong *below*
porter:
brewed: 14.4.94, 12.4.96, 15.4.96, 19.4.96, 1.5.97, 3.5.97, 5.5.97
cleansed: 17.4.94, 16.4.96, 4.5.97, 6.5.97
drawn off: 21–22.2.94, 3.4.94, 30.4.95, 7.5.95, 24.4.96, 27.4.97, 4.5.97, 6.5.97, 8.5.97
malt: dried off, 10.4.95, 14.4.95, 8.2.96, 10.2.96; ground, 11.4.96:
see also beer, types, strong *below*
sixpenny:
bottled: 10.9.94
drawn off: 5.12.93, 27.9.94
orders for one barrel: Mrs Lynes, 9.12.93; William Dobson, 3.1.96
small beer: ordered by Henry Crafer, 3.2.96: *see also* beer, types, '// *below*
strong: cleansed, 18.7.94, 29.7.94, 5.8.94; barrelage figures for production by Norwich's common brewers, HR's endnotes: *see also* beer, types, best, nog, porter, sixpenny, X, XX *above and below*
'//: one barrel ordered by John Lynes of Cley, 22.11.93; 18 barrels ordered by William Chapman of Hindringham,

beer, types, '// (*cont.*)
21.12.93; one barrel delivered to Thomas Atwood at Holt, 29.1.94; delivered to Corpusty and Edgefield, 30.7.94 one barrel delivered to Sharrington, 3.6.97
cleansed:
1794: 9.7.94, 18.7.94, 29.7.94, 5.8.94, 12.8.94, 19.8.94, 26.8.94, 2.9.94, 9.9.94, 16.9.94, 23.9.94, 7.10.94, 14.10.94, 5.11.94, 18.11.94, 27.11.94, 5.12.94, 21.12.94, 30.12.94
1795: 8.1.95, 15.1.95, 27.1.95, 3.2.95, 10.2.95, 17.2.95, 27.2.95, 7.3.95, 17.3.95, 24.3.95, 11.4.95, 21.4.95, 25.4.95, 17.5.95, 26.5.95, 30.5.95, 12.6.95, 18.6.95, 2.7.95, 9.7.95, 17.7.95, 23.7.95, 30.7.95, 7.8.95, 14.8.95, 20.8.95, 27.8.95, 3.9.95, 13.9.95, 23.9.95, 29.9.95, 3.10.95, 8.10.95, 14.10.95, 21.10.95, 27.10.95, 3.11.95, 14.11.95, 20.11.95,25.11.95, 5.12.95, 10.12.95, 17.12.95, 25.12.95
1796: 1.1.96, 9.1.96, 13.1.96, 19.1.96, 26.1.96, 2.2.96, 9.2.96, 13.2.96, 18.2.96, 23.2.96, 3.3.96, 16.3.96, 20.3.96, 25.3.96, 6.4.96, 27.4.96, 3.5.96, 10.5.96, 17.5.96, 24.5.96, 31.5.96, 8.6.96, 14.6.96, 21.6.96, 29.6.96, 5.7.96, 12.7.96, 19.7.96, 26.7.96, 2.8.96, 9.8.96, 16.8.96, 23.8.96, 31.8.96, 8.9.96, 15.9.96, 23.9.96, 29.9.96, 6.10.96, 12.10.96, 20.10.96, 27.10.96, 11.11.96, 18.11.96, 24.11.96, 3.12.96, 10.12.96, 21.12.96, 29.12.96
1797: 10.1.97, 20.1.97, 28.1.97, 3.2.97, 12.2.97, 23.2.97, 28.2.97, 4.3.97, 10.3.97, 17.3.97, 22.3.97, 7.4.97, 21.4.97, 29.4.97, 11.5.97, 19.5.97, 24.5.97, 1.6.97, 9.6.97, 15.6.97, 21.6.97, 29.6.97, 7.7.97, 13.7.97, 27.7.97, 3.8.97, 10.8.97, 18.8.97, 24.8.97, 2.9.97, 12.9.97, 20.9.97, 29.9.97, 5.10.97, 12.10.97, 19.10.97
X:
cleansed:
1794: 25.6.94, 12.8.94, 19.8.94, 2.9.94, 16.9.94, 23.9.94, 8.10.94, 12.11.94, 28.11.94, 31.12.94
1795: 9.1.95, 4.2.95, 11.2.95, 18.2.95, 28.2.95, 28.2.95, 8.3.95, 1.4.95, 18.5.95, 27.5.95, 31.5.95, 4.6.95, 13.6.95, 17.7.95, 30.7.95, 7.8.95, 14.8.95, 20.8.95, 27.8.95, 3.9.95, 18.9.95, 30.9.95, 3.10.95, 15.10.95, 22.10.95, 28.10.95, 4.11.95, 26.11.95, 11.12.95, 18.12.95, 26.12.95

beer, types, X, cleansed (*cont.*)
1796: 2.1.96, 14.1.96, 20.1.96, 27.1.96, 3.2.96, 19.2.96, 29.2.96, 17.3.96, 21.3.96, 26.3.96, 3.4.96, 28.4.96, 4.5.96, 11.5.96, 17.5.96, 1.6.96, 9.6.96, 22.6.96, 29.6.96, 5.7.96, 19.7.96, 26.7.96, 3.8.96, 9.8.96, 16.8.96, 31.8.96,8.9.96, 16.9.96, 24.9.96, 29.9.96, 13.10.96, 21.10.96, 28.10.96, 7.11.96, 11.11.96, 18.11.96, 3.12.96, 10.12.96, 21.12.96, 29.12.96
1797: 21.1.97, 13.2.97, 18.2.97, 1.3.97, 11.3.97, 15.3.97, 3.4.97, 7.4.97, 21.4.97, 6.5.97, 19.5.97, 2.6.97, 29.6.97, 13.7.97, 27.7.97, 3.8.97, 10.8.97, 18.8.97, 20.9.97, 5.10.97, 19.10.97
drawn off: 21.4.96; 13 barrels into home cask, 18.2.96
XX:
cleansed:
1794: 26.8.94, 19.11.94, 22.12.94
1795: 16.1.95, 28.1.95, 18.3.95, 25.3.95, 12.4.95, 2.7.95, 9.7.95, 23.7.95, 14.9.95, 24.9.95, 21.11.95
1796: 15.2.96, 24.2.96, 4.3.96, 24.5.96, 15.6.96, 23.8.96, 24.11.96
1797: 4.2.97, 24.2.97, 5.3.97, 8.3.97, 18.3.97, 23.3.97, 27.3.97, 29.4.97, 2.5.97, 4.5.97, 11.5.97, 24.5.97, 10.6.97, 16.6.97, 21.6.97, 7.7.97, 20.7.97, 24.8.97, 2.9.97, 12.9.97, 29.9.97, 12.10.97:
see also brewing; carts, beer; cleansing; grains
bees, taken up by WHj, HR and Gunton Thompson, 11.9.94
Bell's Acre, Letheringsett field farmed by Hs; ploughed, 31.10.93, 27.3.95, 6.5.96, 28.5.96, 28.2.97, 12.4.97; muck spreading, 16–17.1.94, 13.3.95; wheat harvested, 14.8.94, 18.8.94; raked, 20.8.94; sown, 23.6.96, 12.4.97; harrowed, 10.4.97; barley harvested, 30.8.97
Ben [no surname], William Tinker's assistant; with William Tinker working on bottom of Hs' mash tun, 28–30.12.95; working with William and James Tinker, 22.3.96; working with William Tinker, 14.5.96, 10.8.96, 17.8.96; sawing with William Tinker, 7.1.97, 19.1.97, 21.1.97
Benfield, Mr, musician and piano tuner; at Hs', 11.6.97
Betts, Mr, dines with Hs, 12.7.94
Bignold, John (d.1837 aged 64), of Cromer; with John Smith to dinner at Hs', 25.10.96; with John Edwards to dinner at Hs', 7.3.97
Billing (Billings), Miss, Guestwick farmer; with Messrs Everitt and Keeler to dinner and supper at Hs' and to Weybourne Camp, 26.6.95
bins, *see* malt
Bintree, Norf., **167**, **170**, **171**, WH and WHj to, 7.5.95
Bird (Barde, Birde), John Rash, Rudham surgeon; with Nathaniel Raven jnr and Mary Raven to Hs, 9.8.97; with Hs and Ravens to tea at Sheringham, 10.8.97; with Ravens to Whissonsett, 11.8.97
Bird, Mr, of Thornage; with WH to Aldborough, 27.11.93
birds, *see* shooting
Bissell, Mr, of Briningham; HR reckons with, 10.3.95
Black Boys, *see* Aldborough; Holt, public houses; Thornage
Blakeney (Balkny, Blakeny), Norf., **8**, **72**, **225**, WH to, 4.8.94; Robert Bye takes beer to for shipping to London, 15.11.94, 22.5.95; Thomas Boyce collects hops, 8.1.95; Thomas Boyce to, 27.11.95; Thomas Boyce collects empty barrels, 30.1.96; Thomas Baldwin collects barrel oak, 19.8.96; William Lamb collects 10 bags of hops, 2.1.97; Mr Temple to tea at Hs', 30.1.97, 12.5.97; Mr Temple to dinner with Hs, 25.4.97; William Lamb delivers peas, 18.5.97; WH and WHj to Mr Farthing's sale, 16.8.97
cinders collected from merchants: unnamed, 17.5.94; Robert Farthing, 7–8.11.94, 12.12.94, 18.12.94, 2.3.95, 5.3.95, 14.3.95, 31.3.95, 14.4.95, 27.4.95, 8.5.95, 16.10.95, 18.11.96; Thomas William Temple, 21.12.96, 29.12.96
coal collected from merchants, **382**: Henry Chaplin, 6.2.94; unnamed, 4–6.8.94, 8.8.94; Robert Brereton, 9.8.94; Zebulon Rouse, 4.2.95; Thomas Bond, 29.8.95; for Gunton Thompson, 3.10.96; Robert Farthing, 1.6.95, 6.6.95, 13.8.95, 1.8.97; Thomas William Temple, 18.5.97, 26.9.97
WHj to: 9.4.94, 4.8.94, 22.5.95, 17.10.96, 31.7.97; with Nathaniel Raven of Whissonsett Hall, 18.12.94; with Robert Staff, 17.3.95; with Nathaniel Raven, 26.11.95
bleeding, Hs' horse by Mr Hammond, 28.1.95
Blomfield, Mr, sells barley to WHj, 14.10.93
Bodham, Norf., WHj to, 16.4.94; HR to, 2.7.94, 11.8.96
Bond, Thomas, Blakeney coal merchant; Hs' men collect coal, 29.8.95
books, **248**, WHj dines at Holt book club, 10.1.97: *see also* diary
Booth, Matthew, of Holt, plumber, glazier and pump engineer; with man at work at Hs', 15.7.95; with Edmund Devereux and William Hase installs Hs' new pump, 9.9.95; repairs pipes, 7.5.96

Booty, Mrs, **276**, **277**, Binham brewer; her drayhorses rescued by Hs' men from flooded Glaven, one mare drowns, 4.6.96
Boswell (Bozwell), Andrew (d.1815 aged 80), Edgefield farmer; at Hs', 14.10.93; Hs' men collect barley, 5.3.94, 14.11.94, 18.4.97; Robert Bye delivers malt, 22.5.94; orders malt, 17.11.95
bottling, sixpenny beer by HR, 10.9.94; wine from pipe [cask] by WH, WHj and HR at Cley, 10.12.94
bowling green, at Holt; WHj to feast, 29.10.95
box [iron sleeve], *see* carts; pumps
Boyce, Mrs Sarah (1766–1857), née Jeckell, wife of Thomas; haymaking for Hs, 3.10.96, 7.10.96, 7–8.7.97, 10.7.97, 14.7.97
Boyce, Thomas (d.1855 aged 89), **49**, of Letheringsett, Hs' labourer, builder, gardener and temporary farm servant; attends his club, 12.1.95, 11.1.96; with MH to meetings, 26.4.95, 14.6.95, 27.12.95; not at work, 18.6.95, 26.5.97; employed as Hs' gardener for £10 a year, 10.10.96; to Whit Monday dinner at Hs', 5.6.97; his work for James Cobon temporarily undertaken by Robert Bye, 28.8.97
brewing: 13–14.1.95, 26.1.95, 9.2.95, 26.2.95, 6.3.95, 11.5.95, 13.10.95, 27–28.11.95, 4.12.95, 9.12.95, 13.2.96, 27.2.96, 24.3.96, 28.8.97
cleaning vessels: 1.11.94, 8.10.95
cleansing beer: 6.3.94, 6.11.94, 30.12.94, 9.1.95, 10.2.95, 6.4.95, 6.12.95
drawing off beer: 6.3.94, 9.3.96, 24.4.96, 12.12.96
working in brewery: fetches malt, 12.2.95; moves beer into white hall, 22.4.95; fetches coal, 3.12.95
building work: helping bricklayers, 24.2.94; casting sand, 25.2.94, 17.3.94; cleaning bricks, 26–27.2.94, 1.3.94; laying foundations for stable, 3.3.94; at work in yards, 5.3.94, 8.3.94, 10.3.94, 13.3.94, 15.3.94, 17.3.94, 19–20.3.94, 22.3.94, 24.3.94, 28.3.94, 31.3.94, 1–5.4.94, 23–28.6.94, 5.7.94, 8–9.7.94, 11–12.7.94, 14–19.7.94, 21–26.7.94, 28.7.94; lays foundations of yard at King's Head, Letheringsett, 11.3.94; digging sand, 25.3.94; barrowing bricks, 25.3.94; finishes brewhouse yard, 29.7.94; unloading tiles, 6.11.94; carting gravel, 31.12.94; carries wood into malt chamber, 1.1.95; collects tiles, 15.1.95; at work behind stable, 6.4.95; carting stones, 15.4.95; repairs road, 4.2.96; cleans road, 13–14.6.97
collecting goods: barley, 12.2.95; clay, 9–10.1.95, 10.12.96; coal, 4.2.95; cinders, 13.2.95; furze, 2.1.95, 6.1.95, 27.1.97; hay, 14.3.94, 24.9.94, 29.9.94, 18–19.2.95, 23.4.95;
Boyce, Thomas, collecting goods (*cont.*)
hops, 8.1.95; turnips, 26.12.94, 10.1.95, 31.1.95, 20.2.95; wood, 8.11.95
delivering beer: 24.10.94, 24.12.94, 5.1.95, 15.1.95, 20–21.1.95, 27.1.95, 29–30.1.95, 2–6.2.95, 9.2.95, 11.2.95, 13–17.2.95, 21.2.95, 23.2.95, 27.2.95, 24.12.95, 26.12.95, 11.10.96, 24.12.96, 26.12.96
loading: 29.1.95, 10.2.95, 12.2.95
gardening:
1794: 29–31.7.94, 1–2.8.94, 19–20.9.94, 22–25–27.9.94, 30.9.94, 1–4.10.94, 6–8.10.94, 10–11.10.94, 13.10.94, 15–18.10.94, 20–23.10.94, 25.10.94, 28–31.10.94, 1.11.94, 3–4.11.94, 7–8.11.94, 11–15.11.94, 17–22.11.94, 24.11.94, 27.11.94
1795: 26.2.95, 5.3.95, 7.3.95, 9–12.3.95, 17–19.3.95, 21.3.95, 25–26.3.95, 28.3.95, 9–10.4.95, 13–14.4.95, 16–18.4.95, 7–9.5.95, 12–16.5.95, 18–19.5.95, 22–23.5.95, 25.5.95, 28–30.5.95, 1–5.6.95, 8–13.6.95, 15–16.6.95, 20.6.95, 22.6.95, 24–27.6.95, 29–30.6.95, 1–3.7.95, 6–7.7.95, 14–15.7.95, 18.7.95, 20.7.95, 29–30.7.95, 1–2.10.95, 5–8.10.95, 10.10.95, 12.10.95, 20–21.11.95, 23–26.11.95, 2–3.12.95, 5.12.95, 7–10.12.95, 12.12.95, 14–16.12.95
1796: 29.1.96, 2–3.2.96, 5–6.2.96, 12.2.96, 19–20.2.96, 4.3.96, 29.3.96, 5.4.96, 14–15.4.96, 19–23.4.96, 25–30.4.96, 2–7.5.96, 9–14.5.96, 16.5.96, 18–19.5.96, 23–25.5.96, 27.5.96, 29.6.96, 6–9.7.96, 11.7.96, 15–16.7.96, 19.7.96, 19–20.8.96, 27.8.96, 26–28.9.96, 30.9.96, 1.10.96, 3.10.96, 5–8.10.96, 18–21.10.96, 4.11.96, 14–17.11.96, 1.12.96, 5–9.12.96, 12.12.96, 20–21.12.96
1797: 16.1.97, 23–24.1.97, 13.2.97, 27–28.2.97, 1–2.3.97, 9.3.97, 13.3.97, 20–21.3.97, 15.4.97, 19–20.4.97, 22.4.97, 24–29.4.97, 1.5.97, 15–18.5.97, 23–24.5.97, 30–31.5.97, 1.6.97, 5.6.97, 8.6.97, 10.6.97, 12.6.97, 15–17.6.97, 17–19.7.97, 1–5.8.97, 25.9.97, 5.10.97
cutting drain in garden, 20.3.95; in plantations, 5–6.6.95, 13.6.97; planting trees, 11.1.96; painting in garden, 18.3.96; props up cherry tree, 2.7.96; clipping hedge, 27.8.96; working in MH's bath, 20.9.96; gathering apples, 13.10.96; digging potatoes, 2.12.96; in shrubbery, 29.5.97
harrowing: 26–27.3.94, 21–22.4.95, 27–28.4.95, 6–7.5.95, 20–21.10.95, 27.10.95
harvesting: 22–26.8.96, 11–12.8.97, 14.8.97, 28.8.97
haymaking: 1–2.7.94, 4–5.7.94, 7.7.94, 9–11.7.94, 6–11.7.95, 13–14.7.95, 16.7.95, 12–13.7.96, 18.7.96, 20–23.7.96, 4.10.96, 28–

Boyce, Thomas, haymaking (*cont.*)
30.6.97, 1.7.97, 4.7.97, 6–8.7.97, 11–14.7.97, 17.7.97, 20–22.7.97
hedging: 18–19.3.94, 28.7.94, 26.11.94, 31.3.95, 1–4.4.95, 7–8.4.95, 11.4.95, 19.11.95
hoeing turnips: 26–30.7.96, 3.8.96, 6.8.96, 11–12.8.96, 15–18.8.96, 26–28.7.97, 31.7.97, 7–9.8.97
jobs: 27.10.94, 29–30.12.94, 1.1.95, 7.1.95, 19–20.1.95, 22–24.1.95, 28.1.95, 28.2.95, 26.5.95, 17.6.95, 13.10.95, 31.10.95, 3.11.95, 6.11.95, 30.11.95, 6–8.1.96, 26.5.96, 8.8.96, 10.12.96, 12.12.96, 25.1.97; repairing ditch in Brewhouse Pightle, 18–20.2.94; screening wheat, 21.2.94; with WHj inspects hay at Holt, 9.7.94; loading coal, 5–6.8.94; mucking out pigs, 23.10.94; treats horse, 31.10.94; cleans chaise harness, 5.11.94; chopping sticks, 6.1.95; tying faggots, 2–3.3.95, 14.11.95; at mould cart, 23.4.95, 13–14.12.96; at work in river, 4.7.95, 20.7.95, 2–3.6.97, 14.6.97; raking couch grass, 27–28.10.95, 31.10.95; to Blakeney, 27.11.95; unloading cinders, 10.12.95; delivering malt, 16.12.95; carting gravel, 30.3.96, 2.4.96, 4.2.97, 8–9.2.97; dams river, 20–21.5.96; dressing grass seed, 25.7.96; thatching haystack, 1–2.8.96, 4–6.8.96; at clay cart, 15.12.96, 17.12.96, 19.12.96; topping trees in meadow, 22–23.12.96; delivers fir trees, 24.2.97; hoeing furrows, 19–20.5.97, 22.5.97
malting: 15–16.4.96, 7.5.96, 24–25.5.96, 28.5.96, 30–31.5.96, 1–4.6.96, 6–11.6.96, 13–18.6.96, 20–23.6.96, 25.6.96, 27–28.6.96, 30.6.96, 1–2.7.96, 4.7.96; dressing culms, 21.2.94; screening malt, 22.4.95; drying porter malt, 8.2.96
muck carting/spreading: 22.2.94, 29.1.95, 6–7.2.95, 21.2.95, 28.2.95, 13.3.95, 18.3.95, 30.10.95, 4–5.11.95, 7.11.95, 10–11.11.95, 18.2.96, 24–25.2.96, 31.10.96, 1.11.96, 3–4.11.96, 7–8.11.96, 15–16.12.96, 27.1.97, 23–24.6.97, 28.6.97; his boy collects muck off Brewhouse Pightle, 6.9.94, 8.9.94; turning muck, 2.3.95, 25–26.2.96
ploughing: 17.2.95, 24.2.95, 17.4.95, 20.4.95, 22.4.95, 24–25.4.95, 29–30.4.95, 1–2.5.95, 4–6.5.95, 14–17.10.95, 19.10.95, 22–24.10.95, 26.10.95, 9.11.95, 12–13.11.95, 7–8.3.96, 8.11.96
sowing: 21.4.95, 24.4.95, 30.4.95, 1–2.5.95, 5.5.95, 7.5.95, 12.11.95, 4.4.96
working in fields: 2–6.5.97, 8–12.5.97
Five Acres: 15.3.97
Furze Closes: 29.11.94, 1–6.12.94, 8–10.12.94, 13.12.94, 19–20.12.94, 31.3.97, 1.4.97, 4–7.4.97, 10–14.4.97, 17–18.4.97

Boyce, Thomas, working in fields (*cont.*)
meadow: 17.1.97, 19.1.97, 26.1.97, 28.1.97, 30–31.1.97, 1.2.97, 3.2.97, 10–11.2.97, 15–17.2.97, 23–24.2.97, 3–4.3.97, 6–7.3.97, 16–17.3.97
Six Acres: 10–12.3.96, 14.3.96
working in yards: 4.3.95, 22.5.95, 2.11.95, 16–17.11.95, 24–26.3.96, 31.3.96, 1–2.4.96, 4.4.96, 6–7.4.96, 18.3.97, 3.4.97, 13.5.97, 12.6.97, 19.6.97; cleaning pig yard, 17.11.95
boys (lads):
employed by Hs:
boy 17, [unnamed], 1793–94: starts work, 12.10.93; to Holt Fair, 25.4.94; to Holt Sessions, 27.9.94, 4.10.94; departs from Hs, 10.10.94
brewing:
1793: 16.10.93, 23.10.93, 30.10.93, 6.11.93, 13.11.93, 22–23.11.93, 29–30.11.93, 2–3.12.93, 9.12.93, 16.12.93, 23.12.93, 30.12.93
1794: 6.1.94, 13.1.94, 20.1.94, 3.2.94, 10.2.94, 13.2.94, 17.2.94, 24.2.94, 3.3.94, 11.3.94, 17.3.94, 24.3.94, 31.3.94, 7.4.94, 14.4.94, 21.4.94, 28.4.94, 10.5.94, 14.5.94, 20.5.94, 24.5.94, 3.6.94, 7.6.94, 16.6.94, 23.6.94, 30.6.94, 8.7.94, 17.7.94, 28.7.94, 4.8.94, 11.8.94, 18.8.94, 1.9.94, 8.9.94, 15.9.94, 22.9.94, 29.9.94, 6.10.94
cleaning vessels: 27.3.94, 3.4.94, 31.7.94
cleansing beer: 26.11.93, 23.1.94, 6.3.94, 27.3.94, 3.4.94, 10.4.94, 12.8.94, 2.9.94
drawing off beer: 6.1.94, 21.1.94, 16.2.94, 25.2.94, 6.3.94, 19.3.94, 27.3.94, 2–3.4.94, 6.4.94, 22.4.94, 3.5.94, 2.8.94
collecting goods: cement, 15.7.94; fish for pond, 21.7.94; lime, 25.3.94, 1.4.94, 14.4.94, 26.5.94; sand, 21.12.93, 25.3.94; stones, 7.1.94; tiles, 16.11.93, 21.3.94; turnips, 21.12.93, 15.2.94, 22.2.94, 27.2.94; window frames, 10.4.94; wood, 26.2.94
delivering goods:
beer: 5.12.93, 7.1.94, 11.9.94, 17.9.94, 19–20.9.94
malt: 5.3.94, 24.4.94, 20.9.94
harrowing: 14–15.10.93, 19.3.94, 26.3.94, 2.4.94, 18.4.94, 26.4.94, 5–6.5.94, 30–31.5.94, 14.7.94
harvesting: 13–16.8.94, 18.8.94, 20–22.8.94, 25–26.8.94, 28.8.94; gathering largess, 30.8.94
haymaking: 4.7.94, 9–11.7.94
illness: 25.1.94, 27.1.94

boys, employed by Hs, boy 17 (*cont.*)
jobs: sowing, 11.1.94; moves stack into barn, 8.3.94; fetching malt over to brewery, 27.3.94; burning couch grass, 28.3.94, 25.4.94; takes thorns to meadow, 8.4.94; carting gravel, 2.5.94, 25.7.94, 2.8.94; mucking out pigs, 2.5.94, 26.5.94; returns from Whissonsett, 10.6.94; to Briningham, 16.7.94; cleans barn, 31.7.94; loading coal, 2.8.94, 5–7.8.94; gathering apples, 12.9.94, 19.9.94, 3.10.94; muck spreading, 18.9.94
ploughing: 30.11.93, 7.12.93, 11.12.93, 5.4.94, 9.4.94, 2.6.94, 18.9.94
boy 18, [unnamed], 1794: brewing, 13.10.94, 17.10.94, 22.10.94, 29.10.94, 4.11.94, 10.11.94; collects turnips for cows, 8.11.94; runs away, 12.11.94
boy 19, [unnamed], 1794–95: starts work, 24.11.94; given notice by WHj, 20.9.95; departs, 10.10.95
brewing:
1794: 26.11.94, 4.12.94, 11.12.94, 20.12.94
1795: 7.1.95, 9.2.95, 16.2.95, 26.2.95, 16.3.95, 23.3.95, 10.4.95, 20.4.95, 24.4.95, 29.4.95, 6.5.95, 11.5.95, 16.5.95, 21.5.95, 25.5.95, 29.5.95, 3.6.95, 11.6.95, 17.6.95, 23.6.95, 1.7.95, 8.7.95, 16.7.95, 22.7.95, 29.7.95, 13.8.95, 19.8.95, 26.8.95, 2.9.95, 12.9.95, 16.9.95, 28.9.95, 2.10.95, 7.10.95
cleaning vessels: 29.4.95, 8.10.95
cleansing beer: 31.12.94, 27.2.95, 17.5.95, 31.5.95
collecting goods: cinders, 2.3.95; furze, 2.1.95; hay, 21.7.95, 24–25.7.95; pigs, 8.8.95; stones, 24.3.95, 15.4.95, 22.6.95, 27.6.95; turnips, 29.11.94, 2.12.94, 5.1.95, 9.3.95, 12.3.95, 4.4.95, 8.4.95, 18.4.95
delivering goods:
beer: 11.7.95, 11-12.8.95, 28.8.95, 30.9.95
malt: 5.1.95, 25.3.95, 15.8.95
harrowing: 21.3.95, 28.3.95, 30.3.95, 10.4.95, 17.4.95, 25.4.95, 2.5.95
harvesting: 8–10.9.95, 19.9.95
haymaking: 7.7.95, 10.7.95, 13.7.95, 19.9.95
illness: 8.1.95; goes home when gravely ill, 9.1.95; asleep all day, 4.3.95; very ill, 5–6.3.95
jobs: 23.2.95; gardening, 11.2.95; unloading hay, 23.2.95; carting thorns, 2.4.95; to Holt, 4.4.95; screening malt, 14.4.95; digging hole for tree, 14.4.95; placing

boys, employed by Hs, boy 19, jobs (*cont.*)
hurdles in Brewhouse Pightle, 17.4.95; at mould cart, 23.4.95; to Cley, 4.9.95; in barn, 7.9.95
muck carting/spreading: 7.2.95, 21.2.95, 13.3.95, 21.8.95
boy 20, [unnamed], 1795:
brewing: 13.10.95, 20.10.95, 26.10.95, 2.11.95, 13.11.95, 19.11.95
muck carting/spreading: 30.10.95, 9–10.11.95
boy 21, William [no surname], 1795–96: starts work, 27.12.95; departs, 1.2.96
brewing: 31.12.95, 8.1.96, 12.1.96, 18.1.96, 25.1.96, 1.2.96; drawing off beer, 13.1.96
jobs: 29.12.95; clears mash tun, 28.12.95; cleans yard, 29.12.95
muck carting/spreading: 4–5.1.96, 27.1.96, 29.1.96
boy 22, Nicholas Woodhouse (Wodehouse, Woodehouse), Hs' 'great boy' 1795–96: leaves work with swollen legs, 4.12.95; to Cley Fair, 29.7.96; departs, 10.10.96
brewing: 28.11.95, 20.6.96, 28.6.96, 11.7.96, 18.7.96, 25.7.96, 1.8.96, 15.8.96, 22.8.96, 30.8.96, 7.9.96, 14.9.96, 22.9.96, 28.9.96, 5.10.96
gardening: 9.6.96, 22.6.96, 27.8.96; carts gravel from Hs' garden, 15.6.96, 21.6.96
general brewery work: drawing off beer, 30.11.95; tidying malt, 31.5.96; screening wheat, 29.6.96; clears vat, 30.6.96; delivers malt to Bayfield, 27.7.96; delivers mild to Hunworth, 29.7.96; unloads coal, 4.8.96; delivers malt to Guestwick, 15.8.96; in brewhouse, 26.9.96
general farm work: harrowing, 1.2.96; in river, 6.6.96, 27.7.96, 18.8.96; carts iron cinders into Glaven, 9.6.96; ploughing, 1–2.7.96, 30.9.96; moves part of stack into hay chamber, 23.7.96; collects sand, 29.7.96; repairs river bank, 4.8.96; harrowing turnips, 9.8.96; in barn, 5.9.96
harvesting: 20.8.96, 23–27.8.96, 2–3.9.96, 6.9.96, 8.9.96, 12–14.9.96
haymaking: 5.7.96, 7–8.7.96, 12–13.7.96, 15–16.7.96, 18.7.96, 20.7.96, 22.7.96, 3–5.10.96
jobs: 25.6.96, 9.7.96, 5.8.96, 13.8.96, 16.8.96, 19.8.96, 29.8.96, 31.8.96, 9–10.9.96, 17.9.96, 21.9.96, 23.9.96, 27.9.96, 29.9.96, 1.10.96, 4.10.96, 7–8.10.96; at work in yard, 23.6.96; collects barley from Edgefield, 24.6.96; collects sow and pigs from Thursford, 1.9.96; cleans MH's bath, 15.9.96, 20.9.96

boys, employed by Hs, boy 22, Nicholas Woodhouse (*cont.*)
muck carting/spreading and muck turning: 25–26.5.96, 28.5.96, 10–11.6.96, 16.6.96, 18.6.96, 24.4.96, 9–10.9.96, 19–20.9.96
boy 23, [unnamed], 1796: collected by HR from Weybourne, 31.1.96
brewing: 8.2.96, 13.2.96, 17.2.96, 27.2.96, 2.3.96, 8.3.96, 15.3.96, 19.3.96, 24.3.96, 29.3.96, 1.4.96, 5.4.96, 9.4.96, 12.4.96, 15.4.96, 19.4.96, 26.4.96, 2.5.96, 9.5.96, 16.5.96, 23.5.96, 30.5.96, 7.6.96, 13.6.96, 4.7.96, 11.7.96, 8.8.96
cleansing beer: 13.4.96, 16.4.96, 3.5.96
drawing off beer: 22.2.96, 26.2.96, 9.3.96, 2.4.96, 13.4.96, 16.4.96, 20.4.96, 23–24.4.96; clearing vat, 19.5.96
collecting goods: wheat, 16.2.96; barrel materials, 30.4.96; cement, 6.5.96; fir trees, 12.5.96
jobs: moves stack into barn, 11.2.96; carting bricks, 26.3.96; filling gravel cart, 30–31.3.96; ploughing, 22.4.96, 13–14.5.96; carting gravel, 5–6.5.96; takes gates to Furze Closes, 12.5.96; sets gates in place, 13.5.96; tidying malt, 2.6.96; haymaking, 4.7.96
muck carting/spreading: 8.4.96, 25.7.96; turning muck, 4–5.5.96, 19.5.96, 24.5.96
boy 24, 1796–?97 ('John Ramm's boy'): starts work, 30.8.96; riding horse during harvest, 5.9.96; tends pigs, 6.9.96, 8.9.97
boy 25, [unnamed], 1797: haymaking, 14.7.97; working at Holt Heath Farm, 28.7.97, 8.8.97, 15–16.9.97, 18.9.97, 23.9.97, 25.9.97; harrowing, 29.7.97, 21.9.97; jobs, 19.8.97, 24–26.8.97, 28.8.97, 30.8.97, 1–2.9.97, 12–13.9.97, 20.9.97, 27.9.97, 29–30.9.97, 3–4.10.97; riding horse in barn, 31.8.97; riding horse on goaft, 6.9.97; harvesting, 7–8.9.97; in brewhouse, 9.9.97; barrowing bricks, 11.9.97; collects lime and sand, 2.10.97; departs, 5.10.97
boy 26, William [no surname], 1797–98: starts work, 12.10.97; collects nails, 14.10.97
employed by others:
Joseph Baker's: at work, 15.4.95, 17.4.95
James Bambry's: with master at work, 18–19.11.93
Luke Basham's: cleaning Hs' chaise and mending harness, 17–18.3.95; with master mending harness, 21.5.95
Thomas Boyce's: collecting muck off Brewhouse Pightle, 6.9.94, 8.9.94

boys, employed by others (*cont.*)
John Bunnett's: at work, 11.8.96; with master installs sash windows, 23.3.97; two at work, 24.3.97; with master at work, 29.3.97
'Boy Cornwall': helping with harvest, 28.8.94
George Dawson's: painting, 22–24.3.96, 4–6.5.96, 23.5.96, 26–27.5.96, 1.8.97
John Ramm's: threshing with master, 21.10.96: *see also* boy 24 above
William Tinker's: with master at work, 19–21.6.97
Thomas Youngman's: at work, 14.1.94, 30.4.94, 10.5.94, 29.1.95; with master mending waterwheel, 18.2.94; with master hangs gate, 3.5.94; with master sets waterwheel to work, 6.5.95; painting, 12–14.5.94, 21–23.7.94, 28.7.94, 13.9.94; cleansing beer, 13.5.94; makes wooden support for bricklayers' arch, 26.5.94; fetching barley, 28.8.94; planing deals, 22–24.1.95, 26–28.1.95; sawing, 12–13.3.95

Braeton, *see* Brereton

brakes, *see* hedges

Brampton (Branton), Norf., Robert Bye hurts leg returning from, 15.10.93; WHj to, 22.6.96
beer deliveries:
1793: 14–15.10.93, 21.11.93, 21.12.93
1794: 5.2.94, 13.3.94, 12.4.94, 13.5.94, 31.5.94, 21.6.94, 25.7.94, 16.8.94, 19.9.94, 27.10.94, 28.11.94
1795: 5.1.95, 2.3.95, 4.5.95, 26.5.95, 13.7.95, 17.8.95, 28.9.95, 30.11.95
1796: 11.1.96, 5.3.96, 7.5.96, 18.6.96, 15.8.96, 26.9.96, 6.10.96, 9.11.96, 22.12.96
1797: 21.1.97, 18.3.97, 29.4.97, 13.5.97, 3.6.97, 26.6.97, 13.7.97, 2.9.97, 12.9.97, 16.10.97
loading for: 13.10.93, 26.10.94, 1.3.95, 3.5.95, 10.1.96, 25.9.96, 15.10.97:
see also Ives, Mrs Ann; Ives, Meshack

bran, *see* flour, lower grades

Branford, John Bell (d.1861 aged 98), Godwick farmer, later of Oxwick; at Hs', 17.2.94

Bransby, Joseph, Letheringsett labourer; dressing, 9.2.96, 26.3.96; in barn, 11.2.96; at jobs, 5.3.96; hedging, 21.3.96; stacking hay, 21.7.96
muck carting/spreading: 4–5.1.96, 7.1.96, 9.1.96, 25.2.96
threshing: 6.1.96, 11-16.1.96, 18–23.1.96, 25–30.1.96, 1–6.2.96, 8.2.96, 10.2.96, 12–13.2.96, 15–19.2.96, 22–23.2.96, 25–26.2.96, 29.2.96, 2–4.3.96, 12.3.96, 15–19.3.96, 21.3.96, 25.3.96, 5–8.4.96, 13.4.96, 16.4.96, 18–23.4.96, 25–29.4.96

bread riots, *see* Sharrington

Brereton (Braeton), Robert (1759–1831), Blakeney merchant; Robert Bye collects coal from, 9.8.94

breweries, **272**, **286**, **352**, **419**, **421**:
Binham: *see* Booty, Mrs
E. Dereham: Mr Carr at Hs', 22.11.93
Letheringsett, **116**, **303**: *see* beer; brewhouse; brewing
Norwich, **167**, **170**, **171**, **408**, **411**: list of common brewers and annual strong-beer production, HR's endnotes

brewhouse, Hs', **3**, **11**, **37**, **49**, **77**, **88**, **94**, **95**, **96**, **359**, **393**, **397**, **402**; whitewashed, 8.9.95, 8.10.95; small-beer house whitewashed, 10.11.95; WH walks into, 21.11.95; 'flappers' [?louvres] painted by WHj and HR, 5.8.96; Gunton Thompson and HR clean vat, 14.10.96; HR takes brewery horse to Mr Love at Holt, 16.11.96; great cask cleaned, 3.5.97
counting house, **3**, **96**, **391**: interior dismantled by HR, 18.9.97; roof built by William Tinker, 25.9.97; chamber door made by Thomas Youngman's two men, 14.10.97; HR begins selling goods in new counting house, 20.10.97
Hs' men at work:
1793: 14.10.93, 31.10.93, 2.11.93, 9.11.93, 18.11.93, 21–23.11.93, 30.11.93, 2.12.93, 4.12.93, 6.12.93, 10.12.93, 13.12.93, 19.12.93, 27.12.93
1794: 2.1.94, 9–10.1.94, 21.1.94, 24.1.94, 6.2.94, 17–18.2.94, 20.2.94, 12.3.94, 25.3.94, 30.4.94, 15.5.94, 17.5.94, 21.5.94, 23.5.94, 11.10.94, 14–15.10.94, 29.12.94
1795: 13.1.95, 19.5.95, 22–23.5.95, 5.6.95, 15.8.95, 23–24.9.95, 26.9.95, 13.10.95, 27.11.95, 11.12.95, 14.12.95, 26.12.95
1796: 6.5.96, 5–6.9.96, 9.9.96, 17.9.96, 19.9.96, 26.9.96, 1.10.96, 15.10.96, 22.10.96, 24.10.96, 29.10.96, 31.10.96, 2.11.96, 8–9.11.96, 12.11.96, 14.11.96, 19.11.96, 21.11.96, 28.11.96, 30.11.96, 24.12.96, 26.12.96, 29–30.12.96
1797: 2.1.97, 10–11.1.97, 13.1.97, 20.1.97, 24.1.97, 31.1.97, 6.2.97, 8.2.97, 14–15.2.97, 21.2.97, 7.3.97, 10–11.3.97, 15.3.97, 20.3.97, 23.3.97, 27–29.3.97, 31.3.97, 5.4.97, 8.4.97, 12.4.97, 14.4.97, 18–19.4.97, 21.4.97, 25–26.4.97, 29–30.4.97, 2.5.97, 4.5.97, 9.5.97, 11.5.97, 13.5.97, 16–17.5.97, 19–20.5.97, 22.5.97, 24–25.5.97, 27.5.97, 30.5.97, 3.6.97, 7.6.97, 12.6.97, 15–17.6.97, 21–22.6.97, 24.6.97, 26–27.6.97, 29.6.97, 10–12.7.97, 14–15.7.97, 18.7.97, 21–22.7.97, 24–25.7.97, 29.7.97, 31.7.97, 1.8.97, 3–5.8.97, 12.8.97, 22.8.97, 26.8.97, 28.8.97, 30–31.8.97, 4–7.9.97, 9.9.97, 12–14.9.97,

brewhouse, Hs' men at work (*cont.*)
20–21.9.97, 23.9.97, 25.9.97, 2–3.10.97, 5–7.10.97, 16.10.97, 20–21.10.97
tun room, **3**, **11**, **15**, **37**, **49**, **61**, **77**, **94**, **96**, **201**, **397**: Robert Bye and Thomas Baldwin at work, 14.11.93; Thomas Youngman installs trough, 10.1.94; whitewashed by Gunton Thompson, 8.6.95
white hall, **3**, **11**, **49**, **94**, **96**, **359**, **396**, **397**: cleanse beer stored in great cask, 2.11.93, 28.1.94, 3.5.94, 30.11.95; small cask cleaned, 9.12.93; great cask emptied, 10.12.93; great cask cleaned, 16.12.93; great cask measured, 17.12.93; 10 barrels of beer stored in great cask, 21.12.93; 22 barrels of beer stored in great cask, 23.12.93; 18 barrels of beer stored in great cask, 25.12.93; cleanse beer stored, 28.12.93, 15.1.94, 11.2.94, 22.4.94, 29.4.94, 16.4.96, 23.4.96; beer drawn off, 14.1.94; beer stored in wine pipes, 22.4.95; beer stored, 13.1.96, 17.2.97; beer stored in cask, 13.1.96, 2.4.96; great cask cleaned, 16.2.97; beer drayed, 27.4.97; WHj draws off porter, 27.4.97; cleaned by HR, 12.5.97
workshop: put in order by WHj, Gunton Thompson and HR, 21.1.95
yard, **3**, **66**, **74**, **75**, **77**, **96**, **359**: John Ramm removing stones, 14.7.94; Thomas Boyce finishes work, 29.7.94:
see also beer; brewing; brewing equipment; cleansing; drawing off; malt-mill

Brewhouse Pightle (Brewing Meadow, Phitle, Pitol), **37**, **49**, **80**, **228**, **230**, Hs' field adjoining brewery; muck collected, 15.1.94, 6.9.94, 8.9.94; ditch maintained, 18–20.2.94; scour from ditch spread over, 23.4.94; Thomas Hall at work, 2.6.94, 18.6.94; Jeremiah Moore at work in river, 5.6.94; WHj and HR plant chestnut tree, 20.3.95; Thomas Hall plants thorns around chestnut, 21.3.95; hurdles arranged, 17.4.95; HR paints gate, 14.12.95; WHj planting in, 7.1.96; John Ramm and boy spread dung, 25.7.96: *see also* pond

brewing, Thomas Boyce fetches coal for, 3.12.95
by Hs' men under WHj as brewer:
1793: 16.10.93, 23.10.93, 30.10.93, 6.11.93, 13.11.93, 20.11.93, 29.11.93, 3.12.93, 9.12.93, 16.12.93, 23.12.93, 30.12.93
1794: 6.1.94, 13.1.94, 20.1.94, 27.1.94, 3.2.94, 10.2.94, 13.2.94, 24.2.94, 3.3.94, 11.3.94, 17.3.94, 24.3.94, 31.3.94, 7.4.94, 14.4.94, 21.4.94, 28.4.94, 5.5.94, 10.5.94, 14.5.94, 20.5.94, 24.5.94, 26.5.94, 3.6.94, 7.6.94, 16.6.94, 23.6.94, 30.6.94, 8.7.94, 17.7.94, 28.7.94, 4.8.94, 11.8.94, 18.8.94, 25.8.94, 1.9.94, 8.9.94, 15.9.94, 22.9.94,

brewing, by Hs' men under WHj as brewer, 1794 (*cont.*)
29.9.94, 6.10.94, 13.10.94, 17.10.94, 22.10.94, 29.10.94, 4.11.94, 10.11.94, 17.11.94, 26.11.94, 4.12.94, 11.12.94, 20.12.94
1795: 7.1.95, 14.1.95, 26.1.95, 2.2.95, 9.2.95, 16.2.95, 26.2.95, 6.3.95, 16.3.95, 23.3.95, 30.3.95, 10.4.95, 20.4.95, 24.4.95, 29.4.95, 2.5.95, 6.5.95, 11.5.95, 16.5.95, 21.5.95, 25.5.95, 29.5.95, 3.6.95, 11.6.95, 17.6.95, 23.6.95, 1.7.95, 8.7.95, 16.7.95, 22.7.95, 29.7.95, 6.8.95, 13.8.95, 19.8.95, 26–27.8.95, 2.9.95, 12.9.95, 16.9.95, 22.9.95, 28.9.95, 2.10.95, 7.10.95, 20.10.95, 26.10.95, 2.11.95, 13.11.95, 19.11.95, 24.11.95, 28.11.95, 4.12.95, 9.12.95, 16.12.95, 24.12.95, 31.12.95
1796: 8.1.96, 12.1.96, 18.1.96, 25.1.96, 8.2.96, 13.2.96, 17.2.96, 27.2.96, 2.3.96, 8.3.96, 15.3.96, 19.3.96, 24.3.96, 29.3.96, 1.4.96, 5.4.96, 9.4.96, 12.4.96, 15.4.96, 26.4.96, 2.5.96, 9.5.96, 16.5.96, 23.5.96, 30.5.96, 7.6.96, 13.6.96, 20.6.96, 28.6.96, 4.7.96, 11.7.96, 18.7.96, 25.5.96, 1.8.96, 8.8.96, 15.8.96, 22.8.96, 30.8.96, 7.9.96, 14.9.96, 22.9.96, 28.9.96, 5.10.96, 11.10.96, 19.10.96, 26.10.96, 5.11.96, 10.11.96, 17.11.96, 23.11.96, 2.12.96, 9.12.96, 20.12.96, 28.12.96
by Hs' men under HR as brewer, **332**, **334**, **357**, **411**: 9.1.97, 19.1.97, 27.1.97, 2.2.97, 11.2.97, 16.2.97, 22.2.97, 27.2.97, 3.3.97, 6.3.97, 9.3.97, 13.3.97, 16.3.97, 21.3.97, 25.3.97, 1.4.97, 6.4.97, 13.4.97, 20.4.97, 28.4.97, 10.5.97, 15.5.97, 18.5.97, 23.5.97, 31.5.97, 8.6.97, 14.6.97, 20.6.97, 28.6.97, 6.7.97, 12.7.97, 19.7.97, 26.7.97, 2.8.97, 9.8.97, 17.8.97, 23.8.97, 1.9.97, 11.9.97, 19.9.97, 28.9.97, 4.10.97, 11.10.97, 18.10.97, 25.10.97
porter: brewed by WHj and men, 14.4.94, 12.4.96, 15.4.96, 19.4.96; brewed by HR and men, 1.5.97, 3.5.97, 5.5.97:
see also beer, types; brewhouse, Hs' men at work; cleansing; drawing off; draying off; malt
brewing equipment, **94**, **95**, **96**, **109**, **184**, **191**, **247**, **272**, made ready by Gunton Thompson and Henry Raven, 21.9.95
backs: dismantled by William Tinker and men, 9.7.95; Mr Haddon's men repair pipes, 10.5.97
copper, **118**, **338**, **339**: cleaned by Hs' men, 1.2.95, 8.12.95
mash tun (M T): cleared by Hs' men, 28.12.95, 6.1.96; William Tinker and Ben working on bottom, 28.12.95, 30.12.95
brewing equipment (*cont.*)
troughs (thoughs, througfs, throughfs, throughs): installed by Thomas Youngman in tun room, 10.1.94; cleared by Hs' men, 26.5.95, 18.2.96, 20.3.96, 28.3.96, 5.3.97; men carrying off beer from, 12.12.96
vat (fat, fatt): cleared by Hs' men, 27.3.94, 3.4.94, 31.7.94, 27.8.94, 1.11.94, 15.12.94, 8.10.95, 26.11.95, 19.5.96, 30.6.96, 17.9.96, 4.3.97, 14.3.97; cleaned by Hs' men, 12.7.94, 14.10.96; mash vat cleared by Robert Bye, 21.12.95:
see also fires; pumps
bricklayers (labourers, trowelmen) [builders], helped by Thomas Boyce, 24.2.94; Mr Bunnett's two trowelmen and two labourers demolishing counting house, 16.3.96; Mr Bunnett's two trowelmen and two labourers building bridge walls, 9.8.96; James Bambry and Mr Bunnett's other trowelman at work, 25.9.97
skilled men (trowelmen) working for Hs:
1794: 3.3.94, 6–8.3.94, 10–15.3.94, 17–22.3.94, 24–29.3.94, 31.3.94, 1–5.3.94, 7–12.4.94, 14–19.4.94, 21–26.4.94, 28–30.4.94, 1–3.5.94, 5–8.5.94, 30–31.5.94, 18–20.9.94, 22–25.9.94, 15–18.10.94, 20–22.10.94, 12–13.11.94, 4.12.94
1796: 17–19.3.96, 21–26.3.96, 10–13.8.96
1797: 21–23.9.97, 27–30.9.97, 2–7.10.97, 9.10.97, 11.10.97, 14.10.97, 12–13.10.97, 16–21.10.97, 23.10.97, 25.10.97
unskilled/semi-skilled men (labourers) working for Hs:
1794: 4.3.94, 6–8.3.94, 10–15.3.94, 17–22.3.94, 24–29.3.94, 31.3.94, 1–5.4.94, 7–12.4.94, 14–19.4.94, 21–26.4.94, 28–30.4.94, 1–3.5.94, 5–7.5.94, 30–31.5.94, 18.9.94, 20.9.94, 22–25.9.94, 15–18.10.94, 20.10.94, 13.11.94
1796: 17–19.3.96, 21–26.3.96, 10.8.96, 12–13.8.96, 5-6.10.96
1797: 25.3.97, 20–23.9.97, 27–30.9.97, 2–7.10.97, 9–14.10.97, 16–21.10.97, 23.10.97, 25.10.97:
see also bricks; Bunnett, John
bricks, **163**, **350**, barrowed by R. Barton, 11.10.93; collected by Hs' men, 14.10.93, 29.5.94, 4.6.95, 6.8.96; collected by Hs' men from John Dawson, 12.2.94, 24.2.94, 20.9.97; loaded by Thomas Hall, 24.2.94; cleaned by Hs' men, 26–27.2.94, 1.3.94, 28–29.5.94; barrowed by Thomas Boyce, 25.3.94; gutter bricks laid by WHj, 19.7.94; carted by boy from yard, 26.3.96; collected by Robert Bye from Holt, 22.12.96; collected by William Lamb from Cremer Cremer's kiln, 28.3.97;

bricks (*cont.*)
delivered by Thomas Baldwin to Black Boys, Holt, 5.7.97; collected by Thomas Baldwin from Holt, 2.9.97; small bricks (clinkers) barrowed by boy to cistern, 11.9.97; cut by James Bambry, 26.9.97: *see also* arches; bricklayers; tiles

bridges, **77**, **143**, **179**, **252**, **276**, **277**, **281**, **372**, **373**, Mrs Booty's drayhorses swept under Glaven footbridge, one mare drowned, 4.6.96; Mr Bunnett's bricklayers building walls for Hs' garden bridge, William Tinker and two men working on bridge, 9.8.96

Briningham (Barningham, Birmingham, Birmmingham, Birninham), Norf., **233**, Gunton Thompson to, 8.6.94; Hs' boy to, 16.7.94; HR to, 2.9.94, 14.10.94; HR reckons with Mr Bissell, 10.3.95; WHj and MA meet regiment of Artillery at, 9.6.95

Brinton (Brunton), Norf., **79**, **233**, WHj to, 15.10.93, 15.4.94; HR takes horse to, 16.10.93; Mr Mason orders two loads of bark from Hs, 8.11.93; Mr Sharpe [?Sharpens] at Hs', 10.11.94; HR to, 15.3.96, 19.5.97; HR collects clover seed, 28.3.97

Brisley, Norf., **200**, Thomas Baldwin collects hop-presser, 13.1.96

Briston, Norf., Mr Sharpens exchanges horses with Hs, 1.7.94; WH to, 26.11.94; Robert Bye and Thomas Boyce collect hay, 18–19.2.95; HR and Nathaniel Raven jnr to, 10.3.97
beer deliveries, **161**:
1793: 18.10.93, 5.11.93, 27.11.93, 11.12.93, 31.12.93
1794: 10.1.94, 25.1.94, 7.2.94, 20.2.94, 7.3.94, 24.3.94, 5.4.94, 18.4.94, 17.5.94, 5.6.94, 23.6.94, 7.7.94, 30.7.94, 12.8.94, 29.8.94, 15.9.94, 30.9.94, 10.10.94, 28.10.94, 25.11.94
1795: 3.1.93, 26.1.95, 26.3.95, 17.4.95, 7.5.95, 29.5.95, 18.6.95, 14.7.95, 7.8.95, 26.8.95, 22.9.95, 13.10.95, 17.11.95, 14.12.95
1796: 6.1.96, 25.1.96, 12.4.97, 4.5.96, 19.5.96, 2.6.96, 1.7.96, 23.7.96, 18.8.96, 5.9.96, 19.9.96, 20.10.96, 23.11.96, 27.12.96
1797: 20.1.97, 17.2.97, 14.3.97, 6.4.97, 24.4.97, 19.5.97, 7.6.97, 23.6.97, 11.7.97, 2.8.97, 24.8.97, 18.9.97, 7.10.97, 24.10.97
Methodist meeting, **139**, **161**, **188**, **263**, [? Calvinistic Methodist until mid-1795, then Wesleyan Methodist], attended by MH with: WHj, 4.1.95; HR, 11.1.95, 1.3.95, 8.3.95, 22.3.95, 5.4.95, 12.4.95, 17.5.95, 24.5.95, 31.5.95, 7.6.95, 21.6.95, 28.6.95, 12.7.95, 19.7.95, 16.8.95, 23.8.95, 30.8.95, 6.9.95, 13.9.95, 20.9.95, 27.9.95, 25.10.95;

Briston, Methodist meeting, attended by MH with: (*cont.*)
Thomas Boyce, 26.4.95, 14.6.95; Mrs Phillis Goggs, 10.5.95, 13.9.95, 20.9.95; alone, 5.7.95, 9.8.95, 27.8.97, 24.9.97; MA, 8.10.97: *see also* Longden, Francis

Brooke (Brook), Norf., WHj to, 3.11.95; WHj from, 7.11.95

Broughton, James snr (d.1813)/jnr, Letheringsett labourer; carting and screening culms, 30.1.95; at jobs, 31.1.95, 3–5.2.95, 9.2.95, 23.2.95; brewing, 2.2.95; at work in garden, 6.2.95, 10–11.2.95; muck carting/spreading muck, 7.2.95, 12–14.2.95, 21.2.95, 24.2.95; unloading hay, 23.2.95 *see also* Broughton, James jnr

Broughton, James jnr; starts work as Hs' labourer at 7*s* 6*d* a week, 16.10.97; ploughing, 17.10.97, 19.10.97, 21.10.97, 23.10.97; harrowing, 17.10.97; brewing, 18.10.97, 25.10.97: *see also* Broughton, James snr/jnr

Brunton, *see* Brinton

Buck, Mr, Foulsham farmer; brings sample of barley to Hs, 18.9.94

Buckle, John (d.1818 aged 70), ironmonger, tobacconist and colourman, Sheriff of Norwich 1787, Mayor of Norwich 1793; with Mr Herring at Hs', 19.8.95

builders, *see* bricklayers

Bull, Holt, *see* Baker, Joseph; Bulling, William; Holt, public houses

Bulling, Mr T., kills 52 rats in Hs' barn, 20.2.94; moves stack into barn, 8.3.94

Bulling (Bullin), William (d.1805 aged 51), **59**, **317**, **330**, innkeeper of Bull, Holt; beer deliveries, 30.10.93, 16.11.93, 19.4.94, 27.8.94; sells sow and pigs to Hs, 16.4.94; orders five barrels of nog, 4.7.94

Bulling's Farm, *see* Holt Heath Farm

Bumpstead (Bumpsted), John, pig dealer; collects pigs from Hs, 8.5.94, 18.11.96; removes pig's entrails, 23.11.96

Bunnett (Bunnet), John (?d.1829 aged 83), Holt builder; his men demolishing King's Head stables, Letheringsett, 24.2.94; four men turn arch over river, 28.5.94; with men at work, 29.5.94, 29.3.97, 19–20.9.97; his men at work for Hs at Weybourne public house, 18–19.11.94; two men at work in Hs' kitchen, 3.12.94; two men working at King's Head, Letheringsett, 11.3.95; three men sinking well, 20–21.8.95; four men demolishing Hs' counting house, 16.3.96; four men building walls for bridge in Hs' garden, 9.8.96; man installs door to King's Head, Letheringsett, 10.11.96; with boy installs sash windows in Hs' frontage, 23.3.97; James Bambry and second man at work, 25.9.97

Bunnett, John (*cont.*)
men's unspecified work for Hs: 1.3.94, 4–5.3.94, 18.9.94, 18–19.6.95, 23–27.6.95, 9–11.7.95, 13–14.7.95, 4–5.9.95, 17–19.3.96, 21–26.3.96, 28–31.3.96, 1–2.4.96, 7–9.4.96, 11–16.4.96, 18.4.96, 10–12.8.96, 5–6.10.96, 25.3.97, 23–26.8.97, 20–23.9.97, 27–30.9.97, 2–7.10.97, 9–14.10.97, 16–21.10.97, 23–25.10.97:
see also bricklayers; labourers

Burnham Market, Norf., WH and John Howard to, 5–6.1.95; Thomas Baldwin breaks leg under wagonwheel on return journey from, 9.12.96
beer deliveries, **ix**, **264**:
1795: 14.1.95, 11.2.95, 28.2.95, 14.4.95, 22.4.95, 23.6.95, 31.8.95, 24–25.9.95, 5.10.95, 31.10.95, 23–24.11.95, 29–30.12.95
1796: 28.1.96, 15.2.96, 29.2.96, 14.3.96, 29.3.96, 18.4.96, 4.5.96, 8.6.96, 6.7.96, 15.9.96, 13.10.96, 16.11.96, 9.12.96
1797: 7.1.97, 21.1.97, 10.2.97, 4.3.97, 25.3.97, 15.4.97, 13.5.97, 30.5.97, 8.7.97, 29.7.97, 26.9.97, 24.10.97
loading: 13.1.95, 10.2.95, 27.2.95, 22.6.95, 30.8.95, 4.10.95, 27.1.96, 14.2.96, 13.3.96, 17.4.96, 3.5.96, 15.11.96, 8.12.96, 24.3.97, 14.4.97, 29.5.97, 23.10.97:
see also Howard, John

Burrell, Mrs Elizabeth Anna Maria (d.1795), **222**, née Garrett, 1st wife of Revd John; with husband at Hs', 17.7.94, 2.9.94, 2.1.95

Burrell, Revd John (1761–1825), **11**, **222**, **262**, **294**, **295**, **364**, Rector of Letheringsett 1786–1825, Curate of Hunworth with Stody 1786–?, Curate of Wiveton 1808–23, Curate of Langham; Hs to, 28.11.93, 13.4.95; Hs to tea, 10.5.94, 6.8.94, 2.3.95, 2.6.95, 14.12.95, 26.5.96, 23.5.97; with wife to large tea party at Hs', 17.7.94; reads lecture, 3.8.94; with wife to tea at Hs', 2.9.94, 2.1.95; to tea at Hs', 5.11.94, 15.6.95, 1.12.95; WH to his audit, 12.1.95; with Garretts tours Hs' garden, 11.4.95; with WH to Cley, 28.12.95; marriage at Holt, passes through village to Fakenham, 2.8.96; with family and Hs to tea at new workhouse in Letheringsett, 9.8.96; prevented by illness from taking Easter service, 16.4.97; with wife, brother, Moys and Mr Sheldrake to tea at Hs', 24.5.97
preaches at Letheringsett: 23.3.94, 16.11.94, 14.12.94, 25.12.94, 8.3.97

Burrell, Mrs Mary (d.1833 aged 66), **70**, **222**, **376**, Holt milliner, 2nd wife of Revd John, daughter of Revd William Tower Johnson; at large party at Hs', 1.1.94; Hs to tea, 16.8.96; with husband and others to tea at Hs', 24.5.97

Burrell, Nathaniel (1762–1818), Holt surgeon; with brother and others to tea at Hs', 24.5.97

Byburch, *see* Ryburgh

Bye, Robert, Hs' farm servant, brewer and drayman; leaves Hs' team, 23.12.95, 10.10.97; takes long dinner break at Holt, 17.6.94; to Holt Fair, 25.4.97; not at work, 6.7.95, 21.2.97, 5–6.6.97; works for James Cobon in place of Thomas Boyce, 28.8.97
brewing:
1793: 29.11.93, 4.12.93, 23.12.93
1794: 6.1.94, 20.1.94, 3.2.94, 3.3.94, 31.3.94, 21.4.94, 5.5.94, 24.5.94, 26.5.94, 7.6.94, 23.6.94, 8.7.94, 28.7.94, 11.8.94, 1.9.94, 8.9.94, 22.9.94, 6.10.94, 29.10.94, 10.11.94, 26.11.94, 11.12.94
1795: 7.1.95, 16.2.95, 6.3.95, 23.3.95, 10.4.95, 24.4.95, 6.5.95, 16.5.95, 26.5.95, 29.5.95, 11.6.95, 23.6.95, 16.7.95, 22.7.95, 6.8.95, 13.8.95, 19.8.95, 27.8.95, 2.9.95, 2.10.95, 26.10.95, 13.11.95, 16.12.95
1796: 28.12.96
1797: 19.1.97, 3.2.97, 16.2.97, 6.3.97, 13.3.97, 21.3.97, 1.4.97, 20.4.97, 28.4.97, 1.5.97, 3.5.97, 5.5.97, 10.5.97, 15.5.97, 18.5.97, 23.5.97, 31.5.97, 8.6.97, 14.6.97, 20.6.97, 28.6.97, 6.7.97, 19.7.97, 26.7.97, 2.8.97, 9.8.97, 17.8.97, 23.8.97, 1.9.97, 11.9.97, 19.9.97, 28.9.97, 4.10.97
cleaning vessels: 15.11.93, 9.12.93, 16.12.93, 3.4.94, 14.5.94, 12.7.94, 31.7.94, 1.2.95, 21.12.95, 16.2.97, 5.3.97, 3.5.97
working in brewery: in tun room, 14.11.93; fetching malt, 16.10.94, 12.2.95; lighting fire, 17.10.94
1793: 31.10.93, 2.12.93, 4.12.93, 6.12.93, 10.12.93
1794: 2.1.94, 24.1.94, 17–18.2.94, 20.2.94, 30.4.94, 21.5.94, 23.5.94, 29.12.94
1795: 19.5.95, 22–23.5.95, 5.6.95, 23.9.95, 13.10.95
1796: 29.12.96
1797: 11.1.97, 7.3.97, 15.3.97, 21.4.97, 26.4.97, 29.4.97, 2.5.97, 4.5.97, 11.5.97, 13.5.97, 17.5.97, 19–20.5.97, 22.5.97, 24–25.5.97, 12.6.97, 15–17.6.97, 21.6.97, 26–27.6.97, 29.6.97, 11.7.97, 18.7.97, 24–25.7.97, 31.7.97, 3.8.97, 22.8.97, 12–13.9.97, 15.9.97, 20.9.97, 25.9.97, 2–3.10.97, 5.10.97
cleansing beer:
1794: 14.1.94, 1.4.94, 3.4.94, 6.5.94, 6.6.94, 2.9.94, 9.9.94, 19.10.94, 23.10.94, 11.11.94
1795: 17.5.95, 30–31.5.95, 23.7.95, 14.8.95, 14.11.95, 6.12.95
1797: 28.1.97, 4.2.97, 18.2.97, 1.3.97, 5.3.97, 8.3.97, 6.5.97, 2.6.97, 2.9.97

Bye, Robert (*cont.*)
collecting coal and cinders from ports:
1793: 29.10.93, 5–6.11.93, 10.12.93
1794: 4.1.94, 18.1.94, 18–19.3.94, 1.4.94, 4.6.94, 6.6.94, 13.6.94, 30.6.94, 23.7.94, 1.8.94, 4–6.8.94, 9.8.94, 7–8.11.94, 18.12.94
1795: 14.4.95, 6.6.95, 17.6.95, 4.7.95, 13.8.95, 29.8.95, 15.9.95, 20.10.95, 3.11.95, 28.11.95, 4.12.95, 10.12.95, 15.12.95
1796: 21.12.96, 29.12.96
1797: 9.1.97, 6.4.97
collecting other goods: barley, 7.12.93, 5.3.94, 19.4.94, 12.2.95; barrels, 24.2.97; bricks, 24.2.94, 4.6.95, 22.12.96; cement, 15.7.94, 17.7.94; clay, 26.9.94, 18.1.97; furze, 14.11.94, 12–13.1.97, 17–18.1.97, 27.1.97, 18.2.97; grass, 9.6.97; hay, 29.1.94, 14.3.94, 18.4.94, 18–19.2.95, 23.2.95, 21.7.95, 25.7.95, 5.8.95; heather, 26.1.97; hedging, 9.8.97; hops, 23.11.95; lime, 5.11.93, 19.2.94, 17.3.94, 17.4.94, 25.6.95, 24.10.95; oats, 21.11.94; sale goods, 4.10.94, 14.1.97; sand, 25.2.94, 17.4.94, 21.5.95, 22.6.95; stones, 19.2.94, 9.8.94, 5.6.95; thorns, 15.3.97, 17.3.97; tiles, 24.2.94; turnips, 3.1.94, 21.11.94, 25.11.94; vetches, 27.7.95; wheat, 20.2.94; wood, 12.11.94, 1.7.95, 30.7.95, 18.11.95, 22.12.96, 10.1.97, 26.1.97
delivering beer: cart breaks down, 25.1.94, 27.1.94, 9.6.95; barrel lost, 24.6.94
1793: 11–12.10.93, 14.10.93, 19.10.93, 21.10.93, 29–30.10.93, 1.11.93, 5–9.11.93, 11–13.11.93, 16.11.93, 18–22.11.93, 25–26.11.93, 28.11.93, 30.11.93, 4.12.93, 10.12.93, 13–14.12.93, 17–21.12.93, 24.12.93, 30–31.12.93
1794: 3–4.1.94, 9–10.1.94, 13.1.94, 15–18.1.94, 21.1.94, 24–25.1.94, 27.1.94, 29.1.94, 1.2.94, 4.2.94, 7–8.2.94, 10–11.2.94, 13.2.94, 18.2.94, 21–22.2.94, 26–27.2.94, 1.3.94, 4–5.3.94, 8.3.94, 10.3.94, 13.3.94, 15.3.94, 18–19.3.94, 21–22.3.94, 24.3.94, 28–29.3.94, 1.4.94, 4–5.4.94, 7.4.94, 10–16.4.94, 18–20.4.94, 23.4.94, 25.4.94, 27.4.94, 1–4.5.94, 10.5.94, 12–13.5.94, 15–22.5.94, 24–26.5.94, 31.5.94, 2.6.94, 4–5.6.94, 9.6.94, 11–12.6.94, 14.6.94, 18.6.94, 20–21.6.94, 24–25.6.94, 27.6.94, 30.6.94, 3–5.7.94, 7.7.94, 9–10.7.94, 12.7.94, 14–15.7.94, 18–19.7.94, 21–26.7.95, 29–30.7.94, 1–2.8.94, 7–8.8.94, 11.8.94, 13–16.8.94, 18.8.94, 20.8.94, 25.8.94, 27.8.94, 29–30.8.94, 1–5.9.94, 9–13.9.94, 15–18.9.94, 23–26.9.94, 29.9.94, 1–3.10.94, 10–11.10.94, 13–18.10.94, 20.10.94, 22–25.10.94, 27–28.10.94,

Bye, Robert, delivering beer, 1794 (*cont.*)
31.10.94, 3–4.11.94, 6–7.11.94, 11–13.11.94, 15.11.94, 17.11.94, 19–20.11.94, 24–25.11.94, 27–29.11.94, 4–6.12.94, 10.12.94, 15–17.12.94, 20.12.94, 22–24.12.94, 26–27.12.94, 29–31.12.94
1795: 1–3.1.95, 5–6.1.95, 8–10.1.95, 12.1.95, 14–17.1.95, 19–22.1.95, 26–27.1.95, 29–31.1.95, 3–7.2.95, 9.2.95, 11.2.95, 13–15.2.95, 17.2.95, 20–21.2.95, 23–24.2.95, 26–28.2.95, 2.3.95, 4–6.3.95, 10.3.95, 14.3.95, 18–21.3.95, 23–24.3.95, 26.3.95, 31.3.95, 2.4.95, 4.4.95, 6.4.95, 11.4.95, 15.4.95, 17–18.4.95, 22–23.4.95, 27.4.95, 29.4.95, 1–2.5.95, 4.5.95, 7.5.95, 9.5.95, 11–15.5.95, 18–20.5.95, 22–23.5.95, 25–30.5.95, 1–2.6.95, 5–6.6.95, 8–10.6.95, 12–13.6.95, 15–16.6.95, 18–20.6.95, 24–27.6.95, 29–30.6.95, 2–4.7.95, 7.7.95, 9–11.7.95, 14–15.7.95, 17–18.7.95, 20.7.95, 23–25.7.95, 27.7.95, 29.7.95, 31.7.95, 1.8.95, 3.8.95, 7–8.8.95, 10–12.8.95, 14–15.8.95, 18.8.95, 20.8.95, 22.8.95, 24–28.8.95, 31.8.95, 1.9.95, 3–5.9.95, 8.9.95, 11–12.9.95, 14–16.9.95, 18–19.9.95, 21–23.9.95, 25–26.9.95, 29–30.9.95, 1.10.95, 3.10.95, 5–10.10.95, 12–17.10.95, 19.10.95, 21–24.10.95, 27–29.10.95, 31.10.95, 2–4.11.95, 6.11.95, 12.11.95, 14.11.95, 16–18.11.95, 20–21.11.95, 23–24.11.95, 26–27.11.95, 30.11.95, 1–2.12.95, 4–5.12.95, 7.12.95, 11–12.12.95, 14–15.12.95, 19.12.95, 22–23.12.95
1796: 16.12.96, 23–24.12.96, 26–27.12.96
1797: 2.1.97, 5.1.97, 7.1.97, 9.1.97, 13–14.1.97, 16.1.97, 20–21.1.97, 23–25.1.97, 28.1.97, 30–31.1.97, 4.2.97, 10.2.97, 13.2.97, 17.2.97, 18.2.97, 20.2.97, 27.2.97, 2–4.3.97, 14.3.97, 18.3.97, 20.3.97, 22.3.97, 24–25.3.97, 3–8.4.97, 3.6.97
drawing off beer:
1793: 23.12.93, 28.12.93
1794: 6.1.94, 14.1.94, 28.1.94, 11.2.94, 16.2.94, 25.2.94, 19.3.94, 2–3.4.94, 6.4.94, 22.4.94, 6.5.94, 14.5.94, 16.5.94, 1.6.94, 8.6.94, 15.6.94, 2.8.94, 13.9.94, 27.9.94, 4.10.94, 23.10.94, 23.11.94
1795: 10.2.95, 17.3.95, 29.3.95, 19.4.95, 7.6.95, 6.9.95, 7.11.95
1797: 25.1.97, 18.2.97, 1.3.97, 8.3.97, 20.3.97, 23.3.97, 2.4.97, 27.4.97, 4.5.97, 6.5.97
drunkenness, **226**: 22–23.1.94, 19.6.94, 1–2.12.94, 28.1.95, 11.5.95, 17.12.95; at King's Head, Letheringsett all day, 19.9.94; does no work, 20.9.94; arrives late for work, 12.5.95; drinking all day, 3.12.95

Bye, Robert (*cont.*)
harrowing: 28.10.93, 5–6.2.94, 25–27.3.94, 29.5.94, 13.6.94, 17.3.95, 24.9.95, 14–15.2.97, 10.3.97, 10.4.97, 14.4.97, 18.4.97, 29.7.97, 27.9.97
harvesting: dines with Hs on first day, 10.8.94, 13.8.97; gathers largess, 30.8.94, 9.9.97
1794: 15.8.94, 19–20.8.94, 25–26.8.94, 28–29.8.94
1795: 5.9.95, 7–9.9.95, 17.9.95
1797: 15.8.97, 18–19.8.97, 21–26.8.97, 30.8.97, 1–2.9.97, 4–9.9.97, 13.9.97
haymaking: 3.7.94, 9.7.94, 11.7.94, 8.7.97, 10.7.97, 12–14.7.97, 17.7.97, 20–22.7.97, 6.10.97
illness: 12.2.94, 9.4.94, 21.8.94, 23.8.94, 29.9.94, 3.12.94, 23–24.1.95, 16.3.95, 7–9.2.97, 9.5.97
injuries: hurts leg on beer delivery and unable to work, 15–17.10.93; not at work, 22–25.10.93
jobs:
1794: 1.1.94, 27.9.94, 5.11.94, 14.11.94
1795: 12–13.1.95, 5.3.95, 3.4.95, 8.5.95, 4.6.95, 20.8.95, 25.11.95
1796: 21.12.96
1797: 5.4.97, 22.4.97, 16.5.97, 26–27.5.97, 30.5.97, 1.6.97, 3.6.97, 5.6.97, 9–10.6.97, 13.6.97, 19.6.97, 22–23.6.97, 3.7.97, 5.7.97, 7–8.7.97, 10.7.97, 15.7.97, 17.7.97, 27.7.97, 4–5.8.97, 7–8.8.97, 10–12.8.97, 14–15.8.97, 14–15.9.97, 26.9.97, 29–30.9.97, 9–10.10.97
at home, 10.10.93, 22.11.94; delivering lime, 5.11.93; to Whissonsett and to Winch with HR to collect colts, 23–24.11.93; delivering flour, 5.12.93; collects flag harrow from Thomas Forster, 5.2.94; delivering osiers, 21.2.94; loading cinders, 1.4.94, 5.6.94; his horse taken to Saxlingham by HR, 6.5.94; carting stones, 7.5.94; delivering malt, 22.5.94, 18.7.97, 12.9.97; loading and unloading coal, 13.6.94, 3.6.95, 1.8.97; carting mud, 27–28.6.94, 1.7.94; takes wagon to Holt for repair, 15.7.94; at work in yards, 16.7.94, 4.8.95; collects wagon from Holt, 17.7.94; carting gravel, 24.7.94, 11.1.97, 1.2.97, 3.2.97, 9.2.97; cleans barn, 31.7.94; hedging, 4.8.94, 8.5.97; exchanges Hs' horses at Wells, 18.9.94; ringing pigs, 25.9.94; unloading tiles, 6.11.94; sets up furze in yard, 21.11.94; takes barrel staves to Holt and collects new wagon, 21.11.94; fetches injured Thomas Baldwin following accident, 23.12.94; collects harness, 21.5.95; rolling, 3.6.95; unloading hay, 4.8.95; hoeing turnips, 10.9.95; carting clay, 15.12.96, 17.12.96, 19.12.96; unloading cinders, 22.12.96,

Bye, Robert, jobs (*cont.*)
30.12.96, 8.4.97; takes wheels to Holt, 12.1.97; stacks furze, 1.2.97; collects peas from barn, 1.2.97; collects wagon from Saxlingham, 6.2.97; unloading furze, 20.2.97; greases beer carts, 5.3.97; turns barley, 8.3.97; dressing grass seed, 14.4.97; cutting wood, 24.4.97; carting thorns, 25.4.97; takes WH's horse to Field Dalling, 9.5.97; at work in river, 1.6.97; mucking out pigs, 16.6.97; carts millstones from Mr Rouse's mill, 24.7.97; cutting vetches, 12.8.97; to Kelling and Guestwick, 16.8.97; in barn, 29.8.97, 31.8.97; fences round stack, 13.9.97; carting away rubbish from pea stubble, 27.9.97
loading beer carts and wagons:
1793: 13.10.93
1794: 14.1.94, 13.4.94, 11.5.94, 3.7.94, 2.9.94, 10.9.94, 30.9.94, 23.10.94, 30.10.94, 26.12.94
1795: 2.1.95, 13.1.95, 19.1.95, 29.1.95, 8.2.95, 10.2.95, 12.2.95, 27.2.95, 1.3.95, 3.3.95, 19.3.95, 1.4.95, 3.4.95, 3.5.95, 22.6.95, 25.6.95, 28.6.95, 11.8.95, 30.8.95, 3.9.95, 20.9.95, 19.11.95, 18.12.95
1796: 22.12.96
1797: 24.3.97
malting: 20.3.94, 26.3.94, 11.4.94, 18.11.94; screening malt, 12.11.93, 27.11.93; lighting fire in maltings, 17.10.94
muck carting/spreading: 1–3.1.94, 29–31.1.94, 3–5.6.94, 14.6.94, 16.6.94, 4.9.94, 6.9.94, 10.9.94, 19.12.94, 29.1.95, 7.2.95, 21.2.95, 13.3.95, 14.8.95, 21.8.95, 30.10.95, 7.11.95, 9.11.95, 30.12.96, 3.1.97, 5–6.1.97, 12.1.97, 17.1.97, 26–27.1.97, 6.2.97, 22.4.97, 24.4.97, 10.6.97, 13.6.97, 24.6.97, 30.6.97
ploughing:
1793–94: 2.11.93, 4.11.93, 14–15.11.93, 3.12.93, 7.12.93, 11–12.12.93, 14.12.93, 27–28.12.93, 14–15.2.94, 20.2.94, 6–8.3.94, 11–12.3.94, 2.4.94, 9.4.94, 12.4.94, 24.4.94, 26.4.94, 29.4.94, 8–9.5.94, 27–30.5.94, 16–17.6.94, 26.6.94, 2.7.94, 14.7.94
1794–95: 30.9.94, 7–10.10.94, 21.10.94, 8–9.12.94, 12–13.12.94, 7.3.95, 9–12.3.95, 25–28.3.95, 30–31.3.95, 1.4.95, 7–9.4.95, 13.4.95, 15–16.4.95, 20–21.4.95, 23.4.95, 30.4.95, 5.5.95, 28.7.95, 17.8.95
1795–96: 10-11.11.95, 19.11.95, 8–9.12.95, 18.12.95, 22.12.95
1796–97: 20.1.97, 24.1.97, 22–23.2.97, 25.2.97, 28.2.97, 1.3.97, 10.3.97, 16–17.3.97, 23.3.97, 27–29.3.97, 1.4.97, 3.4.97, 11–13.4.97, 15.4.97, 17.4.97, 15.6.97, 30.6.97, 1.7.97, 4.7.97, 30.8.97
1797–98: 2.10.97, 7.10.97

Bye, Robert (*cont.*)
sowing: 11.1.94, 28.4.94, 30.4.94, 17.6.94, 30.10.94, 1.11.94, 15–16.4.95, 20–21.4.95, 25.4.95, 30.4.95, 5.5.95, 7.5.95, 30–31.3.97, 14–15.4.97, 17.4.97, 1.7.97, 4.7.97
working in fields: meadow, 17.2.97, 29–30.5.97, 2.6.97; Holt Heath Farm, 28.7.97, 16.9.97, 18.9.97, 21–23.9.97

C

Cademy, John, of Letheringsett; delivers timber to Hs, 28.11.93, 30.11.93
camp, *see* Weybourne Camp
Canfor (Chamfer), James, Holt basketmaker; Robert Bye delivers osiers, 21.2.94
Cappa [? Capps], Mr, with WH to Salthouse, 4.8.95
Carafor, *see* Crafer, Henry
carpenters, Mr Dawson's at work, 6–7.6.94, 9.6.94; at work, 4–5.12.94, 1–3.1.95: *see also* sawyers; Tinker, James; Tinker, William
Carr, Mr, E. Dereham brewer; at Hs', 22.11.93
carriages, *see* chaises; coach
carrying off, *see* draying off
carts, **30**, men carting grasses, 15.10.93, 29.10.95, 21.2.97; foundations laid for cart house, 8.2.94, 12.2.94; Thomas Baldwin collects new cart from Holt and takes cartwheels to Hunworth, 9.6.94; men carting cement, 24.7.94, 16.5.96; men carting thorns, 2.4.95, 25.4.97; Thomas Baldwin carts iron cinders [clinkers] into Glaven, 9.6.96; WHj and HR try colt in, 19.9.96; Mr Wilcocks injured in overturning his cart, 17.1.97; Hs' borrowed cart returned by Mr Wilcocks' servant, 18.1.97; new cart delivered by Mr Dawson, 14.3.97; Robert Bye and Gunton Thompson cart millstones from Mr Rouse's mill, 24.7.97; Robert Bye carts away rubbish after harrowing, 27.9.97
beer cart [dray], **47**: loaded, 13.10.93, 6.12.93, 19.1.94, 11.5.94, 3.7.94, 20.8.97; deliveries ordered by innkeepers, 25.11.93, 13.10.94, 25.8.94, 10.9.96; collected by William Lamb from Holt and taken to Hunworth, 10.8.96; taken by Baldwin to Mr Dawson, 13.3.97
accidents, **276**, **277**: breaks down on Robert Bye's delivery to Wells, 25.1.94; collected by Bye, John Jex and Abraham Dobson, 27.1.94; breaks down on Thomas Baldwin's delivery to Cromer, 22.12.94; Baldwin breaks arm falling under wheel on delivery to Beckhithe, 23.12.94; breaks down on Robert Bye's delivery to Holt, 9.6.95; Mrs Booty's beer cart swept under Glaven bridge in floods, horse drowns, 4.6.96

carts, beer cart (*cont.*)
repairs: by William Tinker, 29-31.1.94, 11.6.96; John Jex installs iron arm, 29.1.94; alterations made by John Dawson, 26.6.94; John Dawson removes axle sleeves, 4.8.94; by George Dawson, 20.8.95; greased by William Lamb and Robert Bye, 5.3.97
clay cart: men at, 9.10.94, 15.12.96; in use at Holt Heath Farm, 15.12.96, 17.12.96, 19.12.96
gravel cart: *see* carts, stone cart
hay cart: Hs' men at, 21.7.97
little cart: repaired by William Tinker and his man, 4.12.93; William Tinker installs iron sleeve, 23.12.93; WH and MH to Furze Closes, 5.7.94
malt cart: WHj and HR to Wells, 31.1.94; little mare harnessed, 3.7.94
mould cart: men at, 23.4.95; in use at Holt Heath Farm, 13–14.12.96
muck cart: Thomas Temple's men at, 9.6.94, 11–14.6.94, 16–18.6.94; Charles Kendle's men at, 6.1.95, 10.1.95; Mr Williams carts muck from Hs, 27–28.11.95, 7–11.12.95, 23–24.12.95; Hs' men carting muck to Holt Heath Farm, 30.11.96, 26.1.97
Hs' men at:
1793: 17–18.10.93, 2–3.12.93
1794: 1–3.1.94, 29–31.1.94, 3–4.6.94, 14.6.94, 16.6.94, 4.9.94, 6.9.94, 10.9.94, 19.12.94
1795: 29.1.95, 7.2.95, 21.2.95, 14.8.95, 21.8.95, 30.10.95, 7.11.95, 9.11.95
1796: 4–5.1.96, 27.1.96, 29.1.96, 24.1.96, 18.3.96, 7.4.96, 26.5.96, 28.5.96, 10.6.96, 16–17.6.96, 28–29.10.96, 31.10.96, 1.11.96, 1.12.96, 3.12.96
1797: 31.1.97, 5.1.97, 3–6.1.97, 24.4.97, 23–24.6.97, 28.6.97
mud cart: Thomas Hall carting mud from pond, 23–26.6.94; men at, 27–28.6.94, 30.6.94, 1–3.7.94, 11–12.7.94
sand cart: men at, 21.5.95, 26.3.96
stone cart: men carting gravel, 2.5.94, 24.7.94, 31.12.94, 31.3.96, 2.4.96, 5–6.5.96, 8–9.2.97; Hs' men at, 7–8.5.94, 2.8.94, 15.4.95, 11.1.97, 3–4.2.97, 8.2.97; men cart rocks to repair Sheringham jetty, 28.12.95; William Lamb carting gravel from pit, 30.3.96; Nicholas Woodhouse carting gravel from Hs' garden, 15.6.96; William Lamb carting gravel into meadow, 3–4.2.97
tumbril, **308**: collected by Thomas Baldwin from Thomas Forster's sale, 8.10.96; repaired by William Tinker, 19.12.96
turnip cart: men at, 24.1.97, 30.1.97, 4.3.97: *see also* wagons; wheels

casks, for storing and conditioning Hs' beer; beer drawn off into, 10.10.93, 26.11.93, 15.1.94, 4.2.94, 25.2.94, 22.4.94, 29.4.94, 13.9.94, 13.1.96, 26.2.96, 2.4.96, 16.4.96, 1.3.97, 8.3.97, 23.3.97, 27.4.97; porter drawn off into, 24.4.96, 4.5.97, 8.5.97
great cask in white hall, **29**: beer drawn off into, 2.11.93, 21.12.93, 23.12.93, 25.12.93, 28.12.93, 28.1.94, 11.2.94, 3.5.94, 13.9.94, 30.11.95, 9.3.96, 13.4.96, 20.4.96, 18.2.97, 15.3.97, 2.4.97, 4.5.97, 6.5.97, 8.5.97; emptied, 10.12.93; cleaned, 16.12.93, 29.4.95, 3.5.97; measured by WH, 17.12.93; Thomas Youngman removes plug, 13.5.94; porter drawn off into, 6.5.97
home cask, **21**: cleaned, 15.11.93, 14.5.94, 13.2.96; beer drawn off into, 30.11.93, 4.12.93, 10.12.93, 18.12.93, 6.1.94, 8.1.94, 16.2.94, 6.3.94, 12.3.94, 19.3.94, 27.3.94, 2.4.94, 6.4.94, 14.5.94, 23.5.94, 18.2.96, 22–23.2.96, 11.11.96; Hs' men pumping beer into, 21.1.94; porter drawn off into, 30.4.95, 7.5.95
small cask in white hall: cleaned, 9.12.93: *see also* barrels; drawing off
cattle, *see* cows
cement (mergin, mirgin, murgen), collected by Robert Bye and boy from lime-kiln, 15.7.94; collected by Hs' men, 17.7.94, 22.3.96, 6.5.96, 17.6.96; carted by Hs' men, 24.7.94, 16.5.96
chairs, *see* furniture
chaises (coaches, shaises):
gig (gid): WHj's breaks down on journey to seaside, 14.8.97
Hs', **76**: bought by WHj in Norwich, 2.6.94; WH and MH meet with accident at Swanton Novers when horse falls, shaft broken, 3.7.94; harness cleaned by Thomas Boyce, 5.11.94; WHj and MA to Holt, 24.2.95; repaired by George Dawson at John Jex's, 16.3.95; cleaned by Luke Basham and boy, harness repaired, 17–18.3.95; chaise horse trimmed by WHj and HR, 10.12.95; Leader the colt harnessed by HR, 22.9.96
King's Head's, Holt: hired by Hs, 10.9.96
postchaises: Hs to Norwich in Charles Banyard's, 6.9.94; Hs and Mrs Phillis Goggs to Southrepps, 23.9.95
whiskey: Robert Raven drives hobby to Holt in, 23.1.94
chamber, *see* brewhouse, counting house
Chamfer, *see* Canfor, James
chapel service, MH to, 11.6.97: *see also* Briston, Methodist meeting; Cley, Methodist meeting
Chaplin, Henry (d.1794), Blakeney and Cley merchant; Thomas Baldwin collects coal at Blakeney, 6.2.94
Chapman, William, innkeeper of Falgate, Hindringham, tied house; orders beer, 21.12.93; brings 20 geese to Hs, 25.7.94
Chasteney (Chastney) Elizabeth; at work in barn, 5.9.96
cherries, *see* fruit
chimneys (chymnays, chymneys), *see* house
Christmas (Chrismas), William, former Coltishall and Harleston attorney; with Charles Banyard at Hs', 8.2.95
cinders [coke], Thomas Baldwin carts iron cinders [clinkers] into Glaven, 9.6.96
collected by Hs' men from:
Blakeney: 17.5.94, 7–8.11.94, 12.12.94, 18.12.94, 2.3.95, 5.3.95, 14.3.95, 31.3.95, 14.4.95, 27.4.95, 8.5.95, 16.10.95, 18.11.96, 21.12.96, 29.12.96
Cley:
1793: 1.11.93, 23.11.93, 2.12.93, 10.12.93
1794: 4.1.94, 18.1.94, 1.2.94, 14.2.94, 26.2.94, 7.3.94, 18–19.3.94, 1.4.94, 1.5.94, 4.6.94, 6.6.94, 13.6.94, 23.6.94, 23.7.94, 1.8.94, 5.12.94
1795: 13.2.95, 20.10.95, 3.11.95, 28.11.95, 4.12.95, 12.12.95, 15.12.95
1796: 23.1.96, 30.1.96, 9.2.96, 25.2.96, 1.3.96, 12.3.96, 4–5.4.96, 3.5.96, 30.5.96, 20.6.96, 24.10.96, 26.11.96, 3.12.96
1797: 9.1.97, 7.2.97, 21.2.97, 24.3.97, 6.4.97, 10.5.97, 17.5.97, 6.6.97, 14.6.97, 30.6.97, 10.7.97, 21.9.97
unloaded by Hs' men: 1.4.94, 5.6.94, 16.3.95, 16.4.95, 28.4.95, 3.12.95, 10.12.95, 19.12.95, 1.6.96, 27.10.96, 22.12.96, 30.12.96, 8.4.97, 14.6.97, 26.9.97:
see also coal
cistern, boy barrowing small bricks to, 11.9.97: *see also* steeping
Clark, John, **73**, collects pigs from Hs, 22.5.94
Clark/Clarke, Mr, innkeeper of Black Boys, Holt, tied house; orders beer from Hs, 27.3.95; beer deliveries, 22.4.95, 13.5.95
Clarkson, *see* Claxton
Claxton (Clarkson), Thomas, **380**, **381**, innkeeper of Angel, Bale, tied house; at Hs', 10.6.95: *see also* Bale, beer deliveries
Clay, *see* Cley-next-the-Sea
clay, John Fox digging for in Furze Closes, 2.6.94; collected by Robert Bye from Charles Kendle's pit, 26.9.94, 18.1.97; carted by Hs' men, 9.10.94, 17.12.94, 9–10.1.95, 15.12.96; collected by Hs' men for Hs' garden, 30.1.96; collected by Hs' men, 10.2.96, 29.8.96, 10.12.96; collected from Holt, 6.8.96; cast by J. Herring and W. Duffield, 15.12.96; carted by Robert Bye at Holt Heath Farm, 19.12.96: *see also* marl

cleansing (clensing), of beer by Hs' men, **332**:
1793: 12.10.93, 19.10.93, 24.10.93, 26.10.93, 31.10.93, 2.11.93, 7.11.93, 9.11.93, 14.11.93, 16.11.93, 21.11.93, 23–24.11.93, 26.11.93, 30.11.93, 2.12.93, 4.12.93, 6.12.93, 12.12.93, 17.12.93, 19.12.93, 24.12.93, 26.12.93, 31.12.93
1794: 2.1.94, 7.1.94, 9.1.94, 14.1.94, 23.1.94, 28.1.94, 30.1.94, 4.2.94, 6.2.94, 13.2.94, 18.2.94, 20.2.94, 27.2.94, 4.3.94, 6.3.94, 12.3.94, 18.3.94, 20.3.94, 25.3.94, 27.3.94, 1.4.94, 3.4.94, 8.4.94, 10.4.94, 15.4.94, 17.4.94, 30.4.94, 6–7.5.94, 13.5.94, 15.5.94, 17.5.94, 27.5.94, 4.6.94, 6.6.94, 10.6.94, 17.6.94, 19.6.94, 24.6.94, 26.6.94, 1–2.7.94, 18.7.94, 29.7.94, 5.8.94, 12.8.94, 19.8.94, 26.8.94, 2.9.94, 9.9.94, 16.9.94, 23.9.94, 30.9.94, 1.10.94, 7–8.10.94, 14–15.10.94, 18–19.10.94, 23–24.10.94, 30-31.10.94, 5–6.11.94, 11–12.11.94, 18–19.11.94, 27–28.11.94, 5–6.12.94, 21–22.12.94, 30–31.12.94
1795: 8–9.1.95, 15–16.1.95, 27–28.1.95, 3–4.2.95, 10–11.2.95, 17–18.2.95, 27–28.2.95, 7–8.3.95, 17–18.3.95, 24–25.3.95, 1.4.95, 11–12.4.95, 21.4.95, 25.4.95, 8.5.95, 17–18.5.95, 26–27.5.95, 30–31.5.95, 4.6.95, 12–13.6.95, 18.6.95, 2.7.95, 9.7.95, 17.7.95, 23.7.95, 30.7.95, 7.8.95, 14.8.95, 20.8.95, 27.8.95, 3.9.95, 13–14.9.95, 18.9.95, 23–24.9.95, 29–30.9.95, 3.10.95, 8.10.95, 14–15.10.95, 21–22.10.95, 27–28.10.95, 3–4.11.95, 14.11.95, 20–21.11.95, 25–26.11.95, 30.11.95, 5–6.12.95, 10–11.12.95, 17–18.12.95, 25–26.12.95
1796: 1–2.1.96, 9.1.96, 13–14.1.96, 19–20.1.96, 26–27.1.96, 2–3.2.96, 9.2.96, 14–15.2.96, 18–19.2.96, 23–24.2.96, 29.2.96, 3–4.3.96, 16–17.3.96, 20–21.3.96, 25–26.3.96, 3.4.96, 6.4.96, 13.4.96, 16.4.96, 27–28.4.96, 3–4.5.96, 10–11.5.96, 17.5.96, 24.5.96, 31.5.96, 1.6.96, 8–9.6.96, 14–15.6.96, 21–22.6.96, 29.6.96, 5.7.96, 12.7.96, 19.7.96, 26.7.96, 2–3.8.96, 9.8.96, 16.8.96, 23.8.96, 31.8.96, 8.9.96, 15–16.9.96, 23–24.9.96, 29.9.96, 6.10.96, 12–13.10.96, 27–28.10.96, 7.11.96, 11.11.96, 18.11.96, 24.11.96, 3.12.96, 10.12.96, 21.12.96, 29.12.96
1797: 10.1.97, 20–21.1.97, 28.1.97, 3–4.2.97, 12–13.2.97, 18.2.97, 23–24.2.97, 28.2.97, 1.3.97, 4–5.3.97, 8.3.97, 10–11.3.97, 15.3.97, 17–18.3.97, 22–23.3.97, 27.3.97, 3.4.97, 7.4.97, 21.4.97, 29.4.97, 2.5.97, 4.5.97, 6.5.97, 8.5.97, 11.5.97, 19.5.97, 24.5.97, 1–2.6.97, 9–10.6.97, 15–16.6.97, 21.6.97, 29.6.97, 7.7.97, 13.7.97, 20.7.97, 27.7.97, 3.8.97, 10.8.97, 18.8.97, 24.8.97, 2.9.97, 12.9.97, 20.9.97, 29.9.97, 5.10.97, 12.10.97, 19.10.97

cleansing (*cont.*)
pump: *see* pumps:
see also beer, types; drawing off

clergy, *see individual Anglican clergy* Burrell, John; Collyer, Charles; Cory, James; Crofts, John; Fisher, Thomas jnr; Johnson, William Tower; Thomas, William; Wilcocks, William Wright

Cley-next-the-Sea (Clay), Norf., **8**, **72**, **115**, **146**, **178**, Robert Bye collects lime from Mr Johnson, 5.11.93, 24.10.95; Robert Bye delivers lime to John Lynes, 5.11.93; HR to, 16.3.94, 14.2.97; MH to, 29.9.94, 10.7.97; WH, WHj and HR bottle off pipe of wine, 10.12.94; Hs' men collect tiles, 1.10.94, 25.10.94, 31.10.94, 15.1.95; Hs, Nathaniel Raven, Ann Raven and Nathaniel Raven of Whissonsett Hall to, 25.3.95; Thomas Baldwin collects wheels, 16.6.95; Baldwin delivers wheels, 18.5.95; Mr Smith to tea with Hs, 6.8.95; Hs' boy to, 4.9.95; John Ellis to tea with Hs, 15.9.95; Mrs Harrison to dinner with Hs, 8.10.95; WH to with Mr Burrell, 28.12.95; William Lamb collects lime, 24.3.96; Thomas Baldwin collects malt from John Ellis, 18.10.96; William Lamb collects oats from Mr Rouse, 14.2.97
beer deliveries:
1793: 11.10.93, 29.10.93, 5.11.93, 23.11.93, 10.12.93
1794: 18.1.94, 14.2.94, 28.3.94, 1.4.94, 24.4.94, 15.5.94, 4.6.94, 30.6.94, 21.7.94, 15.8.94, 11.9.94, 1.10.94, 25.10.94, 27.11.94, 24.12.94
1795: 15.1.95, 13.2.95, 23.3.95, 17.4.95, 13.5.95, 5.6.95, 4.7.95, 29.7.95, 27.8.95, 8.10.95, 3.11.95, 12.12.95, 15.12.95
1796: 30.1.96, 1.3.96, 20.4.96, 30.5.96, 13.7.96, 10.9.96, 22.10.96, 3.12.96
1797: 9.1.97, 21.2.97, 5.4.97, 10.5.97, 15.7.97, 16.8.97, 27.9.97
cinders collected from merchants: 10.12.93, 6.6.94, 23.7.94, 1.8.94, 3.5.96
John Ellis: 13.6.94, 13.2.95, 20.10.95, 3.11.95, 28.11.95, 4.12.95, 12.12.95, 15.12.95, 23.1.96, 30.1.96, 9.2.96, 25.2.96, 1.3.96, 12.3.96, 4–5.4.96, 30.5.96, 20.6.96, 24.10.96, 26.11.96, 3.12.96, 9.1.97, 7.2.97, 21.2.97, 24.3.97, 6.4.97, 10.5.97, 17.5.97, 6.6.97, 14.6.97, 30.6.97, 10.7.97, 21.9.97
Robert Farthing: 5.12.94
John Mann: 1.11.93, 5.11.93, 23.11.93, 4.1.94, 18.1.94, 1.2.94, 14.2.94, 26.2.94, 7.3.94, 18–19.3.94, 1.4.94, 1.5.94, 4.6.94
coal collected from merchants: 29.10.93, 30.6.94, 31.10.95, 4.8.96
Corbett Cooke: 17.6.95, 4.7.95, 27.8.95, 19.10.95, 13.7.96, 28.7.96, 30.7.96, 2.8.96

Cley-next-the-Sea, coal collected from merchants (*cont.*)
John Ellis: 1–2.11.93, 6.11.93, 21.7.94
Thomas Jackson: 15.9.95, 20.4.96, 9.5.96, 25.5.96, 2.6.96, 9.6.96, 8.8.96, 11.8.96, 19.8.96, 24.8.96, 12.5.97, 17.6.97, 15.7.97, 16.8.97, 27.9.97
fair: *see* fairs
King's Head: *see* beer deliveries *above*; Lynes, Mrs Edny; Lynes, John
Methodist meeting [Wesleyan] attended by MH, **136**, **218**, **289**:
1795: 8.11.95, 29.11.95, 20.12.95
1796: 3.1.96, 17.1.96, 24.1.96, 31.1.96, 14.2.96, 21.2.96, 20.3.96, 27.3.96, 3.4.96, 10.4.96, 17.4.96, 24.4.96, 1.5.96, 15.5.96, 22.5.96, 29.5.96, 5.6.96, 12.6.96, 19.6.96, 26.6.96, 10.7.96, 7.8.96, 14.8.96, 21.8.96, 28.8.96, 4.9.96, 18.9.96, 2.10.96, 9.10.96, 23.10.96, 30.10.96, 13.11.96, 11.12.96, 25.12.96
1797: 8.1.97, 22.1.97, 5.2.97, 12.2.97, 19.2.97, 26.2.97, 19.3.97, 26.3.97, 2.4.97, 16.4.97, 23.4.97, 30.4.97, 7.5.97, 14.5.97, 28.5.97, 4.6.97, 25.6.97, 2.7.97, 16.7.97, 23.7.97, 30.7.97, 6.8.97, 20.8.97, 3.9.97, 10.9.97, 17.9.97, 1.10.97, 15.10.97
attended by MH with: HR, 22.11.95, 25.12.95; Thomas Boyce, 27.12.95; Miss Custance, 28.2.96, 6.3.96; MA, 9.3.96, 26.3.96, 9.7.97, 22.10.97; WH, 17.7.96; Mrs Phillis Goggs, 24.7.96; William Thackwray, 20.11.96, 27.11.96
sales: Hs to, 29–30.9.94, 1–4.10.94; Robert Bye collects furniture, 4.10.94
WH to: 10.10.93, 16.10.93, 29–30.9.94, 1–4.10.94, 6.8.95, 5–6.10.95, 1.1.96, 11.1.96, 3.3.96, 7.2.97
WHj to: 29.10.93, 17.4.94, 30.9.94, 1–2.10.94, 4.10.94, 6.6.95, 19.10.95, 24.10.95, 30.11.95, 6.3.96, 6.10.96, 2.11.96, 14.12.96, 13.2.97, 10.7.97:
see also Smith, Mrs Elizabeth; Smith, John
clinkers, *see* bricks
clock, brought to Hs by Edward Hall, 3.1.95
closes, *see* Furze Closes
clover, sown, 7.5.95; seed collected by HR from Brinton, 28.3.97
cloves, used in recipe for destroying rats, HR's endnotes
clubs:
Holt: WHj dines at book club, 10.1.97
Letheringsett: purse club feast at King's Head, dispute ends in removal of club to Holt, 13.1.94; Thomas Boyce to, 12.1.95, 11.1.96
coach, Hs depart in Mrs Sheppard's, 25.3.94: *see also* chaises
coal, **382**, **383**, Thomas Youngman puts lock on coalhouse door, 12.9.94; fetched by Thomas Boyce for brewing, 3.12.95
collected by Hs' men from:
Blakeney: 6.2.94, 4–6.8.94, 8–9.8.94, 4.2.95, 1.6.95, 6.6.95, 13.8.95, 29.8.95, 3.10.96, 18.5.97, 1.8.97, 26.9.97
Cley: 29.10.93, 1–2.11.93, 6.11.93, 30.6.94, 21.7.94, 16–17.6.95, 4.7.95, 27.8.95, 15.9.95, 19.10.95, 31.10.95, 10.12.95, 20.4.96, 9.5.96, 25.5.96, 2.6.96, 9.6.96, 21.6.96, 13.7.96, 28.7.96, 30.7.96, 2.8.96, 4.8.96, 8.8.96, 11.8.96, 19.8.96, 24.8.96, 12.5.97, 17.6.97, 15.7.97, 16.8.97, 27.9.97
collected by Hs' men for Gunton Thompson: 8.8.94, 31.10.95, 3.10.96
unloaded by Hs' men: 13.6.94, 2.8.94, 5–7.8.94, 3.6.95, 11.12.95, 4.8.96, 12.5.97, 1.8.97, 3.8.97, 27.9.97:
see also cinders
Cobb, John [?Cobon, John], helps men to draw off cleanse beer into cask, 11.2.94
Cobon, James (d.1840 aged 84), **113**, **127**, **197**, **211**, **238**, **341**, of Letheringsett Hall Farm [then Letheringsett Hall]; Robert Bye undertakes Thomas Boyce's work for, 28.8.97
Cobon, John (d.1812), of Letheringsett; kills pig for Hs, 13.2.94: *see also* Cobb, John
Coke, Mrs Jane (1753–1800), **282**, **283**, née Dutton, 1st wife of Thomas William; with husband at Hs', 23.6.96
Coke (Cooke), Thomas William (1754–1842), **283**, JP, MP, 1st Earl of Leicester of the 2nd creation 1837, of Holkham Hall; WH and WHj to supper at King's Head, Letheringsett with election supporters, 1.6.96; with wife at Hs', 23.6.96
coke, *see* cinders
Coker, Samuel, innkeeper of Crown, Field Dalling; refuses to accept beer delivery from Thomas Baldwin, 7.10.97
colds, *see* illness
Collyer (Clollier, Collier, Colyer), Charles (d.1830 aged 75), **234**, JP, [Revd Charles 1796], of Gunthorpe Hall, Rector of Gunthorpe with Bale 1798–1830, Rector of Thornage with Brinton 1803–26, Rector of Cley 1828–30; Hs' boy delivers beer, 5.12.93; WHj to, 25.6.95; WHj to tea and buys timber, 30.6.95; William Lamb and Robert Bye collect timber, 10.1.97
Collyer (Collier), Master, [?son of Revd Charles]; with Master Forsters to tea at Hs', 23.5.97; with Masters Herring and Shearing to tea at Hs', 1.6.97
Coltishall, Norf., **124**, **190**, **251**, **272**, **352**, **354**, WH and HR to, 3.4.97

colts, *see* horses
combs, *see* malt, culms
Communion, *see* Letheringsett Church, Sacraments
confirmation, MA and HR at Holt, 4.7.94
Cook, Mr, of London; with Henry Goggs from Whissonsett to Hs, 25.7.96, 14.8.97; with Hs and Goggs family to Salthouse, 25.7.96; with Henry Goggs departs , 25.7.96, 15.8.97; with Hs to seaside, 14.8.97
Cook/Cooke, William (d.1826), Thornage miller; Gunton Thompson collects pollard from, 25.6.96
Cooke (Cook), Corbett, Cley coal merchant; Hs' men collect coal, 17.6.95, 4.7.95, 27.8.95, 19.10.95, 10.12.95, 21.6.96, 13.7.96, 28.7.96, 30.7.96, 2.8.96
Cooke, *see* Coke, Thomas William
coombs, *see* malt, culms
coopers, Thomas Baldwin collects barrels from at Holt, 3.12.94: *see also* barrels; hoops; staves
copper, *see* brewing equipment
corn, John Ramm threshes Gunton Thompson's, 25.9.94; Thomas Hall dresses and collects his, 12.2.95; Hs' men gather dwarf corn, 17.9.95: *see also* barley; goaft; granaries; mills; oats; wheat
Cornwall, Master ('Boy Cornwall'), helps Hs with harvest, 28.8.94
Corpusty (Corpusta), Norf., Thomas Baldwin delivers brewer's grains, 30.7.94; Thomas Baldwin delivers pantiles, 6.11.94; WHj to, 19.9.97, 23.10.97
beer deliveries:
1793: 29.10.93, 20.11.93, 18.12.93
1794: 13.1.94, 10.2.94, 10.3.94, 15.4.94, 16.5.94, 12.6.94, 30.6.94, 15.7.94, 27.7.94, 30.7.94, 20.8.94, 6.9.94, 25.9.94, 16.10.94, 6.11.94, 10.12.94
1795: 6.1.95, 6.2.95, 12.3.95, 17.4.95, 12.5.95, 27.5.95, 15.6.95, 10.7.95, 10.8.95, 1.9.95, 26.9.95, 2.11.95, 14.12.95
1796: 7.1.96, 2.2.96, 1.3.96, 31.3.96, 23.4.96, 21.5.96, 6.6.96, 23.6.96, 11.7.96, 10.8.96, 31.8.96, 24.9.96, 11.10.96, 9.11.96
1797: 2.1.97, 30.1.97, 1.3.97, 20.3.97, 21.4.97, 9.5.97, 26.5.97, 13.6.97, 10.7.97, 26.7.97, 21.8.97, 28.9.97, 10.10.97
loading: 25.9.95:
see also Wagstaff, Robert
Cory, Mr C., with Mr and Mrs Cory, Miss Gooderson and Joseph Erratt at Hs', 30.7.96
Cory, Mr [? Revd James, of Kettlestone], with wife, Mr C. Cory, Miss Gooderson and Joseph Erratt at Hs', 30.7.96
Cory, Mrs, with husband and others at Hs', 30.7.96
couch grass (quicks), *see* grasses
counting houses (counting rooms), *see* brewhouse; house
courts, *see* assizes; justices; sessions
cowl, **23**, painted by WHj, 22.11.93
cows, **166**, boy collects turnips for, 8.11.94; calving, 2.1.95; WH sells two and buys one at Holt Fair, 27.4.95
Cozens, Mrs Mary (d.1842 aged 75), **285**, née Hawkins, of Norwich and Sprowston; with Nathaniel Raven and Mary Raven dines at Hs', with Hs to Weybourne Camp and Sheringham, 29.6.96; departs, 30.6.96
Crafer (Carafor, Craffer, Crawfer, Creffer), Henry, **59**, **335**, innkeeper of King's Head, Holt; beer deliveries, 12.12.93, 7.6.94, 11.4.95, 22.4.95, 24.10.95; orders small beer, 3.2.96; chaise hired by Hs, 10.9.96: *see also* Holt, public houses, King's Head
crane, Hs', repaired by Thomas Youngman, 24.12.93
Crawfer, **Creffer**, *see* Crafer, Henry
Cremer (Creamer), Cremer (1768–1808), **350**, of Beeston Hall, Beeston Regis; William Lamb collects bricks from kiln, 28.3.97
Crofts, Revd John (d.1828 aged 80), of Fakenham, Curate of Hitcham, Suff. 1771, Curate of Mileham 1772, Curate of Brisley 1777, Curate of Fakenham 1777–1810, Vicar of E. Bradenham 1782–97, Curate of Shereford 1784, Rector of Stratton Strawless 1784–1828, Rector of Whissonsett 1797–1828; with wife and large party to Weybourne Camp, 24.8.95; with wife departs for Fakenham, 25.8.95
Crofts, Mrs Susanna (1765–1845), née Oxenborow, 2nd wife of Revd John; with husband and large party to Weybourne Camp, 24.8.95; with husband departs for Fakenham, 25.8.95
Cromer, Norf., **158**, **271**, **304**, **386**, Thomas Baldwin collects window frames, 26.3.94; beer cart breaks down on Thomas Baldwin's delivery, 22.12.94; HR to, 20.8.97, 6–7.10.97
beer deliveries:
1793: 17.10.93, 12.11.93, 29.11.93, 26.12.93
1794: 11.1.94, 3.2.94, 22.3.94, 19.4.94, 24.5.94, 25.6.94, 1.8.94, 1.9.94, 20.9.94, 3.10.94, 15.10.94, 27.10.94, 10.11.94, 25.11.94, 16.12.94, 22.12.94
1795: 8.1.95, 17.1.95, 3.2.95, 26.2.95, 11.3.95, 24.3.95, 11.4.95, 27.4.95, 9.5.95, 20.5.95, 8.6.95, 6.7.95, 15.7.95, 6.8.95, 22.8.95, 14.9.95, 23.9.95, 25.9.95, 6.10.95, 27.10.95, 4.11.95, 7.12.95, 23.12.95
1796: 8.1.96, 26.1.96, 27.2.96, 26.3.96, 18.4.96, 21.5.96, 8.7.96, 3.8.96, 23.8.96, 30.9.96, 22.11.96
1797: 13.2.97, 7.4.97, 8.5.97, 6.6.97, 18.7.97, 26.8.97, 9.10.97

Cromer (*cont.*)
Hs to: WHj, 14.7.94, 14.1.96, 19.2.96, 13.5.96, 23.1.97; WHj and MA, 4.9.94, 5.9.97; WH and WHj, 19.9.94, 9.3.95; WHj and Mr Bartell, 2.8.96; WH, MH, WHj and MA, 16.9.96; WH, 6–7.10.97:
see also Sanderson, Mrs Mary
Cross, Miss, at large party at Hs' for tea, 18.8.95
Crown, *see* Sheringham; Southrepps
Cubitt, Mr, dines with Hs, 28.7.96
culms, **cumbs**, *see* malt, culms
Custance, Frances (b.1771), of Fakenham, daughter of William; with Ann Raven and Nathaniel Raven jnr to Hs from Whissonsett, 26.12.93; with Ann Raven, WHj and MA to Holt ball, 30.12.93; with Ann Raven and WHj to Holt, 12.1.94; with MA, Ann Raven and James Moore to tea at Mr Baker's, 13.1.94; with Bakers at Hs', 18.1.94, 14.3.96; dines with Hs, with WHj and MA to Mr Forster, 7.2.94; with WHj and MA to Holt market, 8.2.94; with George Custance at Hs', 19.2.94; with Hs to Holt, 22–24.2.96, 27.2.96, 5.3.96; ? makes entry in HR's diary, 25.2.96; with MH to Cley, 28.2.96, 6.3.96
Custance, George (b.1767), son of William; with Miss Custance at Hs', 19.2.94
Custance, Mrs Martha (d.1857 aged 88), née Holman, wife of William jnr; with mother-in-law to tea at Hs', 7.2.97
Custance, Myles (b.1769), of Portsmouth, son of William; with Misses Baker and Bartell to tea at Hs', 24.10.97
Custance, Mrs Phillis (1737–1812), née Myles, wife of William; with daughter-in-law to tea at Hs', 7.2.97

D

dales, *see* wood, deals
Dalling, *see* Field Dalling
dancing, *see* assemblies; balls
Darby, John, Edgefield farmer; sells grass to WHj for £19, 22.6.96
Davy, Elizabeth, *see* Robinson, Mrs
Davy, Mrs Elizabeth (d.1798), 1st wife of John jnr; with husband to tea at Hs', 21.9.95
Davy, John (d.1805 aged 69/70), Holt draper and grocer; WHj to, 21.11.93; with family to tea at Hs', 9.1.94, 5.9.94, 17.8.97; Ann Raven, WHj and MA to tea, 17.1.94; with family to dinner at Hs', 5.9.94; to tea at Hs', 18.11.94; with son John dines at Hs' while out shooting, 23.9.95; MA to tea, 8.2.97
Davy, John jnr, London linen draper; with wife and stepmother to tea at Hs', 21.9.95; with father dines at Hs' while out shooting, 23.9.95
Davy, Joseph, son of John; with family to tea at Hs', 9.1.94; to tea at Hs', 23.7.94
Davy, Mary (d.1820 aged 43), of Holt, daughter of John; with sister to tea at Hs', 25.5.95, 18.8.95, 10.3.97; at Hs', 19.8.95; with mother to tea at Hs', 29.4.96: *see also* Davy, Misses
Davy, Mrs Mary (d.1820 aged 80), née Starling, 2nd wife of John; with family to tea at Hs', 9.1.94, 19.5.94, 21.9.95, 29.4.96, 6.1.97, 17.8.97
Davy, Matthew, of London, son of John; at large party at Hs' for tea, 18.8.95
Davy, Misses, of Holt, unnamed daughters of John; to tea at Hs', 12.8.96, 6.1.97, 9.2.97, 27.2.97, 27.6.97: *see also* Davy, Mary; Davy, Susanna
Davy, Susanna (Susan), of Holt, daughter of John; with family to tea at Hs', 19.5.94, 25.5.95, 18.8.95, 10.3.97; at Hs', 19.8.95
Dawlin, **Dawling**, *see* Field Dalling
Dawson (Dauson), George (d.1809 aged 78), Holt builder and cartwright; Hs' boy collects tiles, 16.11.93; Thomas Baldwin collects bricks, 12.2.94; his carpenter at work at Hs', 6–7.6.94; takes sleeves for axles from beer carts, 4.8.94; contract for building Letheringsett House of Industry awarded, 15.1.96; his lad painting at Hs', 22–24.3.96, 4–6.5.96, 23.5.96, 26–27.5.96, 1.8.97; his man installs door in King's Head, Letheringsett, 10–12.11.96; Robert Bye takes wheels to, 12.1.97; Thomas Baldwin takes beer cart to, 13.3.97; delivers new cart to Hs, 14.3.97; his man at work for Hs, 23–25.3.97, 29–30.3.97, 29–30.5.97, 21–22.9.97, 12–13.10.97, 16–20.10.97; William Lamb collects bricks, 20.9.97
Dawson, George jnr (d.1840 aged 80), Holt cartwright; to Whissonsett and Setchey, 17–18.5.94; repairs Hs' chaise at John Jex's, 16.3.95; repairs Hs' beer dray, 20.8.95
Dawson (Dawsin), John, Holt cartwright and brickmaker; Robert Bye collects bricks and tiles, 24.2.94; alters Hs' beer cart, 26.6.94
dealers (jobbers), six pigs sold by Hs to, 1.7.95
deals (dales), *see* wood
Dereham, *see* East Dereham
Devereux (Deverich, Deverichs, Devericks, Deverrech), Edmund (d.1814 aged 63/64), Norwich plumber, painter and glazier; with Matthew Booth and William Hase installs Hs' new pump, 9–11.9.95; with HR to Aylsham, 12.9.95
Dew, James, innkeeper of Maid's Head, N. Walsham, tied house; with WH to N. Walsham, 11.5.95
Dewson, Miss, see Dowson
diary, HR's, **2**, **32**, **67**, **103**, **120**, **164**, **177**, **226**, entries by others:
? Frances Custance: 24.2.96

diary, HR's, entries by others (*cont.*)
Nathaniel Raven of Whissonsett Hall, **84**: 30.6.94, ? 24.2.96
WHj, **2**, **4**: 10–17.10.93, 22–26.11.93, 12–19.1.94, 23.3.94, 21–29.6.94, 11–13.8.94, 28.12.94–3.1.95, 23.12.95, 26–29.12.95, 14–15.1.96, 21–25.6.96, 1–7.1.97
dibbling, **254**, peas for Hs by Edmund Balls and man, 11–12.3.96, 14.3.96
Dissent/Nonconformity, *see* meetings *under* Briston; Cley-next-the-Sea; Hunworth
ditches, maintained by Thomas Boyce in Brewhouse Pightle, 18–20.2.94; scour spread by John Fox over Brewhouse Pightle, 23.4.94: *see also* drains
ditching, *see* hedges
doctors, surgeons, *see* Bartell, Edmund; Bartell, Edmund jnr; Bird, John Rash
Dobson, Abraham (1753–1807), Holt blacksmith; repairs Hs' furnace bars, 15.1.94; with Robert Bye and John Jex collects Hs' broken-down beer cart, 27.1.94; cutting straw, 7.3.94; in Hs' malthouse, 5.6.96
Dobson, Mrs, wife of William; to tea with Hs, 29.3.97
Dobson, William (1741–1820), **54**, **61**, **80**, innkeeper of King's Head, Letheringsett, tied house; from Holt to view King's Head, 29.1.94; takes over business, 25.3.94; Charles Banyard at, 26.6.94; Robert Bye drinking at, 19.9.94; Hs' harvest supper, 26.9.95; cleans MH's bath, 15.9.96; town meeting at, 18.4.97
beer deliveries: 4.4.94, 20.4.94, 27.4.94, 4.5.94, 18.5.94, 25.5.94, 31.1.95, 13.1.96, 16.8.97; four barrels of nog delivered to his keeping room, 15.2.95
Hs to: WHj to supper, 21.4.94; WH and WHj to dinner party, 18.6.94; WHj and HR to men's harvest supper, 6.9.94; WH to, 10.2.95; Hs to tea, 19.8.96; WH and WHj with party to tea, 18.8.97
public-house fabric: dining room painted by WHj and HR, 2.5.94; Thomas Baldwin carts stones from yard into road, 8–9.5.94; Mr Bunnett's men at work, 11.3.95
working on Hs' farm: sowing turnips, 21.6.94; mowing in Bell's Acre, 18–19.8.94; stacking hay, 18.7.96; cutting peas, 20.8.96, 14.8.97; turning peas and wheat, collecting and reaping wheat, 2.9.96; collects piglets from Sheringham, 22.9.96; in barn, 29.8.97, 31.8.97: *see also* Letheringsett, King's Head
doors, collected by William Lamb from Cley, 5.11.96; installed by Messrs Dawson and Bunnett's men in King's Head, Letheringsett, 10.11.96; made by Thomas Youngman's men for counting-house chamber, 14.10.97
Dowson [? Dewson], Miss, with Miss Wymer dines at Hs', 11.1.96; with Bartells and Miss Wymer to tea at Hs', 15.1.96, 8.2.96; with WHj and Miss Wymer to Holt, 29.1.96; with Misses Bartell and Wymer at Hs', 17.2.96; with Bartells to tea at Hs', 5.10.96
Dowson, Mr, with Bartells to tea at Hs', 27.5.96
drag raking, *see* raking
drains, **337**, WHj lays down gutter bricks, 19.7.94; Thomas Boyce making underdrain in Hs' garden, 20.3.95; Robert Bye collects ling heather for underdrain from Holt Heath Farm, 26.1.97: *see also* ditches
drawing off, of beer by Hs and men after brewing:
1793: 14.11.93
1794: 14.1.94, 19.1.94, 6.5.94, 16.5.94, 8.6.94, 15.6.94, 5.7.94, 2.8.94, 9.9.94, 13.9.94, 27.9.94, 4.10.94, 23.10.94, 23.11.94
1795: 10.2.95, 17.3.95, 29.3.95, 6.4.95, 19.4.95, 7.6.95, 6.9.95, 25.10.95, 7.11.95
1796: 28.3.96, 21.4.96, 8.5.96, 15.5.96, 20.9.96, 12.12.96
1797: 25.1.97, 17.2.97, 27.4.97, 19.6.97: *see also* casks; draying off
draying off (carrying off), of beer within brewery, 28.1.94, 22.4.94, 6.5.94, 1.6.94, 28.1.94, 22.4.94, 13.1.96, 23.3.96, 20.3.97, 27.4.97: *see also* drawing off
drays, *see* carts, beer cart; wagons
dressing, by Hs' men; 10–11.2.95, 13–14.3.95, 16.3.95, 2–3.4.95, 10.11.95, 9.2.96, 26.3.96
barley: 10.1.95, 5.10.95
flour:
1793: 8.11.93, 23.11.93, 6.12.93, 24.12.93, 26.12.93
1794: 3.2.94, 4.3.94, 19.5.94, 11.6.94, 14.8.94, 6.9.94, 24.9.94, 7.10.94, 11.10.94, 11.11.94
1795: 23.2.95, 9–10.3.95, 14–15.4.95, 18.7.95, 24.8.95, 4.9.95, 12.10.95, 16.10.95, 1.12.95
1796: 16.3.96, 1.6.96, 11.8.96, 1.9.96, 26.9.96, 22.12.96, 31.12.96
1797: 23.1.97, 26.1.97, 23.2.97, 10.4.97, 12.5.97, 23.6.97, 8.7.97, 26.7.97, 8–9.8.97, 25.8.97, 27.9.97, 9.10.97, 23.10.97: *see also* meal *below*
grass seed: 22.4.95, 25.7.96, 14.4.97
malt culms: 25.10.93, 21.2.94, 3.7.94
meal (male): stripped, 6.12.94, 11.2.95, 13.4.95, 10.8.96
millstones:
Hs' corn mill: 15.10.93, 13.11.93, 12.12.93, 2.1.94, 17.2.94, 26.3.94, 7.5.94, 1–3.7.94, 13.8.94, 10–11.9.94, 9.10.94, 15.11.94, 6–7.1.95, 26.6.95, 13.8.95, 19.12.95, 6.1.96, 4–5.2.96, 17–19.5.96, 18.8.96, 1.11.96,

dressing, millstones, Hs' cornmill (*cont.*)
13–14.12.96, 17.1.97, 13.3.97, 5–6.7.97, 11.8.97, 21.8.97, 20.9.97, 13–14.10.97
Hs' malt-mill: 11.10.93, 21–22.7.95, 3.12.95, 5.12.95, 10–12.5.96, 19–20.8.96, 21–22.4.97, 30.6.97, 19.8.97, 30.9.97
peas: 7.12.96, 31.1.97
wheat: 16.9.94, 6.10.94, 18.10.94, 12.2.95: *see also* malt, screening
drum, collected by Thomas Baldwin from Weybourne, 16.4.95
drunkenness, of Hs' men, **226**:
Thomas Baldwin: drunk all day, 23.1.94, 19.6.94, 20.1.96
Robert Bye: 1–2.12.94, 28.1.95; drunk all day, 22–23.1.94, 19.6.94, 17.12.95; at Weybourne, 11.5.95; arrives late for work, 12.5.95; drinking, 3.12.95
Duffield, W., casting clay, 15–16.12.96
dung, *see* muck
Dyball (Dybal), James, innkeeper of Three Pigs, Edgefield; at Hs', 29.5.94; orders beer, 4.9.94, 6.12.96; Thomas Baldwin collects hay, 23.4.96: *see also* Edgefield

E

East Dereham, Norf., **69**, **177**, Mr Carr, brewer, at Hs', 22.11.93
East Runton (Runcton), Norf., **350**, William Lamb collects money from public house, 6.6.97
beer deliveries, **6**:
1793: 10.10.93, 13.11.93, 17.12.93
1794: 24.1.94, 3.3.94, 26.3.94, 17.4.94, 2.5.94, 16.5.94, 24.5.94, 6.6.94, 1.7.94, 21.7.94, 9.8.94, 10.9.94, 23.9.94, 18.10.94, 13.11.94, 17.12.94
1795: 17.1.95, 10.3.95, 18.4.95, 14.5.95, 9.6.95, 24.6.95, 9.7.95, 1.8.95, 25.8.95, 12.9.95, 29.9.95, 2.10.95, 28.10.95, 2.12.95, 23.12.95
1796: 21.1.96, 26.2.96, 14.3.96, 16.4.96, 7.5.96, 27.5.96, 14.6.96, 7.7.96, 11.8.96, 1.9.96, 21.9.96, 12.10.96, 22.11.96, 26.12.96
1797: 3.3.97, 17.4.97, 8.5.97, 30.5.97, 16.6.97, 6.7.97, 24.7.97, 19.8.97, 29.9.97, 23.10.97: *see also* Hill, Robert
East Winch, *see* Winch
Edgefield (Edgfield), Norf., Gunton Thompson to, 30.6.94; brewer's grains delivered to, 30.7.94
barley collected: 20.11.95, 24.6.96, 24.10.96, 7.12.96; from Mr Boswell, 18.4.97
beer deliveries:
1793: 30.10.93, 20.11.93, 30.11.93, 18.12.93, 24.12.93

Edgefield, beer deliveries (*cont.*)
1794: 18.1.94, 24.1.94, 18.2.94, 5.3.94, 3.4.94, 12.4.94, 26.4.94, 22.5.94, 31.5.94, 17.6.94, 3.7.94, 16.7.94, 23.7.94, 30.7.94, 11.8.94, 4.9.94, 17–18.9.94, 3.10.94, 14.10.94, 18.10.94, 4.11.94, 14.11.94, 29.11.94, 16.12.94
1795: 1.1.95, 16.1.95, 6.2.95, 17.2.95, 18.3.95, 17.4.95, 1.5.95, 18.5.95, 28.5.95, 13.6.95, 20.6.95, 7.7.95, 15.8.95, 10.9.95, 26.9.95, 29.9.95, 16.10.95, 20.11.95, 8.12.95
1796: 2.1.96, 26.1.96, 3.2.96, 4.3.96, 19.3.96, 28.3.96, 27.4.96, 21.5.96, 27.5.96, 16.6.96, 7.7.96, 26.7.96, 12.9.96, 26.9.96, 7.10.96, 20.10.96, 10.11.96, 7.12.96, 16.12.96
1797: 17.1.97, 31.1.97, 25.2.97, 9.3.97, 3.4.97, 18.4.97, 26.4.97, 27.5.97, 8.6.97, 15.6.97, 29.6.97, 11.7.97, 29.7.97, 21.8.97, 26.8.97, 14.9.97, 27.9.97, 16.10.97, 23.10.97
hay: inspected by WH and WHj, 18.6.94; bought by WH and WHj, 31.7.95; collected by Hs' men, 5.8.95, 20.7.96; WHj buys grass from Mr Darby, 22.6.96
HR to: 15.7.94, 21.7.94, 2.9.94, 10.10.94, 23.4.96, 12.9.96, 14.8.97; with Nathaniel Raven jnr, 10.3.97
malt deliveries: 12.10.93, 13.1.95, 25.3.95, 20.11.95, 26.7.96, 16.8.96, 8.6.97, 18.7.97; to Mr Boswell, 22.5.94
WHj to: 11.10.93, 5.8.95, 1.7.96, 6.7.96, 12.7.96; with James Moore, 8.11.93; with Mr Savory, 2.1.97:
see also Dyball, James
Edwards, John, innkeeper of Crown, Sheringham, tied house; with Mr Bignold to dinner at Hs', 7.3.97: *see also* Sheringham
Ellis, John (d.1836 aged 67), Cley merchant; at Hs, 24.7.94, 15.9.95, 20.7.96, 14.7.97, 13.10.97, 16.10.97; dines with Hs, 9.12.94, 14.5.96, 17.10.96; stays overnight, 10.3.96; with WHj to Thetford, 11.3.96; to supper with Hs, 14.5.96, 14.7.97; Thomas Baldwin collects malt, 18.10.96
Hs' men collect cinders:
1795: 13.6.95, 13.2.95, 20.10.95, 3.11.95, 28.11.95, 4.12.95, 12.12.95, 15.12.95
1796: 23.1.96, 30.1.96, 9.2.96, 25.2.96, 1.3.96, 12.3.96, 4–5.4.96, 30.5.96, 20.6.96, 24.10.96, 26.11.96, 3.12.96
1797: 9.1.97, 7.2.97, 21.2.97, 24.3.97, 6.4.97, 10.5.97, 17.5.97, 6.6.97, 14.6.97, 30.6.97, 10.7.97, 21.9.97
Hs' men collect coal: 1–2.11.93, 6.11.93, 21.7.94, 16.6.95
engines, *see* pumps
entertainments, *see* assemblies; balls; bowling green; clubs; feasts; frolics; music; plays; shooting; skating

Erratt, Joseph, **248**, Holt printer, bookseller, stationer, bookbinder, perfumer and ironmonger; orders beer from Hs, 24.2.96; at Hs' with Cory family and Miss Gooderson, 30.7.96; stays overnight at Hs', with HR to Holt, 30.9.97

Everitt (Everett), Robert, Guestwick farmer; to supper with Hs and reckons, 23.6.94; with Mr Keeler dines at Hs', 25.11.94; with Mr Keeler and Miss Billing to dinner and supper at Hs' and to Weybourne Camp, 26.6.95; with Mr Keeler at Hs' to reckon for year's barley, 27.6.96

examiners, *see* excise

excise, **29**, **191**, **270**, examiner at Hs' with Mr Sheldrake, 13.10.95: *see also* Sheldrake, John; Todhunter, William

faggots, *see* wood

fairs:
- Cley: Mr and Mrs Gunton Thompson to, 25.7.94; Gunton Thompson to, 31.7.95, 29.7.96, 28.7.97; Nicholas Woodhouse to, 29.7.96
- Hempton Green: HR to, 17.5.96
- Holt: WH and WHj to, Gunton Thompson to, WHj buys wheat, 25.11.93; Hs' boy to, 25.4.94; Hs, Ravens, Cook Flower and John Walden to, WH sells two cows and buys one, 27.4.95; Nathaniel Raven and WHj to, 25.11.95; William Lamb to, 25.4.96, 25.4.97; Robert Bye to, Hs and HR to, 25.4.97
- Weybourne: William Lamb, Thomas Baldwin and Gunton Thompson to, 17.5.96

Fakenham, Norf., **140**, **153**, **173**, WHj to, 13.2.94, 18.12.95, 26–28.1.96; HR to with family, 1.6.94; Nathaniel Raven to, 6.11.94; Revd John and Mrs Crofts at Hs', 25.8.95; HR takes MA to, 21.1.96; William Lamb collects hoops, 7.6.96; Mr and Mrs Burrell to after marriage, 2.8.96; MH and WHj to, 20.4.97; HR to, 6.6.97
- beer deliveries:
  - 1793: 23.10.93, 9.11.93, 25.11.93, 13.12.93
  - 1794: 9.1.94, 4.2.94, 6.3.94, 28.3.94, 16.4.94, 30.4.94, 15.5.94, 2.6.94, 18.6.94, 21.6.94, 8.7.94, 22.7.94, 7.8.94, 22.8.94, 5.9.94, 26.9.94, 14.10.94, 20.10.94, 3.11.94, 24.11.94, 15.12.94
  - 1795: 3.1.95, 2.2.95, 23.2.95, 14.3.95, 9.4.95, 4.5.95, 15.5.95, 28.5.95, 20.6.95, 18.7.95, 7.8.95, 29.8.95, 19.9.95, 14.10.95, 23.10.95, 14.11.95, 15.12.95, 22.12.95
  - 1796: 12.1.96, 19.2.96, 1.4.96, 10.5.96, 7.6.96, 29.6.96, 27.7.96, 23.8.96, 24.9.96, 14.10.96, 24.10.96, 16.11.96, 5.12.96, 27.12.96

Fakenham, beer deliveries (*cont.*)
  - 1797: 16.1.97, 18.2.97, 11.3.97, 7.4.97, 28.4.97, 25.5.97, 12.6.97, 27.6.97, 28.7.97, 22.8.97, 14.9.97, 2.10.97, 17.10.97
  - loading: 2.1.95, 3.5.95, 26.7.96, 15.11.96, 4.12.96:
- *see also* Gathercole, John

farms, **232**, **233**, **238**, **376**, large party of farmers joined by WH passes through Letheringsett to Sharrington, 21.12.95: *see also* barley; barns; Cobon, James; corn; cows; Forster, Thomas; fences; fields; furze; goaft; Goggs, Henry jnr; granaries; grasses; harvests; hay; hedges; Holt Heath Farm; horses; Kendle, Charles; labourers; livestock; marl; meadows; mould; muck; oats; peas; pigs; ploughing; raking; sowing; threshing; turnips; vetches; wheat; workforce

farm servants, *see* workforce

Farthing (Farthin, Fathing), Robert (d.1806 aged 65), Blakeney coal and cinder merchant; WH and WHj to sale at Blakeney, 16.8.97
- Hs' men collect cinders: 7–8.11.94, 5.12.94, 12.12.94, 18.12.94, 2.3.95, 5.3.95, 14.3.95, 31.3.95, 14.4.95, 27.4.95, 8.5.95, 16.10.95, 18.11.96
- Hs' men collect coal: 1.6.95, 6.6.95, 13.8.95, 1.8.97

fasts, public, by royal proclamation in support of British troops in wartime; no work done, MA and HR to Letheringsett Church, 25.2.95; no work done in afternoon, 9.3.96; sermon given by Mr Burrell, 8.3.97

fat, fatt, *see* brewing equipment, vat

fattening, *see* pigs

feasts:
- Holt: WH to venison feast, 30.7.94; WHj to turtle feast, 3.9.94; WHj to bowling-green feast, 29.10.95
- Letheringsett: purse club at King's Head, 13.1.94: *see also* harvest

fences, placed by Robert Bye around stack, 13.9.97: *see also* furze; hurdles; palisade

Field Dalling (Dawlin, Dawling), Norf., HR to with Mr Hammond's bill, 8.9.96; Robert Bye takes WH's horse to, 9.5.97; WH and WHj to, 9.5.97; Samuel Coker refuses to accept beer delivery from Thomas Baldwin, 7.10.97; WHj to, 13.10.97
- beer deliveries, **361**:
  - 1793: 1.11.93, 7.11.93, 17.12.93
  - 1794: 22.2.94, 19.5.94, 18.6.94, 14.7.94, 7.8.94, 25.8.94, 15.9.94, 23.10.94, 7.11.94, 6.12.94
  - 1795: 27.1.95, 19.3.95, 28.4.95, 29.5.95, 11.7.95, 18.7.95, 12.8.95, 28.8.95, 10.10.95, 27.10.95

Field Dalling, beer deliveries (*cont.*)
1796: 2.1.96
1797: 7.10.97, 13.10.97:
see also Reeve, James
fields, Hs', **101**, *see* Bell's Acre; Brewhouse Pightle; Five Acres; Furze Closes; Hill Close; meadows; Six Acres; *see also* Holt Heath Farm; Lime Kiln Field
Finch, Peter, **408**, **411**, Norwich common brewer, Clerk of the Peace for Norfolk; annual production figures, HR's endnotes
fires:
accidental: John Wade's mill at Holt burns down, 8.5.94; Hs' chimney catches fire, 15.2.95
furnaces for malting/brewing, **215**: kindled by Hs' men, 17.10.94, 9.2.95; bars repaired by Abraham Dobson, 15.1.94; new bars installed by John Rolfe, 11.7.95
firewood, *see* wood
fir trees, *see* trees
fish, 300 collected by Hs' boy from Sharrington, 21.7.94; removed when WHj drains river and pond, 20.5.96
Fisher, Misses, of Holt; with Mr Fisher to tea at Hs', 29.9.94; with Mr and Mrs Cook Flower at Hs', 2.12.94
Fisher, Revd Thomas jnr (1768–1806), of Holt, Curate of Linton, Cambs 1792, Officiating Minister at Holt 1794, Curate of Chesterford, Essex 1795, Rector of Girton, Cambs 1800–06; with Misses Fisher to tea at Hs', 29.9.94
Five Acres, Letheringsett field farmed by Hs; harrowed, 21.4.94, 1.7.96, 10.4.97, 19.4.97; men at mould cart, 23.4.95; barley sown, 30.4.95, 15.4.97, 17.4.97; men mowing barley, 11.9.95, 25.8.97; rakings gathered, 22.9.95; men turning over muck heap, 24–25.5.96; muck spreading, 24.6.96; rolled, 1.7.96; men at work, 15.3.97; seeds sown, 19.4.97; men gathering barley, 7.9.97
ploughed: 30.11.93, 3.12.93, 11.12.93, 20.2.94, 18.9.94, 7.3.95, 30.4.95, 4.5.95, 28.7.95, 18.12.95, 24.2.96, 14.5.96, 18.6.96, 7.4.97, 10.4.97, 15.4.97, 17.4.97
flag harrow, *see* harrowing
floods, *see* Glaven, River
flour (flower, flowr), **231**, **232**, **233**, **234**, used in recipe for destroying rats, HR's endnotes
dressed:
1793: 8.11.93, 19.11.93, 23.11.93, 6.12.93, 24.12.93, 26.12.93
1794: 3.2.94, 4.3.94, 19.5.94, 11.6.94, 14.8.94, 6.9.94, 24.9.94, 7.10.94, 11.10.94, 11.11.94
1795: 23.2.95, 9–10.3.95, 14–15.4.95, 18.7.95, 24.8.95, 4.9.95, 12.10.95, 1.12.95

flour, dressed (*cont.*)
1796: 16.3.96, 1.6.96, 11.8.96, 1.9.96, 26.9.96, 22.12.96, 31.12.96
1797: 23.1.97, 26.1.97, 23.2.97, 10.4.97, 12.5.97, 23.6.97, 8.7.97, 26.7.97, 8–9.8.97, 25.8.97, 27.9.97, 9.10.97, 23.10.97
hopper: filled by Thomas Baldwin during dressing, 23.2.95
lower grades:
2nd-grade (male, meal): stripped by Gunton Thompson, 15.4.94, 10.8.96; stripped by HR, 6.12.94, 11.2.95, 13.4.95
3rd/4th-grade coarse flour (bran, pollard, sharps): delivered by Mr Skelton, 8.9.94; collected by Gunton Thompson from William Cook, 25.6.96; ground by Gunton Thompson, 16.9.97
shipping, **231**: prepared for, 8.11.93, 19.11.93; 15 sacks delivered to Wells, 5.12.93:
see also mills; millstones
Flower (Flour), Cook (d.1842 aged 77), **10**, **227**, of Sheringham [Old] Hall; WHj and MA to, 4–5.12.93, 5–6.1.95; Hs to dinner, 24.6.94; with wife, WHj and MA to Holkham, 7.10.94; departs, 8.10.94; with wife and Miss Fisher at Hs', 2.12.94; to dinner, 27.4.95; with wife to dinner, 4.5.95, 23.6.96, 17.8.97; Hs spend day at, 31.8.95; orders trees, 2.12.95, 29.12.95; with wife spends day at Hs', 26.2.96; WHj, MA, Ann and Rose Raven spend day at, 27.4.96; Thomas Baldwin and William Dobson collect pigs, 22.9.96
Flower, Miss, at large tea party at Hs', 17.7.94
Flower, Samuel, of Sheringham; with Mrs Cook Flower at Hs', with WHj and MA to Holt assembly, 18.12.93; departs, 19.12.93
Flower, Mrs Sarah Ditchell (1772–1819), **10**, née Sibbs, wife of Cook; with Samuel Flower at Hs', with WHj and MA to Holt assembly, 18.12.93; with husband, WHj and MA to Holkham, 7.10.94; departs, 8.10.94, 27.12.94; with husband and Miss Fisher at Hs', 2.12.94; to dinner, 24.12.94, 21.11.95, 25.11.95; with husband to dinner, 4.5.95,23.6.96, 17.8.97; with husband spends day at Hs', 26.2.96
Forster, Masters, [? sons of Thomas]; collect parcel from Hs brought by WHj from Ashwicken, 14.5.97; with Master Collyer to tea at Hs', 23.5.97: *see also* Forster, Thomas jnr
Forster, Miss, [? daughter of Thomas]; at Hs', 9–10.4.97
Forster, Mrs, née Buckle, wife of Thomas; with William Herring to tea, 18.1.94; with Mrs Herring to tea, 18.7.94, 15.8.95; with family at Hs', 24.8.94, 9–10.4.97; with MA to Holt, 26.8.94; with family to tea, 30.11.94, 25.2.95, 24.4.95; to tea at Hs', 2.3.95, 2.10.95, 27.7.96;

Forster, Mrs (*cont.*)
Hs, Mrs Phillis Goggs and Mary Raven to, 13.5.95; with husband and Herrings to tea, 2.5.96, 2.9.96
Forster, Thomas, of Bayfield Hall and Holt House, Leziate, farmer:
Bayfield Hall estate, **308**: Hs' men collect lime from kiln, 16.10.93, 26.5.94; Robert Bye borrows flag harrow, 5.2.94; Robert Bye collects hay, 18.4.94; Hs' boy collects wheat, 16.2.96; three teams sent with hay from Lime Kiln Field to Hs, 20–22.7.96; men sent to Hs to help with stacking hay, 20–22.7.96; WH and William Lamb inspect crops, 29.7.96: *see also* Bayfield
at Hs': with family, 24.8.94, 30.11.94, 24.4.95, 9–10.4.97; to tea, 9.11.94, 10.2.95, 25.2.95; with Sheldrakes to tea, 13.11.95; with wife and Herrings to tea, 2.5.96, 2.9.96; with James Moore to supper, 6.11.96; with Miss Riches departs, 14.8.97
Hs at: 22.4.95; Miss Custance, WHj and MA, 7.2.94, 13.5.97; to tea, 23.4.94, 11.11.94, 19.1.96, 20.6.96; Miss Symonds, WHj and MA, 27.5.94; WH, 21.10.94, 11.7.96; WHj to tea, 6.2.95; WH and MA, 26.2.95; MH and MA, 29.4.95; MA to tea, 17.8.95; Hs and Mrs Phillis Goggs to tea, 17.9.95, 21.7.96; Hs and Misses Raven to tea, 22.4.96; WHj and MA from, 13.5.97:
Forster, Thomas jnr, with family to tea at Hs', 25.2.95; leaves Miss Richards at Hs', 25.9.97: *see also* Forster, Masters
Foulger, Robert (d.1795), innkeeper of Crown, Southrepps, tied house; orders beer, 21.10.94: *see also* Southrepps
Foulsham, Norf., William Platten collects barrels, 25.10.93; WHj to, 3.1.94; Mr Buck brings sample of barley to Hs, 18.9.94
Fox, John (b.*c.*1751, d.1832 'aged 83'), of Letheringsett, Hs' labourer; hedging, 8–12.4.94; in yard, 15–16.4.94, 18–19.4.94, 23.4.94; casting gravel, 17.4.94; burning couch grass, 18.4.94; draws off beer into cask, 22.4.94; spreading scour from ditch over Brewhouse Pightle, 23.4.94; spreading gravel in yard, 24.4.94; at work in shrubbery, 19–20.5.94, 24.5.94; at work, 27–29.5.94; covers new-laid arch, 30.5.94; digging for clay in Furze Close, 2.6.94
Fox, Mr, Hindolveston farmer; brings sample of barley to Hs, 17.9.94
Fox, Thomas (1740–1826), **200**, Brisley grocer and draper; with large party to Weybourne Camp, 24.8.95; with Nathaniel Raven to Whissonsett, 25.8.95
frolics, William Lamb and Thomas Baldwin to harvest frolic, 17.9.96: *see also* audit; feasts
fruit, **259**:
apples, gathered by: HR and Gunton Thompson, 18.10.93, 17.10.95; HR and Gunton Thompson jnr, 19.10.93; HR and boy, 12.9.94, 3.10.94; boy, 19.9.94; Thomas Boyce, 13.10.96; WH, HR and William Thackwray, 27.10.96
cherries: Thomas Boyce supports Hs' tree with truss, 2.7.96
figs: used for destroying rats, HR's endnotes
trees: Hs' inspected by Henry Jodrell's gardener, 9.6.96
furnaces, *see* fires
furniture, **248**, **257**, collected by Robert Bye from Cley, 4.10.94; chairs and other items collected by Robert Bye from Weybourne, 14.1.97
furrows, hoed by Thomas Boyce, 19–20.5.97, 22.5.97
furze (furrze), **337**, collected by Thomas Baldwin and Robert Bye, 14.11.94; set up in yard by Robert Bye, 21.11.94; collected by Thomas Boyce and boy from Henry Jodrell's hill, 2.1.95; unloaded by Hs' men, 6.1.95, 13.1.97, 17.1.97, 20.2.97; planted by WHj and HR, 12.3.95; furze trees ordered by Cook Flower from Hs, 2.12.95, 29.12.95; collected by Hs' men from Holt Heath Farm, 12.1.97, 16–17.1.97, 26–28.1.97, 18.2.97; stacked by Hs' men, 18.1.97, 1.2.97; pitched by Robert Bye, 18.1.97
Furze Closes (Furrze Closes), Saxlingham fields farmed by Hs; WH to, 18.8.94; WHj to, 13.3.95, 2.4.95; HR to, 22.5.97
harrowing, **43**: 5.2.94, 25.3.94, 21.4.94, 9.3.95, 10.4.95, 24.9.95, 14–15.2.97, 10.4.97, 18.4.97, 25.10.97
harvesting: mowing barley, 18.8.94, 31.8.95, 24.8.97; raking, 20.8.94; barley collected, 7.9.95, 12.9.96, 31.8.97; stubble collected, 12.11.96
haymaking: 19.9.95, 16.7.96, 20.7.96, 9.6.97
hedging: 31.3.95, 7.4.95, 17–18.4.95, 20–21.4.95, 24.4.95, 19.11.95; thorns carted, 2.4.95
Hs' men at work: 29.11.94, 1–6.12.94, 8–10.12.94, 13.12.94, 19–20.12.94, 23.1.97, 31.3.97, 1.4.97, 4–7.4.97, 10–14.4.97, 17–22.4.97; boy collects sand, 21.12.93; John Fox digging for clay, 2.6.94; stones carted, 15.4.95; couch grass raked, 31.10.95; gates delivered and set in place, 12–13.5.96, 26.7.96; gates collected, 12.12.96; timber collected, 31.12.96; William Holman ditching, 17.4.97; Thomas Baldwin rolling, 19.4.97
muck carting/spreading: 3.2.94, 13.3.95, 5.11.95, 3–5.1.97, 24.6.97

Furze Closes (*cont.*)
ploughing: 15.2.94, 17.2.94, 5.4.94, 11.4.94, 25.4.94, 26.6.94, 11.11.94, 9.3.95, 27.3.95, 7.4.95, 15–16.10.95, 23.10.95, 8.12.95, 4.2.96, 5.6.96, 22–23.2.97, 28.2.97, 1.4.97, 3.4.97, 12.4.97, 2.5.97, 1.7.97, 4.7.97; in wheat stubble, 2.11.93, 9.11.93, 14–16.11.93, 15.4.95, 20.4.95; in Lower Furze Close, 12.3.95, 21.4.95, 29.3.97
sowing: barley in wheat stubble, 15.4.95, 20.4.95; barley in Lower Furze Close, 21.4.95; barley, 24.4.95, 12.4.97; turnips, 1.7.97, 4.7.97
turnips: collected, 21.12.93; hoed, 16.7.94; sown, 1.7.97, 4.7.97:
see also Hill Close

G

Gallant, M. [?Mary], gathering wheat for Hs, 18.8.94
game, *see* shooting; venison
games, *see* bowling green; entertainments
Ganning, Daniel (d.1810 aged 63), **170**, **171**, **408**, **411**, Norwich common brewer; annual production figures, HR's endnotes
gaps, stopping, *see* hedges
garden, Hs', **86**, **87**, **143**, **154**, **157**, **163**, **211**, **230**, **235**, **238**; WH at work, 12.3.95; toured by Mr Burrell and Garretts, 11.4.95; pump played, 21.5.95; William Lamb and Thomas Baldwin collect clay for, 30.1.96; Thomas Boyce painting in, 18.3.96; Henry Jodrell's gardener inspects fruit trees, 9.6.96; Nicholas Woodhouse carts gravel from, 15.6.96, 21.6.96; Mary Loades at work, 15.8.96; hedge cut by Thomas Boyce, 27.8.96; Thomas Boyce employed as Hs' gardener for £10 a year, 10.10.96
Thomas Boyce at work: *see* Boyce, Thomas, gardening
men at work, **52**, **92**: John Ramm, 11–12.10.93, 23–26.7.94, 30.8.94, 20.9.94, 22–24.9.94, 13–14.6.96, 28.6.96; two soldiers, 18.3.94; Thomas Atwood, 1–2.4.94; James Skiffins, 1.4.94, 23.5.94, 30.5.94, 25.8.94, 19.9.94; James Broughton, 6.2.95, 10–11.2.95; boy, 11.2.95; Thomas Hall, 16.2.95, 7–8.4.95; Mr Smith, 7.3.95; Nicholas Woodhouse, 9.6.96, 22.6.96, 27.8.96; Thomas Baldwin, 22.6.96; William Lamb, 22.6.96; Jeremiah Moore and son, 14.6.96
River Glaven beside: Jeremiah Moore and son at work, 21–22.5.94; William Tinker and two men at work on bridge, 9.8.96
shrubbery: HR collects shrubs from James Moore, 10.4.95, 24.10.96; toured by Mr Burrell and Garretts, 11.4.95; Thomas Hall and boy dig hole for tree, 14.4.95; Thomas Hall barrowing muck into and digging up stumps, 28.4.95; underdrained by Thomas Boyce, 20.3.95
men at work: John Fox, 19–20.5.94, 24.5.94; Thomas Hall, 8–9.5.95, 11–12.5.95, 14–16.5.95; John Ramm, 21–22.5.95, 30.5.95, 14–15.7.95, 21–23.7.95, 28–29.7.95, 31.7.95, 1.8.95, 3–4.8.95, 7–8.8.95, 10–12.8.95, 22.8.95, 28–29.8.95; Thomas Boyce, 4.5.96, 29.5.97:
see also bath; fruit; palisade; trees; vegetables
gardeners, Hs', *see* garden, men at work
Garrett (Garratt), Mrs, wife of Robert; with husband and Mr Burrell tours Hs' garden, 11.4.95
Garrett (Garratt), Robert, with wife and Mr Burrell tours Hs' garden, 11.4.95
gates, hung by Thomas Youngman's man and boy, 3.5.94; painted by HR, 17.6.95; painted by HR in Brewhouse Pightle, 14.12.95
temporary field gates (lifts): installed in Furze Closes, 12–13.5.96, 26.7.96; collected from Furze Closes, 12.12.96
Gathercole, John (d.1802), innkeeper of Bell, Fakenham, tied house; at Hs', 12.5.94, 22.8.97; orders beer, 6.6.96: *see also* Fakenham, beer deliveries
Gay, Miss, of Edgefield; with Miss Davy to tea at Hs', 10.3.97
gears, of Hs' mill, trimmed by Thomas Youngman, 27.2.95
geese, 20 brought to Hs by William Chapman, 25.7.94
Gidney, John jnr (1761–1822), Letheringsett labourer; at work in river, 13.6.94
gig, *see* chaises
gill (gil), *see* wheels
Glandford (Glamford), Norf., **8**, WHj and Nathaniel Raven jnr to, 1.11.96
Glaven, River (the river), **8**, **11**, **62**, **65**, **66**, **74**, **77**, **112**, **113**, **116**, **143**, **144**, **146**, **149**, **157**, **197**, **238**, **276**, **277**, **280**, **329**, **372**, **373**; Thomas Hall, Gunton Thompson and Jeremiah Moore throw mould from, 7–8.2.94; Jeremiah Moore and son at work downstream, 19–20.5.94; Jeremiah Moore and son at work in Hs' garden, 21–22.5.94, 14.6.96; Jeremiah Moore and son at work in yard, 26–28.5.94; Mr Bunnett's men build arch, 28.5.94; dammed by Thomas Boyce, water drawn from by WHj and fish removed, 20.5.96; Thomas Boyce working in while William Tinker and Thomas Youngman repair sluice and waterwheel, 21.5.96; Hs' men rescue Mrs Booty's horses in floods, one mare

Glaven, River (*cont.*)
drowned, 4.6.96; Thomas Baldwin carts iron cinders into, 9.6.96; bank repaired by Nicholas Woodhouse, 4.8.96
work unspecified by: Jeremiah Moore, 23.5.94, 29.5.94, 31.5.94, 2–4.6.94, 6–7.6.94, 12–14.6.94, 17–20.6.94; Jeremiah Moore and son, 30.5.94, 11.6.96, 15–18.6.96, 20.6.96; John Gidney jnr and William Parsons, 13.6.94; William Platten, 13–14.6.94; Thomas Boyce, 4.7.95, 20.7.95, 2–3.6.97, 14.6.97; Nicholas Woodhouse, 6.6.96, 27.7.96, 18.8.96; Robert Bye, 1.6.97

goaft (goft), stack of corn removed from fields; John Thompson rides mare on, 21.8.94, 28.8.94; boy rides horse on, 6.9.97

Goggs, Henry (1731–95), Whissonsett farmer; burial, 16.2.95

Goggs, Henry jnr (1767–1827), **150**, **151**, **153**, Whissonsett farmer; with WHj to Letheringsett, 13.12.93; at Hs', 8–9.9.94, 20–21.12.94, 24–25.4.96; with WHj to Holt market, 20.12.94; with farm steward and Hs to Weybourne Camp, 8.7.95; to Holt Quarter Sessions, 15.10.95; with Hs to Holt, 25.4.96; takes mother to Hs, 19.7.96; with Mr Cook to Hs, 25.7.96, 14.8.97; with mother and Hs to Salthouse, 25.7.96; with Hs to seaside, 14.8.97; departs, 15.8.97

Goggs, Mrs Phillis (1731–1806), née Raven, wife of Henry, MH's sister; with niece Mary to Hs, 5.5.95; with MH and niece Mary to Letheringsett Church, with MH to Briston, 10.5.95; with Hs to Forsters, 13.5.95, 17.9.95, 21.7.96; departs, 16.5.95; with MH and HR to Briston, 13.9.95, 20.9.95; with WH to Weybourne Camp, 18.9.95; with Hs to tea at Holt, 22.9.95; with Hs to Southrepps, 23.9.95; with son Henry to Hs, 19.7.96; with MH to Cley, 24.7.96; with family to Salthouse, 25.7.96; with Hs to Holt, 1.8.96

Gooderson, Miss, at Hs' with Cory family and Joseph Erratt, 30.7.96

Goulty, Miss [? Elizabeth Page (d.1862 aged 85)], with Flowers to dinner at Hs', 23.6.96

gout (gught), *see* illness

grains, brewer's, delivered by Thomas Baldwin to Corpusty and Edgefield, 30.7.94

granaries, in Hs' maltings and corn mill, **212**; HR at work, 11.10.93; John Ramm at work, 24–26.10.93, 6.10.94; John Ramm stores dressed barley, 5.10.95; Gunton Thompson and HR clean wheat chamber, 30.1.96:
see also barn

grasses, carted from Hill Close, 15.10.93; mown, 1–2.7.94, 6–11.7.95, 14–15.9.95, 21.9.95, 23.9.95, 30.9.96, 1.10.96, 3–4.10.96, 28–30.6.97, 1.7.97, 4.7.97, 6–8.7.97, 14.7.97, 17.7.97; WHj buys nine acres from Mr Darby for £19, 22.6.96; collected from Furze Closes, 9.6.97; mown at Holt Heath Farm, 11–13.7.97; second crop, 28.9.97
couch grass (quicks): burnt, 28.3.94, 18.4.94, 25.4.94; raked, 27–28.10.95; carted away, 29.10.95, 21.2.97; raked from Furze Closes, 31.10.95; harrowed and heaped, 17.3.97
seed: dressed, 22.4.95, 25.7.96, 14.4.97; sown in meadow, 25.3.97:
see also clover; hay; meadows; vetches; weeding

gravel, *see* stones

Graveland, J., Hs' labourer; turning over muck, 6–7.1.94, 25–28.8.95, 31.8.95, 22–25.9.95; threshing, 23–24.9.95

greasing, *see* oiling

Great Ryburgh, *see* Ryburgh

Great Yarmouth, Norf., **170**, **171**, Mr and Miss Symonds to Hs from, 18.5.94

Gresham (Gressham), Norf., WHj to, 13.1.95; beer deliveries, 15.7.97, 14.8.97, 11.9.97, 2.10.97

Gressenhall (Gressinghall), Norf., **73**, **163**, **166**, **198**, **326**, **366**, chaise accident with WH and MH on journey to, 3.7.94; WHj and James Moore to, 6.4.96

grinding, *see* malt; millstones

Guestwick (Gueastwick, Gustwick), Norf., Phillis Raven, WHj and MA to, 17.6.94; HR delivers malt, 28.8.94, 9.5.96, 23.7.96; HR to, 25.6.95, 11.7.95, 22.3.97; boy delivers malt, 15.8.95; WH to, 25.9.95; Mr Jarvis disputes barley measurement, 16.10.95; Nicholas Woodhouse delivers malt, 15.8.96; Robert Bye to, 16.8.97

Guist, Norf., **167**, **170**, **171**, WH and WHj to, 7.5.95

Gunthorpe (Gunthorp), Norf., **27**, **233**, WH to, 20.11.93, 22.1.96; Thomas Baldwin delivers barley and hops, 21.11.93; boy delivers beer to Charles Collyer, 5.12.93; WHj and HR to, 4.2.94; WH and WHj to, 23.9.94; WHj to, 17.2.95, 2.7.95, 18.11.95, 3.3.96, 14.3.96; HR to, 22.6.95; WHj to Charles Collyer, 25.6.95; Robert Bye collects barley, 9.10.95; HR to, 15.3.96; HR with cousins and Mr Bird to, 11.8.97
beer deliveries, **322**, **323**:
1793: 21.10.93, 21.11.93, 20.12.93
1794: 4.1.94, 25.1.94, 21.2.94, 18.3.94, 9.5.94, 14.6.94, 22.7.94, 4.9.94, 20.9.94, 11.10.94, 12.11.94, 24.12.94
1795: 7.2.95, 27.2.95, 20.3.95, 23.4.95, 30.5.95, 25.7.95, 20.8.95, 9.10.95, 18.11.95
1796: 22.1.96, 16.3.96, 15.4.96, 24.5.96, 12.8.96, 29.9.96, 6.12.96
1797: 27.2.97, 12.5.97, 21.6.97, 11.8.97

Gunthorpe (*cont.*)
malt deliveries: 5.3.94, 24.4.94, 27.6.94, 20.9.94
timber collected: 12.11.94, 2.7.95, 30.7.95, 18.11.95, 22.1.96; from Charles Collyer, 10.1.97:
see also Pleasance, David; Pleasance, Robert
gutter bricks, *see* bricks
Gwynn (Gwiyn), A., with Robert Bartell at Hs', 24.8.94

H

Haddon (Hadden), William (?d.1809 aged 61), Holt plumber, glazier and painter; his two men repair pipe to backs, 10.5.97; with his man paints Hs' keeping room, 18.7.97
Hall, Captain, *see* Hall, 'Captain' Thomas
Hall, Edward (d.1797), innkeeper of Crown, Weybourne, tied house; brings clock to Hs, 3.1.95; at Hs', 28.12.95: *see also* Weybourne, beer deliveries
Hall, Mrs Elizabeth (d.1818 aged 56), née Frary, wife of 'Captain' Thomas; haymaking for Hs, 10.7.94, 25.7.95
Hall, Mrs Martha, née Hardy, 2nd wife of Edward; Thomas Baldwin collects beer, 9.10.97
Hall, 'Captain' (Capt.) Thomas (d.1808 aged 86), Hs' labourer; off work, 25.5.95, 29.5.95
brewing: 13.2.94; drawing off beer, 16.2.94, 30.4.95
building work [as 'Captain' Hall]: laying foundations for cart house, 12.2.94; loading bricks, 24.2.94; carting gravel, 8.5.94; cleaning bricks, 28–29.5.94
building work [as Thomas Hall]: collecting bricks, 14.10.93; laying foundations for cart house, 8.2.94
dressing barley: 10.1.95, 10–11.2.95, 13–14.3.95, 16.3.95, 2–3.4.95; dresses and collects own corn, 12.2.95
gardening: 16.2.95, 7–8.4.95, 14.4.95, 28.4.95, 30.4.95, 8–9.5.95, 11–12.5.95, 14.5.95, 16.5.95
harrowing: 21.4.94, 5–6.5.94, 16.4.95
harvesting: 31.8.95, 1–5.9.95, 8–9.9.95, 11–2.9.95, 17.9.95, 19.9.95
hedging: 7–11.4.95, 13.4.95, 17–18.4.95, 21–22.4.95, 24–25.4.95, 27.4.95
jobs [as 'Captain' Hall]: 25.10.93, 31.10.93, 30–31.5.94, 26.1.95, 2.5.95, 4.5.95; collects turnips, 18.10.93; at work in yards, 1.11.93, 9.5.94; loading bark, 7.11.93; throwing mould from river, 7.2.94; burning couch grass, 28.3.94; collects hay, 18.4.94; at work in Brewhouse Pightle, 2.6.94; weeding, 4–5.6.94; carting mud from pond, 23–28.6.94,

Hall, 'Captain', jobs (*cont.*)
30.6.94, 11.7.94; mucking out pigs, 27.1.95; sets thorns round newly planted tree, 21.3.95; collects stones, 15.4.95; unloading cinders, 16.4.95, 28.4.95; dressing grass seed, 22.4.95; at mould cart, 23.4.95; tying faggots, 1.5.95; in meadow, 18–23.5.95, 28.5.95; hoeing turnips, 10.9.95; laying barley stack, 16.9.95; haymaking, 19.9.95
jobs [as Thomas Hall]: at work in yards, 29.10.93, 5.7.94; moves stack into barn, 8.3.94; hedging, 20.4.95; harrowing, 21–22.4.94; ploughing, 25.4.94, 12.6.94; sowing, 28.4.94; carting stones, 7.5.94; ? at work in Brewhouse Meadow, 18.6.94; at mud cart, 1–3.7.94, 12.7.94; haymaking, 4.7.94, 10.7.94; chopping sticks, 3.7.94; gardening, 15.5.95; harvesting, 7.9.95; thatches Hs' wheat stack, 6.9.97
muck carting/spreading [as 'Captain' Hall]: 17–19.10.93, 21–22.10.93, 2–3.12.93, 3.2.94, 4.6.94, 14.6.94, 13.4.95
muck carting/spreading [as Thomas Hall]: 15–17.1.94, 3.6.94, 11.6.94, 16.6.94
ploughing: 23.10.93, 26.4.94, 29.4.94, 21.6.94, 7.3.95, 29.4.95
screening: malt, 14.4.95, 16.4.95; wheat, 5.5.95
threshing, **132**:
1794: 14–15.11.94, 17–19.11.94, 27–29.11.94, 1–6.12.94, 10–13.12.94, 15–20.12.94, 22.12.94, 24.12.94, 26–27.12.94, 29.12.94, 31.12.94
1795: 1–2.1.95, 6–9.1.95, 13–17.1.95, 19–24.1.95, 28–29.1.95, 2.2.95, 17–21.2.95, 24.2.95, 9–12.3.95, 17.3.95, 19–20.3.95, 23–28.3.95, 30–31.3.95, 1.4.95, 14–16.9.95, 18.9.95
Hammond (Hammon), John, Field Dalling/Saxlingham horse doctor; bleeds one of Hs' horses, 28.1.95; his bill taken to Field Dalling by HR, 8.9.96; summoned from Saxlingham by Gunton Thompson, 22.3.97
Hanault (Hannant), Miss, part of large party at Hs', 1.1.94
harness, *see* horses
Hardy, Mary Ann (1773–1864) (Miss H.), **257**, **284**, **287**, **388**, daughter of William, sister of WHj, HR's cousin; wallpapers bedroom, 26–27.5.96; ill, 2.7.96
church and meeting attendance:
Briston meeting, **188**: 8.10.97
Cley meeting: 9.3.96, 26.3.96, 9.7.97, 22.10.97
Holt Church: 19.1.94, 16.3.94, 21.6.95, 29.11.95, 1.5.96, 13.8.97; confirmed, 4.7.94
Letheringsett Church: 15.2.95, 25.2.95, 3.4.95, 23.10.96, 1.1.97, 19.2.97, 14.5.97,

Hardy, Mary Ann, church and meeting attendance, Letheringsett Church (*cont.*)
21.5.97, 28.5.97, 2.7.97, 23.7.97, 6.8.97, 3.9.97, 17.9.97, 15.10.97
helping with family business: with family to Bayfield, 7.10.96
to Holt:
1794: 31.1.94, 17.3.94, 5.4.94, 19.4.94, 25–26.4.94, 3.5.94, 10.5.94, 17.5.94, 26.5.94, 31.5.94, 12.7.94, 30.7.94, 2.8.94, 26.8.94, 12–13.9.94, 25–27.9.94, 18.10.94
1795: 10.1.95, 19–20.1.95, 29.1.95, 14.2.95, 24.2.95, 28.2.95, 27.3.95, 18.4.95, 15.5.95, 23.5.95, 8.6.95, 10.6.95, 11.8.95, 29.8.95, 19.9.95, 22.9.95, 3.10.95, 14.11.95, 16.11.95, 24.11.95, 5.12.95, 15.12.95, 16.12.95, 26.12.95
1796: 22–24.2.96, 27.2.96, 5.3.96, 7.3.96, 12.3.96, 24.3.96, 11.4.96, 16.4.96, 23–24.4.96, 26.4.96, 7.5.96, 14.5.96, 1.8.96, 5.8.96, 20.8.96, 29.8.96, 1.10.96, 11.10.96, 13.10.96, 29.10.96, 3.11.96, 5.11.96
1797: 14.1.97, 24.1.97, 4.2.97, 10.2.97, 3.3.97, 8.4.97, 22.4.97, 8.7.97, 29.7.97, 31.7.97, 4.8.97, 8.8.97, 26.8.97, 23.9.97, 25.10.97
fair: 25.4.97
market: 16.11.93, 30.11.93, 14.12.93, 8.2.94, 1.3.94, 3.5.94, 24.5.94, 15.8.95, 20.9.94, 7.3.95, 16.1.96, 25.6.96, 16.9.97
social activities: rides out with family, 12.11.93, 13.5.94, 16.5.94, 3.5.96, 10.9.96; with family at Thomas Temple's, 13.12.93, 1.5.94, 10.9.94, 19.12.94, 13.1.97; with family and friends to Holt ball, 30.12.93; Mr Baker's, 13.1.94, 3.2.94; with family and friends to Mr Davy, 17.1.94, 8.2.97; with family at Mr Forster's, 7.2.94, 23.4.94, 27.5.94, 11.12.94, 26.2.95, 22.4.95, 29.4.95, 13.5.95, 17.9.95, 19.11.95, 19.1.96, 22.4.96, 20.6.96, 21.7.96; with family and friends to Sheringham, 21.3.94, 20.5.94, 27.7.95, 24.9.95, 29.6.96, 19.6.97, 10.8.97; with family to Guestwick, 17.6.94; with family at Cook Flower's, 24.6.94, 31.8.95, 27.4.96; with family to dinner at Mr Baker's, 15.7.94; with family at Mr Burrell's, 6.8.94, 13.4.95, 14.12.95, 26.5.96, 16.8.96; with family to Cromer, 4.9.94, 16.9.96, 5.9.97; with WHj and Flowers to Holkham, 7.10.94; with family at Mr Johnson's, 12.1.95, 23.2.97; with family to Cley, 25.3.95; with WHj to Stody, 3.4.95; Mr Sheldrake's, 14.5.95, 22.2.97; with family to Weybourne, 11.6.95; with family to Southrepps, 23.9.95; with family to Mr Bartell, 20.1.96, 24.8.96, 30.12.96; with family to tea at King's Head, Letheringsett, 19.8.96; with

Hardy, Mary Ann, social activities (*cont.*)
family to seaside, 9.11.96, 14.8.97; Mr Savory's, 22.12.96, 3.1.97; with family to Saxlingham, 21.4.97; with family to Mr Sales, 3.10.97
Weybourne Camp: with WHj welcomes Artillery at Briningham, 9.6.95; with family and friends to, 17.6.95, 14.7.95, 12.8.95, 28.4.95
visits: with Charlotte Bartell to Norwich, 8.8.94; with family to Norwich, 6.9.94, 8–10.5.95, 7–9.10.95, 21.5.96; Whissonsett, 13.11.94–7.12.94, 26.5.95, 18–19.5.96, 20–22.10.96, 14.12.96, 28–31.3.97, 30.5.97–13.6.97; with WHj to Cook Flower, 5–6.1.95; with WHj and Mary Raven to Sheringham, 11–12.12.95; to Fakenham, 21.1.96; returns from Mr Forster, 13.5.97

Hardy, Mrs Mary (1733–1809) (Mrs H.), **21**, **52**, **110**, **136**, **160**, **177**, **195**, **232**, **262**, **289**, **298**, **357**, **388**, **406**, née Raven, wife of William, mother of William jnr, aunt of HR; washing, 14.1.94
church and meeting attendance:
Briston Chapel [Briston meeting]: 11.6.97
Briston meeting, **188**, [? Calvinistic Methodist until mid-1795, then Wesleyan Methodist]: 4.1.95, 11.1.95, 1.3.95, 8.3.95, 22.3.95, 5.4.95, 12.4.95, 26.4.95, 10.5.95, 17.5.95, 24.5.95, 31.5.95, 7.6.95, 14.6.95, 21.6.95, 5.7.95, 12.7.95, 19.7.95, 16.8.95, 13.9.95, 20.9.95, 27.9.95, 25.10.95, 27.8.97, 24.9.97, 8.10.97
Cley meeting [Wesleyan Methodist]:
1795: 8.11.95, 22.11.95, 29.11.95, 20.12.95, 25.12.95, 27.12.95
1796: 3.1.96, 17.1.96, 24.1.96, 31.1.96, 14.2.96, 21.2.96, 28.2.96, 6.3.96, 9.3.96, 20.3.96, 26.3.96, 27.3.96, 3.4.96, 10.4.96, 17.4.96, 24.4.96, 1.5.96, 15.5.96, 22.5.96, 29.5.96, 5.6.96, 12.6.96, 19.6.96, 26.6.96, 10.7.96, 17.7.96, 24.7.96, 7.8.96, 14.8.96, 21.8.96, 28.8.96, 4.9.96, 18.9.96, 2.10.96, 9.10.96, 23.10.96, 30.10.96, 13.11.96, 20.11.96, 27.11.96, 11.12.96, 25.12.96
1797: 8.1.97, 22.1.97, 5.2.97, 12.2.97, 19.2.97, 26.2.97, 19.3.97, 26.3.97, 2.4.97, 16.4.97, 23.4.97, 30.4.97, 7.5.97, 14.5.97, 28.5.97, 4.6.97, 25.6.97, 2.7.97, 16.7.97, 23.7.97, 30.7.97, 6.8.97, 20.8.97, 3.9.97, 10.9.97, 17.9.97, 1.10.97, 15.10.97, 22.10.97
Hunworth meeting: 15.11.95, 6.12.95, 13.12.95, 13.3.96
Letheringsett Church: 23.3.94, 9.11.94, 3.4.95, 10.5.95, 1.1.97

Hardy, Mrs Mary (*cont.*)
helping with family business: with WH and WHj to Hindolveston, 24.10.93; with WH and WHj out for day, 25.3.94; with family to Cley, 29.9.94, 2.10.94; with family to Bayfield, 7.10.96; with WH to Holt Heath Farm, 4.1.97, 23.2.97; with WHj to Cley, 10.7.97
to Holt with family:
1793: 5.11.93
1794: 17.1.94, 1.3.94, 7.3.94, 5.4.94, 26.4.94, 10.5.94, 17.5.94, 4.7.94, 12.7.94, 2.8.94, 29.8.94, 12–13.9.94, 8.11.94, 22.11.94, 1–2.12.94
1795: 10.1.95, 29.1.95, 27.3.95, 23.5.95, 9–10.6.95, 29.8.95, 22.9.95, 3.10.95, 26.12.95
1796: 20.2.96, 24.2.96, 26.4.96, 7.5.96, 14.5.96, 1.8.96, 29.8.96, 1.10.96, 29.10.96, 12.11.96, 6.12.96
1797: 14.1.97, 4.2.97, 10.2.97, 3.3.97, 8.4.97, 29.7.97, 23.9.97
fair: 25.4.97
market: 3.5.94, 24.5.94, 16.1.96, 23.1.96: *see also* to Holt *above*
illness: 27.6.94, 9.11.94, 31.12.94, 14.7.95; injured in chaise accident at Swanton Novers, 3.7.94
social activities with family: Thomas Temple's, 3.2.94, 1.5.94, 10.9.94, 19.12.94, 28.1.96, 13.1.97; Mr Forster's, 23.4.94, 11.11.94, 22.4.95, 29.4.95, 13.5.95, 17.9.95, 19.1.96, 22.4.96, 20.6.96, 21.7.96; rides out, 16.5.94, 2.1.95, 10.9.96; Cook Flower's, 24.6.94, 31.8.95; Mr Baker's, 15.7.94; Mr Burrell's, 6.8.94, 13.4.95, 14.12.95, 16.8.96, 23.5.97; Cley, 25.3.95; Weybourne, 11.6.95; Weybourne Camp, 8.7.95; Southrepps, 23.9.95; Mr Bartell's, 20.1.96, 24.8.96, 30.12.96; Lower Sheringham, 29.6.96; Salthouse, 25.7.96; King's Head, Letheringsett, 19.8.96; Cromer, 16.9.96; Mr Savory's, 22.12.96; Fakenham, 20.4.97; Mr Sales's, 3.10.97
visits: to Whissonsett with family, 28.10.93–2.11.93, 9–14.6.94, 15–23.2.95, 19–21.5.95, 17–22.8.95, 3.9.95, 5–9.1.96, 24–28.5.96, 13–18.3.97, 17–22.7.97; to Norwich with family, 6.9.94

Hardy, William (1732-1811) (Mr H.), **vii**, **76**, **158**, **257**, **303**, Letheringsett farmer, maltster and brewer, father of WHj, 10.10.93 *and throughout*

Hardy, William jnr (1770–1842) (WH), **82**, **113**, **188**, **197**, **332**, **363**, **372**, **374**, **391**, **404**, Letheringsett farmer, maltster and brewer, HR's cousin, 10.10.93 *and throughout*

harness, *see* horses

Harris (Harriss), Mr, [?London hop-factor]; with Mr Roxby to tea at Hs', 29.4.96

Harrison (Harison), Mrs, of Cley; dines with Hs, 8.10.95

Harron, *see* Herring, Mrs

harrowing, by Hs' men, **43**; flag harrow collected by Robert Bye from Mr Forster, 5.2.94; William Lamb and Thomas Baldwin laying flags, 10.3.96; in turnips, 9.8.96; in wheat stubble, 12.11.96; heaping couch grass, 17.3.97; yard, 21.9.97; in pea stubble, 27.9.97
1793–94: 14.10.93, 6.2.94, 13.2.94, 19–20.3.94, 26–27.3.94, 2.4.94, 18.4.94, 21.4.94, 22.4.94, 26.4.94, 5.5.94, 29–31.5.94, 13–14.6.94, 14.7.94
1794–95: 16.10.94, 29.10.94, 17.3.95, 21.3.95, 28.3.95, 30.3.95, 16–17.4.95, 21–22.4.95, 25.4.95, 27–28.4.95, 2.5.95, 6–7.5.95
1795–96: 20–21.10.95, 27.10.95, 1.2.96, 16.2.96, 24.3.96, 25.3.96, 2.4.96, 7.4.96, 25.4.96, 27.4.96, 6.5.96, 26.5.96, 23.6.96, 29.6.96
1796–97: 20.9.96, 3.10.96, 13.10.96, 27.10.96, 31.10.96, 11.11.96, 18.1.97, 16.2.97, 21.2.97, 10–11.3.97, 30–31.3.97, 7–8.4.97, 14–15.4.97, 6.5.97, 23.6.97
1797–98: 5.10.97, 17.10.97
Bell's Acre: 10.4.97
Five Acres: 21.4.94, 1.7.96, 10.4.97, 19.4.97
Furze Closes: 5.2.94, 25.3.94, 21.4.94, 9.3.95, 10.4.95, 24.9.95, 14–15.2.97, 10.4.97, 18.4.97, 25.10.97; Hill Close: 28.10.93
Holt Heath Farm: 23.3.97, 29.3.97, 1.7.97, 29.7.97
Six Acres: 10.3.96

harvests, **101**:
1794: men dine at Hs' on first day, 10.8.94; men reaping wheat in Hill Close, 11–12.8.94; men reaping, 13.8.94; men reaping in Bell's Acre, 14.8.94; WHj and men carrying wheat and barley, 15.8.94; men getting up wheat, men mowing wheat in Bell's Acre and barley in Furze Closes, M. Gallant gathering, 18.8.94; men collecting wheat and mowing, 19.8.94; men mowing and collecting, boy raking in Bell's Acre, 20.8.94; men mowing and collecting barley, John Thompson driving mare from top of stack, 21.8.94, 28.8.94; men mowing and collecting, 22–23.8.94, 25.8.94; men raking, 23.8.94, 28.8.94; wheat stored in barn, 25.8.94; men turning and collecting barley and raking, 27.8.94; WHj driving mare, 28.8.94; men gathering largess, 30.8.94; WHj and HR at men's harvest supper at King's Head, Letheringsett, 6.9.94
1795: men mowing barley in Furze Closes, 31.8.95, 1–2.9.95; men gathering and carrying barley, 5.9.95; men and Susan Lamb

harvests, 1795 (*cont.*)
gathering barley in Furze Closes, 7.9.95; men working in barn, 7.9.95; men raking, 8.9.95, 10.9.95, 19.9.95; men collecting barley, 8–9.9.95, 17.9.95; men mowing barley in Five Acres, 11-12.9.95; men get up rakings in Five Acres, 22.9.95; John Ramm gathering largess, 26.9.95; harvest supper at King's Head, 26.9.95
1796, **296**: men reaping wheat, 20.8.96, 22–26.8.96, 2–3.9.96; William Dobson cutting peas, 20.8.96; men cutting peas, 23–27.8.96; men turning sheaves, 29.8.96; men turning peas, 31.8.96; men turning wheat and peas, 2.9.96; men collecting wheat, 2–3.9.96, 8.9.96; men collecting peas, 5–6.9.96, 8.9.96; Gunton Thompson pitching peas, Nicholas Woodhouse and Elizabeth Chasteney in barn, boy riding horse, 5.9.96; men finish reaping wheat, 6.9.96; men mowing barley, 7–10.9.96; men collecting barley, 12.9.96, 14.9.96; barley collected from field and Furze Closes, 12.9.96; men drag raking and gathering up rakings, harvest finishes, 16.9.96; William Lamb and Thomas Baldwin gathering largess and to harvest frolic, 17.9.96
1797: men reaping wheat, 11–12.8.97, 14.8.97, 23.8.97, 26.8.97; men dine at Hs' on first day, 13.8.97; William Dobson cutting peas, 14.8.97; men mowing barley, 18–19.8.97, 21.8.97, 26.8.97; men collecting wheat, 22–23.8.97; men mowing barley in Furze Closes, 24.8.97; men mowing barley in Five Acres, 25.8.97; men mowing barley at Holt Heath Farm, 28.8.97; men gathering and pitching peas and in barn, 29.8.97; men collecting barley, 30.8.97; Gunton Thompson turning peas and barley, Mrs Thompson gathering barley in Bell's Acre, 30.8.97; men driving barley home from Furze Closes, Gunton Thompson pitching barley, men in barn, boy riding horse in barn, Mary Parr raking behind wagon, 31.8.97; men turning barley, 1–2.9.97; men turning wheat, 2.9.97; men loading wheat, Thomas Youngman pitching wheat, men stacking wheat, Mr Sheldrake helping, wheat harvest finished, 4.9.97; men collecting peas, 4–5.9.97; men collecting barley, 5–6.7.97; Mrs Thompson gathering barley, 6–7.9.97; boy riding horse on goaft, Thomas Hall thatching wheat stack, 6.9.97; men collecting barley from Five Acres, 7.9.97; men driving barley from Holt Heath Farm, boy raking behind wagon, 8.9.97; men drag raking, 9.9.97; Robert Bye and Gunton Thompson gathering largess, 9.9.97; men collect rakings from Six Acres, 13.9.97

Hase, William (1767–1841), Saxthorpe blacksmith, ironfounder, clockmaker and water-pump engineer; at Hs', 29.8.95; at work on brewery pump, 8–10.9.95; with Edmund Devereux puts new pump to work, 11.9.95
hase, *see* hedges
Hawkins, Mr, of King's Lynn; with wife, Mr and Mrs Savory and Miss Howard to tea at Hs', 5.5.97
Hawkins, Mrs, of King's Lynn; with husband, Mr and Mrs Savory and Miss Howard to tea at Hs', 5.5.97
hay:
carting: on wagon by Hs' men and Elizabeth Hall, 10.7.94; by men, 11.7.94; Thomas Baldwin driving and unpitching hay wagon, 18.7.96; Mrs Thompson raking behind wagon, 21.7.96; men loading, carting and unpitching hay, 21.7.97; unloaded, 14.10.97
collection: by Hs' men, 29.1.94, 3.7.94, 24.9.94, 29.9.94, 21.7.95, 24–25.7.95, 16.7.96, 18.7.96, 22.7.96, 19.7.97, 22.7.97; from Furze Closes, 20.7.96; from Holt Heath Farm, 12.10.97
cutting: 18.10.97
making: by Hs' men, 2.7.94, 4–5.7.94, 7.7.94, 9.7.94, 6–7.7.95, 10.7.95, 13–14.7.95, 16.7.95, 19.9.95, 29.9.95, 4–5.7.96, 7–8.7.96, 12–13.7.96, 15.7.96, 18.7.96, 3–5.10.96, 7–8.10.96, 10.10.96, 8.7.97, 10.7.97, 12–15.7.97, 17.7.97, 19–20.7.97, 6.10.97; by village women, 25.7.95, 4–5.7.96, 7–8.7.96, 12–13.7.96, 3.10.96, 7.10.96, 7–8.7.97, 10.7.97, 12.7.97, 14.7.97, 6.10.97; by Hs' maids, 5.7.96; prevented by bad weather, 6.7.96; John Ramm drag raking, 15.7.96; WHj gives haymakers beer after work, 20.7.97
purchase: collected by Hs' men from Mr Forster, 14.3.94, 18.4.94; viewed by WH and WHj at Edgefield, 18.6.94; by WH from Mr King of Holt, viewed by WHj and Thomas Boyce, 9.7.94; brought by Hs' men from Briston, 18–19.2.95; unloaded by men, 23.2.95, 3–5.8.95; brought by Hs' men from Thomas Temple, 23.4.95; bought by WHj, 21.7.95; bought by WH and WHj at Edgefield, 31.7.95; brought by Hs' men from James Dyball of Edgefield, 23.4.96; collected by Hs' men from Edgefield, 20–21.7.96; 11 loads sent by Mr Forster, 20.7.96; 18 loads sent by Mr Forster from Lime Kiln Field, 21.7.96; Mr Forster finishes sending hay, 22.7.96; Mr Forster's crop viewed by WH and William Lamb, 29.7.96
sale: load carried to Thomas Atwood at Holt, 16.4.96
stacking: by Hs' men, 15.7.96, 18.7.96, 20–21.7.96, 20–22.7.97; Mr Forster's men help-

hay, stacking (*cont.*)
ing, 20–22.7.96; Thomas Boyce thatches stack, 1.8.96
storage: John Ramm working in hay house, 25.8.94; hay house cleaned, 13.7.96, 15.7.96; loose hay from stack brought to hay chamber, 23.7.96:
see also grasses

heather (ling), collected from Holt Heath Farm by Robert Bye for underdrain, 26.1.97

hedges, hase clipped by Thomas Boyce, 27.8.96; William Holman ditching in Furze Closes, 17.4.97; brakes collected by Hs' men, 9–10.8.97
repair (stopping gaps) by Hs' men:
Furze Closes: 31.3.95, 7.4.95, 17–18.4.95, 20–21.4.95, 24.4.95, 19.11.95
meadow: 11.4.95
Six Acres: 7–9.4.95
unspecified fields: 18–19.3.94, 8–12.4.94, 28.7.94, 4.8.94, 26.11.94, 1–4.4.95, 8.4.95, 10–11.4.95, 13.4.95, 22.4.95, 25.4.95, 27.4.95, 21.3.96, 19.9.96, 4.4.97, 8.5.97:
see also furze; thorns

Hempstead-by-Holt (Hempsted), Norf., Thomas Boyce and boy collect stones, 7.1.94; WHj to, 25.6.94; WHj and HR go skating, 25.1.95

Hempton Green Fair, Norf., HR to, 17.5.96

Henderson, Mr, Newcastle upon Tyne flour merchant; out with WHj on business, 9–10.9.95; with WH to Ryburgh and Whissonsett, 11.9.95; with WH to Wells, 12.9.95

Herring, J., Hs' labourer; threshing, 17–18.11.96; casting clay, 15–16.12.96; filling clay cart at Holt Heath Farm, 17.12.96, 19.12.96; planting fir trees at Holt Heath Farm, 25.2.97; sowing oats, 23.3.97; working at Holt Heath Farm, 24.3.97; cutting hay, 18.10.97

Herring, John (d.1810 aged 61), **107**, Norwich merchant and shawl manufacturer, Sheriff of Norwich 1786, Mayor of Norwich 1799; with John Buckle at Hs', 19.8.95

Herring, John jnr, of Norwich; with mother and Forsters to tea at Hs', 2.5.96: *see also* Herring, Master

Herring, Master, [? son of John]; to tea at Hs', 30.4.95, 1.6.97: *see also* Herring, John jnr; Shearing, Master

Herring (Harron), Mrs [? Rebecca (d.1827 aged 81), née Buckle, wife of John]; with Forsters to tea at Hs', 18.7.94, 24.4.95, 15.8.95, 2.5.96, 2.9.96; with Bartells to tea at Hs', 6.5.95

Herring, William jnr (? d.1853), with Mrs Forster to tea at Hs', 18.1.94

Hildolwestone, *see* Hindolveston

Hill, Robert, **6**, innkeeper of Fishing Boat, E. Runton; orders four barrels of nog, 9.9.94: *see also* East Runton

Hill Close, Saxlingham field in Furze Closes, farmed by Hs; grasses carted, 15.10.93; muck carted from heap, 17–18.10.93; men collect turnips, 18.10.93; ploughed by Hs' men, 23.10.93, 17–19.8.95, 14.10.95; Robert Bye harrowing, 28.10.93; Hs' men reaping wheat, 11–12.8.94: *see also* Furze Closes

Hindolveston (Hildolwestone, Hindolvestone, Hindonvestone), Norf., WH, MH and WHj to, 24.10.93; John Cademy fetches timber, 30.11.93; Mr Bare tries to hire public house, 11.7.94; Mr Fox at Hs' with barley sample, 17.9.94; WHj to, 4.4.95, 24.10.96
beer deliveries, **12**, **13**:
1793: 25.10.93, 26.11.93, 31.12.93
1794: 4.3.94, 10.4.94, 2.6.94, 12.7.94, 15.8.94, 16.9.94, 29.9.94, 13.10.94, 18.10.94, 3.11.94, 26.11.94, 4.12.94
1795: 2.1.95, 15.1.95, 5.2.95, 27.2.95, 19.3.95, 18.4.95, 27.5.95, 10.6.95, 17.7.95, 1.8.95, 26.9.95, 1.10.95, 17.10.95, 26.11.95, 5.12.95
1796: 16.1.96, 23.1.96, 22.3.96, 3.5.96, 12.5.96, 12.7.96, 27.7.96, 23.9.96, 27.10.96, 6.12.96
1797: 23.1.97, 24.2.97, 5.4.97, 8.5.97, 13.6.97, 22.7.97, 13.9.97
loading: 25.9.95

Hindringham (Hinderingham), Norf., **233**,
beer deliveries:
1793: 30.10.93, 23.12.93
1794: 8.2.94, 21.3.94, 3.5.94, 25.6.94, 25.7.94, 28.8.94, 14.10.94, 20.11.94
1795: 14.2.95, 21.4.95, 2.7.95, 22.8.95, 12.10.95, 26.12.95
1796: 27.2.96, 11.5.96, 23.7.96, 29.8.96, 4.11.96
1797: 28.1.97, 12.4.97, 1.6.97, 24.7.97, 21.8.97, 10.10.97:
see also Chapman, William

hobbies, *see* horses

hoeing (howing), by Hs' men:
furrows: 19.5.97, 22.5.97; in Six Acres, 20.5.97
turnips:
1794: 7–8.7.94, 15–19.7.94, 21–24.7.94, 28.7.94, 29–31.7.94, 1–2.8.94, 4–9.8.94, 26.8.94, 1–2.9.94, 4–6.9.94, 8.9.94
1795: 22.8.95, 24–27.8.95, 10.9.95
1796: 26–30.7.96, 3.8.96, 6.8.96, 11–12.8.96, 15–18.8.96, 27–28.9.96, 26–28.7.97, 31.7.97, 7–9.8.97

hogs, *see* pigs

Holkham, Norf., **117**, **283**, WHj, MA and Mr and Mrs Cook Flower to, 7.10.94; Mr and Mrs Thomas William Coke at Hs', 23.6.96

Holman (Hollman), William, Hs' labourer;
brewing:
1796: 11.10.96, 19.10.96, 26.10.96, 5.11.96, 10.11.96, 17.11.96, 23.11.96, 2.12.96, 9.12.96, 20.12.96, 28.12.96
1797: 10.1.97, 19.1.97, 27.1.97, 2.2.97, 11.2.97, 16.2.97, 22.2.97, 27.2.97, 3.3.97, 6.3.97, 9.3.97, 13.3.97, 21.3.97, 25.3.97, 1.4.97, 6.4.97, 13.4.97
cleaning vessels: 16.2.97, 4–5.3.97
working in brewery: 9.11.96, 2.1.97, 10.1.97, 20.1.97, 15.2.97, 7.3.97, 10.3.97, 20.3.97, 27.3.97, 31.3.97, 5.4.97, 12.4.97, 14.4.97
cleansing: 11.11.96, 1.3.97, 5.3.97, 8.3.97, 3.4.97
drawing off beer: 11.11.96, 1.3.97, 8.3.97, 2.4.97
harrowing, 27.10.96, 17.3.97, 29–31.3.97, 7–8.4.97, 15.4.97
haymaking, 30.9.96, 1.10.96, 3–4.10.96
jobs:
1796: 12–15.10.96, 17–18.10.96, 20–22.10.96, 24–25.10.96, 28.10.96, 2–4.11.96, 7–8.11.96, 14–16.11.96, 18–19.11.96, 21–22.11.96, 24–26.11.96, 28–30.11.96, 3.12.96, 5–8.12.96, 10.12.96, 12.12.96, 15–17.12.96, 19.12.96, 22–24.12.96, 26–27.12.96, 29–31.12.96
1797: 2.1.97, 7.1.97, 10–11.1.97, 16.1.97, 21.1.97, 24–25.1.97, 31.1.97, 1.2.97, 7.2.97, 10.2.97, 13.2.97, 20.2.97, 23–25.2.97, 28.2.97, 2.3.97, 17–18.3.97, 22–23.3.97, 3.4.97, 7–8.4.97, 10.4.97, 15.4.97
hoeing turnips, 27–28.9.96; threshing, 5–8.10.96; unloading cinders, 27.10.96; malting, 5.11.96; collects stubble, 12.11.96; working at Holt Heath Farm, 29.11.96; filling mould cart at Holt Heath Farm, 13–14.12.96; scraping road, 7.1.97; collects sash windows from Weybourne, 14.1.97; collects and unloads furze from Holt Heath Farm, 17.1.97, 28.1.97, 18.2.97; collects barrels from Holt, 20.1.97; delivers malt to Thornage, 20.1.97; working in Furze Closes, 23.1.97, 11.4.97, 18–22.4.97; carting turnips, 24.1.97, 30.1.97, 4.3.97; working in meadow, 26.1.97, 6.2.97, 17.2.97, 21.2.97, 14.3.97, 16.3.97; collects wood, 28.1.97, 30.1.97, 29.3.97; filling gravel cart, 3–4.2.97, 8–9.2.97; spreading gravel in meadow, 7.2.97; heaping couch grasses, 17.3.97; sowing seeds in meadow, 20.3.97; sowing grass seeds, 25.3.97; collecting stones off Holt Heath Farm land, 27.3.97; rolling at Holt Heath Farm, 29.3.97; unloads straw, 29.3.97; hedging, 4.4.97, 17.4.97; cleaning yard, 11.4.97

Holman, William (*cont.*)
muck carting/spreading: 28–29.10.96, 31.10.96, 1.11.96, 1.12.96, 3.12.96, 15–17.12.96, 19.12.96, 3–6.1.97, 17.1.97, 28.1.97

Holt, Norf., **7**, **8**, **20**, **39**, **70**, **88**, **112**, **160**, **248**, Mr Margetson at Hs', 13.10.93; WHj to Mr Johnson, 16.10.93; WHj to supper with Mr Thomas, 26.11.93; Letheringsett Purse Club moves to, 13.1.94; Robert Raven to, 23.1.94; William Dobson views King's Head, Letheringsett, 29.1.94; WHj with Mr Symonds to, 20.5.94; Hs with Miss Symonds to, 23.5.94, 26.5.94, 31.5.94; Robert Bye takes long dinner break, 17.6.94; Hs with Mr Watson to, 8.8.94; MA with Mrs Forster to, 26.8.94; HR drives Davys to, 19.8.95; Nathaniel Raven jnr to, 11.11.95; Hs with Ravens to, 5.12.95, 15–17.12.95, 2.4.96, 16.4.96, 23–24.4.96, 26.4.96, 3.11.96, 5.11.96, 4.8.97, 8.8.97; contract for building Letheringsett House of Industry awarded to Mr Dawson, 15.1.96; WHj with Misses Wymer and Dowson to, 29.1.96; WHj draws off wine, 2.2.96; Hs with Miss Custance to, 22–24.2.96, 27.2.96, 5.3.96; Ann and Rose Raven to Hs from, 15.4.96; Hs with Henry Goggs to, 25.4.96; Artillery arrives, 15.6.96; WHj with John Smith to, 25.6.96; Ravens and Miss Rowden to, 7.7.96; Hs with Mrs Phillis Goggs to, 1.8.96; Hs with William Thackwray to, 4.10.96, 8.10.96, 29.10.96, 5.11.96; WH discusses Robert Johnson's affairs with Messrs Bignold and Smith, 14.10.96; HR takes brewery horse to Mr Love, 16.11.96; Gunton Thompson to, 25.11.96; WHj and William Thackwray go skating, 5.12.96; WH to meeting for augmentation of Militia, 7.12.96; Robert Bye takes wheels for Mr Dawson to, 12.1.97; Hs and Ravens to Mr Johnson, 23.2.97; William Raven to, 2.7.97; HR and Joseph Erratt to, 30.9.97
assemblies: *see* Holt, balls *below*
balls and dances: WHj to assembly, 10.11.94; WHj to Mrs Overton's benefit, 31.12.94; HR to, 3.10.95, 20.4.96, 29.9.96, 29.9.97; WHj to, 29.9.96
beer deliveries:
1793: 12.10.93, 16.10.93, 22.10.93, 30.10.93, 12.11.93, 4–5.12.93, 12.12.93, 19.12.93, 23.12.93
1794: 7.1.94, 9.1.94, 21.1.94, 7.2.94, 12.2.94, 25.2.94, 27.2.94, 5.3.94, 15.3.94, 24.3.94, 8.4.94, 10.5.94, 16.5.94, 22.5.94, 7.6.94, 17.6.94, 27.6.94, 4.7.94, 23.7.94, 29.7.94, 12.8.94, 27.8.94, 1.9.94, 3.9.94, 9.9.94, 11.9.94, 22–23.9.94, 30.9.94, 9–10.10.94, 13.10.94, 21.10.94, 25.10.94, 8.11.94, 11.11.94, 19.11.94, 21.11.94, 29.11.94,

Holt, beer deliveries, 1794 (*cont.*)
13.12.94, 16.12.94, 20.12.94, 23.12.94, 29.12.94
1795: 12.1.95, 20.1.95, 22.1.95, 29.1.95, 6.2.95, 14.2.95, 17.2.95, 20.2.95, 23.2.95, 10.3.95, 21.3.95, 27.3.95, 4.4.95, 6.4.95, 11.4.95, 17–18.4.95, 2.5.95, 5.5.95, 13.5.95, 19.5.95, 26.5.95, 29.5.95, 5.6.95, 20.6.95, 25–26.6.95, 7.7.95, 11.7.95, 16.7.95, 18.7.95, 23.7.95, 29.7.95, 1.8.95, 10.8.95, 12.8.95, 18.8.95, 24–25.8.95, 2.9.95, 5.9.95, 10.9.95, 12.9.95, 18.9.95, 21–22.9.95, 1.10.95, 3.10.95, 10.10.95, 16.10.95, 24.10.95, 26.10.95, 28–29.10.95, 4–5.11.95, 14.11.95, 17.11.95, 20–21.11.95, 1.12.95, 3.12.95, 5.12.95, 7.12.95, 11.12.95, 15.12.95, 19.12.95, 21–22.12.95, 26.12.95, 29.12.95, 31.12.95
1796: 6.1.96, 9.1.96, 14.1.96, 19.1.96, 27.1.96, 3.2.96, 11.2.96, 17.2.96, 22–24.2.96, 27.2.96, 2.3.96, 7.3.96, 17.3.96, 21.3.96, 24.3.96, 31.3.96, 4.4.96, 8.4.96, 11.4.96, 14.4.96, 19.4.96, 22.4.96, 28–29.4.96, 3.5.96, 9.5.96, 19.5.96, 21.5.96, 24.5.96, 8.6.96, 11.6.96, 21.6.96, 27.6.96, 4.7.96, 6.7.96, 19.7.96, 27–28.7.96, 4.8.96, 10.8.96, 12.8.96, 22.8.96, 29.8.96, 10.9.96, 16.9.96, 26.9.96, 3.10.96, 10.10.96, 19–20.10.96, 24.10.96, 28.10.96, 1.11.96, 10–11.11.96, 15.11.96, 24.11.96, 3.12.96, 7.12.96, 26.12.96
1797: 2.1.97, 5.1.97, 7.1.97, 11.1.97, 14.1.97, 25.1.97, 7.2.97, 14.2.97, 18.2.97, 24–25.2.97, 16.3.97, 8.4.97, 12.4.97, 17–18.4.97, 21.4.97, 27.4.97, 29.4.97, 1.5.97, 6.5.97, 12.5.97, 19.5.97, 27.5.97, 29.5.97, 1.6.97, 9.6.97, 19.6.97, 22.6.97, 26.6.97, 5–6.7.97, 12–13.7.97, 22.7.97, 27.7.97, 3.8.97, 10.8.97, 14.8.97, 30.8.97, 2.9.97, 12.9.97, 18.9.97, 20.9.97, 2–3.10.97, 6.10.97, 10-11.10.97, 21.10.97, 24.10.97: *see also* Holt, public houses, *below*
bowling green: *see* Holt, public houses, *below*
club: *see* Holt, public houses, *below*
fair: *see* fairs
farm: *see* Holt Heath Farm
goods collected from by Hs' men: barley, 30.10.93; empty barrels, 12.12.93; window frames, 10.4.94; new cart, 7.6.94; wagon after repair, 17.7.94; oats and new wagon, 21.11.94; six barrels from coopers, 3.12.94; goods bought by Hs at Mrs Jewell's sale, 3.12.94; shrubs from James Moore's, 10.4.95, 24.10.96; wheels for delivery to Cley, 18.5.95; clay and bricks, 6.8.96; beer cart, 10.8.96; wagon, 12.8.96; bricks, 22.12.96, 2.9.97; barrels, 20.1.97; lime, 21.9.97; nails, 14.10.97

Holt (*cont.*)
goods delivered to by Hs' men: lime to Black Boys, 22.10.93; beer to Mr Johnson, 20.11.93; gravel to Black Boys, 9.1.94; wagon for repair, 15.7.94; barrel staves, 21.11.94; wagon wheels, 9.12.94; hay to Thomas Atwood, 16.4.96; beer cart to Mr Dawson for repair, 13.3.97; lime, sand and bricks to Black Boys, 5.7.97: *see also* Holt, beer deliveries *above*
HR to: 25.12.93, 19.3.94, 8.5.94, 25.11.94, 13.2.95, 4.3.95, 29.3.95, 10.4.95, 16.4.95, 16.6.95, 31.8.95, 16.11.95, 25.11.95, 16.12.95, 26–27.4.96, 29.4.96, 12.5.96, 3.7.96, 15.11.96, 18.1.97, 10.10.97, 16.10.97
Hs to:
1793: 11.10.93, 16–17.10.93, 4–5.11.93, 18–19.11.93, 21.11.93, 27.11.93, 12.12.93, 17.12.93, 20.12.93, 25.12.93
1794: 6–7.1.94, 10.1.94, 12.1.94, 17–18.1.94, 21–22.1.94, 25.1.94, 27.1.94, 31.1.94, 3.2.94, 6.2.94, 11.2.94, 14.2.94, 18–19.2.94, 1.3.94, 7.3.94, 17.3.94, 21.3.94, 3.4.94, 5.4.94, 8.4.94, 19.4.94, 25–26.4.94, 3.5.94, 5.5.94, 8.5.94, 10.5.94, 17.5.94, 20.5.94, 23.5.94, 26.5.94, 31.5.94, 4.6.94, 16.6.94, 20.6.94, 30.6.94, 4–5.7.94, 10.7.94, 12.7.94, 14.7.94, 26.7.94, 29.7.94, 30.7.94, 2.8.94, 8.8.94, 26.8.94, 29.8.94, 30.8.94, 3.9.94, 7.9.94, 9–10.9.94, 12–13.9.94, 23–27.9.94, 3.10.94, 11.10.94, 18.10.94, 25.10.94, 8.11.94, 22.11.94, 25.11.94, 1–2.12.94, 9.12.94, 12.12.94, 26.12.94
1795: 8–10.1.95, 18–20.1.95, 22.1.95, 29.1.95, 31.1.95, 3.2.95, 7.2.95, 14.2.95, 24–25.2.95, 28.2.95, 11.3.95, 16.3.95, 27–28.3.95, 31.3.95, 1.4.95, 4.4.95, 7.4.95, 9.4.95, 11.4.95, 13.4.95, 18.4.95, 25.4.95, 14–15.5.95, 20.5.95, 23.5.95, 31.5.95, 8–10.6.95, 13.6.95, 16.6.95, 20.6.95, 27.6.95, 4.7.95, 9.7.95, 11.7.95, 8.8.95, 11.8.95, 27.8.95, 29.8.95, 3.9.95, 19–20.9.95, 22.9.95, 3.10.95, 10.10.95, 16–17.10.95, 2.11.95, 11.11.95, 14–16.11.95, 24.11.95, 3.12.95, 12.12.95, 14.12.95, 19.12.95, 22.12.95, 26.12.95
1796: 20–21.1.96, 13.2.96, 20.2.96, 7–8.3.96, 12.3.96, 21.3.96, 24.3.96, 26.3.96, 2.4.96, 11.4.96, 7.5.96, 9.5.96, 12.5.96, 14.5.96, 28.5.96, 30–31.5.96, 6.6.96, 8.6.96, 11.6.96, 15.6.96, 18.6.96, 2.7.96, 11.7.96, 16.7.96, 23.7.96, 30.7.96, 4–5.8.96, 15.8.96, 20.8.96, 24.8.96, 27.8.96, 29.8.96, 1.9.96, 3.9.96, 15.9.96, 17.9.96, 24.9.96, 1.10.96, 11.10.96, 13–15.10.96, 22.10.96, 27.10.96, 5.11.96, 7.11.96, 9.11.96, 12.11.96, 14–15.11.96, 19.11.96, 25–26.11.96, 3.12.96, 6–7.12.96, 10.12.96, 21.12.96, 23–24.12.96, 31.12.96

Holt, Hs to (*cont.*)
1797: 14.1.97, 16.1.97, 21.1.97, 24.1.97, 28.1.97, 4.2.97, 10–11.2.97, 16.2.97, 25.2.97, 1.3.97, 3.3.97, 8.3.97, 11.3.97, 13.3.97, 18.3.97, 21.3.97, 24.3.97, 1.4.97, 7–8.4.97, 10.4.97, 15.4.97, 22.4.97, 26.4.97, 28–29.4.97, 4.5.97, 6.5.97, 13.5.97, 15.5.97, 20.5.97, 22.5.97, 27.5.97, 2–3.6.97, 5.6.97, 7.6.97, 22.6.97, 24.6.97, 1.7.97, 4–5.7.97, 8.7.97, 15.7.97, 22.7.97, 24.7.97, 27–29.7.97, 31.7.97, 2.8.97, 5.8.97, 12.8.97, 19.8.97, 26.8.97, 2.9.97, 9.9.97, 11.9.97, 23.9.97, 30.9.97, 3.10.97, 7.10.97, 14.10.97, 19–20.10.97, 25.10.97:
see also HR to *above*
market: *see* markets; *also* Holt, Hs to *above*
postchaises: *see* chaises, postchaises
public houses, **59**: WH to venison feast, 30.7.94; WHj to turtle feast, 3.9.94; WHj to bowling-green feast, 29.10.95; James Skiffins orders beer, 24.4.96; WHj dines at Holt book club, 10.1.97
Black Boys, **38**: beer delivered, 16.10.93, 22.10.93; lime delivered, 5.7.97; gravel delivered, 9.1.94; sand and bricks delivered, 5.7.97: *see also* Clark/Clarke, Mr; Skiffins, James William; Wakefield, Francis
Bull: *see* Baker, Joseph; Bulling, William
Dolphin: *see* Atwood, Thomas
Feathers: *see* Banyard, Charles; Sheppard, Mrs Elizabeth
King's Head: *see* Crafer, Henry
White Lion: *see* Howard, John; Skiffins, James William
see also Holt, beer deliveries
races: WH and WHj to horse race, 27.9.97
roads: Robert Bye's beer cart breaks down, 9.6.95; Hs' boy removes stones from Holt–Letheringsett lane, 22.6.95
school: *see* school
sessions: *see* justices; sessions
theatre: *see* plays
windmill: *see* mills
Holt Church, St Andrew, **121**, **129**; Ann Raven to, 19.1.94, 24.4.96; MA and HR confirmed, 4.7.94; Mary Raven to, 30.11.94, 6.12.95; Rose Raven to, 24.4.96; marriage of Mr Burrell, 2.8.96; Hs to, 4.12.96; Nathaniel Raven jnr to, 12.3.97, 3.9.97; Miss Riches to, 13.8.97
HR to:
1793: 13.10.93
1794: 11.5.94, 8.6.94, 20.7.94, 3.8.94, 30.11.94
1795: 15.3.95, 29.3.95, 11.10.95
1796: 17.1.96, 28.2.96, 15.5.96, 12.6.96, 19.6.96, 3.7.96, 14.8.96, 21.8.96, 4.9.96, 18.9.96, 25.9.96, 2.10.96, 30.10.96, 6.11.96, 27.11.96
Holt Church, HR to (*cont.*)
1797: 15.1.97, 29.1.97, 26.2.97, 19.3.97, 9.4.97, 23.4.97, 4.6.97, 11.6.97, 30.7.97, 13.8.97, 3.9.97, 1.10.97, 8.10.97
MA to: 19.1.94, 16.3.94, 21.6.95, 29.11.95, 24.4.96, 1.5.96, 13.8.97
WH to: 11.1.95, 21.6.95, 24.4.96, 1.5.96, 22.5.96, 19.6.96
WHj to:
1793: 13.10.93
1794: 19.1.94, 16.2.94, 16.3.94, 27.4.94, 11.5.94, 8.6.94, 20.7.94, 3.8.94, 31.8.94, 14.9.94, 26.10.94, 30.11.94, 28.12.94
1795: 11.1.95, 1.3.95, 15.3.95, 29.3.95, 5.4.95, 24.5.95, 21.6.95, 16.8.95, 30.8.95, 13.9.95, 11.10.95, 15.11.95, 22.11.95, 29.11.95, 6.12.95, 27.12.95
1796: 3.1.96, 10.1.96, 17.1.96, 24.1.96, 14.2.96, 21.2.96, 28.2.96, 27.3.96, 24.4.96, 1.5.96, 22.5.96, 5.6.96, 12.6.96, 19.6.96, 26.6.96, 3.7.96, 17.7.96, 24.7.96, 31.7.96, 14.8.96, 11.9.96, 18.9.96, 25.9.96, 23.10.96, 30.10.96, 20.11.96, 27.11.96, 11.12.96
1797: 1.1.97, 15.1.97, 29.1.97, 12.2.97, 26.2.97, 12.3.97, 26.3.97, 23.4.97, 7.5.97, 14.5.97, 21.5.97, 28.5.97, 4.6.97, 11.6.97, 18.6.97, 2.7.97, 16.7.97, 13.8.97, 20.8.97, 27.8.97, 3.9.97, 10.9.97, 24.9.97, 8.10.97, 15.10.97, 22.10.97
Holt Heath Farm (Bulling's Farm, Holt Farm, the new farm), **317**, **330**:
clay spreading: 15.12.96, 17.12.96, 19.12.96
furze collected: 12.1.97, 17.1.97, 26–28.1.97, 18.2.97
harrowed: 23.3.97, 29.3.97, 1.7.97, 29.7.97
harvesting barley: 28.8.97, 8.9.97
haymaking: 11–14.7.97, 6.10.97, 12.10.97
Hs to: MH, 4.1.97, 23.2.97; WH, 21.11.96, 4.1.97, 23.2.97, 23.3.97, 28.3.97, 2.6.97, 15.9.97, 22.9.97; WHj, 21.11.96, 2.1.97, 30.1.97, 25.2.97
muck delivery/spreading: 29–30.11.96, 1.12.96, 5–6.12.96, 8.12.96, 15–17.12.96, 19.12.96, 30–31.12.96, 4.1.97, 12.1.97, 16–17.1.97, 27–28.1.97, 6.2.97, 11.2.97, 22.4.97, 24.4.97, 26.4.97
ploughed: 29.11.96, 6.2.97, 22–23.2.97, 28.2.97, 10.3.97, 15–18.3.97, 20–23.3.97, 25.3.97, 27–28.3.97, 27.7.97, 29.7.97, 31.7.97, 3–4.8.97, 7.8.97, 18.9.97, 21.9.97; William Lamb unable to plough when tack breaks, 20.2.97; Robert Bye ploughing in barley, 27.3.97; Robert Bye ploughing on old ground, 28.3.97; William Lamb collects plough, 5.10.97
sowing: oats, 27.3.97; barley, 28.3.97

Holt Heath Farm (*cont.*)
special tasks: mould spreading, 13.12.96; heather for underdrain collected, 26.1.97; fir trees planted, 25.2.97; William Holman collecting stones off land, 27.3.97; rolling, 29.3.97
work unspecified: 29.11.96, 24.3.97, 22–24.5.97, 26.5.97, 1–2.6.97, 5.6.97, 4.7.97, 7.7.97, 27–28.7.97, 3.8.97, 5.8.97, 8.8.97, 11–12.8.97, 14.8.97, 15–16.9.97, 18.9.97, 20.9.97, 21–23.9.97, 25.9.97

Hooper, Mr, with wife at large tea party at Hs', 18.8.95

Hooper, Mrs, with husband at large tea party at Hs', 18.8.95; at Hs', 19.8.95

hoops, for barrels, **179**, **421**; Mr Webb of Pattesley sends bunches to Hs, 6.6.95; Thomas Baldwin collects 18 bunches from Fakenham, 7.6.96: *see also* barrels

hoppers, *see* flour

hops, **184**, 42 lb delivered by Thomas Baldwin to Gunthorpe, 21.11.93; WHj, HR and Gunton Thompson clean hop chamber, 5.7.94; seven bags collected by Thomas Boyce from Blakeney, 8.1.95; 10 bags collected by Robert Bye from Wells, 23.11.95; seven bags collected by William Lamb from Wells, 2.1.96; weighed by Thomas Baldwin, 6.1.96; hop merchant at Hs', 12.1.96, 17.10.97; hop-presser from Brisley collected by Thomas Baldwin at Fakenham, 13.1.96; 10 bags collected by William Lamb from Blakeney, 2.1.97; 10 bags weighed by HR, 16.1.97

horses:
accidents, **7**, **276**, **277**: Hs' horse falls while pulling chaise at Swanton Novers, 3.7.94; Mrs Booty's swept under footbridge when Glaven floods, one mare drowned, 4.6.96; William Lamb unable to plough when tack breaks, 20.2.97
borrowed: Hs' old mare lent to Mr Sheldrake, 30.8.95
care: horse taken by HR to Brinton, 16.10.93; Minor seen by Daniel Jex, 3.1.94; Robert Bye's cart horse taken by HR to Saxlingham, 6.5.94; Thomas Boyce treats horse from John Walden, 31.10.94; horse bled by Mr Hammond, 28.1.95; Thomas Baldwin's shod, 22.8.95; Gunton Thompson grinding barley for, 12.11.95; chaise horse trimmed by WHj and HR, 10.12.95; sick filly seen by Love, 30.12.95; mare taken to Love, 14.4.96; Love docks Hs' colt, 1.9.96; HR takes brewery horse to Love, 16.11.96
foaling, **366**: mare's foal dies, 1.6.97
harness, **326**: repaired by Luke Basham, 10.10.93, 22.4.94, 17–18.3.95, 21.5.95;

horses, harness (*cont.*)
chaise harness cleaned, 5.11.94; collected, 21.5.95; cleaned by William Pinchin, 12.11.96; oiled by William Lamb, 20.12.96; repaired by Mr Scott and man, 20.12.96
pasturing, **168**: colts collected by HR and Robert Bye from Winch, 23–24.11.93
purchase: Hs sell Molly to Mr Sharpens in exchange for black filly, 1.7.94; James Skiffins offers mare for sale, 18.11.94; WHj takes Mr Webster's on trial, 23.2.95; WHj buys Mr Sharpens', 25.2.95; Mr Love brings mare for sale, 31.8.96; Mr Love exchanges mare with WH for William Lamb's old horse, 1.9.96
race: WH and WHj to at Holt, 27.9.97
riding horses: HR to Whissonsett on Minor, 12.1.94; HR to Bodham on colt, 11.8.96; WHj on horseback while family in chaise, 10.9.96; WH's taken to Field Dalling, 9.5.97
sale: Robert Bye takes Jack to Wells and brings back horse from John Walden, 18.9.94
teams: John Ramm to Cromer with head team, 17.10.93; Robert Bye's place taken by William Lamb, 23.12.95, 27.12.95; Mr Forster's three teams bring hay to Hs, 20–21.7.96
working horses, **26**, **47**, **48**, **76**, **152**, **306**: Robert Raven puts hobby into whiskey, 23.1.94; Molly pulls WHj and HR to Wells in malt cart, 31.1.94; WHj puts little mare into malt cart, 3.7.94; mare pulls harvest wagon with barley stack, 21.8.94, 28.8.94; black filly pulls beer cart, 25.9.94; colt put to plough and harrow, 22.4.95; colt put to beer cart, 20.5.95; boy rides horse during harvest, 5.9.96, 31.8.97, 6.9.97; WHj and HR put colt to cart, 19.9.96; HR puts Leader the colt into chaise, 22.9.96:
see also stables

Horstead (Horstd), Norf., Mr Nash to dinner with Hs, 21.3.97

house, Hs', **11**, **18**, **37**, **61**, **157**, **230**, **235**, **257**, **349**, **393**, **404** [Rawlings, later Letheringsett Hall from *c.*1800]; best parlour painted by WH, 8.7.94; Mr Bunnett's men working in kitchen, 3.12.94; lumber room cleaned by HR, 15.1.96; counting house in yard demolished by Mr Bunnett's bricklayers and labourers, 16.3.96; HR helps MA to wallpaper her room, 26–27.5.96; sash windows installed at front by Mr Bunnett and boy, 23.3.97; keeping room painted by Mr Haddon and man, 18.7.97
chimneys (chymnays, chymneys), **406**: on fire, 15.2.95; swept by stonemason in keeping room, 16.2.95
see also garden; yards, front

house of industry, *see* Letheringsett
Howard, John, **59**, **138**, innkeeper of White Lion, Holt and Pitt Arms, Burnham Market; with WH to Burnham, 5.1.95; his son orders beer and brings £30, 10.9.96
Howard, Miss, of W. Rudham; with Savorys to tea at Hs', 6.1.97, 20.1.97, 2.2.97, 9.2.97, 5.5.97; to supper, 12.7.97; to tea, 27.8.97, 30.8.97, 17.9.97
Howlett (Howlet), Mrs Ann, **380**, **381**, innkeeper of Angel, Bale, tied house; orders beer from Hs, 17.6.94: *see also* Bale, beer deliveries
HR, *see* Raven, Henry
Humphrey, Thomas 'Duke' (d.1795), Letheringsett labourer; reaping for Hs in Bell's Acre, 14.8.94; tying faggots, 1.4.95
Hunworth, Norf., Thomas Baldwin delivers cartwheels, 7.6.94; HR to, 7.6.94; Thomas Baldwin collects cartwheels, 9.6.94; WHj to, 24.6.96; Nicholas Woodhouse delivers half barrel of mild, 29.7.96; William Lamb takes beer cart for repair, 10.8.96
  meeting: MH to, 15.11.95, 13.3.96; MH and HR to, 6.12.95, 13.12.95
hurdles (hurdels), arranged by WHj, HR and boy in Brewhouse Pightle, 17.4.95
Huson, Mr, at Hs', 16.5.95, 22.8.95, 1.6.96

I

illness, **298**:
  bruising: of MH's face in road accident, 3.7.94
  gout (gught): WH, 4.2.94, 6–8.2.94, 31.12.94, 10–11.11.95, 14.11.95, 16.11.95, 27–30.1.96, 1–6.2.96, 8.2.96, 21.10.96; recovers, 9–12.2.96, 15.2.96; in hand, 19.2.97
  swelling in legs: Nicholas Woodhouse, 4.12.95
  toothache: Thomas Baldwin, 1.9.96
  unspecified:
    MA: 2.7.96
    MH: 27.6.94, 9.11.94, 31.12.94, 14.7.95
    WH: 10.10.94, 31.7.96, 10.2.97
    others: Miss Symonds, 28.5.94; Mr Burrell, 16.4.97
    workforce:
      Thomas Baldwin, 14.1.94, 17.1.94, 29.7.94, 31.7.94, 13–14.8.94, 23.10.94, 20.7.95, 7.11.95, 25.5.96, 12.8.96, 26.4.97, 21–22.6.97, 18–19.10.97
      boy, 25.1.94, 27.1.94, 8–9.1.95, 4–6.3.95
      Robert Bye, 12.2.94, 9.4.94, 21.8.94, 23.8.94, 29.9.94, 3.12.94, 23–24.1.95, 16.3.95, 7–9.2.97, 9.5.97
      John Ramm, 20.3.94, 3.11.94, 3.12.94, 5–6.2.95, 6.3.95, 31.3.95, 1.9.95, 6.10.95, 26–27.1.96, 14.3.96, 13.4.96, 15–16.4.96, 28.4.96, 5.5.96
illness, unspecified, workforce (*cont.*)
      Gunton Thompson: 27.4.97
industrial accidents, *see* accidents, industrial
industry, house of, *see* Letheringsett
injuries, *see* accidents
inns, *see* Holt, public houses; public houses
iron, Thomas Baldwin carts iron cinders into Glaven, 9.6.96
Ives, Mrs Ann (d.1836 aged 75), wife of Meshack; orders beer from Hs, 18.9.94
Ives, Meshack (Meach) (d.1816 aged 64), innkeeper of Queen's Head, Brampton, tied house; at Hs', 4.11.94

J

Jack, *see* horses
Jackson, Thomas, Cley coal merchant; Hs' men collect coal, 15.9.95, 20.4.96, 9.5.96, 25.5.96, 2.6.96, 9.6.96, 8.8.96, 11.8.96, 19.8.96, 24.8.96, 12.5.97, 17.6.97, 15.7.97, 16.8.97, 27.9.97
Jacobs [?Jacob], Mr [?Clement], with stranger at Hs', 27.7.96
James [no surname], miller, helps Hs with harvest, 17.9.95
Jarvis (Jarves), Mr, Guestwick farmer; to supper with Hs, 23.6.94; reckons with Hs, 23.6.94, 7.7.95; disputes barley measurement, 16.10.95; dines with Hs, 18.9.97
Jeckell, Francis, helps Hs with harvest, 7.9.95
Jeckell (Jickell), Mr T., helps Hs with harvest, 17.9.95
Jennis, Misses Mary Pleasance (b.*c.*1774) and Elizabeth (b.1779), of Holt; to tea at Hs', 13.6.94, 3.5.95, 2.10.95, 29.4.96, 4.11.96; with Mary Raven to Hs, 13.11.95
Jewell (Juell), Mrs Sarah (d.1794 aged 70/76), **129**, née March, of Holt; Thomas Baldwin collects Hs' purchases from her sale, 3.12.94
Jex, Daniel, Letheringsett blacksmith/farrier; sees Hs' horse Minor, 3.1.94
Jex, John (d.1797 aged 52), Letheringsett blacksmith; collects Hs' beer cart after breakdown, 27.1.94; lays iron arm in beer cart, 29.1.94; George Dawson repairs Hs' chaise at, 16.3.95
jobbers, *see* dealers
Jodrell (Joddrel), Henry (1752–1814), JP, **111**, **137**, **165**, **234**, of Bayfield Hall, barrister, Recorder of Gt Yarmouth 1792–1813, MP for Gt Yarmouth 1796–1802, MP for Bramber, Suss. 1802–12, Deputy Lieutenant of Norfolk 1803; Thomas Boyce and boy collect furze from his hill, 2.1.95; his gardener inspects Hs' fruit trees, 9.6.96
Johnson, Anna (Ann) (1769–1829), Holt milliner, daughter of Revd William Tower; with

Johnson, Anna (*cont.*)
sister Deborah and Miss Davy to tea at Hs', 27.6.97: *see also* Johnson, Miss

Johnson, Deborah Judith (b.1772), Holt milliner, daughter of Revd William Tower; to tea at Hs', 3.5.95, 27.6.97

Johnson, John, Cley merchant; Hs' men collect lime, 5.11.93, 18.5.95, 24.10.95, 24.3.96

Johnson, Mary, *see* Burrell, Mrs

Johnson, Miss [?Anna]; with Mary Raven at Hs', 23.11.95

Johnson, Robert, innkeeper of Crown, Sheringham, tied house, formerly of Attleborough; dines with Hs, 16.3.95

Johnson, Revd William Tower (d.1799 aged 61/62), LLB, of Holt, formerly of Plumstead-by-Holt, Curate of Twyford 1766, Vicar of N. Barningham 1769–99, Rector of Beeston Regis 1772–99, Curate of Bessingham 1784, Curate of Runton 1784; WHj to, 16.10.93; Thomas Baldwin delivers beer, 20.11.93; WHj and MA to tea, 12.1.95, 23.2.97; Mr and Mrs Nathaniel Raven to tea, 23.2.97

Jordan (Jorden), John (d.1795 aged 52), **181**, innkeeper of Blue Bell, Wiveton, formerly of Edgefield; Robert Bye delivers beer, 6.11.93: *see also* Wiveton

jury, WHj on grand jury at Holt Quarter Sessions, 21.1.96

justices, **191**, **231**, **232**, **234**, **325**, WHj takes Gunton Thompson jnr before at Holt, 28.7.94: *see also* sessions; *also individual justices* Collyer, Charles; Coke, Thomas William; Jodrell, Henry

K

Keeler (Keeller), Thomas, Guestwick farmer; to supper with Hs and reckons, 23.6.94; with Mr Everitt to dinner at Hs', 25.11.94; with Mr Everitt and Miss Billing to dinner and supper at Hs' and to Weybourne Camp, 26.6.95; with Mr Everitt settles for year's barley, 27.6.96

keeping rooms, *see* Dobson, William, beer deliveries; house

Kelling, Norf., **316**, **363**, WH and WHj to, 28.7.96; WHj and HR to, 13.8.96, 23.7.97; WHj and William Lamb to, 17.5.97, 23.5.97; WHj to, 2.6.97; Robert Bye to, 16.8.97; Hs' men collect straw, 28–29.8.97

Kendle (Kendal), Charles, **113**, Thornage and Letheringsett farmer and later auctioneer; Robert Bye collects clay from his pit, 26.9.94, 18.1.97; his men cart muck from Hs' yard, 6.1.95, 10.1.95; at Hs', 29.5.96; with WHj to Norwich, 2.6.96; goes shooting with William Thackwray, 11.10.96, 19.10.96, 6.12.96; buys two pigs from Hs, 20.10.96

Kendle, J., with HR to Sharrington, 2.8.95

Kendle, Thomas, **221**, [?Thomas jnr (b.1777), of Sharrington Hall]; to tea with WHj, 26.4.96

Kettlestone, Norf., William Lamb collects 200 fir trees, 14.1.97
beer deliveries:
1793: 28.10.93, 17.12.93
1794: 13.2.94, 29.3.94, 2.5.94, 21.5.94, 18.6.94, 7.7.94, 22.7.94, 2.8.94, 22.8.94, 16.9.94, 11.10.94, 20.11.94
1795: 9.1.95, 6.3.95, 30.4.95, 15.6.95, 20.7.95, 27.8.95, 30.9.95, 16.11.95
1796: 8.2.96, 2.5.96, 13.6.96, 20.7.96, 18.8.96, 21.9.96, 26.10.96
1797: 14.1.97, 16.5.97, 26.6.97, 19.7.97, 16.8.97, 28.9.97:
see also Pearce, Matthew

Kilburn (Killburn), Mrs, with Mrs Mendham to tea at Hs', 2.6.95

kilns, *see* bricks; lime; malt-kiln

King, Robert, **298**, Holt farmer; sells six loads of hay to WH, 9.7.94

King's Head, *see* Holt, public houses; Letheringsett

kitchen, *see* house

labourers, employed by Hs; James Broughton jnr starts work at 7*s* 6*d* a week, 16.10.97: *see also* bricklayers; harvests; hay, making; workforce; *also individual labourers* Bransby, Joseph; Boyce, Thomas; Broughton, James; Broughton, James jnr; Fox, John; Hall, 'Captain' Thomas; Herring, J.; Holman, William; Moore, Charles; Moore, Jeremiah; Parsons, William; Pinchen, William; Platten, William; Starling, Samuel; Thompson, Gunton Chapman

lads, *see* boys

Lamb, Charles (b.1766), **178**, Cley tidewaiter and Letheringsett cordwainer, son of William; Robert Bye collects stones from, 5.6.95; works for Hs, 5.8.95; helps Hs with harvest, 17.9.95; working in malthouse, 5.6.96; helps Hs with haymaking, 18.7.96, 20–21.7.96

Lamb, Mrs Susan, née Ward, 2nd wife of William; helps Hs with harvest, 7.9.95

Lamb, William (d.1814 aged 73), **363**, Hs' farm servant, maltster, brewer and drayman; to Holt Fair, 25.4.96, 25.4.97; to Whit Monday dinner at Hs', 16.5.96, 5.6.97; to Weybourne Fair, 17.5.96; off work, 18.5.96, 23–24.12.96, 2.2.97, 5.6.97; leaves post as maltster to take Robert Bye's place in Hs' team, is replaced by John Ramm in malthouse, 27.12.95; his old horse exchanged for mare, 1.9.96; unable to plough

Lamb, William (*cont.*)
when tack breaks, 20.2.97; with WHj to Kelling, 17.5.97, 23.5.97
brewing:
1796: 8.1.96, 18.1.96, 1.2.96, 13.2.96, 15.3.96, 1.4.96, 9.4.96, 15.4.96, 26.4.96, 9.5.96, 23.5.96, 7.6.96, 20.6.96, 28.6.96, 18.7.96, 1.8.96, 15.8.96, 30.8.96, 14.9.96, 28.9.96, 5.10.96, 26.10.96, 10.11.96, 9.12.96
1797: 9.1.97, 27.1.97, 11.2.97, 22.2.97, 27.2.97 , 9.3.97, 16.3.97, 25.3.97, 20.4.97, 1.5.97, 5.5.97, 15.5.97, 23.5.97, 8.6.97, 20.6.97, 6.7.97, 2.8.97, 9.8.97, 17.8.97, 19.9.97, 4.10.97, 18.10.97
cleaning vessels: 6.1.96, 17.9.96, 5.3.97, 14.3.97
working in brewery: 29.12.96, 11.3.97, 29.4.97, 2.5.97, 5.5.97
cleansing beer: 26.1.96, 17.5.96, 24.5.96, 1.6.96, 22.6.96, 19.7.96, 11.11.96, 24.11.96, 5.3.97, 8.3.97, 23.3.97
collecting coal and cinders from ports:
1796: 23.1.96, 30.1.96, 9.2.96, 25.2.96, 1.3.96, 12.3.96, 5.4.96, 3.5.96, 25.5.96, 30.5.96, 20–21.6.96, 13.7.96, 28.7.96, 2.8.96, 8.8.96, 24.8.96, 3.10.96, 24.10.96, 18.11.96, 21.12.96, 29.12.96
1797: 7.2.97, 21.2.97, 24.3.97, 10.5.97, 14.6.97, 17.6.97, 30.6.97, 10.7.97, 1.8.97, 16.8.97
collecting other goods: barley, 24.10.96, 18.4.97; bricks, 6.8.96, 28.3.97, 20.9.97; cement, 17.6.96; clay, 30.1.96, 6.8.96, 29.8.96, 10.12.96; fir trees, 12.5.96, 14.1.97; furze, 16.1.97, 26.1.97, 28.1.97; hedging, 9–10.8.97; hops, 2.1.96, 2.1.97; lime, 24.3.96, 22.5.97, 17.10.97; malt, 16.8.96; oats, 14.2.97; sand, 21.3.96, 29.7.96, 22.5.97, 6.10.97, 17.10.97; stones, 3.2.96, 30.3.96, 8.6.96; straw, 25.3.97, 12.5.97, 28–29.8.97; turnips, 12.12.96; vetches, 19.7.96, 14.6.97, 26.7.97, 8.8.97; wood, 22.1.96, 31.12.96, 10.1.97, 28.1.97, 29.3.97
delivering beer:
1795: 28–31.12.95
1796: 2.1.96, 6–7.1.96, 9.1.96, 11.1.96, 14–16.1.96, 19.1.96, 20–23.1.96, 25–28.1.96, 30.1.96, 2–3.2.96, 6.2.96, 8–12.2.96, 15.2.96, 19–20.2.96, 22–23.2.96, 26–27.2.96, 29.2.96, 1–5.3.96, 12.3.96, 14.3.96, 16–17.3.96, 19.3.96, 21–23.3.96, 25.3.96, 28–29.3.96, 31.3.96, 4–5.4.96, 8–9.4.96, 11–14.4.96, 16.4.96, 18–19.4.96, 22–23.4.96, 27–30.4.96, 2–4.5.96, 7.5.96, 9–11.5.96, 13–14.5.96, 19–21.5.96, 24–25.5.96, 27.5.96, 30–31.5.96, 2.6.96, 7–

Lamb, William, delivering beer, 1796 (*cont.*)
8.6.96, 13–15.6.96, 18.6.96, 20–22.6.96, 25.6.96, 27.6.96, 29–30.6.96, 1–2.7.96, 4–9.7.96, 11–13.7.96, 16.7.96, 19.7.96, 22–23.7.96, 25–28.7.96, 30.6.96, 3–5.8.96, 10–13.8.96, 17–19.8.96, 22–24.8.96, 27.8.96, 29.8.96, 31.8.96, 1.9.96, 5.9.96, 7.9.96, 10.9.96, 12–13.9.96, 15–16.9.96, 19.9.96, 21–24.9.96, 26–27.9.96, 29–30.9.96, 3–4.10.96, 6–8.10.96, 10–12.10.96, 14.10.96, 18–20.10.96, 22.10.96, 24–25.10.96, 27–29.10.96, 1–2.11.96, 4–5.11.96, 9.10.96, 14–18.11.95, 21–22.11.96, 24–26.11.96, 28.11.96, 2.12.96, 5–7.12.96, 16.12.96, 19–20.12.96, 22.12.96, 27–28.12.96, 31.12.96
1797: 2–3.1.97, 7.1.97, 11.1.97, 13–14.1.97, 17.1.97, 21.1.97, 23.1.97, 25.1.97, 30–31.1.97, 7.2.97, 10.2.97, 13–14.2.97, 18.2.97, 21.2.97, 24–25.2.97, 27.2.97, 1–4.3.97, 6–7.3.97, 14.3.97, 16–17.3.97, 23–24.3.97, 28.3.97, 3.4.97, 5.4.97, 7–8.4.97, 11.4.97, 13–14.4.97, 18.4.97, 21.4.97, 24.4.97, 26–29.4.97, 1.5.97, 3.5.97, 8–13.5.97, 15–17.5.97, 19–20.5.97, 25–27.5.97, 29–31.5.97, 3.6.97, 6–10.6.97, 12–15.6.97, 17.6.97, 19.6.97, 21–24.6.97, 26–27.6.97, 29.6.97, 5–6.7.97, 8.7.97, 10–13.7.97, 15.7.97, 17–18.7.97, 22.7.97, 24–26.7.97, 28–29.7.97, 4.8.97, 8.8.97, 11.8.97, 15–16.8.97, 19.8.97, 21–22.8.97, 26.8.97, 30.8.97, 2.9.97, 8–9.9.97, 11–14.9.97, 18.9.97, 20.9.97, 22.9.97, 26–30.9.97, 2–3.10.97, 6–7.10.97, 9–14.10.97, 16.10.97, 20–21.10.97, 23–24.10.97
delivering other goods: gates, 12.5.96; hay, 16.4.96; lime, 27.5.97; malt, 8.6.97; straw, 9.2.96, 25.2.96; wood, 25.2.96
drawing off beer: 30.11.95, 13.1.96, 9.3.96, 28.3.96, 2.4.96, 24.4.96, 8.5.96, 15.5.96, 3.6.96, 20.9.96, 11.11.96, 12.12.96, 1.3.97, 8.3.97, 15.3.97, 2.4.97, 27.4.97, 4.5.97, 6.5.97, 19.6.97
harrowing: 16.2.96, 25.3.96, 7.4.96, 25.4.96, 27.4.96, 6.5.96, 23.6.96, 20.9.96, 3.10.96, 13.10.96, 31.10.96, 18.1.97, 16.2.97, 21.2.97, 11.3.97, 29.3.97, 19.4.97, 6.5.97, 1.7.97, 5.10.97, 25.10.97
harvesting: 20.8.96, 24–26.8.96, 2–3.9.96, 5–10.9.96, 14.9.96, 16.9.96, 18.8.97, 24–25.8.97, 28–31.8.97, 4–7.9.97, 13.9.97; gathers largess and to harvest frolic, 17.9.96; dines with Hs on first day, 13.8.97
haymaking: 4.7.96, 15.7.96, 18.7.96, 20–21.7.96, 8.10.96, 10.10.96, 12.7.97, 14–15.7.97, 19–21.7.97, 28.9.97, 12.10.97, 14.10.97
jobs, **326**: 31.12.95, 12.1.96, 1.3.96, 6.8.96,

Lamb, William, jobs (*cont.*)
9.8.96, 12.8.96, 20.9.96, 13.10.96, 3.12.96, 10.12.96, 21.12.96, 12.1.97, 18.3.97, 12.5.97, 20.5.97, 13.6.97, 3.7.97, 11.7.97; carting rocks to repair Sheringham jetty, 28.12.95; moves stack into barn, 11.2.96; carting sand, 26.3.96; carting stones and gravel, 2.4.96, 11.1.97, 1.2.97, 3.2.97, 8–9.2.97; carting cement, 16.5.96; unloading coal and cinders, 1.6.96, 30.12.96, 14.6.97, 27.9.97; working in garden, 22.6.96; cleans hay house, 13.7.96, 15.7.96; installs field gates, 26.7.96; with WH inspects Mr Forster's crops, 29.7.96; collects beer cart from Holt and takes it to Hunworth, 10.8.96; collects wagon from Holt, 12.8.96; collects door from Cley, 5.11.96; collects stubble from Furze Closes, 12.11.96; collects beer from Weybourne Camp, 17.11.96; takes ploughs to Holt Heath Farm, 29.11.96; collects gates from Furze Closes, 12.12.96; carting mould, 13–14.12.96; oils harness, 20.12.96; takes wagon to Saxlingham, 12.1.97; stacking furze, 18.1.97, 1.2.97; removes peas from barn, 20.1.97, 1.2.97; at work in meadow, 15.2.97, 17.2.97, 14.3.97; carting away couch grass, 21.2.97; greases beer carts, 5.3.97; turning barley, 8.3.97; unloading straw, 29.3.97, 29.8.97; to Coltishall, 4.4.97; carting thorns, 25.4.97; collects piano from Southrepps, 3.5.97; working in yard, 5.5.97; collects money from public houses at E. Runton and Sheringham, 6.6.97; cutting vetches, 10.8.97; collects plough from Holt Heath Farm, 5.10.97; tends livestock, 14.10.97

loading beer carts and wagons: his wagon loaded by Thomas Baldwin, 19.1.96
1796: 10.1.96, 14.1.96, 14.2.96, 2.3.96, 13.3.96, 22.3.96, 12.4.96, 29.4.96, 1.5.96, 3.5.96, 5.6.96, 13–14.6.96, 24.7.96, 29.7.96, 12.8.96, 12.9.96, 10.10.96, 13.11.96, 15.11.96, 4.12.96, 6.12.96
1797: 10.5.97, 29.5.97, 16.7.97, 20.8.97, 8.10.97, 15.10.97, 23.10.97

malting, **214**: 12.10.95, 14–17.10.95, 19–24.10.95, 26–31.10.95, 2–7.11.95, 10–11.11.95, 16–18.11.95, 20–21.11.95, 23–28.11.95, 30.11.95, 1–5.12.95, 7–12.12.95, 14–19.12.95, 21–24.12.95, 26.12.95; screening malt, 5.2.96

muck carting/spreading:
1796: 4–5.1.96, 27.1.96, 29.1.96, 18.2.96, 18.3.96, 7–8.4.96, 26.5.96, 28.5.96, 10.6.96, 17.6.96, 28.10.96, 31.10.96, 1.11.96, 28–30.11.96, 1.12.96, 3.12.96, 8.12.96, 15–17.12.96, 30.12.96
1797: 4–6.1.97, 16.1.97, 26.1.97, 28.1.97, 22.4.97, 24.4.97, 26.4.97, 23.6.97, 28.6.97

Lamb, William (*cont.*)
ploughing:
1795–96: 1.1.96, 6.1.96, 9.1.96, 4–5.2.96, 16–17.2.96, 20.2.96, 24.2.96, 8.3.96, 10–11.3.96, 4.4.96, 6.4.96, 20–21.4.96, 5–6.5.96, 14.5.96, 26.5.96, 23–24.6.96
1796–97: 1.10.96, 15.10.96, 17.10.96, 21.10.96, 3–5.11.96, 7–8.11.96, 15.11.96, 17.11.96, 19.11.96, 22.11.96, 24.11.96, 26.11.96, 29.11.96, 19–20.1.97, 24.1.97, 6.2.97, 23.2.97, 28.2.97, 10.3.97, 15.3.97, 18.3.97, 20–22.3.97, 27.3.97, 30–31.3.97, 10.4.97, 12.4.97, 14–15.4.97, 17.4.97, 1.5.97, 16.6.97, 30.6.97, 27.7.97, 29.7.97, 31.7.97, 3.8.97, 7.8.97, 30.8.97, 1.9.97, 21.9.97
1797–98: 5–6.10.97, 17.10.97, 19.10.97, 23.10.97

rolling: 11.3.96, 19.4.96, 1.6.96, 11–12.11.96, 29.3.97, 1.4.97

sowing: 11.3.96, 17.3.96, 8.4.96, 20–21.4.96, 27.4.96, 3.11.96, 8.11.96, 1.4.97, 12.4.97, 15.4.97, 17.4.97, 19.4.97

working at Holt Heath Farm: 22.5.97, 24–26.5.97, 1–2.6.97, 5.6.97, 4.7.97, 7.7.97, 5.8.97, 11–12.8.97, 14.8.97, 15–16.9.97, 23.9.97, 25.9.97

largess (larges, largis), tips collected at end of harvest by: Robert Bye, Thomas Baldwin, John Ramm and boy, 30.8.94; John Ramm, 26.9.95; William Lamb and Thomas Baldwin, 17.9.96; Robert Bye and Gunton Thompson, 9.9.97

Latten, William, **408**, **411**, Norwich common brewer; annual production figures, HR's endnotes

laundry, *see* washing

Leak (Leake), Ann (d.1803 aged 61), **70**, Holt milliner; goes out for ride with WHj, 24.4.97: *see also* Leak, Misses

Leak (Leake, Leek), Misses, Holt milliners; to tea with Hs, 17.7.94, 3.8.96, 29.9.96, 7.11.96, 22.11.96, 21.12.96, 22.1.97, 24.4.97, 2.6.97, 19.7.97, 4.9.97, 22.9.97, 2.10.97; to dinner with Hs, 25.11.96; to supper with Hs, 22.1.97

lectures, in evening at Letheringsett Church by Revd John Burrell, 6.9.94, 3.8.94, 17.8.94, 31.8.94, 14.9.94, 28.9.94, 23.11.94

Lee, James, collects fattening pig from Hs, 24.4.94

Lee, Mr, of Sharrington; William Lamb collects straw, 12.5.97

Letheringsett, Norf., **8**, **11**, **88**, **101**, **127**, **238**, **303**, **317**, Mary Raven and Misses Jennis walk to from Holt, 13.11.95; soldiers pass through on way to Sharrington, 20.12.95; large party of farmers passes through on way to Sharrington,

Letheringsett (*cont.*)
21.12.95; Mr Burrell passes through on way to Fakenham on wedding day, 2.8.96; Thomas Baldwin able to walk to, 17.2.97
house of industry, **197**, **294**, **295**: building contract awarded to Mr Dawson of Holt, 15.1.96; Hs and Burrell family to tea, 9.8.96
King's Head, **37**, **49**, **51**, **54**, **61**, **80**, **325**: viewed by William Dobson, 29.1.94; WH and WHj to election supper for Mr Coke's supporters, 1.6.96; door installed by builders, 10.11.96: *see also* Dobson, William; Mayes, Richard
parish (town) government: townspeople beat bounds of parish, 29.5.94; town meeting at King's Head, 18.4.97
road (rode), **3**, **51**, **77**, **99**, **165**, **230**, **233**, **372**, **373**, **393**, **397**: Thomas Hall carting muck out of street, 2.12.93; Hs' boy collects building stones from Holt Lane, 22.6.95; Hs' men remove stones from street, 27.6.95, 8.6.96; repaired by Thomas Boyce outside Hs' house, 4.2.96; scraped by William Holman, 7.1.97; cleaned by Thomas Boyce, 13.6.97; Thomas Boyce at work, 14.6.97:
see also accidents, road; brewhouse; farms; fields; Glaven, River; house; Letheringsett Church; malthouse; malt-kiln; malt-mill; mills
Letheringsett Church, St Andrew, **11**, **61**, **137**, **206**, **207**, **218**, **246**, **400**, services regularly attended by Hs and HR:
preacher: *see* Burrell, Revd John
services: Mr and Mrs Sales to, 24.8.94; Mr and Mrs Savory to, 15.1.97; none held, 11.1.95, 18.1.95, 15.11.95, 22.11.95, 29.11.95, 27.11.96, 16.4.97:
see also Burrell, Revd John; lectures; Letheringsett, parish government
Letheringsett Hall [Rawlings], *see* house
Letheringsett Hall Farm [Old Hall], *see* Cobon, James
lifts, *see* gates
lime, **365**, Robert Bye collects cement from kiln, 15.7.94
collected by Hs' men from:
Bayfield Hall estate: Mr Forster's, 16.10.93, 17.3.94, 26.5.94
Cley: from Mr Johnson, 5.11.93, 18.5.95, 24.10.95, 24.3.96
Holt: 21.9.97
kilns not specified: 19.2.94, 1.3.94, 11.3.94, 25.3.94, 1.4.94, 4.4.94, 14.4.94, 17.4.94, 25.6.95, 22.5.97, 2.10.97, 17.10.97
delivered by Hs' men to: John Lynes at Cley, 5.11.93; Sheringham public house, 27.5.97; Black Boys at Holt, 5.7.97:
see also cement; marl
Lime Kiln Field, Bayfield Hall; Mr Forster's teams bring hay to Hs from, 21.7.96
Lines, *see* Lynes
ling, see heather
liquor, for malting and brewing, *see* water
Little Snoring, *see* Snoring
Little Walsingham, *see* Walsingham
livestock, tended by William Lamb, 14.10.97: *see also* cows; geese; horses; pigs
Loades (Loads), Mary (d.1824 aged 68), **295**, of Letheringsett; at work in Hs' garden, 15.8.96
lock, installed by Thomas Youngman on Hs' coal house door, 12.9.94
London, **70**, **123**, **412**, beer delivered to Blakeney for shipping to, 15.11.94; rider at Hs', 16.10.95
Longden, Francis, **161**, innkeeper of Three Horseshoes, Briston, tied house; orders beer from Hs at Holt Fair, 25.11.93; Thomas Baldwin resolves problem with bill, 26.8.95: *see also* Briston, beer deliveries
Love, Mr [? Samuel (d.1822 aged 59)], Holt horse doctor; visits Hs' sick filly, 30.12.95; Thomas Baldwin takes mare to, 14.4.96; at Hs' with mare for sale, 31.8.96; docks Hs' colt and exchanges mare with WH for William Lamb's old horse, 1.9.96; HR takes brewery horse to, 16.11.96; with Balls family and Miss Bartell to tea at Hs', 18.4.97
Lower Sheringham, *see* Sheringham
Lynes (Lines), Mrs Edna/Edny (d.1800 aged 62), wife of John; orders four barrels of nog and one of sixpenny, 9.12.93; orders beer, 13.6.97: *see also* Cley, beer deliveries
Lynes (Lines), John (d.1800 aged 63), innkeeper of King's Head, Cley, tied house; Robert Bye delivers lime from Mr Johnson, 5.11.93; orders four barrels of nog and one of small beer from Hs, 22.11.93: *see also* Cley, beer deliveries

M

Mack, Miss, with Mrs Sheldrake and Miss Baker to tea at Hs', 8.7.97
magistrates, *see* justices
maidservants, Hs', **218**, **406**, maids depart, 10.10.94; two maids haymaking, 5.7.96; Sarah Turner departs, 10.10.96; maid starts work, 12.10.97
Maid's Head, *see* Hindolveston; North Walsham; Stalham
malt, **16**:
brought over to brewery: 27.3.94, 25.9.94, 9.10.94, 16.10.94, 24.10.94, 20.11.94, 15.12.94, 26.12.94, 12.2.95, 24.9.95, 6.10.95

malt (*cont.*)
cart: driven to Wells, 31.1.94; little mare put to, 3.7.94
culms (combs, cumbs): dressed by Hs' men, 25.10.93, 21.2.94, 3.7.94; sown by Thomas Baldwin, 10.1.94, 4.4.96; cast and screened by James Broughton, 30.1.95
ground by Hs' men for brewing:
1793: 14.10.93,21.10.93, 28.10.93, 4.11.93, 12.11.93, 18.11.93, 21.11.93, 27.11.93, 2.12.93, 7.12.93, 13.12.93, 19–20.12.93, 27.12.93
1794: 3.1.94, 10.1.94, 18.1.94, 24.1.94, 30–31.1.94, 6.2.94, 8.2.94, 13–14.2.94, 21.2.94, 27.2.94, 14.3.94, 21.3.94, 27.3.94, 28.3.94, 3–4.4.94, 10–11.4.94, 18.4.94, 24.4.94, 1–2.5.94, 8.5.94, 12–13.5.94, 17–18.5.94, 22.5.94, 31.5.94, 5.6.94, 13–14.6.94, 19–20.6.94, 26–27.6.94, 4.7.94, 14–16.7.94, 23–24.7.94, 1–2.8.94, 8.8.94, 15–16.8.94, 22–23.8.94, 29–30.8.94, 11–12.9.94, 18–20.9.94, 25.9.94, 2–3.10.94, 9–10.10.94, 14–15.10.94, 20–21.10.94, 25.10.94, 27.10.94, 1.11.94, 3.11.94, 8.11.94, 13–14.11.94, 20–21.11.94, 1–2.12.94, 9–10.12.94, 16.12.94, 26.12.94; all night by Gunton Thompson, 29.12.94
1795: 1–2.1.95, 12.1.95, 23.1.95, 30.1.95, 5–6.2.95, 12–13.2.95, 19–20.2.95, 4.3.95, 12.3.95, 20.3.95, 26–27.3.95, 16–17.4.95, 4.5.95, 9.5.95, 13–14.5.95, 19–20.5.95, 23.5.95, 27–28.5.95, 1–2.6.95, 15.6.95, 19–20.6.95, 26.6.95, 4.7.95, 13–14.7.95, 20.7.95, 27.7.95, 3.8.95, 12.8.95, 18.8.95, 25.8.95, 31.8.95, 9.9.95, 15.9.95, 19.9.95, 26.9.95, 1.10.95, 6.10.95, 9–10.10.95, 19.10.95, 24.10.95, 30.10.95, 7.11.95, 17–18.11.95, 23.11.95, 27.11.95, 2.12.95, 8.12.95, 14.12.95, 22–23.12.95, 30.12.95
1796: 6–7.1.96, 11.1.96, 15.1.96, 22.1.96, 5.2.96, 12.2.96, 16.2.96, 20.2.96, 1.3.96, 5.3.96, 11.3.96, 22.3.96, 28.3.96, 31.3.96, 4.4.96, 7–8.4.96, 11.4.96, 14.4.96, 18.4.96, 30.4.96, 14.5.96, 21.5.96, 27–28.5.96, 3.6.96, 10–11.6.96, 17–18.6.96, 24–25.6.96, 1–2.7.96, 16.7.96, 23.7.96, 28.7.96, 5–6.8.96, 13.8.96, 17–18.8.96, 26–27.8.96, 3.9.96, 13.9.96, 20.9.96, 27.9.96, 4.10.96, 10.10.96, 17–18.10.96, 25.10.96, 3–4.11.96, 9.11.96, 16.11.96, 22.11.96, 29.11.96, 1.12.96, 7.12.96, 27.12.96
1797: 4.1.97, 17.1.97, 25.1.97, 1.2.97, 9–10.2.97, 15.2.97, 20.2.97, 25.2.97, 2.3.97, 4.3.97, 8.3.97, 11.3.97, 20.3.97, 30.3.97, 5.4.97, 12.4.97, 19.4.97, 27.4.97, 2.5.97, 4.5.97, 13.5.97, 17.5.97, 22.5.97, 29.5.97, 5–6.6.97, 13.6.97, 17.6.97, 27.6.97, 4.7.97,

malt, ground by Hs' men for brewing, 1797 (*cont.*)
11.7.97, 17–18.7.97, 25.7.97, 31.7.97, 1.8.97, 7–8.8.97, 14–15.8.97, 22.8.97, 8–9.9.97, 15–16.9.97, 25–26.9.97, 2–3.10.97, 10.10.97, 17.10.97, 24.10.97
ground for retail sale and storage (bin):
1794: 14.7.94, 22.7.94, 9.8.94, 23.8.94, 21.11.94
1795: 6.1.95, 3.3.95, 2.4.95, 14.4.95, 20.5.95, 20.6.95, 21.8.95, 28.8.95, 6.10.95, 14.12.95, 22.12.95
1796: 11.3.96, 27.7.96, 2.8.96, 18.8.96
1797: 22.3.97, 27.4.97, 29.5.97, 17.7.97, 21.8.97, 26.9.97, 24.10.97
porter malt: dried, 10.4.95, 14.4.95, 8.2.96, 10.2.96; ground, 11.4.96
purchase: two last from John Ellis at Cley, 18.10.96
sale: ordered by Andrew Boswell, 17.11.95
delivered by Hs' men to:
Aldborough: 16.8.96
Bale: 20.9.94, 16.8.96
Bayfield: 16.12.95, 27.7.96
Edgefield, 12.10.93, 13.1.95, 25.3.95, 20.11.95, 26.7.96, 16.8.96, 8.6.97, 18.7.97; to Mr Boswell, 22.5.94
Guestwick: 28.8.94, 15.8.95, 9.5.96, 23.7.96, 15.8.96
Gunthorpe: 21.11.93, 5.3.94, 24.4.94, 27.6.94, 20.9.94
Thornage: 10.11.94, 20.1.97, 12.9.97; to Mr Sturley, 21.11.93, 5.1.95
screening by Hs' men: 4.11.93, 12.11.93, 27.11.93, 27.8.94, 3.9.94, 18–19.9.94, 1.11.94, 12.12.94, 14.4.95, 16.4.95, 22.4.95, 8.10.95, 23.10.95, 29.10.95, 6.11.95, 17.11.95, 23.11.95, 5.2.96, 11.2.96
screening tally: kept by Gunton Thompson, 3.9.94
trimmed: 31.5.96, 2.6.96:
see also malthouse; malting; malt-kiln; malt-mill
malthouse (M H), Hs', **3**, **11**, **14**, **19**, **62**, **65**, **74**, **75**, **77**, **135**, **143**, **149**, **212**, **213**, **214**, **329**; tended by John Ramm, 18.10.94; William Lamb leaves work to take Robert Bye's place in Hs' team, is replaced by John Ramm, 27.12.95; Abraham Dobson and Charles Lamb at work, 5.6.96; Thomas Raynor discusses with WH taking up post in, 10.9.97; Thomas Raynor begins steeping, 5.10.97
chamber: Thomas Boyce carries deals into, 1.1.95; John Ramm arranging malt, 29.5.95
pump repairs: by WHj, 22.11.93; by Thomas Youngman, 5.10.97:
see also malt; malting; malt-kiln; malt-mill; steeping

malting, by Hs' men, **86**, **87**, **125**, **344**:
1793-94: 28–29.10.93, 31.10.93, 1–2.11.93, 4.11.93, 6–7.11.93, 9.11.93, 11.11.93, 13–15.11.93, 18.11.93, 20.11.93, 22–23.11.93, 25–30.11.93, 2–7.12.93, 9–14.12.93, 16–21.12.93, 23–24.12.93, 27–28.12.93, 30–31.12.93, 2–4.1.94, 6–11.1.94, 13–18.1.94, 20.1.94, 22–25.1.94, 27.1.94, 29–31.1.94, 1.2.94, 3–8.2.94, 10–22.2.94, 24–27.2.94, 1.3.94, 3–8.3.94, 10–15.3.94, 17–22.3.94, 24–29.3.94, 31.3.94, 1–5.4.94, 7–12.4.94, 14–19.4.94, 21–26.4.94, 28–30.4.94, 1–2.5.94, 5–10.5.94, 12–17.5.94, 20–24.5.94, 26–31.5.94, 2–7.6.94, 9–14.6.94, 16–20.6.94, 30.6.94
1794–95: 20–25.10.94, 27–31.10.94, 1.11.94, 3–8.11.94, 11–15.11.94, 17–22.11.94, 24.11.94, 26–29.11.94, 2–6.12.94, 8–13.12.94, 15–20.12.94, 22–24.12.94, 26–27.12.94, 29–30.12.94, 1–3.1.95, 5–10.1.95, 12–17.1.95, 19–24.1.95, 26–31.1.95, 2–4.2.95, 6–7.2.95, 9–14.2.95, 16–21.2.95, 24.2.95, 28.2.95, 2–7.3.95, 9–14.3.95, 16–21.3.95, 23–28.3.95, 30–31.3.95, 1–4.3.95, 7–11.4.95, 13–15.4.95, 17–18.4.95, 20–22.4.95, 24–25.4.95, 28.4.95, 1.5.95, 4–7.5.95, 9.5.95, 12–14.5.95, 16.5.95, 18–23.5.95, 8–9.6.95, 11–12.6.95
1795–96: 12.10.95, 14–17.10.95, 19–24.10.95, 26–31.10.95, 2–7.11.95, 10–11.95, 16–18.11.95, 20–21.11.95, 23–28.11.95, 30.11.95, 1–5.12.95, 7–12.12.95, 14–19.12.95, 21–24.12.95, 26.12.95, 28–31.12.95, 1–2.1.96, 4–9.1.96, 11–16.1.96, 18–23.1.96, 25–30.1.96, 1–6.2.96, 8–13.2.96, 15–19.2.96, 22–26.2.96, 29.2.96, 1–5.3.96, 7–8.3.96, 10–12.3.96, 14–19.3.96, 21–23.3.96, 25–26.3.96, 28–31.3.96, 1.4.96, 4–9.4.96, 11–12.4.96, 15–16.4.96, 18–23.4.96, 25–30.4.96, 2–7.5.96, 24–25.5.96, 28.5.96, 30–31.5.96, 1–4.6.96, 6–11.6.96, 13–18.6.96, 20–23.6.96, 25.6.96, 27–30.6.96, 1–2.7.96, 4.7.96, 7.7.96, 9.7.96
1796–97: 24.10.96, 26.10.96, 28–29.10.96, 31.10.96, 1–5.11.96, 7–9.11.96, 11–12.11.96, 14–19.11.96, 21–26.11.96, 28.11.96, 30.11.96, 1–3.12.96, 5–10.12.96, 12–16.12.96, 19–24.12.96, 26–31.12.96, 2–7.1.97, 9–14.1.97, 16–19.1.97, 21.1.97, 23–28.1.97, 30–31.1.97, 1–2.2.97, 4.2.97, 6–11.2.97, 13–15.2.97, 17–18.2.97, 20–25.2.97, 27–28.2.97, 1–4.3.97, 6–11.3.97, 13.3.97, 15–18.3.97, 20–25.3.97, 29–31.3.97, 1.4.97, 4–8.4.97, 10–15.4.97, 17–22.4.97, 25–29.4.97, 1–6.5.97, 8–13.5.97, 15–20.5.97, 22–27.5.97, 29–31.5.97, 1–3.6.97, 5–8.6.97, 10.6.97, 12–17.6.97, 19–22.6.97, 24.6.97, 26–30.6.97, 1.7.97, 3–8.7.97, 10–14.7.97; Thomas Raynor finishes malting, 15.7.97

malting, by Hs' men *(cont.)*
1797–98: 9–11.10.97, 13–14.10.97, 16.10.97, 18–21.10.97, 24–25.10.97:
see also malt; malthouse; malt-kiln; malt-mill; steeping; water

malt-kiln, Hs', **23**, **37**, **49**, **62**, **75**, **77**, **86**, **87**, **143**, **149**, **215**, **374**; cowl painted by WHj, 22.11.93; tended by HR, 1.7.94; Hs' men sowing malt-kiln culms, 4.4.96

malt-mill, Hs', **75**, **359**:
rollers: repaired by Thomas Youngman, 15–18.1.94; used by Gunton Thompson for grinding malt, 18.1.94
stones:
dressed: 11.10.93, 21–22.7.95, 25.7.95, 3.12.95, 5.12.95, 10–12.5.96, 19–20.8.96, 21–22.4.97, 30.6.97, 19.8.97, 30.9.97
laid down: 30.7.94, 7.12.95, 13.5.96, 24.8.96, 24.4.97, 1.7.97, 2.10.97

Mann, Isaac (1777–1828), **196**, of Holt, Curate of Holt 1800–01, Curate of Aylmerton 1801–*c.*1805, Curate of Hemsby 1805–06, Rector of Vere, Jamaica 1807, Rector of St Catherine's, Jamaica 1808, Rector of Kingston, Jamaica 1813–28, son of John; to tea at Hs', 20.7.95, 4.8.95, 20.9.95

Mann, John (d.1794 aged 44), **115**, Cley merchant; Hs' men collect cinders, 2.11.93, 23.11.93, 2.12.93, 10.12.93, 4.1.94, 18.1.94, 1.2.94, 14.2.94, 7.3.94, 18–19.3.94, 1.4.94, 1.5.94, 4.6.94, 23.6.94

Mann (Man), Miss [? Sarah Anne (b.1782), of Holt, daughter of John]; to tea at Hs', 20.7.95, 4.8.95

manure, *see* muck

mares, *see* horses

Margetson, Mr, of Holt; with friend at Hs' to apply for tenancy of Maid's Head, North Walsham, 13.10.93

market, at Holt; Hs to, 13.8.96
MA to: .16.11.93, 30.11.93, 14.12.93, 8.2.94, 1.3.94, 3.5.94, 24.5.94, 20.9.94, 7.3.95, 15.8.95, 16.1.96, 25.6.96, 16.9.97
MH to: 3.5.94, 24.5.94, 16.1.96, 23.1.96
WH to:
1793: 12.10.93, 19.10.93, 26.10.93, 9.11.93, 16.11.93, 23.11.93, 30.11.93, 7.12.93, 14.12.93, 21.12.93, 28.12.93
1794: 4.1.94, 11.1.94, 3.5.94, 24.5.94, 31.5.94, 28.6.94, 26.7.94, 9.9.94, 6.12.94, 13.12.94, 20.12.94, 27.12.94
1795: 3.1.95, 17.1.95, 24.1.95, 31.1.95, 14.2.95, 18.7.95, 5.9.95, 26.9.95, 24.10.95, 26.12.95
1796: 2.1.96, 16.1.96, 23.1.96, 9.4.96, 7.5.96, 25.6.96, 9.7.96, 23.7.96, 30.7.96, 20.8.96, 29.10.96, 17.12.96

market, at Holt, WH to (*cont.*)
1797: 7.1.97, 4.2.97, 4.3.97, 22.4.97, 13.5.97, 29.7.97, 16.9.97, 7.10.97
WHj to:
1793: 9.11.93, 16.11.93, 30.11.93, 7.12.93, 14.12.93, 21.12.93, 28.12.93
1794: 4.1.94, 11.1.94, 8.2.94, 15.2.94, 22.2.94, 1.3.94, 8.3.94, 15.3.94, 29.3.94, 12.4.94, 31.5.94, 28.6.94, 19.7.94, 26.7.94, 9.9.94, 23.8.94, 6.9.94, 20.9.94, 13.12.94, 27.12.94
1795: 3.1.95, 10.1.95, 17.1.95, 24.1.95, 31.1.95, 14.2.95, 7.3.95, 18.7.95, 1.8.95, 15.8.95, 22.8.95, 26.9.95, 24.10.95, 7.11.95, 21.11.95, 28.11.95
1796: 2.1.96, 9.1.96, 16.1.96, 23.1.96, 30.1.96, 9.4.96, 7.5.96, 25.6.96, 9.7.96, 23.7.96, 20.8.96, 26.11.96, 17.12.96
1797: 7.1.97, 4.2.97, 18.2.97, 25.2.97, 4.3.97, 11.3.97, 22.4.97, 10.6.97, 29.7.97, 16.9.97, 23.9.97
others to with Hs: Clara Wymer and Charlotte Bartell, 14.12.94; Miss Custance, 8.2.94; Rose Raven and Miss Symonds, 24.5.94; Henry Goggs, 20.12.94; Robert Raven, 14.2.95; Nathaniel Raven jnr, 11.3.97; Mr Balls, 23.9.97
marl, collected by Thomas Baldwin, 1.3.94: *see also* clay; lime
marriages, Deborah Ramm, 27.1.95; Gunton Thompson jnr before breakfast, 5.11.95; Revd John Burrell, 2.8.96
Mason, John, Brinton tanner; sends load of barley to Hs and collects load of bark, 7.11.93; sends for more bark, 8.11.93; to tea at Hs', 2.11.95
Massingham, Miss, of Holt; with Phillis Raven to tea at Hs', 3.9.97
Mayes (Mays), David (b.1735), Letheringsett cordwainer; helps Hs with harvest, 17.9.95
Mayes (Mays), Richard (1717–1800), **37**, **54**, innkeeper of King's Head, Letheringsett, tied house; beer delivered, 20.10.93, 3.1.94; Purse Club feast, dispute forces club to move to Holt, 13.1.94; stables demolished, 24.2.94; yard foundations laid by Thomas Boyce, 11.3.94: *see also* Dobson, William
meadow, Hs', boy carts thorns to, 8.4.94; John Fox repairing hedges, 8.4.94; Thomas Hall repairing hedges, 11.4.95, 18–23.5.95, 28.5.95; Thomas Boyce topping trees, 22–23.12.96; Hs' men collect wood, 22.12.96, 26.1.97, 28.1.97, 30.1.97; Hs' men take gravel to, 1.2.97, 3–4.2.97, 8–9.2.97; William Holman spreading gravel, 7.2.97; Holman sowing seeds, 20.3.97; Holman sowing grass seeds, 25.3.97; John Ramm mowing weeds, 1.7.97, 5.7.97
meadow, Hs' (*cont.*)
Hs' men at work: 17.1.97, 19.1.97, 26.1.97, 28.1.97, 30-31.1.97, 1.2.97, 3.2.97, 6.2.97, 11.2.97, 15–17.2.97, 21.2.97, 23–24.2.97, 3–4.3.97, 6–7.3.97, 14.3.97, 16–17.3.97, 29–31.5.97
meal, *see* flour, lower grades
measuring, **29**, of great cask by WH in white hall, 17.10.93
meetings [Nonconformist services], *see under individual towns and villages* Briston; Cley-next-the-Sea; Hunworth
Mendham, Mr, *see* Mindham, William
Mendham, Mrs [? Elizabeth, of Briston], with Mrs Kilburn to tea at Hs', 2.6.95
mercury, used in recipe for destroying rats, HR's endnotes
mergin, *see* cement
Methodism, **136**, **139**, **153**, **245**, **289**, *see* meetings *under* Briston; Cley-next-the-Sea; Hunworth
mild, *see* beer
millers, *see individual millers and millwrights* Cook, William; James; Rouse, Mr; Thompson, William Gunton; Thompson, Gunton Chapman; Wade, John; Youngman, Thomas; *see also* mills
Mills, Miss, with Thomas Balls and sister and Miss Mundham [? Mindham] at Hs', 2.2.97
mills, **34**, **35**:
Holt Windmill, **69**: John Wade's burns down in four hours, 8.5.94
Hs' corn watermill: repaired by Thomas Youngman, 6.11.93; Thomas Youngman adjusts gears, 27.2.95, 17.1.97; Thomas Youngman at work, 21.8.97: *see also* flour; malt-mill; millstones; waterwheel
Letheringsett Watermill, **116**, **135**, **142**, **280**, **281**: Robert Bye and Gunton Thompson cart millstones from, 24.7.97:
see also millers; millstones
millstones, Hs':
maltstones:
dressed: by Gunton Thompson snr and jnr, 11.10.93; by HR, 21–22.7.95, 25.7.95; by Gunton Thompson and HR, 3.12.95, 5.12.95, 10–12.5.96, 19–20.8.96, 21–22.4.97, 19.8.97; by Gunton Thompson, 30.6.97, 30.9.97
laid down: by Gunton Thompson snr and jnr, 30.7.94; by Gunton Thompson, 7.12.95, 13.5.96, 24.8.96, 1.7.97, 2.10.97; by Gunton Thompson and HR, 24.4.97: *see also* malt-mill, rollers
wheatstones:
dressed, **33**: by Gunton Thompson, 15.10.93, 13.11.93, 12.12.93, 2.1.94, 17.2.94, 26.3.94,

millstones, wheatstones, dressed, by Gunton Thompson (*cont.*)
7.5.94, 1–3.7.94, 13.8.94, 10–11.9.94, 9.10.94, 15.11.94, 6–7.1.95, 26.6.95, 13.8.95, 19.12.95, 6.1.96, 4–5.2.96, 17–19.5.96, 18.8.96, 1.11.96, 13–14.12.96, 17.1.97, 13.3.97, 5–6.7.97, 11.8.97, 21.8.97, 20.9.97, 13–14.10.97
laid down (bedded): by Gunton Thompson, 17.10.93, 14.11.93, 3.1.94, 18.2.94, 9.5.94, 12.9.94, 10.10.94, 27.2.95, 27.6.95, 7.1.96, 11.3.96, 20.5.96, 18.1.97, 14.3.97, 21.9.97
purchase: Robert Bye and Gunton Thompson cart millstones from Mr Rouse's mill, 24.7.97
taken up: by Gunton Thompson, 31.3.95, 5.11.95, 10.3.96, 17.8.96, 12.12.96

Mindham (Mundham), Miss, with Thomas Balls and sister and Miss Mills at Hs', 2.2.97

Mindham (Mendham), William (1771–1843), **94**, **95**, **96**, **372**, **373**, **374**, **391**, **396**, of Wells, paperhanger, later Holt organ-builder, architect and builder; with Messrs T. and E. Balls to tea at Hs', 29.6.97 repairs Hs' organ, 5–8.9.97

Minns (Minn), John (d.1819 aged 85), Edgefield farmer; dines with Hs, 13.8.96

Minor, *see* horses

mirgin, *see* cement

Miss H, *see* Hardy, Mary Ann

mob, HR to at Sharrington, 17.12.95

moles, recipe for destroying, HR's endnotes

Molly, *see* horses

Moore, Charles, Letheringsett labourer; fills Hs' gravel cart, 30–31.3.96; carting gravel, 2.4.96

Moore (Moor), James (d.1815 aged 52), **163**, Holt attorney; to Edgefield with WHj, 8.11.93; dines with Hs, 20.12.93, 13.1.94, 5.2.94, 15.2.94, 3.4.94, 1.7.95, 7.7.97, 18.9.97; with MA and party to tea at Mr Baker's, 13.1.94; to tea at Hs', 23.3.94, 31.3.94; HR collects shrubs, 10.4.95, 24.10.96; with WHj to Gressenhall, 6.4.96; to supper with Hs, 26.10.96, 6.11.96; with WH to Norwich, 6.8.97; goes shooting with WHj, 18.9.97

Moore (Moor, More), Jeremiah (Jere) (d.1818 aged 68), of Letheringsett, river engineer and dredger; at Hs' 14.10.94
building work for Hs: lays foundations for cart house, 8.2.94, 12.2.94
pond work for Hs: heaving mud, 21.6.94; at work, 23–26.6.94, 1–2.7.94
river work for Hs, **74**, **75**, **280**: 24.5.94, 29.5.94, 31.5.94, 2–4.6.94; throwing mould out of Glaven, 8.2.94; at work in Glaven downstream, 19.5.94; with son at work, 21.5.94, 30.5.94, 11.6.96, 15–18.6.96, 20.6.96; with son at work in Glaven in Hs' garden, 21–

Moore, Jeremiah, river work for Hs (*cont.*)
22.5.94, 14.6.96; in Glaven, 23.5.94; with son at work in river in yard, 26–28.5.94; at work in river in Brewhouse Pightle, 5–7.6.94, 12–14.6.94, 17–20.6.94

Morston, Norf., **216**, beer deliveries, 10.10.95, 12.12.95, 25.1.96, 5.3.96, 14.5.96, 22.6.96, 19.7.96, 1.8.96, 10.9.96, 19.10.96, 31.12.96, 9.3.97, 23.3.97, 29.5.97, 18.8.97, 26.9.97, 10.10.97

mould [earth/silt], thrown from Glaven by Thomas Hall and Gunton Thompson, 7.2.94; thrown from Glaven by Jeremiah Moore, 8.2.94; Thomas Hall, Thomas Boyce and boy at mould cart in Five Acres, 23.4.95; Hs' men at mould cart at Holt Heath Farm, 13–14.12.96

mowing, by Hs' men: 17-19.9.94, 15.8.97
barley: *see* barley; harvests
borders: by John Ramm, 30.6.94
grass, by Hs' men: 1–2.7.94, 7.7.94, 14–15.9.95, 21.9.95, 23.9.95, 28–30.6.97, 1.7.97, 4.7.97, 6–8.7.97, 14.7.97, 17.7.97; at Holt Heath Farm, 11–13.7.97: *see also* haymaking
vetches: 31.7.97
weeds: in meadow, 1.7.97, 4–5.7.97

Moy, John (d.1806 aged 75), **274**, Horningtoft farmer and maltster; with wife, Burrells and Mr Sheldrake to tea at Hs', 24.5.97

Moy, Mrs Judith (1738–1814), née Fox, wife of John; with husband, Burrells and Mr Sheldrake to tea at Hs', 24.5.97

Mr H, *see* Hardy, William

Mrs H, *see* Hardy, Mrs Mary

muck:
carted by Hs' men: 1–3.1.94, 29–31.1.94, 3–4.6.94, 14.6.94, 16.6.94, 4.9.94, 6.9.94, 10.9.94, 19.12.94, 29.1.95, 6–7.2.95, 21.2.95, 13.3.95, 14.8.95, 21.8.95, 30.10.95, 5.11.95, 7.11.95, 9.11.95, 4–5.1.96, 27.1.96, 29.1.96, 18.2.96, 24–25.2.96, 18.3.96, 7.4.96, 26.5.96, 28.5.96, 10.6.96, 16–17.6.96, 29.10.96, 31.10.96, 1.11.96, 3.12.96, 6.1.97, 23–24.6.97, 28.6.97; from Hill Close, 17.10.93; in Six Acres, 28.10.96; to Holt Heath Farm, 30.11.96, 1.12.96, 6.12.96, 4.1.97, 26.1.97, 28.1.97, 11.2.97, 22.4.97, 24.4.97, 26.4.97; in Furze Closes, 3–5.1.97, 24.6.97
collected by Hs' men: out of street, 2.12.93; from Brewhouse Pightle, 15.1.94, 6.9.94, 8.9.94; from yards, 13.4.95
heaping: muck carted from heap in Hill Close, 17.10.93; by men, 7.1.96; turned by men in Five Acres, 24–25.5.96; muck carted from heap in Six Acres, 16.6.96
sale: collected by Thomas Temple's men, 7.6.94, 9.6.94, 11–14.6.94, 16–18.6.94; collected by Charles Kendle's men from

muck, sale (*cont.*)
yard, 6.1.95, 10.1.95; carted away by Mr Williams, 27–28.11.95, 7–11.12.95, 23–24.12.95
spreading by Hs' men: 5.6.94, 11.6.94, 14.6.94, 16.6.94, 2.9.94, 18.9.94, 12–14.2.95, 24.2.95, 28.2.95, 18.3.95, 4.11.95, 10–11.11.95, 7.1.96, 9.1.96, 25.2.96, 8.4.96, 28.5.96, 11.6.96, 16.6.96, 18.6.96, 28.10.96, 1.11.96, 3–4.11.96, 7–8.11.96, 28–30.6.97, 1.7.97; in Hill Close, 18–19.10.93, 21–22.10.93; in Bell's Acre, 16–17.1.94, 13.3.95; in Furze Close, 3.2.94, 13.3.95, 5.11.95; in garden, 28.4.95; in Five Acres, 24.6.96; in Brewhouse Pightle, 25.7.96; at Holt Heath Farm, 15–16.12.96, 19.12.96
turned:
by Hs' men: 6–7.1.94, 2.3.95, 25–28.8.95, 31.8.95, 22–25.9.95, 26.5.96, 9–10.9.96, 19–20.9.96; in yard, 25.2.96, 26.2.96, 4–5.5.96, 19.5.96, 10.6.97, 13.6.97
by Thomas Temple's men, 28.4.94
wagon: loaded, 28–29.11.96, 15.12.96, 17.12.96; to Holt Heath Farm, 29.11.96, 5.12.96, 8.12.96, 15–17.12.96, 30–31.12.96, 12.1.97, 16–17.1.97, 26–27.1.97, 6.2.97
mucking out, of pigs by: boy, 2.5.94, 26.5.94; Thomas Boyce, 23.10.94; Thomas Hall, 27.1.95
mud, thrown from pond by Jeremiah Moore, 21.6.94; carted by Thomas Hall from pond, 23–26.6.94, carted by Hs' men, 27–28.6.94, 30.6.94, 1–3.7.94, 11–12.7.94, 14.7.94
Mundham, Miss, *see* Mindham
murgen, *see* cement
music, William Lamb collects piano from Southrepps, 3.5.97; Mr Mindham repairs Hs' organ, 5–8.9.97

N

nails, collected by boy from Holt, 14.10.97
Nash, Spooner (d.1810 aged 72), Horstead farmer; dines with Hs, 21.3.97
New Farm, *see* Holt Heath Farm
Nicholas, *see* boys, boy 22, Nicholas Woodhouse
Nobbs, Mr, farmer or merchant; to supper with Hs and reckons, 23.6.94
nog, *see* beer
Nonconformity/Dissent, *see* meetings *under* Briston; Cley-next-the-Sea; Hunworth
North Walsham, Norf., **269**, WHj to, 26.10.93, 22.1.96, 17.3.96; Gunton Thompson to, 28.5.94, 19.4.95, 13–15.5.95, 4.5.95, 24–26.5.97; HR to, 2.5.95, 7.3.97; William Lamb delivers two barrels to Mr Thaxter, 2.5.96
beer deliveries: 30.10.93, 21–22.11.93, 20–21.12.93, 1.2.94, 17.3.94, 16.4.94, 20.5.94, 26.7.94, 12.5.95, 26.6.95, 14.10.95, 14.3.97, 29.5.97, 3.10.97; loading, 16.3.94, 11.5.95, 25.6.95, 28.5.97
tenancy of Maid's Head: Mr Margetson of Holt and friend apply, 13.10.93; Mr Raven of Walsingham applies, 10.9.94; James Dew installed by WH, 11.5.95
Norwich, Norf., **64**, **89**, **170**, **171**, **174**, **285**, **408**, **411**, Mr Webster at Hs', 22.2.95; Edmund Devereux at work on Hs' new pump, 9.9.95; Thomas Baldwin collects wheat, 28.6.96; production figures by common brewers, HR's endnotes
beer deliveries, **107**: 11–12.9.94, 2–3.3.94, 14–15.5.95, 22–23.10.95, 4–5.12.95, 2–3.3.96, 31.5.96–1.6.96, 27–28.6.96, 28–29.9.96; loading, 10.9.94, 1.3.95, 3.12.95, 1.3.96, 27.9.96
Hs to: with John Smith for day, 21.5.96
MA: with Charlotte Bartell, 8.8.94; with family, 6.9.94, 8–10.5.95, 7–9.10.95
MH: with family, 6.9.94
WH, **99**: with HR to assizes, 12–13.8.94; with family, 6.9.94, 8–10.5.95, 7–9.10.95; with Mr Bartell, 11–12.4.96; with James Moore, 6.8.97
WHj, **76**: 26–27.2.94, 10.3.94; to buy chaise, 2.6.94; with family, 8–10.5.95; with Charles Kendle, 2–3.6.96

O

oak, *see* wood
oats, collected by Robert Bye from Holt, 21.11.94; collected by William Lamb from Mr Rouse at Cley, 14.2.97; sown by J. Herring, 23.3.97; sown at Holt Heath Farm, 27.3.97
oiling (greazing), by William Lamb of his harness, 20.12.96; by William Lamb and Robert Bye of beer carts, 5.3.97
organ, *see* music
Osborne (Orsborn), Mr, orders beer from Hs, 14.3.94
osiers, delivered by Robert Bye to Mr Chamfer, 21.2.94
Overstrand, Norf., beer deliveries, 26.10.93, 28.10.93, 21.1.94, 1.3.94, 15.3.94, 31.7.95, 14.6.96, 23.7.96, 24.8.96, 27.9.96, 25.10.96, 28.12.96, 13.2.97, 4.4.97, 15.5.97, 20.6.97, 19.9.97, 21.10.97; loading, 13.6.96: *see also* Beckhithe; Thirst, Thomas
Overton, Mrs Mary, née Hayton, of Holt, formerly of King's Head, Holt; her benefit ball attended by WHj, 31.12.94
outholling, *see* ditches

P

painting, by WHj of malt-kiln cowl, 22.11.93; by WHj and HR of dining room at King's Head, Letheringsett, 2.5.94; by WHj of palisade, 10.5.94; by Thomas Youngman's boy, 12–14.5.94, 21–23.7.94, 28.7.94, 13.9.94; by WH of best parlour, 8.7.94; by HR of gate, 17.6.95; by HR of Gunton Thompson's house, 28.8.95; by HR of gate in Brewhouse Pightle, 14.12.95; by Thomas Boyce in garden, 18.3.96; by Mr Dawson's boy, 22–24.3.96, 4–6.5.96, 23.5.96, 26–27.5.96, 1.8.97; by HR, 4.8.96, 22.9.97; by WHj and HR of louvres ('flappers'), 5.8.96; by Mr Haddon and man of keeping room, 18.7.97: *see also* whitewashing

palisade, Thomas Youngman at work on, 9.5.94; painted by WHj, 10.5.94

pamments, *see* tiles

paper, *see* wallpaper

parlour, *see* house

Parr, Mary, raking behind harvest wagon, 31.8.97

parsnips, *see* vegetables

Parsons, William (d.1842 aged 75), Letheringsett labourer; at work in river, 13.6.94

Pattesley (Pattisley), Norf., **179**, hoops sent to Hs by Mr Webb, 6.6.95

Patteson (Patterson), John (1755–1833), **408**, **411**, Norwich common brewer; annual production figures, HR's endnotes

pavements (pamments), *see* tiles

paving, by Thomas Boyce of pigs' yard, 17.11.95; Thomas Boyce collects paving stones from Sheringham, 21.3.96, 9.4.96

Pearce (Peirce), Matthew, innkeeper of Plough, Kettlestone, tied house; orders nog from Hs, 16.6.94; orders beer, 7.2.96

peas, Hs' farm crop:
- cutting: by William Dobson, 20.8.96, 14.8.97; by Hs' men, 23–27.8.96
- dressing: by John Ramm, 7.12.96, 31.1.97; screened and preserved by Gunton Thompson, 18.5.97
- harrowing: in stubble, 27.9.97; rubbish carted away, 27.9.97
- harvesting: by Hs' men, 2.9.96, 5–6.9.96, 8.9.96, 29.8.97, 4–5.9.97
- removal: taken from barn, 20.1.97, 1.2.97; taken to Blakeney, 18.5.97
- sowing, **254**: ground rolled by Hs' men, 11–12.3.96, 1.4.97; bushed into ground by Hs' men, 11.3.96, 14.3.96, 17.3.96, 1.4.97; Edmund Balls and man dibbling, 11–12.3.96, 14.3.96; Hs' men ploughing for, 30–31.3.97; by Robert Bye, 30–31.3.97
- turning after cutting: by Hs' men, 31.8.96, 2.9.96, 30.8.97

peat, *see* mould

piano, *see* music

pigs (hogs, piggs):
- care: mucked out, 2.5.94, 26.5.94, 20.10.94, 27.1.95, 16.6.97; yard paved by Thomas Boyce, 17.11.95; tended by boy, 6.9.96, 8.9.97; barley ground for fattening pigs, 18.9.97
- killed: by John Cobon, 13.2.94; weighing watched by HR, 25.4.94; drawn by Mr Bumpstead, 23.11.96
- purchase: sow and seven pigs from William Bulling, 17.4.94; two from Salthouse, 8.8.95; sow and pigs from Thursford, 1.9.96; six pigs from Cook Flower, 22.9.96
- ringed: by Gunton Thompson and William Platten, 30.10.93; by Robert Bye and Thomas Baldwin, 25.9.94
- sale, **73**: fattening pig collected by James Lee, 24.4.94; to Mr Bumpstead, 8.5.94, 18.11.96; to John Clark, 22.5.94; six sold to dealers, 1.7.95; two to Charles Kendle, 20.10.96

Pinchen, William, Letheringsett labourer; cleans harness, 12.11.96; at jobs, 19.11.96, 21.11.96

pipes:
- conduits: repaired by Matthew Booth, 7.5.96; installed by WHj for pump, 29.7.96; for brewery backs, repaired by Mr Haddon's men, 10.5.97: *see also* pumps
- wine casks: *see* barrels

pits, clay collected by Robert Bye from Charles Kendle's, 26.9.94, 18.1.97; gravel carted by William Lamb from Mr Williams', 30.3.96: *see also* sand

plantations, *see* trees

Platten (Platton), Samuel (d.1817 aged 75), Bayfield Hall gamekeeper; helps Hs with harvest, 16.8.94

Platten (Platton), William, Hs' drayman and labourer; delivering malt, 12.10.93; harrowing, 14.10.93; carting grasses, 15.10.93; collecting lime and at jobs, 16.10.93; at muck cart, 17–18.10.93; collecting turnips, 18.10.93; collecting barrels from Foulsham, 25.10.93; at work in yards, 29.10.93; brewing, 30.10.93, 2.11.93; ringing pigs, 30.10.93; at work in river, 13–14.6.94
- delivering beer: 10–12.10.93, 16.10.93, 20.10.93, 22–26.10.93, 28.10.93
- ploughing: 19.10.93, 21.10.93, 31.10.93, 1.11.93

plays, at Holt; WHj to, 21.3.95; WH and WHj to, 11.4.95; WHj, HR and Nathaniel Raven jnr to, 28.4.95

Pleasance (Pleasence), David, of Cross Keys, Gunthorpe, tied house; orders beer from Hs, 4.9.94, 11.12.94, 23.7.95; at Hs', 17.9.94

Pleasance, Robert, **322**, **323**, innkeeper of Cross Keys, Gunthorpe, tied house; orders beer from Hs, 9.5.94, 13.6.94, 21.7.94, 8.10.95; at Hs', 2.6.94

ploughing (plowing), by Hs' men, **26**, **152**:
- 1793–94: 19.10.93, 21–23.10.93, 31.10.93, 1–2.11.93, 4.11.93, 9.11.93, 14–16.11.93, 18–19.11.93, 25.11.93, 30.11.93, 3.12.93, 6–7.12.93, 11–12.12.93, 14.12.93, 27–28.12.93, 14–15.2.94, 17–18.2.94, 20–21.2.94, 6–8.3.94, 11–13.3.94, 19.3.94, 28.3.94, 1–2.4.94, 5.4.94, 9.4.94, 11–12.4.94, 21–26.4.94, 29.4.94, 6.5.94, 9.5.94, 27–30.5.94, 2.6.94, 4.6.94, 11–12.6.94, 16–17.6.94, 20–21.6.94, 26.6.94, 2–3.7.94, 14.7.94
- 1794–95: 18.9.94, 30.9.94, 7–10.10.94, 16.10.94, 21.10.94, 11.11.94, 21.11.94, 27.11.94, 8–9.12.94, 11–13.12.94, 17.2.95, 24.2.95, 7.3.95, 10–12.3.95, 25–28.3.95, 30–31.3.95, 1–2.4.95, 7–9.4.95, 13.4.95, 15–17.4.95, 20–25.4.95, 29–30.4.95, 1–2.5.95, 4.5.95, 6.5.95, 27–28.7.95, 17–19.8.95
- 1795–96: 14–17.10.95, 19.10.95, 22–24.10.95, 26.10.95, 9–13.11.95, 19.11.95, 8–9.12.95, 16.12.95, 18.12.95, 22.12.95, 1.1.96, 6.1.96, 9.1.96, 4–6.2.96, 13.2.96, 16–17.2.96, 20.2.96, 24.2.96, 29.2.96, 7–8.3.96, 10.3.96, 15–16.3.96, 4.4.96, 6–7.4.96, 20–22.4.96, 5–6.5.96, 13–14.5.96, 26.5.96, 28.5.96, 11.6.96, 16.6.96, 18.6.96, 23–24.6.96, 29.6.96, 1–2.7.96
- 1796–97: 30.9.96, 1.10.96, 3.10.96, 6.10.96, 8.10.96, 12.10.96, 14–15.10.96, 17.10.96, 21.10.96, 3–5.11.96, 7–8.11.96, 12.11.96, 15.11.96, 17–19.11.96, 22.11.96, 24–26.11.96, 28–29.11.96, 19–20.1.97, 24.1.97, 6.2.97, 20.2.97, 22–23.2.97, 25.2.97, 28.2.97, 1.3.97, 10.3.97, 13.3.97, 15–18.3.97, 20–23.3.97, 27–29.3.97, 31.3.97, 1.4.97, 3–4.4.97, 7–8.4.97, 10–15.4.97, 17–18.4.97, 1–2.5.97, 5–6.5.97, 15–17.6.97, 28–30.6.97, 1.7.97, 4.7.97, 27.7.97, 29.7.97, 31.7.97, 3–4.8.97, 7.8.97, 30.8.97
- 1797–98: 1.9.97, 14.9.97, 18.9.97, 21.9.97, 27.9.97, 2.10.97, 4–7.10.97, 16–17.10.97, 19–21.10.97, 23.10.97:

see also furrows; harrowing; ploughs

ploughs, **320**, taken by William Lamb and Thomas Baldwin to Holt Heath Farm, 29.11.96; William Lamb unable to plough when tack breaks, 20.2.97; William Lamb collects plough from Holt Heath Farm, 5.10.97

poison, laid for rats, 14.1;96: *see also* arsenic; mercury

pollard, *see* flour, lower grades

pond, in Brewhouse Pightle; Jeremiah Moore heaving out mud, 21.6.94; Jeremiah Moore at

pond, in Brewhouse Pightle (*cont.*)
work in, 23–26.6.94, 1–2.7.94; John Ramm clears wood from, 14.7.94; drained by WHj, and fish removed, 20.5.96

poor, *see* Sharrington, riots

porter, *see* beer

porter malt, *see* malt

Portsmouth, Hants, Myles Custance of at Hs', 24.10.97

postchaises, *see* chaises, postchaises

potatoes (pittatoes), *see* vegetables

Press, Thomas (*c.*1762–1836), Letheringsett farmer; to tea with Hs, 17.11.94

Price, Mr, at Hs', 23.12.96

Prior (Prier), Mrs, **12**, **13**, innkeeper of Maid's Head, Hindolveston, tied house; at Hs', 5.6.94

proclamations, *see* fasts

Proudfoot, Isaac (d.1809 aged 58), Wells limeburner; with wife and Mrs Smith to tea at Hs', 5.6.97

Proudfoot, Mrs Mary (d.1833 aged 90), **289**, née Vaux, Wesleyan Methodist local preacher, wife of Isaac; with husband and Mrs Smith to tea at Hs', 5.6.97

public houses, hire and purchase, **170**, **171**, **271**, **272**, **335**; Mr Margetson and friend apply for tenancy of Maid's Head, N. Walsham, 13.10.93; William Dobson takes over King's Head, Letheringsett, 25.3.94; Mr Bare applies for tenancy of house at Hindolveston, 11.7.94; Mr Raven applies for tenancy of Maid's Head, N. Walsham, 10.9.94: *see also under individual towns and villages* Aldborough; Bale; Brampton; Briston; Burnham Market; Cley-next-the-Sea; Corpusty; Cromer; East Runton; Edgefield; Fakenham; Field Dalling; Gresham; Gunthorpe; Hindolveston; Hindringham; Holt; Hunworth; Kettlestone; Letheringsett; Morston; North Walsham; Overstrand; Salthouse; Sharrington; Sheringham; Southrepps; Stalham; Stody; Syderstone; Thornage; Thursford; Walsingham; Wells-next-the-Sea; Weybourne; Wiveton

pumps (engines), pipe installed by WHj, 29.7.96
- brewery, **94**, **96**: Gunton Thompson jnr pumping, 26.8.94; new pump installed by William Hase, Edmund Devereux and Matthew Booth, 8–11.9.95
- cleansing: repaired by Thomas Youngman's man, 26.10.95; box removed by Thomas Youngman, 15.2.96; removed by Gunton Thompson and HR for repair, 3.8.96
- garden, for display: played, 21.5.95
- malthouse: John Ramm pumping liquor into steep, 18.10.93; repaired by WHj, 22.11.93; repaired by Thomas Youngman, 5.10.97

pupillage, brewing, *see* Raven, Henry

purse club, *see* clubs

Q

quarter sessions, *see* sessions
quicks, *see* grasses, couch grass

R

race (rase), horse, WH and WHj to at Holt, 27.9.97
racking, *see* beer, drawing off
raking:
couch grass (quicks): by Hs' men, 27–28.10.95; in Furze Closes, 31.10.95
harvest: by Hs' men in Bell's Acre and Furze Closes, 20.8.94; by Hs' men, 10.9.95, 19.9.95; by Hs' men in Five Acres, 22.9.95; by village women behind wagon, 31.8.97; by Hs' men in Six Acres, 13.9.97
drag raking: by Hs' men, 23.8.94, 27.8.94, 29.8.94, 8.9.95, 16.9.96, 2.9.97, 9.9.97; by boy behind wagon, 28.8.94, 8.9.97
hay: by village women behind wagon, 10.7.94, 21.7.96
drag raking: by Hs' men, 20.9.94, 15.7.96, 8.10.96, 11.7.97
Ralph, Mr, at Hs', 20.4.95
Ramm (Ram), Deborah (Deb) (b.1765), of Letheringsett, daughter of John; marriage, 27.1.95
Ramm (Ram), John (d.1813 aged 86), **295**, Hs' farm servant, maltster, brewer and thresher; takes William Lamb's place in malthouse, 27.12.95
brewing: 16.10.93, 23.10.93, 30.10.93, 17.10.94, 29.5.95, 15.8.95, 22.9.95, 28.9.95, 16.12.95
cleansing beer: 12.10.93, 23.1.94, 26.11.95
drawing off beer: 10.10.93, 23.12.93, 21.1.94, 3.5.94
dressing: 10.11.95; culms, 25.10.93, 3.7.94; wheat, 16.9.94, 6.10.94, 18.10.94; barley, 5.10.95; peas, 7.12.96, 31.1.97
gardening:
1793: 11–12.10.93
1794: 23–26.7.94, 30.8.94, 20.9.94, 22–24.9.94
1795: 21–22.5.95, 30.5.95, 14–15.7.95, 21–23.7.95, 28–29.7.95, 31.7.95, 1.8.95, 3–4.8.95, 7–8.8.95, 10–12.8.95, 22.8.95, 28–29.8.95
1796: 13–14.6.96, 28.6.96
harvesting: 10–16.8.94, 18–23.8.94, 26.8.94, 28–29.8.94, 31.8.95, 2–5.9.95, 8–9.9.95, 11–12.9.95, 22–26.8.96, 23.8.97, 26.8.97; dines at Hs' on first day, 10.8.94; gathers largess, 30.8.94, 26.9.95
haymaking:
1794: 2.7.94, 5.7.94, 7.7.94, 10–11.7.94, 17–20.9.94, 24.9.94, 29.9.94

Ramm, John, haymaking (*cont.*)
1795: 6–8.7.95, 10.7.95, 13–14.7.95, 16.7.95, 18.7.95, 21.7.95, 24–25.7.95, 27.7.95, 5.8.95, 14–15.9.95, 21–23.9.95, 29.9.95
1796: 7–8.7.96, 15.7.96, 20.7.96
1797: 10–11.7.97, 17.7.97, 21–22.7.97
hoeing turnips: 7–9.7.94, 15–19.7.94, 21–24.7.94, 28–31.7.94, 1–2.8.94, 4–9.8.94, 26.8.94, 1–2.9.94, 4–6.9.94, 8.9.94, 22.8.95, 24–27.8.95, 10.9.95
illness: 20.3.94, 3.11.94, 3.12.94, 5–6.2.95, 6.3.95, 31.3.95, 1.9.95, 6.10.95, 26–27.1.96, 14.3.96, 13.4.96, 15–16.4.96, 28.4.96, 5.5.96
jobs: 28.5.95, 29–30.6.95, 10.10.95, 20–21.10.95, 7.12.95, 12.12.95, 17–19.12.95, 26.12.95, 26–27.6.97; carting grasses, 15.10.93; delivering beer, 18.10.93; sowing wheat, 19.10.93; working in granaries, 24–26.10.93, 6.10.94, 5.10.95; portering, 22.2.94; mowing borders, 30.6.94; at mud cart, 1.7.94, 12.7.94, 14.7.94; at work in yards, 5.7.94; clears wood from pond, 14.7.94; removes stones from brew-house yard, 14.7.94; at work in hay house, 25.8.94; carting sand, 21.5.95; arranging malt and wheat, 29.5.95; cleaning barn and steep, 30.5.95; clears vat, 26.11.95; lifting potatoes, 22.12.95; his boy starts work with Hs, 30.8.96; mowing weeds, 1.7.97, 4–5.7.97
malting, **214**:
1793–94: 28–29.10.93, 31.10.93, 1–2.11.93, 4.11.93, 6–7.11.93, 9.11.93, 11.11.93, 13–15.11.93, 18.11.93, 20.11.93, 22–23.11.93, 25–30.11.93, 2–7.12.93, 9–14.12.93, 16–21.12.93, 23–24.12.93, 27–28.12.93, 30–31.12.93, 2–4.1.94, 6–11.1.94, 13–18.1.94, 20.1.94, 27.1.94, 29–31.1.94, 1.2.94, 3–8.2.94, 10–22.2.94, 24–27.2.94, 1.3.94, 3–8.3.94, 10–15.3.94, 17–19.3.94, 21–22.3.94, 24.3.94, 26–29.3.94, 31.3.94, 1–5.4.94, 7–12.4.94, 14–19.4.94, 21–26.4.94, 28–30.4.94, 1–2.5.94, 5–10.5.94, 12–17.5.94, 19–24.5.94, 26–31.5.94, 2–7.6.94, 9–14.6.94, 16–20.6.94, 30.6.94
1794–95: 18.10.94, 20–25.10.94, 27–31.10.94, 1.11.94, 4–8.11.94, 11–15.11.94, 18–22.11.94, 24.11.94, 26–29.11.94, 4–6.12.94, 8–13.12.94, 15–20.12.94, 22–24.12.94, 26–27.12.94, 29–30.12.94, 1–3.1.95, 5–10.1.95, 12–17.1.95, 19–24.1.95, 26–31.1.95, 2–4.2.95, 7.2.95, 9–14.2.95, 16–21.2.95, 24.2.95, 28.2.95, 2–5.3.95, 7.3.95, 9–14.3.95, 16–21.3.95, 23–28.3.95, 30–31.3.95, 4.4.95, 7–11.4.95, 13–15.4.95, 17–18.4.95, 20–22.4.95, 24–25.4.95, 28.4.95, 1.5.95, 4–7.5.95, 9.5.95, 12–14.5.95, 16.5.95, 18–23.5.95; drying off porter malt, 14.4.95

Ramm, John, malting (*cont.*)
1795–96: 21.11.95, 28–31.12.95, 1–2.1.96, 4–9.1.96, 10–16.1.96, 18–23.1.96, 25.1.96, 28–30.1.96, 1.2.96, 3–6.2.96, 8–13.2.96, 15–19.2.96, 22–26.2.96, 29.2.96, 1–5.3.96, 7–8.3.96, 10–12.3.96, 15–19.3.96, 21–23.3.96, 25–26.3.96, 28–31.3.96, 1.4.96, 4–9.4.96, 11–12.4.96, 18–23.4.96, 25–27.4.96, 29–30.4.96, 2–4.5.96, 4.6.96
1796–97: 26.10.96, 28–29.10.96, 31.10.96, 1–4.11.96, 7–9.11.96, 11–12.11.96, 14–19.11.96, 21–26.11.96, 28.11.96
screening malt: 12.11.93
steeping: 18.10.93, 22.10.93, 24.10.93, 14.10.94, 30.5.95, 5.10.95, 9.10.95
muck carting/spreading: 14.8.95, 21.8.95, 5.11.95, 9.11.95, 25.7.96, 23–24.6.97, 28–30.6.97, 1.7.97, 4.7.97
ploughing: 21–22.10.93, 27.7.95, 17–19.8.95
threshing:
1794–95: 3–6.9.94, 15–16.9.94, 25–27.9.94, 30.9.94, 10.10.94, 16.10.94
1795–96: 29–30.9.95, 1–2.10.95, 12.10.95, 14–17.10.95, 19.10.95, 26–31.10.95, 2.11.95, 6–7.11.95, 11.11.95, 16–21.11.95, 23.11.95, 25.11.95, 27–28.11.95, 30.11.95, 1–5.12.95, 8–10.12.95, 15.12.95, 21.12.95, 23–24.12.95
1796–97: 21–22.10.96, 25.10.96, 30.11.96, 5–6.12.96, 8–10.12.96, 12–16.12.96, 19–24.12.96, 26–31.12.96, 10–12.1.97, 14.1.97, 16–19.1.97, 21.1.97, 24–28.1.97, 30.1.97
1797–98: 17.10.97
working in barn: 25.8.94, 1–4.10.94, 7.10.94, 13.10.94, 7.9.95, 24.11.95, 29–30.11.96, 2–3.1.97, 5–7.1.97, 9.1.97, 13.1.97

rats, **215**, T. Bulling kills 52 in Hs' barn, 20.2.94; ratcatcher lays poison, 14.1.96; recipe for poisoning, HR's endnotes

Raven, Mrs Ann (1744–1811), **93**, née Smith, of Whissonsett Hall, farmer, HR's mother; with children to Hs, 17.7.94; departs, 19.7.94

Raven, Mrs Ann (1746–1827), née Fox, wife of Nathaniel; with husband to Hs, 6.3.94, 3.11.94, 24.11.95, 20.2.97; they depart, 8.3.94, 7.11.94, 27.11.95, 24.2.97; with husband, Hs and HR to Weybourne Camp, 14.7.95; with husband and Hs to tea at Mr Sheldrake's, 22.2.97; with husband and Hs to Revd Mr Johnson's, 23.2.97

Raven, Anna (Ann) (1773–1814), daughter of Nathaniel, cousin of HR; with cousin Nathaniel and Miss Custance to Hs, 26.12.93; with Hs and Miss Custance to Holt ball, 30.12.93; with WHj and Miss Custance to Holt, 12.1.94; with MA and party to tea at Mr Baker's, 13.1.94; with Hs to tea at Mr Davy's, 17.1.94; with Hs to Holt Church, 19.1.94; with

Raven, Anna (Ann) (*cont.*)
Ravens departs, 23.1.94, 30.4.96; with father and cousin Nathaniel to Hs, 24.3.95; with family and Hs to Cley, 25.3.95; with Rose Raven to Hs from Holt, 15.4.96, 21.4.96; with Rose and Hs to Holt, 16.4.96, 23–24.4.96, 26.4.96, 3.11.96, 5.11.96; with Rose and Hs to tea at Mr Forster's, 22.4.96; with Hs and Rose spends day at Cook Flower's, 27.4.96; with Rose and HR to Holt, 29.4.96; with Rose Raven to Hs from Whissonsett, 31.10.96; with cousins to seaside, 9.11.96

Raven, Mrs Hannah (1739–94), née Myles, of Tunstead and Norwich; with Bakers to dinner at Hs', 17.7.94

Raven, Henry (HR) (1777–?1825), **2**, **32**, **67**, **103**, **120**, **164**, **228**, of Whissonsett Hall, Hs' brewing pupil 1794–1800, son of Mrs Ann Raven, née Smith, nephew of MH;
brewing:
1794: 17.7.94, 4.8.94, 11.8.94, 18.8.94, 25.8.94, 1.9.94, 8.9.94, 15.9.94, 22.9.94, 29.9.94, 6.10.94, 13.10.94, 17.10.94, 22.10.94, 10.11.94, 26.11.94, 11.12.94, 20.12.94
1795: 7.1.95, 14.1.95, 26.1.95, 2.2.95, 9.2.95, 16.2.95, 26.2.95, 16.3.95, 23.3.95, 30.3.95, 29.4.95, 6.5.95, 11.5.95, 16.5.95, 21.5.95, 25.5.95, 29.5.95, 3.6.95, 17.6.95, 23.6.95, 8.7.95, 16.7.95, 29.7.95, 6.8.95, 13.8.95, 19.8.95, 26.8.95, 2.9.95, 16.9.95, 22.9.95, 28.9.95, 2.10.95, 7.10.95, 13.10.95, 20.10.95, 26.10.95, 2.11.95, 13.11.95, 19.11.95, 24.11.95, 28.11.95, 4.12.95, 9.12.95, 16.12.95, 24.12.95
1796: 8.1.96, 12.1.96, 18.1.96, 25.1.96, 1.2.96, 8.2.96, 13.2.96, 17.2.96, 27.2.96, 2.3.96, 8.3.96, 19.3.96, 24.3.96, 29.3.96, 1.4.96, 5.4.96, 9.4.96, 12.4.96, 19.4.96, 26.4.96, 2.5.96, 6.5.96, 16.5.96, 23.5.96, 30.5.96, 7.6.96, 13.6.96, 20.6.96, 4.7.96, 11.7.96, 18.7.96, 25.7.96, 1.8.96, 8.8.96, 15.8.96, 22.8.96, 30.8.96, 5–7.9.96, 14.9.96, 22.9.96, 28.9.96, 5.10.96, 11.10.96, 26.10.96, 5.11.96, 17.11.96, 23.11.96, 2.12.96, 9.12.96, 20.12.96, 28.12.96
1797, **332**, **334**, **357**, **411**, **412**: as head brewer, 9.1.97, 19.1.97, 27.1.97, 2.2.97, 11.2.97, 16.2.97, 22.2.97, 27.2.97, 3.3.97, 6.3.97, 9.3.97, 13.3.97, 16.3.97, 21.3.97, 25.3.97, 1.4.97, 6.4.97, 13.4.97, 28.4.97, 1.5.97, 3.5.97, 5.5.97, 10.5.97, 15.5.97, 18.5.97, 23.5.97, 31.5.97, 8.6.97, 14.6.97, 20.6.97, 28.6.97, 6.7.97, 12.7.97, 19.7.97, 26.7.97, 2.8.97, 9.8.97, 17.8.97, 23.8.97, 1.9.97, 11.9.97, 19.9.97, 28.9.97, 4.10.97, 11.10.97, 18.10.97, 25.10.97

Raven, Henry (*cont.*)
cleansing beer:
1793: 2.11.93
1794: 2.7.94, 9.7.94, 18.7.94, 29.7.94, 5.8.94, 19.8.94, 26.8.94, 23.9.94, 30.9.94, 1.10.94, 7–8.10.94, 14.10.94, 18–19.10.94, 24.10.94, 5–6.11.94, 11–12.11.94, 19.11.94, 27–28.11.94, 5.12.94, 22.12.94
1795: 8–9.1.95, 15–16.1.95, 27–28.1.95, 3–4.2.95, 17–18.2.95, 27–28.2.95, 8.3.95, 24–25.3.95, 11–12.4.95, 8.5.95, 27.5.95, 3–31.5.95, 4.6.95, 13.6.95, 9.7.95, 17.7.95, 23.7.95, 30.7.95, 7.8.95, 14.8.95, 20.8.95, 27.8.95, 3.9.95, 14.9.95, 18.9.95, 23–24.9.95, 29–30.9.95, 3.10.95, 8.10.95, 14–15.10.95, 21–22.10.95, 27–28.10.95, 3–4.11.95, 14.11.95, 20–21.11.95, 25–26.11.95, 30.11.95, 5–6.12.95, 10–11.12.95, 17–18.12.95, 25.12.95
1796: 13–14.1.96, 19–20.1.96, 26.1.96, 3.2.96, 9.2.96, 15.2.96, 18–19.2.96, 23–24.2.96, 29.2.96, 3–4.3.96, 16–17.3.96, 21.3.96, 26.3.96, 3.4.96, 6.4.96, 13.4.96, 16.4.96, 27–28.4.96, 3–4.5.96, 10.5.96, 24.5.96, 31.5.96, 1.6.96, 8–9.6.96, 14–15.6.96, 29.6.96, 5.7.96, 12.7.96, 19.7.96, 26.7.96, 2–3.8.96, 9.8.96, 16.8.96, 23.8.96, 31.8.96, 8.9.96, 15–16.9.96, 23–24.9.96, 29.9.96, 6.10.96, 12–13.10.96, 20–21.10.96, 27–28.10.96, 7.11.96, 24.11.96, 3.12.96, 10.12.96, 21.12.96, 29.12.96
1797: 10.1.97, 20–21.1.97, 28.1.97,3–4.2.97, 13.2.97, 18.2.97, 23–24.2.97, 28.2.97, 1.3.97, 4–5.3.97, 8.3.97, 11.3.97, 15.3.97, 17–18.3.97, 7.4.97, 21.4.97, 29.4.97, 2.5.97, 4.5.97, 6.5.97, 11.5.97, 19.5.97, 24.5.97, 1–2.6.97, 9–10.6.97, 15–16.6.97, 29.6.97, 7.7.97, 13.7.97, 20.7.97, 27.7.97, 3.8.97, 24.8.97, 2.9.97, 12.9.97, 20.9.97, 29.9.97, 5.10.97, 12.10.97, 18.10.97
church and meeting attendance, **246**:
Briston meeting [Methodist]: 11.1.95, 1.3.95, 8.3.95, 22.3.95, 5.4.95, 12.4.95, 17.5.95, 24.5.95, 7.6.95, 21.6.95, 28.6.95, 12.7.95, 19.7.95, 16.8.95, 23.8.95, 30.8.95, 6.9.95, 13.9.95, 20.9.95, 27.9.95, 25.10.95
Cley meeting [Wesleyan Methodist]: 22.11.95, 25.12.95
Holt Church:
1793: 13.10.93
1794: 11.5.94, 8.6.94, 20.7.94, 3.8.94, 30.11.94; with MA confirmed, 4.7.94
1795: 15.3.95, 29.3.95, 11.10.95
1796: 17.1.96, 28.2.96, 15.5.96, 12.6.96, 19.6.96, 3.7.96, 14.8.96, 21.8.96, 4.9.96, 18.9.96, 25.9.96, 2.10.96, 30.10.96, 6.11.96, 27.11.96

Raven, Henry, church and meeting attendance, Holt Church (*cont.*)
1797: 15.1.97, 29.1.97, 26.2.97, 19.3.97, 9.4.97, 23.4.97, 4.6.97, 11.6.97, 30.7.97, 13.8.97, 3.9.97, 1.10.97, 8.10.97
Hunworth meeting [Methodist]: 6.12.95, 13.12.95
Letheringsett Church: 15.2.95, 25.2.95, 10.7.96, 24.7.96, 14.5.97, 6.8.97, 15.10.97
diary, entries by others: *see* diary
drawing off beer: 2.11.93, 10.12.93, 25,12.93, 28.1.94, 11.2.94, 3.5.94, 13.9.94, 30.4.95, 7.5.95, 30.11.95, 13.1.96, 18.2.96, 22–23.2.96, 26.2.96, 9.3.96, 2.4.96, 13.4.96, 16.4.96, 20.4.96, 24.4.96, 18.2.97, 1.3.97, 8.3.97, 15.3.97, 2.4.97, 4.5.97, 6.5.97, 8.5.97
general brewery work, **391**: 21.9.96, 15.10.96, 29.10.96, 2.11.96, 14.11.96, 30.11.96, 13.1.97, 24.1.97, 31.1.97, 18.4.97, 26.4.97, 30.5.97, 26.6.97, 3.7.97, 10.7.97, 14–15.7.97, 21–22.7.97, 1.8.97, 12.8.97, 30–31.8.97, 4–7.9.97, 14–15.9.97, 21.9.97, 23.9.97, 16.10.97; cleans hop chamber, 5.7.94; bottles sixpenny beer, 10.9.94; brings malt over to brewery, 20.11.94, 15.12.94, 26.12.94, 24.9.95; tidies workshop, 21.1.95; drying porter malt, 14.4.95; draws beer into wine pipes, 22.4.95; cleans cask, 29.4.95; prepares for brewing, 21.9.95; cleans troughs, 18.2.96, 5.3.97; draying off beer, 23.3.96, 16.4.96; removes cleansing pump, 3.8.96; with WHj paints louvres ('flappers'), 5.8.96; delivers beer to Holt, 29.8.96; cleans vat, 14.10.96, 21.2.97; weighs hops, 16.1.97; cleans white hall, 12.5.97; dismantles interior of counting house, 18.9.97; begins to sell goods in new counting house, 20.10.97
general farm work: at work in granaries, 11.10.93; gathering apples, 18–19.10.93, 12.9.94, 3.10.94, 17.10.95, 27.10.96; portering, 22.2.94; collects hay from Mr Forster, 14.2.94; burning couch grass, 28.3.94; watches pig-weighing, 25.4.94; walks a-farming with WHj and Gunton Thompson, 13.7.94; gathers bees, 11.9.94; replants chestnut tree in Brewhouse Pightle, 20.3.95; arranges hurdles in Brewhouse Pightle, 17.4.95; cleans wheat chamber, 30.1.96; removes stack into barn, 11.2.96; collects clover seed from Brinton, 28.3.97; collects straw from Mr Temple, 11.5.97; to Furze Closes, 22.5.97
work with horses: takes horse to Brinton, 16.10.93; with Robert Bye collects colts from Winch, 23–24.11.93; takes Robert Bye's horse to Saxlingham, 6.5.94; trims chaise horse, 10.12.95; with WHj drives

Raven, Henry, general farm work, work with horses (*cont.*)
colt in cart, 19.9.96; puts colt to Hs' chaise, 22.9.96; takes brewery horse to Mr Love at Holt, 16.11.96
harvesting: 18.8.94, 21.8.94, 22.9.95
haymaking: 10.7.94, 10.7.95, 13.7.95, 4–5.7.96
to Holt: 25.12.93, 19.3.94, 8.5.94, 25.11.94, 13.2.95, 4.3.95, 29.3.95, 16.4.95, 16.6.95, 31.8.95, 16.11.95, 25.11.95, 16.12.95, 26–27.4.96, 29.4.96, 12.5.96, 3.7.96, 15.11.96, 18.1.97, 10.10.97, 16.10.97
jobs: to Sheringham, 6.12.93; with WHj in malt cart to Wells, 31.1.94; to Gunthorpe, 4.2.94, 22.6.95, 15.3.96; to Cley, 16.3.94, 24.5.96, 14.2.97; to Thornage, 19.3.94; painting dining room at King's Head, Letheringsett, 2.5.94; to Hunworth, 7.6.94; to Bodham, 2.7.94, 11.8.96; to Edgefield, 15.7.94, 21.7.94, 2.9.94, 10.10.94, 23.4.96, 12.9.96, 14.8.97; delivers malt to Guestwick, 28.8.94, 9.5.96, 23.7.96; to Briningham, 2.9.94, 14.10.94; delivers malt to Thornage, 10.11.94; with Hs bottles pipe of wine at Cley, 10.12.94; delivers malt to Edgefield, 13.1.95; collects Hs from Bayfield, 26.2.95, 29.4.95; reckons with Mr Bissell at Briningham, 10.3.95; collects shrubs from James Moore, 10.4.95, 24.10.96; to N. Walsham, 2.5.95, 7.3.97; to Stody, 10.6.95; painting gate, 17.6.95, 14.12.95; to Guestwick, 25.6.95, 11.1.95, 22.3.97; drives Davys to Holt, 19.8.95; to Saxthorpe, 21.8.95; paints Gunton Thompson's house, 28.8.95; with Edmund Devereux to Aylsham, 12.9.95; to Sharrington, 8.11.95, 7.8.96, 16.10.96, 18.12.96; meets mob at Sharrington, 17.12.95; cleans lumber room, 15.1.96; takes MA to Fakenham, 21.1.96; collects boy from Weybourne, 31.1.96; delivers malt to Sharrington, 7.2.96; to Brinton, 15.3.96, 19.5.97; helps MA to wallpaper her room, 26–27.5.96; painting, 4.8.96, 22.9.97; to Field Dalling with Mr Hammond's bill, 8.9.96; to Thursford, 11.9.96, 4.2.97; to Weybourne, 18.11.96; with Nathaniel Raven jnr to Edgefield and Briston, 10.3.97; to Saxlingham, 27.3.97,21.5.97; at home, 10.9.97, 16.9.97; to Bale, 13.9.97
malting:
1793–94: 29.10.93, 31.10.93, 1.11.93, 25–30.11.93, 2–5.12.93, 7.12.93, 9.12.93, 11.12.93, 13–14.12.93, 16–21.12.93, 23–24.12.93, 27–28.12.93, 30–31.12.93, 2–4.1.94, 6–11.1.94, 22–25.1.94, 27.1.94, 29–30.1.94, 1.2.94, 3.2.94, 5–8.2.94, 10.2.94, 12–15.2.94, 17–22.2.94, 24–26.2.94, 1.3.94, 3.3.94, 5–6.3.94, 12.3.94,

Raven, Henry, malting, 1793–94 (*cont.*)
17–18.3.94, 20.3.94, 24.3.94, 26–29.3.94, 31.3.94, 1–5.4.94, 7–12.4.94, 14–19.4.94, 21–24.4.94, 26.4.94, 28–30.4.94, 1–2.5.94, 5–7.5.94, 9–10.5.94, 12–16.5.94, 20–24.5.94, 26–27.5.94, 31.5.94, 2.6.94, 4–7.6.94, 9.6.94, 12–14.6.94, 16–20.6.94, 1.7.94
1794–95: 3–4.11.94, 17–18.11.94, 2–4.12.94, 6.2.95, 6.3.95, 1–3.4.94, 10.4.95, 8–9.6.95, 11–12.6.95
1795–96: 11.1.96, 26–27.1.96, 2.2.96, 15.4.96, 28.4.96, 5–7.5.96, 6.6.96, 29.6.96, 7.7.96, 9.7.96
1796–97: 24.10.96, 21.11.96
screening malt: 18–19.9.94, 12.12.94, 8.10.95, 23.10.95, 6.11.95, 17.11.95, 23.11.95, 11.2.96
milling:
dressing flour, 24.9.94, 7.10.94, 11.10.94, 11.11.94, 9.3.95, 24.8.95, 16.10.95, 1.12.95, 16.3.96, 1.6.96, 23.2.97
dressing maltstones: 21–22.7.95, 25.7.95, 3.12.95, 5.12.95, 10–12.5.96, 19–20.8.96, 21–22.4.97, 19.8.97; lays down maltstones, 24.4.97
grinding malt for brewing and storage:
1794: 15–16.8.94, 22–23.8.94, 11.9.94, 18–20.9.94, 25.9.94, 2.10.94, 9–10.10.94, 14–15.10.94, 21.10.94, 1.11.94, 1.12.94, 26.12.94
1795: 6.1.95, 13–14.5.95, 26.6.95, 25.8.95, 31.8.95, 9.9.95, 15.9.95, 19.9.95, 26.9.95, 1.10.95, 6.10.95, 9–10.10.95, 24.10.95, 30.10.95, 17–18.11.95, 23.11.95, 27.11.95, 2.12.95, 8.12.95, 14.12.95, 22–23.12.95
1796: 7.1.96, 29.1.96, 5.2.96, 1.3.96, 5.3.96, 11.3.96, 22.3.96, 28.3.96, 31.3.96, 4.4.96, 7.4.96, 11.4.96, 14.4.96, 18.4.96, 30.4.96, 14.5.96, 16.7.96, 2.8.96, 18.8.96, 26–27.8.96, 3.9.96, 13.9.96, 20.9.96, 27.9.96, 4.10.96, 10.10.96, 16.11.96, 22.11.96, 1.12.96, 7.12.96, 27.12.96
1797: 17.1.97, 2.3.97, 4.3.97, 11.3.97, 27.4.97, 2.5.97, 21–22.8.97, 8–9.9.97
stripping meal: 6.12.94, 11.2.94, 13.4.95
social activities, **221**, **244**, **386**: goes walking with Gunton Thompson, 16.2.94; with brother and sister to Fakenham, 1.6.94; with family to Thursford, 19.7.94; to men's harvest supper at King's Head, Letheringsett, 6.9.94; with Hs to Snoring, 13.11.94, 5.12.94; goes skating with WHj at Hempstead, 25.1.95; to tea at Mr Bartell's, 25.1.95; to play at Holt, 28.4.95; to Weybourne Camp,

Raven, Henry, socal activities (*cont.*) 14.6.95, 14.7.95, 26.7.95, 10.8.95, 8.7.96; with J. Kendle to Sharrington, 2.8.95; to ball at Holt, 3.10.95, 20.4.96, 29.9.96, 29.9.97; with MH to tea and supper at Thomas Temple's, 28.1.96; with WHj to Mr Bartell, 3.2.96; with party to Sheringham, 10.4.96, 8.7.96; dines at Sharrington, 8.5.96, 25.7.97; to Hempton Green Fair, 17.5.96; with WHj to Kelling, 13.8.96, 23.7.97; with Hs to Holt Fair, 25.4.97; to tea at Thomas Temple's, 28.5.97; to Fakenham, 6.6.97; meets family at Sharrington, 18.6.97; with family to tea at Sheringham, 19.6.97, 10.8.97; with cousins and Mr Bird to Gunthorpe, 11.8.97; to Cromer, 20.8.97; with Joseph Erratt to Holt, 30.9.97

visits, **353**, **354**: with WH to Norwich Assizes, 12–13.8.94; stays overnight at Alethorpe, 22.1.96; with WH to Coltishall and Aldborough, 3–4.4.97; with WH to Southrepps and Cromer, 6–7.10.97

at Whissonsett, **130**: 22.11.93, 12.1.94–20.1.94, 23.3.94, 12–13.4.94, 21.6.94–30.6.94, 26–27.7.94, 25–26.10.94, 28.12.94–4.1.95, 22–23.2.95, 27.4.95, 19–20.5.95, 5.7.95, 9–10.8.95, 17–18.10.95, 26.12.95–3.1.96, 5–6.1.96, 8–9.1.96, 21.6.96–28.6.96, 28.8.96, 10–11.11.96, 13–14.12.96, 1–8.1.97, 11–12.3.97, 16.4.97, 25.6.97

Raven, John, son of Mrs Hannah Raven; with Adam Baker and Misses Wigg and Bartell to dinner and tea at Hs', 15.9.94

Raven, Mary (1772–1855), daughter of Nathaniel, cousin of HR; with father to Hs, 17.10.93, 17.3.96; with Hs to Holt, 17.10.93, 15.5.95, 11.8.95, 5.12.95, 15–17.12.95; with cousins to Hs, 20.1.94; departs, 23.1.94, 30.6.96; at Hs' with Bartells, 4.5.94; at Hs', 1.4.95; with aunt Phillis to Hs, 5.5.95; to Holt, 8.5.95; with aunts to Letheringsett Church, 10.5.95; with Hs to Mrs Forster, 13.5.95; with MA to Mr Sheldrake, 14.5.95; departs with aunt, 16.5.95; with brother and HR to Hs, 10.8.95; with brother and Hs to Weybourne Camp, 10.8.95, 12.8.95; with Misses Jennis to Hs from Holt, 13.11.95; with Miss Bartell to dinner and supper at Hs', 20.11.95; with Miss Johnson to Hs, 23.11.95; with WHj to Holt Church, 6.12.95; with WHj and MA to Sheringham, 11–12.12.95; with Hs to tea at Mr Burrell's, 14.12.95; with brother departs for Whissonsett, 18.12.95, 11.8.97; with father and Mrs Cozens dines at Hs', with Hs to Weybourne Camp and Sheringham, 29.6.96; with brother and Mr Bird to Hs, 9.8.97; with family and Hs to tea at Sheringham, 10.8.97

Raven, Mary (1780–1846), of Whissonsett Hall, daughter of Mrs Ann Raven, née Smith, future wife of WHj, sister of HR; with family to Hs, 17.7.94, 7.7.96; with WHj to Hs, 15.11.94; with Hs to Holt, 22.11.94, 1–2.12.94, 7.7.96; with HR to Holt, 25.11.94; with WHj and HR to Holt Church, 30.11.94; departs with WHj for Whissonsett, 5.12.94; with family to Weybourne Camp and Sheringham and departs, 8.7.96

Raven, Mr, of Walsingham; applies for tenancy of Maid's Head, N. Walsham, 10.9.94

Raven, Nathaniel (1735–99), **79**, **241**, Whissonsett grocer, draper, farmer and maltster, uncle of HR; with daughter Mary to Hs, 17.10.93, 17.3.96; with Hs to Holt, 17.10.93, 7.3.94; with wife to Hs, 6.3.94, 14.7.95, 24.11.95, 20.2.97; departs, 8.3.94, 16.5.94, 7.11.94, 26.3.95, 27.11.95, 30.6.96, 10.11.96, 24.2.97; with niece Rose to Hs, 15.5.94; with wife to dinner at Hs', 3.11.94; to Fakenham, 6.11.94; with daughter Ann and nephew Nathaniel to Hs, 24.3.95; with family and Hs to Cley, 25.3.95; with wife, Hs and HR to Weybourne Camp, 14.7.95; with large party to Weybourne Camp, 24.8.95; with Thomas Fox departs, 25.8.95; with WHj to Holt Fair, 25.11.95; with WHj to Blakeney sale, 26.11.95; with daughter Mary and Mrs Cozens dines with Hs, with Hs to Weybourne Camp and Lower Sheringham, 29.6.96; with MH to Hs, 7.11.96; with family to seaside, 9.11.96; with wife and Hs to tea at Mr Sheldrake's, 22.2.97; with wife and Hs to tea at Revd Mr Johnson's, 23.2.97; to Hs, 28.9.97

Raven, Nathaniel jnr (1774–1851), Whissonsett grocer and draper, cousin of HR; with cousin Robert and large party at Hs', 1.1.94; with cousins departs, 3.1.94, 16.6.94, 13.11.95, 18.12.95, 13.3.97, 11.8.97; to Hs, 17.2.94, 27.4.95, 11.1.95, 16.12.95, 9.3.97, 18.3.97, 9.8.97; with Hs to Holt, 18.2.94, 8.8.94, 11.8.95, 11.11.95, 17.12.95; departs, 19.2.94, 9.8.94, 29.4.95, 20.3.97; with Hs to Letheringsett, 14.6.94; with Mr Watson to Hs, 8.8.94; to play at Holt, 28.4.95; with sister Mary and HR to Hs, 10.8.95; with sister and Hs to Weybourne Camp, 10.8.95, 12.8.95; with WHj to Glandford, 1.11.96; with HR to Edgefield and Briston, 10.3.97; with WHj to Holt market, 11.3.97; with cousins to Holt Church, 12.3.97, 3.9.97; with family and Hs to tea at Sheringham, 10.8.97

Raven, Nathaniel (b.1781), **82**, **84**, of Whissonsett Hall, son of Mrs Ann Raven, née Smith, brother of HR; with family to Hs, 26.12.93, 17.7.94, 24.3.95; departs, 3.1.94, 28.12.94, 26.3.95, 25.2.96, 30.4.96, 8.7.96; with Hs to

Raven, Nathaniel (b.1781) (*cont.*)
Holt, 16.6.94; collects brother and sister from Hs, 21.6.94; makes entries in HR's diary, 30.6.94, 24.2.96; to Hs, 16.12.94; with Hs to Sheringham, 17.12.94; with WHj to Blakeney, 18.12.94; with Hs to Thomas Temple, 19.12.94; with family and Hs to Cley, 25.3.95; with family to Weybourne Camp and Sheringham, 8.7.96

Raven, Phillis (1779–1844), **384**, of Whissonsett Hall, Holt schoolteacher, daughter of Mrs Ann Raven, née Smith, sister of HR; with Hs to Guestwick, 17.6.94; with family departs, 21.6.94, 8.7.96, 20.6.97; with family to Hs, 7.7.96, 18.6.97, 4.8.97, 8.8.97; with Hs to Holt, 7.7.96, 4.8.97; with family to Weybourne Camp and Sheringham, 8.7.96; with family to tea at Sheringham, 19.6.97; with WHj and MA to Miss Alpe, 8.8.97; with Miss Massingham to tea at Hs', 3.9.97; with Sheldrakes to tea at Hs', 23.10.97

Raven, Robert (b.1771), **175**, **194**, of Whissonsett Hall, farmer, son of Mrs Ann Raven, née Smith, brother of HR; with large party at Hs', 1.1.94; with family departs, 3.1.94, 23.1.94, 1.6.94, 15.2.95, 8.7.96, 20.6.97; at Hs', 22.1.94; drives his hobby in whiskey to Holt, 23.1.94; to Hs, 20.1.94, 1.2.94, 17.2.94, 13.4.94, 25.5.94, 6.7.94, 21.9.94, 25.4.96, 7. 7.96, 19.6.97, 4.8.97; with Hs to Letheringsett, 7.12.94; with Hs to Holt market, 14.2.95; to Holt, 7.7.96, 4.8.97; with family to Weybourne Camp and Sheringham, 8.7.96; with family to tea at Sheringham, 19.6.97

Raven, Rose, *see* Skrimshire, Mrs

Raven, William (b.1776), formerly of Whissonsett Hall, Hs' former brewing pupil, son of Mrs Ann Raven, née Smith, brother of HR; to dinner and supper at Hs' and stays overnight, 2.7.97; departs for Whissonsett, 3.7.97

Raynor (Rayner), Thomas (John), Hs' maltster; hired for malting season, 29.11.96; has Whit Monday dinner at Hs', 5.6.97; brewing, 12.7.97; jobs, 13–14.7.97, 12.10.97; calls on WH to arrange working in malthouse, 10.9.97; at Hs', 4.10.97; begins steeping, 5.10.97; collects hay from Holt Heath Farm, 12.10.97
malting, **344**: 30.11.96, 1–3.12.96, 5–10.12.96, 12–16.12.96, 19–24.12.96, 26–31.12.96, 2–7.1.97, 9–14.1.97, 16–19.1.97, 21.1.97, 23–28.1.97, 30–31.1.97, 1–2.2.97, 4.2.97, 6–11.2.97, 13–15.2.97, 17–18.2.97, 20–25.2.97, 27–28.2.97, 1–4.3.97, 6–11.3.97, 13.3.97, 15–18.3.97, 20–25.3.96, 29–31.3.97, 1.4.97, 4–8.4.97, 10–15.4.97, 17–22.4.97, 25–29.4.97, 1–6.5.97, 8–13.5.97, 15–20.5.97, 22–27.5.97, 29–31.5.97, 1–3.6.97, 5–8.6.97, 10.6.97, 12–17.6.97, 19–22.6.97, 24.6.97, 26–30.6.97,

Raynor, Thomas, malting (*cont.*)
1.7.97, 3–8.7.97, 10–15.7.97, 9–11.10.97, 13–14.10.97, 16.10.97, 18–21.10.97, 24–25.10.97

reaping, *see* harvests

Reepham (Reefham), Norf., **106**, **286**, WHj to, 12.10.93, 13.7.96; WH and Mr Bartell to, 24.9.94, 20.2.97; WHj and Thomas Balls jnr to, 27.3.97

Reeve, James, innkeeper of Hart, Field Dalling; Thomas Baldwin delivers beer, 14.1.94

Reeve, Jane, of Hart, Field Dalling; orders beer from Hs, 25.8.94

rent, paid to Hs by Mr Williams of Weybourne, 14.10.93

reservoir, *see* pond

rhodium (rodum), used in recipe for poisoning rats, HR's endnotes

Rice, Mr, barrel materials collected by boy from, 30.4.96

Richards (Riches), Miss, dines with Hs, 13.11.95, 20.1.96; with Hs to Holt Church, 13.8.97; with Mr Forster departs from Hs, 14.8.97; left by Mr Forster at Hs', 25.9.97

riddling, *see* screening

riders, at Hs'; Mr Wood's, 12.1.95, 10.11.95; London rider, 16.10.95; hop rider, 12.1.96

ringing, *see* pigs

riots, *see* Sharrington

river, Jeremiah Moore at work in river in Brewhouse Pightle, 5.6.94: *see also* Glaven, River

road (rode), *see* accidents, road; carts; chaises; coach; Letheringsett, road; wagons

Roberts, Mr, of Salthouse; orders beer, 24.2.96

Robinson (Robbinson), Edward, **123**, London linen draper; at large tea party at Hs', 18.8.95

Robinson, Mrs Elizabeth, **123**, née Davy, wife of Edward, daughter of John Davy; with family to tea at Hs', 9.1.94, 19.5.94; with sisters and Mrs Hooper to Hs, 19.8.95

Rolfe, John, **190**, Coltishall builder; at Hs', 8.7.95; installs furnace bars in brewery, 11.7.95

rollers, *see* malt-mill

rolling (rowling), of fields; newly sown barley, 9.5.95; by Hs' men, 18.5.95, 3.6.95, 11.3.96, 19.4.96, 1.6.96, 11.11.96; newly sown peas, 12.3.96, 1.4.97; by John Thompson in Five Acres, 1.7.96; by Hs' men at Holt Heath Farm, 29.3.97; by Thomas Baldwin in Furze Closes, 19.4.97; of newly sown ground, 20.4.97

roof, of Hs' counting house, built by William Tinker, 25.9.97

Rouse, Mr [?Richard (d.1816 aged 84)], **116**, **135**, of Letheringsett and Glandford, miller; his men at work, 10.6.96; Robert Bye and Gunton Thompson cart millstones from his mill, 24.7.97

Rouse, Peter (d.1830 aged 58), farmer, son of Richard; with sister to tea at Hs', 5.10.94

Rouse, Sarah (b.1777), daughter of Richard; with brother to tea at Hs', 5.10.94

Rouse, Zebulon (d.1840 aged 75), **116**, **135**, **142**, 146, Blakeney coal merchant, Glandford and Letheringsett miller and Cley land surveyor, son of Richard; Thomas Boyce collects coal, 4.2.95; William Lamb collects oats from at Cley, 14.2.97

Rowden, Miss [?Julia], with Ravens to Hs, 7.7.96, 19.6.97; to Holt, 7.7.96; departs, 8.7.96, 20.6.97

Roxby, Mr, London hop-factor; with Mr Harris to tea at Hs', 29.4.96

Rudham, *see* West Rudham

Runton, *see* East Runton

Ryburgh (Ryburch, Ryburch), Norf., **252**, Mr Sheldrake on Hs' mare to, 30.8.95; WH and Mr Henderson to, 11.9.95; WHj to, 7.3.96: *see also* Wade, John

S

Sales, Mrs Ann (d.1821 aged 65), née Legge, wife of Charles; with husband to tea at Hs' and to Letheringsett Church, 24.8.94; with Forsters and Mrs Herring to tea at Hs', 2.9.96

Sales, Charles (d.1821 aged 68), Holt draper and grocer; with wife to tea at Hs' and to Letheringsett Church, 24.8.94; to tea at Hs', 13.3.95; at Hs', 22.4.96, 5.8.96; Hs to, 3.10.97

sales, **308**, man injured returning from Thomas Atwood's, 22.5.95; WHj and Nathaniel Raven to at Blakeney, 26.11.95; WH to Mr Forster's at Bayfield, 6.10.96, 8.10.96; Thomas Baldwin collects tumbril from at Bayfield, 8.10.96; Robert Bye collects chairs from at Weybourne, 14.1.97; WH and WHj to Mr Farthing's at Blakeney, 16.8.97; HR begins to sell goods in new counting house, 20.10.97

Salthouse, Norf., **8**, WH to with Mr Cappa/Capps, 4.8.95; Hs' boy collects two pigs, 8.8.95; WHj to, 24.10.95, 25.2.96, 12.10.96; William Lamb delivers straw, 9.2.96, 25.2.96; Mr Roberts orders beer, 24.2.96; William Lamb delivers spars, 25.2.96; WH, MH, Mrs Phillis Goggs, Henry Goggs and Mr Cook to, 25.7.96
beer deliveries:
1793: 18.12.93
1794: 22.1.94, 19.3.94, 23.4.94, 24.5.94, 23.6.94, 23.7.94, 30.8.94, 26.9.94, 31.10.94, 6.12.94
1795: 5.1.95, 9.2.95, 18.3.95, 29.4.95, 10.6.95, 24.7.95, 24.8.95, 30.9.95, 6.10.95, 24.10.95, 17.11.95, 12.12.95

Salthouse, beer deliveries (*cont.*)
1796: 16.1.96, 9.2.96, 12.3.96, 22.4.96, 25.5.96, 20.6.96, 22.7.96, 11.8.96, 5.9.96, 7.10.96, 15.10.96, 5.11.96, 26.11.96
1797: 9.1.97, 7.2.97, 6.4.97, 17.6.97, 10.7.97, 22.8.97, 21.9.97, 14.10.97

samples, *see* barley

sand, spread, 25.2.94, 17.3.94; dug, 25.3.94; carted, 21.5.95, 26.3.96; delivered by Thomas Baldwin to Black Boys, Holt, 5.7.97
collected: 25.2.94, 27.2.94, 1.3.94, 25.3.94, 4.4.94, 17.4.94, 21.5.95, 22.6.95, 31.10.95, 21–22.3.96, 29.7.96, 22.5.97, 2.10.97, 6.10.97, 17.10.97; from Furze Closes, 21.12.93

Sanderson, Samuel, innkeeper of Crown, Sheringham, tied house, and keeper of Weybourne Camp canteen; at Hs', 10.3.95, 15.12.95; dines with Hs, 16.3.95, 9.4.96; beer delivered, 24–25.11.95, 13.6.96; beer collected from Weybourne, 17.11.96: *see also* Sheringham, Crown; Weybourne Camp

sashes, *see* windows

sassafras (sasafax), used in recipe for destroying moles, HR's endnotes

Savory, John Claxton (d.1819), **317**, of Bayfield Hall and Bayfield Lodge [later Bayfield Brecks], farmer; Hs to tea, 22.12.96, 3.1.97, 25.5.97; with WHj to Edgefield, 2.1.97; with wife to Hs and to Letheringsett Church, 15.1.97; with family to tea at Hs', 20.1.97; WHj to, 3.2.97, 28.4.97; with wife, Miss Howard and Hawkins family to tea at Hs', 5.5.97

Savory, Mrs Mary (d.1805 aged 32), **400**, née Howard, wife of John Claxton; with husband to Hs and to Letheringsett Church, 15.1.97; with family to tea at Hs', 20.1.97, 5.5.97

Savory, Miss, [?sister of John Claxton]; to tea at Hs', 6.1.97, 20.1.97, 2.2.97, 9.2.97, 27.2.97

sawing (sawying), **34**, **35**, by carpenters, 1.1.95; by Thomas Youngman's man and boy, 12–13.3.95; by William Tinker and Ben, 27.1.96, 7.1.97, 19.1.97, 21.1.97; by William Tinker and man, 18.1.97, 6.7.97: *see also* wood

sawyers (sawers), **34**, **35**, at work for Hs, 20–21.12.93, 23–24.12.93, 27–28.12.93, 30–31.12.93, 2–4.1.94, 7–9.1.94, 11.1.94, 13–17.1.94, 22.9.97, 5.10.97, 17.10.97: *see also* carpenters

Saxlingham [Saxlingham-by-Holt], Norf., HR takes Robert Bye's horse to, 6.5.94; Mr Hammond bleeds horse at Hs', 28.1.95; WHj to tea with Mr Balls, 23.9.96; WHj to, 24.11.96; WHj dines at, 26.11.96; William Thackwray to, 13.12.96; William Lamb takes wagon to, 12.1.97; WHj to supper at, 1.2.97; Robert Bye collects wagon, 6.2.97; Gunton Thompson summons Mr Hammond, 22.3.97; HR to, 27.3.97,

Saxlingham (*cont.*)
21.5.97; WHj and MA to tea, 21.4.97: *see also* Balls, Thomas; Balls, Thomas jnr; Furze Closes; Hill Close
Saxthorpe, Norf., HR to, 21.8.95
school, **384**, Phillis Raven starts as teacher at Miss Alpe's at Holt, 8.8.97
Scott, Gateson/Gatzon, **326**, Holt saddler and collarmaker; with man repairs Hs' harness, 20.12.96
screening (riddling, skreening, skreining, skrening, striping), by Hs' men, **109**:
culms: 30.1.95
gravel: 13.9.94
malt: 4.11.93, 12.11.93, 27.11.93, 27.8.94, 3.9.94, 18–19.9.94, 14.4.95, 16.4.95, 22.4.95, 8.10.94, 23.10.95, 29.10.95, 6.11.95, 23.11.95, 5.2.96, 11.2.96
meal: 6.12.94, 11.2.95, 13.4.95, 10.8.96
peas: 18.5.97
wheat: 22.11.93, 21.2.94, 5.5.95, 29.6.96: *see also* dressing
sea, **184**, **185**, **189**, **227**, **271**, **363**:
damage by: Hs' men cart rocks to repair jetty at Sheringham, 28.12.95
pleasure trips to: by Nathaniel Raven, Ann and Rose Raven, WHj and MA, 9.11.96; by Henry Goggs, Mr Cook, WHj and MA, 14.8.97: *see also* Salthouse; Sheringham: *see also* shipping
seed, grass seed dressed by Hs' men, 22.4.95, 25.7.96, 14.4.97; clover seed sown by Robert Bye, 7.5.95; grass seed sown in meadow, 25.3.97; HR collects clover seed from Brinton, 28.3.97; sown in Five Acres, 19.4.97: *see also* rolling; sowing
sermon, preached by Mr Burrell at Letheringsett Church on fast day, 8.3.97: *see also* lectures
servants, *see* maidservants; *see also farm servants under* boys; workforce; *also* labourers
servants in husbandry, Hs', *see* workforce
sessions, at Holt; WH to justices' sitting, 11.4.95
hiring: Hs' boy to, 27.9.94, 4.10.94
quarter: WH to, 17.10.93, 23.1.94, 13.10.96; Henry Goggs to, 15.10.95; WHj on grand jury, 21.1.96: *see also* assizes; justices
Setchey (Setch), Norf., **281**, George Dawson to, 17–18.5.94
shafts, *see* chaises
Sharpe, Mr S., of Brinton; with WHj from Holt assembly, stays overnight at Hs', 10.11.94; at Hs', 10.10.95
Sharpens (Sharpan, Sharpen), Mr, of Briston; buys Hs' mare Molly in exchange for filly, 1.7.94; sells horse to WHj, 25.2.95
Sharrington (Sarrington, Sherington, Sherrington), Norf., **221**, **270**, Hs' boy collects 300 fish, 21.7.94; WHj to, 21.7.94, 20.12.95, 15.6.97; HR and J. Kendle to, 2.8.95; HR to, 8.11.95, 7.2.96, 7.8.96, 16.10.96, 18.12.96; HR dines at, 8.5.96, 25.7.97; William Lamb collects straw from Mr Lee, 12.5.97; HR meets family party, 18.6.97
beer deliveries:
1793: 7.11.93
1794: 8.2.94, 15.3.94, 2.5.94, 4.6.94, 27.6.94, 24.7.94, 23.8.94, 24.9.94, 6.11.94, 20.12.94
1795: 6.3.95, 11.4.95, 18.5.95, 1.8.95, 16.9.95, 4.11.95, 17.12.95, 19.12.95, 21.12.95
1796: 11.1.96, 16.2.96, 23.4.96, 2.6.96, 28.7.96, 24.9.96, 28.10.96, 26.12.96
1797: 31.1.97, 27.2.97, 22.3.97, 13.4.97, 28.4.97, 9.5.97, 17.5.97, 25.5.97, 3.6.97, 9.6.97, 14.7.97, 25.7.97, 23.9.97
riots, **228**, **231**, **232**, **233**, **234**, **235**: HR meets mob, 17.12.95; WH to, 18.12.95; soldiers sent to, 20.12.95; WH joins large party of farmers riding to quell, 21.12.95
Shearing (Herring), **346**, Master, with Master Collyer to tea at Hs', 1.6.97
shearing, *see* harvests
Sheldrake, John, Holt excise officer and Inspector of Weights and Balances, Holt hundred; with wife to tea at Hs', 9.1.94, 22.5.94, 6.11.94, 3.12.94, 7.1.95, 6.3.95, 10.4.95, 6.8.95, 16.9.95, 13.10.95, 13.11.95, 6.1.96, 4.2.96, 8.3.96, 9.1.97, 21.2.97, 23.3.97, 18.5.97, 25.8.97, 23.10.97; to supper at Hs', 4.11.94, 6.4.96, 3.7.96, 12.7.97, 1.9.97; to tea, 15.6.95, 24.5.97, 25.10.97; borrows Hs' mare to Ryburgh, 30.8.95; calls with examiner at Hs', 13.10.95; to dinner, 25.4.96, 12.7.97; Hs and Mr and Mrs Nathaniel Raven to tea, 22.2.97; helps Hs with wheat harvest, 4.9.97
Sheldrake, Miss M., daughter of John; with parents to tea at Hs', 6.11.94, 3.12.94, 9.1.97
Sheldrake, Mrs, Holt dressmaker, wife of John; with husband to tea at Hs', 9.1.94, 22.5.94, 6.11.94, 3.12.94, 7.1.95, 6.3.95, 10.4.95, 6.8.95, 16.9.95, 13.10.95, 13.11.95, 6.1.96, 4.2.96, 8.3.96, 9.1.97, 21.2.97, 23.3.97, 18.5.97, 25.8.97, 23.10.97; MA and Mary Raven to tea, 14.5.95; with husband to supper at Hs', 6.4.96; with Miss Baker and Miss Mack to tea, 8.7.96
Sheppard (Shephard), Mrs Elizabeth (d.1816 aged 77), **20**, **59**, née Main, innkeeper of the Feathers, Holt, and excise officekeeper; her coach hired by Hs, 25.3.94: *see also* Holt, public houses, Feathers
Sheringham (Sharringham, Sherringham), Norf., **227**, HR on errand to, 6.12.93; William Lamb and Robert Bye cart rocks to repair

Sheringham (*cont.*)
jetty, 28.12.95; Thomas Baldwin collects paving stones, 21.3.96, 9.4.96; HR with party to, 10.4.96
beer deliveries to Upper Sheringham [?to Cook Flower]: 26.12.94, 4.2.95, 23.7.95, 29.10.95, 28.12.95, 21.6.96
Crown at Lower Sheringham: William Lamb delivers lime, 27.5.97; William Lamb collects money, 6.6.97
beer deliveries:
1793: 12.10.93, 22.10.93, 8.11.93, 30.11.93, 14.12.93, 30.12.93
1794: 17.1.94, 22.2.94, 18.3.94, 29.3.94, 11.4.94, 23.4.94, 2.5.94, 16.5.94, 30.5.94, 18.6.94, 5.7.94, 18.7.94, 29.7.94, 16.8.94, 27.8.94, 17.9.94, 22.9.94, 25.9.94, 4.10.94, 17.10.94, 1.11.94, 7.11.94, 22.11.94, 22.12.94
1795: 10.1.95, 14.2.95, 23.3.95, 16.4.95, 1.5.95, 11.5.95, 25.5.95, 1.6.95, 11.6.95, 19.6.95, 29.6.95, 3.7.95, 17.7.95, 28.7.95, 3.8.95, 8.8.95, 1.9.95, 14.9.95, 18.9.95, 26.9.95, 7.10.95, 22.10.95, 12.11.95, 26.11.95, 14.12.95, 28.12.95
1796: 7.1.96, 19.1.96, 28.1.96, 12.2.96, 21.3.96, 9.4.96, 23.4.96, 29.4.96, 11.5.96, 23.5.96, 7.6.96, 20.6.96, 30.6.96, 8.7.96, 16.7.96, 5.8.96, 17.8.96, 29.8.96, 23.9.96, 4.10.96, 10.10.96, 22.10.96, 29.10.96, 14.11.96, 21–22.11.96, 2.12.96, 19.12.96
1797: 25.1.97, 4.2.97, 4.3.97, 28.3.97, 14.4.97, 1.5.97, 19.5.97, 27.5.97, 3.6.97, 15.6.97, 24.6.97, 8.7.97, 25.7.97, 8.8.97, 26.8.97, 12.9.97, 29.9.97, 12.10.97
loading: 13.11.96:
see also Edwards, John; Johnson, Robert; Sanderson, Samuel
Mr and Mrs Cook Flower of [Old] Hall, **10**: WHj and MA to, 4.12.93; Hs to dinner, 24.6.94; Thomas Baldwin and William Dobson collect pigs, 22.9.96: *see also* Flower, Cook; Flower, Mrs Sarah
Hs to: WHj and MA, 21.3.94, 27.7.95; WH, MA, Rose Raven and Mr and Miss Symonds, 20.5.94; WHj, MA, Phillis Raven and Miss Symonds, 6.6.94; WHj, MA and Nathaniel Raven, 17.12.94; WH and WHj, 4.2.95, 1.6.95, 31.10.96, 16.6.97; WH and WHj to Lower Sheringham, 6.4.95; WHj, MA and Mary Raven, 12.5.95, 11–12.12.95; WHj and MA with party of friends, 24.9.95; Hs with Nathaniel Raven, daughter Mary and Mrs Cozens for tea, 29.6.96; WHj and Raven cousins, 8.7.96; Hs to dinner, 10.8.96; WH, WHj and William Thackwray, 27.9.96, 1.10.96; WHj, MA, Messrs Skrimshire, Rose,

Sheringham, Hs to (*cont.*)
Phillis and Robert Raven and HR to tea, 19.6.97; WHj, MA, Mr Bird, Nathaniel Raven jnr, Mary Raven and HR to tea, 10.8.97
WHj to: 24.4.94, 27.10.94, 13.1.95, 18.2.95, 20.6.95, 14.9.95, 9.11.95, 16.11.95, 20.11.95, 27.11.95, 1.12.95, 28.12.95, 9.3.96, 1.6.96, 21.9.96, 14–15.11.96, 28.11.96, 23.1.97, 22.3.97, 29.5.97, 9–10.6.97, 14.6.97, 26.6.97, 13.9.97, 21.10.97
Sherington, *see* Sharrington
shipping, **227**, flour dressed for, 8.11.93, 19.11.93; beer delivered to Blakeney for London, 15.11.94; beer delivered to Blakeney for, 22.5.95
shooting (shootting), **165**, John Davy snr and jnr to dinner at Hs' while, 23.9.95; by William Thackwray and Charles Kendle, 11.10.96, 19.10.96, 6.12.96; by William Thackwray, 13.10.96; by WHj and James Moore, 18.9.97
shrubbery, *see* garden
Siderstone, *see* Syderstone
sieving (riddling), *see* screening
Silence (Silance, Silense), William, innkeeper of Fighting Cocks, Wells, tied house; at Hs' with John Walden, 10.9.96, 18.10.96; at Hs', 3.10.97: *see also* Wells, beer deliveries
Six Acres (Six Acars), Letheringsett field farmed by Hs; Thomas Hall hedging in, 7–9.4.95; ploughed by Hs' men, 1.1.96, 7.3.96, 10.3.96, 1.10.96; Thomas Boyce working in, 11–12.3.96, 14.3.96; William Lamb carts muck from heap in, 16.6.96; men filling muck cart, 28.10.96; Thomas Boyce hoeing furrows, 20.5.97; men raking, 13.9.97
sixpenny, *see* beer
skating (scating), by WHj and HR at Hempstead, 25.1.95; by WHj and William Thackwray at Holt, 5.12.96
Skelton, Mr, delivers coarse flour to Hs, 8.9.94
Skiffins (Skiffings), James William, innkeeper of Black Boys, Holt, tied house, and White Lion, Holt; calls at brewery, 2.1.94; William Tinker and man at work at, 3.1.94; offers mare for sale to Hs, 18.11.94
beer deliveries, **39**, **59**, **138**: 16.11.93, 4.12.93, 19.4.94
gardening for Hs: 1.4.94, 23.5.94, 30.5.94, 25.8.94, 19.9.94
orders beer: 20.1.94, 21.1.95, 24.2.96:
see also Holt, beer deliveries; Holt, public houses
Skrimshire, George, later Fakenham shopkeeper, son of William snr; with family and Ravens to Hs, 18.6.97; with Hs and family party to tea at Sheringham, 19.6.97; with

Skrimshire, George (*cont.*)
family and Ravens departs for Whissonsett, 20.6.97

Skrimshire, Mrs Rose (1773–1829), née Raven, wife of Thomas, daughter of Mrs Ann Raven, née Smith, sister of HR; with uncle Nathaniel to Hs, 15.5.94; goes out with Hs, 16.5.94, 21.5.94; with Hs to Holt, 17.5.94, 26.5.94, 31.5.94, 16.4.96, 23–24.4.96, 26.4.96, 7.7.96, 3.11.96, 5.11.96; with Hs to Sheringham, 20.5.94; with Hs to Holt market, 24.5.94; with family departs for Whissonsett, 1.6.94, 30.4.96, 8.7.96; with cousin Ann to Hs from Holt, 15.4.96, 21.4.96; with Ann and Hs to tea at Mr Forster's, 22.4.96; with Ann, WHj and MA spends day at Cook Flower's, 27.4.96; with Ann and HR to Holt, 29.4.96; with family to Hs, 7.7.96; with family to Weybourne Camp and Sheringham, 8.7.96; with Ann to Hs, 31.10.96; with cousins to seaside, 9.11.96; with sister Phillis and Skrimshires to Hs, 18.6.97; with Hs and family party to tea at Sheringham, 19.6.97; with family and Skrimshires departs for Whissonsett, 20.6.97

Skrimshire, Thomas (d.1836 aged 61), LLB [Revd Thomas 1798], of Wisbech, Master of Fakenham Academy, Curate of Whissonsett 1798, Curate of Houghton juxta Harpley 1814–17, 1822– ?, Rector of Testerton and Vicar of Gt and Lt Hockham 1800–36, Vicar of Houghton juxta Harpley and Vicar of S. Creake 1817–24, Chaplain to Marquess of Cholmondeley, Master of Syderstone School, son of William snr; with family, Rose and Phillis Raven to Hs, 18.6.97; with Hs and family party to tea at Sheringham, 19.6.97; with family and Ravens departs for Whissonsett, 20.6.97

Skrimshire, William [? snr, Wisbech surgeon, ? jnr], with family and Ravens to Hs, 18.6.97; with Hs and family party to tea at Sheringham, 19.6.97; with family and Ravens departs for Whissonsett, 20.6.97

sluice (watergate), **65**, **77**, **144**, repaired by Thomas Youngman, 31.7.94, 21.5.96; repaired by William Tinker, 21.5.96

small beer, *see* beer

Smith, Mrs Elizabeth (d.1803), formerly Mrs Hunt, 1st wife of John; to tea at Hs', 20.7.95; with Proudfoots to tea at Hs', 5.6.97

Smith, John, Cley attorney; with Bartells and Sheldrakes to tea at Hs', 3.12.94; with Sheldrakes to tea at Hs', 6.8.95; with Hs to Norwich for day, 21.5.96; goes out with WH, 29.8.96; with Mr Bignold spends day at Hs', 25.10.96; dines at Hs', 22.11.96; with WH to Thursford, 29.3.97; to tea at Hs', 7.6.97

Smith, Mr, in Hs' garden, 7.3.95

Snoring, Norf., **244**, HR accompanies family to on their journey to Whissonsett, 13.11.94, 5.12.94

soldiers, *see* Army; Weybourne Camp

soot, sown by Robert Bye and boy, 11.1.94

Southrepps (Southreeps), Norf., two men from to dinner with Hs, 14.3.95; Hs to with Mrs Phillis Goggs, 23.9.95; William Lamb collects piano, 3.5.97
beer deliveries, **55**, **56**, **109**:
1794: 12.9.94, 6.10.94, 22.10.94, 31.10.94, 28.11.94, 31.12.94
1795: 30.1.95, 24.2.95, 26.3.95, 2.4.95, 6.5.95, 30.5.95, 2.6.95, 13.7.95, 18.8.95, 4.9.95, 8.10.95, 6.11.95, 27.11.95, 24.12.95
1796: 18.1.96, 12.2.96, 26.2.96, 30.3.96, 2.5.96, 14.5.96, 6.6.96, 5.7.96, 30.7.96, 22.9.96, 25.10.96
1797: 31.1.97, 2.3.97, 17.3.97, 13.4.97, 21.4.97, 3.5.97, 12.6.97, 27.6.97, 7.8.97, 19.8.97, 30.9.97, 20.10.97
loading: 11.9.94, 30.10.94, 30.12.94, 29.1.95, 25.3.95, 1.4.95, 5.5.95, 3.9.95, 17.1.96, 11.2.96, 1.5.96, 5.6.96, 29.7.96
WH to: 28.10.94, 9.3.95, 5.5.95; with HR, 6.10.97
WHj to: 28.10.94, 9.3.95, 5.5.95, 18.5.95, 20.7.95, 3.8.95, 17.8.95, 1.9.95, 14.10.95, 26.12.95; with Thomas Balls jnr, 13.4.97: *see also* Foulger, Robert; Summers, John

sowing, by Hs' men; 23.4.94, 30.4.94, 14.7.94, 27.4.96; in Bell's Acre, 23.6.96; in meadow, 20.3.97; in Five Acres, 19.4.97; Thomas Baldwin rolling new-laid ground, 20.4.97
barley: 28.4.94, 16.4.95, 25.4.95, 1–2.5.95, 5.5.95, 7.5.95, 20–21.4.96, 11.4.97, 14.4.97, 18.4.97; in Furze Closes, 15.4.95, 20–21.4.95, 24.4.95, 12.4.97; in Five Acres, 30.4.95, 15.4.97, 17.4.97; at Holt Heath Farm, 28.3.97; in Bell's Acre, 12.4.97
clover: 7.5.95
culms: 10.1.94, 4.4.96
grass: in meadow, 25.3.97
oats: 23.3.97; at Holt Heath Farm, 27.3.97
peas, **254**: 30–31.3.97
soot: 11.1.94
turnips: 17.6.94, 21.6.94, 29.6.96, 1–2.7.96, 5.7.96, 29.6.97; in Furze Closes, 1.7.97, 4.7.97
vetches: 29–30.10.94, 1.11.94, 8.4.96, 3.11.96
wheat: 19.10.93, 12.11.95, 3–4.11.96, 8.11.96: *see also* dibbling; rolling; seed

sows, *see* pigs

spars, *see* wood

sports, *see* bowling green; shooting

spices, *see* cloves

stables, **3**, **37**, **77**, doors repaired by William Tinker and man, 31.1.94; demolished at King's Head, Letheringsett, 24.2.94; foundations laid by Thomas Boyce, 3.3.94; Thomas Boyce working behind, 6.4.95
stacks, **133**:
barley: brought in by Hs' men, 8.3.94; foundation laid by Thomas Hall, 16.9.95; removed into barn, 11.2.96: *see also* goaft
hay: foundation laid by Hs' men, 15.7.96; Hs' men at work, 18.7.96, 20–22.7.96, 20–21.7.97; Mr Forster's men help Hs with, 20–22.7.96; propped, 21.7.96; trimmed by Thomas Boyce, 23.7.96, 22.7.97; loose hay removed into hay chamber, 23.7.96; thatched by Thomas Boyce, 1.8.96
wheat: Hs' men at work, 4.9.97; thatched by Thomas Hall, 6.9.97; fenced by Robert Bye, 13.9.97
Staff, Robert, innkeeper of Maid's Head, Stalham, tied house; at Hs', 21–23.1.94, 17.3.95, 16.12.95; orders beer, 13.4.94; with WHj to Blakeney, 18.3.95: *see also* Stalham
Stalham, Norf, Robert Staff to Hs from, 16.12.95
beer deliveries:
1793: 11–12.10.93, 18–19.11.93
1794: 15–16.1.94, 26–27.2.94, 13–15.4.94, 12–13.5.94, 11–12.6.94, 4–5.7.94, 13–14.8.94, 1–2.10.94, 24–25.10.94, 5–6.12.94
1795: 20–21.1.95, 20–21.3.95, 1–2.5.95, 25.5.95, 29–30.6.95, 10–11.8.95, 18–19.9.95, 9–10.10.95, 20–21.11.95
1796: 20–21.1.96, 3–4.3.96, 13–14.4.96, 19–20.5.96, 30.6.96–1.7.96, 3–4.8.96, 5.10.96, 1–2.11.96, 23–24.12.96
1797: 6–7.3.97, 24–25.4.97, 9–10.6.97, 17–18.7.97, 8–9.9.97, 13–14.10.97
loading: 14.1.94, 3.7.94, 30.9.94, 23.10.94, 19.1.95, 19.3.95, 28.6.95, 9.8.95, 19.11.95, 19.1.96, 2.3.96, 12.4.96, 3.10.96, 31.10.96, 22.12.96, 23.4.97, 16.7.97, 12.10.97:
see also Staff, Robert
Stannard, Miss, of Norwich; with Bartells at Hs', 24.8.94; at Hs', 21.6.95
Stannard, Mr, with Mr Bartell at Hs', 2.10.97
Starling, Samuel (Sam), threshing for Hs, 21–22.9.97
staves, *see* barrels
steeping, in Hs' malthouse, **212**, **213**; John Ramm pumping liquor into steep, 18.10.93; by John Ramm, 22.10.93, 14.10.94, 30.5.95, 5.10.95, 9.10.95; John Ramm empties steep, 24.10.93; begun by Thomas Raynor, 5.10.97
steward, Henry Goggs's, with Henry Goggs and Hs to Weybourne Camp, 8.7.95
sticks, *see* wood
stock, *see* cows; geese; horses; livestock; pigs
Stody (Study), Norf., WHj and MA to, 3.4.95; WHj to, 29.4.95; HR to, 10.6.95; Hs' boy to, 11–12.8.95; William Thackwray to, 31.12.96
beer deliveries, **17**:
1793: 1.11.93, 5.11.93, 28.11.93
1794: 1.1.94, 8.2.94, 12.3.94, 18.4.94, 10.5.94, 31.5.94, 25.6.94, 12.7.94, 23.8.94, 17.9.94, 11.10.94, 8.11.94, 10.12.94
1795: 1.1.95, 19.1.95, 5.3.95, 11.4.95, 15.6.95, 18.6.95, 7.8.95, 3.9.95, 9.10.95, 24.10.95, 30.11.95
1796: 9.1.96, 2.2.96, 5.3.96, 19.3.96, 25.3.96, 22.4.96, 25.5.96, 2.7.96, 19.7.96, 18.8.96, 7.9.96, 27.10.96, 8.12.96
1797: 17.1.97, 4.3.97, 8.4.97, 17.5.97, 17.6.97, 21.6.97, 25.7.97, 15.8.97, 23.9.97, 13.10.97
stonemason, sweeps Hs' chimney, 16.2.95
stones:
carted by Hs' men: 7.5.94; into road out of yard at King's Head, Letheringsett, 8.5.94; out of brewhouse yard, 14.7.94; rocks carted to repair jetty at Sheringham, 28.12.95
collected by Hs' men: 10.3.94, 10.6.95, 25.6.95; from Hempstead, 7.1.94; from lime-kiln, 19.2.94; from Charles Lamb, 5.6.95; building stones removed from Holt Lane, 22.6.95; from the street, 27.6.95; paving stones collected from Sheringham, 21.3.96, 9.4.96; from road, 8.6.96; from land at Holt Heath Farm, 27.3.97
gravel: delivered to Black Boys, Holt, 9.1.94; spread by John Fox, 17.4.94; spread in yard, 24.4.94; carted to head yard, 2.5.94; carted, 8.5.94, 24–25.7.94, 2.8.94, 31.12.94, 31.3.96, 2.4.96, 5–6.5.96, 11.1.97, 3–4.2.97; collected, 9.8.94, 17.12.94, 3.2.96; sieved, 13.9.94; collected from Mr Burrell, 24.3.95; carted from Furze Closes, 15.4.95; carted into yard from Mr Williams' pit, 30.3.96; carted from Hs' garden, 15.6.96, 21.6.96; taken to meadow, 1.2.97, 3–4.2.97, 8–9.2.97; spread in meadow, 7.2.97
stopping gaps, *see* hedges
storm, tempest, 15.7.96
straw, cut by Abraham Dobson, 7.3.94; delivered to Salthouse, 9.2.96, 25.2.96; unloaded, 29.3.97, 29.8.97
purchase from: Mr Temple, 25.3.97, 11.5.97; Mr Lee at Sharrington, 12.5.97; Kelling, 28–29.8.97
stubble: collected from Furze Closes, 12.11.96; wheat stubble harrowed, 12.11.96; collected, 12.11.96; barley stubble ploughed, 22.12.96
stripping (striping), *see* screening
stubble, *see* straw

Study, *see* Stody

Sturley, John, of Thornage Hall, farmer and butcher; Hs' men deliver malt, 21.11.93, 5.1.95

sugar, used in recipe for poisoning rats, HR's endnotes

Summers, John, **55**, **109**, innkeeper of Crown, Southrepps, tied house; at Hs', 10.9.94; dines with Hs, 11.10.94: *see also* Southrepps

Swanton Novers, Norf., **27**, WH and MH injured in chaise accident, 3.7.94; Thomas Baldwin collects tiles, 17.9.94

Syderstone (Siderstone), Norf., Robert Bye collects empty barrels, 24.2.97
beer deliveries:
1793: 23.10.93, 11.11.93, 7.12.93
1794: 20.1.94, 4.3.94, 5.4.94, 7.5.94, 12.5.94, 9.6.94, 21.6.94, 10.7.94, 26.7.94, 20.8.94, 3.9.94, 24.9.94, 14.10.94, 20.10.94, 24.11.94, 27.12.94
1795: 3.1.95, 8.2.95, 4.3.95, 4.4.95, 4.5.95, 23.5.95, 16.6.95, 11.7.95, 12.8.95, 4.9.95, 21.9.95, 12.10.95, 6.11.95, 19.12.95
1796: 15.1.96, 22–23.2.96, 30.4.96, 31.5.96, 25.6.96, 25.7.96, 27.7.96, 19.8.96, 13.9.96, 19.9.96, 11.10.96, 22.10.96, 7.12.96
1797: 13.1.97, 3.4.97, 11.5.97, 8.6.97, 17.7.97, 4.8.97, 9.9.97, 13.9.97, 9.10.97
loading: 6.12.93, 19.1.94, 2.9.94, 26.12.94, 2.1.95, 8.2.95, 3.3.95, 3.4.95, 3.5.95, 22.5.95, 10.7.95, 11.8.95, 3.9.95, 20.9.95, 18.12.95, 14.1.96, 29.4.96, 24.7.96, 26.7.96, 12.9.96, 10.10.96, 6.12.96, 10.5.97, 16.7.97, 8.10.97

Symonds, Jonathan (d.1803 aged 65), **71**, of Gt Yarmouth and Ormesby St Margaret, grocer and merchant; with daughter to Hs, 18.5.94; with WHj to Holt, with Hs to Sheringham, 20.5.94

Symonds, Phillis (d. 1805 aged 26), **71**, daughter of Jonathan; with father to Hs, 18.5.94; with Hs to Sheringham, 20.5.94; with Hs to Holt market, 26.5.94; with Hs to Holt, 26.5.94, 31.5.94; with Hs to tea at Mr Forster's, 27.5.94; very ill, 28.5.94

T

tally, kept by Gunton Thompson during malt-screening, 3.9.94

tasking, *see* threshing

teacher, *see* school

teams, *see* horses

Temple, Mrs Mary, née Beverley, wife of Thomas; with family and large party at Hs', 1.1.94; with husband to tea at Hs', 18.12.94; with husband and Bartells to supper at Hs', 3.3.96; with Bartells at Hs', 18.1.97

Temple, Miss, daughter of Thomas; with parents and large party at Hs', 1.1.94

Temple, Richard, Barmer farmer; Thomas Temple orders load of mild from Hs for, 16.12.94; Robert Bye delivers four barrels to, 4.3.95; dines with Hs, 18.6.96; to tea at Hs', 18.9.97: *see also* Barmer

Temple (Tempel, Tempell), Thomas, Thornage farmer; his men turning muck at Hs', 28.4.94; his men carting muck from Hs, 7.6.94, 9.6.94, 11–14.6.94, 16–18.6.94; with WH to Wells, 17.9.94; Hs' men collect hay, 23.4.95; Hs' men collect straw, 25.3.97, 11.5.97
at Hs': with family and large party, 1.1.94; to tea, 21.4.94, 18.12.94, 17.2.97; orders load of mild for Richard Temple, 16.12.94; with wife and Bartells to supper, 3.3.96
Hs to: WH, MA, Clara Wymer and Charlotte Bartell, 13.12.93; WHj and party, 2.1.94; WH and MH, 3.2.94; to tea, 1.5.94, 12.6.94, 10.9.94; with Nathaniel Raven, 19.12.94; MH, WHj and HR to supper, 28.1.96; WH, MH, WHj and MA, 13.1.97; WHj to tea, 13.2.97; WH, 30.3.97; HR to tea, 28.5.97

Temple, Thomas William (d.1816 aged 48), Blakeney coal and cinder merchant; Hs' men collect cinders, 21.12.96, 29.12.96; to tea at Hs', 30.1.97, 12.5.97; to dinner, 25.4.97; Hs' men collect coal, 18.5.97, 26.9.97

Thackwray (Thackwry), William (b.*c.*1779), **310**, of Forest Lane Head, Knaresborough, Yorks, WH's nephew; arrives at Hs', 26.9.96; with Hs to Bayfield, 27.9.96; with WH and WHj to Sheringham, 27.9.96, 1.10.96; with Hs to Holt, 4.10.96, 8.10.96, 29.10.96, 5.11.96; goes shooting with Charles Kendle, 11.10.96, 19.10.96, 6.12.96; out shooting, 13.10.96; with WHj to Wells, 14.10.96; with WHj and MA at Whissonsett, 20–22.10.96; gathers apples, 27.10.96; with Hs to Letheringsett Church, 13.11.96; with MH to Cley meeting, 20.11.96, 27.11.96; with WHj skating at Holt, 5.12.96; to Saxlingham, 13.12.96; to Stody, 31.12.96; to Wells with John Thompson, 1.1.97

thatching (thaching), haystack by Thomas Boyce, 1–2.8.96, 4–6.8.96; wheatstack by Thomas Hall, 6.9.97

Thaxter, Mr, of N. Walsham; William Lamb delivers two barrels, 2.5.96

theatre, at Holt, *see* plays

Thetford, Norf., WHj and John Ellis to, 11.3.96

Thirst, Thomas, innkeeper of White Horse, Overstrand; orders beer from Hs at Holt Fair, 25.11.93

Thomas, Revd William, Curate of Holt *c.*1790–96; WHj to supper, 26.11.93; with James Moore to dinner at Hs', 5.2.94

Thompson, Mrs Ann (d.1800 aged 50), **65**, wife of William Gunton; with husband to Cley, 25.7.94; haymaking with daughter for Hs, 25.7.95, 4–5.7.96, 7–8.7.96, 12–13.7.96; raking behind hay wagon, 21.7.96; gathering barley for Hs, 30.8.97, 6–7.9.97; haymaking at Holt Heath Farm, 6.10.97

Thompson (Tompson), Gunton Chapman, Hs' labourer, son of William Gunton; with father dresses Hs' malt-mill stones, 11.10.93; at muck cart, 17–18.10.93; collects turnips, 18.10.93; gathers apples, 19.10.93; arrested by WHj and taken before justices, 28.7.94; with father lays down maltstones, 30.7.94; pumping, 26.8.94; harvesting, 26.8.94, 28.8.94; married before breakfast, 5.11.95

Thompson, Harriet Gunton, daughter of William Gunton; haymaking with mother for Hs, 25.7.95, 4–5.7.96, 7–8.7.96, 12–13.7.96

Thompson, John, helps Hs with harvest, 21.8.94, 28.8.94; delivers barrel of beer to Cley, 22.10.96; takes William Thackwray to Wells, 1.1.97

Thompson, Messrs [Stackhouse and Timothy], Norwich brewers, *see* Tompson

Thompson (Tompson), William Gunton (Gun, Gunton), **65**, **135**, **148**, Hs' brewer, miller and millwright 1792–98; his coal collected by Hs' men from ports, 8.8.94, 31.10.95, 3.10.96; his corn threshed by John Ramm, 25.9.94; house painted by HR, 28.8.95; does no work, 21.2.97; ill, 27.4.97

brewing:

1793: 23.11.93, 3.12.93, 16.12.93, 23.12.93, 30.12.93

1794: 6.1.94, 13.1.94, 20.1.94, 27.1.94, 10.2.94, 24.2.94, 3.3.94, 11.3.94, 17.3.94, 24.3.94, 31.3.94, 7.4.94, 14.4.94, 5.5.94, 10.5.94, 14.5.94, 20.5.94, 24.5.94, 3.6.94, 7.6.95, 16.6.94, 23.6.94, 30.6.94, 8.7.94, 17.7.94, 4.8.94, 11.8.94, 18.8.94, 25.8.94, 1.9.94, 8.9.94, 15.9.94, 22.9.94, 29.9.94, 6.10.94, 13.10.94, 17.10.94, 22.10.94, 29.10.94, 4.11.94, 10.11.94, 17.11.94, 26.11.94, 4.12.94, 11.12.94, 20.12.94

1795: 14.1.95, 26.1.95, 2.2.95, 16.2.95, 26.2.95, 16.3.95, 23.3.95, 30.3.95, 10.4.95, 20.4.95, 24.4.95, 29.4.95, 2.5.95, 6.5.95, 11.5.95, 16.5.95, 21.5.95, 25.5.95, 29.5.95, 3.6.95, 11.6.95, 17.6.95, 23.6.95, 1.7.95, 8.7.95, 16.7.95, 22.7.95, 29.7.95, 6.8.95, 19.8.95, 26.8.95, 2.9.95, 12.9.95, 16.9.95, 22.9.95, 28.9.95, 2.10.95, 7.10.95, 13.10.95, 20.10.95, 26.10.95, 2.11.95, 13.11.95, 19.11.95, 24.11.95, 28.11.95, 4.12.95, 9.12.95, 16.12.95, 24.12.95, 31.12.95

1796: 8.1.96, 12.1.96, 18.1.96, 25.1.96, 1.2.96, 8.2.96, 13.2.96, 17.2.96, 27.2.96, 2.3.96, 8.3.96, 15.3.96, 19.3.96, 24.3.96, 29.3.96, 1.4.96, 5.4.96, 9.4.96, 12.4.96, 15.4.96, 19.4.96, 26.4.96, 2.5.96, 9.5.96, 16.5.96, 23.5.96, 30.5.96, 7.6.96, 13.6.96, 20.6.96, 28.6.96, 4.7.96, 11.7.96, 25.7.96, 1.8.96, 8.8.96, 15.8.96, 22.8.96, 30.8.96, 7.9.96, 14.9.96, 22.9.96, 28.9.96, 5.10.96, 11.10.96, 19.10.96, 26.10.96, 5.11.96, 10.11.96, 17.11.96, 23.11.96, 2.12.96, 9.12.96, 20.12.96, 28.12.96

Thompson, William Gunton, brewing, 1796 (*cont.*)

1797: 9.1.97, 19.1.97, 27.1.97, 2.2.97, 11.2.97, 16.2.97, 22.2.97, 27.2.97, 3.3.97, 6.3.97, 9.3.97, 16.3.97, 21.3.97, 25.3.97, 1.4.97, 6.4.97, 13.4.97, 20.4.97, 28.4.97, 1.5.97, 3.5.97, 5.5.97, 10.5.97, 15.5.97, 23.5.97, 31.5.97, 8.6.97, 14.6.97, 20.6.97, 28.6.97, 19.7.97, 26.7.97, 2.8.97, 17.8.97, 23.8.97, 1.9.97, 11.9.97, 19.9.97, 28.9.97, 4.10.97, 11.10.97, 18.10.97, 25.10.97

cleansing beer:

1793: 17.10.93, 19.10.93, 24.10.93, 26.10.93, 31.10.93, 7.11.93, 9.11.93, 14.11.93, 16.11.93, 23–24.11.93, 26.11.93, 30.11.93, 2.12.93, 4.12.93, 6.12.93, 12.12.93, 17.12.93, 19.12.93, 24.12.93, 26.12.93, 31.12.93

1794: 2.1.94, 7.1.94, 9.1.94, 14.1.94, 16.1.94, 23.1.94, 28.1.94, 30.1.94, 4.2.94, 6.2.94, 13.2.94, 18.2.94, 20.2.94, 27.2.94, 4.3.94, 6.3.94, 12.3.94, 18.3.94, 20.3.94, 25.3.94, 27.3.94, 3.4.94, 8.4.94, 10.4.94, 15.4.94, 17.4.94, 30.4.94, 6–7.5.94, 13.5.94, 15.5.94, 17.5.94, 27.5.94, 4.6.94, 6.6.94, 10.6.94, 17.6.94, 19.6.94, 24–25.6.94, 1–2.7.94, 9.7.94, 18.7.94, 29.7.94, 5.8.94, 12.8.94, 19.8.94, 26.8.94, 2.9.94, 9.9.94, 16.9.94, 23.9.94, 30.9.94, 1.10.94, 7–8.10.94, 14–15.10.94, 18–19.10.94, 23–24.10.94, 30–31.10.94, 5–6.11.94, 11–12.11.94, 18–19.11.94, 27–28.11.94, 5–6.12.94, 21–22.12.94, 31.12.94

1795: 8–9.1.95, 15–16.1.95, 27–28.1.95, 3–4.2.95, 10–11.2.95, 17–18.2.95, 27–28.2.95, 7–8.3.95, 17–18.3.95, 24–25.3.95, 1.4.95, 11–12.4.95, 21.4.95, 25.4.95, 8.5.95, 17–18.5.95, 26–27.5.95, 30–31.5.95, 4.6.95, 12–13.6.95, 18.6.95, 2.7.95, 9.7.95, 17.7.95, 23.7.95, 30.7.95, 7.8.95, 14.8.95, 20.8.95, 27.8.95, 3.9.95, 13–14.9.95, 18.9.95, 23–24.9.95, 29–30.9.95, 3.10.95, 8.10.95, 14–15.10.95, 21–22.10.95, 27–28.10.95, 3–4.11.95, 14.11.95, 20–21.11.95, 25–26.11.95, 30.11.95, 5–6.12.95, 10–11.12.95, 17–18.12.95, 25–26.12.95

1796: 1–2.1.96, 9.1.96, 13–14.1.96, 19–20.1.96, 26.1.96, 2–3.2.96, 9.2.96, 14–

Thompson, William Gunton, cleansing, 1796 (*cont.*)
15.2.96, 18–19.2.96, 23- 24.2.96, 29.2.96, 3–4.3.96, 16–17.3.96, 20–21.3.96, 25–26.3.96, 3.4.96, 6.4.96, 13.4.96, 16.4.96, 27–28.4.96, 3.5.96, 10–11.5.96, 17.5.96, 24.5.96, 31.5.96, 1.6.96, 8–9.6.96, 14–15.6.96, 21.6.96, 29.6.96, 5.7.96, 12.7.96, 19.7.96, 26.7.96, 2–3.8.96, 9.8.96, 16.8.96, 23.8.96, 31.8.96, 8.9.96, 15–16.9.96, 23–24.9.96, 29.9.96, 6.10.96, 12–13.10.96, 20–21.10.96, 27–28.10.96, 7.11.96, 11.11.96, 18.11.96, 24.11.96, 3.12.96, 10.12.96, 21.12.96, 29.12.96
1797: 10.1.97, 20–21.1.97, 28.1.97,3–4.2.97, 12–13.2.97, 18.2.97, 23–24.2.97, 28.2.97, 1.3.97, 4–5.3.97, 8.3.97, 10–11.3.97, 15.3.97, 17–18.3.97, 22–23.3.97, 27.3.97, 3.4.97, 7.4.97, 21.4.97, 29.4.97, 2.5.97, 6.5.97, 11.5.97, 19.5.97, 1–2.6.97, 9–10.6.97, 15–16.6.97, 21.6.97, 29.6.97, 7.7.97, 13.7.97, 27.7.97, 3.8.97, 10.8.97, 24.8.97, 2.9.97, 12.9.97, 29.9.97, 5.10.97, 12.10.97, 19.10.97
drawing off beer:
1793: 13.10.93, 26.11.93, 30.11.93, 4.12.93, 5.12.93, 18.12.93, 21.12.93, 25.12.93, 28.12.93
1794: 6.1.94, 8.1.94, 14.1.94, 15.1.94, 19.1.94, 28.1.94, 4.2.94, 11.2.94, 16.2.94, 25.2.94, 6.3.94, 12.3.94, 19.3.94, 2.4.94, 6.4.94, 22.4.94, 29.4.94, 3.5.94, 6.5.94, 16.5.94, 23.5.94, 13.9.94
1795: 30.4.95, 7.5.95, 30.11.95
1796: 13.1.96, 18.2.96, 22–23.2.96, 26.2.96, 9.3.96, 2.4.96, 13.4.96, 16.4.96, 20–21.4.96, 24.4.96, 11.11.96
1797: 18.2.97, 1.3.97, 8.3.97, 15.3.97, 23.3.97, 6.5.97, 8.5.97
general brewery work:
1793: 22.11.93,9.12.93
1796: 9.9.96, 17.9.96, 19.9.96, 21.9.96, 1.10.96, 15.10.96, 22.10.96, 24.10.96, 29.10.96, 31.10.96, 2.11.96, 8.11.96, 12.11.96, 14.11.96, 19.11.96, 21.11.96, 28.11.96,30.11.96, 24.12.96, 26.12.96, 30.12.96
1797: 13.1.97, 24.1.97, 31.1.97, 6.2.97, 8.2.97, 14.2.97, 7.3.97, 28–29.3.97, 8.4.97, 11.4.97, 18.4.97, 25–26.4.97, 16.5.97, 20.5.97, 27.5.97, 30.5.97, 3.6.97, 7.6.97, 12.6.97, 22.6.97, 24.6.97, 26.6.97, 3.7.97, 16.7.97, 24.7.97, 29.7.97, 4–5.8.97, 12.8.97, 22.8.97, 26.8.97, 28.8.97, 13–14.9.97, 23.9.97, 6–7.10.97, 16.10.97, 20–21.10.97
delivering beer, 20.10.93, 27.12.94; loading beer cart, 14.1.94, 19.1.94, 5.4.95; fetches

Thompson, William Gunton, general brewery work (*cont.*)
malt over to brewery, 29.5.94, 15.12.94, 26.12.94, 24.9.95; cleans hop chamber, 5.7.94; loading coal, 7.8.94; grinding all night, 29.12.94; tidies workshop, 21.1.95; at work in waterwheel when river frozen, 24.1.95; pumps liquor for brewing, 1.2.95; kindles fire for copper, 9.2.95; draws off beer into wine pipes, 22.4.95; cleans cask, 29.4.95; clearing troughs, 26.5.95, 18.2.96, 20.3.96, 5.3.97; whitewashes tun room, 8.6.95; whitewashes brewhouse, 8.9.95; prepares for brewing, 21.9.95; whitewashes small-beer house, 10.11.95; draying off beer, 23.3.96, 16.4.96, 23.4.96, 17.2.97; repairs cleansing pump, 3.8.96; cleans vat, 14.10.96
general farm work: gathering apples, 18.10.93, 17.10.95; ringing pigs, 30.10.93; throwing mould out of river, 7.2.94; harrowing, 20.3.94; ploughing, 29.5.94; walks a-farming with WHj and HR, 13.7.94; gathers bees, 11.9.94; moves stack into barn, 11.2.96; moves part of haystack into hay chamber, 23.7.96; screening and preserving peas, 18.5.97
harvesting: 15–16.8.94, 18–22.8.94, 28.8.94, 5.9.95, 7.9.95, 17.9.95, 26–27.8.96, 29.8.96, 2–3.9.96, 5–6.9.96, 12–13.9.96, 22.8.97, 28–31.8.97, 1.9.97, 4–9.9.97; gathers largess, 9.9.97
haymaking: 7.7.94, 10.7.94, 24–25.7.95, 5.8.95, 4–5.7.96, 8.7.96, 11–13.7.96, 15–16.7.96, 18.7.96, 20–21.7.96, 7.10.96, 12.7.97, 14.7.97, 19–22.7.97
jobs: 22.9.97; collects window frames from Holt, 10.4.94; collects bricks, 29.5.94; to Briningham, 8.6.94; to Edgefield, 30.6.94; to Thornage, 17.3.96; collects coal, 2.8.96; summons Mr Hammond from Saxlingham, 22.3.97
milling: cleans wheat chamber, 30.1.96; collects coarse flour from Mr Cook, 25.6.96; stripping meal, 15.4.94, 13.4.95, 10.8.96; carts millstones from Mr Rouse's mill, 24.7.97
dressing flour:
1793: 8.11.93, 19.11.93, 23.11.93, 6.12.93, 24.12.93, 26.12.93
1794: 3.2.94, 4.3.94, 19.5.94, 11.6.94, 14.8.94, 6.9.94, 24.9.94, 7.10.94, 11.10.94, 11.11.94
1795: 23.2.95, 9–10.3.95, 14–15.4.95, 18.7.95, 24.8.95, 4.9.95, 12.10.95, 16.10.95, 1.12.95
1796: 16.3.96, 1.6.96, 11.8.96, 1.9.96, 26.9.96, 22.12.96, 31.12.96

Thompson, William Gunton, milling, dressing flour (*cont.*)
1797: 23.1.97, 26.1.97, 23.2.97, 10.4.97, 12.5.97, 23.6.97, 8.7.97, 26.7.97, 8–9.8.97, 25.8.97, 27.9.97, 9.10.97, 23.10.97
dressing maltstones: 11.10.93, 3.12.95, 5.12.95, 10–12.5.96, 19–20.8.96, 21–22.4.97, 30.6.97, 19.8.97, 30.9.97
dressing wheatstones, **33**:
1793: 15.10.93, 13.11.93, 12.12.93
1794: 2.1.94, 17.2.94, 26.3.94, 7.5.94, 1–3.7.94, 13.8.94, 10–11.9.94, 9.10.94, 15.11.94
1795: 6–7.1.95, 26.6.95, 13.8.95, 19.12.95
1796: 6.1.96, 4–5.2.96, 17–19.5.96, 18.8.96, 1.11.96, 13–14.12.96
1797: 17.1.97, 13.3.97, 5–6.7.97, 11.8.97, 21.8.97, 20.9.97, 13–14.10.97
grinding barley for animals: 3.12.94, 12.11.95, 16.1.97, 18.9.97, 9.10.97
grinding coarse flour: 16.9.97
grinding malt for brewing and storage:
1793: 14.10.93, 21.10.93, 28.10.93, 4.11.93, 12.11.93, 18.11.93, 21.11.93, 27.11.93, 2.12.93, 7.12.93, 13.12.93, 19–20.12.93, 27.12.93
1794: 3.1.94, 10.1.94, 18.1.94, 24.1.94, 30–31.1.94, 6.2.94, 8.2.94, 13–14.2.94, 21.2.94, 27.2.94, 14.3.94, 21.3.94, 27–28.3.94, 3–4.4.94, 10-11.4.94, 18.4.94, 24.4.94, 1–2.5.94, 8.5.94, 12–13.5.94, 17–18.5.94, 22–23.5.94, 31.5.94, 5.6.94, 13–14.6.94, 19–20.6.94, 26–27.6.94, 4.7.94, 14–15.7.94, 22–24.7.94, 1–2.8.94, 8–9.8.94, 29–30.8.94, 4.9.94, 12.9.94, 18–20.9.94, 25.9.94, 2–4.10.94, 20–21.10.94, 25.10.94, 27.10.94, 1.11.94, 3.11.94, 8.11.94, 13–14.11.94, 20–21.11.94, 1–2.12.94, 9–10.12.94, 16.12.94, 26.12.94, 29.12.94
1795: 1–2.1.95, 12.1.95, 23.1.95, 30.1.95, 5–6.2.95, 12–13.2.95, 19–20.2.95, 3–4.3.95, 12.3.95, 20.3.95, 26–27.3.95, 2.4.95, 14.4.95, 16–17.4.95, 4.5.95, 9.5.95, 19–20.5.95, 23.5.95, 27–28.5.95, 1–2.6.95, 5–6.6.95, 15.6.95, 19–20.6.95, 4.7.95, 13–14.7.95, 20.7.95, 27.7.95, 3.8.95, 12.8.95, 18.8.95, 21.8.95, 25.8.95, 28.8.95, 31.8.95, 9.9.95, 15.9.95, 19.9.95, 26.9.95, 1.10.95, 6.10.95, 9.10.95, 19.10.95, 24.10.95, 30.10.95, 7.11.95, 17–18.11.95, 23.11.95, 27.11.95, 2.12.95, 8.12.95, 14.12.95, 22–23.12.95, 30.12.95
1796: 6.1.96, 11.1.96, 15.1.96, 22.1.96, 29.1.96, 12.2.96, 16.2.96, 20.2.96, 1.3.96, 5.3.96, 22.3.96, 28.3.96, 31.3.96,

Thompson, William Gunton, grinding malt for brewing and storage, 1796 (*cont.*)
4.4.96, 7–8.4.96, 11.4.96, 14.4.96, 18.4.96, 30.4.96, 14.5.96, 21.5.96, 27–28.5.96, 3.6.96, 10–11.6.96, 17–18.6.96, 24–25.6.96, 1–2.7.96, 23.7.96, 27–28.7.96, 2.8.96, 5–6.8.96, 13.8.96, 17.8.96, 20.9.96, 27.9.96, 4.10.96, 10.10.96, 17–18.10.96, 25.10.96, 3–4.11.96, 9.11.96, 22.11.96, 29.11.96, 1.12.96, 7.12.96, 27.12.96
1797: 4.1.97, 25.1.97, 1.2.97, 9–10.2.97, 15.2.97, 20.2.97, 25.2.97, 2.3.97, 4.3.97, 8.3.97, 11.3.97, 20.3.97, 22.3.97, 30.3.97, 5.4.97, 12.4.97, 19.4.97, 2.5.97, 4.5.97, 9.5.97, 13.5.97, 17.5.97, 22.5.97, 29.5.97, 5–6.6.97, 13.6.97, 17.6.97, 27.6.97, 4.7.97, 11.7.97, 17–18.7.97, 25.7.97, 31.7.97, 1.8.97, 7–8.8.97, 14–15.8.97, 15–16.9.97, 25–26.9.97, 2–3.10.97, 10.10.97, 17.10.97, 24.10.97
taking up and laying down stones:
maltstones: 30.7.94, 7.12.95, 13.5.96, 24.8.96, 24.4.97, 1.7.97, 2.10.97
wheatstones: 17.10.93, 14.11.93, 3.1.94, 18.2.94, 9.5.94, 12.9.94, 10.10.94, 27.2.95, 31.3.95, 27.6.95, 5.11.95, 7.1.96, 10–11.3.96, 20.5.96, 17.8.96, 12.12.96, 18.1.97, 14.3.97, 21.9.97
screening malt: 18–19.9.94, 1.11.94, 12.12.94, 8.10.95, 23.10.95, 29.10.95, 6.11.95, 17.11.95, 23.11.95, 11.2.96; keeps tally during malt screening, 3.9.94
social and family activities, **269**: to Holt Fair, 25.11.93, 25.11.96; goes walking with HR, 16.2.94; goes out on Sunday, 16.3.94; to N. Walsham Fair, 28.5.94, 19.4.95, 13–15.5.95, 4.5.96, 24–26.5.97; with family to Weybourne, 29.6.94; with family to Walsingham, 20.7.94; with wife to Cley Fair, 25.7.94; accompanies son before justices after son's arrest by WHj, 28.7.94; to Cley Fair, 31.7.95, 28.7.97; to Whit Monday dinner at Hs', 16.5.96; to Weybourne Fair, 17.5.96; with William Lamb to Weybourne, 16.8.97

Thornage, Norf., **112**, **259**, **277**, **376**, WHj to, 15.10.93, 24.11.93, 2.11.94; HR to, 19.3.94; Thomas Baldwin doing jobs, 7.10.94; Peter Williams at Hs', 13.10.94; Gunton Thompson to, 17.3.96; WHj to tea with Mr Temple, 13.2.97
beer deliveries, **9**:
1793: 19.10.93, 14.12.93
1794: 8.2.94, 26.2.94, 19.3.95, 8.4.94, 10.4.94, 22.4.94, 10.5.94, 19.5.94, 9.6.94, 25.6.94, 12.7.94, 23.7.94, 12.8.94, 23.8.94, 17.9.94, 1.11.94, 8.12.94, 31.12.94

Thornage, beer deliveries (*cont.*)
1795: 3.2.95, 21.2.95, 25.3.95, 6.4.95, 5.5.95, 22.5.95, 12.6.95, 2.7.95, 3.8.95, 20.8.95, 3.9.95, 23.9.95, 3.10.95, 15.10.95, 27.10.95, 2.12.95, 26.12.95
1796: 14.1.96, 13.2.96, 5.3.96, 25.3.96, 16.4.96, 4.5.96, 10.6.96, 29.7.96, 16.9.96, 7.10.96, 27.10.96, 26.11.96, 27.12.96
1797: 24.1.97, 25.2.97, 23.3.97, 22.4.97, 15.5.97, 6.6.97, 21.6.97, 10.7.97, 25.7.97, 15.8.97, 26.8.97, 18.9.97, 23.9.97, 3.10.97
malt deliveries: 10.11.94, 20.1.97, 12.9.97:
see also Sturley, John; Temple, Thomas; Williams, Peter; Williams, William

thorns, taken to meadow by Hs' boy while John Fox hedging, 8.4.94; set by Thomas Hall around newly planted tree, 21.3.95; carted by Hs' boy in Furze Closes, 2.4.95; collected by Robert Bye, 15.3.97, 17.3.97; carted by Hs' men into field, 25.4.97

threshing (tasking, trashing), for Hs, **132**:
1794–95: 3–6.9.94, 15–16.9.94, 26–27.9.94, 30.9.94, 10.10.94, 16.10.94, 14–15.11.94, 17–19.11.94, 27–29.11.94, 1–6.12.94, 10–13.12.94, 15–20.12.94, 22.12.94, 24.12.94, 26–27.12.94, 29.12.94, 31.12.94, 1–2.1.95, 6–9.1.95, 13–17.1.95, 19–24.1.95, 28–29.1.95, 2.2.95, 17–21.2.95, 24.2.95, 9–12.3.95, 17.3.95, 19–20.3.95, 23–28.3.95, 30–31.3.95, 1.4.95
1795–96: 14–16.9.95, 18.9.95, 24–25.9.95, 29–30.9.95, 1–2.10.95, 12.10.95, 14–17.10.95, 19.10.95, 26–31.10.95, 2–4.11.95, 6–7.11.95, 11.11.95, 16–21.11.95, 23.11.95, 25.11.95, 27–28.11.95, 30.11.95, 1–5.12.95, 8–10.12.95, 15.12.95, 21.12.95, 23–24.12.95, 6.1.96, 11–16.1.96, 18–23.1.96, 25–30.1.96, 1–6.2.96, 8.2.96, 10.2.96, 12–13.2.96, 15–19.2.96, 22–23.2.96, 25–26.2.96, 29.2.96, 2–4.3.96, 12.3.96, 15–19.3.96, 21.3.96, 25.3.96, 5–8.4.96, 13.4.96, 16.4.96, 18–23.4.96, 25–29.4.96
1796–97: 5–8.10.96, 21–22.10.96, 25.10.96, 17–18.11.96, 23.11.96, 30.11.96, 1.12.96, 3.12.96, 5–6.12.96, 8–10.12.96, 12–16.12.96, 19–24.12.96, 26–31.12.96, 10–12.1.97, 14.1.97, 16–19.1.97, 21.1.97, 24–28.1.97, 30.1.97
1797–98: 21–22.9.97, 17.10.97
for Gunton Thompson: his corn threshed by John Ramm, 25.9.94:
see also barn

Thurgarton (Thurgaton), Norf., WHj to, 14.1.96

Thursford, Norf., **27**, WH to, 14.10.93; HR accompanies family as far as on journey to Whissonsett, 19.7.94; Nicholas Woodhouse

Thursford (*cont.*)
collects sow and pigs, 1.9.96; HR to, 11.9.96, 4.2.97; WH and John Smith to, 29.3.97
beer deliveries: 22.8.96, 12.9.96, 8.10.96, 21.11.96, 7.1.97, 20.2.97, 22.3.97, 5.4.97, 16.5.97, 7.6.97, 29.6.97, 24.7.97, 21.8.97, 20.9.97, 11.10.97

tiles, **44**, **86**, **87**:
collected by Hs' men: from John Dawson, 16.11.93, 24.2.94; by boy, 21.3.94; from Swanton Novers, 17.9.94; from Cley, 1.10.94, 25.10.94, 31.10.94; unloaded by Hs' men, 6.11.94
roof, **124**: pantiles delivered by Thomas Boyce to Corpusty, 6.11.94; collected by Hs' men from Cley, 15.1.95

timber, *see* wood

Tinker, James, **404**, Letheringsett carpenter; repairs Hs' wagon, 27.12.93; at work at Hs', 3.3.94, 12.3.94, 8.4.94, 29.7.95, 22–24.11.96; with man at work, 7–8.3.94, 11.3.94; at work with William Tinker, 3.3.94, 11.3.94; at work with Mr Barnes, 2.7.95; at work with William Tinker and Ben, 22.3.96, 10–11.8.96

Tinker, William (d.1830 aged 75), Letheringsett carpenter, at work for Hs:
brewery work: repairs Hs' carts, 29–30.1.94; with man repairs stable doors, 31.1.94; with two men takes down Hs' backs, 9.7.95; with Ben repairs mash-tun bottom, 28–30.12.95; with Thomas Youngman repairs sluice and waterwheel, 21.5.96; building counting-house roof, 25.9.97
bridge work: with two men builds bridge from Hs' garden side, 9.8.96
cart and wagon work: with man repairs wagon, 2-3.12.93; with man repairs little cart, 4.12.93; repairs beer cart, 23.12.93, 31.1.94, 11.6.96; repairs tumbril, 19.12.96
public-house work: with man at Black Boys, Holt, 3.1.94
sawing: with Ben, 27.1.96, 7.1.97, 19.1.97, 21.1.97; with man, 18.1.97, 6.7.97
work unspecified:
alone: 30.4.94, 5.6.95, 8.6.95, 15–16.1.95, 28.7.95, 7.3.96, 18.3.96, 4.4.96, 19.4.96, 25.5.96, 13.6.96, 15.6.96, 6.10.96, 4.11.96, 17.12.96, 22.6.97, 21–23.9.97, 28.9.97, 4–7.10.97, 9.10.97, 11.10.97, 13–14.10.97, 16–21.10.97, 23.10.97
his men or lad at work for Hs: one man, 21.3.96; two men, 2.5.94, 12.8.95, 14–15.8.95, 9.10.95, 5.12.95, 2.3.96, 7.3.96, 14.3.96, 21.6.97; three men, 20.6.97
with named others: James Tinker and man, 3.3.94; son William, 29.4.94; Ben, 22.3.96, 14.5.96, 10.8.96, 17.8.96

Tinker, William, work unspecified (*cont.*)
with one man: 31.10.93, 1–2.11.93, 7.11.93, 16–17.12.93, 30–31.12.93, 2.1.94, 12.2.94, 12.3.94, 10–12.6.95, 3.12.95, 29–30.1.96, 16.3.96, 19.3.96, 24.5.96, 26–27.5.96, 11–13.8.96, 15–16.8.96, 20.8.96, 5.10.96, 1–2.11.96, 21.11.96, 31.1.97, 19.6.97, 28.6.97
with two men: 4.3.94, 6.3.94, 13–15.3.94, 18–22.3.94, 24–29.3.94, 31.3.94, 1–5.4.94, 7.4.94, 9–12.4.94, 14–19.4.94, 21–26.4.94, 28.4.94, 1.5.94, 10–11.7.95, 13–14.7.95, 23–25.7.95, 27.7.95, 13.8.95, 18.8.95, 20–21.8.95, 10.10.95, 19.11.95, 4.12.95, 7–8.12.95, 28.1.96, 1–2.2.96, 8.3.96, 10–12.3.96, 23–26.3.96, 28–31.3.96, 1–2.4.96, 9.4.96, 11–15.4.96, 23.5.96, 8.8.96
with three men, 13.6.95, 15–18.6.95, 3–4.7.95
with four men, 19–20.6.95, 22.6.95
with five men, 23–26.6.95:
see also sawyers
Tinker, William jnr (b.1783), Letheringsett carpenter; with father at work at Hs', 29.4.94
Todhunter, Mrs, with husband dines at Hs', 25.4.96
Todhunter, William, excise supervisor and port surveyor; to tea at Hs', 15.6.95; with wife dines at Hs', 25.4.96
Tompson, Messrs Stackhouse and Timothy, **408**, **411**, Norwich common brewers; annual production figures, HR's endnotes
Tompson, *see* Thompson, William Gunton
trashing, *see* threshing
trees, Thomas Hall and boy dig hole for in shrubbery, 14.4.95; stumps dug up by Thomas Hall, 28.4.95, 30.4.95; planted by WHj in Brewhouse Pightle, 7.1.96
cherry: supported with truss, 2.7.96
chestnut: dug up by WHj and HR and re-planted in Brewhouse Pightle, 20.3.95; thorns set around by Thomas Hall, 21.3.95
firs, **317**, **330**: ordered by Cook Flower from Hs, 2.12.95, 29.12.95; planted by Thomas Boyce, 11.1.95; collected by William Lamb and boy, 12.5.96, 14.1.97; delivered by Thomas Boyce, 24.2.97; planted at Holt Heath Farm, 25.2.97
plantations: Thomas Boyce working in, 5–6.6.95; cleaned by Thomas Boyce, 13.6.97
pruning: by WHj and HR, 12.3.95; topped by Thomas Boyce in meadow, 22–23.12.96:
see also wood
troughs (thoughs, througfs, throughfs, throughs, thwarts), in Hs' brewery; installed by Thomas Youngman in tun room, 10.1.94; cleared by Hs' men, 26.5.95, 20.3.96, 28.3.96, 5.3.97; cleaned by Hs' men, 18.2.96; Hs' men carry off beer from, 12.12.96
trowelmen, *see* bricklayers
tumbril, *see* carts
tun room, *see* brewhouse
Turner, Sarah, Hs' maidservant; departs, 10.10.96
turnips:
carted: 24.1.97, 30.1.97, 4.3.97
collected: 18.10.93, 21.12.93, 3.1.94, 15.2.94, 22.2.94, 27.2.94, 21.11.94, 25.11.94, 29.11.94, 2.12.94, 17.12.94, 26.12.94, 10.1.95, 31.1.95, 20.2.95, 4.3.95, 9.3.95, 12.3.95, 4.4.95, 8.4.95, 18.4.95, 11.4.95, 27.4.96, 12.12.96; for cows, 8.11.94
harrowing: 9.8.96
hoeing: 8–9.7.94, 15–19.7.94, 21–24.7.94, 28–31.7.94, 1–2.8;94, 4–9.8.94, 26.8.94, 1–2.9.94, 4–6.9.94, 8.9.94, 22.8.95, 24–27.8.95, 10.9.95, 26–30.7.96, 3.8.96, 6.8.96, 11–12.8.96, 15–18.8.96, 27–28.9.96, 26–28.7.97, 31.7.97, 7–9.8.97
ploughing: 14.7.94, 5.5.96
sowing: 17.6.94, 21.6.94, 29.6.96, 1–2.7.96, 5.7.96, 29.6.97; in Furze Closes, 1.7.97, 4.7.97
turtles, WHj to turtle feast at Holt, 3.9.94

U

Upper Sheringham, *see* Sheringham

V

vat (fat, fatt), *see* brewing equipment
vegetables, **154**, potatoes lifted, 22.12.95, 2.12.96; parsnip used in recipe for destroying moles, HR's endnotes
venison, WH to feast at Holt, 30.7.94
vetches:
collected: 27.7.95, 9.7.96, 19.7.96, 1.8.96, 6.8.96, 14.6.97, 11.7.97, 26.7.97, 8.8.97, 16.8.97
mown: 18.7.95, 31.7.97, 10.8.97, 12.8.97
sown: 29–30.10.94, 1.11.94, 8.4.96, 3.11.96
Viverton, *see* Wiveton

W

Wade, John, **69**, **252**, Holt and Gt Ryburgh miller; to tea at Hs', 16.1.94, 23.3.94, 9.4.94, 13.6.94, 6.7.94; his windmill burns down at Holt, 8.5.94; to supper with Hs, 6.7.94; dines with Hs, 24.9.94, 25.3.95, 8.5.96, 24.6.96; with Hs and Ravens to Cley, 25.3.95: *see also* Ryburgh
wages, Thomas Boyce paid £10 a year as Hs' gardener, 10.10.96; James Broughton jnr paid 7*s* 6*d* a week as Hs' labourer, 16.10.97

wagons, Hs':
beer wagon: loaded for Stalham, 14.1.94, 19.1.96; loaded, 11.5.94; loaded for Fakenham and Syderstone, 2.1.95; Thomas Baldwin's leg broken when run over by, 9.12.96
harvest wagon, **133**, **349**: Hs' boys raking behind, 28.8.94, 8.9.97; driven by WHj, 28.8.94; Mary Parr raking behind, 31.8.97
hay wagon: Mrs Hall raking behind, 10.7.94; Mrs Thompson raking behind, 21.7.96
muck wagon: loaded, 28–29.11.96, 15–17.12.96; driven to Holt Heath Farm, 29.11.96, 5.12.96, 8.12.96, 15–17.12.96, 31.12.96, 2.1.97, 12.1.97, 16–17.1.97, 26–28.1.97, 6.2.97
new wagon: collected from Holt, 21.11.94
repaired: by William Tinker and man, 2–3.12.93; by James Tinker, 27.12.93; taken to Holt, 15.7.94, 17.7.94; wheels taken to Holt, 9.12.94; collected from Holt, 12.8.96; taken to Saxlingham, 12.1.97; collected from Saxlingham, 6.2.97:
see also carts; horses, teams; wheels

Wagstaff, Robert, innkeeper of Horseshoes, Corpusty, tied house; at Hs', 13.5.94: *see also* Corpusty

Wakefield, Francis, innkeeper of Black Boys, Holt, tied house; Robert Bye delivers beer, 5.10.95, 7.12.95: *see also* Holt, public houses

Walden, John, innkeeper of Fighting Cocks, Wells, tied house; reckons with Hs, 9.12.93; Robert Bye collects horse, 18.9.94; at Hs', 23.9.94; horse treated, 31.10.94; dines with Hs, 27.4.95; with William Silence at Hs', 10.9.96, 18.10.96: *see also* Wells, beer deliveries

wallpaper, HR helps MA to hang her room, 26–27.5.96

Walsingham, Norf., **245**, **270**, Gunton Thompson and family to, 20.7.94; Mr Raven at Hs' to hire Maid's Head at N. Walsham, 10.9.94; WH to, 21.9.95, 13.5.96; WHj with Messrs Ellis and Balls to, 16.12.96; WHj to, 12.9.97
beer deliveries: 8.11.93, 4.12.93, 6.1.94, 7.2.94, 22.3.94, 3.5.94, 13.6.94, 18.7.94, 7.8.94, 9.9.94, 17.10.94

washing, by MH, 14.1.94

water (liquor) **49**, for malting and brewing; pumped by John Ramm into malthouse steep, 18.10.93; pumped by Gunton Thompson for brewing, 1.2.95: *see also* Glaven, River; pond; pumps; river; well

watergate, *see* sluice

watermills, *see* mills

waterwheel, for Hs' malt-mill, brewery and cornmill, **3**, **65**, **66**, **67**, **74**, **75**, **77**, **95**, **96**, **142**, **143**, **144**, **276**; repaired by Thomas Youngman and boy, 18.2.94, 29.5.94, 28.10.94; freed by Thomas Youngman and boy, 6.5.94; frozen up, 23.1.95; Gunton Thompson at work in, 24.1.95; repaired by William Tinker and Thomas Youngman, 21.5.96; repaired by Thomas Youngman's two men, 14.10.97

Watson, Mr, of Mileham; with Nathaniel Raven jnr to Hs, with WH and WHj to Holt, 8.8.94

Waybourn/Wayburn, *see* Weybourne

weather, tempest, 15.7.96

Webb, Mr, sells barley to WHj, 14.10.93

Webb, Mr, of Pattesley; sends hoops to Hs, 6.6.95

Webster, Mr, of Norwich; at Hs', 22.2.95; with WHj tries horse and returns home, 23.2.95

weeding, by Thomas Hall, 4–5.6.94, 12.6.94; by John Ramm in meadow, 1.7.97, 4–5.7.97: *see also* grasses

well, sunk by Mr Bunnett's three men, 20.8.95

Wells-next-the-Sea, Norf., **231**, **289**, Robert Bye delivers flour, 5.12.93; WHj and HR to, 31.1.94; two gentlemen from at Hs', 7.4.94; WHj to, 15.7.94, 17.10.96, 18.11.96; WH to with Thomas Temple, 17.9.94; Robert Bye delivers horse Jack and brings back horse from John Walden, 18.9.94; John Walden dines with Hs, 27.4.95; WH to with Mr Henderson, 12.9.95; WH to, 21.9.95; Hs' men collect hops, 23.11.95, 2.1.96; WHj to with William Thackwray, 14.10.96; WH and WHj to, 26.12.96; William Thackwray and John Thompson to, 1.1.97
beer deliveries, **58**, **210**:
1793: 24.10.93, 11.11.93, 26.11.93, 19.12.93
1794: 7.1.94, 25.1.94, 22.2.94, 10.3.94, 31.3.94, 9.4.94, 1.5.94, 22.5.94, 20.6.94, 18.7.94, 8.8.94, 5.9.94, 18.9.94, 24.10.94, 17.11.94, 30.12.94
1795: 27.1.95, 13.2.95, 24.3.95, 25.4.95, 20.5.95, 18.6.95, 15.7.95, 11.8.95, 24.8.95, 16.9.95, 19.10.95, 16.11.95, 23.11.95
1796: 2.1.96, 1.2.96, 19.2.96, 17.3.96, 8.4.96, 25.4.96, 20.5.96, 9.6.96, 13.7.96, 17.8.96, 15.9.96, 18.10.96, 2.11.96, 25.11.96, 16.12.96
1797: 3.1.97, 23.1.97, 10.2.97, 3.3.97, 24.3.97, 8.4.97, 16.5.97, 10.6.97, 30.6.97, 22.7.97, 22.8.97, 30.9.97
loading: 12.2.95

Weston, Charles, **408**, **411**, of Horsham St Faith, Norwich banker and common brewer; annual production figures, HR's endnotes

West Rudham, Norf., WH and WHj return from, 13.9.96

West Winch, *see* Winch

Weybourne (Waybourn, Wayburn, Weybourn), Norf., Mr Williams pays rent to Hs, 14.10.93; Gunton Thompson and family to, 29.6.94; Mr

Weybourne (*cont.*)
Bunnett's two men at work at public house, 18–19.11.94; Thomas Baldwin collects drum, 16.4.95; Robert Bye drunk, 11.5.95; WH and WHj to, 1.6.95; WHj to, 6.6.95, 22.10.95, 21.6.96, 12–13.1.97; WH, MH and MA to, 11.6.95; HR to, 14.6.95, 26.7.95, 18.11.96, 14.1.97; HR collects boy, 31.1.96; William Lamb, Thomas Baldwin and Gunton Thompson to fair, 17.5.96; WHj follows Artillery to, 17.6.96; Hs' men collect sale goods, 14.1.97; Gunton Thompson to on William Lamb's beer delivery, 16.8.97
beer deliveries:
1793: 13.11.93, 24.12.93
1794: 11.2.94, 25.2.94, 4.4.94, 1.5.94, 19.5.94, 24.6.94, 9.7.94, 30.7.94, 26.8.94, 18.9.94, 2.10.94, 28.10.94, 18.11.94, 24.12.94
1795: 21.1.95, 4.3.95, 31.3.95, 7.5.95, 11.5.95, 2.6.95, 8.6.95, 11.6.95, 13.6.95, 19.6.95, 3.7.95, 14.7.95, 24.7.95, 26.7.95, 3.8.95, 15.8.95, 25.8.95, 5.9.95, 18.9.95, 21.9.95, 28.9.95, 15.10.95, 21.10.95, 26.10.95, 4.11.95, 25.11.95
1796: 1.1.96, 23.1.96, 10.2.96, 16.3.96, 28.3.96, 27.4.96, 9.5.96, 27.5.96, 13.6.96, 22.6.96, 2.7.96, 9.7.96, 22.7.96, 26.7.96, 5.8.96, 30.8.96, 4.10.96, 22.10.96, 17–18.11.96, 28.11.96
1797: 14.1.97, 27.2.97, 24.3.97, 20.5.97, 22.6.97, 16.8.97
beer collected from: by William Lamb and Thomas Baldwin from Mr Sanderson, 17.11.96; by Thomas Baldwin from Mrs Hall, 9.10.97:
see also Hall, Edward; Weybourne Camp

Weybourne Camp (Waybourn Camp), Norf., **177**, **184**, **185**, **189**, **203**, **266**, WH and MA to, 17.6.95; Hs to with Messrs Everitt and Keeler and Miss Billing, 26.6.95; WH, MH, Henry Goggs and farm steward to, 8.7.95; WH, MA, HR and Mr and Mrs Nathaniel Raven to, 14.7.95; Hs, HR, Nathaniel Raven jnr and Mary Raven to, 10.8.95; WHj, MA, Nathaniel Raven jnr and Mary Raven to, 12.8.95; Hs, Nathaniel Raven, Thomas Fox, Revd John and Mrs Crofts to, 24.8.95; WH and Mrs Phillis Goggs to, 18.9.95; Nathaniel Raven, daughter Mary and Mrs Cozens to, 29.6.96; WHj, HR and Ravens to, 8.7.96; WHj to, 29.7.96
beer deliveries:
1795: 6.6.95, 19.6.95, 27.6.95, 7.7.95, 10.7.95, 27.7.95, 8.8.95, 14.8.95, 20.8.95, 28.8.95, 3.9.95, 14.9.95, 16.9.95, 28.9.95, 8.10.95, 21.10.95, 28–29.10.95
1796: 28.4.96, 27.6.96, 2.7.96, 9.7.96, 22.7.96, 6.8.96, 20.8.96, 3.9.96:
see also Sanderson, Samuel; Weybourne

WH, *see* Hardy, William jnr

W H, *see* brewhouse, white hall

wheat, **194**, **296**, Hs' men ploughing in stubble, 2.11.93, 9.11.93, 14–16.11.93, 9-11.11.95; barley sown in stubble, 15.4.95, 20.4.95; arranged by John Ramm, 29.5.95; chamber cleaned by Gunton Thompson and HR, 30.1.96; Thomas Baldwin harrowing stubble, 12.11.96; Thomas Hall thatching stack, 6.9.97; used in recipe for poisoning rats, HR's end-notes
dressing: 16.9.94, 6.10.94, 18.10.94
harvesting: 11.8.94, 14–16.8.94, 18–19.8.94, 2–3.9.96, 6.9.96, 8.9.96, 11–12.8.97, 14.8.97, 22–23.8.97, 26.8.97, 2.9.97, 4.9.97
price: 21*s* per coomb, 25.11.93
purchase by Hs: from John Barwick at Holt Fair, 25.11.93; from Mr Forster, 16.2.96; 10 quarters by Thomas Baldwin in Norwich, 28.6.96
riots: *see* Sharrington
screening: 22.11.93, 21.2.94, 5.5.95, 29.6.96
sowing: 19.10.93, 12.11.95, 3–4.11.96, 8.11.96
storing in and fetching from barn: 11.1.94, 20.2.94, 25.8.94
wheatstones: *see* millstones:
see also corn; flour; milling; straw; threshing

wheels, Thomas Baldwin takes cartwheels to Hunworth, 9.6.94; Thomas Baldwin takes wagonwheels to Holt, 9.12.94; Thomas Baldwin breaks arm falling under cartwheel, 23.12.94; collected by Thomas Baldwin from Holt and taken to Cley, 18.5.95, 16.6.95; Thomas Baldwin breaks leg falling under wagonwheel, 9.12.96; Robert Bye takes wheels to Holt for Mr Dawson, 12.1.97: *see also* waterwheel

whiskeys, *see* chaises

Whissonsett, Norf., **xii**, **5**, **79**, **93**, **130**, **150**, **151**, **175**, **179**, **194**, **195**, **241**, **313**, **314**, **315**, **413**, birthplace of HR and MH; Robert Bye to, 23.11.93; Henry Goggs to Hs from, 13.12.93, 8.9.94; George Dawson to, 17.5.94; Thomas Fox to, 25.8.95; Mr Henderson to, 11.9.95; Henry Goggs and Mr Cook to Hs from, 25.7.96, 14.8.97; William Thackwray with Hs to, 20.10.96; William Thackwray with Hs from, 22.10.96; Messrs Skrimshire and Miss Rowden with Ravens from Hs to, 20.6.97; Mr Bird with Ravens to Hs from, 9.8.97; they return, 11.8.97
Hs from:
MA: 7.12.94, 19.5.96, 22.10.96, 14.12.96, 31.3.97, 13.6.97
MH: 2.11.93, 14.6.94, 23.2.95, 22.8.95, 3.9.95, 28.5.96, 7.11.96, 18.3.97, 22.7.97
WH: 2.11.93, 23.2.95, 22.8.95, 3.9.95, 28.5.96, 18.3.97, 22.7.97

Whissonsett, Hs from (*cont.*)
WHj: 13.12.93, 14.6.94, 12.10.94, 7.12.94, 28.5.95, 6.10.95, 19.12.95, 19.5.96, 22.10.96, 31.3.97, 31.5.97, 13.6.97
Hs to:
MA: 13.11.94, 26.5.95, 18.5.96, 20.10.96, 28.3.97, 30.5.97
MH: 28.10.93, 9.6.94, 15.2.95, 19.5.95, 17.8.95, 5.1.96, 24.5.96, 13.3.97, 17.7.97
WH: 28.10.93, 15.2.95, 19.5.95, 17.8.95, 11.9.95, 5.1.96, 24.5.96, 13.3.97, 17.7.97
WHj: 18.10.93, 11–12.12.93, 16.5.94, 9.6.94, 9.10.94, 13.11.94, 5.12.94, 12.2.95, 26.3.95, 26.5.95, 5.10.95, 15.2.96, 18.5.96, 12.9.96, 20.10.96, 28.3.97, 9.5.97, 30.5.97, 12.6.97, 25.10.97
Ravens from: 26.12.93, 20.1.94, 1.2.94, 6.3.94, 13.4.94, 25.5.94, 14.6.94, 17.7.94, 21.9.94, 3.11.94, 7.12.94, 16.12.94, 24.3.95, 27.4.95, 14.7.95, 10.8.95, 11.11.95, 27.11.95, 17.3.96, 7.7.96, 31.10.96, 7.11.96, 9.3.97, 18.3.97, 20.6.97, 4.8.97, 8–9.8.97, 9.8.97
HR: 20.1.94, 13.4.94, 30.6.94, 27.7.94, 4.1.95, 23.2.95, 27.4.95, 20.5.95, 5.7.95, 10.8.95, 18.10.95, 3.1.96, 6.1.96, 9.1.96, 28.6.96, 28.8.96, 11.11.96, 14.12.96, 8.1.97, 12.3.97, 25.6.97
Ravens to: 16.5.94, 21.6.94, 5.12.94, 28.12.94, 15.2.95, 26.3.95, 25.8.95, 18.12.95, 30.4.96, 10.11.96, 24.2.97, 13.3.97, 3.7.97, 11.8.97
HR: 22.11.93, 12.1.94, 23.3.94, 12.4.94, 21.6.94, 26.7.94, 25.10.94, 28.12.94, 22.2.95, 19.5.95, 9.8.95, 17.10.95, 26.12.95, 5.1.96, 8.1.96, 21.6.96, 28.8.96, 10.11.96, 13.12.96, 1.1.97, 11.3.97, 16.4.97:
see also Raven, Nathaniel; Goggs, Henry jnr

white hall (W H), *see* brewhouse

whitewashing (whitening, whiting), tun room by Gunton Thompson, 8.6.95; brewhouse by Gunton Thompson, 8.9.95; brewhouse by WHj, 8.10.95; small-beer house by Gunton Thompson, 10.11.95: *see also* painting

Wigg, Miss, with Charlotte Bartell, Adam Baker and John Raven to dinner at Hs', 15.9.94

Wilcocks, Revd William Wright (d.1846), **183**, of Holt, Bale and Thornage, Curate of Field Dalling 1801, Curate of Wiveton 1801–04, Curate of Thornage with Brinton 1806, Vicar of Barney 1806–46, Rector of Pudding Norton 1807–46; injured in overturning cart in Hs' field, 17.1.97; his servant returns Hs' borrowed cart, 18.1.97

Wilkin, Mr, at Hs', 22.9.95

William, [no surname], *see* boys, boy 21; boys, boy 26

Williams, Mr, of Weybourne; pays rent to Hs, 14.10.93

Williams, Peter (d.1801 aged 75), **9**, innkeeper of Black Boys, Thornage; orders beer, 18.10.93, 14.1.94; beer deliveries, 16.11.93, 16.1.94; at Hs', 13.10.94: *see also* Thornage, beer deliveries

Williams, William, Thornage attorney; carts away muck from Hs, 27–28.11.95, 7–11.12.95, 23–24.12.95; William Lamb carts gravel from his pit, 30.3.96

Winch, Norf., HR and Robert Bye collect colts, 23.11.93

windmills, *see* mills

windows (winders), **349**, Thomas Baldwin collects window frames from Cromer, 26.3.94; Gunton Thompson and boy collect window frames from Holt, 10.4.94; William Holman collects sash windows from Weybourne, 14.1.97; sash windows installed by Mr Bunnett and boy at Hs' front, 23.3.97

wine, WH, WHj and HR bottle pipe at Cley, 10.12.94; WHj, Gunton Thompson and HR draw off beer into wine pipes, 22.4.95; drawn off by WHj at Holt, 2.2.96

Wiveton (Viverton, Whiverton, Wiverton), Norf., **8**, **33**, **181**, beer deliveries:
1793: 2.12.93
1794: 4.1.94, 1.2.94, 1.5.94, 19.5.94, 24.6.94, 15.7.94, 1.8.94, 2.9.94, 23.9.94, 28.10.94, 12.12.94
1795: 5.1.95, 4.2.95, 31.3.95, 9.5.95, 5.6.95, 9.7.95, 8.8.95, 25.9.95, 31.10.95, 4.12.95
1796: 30.1.96, 5.4.96, 9.5.96, 21.6.96, 24.8.96, 3.10.96:
see also Jordan, John

Wodehouse, *see* Woodhouse

Wood (Woods), Mr [?Matthew], London chemist; at Hs', 12.1.95, 17.6.95, 10.11.95; with wife and Bartells to tea at Hs', 7.6.97; with wife at Hs', 8.6.97

Wood, Mrs, of London; with husband and Bartells to tea at Hs', 7.6.97; with husband at Hs', 8.6.97

wood, collected by boy from Hs' yard, 26.2.94; Thomas Youngman's boy makes centre for brick arch, 26.5.94; cleared from pond, 14.7.94; collected from meadow, 22.12.96, 26.1.97, 28.1.97, 30.1.97; collected by Hs' men, 29.3.97; cut by Robert Bye in yard, 24.4.97
bark: wagonload collected by Mr Mason from Hs, 7.11.93; Mr Mason sends for second load, 8.11.93; used in recipe for destroying moles, HR's endnotes
faggots: collected by Hs' men, 4.12.94; tied by Hs' men, 2–3.3.95, 1.4.95, 1.5.95, 14.11.95
spars: taken to Salthouse, 25.2.96
sticks: chopped by Hs' men, 3.7.94, 6.1.95
timber, **34**, **35**: delivered from Hindolveston by John Cademy, 28.11.93, 30.11.93; deals

wood, timber (*cont.*)
stacked by WH and WHj, 1.2.94; collected by Hs' men from Gunthorpe, 12.11.94, 1–2.7.95, 30.7.95, 18.11.95, 22.1.96, 10.1.97; deals carried into malt chamber, 1.1.95; deals planed by Thomas Youngman's lad, 22–24.1.95, 26–28.1.95; small timber bought by WHj from Mr Collyer, 30.6.95; oak for barrels collected by Thomas Baldwin from Blakeney, 19.8.96; collected from Furze Closes, 31.12.96; sawyers finish work, 17.10.97:
see also barrels; carpenters; sawing; trees
Woodcock, Mr, Briston grocer and draper; at Hs', 13.12.94; his apprentice to tea at Hs', 17.12.94; reckons with Hs, 9.3.95
Woodhouse (Wodehouse, Woodehouse), Nicholas: *see* boys, boy 22
Wordingham, John, Wells carpenter; dines with Hs, 3.1.97
workforce (sarvants, savants), Hs', **402**, men given dinner at Hs' on first day of harvest, 10.8.94, 14.8.97; men given Christmas dinner, 25.12.93, 25.12.94, 25.12.95, 25.12.96; Robert Bye leaves team, 23.12.95; William Lamb leaves malthouse to take Robert Bye's place, is replaced by John Ramm, 27.12.95; men given Whit Monday dinner and have afternoon off work, 16.5.96, 5.6.97; Thomas Boyce employed as Hs' gardener for £10 a year, 10.10.96; Thomas Raynor hired for malting season, 29.11.96; Robert Bye takes Thomas Boyce's place working for James Cobon, 28.8.97; Thomas Raynor arranges to work for Hs, 10.9.97; Robert Bye leaves, 10.10.97
casual: *see* harvests; hay; labourers
regular, hired by year as farm servants and maltsters: *see* Baldwin, Thomas; Boyce, Thomas; Bye, Robert; Lamb, William; Platten, William; Ramm, John; Raynor, Thomas; Thompson, William Gunton; *also hired by year* boys, maidservants
workhouse, *see* Letheringsett, house of industry
workshop, *see* brewhouse
Wymer, Clara, **174**, of Norwich, daughter of George; with Charlotte Bartell at Hs', with WH and MA to Thomas Temple, 13.12.93; with Hs to Holt market, 14.12.93; with Bartells to tea at Hs', 8.1.96, 15.1.96, 8.2.96; with Miss Dowson to dinner at Hs', 11.1.96; with WHj and Miss Dowson to Holt, 29.1.96; with Charlotte Bartell and Miss Dowson at Hs', 17.2.96
Wymer, George (d.1809 aged 72), **174**, Norwich attorney; with Bartells to tea and supper at Hs', 22.6.94; with wife and Bartells to dinner and tea at Hs', 25.8.96
Wymer, George jnr (d.1839 aged 74), **106**, Reepham attorney; at Hs', 14.11.94
Wymer, Mrs, née Harrold, of Norwich, 2nd wife of George; with husband and Bartells to dinner at Hs', 25.8.96

Y

yards, Thomas Hall carting muck, 3.12.93; Hs' men turning muck, 22.2.94, 25–26.2.96, 4.5.96, 19.5.96, 10.6.97, 13.6.97; Hs' boy removing wood, 26.2.94; John Fox spreading gravel, 24.4.94; Jeremiah Moore and son working in river, 26–28.5.94; Robert Bye lays furze, 21.11.94; Charles Kendle's men carting muck, 6.1.95, 10.1.95; Thomas Hall scrapes up muck, 13.4.95; cleaned by Hs' men, 2.11.95, 16.11.95, 29.12.95, 11.4.97; Mr Bunnett's bricklayers and labourers demolish counting house, 16.3.96; boy carting bricks, 26.3.96; William Lamb carts gravel into, 30.3.96; Robert Bye cutting wood, 24.4.97; harrowed by boy, 21.9.97
brewhouse, **3**, **66**, **74**, **75**, **77**, **96**, **359**: John Ramm removing stones, 14.7.94; Thomas Boyce finishes work, 29.7.94
front: Hs' men at work, 5.7.94, 4.3.95, 22.5.95; Thomas Boyce repairs road at entrance, 4.2.96
great yard: paved by Thomas Boyce, 17.11.95
headyard: boy carting gravel to, 2.5.94
Hs' men at work:
1793: 29.10.93, 1.11.93, 10.12.93
1794: 8.3.94, 10.3.94, 13.3.94, 15.3.94, 17.3.94, 19–20.3.94, 22.3.94, 24.3.94, 28.3.94, 31.3.94, 29.3.94, 1.4.94, 2–5.4.94, 15–16.4.94, 18–19.4.94, 23.4.94, 9.5.94, 23–28.6.94, 5.7.94, 8–9.7.94, 11–12.7.94, 14.7.94, 15–19.7.94, 21–26.7.94, 3.9.94, 29–30.12.94
1795: 30.6.95, 4.8.95
1796: 24–26.3.96, 31.3.96, 1–2.4.96, 4.4.96, 6–7.4.96, 23.6.96
1797: 18.3.97, 3.4.97, 5.5.97, 13.5.97, 12.6.97, 19.6.97
King's Head, Letheringsett: foundations laid in, 11.3.94; Thomas Boyce carting stones into road, 8.5.94; Thomas Boyce at work, 9.5.94
pigs': paved by Thomas Boyce, 17.11.95; mucked out by Robert Bye, 16.6.97
Yarmouth, *see* Great Yarmouth
yeast, *see* cleansing
Youngman, Mrs Lydia (d.1828 aged 68), wife of Thomas; with MH to Cley, 29.11.95
Youngman, Thomas (d.1834 aged 76), **67**, Letheringsett millwright; installs trough in

Youngman, Thomas (*cont.*)
tun room, 10.1.94; his man at work for Hs, 30.4.94; his man and boy hanging gate, 3.5.94; at work for Hs, 7.5.94, 28.5.94, 3.2.95; working on palisade, 9.5.94; removes plug from great cask, 13.5.94; puts lock on Hs' coalhouse door, 12.9.94; trims mill gears, 27.2.95, 17.1.97; his man sawing for Hs, 12-13.3.95; helps Hs with harvest, 4.9.97; his men building door for counting-room chamber, 14.10.97

Youngman, Thomas (*cont.*)
his boy (lad): *see* boys, Thomas Youngman's
repair work for Hs: flour mill, 6.11.93; Hs' crane, 24.12.93; malt-mill rollers, 15–18.1.94; waterwheel, 18.2.94, 6.5.94, 29.5.94, 21.5.96; sluice, 31.7.94, 21.5.96; his man working on pump, 26.10.95; removes sleeve from cleansing pump, 15.2.96; mill, 21.8.97; malthouse pump, 5.10.97; his men repairing waterwheel, 14.10.97

The Diary of
Mary Hardy
1773–1809
· 1 ·
Public house and
waterway
edited by
MARGARET BIRD

The Diary of
Mary Hardy
1773–1809
· 2 ·
Beer supply, water power
and a death
edited by
MARGARET BIRD

The Diary of
Mary Hardy
1773–1809
· 3 ·
Farm, maltings and
brewery
with the diary of
Henry Raven
edited by
MARGARET BIRD

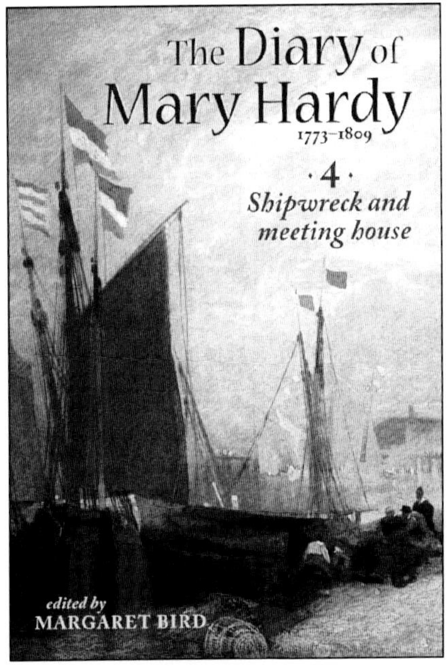
The Diary of
Mary Hardy
1773–1809
· 4 ·
Shipwreck and
meeting house
edited by
MARGARET BIRD

The full Mary Hardy series

Margaret Bird, published by Burnham Press

The Diary of Mary Hardy 1773–1809

PUBLISHED 30 APRIL 2013

Diary 1 · Public house and waterway	*1773–1781*	ISBN 978–0–9573360–0–1
Diary 2 · Beer supply, water power and a death	*1781–1793*	ISBN 978–0–9573360–1–8
Diary 3 · Farm, maltings and brewery	*1793–1797*	ISBN 978–0–9573360–2–5
Diary 4 · Shipwreck and meeting house	*1797–1809*	ISBN 978–0–9573360–3–2
Set of four volumes	*1773–1809*	ISBN 978–0–9573360–4–9

maryhardysdiary.co.uk

Each volume has an editorial introduction, chronology, glossary, bibliography and index

The Remaining Diary of Mary Hardy 1773–1809

PUBLISHED 30 APRIL 2013
ISBN 978–0–9573360–5–6

Entries 1781–1809 not included in the four-volume edition of the diary

maryhardysdiary.co.uk

The
Remaining Diary of
Mary Hardy
1773–1809
MARGARET BIRD

This companion volume is also published in 2013 by Burnham Press, Kingston upon Thames. It contains the remainder of the text of Mary Hardy's diary written in the Letheringsett years, but omitted from Diary 2, Diary 3 *and* Diary 4. (Diary 1, *written at Coltishall 1773–1781, contains the full text.*)

The transcription follows the same editorial method as in The Diary of Mary Hardy, *except that this volume has very few illustrations and is without editorial annotations and index.*

In the editorial notes in the four-volume edition it is cited as Diary MS

Mary Hardy and her World 1773–1809

TO BE PUBLISHED

Volume 1 · A working family

Volume 2 · Barley, beer and the working year

Volume 3 · Spiritual and social forces

Volume 4 · Under sail and under arms

Set of four volumes

maryhardysworld.co.uk

Each volume has a bibliography and index; the chapters and appendices are listed opposite

Mary Hardy and her World 1773–1809 by Margaret Bird

The nine books, with 39 chapters, in the four-volume commentary

Volume 1
A working family

Prologue — The diaries

I. FAMILY BONDS
1. The setting
2. The diarists
3. The shaping time
4. Marriage ventures
5. Nurturing children
6. Pupils

II. AT HOME
7. The comfortable house
8. Maidservant turnover
9. The garden
10. Pleasure grounds

Appendices
1.A Dictionary of Norfolk speech
1.B Mary Ann Hardy's recipes
1.C The Hardys' 90 maidservants
1.D A Hardy chronology 1732–1811

Volume 2
Barley, beer and the working year

I. IMPROVING THE LAND
1. A versatile workforce
2. Small farms
3. Enclosure
4. Climate and crops

II. RURAL MANUFACTURERS
5. Industry structure
6. Malting
7. Brewing and milling
8. Rival brewers

III. BEER AND THE EXCISE
9. The public houses
10. Supplying the beer
11. Debt and taxes

Directory — 35 Norfolk and Suffolk breweries
Gazetteer — The Hardys' 101 public houses

Appendix — 2.A The excise service

Volume 3
Spiritual and social forces

I. FLAMES OF FIRE
1. The parish clergy
2. The Sunday schools
3. Roving preachers
4. The wandering flock

II. TOWN AND VILLAGE
5. Local society
6. Upholding the peace
7. The market town
8. Trades and professions
9. Indoor pursuits
10. Outdoor recreations

Appendix — 3.A Ecclesiastical terms

Volume 4
Under sail and under arms

I. WIDE HORIZONS
1. The roads
2. The new navigation
3. Riverside staithes
4. Keels and wherries
5. The sea

II. HUMAN CONFLICT
6. Politics
7. Civilians at war
8. Deliverance

Epilogue — The enduring record

Glossary — Terms, weights and measures

This analytical study is in course of preparation and will be published by Burnham Press.

The preface, foreword and acknowledgments appear at the beginning of volume 1 only.

The list of figures and tables in each of the nine books appears at the beginning of each book. Each volume has its own bibliography and index

rear endpaper

North-east and north Norfolk: a distribution chart of the towns and villages supplied with beer by the Hardys during some or all of the diary years 1773–1809.

In *Diary 1* and *Diary 3* we are shown the routines underpinning supply to the public houses. We also glimpse the difficulties encountered by the men as they struggled across the county with the horse-drawn beer cart—on top of all their other tasks.

On the chart the overlapping sets of concentric circles are placed at 5, 10 and 15 miles from the brewery base [**B**]: Coltishall, on white, in the north-east; and Letheringsett, on black, in the north. The circles provide a quick way of gauging the distance of any one outlet from the brewery, if going in a straight line, and of assessing the bunching effect.

The winding roads meant that actual mileages were longer, the figures being shown in the lists under the column *road miles*. Faden's *Map of Norfolk* (1797) was used for calculating the precise mileages by road.

The chart locates 93 outlets. Until 1781 supply was from John Wells's brewery at Coltishall, which William Hardy managed (*Diary 1*). The 27 public houses recorded by his wife as taking Wells's beer are enumerated on a white ground.

From 1781 supply was from William Hardy's own brewery at Letheringsett, ownership passing to his son William in 1797. Their 62 recorded outlets, including the military camp by the sea at Weybourne [**59**], are shown on a black ground.

Additionally four outlets transferred from Wells's at Coltishall to Hardy's at Letheringsett. These four are shown as piebald: white and black.

About two-thirds of the 66 Letheringsett outlets are the public houses and camp supplied while the brewery apprentice Henry Raven was writing his diary at Letheringsett 1793–97 (in this volume, *Diary 3*). Supply to any one house was sometimes not sustained; others stayed loyal for many decades.

The brewer's tie is here defined as control of the retail outlet by the wholesale brewer either as owner or leaseholder or by means of a mortgage or innkeeper's bond.

The Maid's Head, near the coast at Stalham, was the most distant of all the houses, being 25 miles from Letheringsett (but only 9 from Coltishall). The Maid's Head was one of the four which William Hardy took with him, and is shown as piebald [**3**].

The Falcon at Limpenhoe [**23**], to the south-east in the valley of the Yare, was the most distant of the Coltishall houses from Wells's brewery: 15 miles.

In 1781–82, until a new manager took over, William Hardy maintained supply to the Coltishall houses from his new brewery base in the north of the county (*Diary 2*)

NORTH SEA

KEY

19 (square)	supplied with brewer's tie from Coltishall
27 (circle)	supplied without tie from Coltishall
43 (black square)	supplied with brewer's tie from Letheringsett
62 (black circle)	supplied without tie from Letheringsett
3 4	transferred from Coltishall to Letheringsett in 1781
B B	Coltishall and Letheringsett breweries
········	5-mile straight-line radius from brewery
· · · · ·	10-mile straight-line radius from brewery
———	15-mile straight-line radius from brewery

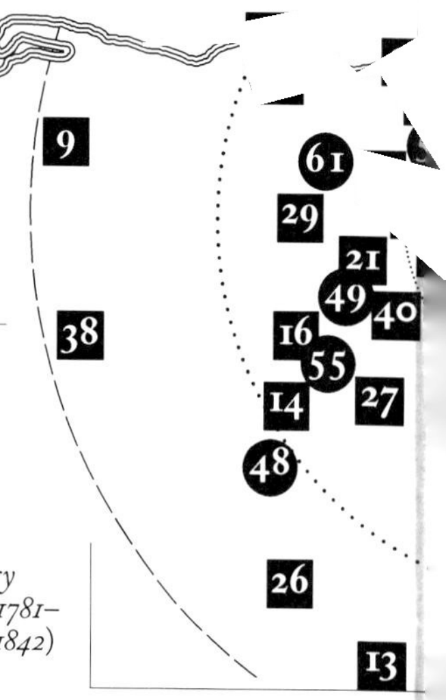

92 PUBLIC HOUSES AND ONE MILITARY CAMP

supplied with and without the brewer's tie by the Hardys 1773–1809, showing each identifying outlet number and road mileage from the brewery

Coltishall 1773–1781

supplied with tie by Wells's brewery (manager William Hardy 1772–1782)

		road miles
1.	Buxton	3·5
2.	Hevingham	4
3.	Horning	5
4.	Horsham St Faith	5
5.	Horsham St Faith	5
6.	Horstead	0·5
7.	Hoveton St John	2·5
8.	Ingworth	7
9.	Little Hautbois	2
10.	Neatishead	7
11.	North Walsham	7
12.	North Walsham	7
13.	North Walsham	7
14.	North Walsham	7
15.	Smallburgh	5
16.	Strumpshaw	11
17.	Tunstead	3
18.	Tuttington	5
19.	Worstead	5

Coltishall 1773–1781

supplied without tie by Wells's brewery

		road miles
20.	East Ruston	10
21.	Horsham St Faith	5
22.	Lessingham	11
23.	Limpenhoe	15
24.	Ludham	8·5
25.	Neatishead	7
26.	Swanton Abbot	5
27.	Upton	12

Letheringsett 1781–1809

supplied with tie by Hardy's brewery (owner-managers William Hardy 1781–1797 and William Hardy jnr 1797–1842)

		road miles
1.	Aldborough	9
2.	Bale	3·5
3.	Bessingham	7
4.	Binham	6·5
5.	Blakeney	4
6.	Bodham	4·5
7.	Brampton	14·5
8.	Briston	4·5
9.	Burnham Market	17·5
10.	Cley	4
11.	Cromer	11·5
12.	Cromer	11·5
13.	East Bilney [1]	15
14.	Fakenham	10·5
15.	Field Dalling	3·5
16.	Great Snoring [1]	9
17.	Gunthorpe	4
18.	Hindolveston	6
19.	Hindolveston	6
20.	Hindolveston	6
21.	Hindringham	6
22.	Holt	1
23.	Holt	1
24.	Holt	1
25.	Holt	1·5
26.	Horningtoft	15
27.	Kettlestone	7
28.	Letheringsett	0
29.	Little Walsingham	8·5
30.	Morston	7

Letheringsett (*cont.*)

supplied with tie by Hardy

		roa
31.	Morston [1]	
32.	North Walsham [1]	
33.	North Walsham	
34.	Salthouse	
35.	Sheringham	
36.	Southrepps	
37.	Stody	
38.	Syderstone	
39.	Thornage	
40.	Thursford	
41.	Wells	
42.	Wells	
43.	Weybourne	

Letheringsett 1781-

supplied without tie by H

		ro
44.	Blakeney	
45.	East Runton	
46.	Field Dalling	
47.	Gresham	
48.	Hempton	
49.	Hindringham	
50.	Holt	
51.	Holt	